Morocco

Paul Clammer

Alison Bing, Anthony Sattin, Paul Stiles

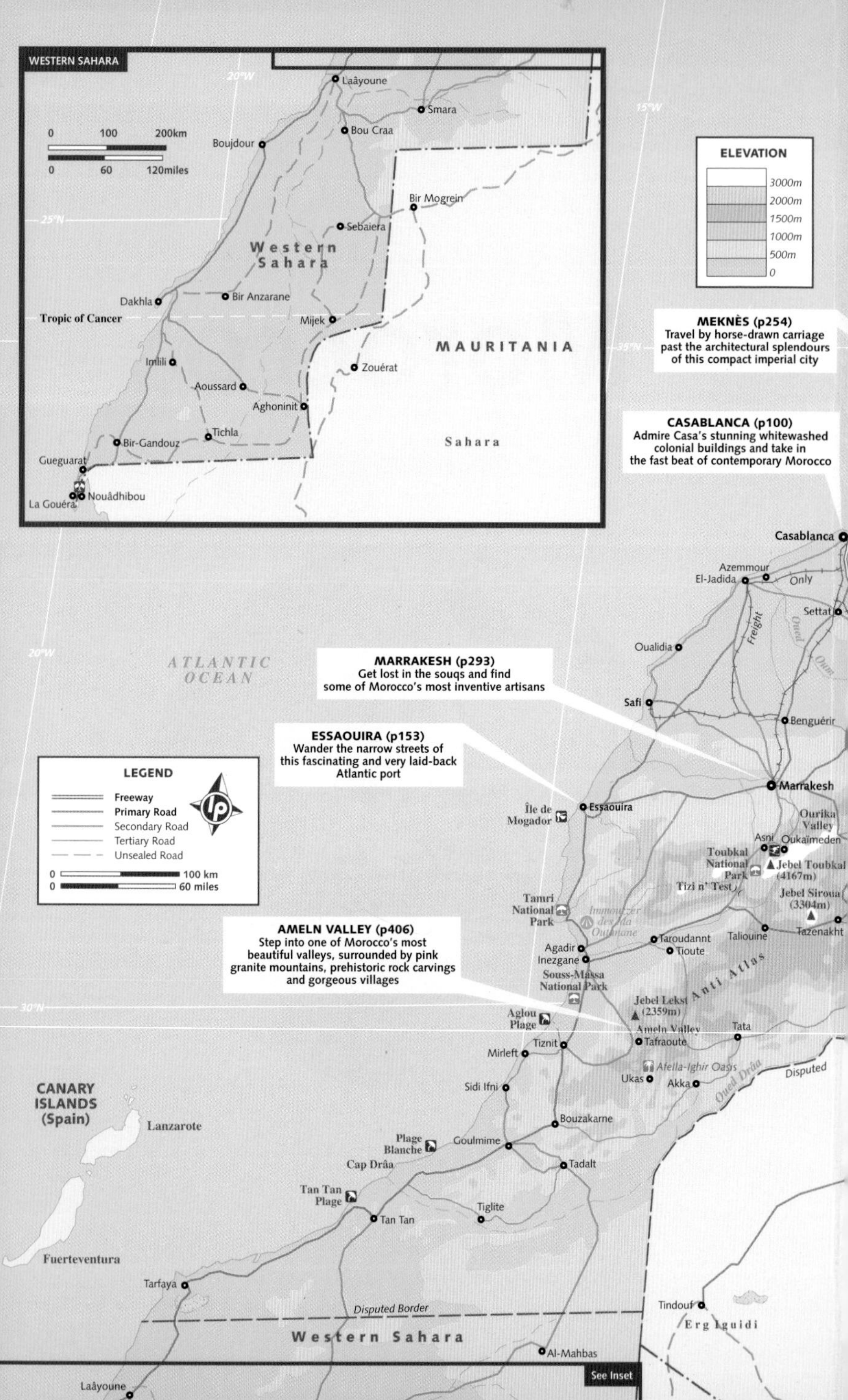
WESTERN SAHARA
Laâyoune
Smara
Bou Craa
Boujdour
Bir Mogrein
Sebaiera
Western Sahara
Bir Anzarane
Dakhla
Tropic of Cancer
Mijek
MAURITANIA
Imlili
Zouérat
Aoussard
Aghoninit
Tichla
Bir-Gandouz
Sahara
Gueguarat
Nouâdhibou
La Gouéra
ELEVATION
3000m
2000m
1500m
1000m
500m
0
MEKNÈS (p254)
Travel by horse-drawn carriage past the architectural splendours of this compact imperial city
CASABLANCA (p100)
Admire Casa's stunning whitewashed colonial buildings and take in the fast beat of contemporary Morocco
MARRAKESH (p293)
Get lost in the souqs and find some of Morocco's most inventive artisans
ESSAOUIRA (p153)
Wander the narrow streets of this fascinating and very laid-back Atlantic port
AMELN VALLEY (p406)
Step into one of Morocco's most beautiful valleys, surrounded by pink granite mountains, prehistoric rock carvings and gorgeous villages
ATLANTIC OCEAN
LEGEND
Freeway
Primary Road
Secondary Road
Tertiary Road
Unsealed Road
100 km
60 miles
Casablanca
Azemmour
El-Jadida
Settat
Oualidia
Safi
Benguérir
Marrakesh
Essaouira
Île de Mogador
Ourika Valley
Asni
Oukaïmeden
Toubkal National Park
Jebel Toubkal (4167m)
Tizi n' Test
Jebel Siroua (3304m)
Tamri National Park
Taliouine
Tazenakht
Agadir
Inezgane
Taroudannt
Tioute
Souss-Massa National Park
Anti Atlas
Jebel Lekst (2359m)
Aglou Plage
Ameln Valley
Tafraoute
Tata
Tiznit
Mirleft
Afella-Ighir Oasis
Ukas
Akka
Sidi Ifni
Disputed
CANARY ISLANDS (Spain)
Lanzarote
Bouzakarne
Plage Blanche
Goulmime
Cap Drâa
Tadalt
Tan Tan Plage
Tan Tan
Tiglite
Fuerteventura
Tarfaya
Disputed Border
Tindouf
Erg Iguidi
Western Sahara
Al-Mahbas
See Inset
Laâyoune

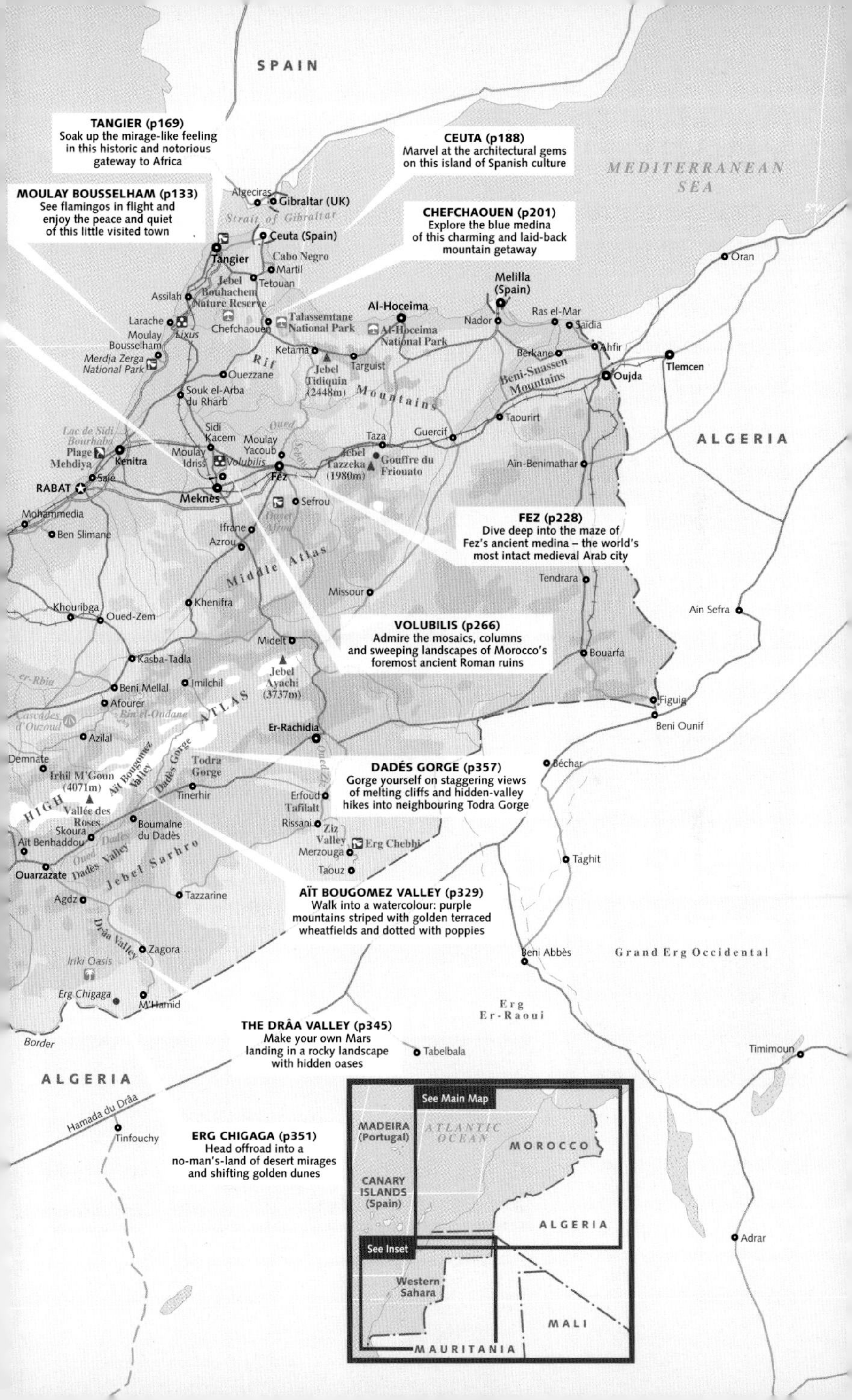

SPAIN

TANGIER (p169)
Soak up the mirage-like feeling in this historic and notorious gateway to Africa

CEUTA (p188)
Marvel at the architectural gems on this island of Spanish culture

MOULAY BOUSSELHAM (p133)
See flamingos in flight and enjoy the peace and quiet of this little visited town

CHEFCHAOUEN (p201)
Explore the blue medina of this charming and laid-back mountain getaway

MEDITERRANEAN SEA

FEZ (p228)
Dive deep into the maze of Fez's ancient medina – the world's most intact medieval Arab city

VOLUBILIS (p266)
Admire the mosaics, columns and sweeping landscapes of Morocco's foremost ancient Roman ruins

DADÉS GORGE (p357)
Gorge yourself on staggering views of melting cliffs and hidden-valley hikes into neighbouring Todra Gorge

AÏT BOUGOMEZ VALLEY (p329)
Walk into a watercolour: purple mountains striped with golden terraced wheatfields and dotted with poppies

THE DRÂA VALLEY (p345)
Make your own Mars landing in a rocky landscape with hidden oases

ERG CHIGAGA (p351)
Head offroad into a no-man's-land of desert mirages and shifting golden dunes

Algeciras
Gibraltar (UK)
Strait of Gibraltar
Ceuta (Spain)
Tangier
Cabo Negro
Martil
Tetouan
Jebel Bouhachem Nature Reserve
Assilah
Larache
Lixus
Chefchaouen
Talassemtane National Park
Al-Hoceima
Al-Hoceima National Park
Melilla (Spain)
Nador
Ras el-Mar
Saïdia
Oran
Moulay Bousselham
Merdja Zerga National Park
Ketama
Jebel Tidiquin (2448m)
Targuist
Rif Mountains
Berkane
Ahfir
Tlemcen
Beni-Snassen Mountains
Oujda
Ouezzane
Souk el-Arba du Rharb
Taourirt
Lac de Sidi Bourhaba
Plage Mehdiya
Kenitra
Sidi Kacem
Moulay Yacoub
Oued Sebou
Taza
Guercif
Moulay Idriss
Volubilis
Jebel Tazzeka (1980m)
Gouffre du Friouato
Aïn-Benimathar
ALGERIA
RABAT
Salé
Fez
Meknès
Sefrou
Mohammedia
Ben Slimane
Dayet Aaoua
Ifrane
Azrou
Middle Atlas
Tendrara
Missour
Khouribga
Oued-Zem
Khenifra
Aïn Sefra
Midelt
Bouarfa
Kasba-Tadla
Jebel Ayachi (3737m)
Oued er-Rbia
Beni Mellal
Imilchil
Afourer
Cascades d'Ouzoud
Bin el-Oudane
Azilal
HIGH ATLAS
Er-Rachidia
Figuig
Beni Ounif
Demnate
Aït Bougomez Valley
Dadès Gorge
Todra Gorge
Irhil M'Goun (4071m)
Tinerhir
Oued Ziz
Erfoud
Tafilalt
Béchar
Vallée des Roses
Skoura
Boumalne du Dadès
Rissani
Ziz Valley
Aït Benhaddou
Oued Dadès
Dadès Valley
Erg Chebbi
Merzouga
Ouarzazate
Jebel Sarhro
Taouz
Taghit
Agdz
Tazzarine
Drâa Valley
Zagora
Beni Abbès
Grand Erg Occidental
Iriki Oasis
Erg Chigaga
M'Hamid
Erg Er-Raoui
Border
Tabelbala
Timimoun
ALGERIA
Hamada du Drâa
Tinfouchy
Adrar

See Main Map
MADEIRA (Portugal)
ATLANTIC OCEAN
MOROCCO
CANARY ISLANDS (Spain)
ALGERIA
See Inset
Western Sahara
MALI
MAURITANIA

On the Road

PAUL CLAMMER Coordinating Author
This photo is actually an echo – I have an almost identical version from 1994, taken in annexe of the Mausoleum of Moulay Ismail in Meknès. In that shot I'm leafing through my Lonely Planet *Morocco, Algeria & Tunisia*. I'm not sure what I was thinking, but I'd be surprised it involved an inkling that I'd be back so many years later on the other side of the page...

ALISON BING That's me at the Kasbah Amerdil in the Skoura Oasis, admiring ancient castle-lock technology. I'm far from photogenic at the end of a 39°C day, but with Sidi Amerdil positively glowing to be showing his favourite family heirloom, grinning for the camera was easy.

ANTHONY SATTIN The area around Tafraoute has so many attractions, but my favourite were the ancient rock carvings south of town. There, in a barren landscape of shattered rocks and dried rivers, are images of elephants, horned cattle, big cats and other reminders that this was once covered with forests and rich savannah.

PAUL STILES The world's strangest national border: the narrow spit from Morocco to the Spanish fortress of El Peñón de Velez de la Gomera. At the end of a long desert canyon, it arises from the Mediterranean as if forgotten in time.

For full author biographies see p516.

Morocco Highlights

Morocco's sights, smells and sounds overload the senses. Selecting highlights is an impossible task as each traveller will walk away with their own version of the country. Below are some experiences that Lonely Planet authors, staff and fellow travellers count among the highlights of their trip. Do you agree with their choices, or have we missed your favourites? Go to www.lonelyplanet.com/morocco and tell us your highlights.

SUNE WENDELBOE

1 FEZ MEDINA

The first time I visited the Fez medina (p232) I got so lost I had to pay a small boy to rescue me and take me back to familiar ground. The second time too. After a while I realised that getting lost was half the point, blindly following alleys into hidden squares and souqs – the constant thrill of discovery. Years on and dozens of visits later, I know my way around pretty well, but those wrong turns are still there, hiding quietly and waiting for me to drop my guard and take me off on another adventure.

Paul Clammer, Lonely Planet author

SARA-JANE CLELAN

2 DJEMAA AL-FNA, MARRAKESH

Physical and metaphysical meld at the evening market on Djemaa el-Fna (p298), where all that seems missing is some magic dust. Instructions in Berber and Arabic emanate from whispering figures cloaked in jellabas, administering herbs and potions while *fakir* (holy men) and storytellers captivate the crowds. Ask a local to accompany you to decipher ancient parables, fathom the use of a dried camel foetus or hear your fortune revealed.

Debra Herrmann, Lonely Planet staff

CHRISTINE OSBORN

3 CASABLANCA NIGHTLIFE

Marrakesh may make the headlines, but Casablanca also has some fabulously varied nightlife (p114). Start the evening over a martini while Sam plays it again (and again) at Rick's Café. Head out to the Corniche in Ain Diab to party with Casablanca's beautiful people in the hip 1950s nightclubs. Then end the night watching the belly dancers strut their stuff at Transatlantique's seedy nightclub or in the raucous bars around downtown Casa's Marché Central.

Anthony Sattin, Lonely Planet author

TRAVELLING BY CAMEL

Gently swaying back and forth on the back of a ship of the desert (p453); the sand dunes endless and enchanting, eternal yet ever-changing; the colours beyond even the wildest imagination.

intrepid_living, traveller

4

JOHN ELK III

BRUNO MORANDI/GETTY IMAGE

5 LEGZIRA

This stretch of Atlantic coast is so wild and beautiful that almost anywhere you stop is a thrill, but Legzira (p398) wins hands down for the whole experience. You start with a huddle of hotels that seem to fall down the steep cliff to the beach. Each has its own café and restaurant that serves a mean grilled fish. Place your order when you arrive and then go for a walk along the beach. Most of the year you'll have the place to yourself – just you, the thundering waves and the ocean spray.

Anthony Sattin, Lonely Planet author

DOUG MCKINLA

6 MOULAY IDRISS

This holy town (p268) cresting two hills is a whitewashed gem. For years, foreigners were barred from spending the night here, but recently there's been a mini-boom in local families opening their homes up as guest houses, allowing you to get away from the nearby cities and drop your pace a gear. Tour groups only ever stop there for an hour during the day, so catching sunset over the town, and watching the locals promenade from the cafés on the main square were real treats.

Paul Clammer, Lonely Planet author

MERDJA ZERGA NATIONAL PARK

Even if you are not a birdwatcher, there are good reasons to head to the Merdja Zerga (p133; Blue Lagoon) at Moulay Bousselham. Relatively undiscovered, it is a laid-back little town with a sweeping beach, plenty of simple fish restaurants, the shrines of two holy men to protect your sanity, and a fleet of small fishing boats to take you out onto the tranquil lagoon, from where you can watch the birds or just lie back and enjoy the scenery.

Anthony Sattin, Lonely Planet author

7

FRANCES LINZEE GORDON

MOROCCO FOR PHOTOGRAPHERS

The blue nomadic Berbers' robes against the orange dunes. The sandstone kasbahs peeking out of bright green oases. The souqs and markets with their pyramids of oranges. The elegant lines and geometric symmetry of Islamic buildings (p470).

travelnut35, traveller

8

CHRIS MELLOR

CHRISTOPHER WOOD

9

CHEFCHAOUEN

The sun rises over the Rif Mountains as we drive. Chefchaouen (p201) is more beautiful than I imagined. The buildings are handcrafted blue-and-white artworks. I decide that I could stay here for a long time. I try my first tajine.

wordage_senhora, traveller

AÏT BOUGOMEZ VALLEY

A wrong turn at Imi-n-Ifri led me into valleys full of swaying golden wheat, dotted with red poppies and striped with purple rock walls. Just when I was thinking this couldn't get more Impressionist, a Berber woman dressed in a pinafore looked up from her work, smiled and waved hello with her scythe.

The live-action Monet took a prehistoric turn when I pulled over at the sign for dinosaur footprints. From nowhere, some kids appeared to help me clamber up rocks to see the faint depressions. We took turns doing T Rex impersonations; a kid named Mustafa was better than me, and he made me promise to practice.

A couple more turns, and I was back on the map and in the 21st century – and I was missing Aït Bougomez (p329) already.

Alison Bing, Lonely Planet author

10

SYLVESTER ADAMS/GETTY IMAGES

DUSHAN COORAY

GOATS!

Catching the bus from Tata to Agadir and looking out the window at the trees (argon trees – they are a bit like olives; p165) and then doing a double take at one tree – filled with goats. Goats: I kid you not (that pun was unintentional). What are goats doing up trees (and not on the lower branches – no no, swaying at the top)? Are there goats here with opposable thumbs?

Jenny Blake, traveller

11

ROAD TRIP: TIZI'N'TEST PASS

Drivers need a strong stomach for Morocco's highest pass (p336) over the aptly named High Atlas mountains, where one-lane hairpin bends take you through awe-inspiring scenery, past ancient mosques and Berber villages, with snow-covered peaks in the distance.

Robyn Dwyer, traveller

12

CHRISTOPHER WOO

MERZOUGA

After travelling in a grand taxi along a dusty road for hours, my boyfriend and I finally reached the remote village of Merzouga (p370). We found the isolated kasbah we were staying at (we were the only people staying there at the time so had the place to ourselves!) and unrolled our sleeping bags on the rooftop. We then sat back and watched the sun go down over the sand dunes and marvelled at the amazing fiery colours the dunes took on as the sun set over the horizon.

Catherine Menzies, Lonely Planet staff

SUNE WENDELBOE

ESSAOUIRA

The bright sun and Atlantic breeze in Essaouira (p153) never fails to blow the cobwebs away, and for me it's just about the perfect place to kick back at the close of a trip. I love poking about the alleys and sea walls, and walking on the sand for miles until you have the entire beach to yourself – before turning for home and choosing the catch of the day from the fish stalls by the port, grilled in front of you and served with a pile of bread and salad. The quintessential Essaouira experience!

Paul Clammer, Lonely Planet author

14

KRISTIN PILJAY

DOUG MCKINLA

15 ROAD TRIP: MARRAKESH TO OUARZAZATE

Driving into the dusty desert where sand obliterates the road, using our rental car as a makeshift bus for travelling salesmen, blind ladies and school kids – with the sun setting over the most amazing kasbah (p342) as you arrive.

Robyn Dwyer, traveller

DOUG MCKINLA

16 TALK DIRTY TO ME: HAMMAM LINGO

After Marrakesh's souqs, everyone needs a good soak. Head to a hammam (p454; bathouse) to get steamed, slimed with *savon noir* (palm soap), roughed up by a *tabbeya* (bath attendant) with a mean *kissa* (pumice glove), and doused with warm water. If the skin-sloughing ever approaches the blood-vessel-breaking point, just say, '*Shwiyya shwiyya*' ('Easy does it'). Some hammams follow this basic service with royal treatments: a soothing, cleansing *rhassoul* clay scalp-rub or full-body *argile* mud-mask with crushed herbs or rose petals, a fragrant orange-flower-water rinse, or a massage with emollient argan oil. Many layers of shed dead skin later – you'll be surprised and slightly aghast to see just how much was clogging your pores – you'll emerge from the hammam relaxed, refreshed and vowing to think clean thoughts, or at least apply more sunscreen.

Alison Bing, Lonely Planet author

RIADS

Behind its pink walls Marrakesh is hiding more authentic mud-brick riads (p310) than any other city in North Africa, including exuberantly ornamented examples from the 17th century. Over the past decade, hundreds of these historic family homes have been sold and reinvented as guest houses, mainly by European owners with Marrakshi staff.

Alison Bing, Lonely Planet author

17

JOHN ELK III

DO IT WITH A MULE!

Go to the Dadès Valley (p354), hire a guide, a muleteer and a mule (p421) to take you deep into its mountains. Your rewards: revealing conversations with your guides, delicious fresh rosemary tea served in man-made caves and landscapes that just don't quit!

alwaysanomad, traveller

18

JANE SWEENEY

SIDI IFNI, SOUSS VALLEY

It's worth the journey to Ifni (p396) and it's enough to come here if only to exhale. This former Spanish colonial outpost evokes exotic art deco. Here, just north of the Western Sahara, women's hijab flutter like flags in the winds that reel off the ocean; while fishermen, children and goats make their way down to the beach.

Debra Herrmann, Lonely Planet staff

OLIVIER CIRENDINI

20

HEMIS/ALAMY

19 IMPERIAL TEA IN FEZ

After a long day of walking and bargaining in Fez, make your evening special by enjoying a cup of tea on the terrace of the Palais Jamaï (p251), overlooking the medina and listening to the last chanting of the day

elsalmondigital, traveller

OLIVIER CIRENDINI

21 SMOKE AND SPECIAL COKE

Once used for public executions, the Djema el-Fna (p315) in Marrakesh is now a stage for the living. At night, clouds of smoke rise overhead, full of mouth-watering odors from grilled lamb, beef and chicken, fried calamari, spicy *harira* (lentil soup) and flaky chicken pastilla. 'Special Coke', cheap red wine in a cola bottle, adds the finishing touch.

thegnomad, traveller

ASSOCIATION DEVELOPMENT HART CHAOU COMMUNITY GARDEN PROJECY, DRÂA VALLEY

Where was this dusty track leading? I couldn't believe that here in the sunburned, bone-dry Drâa Valley was a life-saving organic community garden (p345). But around the turn, there it was: a lush little oasis that now provides 80% of the nutritional needs for 114 families, many of whom were going hungry just two years ago. Families were taking turns using the sole water source and village compost pile.

A man tending his fields waved me over. 'Try my fava beans,' he insisted. 'Take more, maybe you can start your own village garden. I hear in America, they have very big gardens.'

'Yes, but yours is great.'

He shook my hand, proudly. 'Come back next year, and try our tomatoes.'

Alison Bing, Lonely Planet author

22

JOHN ELK III

SAHARAN DUNES

Ride a camel from Morocco to the border of the Western Sahara and gaze into the yellow abyss of the Sahara Desert (p351). The countless sand dunes will greet you as the massive guardians to this unforgiving land, urging you to travel no further. The tiny footprints leading to the horizon and the sheer mystery of what's out in this golden nothing will invite you in.

Michael Veraz, traveller

23

SUNE WENDELBOE

DOUG MCKINL

24 LIFE OF SPICE

In the souqs of Marrakesh (p298), cinnamon, cumin, paprika, coriander, cloves and harissa are an all-you-can-smell buffet for the nose, sculpted into pyramids of red, gold, green and brown. There are spices for the body, too. Verbena, musk, amber, rosemary, eucalyptus and lavender all beckon you to unlock their secrets.

thegnomad, traveller

AMERENS HEDW

25 TOUBKAL TREK

The Kasbah at Toubkal is an island of calm. From every window a view to eternity, it seems. Mountains as far as the eye can see. Bald ridges, sunlit rocky slopes, the faintest blush of green on the nearest slopes. The Berber hosts all smiles even though there is little shared language. Cats bask in the sun, mules and donkeys bray. This is the most popular starting point for trekkers coming to climb Mt Toubkal (p425; a three-day climb). From our sunny living room one sees in the far distance tiny ants – in reality laden mules leading or guiding trekkers. There is a constant roar of water as the last of the winter snow melts and rushes down into the valleys.

Stephanie Alexander, traveller

Contents

Regional Map Contents

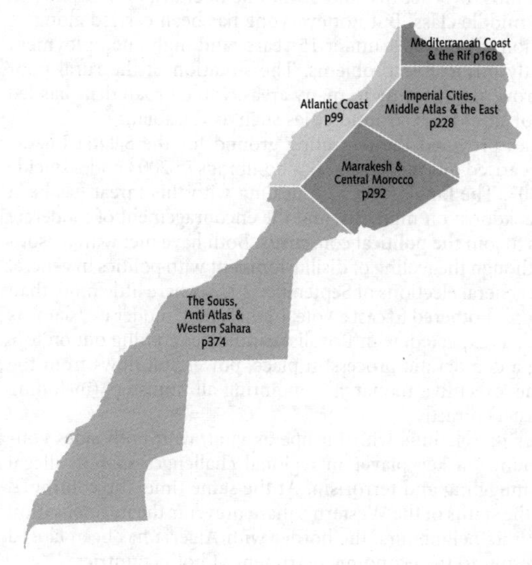

Destination Morocco

Morocco continues to tread a cautious path into the 21st century, facing up to the challenges imposed both by its official willingness to embrace globalisation and its deep traditional roots.

For most visitors, Morocco is primarily a tourist destination, and visitors are beginning to reap the rewards of the huge infrastructural projects driven by the government to meet King Mohammed VI's plan to attract 10 million tourists by the year 2010. Although rumours suggest that the date might be pushed back by a couple of years, recent years have seen an almost exponential rise in visitor numbers. A building boom has seen the great empty spaces that sat between Marrakesh and its airport now thickly planted with water-thirsty tourist hotels and apartments, with ground being broken on similar developments on the outskirts of Fez. The Mediterranean coast has seen even more startling changes, with expanding resorts following a new motorway improving access to this often-forgotten corner of the country. With the announcement of a high-speed rail link between Casablanca and Tangier, and the latter's huge new Renault-Nissan car plant, the signs all firmly declare that Morocco is open for business.

FAST FACTS

Population: 34.33 million

GDP per head: US$4555

External debt: US$19.9 billion

Life expectancy: 70.4 years

Adult literacy rate: 52.3%

Ranking on UN Human Development Index: 126 (of 177)

Population without access to an improved water source: 19%

Share of total world CO_2 emissions: 0.1%

But despite this showy embrace of modernity, the fault lines of Moroccan society are still there to be read by anyone looking beyond the style magazine–friendly riads of the Marrakesh medina, in the often conflicting outlooks of conservative and liberal society, secular and Islamic, urban and rural, Arab and Berber.

Development and investment in schools, roads and health care have been a boon to most Moroccans, and economic liberalisation has helped fuel a growing middle class. But not everyone has been carried along. A young population (nearly 30% under 15 years) and high unemployment remain currently intractable problems. The situation of the rural poor has yet to improve significantly in many areas, while urban drift has led to the growth of slum areas around cities such as Casablanca.

These shanties provided the recruiting ground for the Salafia Jihadia terrorists, who carried out the Casablanca bombings in 2003 and a suicide bombing in 2007. The king's policy on dealing with this threat has been two fold – a crackdown on militants, and the encouragement of moderate Islamist parties to join the political consensus. Both have met with reasonable success, although the feeling of disillusionment with politics in general was seen in the general elections of September 2007, where little more than one in three people bothered to cast a vote. In the ballot, moderate Islamists didn't do as well as expected, with Royalist candidates coming out on top. Despite having a democratic process in place, power still flows from the throne, with the 'executive monarch' appointing all ministers (including the prime minister) directly.

Morocco sees its relations with Europe as vital, with both sides considering the country a key player in regional challenges such as illegal immigration, smuggling and terrorism. At the same time, the continued stalemate over the status of the Western Sahara prevents the normalisation of relations with its neighbours: the border with Algeria has been closed for years as a result, to the economic detriment of both countries.

As a bridge between the Western and the Islamic worlds, Morocco plays an important and often-undervalued role. Careful negotiation between these poles, and the contradictions of its own society will be key challenges in the future.

Getting Started

Every trips bears some preparation time before you travel – not just to get a handle on the country you're visiting, but to give you time to enjoy the daydreams of what you'll do when you get there. This holds true especially for Morocco. The advent of the budget airlines has put it, for many, in the same bracket as just another short-haul destination, only a few hours from the major European capitals. But Morocco is far more than this: it's Africa and the Middle East rolled into one with all the rewards and challenges of the great continent and the culture of Islam. It is both a short ferry hop and a world away from Europe. Whether you're heading to the desert, the mountains or for a chic city break in a riad, forward planning with this guidebook in hand will help you get the most out of one of the most exciting travel destinations there is.

See Climate Charts on p458 for more information.

WHEN TO GO

Morocco is at its best in spring (mid-March to May), when the country is lush and green, followed by autumn (September to November) when the heat of summer has eased.

A popular saying has it that Morocco is a cold country with a hot sun, and you shouldn't underestimate the extremes of summer heat and winter, particularly in the High Atlas, where snowcapped peaks persist from November to July. If you are travelling in winter, head for the south, although be prepared for bitterly cold nights. Morocco's Mediterranean coast and Rif Mountains are frequently wet and cloudy in winter and early spring, and even Fez can be surprisingly cold.

Apart from the weather, it's the timing of Ramadan, the Muslim month of fasting and purification, which is another important consideration. During Ramadan some restaurants and cafés are closed during the day and general business hours are reduced – during the lifetime of this

DON'T LEAVE HOME WITHOUT...

- your ID card or passport and visa if required (p474)
- valid travel insurance (p467)
- driving licence, car documents and appropriate car insurance (p494) if driving
- loose-fitting cotton shirts and long skirts or trousers for women and men
- a universal washbasin plug or a tennis ball cut in half
- a few basic words of Arabic
- a good tent, warm sleeping bag and sturdy walking boots if you plan on trekking (p419)
- some wet-weather gear, preferably Gore-Tex
- a torch
- earplugs for successful sleeping in the noisier cheap hotels
- a water bottle, purification tablets and a medical kit (p499) for longer stays
- an emergency supply of toilet paper
- a sense of perspective – persistent shopkeepers are just trying to make a living and can actually be nice people
- patience – most things do run on time, but the timetable may be elusive to the uninitiated.

guidebook, Ramadan will fall during the hot summer months (for more details see p466).

COSTS & MONEY

Morocco isn't quite as cheap as you might think it is. Taking into account a few small tips, taxi fares, entry charges to museums, and with a willingness to stay in cheap hotels without respite, those carefully counting their dirhams could get by on Dh350 (US$40) per day. At the other end of the scale, if you intend to travel in style in cities like Marrakesh, expect your daily budget to increase dramatically – quality accommodation starts at Dh600, hovers around Dh1100 and then keeps going skyward. Staying in an average-priced riad and enjoying quality restaurants will require a budget of at least Dh1000 a day per person. Outside the major cities most of the better accommodation tends to hover around Dh600.

HOW MUCH?

Pot of mint tea Dh8

Hammam Dh8-12

Petit-taxi ride Dh5-10

City bus ride Dh2-3

Local sim card Dh30

A meal in a cheap restaurant costs as little as Dh30. In a midrange restaurant you'd pay up to Dh200 and in a more upmarket place it will cost around Dh300, including wine; in Marrakesh topping Dh500 to Dh700 wouldn't be uncommon.

If you want to explore the country in your own car, average hire charges for a small car (Renault Clio) are Dh500 per day. Petrol costs about Dh11 per litre, while diesel is cheaper at around Dh8 per litre. For a 4WD you are looking at about Dh1500 per day, with driver. Car hire is significantly cheaper if booked in advance rather than on the spot.

There's not much difference in price between trains and buses – a bus ticket between Casablanca and Marrakesh costs around Dh80, compared to Dh84 for a 2nd-class train ticket. As a general rule, a 100km bus or train journey costs about Dh28.

LANGUAGE

The official languages of Morocco are Moroccan Arabic (Darija) and French. Road signs are bilingual, although in the countryside and mountains French speakers aren't quite so common – Moroccan Berbers have their own languages (notably Tashelhit, Tarafit and Tamazight), and tend to speak Darija as their second language. English speakers tends to be commonplace only where you find tourists.

It repays the little effort needed to learn a few words or phrases in Darija. Other than Olympic tea-pouring skills, there's no better way to make friends and impress people in Morocco than to venture a few words in Darija or the local Berber language. Some Moroccans resent the fact that half a century on from independence, French is still the main language of trade. Even seen-it-all shopkeepers will be charmed by travellers attempting to use those few phrases of Tashelhit, Tarafit or Tamazight – quite a diplomatic coup, not to mention a real advantage when it comes to bargaining.

See the language chapter (p504) to get going with Darija and Berber.

TRAVELLING RESPONSIBLY

Since our inception in 1973, Lonely Planet has encouraged readers to tread lightly, travel responsibly and enjoy the magic independent travel affords. International travel is growing at a jaw-dropping rate, and we still firmly believe in the benefits it can bring – but, as always, we encourage you to consider the impact your visit will have on both the global environment and the local economies, cultures and ecosystems.

The recent boom in Morocco has brought in huge numbers of tourists, many of whom are unaware of the different attitudes to life, dress and behaviour in a Muslim country. To give yourself a head start on how your clothes can make the right or wrong impression, and to pick up a quick bit of local etiquette see boxed texts, p49 and p51.

Part of Morocco's tourist growth has been fuelled by the development of large hotel complexes and golf courses, both with an insatiable thirst for water in this dry country. Plunge pools of the sort found in riads tend to be better than Olympic-sized ones, with the added bonus that traditional architecture is designed to work with the environment rather than against it – thick mudbrick walls provide excellent insulation, and cut the need for energy-gobbling air-conditioning. There are more ideas on creative conservation of resources during your trip on p52.

For specific listings of more sustainable places to stay and activities, see the Greendex at the back of the book.

TRAVEL LITERATURE

The Caliph's House by Tahir Shah is a brilliant account of how a writer and filmmaker left behind London life to renovate the djinn-haunted former home of the caliph of Casablanca – overflowing with insight and Moroccan characters writ large. Check out his more recent *In Arabian Nights* for his delving into Morocco's rich storytelling tradition.

A young hippie takes her children to 1960s Marrakesh to find herself and an alternative life in Esther Freud's delightful and autobiographical *Hideous Kinky*. Famously made into a film starring Kate Winslet, the author's witty lightness-of-touch is even more engaging.

Morocco: In the Labyrinth of Dreams and Bazaars by Walter M Weiss is an ambitious journey through the contradictions of modern Morocco from its polyglot past to its modern liberal-conservative fault lines.

In *The Spider's House*, Paul Bowles presents Fez in the twilight of the French occupation as the arena for this political *tour de force* considered by many to be Bowles' finest. Daily Fez life, with its weblike complexities, provides a fascinating backdrop.

If you fancy living the riad dream, first check out *A House in Fez* by Suzanna Clarke, an excellent recounting of her purchase and restoration of a townhouse in the heart of the Fez medina, and the many challenges therein.

Tangier: City of the Dream by Iain Finlayson is a great book to pack if you're entering Morocco through this 'seedy, salacious, decadent, degenerate' city. There are plenty of insights into the Beat Generation of writers including Paul Bowles, William S Burroughs and Jack Kerouac.

'There are plenty of insights into the Beat Generation of writers including Paul Bowles, William S Burroughs and Jack Kerouac'.

Valley of the Casbahs: A Journey Across the Moroccan Sahara is an account of Jeffrey Taylers' epic modern-day camel journey from the Drâa Valley to the Atlantic, leaving behind tourist Morocco, with Berbers and a harsh desert terrain for company.

If you think your feet felt sore after a short hike in the mountains, you'll appreciate Hamish Brown's *The Mountains Look on Marrakech*, an expert walker's elegant account of his 900-mile 96-day trek from one end of the Atlas to the other.

Gavin Maxwell's *Lords of the Atlas* is a gripping story of intrigue and power amid the rise of the Glaoui family in southern Morocco. 'To call it a travel book is as inadequate as calling a camel a quadruped' wrote one reviewer, and we'd have to agree.

As guidebook writers we always appreciate the best in travel writing, and *Marrakech through Writers' Eyes* edited by Barnaby Rogerson and Rose Baring is like one of those feasts of endless Moroccan dishes that you can dip into again and again.

TOP 10

ESSENTIAL MOROCCAN EXPERIENCES

1. Enjoying a huge serving of couscous washed down with mint tea (p84)
2. Getting lost in any medina
3. Riding a camel into the sunset in the Sahara (p351)
4. Being hypnotised by the spectacle and colour of the Djemma el-Fna in Marrakesh (p298)
5. Pulling into Tangier (p169) by ferry across the Strait of Gibraltar
6. Haggling for carpets (pp67-8)
7. Being entranced while watching Gnawa musicians (p63)
8. Sweating the stress away in a hammam (pp453-4)
9. Watching the sun rise along one of the spectacular treks in the High Atlas Mountains (p423)
10. Lounging in an elegantly trendy riad (p452)

MUST-SEE MOROCCAN MOVIES

Cinematic Morocco comes in many guises from hard-hitting social commentaries, usually the work of contemporary Moroccan filmmakers, to Hollywood fantasy with its illusory idea of exotic North Africa.

1. *Morocco* (1930) Director: Josef von Sternberg
2. *Casablanca* (1942) Director: Michael Curtiz
3. *The Man Who Knew Too Much* (1956) Director: Alfred Hitchcock
4. *A Thousand and One Hands* (1972) Director: Souheil Ben Barka
5. *El Chergui* (1974) Director: Moumem Smihi
6. *Alyam Alyam* (1978) Director: Ahmed el Maanouni
7. *Le Coiffeur du Quartier des Pauvres* (1982) Director: Mohamed Reggab
8. *Hideous Kinky* (1998) Director: Gilles MacKinnon
9. *Ali Zaoua: Prince of the Streets* (2000) Director: Nabil Ayouch
10. *The Wind Horse* (2001) Director: Daoud Aoulad-Syad

FAVOURITE FESTIVALS

Moussems (festivals) honouring local saints are held across Morocco throughout the year, often drawing huge crowds. There is also a host of excellent international cultural events.

1. Almond Blossom Festival (Tafraoute and around; p463) February/March
2. Festival du Desert (Er-Rachidia, Merzouga and Rissani; p464) May
3. Moussem of Ben Aïssa (Meknès; p464) May/June
4. Gnaoua and World Music Festival (Essaouira; p464) June
5. Festival of World Sacred Music (Fez; p464) June/July
6. Festival International de Rabat (Rabat; p464) June/July
7. Marrakesh Popular Arts Festival (Marrakesh; p464) July
8. Timitar World Music Festival (Agadir; p464) July
9. International Cultural Festival (Assilah; p464) July/August
10. Marriage Festival (Imilchil; p464) September

INTERNET RESOURCES

The Lonely Planet website features the **Thorn Tree** (www.lonelyplanet.com/thorntree) bulletin board, where you can post questions and get the latest tips on Morocco.

Al-Bab (www.al-bab.com/maroc) Also called The Moroccan Gateway, Al-Bab has excellent links, especially for current affairs, news and good books about Morocco.

Maghreb Arts (www.maghrebarts.ma, in French) Up-to-the-minute coverage of theatre, film, music, festivals and media events in Morocco.

Maroc Blogs (http://maroc-blogs.com) Useful blog aggregator pulling in feeds from the entire Moroccan 'blogma' – blogging community.

Office National des Chemins de Fer (www.oncf.ma, in French) Official website of the Moroccan rail services with information on timetables and prices.

The View From Fez (http://riadzany.blogspot.com) News and views from Fez, but pulling in countrywide stories of interest to travellers.

Tourism in Morocco (www.tourism-in-morocco.com/index_en.php) Morocco's official tourist information site; user-friendly, with guided tours, links and news.

Itineraries

CLASSIC ROUTES

Covering around 500km, this route dives into the heart of Moroccan history and culture. The trip starts in the grand medieval cities of the north and sweeps through modern seats of power on the coast, before finishing in Marrakesh, the heart of Moroccan tourism.

IMPERIAL CITIES

Two Weeks / Fez to Marrakesh

Immerse yourself in cities once ruled by enlightened dynasties, who crossed the Strait of Gibraltar and pulled Europe out of its Dark Ages. Begin in **Fez** (p228), venerable heart of Morocco's religious and cultural life, and see modern Morocco and its rich antecedent crowd for space in the extraordinary medina. **Meknès** (p254) is embodied in the lavish palace built by Sultan Moulay Ismail. **Volubilis** (p266), easily Morocco's best-preserved ancient city, stands testament to the astonishing breadth of the Roman Empire. Nearby **Moulay Idriss** (p268), home to the shrine of the founder of Morocco's first imperial dynasty, is a wonderful antidote to the clamour of the cities.

Rabat (p117) is enjoying its third period as Morocco's capital. A modern city of elegant French streets, its quiet, 12th-century medina hints at former imperial grandeur. Street-savvy **Casablanca** (p100), Morocco's principal port and most prosperous city, has an energy and anarchy rivalled only by **Marrakesh** (p293), icon of today's Morocco, where centuries of souqs, street performers and imperial architecture form an intoxicating mix.

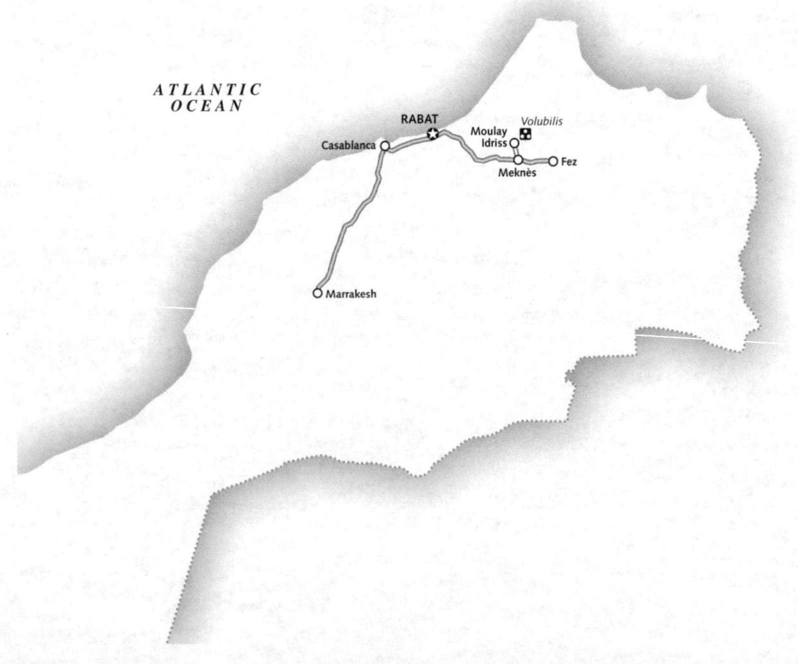

MOROCCAN ODYSSEY

One Month / Imperial Cities & the South

With a month at your disposal and taking little time to rest, you can get a taste of the best Morocco has to offer, by journeying from the sea to the Sahara and back again. Fly in to **Casablanca** (p100) before heading to **Meknès** (p254) and **Fez** (p228).

From Fez, leave behind the noise and hassles of the city and head directly south to the relatively under-visited Middle Atlas around **Azrou** (p272) where the Barbary apes are one of Moroccan wildlife's most mischievous sights. Pretty **Ifrane** (p270) also stands at the heart of some stunning mountain scenery and offers enticing possibilities for hiking in the lush countryside, although continuing south through **Midelt** (p275) is arguably even more scenic. The journey through the delightful palm-and-*ksar* (fortified stronghold) terrain of the **Ziz Valley** (p363) is one of Morocco's most picturesque roads and carries you down towards **Merzouga** (p370), southwestern Morocco's gateway to the Sahara. Lorded over by towering dunes, it's an ideal spot in which to saddle up your camel and sleep under the stars amid Morocco's largest sand sea, the perfectly sculpted **Erg Chebbi** (p370).

Shadowing the High Atlas as you head southwest brings you to the sharp cleft of the **Todra Gorge** (p360). From here, you can travel through dramatic boulder-strewn valleys, full of nomad camps in springtime, into the **Dadès Gorge** (p357). If time allows, strike out from Boumalne du Dadès for some spectacular trekking around the **M'Goun Massif** (p437) before making for **Aït Benhaddou** (p339) which seems like an evocation of a fairytale.

En route to the coast, check into a luxurious riad in **Marrakesh** (p293), stay as long as you can, and then don't stop until you reach artsy **Essaouira** (p153).

You could get from Casablanca to Essaouira in a few hours. But it's far more fun to take in a thorough picture of Morocco en route. A month-long diversion takes in the best of the imperial cities, the Atlas mountains and the Saharan sand dunes.

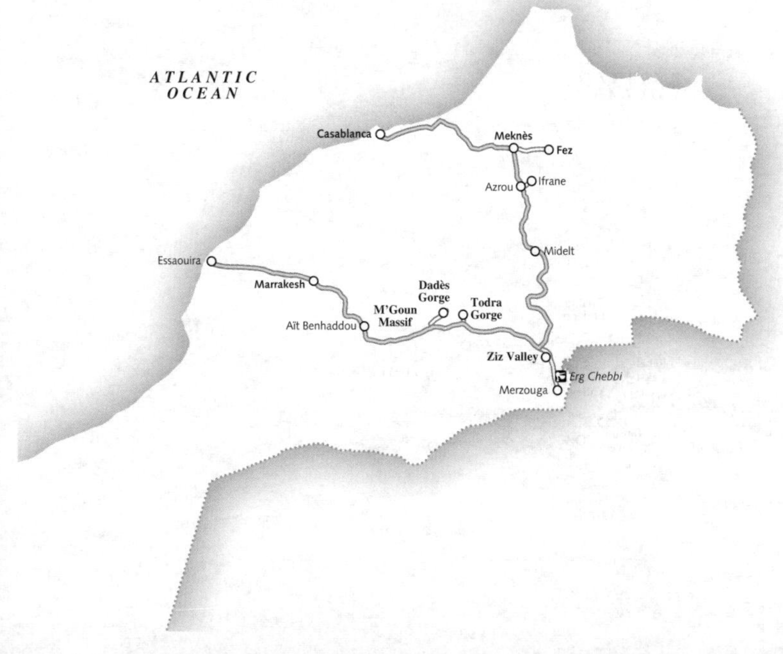

CIRCLING THE SOUTH

Three Weeks / Agadir & the Souss

This 1000km journey will sweep you through the cream of Morocco's landscapes: the peaks of the Atlas mountains, the sandscapes of the desert and the kasbah-studded valleys of the south. Parts of the trip can be hard to access, so having you own wheels, and three weeks on the calendar will help you get the most out of this itinerary.

Morocco is far more than trendy riads (town houses) and tourist hordes shuttling between hotel, souq and sun lounger. This itinerary will take you deep into the south for wild mountain and desert landscapes, far from the madding crowds and with plenty of activities to keep mind and body exercised.

Agadir is a handy entry point to Morocco, but adventurers will want to leave quickly. Head first to tiny **Tafraoute** (p402) encircled by the beautiful **Ameln Valley** (p406) with its lush, green *palmeraies* (palm groves) and pink-hued houses. Hire a bike and camp by the painted rocks, spend three days climbing **Jebel Lekst** (p406), or trek through the **Aït Mansour Gorges** (p405) where the beautiful scenery contrasts poignantly with the ancient slave routes that once passed this way. Stay in **Tiwadou** (p405) then journey overland to see the rock engravings at **Ukas** (p406) before returning to Tafraoute.

By now you've a taste for the Moroccan wilderness so head east to the magnificent rock engravings around **Akka** (p407) and **Tata** (p407), then down to **Erg Chigaga** (p351), dunes that see few tourists. Leave your vehicle in M'Hamid and find yourself a camel to lead you north into the kasbah-littered **Drâa Valley** (p345).

At **Ouarzazate** (p340), go quad biking in the stony desert landscape famous for its film studios, then loop back through the saffron capital of **Taliouine** (p391) with a detour for a trekking reprise on the **Tichka Plateau** (p435). Forge on to **Taroudannt** (p387) with its red walls, backdrop of snow-capped peaks and hassle-free echoes of Marrakesh, before heading back to **Agadir** (p379) for the much-needed robust pampering of a hammam.

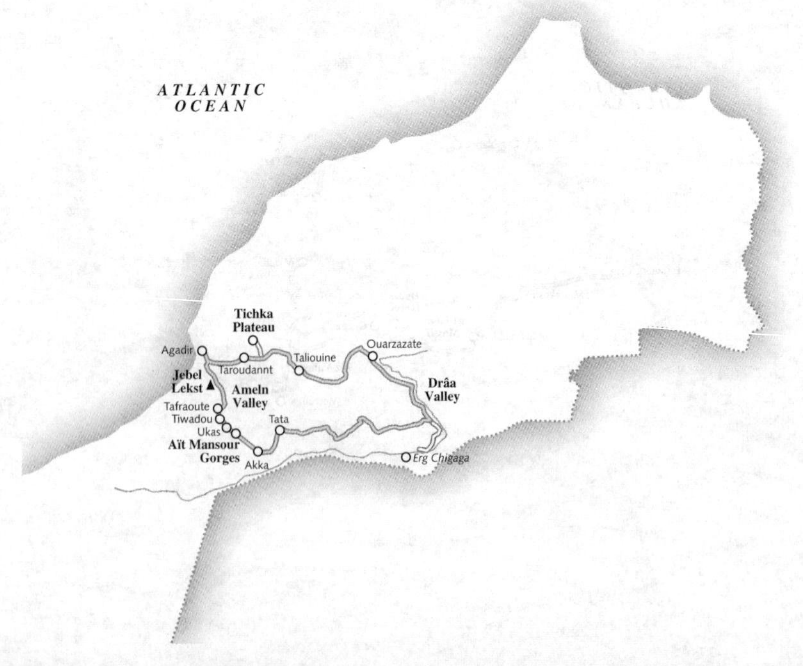

THE MED & THE MOUNTAINS

Three Weeks / Mediterranean Coast / Rif Mountains & Imperial Cities

While the previous itinerary suggested heading south to escape the crowds, an equally good alternative is to look at Morocco's Mediterranean littoral and Rif Mountains. The region has seen huge investment from the government in recent years and there are big plans to push tourism in the area – but if you get in now you'll be ahead of the curve.

Start out in **Tangier** (p169), ideally arriving by ferry across the Strait of Gibraltar at this legendary port city. After a few days taking in the history, nightlife and restaurants, skip inland to **Tetouan** (p194), the old capital of Spanish Morocco, with its charming blend of Arab medina and Andalusian architecture. The Spanish left a lighter imprint on nearby **Chefchaouen** (p201), nestled in the Rif Mountains with its gorgeous blue-painted medina. It's a good trekking spot too, and you can head deep into the mountains on a five-day trek via **Akchour** (p443) to the tiny fishing village of Bou Ahmed. Continue east along the coast to **Al-Hoceima** (p211), gateway to the **National Park of Al-Hoceima** (p214) where you can also hike and enjoy homestays with local Berber families. There's more fine scenery to be enjoyed further inland at the **Beni-Snassen Mountains** (p225) and the achingly beautiful and flower-filled **Zegzel Gorge** (p226).

From here, head to **Oujda** (p283) to refresh yourself with some city comforts, before taking the train to that grandest of imperial cities, **Fez** (p228). Dive into the medina and relax in a riad, but if you find yourself missing the countryside, you can still make an easy day (or several-day) trip into the cedar-clad Middle Atlas around the Berber market town of **Azrou** (p272).

Northern Morocco has always been low on the traveller's radar, but this three-week trip helps redress the balance. Sea ports, mountain villages and national parks are all part of the itinerary, with plenty of virgin hiking territory to savour on foot.

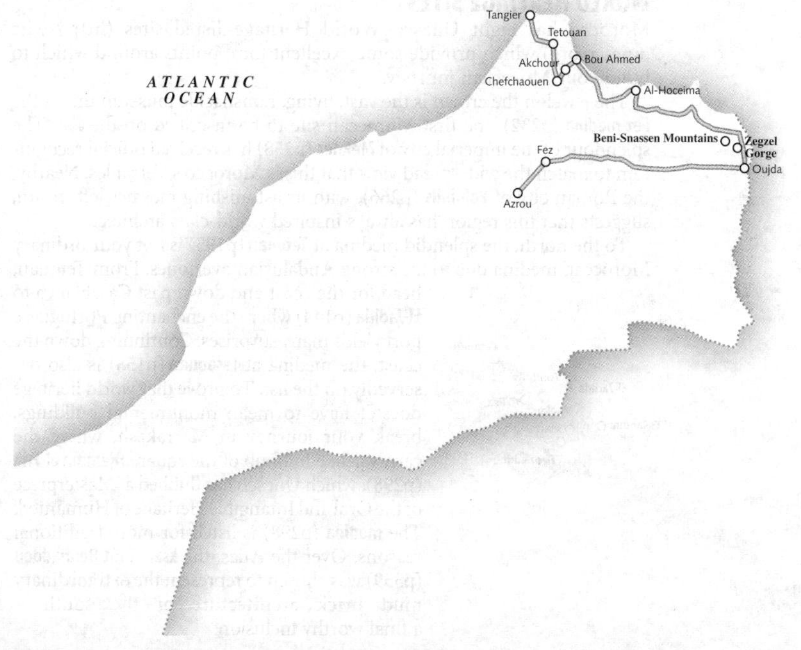

TAILORED TRIPS

ATLANTIC ADVENTURE

Morocco's Atlantic seaboard takes you from the clamour of the north to the deserted coastline of the south.

Take the ferry from Spain to **Tangier** (p169), at once a quintessentially Moroccan mosaic and a decadent outpost of Europe. Catch the train south, first to artsy **Assilah** (p139), which is loaded with whitewashed charms, and then to **Casablanca** (p100) with its melange of art deco and skyscrapers. Follow Casa's suburbanites to **El-Jadida** (p144) then visit **Oualidia** (p149), a St Tropez lookalike grafted onto the African coast and arrayed around a perfect crescent lagoon. Further down the coast, **Essaouira** (p153) may have been discovered long ago, but its white-walled ramparts, bohemian beat and renovated riads have that special something that makes travellers stay longer than they planned. The peaceful beaches of **Diabat** (p166) and **Sidi Kaouki** (p166) are close at hand.

For family-friendly beaches head on to **Agadir** (p375) or escape the crowds further south in **Mirleft** (p395) or **Sidi Ifni** (p396). If you're heading south to Mauritania, break your journey at **Laâyoune** (p411), the biggest city in the Sahara, and then **Dakhla** (p414).

WORLD HERITAGE SITES

Morocco has eight Unesco World Heritage–listed sites (http://whc.unesco.org) which provide some excellent focal points around which to build your Moroccan journey.

The jewel in the crown is the vast, living, ramshackle museum that is the **Fez medina** (p232), the first Moroccan site to be inscribed on the list. The splendour of the imperial city of **Meknès** (p258) has received official recognition to match the widespread view that this is Morocco's Versailles. Nearby, the Roman city of **Volubilis** (p266), with its astonishing mosaics left *in situ*, suggests that this region has always inspired world-class architects.

To the north, the splendid medina at **Tetouan** (p195) is not your ordinary Moroccan medina due to the strong Andalusian overtones. From Tetouan, head for the coast and down past Casablanca to **El-Jadida** (p144) where the enchanting Portuguese port yields many surprises. Continuing down the coast, the medina at **Essaouira** (p158) is also deservedly on the list. To prove that world heritage doesn't have to mean monumental buildings, break your journey in Marrakesh, where the carnival-like hubbub of the square **Djemma el-Fna** (p298), which Unesco has dubbed a 'Masterpiece of the Oral and Intangible Heritage of Humanity'. The **medina** (p298) is listed for more traditional reasons. Over the Atlas, the **ksar of Aït Benhaddou** (p339) was chosen to represent the extraordinary mud brick architecture of the south – a final worthy inclusion.

A MOROCCAN CULINARY TOUR

Morocco's culinary capital of Fez offers pleasures that travellers of all budgets can enjoy, from the local *b'sara* (a butterbean and garlic soup) and snails served at **stalls** (p249) all over town to some of the splendid riad restaurants like **Dar Roumana** (p248). The nearby small Berber town of Sefrou is worth a visit in June for its annual **Cherry Festival** (p254). Marrakesh is a feast in more ways than you can imagine but you can learn how to make your own at one of the **cooking schools** (p307) in the city. As you continue further south, saffron-scented Taliouine does more than produce saffron – at the **Coopérative Souktana du Safran** (p391) there's a saffron museum, saffron tasting and a saffron shop. *Mechoui* (spit-roasted lamb) is a High Atlas speciality, so pause in Taroudannt at **Jnane Soussia** (p390) before continuing on your way. At Tamanar, located 80km north of Agadir, make for **Coopérative Amal** (p165), where they'll tell and show you everything you need to know about argan oil, which is unique to Morocco. Away to the southeast, the villages of the **Ameln Valley** (p406) are known for their food festivals; if you're here in late February, the **almond harvest** (p402) around Tafraoute is a wonderfully food-focused celebration, although the delicious *amlou* (honey-and-almond paste made with argan oil) is available year-round. For regional Moroccan specialities, see Been There, Eaten That, p80.

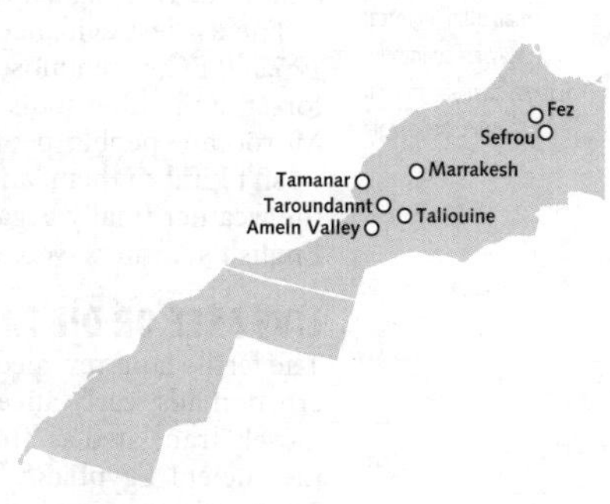

NATIONAL PARKS

Many trips to Morocco revolve around the inevitable axis of the imperial cities, taking in a camel trip to see the Sahara. But Moroccan landscapes revolve around more than just minarets and sand dunes, and there are some great national parks to be explored.

Easy to reach from Marrakesh, the national park at **Jebel Toubkal** (p425) takes you straight into the High Atlas mountains for some dramatic scenery and the chance to climb Mt Toubkal, North Africa's highest mountain. Southeast from here and near Agadir, **Souss-Massa National Park** (p384) is a more varied park, with a mix of estuary, for birdwatching, and forest to hike in. Travelling north along the coast past Rabat, **Lac de Sidi Bourhaba** (p133) has wetlands that attract large numbers of migratory water birds, and you can also take a dip and go swimming yourself. The lagoons of nearby **Merdja Zerga National Park** (p133) at Moulay Bousselham are famous for their flamingo colonies. Heading inland, Chefchaouen is the ideal base from where you can explore **Talassemtane National Park** (p444). The Rif Mountains here are clad in oak and cedar forests, and as you trek through you stand a good chance of seeing a troop of Barbary apes. On the Mediterranean coast, the **National Park of Al-Hoceima** (p214) is also ideal hiking country, with its forests and limestone cliffs, and community-led tourism project. **Tazzeka National Park** (p282) near Taza is the last on the circuit, with striking Middle Atlas scenery of pretty waterfalls, and birdlife.

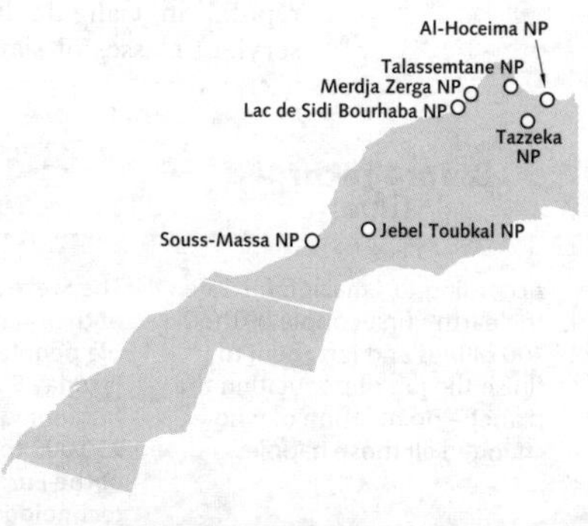

History

PREHISTORIC FLASHBACKS

Even when you see Morocco for the first time, you might experience déjà-vu. Maybe you recognise Morocco's green oases, striped purple canyons and rose-gold sand dunes from paintings by Henri Matisse, Winston Churchill or Jacques Majorelle. But there's a deeper, primordial connection here too. Exposed fossil deposits in the Anti Atlas make prehistory look like it was only yesterday, and High Atlas petroglyphs transmit mysterious messages across millennia. In the Atlas Mountains, Saharan steppes and red-earth valleys you can mark the exact strata where tectonic plates shifted billions of years ago, and civilisation surfaced from a rugged seabed.

The first movie shot in Berber was *Jesus' Film*, but the missionary movie missed its mark: its European distributors received mail from Moroccan viewers suggesting changes to make the film more believable.

The earliest evidence of human settlement here dates from 75,000 to 125,000 BC, when most of North Africa was covered in lush semitropical forest, and stone tools were cutting-edge technology. What the proto-Moroccan 'pebble people' really needed were radiators. The Ice Age wasn't kind to them, and left the country wide open for settlement when the weather finally began to improve around 5000 BC (and you thought English summers were gloomy).

LIVE FREE OR DIE TRYING: THE BERBERS

The fertile land revealed after the great thaw was a magnet for Near Eastern nomads, early ancestors of Morocco's Amazigh (plural Imazighen, loosely translated as 'free people') who may have been distant cousins of the ancient Egyptians. They were joined by Mediterranean anglers and Saharan horse-breeders around 2500 BC. Phoenicians appeared around 800 BC and East Africans around 500 BC, and when the Romans arrived in the 4th century they didn't know quite what to make of this multicultural milieu. The Romans called the expanse of Morocco and Western Algeria 'Mauretania' and the indigenous people 'Berbers,' meaning 'barbarians'. The term has recently been reclaimed and redeemed by the Berber Pride movement (see p35), but at the time it was taken as quite a slur.

For news feeds, links and articles in English and French on Amazigh culture, history and politics, visit www.amazigh-voice.com, an online Berber Pride forum.

The ensuing centuries were one long lesson for the Romans in minding their manners. First the Berbers backed Hannibal and the Carthaginians against Rome in a rather serious spat over Sicily known as the Punic Wars (264–202 BC). Fed up with the persistently unruly Berbers, the new Roman Emperor Caligula finally declared the end of Berber autonomy in the Maghreb (North Africa) in AD 40. True to his ruthless reputation, Caligula divided relatively egalitarian Berber clans into subservient classes of slaves, peasants, soldiers and Romanised aristocrats.

TIMELINE

Before recorded time...

According to Amazigh folklore, the earth's first couple birthed 100 babies and left them to finish the job of populating the planet – no mention of who changed all those nappies.

1–1½ million years ago

The Steve Jobs and Bill Gates of their day, precocious 'pebble people' living near what is today Casablanca begin fashioning stone tools some 250,000 to 700,000 years ahead of the European Stone-Age technology curve.

5000–2500 BC

Once the Ice Age melts away, the Maghreb becomes a melting pot of Saharan, Mediterranean and indigenous people. They meet, mingle and merge into a diverse people: the Amazigh.

WHEN PURPLE WAS PURE GOLD

The port that is today called Essaouira was hot property in ancient times, because it had one thing everyone wanted: the colour purple. Imperial purple couldn't be fabricated, and was the one colour strictly reserved for Roman royalty. This helps explain the exorbitant asking price, which according to Aristotle was 10 to 20 times its weight in gold. The natural dye came from the spiky murex marine snails that clung to the remote Purpuraire (Purple) Islands – as though that could save them from the clutches of determined Roman fashionistas.

Technically the Phoenicians were there first and discovered the stuff, but everyone wanted purple power. Savvy King Juba II established a coastal dye works in the 1st century BC to perform the tricky task of extracting murex dye from the vein of the mollusc, and kept his methods a closely guarded secret. The hue became wildly popular among royal celebrities of the day; Cleopatra loved the stuff so much that she dyed the sails of her royal barge purple to meet Mark Antony.

But violet soon turned to violence. Legend has it that Juba's son Ptolemy was murdered by Emperor Caligula for having the audacity to sport a purple robe, making trendy Ptolemy possibly the world's first fashion victim. The bright, nonfading dye was never successfully produced commercially, and the secret extraction methods were assumed lost in the siege of Constantinople in 1453. But in Essaouira the stuff is mysteriously still available, for a price. The mysteries of the colour purple are still passed down from one generation of murex collectors to the next, and jealously guarded.

This strategy worked with Vandals and Byzantines, but Berbers in the Rif and the Atlas were another story. They drove out the Romans with a campaign of near-constant harassment – a tactic that would later oust unpopular Moroccan sultans, and is still favoured by certain carpet salesmen today. Many Berbers refused to worship Roman gods, and some practiced the new renegade religion of Christianity right under Roman noses. Christianity took root across North Africa; St Augustine himself was a Berber convert.

Ultimately Rome was only able to gain a sure foothold in the region by crowning local favourite Juba II king of Mauretania. The enterprising young king married the daughter of Mark Antony and Cleopatra, supported scientific research and performing arts, and helped foster Moroccan industries still vital today: olive-oil production from the region of Volubilis (near Meknès), fishing along the coasts and vineyards on the Atlantic plains. Today you can still see Roman mosaics that were cut in Italy and assembled by Volubilis artisans into a curvy, sexpot goddess Diana – a hint of the stunning *zellij* (fitted mosaic) masterworks to come under Moroccan dynastic rule.

The most comprehensive Berber history in English is *The Berbers* by Michael Brett and Elizabeth Fentress. The authors leave no stone carving unturned, providing archaeological evidence to back up their historical insights.

The Roman foothold in Mauretania slipped in the centuries after Juba II died, due to increasingly organised Berber rebellions inland and attacks on the Atlantic and Mediterranean coasts by the Vandals, Byzantines and Visigoths. But this new crop of marauding Europeans couldn't manage

1600 BC

Bronze Age petroglyphs in the High Atlas depict fishing, hunting and horseback riding – a versatile combination of skills and cultures that would define the adaptable, resilient Amazigh.

950 BC

Amazigh rebuff Romans and their calendar year, and start tracking Berber history on their own calendar on January 13. Even after the Muslim Hejira calendar is introduced centuries later, the Berber calendar is maintained.

800–500 BC

The Maghreb gets even more multiculti as Phoenicians and East Africans join the Berbers, making the local population makeup as complex as a *ras al hanout* spice blend.

Mauretania, and neither could Byzantine Emperor Justinian. Justinian's attempt to extend his Holy Roman Empire turned out to be an unholy mess of treaties with various Berber kingdoms, who played their imperial Byzantine connections like face cards in high-stakes games. The history of Morocco would be defined by such strategic gamesmanship among the Berbers, whose savvy, competing alliances helped make foreign dominion over Morocco a near-impossible enterprise for more than a millennium.

THE POWER OF CONVICTION

By the early 7th century, the Berbers of Morocco were mostly worshipping their own indigenous deities, alongside Jewish Berbers and a smattering of local Christian converts. History might have continued thus, but for a middle-aged man thousands of miles away who'd had the good fortune to marry a wealthy widow, and yet found himself increasingly at odds with the elites of his Arabian Peninsula town of Mecca. This was no ordinary midlife crisis. Mohammed bin Abu Talib was his given name, but he would soon be recognised as the Prophet Mohammed for his revelation that there was only one God, and that believers shared a common duty to submit to God's will. The polytheist ruling class of Mecca did not take kindly to this new religion that assigned them shared responsibilities and took away their minor-deity status, and kicked the Prophet out of town on 16 July AD 622.

An incisive look at religious life on opposite ends of the Muslim world, anthropologist Clifford Geertz's groundbreaking *Islam Observed: Religious Development in Morocco and Indonesia* reveals complex variations within the vast mosaic of Islam.

This Hejira (exile) only served to spread the Prophet Mohammed's message more widely. By the Prophet's death in AD 632, Arab caliphs – religious leaders inspired and emboldened by his teachings – were carrying Islam east to Central Asia and west to North Africa. But infighting limited their reach in North Africa, and it took Umayyad Arab leader Uqba bin Nafi until 682 to reach the Atlantic shores of Morocco. According to legend, Uqba announced he would charge into the ocean, if God would only give him the signal. But the legendary Algerian Berber warrior Queen Al-Kahina would have none of Uqba's grandstanding, and with her warriors soon forced Uqba to retreat back to Tunisia.

Although an armed force failed to win the Berbers over to Islam, force of conviction gradually began to succeed. The egalitarian premise of Islam and its emphasis on duty, courage and the greater good were compatible with many Berber beliefs, including clan loyalty broadly defined to include almost anyone descended from the Berber equivalent of Adam and Eve. Many Berbers willingly converted to Islam – and not incidentally, reaped the benefits of Umayyad overland trading routes that brought business their way. So although Uqba was killed by his Berber foes before he was able to establish a solid base in Morocco, by the 8th century his successors were able to pull off this feat largely through diplomatic means.

4th–1st century BC

Romans arrive to annex Mauretania and 250 years later, they're still trying, with limited success and some Punic Wars to show for their troubles.

49 BC

North African King Juba I supports renegade General Pompey's ill-fated power play against Julius Caesar. Rome is outraged – but then Roman senators pick up where Pompey left off, and assassinate Caesar a few years later.

25 BC–AD 23

Rome gets a toehold in Mauretania with farms, cities and art, thanks to North African King Juba II. He expands Volubilis into a metropolis of 20,000 mostly Berber residents, including a sizeable Jewish Berber community.

BERBER PRIDE & PREJUDICE

Despite a rich tradition of poetry, music and art dating as far back as 5000 BC, the Amazigh were often misconstrued as uneducated by outsiders, because no standard written language had been consistently applied to their many distinct languages. The Romans tried for 250 years to take over Amazigh territory and institute Roman customs – and when they failed they bad-mouthed them, calling them 'Berbers', or Barbarians. The name stuck, and so did anti-Amazigh prejudice among foreigners.

The Protectorate established French as the official language of Morocco to make it easier to conduct (and hence control) business transactions and affairs of state. Complex Amazigh artistic symbolism and traditional medicine were dismissed as charming but irrelevant superstition by those not privy to the oral traditions accompanying them, and the educated classes were encouraged to distance themselves from their Berber roots.

After independence (1955–6), Arabic became the official language, though French continues to be widely spoken among the elite. Since the Quran was written in Arabic, Moroccan religious instruction was in Arabic, and a hybrid Moroccan Arabic dialect (Darija) emerged in cities as a way to communicate across the many Berber languages. But Amazigh languages and traditions have persisted in Morocco, and the Berber Pride movement has recently reclaimed 'Berber' as a unifying term.

More than 60% of Moroccans now call themselves Amazigh or Berber, and Berber languages are currently spoken by upwards of 12 to 15 million Moroccans. Tashelhit is the most common Berber language, and is widely spoken in central Morocco. You'll also hear Tarifit along the Rif, Tamazight in the Middle Atlas and Tuareg in the Sahara. With the backing of King Mohammed VI – who is part Berber himself – the ancient written Tifinagh alphabet is now being taught in some schools as a standardised written Berber. Within the next decade, Berber will be taught in public schools across Morocco, along with the new lingua franca of trade and tourism: English.

THE CONVICTION OF POWER

The admiration between the Berbers and the Arab Umayyads was not always mutual, however. While the Umayyads respected Jews and Christians as fellow believers in the word of a singular God, they had no compunction about compelling polytheist Berbers to pay special taxes and serve as infantry (read: cannon fodder). The Umayyads greatly admired Berber women for their beauty, but this wasn't necessarily advantageous; many were conscripted into Umayyad harems.

Even the Berbers who converted to Islam were forced to pay tribute to their Arab overlords. A dissident school of Islamic thought called Kharijism critiqued the abuses of power of the Umayyads as a corruption of the faith, and called for a new moral leadership. In the mid-8th century, insurrections erupted across North Africa. Armed only with slings, a special force of Berbers defeated the elite Umayyad guard. The Umayyads were soon cut off from Spain and Morocco, and local leaders took over an increasingly lucrative trade in silver from the Western Sahara, gold from Ghana and slaves from West Africa.

Moulay Ismail was pen pals with England's James II and Louis XIV of France, and tried to convert the Sun King to Islam by mail.

200–429

Vandals and Visigoths take turns forcing one another out of Spain and onto the shores of Morocco, until local Rif warriors convince them to bother the Algerians instead.

533

Justinian rousts the last Vandals from Morocco, but his grand plans to extend the Holy Roman Empire are soon reduced to a modest presence in Essaouira, Tangier and Salé.

662–682

Arabs invade the Maghreb under Umayyad Uqba bin Nafi, introducing Islam to the area. Berber warriors eventually boot out the Umayyads, but decide to keep the Quran.

DYNASTIC DRAMAS

Looking back on early Berber kingdoms, the 14th-century historian Ibn Khuldun noted a pattern that would repeat throughout Moroccan dynastic history. A new leadership would arise determined to do right, make contributions to society as a whole and fill the royal coffers, too. When the pursuit of power and royal comforts began to eclipse loftier aspirations, the powers that be would forfeit their claim to moral authority. A new leadership would arise determined to do right, and the cycle would begin all over again.

So it was with the Idrissids, Morocco's first great dynasty. A descendant of the Prophet Mohammed's daughter Fatima, Idriss I fled Arabia for Morocco in AD 786 after discovering ambitious Caliph Haroun ar-Rashid's plan to murder his entire family. But Idriss didn't exactly keep a low profile. After being proclaimed an imam (religious leader) by the local Berbers, he unified much of northern Morocco in the name of Islam. Just a few days after he'd finally settled into his new capitol at Fez in 792, Haroun ar-Rashid's minions finally tracked down and poisoned Idriss I. Yet death only increased Idriss I's influence; his body was discovered to be miraculously intact five centuries later, and his tomb in the hillside town of Moulay Idriss (p268) remains one of the holiest pilgrimage sites in Morocco.

Queen Al-Kahina had one distinct advantage over the Umayyads: second sight. The downside? She foretold her own death at the hands of her enemy.

His son Idriss II escaped Haroun's assassins and extended Idrissid control across northern Morocco and well into Europe. In perhaps the first (but certainly not the last) approximation of democracy in Morocco, Idriss II's 13 sons shared power after their father's death. Together they expanded Idrissid principates into Spain and built the glorious mosques of Fez: the Kairaouine (p233) and the Andalous.

WARRIORS UNVEILED: THE ALMORAVIDS

With religious leaders and scholars to help regulate trade, northern Morocco began to take shape as an economic entity under the Idrissids. But the south was another story. A dissident prophet emerged near Salé brandishing a Berber version of the Quran, and established an apocryphal Islam called Barghawata that continued to be practised in the region for centuries. The military strongmen who were left in control of trading outposts in the Atlas Mountains and the Sahara demanded what they called 'alms' – bogus religious nomenclature that didn't fool anyone, and stirred up resentments among the faithful.

From this desert discontent arose the Sanhaja, the pious Saharan Berber tribe that founded the Almoravid dynasty. While the Idrissid princes were distracted by disputes over Spain and Mediterranean Morocco, the Sanhaja swept into the south of Morocco from what is today Senegal and Mauritania. Tough doesn't do justice to the Sanhaja; they lived on camels' meat and milk instead of bread, wore wool in the scorching desert and

788–829

Islam takes root in Morocco under Idriss I and Idriss II, who make Fez the epitome of Islamic art, architecture and scholarship and the capital of their Idrissid empire.

8th century

Through shared convictions and savvy alliances, Arab caliphates control an area that extends across the Mediterranean and well into Europe, just 320km shy of Paris.

1062

With the savvy Zeinab as his wife and chief counsel, Berber leader Yusuf ben Tachfin founds Marrakesh as a launching pad for Almoravid conquests of North Africa and Europe.

abstained from wine, music and multiple wives. Their manly habit of wearing dark veils is still practised today by the few remaining Tuareg, the legendary 'blue men' of the desert (and the many tourists who imitate them in camel-riding photo-ops). When these intimidating shrouded men rode into Shiite and Barghawata outposts under the command of Yahya ibn Umar and his brother Abu Bakr, they demolished brothels and musical instruments as well as their opponents.

After Yahya was killed and Abu Bakr was recalled to the Sahara to settle Sanhaja disputes in 1061, their cousin Youssef ben Tachfine was left to run military operations from a camp site that would become Marrakesh the magnificent. To spare his wife hardships of life in the Sahara, Abu Bakr divorced brilliant Berber beauty Zeinab and arranged her remarriage to his cousin. Though an odd romantic gesture by today's standards, it was an inspired match. Between ben Tachfine's initiative and Zeinab's strategic counsel, the Almoravids were unstoppable.

The Almoravids took awhile to warm up to their new capital – too many mountains and rival Berbers around, and too few palm trees. To make themselves more at home, the Almoravids built a mud wall around Marrakesh 5m high and 16km long, and set up the ingenious *khettara* underground irrigation system that still supports the Palmeraie, a vast palm grove outside of Marrakesh (now home away from home for celebrities including Paul McCartney and designer Jean-Paul Gaultier). The Jewish and Andalusian communities in Fez thrived under bin Tachfin, a soft-spoken diplomat and brilliant military strategist. His Spanish Muslim allies urged him to intercede against Christian and Muslim princes in Spain, complaining bitterly of extortion, attacks and debauchery. At the age of almost 80, bin Tachfin launched successful campaigns securing Almoravid control of Andalusia right up to the Barcelona city limits

'The Jewish and Andalusian communities in Fez thrived under bin Tachfin, a soft-spoken diplomat and brilliant military strategist.'

Youssef ben Tachfine was a tough act to follow. Ali was his son by a Christian woman, and he shared his father's commitments to prayer and urban planning. But while the reclusive young idealist Ali was diligently working wonders with architecture and irrigation in Marrakesh, a new force beyond the city walls was gathering the strength of an Atlas thunderstorm: the Almohads.

STICKS & STONES: THE ALMOHADS

Almohad historians would later fault Ali for two supposedly dangerous acts: leaving the women in charge and allowing Christians near drink. While the former was hardly a shortcoming – the mighty ben Tachfine prized his wife Zeinab's counsel – there may be some merit in the latter. While Ali was in seclusion praying and fasting, court and military officials were left to carry on, and carry on they did. Apparently, Almoravid Christian troops were all too conveniently stationed near the wine merchants of Marrakesh.

1069

The Almoravids take Fez by force and promptly begin remodelling the place, installing mills and lush gardens and cleaning up the city's act with running water and hammams.

1147

The Almohads finally defeat the Almoravids and destroy Marrakesh after a two-year siege, paving the way for Yacoub al-Mansour and his architects to outdo the Almoravids with an all-new Marrakesh.

1276

The winds of change blow in from the Atlas with the Zenata Berbers, who oust the Almohads and establish the Merenid dynasty with strategic military manoeuvres and even more strategic marriages.

None of this sat well with Mohammed ibn Tumart, the Almohad spiritual leader who'd earned a reputation in Meknès and Salé as a ninja-style religious vigilante, using his walking stick to shatter wine jars, smash musical instruments and smack men and women with the audacity to walk down the street together. Ibn Tumart finally got himself banished from Marrakesh in the 1120s for knocking Ali's royal sister off her horse with his stick. But though ibn Tumart died soon after, there was no keeping out the Almohads. They took over Fez after a nine-month siege in 1145, but reserved their righteous furore for Marrakesh two years later, razing the place to the ground and killing what was left of Ali's court (Ali died as he lived, quietly, in 1144). Their first projects included rebuilding the Koutoubia Mosque – which Almoravid architects, not up on their algebra, had misaligned with Mecca – and adding the soaring, sublime stone minaret that became the template for Andalusian Islamic architecture (see p233).

What ever happened to Barbary pirates, how did Islam mesh with Berber beliefs, and why was Morocco the exception to Ottoman rule? Jamil Abun-Nasr unravels these and other Moroccan mysteries in *A History of the Maghreb in the Islamic Period*.

A bloody power struggle ensued between the sons of ibn Tumart and the sons of his generals that wouldn't be settled definitively until 1185, when Abu Youssef Yacoub, the young son of the Muslim governor of Seville and Valencia, rode south into Morocco and drove his foes into the desert. But he also kept and expanded his power base in Spain, winning so many victories against the princes of Spain that he earned the moniker Al-Mansour, 'the victorious'. He modelled Seville's famous La Giralda after Marrakesh's Koutoubia minaret, and reinvented Marrakesh as an Almohad capital and learning centre to rival Fez. Yacoub's urban-planning prowess also made Fez arguably the most squeaky-clean city of medieval times, with 93 hammams, 47 soap factories and 785 mosques complete with ablutions facilities. Yacoub al-Mansour was also a patron of great thinkers, including Aristotle scholar Ibn Rashid – whose commentary would help spark a Renaissance among Italian philosophers – and Sufi master Sidi Bel-Abbes. Yacoub's enlightenment and admiration of architecture was apparently not all-encompassing; several synagogues were demolished under his rule.

Similar thinking (or lack thereof) prevailed in 12th-century Europe, where a hunt for heretics turned to officially sanctioned torture under the egregiously misnamed Pope Innocent IV. Bishop Bernard of Toledo, Spain, seized Toledo's mosque, and rallied Spain's Castilian Christian kings in a crusade against their Muslim rulers. The Almohads were in no condition to fight back. When Yacoub's 16-year-old son was named caliph, he wasn't up to the religious responsibilities that came with the title. He was obsessed with bullfighting, which was the PlayStation of the day, only considerably more dangerous; he was soon gored to death. Yacoub al-Mansour must've done pirouettes in his grave around 1230, when his next son tapped as caliph, al-Mamun, allied with his Christian persecutors and turned on his fellow Almohads in a desperate attempt to hang onto his father's empire. This short-lived caliph added the ultimate insult to Almohad injury when he climbed the Koutoubia *minbar* (pulpit)

1348

The bubonic plague strikes Mediterranean North Africa, and Merenid alliances and kingdoms crumble. Rule of law is left to survivors and opportunists to enforce, with predictably disastrous consequences.

1377

At Kairaouine University in Fez, Ibn Khaldun examines Middle Eastern history with scientific methods in his groundbreaking *Muqaddimah*, explaining how religious propaganda, taxation and revisionist history can make and break states.

1415

In search of gold and the fabled kingdom of Prester John – location of the Fountain of Youth, at the border of Paradise – Portuguese Prince Henry the Navigator begins his conquests of Moroccan seaports.

and announced that ibn Tumart wasn't a true Mahdi, or leader of the faithful. That title, he claimed, rightfully belonged to Jesus.

BY MARRIAGE OR MURDER: THE MERENIDS

When Zenata Berbers from the Anti Atlas invaded the Almohad capital of Marrakesh in 1269, the Almohad defeat was complete. The Zenata had already ousted the Almohads in Meknès, Salé, Fez and most of the Atlantic Coast. To win over religious types, they promised moral leadership under their new Merenid dynasty. Making good on the promise, the Merenids undertook construction of a *medersa* (school of religious learning) in every major city they conquered, levying special taxes on Christian and Jewish communities for the purpose. In exchange, they allowed these communities to practise key trades, and hired Christian mercenaries and Jewish policy advisors to help conduct the business of the Merenid state.

But this time the new rulers faced a tough crowd not easily convinced by promises of piety. Fez revolted, and the Castilian Christians held sway in Salé. To shore up their Spanish interests, the Merenids allied with the Castilian princes against the Muslim rulers of Granada. Once again, this proved not to be a winning strategy. By the 14th century, Muslim Spain was lost to the Christians, and the Strait of Gibraltar was forfeited. The Merenids also didn't expect the Spanish Inquisition, when over one million Muslims and Jews would be terrorised and forcibly expelled from Spain.

Without military might or religious right to back their imperial claims, the Merenids chose another time-tested method: marriage. In the 14th century, Merenid leaders cleverly co-opted their foes by marrying princesses from Granada and Tunis, and claimed Algiers, Tripoli and the strategic Mediterranean port of Ceuta. But the bonds of royal marriage were not rat-proof, and the Merenid empire was soon devastated by plague.

'Without military might or religious right to back their imperial claims, the Merenids chose another time-tested method: marriage.'

Abu Inan, son of the Merenid leader Abu Hassan, glimpsed opportunity in the Black Death, and proclaimed himself the new ruler despite one minor glitch: his father was still alive. Abu Hassan hurried back from Tripoli to wrest control from his treacherous son in Marrakesh, but to no avail. Abu Inan buried his father in the royal Merenid necropolis outside Rabat in 1351, but he too was laid to rest nearby after he was strangled by one of his own advisors in 1358.

The Merenids had an unfortunate knack for hiring homicidal bureaucrats. To cover his tracks, Abu Inan's killer went on a royal killing spree, until Merenid Abu Salim Ibrahim returned from Spain and terminally terminated this rampaging employee. Abu Salim's advisor sucked up to his boss by offering his sister in marriage, only to lop off Abu Salim's head after the wedding. He replaced Abu Salim with a Merenid patsy before thinking better of it and strangling the new sultan, too. This slippery advisor was assassinated by another Merenid, who was deposed a scant few

1498

Church Inquisitors present European Muslims and Jews with an unenviable choice: a) conversion and persecution or b) torture and death. Many choose c) none of the above, and escape to Morocco instead.

1525

Like a blast of scorching desert wind, the Beni Saad Berbers blow back European and Ottoman encroachment in Morocco, and establish a new Saadian dynasty in Marrakesh.

1549

Ahmed el-Mansour ed-Dahbi discovers Europe's sweet tooth, and makes a killing in the sugar trade – sometimes literally. With the proceeds, the Midas of Marrakesh gilds everything in sight.

years later by yet another Merenid – and so it continued for 40 years, with new Merenid rulers and advisors offing the incumbents every few years. While the Merenids were preoccupied with murderous office politics in Meknès and Fez, the Portuguese seized control of coastal Morocco.

VICTORY IS SWEET: THE SAADIANS

Much of Portugal (including Lisbon) had been under Muslim rule during the 12th century, and now the Portuguese were ready for payback – literally. The tiny, rugged kingdom needed steady supplies of food for its people and gold to fortify its growing empire, but Morocco stood in the way. No nation could wrest overland Saharan trade routes from the savvy Berber warriors who'd controlled key oases and mountain passes for centuries. Instead, the Portuguese went with tactics where they had clear technical advantages: naval warfare and advanced firearms. By systematically capturing Moroccan ports along the Mediterranean and Atlantic coasts, Portuguese gunships bypassed Berber middlemen inland, and headed directly to West Africa for gold and slaves.

'The Saadians satisfied European sugar cravings at prices that make today's oil and cocaine cartels look like rank amateurs.'

Once trade in the Sahara began to dry up, something had to be done. Entire inland communities were decimated, and formerly flush Marrakesh was wracked with famine. The Beni Saad Berbers – now known to history as the Saadians – from the desolate Drâa Valley took up the fight against the Portuguese. With successive wins against European, Berber and Ottoman rivals, the Saadians were able to reinstate inland trade. Soon the Saadians were in control of such sought-after commodities as gold, slaves, ivory, ostrich feathers and the must-have luxury for trendy European royals: sugar.

The Saadians satisfied European sugar cravings at prices that make today's oil and cocaine cartels look like rank amateurs. With threats of full-scale invasion, the Saadians had no problem scaring up customers and suppliers. The most dangerous sugar-dealer of all was Saadian Sultan Ahmed al-Mansour ed-Dahbi, who earned his names al-Mansour (the Victorious) for defeating foes from Portugal to the Sudan, and ed-Dahbi (the Golden) for his success in bilking them. This Marrakshi Midas used the proceeds to line the floor to ceiling of his Badi Palace (see p302) in Marrakesh with gold and gems. But after the sultan died, his short-lived successor stripped the palace down to its mudbrick foundations, as it remains today. The Saadian legacy is most visible in the Saadian Tombs (see p300), decked out for a decadent afterlife with painted Carrara marble and gold leaf. The Saadians died as they lived: dazzling beyond belief and a touch too rich for most tastes.

PIRATES & POLITICS: THE EARLY ALAWITES

The Saadian empire dissolved in the 17th century like a sugar cube in Moroccan mint tea, and civil war prevailed until the Alawites came along. With illustrious ancestors from the Prophet Mohammed's family and descendents extending to the current King Mohammed VI, the Alawites

1578

The Saadians fight both alongside and against Portugal at the infamous Battle of Three Kings, which ends with more than 8000 dead, a scant 100 survivors and the decimation of Portugal's ruling class.

1659–66

The Alawites end years of civil war, and even strike an uneasy peace with the Barbary pirates controlling Rabati ports

1684

Barbary pirates take English captives and England seizes Tangier, leading Morocco and England to argue over who stole what from whom first. The prisoners are released when England finally relinquishes Tangier – after destroying its port.

SUGAR & SALT: JEWISH MOROCCO

By the 1st century AD, Jewish Berber communities already well established in Morocco included farmers, metalworkers, dyers, glassblowers, bookbinders and cowboys. Jewish entrepreneurs excluded from trades and guilds in medieval Europe also took up crucial roles as dealers of the hottest Moroccan commodities of the time: salt and sugar. Jewish Moroccans were taxed when business went well for the ruling dynasty and sometimes blamed when it didn't, yet they managed to flourish even while European Jews faced escalating persecution.

Inquisition, forced conversions and summary executions were all the rage in Europe in the 14th to 16th centuries, and not surprisingly many European Jews fled to Morocco. Unlike European rulers, the comparatively tolerant Merenid and Saadian dynasties provided Jewish communities with some security, setting aside sections of Fez and Marrakesh as the first Jewish quarters, or *mellahs* – a name derived from the Arabic word for salt. This protection was repaid many times over in taxes levied on Jewish and Christian businesses, and the royally flush Saadians clearly got the sweet end of the deal. Yet several Jewish Moroccans rose to prominence as royal advisors, and in the Saadian Tombs of Marrakesh, trusted Jewish confidantes are buried even closer to the kings than royal wives.

By day, Jewish merchants traded alongside Christian and Muslim merchants, and were entrusted with precious salt, sugar and gold brought across the Sahara; by night they were under official guard in their quarters. Once the *mellahs* of Fez and Marrakesh became overcrowded with European arrivals, other notable *mellahs* were founded in Essaouira, Safi, Rabat and Meknès, and the traditions of skilled handicrafts that flourished there continue to this day. The influence of the *mellahs* spread throughout Morocco, especially in tangy dishes with the signature salted, pickled ingredients of Moroccan Jewish cuisine.

Under Alawite rule in the 17th to 19th centuries, the official policy toward Jewish Moroccans was one of give and take: on the one hand were opportunities as tradespeople, business leaders and ambassadors to England, Holland and Denmark in the 19th century; on the other were taxes, surveillance and periodic scapegoating. But in good times and bad, Jewish Moroccans remained a continuous presence. By 1948, some 250,000 to 300,000 Jewish Moroccans lived in Morocco. Many left after the founding of the states of Morocco and Israel, and today only an estimated 8000 to 10,000 remain, mostly in Casablanca. A Jewish community centre in Casablanca was a bombing target in 2003, and though no one was harmed at the community centre, the trade-centre blasts killed 33 and wounded 100. Yet the community remains intact, with a modest renaissance under the current king. Jewish schools now receive state funding; a few Jewish expatriates have responded to a royal invitation to return and are contributing to the revival of Essaouira's *mellah;* and like his Alawite predecessors, King Mohammed VI counts Jewish advisors among his confidantes.

were quite a change from the free-wheeling Saadians and their anarchic legacy. But many Moroccans might have preferred anarchy to the second Alawite ruler, the dreaded Moulay Ismail (1672–1727).

A despot whose idea of a good time included public disembowelments and amateur dentistry on courtiers who peeved him, Moulay Ismail was

1777

A century after the English leave Tangier a royal wreck, Morocco gets its revenge on the English, and becomes the first country to recognise the breakaway British colony calling itself the United States of America.

1830

France seizes the Algerian coast, increasing pressure on the Moroccan sultan to cede power in exchange for mafia-style protection along Morocco's coasts from the advancing Ottomans.

1860

If at first you don't succeed, try for seven centuries: Spain takes control of a swath of northern Morocco reaching into the Rif.

also a scholar, dad to hundreds of children and Mr Popularity among his royal European peers. European nobles gushed about lavish dinner parties at Moulay Ismail's palace in Meknès, built by conscripted Christian labourers. Rumour has it that when these decidedly nonunion construction workers finished the job, some were walled in alive. The European royal party tab wasn't cheap, either, but Moulay Ismail wasn't worried: piracy would cover it.

'European nobles gushed about lavish dinner parties at Moulay Ismail's palace in Meknès...'

Queen Elizabeth I kicked off the Atlantic pirate trade, allying against her arch-nemesis King Phillip II of Spain with the Saadians and specially licensed pirates known as privateers. The most notoriously effective hires were the Barbary pirates, Moriscos (Spanish Muslims) who'd been forcibly converted and persecuted in Spain and hence had an added motivation to shake down Spaniards. James I outlawed English privateering in 1603, but didn't seem to mind when his buddy Moulay Ismail aided and abetted the many British and Barbary pirates who harboured in the royal ports at Rabat and Salé – for a price. Business and tax revenues soared, and in the 17th century, Barbary pirates attacked Ireland, Wales, Iceland and even Newfoundland.

Barbary pirates also took prisoners, who were usually held for ransom and freed after a period of servitude – except for those who joined the pirates or the Moroccan government. Captives were generally better off with Barbary pirates than French profiteers, who typically forced prisoners to ply the oars of slave galleys until death. When the Portuguese were forced out of Essaouira in the 17th century, the city was rebuilt by European captives under the leadership of a French profiteer and a freed British prisoner who'd converted to Islam.

After Moulay Ismail's death, his elite force of 50,000 to 70,000 Abid, or 'Black Guard', ran amok, and not one of his many children was able to succeed him. The Alawite dynasty would struggle on until the 20th century, but the country often lapsed into lawlessness when rulers overstepped their bounds. Piracy and politics became key ways to get ahead in the 18th and 19th centuries – and the two were by no means mutually exclusive. By controlling key Moroccan seaports and playing European powers against one another, officials and outlaws alike found they could demand a cut of whatever goods were shipped through the Strait of Gibraltar and along the Atlantic Coast. In the late 18th century, when Sidi Mohammed ben Abdullah ended the officially condoned piracy of his predecessors and nixed shady side deals with foreign powers, the financial results were disastrous. With added troubles of plague and drought, Morocco's Straits were truly dire.

WITH FRIENDS LIKE THESE: EUROPEAN ENCROACHMENT

For all their successful European politicking, the early Alawites had apparently forgotten a cardinal rule of Moroccan diplomacy: never neglect

1880

France, Britain, Spain and the US meet in Madrid and agree among themselves that Morocco could retain nominal control over its territory – after granting themselves tax-free business licenses and duty-free shopping.

1906

The controversial Act of Algeciras divvies up North Africa among European powers like a *bastilla* pigeon pie, but Germany isn't invited to the feast – a slight that exacerbated tensions among European powers.

1912

The Treaty of Fès hands Morocco to the misnamed French Protectorate, which mostly protects French business interests at Moroccan taxpayer expense with the ruthless assistance of Berber warlord Pasha el-Glaoui.

Berber alliances. Sultan Moulay Hassan tried to rally support among the Berbers of the High Atlas in the late 19th century, but by then it was too late. France had taken an active interest in Morocco around 1830, and allied with Berbers across North Africa to fend off the Ottomans. After centuries of practise fighting Moroccans, Spain finally managed to occupy areas of northern Morocco in 1860 – and not incidentally, generated lasting resentment for desecrating graveyards, mosques and other sacred sites in Melilla and Tetouan. While wily Queen Victoria entertained Moroccan dignitaries and pressed for Moroccan legal reforms, her emissaries were busy brokering deals with France and Spain.

Order became increasingly difficult to maintain in Moroccan cities and in Berber mountain strongholds, and Moulay Hassan employed powerful Berber leaders to regain control – but accurately predicting Moulay Hassan's demise, some Berbers cut deals of their own with the Europeans. By the time Moulay Hassan's teenage successor Sultan Moulay Abdelaziz pushed through historic antidiscrimination laws to impress Morocco's erstwhile allies, the Europeans had reached an understanding: while reforms were nice and all, what they really wanted were cheap goods. By 1880, Europeans and Americans set up their own duty-free shop in Tangier, declaring it an 'international zone' where they were above the law and beyond tax collectors' reach.

But the lure of prime North African real estate proved irresistible. By 1906, Britain had snapped up strategic waterfront property in Egypt and the Suez; France took the prize for sheer acreage from Algeria to West Africa; Italy landed Libya; Spain drew the short stick with the unruly Rif and a whole lot of desert. Germany was incensed at being left out of this arrangement and announced support for Morocco's independence, further inflaming tensions between Germany and other European powers that would culminate in WWI.

In *The Conquest of Morocco*, Douglas Porch describes a controversial colonial war promoted as a 'civilising mission' and supported by business interests – an eerie echo of today's headlines, as Porch observes in the 2005 edition.

FRANCE OPENS A BRANCH OFFICE: THE PROTECTORATE

Whatever illusions of control Morocco's sultanate might've been clutching slipped away at the 1906 Conference of Algeciras, when control of Morocco's banks, customs and police force was handed over to France for 'protection'. The 1912 Treaty of Fès establishing Morocco as a French Protectorate made colonisation official, and the French hand-picked a new sultan with all the backbone of a sock puppet. More than 100,000 French administrators, outcasts and opportunists arrived in cities across Morocco to take up residence in French villes nouvelle (new cities).

Résident-Général Louis Lyautey saw to it that these new French suburbs were kitted out with all the mod cons: electricity, trains, roads and running water. Villes nouvelle were designed as worlds apart from adjacent Moroccan medinas (historic city centres), with French schools, churches, villas and grand boulevards named after French generals. No

1921–26

Under the command of Abd el-Krim, Berber leaders rebel against Spanish rule of the Rif, and Spain loses its foothold in the mountains.

1943–45

When the Allies struggle in Italy against the Axis powers, US General Patton calls in the Goums, Morocco's elite force of mountain warriors. With daggers and nighttime attacks, they overcome the Fascists and terrify unsuspecting Tuscans.

1942

In defiance of Vichy France, Casablanca hosts American forces staging the Allied North African campaign. This move eventually yields US support for Moroccan independence and the classic Humphrey Bogart film *Casablanca*.

Impress Moroccans with your knowledge of the latest developments in Moroccan society, Amazigh culture, and North African politics, all covered in English at www.magharebia.com/cocoon/awi/xhtml1/en_GB/homepage/default.

Read first-hand accounts of Morocco's independence movement from Moroccan women who rebelled against colonial control, rallied and fought alongside men in Alison Baker's *Voice of Resistance: Oral Histories of Moroccan Women*.

expense or effort was spared to make the new arrivals feel right at home – which made their presence all the more galling for Moroccans footing the bill through taxes, shouldering most of the labour and still living in crowded, poorly serviced medinas. Lyautey had already set up French colonial enterprises in Vietnam, Madagascar and Algeria, so he arrived in Morocco with the confidence of a CEO and a clear plan of action: break up the Berbers, ally with the Spanish when needed and keep business running by any means necessary.

Once French-backed Sultan Yusuf died and his French-educated 18-year-old son Mohammed V became sultan, Lyautey expected that French business in Morocco would carry on as usual. He hadn't counted on a fiery young nationalist as sultan, or the staunch independence of ordinary Moroccans. Mining strikes and union organising interfered with France's most profitable colonial businesses, and military attention was diverted to force Moroccans back into the mines. Berbers had never accepted foreign dominion without a fight, and they were not about to make an exception for the French. By 1921 the Rif was up in arms against the Spanish and French under the leadership of Ibn Abd al-Krim al-Khattabi. It took five years, 300,000 Spanish and French forces and two budding Fascists (Francisco Franco and Marshal Pétain) to capture Ibn Abd al-Krim and force him into exile.

The French won a powerful ally when they named Berber warlord Thami el-Glaoui pasha of Marrakesh, but they also made a lot of enemies. The title gave the pasha implicit license to do as he pleased, which included mafia-style executions and extortion schemes, kidnapping women and children who struck his fancy, and friendly games of golf at his Royal Golf Club with Ike Eisenhower and Winston Churchill. The pasha forbade talk of independence under penalty of death, and conspired to exile Mohammed V from Morocco in 1953 – but as fate and perhaps karma would have it, Pasha Glaoui ended his days powerless, wracked with illness and grovelling on his knees for King Mohammed V's forgiveness.

A ROUGH START: AFTER INDEPENDENCE

Although the French Protectorate of Morocco was nominally an ally of Vichy France and Germany in WWII, independent-minded Casablanca provided ground support for the Allied North African campaign. So when Morocco's renegade Istiqlal (Independence) party demanded freedom from French rule in 1944, the US and Britain were finally inclined to agree. Under increasing pressure from Moroccans and the Allies, France allowed Mohammed V to return from exile in 1955. Morocco successfully negotiated its independence from France and Spain between 1956–58.

When Mohammed V died suddenly of heart failure in 1961, King Hassan II became the leader of the new nation. Faced with a shaky power base, an unstable economy and elections that revealed divides

1944–53

Moroccan nationalists demand independence from France with increasing impatience. Sultan Mohammed V is inclined to agree, and is exiled to Madagascar by the Protectorate for the unspeakable crime of independent thought.

1955–56

Morocco successfully negotiates its independence from France, Spain cedes control over most of its colonial claims within Morocco, and exiled nationalist Mohammed V returns as king of independent Morocco.

1961

When Mohammed V dies suddenly, young Hassan II becomes king. He transforms Morocco into a constitutional monarchy in 1962, but in 1965 ushers in the 'Years of Lead', dealing heavy punishments for dissent.

MARCHING TO THE KING'S TUNE

Talk of 'Greater Morocco' began idly enough in the 1950s, but in the 1970s it became the official explanation for Morocco's annexation of phosphate-rich Spanish Sahara. But there was a snag: the Popular Front for the Liberation of the Sahara and the Rio di Oro (Polisario – Saharawi pro-independence militia) declared the region independent. Putting his French legal training to work, Hassan II took up the matter with the International Court of Justice (ICJ) in the Hague in 1975, expecting the court would provide a resounding third-party endorsement for Morocco's claims. Instead the ICJ considered a counter-claim for independence from the Polisario, and dispatched a fact-finding mission to Spanish Sahara.

The ICJ concluded that the ties to Morocco weren't strong enough to support Moroccan sovereignty over the region, and the Western Sahara was entitled to self-determination. In a highly creative interpretation of this court judgment, Hassan II declared that Morocco had won its case and ordered a celebratory 'peace march' of more than 350,000 Moroccans from Marrakesh into Western Sahara in 1975 – some never to return. This unarmed 'Green March' underlined Morocco's regional presence, which was soon fortified by military personnel and land mines, and was vehemently resisted by armed Polisario fighters.

The Green March is no longer the symbol of national pride it once was in Morocco. The Green March murals that once defined café decor across southern Morocco have been painted over with trendier dunescapes and Amazigh pride symbols. Meanwhile, phosphate profits have dwindled, due to falling prices, mining sabotage and spiralling costs for Moroccan military operations, exceeding US$300 million annually by 1981. A truce was finally established in 1991 between Morocco and the Polisario, but Morocco's 2008 purchase of 24 F-26 fighter jets as part of a US$2.4 billion deal with US military contractors signals continuing regional tensions. UN efforts remain deadlocked, and the status of the Western Sahara is unresolved – a rallying cry for many Saharawi, and an awkward conversation nonstarter for many deeply ambivalent Moroccan taxpayers.

even among nationalists, Hassan II consolidated power by crackdowns on dissent and suspending parliament for a decade. With heavy borrowing to finance dam-building, urban development and an ever-expanding bureaucracy, Morocco was deep in debt by the 1970s. Attempts to assassinate the king underscored the need to do something, quickly, to turn things around – and then in 1973, the phosphate industry in the Spanish-controlled Western Sahara started to boom. Morocco staked its claim to the area and its lucrative phosphate reserves with the Green March (see boxed text, above), settling the area with Moroccans while greatly unsettling indigenous Saharawi people agitating for self-determination.

In Morocco's second parliamentary elections in 2007, 34 women were elected, representing 10.4% of all seats – that's just behind the US at 12.5% female representation after 110 elections.

RENOVATIONS IN PROGRESS: MOROCCO TODAY

With a growing gap between the rich and the poor and a mounting tax bill to cover Morocco's military debt from the Western Sahara, King Hassan II's suppression of dissent fuelled further resentment among his subjects. By the 1980s, the king's critics included journalists, trade

1975

The UN concludes that the Western Sahara is independent, but Hassan II concludes otherwise, ordering the Green March to enforce Morocco's claims to the region and its phosphate reserves.

1981

After the Casablanca Uprising, the military rounds up the usual suspects of dissenters and unionists nationwide. But demands for political reforms increase, and many political prisoners are later exonerated.

1999

Soon after taking the exceptional step of initiating a Truth and Reconciliation Commission to investigate abuses of power under his own rule, Hassan II dies. All hail Mohammed VI, and fresh hopes for a constitutional monarchy.

BROUHAHA IN THE BLOGOMA

Mobile phones chime in with the call to prayer, royal rose gardens are lined with internet kiosks, and cybercafé screens shield couples smooching via webcam: welcome to Morocco, home of techie trend-setters. Over the past decade, Moroccan women have become the most avid internet users in the Arab world, and with Morocco's youthful population obsessively texting one another, Moroccan mobile-phone usage soon rivalled Europe's. When Mohammed VI married computer engineer Salma Bennani in 2002, tech-savvy Moroccans rejoiced at the merger of modern monarchy and new technology. Soon after the happy event, the blogoma was born.

The Moroccan blogosphere (known by its pet nickname: Blogoma) now consists of hundreds of bloggers and online commentators posting on subjects ranging from cinema to neo-colonialism. After initially limiting access to YouTube, Google Earth, LiveJournal and Western Sahara sites, Morocco has eased up somewhat on online controls. Bloggers have found workarounds in any case, shifting screen names and locations for their commentary to stay clear of filters – whether parental or political. But in his early-adopter enthusiasm, one 26-year-old neglected the cardinal rule of Facebook: be careful what you post, for it will surely haunt you.

Taking his cue from the many satirical, faux-Facebook pages for George Bush and other public figures, Fouad Mourtada posted a fake page for Crown Prince Moulay Rachid of Morocco in February 2008, and promptly got himself arrested and sentenced to three years in prison. The blogoma immediately launched a protest site and an email campaign, and one month later a shaken, repentant Mourtada was released from prison with a royal pardon. Bloggers around the world briefly exulted in a flurry of cross-postings, and then turned their attention back to the usual subjects: movie spoilers, political scandals and Microsoft-bashing. To see what the blogoma is up to lately, visit the Moroccan Blog Aggregator at http://maroc-blogs.com.

unionists, women's rights activists, Marxists, Islamists, Berbers advocating recognition of their culture and language, and the working poor – in other words, a broad cross-section of Moroccan society.

The last straw for many came in 1981, when official Moroccan newspapers casually announced that the government had conceded to the International Monetary Fund to hike prices for staple foods. For the many Moroccans subsisting on the minimum wage, these increases meant that two-thirds of their income would be spent on a meagre diet of sardines, bread and tea. When trade unions organised protests of the measure, government reprisals were swift and brutal. Tanks rolled down the streets of Casablanca and hundreds were killed, at least 1000 wounded, and an estimated 5000 protesters arrested in a nationwide *laraf*, or roundup.

A Travellers History of North Africa by Barnaby Rogerson is a handy and accessible guide that puts Morocco into the wider currents of regional history.

Far from dissuading dissent, the Casablanca Uprising galvanised support for government reform. Sustained pressure from human-rights activists throughout the 1980s achieved unprecedented results in 1991, when Hassan II founded the Truth and Reconciliation Commission to investigate human-rights abuses that occurred during his own reign – a first for a king. In his very first public statement as king upon his

2002

Tensions with Spain flare over policing smuggling on the desert island in the Strait of Gibraltar known to Spanish as Perejil and Moroccans as Leila or Tura, compounding centuries-old sovereignty disputes over Ceuta and Melilla.

2002–04

Historic reforms initiated under Mohammed VI include regular parliamentary and municipal elections across Morocco, plus the Mudawanna legal code offering unprecedented protections for women.

2004–05

Morocco's Truth and Reconciliation Commission televises testimonies of the victims of Moroccan human-rights abuses during the 'Years of Lead', and the shows become the most watched in Moroccan TV history.

father's death in 1999, Mohammed VI vowed to right the wrongs of the era known to Moroccans as the Years of Lead.

Today Morocco's human-rights record is arguably the cleanest in Africa and the Middle East, though still not exactly spotless. Repressive measures were revived after 9/11 and the 2003 Casablanca bombings, when suspects were rounded up – many of whom, according to Human Rights Watch, were subjected to threats and abuse. But since that time, the commission has helped cement human-rights advances by awarding reparations to 9280 victims of the Years of Lead. The new parliament elected in 2002 set aside 30 seats for women members of parliament, and has implemented some promising reforms. Foremost among these are Morocco's first-ever municipal elections, the introduction of Berber languages in some state schools and the much-anticipated Mudawanna, a legal code protecting women's rights to divorce and custody.

As Moroccans will surely tell you, there's still room for improvement. While Morocco's economic growth rate topped 6.5% for 2007, unemployment remains high, and a 2007 suicide bombing in a cybercafé in a working-class Casablanca suburb tragically underlined economic and cultural tensions. Municipal councils remain subject to Rabat's control, and the historically low 37% turnout in 2007 parliamentary elections have been construed by pundits as a lack of confidence in the pace of democratic reform. Most seats were won by the moderate Islamist Justice & Development Party (PJD) on a platform of improved government responsiveness. The state seems to be taking the critique on board, or at least lightening up. After cracking down on Morocco's most popular magazine *TelQuel* for reporting mild jokes about the royal family in August 2007, the state pardoned a blogger who subtly mocked the crown prince in April 2008 (see boxed text, opposite). While state reforms are in the works, Moroccans are taking the initiative to address poverty and illiteracy with enterprising projects from village associations and nonprofit organisations.

This is the state of modern Morocco today: home to rich and poor, old and new, deep contradictions and the courage to confront them. Tourism is flourishing in this nation of moderate climates and politics, and though tourism stretches available resources, it also helps support a middle class emerging between royalty and subsistence farmers. In new village self-help initiatives, the emerging Moroccan blogosphere and traditional free-form poetry, Moroccans are making their voices heard and staying true to their Berber roots as 'the free people'.

Global Voices Morocco provides a roundup of Moroccan news and opinion online, including English translations of bloggers' responses to Moroccan news at www.globalvoicesonline.org/-/world/middle-east-north-africa/morocco/.

Western Sahara Info at http://w-sahara.blogspot.com offers perspectives on the Western Sahara you won't find in officially sanctioned Moroccan newspapers, plus a plethora of live links to North African news sources.

The Moroccan Mirror offers frank, irreverent commentary about Moroccan democracy plus critical perspectives on international politics in English at http://almiraatblog.blogspot.com.

2004

Morocco signs free trade agreements with the EU and the US and gains status as a non-NATO ally. Morocco was turned down for EU membership in 1987, but special status is under consideration since 2006.

2006

Morocco proposes 'special autonomy' for the Western Sahara, and holds the first direct talks with Polisario in seven years – which end in a stalemate.

2007

The state bans Moroccan publication *Nichane* for a cover article called 'Jokes: How Moroccans Laugh at Religion, Sex and Politics', and an issue of Moroccan weekly *TelQuel* is pulped for 'failing to respect' the king.

The Culture

Forget for a moment the glossy travel brochures about Marrakesh, movies filmed in the Moroccan Sahara, urban legends about decadent Tangier: as anyone who's been there knows, the best way to get to know Morocco is through Moroccans. So to introduce you to Morocco, meet Fatima, Driss, Amina and Rashid, four characters who are composites of people you're likely to encounter on your travels. Each is representative of a segment of Moroccan society in some ways, and atypical in others; this chapter will describe how their experience maps onto Moroccan culture as a whole. Once you visit Morocco, you'll appreciate where these characters are coming from, and where they're headed in modern Morocco.

Meet Fatima

Fatima grew up working on a farm and making carpets for sale on the side just to put bread on the family table, but now she has a steady income collecting argan nuts at a Fair Trade women's cooperative near Agadir. The few times she's been into town, she was surprised how informal young people were towards their elders, though not offended – she thinks it's good for young people to think for themselves – and truly shocked by the prices. She lives frugally, saving every dirham to cover school fees for her five grandchildren. All her four children are married, and she always has stories and sweets for her grandchildren when they visit. Her arthritis is beginning to interfere with her work, though, and she worries about the family that now depends on her; her husband passed away a few years ago. She speaks Tashelhit (a Berber language) at home, can get by in Moroccan Arabic, and knows how to say 'hello' and 'welcome' in French and English to foreigners who sometimes visit the argan cooperative, but she doesn't read or write. Her dream is to make the pilgrimage to Mecca, *inshallah* (God willing).

In *Stolen Lives: Twenty Years in a Desert Jail*, Malika Oufkir describes her demotion from courtier to prisoner after her father's plot to assassinate Hassan II. The movie version is being filmed by Moroccan-French director Morjana Alaoui.

Meet Driss

Six days a week, Driss wakes at 6am to ride his scooter from his family's apartment in a new suburb of Marrakesh to the riad (courtyard house, converted into a guest house) where he works as assistant manager, dropping off his little sister at school on the way. He knows enough Spanish and English to explain the riad's breakfast menu to guests and speaks fluent Moroccan Arabic, French and classical Arabic (mostly from watching the news on Al-Jazeera) – though his native Berber language of Tashelhit is getting a little rusty. Driss's father owns a small *hanout* (corner grocery) and doesn't read or write that well himself, but insisted that Driss and his four siblings attend school. Driss takes a computer course on his weekly day off, and is saving up for a mobile phone. He knows his parents will start pressuring him to get married now that he's pushing 30, but he's in no rush and not especially interested in the village girls they have in mind. He'd rather have a girlfriend in the city first, and take things from there. He already has someone in mind, actually: she works at a cybercafé near the riad.

Meet Amina

Amina is a 22-year-old French-literature student, and she'd like to work in the Moroccan government – maybe even the foreign service. Her dad works for the state, and they live in a newer suburb of Rabat. Amina hasn't been to France yet, but a couple of her relatives who live there are financing her education. They keep in touch through email in French and Moroccan Arabic, and she keeps up on world news in French, Arabic and English through the internet and watching satellite TV with her cousins. On weekends, she often goes to restaurants with friends as one big group. She doesn't drink alcohol personally, but some people she knows do, and she doesn't judge them for it. As far as dating goes, she met a guy in an internet chat room a while back, but that was nothing serious. She hasn't yet met anyone she'd consider chatting with via webcam, though some of her friends do. She's not ready to settle down yet – there's too much else to do first.

Meet Rashid

Rashid's sisters tease him that he's such a dreamer, he always lets the goats get away. They used to walk 4km each way to school together, but last year's drought hit his Middle Atlas village hard. His family had to sell their donkey, and make tough choices about who they could spare this harvest season. Eleven-year-old Rashid is a better student and worse goatherd than his sisters, so he gets to go to school – for now, anyway. He likes to surprise his sisters by bringing something home from school: a lazy lizard, beans from the school garden, and one time, a foreign trekker for tea. His family served their best bread and butter, and though no one understood a word the guy was saying, he wasn't bad at *koura* (football). The postcard the trekker sent through the village association is on the family-room shelf, and Rashid is sure that if he can go to the regional middle school, one day he'll write back in perfect English.

To help keep kids in school, make purchases only from adults, and don't give children money, pens or sweets – it encourages them to skip school and hassle tourists.

LIFESTYLE

Family Values

As different as they may seem, Fatima, Driss, Amina and Rashid have one thing in common: a profound attachment to family. While they each have careers and ideas of their own, their aspirations and ambitions are tied in some way to family – which makes them each quintessentially Moroccan.

MOROCCAN SOCIAL GRACES

Many visitors are surprised at how quickly friendships can be formed in Morocco, and often a little suspicious. True, carpet sellers aren't necessarily after your friendship when they offer you tea, and an unexpected introduction to your new Moroccan friend's single cousin can be awkward. If you find yourself in these situations, just claim an obligation elsewhere, smile, and leave – no hard feelings.

But notice how Moroccans behave with one another, and you'll see that friendly overtures are more than a mere contrivance. People you meet only in passing are likely to remember you and greet you warmly the next day, and it's considered polite to stop and ask how they're doing. Greetings among friends can last 10 minutes in Morocco, as each person enquires after the other's happiness, well-being and family. To make friends in Morocco, shake hands and then touch your heart with your right hand, which shows you're taking the meeting to heart. Good friends tack up to four air kisses on after a handshake.

Moroccans are generous with their time, and extend courtesies that might seem to you like impositions, from walking you to your next destination to inviting you home for lunch. (At the risk of stating the obvious, anyone who suddenly demands payment for services rendered is not your friend). To show your appreciation, stop by the next day to say hello, and be sure to compliment the cook (see p88).

With the possible exception of the royal family (see Economy, p52), status is gained in Morocco not so much by displaying wealth or privilege but from sharing it with family. Even major status symbols (like Driss' motor scooter and the satellite TV at Amina's house) are valued less as prized possessions than as commodities benefiting the family as a whole. This is beginning to change, as the emerging middle class Driss represents moves out of large family homes and into smaller apartments in the suburbs, where common property is not such a given. But family connections remain paramount in Morocco, and remittances from Moroccans living abroad are essential to family back home.

Catch Moroccan Arabic jokes you might otherwise miss with *Humour and Moroccan Culture*, a treasury of Moroccan wit in translation collected by American expat Mathew Helmke.

Since family is a focal point for Moroccans, expect related questions to come up in the course of conversation: where is your family? Are you married, and do you have children? How are they doing? This might seem a little nosey, and a roundabout way of finding out who you are and what interests you. But to Moroccans, questions about where you work or what you do in your spare time are odd ice-breakers, since what you do for a living or a hobby says less about you than what you do for your family.

Education

Next to family, education is the most important indicator of social status in Morocco. Driss and Amina read and write, like 55.3% of Morocco's urban population. While Driss is like most Moroccan men in this respect, Amina is in the minority of Moroccan women, 60% of whom were illiterate as of 2003. But even with her college degree, Amina may find her employment options limited: 40% of Moroccan humanities graduates were unemployed in 2008.

At rural girls' school Dar Taliba, 14-year-old students have assisted international ethnobotanists in compiling the most thorough catalogue of Berber medicinal plants and their uses in North Africa.

Rashid's ability to read makes him an exception in rural Morocco, where illiteracy still tops 70% – and if he does enrol in middle school, he will be among just 12% of rural boys to have that opportunity. Like Rashid's sisters, Moroccan girls account for almost two-thirds of the half-million Moroccan kids under 15 who work instead of getting an education. Schooling to age 14 is now an official mandate, and positive social pressure and local initiatives have dramatically improved opportunities for education in the Moroccan countryside. But for vulnerable rural families like Rashid's, just getting the children fed can be difficult, let alone getting them to school. According to the Food and Agriculture Organization (FAO) of the United Nations, child malnourishment is on the rise in Morocco, doubling from 4% in the mid-1990s to 8% in 2006. Innovative school programs like Rashid's that provide food as well as literacy are much needed to build a healthier, brighter future for Morocco.

Social Norms

Explore the world of Moroccan haute couture online at http://marocfashion.canalblog.com (in French) with photos of models working chic belted caftans and gauzy *gandouras* (gowns).

As you will probably notice in your travels through Morocco, behaviour that is considered unacceptable outdoors, in full public view – such as drinking alcohol, or making kissy faces at someone of the opposite sex – is often tolerated in the relative privacy of a restaurant terrace, riad, or internet café. In this context, Amina's views on drinking and internet dating are not so radical, and Driss may stand a chance with his cybercafé cutie. While there are still laws in Morocco restricting sale of alcohol in view of a mosque, sex outside of marriage and homosexuality, enforcement of these laws is very rare. With proper discretion, there is generally plenty of latitude when it comes to socially acceptable behaviour.

VISITORS: DRESS TO IMPRESS

Since they've had contact with Europeans for the last couple of millennia and satellite TV for a decade, Moroccans are not likely to be shocked by Western attire. If you pull a Lawrence of Arabia and don robes and headgear, you'll get puzzled stares in Morocco, and possibly a smirk or two. This is not Saudi Arabia, and who wears a scimitar to work anymore? A head-covering is handy protection against sandstorms in the desert, but nobody expects you to wear a headscarf or Tuareg blue turban – and these days, even Tuaregs wear Adidas.

That said, your choice of attire still may be perceived as a sign of respect (or lack thereof) for yourself, your family and your hosts. Mostly likely no one will say anything to you if your clothing is on the skimpy side – but in this sociable society, nothing indicates disapproval like the cold shoulder. Some people will be embarrassed for you and the family that raised you, and either give you pitying glances or avoid eye contact altogether. So if you don't want to miss out on some excellent company – especially among older Moroccans – do make a point of dressing modestly.

For men and women alike, this means not wearing shorts and sleeveless tops. Even in trendy nightclubs, clingy clothing, short skirts, and low-cut and midriff tops could be construed as, ahem, the oldest kind of professional attire. Anything you could wear to the supermarket back home without attracting attention should do, taking into consideration the local climate, which can range from desert-scorching to mountain-chilly.

Fashion, Moroccan Style

Many Moroccan men and women wear the jellaba, an ankle-length robe with a pointy hood and silk buttons down the front. It's roomy, cosy and intended to be modest, though some of the leopard-print and hypnotic-swirl jellabas women wear may strike you as more eye-catching than a miniskirt. Many younger Moroccans mix up their wardrobe: urbanites like Amina and Driss might pair a chic hip-length tunic or buttoned shirt with jeans or ankle-length pants and Moroccan *babouches* (slippers) or trendy shoes. Logo T-shirts and trainers are all the rage – if copyright were enforced here, the populations of major Moroccan cities would be half naked.

Head coverings are not nearly such a fixation in Morocco as they are in France, where laws attempt to regulate where women can and can't wear them. Some Moroccan women wear the *hijab* (headscarf) for religious or cultural reasons, and some don't, depending on the locale and the individual woman. Women in Casablanca are more likely to wear headscarves (colour-coordinated with their outfits, naturally) than Marrakshiyyas (women from Marrakesh). A full face-covering veil is unusual in cities, and even rarer for rural women working in the fields. Young women like Amina often choose not to wear a headscarf at all, try it for a while to see if it suits them, or alternate, wearing a head covering in the streets but taking it off at home and work.

Keep tabs on the welfare of Morocco's street children and find out what you can do to help at http://gvnet.com/streetchildren/Morocco.htm, an information clearing house on at-risk youth.

ECONOMY

Economic Status

Fatima, Driss and Amina would be considered fortunate in Morocco, where the World Bank cites 19% of the population living below the poverty line and unemployment tops 13%. Although the national economy grew at an impressive rate of 5.8% in 2007, 7% of the population still makes less than US$1 a day and the average annual income is US$1677. The hospitality Rashid's family offer their visitor is especially generous, considering most rural Moroccans are working hard just to put food on the table. Bread and butter may not seem like a lavish meal to you, but

35% of the average Moroccan income is spent to cover basic foodstuffs. Only 10% of Moroccans have the means to buy imported foods at the supermarket, let alone eat at restaurants like Amina.

While the gap between rich and poor is growing in Morocco, a new middle class is emerging. Driss and Fatima belong to this class, even though they almost certainly make less in a day than you do in an hour. Still, the economic class that's head, shoulders and tiaras above all others is the Moroccan royal family, whose wealth was estimated by a (now-estranged) royal family member at between US$4 billion and US$20 billion. In response, an officially sanctioned Moroccan magazine published the king's salary: about US$45,000 a month, described as 'less than a Western CEO's salary' – not including expenses like US$190,000 per month spent on tune-ups for the royal car collection.

Products & Prospects

Driss, Amina and Fatima's incomes come from foreign trade, tourism, remittances from relatives living abroad, and hard work – fairly representative for the country as a whole. Your visit to Morocco makes a positive impact on all of their career prospects, but especially Rashid's. The UN estimates that for every for every eight to 10 tourists who visit an urban area, one job is created locally, and in rural areas those tourists represent six or seven essential new job opportunities.

With a boost from tourism and a growing Moroccan middle class, services are now the fastest-growing sector of the Moroccan economy at 56% of GDP in 2005. Another estimated 17% of GDP comes from industry, mostly from textiles, food processing, and phosphate mining in the Western Sahara (see Marching to the King's Tune, p45). Agriculture and forestry account for 12% to 20% of GDP, depending on the harvest, and 40% of the country's workforce. Fishing is not the pivotal industry it once was, with low fish stocks in the Mediterranean. Hashish is still a key cash crop in Morocco, though periodic police crackdowns have made it more of a high-risk, export-only product.

Morocco is the world's number two producer of cannabis, behind the US. So who's buying? At 60% markup, the UK spends £5 billion annually on kif.

Social security is provided by the family in Morocco, not the government, and workers' compensation and private-sector pensions are nonexistent. But with pressure from activists and unions, some industries are establishing regulations and licensing to ensure workers' well-being. Working conditions are under increased public scrutiny since 2008, when fires in a Casablanca mattress factory killed 55 workers who were allegedly locked inside by management.

Creative Conservation

So what does the economic future hold for our Moroccan friends, beyond farming and tourism? In short: sun, wind and dung. Drilling oil off the coast of the Western Sahara has proved expensive and environmentally messy, and Morocco is now turning towards more reliable energy sources for its own use and for export. The pioneering nation is already harnessing wind power in the Rif, and has partnered with British Petroleum to explore solar energy near Marrakesh. Morocco is the world's largest exporter of what is referred to as 'crude fertiliser', and redirecting resources towards intensive animal-dung collection could mean a shift away from dangerous mining and processing of phosphates into chemical fertiliser – not to mention a whole new meaning for the term 'gross national product'.

The water situation is less promising. Due to the demands of city dwellers and tourist complexes, Moroccan water reserves are at a historic low, and existing water is already being redirected away from subsistence farmers like Rashid's family in the Atlas. According to the Centre for Environmental Systems Research, Morocco is now under severe water stress, and per capita water availability for Moroccans is less than half World Health Organization–recommended levels. With splashy inland water parks and golf courses draining water resources and 17 large coastal resort developments in the works, Morocco is now having to rethink its resource-intensive tourism strategy.

But here Morocco is in a fortunate position: to envision a more sustainable future, it can look to its recent past. Ancient *khettara* irrigation systems, still in use, transport water from natural springs to fields and gardens in underground channels, without losing precious water to evaporation. Although certification is still a novel concept, most small-scale Moroccan farming practices are organic by default, since chemical fertilizers are costly and donkey dung pretty much comes with the territory. Community hammams use power and water for steamy saunas more efficiently than individual showers or baths. Locally made, detergent-free *savon noir* ('black soap' made from natural palm and olive oils) is gentle enough for a hammam or shave, and effective as laundry soap and household cleaner, without polluting run-off. The leftover 'grey water' can be used for gardens and courtyard fountains. There's more to Morocco's traditional courtyard architecture than just its dashing good looks, too. The metre-thick mudbrick walls provide

BUYING SUSTAINABLE SOUVENIRS

- **Most sustainable: tyre crafts** Used tyres don't biodegrade, and burning them produces toxic fumes – but, cleverly repurposed by Moroccan artisans, they make fabulous home furnishings. Tyre-tread mirrors make any entryway look dashingly well-travelled, and inner-tube tea trays are ideal for entertaining motorcycle gangs. For the best selection, visit the tyre-craft *mâalems* lining the south end of Rue Riad Zitoun el-Kedim in Marrakesh (p321).
- **Quite sustainable: argan oil** The finest cosmetic oil to ever pass through the business end of a goat – no, really. Outside Essaouira, goats climb low argan trees to eat the nuts, digesting the soft, fuzzy outer layer and passing the pit. Traditionally, women then collect the dung, extract and clean the pit, crack it to remove the nut, and press the nut to yield a tiny quantity of the orange-tinted, vitamin-E-rich oil. This is arduous handwork, and buying from a collective is the best way to ensure that the women are paid fairly and no additives are included in the end product (no pun intended). Check out **Cooperative Amal** (p165) north of Agadir, **Cooperative Tiguemine** (p166) outside Essaouira, or **Assouss Cooperative d'Argane** (p322) at their retail outlet in Marrakesh.
- **Possibly sustainable: Berber carpets and blankets** Berber blankets are your best bet, made with wool so all-natural that you can feel the lanolin on them. Despite claims to use only vegetable dyes, most carpet weavers use a combination of natural and artificial dyes to achieve the desired brilliance and lightfastness. Some cooperatives card and dye their own wool for natural colours (mostly browns, yellows and pale greens), but for bright colours it's better that they source their wool from reputable industrial dyers instead of handling chemical dyes and pouring used dye down drains. Check out Middle Atlas weaving cooperatives such as **Kasbah Myriem** (p275) and **Atelier du Tissages de l'Association du Zaouiat Ahsal** (p331).
- **Not so sustainable: thuyya wood** The root of a juniper that grows only in Morocco, this caramel-coloured knotty burl is at risk of being admired to extinction. Buy carved thuyya bowls and jewellery boxes only from artisans' collectives more likely to practice responsible collection and reforesting, such as the **Cooperative Artisanal des Marqueteurs** (p164) and the **Cooperative Artisanale Femmes de Marrakesh** (p321).

natural insulation against heat in summer and chill in winter, eliminate most street noise, and don't trap humidity like concrete so that you can literally breathe easier.

Morocco is also thinking fast on its feet, becoming an early adopter of resource-saving new technologies. Solar water heaters provide hot water instantly for showers in the afternoon and evening, saving water that might otherwise be wasted by running the tap while gas heaters warm up. Small, salt-filtered plunge pools offer a quick way to cool down without the need for air-conditioning or Olympic-size, chlorine-laced pools. Add these new and traditional resource-saving practices together, and you'll see why Morocco is poised not only to make the switch to sustainable tourism, but to show Europe how it's done. To do your part to promote responsible travel, check out the Greendex (p1) and Buying Sustainable Souvenirs (p53).

POPULATION

For a millennia-old civilisation, Morocco looks young. There's a reason for this, beyond all those rejuvenating hammams: 55% of the population is under 25, and almost a third of Morocco's population is under 15. Back in 1971, when Moroccan child-mortality rates were high and life expectancy low, Moroccan women had an average of 7.8 children. But with improved health care and young Moroccans like Driss and Amina delaying marriage for careers and dating, Morocco's baby boom is winding down. The average number of births per woman is now 2.7, and population growth has dipped below 1.6%. Less than 5% of Morocco's population of almost 33 million is over 65, and most of these are women – often, working widows like Fatima.

Médecins Sans Frontières (www.doctorswithoutborders.org) and Amnesty International (www.amnesty.org) provide essential aid to Moroccan migrants stranded between borders without family, funds or legal protection.

Like many Moroccans born and raised in rural villages, 11-year-old Rashid probably won't be able to stay home much longer. Since 55% of rural Moroccan families struggle to meet subsistence-level needs, rural teens often must move to larger towns and cities to find work and educational opportunities.

Most Moroccans you'll meet are of Berber-Arab origin, but you'll also probably interact with some of Morocco's 100,000-plus foreign residents. The majority are French, and many work in the tourism trade – especially in Marrakesh, Morocco's number-one tourism destination.

Emigration & Immigration

You've probably read about Moroccans swimming across the Strait of Gibraltar to seek agricultural work in Spain (see A Brisk Trade in Dreams, opposite), but that's not even half the story of migration in Morocco. With most of Morocco's population now hitting puberty, competition is fierce for coveted spots in Morocco's state-supported universities. Those who succeed face limited opportunities after graduation, given 2008 nationwide unemployment rates approaching 34% for urban Moroccans aged 15 to 34.With limited state resources to remedy this situation, Moroccans like Amina are turning to family for help. Moroccan residents and naturalised citizens in France, Germany, Spain and the US – whose combined remittances to family back home represent as much as 20% of GDP – are increasingly sponsoring family members to pursue studies and careers abroad.

Émigrés, Expats and Internationals

The growing numbers of Moroccan emigrants returning to Morocco to live, retire or start businesses are becoming an upper-middle economic

A BRISK TRADE IN DREAMS

Uninhabited islands off the coast of Morocco have long been used as ports for cocaine en route from South America to Europe and international trade in Moroccan hashish, especially Spanish-administered islands Ceuta, Melilla and Isla del Perejil (aka Leila). Now smugglers are earning as much or more promising to lead undocumented immigrants along these stepping stones to Europe – though many don't quite deliver on their promises. Migrants are often expected to swim for miles through the treacherous waters, or are simply abandoned in the Strait. With funding from Spain and the EU, Ceuta and Melilla have recently constructed razor-wire barriers at a combined cost of about €338 million, but smuggling continues.

Such as they are, smugglers' services are generally priced at anywhere between €300 to €3500 – which is as much as three years' income for the average Moroccan – but the human costs are considerably higher. According to recent human-rights reports, over a five-year period as many as 4000 North African migrants have died in their attempts to reach Spanish shores. But given daunting unemployment rates, limited educational opportunities and the need to support their families, many Moroccans continue to take the risk, convinced that all they have left to lose is their lives.

class of their own, since their euros and dollars have considerably more buying power than nontransferable dirhams. The carefree spending of Moroccan emigrants is a source of both revenue and resentment for Moroccans, who grumble openly about returnees driving up costs and importing a culture of conspicuous consumption that's unattainable and shallow.

Morocco hosted over seven million visitors in 2007 – that's about one visitor for every five Moroccans, up from 2.5 million in 2002 – but it hadn't counted on quite so many staying. To many Moroccans who remember the hard-fought Independence movement, international chain resorts and European holiday apartment complexes along the Atlantic coast bring to mind colonial French-only villes nouvelles (see France Opens a Branch Office, p43). Swimming pools, air-conditioning and green lawns strain scarce local water and energy resources, making most tourist complexes a very mixed blessing.

Farida ben Lyzaid's film *A Door to the Sky* tells the story of an émigré's return to Morocco, and her delicate balancing act between activism and tradition.

Meanwhile, the European rage for buying riads (traditonal courtyard houses) has spread from Marrakesh to medinas (old cities) across Morocco, pricing Moroccans out of the market for homes in their hometowns. As Moroccans move to the peripheries, suburban sprawl and traffic has increased, and historic medina neighbourhoods can seem strangely empty and lifeless off-season. To make foreign-owned real-estate investments still more complicated, European and American expatriates living and working in Morocco often earn income in euros and pay expenses in dirhams, giving them a competitive advantage over local businesses – and many stand accused of not paying fair wages and taxes.

But as expat riad-owners are quick to point out, there is a flipside to this real-estate equation. Increased foreign investment can create employment opportunities in the growing tourism sector, help preserve historic homes, generate increased appreciation and demand for local artisanship, and provide Moroccans with the contacts and hard currency needed to start their own businesses. Additional taxes were levied on guest houses in 2008, and with increased competition for talented multilingual employees, riad-owners are beginning to offer better salaries, employee health benefits, and weekends off to retain employees. Lonely Planet recommends licensed riad guest houses that provide fair pay and working conditions to employees and promote positive cultural exchange; you can help by sharing feedback from your experience at talk2us@lonelyplanet.com.

In Morocco, cultural differences are not insurmountable – witness the many intercultural married couples you'll meet running riads, restaurants and other businesses in Morocco. In response to claims that their mere presence is changing the local culture, some expats and internationals point to the satellite dishes on their neighbours' houses, and claim that globalisation is inevitable. Maybe, but travellers can make the exchange more equitable by making an effort to venture beyond their hotels to explore Moroccan culture and meet Moroccans on their home turf.

WOMEN IN MOROCCO

Nineteenth-century Swiss adventurer Isabelle Eberhardt dressed as a Berber man, became a Sufi, smoked kif, operated as a triple agent, married an Algerian dissident and wrote her memoir *The Oblivion Seekers* – all before 30.

A generation or two ago, you might not have had a chance to meet Fatima or Amina. Most of the people you'd see out and about, going to school, socialising and conducting business in the souqs would have been men. But while the public sphere was mostly a male domain, the private sphere belonged to women. Women have long been the backbone of Moroccan households – and, traditionally, performed most of the back-breaking domestic labour. In poorer rural households, women typically had the burden of animal husbandry and tending crops in addition to child care, cooking, cleaning, and fetching water and kindling. In well-to-do urban households, girls as young as 10 were hired as indentured servants, isolated from their families and receiving little more than a place to sleep for their efforts. A woman had no guarantee of support after marriage, either: women abandoned by their husbands could lose their homes to their husband's family, and be left to fend for themselves and their children.

But thanks to the bold efforts made by many pioneering Moroccans, women such as Fatima and Amina now have choices open to them unthinkable just a generation or two ago. As of 2004, Morocco's Mudawanna legal code guarantees women crucial rights to custody, divorce, property ownership and child support, among other protections. Positive social pressure has nearly eradicated the practice of hiring girls under 14 years of age as domestic workers, and initiatives to eliminate illiteracy are giving girls a considerably better start in life. Women have asserted their rights in the workplace, too, joining industrial unions and forming agricultural and artisans' collectives. More than 10% of the winners in Morocco's second parliamentary elections in 2007 were women, and women have been elected to municipal offices across the country.

Best selling Moroccan author and academic Fatima Mernissi exposes telling differences and uncanny similarities in ideals of women in Europe and the Middle East in *Scheherazade Goes West: Different Cultures, Different Harems*.

The modern Moroccan woman's outlook extends far beyond her front door, especially for urban and middle-class women with access to satellite TV, mobile phones and the internet. Women visitors may meet urban Moroccan women eager to chat, and compare life experiences and perspectives on world events. Men visiting Morocco have less opportunity to befriend Moroccan women, since male–female interactions are still somewhat stifled by social convention. But despite customs that typically limit male–female interactions to large group outings, you'll surely notice some jittery internet daters meeting in parks, at cafés and via webcam. Moroccan women are on the move and making their presence known, whipping past on their motor scooters, tunics and headscarves billowing in the breeze, and taking over sidewalks on arm-in-arm evening strolls.

RELIGION

Like nearly 99% of Moroccans today, Driss, Fatima, Amina and Rashid are Muslim. Christian and Jewish communities have been established in Morocco for 1700 years or more, but in recent years their numbers have dwindled. Along with a few Protestants and Hindus, there are about 23,000 Catholics and 65 Catholic priests in the country, mostly in major urban centres. Emigration to France, Israel and the US has reduced Morocco's once-robust Jewish community to about 7000, and the Jewish communities that once inhabited the historic *mellahs* (Jewish quarters) of Fez, Marrakesh, Safi, Essaouira and Meknès have relocated to Casablanca. (For more on this subject, see Sugar and Salt: Jewish Morocco, p41).

About Islam

Soaring minarets, shimmering mosaics, intricate calligraphy, the muezzin's mesmerising call to prayer: much of what thrills visitors in Morocco today is inspired by Moroccans' deep and abiding faith in Islam. It all began in AD 610, when a middle-aged merchant from Mecca named Mohammed began to receive revelations that there was one God, and that believers shared a common responsibility to submit to God's will. Based on the teachings of the Old and New Testaments, this new religion would be built on five pillars: *shahada*, the affirmation of faith in God and God's word entrusted to the Prophet Mohammed; *salat*, or prayer, ideally performed five times daily; *zakat* or charity, a moral obligation to give to those in need; *sawm*, the daytime fasting practised during the month of Ramadan; and *haj*, the pilgrimage to Mecca that is the culmination of lifelong faith for Muslims.

To avoid conflict, French Général Lyautey banned non-Muslims from mosques in Morocco. Moroccans appreciated the privacy so much that they ousted the French from Morocco, and kept the ban.

While all Muslims agree on these basic tenets received by the Prophet Mohammed, some doctrinal disagreements ensued after his death. The Umayyads challenged his son-in-law Ali's claim to the title of caliph, or leader of the faithful. Despite the Umayyads' considerable conviction and military might, some Muslims continued to recognise only successors of Ali; today they are known as Shiites. But in sheer numbers of followers, the Umayyad caliphate's Sunni Muslim practice is more mainstream today.

ISLAM IN MOROCCO

Like many Muslim countries, Morocco is mostly Sunni. There are four main schools of thought among the Sunnis emphasising different aspects of doctrine, and today the one most commonly followed in Morocco is the Maliki school. Historically this school has been less strict, with Maliki *qaids* (judges) applying the sharia, or religious code, according to local custom instead of absolutist rule of law.

During Ramadan, believers are expected to abstain from sex, and nothing should pass their lips from sunup to sundown.

One local tradition to emerge over centuries of Islamic practice in Morocco is the custom of venerating *marabouts*, or saints. *Marabouts* are devout Muslims whose acts of devotion and professions of faith were so profound, their very presence is considered to confer *baraka*, or grace, even after their death. Moroccans go out of their way to visit *marabouts'* tombs and *zawiyas* (shrines) – and many claim that for the faithful, the right *zawiya* can fix anything from a broken heart to arthritis.

This practice of honouring *marabouts* is more in line with ancient Berber beliefs and Sufi mysticism than orthodox Islam, which generally discourages anything resembling idol worship. Visits to *zawiyas* are side trips for the many devout Moroccans who – like Fatima – spend a lifetime preparing and planning for the *haj*. Moroccans do not necessarily see a conflict between *baraka* and belief, or local customs and universal understanding.

SPORT

Football

If it's a rousing game of *koura* (football, aka soccer) you're after, you won't have to look far: you'll find a football skidding across virtually every patch of *piste* (hard-packed dirt) in Morocco. Opportunities for a game abound in rural areas like Rashid's village and in urban parks, but mind the cactus – and don't get too cocky if you're assigned to guard a scrawny preteen like Rashid. You're in for a workout, if not public humiliation.

If you prefer other people to do the kicking for you, you'll find plenty of company among fellow football fans in 320 stadiums across Morocco. A ticket will only set you back a few dirhams, so you can invest in the roasted pumpkin and sunflower seeds that hyped-up fans chomp throughout the game. Offer some to your neighbour, and maybe your new friend will explain to you what people are yelling at the referee. Probably it's *'Seer al muk!'* – loosely translatable as 'How can you face your mother?!'

Football-fan behaviour in Morocco is generally more genteel than in, ahem, England, though it always helps if you're rooting for the same team as the people sitting next to you. Usually this is Morocco's own 'Lions of the Atlas', who often make it to the World Cup qualifiers – otherwise, it's any team but Tunisia, Morocco's archrival. Local teams to watch include Marrakesh's Kawkab, Raja Casablanca, MAS Fez and Rabat's Fath. Star players on these teams often get recruited for the national team (the Lions) and sometimes for teams in France, Spain and Germany.

THE TOUGHEST FOOT RACE ON EARTH *Brendan Sainsbury*

The steep Saharan dunes rose like ghostly sentinels out of the shimmering desert mirage. Instinctively, I readjusted my backpack, took a quick sip of insipid electrolyte drink and floundered towards them like a punch-drunk boxer struggling to stay lucid.

It was 48°C, I hadn't showered or eaten properly in five days, and the blisters on my feet were starting to look like hideously deformed golf balls. For close on 100 miles I had half-run, half-staggered across a back-breaking mix of barren moonscapes, vertiginous mountains and arid salt flats. Rather forebodingly, I still had another 50 to go.

It was March 2008 and I was taking part in the legendary Marathon des Sables, a 150-mile, seven-day pain fest across the scorching deserts of Southern Morocco, popularly considered by ultra-athletes to be 'the toughest footrace on earth'. Dreamt up by pioneering Frenchman, Patrick Bauer, in 1986, the route takes gung-ho participants through some of the most breathtaking and brutal landscapes on the planet in an event that makes training for the French Foreign Legion seem like a relaxing vacation.

In keeping with the extreme conditions, competitors must shoulder all their own food, carry a distress flare in case of emergencies, and sleep in open-sided sack-cloth tents that provide little shelter from the blinding sandstorms.

Yet, despite its fearsome reputation, the race – now in its 24th year – regularly attracts over 800 participants. Some run to raise money for charity; others arrive hungry for adventure and the thrill of living dangerously. My own motives were similarly ambitious. Pricked by curiosity and inspired by the notoriously extreme conditions, I had long dreamt of the life-changing epiphanies and rugged psychological battles that I might encounter en route.

I wasn't to be disappointed. But, while the epiphanies were suitably vivid and the dusty terrain ingrained with plenty of painful memories, the surprise star of the race for me was not the heroic runners or the cheery organisers, but the sultry Moroccan desert – a landscape so barren and hostile yet, at the same time, so eerily beautiful.

Athletics

Think your workout routine is tough? Try comparing notes with Moroccan marathoners. Runners literally feel the burn each April in the annual Marathon des Sables (see opposite), which lasts seven days and covers 243km of scorching Sahara – 78 of them in a single stretch. Once they're warmed up, runners hit their high in May with the high-altitude Berber Marathon through the Atlas Mountains.

With training like this, Moroccans have been giving Kenyan frontrunners reason to watch their backs in international track events. Moroccan Nawal el-Moutawakel became the first Arab woman to win Olympic gold in 1984, when she nabbed the medal for the 400m hurdles. Middle-distance maverick Hicham el-Guerrouj became the first man to hold the world records for the mile and 1500m in 1999, and a national hero in Morocco when he took home Olympic gold for both the 1500m and 5000m events in 2004.

Even if you're no el-Moutawakel or el-Guerrouj yourself and ultramarathons aren't exactly your dream vacation, you can still enjoy a decent jog in Morocco. The annual Marrakesh Marathon in January gives runners a chance to run a lap around the city ramparts, through the *palmeraie,* and back again. Then again, somebody has to cheer on 50,000 runners from the comfort of a Djemaa el-Fna café, fresh-squeezed orange juice in hand…

Golf

Golf courses have become a royal nuisance in Morocco, and not just because of the killer sand traps. Given how much water and chemical fertilizer it takes to keep a fairway green in the desert, courses built by Pasha Glaoui and King Hassan II are a strain on Morocco's environment – not to mention private golf courses recently built outside Marrakesh, and others in the works near Essaouira and Oukaïmeden. Golfers who want to improve their game in more ways than one can head instead to La Pause (p314), an eco-friendly, turfless 'all-terrain' golf and disc-golf course in the desert outside Marrakesh.

Arts & Architecture

If it's true that we normally only use 10% of our brains, Morocco gives the other 90% something to do for a change. The stimulation doesn't stop, from mornings waking in awe in an authentic mudbrick *ksar* (castle) to wee hours spent entranced by a late-night Gnaoua *leila* (jam session). The mind reels trying to make sense of it all: ancient becomes avant-garde and vice versa, as traditions of Arabo-Andalusian music and Amazigh storytelling merge with Moroccan hip hop and independent cinema. Getting you good and gobsmacked is all part of the Moroccan master plan, so feel free to gawk. Moroccan artists are flattered by the attention, and after millennia of artistic accomplishment, they know full well they have it coming.

Author Tahir Shah moved his family from London to Casablanca to become a Moroccan storyteller groupie, collecting tales for his *In Arabian Nights: In Search of Morocco Through its Stories and Storytellers*.

ARTS

LITERATURE

Morocco has an ancient literary tradition that has only been recently recognised as such. Poetry and stories have traditionally been passed along by storytellers and singers, and in manuscripts circulated from one person to the next. As the population for the most part couldn't read or afford books, Morocco's oral tradition has helped keep shared legends and histories alive. Watch the storytellers, singers and scribes in Marrakesh's Djemaa el-Fna in action and you'll understand how Morocco's literary tradition has remained so vital and irrepressible – even with a long-standing policy of press censorship.

A Different Beat

The international spotlight first turned on Morocco's literary scene in the 1950s and '60s, when Beat Generation authors Paul and Jane Bowles took up residence in Tangier and began recording the stories of Moroccans they knew. From these efforts came Larb Layachi's *A Life Full of Holes* (written under the pseudonym Driss ben Hamed Charhadi), Mohammed Mrabet's *Love with a Few Hairs,* and Mohammed Choukri's *For Bread Alone.* Like a lot of Beat literature, these books are packed with sex, drugs and unexpected poetry – but if anything, they're more streetwise, humorous and heartbreaking.

The World's Embrace: Selected Poems is a collection of poems by Abdellatif Laâbi, founder of *Anfas/Souffles* (Breath), the poetry magazine that landed Laâbi eight years in prison for 'crimes of opinion'.

Coming up for Air

Encouraged by the outspoken 'Tangerine' authors, a Moroccan poet named Abdellatif Laâbi founded the free-form, free-thinking poetry magazine *Anfas/Souffles* (Breath) in 1966, not in the anything-goes international zone of Tangier, but in the royal capital of Rabat. What began as a journal soon became a movement of writers, painters and filmmakers heeding Laâbi's outcry against censorship: '*A la poubelle poème/ A la poubelle rythme/A la poubelle silence*' ('In the trash, poetry/In the trash, rhythm/In the trash, silence'). *Anfas/Souffles* published 21 more daring issues, until the censors shut it down in 1972 and sent Laâbi to prison for eight years for 'crimes of opinion'. Government censorship notwithstanding, the complete French text of *Anfas/Souffles* is now available online at http://clicnet.swarthmore.edu/souffles/sommaire.html.

The literary expression that the magazine equated to breathing has continued unabated. In 1975, *Anfas/Souffles* co-founder and self-proclaimed 'linguistic guerrilla' Mohammed Khaïr-Eddine published his confrontational *Ce Maroc!*, an anthology of revolutionary writings. A Souss Berber himself, Khaïr-Eddine also called for the recognition of Berber identity and culture in his 1984 *Legend and Life of Agoun'chich*, which has emerged as a rallying cry for today's Berber Pride movement (see p35).

Living to Tell

Still more daring and distinctive Moroccan voices have found their way into print over the past two decades, both at home and abroad. Among the most famous works to be published by a Moroccan author are *Dreams of Trespass: Tales of a Harem Girlhood* and *The Veil and the Male Elite: A Feminist Interpretation of Islam*, both by Fatima Mernissi, an outspoken feminist and professor at the University of Rabat. In Rabati author Leila Abouzeid's *The Year of the Elephant* and *The Director and Other Stories from Morocco*, tales of Moroccan women trying to reinvent life on their own terms become parables for Morocco's search for independence after colonialism.

In *Moroccan Folk Tales*, Jilali El Koudia presents 31 classic legends ranging from a Berber version of Snow White to a tale of a woman who cross-dresses as a Muslim scholar.

The past few years have brought increased attention to individual Moroccan writers and their dissenting opinions – an encouraging sign of openness under King Mohammed VI, and a positive counter-reaction to a war on terror that seems dangerously all-encompassing. Inspired by *Anfas/Souffles*, Fez-born expatriate author Tahar ben Jelloun combined poetic devices and his training as a psychotherapist in his celebrated novel *The Sand Child*, the story of a girl raised as a boy by her father in Marrakesh. He won France's Prix Goncourt for his book *The Sacred Night*. Several recent Moroccan novels have explored the promise and trauma of emigration, notably Mahi Binebine's harrowing *Welcome to Paradise* and Laila Lalami's celebrated *Hope and Other Dangerous Pursuits*.

CINEMA & TV

Until recently Morocco has been seen mostly as a stunning movie backdrop, easily upstaging the actors in such dubious cinematic achievements

BOLLYWOOD IN THE SAHARA

'*Namaste, mohabbat!*' (Greetings, my love!). If you're South Asian, you may be met with a warbling chorus of Hindi hellos even in remote Moroccan oases. If this strikes you as a scene straight from a movie, you're exactly right: for 50 years, Morocco has been completely besotted with Bollywood.

When Morocco gained its independence in the 1950s, the anti-colonial themes and social realism of Indian cinema struck a deep chord. Morocco's small but influential resident Indian community began distributing Indian films that soon earned a loyal local following. Top Moroccan acting talents were recruited to dub and subtitle Indian movies into Darija and French, and generations of 'Bollyphiles' learned to sing along with the movie themes in Hindi. Not surprisingly, Bollywood stars were among the first honourees at the Marrakesh Film Festival, and at open-air screenings in the Djemaa el-Fna, there's no mistaking the Indian-import crowd favourites.

In 2005, more than a third of the movies shown on Morocco's 105 screens were Bollywood films, and 264 Hindi films were screened in Morocco in the first six months of 2006. Among the biggest Moroccan marquee draws are Salman Khan, Aishwarya Rai and Shah Rukh Khan – a 2008 Casablanca screening of *Chalte Chalte* starring Shah Rukh Kahn with an in-person appearance by co-star Rani Mukherjee drew 50,000 devoted fans. After half a century of ardent admiration, Bollywood is finally returning the love: in 2008, two Bollywood productions filmed scenes in Morocco. While you're visiting, maybe you can be an extra in that mountain-top dance sequence...

as *Alexander, Ishtar, Hideous Kinky, The Four Feathers, The Mummy, Troy* and *Sahara*. But while there's much to cringe about in Morocco's filmography, the country had golden moments on the silver screen in Hitchcock's *The Man Who Knew Too Much,* Orson Welles' *Othello* and David Lean's *Lawrence of Arabia.* Morocco has certainly proved its versatility: it stunt-doubled for Somalia in Ridley Scott's *Black Hawk Down*, Tibet in Martin Scorsese's *Kundun,* Lebanon in Stephen Gaghan's *Syriana,* and India in the BBC's 2008 production of *Brideshead Revisted.* Morocco also stole the show right out from under John Malkovich by playing itself in Bernardo Bertolucci's *The Sheltering Sky*, and untrained local actors Mohamed Akhzam and Boubker Ait El Caid held their own with the likes of Cate Blanchett and Brad Pitt in the 2006 Oscar- and BAFTA-nominated *Babel.* And talk about hard-working: Morocco serves as the location for more than 1000 French, German and Italian productions each year.

Profiles of Moroccan stars, movie-festival announcements, and free-speech updates are covered in expressive English on filmmaker Allal El Alaoui's blog: http://allal-cinemagoer.blogspot.com.

The movies Morocco gets paid to help make are not always the movies Moroccans pay to see. Traditionally, Moroccans prefer Bollywood and Egyptian movies to French dramas and Hollywood popcorn fare. But lately, Moroccans are getting greater opportunity to see films shot in Morocco that are actually by Moroccans and about Morocco. In 2006 and 2007, more than 50 Moroccan features and 100 short films were produced.

Lately Franco-Moroccan films have become serious contenders on the international festival circuit. Director Leila Marrakchi was awarded 'Un Certain Regard' at the 2005 Cannes Film Festival for her first feature, *Marock,* about a Muslim girl and Jewish boy who fall in love. Nabil Ayouch's light-hearted story, *Whatever Lola Wants,* filmed in Morocco and about an American attempting to learn old-school Egyptian belly dance, was a crowd-pleaser at New York's 2008 Tribeca Film Festival. Also making waves are Moroccan neo-realist films, including Jilali Ferhati's *Mémoire en Détention* (Memory in Detention), about an ex-con's attempts to track down relations of an inmate who lost his memory during his long detention, and Narjiss Nejjar's controversial *Les Yeux Secs* (Cry No More), about a former prostitute who returns to her Berber village to stop her daughter from being drawn into the local flesh trade.

None of the 1942 classic *Casablanca* was actually shot in Casablanca. It was filmed on a Hollywood backlot, and the Rick's Café Américain set was based on the historic El-Minzah hotel in Tangier (see p181).

Despite this creative boom, cinephiles have begun to fear for Morocco's movie palaces, since ticket prices can't compete with cheap pirated DVDs. In 2007, only 5% of Morocco's population went to the movies, while more than 400,000 pirated DVDs were symbolically seized from souq stalls in Rabat and Casablanca. But with the success of the Marrakesh International Film Festival, movie festivals are springing up across Morocco; check www.maghrebarts.ma/cinema.html for schedules. Morocco's deco movie palaces are becoming major tourist attractions for visiting movie buffs and architecture aficionados alike, and Tangier's historic 1930s Cinema Rif reopened in 2006 as Tangier Cinematheque, a nonprofit cinema featuring international independent films and documentaries. The Moroccan government is showing initiative, too: in 2008, the state launched Aflam, a new, free, national TV channel showcasing Moroccan-made movies, and films dubbed or subtitled in French, Darija and Tamazight.

MUSIC

Any trip to Morocco comes with its own syncopated soundtrack: women tapping out a beat with tea glasses on brass trays, hawkers singing the praises of knock-off Armani right over the early evening *adhan* (call to prayer), and the ubiquitous donkey-cart-drivers' chants of *'Balek!'* – fair

NOW HEAR THIS: MOROCCAN MUSIC FESTIVALS

Dates and locations may vary, so check www.maghrebarts.ma/musique.html for updates.

- January: Fez Andalusian Music Festival
- February: SidiRock (Metal Fest, Sidi Kacem, p64)
- March: Rencontres Musicales de Marrakesh (Classical)
- April: Magic Drâa (African Music Festival, Zagora), Festival of Sufi Culture (Fez, p242), Jazzablanca (Casablanca)
- May: Festival du Desert (Er-Rachidia, p464), Jazz aux Oudayas (Rabat), Tanjazz (Tangier, p179)
- June: Festival of World Sacred Music (Fez, p242), Gnaoua and World Music Festival (Essaouira, p161), Jazz du Chellah (Rabat)
- July: Marrakesh Popular Arts Festival (p464), Voix des Femmes (Women's Voices, Tetouan), Trance Atlantic (Safi), Festival Timitar (Amazigh Music, Agadir)
- August: Marriage Festival (Imilchil, p332)
- September: Atlantic Andalusian Music Fest (Essaouira)
- October: Rap MedinFes (Fez)
- December: Rencountres Casandalous (Andalusian Encounters, Casablanca)

warning that since donkeys don't yield, you'd better, and quick. As if this weren't enough to start you humming maniacally, there's also music booming out of taxis, ham radios and roadside stalls. For a memory bank of Maghrebi music any DJ would envy, sample these varieties.

Classical Arab-Andalusian Music

Leaving aside the thorny question of where exactly it originated (you don't want be the cause of the next centuries-long Spain–Morocco conflict, do you?) this music combines the flamenco-style strumming and heartstring-plucking drama of Spanish folk music with the finely calibrated stringed instruments, complex percussion and haunting half-tones of classical Arab music. Add poetic lyrics and the right singer at dinner performances, and you may find that lump in your throat makes it hard to swallow your *bastilla* (pigeon pie). Listen for it at classical-music festivals in Casablanca and Fez, and in concerts and fine restaurants across Morocco. Popular interpreters include Abdelkrim Rais and Amina Alaoui.

Check out Morocco's latest top 10 hits and hear Darija DJ stylings on RealPlayer audio at Radio Casablanca online: www.maroc.net/newrc.

Gnawa

Joyously bluesy with a rhythm you can't refuse, this music may send you into a trance – and that's just what it's meant to do. Gnawa began among freed slaves in Marrakesh and Essaouira as a ritual of deliverance from slavery and into God's graces. Watch the musicians work themselves into a state of ecstasy, with fezzes spinning and sudden backflips, and let their music set you free.

Join the crowds watching in Marrakesh's Djemaa el-Fna or at the annual Gnaoua and World Music Festival in Essaouira (p161), and hear Gnawa on Peter Gabriel's Real World music label. Gnawa *maâlems* (master musicians) include Abdeslam Alikkane and his Tyour Gnaoua, famed fusion musician Hassan Hakmoun, Indian-inflected Nass Marrakech and reggae-inspired Omar Hayat. Since Gnawa are historically a brotherhood, historically most renowned Gnawa musicians have been men – but the all-women group Haddarates plays Gnawa trances traditionally reserved for women.

MOROCKIN' HARD: HEAVY METAL ROARS BACK

Not since Ozzy bit a live bat onstage has hard rock caused such an uproar. In 2003, police who didn't appreciate being rocked like a hurricane arrested 11 Moroccan metalheads for making their audiences 'listen, with bad intent, to songs which contravene good morals or incite debauchery'. Despite widespread protests that authorities were driving the crazy train, the rockers were ultimately sentenced to one year in jail for 'employing seductive methods with the aim of undermining the faith of a Muslim'.

But diehard Moroccan metalheads got organised, calling all rockers to the mosh pit in Sidi Kacem, an inland agricultural centre near Meknès better known for braying donkeys than wailing guitars. The second SidiRock festival was held in February 2008, showcasing bands from the area with names sure to warm any true metalhead's heart, if not a mullah's: Despotism from Casablanca, Krematorium from Kenitra, and Sidi Kacem's own Damned Creation. Far from pleather-clad '80s hair bands, these Moroccan groups write their own rebellious lyrics in English, and rock hardcore in black jeans and dreadlocks.

To see clips of the headbanging action, check out SidiRock's official MySpace page and YouTube channel at www.youtube.com/user/SidiRock – and for those about to SidiRock come February, we salute you.

Berber Folk Music

There's plenty of other indigenous Moroccan music besides Gnawa, thanks to the ancient Berber tradition of passing along songs and poetry from one generation to the next. You can't miss Berber music at village *moussems* (festivals in honour of a local saint), Agadir's Timtar Festival of Amazigh music, the Marrakesh Popular Arts Festival and Imilchil's Marriage Festival, as well as weddings and other family celebrations.

The most renowned Berber folk group is the Master Musicians of Joujouka, who famously inspired the Rolling Stones, Led Zeppelin and William S Burroughs, and collaborated with them on experimental fusion with lots of clanging and crashing involved. Lately the big names are women's, including the all-women group B'net Marrakech and the bold Najat Aatabou, who sings protest songs in Berber against restrictive traditional roles. For more women vocalists, head to Tetouan for Voix des Femmes (Women's Voices) Festival.

To explore Amazigh music in a variety of styles, languages, and regions, check out samples, musician bios and CDs from basic bluesy Tartit to '70s-funky Tinariwen at www.azawan.com.

From Marock to Hibhub

Like the rest of the Arab world, Moroccans listen to a lot of Egyptian music, but Moroccopop is gaining ground. A generation of local DJs with cheeky names like Ramadan Special and DJ Al Intifada have mastered the art of the remix, and so have a few pop acts. Some of the more intriguing talents to emerge in recent years are Darga, a group that blends ska, Darija rap, and a horn section into Moroccan surf anthems; British-Moroccan U-Cef, who mixes Arab pop and hip hop with Gnawa to slick electronica effect; Moroccan singer-songwriter Hindi Zahra, Morocco's answer to Tori Amos with bluesy acoustic-guitar backing; and the bluntly named Ganga Fusion and Kif Samba, who both pound out a groovy mix of funk, Moroccan folk music, reggae and jazz. For something completely different, check out the burgeoning Megadeth-inspired Moroccan metal scene at annual SidiRock (see above).

But ask any guy on the street with baggy cargo shorts and a T-shirt with the slogan MJM (*Maroc Jusqu'al Mort,* Morocco 'Til Death) about Moroccan pop, and you'll get a crash course in *hibhub* (Darija for hip

(Continued on page 73)

Moroccan Crafts

Pick up a hand-embroidered piece in Fez

DOUG MCKINLAY

Glass towers, steel elevators, tight suits, plastic surgery: all the mechanically engineered seamlessness of the modern world is enough to make a person claustrophobic. But Morocco breaks up the modern monotony with the imprint of the human hand at every turn, from *pisé* (mud-brick) walls to hand-knotted silk buttons.

Meticulous handiwork on display, Marrakesh
DOUG MCKINLAY

Moroccan crafts range dramatically in organic appeal and polished refinement, and have one thing in common: even at their most splendid, they're still approachable, and even at their most approachable, they're still splendid.

The media and methods that Morocco is most famous for are highlighted in this section, but don't be surprised to find Moroccan *maâlems* (master artisans) inventing entirely new ones in closet-sized studios. The riad guest-house craze has revitalised many Moroccan home-decor traditions, from intricately worked pierced-brass chandeliers to recycled-tyre tea tables. As a point of comparison for the quality and prices of crafts you see in the souqs, hit museums, cooperatives and the local Ensemble Artisanal (state-run showroom) before you shop.

KNOW YOUR MAÂLEMS

European designers are known by their logos, but in Morocco you can recognise a true *maâlem* by the hands. The most meticulous artisans work clean to avoid staining their work, but they may have calluses from specialised handiwork that don't come with, say, pointing and clicking a computer mouse. Most of Morocco's design wonders are created without computer models or even an electrical outlet, relying instead on imagination, an eye for colour and form, and steady hands you'd trust to take out a tonsil. When you watch a *maâlem* at work, it's the confidence of the hand movements, not the speed, that indicates a major work in the making.

Location is another give-away. City souqs are traditionally organised by trade, including specific crafts – leather saddles, musical instruments, slippers – and a village might be known primarily by its style of embroidery. In these specialised craft zones, techniques and tools are traditionally handed down from one generation to the next, and you'll notice *maâlems* in the same family or neighbourhood working side by side, pausing to consult, commiserate and gossip. There's friendly competition and bravado too, as the *maâlem* try to impress and outdo one another. During the long hours it can take to finish an *oud* (lute) or knot a carpet, stories, motifs and techniques are shared, so that the end result is its own piece of folklore.

You can't always tell a *maâlem* by gender or age. Most of the artisans you'll see in city souqs are men, but you're likely to glimpse women *maâlems* knotting carpets in Middle Atlas villages, weaving textiles along the Southern coast, and painting ceramics in Fez, Salé and Safi. Age is not necessarily an indicator either, though many Moroccan art forms take years and the patience of a *marabout* (saint) to master. A single shape of *zellij* mosaic tile can take two to three months to learn to shape without a fatal slip of the chisel, and there are 360 standard shapes to learn – so that splendid mosaic wall in your riad isn't the product of a sudden creative whim.

Just You Try It

A *maâlem* with saintly patience or a devilish sense of humour may invite to try your hand at their craft, and you'll never know how many thumbs you have until you try to mimic the acute hand–eye coordination required to work that loom or leather awl. Now that you fully appreciate the craftsmanship, naturally you'll want to bring home a sample – clever ploy, eh? Just don't forget to bargain a little (see Rules to Remember, p472, for tips).

To really learn how it's done, consider taking a course; many guest houses offer crafts workshops with local *maâlem*, and the index covers crafts courses recommended in this book. So what if your first try at carpet weaving isn't a Middle Atlas masterpiece? Any *maâlem* knows that giving modern life your own personal touch is its own satisfaction. As your Moroccan teacher might say, '*tbarakallalek*' (blessings on your accomplishment).

CARPETS

If you manage to return from Morocco without a carpet, you may well congratulate yourself on being one of few travellers to have outsmarted the wiliest salespeople on the planet. Huzzah! But then it sets in: they've got lush piles of colourful, one-of-a-kind carpets underfoot, and you're stuck with your faded acrylic doormat. Hmmm.

Moroccan carpets hook travellers almost every time because there's a perfect carpet out there for everyone – and if that sounds like something your mother once said to you about soul mates, it's not entirely a coincidence. Women in rural Morocco traditionally created carpets as part of their dowries, expressing their own personalities in exuberant colours and patterns, and weaving in symbols of their hopes for health and married life. Now carpets are mostly made as a way to supplement household income and are sold to middlemen who resell them at a hefty mark-up. Consider buying directly from a cooperative or state-run showroom instead – the producer is more likely to get their fair share of the proceeds, you'll get a better deal, and you may meet the artisan who gave your new rug so much personality, that it could never be mistaken for a mere doormat.

top five CARPET COOPERATIVES

Kasbah Myriem, Midelt, Middle Atlas (p275)

Coopérative de Tissage, Ouarzazate (p344)

Atelier du Tissages de l'Association du Zaouiat Ahsal, Zaouiat Ahansal (p331)

Ensemble Artisanal, Marrakesh (p322)

Iklane Association, Tazenakht (p353)

A CRASH-COURSE IN CARPETS

Once you begin to check out Moroccan carpets – casually of course, betraying no purchasing interest until the last minute – you'll begin to distinguish some key types.

- **Rabati carpets** Plush pile carpets in jewel tones feature an ornate central motif balanced by fine detail along the borders. Many of the patterns may remind you of a formal garden, though you may see some newer animal motifs and splashy modern abstract designs. Rabati carpets are highly prized, and could cost you Dh2000 per sq metre.
- **Hanbels** (aka kilims) Flat-woven rugs with no pile, where character makes up for a lack of cushiness. Chichaoua rugs are among the most striking, with zigzags, diamond patterns, and horizontal stripes in yellow, black and white on a red background (about Dh700 per sq metre). Some hanbels include Berber letters and auspicious symbols such as the Evil Eye, Southern Cross and Berber *fibule* (brooch) in the weave. Ask the seller to explain them for you – whether it's folklore or fib, the carpet-seller's interpretation is sure to intrigue.
- **Zanafi** (aka glaoua) Kilims and shag carpeting, together at last. Opposites attract in these rugs, where sections of fluffy pile alternate with flat-woven stripes or borders. These are usually in the Dh1000 to Dh1750 per sq-metre price range.
- **Shedwi** Flat-woven rugs or blankets with bold black patterns on off-white wool, so au naturel you can still feel the lanolin between your fingers when you rub it. At as little as Dh400 for a smaller rug, they're impressive yet inexpensive gifts.

TEXTILES

Anything that isn't nailed down in Morocco is likely to be woven, sewn or embroidered – and even then, it might be upholstered. Moroccan women are the under-recognised *maâlems* of Moroccan textiles, and the tradition they've established has recently helped attract emerging fashion enterprises and global brands to Morocco. One third of Moroccan women are now employed in Morocco's industrial garment industry. But for something produced with individual flair and hands-on expertise, check out these traditional textile handicrafts.

Embroidery

Ranges from simple Berber designs to minutely detailed *terz Fezzi*, the elaborate nature-inspired patterns stitched in blue upon white linen that women in Fez traditionally spent years

In deep concentration while working a loom, Fez medina

DOUG MCKINLAY

mastering for their dowries…practise for the delicate art of mastering their husbands, perhaps? Rabati embroidery is a riot of colour, with bold, graphic flowers in one or two colours that almost completely obscures the plain-cotton backing. But the ladies of neighbouring Salé also deserve their due for their striking embroidery in one or two bold colours along the borders of crisp, white linen. Though you might not be able to bring yourself to wipe your mouth or nose on anything this spectacular, it makes a lovely pillow case or table runner – and clumsy dinner guests don't have to know why they're being served white wine with their steaks.

Weaving

Beyond the sea of synthetic jellabas (popular flowing garments) and imported cotton tunics in the souqs, fabrics with exceptional sheen and texture may catch your eye: nubby organic cotton from the Rif, linens from the Atlantic Coast, and 'cactus silk' (cactus fibres woven with cotton and synthetic materials) from the south. Most of these are industrially produced, some quite well – but connoisseurs seek out the subtly plusher nap, tighter weave, and elegant drape of handwoven Moroccan fabric.

Weaving is time-consuming, meticulous labour that takes years of practice to perfect, and you may be able to see two women working the loom at once in a village co-operative or state-run Ensemble Artisanal. In souqs and cooperative showrooms, you may find handwoven textiles fashioned into bedspreads, table linens, or ready-made garments. But you can also buy handwoven fabric by the bolt or metre, and have Moroccan couture or household linens custom-made. Tailors can be found in any city, but leave time for the initial consult plus one or two fittings.

top five
MOROCCAN FASHION STATEMENTS

Caftan
Bell-sleeved gown, often belted

Jellaba
Pointy-hooded unisex robe

Hendira
Moroccan poncho

Ghandoura
Casual embroidered, open-necked gown

Burnous
Short hooded jacket

Passmenterie

In a single cupboard-sized Moroccan *passmenterie* (trims) shop, you'll find enough gold braid to decorate an army of generals, and more tassels than a burlesque troupe could spin in a lifetime. Trimming has become its own art form in Morocco, with silk thread wrapped around wire to make mod napkin holders, hand-knotted into silk buttons for trendy tunics, and tied into tassels for cushions, hooded pullovers and keychains.

Felt

Makers of handmade felt hats, slippers, coats and rugs really put wool through the wringer: it's dyed, boiled and literally beaten to a pulp. Instead of being woven or sewn, felt is usually formed into shape on a mould and allowed to dry gradually to hold its shape. Felt *maâlem* are usually found in the wool souq, perfect if a bad hair day calls for a fez fix (around Dh100 to Dh150) or a dapper beanie (Dh80 to Dh200) and a tote bag to carry your finds (Dh120 to Dh200).

LEATHERWORK

Now that there's not much call for camel saddles anymore, you're more likely to find Moroccan leather artisans fashioning must-have handbags with what looks like medieval dentistry tools. Down unpaved medieval *derbs* (alleys), you may discover lime-green leather being sculpted into fashion-forward square poufs (aka ottomans, Dh200 to Dh450 or more, depending on leather quality); yellow pom-poms stitched onto stylish fuchsia kidskin gloves (Dh150 to Dh200); and silver leather crafted into glam-rock bedroom slippers (Dh80 to Dh200, depending on decoration). Nearby you might notice an artisan carefully painting henna onto stretched goatskin to create 'tattooed' leather candleholders, lampshades, or even avant-garde abstract artworks. If you're in town for a couple of days, you might commission an artisan to make you a custom-made lambskin leather jacket, jodhpurs or whatever else you might imagine in leather (ahem).

CERAMICS

If Moroccan ceramics don't convince you to upgrade from Tupperware, nothing will. Blue-and-white pottery from Fez might even top your grandmother's china as the new family heirloom, only less expensive to replace – a plate runs Dh20 to Dh500, depending on size and decoration. Among the espresso cups and coffee mugs made for export in Moroccan ceramics studios, you might spot the traditional *harira* (soup) pot, shaped rather like a cookie jar. But there's no mistaking the iconic tajine, the pot with the round base and conical top found on every self-respecting stove top across Morocco. Plain terracotta cooking tajines are oven-safe, fine for stove-top cooking and cost less than Dh100; elaborate painted and glazed tajines are just for presentation. Miniature versions are for spices, and those tiny conjoined-twin tajines are used for salt and cumin.

Exquisite hand-painted ceramics, Marrakesh

SARA-JANE CLELAND

Zellij

To make a Moroccan fountain, grab your hammer and screwdriver-sized chisel, and sculpt a *zellij* tile into a geometrically precise shape. Good job – now only 6000 more to go to finish that fountain. Then again, you might leave it to the Moroccan masters. Since a fountain probably won't fit in your carry-on luggage, you might consider a *zellij* mirror, picture frame or small tabletop instead; the asking price depends on the quality of the work involved. Many consider the trademark blue-and-white *zellij* of Fez the masterworks of Moroccan artisans. Meknès' *zellij*-makers are quick to point out that Morocco's mosaics tradition got its start nearby, in the Berber/Roman town of Volubilis. But thanks to the current riad craze, Marrakshi *maâlems* now have greater opportunities to practise and hone their craft than *maâlems* in other towns, whose skills are mostly used for historical restoration.

top five REGIONAL CERAMIC STYLES

Safi
Polychrome and black/white Berber symbols

Fez
Traditional blue on white

Marrakesh
Modern monochrome

Meknès
Graphic black on green

Salé
Yellow and turquoise

BRASS, COPPER AND SILVER

Entertaining guests is a performance art in Morocco, requiring just the right props. As though tea poured from over your head weren't dramatic enough, gleaming brass teapots (from Dh200) and copper tea trays (from Dh500) are hammered by hand to catch the light and engraved with calligraphy to convey *baraka* (blessings). Unless it's stamped with 925 for sterling, most 'silver' tea services are actually nickel silver, and should cost accordingly (Dh50 to Dh200). But if you're having a motorcycle gang over for tea, skip the silver service and trot out a studded recycled-tyre tea tray made by Marrakshi recycling *maâlems* (Dh100 to Dh200). If all else fails to impress, brandish an antique inlaid dagger to serve your guests cake (Dh80 to Dh600).

Copper worker, Marrakesh

DOUG MCKINLAY

To set the mood and make an impression on guests, a lantern usually lights the entryway in Moroccan riads and restaurants. These start at Dh150 for a basic wall sconce, but the sky's the limit for intricately worked pierced-brass chandeliers. In Berber tents and remote mountain villages, the main source of light is often the classic Moroccan tin lantern, a rectangular base capped with a dome. But lately, clever Moroccan recycling *maâlems* have reinvented these iconic lanterns by making them with salvaged metal.

Jewellery

Not all that glitters is gold in Morocco, since traditionally Berbers consider gold evil and prefer silver as a dowry payment method (Amex not accepted). You may spot jewellers working a tricky bit of gold filigree, but most gold you see in the souqs is imported from India and Bali. Sterling will be marked with 925, and is often sold by weight rather than design – check the going world price for silver before you shop, watch those scales and calculate accordingly. Prized Saharan dowry necklaces feature rough-hewn coral, agate, carnelian and amber, but most 'amber' you'll see in city souqs is plastic, and lacks the waxy feel and incense scent of the genuine article.

But Moroccan *maâlem*s don't need precious materials to create a thing of beauty. Ancient fossils make cutting-edge pendants in the Anti Atlas around Rissani, and a combination of leather, wood and nickel silver give Berber amulets their unmistakable magic. For Berber folkloric *fibule*s with modern minimalist impact, make a trip to Tiznit, or see what the *maâlem* of Marrakesh are up to this week.

top five
LUCKY LOCAL BLING

Croix du Sud
A cross topped with a circle, almost a stick figure

Traveller's Spiral
Silver spiral with a North Star to guide your caravan home

Fibule
Crescent-shaped brooch with a long pin

Trilobite pendant
Prehistoric cool for Essaouira surfer dudes

Hand of Fatima
All-purpose charm amulet

WOODWORK

The most pleasingly aromatic area of the souq is the woodworker's area, with scents of orangewood, cedar, lemonwood and pine rising from the curls of wood-carpeting workshop floors. These are the *maâlems* responsible for those brass-studded cedar doors you've been obsessively photographing, and the carved cedar ceilings that cause neck cramps in Moroccan palaces. Tetouan, Meknès and Fez have the best reputations for carved-wood ornament, but you'll see impressive woodworking in most Moroccan medinas.

For the gourmets on your gift list, handcarved orangewood *harira* spoons (Dh6 to Dh12) are small ladles with long handles that make ideal tasting spoons. Cedar is used for carved jewellery boxes and hefty chip-carved chests to keep the moths at bay (priced according to size and ornament). The most prized wood is thuja wood, knotty burl from an endangered tree indigenous to Essaouira – buy from artisans' collectives, which are more likely to practise responsible collection and reforesting. Lutes, banjos, and guitars are made from a combination of woods chosen for their flexibility, resonance and durability to withstand a proper all-night Gnawa thrashing.

WHAT ARE THEY DOING?

A man ties a thread to a nail 1.5m up a wall and runs the thread tautly along the wall for about 15m. A small motor whirrs in his hands. Curious. In fact he's spinning thread for the embroiderers of caftans and jellabas, and for the tiny buttons that adorn these garments. There's a great tradition of making *passementerie* in Fez: tassels for cushions, buttons for clothing and to decorate babouches, embroidered belts for caftans, and to add to prayer beads. Be careful not to walk too close to the wall!

(Continued from page 64)

hop). Meknès' H-Kayne rap gangsta-style, while Fez City Clan features a talented but annoying kid rapper, extravagantly rolled Rs and an Arabic string section. But the acts that consistently work the crowd into a frenzy are Agadir's DJ Key, who remixes hip-hop standards with manic scratching, and Marrakesh's Fnaire, mixing traditional Moroccan sounds with staccato vocal stylings. To get in the know before you go, check out video clips of these and other Moroccan hip-hop groups online and the soundtrack for the 2008 documentary *I Love HipHop in Morocco* (www.ilovehiphopinmorocco.com), which shows how groups struggle to get gigs and respect.

Author Laila Lalami tracks the latest developments in Moroccan pop culture from Moroccan hip hop to political scandals on her English-language blog at www.lailalalami.com/blog/archives/cat_all_things_moroccan.html

THEATRE & DANCE

When Shakespeare wrote 'All the world's a stage,' he must've had Morocco in mind. Every square, souq and sidewalk is action-packed, with lovers starring in mobile-phone-assisted dramas, shopkeepers wisecracking that you won't find better prices at an insane asylum, and passers-by pausing to supply the chorus on a ballad blasting out of a boom box. But if you think this opening scene is exciting, wait until you see Morocco's main act, *halqa* (Moroccan street theatre).

Enter storytellers, stage left, to parry with imaginary daggers and die countless fake deaths in battles worthy of Don Quixote. Look up, and you'll notice a human pyramid performing carefully synchronised dance movements, as an acrobat steadies his nerves for a flying leap to the top. As sun sets, cross-dressing belly dancers twirl their hands to distract from their five-o'clock shadows – and with an inviting flick of a spangled scarf, you could be the next on stage.

The show begins around dusk in the main square of any sizable Moroccan town, but the best venue is Marrakesh's legendary Djemaa el-Fna. After a 1000-year run, the Djemaa was finally given its due in 2001 as Unesco's first World Heritage Site for Oral Tradition. Morocco offers more formal performances in urban cultural centres and theatres, and Fez tries to organise the chaos into the Festival Populaire de l'Art de la Halqa each April; see www.maghrebarts.ma/theatre.html for upcoming events.

Dinner Theatre

Programmed folk entertainment can't always match the nightly improvised drama in the Djemaa. This is certainly true of *fantasias*, faux-folkloric theatre-restaurant spectacles big on chaotic horseback charges, blaring musket salutes and other noisy displays thwarting attempts to digest the cold grilled meats on offer. Some restaurants also offer a 'dinner spectacle', complete with belly dancers (not part of Morocco's dance tradition, but a Turkish import), Gnawa gamely trying to compete with clattering dishes, and 'candle dancers' balancing brass trays of lit candles on their heads like Dr Seuss characters. For better entertainment value, all you need is a café seat with a view of the town square, and a handful of coins to show appreciation for the talents on display.

No, that's not a musical rugby scrum: the *haidous* is a complex circle dance with musicians in the middle, often performed in celebration of the harvest.

VISUAL ART

The usual arts and crafts hierarchy is reversed in Morocco, where the craft tradition (see p65) is ancient and revered, while visual art is something of a minor, more recent development. Ornament is meant to be spiritually uplifting, while nonfunctional objects and representational images are often considered pointless – or worse, vanity verging on idolatry, as it is perceived in orthodox Judaism and some (though not all) Muslim societies. No doubt you will see paintings of eyelash-batting veiled women and scowling turbaned warriors, but these come from a 19th-century French Orientalist tradition and are mostly made for export – they're not generally considered the finest art Morocco has to offer.

Artworks dubbed 'Orientalist' are trying too hard to fit the 'exotic Moroccan' mould – not exactly a compliment, as Edward Said explains in *Orientalism*, his breakthrough critique of Western distortions of Middle Eastern culture.

In the 1950s and '60s, folk artists in Essaouira and Tangier made painting and sculpture their own by incorporating Berber symbols and locally scavenged materials. Landscape painting also became a popular way to express pride of place in Essaouira and Assilah, and abstract painting became an important means of poetic expression in Rabat and Casablanca. The emerging Marrakesh art scene combines abstract expressionism with traditional media, and is reinventing calligraphy as an expressive art form. Photography had no such luck, and is still mostly stuck in documentary mode in Morocco – unless you count all those glamour shots of the king on display everywhere.

Calligraphy

Calligraphy is Morocco's most esteemed visual-art form, practised and perfected in Moroccan *medersas* (Quranic schools) over the last 1000 years. In Morocco, calligraphy isn't just in the Quran: it's on tiled walls, inside stucco arches, and literally coming out of the woodwork. Look carefully, and you'll notice that the same text can have an incredibly different effect in another calligraphic style. One calligrapher might take up a whole page with a single word, while another might turn it into a flower, or fold and twist the letters origami style into graphic patterns.

You too can read Islamic calligraphy: vertical lines are usually consonants, smaller marks above and below are vowels, and that tall letter that looks like the letter 'l' is probably an *alif*, the first letter in Allah.

The style most commonly used for Qurans is Naskh, a slanting cursive script introduced by the Umayyads. Cursive letters ingeniously interlaced to form a shape or dense design are hallmarks of the Thuluth style, while high-impact graphic lettering is the Kufic style from Iraq. You'll see three main kinds of Kufic calligraphy in Morocco: angular, geometric letters are square Kufic; ones bursting into bloom are foliate Kufic; and letters that look like they've been tied by sailors are knotted Kufic.

ARCHITECTURE

Stubbed toes come with the territory in Morocco: with so much intriguing architecture to gawp at, you can't always watch where you're going. Some buildings are more memorable than others – as in any developing country, there's a fair amount of makeshift housing and cheap concrete here – but it's the striking variation in architecture that keeps you wondering what could possibly be down the block and over that mountain range. Here is a brief catalogue of Moroccan landmarks most likely to leave your jaw on tiled floors, and your toes in constant jeopardy.

LANDMARKS

Mosque

Even small villages may have more than one mosque, built on prime real estate in town centres with one wall facing Mecca. Mosques provide moments of sublime serenity in chaotic cities and busy village market days, and though non-Muslims are not allowed to enter (except in Rabat's Hassan II Mosque), even passers-by can sense their calming influence.

Towering minarets not only aid the acoustics of the call to prayer, but provide a visible reminder of God and community that puts everything else – spats, dirty dishes, office politics – back in perspective.

Muslim visitors claim that no Moroccan architecture surpasses buildings built for the glory of God, especially mosques in the ancient Islamic spiritual centre of Fez. With walls and ablutions fountains covered in lustrous green and white Fassi *zellij* (ceramic-tile mosaic) and a mihrab (niche indicating the direction of Mecca) elaborately outlined in stucco and marble, Fez mosques are purpose-built for spiritual uplift. Non-Muslims can see Morocco's most historic *minbar* (pulpit): the 12th-century Koutoubia *minbar,* inlaid with silver, ivory and marquetry by Cordoba's finest artisans, and housed in Marrakesh's Badi Palace (p302).

The only mosque non-Muslims are allowed to visit in Morocco is Casablanca's Hassan II Mosque (p105). It's the world's third-largest mosque, so you won't be cramping anyone's style.

Souq

As thrillingly chaotic as Morocco's ancient cities seem, there is a certain logic to their zoning that you can still discern today in Fez, Meknès and Marrakesh. At the centre of the medina (old city), you'll find labyrinthine souqs (covered market streets) beneath lofty minarets, twin symbols of the ruling power's worldly ambitions and higher aspirations. Souq means 'market', and the same word is used to describe weekly village farmers markets – but once you've gotten lost in the souqs of Marrakesh or Fez, you'll agree there's no comparison. In these ancient medinas you can still see how souqs were divided into zones by trade, so that medieval shoppers would know exactly where to head for pickles or camel saddles. The smelliest, messiest trades were pushed to the peripheries, so you'll know you're near the edge of the medina when you arrive at tanneries, livestock markets and egg souqs.

In Morocco, souqs are often covered with palm fronds for shade and shelter, and criss-crossed with smaller streets lined with food stalls, storerooms, and cubby-hole-sized artisans, studios carved into thick mudbrick walls. Unlike souqs, these smaller streets often do not have names, and are collectively known as *qissaria.* Most *qissariat* are through streets, so when (not if) you get lost in them, keep heading onward until you intersect the next souq or buy a carpet, whichever happens first.

Ramparts

Dramatic form follows defensive function in many of Morocco's trading posts and ports. The Almoravids took no chances with their trading capital, and wrapped Marrakesh in 16km of pink *pisé* (mudbrick reinforced with clay and chalk), 2m thick. Coastal towns like Essaouira and Assilah have witnessed centuries of piracy and fierce Portuguese–Moroccan trading rivalries – hence the heavy stone walls dotted by cannons, and crenellated ramparts that look like medieval European castles.

Spain and Morocco still dispute sovereignty over the coastal towns of Ceuta and Melilla, and the local architecture does nothing to resolve the conflict. Those siding with Spain point out Andalusian elements, which Moroccans will certainly remind you developed under Almohad rule (for more on Almohad accomplishments, see p37).

Kasbah

Wherever there were once commercial interests worth protecting in Morocco – salt, sugar, gold, slaves – you'll find a kasbah. These fortified quarters housed the ruling family, its royal guard, and all the necessities for living in case of siege. The *mellah* (Jewish quarter) would be positioned within reach of the kasbah guard and the ruling power's watchful eye (for more on Moroccan *mellahs*, see p41). One of the largest remaining kasbahs is Marrakesh's 11th-century kasbah, which still houses a royal palace and acres of gardens and abuts Marrakesh's *mellah*. Among the most scenic are the red kasbah overlooking all-blue Chefchaouen, and Rabat's whitewashed seaside kasbah (p120) with its elegantly carved gate, the Bab Ouidia.

The most famous kasbah is Aït Benhaddou (p339), the rose-coloured mudbrick fortification complete with impressive crenellated watchtowers, an *agadir* (fortified granary), and a prime desert location overlooking a river valley. Don't be surprised if you recognise the place on sight; it's frequently used by nearby Ouarzazate movie studios as a romantic film backdrop. Some historians date Aït Benhaddou to the 11th century, but like a true movie star, this kasbah is high maintenance and constantly retouched.

Other kasbahs have not been so lucky. Unesco saved the Glaoui Taourirt kasbah in Ouarzazate, which is now used as a film backdrop, but the once-spectacular Glaoui kasbahs at Taliouine, Tamdaght and Telouet have been largely abandoned to the elements – go and see them now, before they're gone. These are deeply ambivalent monuments: they represent the finest Moroccan artistry (no one dared displease the Glaoui despots) but also the betrayal of the Alawites by the Pasha Glaoui, who collaborated with French colonists to suppress his fellow Moroccans. But locals argue Glaoui kasbahs should be preserved, as visible reminders that even the grandest fortifications were no match for independent-minded Moroccans.

'From the austere metre-thick mudbrick walls, you'd never guess what splendours await beyond those brass-studded doors'

Riad

Near the palace in Morocco's imperial cities are grand riads, courtyard mansions where families of royal relatives, advisors and rich merchants whiled away idle hours gossiping in *bhous* (seating nooks) around arcaded courtyards paved with *zellij* and filled with songbirds twittering in fruit trees. Not a bad setup, really, and one you can enjoy today as a guest in one of the many converted riad guest houses in Marrakesh and Fez. So many riads have become B&Bs over the past decade that riad has become a synonym for guest house – but technically, an authentic riad has a courtyard garden divided in four parts, with a fountain in the centre (for more on riad ownership, see p54). With more than 1000 authentic riads, including extant examples from the 15th century, Marrakesh is the riad capital of North Africa.

From the austere metre-thick mudbrick walls, you'd never guess what splendours await beyond those brass-studded doors: painted cedar ceilings, ironwork balconies and archways dripping with stucco. Upkeep on these architectural gems isn't easy, and modernising mudbrick structures with plumbing and electricity without destabilising the foundations is especially tricky. But for all its challenges, this ancient material may be the building material of the future. Mudbrick insulates against street sound, keeps cool in summer and warm in winter, and wicks away humidity instead of trapping it like mouldy old concrete – no wonder green builders around the world are incorporating it into their construction methods.

Hammam

Talk about neat freaks: the first thing the Almohads did after they seized power was raze unruly Marrakesh and its misaligned Koutoubia mosque, and start building 83 hammams (public bathhouses) in Fez. These domed buildings have been part of the Moroccan urban landscape ever since, and every village aspires to a hammam of its own. Traditionally they are built of mudbrick, lined with *tadelakt* (hand-polished limestone plaster that traps moisture) and capped with a dome with star-shaped vents to let steam escape. The domed main room is the coolest area, with side rooms offering increasing levels of heat to serve the vaguely arthritic to the woefully hungover.

The boldly elemental forms of traditional hammams may strike you as incredibly modern, but actually it's the other way around. The hammam is a recurring feature of landscapes by modernist masters Henri Matisse and Paul Klee, and Le Corbusier's International Style modernism was inspired by the interior volumes and filtered light of these iconic domed North African structures. *Tadelakt* has become a sought-after surface treatment for pools and walls in high-style homes, and pierced domes incorporated into the 'Moroccan Modern' style feature in umpteem coffee-table books. To see these architectural features in their original context, pay a visit to your friendly neighbourhood hammam – there's probably one near the local mosque, since hammams traditionally shared a water source with ablutions fountains.

Why'd they build it that way? Eight of the world's leading Islamic architectural scholars give you their best explanations in *Architecture of the Islamic World: Its History and Social Meaning*, by Oleg Grabar et al.

Zawiya

Don't be fooled by modest appearances or remote locations in Morocco: even a tiny village teetering off the edge of a cliff may be a major draw across Morocco because of its *zawiya* (shrine to a *marabout*). Just being in the vicinity of a *marabout* (saint) is said to confer *baraka* (a state of grace). Zawiya Naciria in Tamegroute is reputed to cure the ill, and the *zawiya* of Moulay Ismail on the Kik Plateau in the High Atlas is said to increase the fertility of female visitors (consider yourself warned). Most *zawiyas* are closed to non-Muslims – including the famous Zawiya Moulay Idriss II in Fez, and all seven of Marrakesh's *zawiyas* – but you can often recognise a *zawiya* by its ceramic green-tiled roof and air of calm even outside its walls. To boost your *baraka*, you can visit the *zawiya* of Moulay al-Sherif in Rissani (p368), which is now open to non-Muslims.

Medersa

More than schools of rote religious instruction, Moroccan *medersas* have been vibrant centres of learning about law, philosophy and astrology since the Merenid dynasty. For enough splendour to lift the soul and distract all but the most devoted students, visit the *zellij*-bedecked 14th-century Medersa el-Attarine (p236) in Fez and its rival for top students, the intricately carved and stuccoed Al-Ben Youssef Medersa (p298) in Marrakesh. Now open as museums, these *medersas* give some idea of the austere lives students led in sublime surroundings, with long hours of study, several room-mates, dinner on a hotplate, sleeping mats for comfort, and one bathroom for up to 900 students.

Most *medersas* remain closed to non-Muslims, but at Zawiya Naciria in Tamegroute, visitors can glimpse the still-functioning *medersa* while visiting the library of handwritten texts dating from the 13th century. Muslim visitors can stay overnight in Moroccan *medersas*, though arrangements should be made in advance and a modest donation is usually appreciated.

Fondouq

Since medieval times, these creative courtyard complexes featured ground-floor artisans' workshops and rented rooms upstairs – from the nonstop *fondouq* flux of artisans and adventurers emerged cosmopolitan ideas and new inventions. *Fondouqs* once dotted caravan routes, but as trading communities became more stable and affluent, most *fondouqs* were gradually replaced with private homes and storehouses. Happily, 140 *fondouqs* remain in Marrakesh, including notable ones near Place Bab Ftueh and one on Rue Mouassine (p303) featured in the film *Hideous Kinky*. The king recently announced a Dh40 million plan to spruce up 98 *fondouqs*, so now's the time to see them in all their well-travelled, shop-worn glory.

Ksar

The location of *ksour* (mudbrick castles, plural of *ksar*) are spectacularly formidable: atop a rocky crag, against a rocky cliff, or rising above a palm oasis. Towers made of metres-thick, straw-reinforced mudbrick are elegantly tapered at the top to distribute the weight, and capped by zigzag *merlon* (crenellation). Like a desert mirage, a *ksar* will play tricks with your sense of scale and distance with its odd combination of grandeur and earthy intimacy. From these watchtowers, Timbuktu seems much closer than 52 days away by camel – and in fact, the elegant mudbrick architecture of Mali and Senegal is a near relative of Morocco's *ksour*.

'Like a desert mirage, a *ksar* will play tricks with your sense of scale and distance...'

To get the full effect of this architecture in its natural setting, visit the *ksour*-packed Drâa and Dadès valleys. Of particular note are the ancient Jewish *ksar* in Tamnougalt (p346) and the three-tone pink/gold/white *ksar* of Aït Arbi, teetering on the edge of a gorge. Between the Drâa Valley and Dadès Valley, you can stay overnight in an ancient *ksar* in the castle-filled oases of Skoura and N'Kob. But don't stop there: the Middle Atlas also has spectacular *ksour* rising between snowcapped mountain peaks, including a fine hilltop tower that once housed the entire 300-person community of Zaouiat Ahnsal (p331).

Deco Villa

When Morocco came under colonial control, villes nouvelles (new cities) were built outside the walls of the medina, with street grids and modern architecture imposing new order. Neoclassical facades, Mansard roofs and high-rises must have come as quite a shock when they were introduced by the French and Spanish – especially for the Moroccan taxpayers footing colonial construction bills.

But one style that seemed to bridge local Islamic geometry and streamlined European modernism was art deco. Painter Jacques Majorelle brought a Moroccan colour sensibility to deco in 1924, livening up the spare surfaces of his villa and garden with bursts of blue, green and acid yellow (see Jardin Majorelle, p304). In its 1930s heyday, Casablanca cleverly grafted Moroccan geometric detail onto whitewashed European edifices, adding a signature Casablanca deco (also called Mauresque) look to villas, movie palaces and hotels. Today you'll see elements of Casablanca deco all over Morocco – in architecture and in everyday life, Morocco is making a noteworthy effort to balance its indigenous traditions and global outlook.

Food & Drink

Moroccan cuisine is the stuff of myth and legend – and sometimes sheer befuddlement, thanks to many seemingly indecipherable menus. Awkwardly phrased English and French menu descriptions often appear to require a special decoder ring, so visitors end up sticking to what they already know of Moroccan cuisine: couscous and tajines. Many other scrumptious Moroccan breakfast, lunch and dinner options are described in this chapter to take some of the mystery out of the menu, and help you explore your full range of dining options in Morocco.

Casablanca-raised Kitty Morse shows how a *diffa* is done in *Cooking at the Kasbah: Recipes from My Moroccan Kitchen*, from soup (*harira* savoury bean potage) to nuts (in almond *kaab al-ghazal* cookies).

Get adventurous with the menu in Morocco, and your tastebuds will thank you. Have no fear of the salad course, since these vegetable dishes are mostly cooked or peeled and among Morocco's finest culinary offerings. Entrées ominously described as 'spicy' on Moroccan menus are probably not overly hot or piquant – there could just be an extra pinch of delicate saffron or savoury-sweet cinnamon involved. Dessert is a temptation you won't want to resist, and includes flaky pastries rich with nuts and aromatic traces of orange-flower water. In other words, come hungry.

GET FRESH IN MOROCCO

The food you find in Morocco is likely to be fresh, locally grown and homemade, rather than shipped in from Brazil, microwaved and served semi thawed. Most Moroccan produce is cultivated in small quantities the old-fashioned way, without GMOs (genetically modified organisms), chemical pesticides or even mechanisation. These technologies are far too costly an investment for the average small-scale Moroccan farmer, as is

VEGETARIANS: GRAZE THE DAY AWAY IN MOROCCO

- **Breakfast** Load up on Moroccan pastries, pancakes, fresh fruit and the inimitable orange juice. Fresh goat's cheese and olives from the souq are solid savoury choices with fresh-baked *khoobz* (bread). Steer clear of bubbling roadside vats if you're squeamish – they probably contain snails or sheep's-head soup.
- **Lunch** After a filling breakfast, try the *mezze* of salads, which come with fresh bread and may range from delicate cucumbers in orange-blossom water to substantial herbed beets laced with kaffir lime. In wintertime, couscous with seven vegetables or Berber tajine with pumpkin and onions are warming, filling alternatives. Pizza is another widely available and inexpensive menu option, best when spiked with local herbs and olives.
- **Snacks** Here's where vegetarians go wild. Dried fruit and nuts are scrumptious and ubiquitous in market stalls featuring cascades of figs, dates and apricots alongside towering cones of roasted nuts with salt, honey, cinnamon, cane sugar or hot pepper. Chickpeas and other pulses are roasted, served hot in a paper cone with cumin and salt, and not to be missed. Tea-time menus at swanky restaurants may feature *broiuats,* cigar-shaped pastries stuffed with goat's cheese or egg and herbs, plus finger sandwiches, pastries and cakes. If that's not enough, there's always ice cream, and mint tea with cookies or nuts are hardly ever more than a carpet shop away.
- **Dinner** For a hearty change of pace from salads and couscous, try a vegetarian pasta (anything with eggplant is especially tasty) or omelette (usually served with thick-cut fries). If you're staying in a Moroccan guest house, before you leave in the morning you can usually request a vegetarian tajine made to order with market-fresh produce. Pity you can't do that at home, right?

More than 138 reader-rated Moroccan recipes from foodie magazines *Gourmet* and *Bon Appétit* are online at www.epicurious.com, including quick and healthy options and suggested wine pairings.

organic certification and labelling – so though you may not see a label on it to this effect, much of the Moroccan produce you'll find in food markets is pesticide-free and GMO-free.

The splendid appearance, fragrance and flavour of Moroccan market produce will leave you with a permanent grudge against those wan, shrivelled items trying to pass themselves off as food at the supermarket. There's a reason for this: Moroccan produce is usually harvested by hand when ripe, and bought directly from farmers in the souqs. Follow the crowds of Moroccan grandmothers and restaurant sous-chefs to the carts and stalls offering the freshest produce. Just be sure to peel, cook, or thoroughly wash produce before you eat it, since your stomach may not yet be accustomed to local microbes.

Here's what to look for on the menu and in the market, at its most ripe and delicious:

Autumn Figs, pomegranates, grapes.
Spring Apricots, cherries, strawberries, peaches.
Summer Watermelon, wild artichokes, tomatoes.
Winter Oranges, mandarins, onions, beets, carrots, potatoes and other root vegetables.
Year-round Almonds, walnuts, bananas, squash, pumpkin, fava beans, green beans, lentils, eggplant, peppers, lemons (fresh and preserved).

For Moroccan recipes, a glossary of Arabic ingredients, and Moroccan cooking tips and anecdotes, surf Moroccan Gateway's foodie links at www.al-bab.com/maroc/food.htm.

Carnivores and sustainability-minded eaters can finally put aside their differences and chow down in Morocco. As you may guess, watching sheep and goat scamper over mountains and valleys in Morocco, herds live a charmed existence here – until dinner time, that is. Consequently, most of the meat you'll enjoy in Morocco is free-range, antibiotic-free, and raised on a steady diet of grass and wild herbs. If you wonder why lamb and mutton is so much more flavourful in Morocco than the stuff back home, there's your answer.

PLAYING FAVOURITES

If there is one food you adore or a dish you detest, you might want to plan your visit to Morocco accordingly. Morocco offers an incredible bounty of produce, meats and fish, but these vary seasonally. The country's relative lack of infrastructure and hard currency can be advantageous to visitors – hence the picturesque mountain villages that seem untouched

BEEN THERE, EATEN THAT

Eat your way across Morocco north to south with these outstanding regional dishes:

Casablanca *Seksu bedawi* (couscous with seven vegetables)
Chefchaouen *Djaj bil berquq* (chicken with prunes)
Demnate *Seksu Demnati* (couscous made with corn or barley instead of semolina)
Essaouira *Hut Mqalli (*fish tajine with saffron, ginger and preserved lemons), *djej kadra toumiya* (chicken with almonds, onions and chickpeas in buttery saffron sauce).
Fez *Kennaria* (stew with wild thistle/artichoke, with or without meat), *hut bu'etob* (baked shad filled with almond-stuffed dates).
High Atlas *Mechoui* (slow-roasted stuffed lamb or beef).
Marrakesh *Bessara* (fava beans with cumin, paprika, olive oil and salt), *tangia* (crockpot stew of seasoned lamb, vegetables and onions cooked eight to 12 hours in a hammam, or sauna).
Meknès *Kamama* (lamb stewed with ginger, *smen*, saffron, cinnamon and sweet onions).
Southern Coast *Amelou* (argan-nut paste with honey and argan oil).
Tangier Local variations on tapas and *paella* (Spanish dish made from rice, shellfish, chicken and vegetables).

LOCAL TREATS

Agadir Oranges, lemons, argan oil
Casablanca Cactus fruit
Dades Edible rosebuds, rosewater
Doukkala Melons
Erfoud Dates
Essaouira Fish, argan oil
Fez Wild artichokes, olive oil, oranges, orange-flower water, lemons
Marrakesh Pomegranates
Meknès Mint, olives, olive oil
Oualidia Oysters
Rif Walnuts, chestnuts, citrus, goat's cheese
Safi Shellfish
Sebou Shad, shad-roe caviar
Sefrou Cherries
Souss Almonds, lamb, dates
Tagoundaft Honey

by time, and the jackpot of dirhams you get for your euros – but this also makes importing produce tricky at best. This means that if you're visiting in the fall, you may have to enjoy fresh figs instead of kiwi fruit (not exactly a hardship).

When you consider your menu options, you'll also want to consider geography. Oualidia oysters may not be so fresh by the time they cross mountain passes to Ouarzazate, and Sefrou cherries can be hard to come by in Tiznit. So if your vacation plans revolve around lavish seafood dinners, head for the coasts; vegetarians visiting desert regions should have a high tolerance for dates. For hints on where to find your favourite foods, see Local Treats (above).

BUT WAIT, THERE'S MORE...

One final and important tip: pace yourself. Moroccan meals can be lengthy and generous, and might seem a bit excessive to an unyielding waistband. Take your time and drink plenty of water throughout your meal, especially with wine and in dry climates, instead of pounding a drink at the end. There are better ways to end a meal than dehydration and bloating – namely, a dessert *bastilla* (multilayered pastry) with toasted almonds, cinnamon and cream. Your Moroccan hosts may urge you on like a cheerleading squad in a pie-eating contest, but obey your instincts and quit when you're full with a heartfelt '*alhamdulallah*!' (Thanks to God!)

Ignore the search engine ads and scroll your way to culinary inspiration at www.astray.com/recipes/?search=moroccan, which lists more than 350 Moroccan-themed recipes with varying levels of difficulty and authenticity.

WHAT'S FOR AL-FTOUR (BREAKFAST)?

Even if your days back home begin with just coffee, it would be a culinary crime to skip breakfast in Morocco. Whether you grab yours on the go in the souqs or sit down to a leisurely repast, you are in for a treat. Breakfasts are rarely served before 9am in guest houses and hotels, so early risers in immediate need of coffee will probably have to head to a café or hit the souqs.

Street Eats

Sidewalk cafés and kiosks put a local twist on Continental breakfast, with Moroccan pancakes and doughnuts, French pastries, coffee and mint tea.

ALL HAIL THE DADA

There's a reason why breakfasts at many Moroccan homes and guest houses are so much better than in big hotels, and you'll find her presiding over the kitchen. *Dadas* (cooks) used to spend their entire careers in the service of just one Moroccan family – sometimes a royal one. The royal *dadas* of yore were brought from as far away as Mali and Senegal, and rarely left the palace. But with increased competition for their services from guest houses, restaurants and a growing middle-class, they are now free agents who command respect, real salaries and creative control.

At mealtimes, you might glimpse the *dada* cooking up royal feasts with whatever looked freshest in the market that morning, usually without a recipe or a measuring cup. If those dreamy figs poached in honeyed orange-flower water gave you a whole new reason to get up in the morning, ask to thank the *dada* personally – this is your chance for a brush with culinary greatness.

Follow your nose and rumbling stomach into the souqs, where you'll find tangy olives and local *jiben* (fresh goat's or cow's milk cheese) to be devoured with fresh *khoobz* (Moroccan-style pita bread baked in a wood-fire oven until it's crusty on the outside, yet fluffy and light on the inside). *Khoobz* can be found wrapped in paper at any *hanout* (cupboard-sized corner shops found in every neighbourhood).

In the souqs, you can't miss vendors with their carts piled high with fresh fruit, singing their own praises. They're right: you'll never know how high oranges can be stacked or how delicious freshly squeezed *aseer limoon* (orange juice) can be until you pay a visit to a Moroccan juice-vendor's cart. Drink yours from a disposable cup or your own water bottle, because the vendor's glasses are rinsed and reused dozens of times daily.

For tips on Moroccan street food and foodie adventures to get you salivating, visit Lydia Beyoud's blog at http://lallalydia.blogspot.com.

One savoury southern breakfast just right for chilly mornings is *bessara* (a steaming hot fava-bean puree with cumin, olive oil, and a dash of paprika) best when mopped up with *khoobz* still warm from the communal oven right down the street. For a twist on the usual French breakfast pastries, try *rghaif* (flaky, dense Moroccan pastries like flattened croissants), usually served with warm honey or apricot jam. Protein fiends will enjoy *rghaif* stuffed with *khlii* (sundried strips of spiced beef, like beef jerky). The truly adventurous can start their day with a rich stew of lamb's head or calves' feet, generously ladled into an enamel bowl from a huge vat precariously balanced on a makeshift Buddha gas burner.

Breakfast of Champions

As a guest in a Moroccan home, you'd be treated to the best of everything, and the best guest houses scrupulously uphold this Moroccan tradition each morning. You'll carbo-load like a Moroccan marathoner, with some combination of the following to jumpstart your day:

Ahwa (Coffee) is one option, but also *café au lait*, *thé b'na na* (tea with mint) or *thé wa hleb* (tea with milk), *wa* (with) or *bla* (without) *sukur* (sugar).
Aseer limoon (Orange juice)
Bayd (Eggs) in omelettes, cooked with a dash of *kamun* (freshly ground cumin) or *zataar* (cumin with toasted sesame seeds).
Beghrir Moroccan pancakes with an airy, spongy texture like crumpets, with honey or jam.
French pastries Croissants, *pain au chocolat* and others.
Khoobz Usually served with butter and jam or olive oil and *zataar*.
Rghaif Flat, buttery Moroccan pastries.
Seasonal fruit (see p79).
Sfenj Moroccan doughnuts.

LET'S DO EL-GHDA (LUNCH)

Lunch is traditionally the biggest meal of the day in Morocco, followed by a nice nap through the heat of the day. The lunch hour here is really a three- to four-hour stretch from noon to 3pm or 4pm, when most shops and facilities are closed, apart from a few stores catering to tourists.

For speed eaters this may seem inconvenient, but especially in summer it's best to do as the locals do, and treat lunchtime as precious downtime. Tuck into a tajine, served à la carte with crusty bread, or upgrade to a *prix fixe*, three-course lunch at a fancy restaurant. Afterwards, you'll have a whole new appreciation for mint tea and afternoon naps.

Join the conversation about Moroccan cooking already in progress at http://groups.yahoo com/group/bstilla, an English-language online forum covering bastilla, tajine, and other Moroccan dishes.

Snak Attack

If you're still digesting your lavish guest-house breakfast come lunchtime, try one of the many *snaks* (kiosks) and small restaurants offering lighter fare – just look for people clustered around sidewalk kiosks, or a sign or awning with the word *snak*. Many hard-working locals do not take afternoon siestas, and instead eat sandwiches on the go. At the risk of stating the obvious, always join the queue at the one thronged with locals: Moroccans are picky about their *snaks*, preferring the cleanest establishments that use the freshest ingredients.

Here's what you'll find on offer at a *snak*:

Brochettes Kebabs rubbed with salt and spices, grilled on a skewer and served with *khoobz* and *harissa* (capsicum-pepper sauce), cumin and salt. Among the most popular varieties are lamb, chicken, *kefta* (spiced meatballs of ground lamb and/or beef) and the aggressively flavourful 'mixed meat' (usually lamb or beef plus heart, kidney and liver).

Merguez Hot, spicy, delicious homemade lamb sausage, not to be confused with *teyhan* (stuffed spleen) – *merguez* is usually reddish in colour, while *teyhan* is pale.

Pizza Now found at upscale *snaks* catering to the worldly Moroccan middle-class. Look for *snaks* boasting wood-fire ovens, and try tasty local versions with olives, onions, tomatoes, Atlantic anchovies and wild thyme.

Shawarma Spiced lamb or chicken roasted on a spit and served with *tahina* (sesame sauce) or yoghurt, with optional onions, salad, *harissa* and a dash of *sumac* (a tart, pickle-ish purple spice; highly recommended).

Tajines The famous Moroccan stews cooked in conical earthenware pots that keep the meat unusually moist and tender. The basic tajines served at a roadside *snak* are usually made with just a few ingredients, pulled right off a camping stove or *kanun* (earthenware brazier), and plonked down on a ramshackle folding table. Don't let appearances fool you: these can be some of the best tajines you'll eat in Morocco. So pull up a stool and dig in, using your *khoobz* as your utensil instead of rinsed-and-reused flatware.

Expand your Moroccan cooking repertoire beyond the obligatory cinnamon-dusted orange slices with Fatema Hel's *Authentic Recipes from Morocco: 60 Simple and Delicious Recipes from the Land of the Tagine*.

The Moroccan Power Lunch

Some upscale Moroccan restaurants that serve an evening *diffa* (feast) to tourist hordes serve a scaled-down menu at lunch, when wait staff

NAME THAT SAUCE

What's in your dish that makes it so tasty? Probably one of four main kinds of stock, which you can distinguish by colour:

- light yellow *mqalli* is a base of saffron, oil and ginger
- golden *msharmal* has saffron, ginger and a dash of pepper
- orange or reddish *mhammar* includes paprika, cumin and butter
- beige *qadra* is made of *smen* (aged, seasoned clarified butter) with vegetable stock, chickpeas and almonds.

SEXY SEKSU

Berbers call it *seksu*, *New York Times* food critic Craig Claiborne called it one of the dozen best dishes in the world, and when you're in Morocco, you can call couscous lunch. You know that yellowish stuff that comes in a box, with directions on the side instructing you to add boiling water and let stand for three minutes? That doesn't count. What Moroccans call couscous is a fine, pale, grain-sized, hand-rolled pasta lightly steamed with aromatic broth until toothsome and fluffy, served with a selection of vegetables and/or meat or fish in a delicately flavoured reduction of stock and spices.

Couscous isn't a simple side dish but rather the main event of a Moroccan meal, whether tricked out Casablanca-style with seven vegetables, heaped with lamb and vegetables in Fez, or served with tomatoes, fish and fresh herbs in Essaouira. Many delicious couscous dishes come without meat, including the pumpkin couscous of Marrakesh and a simple yet savoury High Atlas version with stewed onions, but scrupulous vegetarians will want to enquire in advance whether that hearty stock is indeed vegetarian. On occasion a couscous dish can be ordered à la carte, but usually it's a centrepiece of a multicourse lunch or celebratory *diffa* – and when you get a mouthful of the stuff done properly, you'll see why.

are more relaxed, the clientele is more local and the meal is sometimes a fraction of the price you'd pay for dinner. You might miss the live music and inevitable belly dancing that would accompany your supper – but then again, you might not. Three courses may seem a bit much for lunch, but don't be daunted: what this usually means is a delightful array of diminutive vegetable dishes, followed by a fluffy couscous and/or a small meat or chicken tajine, capped with the obligatory mint tea.

Hold the hot sauce: dousing your tajine with *harissa* (capsicum-pepper sauce) is generally done in Tunisia, Morocco's rival in the kitchen and football field.

MEZZE (SALAD COURSE)

The salad course is a bonanza for vegetarians, with fresh bread and three to five small plates that might include lemony beet salad with chives, herbed potatoes, cumin-spiked chickpeas, a relish of roasted tomatoes and caramelised onions, pumpkin puree with cinnamon and honey, and roasted, spiced eggplant dip so rich it's often called 'aubergine caviar'.

TAJINE & COUSCOUS

The main course is usually a tajine and/or couscous – a quasi-religious experience in Morocco not to be missed (see Sexy Seksu, above). The most common tajine choices are *dujaj mqalli bil hamd markd wa zeetoun* (chicken with preserved lemon and olives, zesty in flavour and velvety in texture); *kefta bil matisha wa bayd* (meatballs in a rich tomato sauce with a hint of heat from spices and topped with a sizzling egg); and *lehem bil berquq wa luz*, (lamb with prunes and almonds served sliding off the bone into a saffron-onion sauce).

Before dinner, your host may appear with a pitcher and a deep tray. Hold out your hands, and your host will pour rosewater over them.

If you're in Morocco for a while, you may tire of the usual tajine options – until you come across one regional variation that makes all your sampling of chicken tajine with lemon and olives worthwhile. That's when you cross over from casual diner to true tajine connoisseur, and fully appreciate the passionate debates among Moroccans about such minutiae as the appropriate thickness of the lemon rind and brininess of the olives. Every region, city, restaurant and household has pronounced opinions you can actually taste in your tajine. No self-respecting Moroccan restaurant should ever serve you a tajine that's stringy, tasteless, watery or overcooked. Vegetarians can sometimes, but not always, request a vegetable tajine instead; ingredients are bought fresh daily in small quantities, and the chef may not have factored vegetarians into the restaurant's purchases.

MECHOUI

The most powerful power lunch of all features *mechoui*, an entire lamb or calf that may be stuffed with couscous and some combination of almonds (or other nuts) and prunes (or other dried fruit). The whole beast is basted with butter, garlic, cumin and paprika, and slow-roasted until it's ready to melt into the fire or your mouth, whichever comes first. Sometimes *mechoui* is accompanied by kebabs or *kwa* (grilled liver kebabs with cumin, salt and paprika). Do not attempt to operate heavy machinery or begin a whirlwind museum tour post-*mechoui*; no amount of post-prandial mint tea will make such exertions feasible without a nap.

Vitamin-rich Moroccan argan oil is popular as a cosmetic, but also as a gourmet treat: the toasted-hazelnut flavour makes an intriguing dipping oil and exotic salad dressing.

DESSERT

At lunchtime, dessert is usually sweet mint tea served with almond cookies. You may not think you have room, but one bite of a dreamy *kaab al-ghazal* (crescent-shaped 'gazelle's horns' cookie stuffed with almond paste and laced with orange-flower water) will surely convince you otherwise. A light, refreshing option is the tart-sweet *orange a canelle* (orange slices with cinnamon and orange-flower water),

SNACKTIME (5-ISH)

Missed the *mechoui* at lunch? Follow your nose and growling stomach to a street vendor for these treats:

- roasted corn fresh off the brazier
- dry-roasted chickpeas with salt and cumin
- sweet or salty roasted almonds
- roasted sunflower seeds and pumpkin seeds
- hard-boiled eggs with fresh cumin
- sandwiches of brochettes or *merguez* with cumin, salt and *harissa*
- escargot (snails) in hot, savoury broth, ladled into a tin bowl or cup.

Even top chefs consult Paula Wolfert's *Couscous and Other Good Food from Morocco*, which includes 20 tantalising recipes for the titular dish and won the 2008 James Beard Cookbook Hall of Fame Award.

Other popular late-afternoon treats are coffee or mint tea at a café, ice cream at a *glacier* (ice-cream parlour), or Moroccan and French sweets from your local patisserie.

A LATE L'ASHA (DINNER)

Dinner in Morocco doesn't usually start until around 9pm, after work and possibly a sunset stroll. Most Moroccans eat dinner at home, but you may notice young professionals, students and bachelors making a beeline for the local *snak* or pizzeria. In the winter, you'll see vendors crack open steaming vats of *harira* (a hearty soup with a base of tomatoes, onions, saffron and cilantro and often lentils, chickpeas, and/or lamb). Dinner at

WHERE IN THE WORLD?

Can't quite place that taste? Here's where some of the distinctive flavours of modern Moroccan cuisine originate:

Essaouira Portuguese and Jewish origins.
Fez Andalucía (Spain) and Persia.
Marrakesh Senegal, France, Berber North Africa and Italy.
Tetouan Andalucía and Turkey.

home is probably *harira* and lunch leftovers, with the notable exception of Ramadan and other celebrations.

Do the Diffa

With enough hard currency and room in your stomach, you might prefer Moroccan restaurant dining to *snak* fare for dinner. Most upscale Moroccan restaurants cater to tourists, serving an elaborate *prix fixe* Moroccan *diffa* (feast) in a palatial setting. This is not a dine-and-dash meal, but an evening's entertainment that often includes belly dancing, live music and wine or beer. It's a novel experience worth trying at least once.

Fair warning about palace restaurants: your meal may come with a side order of kitsch. Many palace restaurants appear to have been decorated by a genie, complete with brass lamps, mirrors, tent fabric and cushions as far as the eye can see. Often it's the ambience you're paying for rather than the food, which can vary from exquisitely prepared regional specialties to mass-produced glop. Here's a rule of thumb: if the place is so cavernous that your voice echoes and there's a stage set up for a laser show, don't expect personalised service or authentic Moroccan fare.

Bloggers Samira and Sabah dish foodie secrets in English and French at http://moroccankitchen.blogspot.com, including recipes from their hometown of Fez.

Whether you're in for a *diffa* at a Moroccan home (lucky you) or a restaurant, your lavish dinner will include some combination of the following:

Mezze Up to five different small salads (though the most extravagant palace restaurants in Marrakesh and Fez boast seven to nine).
Briouat or brik Buttery cigar-shaped or triangular pastry stuffed with herbs and goat's cheese, savoury meats, or egg, then fried or baked.
Bastilla The justly famed savoury-sweet pie made of *warqa* (sheets of pastry even thinner than filo), painstakingly layered with pigeon or chicken cooked with caramelised onions, lemon, eggs and toasted sugared almonds, then dusted with cinnamon and sugar.
Couscous Made according to local custom (see p84); couscous variations may be made of barley, wheat or corn.
Tajine Often your choice of one of a couple of varieties.
Mechoui And/or some regional speciality (see p80).
Dessert This may be *orange a canelle*, a dessert *bastilla* (with fresh cream and toasted nuts), *briouat bil luz* (*briouat* filled with almond paste), *sfaa* (sweet cinnamon couscous with dried fruit and nuts, served with cream) or *kaab al-ghazal*.

EATING DURING RAMADAN

During Ramadan, most Moroccans observe the fast during the day, eating only before sunup and after sundown. Dinner is eaten later than usual – around 11pm – and many wake up early for a filling breakfast before dawn. Another popular strategy is to stay up most of the night, sleep as late as possible, and stretch the afternoon nap into early evening. Adapt to the local schedule, and you may thoroughly enjoy the leisurely pace, late-night festivities and manic feasts of Ramadan.

Although you will not be expected to observe the fast, eating in public view is generally frowned upon. Hence many restaurants are closed during the day and around *lftour*, the evening meal when the fast is broken. But with a little planning, there are plenty of workarounds: load up on snacks in the market to eat indoors, make arrangements for breakfast or lunch in the privacy of your guest house, and ask locals about a good place to enjoy *lftour*.

Lftour comes with all the traditional Ramadan fixings: *harira*, dates, milk, *shebbakia* (a sweet, coiled pastry that's guaranteed to shift your glucose levels into high gear), and *harsha* (buttery bread made of semolina and fried for maximum density). You may find that *harira* is offered free; even Moroccan McDonald's offers it as part of their special Ramadan Happy Meal.

CARE FOR SOMETHING STRONGER?

Yes, you can drink alcohol in Morocco without offending local sensibilities, as long as you're out of sight of a mosque and inside a restaurant, club, hotel, guest house or private home. One note of caution: quality assurance is tricky in a Muslim country where mixologists, micro-brewers, and licensed sommeliers are in understandably short supply, and your server may not be able to make any personal recommendations from the wine menu. Don't hesitate to send back a drink if something about it seems off; your server will likely take your word for it. Your best bets:

- **Casa** is a fine local pilsner beer, and **Flag** is a faintly herbal second-best.
- Admirable Moroccan white wines include crisp **Coquillages** and citrusy **Sémillant Blanc**.
- Reliable reds include the mellow **President Cabernet**, spicier **Medallion Cabernet** and zesty **Siroua S Syrah**.
- **Mojitos, caipirinhas**, and **negronis** are three imported cocktails that become local nightclub favourites when made with (respectively) Moroccan mint, local kaffir lime, and orange juice/orange-blossom water. These Moroccan twists can make even low-end alcohol seem top-shelf...at least until tomorrow morning.

DRINK UP

To wash your *diffa* down and stay hydrated, you'll need a good amount of liquid. Serving alcohol within many Moroccan medinas or within view of a mosque may be frowned upon, and liquor licences can cost an astronomical Dh20,000 – but many Moroccan guest houses and restaurants get around these hurdles by offering booze in a low voice, and serving it out of sight indoors or on a terrace. So if you're in the mood for a beer and don't find it on the menu, you might want to ask the waiter in a low voice, speakeasy-style.

Moroccan tap water is often potable, though not always – so stick with treated water or local mineral water. Best bets are Sidi Ali and sparkling Oulmes; others have a chalky aftertaste.

Day and night, don't forget to drink plenty of bottled water. Vying to quench your thirst are orange-juice vendors loudly singing their own praises, and water vendors in fringed tajine-shaped hats clanging brass bowls together. If you want to take up these appealing offers, ask the vendors to pour right into your water bottle or a disposable cup – the glass cups and brass bowls are often reused, and seldom thoroughly washed.

When you're offered Moroccan mint tea, don't expect to bolt it and be on your way. Mint tea is the hallmark of Moroccan hospitality, and a sit-down affair that takes around half an hour. If you have the honour of pouring the tea, pour the first cup back in the teapot to help cool it and dissolve the sugar. Then starting from your right, pour each cup of tea from as high above the glass as you can without splashing. Your hosts will be most impressed.

Foodies who equate Middle Eastern food with Lebanese cuisine stand corrected by Claudia Roden's *Arabesque: A Taste of Morocco, Turkey and Lebanon*, which showcases Moroccan cuisine and won the 2007 James Beard Award (the culinary Oscar).

Moroccan mint tea may be ubiquitous, but you can find a mean cup of coffee in Morocco too. Most of it is French-pressed, and delivers a caffeine wallop to propel you through the souqs and into the stratosphere.

MOROCCO TO GO

Want to fix Moroccan feasts at home? Consider a cooking course (the best ones are in Marrakesh; see p307 for details) and give your home kitchen a Moroccan makeover with these kitchen supplies:

Harira pot A deep ceramic pot with a lid to keep soup hot.
Mortar and pestle Used to crush herbs, garlic and spices.
Tajine slaoui The earthenware cooking tajine in basic terracotta (fancy painted ones are for presentation only).
Tbiqa A basket with a pointed lid for storing bread and pastries.

EAT YOUR WORDS

Begin your taste adventure by picking up some Moroccan food lingo – for a pronunciation guide, see the Language chapter (p504).

Useful Phrases

Table for..., please.	*tabla dyal... 'afak*
Can I pay by credit card?	*wash nkder nkhelles bel kaart kredee?*
Can I see a menu please?	*nazar na'raf lmaakla lli 'andkum?*
I'm a vegetarian.	*makanakoolsh llehem*
What do you recommend?	*shnoo tansaani nakul?*
I'll try what she/he is having.	*gha nzharrab shnoo kaatakul hiyya/huwwa*
Without..., please.	*bla..., 'afak*
I'd like something to drink.	*bgheet shi haazha nashrubha*
I didn't order this.	*tlabtsh had shshi*
Please bring me...	*llaa ykhalleek zheeb li...*
some water	*shwiyya dyaal lmaa*
some salt	*shwiyya dyaal lmelha*
some pepper	*shwiyya dyaal lebzaar*
some bread	*shwiyya dyaal lkhoobz*
a napkin	*mandeel*
a beer	*birra*
a glass/bottle of red/white/rose wine	*kaas/qar'a dyal hmar/byad/roozi shshrab*
This is...	*Had shshi...*
brilliant!	*ldeed bezzef!*
burnt	*mahruqa*
cold	*barda*
undercooked	*ma taybash mazyan*
Cheers! (To your health!)	*Bsaha!*
The bill, please.	*Lahsaab, 'afak.*
Thank you.	*Shukran.*

Food glossary

MEAT

baqree	beef
farooj/dujaj	chicken
lehem	meat
kebda	liver
kelawwi	kidneys
lehem ghenmee	lamb
lehem jemil	camel

SEAFOOD

hut	fish
laangos	lobster
lamoori	cod
merla	whiting
qaimroon	shrimp
serdeen	sardines
shton	anchovies

sol	sole
ton	tuna

VEGETABLES & PULSES

'aads	lentils
batatas	potatoes
besla	onion
fasooliya	white beans
fegg'a	mushroom
khess	lettuce
khiyaar	cucumber
lbdanzhaal	aubergine
loobeeya	green beans
mataisha tamatim	tomato
qooq	artichoke
tooma	garlic
khoodar	vegetables
zeetoun	olives
zelbana bisila	peas

FRUIT

'eineb	grapes
banan/moz	banana
dellah	watermelon
fakiya	fruit
kermoos	figs
limoon	orange
meshmash	apricot
reman	pomegranate
teffah	apple
tmer	dates

OTHER FOODS

bayd	eggs
shorba	soup
filfil/lebzaar	pepper
fromaj/jiben	cheese
khoobz	bread
melha	salt
ships	chips
sukur	sugar
zabadee/laban/danoon	yoghurt
zebda	butter
zit	oil

Environment

ENVIRONMENTAL ISSUES

More than the fully industrialised West, Morocco is a country where land and people live in close interdependence, and environmental challenges are part of everyday life rather than topics of discussion for pundits and campaigning groups. While urban drift presents its own developmental problems, around a quarter of the country's revenue still come from agriculture. Trade agreements with Europe have seen Morocco charging forward as a food exporter to a global market, but the country remains highly prone to other globalised environmental problems.

The World Bank's website (http://web.worldbank.org/morocco) reports in detail on the problems Morocco faces with water use and management.

North Africa has been slowly drying out for centuries. In the south, many rivers have been dry for over a decade and the subsequent burning of date palms and almond groves is nearly irreparable, while global warming has stolen valuable snowfall from mountain regions whose rivers depend upon the melt. Overgrazing is picking the land clean, thereby accumulating the pressures heaped upon the land by global environmental change. Desertification is the result, rendering crops defenceless against whipping sandstorms or torrential flooding. As the Sahara eats away at ever-growing tracts of southern Morocco, oases are left without natural defences and are in danger of drowning beneath the desert. In the end, the ravaged villages confront a crisis in their food and water supplies: poor health and sanitation fester, land becomes unsuitable for farming, and pristine environments are lost forever. The situation is better in the greener plain of the north – a breadbasket since Roman times – but even here the land is becoming pressured for more and more intensive farming.

The North African Environment at Risk, by Will D Swearingen and Abdellatif Bencherifa (eds) can be hard to find but it's worth hunting down as it deals comprehensively with the regional causes of environmental degradation.

Forests are constantly under threat with around 25,000 hectares of forest lost each year. The Atlantic pistachio and wild olive have already perished. The Moroccan pine, thuja and Atlas cedar are seriously at risk. Argan, red juniper, holm oak, canary oak and tauzin oak are very degraded. Damming for irrigation frequently diverts water from these environments, or strips downstream water of valuable silts needed to sustain coastal wetlands.

Although conservation practices are slowly improving, attempts to protect these ecosystems haven't always been a great success. In response to loss of ground cover from overgrazing, the Moroccan forestry department initially reacted by employing methods intended for temperate forest climates, with disastrous results: in the Forest of Mamora near Rabat, broom was thinned from under the cork oaks, leading to serious soil erosion – the trees later died from dehydration. Plantation programs are under way, some with international backing. Every year, two million fruit trees are distributed as the south fights to restore its palm groves. The Plan National de Replanter promised to meet the demand for timber by the year 2000, but has been criticised for planting rapidly growing trees – often foreign varieties, such as the increasingly ubiquitous eucalyptus – without considering suitability.

Want some suggestions on leaving light footprints during your trip? See 'Creative Conservation', p52.

Pollution is another problem that threatens to choke Morocco's environment. Industrial waste is routinely released into the sea, soil and waterways, thereby contaminating water supplies used for drinking and irrigation. Morocco's cities alone produce an annual harvest of 2.4 million tonnes of solid waste, while the draining of coastal wetlands – which provide important habitats for endangered species – continues apace to address the rising demand and falling supply of water for irrigation.

Those water supplies are also being drunk by thirsty tourism developments – either along the coast in places like Agadir or Saïdia or booming Marrakesh and Fez, where hotel complexes with giant pools and golf courses thirstily suck up a finite resource.

The coastal environment is being increasingly challenged, particularly along the Mediterranean shore where in recent years Morocco has been pushing the development of concrete megatourism projects. In a bid to outdo Spain's 'Costa' coast, apartment blocks, 1000-bed hotels and golf courses are being thrown up. Places like Saïdia have seen delicate sand-dune ecosystems torn up and paved over, juniper forest uprooted and the internationally important Moulouya wetlands (home to around 200 bird species) threatened with drying out as a result of building works. According to the European Environment Agency, nearly one in seven of Morocco's beaches have completely disappeared in the last few years.

If you're going for a dip, be aware that the Atlantic rollers can hide some fearsome riptides, and once you're in the waters there's nothing between you and the Americas (or at best, the Canary Islands).

LANDSCAPES

For those whose mental picture of Morocco is formed of palm-fringed oases and plenty of sand, the geographical variety of the country comes as a surprise. The desert is there of course, but you might not expect the dramatic and often snowy crags of the High Atlas, the green rolling plains of the north, the cliffs of the Mediterranean or the wide sweep of the Atlantic coast – all part of North Africa's most varied topography.

And everywhere, there are people interacting with their environment, be they olive farmers in the north, or shepherds leading their flocks to mountain pastures. Over half of all Moroccans still live in rural areas, and the land can in no way be separated from the people who inhabit it.

Coast

When the Arabs first arrived in Morocco, they rode their horses into the Atlantic and dubbed the country *Al-Maghreb* (where the sun sets),

ENVIRONMENTALLY PISTE-OFF

The dire state of the Moroccan environment is something in which we are all implicated. An example of this is in the invasion of the desert by tourist 4WD vehicles in a process known as the 'Toyotarisation' of the Sahara. With their large wheels, 4WDs break up the surface of the desert, which is then scattered into the air by strong winds. By one estimate, the annual generation of dust has increased by 1000% in North Africa in the last 50 years. And in case you thought that your 4WD tracks across the sands would soon be erased by the winds, remember that tracks from WWII vehicles are still visible in the Libyan desert six decades after the cessation of hostilities. Airborne dust is a primary cause of drought far more than it is a consequence of it, as it shields the earth's surface from sunlight and hinders cloud formation.

The consequences of our impatience in the desert extend far beyond Morocco and its desert communities. The stirred-up sand threatens to envelop the world in dust, with serious consequences for human health, coral reefs and climate change. Plankton on the surface of the world's oceans is also being smothered by sand, with devastating implications for marine life. Dust storms are increasingly common in cities like Madrid and the dust-laden winds threaten to transform 90% of Spain's Mediterranean regions into deserts. Once these deserts gain a European foothold, the process of desertification will be extremely difficult and costly to reverse. Sand from the Sahara has even reached as far away as Greenland, settling on icebergs and causing them to melt faster.

Exploring the desert by camel is infinitely more friendly to the environment, quite apart from the fact that it forces you to slow down to a desert pace, free from the intrusions of the modern world. It's also the best way to ensure that you leave behind nothing but easily erasable footprints in the sand.

knowing that the sea marked the western-most limit of their conquests. The coast has defined swathes of Moroccan history, from the Barbary pirates to the Allied landings of WWII, and is currently a key motor for the tourist industry. During the French Protectorate the Atlantic coast was simply dubbed *Maroc utile* (useful Morocco), compared to the relative dryness of the interior. The coastal strip from Casablanca to Rabat was subject to the largest development and today still dominates the country politically, economically and industrially. By contrast, the craggy Mediterranean coast has remained relatively undeveloped until recently, due to its location on the other side of the politically marginalised Rif Mountains. In the past few years, huge government investment has improved access, revealing it as home to some of Morocco's least known, yet loveliest landscapes.

Sahara: An Immense Ocean of Sand, by Paolo Novaresio and Gianni Guadalupi, has stunning Saharan images and informative text that'll have you dreaming of the desert.

While Mediterranean Morocco is mainly a coastline of sheltered coves and plunging cliffs, the long Atlantic littoral is more varied. The north is punctuated by raw and rocky beaches around Assilah, and wetland habitats like the lagoon of Merdja Zerga National Park, famed for its flamingos and wildfowl. From here, things gets more built up, with a concrete strip spreading along the sea from the big cities. South of Casablanca are the ports of Safi and Essaouira, both important tourist towns as well as fishing ports, and then the commercialised boardwalks of Agadir. Further south, the beaches empty into great sandy expanses stretching through Western Sahara to Mauritania.

The Anti Atlas Mountains were part of a chain of mountains formed when Africa and America collided 300 million years ago. The western half of the chain can be found in the Appalachian Mountains in the USA.

Fishing and trade continue to play important roles in the coastal economy. Lixus was an important port for the Phoenicians and Romans, while the cold Atlantic currents are rich in fish. More recently, Morocco's Atlantic coast has become notorious for a darker trade – smuggling sub-Saharan African immigrants to the Canary Islands.

Coastal weather is mild, with a tendency in the north to become cool and wet. Average daily temperatures range from 12°C in winter to 25°C in summer, but the humidity is constant and makes drying laundry nearly impossible. The southern Atlantic and eastern Mediterranean coasts are noticeably more barren.

Mountains

The topographical map of Morocco shows a series of mountain ranges rippling south and growing in size from the Mediterranean – the Rif, the Middle Atlas and the High Atlas, with the subchain of the Anti Atlas eventually petering out towards the desert. The monumental force of plate tectonics brought them into being, the most awesome of events being the collision of Africa and Eurasia around 60 million years ago, which not only forced up the High Atlas, but also closed the Strait of Gibraltar and raised the Alps and Pyrenees. In human times, the mountains have provided shelter for the self-contained Berbers and others who would escape (or rebel against) the invaders of Morocco.

The Sahara Conservation Fund (www.saharaconservation.org), which is dedicated to preserving the wild creatures of the Sahara, is a useful place for learning more about desert wildlife

In the north, the low Rif Mountains form a green and fertile arc that protects the coast from the arid West African interior. The independent-minded Tamazight Berbers have historically held themselves apart from the Moroccan state, and although this has led to the region being ignored and underdeveloped by the government, it's a situation they've turned to their advantage, turning the rough terrain over to kif (marijuana) cultivation. Summers here are comfortably sunny but come October the temperature begins to fall as steeply as the land itself. When the merciless winter gives way around April and May, an intensive and humid rainy season begins.

The Middle Atlas is the Moroccan heartland, with a patchwork of farmland riven with quiet country roads. Running northeast to southwest from the Rif, the range soars to 3340m at its highest point. Agriculture drives the daily routine of the inhabitants of this interior territory, and the plains at the feet of the mountains have grown many of Morocco's major cities, from Volubilis to Fez. The peaks themselves remain mostly forested, ideal trekking country, and home to the Barbary ape, Morocco's only (nonhuman) primate.

The low hills east of Agadir rise to form the gloriously precipitous High Atlas which towers over the villages of Marrakesh and reach the dizzy heights of Jebel Toubkal, North Africa's highest summit (4167m). These High Atlas peaks, some sculpted red, others cloaked in moss and pine, nurture wheat, walnuts and almonds but do little to shield the blistering sun. The temperature is stifling in summer, easily exceeding 40°C. Where the High Atlas drops away to the southeast, deep and winding gorges give way to the Sahara.

Lastly, further south, the low and calloused Anti Atlas drops into the Sahara and protects the Souss Valley from the hot desert winds.

Look out for storks nesting on minarets in old medinas – the way they perch and then bend to sit on their nests is regarded as symbolic of the Muslim prayer, with storks seen as auspicious and pious birds as a result.

Desert

South of the Anti Atlas, the barren slopes, slashed with more gorges, trail off into the stony, almost trackless desert of the Western Sahara. This sparsely populated and unforgiving region is bounded to the east and south by Algeria and Mauritania.

Cresting the Middle Atlas in the Zagora region draws you down through the clustered palms of the chiselled Drâa Valley and into the desolate dunes known as Tinfou and Erg Chigaga. Southeast in Er-Rachidia province are the saffron dunes of Merzouga, entry point to the great sand seas of the Sahara. This region is rich in kasbahs, remnants of the days of the trans-Saharan trade routes that made cities like Marrakesh so rich. Today, dates from the many palm groves provide the population's economic mainstay.

Even in winter the lowlands sizzle by day, with temperatures around 30°C, but the dry atmosphere lowers temperatures quickly in the evening and the nights can be frightfully cold, demanding layered clothing and good humour. The wild environment of the Moroccan deserts has also left its mark upon the people – the pace of life here is slower and the

COLD-BLOODED CAPITALISM

Sadly, the easiest way to encounter Morocco's wildlife, particularly its reptiles, is in the anything-but-natural surrounds of a souq. Snake charmers, stalls selling various reptiles (or parts of reptiles) for use in folk medicine, and tortoise shells turned into decorative fire bellows or banjolike musical instruments for souvenir-hungry tourists are common sights and, sadder still, common purchases made by tourists.

Take a close look at the snakes and you'll discover that their mouths are stitched closed, leaving tiny gaps for their tongues to flicker though. The snakes frequently develop fatal mouth infections and are unable to feed, requiring replacement by freshly caught specimens. As a result of the unceasing demand for tourist-charming snakes, numbers of Egyptian cobra have plummeted.

An estimated 10,000 tortoises are also killed annually for the tourist trade, which, when combined with large-scale habitat loss, helps explain why one of Morocco's tortoises *(Testudo graeca graeca)* is on the UN's Convention on the International Trade of Endangered Species list. Current legislation doesn't prohibit their sale (or the sale of their shells) within Morocco, but try to take an endangered tortoise out of the country and you'll be breaking the law.

conversations are less garrulous, with every aspect of life dictated by the daytime heat and by the need to draw near around the campfire at night.

For more information on birdwatching in Morocco, see p453.

WILDLIFE

An old overlanding hand once commented to us that Morocco was almost the perfect African country as it had mountains, deserts, historic cities and culture. Everything in fact, except wildlife. Well, Morocco teems with wildlife, although you'll generally need to get away from well-travelled routes to catch a glimpse of it. There are more than 40 different ecosystems that provide habitat for many endemic species. Unfortunately, the pressure upon these ecosystems from sprawling urban areas and the industrialisation upon Morocco's wilderness has ensured that much of the country's iconic plant and animal life is endangered.

Animals

COASTAL WILDLIFE

The camel – synonymous with Morocco's deserts – isn't a native species, but was introduced from Arabia around AD 600.

As cities like Casablanca and Tangier and Agadir-style resorts spread along the littoral, Morocco's marine life has come under increasing pressure. However, away from the urban sprawl, there are still long stretches of coastline free from an intensive human presence, with abundant bird populations and marine mammals such as dolphins and porpoises. Important bird species include white-eyed gulls, Moroccan cormorants and sandwich terns found along the beaches. On the Mediterranean coast, a remnant population of the Mediterranean monk seal, one of the world's most endangered mammals, is thought to still be clinging to existences.

Seabirds and freshwater birds are abundant in places like Souss-Massa National Park, with many species of duck and waders often migrating from Europe to spend winter in warmer Moroccan climes. This region also hosts a population of the endangered bald ibis.

DESERT

At first glance, the Sahara seems an impossible place to make a living, but its home to a surprising number of animal species. There are plenti-

LION KING

When the Romans took to feeding Christians to the lions, they looked to Morocco for their dinner companions. The Barbary lion, once found across the Atlas and Rif Mountains was a distinct subspecies, larger than savannah lions, with a thick black mane and a solitary habit adapted to its forested home. It preyed mainly on Barbary sheep, wild boar and deer. The last wild Barbary lion was shot in 1921.

Legend has it that the king of Morocco himself had been happily feeding wrongdoers to his personal collection of felines as late as 1914. The last dissident to meet this fate was apparently offered a short reprieve by the king, but instead retorted that, 'It's better to be eaten by lions than bitten by a dog', and was dispatched *tout de suite*.

The Parc Zoologique National in Rabat, along with European partner zoos has established a small captive-breeding program with the descendants of the king's man-eaters, now about 80% Barbary lion. Genetic markers are being used to determine the lions' pedigree, although claims by some zoos to have pure Barbary lions remain unverified.

This slow but genuine progress has some naturalists dreaming of a release program, although it's unlikely to find much favour with rural populations faced with such a feline neighbour.

BUSTARDS TAKE TO THE WING AGAIN

The spring of 2008 saw the culmination of a years-long project to increase the population of the endangered Houbara bustard, with the release of 5000 captive-bred birds into the eastern desert – believed to be the largest single reintroduction of any endangered species in the world.

The project is based at the Emirates Centre for Wildlife Propagation (ECWP) in Missour on the eastern edge of the Middle Atlas, and funded by the UAE, which has been leading the way in bustard captive-breeding since the early 1980s. Many feel this is especially appropriate as Houbara-bustard populations across the Middle East and North Africa have come under severe pressure, in large part due to their popularity as prey for falcon-hunting by wealthy Gulf Arabs. The ECWP is regarded as a model for captive-breeding of this flagship conservation species – bustards have been notoriously regarded as difficult to breed in captivity, due to their intricate mating behaviour and nervous disposition.

A third of the released birds were fitted with satellite transmitters to allow them to be monitored and studied within the total protected area of nearly 40,000 sq km.

ful rodents, including numerous varieties of gerbils and jerboas, and the desert hedgehog. Lizards such as skinks, spiny-tailed lizards, thrive, along with the horned viper. Higher up the food chain is the delightful fennec fox, an iconic desert species with fur-soled feet and huge batlike ears. It's nocturnal, but if you're staying overnight in the desert you might be lucky enough to catch a brief glimpse. Golden jackals are the most common large predator; in the remoter parts of the Western Sahara there are thought to still be some desert-adapted cheetahs, but their status is unknown. Dorcas and Cuvier's Gazelle are its main prey. The Addax, a larger antelope is almost certainly locally extinct, sadly following Morocco's oryx into the history book.

MOUNTAINS

The forested slopes of the mountains are Morocco's richest wildlife habitats. Their most famous denizen, in parts of the Middle Atlas and the Rif, is the sociable Barbary macaque (also known as the Barbary ape), most easily spotted around Azrou. Less easy to track are mountain gazelles, lynx and Barbary sheep. The last has benefited from governmental protection, good news for its top predator, the critically endangered Barbary leopard – the last population of leopards in North Africa.

Sahara: A Natural History, by Marq de Villiers and Sheila Hirtle, is a highly readable account of the Sahara's wildlife, its people and geographical history.

Although outshone by the beautiful golden eagle, birds of this area include red crossbills, horned larks, acrobatic booted eagles, Egyptian vultures, and both black and red kites. Butterflies, too, are abundant, although you will probably only come across them in the spring. Species common to the area include the scarlet cardinal and bright-yellow Cleopatra.

Plants

Morocco is particularly colourful in April and May when the country is briefly in bloom before the summer swelter. Highlights include irises, thyme, orchids, geraniums, cedar forests, oaks, thuja, pines, and, at higher altitudes, even juniper. The flower-studded pastures of the Rif Mountains are a particular delight. But the more appetising of Morocco's plant life are its fruits and legumes, particularly abundant in the south due to the semitropical climate. While pomegranate and fig trees are found throughout the country, you'll find orange groves in Agadir, walnut trees in Marrakesh, almond trees in Ouarzazate and date palms in Zagora.

NATIONAL PARKS

Morocco's record on environmental protection may be far from perfect, but the government has begun to set aside protected areas to arrest the alarming loss of habitat and the resulting disappearance of plant and animal species. Toubkal National Park in the Atlas Mountains was the first national park to be created in 1942, while Morocco's most impressive park, Souss-Massa National Park, was carved out in 1991 outside Agadir.

Evidence that Morocco is taking its environmental responsibilities seriously came in 2004 with the creation of four new national parks: Talassemtane (58,950 hectares) in the Rif; Al-Hoceima (48,460 hectares) in the Mediterranean, which protects outstanding coastal and marine habitats along the Mediterranean and one of the last outposts of osprey; Ifrane National Park (51,800 hectares) in the Middle Atlas, with cedar forests and Barbary macaques; and the Eastern High Atlas National Park (55,252 hectares). During this flurry of national-park creation, the Tazekka National Park was also enlarged.

In all, Morocco has 12 fully fledged national parks, as well as 35 nature reserves, forest sanctuaries and other protected areas which are overseen by Morocco's Direction des Eaux et Forêts. The parks have also provided a sphere for research into the region's biodiversity (including botanical inventories, bird censuses, primate studies and sediment analyses) and the causes of habitat loss that could have implications for unprotected areas beyond the parks' boundaries. Lately, the international community has also shown interest; the Spanish and American Park Services have used Morocco's protected areas as a base for their own research into broader biodiversity issues.

NOTABLE NATIONAL PARKS

National park	Location	Features	Activities	Best time to visit
Toubkal National Park (p425)	near Marrakesh	highest peak in North Africa	hiking, climbing	May-Jun
Souss-Massa National Park (p384)	south of Agadir	coastal estuaries and forests; 275 species of birds, including endangered bald ibis, mammals & enclosed endangered species	hiking, wildlife-watching birdwatching,	Mar-Oct
Lac de Sidi Bourhaba (p133)	Mehdiya	lake & wetlands; 200 migratory bird species, including marbled duck, African marsh owl & flamingo	swimming, birdwatching, hiking	Oct-Mar
Merdja Zerga National Park (p133)	Moulay Bousselham	lagoon habitats; 190 species of waterfowl, including African marsh owl, Andouin's gull, flamingo & crested coot	wildlife-watching	Dec-Jan
Talassemtane National Park (p444)	Chefchaouen	cedar & fir forests; Barbary macaque, fox, jackal & bats in the cedar forest	wildlife-watching, hiking	May-Sep
Bouarfa Wildlife Sanctuary (p288)	Bouarfa	red rock steppe	hiking, climbing	Apr-Oct
Tazzeka National Park (p282)	near Taza	oak forests & waterfalls	hiking	Jun-Sep
National Park of Al-Hoceima (p214)	Al-Hoceima	thuya forest, limestone escarpments, fish eagles	hiking, birdwatching	May-Oct

Of the parks that do exist, the age-old tension between increasing tourist revenues from national parks, and frustration over the parcelling of land and inattention to concerns like water shortages and health care, means that support among local communities for the new protected areas is patchy at best. Though the parks' missions are perceived as valuable, local communities have often not benefited quickly and directly enough from initiatives. The Ministries of Tourism and Agriculture temper this sentiment by reasoning that tourist activity means profits to fund future environmental programs – the very initiatives that will return plant and animal life to their original, more productive state, restore arable land and ultimately benefit the surrounding communities.

Africa & the Middle East: A Continental Overview of Environmental Issues, by Kevin Hillstrom, contains an excellent exploration of North Africa's environmental past and future, focusing on how human populations impact upon the environment.

For all their problems, Morocco's national parks are becoming a major tourist drawcard, particularly for the opportunities they present for recreational activities in pristine wilderness areas. Toubkal National Park, for example, encompasses North Africa's highest mountain range and has rich camping, hiking and rock-climbing possibilities. As the parks' popularity grows, and with it Morocco's reputation as a venue for environmental tourism, the government has plans to make the parks self-supporting, mostly by charging admission.

The Al-Hoceima and Talassemtane parks in particular are examples of how far Moroccan nature conservation has come, integrating plans for promoting rural tourism and developing hiking routes. At the same time, the parks' authorities are working with local communities to allay their concerns and enable them to view the parks as a profitable alternative to kif cultivation.

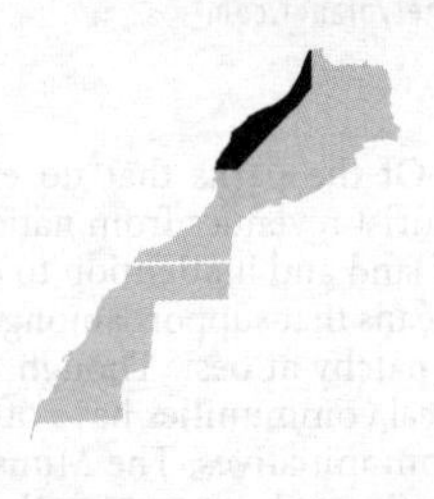

Atlantic Coast
شاطئ الأطلنطي

It was once literally the end of the earth: those living around the ancient Mediterranean believed there was no land beyond Morocco's Atlantic Coast. Now it's one of Morocco's most prosperous regions, home to the nation's capital, to its major city and some of its finest sights.

Miles of glorious sands peppered with small fishing villages, historic ports and fortified towns weave along Morocco's blustery coast. Throughout history, control of this coast was imperative for both invading forces and local tribes hoping to expand their empires. The Phoenicians, Romans, Portuguese, Spanish and French all fought to control the region and left a legacy in the beautiful walled towns, wide boulevards and relaxed attitude of this part of Morocco.

The coast has its beauty and its eyesores. A large chunk of Morocco's population lives in this area and the modern cities are far more cosmopolitan than those of the interior – their art-deco and neo-Moorish architecture, stylish cafés and liberal attitudes a far cry from traditional Morocco, but increasingly valued by locals and visitors.

Beyond these two cities lie Assilah and other fortified towns, and around these are several reserves that showcase the coast's rich birdlife. But the developers are arriving with their plans for mega-resorts, golf courses and huge marinas, hoping in the process to transform a region that, for many, already has more than enough attractions.

HIGHLIGHTS

- Dress to the nines and join the in-crowd at the hip Blvd de la Corniche in **Casablanca** (p114)
- Revel in the whitewashed colonial 1920s architecture in the spotless streets of **Rabat** (p120)
- Wander the ramparts, gorge on fresh fish or just sit back and soak up the atmosphere in laid-back **Essaouira** (p153)
- Drive along the coastal road from **El-Jadida** (p144) to **Essaouira** (p153), where the fields go down to the wild shores of the Atlantic
- Gorge on oysters or a fresh seafood platter and catch a wave at the idyllic, crescent-shaped bay of **Oualidia** (p149)
- Enjoy the quiet pace and authenticity of the old medina in **Azemmour** (p148), between the sea and the Oum ar-Rabia river
- See a cloud of pink flamingos fluttering like huge butterflies in the sunset while boating on the waters of the **Merdja Zerga National Park** (p133)

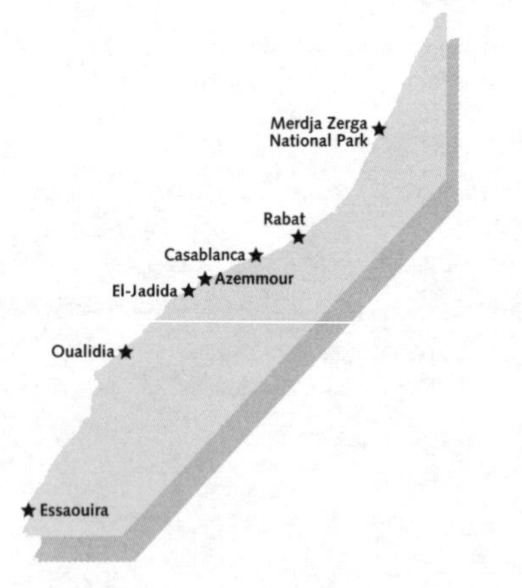

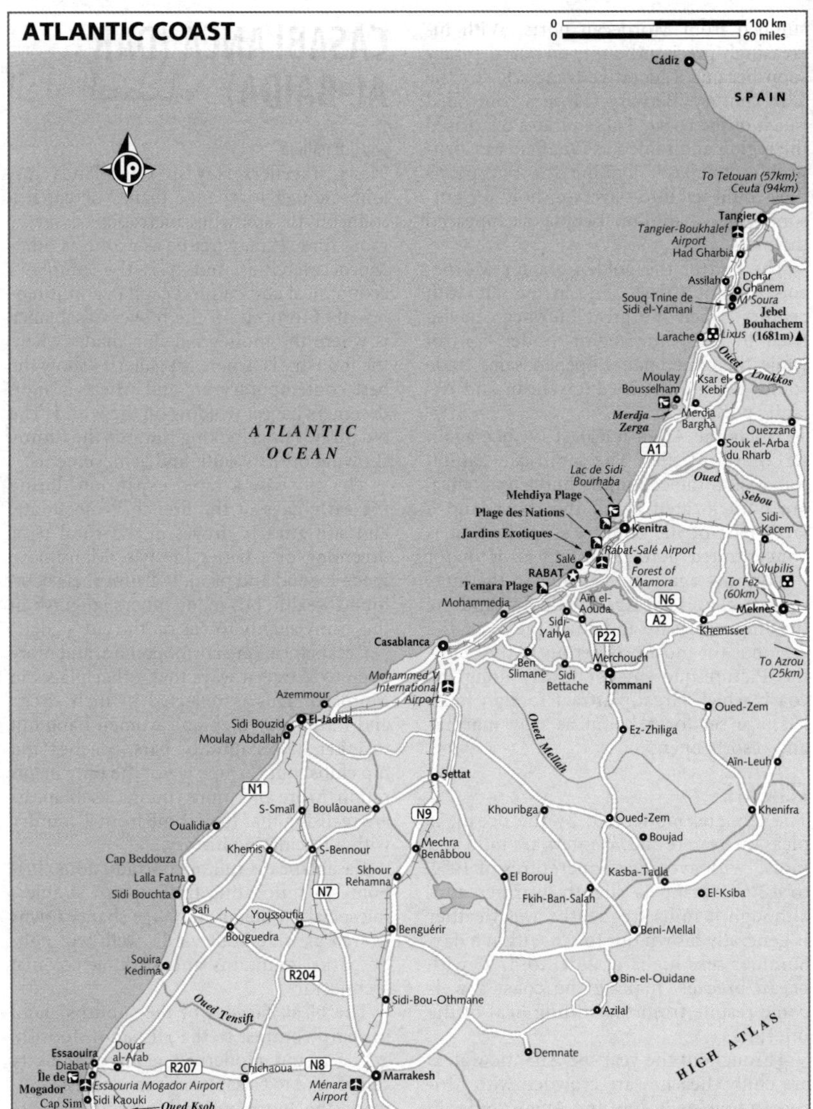

HISTORY

The French called it Le Maroc Utile (useful Morocco), and throughout the country's history, this stretch of the Atlantic Coast has remained crucial to its prosperity. From the 10th to 6th century BC, seafaring Phoenicians found it useful to run trading posts – including Liks (Lixus), Essaouira and Chellah – along the coast. Some of these settlements went on to become the westernmost outposts of the Roman Empire.

The Portuguese established several trading posts from Assilah to Agadir in the late 15th and early 16th centuries. A period of great prosperity followed, as the spoils from the trans-African caravan routes were shipped from Moroccan ports. With increasingly precious bounty on board, piracy soon became a lucrative trade and, by the 18th century, Barbary Corsairs controlled much of the coast. These pirates terrorised the region and raided as far afield as Cornwall in England, looking for Europeans they could sell into slavery or hold for ransom. Over a million people disappeared this way.

The end of the golden era for Morocco's Atlantic Coast came in the late 18th century, when the great European navies tried to bring the region under control while their merchants opened safer trade routes beyond the Mediterranean and Atlantic ports.

Today the Atlantic Coast is once again Le Maroc Utile. The political capital Rabat, and the economic hub Casablanca, are both located along the coast, and a large part of the country's production is concentrated here. Shipping is of major importance again, and thanks to the huge industrial ports at Agadir and Safi and the thriving resorts up and down the coast, the region is the most prosperous in the country. Picturesque smaller towns along the coast, which already attract foreign tourists, are set for a boom as new marinas and resorts open.

CLIMATE

The climate, moderated by the ocean, is pleasant year-round. Winters are mild and moist, with average temperatures of 10°C to 12°C. Spring is slightly warmer and, although it rains frequently, wet weather is generally blown out to sea within a day. Summer sees highs of 25°C to 27°C with ocean breezes, making the coast a welcome respite from the stifling heat of the interior.

Throughout the year the Atlantic waters are chilly. Beaches are crowded with Moroccan tourists in July and August only.

GETTING THERE & AWAY

Casablanca and Rabat are transport hubs for the region. Both are on the national train line with direct links to Tangier, Oujda, Fez, Meknès and Marrakesh. Both also have international airports, though Casablanca has a far greater number of international flights.

CASABLANCA (DAR AL-BAÏDA) الدار البيضاء

pop 3.8 million

Many travellers stay in Casablanca just long enough to change planes or catch a train, but the sprawling metropolis deserves more time. It may not be as exotic as other Moroccan cities, but it is the country's economical and cultural capital, and it represents Morocco on the move: Casablanca is where the money is being made, where the industry is, where art galleries show the best contemporary art and where fashion designers have a window on the world. The old pirate lair is looking towards the future, showing off its wealth and achievements.

The city saw a rapid expansion during the early days of the French Protectorate, and still attracts droves of the rural poor dreaming of a better lifestyle. Many have made it good and proudly flaunt their newfound wealth, but many others languish in the grimy shanty towns on the city's edge.

Casablancais are cosmopolitan, and more open to Western ways than other places in Morocco. This is reflected in their dress, and in the way men and women hang out together in restaurants, bars, beaches and hip clubs. But Europe is not the only inspiration. More and more young Casablancais are realising that they come from a country with a fascinating history.

Casablanca is full of contradictions. It is home to suffocating traffic jams, simmering social problems and huge shanty towns as well as wide boulevards, well-kept public parks, fountains and striking colonial architecture.

The bleak facades of the suburbs stand in sharp contrast to the Hispano-Moorish, art-deco and modernist gems of the city centre, and to Casablanca's modernist landmark, the enormous and incredibly ornate Hassan II Mosque.

HISTORY

The Phoenicians established a small trading post in the now upmarket suburb of Anfa from the 6th century BC onwards. In the 7th century AD, Anfa became a regional capital under the Barghawata, a confederation of Berber tribes. The Almohads destroyed it in 1188, and 70 years later, the Merenids took over.

In the early 15th century, the port became a safe haven for pirates and racketeers. Anfa pirates became such a serious threat later in the century that the Portuguese sent 50 ships and 10,000 men to subdue them. They left Anfa in a state of ruins. The local tribes however continued to terrorise the trade routes, provoking a second attack by the Portuguese in 1515. Sixty years later the Portuguese arrived to stay, erecting fortifications and renaming the port Casa Branca (White House).

The Portuguese abandoned the colony in 1755 after a devastating earthquake destroyed Lisbon and severely damaged the walls of Casa Branca. Sultan Sidi Mohammed ben Abdallah subsequently resettled and fortified the town, but it never regained its former importance. By 1830 it had few more than 600 inhabitants.

By the mid-1800s Europe was booming and turned to Morocco for increased supplies of grain and wool. The fertile plains around Casablanca were soon supplying European markets, and agents and traders flocked back to the city. Spanish merchants renamed the city Casablanca and by the beginning of the 20th century the French had secured permission to build an artificial harbour.

Increased trade brought prosperity to the region, but the activities and influence of the Europeans also caused resentment. Violence erupted in 1907 when Europeans desecrated a Muslim cemetery. The pro-colonialist French jumped at the chance to send troops to quell the dispute; a French warship and a company of marines soon arrived and bombarded the town. By 1912 it was part of the new French Protectorate.

Under the first French resident-general, Louis Hubert Gonzalve Lyautey, architect Henri Prost redesigned Casablanca as the economic centre of the new protectorate. His wide boulevards and modern urban planning still survive, and mark the city as more European than Moroccan. However, Lyautey underestimated the success of his own plans and the city grew far beyond his elaborate schemes. By the end of the WWII, Casablanca had a population of 700,000 and was surrounded by heaving shanty towns.

Casablanca still has huge disparities of wealth, and the shanty towns (see p105) are easily visible on the train journey in from the airport. New migrants arrive daily and for every one that finds success, others continue to struggle.

ORIENTATION

Casablanca is a sprawling modern city. The medina – the oldest part of town – is tiny and sits in the north of the city close to the port. To the south of the medina is Place des Nations Unies, a large traffic junction that marks the heart of the city.

The city's main streets branch out from here: Ave des Forces Armées Royales (Ave des FAR), Ave Moulay Hassan I, Blvd Mohammed V and Blvd Houphouët Boigny.

Ave Hassan II leads to Place Mohammed V, easily recognised by its grand art-deco administrative buildings. Quartier Gauthier and Maarif, west and southwest of the Parc de la Ligue Arabe, are where most of the action is, with shops, bars and restaurants.

To the southeast is the Quartier Habous (also know as the nouvelle medina) and to the west is Aïn Diab, the beachfront suburb home to upmarket hotels and nightclubs.

The CTM bus station and Casa Port train station are in the centre of the city. Casa Voyageurs station is 2km east of the centre

CASABLANCA IN...

24 hours

Start your day with breakfast at **Paul** (p113) in the stunning Zevaco building filled with local yummy mummies. Take a taxi to the **Hassan II Mosque** (p105), then head to **Café Maure** (p112), in the ramparts, for lunch. Follow the **walking tour** (p106), taking in the best of Casa's art-deco heritage, before making your way to the **Quartier Habous** (p104) for shopping and cakes the French-Moroccan way. Treat yourself to stunning views over the ocean by dining at one of the **cliff-top restaurants** (p113) by Phare el-Hank before joining the city's pretty young things in the bars and clubs along **Blvd de la Corniche** (p114).

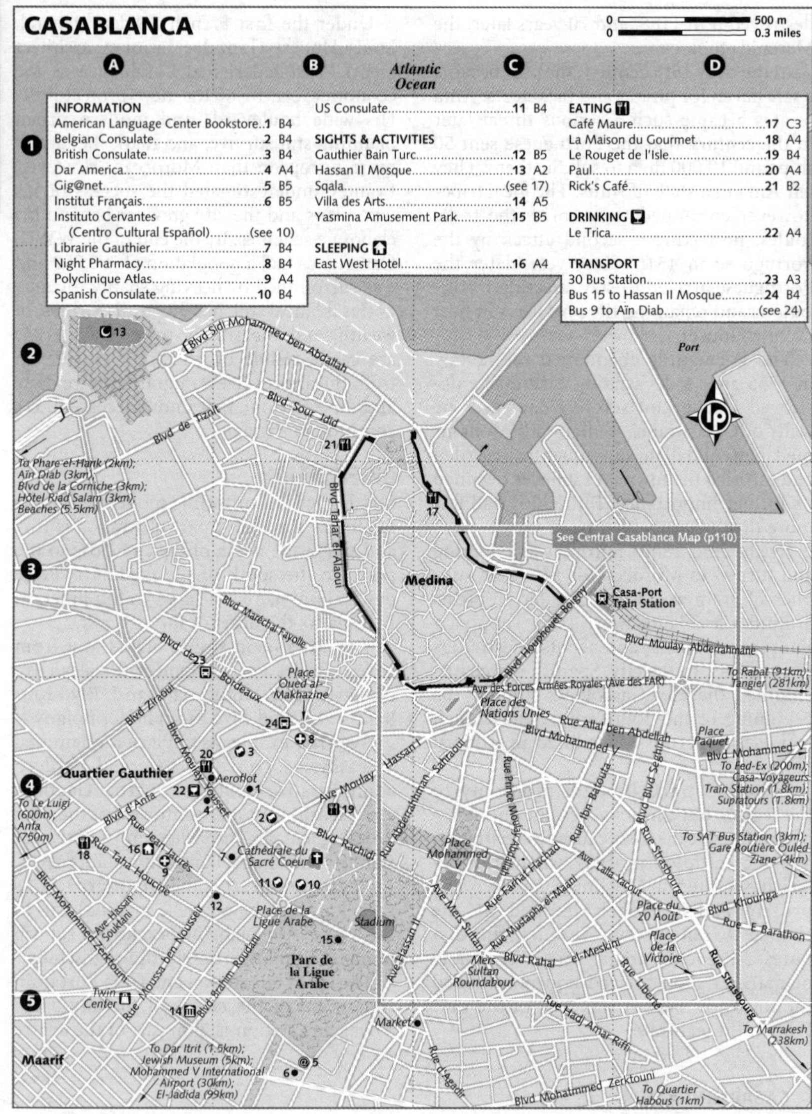

and the airport is 30km southeast of town. See p128 for more transport information.

Street Names

Casablanca's French street names are slowly being replaced with Moroccan names. Be very specific when asking for directions, as many people (and some local street directories) have yet to make the transition. You'll often see several different names for one street.

INFORMATION

Bookshops

American Language Center Bookstore (Map p102; ☎ 022 277765; 1 Place de la Fraternité) A good selection of English-language classics as well as books on Morocco, North Africa and Islam. Just off Blvd Moulay Youssef.

Librairie Gauthier (Map p102; ☎ 022 264426; 12 Rue Moussa ben Nousseir) Books by French and Moroccan writers, as well as road maps.

Cultural Centres

Dar America (Map p102; ☎ 022 221460; http://casablanca.aca.org.ma; 10 Place Bel Air; 🕑 8am-5pm Mon-Fri) The cultural centre of the American Language Center and library; bring ID to get in.

Goethe Institut (Map p110; ☎ 022 200445; www.goethe.de/casablanca, in German; 11 Place du 16 Novembre; 🕑 10am-noon & 3-6pm Tue-Sat) Conducts German classes and presents the occasional film screening, cultural event and exhibition.

Institut Français (Map p102; ☎ 022 779870; www.ambafrance-ma.org, in French; 121-123 Blvd Mohammed Zerktouni; 🕑 9am-2.30pm Tue-Sat) Offers a good library, films, lectures, exhibitions and other events.

Instituto Cervantes (Centro Cultural Español; Map p102; ☎ 022 267337; http://casablanca.cervantes.es, in Spanish; 31 Rue d'Alger; 🕑 10am-noon & 3-6pm Tue-Sat) Hosts film screenings and cultural events and has a library.

Emergency

Emergency services (☎ 15; 🕑 24hr)

Service d'Aide Médicale Urgente (SAMU; ☎ 022 252525; 🕑 24hr) Private ambulance service.

SOS Médecins (☎ 022 444444, 022 202020; house call Dh350; 🕑 24hr) Private doctors who make house calls.

Internet Access

EuroNet (Map p110; ☎ 022 265921; 51 Rue Tata; per hr Dh10; 🕑 8.30am-11pm)

G@.net (Map p110; ☎ 022 229523; 29 Rue Abdelkader al-Moftaker; per hr Dh8; 🕑 9am-midnight) Very clean and modern, with fast connection.

Gig@net (Map p102; ☎ 022 484810; 140 Blvd Mohammed Zerktouni; per hr Dh10; 🕑 24hr)

LGnet (Map p110; ☎ 022 274613; 81 Blvd Mohammed V; per hr Dh6; 🕑 9am-midnight)

Medical Services

Night Pharmacy (Map p102; cnr Place Oued al-Makhazine & Blvd d'Anfa; 🕑 24hr)

Polyclinique Atlas (Map p102; ☎ 022 274039; 27 Rue Mohammed ben Ali, Quartier Gauthier; 🕑 24hr) Off Rue Jean Jaures.

Money

There are banks – most with ATMS and foreign-exchange offices – on almost every street corner in the centre of Casablanca.

BMCE (Map p110; Hôtel Hyatt Regency, Place des Nations Unis; 🕑 9am-9pm) Good for after-hours and weekend services.

Crédit du Maroc (Map p110; ☎ 022 477255; 48 Blvd Mohammed V) Separate bureau de change that is very central; American Express (Amex) travellers cheques cashed for free.

Voyages Schwartz (Map p110; ☎ 022 376330; schwartz@mbox.azure.net; 112 Rue Prince Moulay Abdallah) Amex representative; does not cash or sell travellers cheques.

Wafa Cash (Map p110; ☎ 022 208080; 15 Rue Indriss Lahrizi; 🕑 8am-8pm Mon-Sat) Open longer hours; has an ATM and cashes travellers cheques.

Post

Central Market post office (Map p110; cnr Blvd Mohammed V & Rue Chaouia; 🕑 8am-4.15pm Mon-Fri)

FedEx (☎ 022 541212; 313 Blvd Mohammed V)

Main post office (Map p110; cnr Blvd de Paris & Ave Hassan II; 🕑 8am-6pm Mon-Fri, 8am-noon Sat)

Medina post office (Map p110; Place Ahmed el-Bidaoui; 🕑 8am-6pm Mon-Fri, 8am-noon Sat) Near the youth hostel.

Tourist Information

Although the staff are polite, tourist offices in Casablanca are of very little practical use. Try www.visitcasablanca.ma for information before you travel or ask the receptionist at your hotel for help.

Office National Marocain du Tourisme (ONMT; Map p110; ☎ 022 279533; 55 Rue Omar Slaoui; 🕑 8.30am-noon & 2.30-6.30pm Mon-Fri)

Syndicat d'Initiative (Map p110; ☎ 022 221524; 98 Blvd Mohammed V; 🕑 8.30am-4.30pm Mon-Fri, 9am-12.30pm Sat)

Travel Agencies

Carlson Wagonlit (Map p110; ☎ 022 203051; www.carlsonwagonlit.com/en/countries/ma; 60-62 Rue Araibi Jilali) A respected international chain of travel agencies.

Supratours (off Map p102; ☎ 022 248172; www.supratourstravel.com; Casa Voyageurs train station) Organises rail and bus connections.

Voyages Wasteels (Map p110; ☎ 022 541010; www.wasteels.fr, in French; 26 Rue Léon L'Africain) A good place for cheap intercontinental rail tickets.

DANGERS & ANNOYANCES

Although Casablanca can feel pretty rough around the edges, it's relatively safe for tourists. However, there are huge disparities of wealth – as in any large city, you need to keep your wits about you. Travellers should take care when walking around the city centre at night and be extra vigilant in and around the old medina. Coming home late from a bar or club, it's best to take a taxi.

SIGHTS

Casablanca is Morocco's commercial hub and locals are far more interested in big international business than in tourism. Tourists are few in town and it's very much a workaday place with remarkably few traditional tourist attractions. Apart from the grand Hassan II Mosque, the city's main appeal is in strolling around its neighbourhoods: the wonderful art-deco architecture of the city centre, the peaceful Parc de la Ligue Arabe, the gentrified market district of the Quartier Habous and the beachfront views of the Corniche. Join the Casablancais in enjoying the cosmopolitan pleasures of their city, go out for dinner, visit an art gallery, shop till you drop in Maarif, try out the funky nightlife or go roller skating outside the Hassan II Mosque.

Downtown Casa

It is often said that Casablanca has no sights apart from the Hassan II Mosque, but the French-built city centre is packed with grand colonial buildings, some of which are being restored. The best way to take it all in is by strolling in the area around the **Marché Central**, or by doing the walking tour (see p106). The run-down Marché Central quarter is slowly being revived, particularly around the pedestrian street of Rue Prince Moulay Abdallah. The **Place Mohammed V** is where the architect Henri Prost really went to town. The grand square is surrounded by public buildings whose designs were later copied in buildings throughout Morocco, including the law courts, the splendid *wilaya*, the Bank al-Maghrib, the post office and the Ministry of Defense building. Many grand boulevards lined with wonderful architecture go off this square. To the south is the **Parc de la Ligue Arabe**, designed in 1918 with a majestic palm tree–lined promenade.

Located in a converted art-deco building near the Parc de la Ligue Arabe, the gorgeous 1930s **Villa des Arts** (Map p102; ☎ 022 295087; 30 Blvd Brahim Roudani; admission Dh10; ⏲ 9am-7pm Tue-Sat) holds exhibitions of contemporary Moroccan and international art.

Ancienne Médina

Casablanca's small and dilapidated **medina** (Map p110) gives an idea of just how small the city was before the French embarked on their massive expansion program. Most of the buildings date from the 19th century, so it lacks the medieval character of other medinas.

Enter the medina from the northeast corner of the Place des Nations Unies near the restored **clock tower** (Map p110). The narrow lanes to the east are piled high with cheap shoes, high-sheen underwear, household goods and, reputedly, stolen goods. The rest of the medina remains largely residential. The old city's main Friday mosque is the **Jemaa ash-Chleuh** (Map p110) along Rue Jemaa ash-Chleuh Arsalane.

On the north side of the medina, facing the port, you'll see the last remains of Casablanca's 18th-century fortifications. Known as the **sqala** (Map p102), the bastion offers panoramic views over the sea.

Maarif

Southwest of the Parc de la Ligue Arabe is the city's business centre and the place to head for international designer brands. At the time of writing, the **Twin Center** (Map p102; cnr Blvd Mohammed Zerktouni & Al-Massira al-Khadra) – marking the high-end of the chic shopping area – was about to open a shopping mall, luxury hotel and office spaces. Smaller boutiques on the side streets and around the covered Maarif market are more atmospheric and good for bargains.

Quartier Habous (Nouvelle Medina)

The Quartier Habous, or nouvelle medina, is Morocco-lite – an idealised, almost Disney version of a traditional medina, with neat rows of streets and shop stalls. Built by the French in the 1930s it was a unique experiment: a medina built to Western standards to accommodate the first rural exodus in the 1920s. As such, it blends Moroccan architecture with French ideals, epitomised by a mosque and a strip of grassy lawn, reminiscent of European village churches.

However sanitised it may feel, if you have some last-minute souvenir shopping to do, Habous is more peaceful than most souqs and has a decent selection of bazaars, craft shops, bakeries and cafés.

The **Royal Palace** (closed to the public) is to the north of the district, while to the south is the old **Mahakma du Pasha** (courts & reception hall; admission free; 8am-noon & 2-6pm Mon-Sat), which has more than 60 rooms decorated with sculpted wooden ceilings, stuccowork, wrought-iron railings and earthenware floors.

The Quartier Habous is located about 1km southeast of town. Take bus 81 from Blvd de Paris, across from the main post office.

Hassan II Mosque

The late King Hassan II wanted to make his mark, and give Casablanca the landmark it so sorely missed. This most ambitious building project started in 1980 to commemorate the king's 60th birthday and was completed in 1993, although work continues on reshaping the boulevards and area around the mosque, also part of the grand plan.

Designed by French architect Michel Pinseau the **mosque** (Map p102) rises above the ocean on a rocky outcrop reclaimed from the sea, echoing the verse from the Quran that states that God's throne was built upon the water. The 210m-high minaret, the tallest building in the country, is topped by a spectacular laser beam that shines towards Mecca. It is the world's third-largest mosque, accommodating 25,000 worshippers inside, and a further 80,000 in the courtyards and squares around it. Believers can enjoy praying on a centrally heated floor, seeing the Atlantic washing the rocks underneath the glass floor and feel the sunlight through the retractable roof.

Above all, the vast size and elaborate decoration of the prayer hall is most striking. Large enough to house Paris' Notre Dame or Rome's St Peter's, it is blanketed in astonishing woodcarving, *zellij* (tilework) and stucco moulding. A team of over 6000 mastercraftsmen was assembled to work on the mosque, delicately carving intricate patterns and designs in cedar from the Middle Atlas, marble from Agadir and granite from Tafraoute.

The project cost more than half a billion dollars and was paid for largely by public subscription. Most Casablancais are proud of their monument, but some feel this vast sum might have been better spent. There is also a dispute over who is going to pay for the upkeep of the mosque, as the exterior is already showing serious distress under the extreme weather conditions so close to the ocean.

The mosque of Tin Mal in the High Atlas (see p336) and Hassan II Mosque are the only two mosques open to non-Muslims in Morocco. To see the interior you must

THE SHANTY TOWNS

In May 2003, 13 suicide bombers blew themselves up at public places in Casablanca, killing themselves and 32 other people. They belonged to Salafia Jihadia, a radical Islamic group whose founding members trained in Afghanistan. The bombers were all young Moroccan men living in Casablanca's worst slums, less than half an hour from the city centre.

In 2007, 24 Islamists were arrested for plotting another wave of bombings after their leader blew himself up at an internet café. Many came from the same slums.

Most Casablancais openly condemn the killings, and claim their city is the most tolerant in the country. But a quarter – perhaps even a third – of the city's population lives in shanty towns, where living conditions are harsh: makeshift houses are made of cardboard and plastic, there is no running water, sewage system or electricity, no schools, no work and no hope. Many youngsters feel they have nothing to lose.

After the bombings, many charities were set up to improve the conditions, and the government has become more aware of the problems. The Housing Ministry has a plan to abolish all slums in Casablanca by 2012 and several slums have already been destroyed, with residents moved to new housing. Tens of thousands of houses are under construction, but slum residents complain that the new housing is too expensive and too small for extended families. There has been a serious improvement, but many feel it's not enough, and unless the government addresses the underlying problems there will be no improvement in conditions. It is hoped this will happen before anger and frustration boil over into support for violent alternatives.

take a **guided tour** (☎ 022 222563; adult/child/student Dh120/30/60; ⏲ 9am, 10am, 11am & 2pm Sat-Thu). Visitors must be 'decently and respectfully dressed' and, once inside, will be asked to remove their shoes. Hour-long tours are conducted in French, English, German and Spanish, and take in the prayer hall, ablutions rooms and hammam.

It is possible to walk to the mosque in about 20 minutes from Casa Port train station, but Blvd Moulay Youssef is busy with traffic, there are hardly any pedestrians, and there have been some reports of muggings here. It's certainly not advisable for lone women. Take a petit taxi from the town centre (around Dh10 on the meter). Bus 15 leaves from Place Oued al-Makhazine (Dh4).

Jewish Museum

Set in a beautiful villa surrounded by lush gardens, this is Casablanca's only **museum** (off Map p102; ☎ 022 994940; 81 Rue Chasseur Jules Gros, Quartier Oasis; admission Dh20, with guide Dh30; ⏲ 10am-6pm Mon-Fri) and the only Jewish museum in the Islamic world. It relates the history of the once-thriving Jewish community and its influence on modern Moroccan society, with more than 1500 historical artefacts including documents, traditional clothing, ceremonial items and a vast collection of photographs. The museum is in the suburb of Oasis, a 15-minute taxi ride (Dh20) from the city centre.

Aïn Diab

This affluent suburb on the Atlantic beachfront, west of the centre, is home to the happening **Blvd de la Corniche**. Lined with beach clubs, upmarket hotels, restaurants, bars and clubs, it is the city's entertainment hub and *the* place for young, chic professionals to see and be seen.

However, the promenade packed with walkers and joggers is really a potholed pavement. In between the busy beach clubs, the view is spoiled by abandoned pleasure grounds and concrete swimming pools filled with construction rubbish. Nevertheless, the beach remains extremely popular. The easiest way to find space in the sand is to visit one of the beach clubs. Two of the better ones, **Miami Plage** (per day Dh80-150) and **Tahiti** (per day Dh80-150) have beach umbrellas, a pool, restaurant and bar.

Bus 9 goes to Aïn Diab from Place Oued al-Makhazine. A taxi from the centre costs around Dh25 (Dh60 at night).

ACTIVITIES

Hammams

Sparkling clean and decidedly modern, **Hammam Ziani** (Map p110; ☎ 022 319695; 59 Rue Abou Rakrak; Mon-Fri Dh40, Sat & Sun Dh50; ⏲ 7am-10pm) is an upmarket hammam offering the traditional steam room and *gommage* (scrub) and massage, as well as a Jacuzzi and gym. Its off Rue Verdin.

You'll find similar facilities at the ultra-modern **Gauthier Bain Turc** (Map p102; ☎ 061 145926; 25 Rue Jean Jaures; Mon-Fri Dh50, Sat & Sun Dh60; ⏲ 7am-10pm), where a scrub costs about Dh20 and a 30-minute massage Dh100.

For a traditional hammam, a Japanese bath, a Balinese massage or an ayurvedic treatment head for the trendy **Spa 5 Mondes** (off Map p102; ☎ 022 996608; 18 Rue Ibrahim En-Nakhai, Maarif; ⏲ 10am-8pm).

WALKING TOUR

Central Casablanca has a rich architectural heritage, particularly with its Mauresque architecture – a blend of French-colonial design and traditional Moroccan style, popular in the 1930s. Heavily influenced by the art-deco movement, it embraced decorative details such as carved friezes, ornate tilework and wrought-iron balconies. Some gems have been beautifully restored, others remain shamefully neglected. This walking tour takes in the best Mauresque buildings, and some other Casa treasures.

Start on the northwest edge of the Parc de la Ligue Arabe, where you can't miss the imposing **Cathédrale du Sacré Coeur (1)**, a graceful cathedral designed by Paul Tornon in 1930. It has been used as a school, theatre and cultural centre, and is due to be restored. The rundown interior is only open for special events.

From here, walk two blocks east to Place Mohammed V, which is the grand centrepiece of the French regeneration scheme. The vast square is surrounded by an impressive array of august administrative buildings, most designed by Robert Marrast and Henri Prost. The **wilaya** (**2**; old police headquarters), dating from 1930, dominates the south side of the square and is topped by a modernist clock tower.

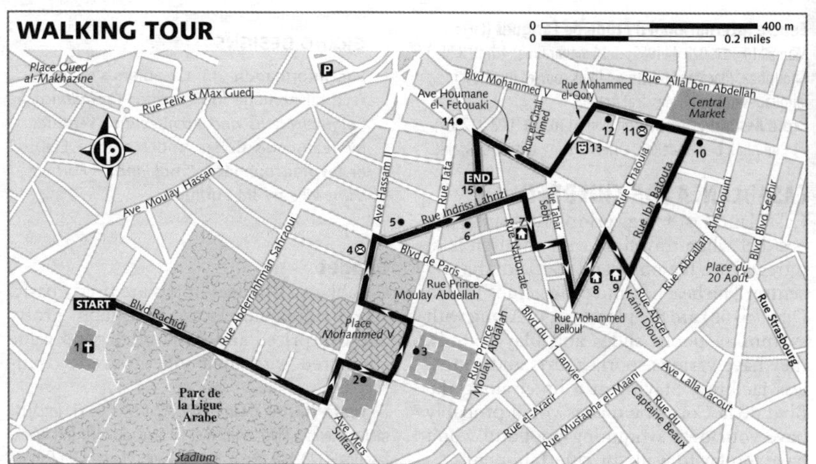

WALK FACTS

Start Parc de la Ligue Arabe, Blvd Rachidi
End Rue Prince Moulay Abdellah
Distance 3km
Duration 45 minutes

The nearby **palais de justice** (**3**; law courts) was built in 1925. The huge main door and entrance were inspired by the Persian *iwan,* a vaulted hall that usually opens into the central court of the *medersa* (theological college) of a mosque.

Stroll across the grand square and admire the 1918 **main post office (4)**, a wonderful building fronted by arches and stone columns and decorated with bold mosaics. More in the style of traditional Moroccan architecture is the **Banque al-Maghrib (5)**, on Blvd de Paris. Fronted with decorative stonework, it was the last building constructed on the square.

From here, walk east on Rue Indriss Lahrizi, where impressive facades line both sides of the street, the best being **La Princière Salon de Thé (6)**, easily recognised by the huge stone crown on the roofline. Turn right into Rue Mohammed Belloul to see **Hotel Guynemer** (**7**; p109) with its art-deco panelling, then walk one block east and turn right down Rue Tahar Sebti, which is lined with colonial buildings.

Turn left into Rue Chaouia and look out for **Hotel Transatlantique** (**8**; p109), which dates from 1922 and has been beautifully restored. Just around the corner, another restored gem, the **Hotel Volubilis (9)**, has a great facade.

Turn left up Rue Ibn Batouta and continue to the corner of Blvd Mohammed V. On your right is the derelict shell of the **Hôtel Lincoln (10)**, an art-deco masterpiece built in 1916 and patiently awaiting a long-talked-about restoration.

Turn left into Blvd Mohammed V and look out for an array of wonderful facades along the south side of the street. The Central Market **post office (11)**, with its delicate, carved motifs, and the **Le Matin/Maroc Soir (12)** building, with its classic style, are two of the most impressive.

At the end of this block turn left into Rue Mohammed el-Qory to find the **Cinema Rialto** (**13**; p115), a classic art-deco building with some wonderful touches. Continue south to the junction with Ave Houmane el-Fetouaki and turn right to reach **Place 16 Novembre (14)**, which is home to an array of art-deco buildings. Finally, continue to the south along pedestrianised **Rue Prince Moulay Abdellah (15)**, where you'll find a selection of interesting facades with decorative doorways and ironwork.

COURSES

Casablanca has a multitude of language schools, almost all of which have French classes. Many, including the Institut Français (p103), only run semester-long courses. Some options for short-term lessons:

Centre International d'Étude de Langues (CIEL; Map p110; ☎ 022 441959; ciel@menara.ma; 4th fl, 8 Blvd Khouribga, Place de la Victoire) Runs courses in a host of languages including classical Arabic.

École Assimil-Formation (Map p110; ☎ 022 312567; 71 Rue Allah ben Abdellah) Offers private tuition in Arabic.

CASABLANCA FOR CHILDREN

Casablanca is a big, grimy city and your best bet when travelling with children is to retreat from the noise and traffic of the city centre. The beaches and beach clubs in Aïn Diab (p106) are the places to go. Along with swimming pools, slides and playgrounds, they have various sports courts and countless facilities. Staying at a hotel along the Blvd de la Corniche means you'll probably have your own swimming pool and won't have too far to walk for entertainment.

Back in town, Casa's biggest open space is the **Parc de la Ligue Arabe**. It's a good place for games and walks, and has a choice of small cafés and the **Yasmina amusement park** (Map p102; admission Dh150; 🕑 10am-7pm), with plenty of small-scale rides and fun-fair atmosphere.

TOURS

Both tourist offices (p103) offer a three-hour walking tour of the city (Dh450 for up to three people) that can be customised to suit the client's interests. **Olive Branch Tours** (Map p110; ☎ 022 220354; www.olivebranchtours.com; 35 Rue el-Oraïbi Jilali) offers a 'Grand Tour of Casablanca', which takes in the main squares in the city centre, the medina and Quartier Habous, as well as a stroll along the Corniche.

FESTIVALS

The **L'Boulevard Festival of Casablanca** (www.boulevard.ma) takes places every year in June. It's a three-day urban-music festival with hip-hop, electro, rock, metal and fusion music, with bands from Morocco, France, the USA and the UK.

SLEEPING

Most of Casablanca's hotels are in the centre of town with the exception of the youth hostel, which is in the medina, and the upmarket hotels along the Blvd de la Corniche. Hotels fill up fast during the summer months, particularly in August, so it's a good idea to make reservations in advance.

> **GRAND DESIGNS**
>
> For information on Casablanca's architectural heritage look out for *Casablanca: Colonial Myths and Architectural Ventures* by Jean-Louis Cohen and Monique Eleb, or for francophones, *Casablanca – Portrait d'une ville* by JM Zurfluh.

Budget

Casablanca's budget hotels are pretty basic. The medina hotels are invariably grotty and overpriced and don't offer good value compared with their ville-nouvelle counterparts.

Youth Hostel (Map p110; ☎ 022 220551; frmaj1@menara.com; 6 Place Ahmed el-Bidaoui; dm/d/tr incl breakfast Dh45/120/180; 🕑 8-10am & noon-11pm; 💻) Clustered around a bright central lounge area, the rooms are basic but well kept and quiet, with high ceilings and a lingering smell of damp in winter. There are good hot showers in the morning and a small kitchen for guests use. No IYHF or YHA cards are required. Sheet hire is Dh5.

Hôtel du Palais (Map p110; ☎ 022 276191; 68 Rue Farhat Hachad; s/d Dh80/120, with bathroom Dh140/240) At the lower end of the price range, this basic hotel is a good choice, offering clean, spacious rooms with large windows. Although recently upgraded, it's still fairly spartan and can be noisy. A hot shower costs Dh10.

Hotel de Foucauld (Map p110; ☎ 022 222666; 52 Rue el-Oraïbi Jilai; s/d Dh80/130, s/d/tr with bathroom Dh130/160/190) Rooms in this simple hotel in the centre of town don't live up to the plasterwork decoration in reception, but they're much bigger than average and have a certain faded charm. Some rooms have en-suite bathrooms. Streetside rooms can be noisy.

Hôtel Mon Rêve (Map p110; ☎ 022 411439; 7 Rue Chaouia; s/d Dh100/130, with bathroom Dh150/180) This charming old-style hotel has been a favourite with budget travellers for years. It is centrally located (off Rue Colbert) but can be quite noisy, and the rooms painted in blue are spartan but clean. Choose a higher room to avoid the noise.

Hôtel Oued-Dahab (Map p110; ☎ 022 223866; oueddahab@yahoo.com; 17 Rue Mohamed Belloul; s/d bathroom Dh120/180, s/d/tr with bathroom Dh150/250/295) Run by the same family as the Guynemer, this hotel with spacious rooms is cheap and clean and offers rooms with shower or bathroom. Rooms facing inwards are quieter but a bit darker. Very good value.

Hôtel Galia (Map p110; ☎ 022 481694; galia_19@hotmail.fr; 19 Rue Ibn Batouta; s/d/tr Dh150/220/300, with shower Dh170/250/330;) Tiled floors, gold tasselled curtains and matching bedspreads adorn the homy, spacious and well-kept rooms at the Galia, a top-notch budget option offering excellent value. Management is friendly and helpful, and it's in a convenient location, although the bar underneath can be quite rowdy at times. There's free internet in the lobby.

Hôtel Astrid (Map p110; ☎ 022 277803; hotelastrid@hotmail.com; 12 Rue 6 Novembre; s/d/tr Dh256/309/405) Tucked away on a quiet street south of the centre, the Astrid offers the most elusive element of Casa's budget hotels – a good night's sleep. There's little traffic noise here and the spacious, well-kept rooms are all en suite, with TV, telephone and frilly decor. There's a friendly café downstairs.

our pick Hôtel Guynemer (Map p110; ☎ 022 275764; www.guynemerhotel.com; 2 Rue Mohammed Belloul; s/d/tr incl breakfast Dh398/538/676; wi-fi) The friendly and super-efficient family-run Guynemer, in a gorgeous art-deco building, just goes from strength to strength. The 29 well-appointed and regularly updated rooms are tastefully decked out in cheerful colours. Fresh flowers, plasma TVs, wi-fi access and firm, comfortable beds make them a steal at these rates and the service is way above average: staff will happily run out to get anything you need. There's an airport pick-up service (Dh200) and city tours. The small restaurant serves a range of top-notch Moroccan specialities and has live oud (lute) music every night. There is also an interactive info post in the lobby, a dedicated PC for guest use and a phone to call the USA and Canada free.

The hotel also rents out two contemporary, fully equipped flats on the same street, which are ideal for longer stays and for families.

Hôtel de Paris (Map p110; ☎ 022 274275; fax 022 298069; cnr Rue Ech-Cherif Amziane & Rue Prince Moulay Abdallah; s/d/tr Dh400/450/450) Flowered carpet and flashy textiles in the corridors reveal dubious taste, but the renovated, spacious rooms at this small hotel are clean and relatively quiet. Rooms are decorated with dark wood and equipped with good mattresses, satellite TV and direct phone line. There's a swish café downstairs on the pedestrian street, and the hotel is in a good central location.

Hôtel Maamoura (Map p110; ☎ 022 452967; www.hotelmaamoura.com; 59 Rue Ibn Batouta; s/d Dh420/550, ste Dh650-750;) This newly opened modern hotel offers excellent value for money. The spotless and spacious rooms may lack period detail, but they are very quiet for this central location, tastefully decorated in muted colours and have neat bathrooms. There is a Moroccan and international restaurant, and friendly, helpful staff.

Midrange

Casablanca has a good selection of midrange accommodation scattered around the city centre. You'll also find some nice alternatives with ocean views and easy access to the beach along Blvd de la Corniche.

Hôtel Transatlantique (Map p110; ☎ 022 294551; www.transatcasa.com; 79 Rue Chaouia; s/d/tr Dh600/750/950;) Set in one of Casa's art-deco gems, this 1922 hotel, shaped like a boat, has buckets of neo-Moorish character. The grand scale, decorative plaster, spidery wrought iron and eclectic mix of knick-knacks, pictures and lamps give the Transatlantique a whiff of colonial-era decadence crossed with '70s retro. It has a lovely outdoor seating area and comfortable, but fairly plain, bedrooms. Avoid the 1st floor, as it gets the brunt of noise from the popular and very rowdy piano bar and nightclub. There are several newly decorated suites. Edith Piaf lived in rooms 303, 304 and 315.

Dar Itrit (off Map p102; ☎ 022 360258; www.daritrit.ma; 9 Rue de Restinga; d Dh850) There are only three double rooms in this charming B&B, each decorated in a different Moroccan style – Marrakesh, Berber and Mogador. A delicious breakfast is served in a bright living room or on the terrace, in this slightly out of the centre location.

East-West Hotel (Map p102; ☎ 022 200210; www.eastwest-hotel.com; 10 Ave Hassan Souktani, Quartier Gauthier; s/d Dh400/626;) Several readers have recommended this bright and cheerful three-star hotel. All rooms have clean bathrooms with modern fittings, free internet and a safe, and the hotel boasts a good restaurant and a lounge bar. The hotel,

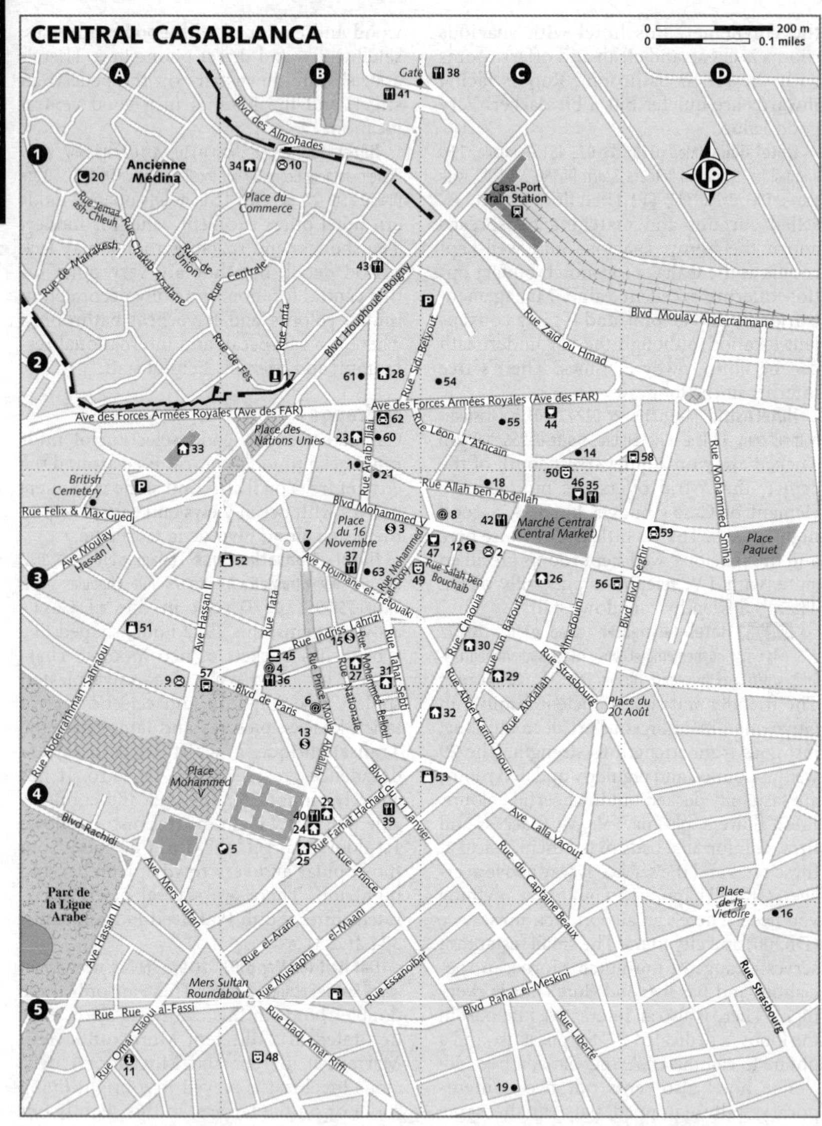

in the residential but upcoming Quartier Gauthier, is very quiet.

Hôtel Bellerive (off Map p102; ☎ 022 797504; www.belleriv.com; 38 Blvd de La Corniche, Aïn Diab; s/d/tr/q Dh570/720/950/1200;) The lovely terrace, pool and garden make up for the dated, standard rooms at this small, family-run hotel. Many rooms have ocean views though, and it's cheaper than most along this waterfront strip. There's plenty of space and a playground, which makes it a good bet if you're travelling with children.

Hôtel le Littoral (off Map p102; ☎ 022 797373; fax 022 797374; Blvd de l'Océan Atlantique, Aïn Diab; s/d Dh699/850;) This cavernous, well-kept hotel is rather dark, with rooms that

INFORMATION
- BMCE (see 33)
- Carlson Wagonlit 1 B2
- Central Market Post Office 2 C3
- Crédit du Maroc 3 B3
- EuroNet 4 B3
- French Consulate 5 B4
- G@.net 6 B4
- Goethe Institut 7 B3
- LGnet 8 C3
- Main Post Office 9 A3
- Medina Post Office 10 B1
- Office National Marocain du Tourisme 11 A5
- Syndicat d'Initiative 12 C3
- Voyages Schwartz 13 B4
- Voyages Wasteels 14 C2
- Wafa Cash 15 B3

SIGHTS & ACTIVITIES
- Centre International d'Etude de Langues 16 D5
- Clock Tower 17 B2
- École Assimil-Formation 18 C3
- Hammam Ziani 19 C5
- Jemaa ash-Chleuh 20 A1
- Olive Branch Tours 21 B3

SLEEPING
- Hôtel Astrid 22 B4
- Hotel de Foucauld 23 B2
- Hotel de Paris 24 B4
- Hôtel du Palais 25 B4
- Hôtel Galia 26 C3
- Hôtel Guynemer 27 B3
- Hotel les Saisons 28 B2
- Hôtel Maamoura 29 C3
- Hôtel Mon Reve 30 C3
- Hotel Oued-Dahab 31 B3
- Hôtel Transatlantique 32 C4
- Hyatt Regency Hotel 33 A2
- Youth Hostel 34 B1

EATING
- Brasserie La Bavaroise 35 C3
- Epsom 36 B3
- La Petite Perle 37 B3
- Ostréa 38 C1
- Pâtisserie de l'Opéra 39 B4
- Restaurant al-Mounia 40 B4
- Restaurant du Port de Peche 41 B1
- Rotisseries 42 C3
- Snack Amine (see 42)
- Taverne du Dauphin 43 B2

DRINKING
- Black House (see 33)
- Caesar 44 C2
- Café Alba 45 B3
- La Bodéga 46 C3
- Petit Poucet 47 C3

ENTERTAINMENT
- Cinéma Lynx 48 B5
- Cinéma Rialto 49 B3
- Complex Cultural Sidi Belyout 50 C3

SHOPPING
- Disques GAM 51 A3
- Exposition Nationale d'Artisinat 52 B3
- Le Comptoir Marocain de Distribution de Disques 53 C4

TRANSPORT
- Avis 54 C2
- Budget 55 C2
- Bus 10 & 36 to Gare Routière Ouled Ziane 56 C3
- Bus 81 to Nouvelle Medina 57 A3
- CTM Bus Station 58 D2
- Grands Taxi Stand 59 D3
- Hertz 60 B2
- National 61 B2
- Petits Taxis 62 B2
- President Car 63 B3

were once the height of fashion but now look dangerously '80s. However, there are large balconies and wonderful views over the waterfront. The hotel has several restaurants, a discotheque and a private beach with umbrellas.

Hôtel les Saisons (Map p110; ☎ 022 490901; www.hotellessaisonsmaroc.ma; 19 Rue el Oraïbi Jilali; s/d Dh900/1100) This small hotel offers extremely comfortable, well-appointed and quiet rooms with all the usual facilities: a safe, minibar, satellite TV and direct dial phone. It's a more personal place than the larger international hotels and offers good value for money. The staff speak English.

Top End

Casablanca has a glut of top-end hotels, with all the major international chains represented in town. Most are along Ave des FAR, with a few others along the Blvd de la Corniche. For something less generic try one of the following:

Hôtel Riad Salam (☎ 022 391313; fax 022 391345; Blvd de la Corniche; r Dh2325) Although not as swish as it once was, and with rather erratic service, the Riad Salam is still the top spot along the waterfront. The Moroccan-style, nonsmoking rooms with low couches, woven rugs and decorative tiling are centred on the hotel's three swimming pools and landscaped terrace. It has a thalassotherapy centre, a health club and tennis courts, and substantial discounts in the off-season. It's located 3km south of Casablanca.

Hôtel Hyatt Regency (Map p110; ☎ 022 431234; www.casablanca.hyatt.com; Place des Nations Unis; r Dh3500) The best and the most central of all the five-star hotels, the Hyatt is a favourite meeting place for Casablancais for a meal in one of the many restaurants, or a drink at the bar. The spacious rooms are equipped with modern amenities and decorated in an elegant contemporary style, and have magnificent views of Casablanca, the old medina, the ocean and the Hassan II Mosque. The hotel also has a discotheque and spa.

EATING

Restaurants

Casablanca has a great selection of restaurants, and you can eat anything from excellent tajine to French pâté and Thai dumplings. However as elsewhere along the ocean, fresh fish and seafood are the local speciality and it's worth checking out the restaurants at the port or on the way to Aïn Diab for a culinary treat.

CENTRAL CASABLANCA

Le Luigi (off Map p102; ☎ 022 390271; cnr Rue de Normandie & Blvd Abou Yalaa al-Ifrani; mains Dh55-90) One of the most popular Italian restaurants, Le Luigi makes for a welcome break from tajine if you've been in Morocco for some time. The decor is nothing special but the pizzas are worth the journey. Book ahead.

Taverne du Dauphin (Map p110; ☎ 022 221200; 115 Blvd Houphouet Boigny; 3-course set menu Dh110, mains Dh70-90; ⌚ Mon-Sat) A Casablanca institution, this traditional Provençal restaurant and bar has been serving up *fruits de mer* (seafood) since it opened in 1958. This is an old-fashioned family-run place, and one taste of the succulent grilled fish, fried calamari and *crevettes royales* (king prawns) will leave you smitten.

Sqala Restaurant (Map p102; ☎ 022 260960; Blvd des Almohades; mains Dh70-160; ⌚ 8am-10.30pm Tue-Sun, daily in summer) Nestled in the ochre walls of the *sqala*, an 18th-century fortified bastion, this lovely restaurant is a tranquil escape from the city. The café has a rustic interior and a delightful garden surrounded by flower-draped trellises. No alcohol is served, but there's a good selection of teas and fresh juices. It's a lovely spot for a Moroccan breakfast (Dh70) or a selection of salads for lunch (Dh68). Tajines are a speciality (the goat tajine with argan oil being particularly good), but the menu features plenty of fish, as well as a selection of meat brochettes.

our pick Restaurant du Port de Pêche (Map p110; ☎ 022 318561; Le Port de Pêche; mains Dh80-140) This authentic and rustic seafood restaurant in the middle of the fishing harbour is packed to the gills at lunch and dinner as happy diners tuck into fish freshly whipped from the sea and cooked to perfection. The fish and tangy paella are some of the best in town. The decor is very 1970s with red-and-white gingham tablecloths. Service is professional and swift. Book ahead as this place is very popular with Casablancais from all walks of life.

Le Rouget de l'Isle (Map p102; ☎ 022 294740; 16 Rue Rouget de l'Isle; mains Dh110-130; ⌚ lunch Mon-Fri, dinner Mon-Sat) Sleek, stylish and charming, renowned for its simple but delicious and light French food, Le Rouget is one of Casa's top eateries. Set in a renovated 1930s villa, it is an elegant place filled with period furniture and contemporary artwork. The impeccable food is reasonably priced though, and there's a beautiful garden. Book in advance.

Ostréa (Map p110; ☎ 022 441390; Le Port de Pêche; dozen oysters Dh74, mains Dh120-250; ⌚ 11am-11pm) Across the road from Restaurant du Port de Pêche is this more upmarket seafood restaurant specialising in Oualidia oysters and fresh lobster.

Rick's Cafe (Map p110; ☎ 022 274207; 248 Blvd Sour Jdid; mains Dh130-160; ⌚ noon-3.30pm, 6pm-midnight) 'Here's looking at you kid!' Cashing in on the Hollywood hit Casablanca, this beautiful bar, lounge and restaurant is run by a former American diplomat, with furniture and fittings inspired by the film, and serving a taste of home for the nostalgic masses. Lamb chops, chilli, hamburgers and American breakfasts as well as a few excellent French and Moroccan specialities are all on the menu. There's also an in-house pianist, a Sunday jazz session, wi-fi access and, inevitably, souvenir T-shirts. It's a stunning setting and a good place for late-night drinks. You can watch the film again and again on the 1st floor.

Restaurant al-Mounia (Map p110; ☎ 022 222669; 95 Rue Prince Moulay Abdallah; mains Dh130-170) Eat the best Moroccan food in the centre of Casablanca at this delightful traditional restaurant where you can choose to sit in the Moroccan salon elegantly decorated with *zellij* (tilework) and sculpted wood, or under the pepper tree in the cool, leafy garden. There's a selection of salads worthy of any vegetarian restaurant and an array of exotic delicacies such as pigeon *pastilla* (rich, savoury pie) and sweet tomato tajine.

La Brasserie la Bavaroise (Map p110; ☎ 022 311760; 129 Rue Allah ben Abdellah; mains Dh140-200) Locals and expats like to hang out in this upmarket brasserie behind the Marché Central, partly for the French cuisine, partly to see and be seen. It offers a good selection of fish as well as French classics such as veal, steak and pheasant cooked to perfection. Meat is grilled on a wood fire. It has a pleasant atmosphere and a friendly welcome. Every month the menu features specialities from a different region of France. The same owners also run La Bodega (p114) next door, a great tapas bar.

Thai Gardens (☎ 022 797579; Ave de la Côte d'Emeraude, Anfa; meals Dh250) Slightly out of the centre in the affluent suburb of Anfa, but worth seeking out for its excellent Thai cuisine, this place is another top-notch option. The vast menu of Thai classics is refreshingly inventive and makes a good choice for vegetarians.

La Maison du Gourmet (Map p102; ☎ 022 484846; Rue Taha Houcine, Maarif; meals Dh400-500; ⏰ lunch Mon-Fri, dinner Mon-Sat) This upmarket gourmet restaurant serves an inventive menu of the finest of French and Moroccan cuisine, run by a couple, he French, she Moroccan, both trained by Paul Bocuse. Specialities include a heavenly *pastilla* with confit of duck and foie gras. The elegant surroundings, excellent service and exceptional food make this the perfect address for a special occasion. Book ahead.

AÏN DIAB

The best of this neighbourhood's restaurants are clustered together on a cliff top overlooking the crashing Atlantic waves near the el-Hank Lighthouse.

La Fibule (☎ 022 360641; Blvd de la Corniche, Phare el-Hank; meals around Dh300) Subtle lighting, warm colours and an elegant decor give La Fibule an inviting atmosphere. The food is a mixture of well-prepared Moroccan and Lebanese, served at low tables overlooking the ocean through large windows.

La Mer (☎ 022 363315; Blvd de la Corniche, Phare el-Hank; meals around Dh300) Right next door to La Fibule, and under the same management, this seafood restaurant is a more refined place with white linen and bone china replacing the ethnic vibe. The menu and service is very French, bordering on stuffy, but the food is divine.

Le Mystic Garden (☎ 022 798877; 33 Blvd de la Corniche; Aïn Diab; meals around Dh350; ⏰ noon-3pm & 7pm-2am) Giant glass walls swathe this sleek, two-storey restaurant-cum-bar in light. Downstairs leads onto a garden; upstairs overlooks the ocean. It's an ultra-cool hang-out for Casa's well-heeled youth but the Mediterranean menu is well worth sampling. Dinner is accompanied by low-key sounds that morph into a full-on disco beat later in the evening, and for once on this strip the beer isn't astronomically priced.

A Ma Bretagne (☎ 022 362112; Sidi Abderrahman, Blvd de la Corniche; meals around Dh500; ⏰ dinner daily) Locally promoted as the best restaurant in Africa, this self-consciously cool establishment is all modern lines and superb food. Although seafood tops the bill here, you can opt for some other French delicacies, cooked by the *maître cuisinier* (master chef) André Halbert. It's 5km out of town.

Cafés, Patisseries & Ice-cream Parlours

CENTRAL CASABLANCA

Paul (Map p102; ☎ 022 366000; www.paul.ma; cnr Blvd d'Anfa & Blvd Moulay Rachid; ⏰ 7am-9pm) The French chain of bakery and patisserie has arrived in Casa, in the gorgeous art-deco Villa Zevaco. There is a constant flow of people here, coming as much for the food and decor as for the pleasure of being seen in this trendy hang-out. Excellent breakfast is served, and there is also a menu of salads, snacks and other Mediterranean delights.

Patisserie Bennis Habous (☎ 022 303025; 2 Rue Fkih el-Gabbas; ⏰ 8am-8pm) One of the city's most famous and traditional patisseries, this place in the Quartier Habous is Casa's best spot for traditional Moroccan treats, including some of the best *cornes de gazelle* (gazelle horns, almond paste) pastries in town, as well as made-to-order *pastillas*.

AÏN DIAB

Palais des Glaces (☎ 022 798013; Blvd de la Corniche, Aïn Diab; ⏰ 7am-9pm) Famous across the city for its excellent ice cream, this is one of the city's oldest sweet-tooth stops, serving up delicious ice creams and sorbets for 125 years. Set across from the beach in Aïn Diab, it makes a glorious retreat on a fine day.

Hediard (☎ 022 797232; Résidence Jardin d'Anfa, Blvd Lido Route Côterie, Aïn Diab; cakes Dh12-28, meals Dh45-60) Slick, new and popular with the young and beautiful, this café in Aïn Diab serves a range of sumptuous cakes as well as light meals and deli-style sandwiches (Dh30 to Dh50).

Quick Eats

Rue Chaouia, located opposite the Marché Central is the best place for a quick eat, with a line of rotisseries, stalls and restaurants serving roast chicken, brochettes and sandwiches (Dh20 to Dh30). It's open until about 2am.

La Petite Perle (Map p110; ☎ 022 272849; 17-19 Ave Houmane el-Fetouaki; mains Dh25-45; ⏰ 11.30am-3pm & 6-11pm) Popular with young professionals and women travelling alone, this spotless, modern café serves up a range of sandwiches, crêpes, pastas and pizzas as well as a great choice of breakfasts.

Epsom (Map p110; ☎ 022 220746; cnr Rue Tata & Mouftakar; mains Dh22-60) Almost always crowded and spilling customers onto the streetside seating, this friendly café serves a choice of grills and brochettes at bargain prices. It's a relaxed place with a mixed clientele and offers hassle-free eating for women.

Snack Amine (Map p110; ☎ 022 541331; Rue Chaouia; mains Dh25-45; noon-10pm) Tucked between the chicken rotisseries by the Marché Central, Snack Amine serves up big plates of simple but tasty fried fish, and platters of the freshest seafood.

Self-Catering

If you're planning a picnic on the beach, head for the **Marché Central** (Central Market; Map p110), located between Blvd Mohammed V and Rue Allah ben Abdellah. It's a fascinating place to just stroll and has a great selection of fresh produce and a couple of good delis.

DRINKING

Although there are plenty of classic French-style drinking dens in the centre of town, they are pretty much a male preserve and are usually intimidating for women.

Cafés

Café Alba (Map p110; ☎ 022 227154; 59-61 Rue Indriss Lahrizi; 8am-1am) High ceilings, swish, modern furniture, subtle lighting and a hint of elegant colonial times mark this café out from the more traditional smoky joints around town. It's hassle-free downtime for women and a great place for watching Casa's up-and-coming.

Sqala Café Maure (Map p102; ☎ 022 260960; Blvd des Almohades; mains Dh60-80; 11am-1am) Another exception to the men-only rule, this lovely café is set behind the *sqala* in the medina wall. The flower-filled garden is quiet all afternoon and makes a great place for coffee or delicious juices.

Bars

Casablanca's bars can be pretty rough around the edges and generally attract a male-only clientele (plus prostitutes). In general, the bars in the larger hotels are more refined places to drink, especially for women.

La Bodéga (Map p110; ☎ 022 541842; 129 Rue Allah ben Abdellah; 12.30-3pm & 7pm-midnight) Hip, happening and loved by a mixed-aged group of Casablanca's finest, La Bodega is essentially a tapas bar where the music (everything from Salsa to Arabic pop) is loud and the Rioja (Spanish wine) flows freely. It's a fun place with a lively atmosphere and a packed dance floor after 10pm.

Petit Poucet (Map p110; Blvd Mohammed V; 9am-10pm) A die-hard relic of 1920s France, this strictly male-only bar was where Saint-Exupéry, the French author and aviator, used to spend time between mail flights across the Sahara. Today, the bar is low-key but is an authentic slice of old-time Casa life.

Le Trica (Map p102; ☎ 022 220706; 5 Rue el-Moutanabi, Quartier Gauthier; noon-1am, closed Sat lunch & Sun) This bar-lounge, set over two levels with brick walls and 1960s furniture, is the place to feel the beat of the new Morocco. The atmosphere is hot and trendy at night, stirred by the techno beat and a flow of beer and *mojitos* (rum cocktails), but things are a lot calmer at lunch.

ENTERTAINMENT

Nightclubs

The beachfront suburb of Aïn Diab is the place for late-night drinking and dancing in Casa. However, hanging out with Casablanca's beautiful people for a night on the town doesn't come cheap. Expect to pay at least Dh100 to get in and as much again for drinks. Heavy-set bouncers guard the doors and practise tough crowd control – if you don't look the part, you won't get in.

The strip of disco joints along the beachfront ranges from Fellini-esque, cabaret-style bar-cum-restaurants such as **Balcon 33** (33 Blvd de la Corniche) to the pastel-coloured pop sensation **Candy Bar** (55 Blvd de la Corniche) and the catch-all **VIP club** (Rue des Dunes). **Le Village** (11 Blvd de la Corniche) has a slightly gay-friendly atmosphere, and the incredibly packed **Armstrong Legend** (41 Blvd de la Corniche) is one of the few places with funky live music.

Other than Aïn Diab, the only real options are clubs at the large international hotels, including **Caesar** (Map p110; Hôtel Sheraton, 100 Ave des FAR) and **Black House** (Map p110; Hôtel Hyatt Regency, Place des Nations Unies). Prostitutes work all of the clubs, men are always expected to pay for drinks and women shouldn't expect hassle-free drinking anywhere. The seedy nightclub at **Hotel Transatlantique** (p109) is good for late night *couleur locale* as the belly dancers and singers provoke the mostly male locals into throwing money at them.

Theatres

Complex Culturel Sidi Belyout (Map p110; 28 Rue Léon L'Africain; performances 9pm) This 200-seat theatre hosts plays (usually in Arabic) and the occasional music recital or dance performance.

Cinema

Most English-language films are dubbed in French, unless it specifically mentions *'version originale'*.

Megarama (022 798888; www.megarama.info, in French; Blvd de la Corniche; afternoon/evening shows Dh35/45) The plushest cinema in town, this huge complex in Aïn Diab has four comfortable theatres that are usually packed.

Cinéma Lynx (Map p110; 022 220229; 150 Ave Mers Sultan; screen/balcony/club Dh25/30/50) A good option if you don't want to trek out to Aïn Diab, this spacious and comfortable cinema has an excellent sound system.

Cinéma Rialto (Map p110; 022 262632; Rue Mohammed el-Kouri; screen/balcony/club Dh25/30/50) A classic, cavernous, single-screen art-deco cinema.

SHOPPING

Although not an artisan centre, Casablanca has a good choice of traditional crafts from around Morocco. The most pleasant place to shop is Quartier Habous (p104), south of the centre. Merchants here are pretty laid-back, but the quality of crafts can vary and hard bargaining is the order of the day.

If you'd rather avoid haggling altogether, head for the **Exposition Nationale d'Artisanat** (Map p110; 022 267064; 3 Ave Hassan II; 8.30am-12.30pm & 2.30-8pm), where you'll find three floors of fixed-price crafts.

For a good selection of traditional Arab and Berber music try **Disques GAM** (Map p110; 022 268954; 99 Rue Abderrahman Sehraoui) or **Le Comptoire Marocain de Distribution de Disques** (Map p110; 022 369153; 26 Ave Lalla Yacout).

GETTING THERE & AWAY

Air

Casablanca's **Mohammed V International Airport** (022 539040; www.onda.ma) is 30km southeast of the city on the Marrakesh road. Regular flights leave here for most countries in Western Europe, as well as to West Africa, Algeria, Tunisia, Egypt, the Middle East and North America. For a list of airlines with flights in and out of Casablanca see p480.

Internally, the vast majority of Royal Air Maroc's (RAM) flights go via Casablanca, so you can get to any destination in Morocco directly from the city. Regional Air Lines flies to over a dozen Moroccan destinations, mostly south along the coast.

Bus

The modern **CTM bus station** (Map p110; 022 541010; www.ctm.ma; 23 Rue Léon L'Africain) is close to the Ave des FAR. It's a pretty efficient place with a café and **left-luggage counter** (per 24hr Dh5; 6am-11.30pm). There are daily CTM departures to the following places:

Destination	Cost (Dh)	Duration (hrs)	No of daily services
Agadir	190	9	10
El-Jadida	40	1½	every 15 min (6.30am-7pm)
Essaouira	130	7	2 with CTM; hourly with private companies
Fez	100	5	10
Laâyoune	340	24	3
Marrakesh	80	3½	10
Meknès	80	4	10
Rabat	30	1¼	every 30 min
Tangier	135	6	5 with CTM; regularly with private companies
Taza	130	7½	5
Tetouan	130	7	3

There are also overnight buses to Ouarzazate (Dh140, 7½ hours) and Er-Rachidia (Dh155, 14 hours) via Tinerhir, as well as one or two buses daily to Oujda (Dh180, 11 hours), Al-Hoceima (Dh160, 11 hours), Nador (Dh170, 13 hours), Taroudannt (Dh165, 10 hours) and Dakhla (Dh520, 28 hours). CTM also operates international buses to Belgium, France, Germany, Italy and Spain from Casablanca (see p483).

The modern **Gare Routière Ouled Ziane** (022 444470), 4km southeast of the centre, is the bus station for almost all non-CTM services. The main reason to trek out here is for destinations not covered by CTM, mainly Ouezzane (Dh60, nine daily) and Chefchaouen (Dh70, two daily). A taxi to the bus station will cost about Dh15, alternatively take bus No 10 or 36 from Blvd Mohammed V near the market.

Also on Route Ouled Ziane, but more than 1km closer to town, is the **SAT bus station** (☎ 022 444470). SAT runs national and international buses of a similar standard to CTM, but fares are slightly cheaper.

Car

Casablanca is well endowed with car-rental agencies, many with offices around Ave des FAR, Blvd Mohammed V and at the airport.

Avis Casablanca (Map110; ☎ 022 312424; 19 Ave des FAR); Mohammed V International Airport (☎ 022 539072)

Budget Casablanca (Map110; ☎ 022 313124; Tours des Habous, Ave des FAR); Mohammed V International Airport (☎ 022 339157)

Hertz Casablanca (Map110; ☎ 022 484710; 25 Rue el-Oraïbi Jilali); Mohammed V International Airport (☎ 022 539181)

National Casablanca (Map110; ☎ 022 277141; 12 Rue el-Oraïbi Jilali); Mohammed V International Airport (☎ 022 539716)

President Car (Map110; ☎ 022 260790, 061 210394; presidentcar@menara.ma; 27 Rue el-Ghali Ahmed) A reliable local agency that has a well-maintained fleet of cars, very competitive rates, and comes much recommended by the local expat community. The Bouayad brothers will do their utmost to help, and can deliver a car to the airport or Marrakesh if requested. It's off Blvd Mohammed V.

Casablanca has parking meters (Dh5, two hours maximum), operating from 8am to noon, and 2pm to 7pm daily, except on Sunday and public holidays. If you don't pay, you may be fined. There is a guarded car park next to the British cemetery (per day/night Dh20) and another just off of Rue Tata (costs Dh5 per hour). Anywhere else a guard will ask for a tip for watching your car; it is common practice to pay Dh5.

Taxi

Grands taxis to Rabat (Dh35) and to Fez (Dh55 to Dh65) leave from Blvd Hassan Seghir, near the CTM bus station. However, the train is more convenient and comfortable.

Train

If your destination is on a train line, it's generally the best way to travel. Casablanca has five train stations, but only two are of interest to travellers.

All long-distance trains as well as trains to Mohammed V International Airport depart from **Casa-Voyageurs train station** (☎ 022 243818), 4km east of the city centre. Catch bus 30 (Dh3.50), which runs along Blvd Mohammed V, or hop in a taxi and pay about Dh10 to get there.

Destinations include Marrakesh (Dh84, three hours, nine daily), Fez (Dh103, 4½ hours, nine daily) via Meknès (Dh86, 3½ hours), Oujda (Dh202, 10 hours, two daily) via Taza (Dh134, seven hours), Tangier (Dh118, 5¾ hours, two daily) and El-Jadida (Dh30, 1½ hours, five daily). For Safi (Dh75.50, five hours, two daily) change at Benguérir.

The **Casa-Port train station** (Map p110; ☎ 022 271837) is a few hundred metres northeast of Place des Nations Unies. Although more convenient, trains from here only run to Rabat (Dh32, one hour, every 30 minutes) and Kenitra (Dh44, 1½ hours, every 30 minutes).

GETTING AROUND

To/From the Airport

The easiest way to get from Mohammed V International Airport to Casablanca is by train (2nd class Dh35, 35 minutes). The trains are comfortable and reliable, and leave every hour from 6.45am to 10.45pm. You can also continue to Rabat (Dh60) or Kenitra (Dh75), though you'll probably have a change of train at Casa-Voyageurs or Aïn Sebaa. The trains leave from below the ground floor of the airport-terminal building.

From Casa-Voyageurs train station to the airport, trains go every hour from 5am to 10pm. A few additional trains go from Casa-Port.

A grand taxi between the airport and the city centre costs Dh300, though you may be asked for Dh350 at unsocial hours. Some taxi drivers receive commissions if they bring clients to particular hotels.

Bus

The local bus system is underfunded and very crowded; unless you're travelling alone and on a very limited budget a petit taxi is generally much easier. Buses cost Dh4 and stop at designated bus stops. At the time of research, the city bus system was about to be overhauled by French transport company RATP. The following routes are useful, but numbers and routes may change in the restructure:

Bus 2 Blvd Mohammed V to Casa-Voyageurs train station.
Bus 4 Along Blvd de Paris and down Ave Lalla Yacout to Nouvelle Medina.
Bus 9 From Blvd d'Anfa to Aïn Diab and the beaches.
Bus 10 From Place de la Concorde, along Blvd Mohammed V to Gare Routière Ouled Ziane.
Bus 15 Northbound from Place Oued al-Makhazine to the Hassan II Mosque.

Taxi

Casa's red petits taxis are excellent value and can generally get you to your destination far faster than any bus. You can hail one anywhere, or there's a petit-taxi stand on Ave des FAR. The minimum fare is Dh7, but expect to pay Dh10 in or near the city centre. Most drivers use the meter without question, but if they refuse to, just get out of the cab. Prices rise by 50% after 8pm.

NORTH OF CASABLANCA

RABAT الرباط

pop 1.7 million

While Rabat, Morocco's political and administrative capital since independence in 1956, has not established itself as a tourist destination, the few visitors who do go find a gem of a city. The colonial architecture is stunning, the palm-lined boulevards are well kept and relatively free of traffic, and the atmosphere is as cosmopolitan as its economic big brother down the coast. All in all, life here is pleasant and civilised. Casablancais say that, with all the bureaucrats, Rabat is dull, and they have a point. Yet the city is more laid-back, pleasant and more provincial than Casablanca, and far less grimy and frantic.

The quiet medina has an authentic feel to it, some good shops and fascinating architecture. You'll be blissfully ignored on the streets and souqs, so it's easy to discover the city's monuments and hidden corners at your own pace. The picturesque kasbah, with its narrow alleys, art galleries and magnificent ocean views, is also worth exploring.

Rabat has a long and rich history, and plenty of monuments to show for it from the Phoenician, Roman, Almohad and Merenid times. The power shifted at times between Rabat and Salé, the whitewashed town across the Bou Regreg river, where time appears to have stood still.

Rabat is also a good place to eat; there are plenty of wonderful restaurants around town. The nightlife is not what it is in Casablanca, but an early afternoon stroll along the main avenues of the happening suburb of Agdal, where local hipsters flaunt their skinny jeans, is entertaining enough. And if city life gets you down, there are beaches further north to escape to.

The mega project of Amwaj – started in 2006 and due for completion by 2010 – aims to link the cities of Rabat and Salé by developing the waterfront on both sides of the river. Thousands of new apartments, offices, shops, theatres, parks and landscaped areas are being built, as well as a new tramway and several bridges.

History

The fertile plains inland from Rabat drew settlers to the area as far back as the 8th century BC. Both the Phoenicians and the Romans set up trading posts in the estuary of the Oued Bou Regreg river in Sala, today's Chellah. The Roman settlement, Sala Colonia, lasted long after the empire's fall and eventually became the seat of an independent Berber kingdom. The Zenata Berbers built a *ribat,* a fortress-monastery after which the city takes its name, on the present site of Rabat's kasbah. As the new town of Salé (created in the 10th century) began to prosper on the north bank of the river, the city of Chellah fell into decline.

The arrival of the Almohads in the 12th century saw the *ribat* rebuilt as a kasbah, a strategic jumping-off point for campaigns in Spain, where the dynasty successfully brought Andalusia back under Muslim rule. Under Yacoub al-Mansour (the Victorious), Rabat enjoyed a brief heyday as an imperial capital, Ribat al-Fatah (Victory Fortress). Al-Mansour had extensive walls built, added the enormous Bab Oudaïa to the kasbah and began work on the Hassan Mosque, intended to be the greatest mosque in all of the Islamic West, if not in all of the Islamic world.

Al-Mansour's death in 1199 brought an end to these grandiose schemes, leaving the great Hassan Mosque incomplete. The city soon lost all significance and it wasn't until the 17th century that Rabat's fortunes began to change.

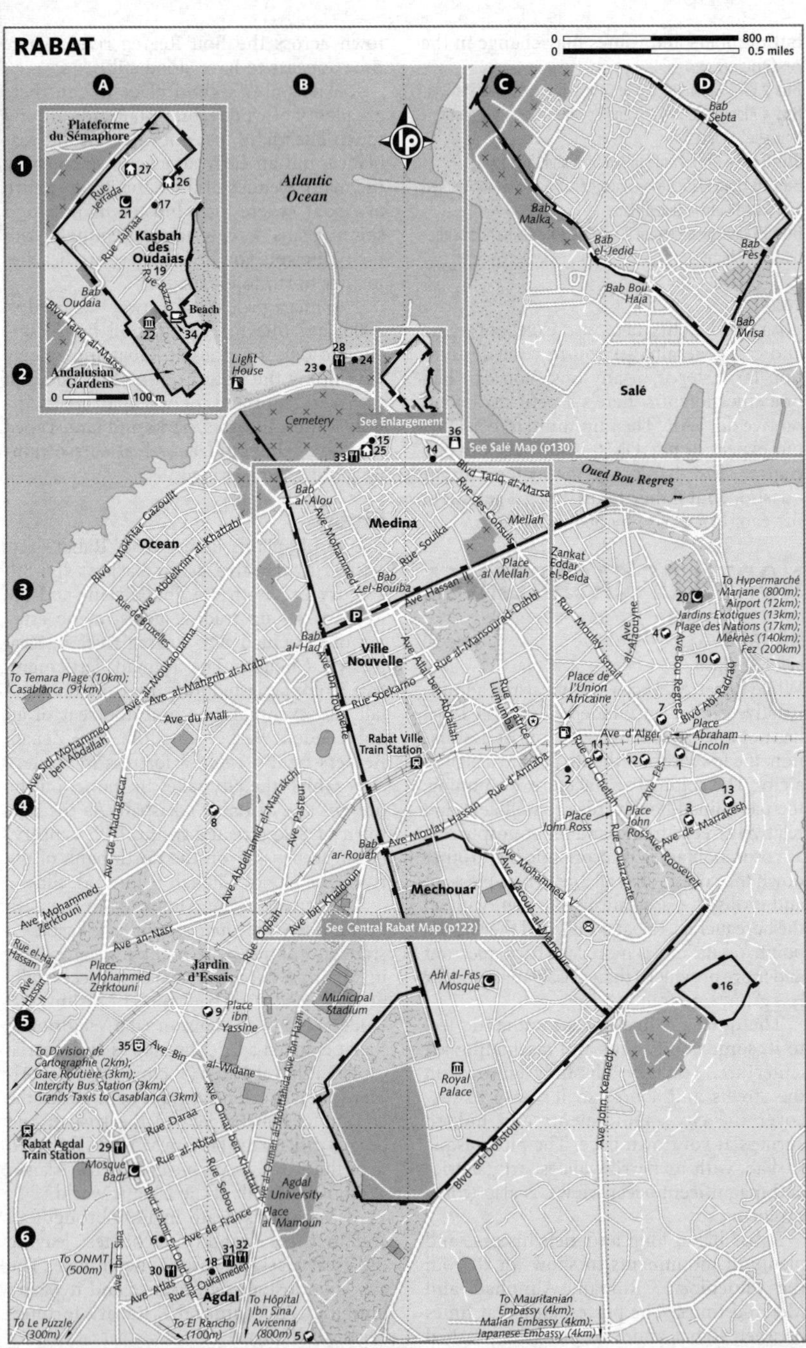
RABAT
0 800 m
0 0.5 miles
Plateforme du Sémaphore
Rue Jerrada
Rue Jamaa
Kasbah des Oudaias
Rue Bazzo
Bab Oudaia
Blvd Tariq al-Marsa
Beach
Andalusian Gardens
0 100 m
Atlantic Ocean
Light House
Cemetery
See Enlargement
See Salé Map (p130)
Bab Sebta
Bab Malka
Bab el-Jedid
Bab Bou Haja
Bab Fès
Bab Mrisa
Salé
Oued Bou Regreg
Bab al-Alou
Medina
Mellah
Ocean
Blvd Mokhtar Gazoulit
Ave Abdelkrim al-Khattabi
Rue de Bruxelles
Ave Mohammed V
Rue Souika
Rue des Consuls
Bab el-Bouiba
Ave Hassan II
Place al Mellah
Zankat Eddar el-Beida
To Hypermarché Marjane (800m); Airport (12km); Jardins Exotiques (13km); Plage des Nations (17km); Meknès (140km); Fez (200km)
Bab al-Had
Ville Nouvelle
Ave Allal ben Abdallah
Rue al-Mansourad-Dahbi
Rue Moulay Ismail
Ave al-Alaouyne
Ave Bou Regreg
Blvd Abi Radraq
To Temara Plage (10km); Casablanca (91km)
Ave al-Moukaouama
Ave al-Mahgrib al-Arabi
Rue Soekarno
Ave Ibn Toumerte
Rue Patrice Lumumba
Place de l'Union Africaine
Ave d'Alger
Place Abraham Lincoln
Ave du Mali
Ave Sidi Mohammed ben Abdallah
Rabat Ville Train Station
Rue du Chellah
Ave Fès
Ave de Madagascar
Ave Abdelhamid el-Marrakchi
Ave Pasteur
Rue d'Annaba
Place John Ross
Rue Ouarzazate
Ave de Marrakesh
Bab ar-Rouah
Ave Moulay Hassan
Ave Roosevelt
Ave Mohammed Zerktouni
Ave Ibn Khaldoun
Mechouar
Ave Mohammed V
Ave Yacoub al-Mansour
Ave an-Nasr
Rue Oqbah
See Central Rabat Map (p122)
Rue el-Haj Hassan
Place Mohammed Zerktouni
Ave Hassan II
Jardin d'Essais
Ahl al-Fas Mosque
Place ibn Yassine
Municipal Stadium
To Division de Cartographie (2km); Gare Routière (3km); Intercity Bus Station (3km); Grands Taxis to Casablanca (3km)
Ave Bin al-Widane
Ave Omar ben Khattab
Ave al-Ouman al-Mouttahida
Ave Ibn Hazm
Royal Palace
Ave John Kennedy
Rabat Agdal Train Station
Rue Daraa
Rue al-Abtal
Mosque Badr
Rue Sebou
Agdal University
Place al-Mamoun
Blvd ad-Doustour
Blvd al-Amir Fal Ould Omar
Ave de France
To ONMT (500m)
Ave Ibn Sina
Ave Atlas
Rue Oukaïmeden
Agdal
To Le Puzzle (300m)
To El Rancho (100m)
To Hôpital Ibn Sina/ Avicenna (800m)
To Mauritanian Embassy (4km); Malian Embassy (4km); Japanese Embassy (4km)

INFORMATION
Algerian Embassy....................1 D4
American Bookshop....................2 C4
Belgian Embassy....................3 D4
British Embassy....................4 D3
Canadian Embassy....................5 B6
DHL....................6 A6
Dutch Embassy....................7 D4
French Consulate....................8 B4
French Embassy....................9 B5
Italian Embassy....................10 D3
Spanish Consulate....................11 C4
Tunisian Embassy....................12 D4
US Embassy....................13 D4

SIGHTS & ACTIVITIES
Carpet Souq....................14 C2
Center for Cross-Cultural Learning....................15 B2
Chellah....................16 D5
Galérie d'Art Nouiga....................17 A1
Institute for Language & Communication Studies....................18 B6
Kasbah des Oudaias....................19 A2
Le Tour Hassan....................(see 20)
Mausoleum of Mohammed V....................20 D3
Mosque el-Atiqa....................21 A1
Musée des Oudaia....................22 A2
Oudayas Surf Club....................23 B2
Sala Colonia....................(see 16)
Surf Club Monde de la Glisse....................24 B2

SLEEPING
Dar Al Batoul....................25 B2
Riad Dar Baraka....................26 A1
Riad Kasbah....................27 A1

EATING
Borj Eddar....................28 B2
Galapagos Café....................29 A6
L'Entrecôte....................30 A6
Les Casseroles en Folie....................31 B6
Paul....................32 B6
Restaurant de la Plage....................(see 28)
Restaurant Dinarjat....................33 B2

DRINKING
Café Maure....................34 A2

ENTERTAINMENT
5th Avenue....................35 A5

SHOPPING
Ensemble Artisanal....................36 C2

As Muslim refugees arrived from Christian Spain, so did a band of Christian renegades, Moorish pirates, freebooters and multinational adventurers. Rabat and Salé became safe havens for corsairs – merciless pirates whom English chroniclers called the Sallee Rovers. At one point they even created their own pirate state, the Republic of Bou Regreg. These corsairs roved as far as the coast of the USA seeking Spanish gold, and to Cornwall in southern England to capture Christian slave labour. The first Alawite sultans attempted to curtail their looting sprees, but no sultan ever really exercised control over them. Corsairs continued attacking European shipping until well into the 19th century.

Meanwhile, Sultan Mohammed ben Abdallah briefly made Rabat his capital at the end of the 18th century, but the city soon fell back into obscurity. In 1912 France strategically abandoned the hornet's nest of political intrigue and unrest in the traditional capitals of Fez and Marrakesh and instead shifted power to coastal Rabat, where supply and defence were more easily achieved. Since then, the city has remained the seat of government and official home of the king.

Orientation

Ave Hassan II divides the medina from the ville nouvelle and follows the line of the medina walls to the Oued Bou Regreg. The river separates the cities of Rabat and Salé.

The city's main thoroughfare – the wide, palm-lined Ave Mohammed V – is where you'll find many hotels and the main administrative buildings. Most embassies cluster around Place Abraham Lincoln and Ave de Fès east of the centre; see p462 for addresses. Rabat Ville train station lies towards the southern end of Ave Mohammed V. Many restaurants and boutiques are in the suburb of Agdal, 3km southwest of the city centre.

MAPS

Rabat is one of the few places in Morocco where you can get a range of topographical Moroccan maps and town plans. The **Division de Cartographie** (off Map p118; ☎ 037 708935; www.acfcc.gov.ma, in French; cnr Ave Moulay Youssef & Ave Moulay Hassan I; 9am-3.30pm Mon-Fri) sells topography maps, but staff can be sensitive about selling some maps; see p417. Take your passport. Most maps need to be ordered and can be picked up 48 hours later.

Information

BOOKSHOPS

American Bookshop (Map p118; cnr Rues Moulay Abdelhafid & Boujaad) A good range of new titles, and a good selection of books on Morocco.

Aux Belles Images (Map p122; ☎ 037 724495; 281 Ave Mohammed V; 9am-noon & 3-8pm Mon-Sat) Good picture books of Morocco.

English Bookshop (Map p122; ☎ 037 706593; 7 Rue al-Yamama) New titles and second-hand English-language novels.

Libraire Kalila Wa Dimma (Map p122; ☎ 037 723106; 344 Ave Mohammed V) Carries a decent collection of trekking and travel guides (in French) to Morocco.

CULTURAL CENTRES

British Council (Map p122; ☎ 037 760836; www.britishcouncil.org.ma; 36 Rue de Tanger; 8.30am-7.30pm Mon-Fri, to 5.30pm Sat) Offers a large library (with English papers) as well as a program of lectures and exhibitions.

Goethe Institut (Map p122; ☎ 037 736544; www.goethe.de/rabat, in German; 7 Rue Sana'a; 🕑 10am-7pm Mon-Fri) Features a library, art and photography exhibitions and the cool Café Weimar (p127).

Institut Français (Map p122; ☎ 037 701122; www.ambafrance-ma.org; 1 Abdou Inane; 🕑 10am-6.30pm Tue-Sat, noon-6.30pm Thu) Films, exhibitions and cultural events as well as a fun restaurant, La Veranda (p126).

EMERGENCY

SAMU (☎ 037 737373) Private ambulance service.

SOS Médecins (☎ 037 202020; house call Dh250; 🕑 24hr) Doctors on call.

INTERNET ACCESS

Internet (Map p122; ☎ 037 346903; Rue Tantan; per hr Dh7; 🕑 9am-7.30pm) Next to La Mamma.

Librairie Livre Service (Map p122; ☎ 037 724495; 46 Ave Allal ben Abdallah; per hr Dh7; 🕑 9am-noon & 3-8pm Mon-Sat)

MEDICAL SERVICES

Town pharmacies open nights and weekends on a rotational basis; check the rota posted in French and Arabic in all pharmacy windows.

Hôpital Ibn Sina/Avicenna (off Map p118; ☎ 037 672871, emergencies 037 674450; Place Ibn Sina, Agdal)

Night Pharmacy (Map p122; Rue Moulay Rachid; 🕑 9.30pm-7.30am)

MONEY

Numerous banks (with ATMs) are concentrated along Ave Mohammed V and the parallel Ave Allal ben Abdallah, including Banque Populaire.

BMCE (Map p122; Ave Mohammed V; 🕑 8am-8pm Mon-Fri)

POST

DHL (Map p118; ☎ 037 779934; Ave de France, Agdal)

Main post office (Map p122; cnr Rue Soékarno & Ave Mohammed V; 🕑 8am-4.30pm Mon-Fri, 8am-noon Sat)

TOURIST INFORMATION

Office National Marocain du Tourisme (ONMT; off Map p118; ☎ 037 674013; visitmorocco@onmt.org.ma; cnr Rue Oued el-Makhazine & Rue Zalaka, Agdal; 🕑 8.30am-noon & 3-6.30pm Mon-Fri) Smiles and vacant faces await at this bureaucratic office. To get here, take bus 3 from the train station or take a taxi.

TRAVEL AGENCIES

CAP Tours (Map p122; ☎ 037 733571; www.captours.ma; 7 Rue Damas) A good place for cheap flights to African destinations; also makes ferry reservations.

Carlson Wagonlit (Map p122; ☎ 037 709625; www.carlsonwagonlit.com; 1 Ave Moulay Abdallah)

Sights

MEDINA

Rabat's walled medina (Map p122), all there was of the city when the French arrived in the early 20th century, is a rich mixture of spices, carpets, crafts, cheap shoes and bootlegged DVDs. Built on an orderly grid in the 17th century, it may lack the more intriguing atmosphere of the older medinas of the interior, but it's a great place to roam, with no aggressive selling.

The main market street is Rue Souika, lined with food and spice shops at the western end, then textiles and silverware as you head east. The **Souq as-Sebbat** (Jewellery Souq; Map p122) specialises in gaudy gold and begins roughly at Rue Bab Chellah. The **Grande Mosquée**, a 14th-century Merenid original that has been rebuilt in the intervening years, is just down this road to the right.

If you continue past the Rue des Consuls (so called because diplomats lived here until 1912), you'll come to the *mellah* (Jewish quarter) with an interesting **flea market** (Map p122) going down to Bab el-Bahr and the river. Turning north along Rue des Consuls is one of the more interesting areas of the medina, with craft shops and some of the grand diplomatic residencies. After the **carpet souq** (Map p118) the street ends in an open area lined with craft shops, which was once the setting for the slave auctions in the days of the Sallee Rovers. From here you can make your way up the hill to the kasbah.

KASBAH DES OUDAIAS

The **kasbah** (Map p118) occupies the oldest part of the city, the site of the original *ribat*, and commands magnificent views over the river and ocean from its cliff-top perch. Predominately residential, with tranquil alleys and whitewashed houses mostly built by Muslim refugees from Spain, this is a picturesque place to wander. Many foreigners are buying up the houses here, and it's easy to see the appeal. Some 'guides' offer their services but there is no need. Ignore anyone who says that the kasbah is 'forbidden' or closed.

The 12th-century Almohad **Bab Oudaia**, the most dramatic kasbah gate, is elaborately decorated with a series of carved arches. Inside the gateway, the main street, Rue Jamaa, runs straight through the kasbah. About 200m ahead on the left is the **Mosque el-Atiqa**, the oldest mosque in Rabat, built in the 12th century and restored in the 18th century. You'll also find a number of low-key tourist shops and a couple of art galleries, such as the **Galerie d'Art Nouiga** (Map p118), along this street.

At the end of the street is the **Plateforme du Sémaphore** (Signal Platform) with sweeping views over the estuary and across to Salé. The elevated position provided an excellent defence against seagoing attackers negotiating the sandbanks below.

Returning from the Plateforme, turn left down Rue Bazzo, a narrow winding street that leads down to the popular **Café Maure** (p127) and a side entrance to the formal **Andalusian Gardens** (sunrise-sunset). The gardens, laid out by the French during the colonial period, occupy the palace grounds and make a wonderful shady retreat.

The palace itself is a grand 17th-century affair built by Moulay Ismail. The building now houses the **Musée des Oudaia** (Map118; ☎ 037 731537; admission Dh10; 9am-5pm Wed-Mon), the national jewellery museum with a beautifully displayed and fascinating collection of prehistoric, Roman and Islamic jewellery found in the different regions of Morocco.

LE TOUR HASSAN & MAUSOLEUM OF MOHAMMED V

Towering above Oued Bou Regreg, and surrounded by well-tended gardens, is Rabat's most famous landmark, **Le Tour Hassan** (Hassan Tower, Map p118). The Almohads most ambitious project would have been the second-largest mosque of its time, after Samarra in Iraq, but sultan Yacoub al-Mansour died before it was finished. He intended a 60m-tall minaret, but the tower was abandoned at 44m. The mosque was destroyed by an earthquake in 1755, and today only a forest of shattered pillars testifies to the grandiosity of Al-Mansour's plans. The tower is built to the same design as the Giralda in Seville, and the Koutoubia in Marrakesh (p299).

Near the tower stands the marble **Mausoleum of Mohammed V** (Map p118; admission free; sunrise-sunset), built in traditional Moroccan style. The present king's father (the late Hassan II) and grandfather have been laid to rest here. The decoration, despite the patterned *zellij* and carved plaster, gives off an air of tranquillity. Visitors to the mausoleum must be respectfully dressed, and can look down into the tomb from a gallery.

CHELLAH

Abandoned, crumbling and overgrown, the ancient Roman city of **Sala Colonia** (Map p118) and the Merenid necropolis of **Chellah** (Map p118; cnr Ave Yacoub al-Mansour & Blvd Moussa ibn Nassair; admission Dh10; 9am-5.30pm) is one of Rabat's most evocative sights.

The Phoenicians were the first to settle on the grassy slopes above the river, but the town grew when the Romans took control in about AD 40. The city was abandoned in 1154 in favour of Salé, but in the 14th century the Merenid sultan Abou al-Hassan Ali built a necropolis on top of the Roman site and surrounded it with the towers and defensive wall that stand today.

This rarely visited site, overgrown by fruit trees and wild flowers, is an atmospheric place to roam around. From the main gate, a path heads down through fragrant fig, olive and orange trees to a **viewing platform** that overlooks the ruins of the Roman city. Making out the structures takes a bit of imagination, but the mystery is part of the magic of this place. A path leads through the ruins of the triple-arched entrance known as the Arc de Triomphe, past the Jupiter Temple (to the left) and to the forum (at the end of the main road), while another goes to the octagonal Pool of the Nymph, part of the Roman system of water distribution.

Far easier to discern are the remains of the **Islamic complex**, with its elegant minaret now topped by a stork's nest. An incredible colony of storks has taken over the ruins, lording over the site from their treetop nests. If you visit in spring, the clacking bills of mating pairs is a wonderful soundtrack to a visit.

Near the ruined minaret is the tomb of Abou al-Hassan Ali and his wife, complete with ornate *zellij* ornamentation. A small *medersa* is nearby, where the remains of pillars, students' cells and scalloped pools – as well as the blocked-off mihrab (prayer niche) – are still discernable.

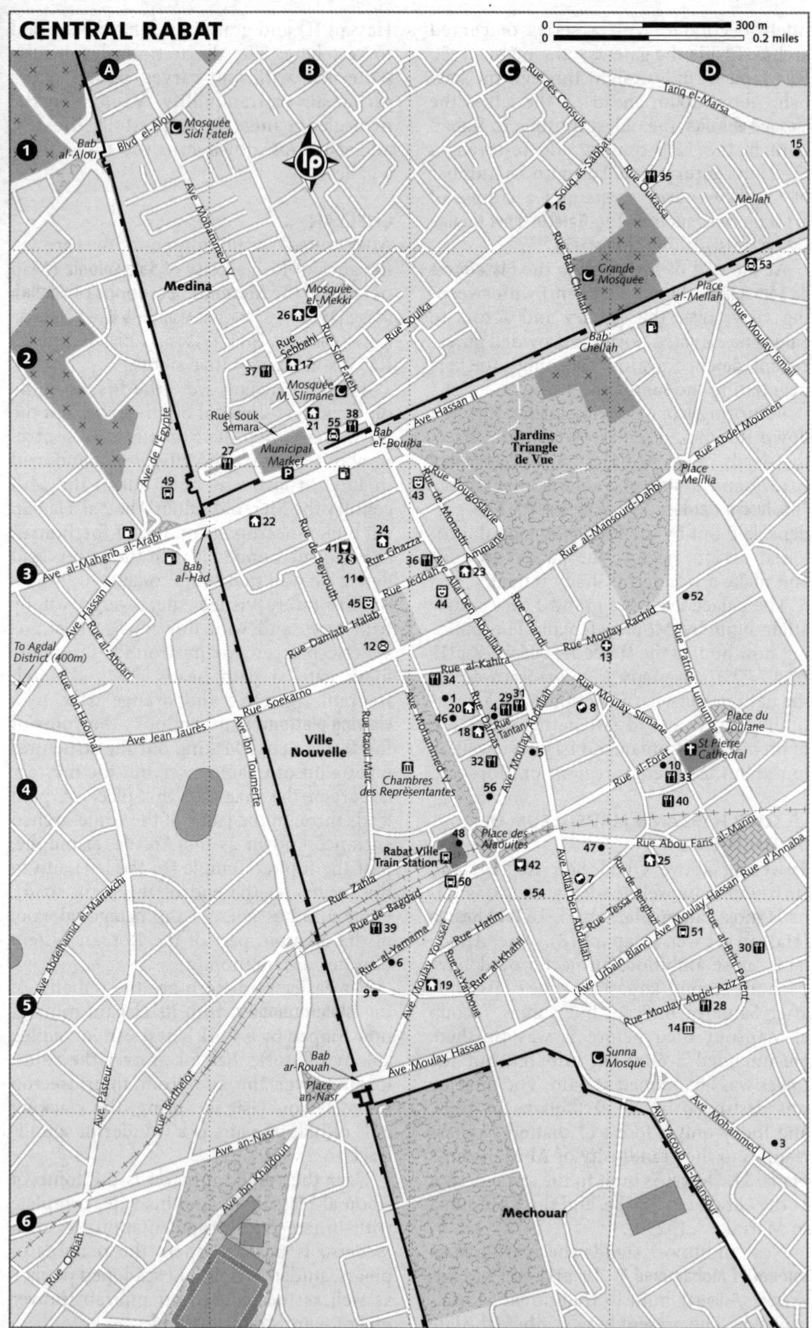
CENTRAL RABAT
0 300 m
0 0.2 miles
Medina
Ville Nouvelle
Mellah
Mechouar
Bab al-Alou
Blvd el-Alou
Mosquée Sidi Fateh
Ave Mohammed V
Rue des Consuls
Tariq el-Marsa
Souq as-Sabbat
Rue Oukassa
Rue Bab Chellah
Grande Mosquée
Place al-Mellah
Rue Moulay Ismail
Mosquée el-Mekki
Rue Sebbahi
Rue Sidi Fateh
Rue Soulka
Bab Chellah
Mosquée M. Slimane
Rue Souk Semara
Municipal Market
Bab el-Bouiba
Ave Hassan II
Jardins Triangle de Vue
Rue Abdel Moumen
Place Melilia
Ave de l'Egypte
Rue Yougoslavie
Rue de Monastir
Ammane
Ave al-Mahgrib al-Arabi
Bab al-Had
Rue de Beyrouth
Rue Ghazza
Rue Jeddah
Ave Allal ben Abdallah
Rue al-Mansourd-Dahbi
Rue Ghandi
Rue Moulay Rachid
Rue Damiate Halab
To Agdal District (400m)
Rue al-Abdari
Rue Ibn Haouhal
Rue al-Kahira
Rue Soekarno
Ave Jean Jaurès
Ave Ibn Toumerte
Rue Raoul Marc
Rue Damas
Rue Tantan
Ave Moulay Abdallah
Rue Moulay Slimane
Rue Patrice Lumumba
Place du Joulane
St Pierre Cathedral
Rue al-Forat
Chambres des Représentantes
Place des Alaouites
Rabat Ville Train Station
Rue Abou Faris al-Marini
Ave Allal ben Abdallah
Rue de Benghazi
Rue Tessa
Rue Zahla
Rue de Bagdad
Rue al-Yamama
Rue Hatim
Ave Moulay Youssef
Rue al-Yanboua
Rue al-Khahil
Ave Moulay Hassan
(Ave Urbain Blanc)
Rue d'Annaba
Rue al-Brihi Patent
Rue Moulay Abdel Aziz
Sunna Mosque
Ave Abdelhamid el-Marrakchi
Bab ar-Rouah
Place an-Nasr
Ave Mohammed V
Ave Yacoub al-Mansour
Ave Pasteur
Rue Berthelot
Ave an-Nasr
Ave Ibn Khaldoun
Rue Oqbah

INFORMATION
Aux Belles Images....1 C4
Banque Populaire....(see 21)
BMCE (ATM)....2 B3
British Council....3 D6
CAP Tours....4 C4
Carlson Wagonlit....5 C4
English Bookshop....6 B5
French Consulate-General....7 C4
German Embassy....8 C4
Goethe Institut....9 B5
Institu Français....10 D4
Internet....(see 31)
Libraire Kalila Wa Dimma....11 B3
Main Post Office....12 B3
Night Pharmacy....13 C3
Spanish Embassy....(see 8)

SIGHTS & ACTIVITIES
Archaeology Museum....14 D5
Flea Market....15 D1
Souq as-Sebbat....16 C1

SLEEPING
Hôtel al-Maghrib al-Jadid....17 B2
Hôtel Balima....18 C4
Hôtel Bélère....19 C5
Hotel Central....20 C4
Hôtel Dorhmi....21 B2
Hôtel Majestic....22 B3
Hôtel Royal....23 C3
Hôtel Splendid....24 B3
Le Pietri Urban Hotel....25 D4
Riad Oudaya....26 B2

EATING
Café Weimar....(see 9)
Fruit & Vegetable Market....27 B2
L'R du Gout....28 D5
La Dolce Vita....29 C4
La Koutoubia....30 D5
La Mamma....31 C4
La Petit Beur - Dar Tajine....32 C4
La Véranda....33 D4
Le Grand Comptoir....34 C3
Le Ziryab....35 D1
Pâtisserie Majestic....36 C3
Restaurant de la Libération....37 B2
Restaurant el-Bahia....38 B2
Riad Oudaya....(see 26)
Tagine wa Tanja....39 B5
Ty Potes....40 D4

DRINKING
Bar de L'Alsace....41 B3
Cafétéria du 7ème Art....(see 44)
Henry's Bar....42 C4
Hôtel Balima....(see 18)

ENTERTAINMENT
Amnesia....43 C3
Cinèma du 7ème Art....44 C3
Cinéma Renaissance....45 B3

TRANSPORT
Air France....46 C4
Avis....47 C4
Budget....48 C4
Bus 12, 13, 14, 16 or 34 to Salé....(see 53)
Bus 17 & 30 to Intercity Bus Station....49 A3
Bus 3 to Agdal....50 C4
Bus Stand (16 & 28)....51 D5
Europcar....52 D3
Grands Taxis for Fez, Meknès & Salé....53 D2
Hertz....54 C4
Petit Taxi Stand....55 B2
Royal Air Maroc....(see 47)
Royal Air Maroc....56 C4
Supratours....(see 48)

On leaving the mosque, the path passes the **tombs** of several saints on the far right. To the left, the murky waters of a walled pool (marked *'bassin aux anguilles'*) still attract women who believe that feeding boiled eggs to the eels here brings fertility and easy childbirth..

ARCHAEOLOGY MUSEUM

Dusty and forlorn but interesting (even if the labels are only in French), the **Archaeology Museum** (Map p122; ☎ 037 701919; 23 Rue al-Brihi Parent; admission Dh10; 9am-4.30pm Wed-Mon) gives a good account of Morocco's history. Prehistoric finds include a beautiful neolithic rock carving of a man surrounded by concentric circles. The highlight of the collection is the **Salle des Bronzes**, which displays ceramics, statuary and artefacts from the Roman settlements at Volubilis, Lixus and Chellah. Look out for the beautiful head of Juba II and the unforgiving realism of the bust of Cato the Younger – both found at Volubilis.

Activities

SURFING

King Mohammed VI was a founding member of the **Oudayas Surf Club** (Map p118; ☎ 037 260683; 3 Plage des Oudayas; 90min surfboard/bodyboard lesson Dh150), below the kasbah. Next door is the **Surf Club Monde de la Glisse** (Map p118; ☎ 061 654362; Plage des Oudayas), offering similar services and equipment rental.

Courses

Rabat has many language schools offering year-long courses, but the following offer short-term classes:

Center for Cross-Cultural Learning (CCCL; Map p118; ☎ 037 202365; www.cccl-ma.com; Ave Laalou, 11 Zankat Hassani) Intensive short courses in French and Moroccan Arabic.

Institute for Language & Communication Studies (Map p118; ☎ 037 675968; www.ilcs.ac.ma; 29 Rue Oukaimeden, Agdal) Offers intensive courses and private tuition in French and Moroccan Arabic.

Festivals & Events

Rabat hosts a number of festivals and events each year, including the popular **Oudayas Jazz Festival** held in the last weekend of May. The **Festival Mawazine** (www.mawazine.ma), also held in May, draws big names from the world-music scene. The biggest drawcard is the **Festival International de Rabat** (www.rabatfilmfestival.org, in French), which attracts hoards of music lovers and film buffs to the capital for two weeks in late June and early July.

Rabat for Children

Hassle-free shopping in the souqs and the impressive kasbah make Rabat a pleasant place to visit with children. However there are few specific attractions in the city for younger visitors The best bet is to head out of town to the beach, or the Jardins Exotiques (p132).

Sleeping

Most of Rabat's better accommodation is in the nouvelle medina between Ave Mohammed V and Ave Abderrahman, while the old medina has a host of low-budget dives and a couple of upmarket riads (town houses set around an internal garden). Rabat caters mainly for business travellers and has a disproportionate number of top-end hotels.

BUDGET

Although the medina is full of budget hotels, they're pretty basic and many lack any kind of creature comforts, including showers. The best medina options are listed here, otherwise pay the extra and head for the ville nouvelle.

Hôtel al-Maghrib al-Jadid (Map p122; ☎ 037 732207; 2 Rue Sebbahi; s/d Dh70/110, hot shower Dh7.50) Although the rooms at this hotel are fairly small and spartan, they are pristinely clean, and have shuttered windows that let in lots of light. You'll either love or hate the shocking pink walls but it's all part of the rather quirky character of this place.

Hôtel Dorhmi (Map p122; ☎ 037 723898; 313 Ave Mohammed V; s/d Dh90/130, hot shower Dh10) Immaculately kept, very friendly and keenly priced, this family-run hotel is the best of the medina options. The simple rooms are bright and tidy and surround a central courtyard on the 1st floor above the Banque Populaire. Despite being in the hub of things, the Dormhi offers quiet rooms.

Hotel Central (Map p122; ☎ 037 707356; 2 Rue Al-Basra; s/d 90/130, with bathroom Dh120/170, hot shower Dh10) Opposite the imposing Balima and right in the heart of town, the Hotel Central has a good-value range of simple rooms. It's a little past its best, but remains a friendly place handy to everything in town.

Hôtel Splendid (Map p122; ☎ 037 723283; 8 Rue Ghazza; s/d Dh104/130, with bathroom Dh130/190) Slap-bang in the heart of the medina, the spacious, bright rooms with high ceilings, big windows, cheerful colours and simple wooden furniture are set around a pleasant courtyard. Bathrooms are new and rooms without bathrooms have a hot-water washbasin.

Hôtel Majestic (Map p122; ☎ 037 722997; www.hotelmajestic.ma; 121 Ave Hassan II; s/d Dh239/279) Another excellent option, though not as palatial as it sounds. This modern place has smallish rooms with sleek, new furniture and fittings – if not a lot of character. Despite the double glazing the rooms can be noisy, so it's best to forego the medina view for a room at the back.

MIDRANGE

Rabat has a limited choice of midrange accommodation, most of it located on or just off Ave Mohammed V.

our pick **Le Piétri Urban Hotel** (Map p122; ☎ 037 707820; www.lepietri.com; 4 Rue Tobrouk; s/d/ste Dh600/650/1050; ❄ 💻) The former Hôtel Oudayas was totally renovated and is now a good-value boutique hotel in a quiet street in a central, but more residential, part of town. The 36 spacious bright rooms with wooden floors are comfortable, well equipped and decorated in warm colours in a contemporary style. The hotel has an excellent restaurant with a small garden for elegant alfresco dining. On the menu are contemporary Moroccan and Mediterranean specialities and there is a good wine list.

Hôtel Balima (Map p122; ☎ 037 707755; www.hotel-balima.com; Ave Mohammed V; s/d Dh450/580; ❄) The grand dame of Rabat hotels is not as grand as she used to be but still offers newly decorated and comfortable en-suite rooms, all immacutely kept and with great views over the city. The hotel has a decent restaurant and nightclub and a glorious shady terrace facing Ave Mohammed V – still the place to meet in Rabat.

Hôtel Royal (Map p122; 1 Rue Jeddah Ammane; s/d Dh400/600) Slightly expensive for what's on offer but in a very central location. The Royal's tastefully renovated rooms are very comfortable, with polished wooden furniture and sparkling clean bathrooms. The rooms on the 4th floor have the best views over the park and city, are quieter and come with a large terrace. The rooms on the lower floors are quite noisy and the staff make a racket cleaning the rooms in the morning. An adequate breakfast is served in the downstairs restaurant by rather surly waiters.

Hôtel Bélère (Map p122; ☎ 037 709689; fax 037 709801; 33 Ave Moulay Youssef; s/d Dh665/864;

) This four-star hotel is a step up from the other options in this price range and offers small but extremely comfortable nonsmoking rooms with tasteful (albeit very 1970s) modern decor, now back in fashion. It has a good bar and restaurant and it's handy to the train station.

TOP END

Rabat offers all the usual top international chain hotels, but for something with a little more local flavour the medina options offer ultra-chic style and service.

Riad Kasbah (Map p118; ☎ 037 705247; www.riadoudaya.com; 49 Rue Zirara; s/d incl breakfast Dh880/980) Set in the heart of the kasbah away from the hubbub of the city, this sublimely peaceful guest house is a sister property to the Riad Oudaya. Although it's not quite as luxurious, this beautiful house has three rooms with elegant traditional decor.

our pick **Riad Dar Baraka** (Map p118; ☎ 037 730362, 061 783361; www.darbaraka-rabat.com; 26 Rue de la Mosquée; s/d incl breakfast Dh990/1430) Recognisable from the blue door at the end of the main street of the kasbah, this most delightful guest house has superb views over the estuary and Salé. There are just two rooms – one small and one large, both decorated in white and electric blue, and bright and airy – so definitely book ahead. Breakfast is served on a terrace in summer or by the fireplace in winter. This really is, in all its simplicity, the dream home-away-from-home.

Dar Al Batoul (Map p118; ☎ 037 727250, 061 401181; www.riadbatoul.com; 7 Derb Jirari; d/ste incl breakfast Dh1100/1600) This grand 18th-century merchant's house has been transformed into a sumptuous hotel with just eight rooms in traditional Moroccan style. Centred on a graceful columned courtyard, each room is different, with stunning combinations of fabrics, stained glass and intricate tilework.

Riad Oudaya (Map p122; ☎ 037 702392; www.riadoudaya.com; 46 Rue Sidi Fateh; r/ste Dh1350/1650) Tucked away down an alleyway in the medina, this gorgeous guest house is a real hidden gem. The rooms around a spectacular courtyard are tastefully decorated with a blend of Moroccan style and Western comfort. Subtle lighting, open fireplaces, balconies and the gentle gurgling of the fountain in the tiled courtyard below complete the romantic appeal. Meals here are sublime but need to be ordered in advance (see below).

Eating

Rabat has a wonderful choice of restaurants from cheap and cheerful hole-in-the-walls to upmarket gourmet pads feeding the city's legions of politicians and diplomats.

RESTAURANTS

Medina

Restaurant de la Libération (Map p122; 256 Ave Mohammed V; mains Dh30) Cheap, cheerful and marginally more classy than the string of other eateries along this road (it's got plastic menus and tablecloths), this basic restaurant does a steady line in traditional favourites. Friday is couscous day when giant platters of the stuff are delivered to the eager masses.

Restaurant el-Bahia (Map p122; ☎ 037 734504; Ave Hassan II; mains Dh50; 6am-midnight, to 10.30pm in winter) Built into the outside of the medina walls and a good spot for people-watching, this laid-back restaurant has the locals lapping up hearty Moroccan fare. Sit on the pavement terrace, in the shaded courtyard or upstairs in the traditional salon.

Le Ziryab (Map p122; ☎ 037 733636; 10 Zankat Ennajar; mains Dh90-140) This chic Moroccan restaurant is in a magnificent building just off Rue des Consuls. The blend of old-world character and stylish contemporary design is reflected in the excellent menu of interesting variations on tajine, couscous, *pastilla*, and grilled meat and fish.

Riad Oudaya (Map p122; ☎ 037 702392; 46 Rue Sidi Fateh; lunch/dinner Dh220/330) This lovely restaurant squirreled away behind a wooden door in the depths of the medina is reason enough to come to Rabat. Set in a gorgeous riad, it dishes up gourmet five-course dinners featuring anything from juicy tajines or *pastilla* to stuffed calamari.

our pick **Restaurant Dinarjat** (Map p118; ☎ 037 724239; 6 Rue Belgnaoui; menu Dh450, bottle wine Dh80) Stylish and the most elegant of medina restaurants, Dinarjat is a favourite with well-heeled locals and visitors alike. It's set in a superb 17th-century Andalusian-style house at the heart of the medina, and has been carefully restored and decorated in a contemporary style but in keeping with tradition. The restaurant is an ode to the Arab-Andalusian art of living with its sumptuous architecture, refined traditional food and peaceful oud (lute) music. The tajines, couscous and salads are prepared with the freshest ingredients, using little fat, and are surprisingly light. Book in advance.

Ville Nouvelle

our pick **Le Petit Beur – Dar Tajine** (Map p122; ☎ 037 731322; 8 Rue Damas; meals Dh66-84; closed Sun) This modest little place is renowned for its excellent Moroccan food, from succulent tajines and heavenly couscous to one of the best *pastillas* in town. It's a little sombre at lunchtime but livens up at night when the waiters double as musicians and play oud music to accompany your meal. Book ahead or get there early as it fills up quickly.

Tajine wa Tanja (Map p122; ☎ 037 729797; 9 Rue de Baghdad; mains Dh70-90; closed Sun) Down-to-earth Moroccan dishes are the speciality at this small, friendly restaurant near the train station. Choose from a range of wood-fired grills or tajines prepared to traditional recipes, or make a special outing for the magnificent Friday couscous. It's a fairly quiet spot, and not so intimidating for women travelling alone.

Ty Potes (Map p122; ☎ 037 707965; 11 Rue Ghafsa; set menu Dh70-105; closed Mon & Tue-Wed dinner) A pleasant and welcoming lunch spot and tea house, serving sweet and savoury crepes, healthy salads and sandwiches. It's popular with well-heeled locals. The atmosphere is more European, with a little garden at the back, and the Sunday brunch is particularly well attended.

La Mamma (Map p122; ☎ 037 707329; 6 Rue Tanta; mains from Dh80) It looks pretty dark from the outside, but this old favourite serves some of the best pizza and pasta in town. The beamed ceilings and candlelit tables add a touch of 1970s romantic atmosphere, and the wood-fired pizzas and grilled meats will leave you planning a return visit.

La Koutoubia (Map p122; ☎ 037 701075; 10 Pierre Parent; mains Dh90-140) Old-fashioned Moroccan restaurant with plenty of traditional *zallij* and colourful painted panels. All the classic Moroccan dishes are on the menu here, including tajines and couscous, but labour-intensive specialities like *pastilla ay pigeon* or *mechoui* (roast lamb) need to be ordered in advance. Good wine list.

La Veranda (Map p122; ☎ 074 841244; Institut Français, 1 Rue Abou Inane; mains Dh90-150; closed Sun) Run by the same owner as Le Grand Comptoir, this loft-style restaurant, in a modernist villa with a pleasant garden under majestic palm trees, is already proving the place to be at lunchtime. It serves good contemporary French-Mediterranean bistro food from a changing menu written on a blackboard. The staff is young and trendy. It's just behind the church.

Le Grand Comptoir (Map p122; ☎ 037 201514; www.legrandcomptoir.ma; 279 Ave Mohammed V; mains Dh95-175) Sleek, stylish and oozing the charms of an old-world Parisienne brasserie, this suave restaurant and lounge bar woos customers with its chic surroundings and classic French menu. Candelabras, giant palms and contemporary art adorn the grand salon while a pianist tinkles in the background. Go for the succulent steaks or be brave and try the *andouillette* (tripe sausage) or veal kidneys. A good place to have breakfast or coffee too, and there is wi-fi.

L'R du Gout (Map p122; ☎ 037 262727; Rue Moulay Abd el-Aziz; mains Dh100-150) This large, new restaurant with a colourful interior – a blend of French bistort and Moroccan flair – is run by young French men. The menu serves traditional French brasserie food such as foie gras, veal kidneys, and steak with a pepper sauce.

Outside the Centre

Borj Eddar (Map p118; ☎ 037 701500; mains from Dh120; closed Oct-Apr) This restaurant overlooking the sea has a menu of excellent fresh fish and seafood dishes. The next door Restaurant de la Plage has a similar menu and the same views, if the Borj Eddar is full. There's little to choose between them: both have glass-fronted terraces overlooking the ocean.

Les Casseroles en Folie (Map p118; ☎ 037 674247; 4 Ave de l'Atlas, Agdal; mains around Dh130) This elegant French restaurant is popular at lunchtime with bureaucrats from the nearby ministries, but more relaxed in the evening. The food is very French with specialities like Salade des Casseroles (a salad with wild mushrooms and duck breast), and steaks with various sauces. Keep some space for the delicious dessert trolley.

L'Entrecôte (Map p118; ☎ 037 671108; 74 Blvd al-Amir Fal Ould Omar, Agdal; mains around Dh140) The menu and attitude at this upmarket old-style restaurant in Agdal are very French but the dark woods and rough plaster are more reminiscent of Bavaria than Bordeaux. Steak, fish and game specialities dominate the classic French menu, and to further confuse the ambience there's jazz or traditional Spanish music at night.

CAFES, PATISSERIES & ICE-CREAM PARLOURS

Cafe Weimar (Map p122; ☎ 063 428101; 7 Rue Sana'a; pizza Dh55) This hip café in the Goethe Institut is where the young and beautiful hang out for cake and coffee or lunch. It also does a simple Mediterranean menu and is a good spot for Sunday brunch. Book ahead, but there are no reservations on Friday and Saturday

Pâtisserie Majestic (Map p122; cnr Rue Jeddah Ammane & Ave Allal ben Abdallah) An excellent and extremely popular patisserie, perfect for breakfast or an afternoon cake and coffee, and right in the centre of town.

Paul (Map p118; ☎ 037 037 672000; 2 Ave al-Oumam al-Muttahida, Agdal; mains from Dh60; 🕑 7.30am-11pm) This French bakery and patisserie is the place to hang out in Rabat, serving the best croissants in town for breakfast, good sandwiches, salads and a light menu throughout the day. Sit in the elegant interior or on the pleasant, if noisy, streetside terrace.

La Dolce Vita (Map p122; ☎ 037 707329; 8 Tanta; cones/tubs Dh7/12; 🕑 7.30am-1am) Delicious homemade Italian gelato next to the Italian La Mamma restaurant, with over 40 flavours.

Galapagos Café (Map p118; ☎ 037 686879; 14 Blvd al-Amir Fal Ould Omar, Agdal; snacks Dh25-45) Slick café-terrace with dark-wood panelling, contemporary furniture and floor-to-ceiling windows. It's popular with young professionals for its ice cream, crêpes, panini and people-watching.

QUICK EATS

The best place for quick, cheap food in Rabat is on Ave Mohammed V just inside the medina gate. Here you'll find a slew of hole-in-the-wall joints dishing out tajines, brochettes, salads and chips for cheap and cheaper. You'll know the best ones by the queue of locals waiting patiently to be served.

Another good spot is around Rue Tanta in the ville nouvelle, where you'll find a selection of fast-food joints serving everything from burgers and brochettes to pizza and panini.

SELF-CATERING

The medina is the best place to go for self-catering supplies. The indoor **fruit and vegetable market** (Map p122; Ave Hassan II) has a fantastic choice of fresh produce, dried fruits and nuts. You should be able to find everything else you need (including booze) at the surrounding stalls or along Rue Souika and near Bab el-Bouiba.

You'll find Western food at the vast **Hypermarché Marjane** (off Map p118; 🕑 7am-7pm) on the road to Salé.

Drinking

CAFÉS

Café Maure (Map p128; Kasbah des Oudaias; 🕑 9am-5.30pm) Sit back, relax and just gaze out over the estuary to Salé from this chilled open-air café spread over several terraces in the Andalusian Gardens. Mint tea is the thing here, accompanied by little almond biscuits delivered on silver trays. It's an easy place to pass time writing postcards, and a relaxed venue for women.

Cafetéria du 7ème Art (Map p122; ☎ 037 733887; Ave Allal ben Abdallah) Set in the shady grounds of a cinema (p128), this popular outdoor café attracts a mixed clientele of students and professionals. It's a relaxed place but the noise of passing traffic makes it less tranquil than Café Maure.

BARS

Most Rabat bars are pretty intimidating for women. The more modern, popular joints are a safer bet.

El Rancho (off Map p118; ☎ 067 330030; 30 Rue Mischliffen, Agdal; 🕑 7pm-1am) Tex-Mex restaurant and bar where Rabat's well-heeled go for a bite and a drink before clubbing. The atmosphere on weekends is electric, when the world-music beat gets turned up a few notches.

Le Puzzle (off Map p118; ☎ 037 670030; 79 Ave ibn Sina, Agdal; beer Dh45; 🕑 7.30pm-1am, closed Sun lunch) A happening bar-restaurant in Agdal, favoured by suburban sophisticates. It has a strange mix of traditional style and modern design but pulls in the punters with half-price beer and daily live gigs (except for Wednesday and Sunday karaoke nights).

Hôtel Balima (Map p122; ☎ 037 707755; Ave Mohammed V; 🕑 8am-11pm) Less self-conscious than the chic town bars and an excellent place to watch Rabat go by, the leafy terrace in front of the Balima is a great place to just see and be seen. It's a relaxed place for women and pleasantly cool on summer nights.

If you're in search of old-time local haunts rather than squeaky-clean trendsetters, try **Henry's Bar** (Map p122; Place des Alaouites) or **Bar de L'Alsace** (Map p122; Ave Mohammed V), both staunch male-only preserves where the smoke is thick and the alcohol neat. These two are open all day but close by about 10pm.

Entertainment

Rabat has a large international community and plenty of young, well-heeled and well-educated locals looking for entertainment so there's usually a good choice of events on offer. Check the French-language newspapers for listings.

NIGHTCLUBS

Rabat's nightlife is a lot more limited – and subdued – than Casablanca's but there's still a fairly good range of clubs to choose from. All the large hotels have their own discos, usually fairly standard fare, and there's a few try-hard theme clubs where you need plenty of booze to numb the decor. Expect to pay about Dh100 to Dh150 to get in and the same for drinks, and dress up or you won't even make it past the door.

Amnesia (Map p122; ☎ 037 701860; 18 Rue de Monastir; admission Mon-Thu Dh100, Fri & Sat Dh150, women free) The hippest club in downtown Rabat, this USA-themed place (complete with a diner-style backroom) buzzes most nights of the week. The music is pretty standard chart pop but the young socialites who come here just lap it up.

5th Avenue (Map p118; ☎ 037 775254; 5 Rue Bin al-Widane, Agdal; cover Dh80; 🕑 until 5am Sat & Sun) Another USA-themed bar, this one styled on a Moroccan impression of New York, it plays a better range of music than the others and features everything from hip hop to techno to Middle Eastern.

CINEMA

Most films are dubbed in French, unless marked as *'version originale'*.

Cinéma Renaissance (Map p122; ☎ 037 722168; 360 Ave Mohammed V; orchestra/balcony Dh30/35) This large cinema complex on the main drag shows mainstream Hollywood flicks.

Cinéma du 7ème Art (Map p122; ☎ 037 733887; Ave Allal ben Abdallah; admission Dh20) A good bet for more local offerings and art-house films, this cinema shows mainly Moroccan, Middle Eastern and European films.

Shopping

Rabat's great shopping secret is its laid-back merchants. There's little pressure to buy, so you can stroll the stalls in relative peace, but there is also less space to bargain. The souqs still have a fair bit of good handicrafts, particularly in and around the Rue des Consuls in the medina and Blvd Tariq al-Marsa towards the kasbah. You'll find everything in this area from jewellery, silks and pottery to *zellij* and carved wooden furniture.

Weaving was one of the most important traditional crafts in Rabat, and the more formal, Islamic style (see p67) is still favoured. On Tuesday and Thursday mornings women descend from the villages to auction their carpets to local salesmen at the carpet souq off Rue des Consuls, a great sight even though tourists are not allowed in on the action.

For fixed prices head for the **Ensemble Artisanal** (Map p118; ☎ 037 730507; Blvd Tariq al-Marsa; 🕑 9am-noon & 2.30-6.30pm), which sells a good selection of crafts. For ceramics, your best bet is to head across to Salé to the Complexe des Potiers (p132).

Getting There & Away

AIR

Tiny **Rabat-Salé Airport** (☎ 037 808090/89), 10km northeast of town, only has direct flights to Paris with **Royal Air Maroc** (RAM; Map p122; ☎ 037 709766; www.royalairmaroc.com; Ave Mohammed V) and **Air France** (Map p122; ☎ 037 707066; www.airfrance.co.ma; 281 Ave Mohammed V). A grand taxi to the airport will cost about Dh100.

BUS

Rabat has two bus stations – the main **gare routière** (off Map p118; ☎ 037 795816; Place Zerktouni) where most buses depart and arrive, and the less chaotic **CTM station** (☎ 037 281488). Both are inconveniently situated about 3km southwest of the city centre on the road to Casablanca. The main station has a **left-luggage service** (per item per day Dh5; 🕑 6am-11pm). To get to the town centre from either station, take bus 30 (Dh4) or a petit taxi (Dh20).

Arriving by bus from the north, you may pass through central Rabat, so it's worth asking if you can be dropped off in town. Otherwise, you could save some time by alighting at Salé and taking a local bus (Dh4) or grand taxi (Dh4) into central Rabat.

CTM has buses to the following:

Destination	Cost (Dh)	Duration (hr)	No of daily services
Agadir	190	10	3
Casablanca	35	1½	every hr
El-Jadida	65	3½	3
Er-Rachidia	145	10	1
Essaouira	115	8	3
Fez	68	3½	every hr
Marrakesh	120	5	every 30min
Nador	150	9½	1
Oujda	145	9½	1
Safi	105	5½	3
Tangier	90	4½	5
Taroudannt	192	10	1
Tetouan	88	5	1
Tiznit	198	10½	2

There are also international services to Barcelona (Dh1190), Madrid (Dh735) and Paris (Dh1480).

CAR

Rabat has no shortage of local car-rental agencies – most of which offer cheaper rates than these international agencies:

Avis (Map p122; ☎ 037 769759; 7 Rue Abou Faris al-Marini)
Budget (Map p122; ☎ 037 705789; Rabat Ville train station, Ave Mohammed V)
Europcar (Map p122; ☎ 037 722328; 25 Rue Patrice Lumumba)
Hertz (Map p122; ☎ 037 707366; 467 Ave Mohammed V).

City centre parking restrictions apply from 8am to noon and 2pm to 7pm Monday to Saturday; meters cost Dh3 per hour. There's a convenient car park near the junction of Ave Hassan II and Ave Mohammed V.

TAXI

Grands taxis leave for Casablanca (Dh35) from just outside the intercity bus station. Other grands taxis leave for Fez (Dh59), Meknès (Dh46) and Salé (Dh4) from a lot off Ave Hassan II behind the Hôtel Bou Regreg.

TRAIN

Train is the most convenient way to arrive in Rabat, as **Rabat Ville train station** (Map p122; ☎ 037 736060) is right in the centre of town (not to be confused with Rabat Agdal train station to the west of the city). The station is in use but was under refurbishment at the time of writing, and only the ticket counter, Budget and **Supratours** (Map p122; ☎ 037 208062; 🕑 9am-12.30pm & 3-7pm Mon-Sat) offices are open.

Trains run every 30 minutes from 6am to 10.30pm between Rabat Ville and Casa-Port train stations (Dh36 to Dh46) and Kenitra (Dh15, 30 minutes). Taking the train to Mohammed V Airport (Dh67, one hour and 40 minutes) in Casablanca requires a change at Casa Voyageurs or at Aïn Sebaa.

On all long-distance routes there's always one late-night ordinaire train among the rapide services (see p497 for information on train classes). Fares for the 2nd-class rapide service include Fez (Dh76, 3½ hours, eight daily) via Meknès (Dh60, 2½ hours), Oujda (Dh182, 10 hours, three daily) via Taza (Dh113, six hours), Tangier (Dh91, 4½ hours, seven daily) and Marrakesh (Dh112, 4½ hours, eight daily).

Getting Around

BUS

Some useful bus routes (Dh4) are listed below:

Buses 2 & 4 Ave Moulay Hassan to Bab Zaer, for the Chellah.
Bus 3 Rabat Ville train station to Agdal.
Buses 12 & 13 Place Melilla to Salé.
Buses 17 & 30 From near Bab al-Had to Rabat's gare routière via the map office; 17 goes on past the zoo to Temara Beach.
Bus 33 From Bab al-Had to Temara Beach.

TAXI

Rabat's blue petits taxis are plentiful, cheap and quick. A ride around the centre of town will cost about Dh15 to Dh20. There's a petit-taxi rank near the entrance of the medina on Ave Hassan II.

SALÉ سلا

pop 400,000

Still a long way from its lively counterpart and old rival on the other bank of the Oued Bou Regreg, Salé is a quiet and traditional kind of place, where time seems to have stood still. But not for too long, as a massive project is underway to bring the city into the 21st century with a new tramway, new bridges and a new development with apartments and shopping malls.

The centre of Salé feels more like a typical Moroccan village with its narrow alleys, old medina houses and beautiful mosques, but beyond it lies a sprawling town with characterless apartment buildings, mostly home to Rabat commuters. People are noticeably more conservative here, and the dress code is a lot tighter .

History

People began to settle in Salé in the 10th century and the town grew in importance as inhabitants of the older settlement at Sala Colonia began to move across the river to the new town. Warring among local tribes was still rampant at this stage and it was the Almohads who took control of the area in the 12th century, establishing neighbouring Rabat as a base for expeditions to Spain.

Spanish freebooters attacked in 1260; in response the Merenids fortified the town, building defensive walls and a canal to Bab Mrisa to allow safe access for shipping. The town began to flourish and established valuable trade links with Venice, Genoa, London and the Netherlands.

As trade thrived so too did piracy, and by the 16th century the twin towns prospered from the activities of the infamous Sallee Rovers pirates (see p117).

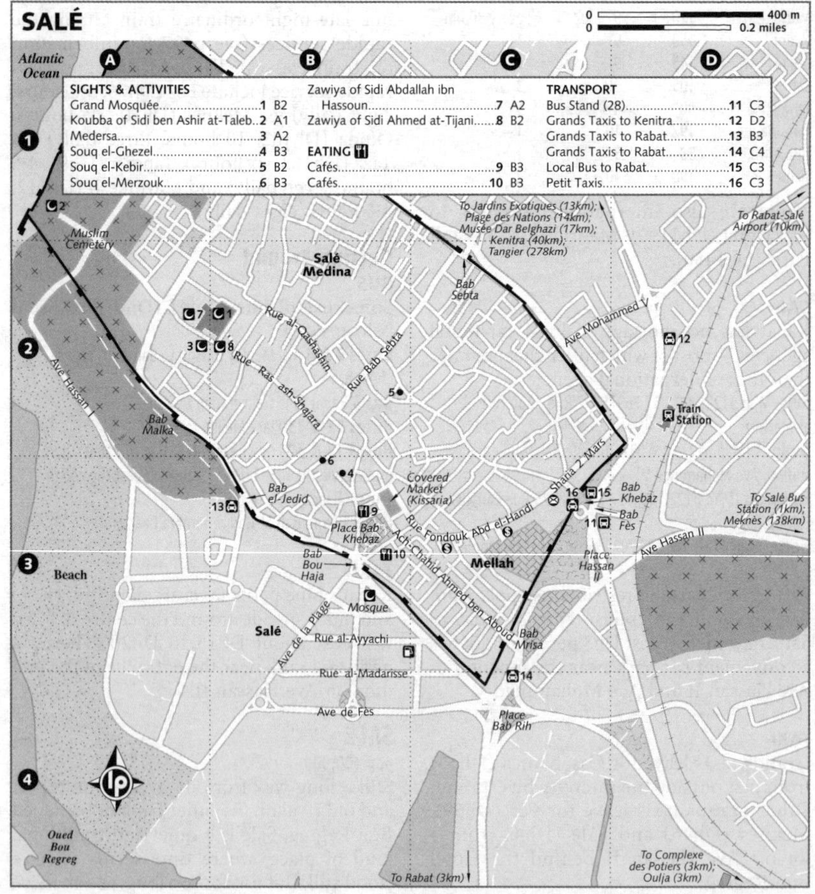

By the 19th century the pirates had been brought under control, Rabat had been made capital and Salé sunk into obscurity.

Orientation & Information

Salé is best seen on an afternoon trip from Rabat. The main entrance to the medina is Bab Bou Haja, on the southwestern wall, which opens onto Place Bab Khebaz. From here walk north to the souqs, and find the Grande Mosquée 500m further northwest along Rue Ras ash-Shajara (also known as Rue de la Grande Mosquée). Alternatively walk along the road that runs inside the city walls past Bab Bou Haja and Bab Malka for a more straightforward approach.

There are a few banks along Rue Fondouk Abd el-Handi. To the south Bab Mrisa was once connected to the ocean by canal, allowing ships to float right into the city. It was here that Robinson Crusoe was brought into the town in Daniel Defoe's novel. The Complexe des Potiers (pottery cooperative, p132) is southeast of the medina on the road to Oulja.

Sights

GRANDE MOSQUÉE & MEDERSA

Central to life in pious Salé and one of the oldest religious establishments in the country, the Grand Mosquée and *medersa* are superb examples of Merenid artistry. They were built in 1333 by Almohad Sultan Abu al-Hassan Ali. The mosque is closed to non-Muslims, but the splendid **medersa** (admission Dh10; 9am-noon & 2.30-6pm) is open as a museum. Similar to those in Fez or Meknès, it takes the form of a small courtyard surrounded by a gallery. The walls are blanketed in intricate decoration from the *zellij* base to the carved stucco and elegant cedar woodwork.

Small student cells surround the gallery on the upper floor, from where you can climb to the flat roof, which has excellent views of Salé and across to Rabat. The guardian who shows you around will expect a small tip.

SHRINES

To the rear of the Grande Mosquée is the **Zawiya of Sidi Abdallah ibn Hassoun**, the patron saint of Salé. This respected Sufi died in 1604 and is revered by Moroccan travellers in much the same way as St Christopher is revered among Christians. An annual pilgrimage and procession in his honour makes its way through the streets of Salé on the eve of Mouloud (the Prophet's birthday, usually in late spring). On this day, local fishermen dress in elaborate corsair costumes, while others carry decorated wax sculptures and parade through the streets, ending up at the shrine of the *marabout* (saint).

There are two more shrines in Salé: the **Zawiya of Sidi Ahmed at-Tijani**, on the lane between the mosque and *medersa*, and the white **Koubba of Sidi ben Ashir at-Taleb** in the cemetery northwest of the mosque.

SOUQS

From the Grande Mosquée, head back to the souqs via the Rue Ras ash-Shajara, a street lined with the houses built by wealthy merchants. Shaded by trees and unchanged for centuries, the atmospheric **Souq el-Ghezel** (Wool Market), makes an interesting stop. Here, men and women haggle over the price and quality of rough white wool as it hangs from ancient scales suspended from a large tripod.

In the nearby **Souq el-Merzouk**, textiles, basketwork and jewellery are crafted and sold. The least interesting souq for travellers is the **Souq el-Kebir**, featuring secondhand clothing and household items.

Sleeping & Eating

There is little point in staying in Salé as there's a much better choice of accommodation in Rabat. There are plenty of hole-in-the-wall cafés in the souqs and surrounding streets, as well as in the area just south of Place Bab Khebaz.

Getting There & Away

BUS

Salé's main bus station is 1km east of the medina, but buses from Rabat also stop outside Bab Mrissa. From Rabat take bus 12, 13, 14, 16 or 34 (Dh4) from Place al-Mellah just off Ave Hassan II, and get off at Bab Kehbaz. This is also the place to take the bus back.

TAXI

The easiest way to get to Salé medina from Rabat is to pick up a taxi close to the Hôtel Bou Regreg, on Ave Hassan II; ask for the

Bab Bou Haja or Bab Mrissa. From Salé there are departures from Bab el-Jedid and Bab Mrisa (Dh4 one way). Note that petits taxis are not permitted to cross into or out of Rabat. Petits taxis are frequent, and there's a taxi stand at Bab Fès. Grands taxis for Kenitra leave from just north of the train station (Dh14).

TRAIN

Trains run to/from Rabat, but buses or grands taxis are probably the simplest options. Trains north to Kenitra run every 30 minutes (Dh15).

AROUND RABAT & SALÉ

Complexe des Potiers

The village of Oulja, 3km southeast of Salé, is home to the **Complexe des Potiers** (Pottery Cooperative; sunrise-sunset) which produces a huge range of ceramics. The potters work at the back of the complex, bringing in clay from a rich seam in the surrounding hills (you'll see it on the left as you drive in), throwing and turning it on kick wheels, then glazing and firing the finished pieces in enormous kilns. A firing takes 15 hours and reaches 900°C. Fine domestic pottery is fired in gas kilns designed to reduce environmental degradation and air pollution, but more rustic pieces are still fired in kilns fuelled by twigs and leaves from nearby eucalyptus forests.

The centre has a café and some workshops used by basket weavers and blacksmiths. To get here take a petit taxi from Salé (about Dh15) or catch bus 35 or 53 (Dh4) from Bab Khebaz.

Jardins Exotiques

The **Jardins Exotiques** (www.jardinsexotiques, in French; adult/child Dh10/5; 9am-5pm winter, to 7pm summer), created by French horticulturist Marcel François in 1951, was declared a Natural Heritage site in 2003 and reopened in 2005 after several years of restoration. The gardens are divided into the Jardin Nature, plantations that evoke the exotic vegetation the horticulturalist encountered on his many travels; the Jardin Culture, referring more to the philosophy of the garden in different cultures; and the Jardin Didactique, with birdcages, an aquarium and a vuivarium. Colour-coded paths lead through overgrown Brazilian rainforest, Polynesian jungle, Japanese pleasure grounds and an Andalusian garden. Jardins Exotiques is managed by the Mohammed VI Foundation for the Protection of the Environment.

The gardens are tranquil on weekend, and are a great place to bring children. It's also a popular spot for courting couples.

The gardens are 13km north of Rabat on the road to Kenitra. Take bus 28 from Ave Moulay Hassan in Rabat, or Bab Fès, the main gate at Salé medina.

Musée Dar Belghazi

The first museum in Morocco, the **Musée Dar Belghazi** (☎ 037 822178; www.museebelghazi.marocoriental.com, in French; admission to main collection Dh40, incl private rooms Dh100; 8.30am-6pm), has a vast collection of traditional Andalusian, Jewish Moroccan and Islamic arts and crafts amassed by the Belghazi family.

Displays include measuring instruments, (one of the first Belghazis was an astrologist at the Qarawiyin court in Fez), 17th-century carpets, exquisitely carved wooden *minbars* (pulpits from a mosque), doors and ceilings dating from the 10th century, intricate gold and silver jewellery, exceptional pottery and embroidery from Fez, and miniature copies of the Quran. The museum has a boutique with souvenirs and a restaurant

The museum is 17km from Salé on the road to Kenitra. Take bus 28 from Ave Moulay Hassan in Rabat or from the main gate of the Salé medina.

Beaches

There are beautiful beaches close to Rabat, such as the wild and sandy **Temara Plage**, 13km southwest of the city, popular with surfers and sunbathers alike. It can be reached on bus 17 from Bab al-Had in Rabat.

The clean, sandy strip of beach at **Plage des Nations**, 17km north of Rabat, is a popular spot with Rabat locals. It gets some serious wave action, good for surfers, but the currents can be dangerous for swimming. Above the beach, the **Hôtel Firdaous** (☎ 037 822131; fax 037 822143; s/d Dh550/670;) is a haven of retro glory with decor largely unchanged since the '70s. Rooms at this resort hotel are comfortable and have ocean views and new bathrooms. Book in advance to have any chance of a room in summer. To get to the beach, drive north as far as the Musée Dar Belghazi and turn left down a road known as Sidi Bouknadel. Bus 28 from Rabat or Salé will drop you at the turn off, from where it's a 2km walk to the beach.

Further north along the coast, 50km from Rabat, is another strip of beach, **Mehdiya Plage**, lined with holiday homes and beach bars, but here again the currents are dangerous for swimmers. It gets busy with day-trippers in summer but is deserted for the rest of the year. There are regular trains from Rabat to Kenitra, from where you take bus 9 or 15 to Mehdiya. Both of these buses (Dh4) and grands taxis (Dh5) leave from the corner of Rue du Souk el-Baladia and Ave Mohammed Diouri in Kenitra.

Lac de Sidi Bourhaba

Inland from Mehdiya is the beautiful freshwater Lac de Sidi Bourhaba, part of a larger protected wetland reserve. As a refuelling stop for thousands of birds migrating between Europe and sub-Saharan Africa, the lake provides some of the best birdwatching in the country, especially between October and March. It's also a great place for gentle hiking, with well-appointed walking trails in the forested hills around the lake.

More than 200 species of birds have been spotted here and many choose to winter or nest here – among them a number of rare or endangered species. This is one of the last places on earth where you can still see large numbers of marbled ducks, distinguished by the dark patch around their eyes. Other birds to look out for include the beautiful marsh owl (seen most often at dusk), the crested coot, black-shouldered kite and greater flamingo.

The **information centre** (☎ 037 747209, 060 383331; ⌚ noon-4pm Sat & Sun) on the northern side of the lake is useful but has limited opening hours.

To get to the lake follow the signposts from the beach road to Mehdiya Plage, 300m past the Cafe Restaurant Belle Vue. If you're on foot, the lake is a 3.3km walk from the turn-off.

MOULAY BOUSSELHAM مولاي بوسلهام

The idyllic fishing village of Moulay Bousselham is a tranquil place, protected by the shrines of two local saints. The village is slowly expanding, as retired Europeans are starting to buy homes here. There is a sweeping beach, (empty for most of the year), friendly people, good fish restaurants and an impressive, internationally important wildfowl reserve. Except for the summer months, this is a great place to spend a few days, with little more to do than birdwatching, fishing or strolling along the beach. Surfers come here for the crashing waves, but the strong currents are dangerous for swimmers. In summer the pace changes dramatically as the village becomes a low-key resort for Moroccans, and the inhabitants swell from around 1000 to 65,000.

Moulay Bousselham is named after a 10th-century Egyptian saint who is commemorated in one of the *koubbas* (shrines) that line the slope down to the sea, and guards the mouth of the river. Moroccans seeking a cure for psychological problems are locked into the tomb for 24 hours. Across the river is another shrine of Sidi Abd el-Galil, believed to cure sterile women. You'll find everything you need along the one main street, including a bank, post office, pharmacy and a couple of internet cafés (Dh8 per hour), but there is no alcohol in town.

Sights & Activities

MERDJA ZERGA NATIONAL PARK

One of the great pleasures in Moulay Bousselham, even for the most unconvinced of twitchers, is to take a boat out on Merdja Zerga (the Blue Lagoon), preferably with a bird guide who will bring the place to life. The 7300-hectare **Merdja Zerga National Park** (4000hectares of water and the rest marshland) attracts thousands of migrant birds, including wildfowl, waders and flamingos in huge numbers, making it one of Morocco's prime birdwatching habitats. The lagoon is between 50cm and 4m deep depending on the tide. Ninety percent of the water comes from the sea, 10% is sweet water from the Oued Dredr, south of the lagoon.

Although the largest flocks are present in December and January, you'll find herons, flamingos, ibises, spoonbills, plovers and egrets here as late as March or April, and there are about 100 species all year round. The calm lagoon is also a good place to see slender-billed and Audouin's gulls, and the

African marsh owl. Shelducks, teals, and numerous terns are frequently seen, as are marsh harriers and peregrine falcons.

There are six villages around the lake, four of which depend on agriculture, two on fishing – the men fish the lagoon and the ocean while the women gather shellfish.

Most of the fishermen take tourists around the lake as a sideline. Boat trips with the local boatmen, who have had some guide training, are easily arranged if you wander down to the small beach where the boats are moored. Expect to pay about Dh100 per hour for the boat. The only officially recognised (and by far the best) guide is **Hassan Dalil** (☎ 068 434110; guide half-day Dh200, plus motorboat per hr Dh100), who can also be contacted at the Café Milano (on the main road into town). Call him rather than ask for him as several people have been known to pretend to be him in order to take his business. Otherwise ask the waiters at the Café Milano to call him. Trips can also be arranged through Villanora (see opposite). The boatmen can also arrange fishing trips (Dh100 per hour, including equipment).

Hardcore birdwatchers may also want to explore **Merdja Khaloufa**, an attractive lake about 8km east of Moulay Bousselham, which offers good viewing of a variety of wintering wildfowl.

HASSAN DALIL

How long have you lived in Moulay Bousselham? I was born on the lagoon, and I started taking tourists in my little rowing boat when I was 12, so I could make money to go to school. People then mostly wanted to see flamingos. In 1987 I finished studying physics and chemistry at the University of Kenitra and decided to become a bird guide. In the summer I take people walking around the lagoon, in winter I take them by boat.

How did you get into birds? People came here to watch birds so I learned a lot from them at first. In 1990 there was a very rare bird, the slender-billed curlew, and I became an expert in finding it. This bird became extinct here in 1995, so then I decided to look for the rare marsh owl, now we have 20 pairs. They nest in April so we leave them alone, but May and June are a great time to see them. I used to go to a village on the other side of the lagoon to spot the slender-billed curlew, but after it became extinct I met my wife there. It's a beautiful story, no?

Has it changed a lot recently? There are a lot more people now than when I started, and less birds. We had thousands of birds and now it is more like hundreds – before 1000 flamingos and now maybe 400. The farmers take over the habitats of the bird, and the new highway hasn't helped as you can actually hear the passing trucks. But look up in the sky – a large flock of flamingos. They must be scared of a falcon or maybe they are just following the tide. Aren't they magnificent? They are like butterflies. I never tire of seeing them.

How do you pass your day? I take people out every day in the season. Birdwatchers from all over the world come and see me, and a lot of people who make documentaries. I have met so many nice people, and I learn a lot from them too. My work is very word of mouth. People say it would be good to have a website but I'm on the internet already! On quiet days I fish and sell the catch to campers or local people.

What is your favourite bird? The slender-billed gull. Its chest is pink like a flamingo.

Favourite monument? I love the sight of the two *marabouts,* shrines of holy men. We are very well protected here.

What do you like about this place? I like the peace and quiet, there is place to think here. I love eating fish. Of course I love the birds. I love seeing people returning happy from a trip on the lake, even if they've just had a picnic and saw flamingos.

What is your favourite restaurant? I always go to Café Milano. I keep my bird log there, which is updated by birders from all over the world.

Where do you go to relax? I take a boat out on the lagoon, or go for a walk on the beach. In summer we don't relax though.

What is your favourite word in the local darija (Moroccan dialect)? All the names of birds. I know them in Arabic, French and English.

Hassan Dalil is an official bird guide and fisherman

Sleeping & Eating

Villanora (☎ 037 432071, 064 872008; http://villanoramorocco.ifrance.com; s/d incl breakfast Dh250/400, with seaview Dh350/500). This B&B, the holiday home of an English family who fell in love with this quiet corner of Morocco, could be somewhere in Brittany, on top of a high dune with glorious ocean views. It's run by the Anglophile Mohammed, a family friend. There are just a few homy rooms (with shared bathroom) where you can fall asleep to the sound of crashing waves, and breakfast is served on the terrace. It is possible to order dinner in advance – ask for the fish. Villanora is at the far northern end of town, about 2km from the main street and it's essential to book in advance. Mohammed can also organise boat trips on the lake. The same family has just opened Farm Nora (same contact), the only accommodation on the nearby lake Merdja Bargha.

Hôtel Le Lagon (☎ 037 432650; fax 037 432649; d Dh250;) The saving grace of this faded '70s hotel is its stunning location overlooking the lagoon below. The rooms are big, bright and clean, but in dire need of updating. The large terrace makes up for that. The restaurant is mediocre, and the swimming pool and nightclub are only open in July and August.

La Maison des Oiseaux (☎ 037 432543, 061 301067; http://moulay.bousselham.free.fr; half board per person Dh350) Another friendly guest house set in a lovely garden with eight simple but beautifully styled traditional rooms. There's a seminar room upstairs for visiting school groups and birding excursions can be arranged for Dh200 to Dh300 for 2½ hours. The guest house is hidden down a maze of sandy lanes to the left as you drive into town. Ask around or call for directions.

The friendly owner of Restaurant l'Ocean (see right) can help to arrange a **house rental** (Sep-May Dh300, Jun-Aug Dh600-700), which sleeps up to six people. During the summer months they fill up quickly, so it's best to call and reserve in advance.

There are two popular camp sites here.

Camping Caravaning International (☎ 037 777226; tent/car/caravan Dh10/20/30 plus per adult/child Dh12/6) Slightly run-down but beautifully situated.

Camping Flamants-Loisirs (☎ 037 432539; http://flamants-loisirs.ifrance.com, in French; camp site per person Dh15, plus per caravan/car/tent Dh50, bungalows Dh240-330;) A large place that's aging badly.

The road down to the seafront is lined with cafés and restaurants serving platters of grilled fish and tajines (Dh45 to Dh60). One of the best is the small **Restaurant l'Ocean** (☎ 078 31 0954, 069 434245), with a terrace and an indoor seating area, serving excellent fish, couscous, tajines and paella.

Getting There & Away

Moulay Bousselham is about 40km due south of Larache. To get here by public transport you'll need to make your way to the little town of Souk el-Arba du Rharb, from where there are frequent grands taxis (Dh17, 45 minutes) and a few buses (Dh12, 45 minutes) to Moulay Bousselham. You can get to Souk el-Arba du Rharb by grand taxi from Kenitra or Larache (Dh30, one hour) and Rabat (Dh40, 1½ hours). Souk el-Arba du Rharb also has a train station with daily trains in either direction. Villanora can arrange a private taxi from Larache to Moulay Bousselham (Dh150, one hour).

LARACHE العرائش

Larache, like the other towns on this stretch of coast, is sleepy and laid-back for most of the year, bursting into life in summer when Moroccan tourists come to the beach. The charming town otherwise sees few visitors. The new town has some grand Spanish-era architecture, particularly around the central Place de la Libération (the former Plaza de España), while the tiny crumbling medina was being renovated at the time of writing. North of the river Loukos, on the edge of town, is the main site, the overgrown ruins of ancient Lixus, the legendary site of the Gardens of Hesperides.

Larache was occupied by the Spanish for most of the 17th century. The port activities were limited because of some dangerous sandbars offshore, but the locals made ships for the corsairs further south. It became the main port of the Spanish protectorate in 1911. Today the whitewashed houses with blue doors, the church, the market, the hotels and bars still reveal the strength of the Spanish influence. The town may be as picturesque as Assilah, but it gets far fewer visitors and has none of the hustle.

All Larachians seem to come out for the *paseo* (evening stroll) in the centre of town. The cafés and few restaurants fill up

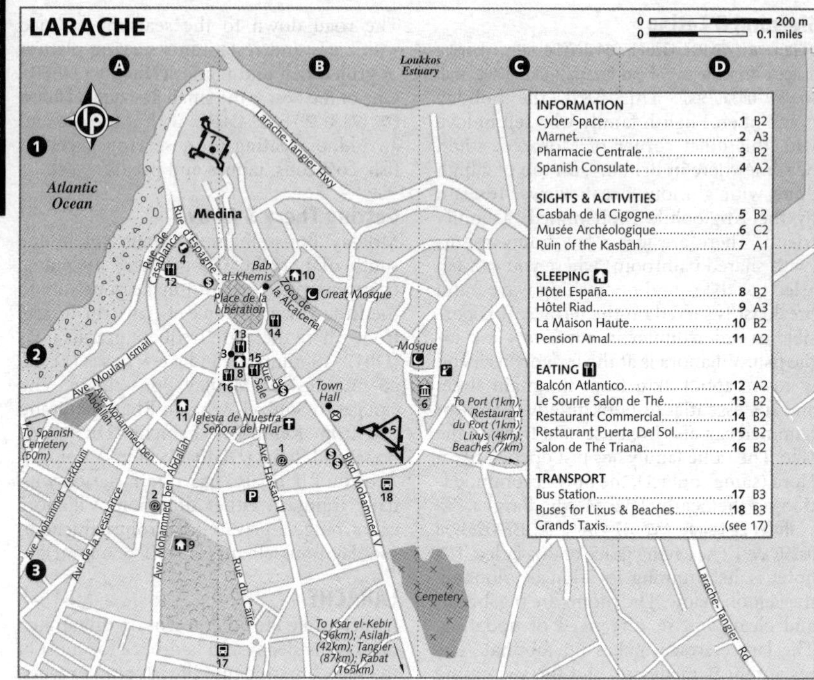

as the locals drink coffee, play cards and chew over the day's events, and by 10pm the streets are again deserted.

The French writer Jean Genet loved the bay of Larache and although he died in France, he was buried here (see right).

Information

The banks cluster at the northern end of Blvd Mohammed V; most accept cash and travellers cheques, and have ATMs. For internet access try **Cyber Space** (☎ 039 914141; Rue 2 Mars; per hr Dh8; 🕑 24hr) or **Marnet** (☎ 039 916884; Ave Mohammed ben Abdallah; per hr Dh8; 🕑 10am-midnight Sat-Thu, 3pm-midnight Fri).

Sights

MUSÉE ARCHÉOLOGIQUE

Housed in a former Merenid palace, and often closed, the tiny **archaeological museum** (admission Dh10; 🕑 10am-noon & 3.30-5.30pm Tue-Sat) has a limited but interesting collection of artefacts, mostly from the nearby Roman ruins of Lixus (p138). The displays include ceramics and utensils from Phoenician and Roman times with explanations in Arabic and French. Look out for the arms of Charles V above the main door.

OLD TOWN

Perched on a cliff top overlooking the ocean are the ruins of the **kasbah** (Qebibat), a 16th-century fortress built by the Portuguese and now in a state of serious disrepair. Head south from here to the old cobbled **medina**, through **Bab al-Khemis**, a large, unmistakable Hispano-Moorish arch on Place de la Libération. You come immediately into a colonnaded market square, the bustling **Zoco de la Alcaiceria**, which was built by the Spaniards during their first occupation of Larache in the 17th century. South of the square, through the medina, is the **Casbah de la Cigogne** (Fortress of the Storks), a 17th-century fortification built by the Spaniards under Philip III. Unfortunately, the building is not open to visitors.

To the west of town, the old Spanish cemetery is the final resting place of French writer Jean Genet (1910–1986). If the gate is not open, ring the bell on the right and the caretaker will let you in. A small tip is expected for showing you to the grave.

BEACHES

Larache has a small strip of sand below the town but the best beach is 7km north across the Loukos Estuary. This strip is now being developed into a huge holiday resort, Port Lixus, with golf course, several resort hotels, villas and a luxury marina. To get there take the hourly bus 4 (Dh5, June to August). Out of season, bus 5 will drop you at the turn-off just before Lixus (Dh5), from where it's a 3km walk to the beach. Both buses leave from opposite the Casbah de la Cigogne.

Sleeping

Larache has a small but decent selection of accommodation, most of which is clustered along the streets just south of the Place de la Libération.

Pension Amal (☎ 039 912788; 10 Rue Abdallah ben Yassine; s/d/tr Dh40/80/120) Dirt cheap, immaculately kept and extremely friendly, this little pension has tiled rooms with shared facilities. The mattresses are renewed every year and the beds are very comfortable. A hot shower is Dh6. The owner, who likes to exchange ideas more than make money, is always happy to meet new people. If you like music, he will jump at the chance to get out his guitar for an impromptu performance.

Hôtel España (☎ 039 913195; hotelespana2@yahoo.fr; 6 Ave Hassan II; s/d/tr/ste Dh220/260/280/350;) A relic of colonial times, this once-grand hotel is now again a great place to stay in town, as the rooms have been redecorated. The decor is still old-style with dark wood furnishings, but the beds are comfortable, the rooms spotless, and the bathrooms have new fittings. Ask for rooms higher up as the noise from the square can be a problem. The service is friendly. There's no breakfast, but the reception will order you breakfast from Café Sourire next door and one of the waiters will bring it up.

Hôtel Riad (☎ 039 912626; Ave Mohammed ben Abdallah; s/d incl breakfast Dh239/314;) This grand old 19th-century mansion, which belonged to the Duchesse de Guise when she was exiled from France, is set in landscaped gardens just south of the centre and offers comfortable rooms and plenty of child-friendly activities. The hotel has lots of character and at the time of writing there were talks of turning it into a luxury boutique hotel. The hotel has tennis courts, bicycle hire, a pool and its own pizzeria.

La Maison Haute (☎ 065 344888; www.lamaisonhaute.com; 6 Derb ben Thami; r Mar-Jun & Sep-Nov Dh350-450, Jul-Sep & public holidays Dh390-550) The most atmospheric accommodation in Larache, this wonderfully restored Hispano-Moorish house has a choice of six charming rooms with modern bathrooms. Traditional Moroccan decor, bright colours, stained-glass windows and mosaic floors give this place a feeling of simplicity, warmth and tradition, while the roof terrace boasts incredible views of the ocean and market square, and offers a nice corner to read a book or sunbathe.

Eating

Eating out in Larache is cheap and cheerful with plenty of little places around Place de la Libération and the Zoco de la Alcaiceria serving simple but substantial meals. The Spanish influence lingers on in the *churros* (a kind of doughnut) stall on the main square.

Restaurant Commercial (☎ 061 682420; Place de la Libération; mains Dh20; noon-9.30pm) The locals' favourite, this basic place on the main square does a roaring trade in simple soup, brochettes and fried fish. It's ultra cheap, packed with happy diners every night and is a great place for people-watching.

Restaurant du Port (☎ 039 417463; Larache Port; mains Dh60; 10am-5pm & 7-11pm) Out of town by the port, but worth the trip, this slightly upmarket place specialises in fresh seafood cooked simply but to perfection.

Restaurant Puerta Del Sol (☎ 039 913641; Rue de Salé; mains Dh20-30; noon-9pm) For more seafood and a choice of Moroccan dishes, this no-nonsense place is a good bet. It's popular but a little quieter than the Restaurant Commercial.

Balcón Atlantico (☎ 039 910110; Rue de Casablanca; pizza Dh40-60, crepes Dh10-15; 6am-10pm) Overlooking the beach, and the nicest spot in town for a relaxed breakfast or simple lunch, this bright, bustling café has plenty of outdoor seating and passable pizzas.

For a quick breakfast or ice cream your best options are the **Salon de Thé Triana**

(☎ 039 500913; Ave Mohammed ben Abdallah), which also serves decent pizza (Dh26 to Dh40) in summer, or, just off the square, **Le Sourire Salon de Thé** (Ave Hassan II; 🕑 6am-10pm).

Getting There & Away

The bus station is south of the town centre on Rue du Caire.

CTM buses include services to Casablanca (Dh90, four hours, three daily) via Kenitra (Dh40, two hours) and Rabat (Dh70, three hours); Fez (Dh80, four hours, three daily) via Meknès (Dh60, three hours); Tangier (Dh30, 2½ hours, four daily); Tiznit (Dh310) via Marrakesh (Dh160, eight hours); and Agadir (Dh225, 12 hours).

Cheaper non-CTM buses also cover these destinations as well as Ouezzane (Dh20), Tetouan (Dh20) and Kenitra (Dh30), and are generally more frequent.

Grands taxis run from outside the bus station to Ksar el-Kebir (Dh12) and occasionally to Assilah (Dh30), Souk el-Arba (Dh25) and Tangier (Dh40).

LIXUS الاوكوس

Set on a hill overlooking the Loukkos Estuary are the Roman ruins of **Lixus** (admission free), a rather mysterious and neglected site that is one of the oldest inhabited places in the country. Only about a quarter of the ancient city has been excavated but the visible ruins, though badly damaged and overgrown, are impressive. Although not as extensive or as well excavated as Volubilis (see p266), the location, size and serenity of Lixus give it a lingering sense of gravitas and with a little imagination you can picture just how grand and important this city once was.

The site is not enclosed, so you're at liberty to wander around. Few visitors make it here outside the summer months, and in winter your only companions will be the wind and the odd goat quietly grazing, but beware that some readers have reported being hassled by local youths. Although some unemployed locals may offer their services as a guide, it's not really necessary and their knowledge of the site is usually sketchy.

History

Megalithic stones found in the vicinity of Lixus suggest that the site was originally inhabited by a sun-worshipping people with knowledge of astronomy and mathematics. However, little more is known about the areas prehistory until the Phoenicians set up the colony Liks here in about 1000 BC. According to Pliny the Elder, it was here that Hercules picked the golden apples of the Garden of Hesperides, thus completing the penultimate of his 12 labours. The golden apples may well have been the famous Moroccan tangerines.

In the 6th century BC the Phoenician Atlantic colonies fell to the Carthaginians. Lixus remained a trading post, principally in gold, ivory and slaves and, by AD 42, had entered the Roman Empire. Its primary exports soon changed to salt, olives, wine and *garum* (an aromatic fish paste) and its merchants also grew rich from the export of wild animals for use in the empire's amphitheatres.

The colony at Lixus rapidly declined as the Romans withdrew from North Africa, and was abandoned completely with the collapse of the Roman Empire sometime in the 5th century. Later, the site became known to Muslims as Tuchummus.

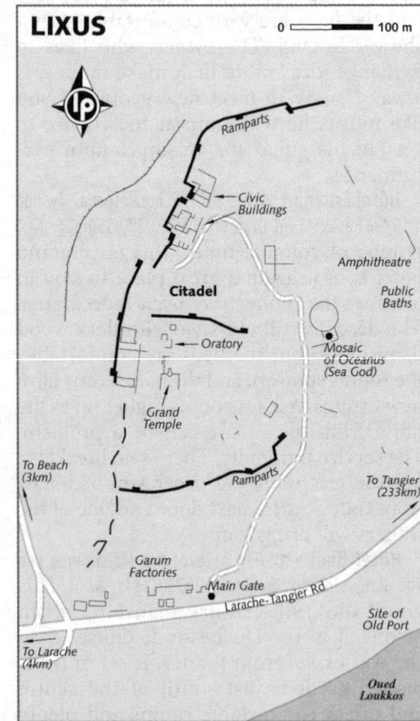

Sights

The main gate to Lixus is in the green railings that border the Larache–Tangier road. Inside the railings to the left are the remains of the *garum* factories, where fish was salted and the prized paste produced. A gravel path leads up the hill from the gate past a number of minor ruins to the **public baths** and **amphitheatre**. The amphitheatre provides impressive views of the surrounding countryside and makes a wonderful place just to sit and relax.

Most mosaics from the site were removed and are now on display at the archaeology museum in Tetouan (see p197). The Grand Temple mosaics depicting Helios, Mars and Rhea, the three Graces, and Venus with Adonis are all there. The only remaining mosaic at Lixus is that of **Oceanus** (the Greek Sea God). Unfortunately, it's been exposed both to the elements and to local vandalism, so is in rough shape.

Continue up the path to the main assembly of buildings, which straddle the crest of the hill. From here there are incredible views down over the Loukos Estuary and salt fields below. The civic buildings, additional public baths and original city ramparts are here, while to the south is the striking citadel, a flurry of closely packed ruins standing stark against the sky. Although most of the antiquities are in an advanced state of decay, you should be able to make out the main temple and associated sanctuaries, an oratory, more public baths and the remains of the city walls.

Getting There & Away

Lixus is approximately 4.5km north of Larache on the road to Tangier. To get there take bus 4 or 5 from outside the Casbah de la Cigogne (Dh4). A petit taxi costs about Dh20 one way.

ASSILAH أصيلا

The gorgeous whitewashed resort town of Assilah feels like somewhere on a Greek Island, but the tapas and paella on the Spanish menus in the restaurants and the wrought-iron windows on the white houses are but a few reminders that the town was Spanish territory for a long time. Arriving here by ferry from Spain, Assilah is an easier and much more hassle-free introduction to Morocco than its northern neighbour Tangier. With a good selection of budget hotels and restaurants, and a small art scene, the town has become a favourite stop on the traveller's trail of the North Atlantic coast.

The town's mayor lives in the picturesque medina and has vowed to make it as clean as Switzerland. The old medina has been seriously gentrified in the last few years as more and more houses have been bought by affluent Moroccans and Europeans, mainly Spanish. Its narrow streets are indeed squeaky clean and a bit empty. Flats and houses are as expensive now as in Marrakesh. The town is sleepy for most of the year, but in the summer months the population grows from 12,000 to 110,000, when Moroccan families descend here, as elsewhere along the coast. The small town is then completely over-run, the beaches are packed and the touts come out in force. Outside the summer months, touts are less imposing, but they are around, waiting for tourists at the train or bus station, offering drugs and cheap accommodation in the holiday homes of absent foreigners in the medina (see p140).

The best time to visit is in spring or autumn when the weather is still pleasant but the crowds are gone.

History

Assilah has had a turbulent history as a small, but strategic port since it began life as the Carthaginian settlement of Zilis. During the Punic Wars the people backed Carthage, and when the region fell to the Romans, the locals were shipped to Spain and replaced with Iberians. From then on, Assilah was inexorably linked with the Spanish and their numerous battles for territory.

As Christianity conquered the forces of Islam on the Iberian peninsula in the 14th and 15th centuries, Assilah felt the knock-on effects. In 1471 the Portuguese sent 477 ships with 30,000 men, captured the port and then built the walls that still surround the medina, a trading post on their famous gold route across Africa. In 1578, King Dom Sebastian of Portugal embarked on an ill-fated crusade from Assilah. He was killed, and Portugal (and its Moroccan possessions) passed into the hands of the Spanish, who remained for a very long time.

Assilah was recaptured by Moulay Ismail in 1691. In the 19th century, continuing piracy prompted Austria and then Spain to send their navies to bombard the town. Its most famous renegade was Er-Raissouli (see p142), one of the most colourful bandits ever raised in the wild Rif Mountains. Early in the 20th century, Er-Raissouli used Assilah as his base, becoming the bane of the European powers. Spain made Assilah part of its protectorate from 1911 until 1956.

Information

Place Mohammed V is crowded with banks, including BMCE and Banque Populaire, both of which will change cash and travellers cheques and have ATMs.

Internet access is available at **Pyramide Net** (Ave Hassan II; per hr Dh8; 9am-midnight) and **Raweya Internet** (Rue Assoussane; per hr Dh6; 10am-midnight). There are a couple of pharmacies in town including **Pharmacie l'Océan** (Place Zellaka) and **Pharmacie Loukili** (Ave Mohammed V).

Dangers & Annoyances

Assilah has a large young population, and unemployment is high. Kif (dope) plays a big role in Assilah: increasingly, tourists are being offered it, often as part of an elaborate scam to fleece them (see drugs, p459). As tourism and kif use have increased in recent years, so too has the number of touts operating in Assilah. Apart from offering drugs, many will tell you that the only place to stay in town is in the medina. There are hardly any official places to stay in the medina, but

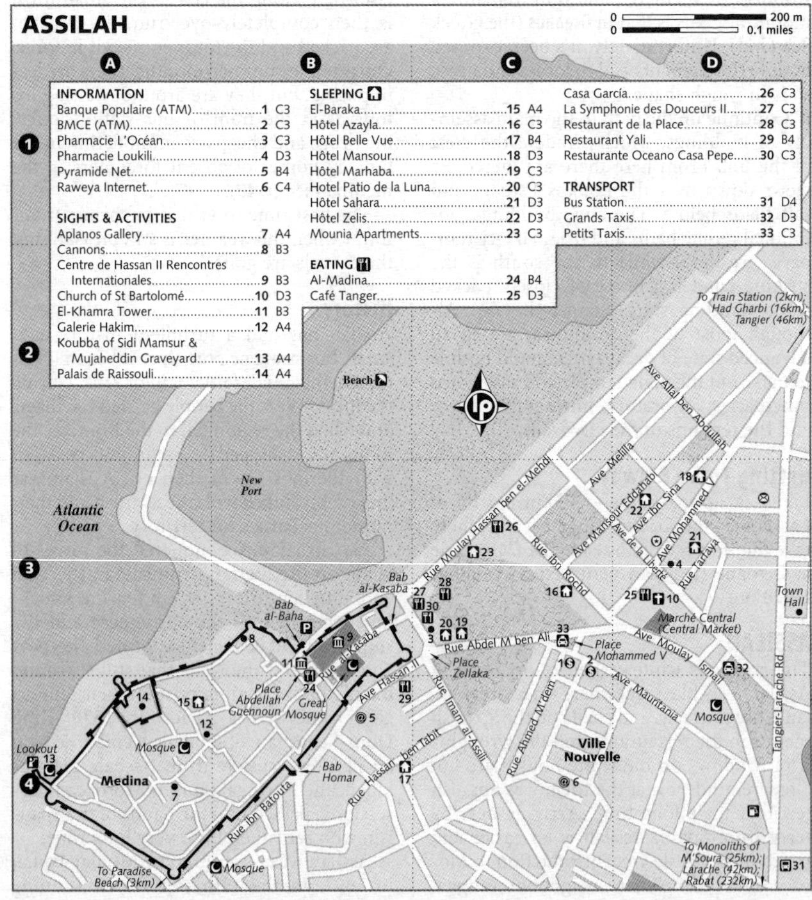

the touts offer rooms in the holiday homes of absent foreigners, or worse, a sleeping mat in a friend's house in the medina at sumptuous prices.

Sights & Activities

RAMPARTS & MEDINA

Assilah's largely residential medina is surrounded by the sturdy stone fortifications built by the Portuguese in the 15th century and it is these walls, flanked by palms, that have become the town's landmark.

The medina and ramparts have been largely restored in recent years and the tranquil narrow streets lined by whitewashed houses are well worth a wander. Although the restoration work has left the medina much sanitised, the ornate wrought-iron window guards and colourful murals (painted each year during the International Cultural Festival, see right) give it a very photogenic quality. Craftsmen and artists have opened workshops along the main streets and invite passers-by in to see them work.

Access to the ramparts is limited. The southwestern bastion is the best spot for views over the ocean and is a popular spot at sunset. It also offers a peek into the nearby **Koubba of Sidi Mamsur** (which is otherwise closed to non-Muslims) and the **Mujaheddin Graveyard**.

The southern entrance to the medina, **Bab Homar** on Avenue Hassan II, is topped by the much-eroded Portuguese royal coat of arms. There are a few **old cannons** just inside the medina's seaward wall, but they are cut off from the walkway below and can only be seen from a distance. The **Bab al-Kasaba** leads to the **Great Mosque** (closed to non-Muslims) and the Centre Hassan II des Rencontres Internationales. The medina is busiest on Thursdays, Assilah's main market day.

ART GALLERIES

With more than 50 resident artists, five galleries and several artist studios and exhibition spaces, Assilah is renowned as a city of arts. It all started in 1978 when several Moroccan artists were invited to hold workshops for local children and to paint some walls in the medina as part of the town's *moussem* (International Cultural Festival) celebrations. Several Zaïlachi artists and some of these children have now made a name in the contemporary-art world, among them the late Abdelilah Bououd, Brahim Jbari, Elina Atencio, Mohamed Lhaloui and several members of the Mesnani family.

Belgian painter Anne-Judith Van Loock created the **Aplanos gallery** (☎ 061 998030; Rue Tijara) with her Moroccan husband Ahmed Benraadiya, where foreign and local artists can exhibit. Zaïlachi artist Hakim Ghaïlan started the **Galerie Hakim** (☎ 039 418896, 061 799535; hakimghailan@yahoo.fr; 14 Place Sidi ben Issa) and exhibits mainly young Moroccan artists.

The main exhibition space in town is the **Centre de Hassan II Rencontres Internationales** (☎ 039 417065; foundationdassilah@yahoo.fr; admission free; 8.30am-12.30pm & 2.30-5pm, to 8pm summer), just inside the medina walls. This centre in a beautiful medina house displays a revolving exhibition of international painting and sculpture in its gallery (and at times, in the nearby **El-Khamra Tower**, a renovated Portuguese fortification on Place Abdellah Guennoun).

The **Palais de Raissouli**, also known as the Palais de Culture (Palace of Culture) on the seaside of the medina, was built in 1909 by Er-Raissouli (see boxed text, p142) and still stands as a testament to the sumptuous life he led at the height of his power. It has been beautifully restored, but is only open during the *moussem* or for temporary exhibitions, although if you can find the caretaker you may be able to persuade him to let you in. The striking building includes a main reception room with a glass-fronted terrace overlooking the sea, from where Er-Raissouli forced convicted murderers to jump to their deaths onto the rocks 30m below.

NEW TOWN

The centre of the small new town is Place Mohammed V. Northwest of the square is the **Church of San Bartolome**, built by Spanish Fransiscans, in a typical colonial Moorish style. It is one of the few churches in Morocco allowed to ring the bells for Sunday Mass. Nearby is the **marché central** (central market).

MOUSSEM

The Centre Hassan II des Rencontres Internationales is the main focus for the annual **moussem** (International Cultural

RASCALLY ER-RAISSOULI

Feared bandit, kidnapper and general troublemaker, Moulay Ahmed ben Mohammed er-Raissouli (or Raisuni) was one of Assilah's most legendary inhabitants. He started life as a petty crook in the Rif Mountains but saw no problem in bumping off unwilling victims and was soon renowned as a merciless murderer, and feared right across the region.

Internationally, Er-Raissouli was best known for kidnapping Westerners. He and his band held various luminaries to ransom, including Greek-American billionaire Ion Perdicaris, who was ransomed in 1904 for US$70,000.

In an attempt to control the unruly outlaw, consecutive sultans appointed him to various political positions, including governor of Assilah and later Tangier. However, Er-Raissouli continued with his wicked ways, amassing great wealth in whatever way he could. He held considerable sway over the Rif tribes and the Spanish funded his arms in the hope of keeping order in the mountains, but Er-Raissouli often used them against his benefactors.

The Spaniards eventually forced Er-Raissouli to flee Assilah after WWI, but he continued to wreak havoc in the Rif hinterland until 1925, when the Rif rebel Abd al-Krim arrested him and accused him of being too closely linked with the Spanish.

Festival) held in August, when artists, musicians, performers and thousands of spectators descend upon the town. Numerous workshops and public art demonstrations, concerts, exhibitions and events are held throughout the month with a strong Spanish and Islamic slant. A three-day horse festival, including a Moroccan *fantasia* (musket-firing cavalry charge) takes place towards the end of the festival.

BEACHES

Assilah's main beach, flanked by camp sites and hotels, stretches north from town. It's a wide sweep of golden sand and although pleasant in low season, the crowds and noise from the nearby road make it much less appealing in summer. For more peace and quiet head 3km south to **Paradise Beach**, a gorgeous, pristine spot that really does live up to its name. It's a pleasant walk along the coast or, alternatively, hop on one of the horse-drawn carriages that ply this route in summer. Assilah Marina, an entire new resort, is planned to open in 2010 south of town with a marina, golf course and several luxury hotels.

Sleeping

Assilah has a choice of decent but uninspiring accommodation options, all in the new part of town. Touts meeting the buses or trains offer basic accommodation in the medina for about Dh75. It's usually a large room sleeping up to seven people on thin mattresses on the floor. Some also offer rooms in unofficial B&Bs at much higher prices. Be careful however when renting through touts: there are many scams. During high season (Easter week and July to September), the town is flooded with visitors so it's advisable to book well in advance.

BUDGET

Assilah has a limited choice of budget hotels.

Hôtel Sahara (☎ 039 417185; 9 Rue de Tarfaya; s/d/tr Dh98/136/204, hot showers Dh5) By far the best budget option, this small, immaculately kept hotel offers simple rooms set around an open courtyard, with a very Moroccan atmosphere. Patterned tiles and potted plants adorn the entrance, and the compact rooms, though fairly spartan, are comfortable and well maintained. Some have tiny windows, so it may be worth checking more than one. The sparkling shared toilets and showers are all new and scrubbed till they gleam.

Hôtel Marhaba (☎ 039 417144; Rue Zellaka; s/d Dh80/120, Jul & Aug Dh100/180) This place has a good central location, next to the Place Zellaka, and a friendly welcome. The rooms have seen better days, though all are spotless. Go for the rooms in the front which are larger and brighter, if a bit noisier. The shared facilities are ancient but there's a nice roof terrace overlooking the medina.

Hôtel Belle Vue (☎ 039 417747; Rue Hassan ben Tabit; d low/high season Dh100/200) A friendly, small hotel in a quiet side street, run by young Moroccans who are very welcoming and up to date on what's happening in town. The rooms have all recently been redecorated; some are entirely painted by local artists. The mattresses are good and everything is immaculately kept, including the shared facilities. A few rooms have their own bathroom (Dh50 extra) and balconies, and there are four pleasant apartments (Dh100 per person), with two double rooms and a sitting area. The rooftop terrace is a great place for an evening drink or to relax. It's particularly popular with Spanish travellers.

MIDRANGE & TOP END

Hôtel Mansour (☎ 039 417390; www.hotelmansour.fr.fm; 56 Ave Mohammed V; s/d Dh180/220) You'll get a hint of traditional character in the tiled public areas at this small hotel, northeast of the centre, but the bedrooms are fairly bland with faded decor and tiny bathrooms. It's still a good deal for the price, but it's worth asking for a room with balcony and sea view.

our pick Hôtel Patio de la Luna (☎ 039 416074; 12 Place Zellaka; s/d Dh300/450) The only accommodation option in Assilah with any local character is this intimate, Spanish-run place secluded behind an unassuming door on the main drag. The simple, rustic rooms have wooden furniture, woven blankets and tiled bathrooms and are set around a lovely leafy patio. It's very popular, so book ahead.

Hôtel Zelis (☎ 039 417069; fax 039 417098; 10 Ave Mansour Eddahabi; s/d/tr Dh300/400/550, Jul-Sep Dh400/500/650;) Packed out in summer and deserted the rest of the year, this big holiday hotel has 65 comfortable, modern rooms with funky blue and white textiles, TV and fridge. You can eat in the traditional Moroccan restaurant with low seating and tables, or the characterless cafeteria-style alternative. The pool is fine and there's a games room for children, a gym, cyber café (Dh10 per hour) and a bar.

Hôtel Azayla (☎ 039 416717; e-elhaddad@menara.ma; 20 Rue ibn Rochd; s/d Dh300/380, Jul-Sep Dh390/480) Big, bright, comfy and well equipped, the rooms here are a good deal. The bathrooms are new, the decor is tasteful with great photographs of Morocco and Moroccans by the owner, and the giant windows bathe the rooms in light. The larger rooms include a spacious seating area where up to three people could easily sleep. The place may lack local character, but the staff is friendly, helpful and reliable.

HOUSES & APARTMENTS

A host of properties in Assilah's medina have been bought by foreigners and wealthy Moroccans and reconstructed as holiday homes. At any time of the year it is possible to rent a flat or house in the medina or near the beach through the agency **el-Baraka** (☎ Miguel 075 722323, Larbi 068 092187; www.elbaraka.net). There are some wonderful three- and four-bedroom houses available with stunning decor and all the comforts you are likely to want. Prices range from about Dh4000 per week in low season to about Dh15,000 per week in high season.

Mounia Apartments (☎ 039 417815; 14 Rue Moulay Hassan ben el-Mehdi; 2-/4-person apt Dh250/350, Jul & Aug Dh450/600) Generally spacious and clean flats, but there are only basic kitchen facilities and well-worn furnishings.

Zaki Apartments (☎ 039 417497; 14 Rue Imam al-Assili; 2-/4-/7-person apt Dh300/450/550) Offers similar accommodation to Mounia Apartments.

Eating & Drinking

Assilah has a string of restaurants clustered around Bab Kasaba and along the medina walls on Ave Hassan II. There are a few other cheap options on Rue Ahmed M'dem near the banks on Place Mohammed V.

La Symphonie des Douceurs II (☎ 039 416633; 26 Place Zellaka) During summer, this French-style patisserie is the best place for breakfast or an afternoon sugar fix. Devour pastries and ice cream in very civilised surroundings; for the rest of the year only drinks are available.

Café Tanger (52 Ave Mohammed V) If the Symphonie is too flashy for you, head for this café north of the square, where the predominantly male clientele sip coffee, suck their teeth and watch over the world.

Restaurant Yali (☎ 071 043277; Ave Hassan II; mains Dh25-50) Although there's little to choose between them, this is one of the most popular of the string of restaurants along the medina walls. It serves up a good selection of fish, seafood and traditional Moroccan staples.

Al-Madina (Place Abdellah Guennoun; mains Dh30-45) The main attraction of this simple little café in the medina is its sunny seating area in the square in front of El-Kamra Tower. It's a great place to sip a coffee, have a snack from the simple, Moroccan menu or drink a delicious freshly squeezed orange juice.

Restaurant de la Place (☎ 039 417326; 7 Ave Moulay Hassan ben el-Mehdi; mains Dh40-80) Friendly, less formal and more varied than its neighbours, this restaurant offers a choice of traditional Moroccan dishes as well as the ubiquitous fish and seafood. The delicious fish tajine provides the best of both worlds.

Casa García (☎ 039 417465; 51 Rue Moulay Hassan ben el-Mehdi; mains Dh55-80) Spanish-style fish dishes and fishy tapas are the speciality at this small restaurant opposite the beach. Go for succulent grilled fish or a more adventurous menu of octopus, eels, shrimp and barnacles, served with a glass of crisp Moroccan rosé wine on the large and breezy terrace. The paella is delicious too.

Restaurante Oceano Casa Pepe (☎ 039 417395; 8 Place Zellaka; mains Dh60-80) Black-tied waiters lure in the punters from the street at this slightly more formal dining option, where fresh seafood tops the bill. Spanish and Moroccan wine, pata-negra ham imported from Spain, low lighting and soft music make it a more refined atmosphere, but the food doesn't entirely live up to it.

Getting There & Away

BUS

Assilah is 46km south of Tangier and has good bus connections to most towns. The tiny bus station is on the corner of Ave Moulay Ismail and the Tanger-Rabat Rd. Since the highway was built, CTM doesn't really stop in Assilah anymore. Several private bus companies offer various services including Rabat (Dh60, 3½ hours), Marrakesh (Dh 130, nine hours), Tangier (Dh10, one hour) and Fez (Dh60, 4½ hours). It's a good idea to book long distance buses in advance as they tend to fill up in Tangier.

Buses to Tangier and Casablanca leave roughly every half-hour, from 6.30am to 8pm. Just wait until a bus pulls in and hope there's a seat available.

CAR

There is guarded parking (Dh10 overnight, Dh15 per 24 hour) outside Bab al-Baha (Sea Gate), near the port.

TAXI

Grands taxis to Tangier (Dh20) and Larache (Dh15) depart when full from Ave Moulay Ismail, across from the mosque. Tangier's airport is only 26km north of here, so taking a taxi from Assilah (Dh250) may save you spending a lot of time and energy in Tangier. The petit-taxi stand is at Place Mohammed V.

TRAIN

The train station is 2km north of Assilah, but a bus (Dh5) generally meets trains and drops passengers at Place Mohammed V and Bab Homar. Three trains run daily to Rabat (Dh77, 3½ hours) and Casablanca (Dh101, 4½ hours), one to Meknès (Dh66, three hours) and Fez (Dh81, four hours) and six daily to Tangier (Dh14, 45 minutes). One overnight train goes direct to Marrakesh (Dh174, nine hours), but this train originates (and fills up) in Tangier, so you may want to buy your ticket in advance.

AROUND ASSILAH

The mysterious **Monoliths of M'Soura** make an interesting half-day trip from Assilah if you've got time to spare. The prehistoric site consists of a large stone circle (actually an ellipse) consisting of about 175 stones, thought to have originally surrounded a burial mound. Although many of the stones have fallen or been broken, the circle is still impressive, its strange presence heightened by the desolation of its location. The tallest stone reaches about 5.5m in height and is known as *El-Uted* (The Pointer).

The stone circle is about 25km (by road) southeast of Assilah. To get there you'll need a sturdy vehicle. Head for the village of Souq Tnine de Sidi el-Yamani, off highway R417, which branches east off the main Tangier to Rabat road. Veer left in the village and follow a poorly maintained, unsealed track 6km north to the site. It can be difficult to find so you may want to ask for directions or hire a guide in the village.

Another interesting trip from Assilah is a visit to the lively Sunday market in the village of **Had Gharbia**, 16km north of town off the road to Tangier.

SOUTH OF CASABLANCA

EL-JADIDA الجديدة

pop 144,000

El-Jadida owes its existence to the exchange between Europeans and Moroccans so it is perhaps not surprising that it

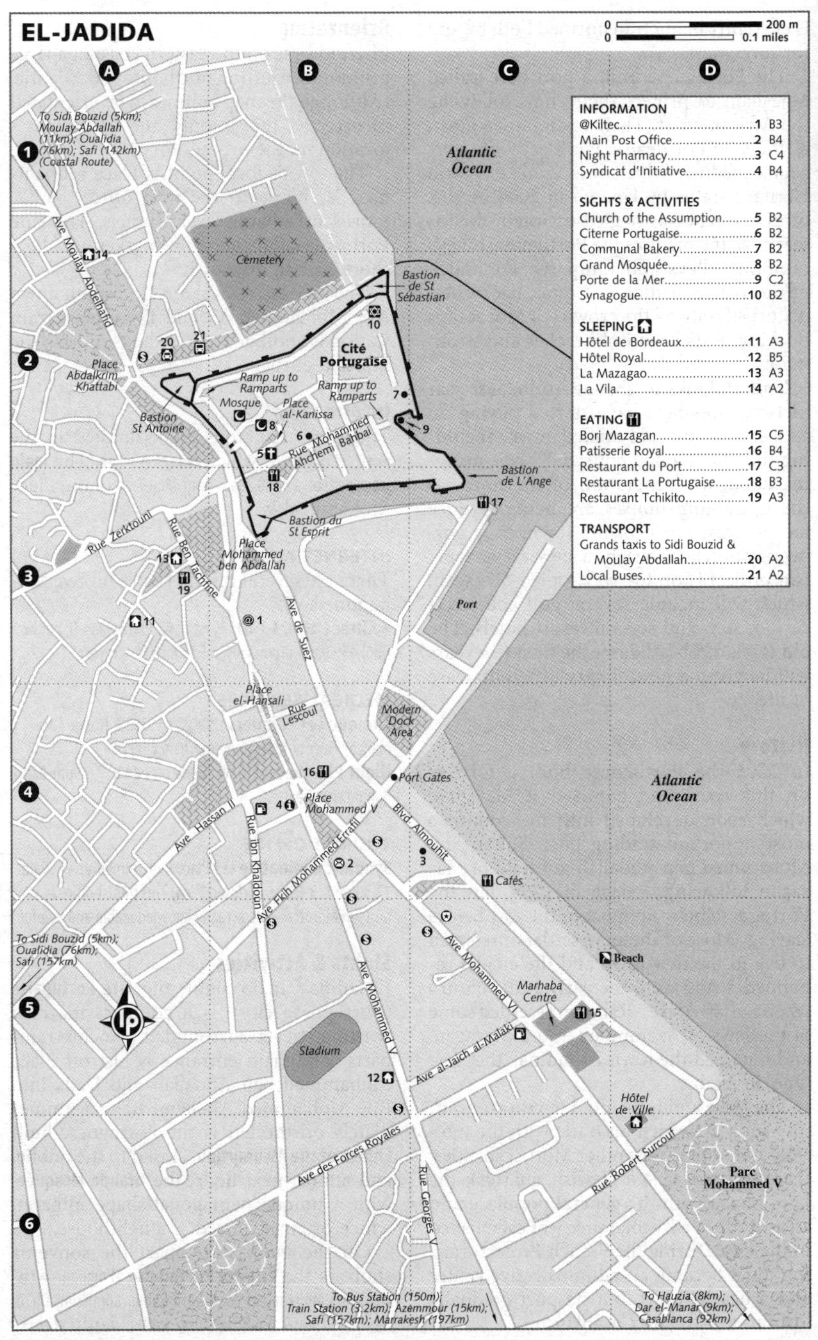
EL-JADIDA
0 200 m
0 0.1 miles
A
B
C
D
1
2
3
4
5
6
INFORMATION
@Kiltec 1 B3
Main Post Office 2 B4
Night Pharmacy 3 C4
Syndicat d'Initiative 4 B4
SIGHTS & ACTIVITIES
Church of the Assumption 5 B2
Citerne Portugaise 6 B2
Communal Bakery 7 B2
Grand Mosquée 8 B2
Porte de la Mer 9 C2
Synagogue 10 B2
SLEEPING
Hôtel de Bordeaux 11 A3
Hôtel Royal 12 B5
La Mazagao 13 A3
La Vila 14 A2
EATING
Borj Mazagan 15 C5
Patisserie Royal 16 B4
Restaurant du Port 17 C3
Restaurant La Portugaise 18 B3
Restaurant Tchikito 19 A3
TRANSPORT
Grands taxis to Sidi Bouzid & Moulay Abdallah 20 A2
Local Buses 21 A2
To Sidi Bouzid (5km); Moulay Abdallah (11km); Oualidia (76km); Safi (142km) (Coastal Route)
Atlantic Ocean
Ave Moulay Abdelhafid
Cemetery
Bastion de St Sébastian
Cité Portugaise
Place Abdalkrim Khattabi
Ramp up to Ramparts
Ramp up to Ramparts
Mosque
Place al-Kanissa
Bastion St Antoine
Rue Mohammed Ahchemi Bahbai
Bastion de L'Ange
Bastion du St Esprit
Rue Zerktouni
Rue Ben Tachfine
Place Mohammed ben Abdallah
Ave de Suez
Port
Place el-Hansali
Rue Lescoul
Modern Dock Area
Port Gates
Atlantic Ocean
Place Mohammed V
Ave Hassan II
Rue Ibn Khaldoun
Ave Fkih Mohammed Errafil
Blvd Almouhit
Cafés
Ave Mohammed VI
Beach
To Sidi Bouzid (5km); Oualidia (76km); Safi (157km)
Marhaba Centre
Ave Mohammed V
Stadium
Ave al-Jaich al-Malaki
Hôtel de Ville
Ave des Forces Royales
Rue Robert Surcouf
Parc Mohammed V
Rue Georges V
To Bus Station (150m); Train Station (3.2km); Azemmour (15km); Safi (157km); Marrakesh (197km)
To Hauzia (8km); Dar el-Manar (9km); Casablanca (92km)

is currently being transformed both by and for foreigners.

The Portuguese built a port here, called Mazagan, to protect their ships following the African coast. Their town, now known as the Cité Portugaise, is a sleepy but gorgeous medina, which was granted World Heritage status by Unesco in 2004. A lack of investment has helped maintain the integrity of the picturesque Portuguese town's rambling alleys and ramparts. For much of the year El-Jadida is a quiet backwater, disturbed only by the crowds of Moroccans flocking to its beautiful beaches and strolling its boulevards.

This all looks to change. In the last year or two, foreigners have started buying up property in the old walled town, including the old colonial church. This is bringing about a regeneration of the town, as the crumbling houses are being given a facelift. Just north of the town, on a gorgeous stretch of beach, a new mega tourism project is on the way, called Mazagan, which will include several golf courses, a casino, spas and several resort hotels. The old town of El-Jadida in the next few years will be given a new, if very different, lease of life.

History

In 1506 the Portuguese built a fortress on this coast and baptised it Mazagan, which soon developed into the country's most important trading post. Sultan Sidi Mohammed ben Abdallah got hold of Mazagan following a siege in 1769, but the Portuguese blew up most of the fort before leaving. Most of the new settlers preferred to live in the new town and the citadel remained a ruin until the early 19th century when Sultan Abd er-Rahman resettled some of the Jews of Azemmour in old Mazagan, and renamed the town Al-Jadida, 'the New One' in Arabic.

The large and influential Jewish community soon grew rich on trade with the interior, and unlike most other Moroccan cities, there was no *mellah* (Jewish quarter); the Jews mixed with the general populace and an attitude of easy tolerance was established in the city. During the French Protectorate, the town became an administrative centre and a beach resort, but its port gradually lost out to Safi and Casablanca.

Orientation

El-Jadida sits on the eastern coast of a large promontory jutting north into the Atlantic. (Although the map appears to be orientated incorrectly, this is only due to the city's location on the promontory.)

The town's focal point is Place Mohammed V, home to the post office, banks, tourist office and several hotels. The Cité Portugaise and the main market area lie a short walk to the north.

The bus station is about 1km south down Ave Mohammed V, and El-Jadida's train station is another 3km further south on the Marrakesh road.

Information

There are numerous banks located in the centre of town which have ATMs. The **main post office** (⌚ 8.30am-4pm Mon-Fri) is on Place Mohammed V.

INTERNET ACCESS

There are several internet cafés on Ave Mohammed VI.

@Kiltec (☎ 023 350487; 1st fl, 62 Place Hansali; per hr Dh6; ⌚ 9am-11pm, closed Fri lunch for prayer).

MEDICAL SERVICES

Clinique Les Palmiers (☎ 023 393939; Rte de Casablanca) Twenty-four-hour emergency service.

Night Pharmacy (off Ave Mohammed VI; ⌚ 9pm-8am) Behind the theatre.

TOURIST OFFICE

Syndicat d'Initiative (33 Place Mohammed V; ⌚ 9am-12.30pm & 3-6.30pm, closed Wed) This tourist office is a rarity in Morocco – it's actually knowledgeable and helpful.

Sights & Activities

El-Jadida's main sight, the **Cité Portugaise** (Portuguese city), is a compact maze of twisting streets, surrounded by ochre ramparts. The main entrance is just off Place Mohammed ben Abdallah and leads into Rue Mohammed Ahchemi Bahbai. Immediately on the left is the Portuguese-built **Church of the Assumption**, closed to the public, and almost next door, the **Grande Mosquée**, with a unique pentagonal-shape minaret, which originally acted as a lighthouse.

On the main street past the souvenir shops is the **Citerne Portugaise** (Portuguese Cistern; Rue Mohammed Ahchemi Bahbai; admission Dh10; ⌚ 9am-1pm & 3-6.30pm), a vast, vaulted cistern lit by a single shaft of light. The spectacularly tranquil spot, with a thin film of water on the floor reflecting a mirror image of the vaulted ceiling and elegant columns, was originally used to collect water. It is famous as the eerie location for the dramatic riot scene in Orson Welles' 1954 *Othello*.

Further down the street are the ramparts with the **Porte de la Mer**, the original sea gate where ships unloaded their cargo and from where the Portuguese finally departed. To the left of the gate, through the archway, is one of the town's **communal bakeries**, where local women bring their bread to be cooked.

To the right of the sea gate, a ramp leads up to the windy ramparts (open 9am to 6pm) and **Bastion de L'Ange** (southeast corner), an excellent vantage point with views out to sea and over the new town and port. Walk along the ramparts to the left to reach **Bastion de St Sebastian** (northeast corner), from where you can see the old Jewish cemetery. Next to the bastion is the abandoned **synagogue** (originally the old prison) with its Star of David.

The **beaches** to the north and south of town are fairly clean and safe, enjoyable out of season, but packed in July and August. The beach at **Hauzia**, northeast of town, use to be pleasant, but the Mazagan mega-resort was being built here at the time of research. **Sidi Bouzid**, 5km southwest of El-Jadida, is a popular spot with sunbathers and surfers. **Le Requin Blue** (☎ 023 348067; set menus from Dh140) overlooking the beach in Sidi Bouzid serves excellent fish.

Local bus 2 runs from El-Jadida to Sidi Bouzid (Dh3) every hour.

Sleeping

A few new hotels near the Cité Portugaise make El-Jadida a nice option to spend a couple of days. The hotels in the new town are modern and comfortable but have less character. At the time of writing, a group of new hotels was under construction near Hauzia beach.

BUDGET

Hôtel de Bordeaux (☎ 023 373921; 47 Rue Moulay Ahmed Tahiri; s/d Dh95/130, hot shower Dh5) The best of the cheapies, this friendly, good-value hotel in a traditional house in the medina has comfortable but compact rooms around a covered courtyard. Only the rooms on the 1st floor have en-suite bathrooms. You'll have use the communal shower downstairs for hot showers. The hotel is well signposted from Rue ben Tachfine.

Hôtel Royal (☎ 023 341100; 108 Ave Mohammed V; s/d Dh100/140, with bathroom Dh140/250) This large hotel has big, bright rooms with cheap furnishings and retro-fitted showers separated from your bed by a sheet of glass panelling. Quality and comfort varies, so check first. The public areas have colourful tiling and a lovely courtyard that becomes a lively bar at night.

MIDRANGE & TOP END

Le Mazagao (☎ 023 350137; 6 Derb el-Hajjar; www.lemazagaocom; s/d Dh484/615; ❄) The rooms are set around the courtyard and on the roof terrace of this welcoming atmospheric 19th-century guest house located in the medina. The large rooms are decorated in a warm Moroccan style with lots of tiling and local textiles, and feel very homy. Half board is obligatory if you stay more than a week. The communal bathrooms are spotless.

La Villa (☎ 023 344423; www.villa-david.com; 4 Ave Moulay Abdelhafid; r Dh700-900, ste Dh1100; ❄ 💻) A charming contemporary-style hotel in an old villa, built using local materials and vegetation, is just outside the old city and run by two Frenchmen. The rooms are set around a white courtyard. Stylish neon lights lead you upstairs, and rooms have plasma screens, wi-fi and *tadelakt* (lime plaster) bathrooms and floors. The effect is very Zen rather than high tech. There is a little bar on the roof with spectacular views over the old city, and the best restaurant in town serving inventive French-Moroccan cuisine.

our pick **Dar el-Manar** (☎ 023 23351645, 061 495411; www.dar-al-manar.com; off the road to Casablanca; r Dh700/900; ❄) Fatima fell in love with this wheat field overlooking the ocean and town while out cycling, and decided to build a lovely house with a vast garden, where it would be good to live and receive guests. Everything is done to make guests feel at ease, in the five simple but stylish and spacious rooms, decorated in a contemporary Moroccan style. Guests can use the garden, where a few cows and a donkey graze, and the bright dining room. Dinner can be ordered in advance, and is cooked with vegetables from the organic garden. You'll get a warm welcome from Fatima and her French husband. Call for directions; it is near the Phare Sidi Mesbah, a lighthouse, and is signposted on the road from El-Jadida north to Azemmour.

Eating

El-Jadida has a handful of reasonable restaurants and a thriving café culture.

Restaurant Tchikito (4 Rue Mohammed Smiha; mixed fish platter Dh25-30) This hole-in-the-wall, just off Place Hansali, is popular for its delicious and cheap fried fish served with a fiery chilli sauce.

Restaurante La Portugaise (☎ 063 037480; Rue Mohammed Ahchemi Bahbai; mains Dh35-60) Just inside the walls of the old city, this characterful little place serves up a decent menu of good-value fish, chicken and tajine dishes.

Restaurant du Port (☎ 023 342579; Port du Jadida; mains Dh60-80; closed Sun evening) Head upstairs for excellent views over the port and ramparts from one of El-Jadida's best restaurants, naturally focused on fish and seafood, cooked simply but well. The atmosphere is pretty mellow making it a comfortable spot for women and – joy of joys – it's licensed.

Borj Mazagan (☎ 023 343435; 4th fl, Marhaba Centre, 54 Ave Mohammed V; mains Dh60-100; 7am-midnight) Sort of slick and stylish, this friendly restaurant is popular with young professionals. Sleek modern furniture, floor-to-ceiling windows and an international menu featuring homemade pasta, wood-fired pizzas and succulent steaks mean it's an ideal place to just feel anonymous once more. It's fantastic for breakfast (Dh18 to Dh28) or luscious afternoon cake on what is easily El-Jadida's finest terrace. It's not licensed.

Patisserie Royale (☎ 061 878354; Place Mohammed V; 6am-8pm) A good spot for breakfast or a quiet coffee, the Royale is an old-style kind of joint where you can blend into the woodwork or chat to the locals without feeling under any pressure.

Getting There & Away

BUS

The **bus station** (☎ 023 373841) is a 10-minute walk from the centre on Ave Mohammed V.

CTM (☎ 023 342662) runs services to and from Casablanca (Dh27, 1½ hours, four daily). There are also services to Oualidia (Dh30, 1½ hours, three daily), Safi (Dh60, 2½ hours, six daily) and Essaouira (Dh80, 4½ hours, one daily).

Cheaper local buses go to all the same destinations as well as Azemmour (Dh5), Rabat (Dh40, four hours, 12 daily) and Marrakesh (Dh40, four hours, hourly). In summer, buses to Casablanca (Dh23) and Marrakesh should be booked at least one day ahead.

Bus 2 for Sidi Bouzid (Dh3) and bus 6 for Moulay Abdallah (Dh4.5), leave from just north of the Cité Portugaise.

TAXI

Grands taxis for Azemmour (Dh6) and Casablanca (Dh35) leave from the side street next to the long-distance bus station. Taxis to Oualidia (Dh25) and Safi (Dh55) depart from a junction on the road to Sidi Bouzid. You'll need to take a petit taxi (Dh5) to get there. The grand-taxi rank for Sidi Bouzid (Dh5) and Moulay Abdallah (Dh6) is beside the local bus station north of the Cité Portugaise.

TRAIN

El-Jadida **train station** (☎ 023 352824) is located 4km south of town. There are five services a day to and from Casablanca (Dh30, one hour). A petit taxi to the centre costs around Dh10. For timetable details ask at the tourist office (p146).

AROUND EL-JADIDA

Azemmour

El-Amine, one of Azemmour's most successful painters, hit it right describing his favourite view of town from his roof terrace, which he has painted numerous times: the old walled medina squeezed in between the Oum er-Rbia (Mother of Spring) river and the ocean, with the fields spread beyond.

The picturesque town has inspired many artists, who have come to live here. Although it is close to the art market of Casablanca, life is still simple, with the farmers and fishermen going door-to-door with their produce. It's a sleepy backwater with a languid charm, a sturdy Portuguese medina and some wonderful accommodation options – a great place to while away a few days overlooking the river.

The Portuguese built the town in 1513 as one of a string of trading posts along the coast. The town's most famous inhabitant was Estevanico the Black. Captured and made a slave, he later became one of the first four explorers to cross the entire mainland of North America from Florida to the Pacific.

Azemmour has several banks, a pharmacy and internet access at **Capsys** (off Place du Souk; per hr Dh7).

The main sight is the medina, an ochre-walled town of narrow winding streets and whitewashed houses. Unlike Assilah, to the north, it is completely unadorned and still gives an authentic glimpse of life in modern Morocco. You can get up onto the **ramparts** near Place du Souk or via steps at the north-eastern corner of the medina. Walk along the walls to see **Dar el Baroud** (the Powder House) a Portuguese gunpowder store of which only the tower remains. To the north of the medina is the *mellah* and further on you'll get wonderful views over the river. All over the medina are walls painted by local artists, artists studios including **Ahmed el-Amine** (☎ 023 358902; 6 Derb el-Hantati) and a few places selling the typical Azemmour embroidery.

Azemmour has two wonderful accommodation options. **Riad Azama** (☎ 023 347516; www.riadazama.com; 17 Impasse Ben Tahar; d Dh500-750) is a grand 19th-century house complete with original carved woodwork and charming rooms surrounding a lovely courtyard. The carved, painted ceilings here are some of the finest and the rooftop terrace has great views of the medina. There's an excellent dinner (Dh200).

Totally different but equally special, **L'Oum Errebia** (☎ 023 347071; www.azemmour-hotel.com; 25 Impasse Chtouka; s/d/tr Dh750/900/1250) blends traditional Moroccan style with chic contemporary design. The simple rooms are delightful and the large lounge, complete with open fireplace and grand piano, acts as a modern art gallery. The large terrace overlooks the river and communal meals (Dh200) are served at the big dining-room table.

There are lots of small restaurants outside the city walls in the new town.

A grand taxi to/from El-Jadida costs Dh7, a bus trip costs Dh5.

OUALIDIA الوالدية

pop 4000

The drive from El-Jadida to Oualidia along the coastal road, where the fields come down to the wild shore of ocean, is spectacular enough, but the view upon arrival is more than pleasing. The delightful small-scale resort of Oualidia spreads around a gorgeous crescent-shaped lagoon fringed with golden sands and protected from the wild surf of the ocean by a rocky breakwater. A quiet backwater for many years, with a good selection of accommodation and great fish restaurants, Oualidia is becoming increasingly chic as a weekend resort for Marrakchis and Casablancais.

Out of season it is still quiet, with little more to do than relax, surf, swim and eat well, but avoid the crowds in summer. A lot of building work is threatening to destroy the tranquil charm of this stunning location.

Orientation & Information

The village sits on an escarpment above the lagoon. Most hotels and restaurants are along the road to the beach (1km) – follow signs down beside the post office. You'll find a bank, CTM office and **internet café** (per hr Dh8; 🕑 8am-midnight) here, and a Saturday souq when people from surrounding villages come to town to sell their wares.

Sights & Activities

The town is named after the Saadian Sultan el-Oualid, who built the atmospherically crumbling **kasbah** on the bluff overlooking the lagoon in 1634. The lagoon also attracted Morocco's royalty and the grand villa on the water's edge was **Mohammed V's summer palace**.

The safe, calm waters of the lagoon are perfect for **swimming**, **sailing** and **fishing**, while the wide, sandy beach on either side of the breakwater is good for **windsurfing** and **surfing**. Signposted left off the road to the beach is **Surfland** (☎ 023 366110; 🕑 Apr–mid-Nov) a well-organised surfing and kitesurfing school offering tuition (Dh250). **Dream Surf Oualidia** (☎ 061 817817, 041 291838; 🕑 year-round), on the beach in town, also offers surfing and kitesurfing lessons, as well as equipment rental, fishing trips and treks in the hinterland. **Plancoët Canoë-Kayak** (☎ 062 2511934; 4 Ave Hassan II; http://canoekayakplancoet.free.fr; per hr Dh80-100;

(Mar-Oct) offers canoe and kayak trips on the lagoon, ideal for birdwatching.

Oualidia is famous for its **oyster beds**, which produce about 200 tonnes of oysters annually. You can visit oyster farm No 7 at **Maison de l'Ostréa II** (023 366324; www.ilove-casablanca.com/ostrea; entrance of Oualidia on the Casablanca road) to see how it all works. You can taste oysters and other seafood at the excellent restaurant attached (meals including wine cost, Dh200 to Dh250).

To explore the splendid countryside around Oualidia you can hire mountain bikes (Dh100 per half-day) and scooters (Dh200 per half-day) from **Oualidia Maroc Adventure** (061 157743) on the main drag.

South of Oualidia the coast road becomes ever more dramatic, passing through green grazing lands that end at precipitous sea cliffs.

Sleeping & Eating

All hotels listed have their own restaurants. There are some slightly cheaper places lining the road down to the beach. For bargain meals there is a selection of cheap eateries on the main road in the village.

Hotel Thalassa (023 366050; r Dh100-150, Jun-Sep Dh150-200) The only hotel on the main drag, this slightly dated place is better than you might expect, with bright, airy whitewashed rooms with old-fashioned bathrooms. It's good value but far from the beach.

Hôtel-Restaurant L'Initiale (023 366246; linitiale@menara.ma; r Dh400, Jun-Sep Dh500, set menu from Dh100) This little, white villa with a warm orange interior and pleasant and comfortable rooms, is well equipped with new fittings, spotless bathrooms and tiny balconies. The popular licensed restaurant is one of the best in town and serves a wide selection of fish dishes and pizzas.

Motel A l'Araignée Gourmande (023 366447; fax 023 366144; s/d Dh200/300, Jun-Sep Dh246/280) A friendly hotel with spacious, comfortable rooms that could do with some modernising. The ones at the back however have views of the lagoon from a balcony. The restaurant downstairs serves up a feast of well-prepared seafood with set menus ranging from Dh110 to Dh250.

L'Hippocampe (023 366108; s/d Dh200/300, Jun-Sep Dh246/280) A friendly hotel with immaculate rooms off a garden filled with flowers, looking over the lagoon. There's an excellent fish restaurant (set menus cost Dh110 to Dh250), and steps down to the beach. It's family friendly.

La Sultana (024 388008; www.lasultanaoualidia.com; Parc à Huîtres No 3; d Dh2100-4200, ste Dh3800-4750;) Spectacularly luxurious, this gorgeous hotel has just 11 rooms with fireplace, private Jacuzzi and terrace overlooking the lagoon. There's a choice of three restaurants (set menu costs Dh200 to Dh350), an indoor pool, and an infinity pool and spa – all set in beautiful landscaped gardens.

Villa La Diouana (066 551646, in UK 00 44 7810 541646; www.ladiouana.com; off Ave Moulay Abdel Salaam; up to 6 people from £1000;) All you can hear at night from this stunning 1930s villa is the crash of the ocean and the wind. High on a cliff with panoramic ocean views, the chic villa is simply but luxuriously decorated in a mixture of traditional and contemporary Moroccan design. There is a three bedroomed villa, a lovely one-bedroom garden cottage and a studio flat with roof terrace, all surrounded by a 25,000-sq-ft garden with palm trees. The accommodation is rented out for the week and prices include a maid and breakfast.

Other apartments and villas can be rented through **www.oualidia.net** (in French; studios per night from Dh300).

Getting There & Away

Local buses and grands taxis run at irregular times to El-Jadida (bus/taxi Dh25/22) and Safi (bus/taxi Dh25/22). They leave from near the post office on the main road. CTM has an office here and has a daily bus (Dh30) in either direction.

SAFI آسفي

pop 415,000

An industrial centre and a thriving port for the export of phosphates, Safi is a lot less picturesque than the neighbouring coastal towns, but it offers an insight into the day-to-day life of a Moroccan city. Most tourists stop here en route to or from Essaouira to visit the giant pottery works that take over a whole city quarter and produce the typical brightly coloured Safi pottery.

The new town is pleasant enough with tree-lined boulevards and whitewashed villas, but the alleys of the walled and fortified medina are more atmospheric to stroll through, and you often have the sites to yourself. The beaches are famous for their impressive surf. The immaculate sands north of town were the location for the 2006 Billabong Challenge and are said to have some of the finest waves in the world. Just south of town the landscape is largely industrial and of no interest to visitors.

History

Safi's natural harbour was known to the Phoenicians and the Romans, but in the 11th century it was known as a port for the trans-Saharan trade between Marrakesh and Guinea, where gold, slaves and ivory were sold. In the 14th century the town became an important religious and cultural centre, when the Merenids built a *ribat* (fortified monastery) here. The Portuguese took the city for a brief spell from 1508 until 1541, when the Saadians took it back. They built the monumental Qasr al-Bahr fortress, a cathedral and generally expanded the town, but destroyed most monuments upon their departure.

In the 16th century, Safi grew wealthy from the trade in copper and sugar, and European merchants and agents flocked to the city, but when the port at Essaouira was rebuilt in the 18th century and all external trade was diverted, Safi was largely forgotten.

Safi's real revival came in the 20th century when its fishing fleet expanded and huge industrial complexes were built to process

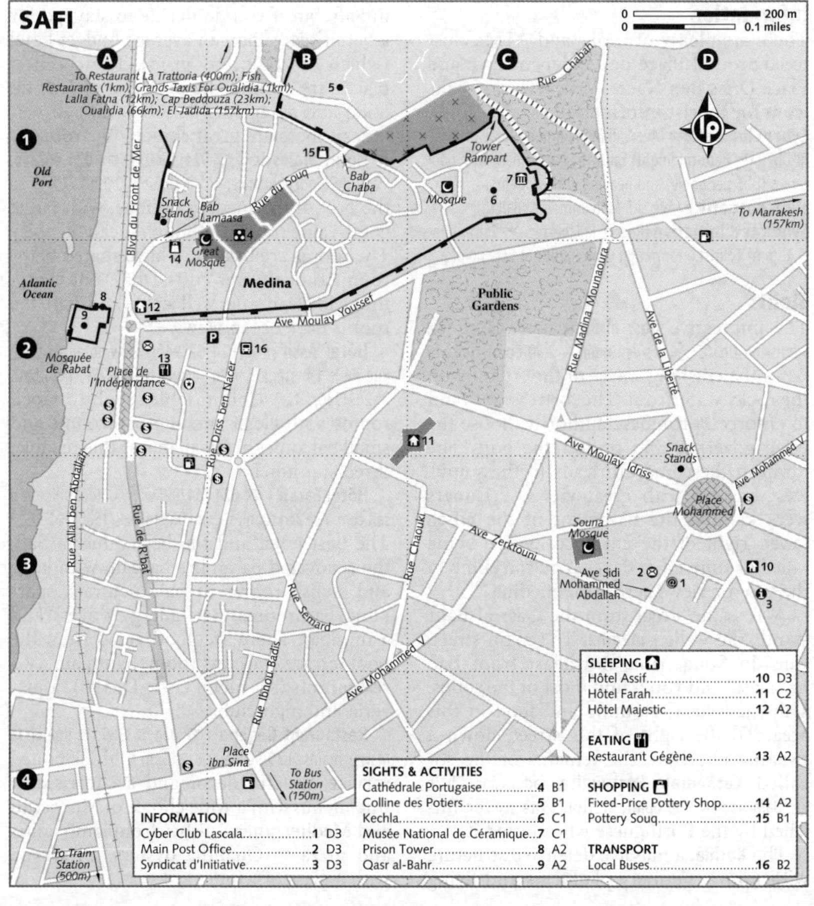

the 30,000 tonnes of sardines caught annually. A major phosphate-processing complex was established south of the town and the city began to expand rapidly. Today, Safi is one of Morocco's largest ports.

Orientation

The fortress, medina and the bulk of cheaper hotels and restaurants are in the lower town, on or around Place de l'Indépendance. The 'new' town – up on the hill to the east – is home to the city's administrative buildings, the more expensive hotels and the smarter residential areas. At the centre is Place Mohammed V.

Safi's bus and train stations are about 1km south of the town centre.

Information

There are plenty of banks and ATMs clustered around Place de l'Indépendance and Place Driss Ben Nacer. Visit www.safi-ville.com for tourist information.

Cyber Club Lascala (Ave Sidi Mohammed Abdallah; per hr Dh7; 8am-midnight) Fantastic games den, with pool tables (Dh5 per game) and heaving with students.

Main post office (Ave Sidi Mohammed Abdallah)

Syndicat d'Initiative (Rue de la Liberté; 9am-noon & 3-7pm) Tourist information centre, but not very helpful.

Sights

The impressive **Qasr al-Bahr** (Castle on the Sea; admission Dh10; 8.30am-noon & 2.30-6pm) dominates the crashing waves of the Atlantic on the rocky waterfront. The fortress was built to enforce Portuguese authority, house the town governor and protect the port. The ramp in the courtyard leads to the southwest bastion with great views. Prisoners were kept in the basement of the **prison tower**, right of the entrance, before being killed or shipped as slaves. You can climb to the top for views across the medina.

Across the street from the Qasr al-Bahr stands the walled **medina**. The main street, Rue du Souq, runs northeast from Bab Lamaasa, and you'll find most of the souqs, stalls, jewellery, clothing and food in this area. To the right of this street, down a twisting alley, are the remains of the so-called **Cathédrale Portugaise** (admission Dh10; 8am-noon & 2.30-6pm), which was never finished by the Portuguese who started it.

The **Kechla**, a massive defensive structure with ramps, gunnery platforms and living quarters, has been restored and opened as the **Musée National de Céramique** (admission Dh10; 8.30am-6pm Wed-Mon). Exhibits include pottery from Safi, Fez and Meknès, and some contemporary pieces by local artists.

Outside Bab Chaba, on the hill opposite the gate, you can't miss the earthen kilns and chimneys of the **Colline des Potiers** (Potters' Hill). The skills used here are predominantly traditional and you can wander around the cooperatives and see the potters at work. If a potter invites you in to watch him at work, you'll be expected to give a small tip or buy an item or two from the shop.

Sleeping & Eating

There is not much reason to spend the night in Safi, but if you do decide to stay, go for a better place than an average budget hotel (which can be pretty grim). The cheapest places are around the port end of Rue du Souq and along Rue de R'bat, though neither of these are great choices for women.

Hôtel Majestic (024 464011; fax 024 462490; Place de l'Indépendance; s/d/tr Dh60/100/130) This is the best of the medina options, with large, good-value rooms, although it can be noisy The rooms are basic and have shared bathrooms (hot shower costs Dh5), but everything is clean and well kept, and half the rooms have ocean views.

Hôtel Assif (024 622940; www.hotel-assif.ma; Rue de la Liberté; s/d with shower Dh198/280, with bath Dh262/330;) Comfortable, slightly faded rooms with clean en-suite bathrooms and small balconies are available at this reliable, three-star hotel.

Hôtel Farah (024 464299; www.goldentulipfarahsafi.com; Ave Zerktouni; s/d/ste Dh514/728/1500;) The best hotel and the best value in Safi, the renovated Farah is a bargain with large and stylish rooms in pale neutrals, sparkling bathrooms, anti-allergy duvets and a minibar. There are good views from the pool terrace, a fitness room, hammam, two restaurants (set menu costs Dh190), a pizzeria and nightclub.

Restaurant Gégène (024 463369; 11 Rue de la Marne; mains Dh70-90; closed Sun) Old-fashioned service, tasteful decor and a surprisingly fine menu, with a wide choice of Moroccan and Mediterranean dishes from lamb tajine and pizza to Oualidia oysters, all served with a glass of wine.

Restaurant La Trattoria (☎ 024 620959; 2 Rue l'Aouinate; meals Dh200, fish Dh150; 🕑 closed Sun) Run by the same management as Gégène, but more upmarket, La Trattoria is a lovely place with a relaxed ambience and surprisingly good Italian food. The menu has a full range of pizzas and pasta, and a good choice of fish and seafood.

Fish and seafood, particularly sardines, are a speciality in Safi, and the best place to sample them are at the **open-air fish restaurants** on the hill at the *rond-point de Sidi Bouzid* (the Sidi Bouzid roundabout). Establish the price before ordering, as fish is charged by weight, or order the fish special – a plate of fish served with bread and a spicy tomato sauce for Dh35. A petit taxi to get there costs about Dh10.

Shopping

Safi is an excellent place to buy pottery of all types. To get a feel for prices visit the **fixed-price pottery shop** (🕑 9am-8pm) on the right-hand side of Rue du Souq as your enter the medina from Bab Lamaasa. To the left, towards the eastern end of the same street, you'll find the colourful **pottery souq**.

Getting There & Away

BUS

Most of the **CTM** (☎ 024 622140) buses stopping in Safi originate elsewhere, so consider booking at least a day in advance. CTM has one daily service to Agadir (Dh97, five hours) and others to Casablanca (Dh81, four hours, 15 daily), El-Jadida (Dh45, two hours, four daily) and Essaouira (Dh30, two hours, nine daily).

Other operators run daily departures to the same destinations as well as to Oualidia (Dh25, one hour, one daily) and Tiznit (Dh90, six hours, one daily).

TAXI

There are grands taxis to Marrakesh (Dh57) and Essaouira (Dh48), among other destinations, which leave from the parking lot beside the bus station. The rank for Oualidia (Dh25) and El-Jadida (Dh45) is a good kilometre north of town on the El-Jadida road.

TRAIN

There are two services from Safi **train station** (☎ 024 462176; Rue de R'bat) for Benguérir, where you change for services to Rabat (Dh109, 5½ hours), Casablanca (Dh84, 4½ hours), Fez (Dh179, 8½ hours) and Marrakesh (Dh63, three hours). They depart at 5.50am and 3.50pm. There are return trains to Safi at noon and 8pm.

Getting Around

Both the **bus station** (Ave Président Kennedy) and the **train station** (Rue de R'bat) are quite a distance south from the centre of town. A metered petit taxi from either will cost around Dh10. Local buses operate from just north of Place Driss ben Nacer.

AROUND SAFI

The wonderfully wild coastline north of Safi, with its dramatic cliffs sheltering gorgeous sandy coves, makes a great drive. The first stop is the headland of Sidi Bouzid, where you'll get a great view back over town. It's a good spot for lunch at the popular fish restaurant **Le Refuge** (☎ 024 464354; Route Sidi Bouzid; set menu Dh150; 🕑 closed Mon).

Driving further on, you'll hit some undeveloped beaches that are up-and-coming surf spots and home to one of the longest tubular right-handers in the world. Professionals such as Gary Elkerton, Tom Carroll and Jeff Hackman come here to train and in 2006 the Billabong Challenge was held here. At 12km from Safi, sheltered **Lalla Fatna** is one of the nicest spots on this stretch. Take a left by the Lalla Fatna café down a series of hairpin bends to the sands beneath the cliffs. Further on you'll reach the headland and lighthouse at **Cap Beddouza** (23km), where there's a wide, sandy beach.

In summer (May to September) bus 15 runs along this route from Rue Driss ben Nacer in Safi.

ESSAOUIRA الصويرة

pop 69,000

Essaouira (pronounced 'essa-weera', or 'es-Sweera' in Arabic) is at once familiar and exotic with its fortified walls, fishing harbour and seagulls soaring and screaming over the town. At first it seems as though this could be a town in Brittany, France – not such a strange thought given that Essaouira was designed by the same Frenchman who designed Brittany's most famous port town, Saint-Malo. And yet once you enter the walls, it is also infinitely Moroccan and mysterious: narrow alleys full of

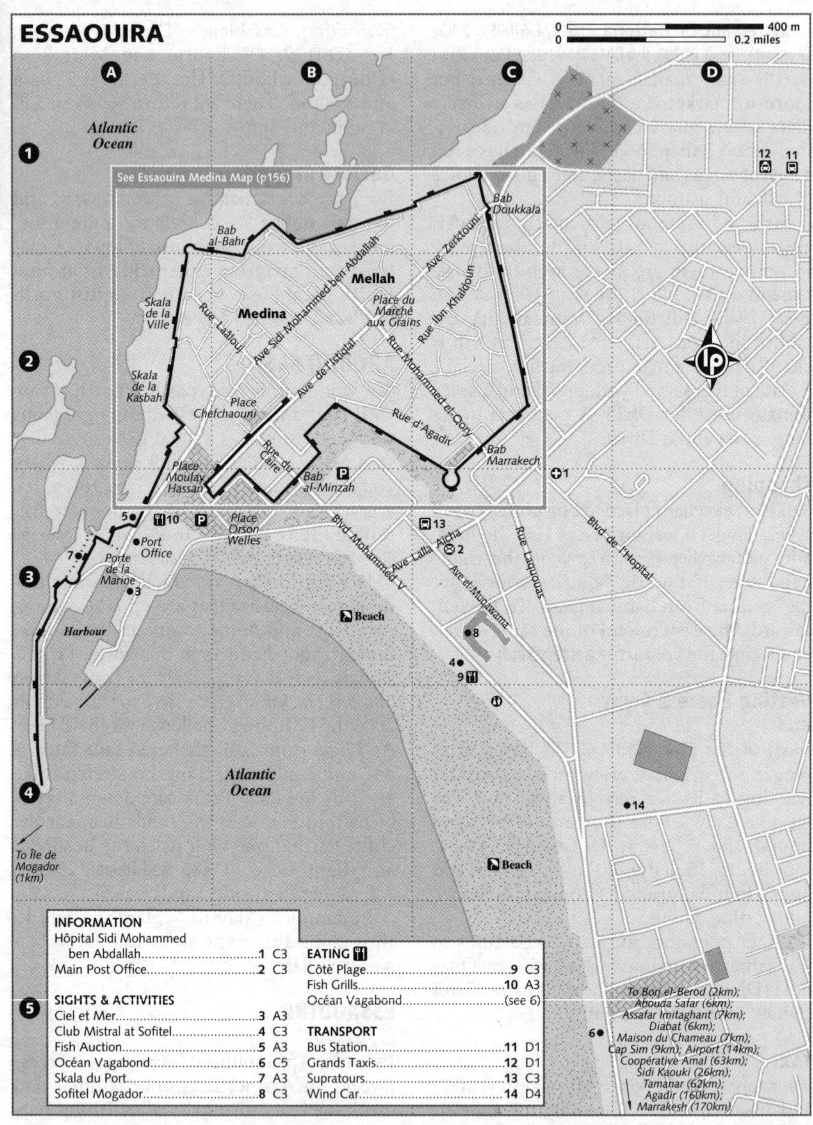

intrigue, the wind that reputedly drives people crazy, the smells of fish guts and damp sea air mixed with the aroma of spices and thuya wood, the women in their white *haiks* (veils), the midday shadow reflection of the palm trees on the red city walls, and the sound of drums and Gnawa singing that reverberates from shops and houses.

With its long history as a coastal trading post, Essaouira has always been a place where Arabs, Africans and Europeans meet. The town has a more laid-back attitude towards newcomers than elsewhere in Morocco, and it's the kind of place where people come and hang out rather than go sightseeing. This is what attracted hippies, including Jimi Hendrix, here in the 1960s and 1970s, and later artists, writers and craftsmen. These days however, as in many places in Morocco, you are more likely to encounter visitors looking to buy a house in the picturesque old medina, dreaming of an easy life in the sun or of opening yet another guest house.

Firmly established on the travellers' trail, Essaouira has become more crowded in recent years and increasingly it is a chic place to be. The 18th-century old town is slowly but surely being tarted up and gentrified. In the late morning, busloads of day-trippers get dropped off at the main square, stroll en masse through the town, and are picked up on the other side of town in the late afternoon. At night however the place becomes itself again, laid-back and calm, when you can hear once again the gentle shuffle of kaftans, the blowing of the wind and the hush of the Souiris (term for locals from Essaouira) crowding the cafés on Place Moulay Hassan.

It is the wind – the beautifully named *alizee* or *taros* in Berber – that, despite the crowds, ensures Essaouira retains its character. It blows too hard to attract sun, sand and sea tourists: for much of the year, you can't sit on the beach at all as the sand blows horizontally in your face. No surprise then that Essaouira has been dubbed 'Wind City of Africa' and attracts so many windsurfers. Sun-seekers head further south to the temperate clime of Agadir. The charm of the town is that it hasn't been entirely taken over by tourism. The fishing harbour is just as busy as it always was, the woodworkers are still amazing at their craft and the medina is just as important for locals as it is popular with tourists.

Essaouira lies on the crossroads between two tribes: the Arab Chiadma to the north and the Haha Berbers in the south. Add to that the Gnawa, who came originally from further south in Africa, and the Europeans and you get a rich cultural mix. The light and beauty have forever attracted artists to Essaouira, and the town has a flourishing art scene. The sculptor Boujemaa Lakhdar started the local museum in the 1950s and, in the process, inspired a generation of artists. Since then, the autodidactic Gnawa painters, who paint their dreams in a colourful palette, have earned international renown, mainly thanks to the efforts of the Galerie Frederic Damgaard (p164).

Winter is the time to get closer to the real Essaouira, when the wind howls at its strongest and the waves smash against the city's defences. In summer the town is invaded by throngs of Moroccan tourists, the beach is crowded and it is hard to find accommodation.

History

Most of the old city and fortifications in Essaouira today date from the 18th century, but the town has a much older history that started with the Phoenicians. For centuries, foreigners had a firm grip over the town, and although Moroccans eventually reclaimed it, the foreign influence lingers on in the way the town looks and feels today.

The Phoenicians founded the settlement of Migdol (meaning watchtower) here around the 7th century BC, and the rocky offshore islands soon supported a large population who extracted a much-prized purple dye from a local mollusc, the murex. For centuries Essaouira served as a safe harbour and freshwater source on the route between the Cap Verde Islands and the equator.

In the late 15th century, Portuguese sailors saw the advantages of the bay, renamed it Mogador, and established a trade and military post. The Jews took an important position in the town, as intermediaries between the sultan and the foreign powers. They were the only ones allowed to sell wheat to the Christians. By 1541, the Portuguese had lost control to the Saadians, the port fell from favour and trade diverted to Agadir. Although trade returned to Mogador when political power shifted to the Alawites, the town never fully recovered.

In 1764 Sultan Sidi Mohammed ben Abdallah installed himself in Essaouira, from where his corsairs could go and attack the people of Agadir who rebelled against him. He hired a French architect, Théodore Cornut, to create a city in the middle of sand and wind, where nothing existed. The combination of Moroccan and European styles pleased the Sultan, who renamed the town Essaouira, meaning 'well designed'. The port soon became a vital link for trade between Timbuktu and Europe. It was a place where the trade in gold, salt, ivory, and ostrich feathers was carefully

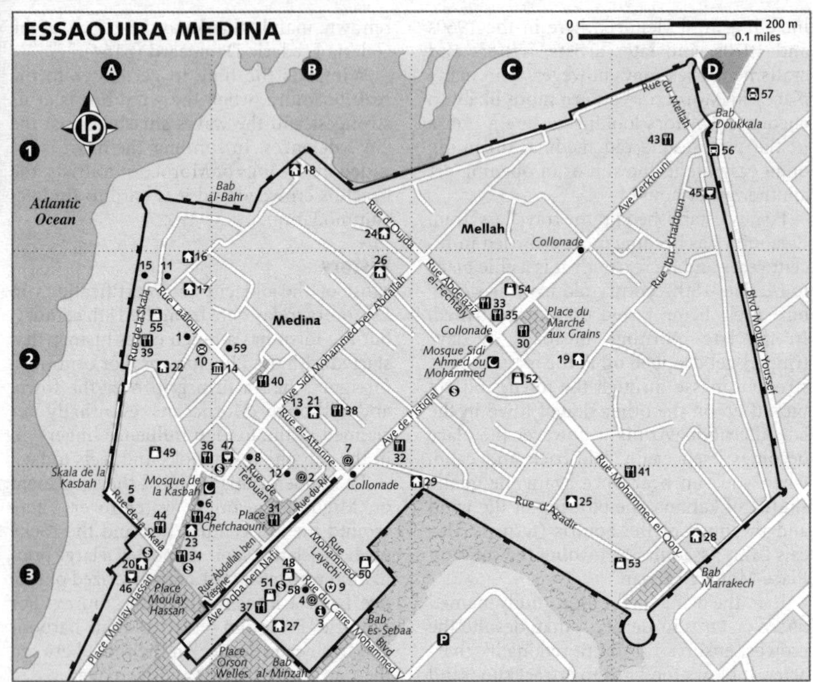

monitored, taxed and controlled by a garrison of 2000 imperial soldiers.

By 1912 the French had established their protectorate, changed the town's name back to Mogador and diverted trade to Casablanca, Tangier and Agadir. It was only with independence in 1956 that the sleepy backwater again became Essaouira. After Orson Welles filmed *Othello* here, and since Jimi Hendrix and the hippies chose Essaouira as a hang out, the town has seen a steady flow of visitors, from artists, surfers and writers to European tourists escaping the crowds of Marrakesh.

Dangers & Annoyances

Essaouira is still mostly a safe, relaxed tourist town but you should be on your guard in the backstreets of the *mellah* after dark. Although the town, and particularly the *mellah*, have been much cleaned up in recent years, there are still problems with drugs and drinking. Drug dealers and junkies hang out in the backstreets in an area east of l'Lunétoile and north of Ave Zerktouni, making this the least salubrious part of town.

Orientation

Almost everything you'll need in Essaouira is in the old walled town, around the port or along the seafront, a pretty compact area that is easy to navigate.

The main thoroughfare in the walled town is Ave de l'Istiqlal, which becomes Ave Zerktouni as you head towards Bab Doukkala to the northeast. At the southwestern end is the main square Place Moulay Hassan, with café-terraces. Beyond the square is the port, fish market and the bastion of Skala du Port.

Intersecting the main thoroughfare is Rue Mohammed el-Qory, which runs from Bab Marrakesh in the southeast to near Bab al-Bahr in the northwest, changing into Rue Abdelaziz el-Fechtaly and then into Rue d'Oujda along the way. Parallel to this is another busy street, Rue Lattarine, merging into Rue Laâlouj.

The new town is fast expanding but most of the hotels and restaurants are along the seafront; the rest of the town is residential. The bus station and grands taxis are 1km northeast in a fairly raggedy part of the new town.

INFORMATION
Alliance Franco-Marocaine......1 A2
Cyber Les Remparts......2 B3
Délégation du Tourisme......3 B3
Espace Internet......4 B3
Galerie Aida......5 A3
Jack's Kiosk......6 A3
Mogador Informatique......7 B2
Pharmacie La Kasbah......8 B2
Police Station......9 B3
Post Office......10 A2

SIGHTS & ACTIVITIES
Entry to Ramparts......11 A2
Hammam Lalla Mira......(see 25)
Hammam de la Kasbah......12 B3
Hammam Riad el-Medina......13 B2
Sidi Mohammed Ben Abdallah Museum......14 B2
Skala de la Ville......15 A2

SLEEPING
Dar Adul......16 A2
Dar Afram......17 A2
Dar Al-Bahar......18 B1
Dar Beida......19 C2
Hôtel Beau Rivage......20 A3
Hôtel Les Matins Bleus......21 B2
Hôtel Smara......22 A2
Jack's Appartments......(see 6)
Karimo......23 A3
La Casa del Mar......24 B1
Lalla Mira......25 C3
Le Grand Large......26 B2
Madada......27 B3
Palais Heure Bleue......28 D3
Riad Nakhla......29 C3

EATING
Au Bonheur des Dames......30 C2
Café Faid......(see 44)
Café d'Horloge......31 B3
Elizir......32 B2
Fish Souq......33 C2
Gelateria Dolce Freddo......34 A3
Grill Stands......35 C2
Le 5......(see 27)
Pâtisserie Driss......36 A2
Restaurant El-Minzah......37 B3
Restaurant Ferdaous......38 B2
Restaurant Les Alizés......39 A2
Restaurant Les Chandeliers......40 B2
Riad Al-Baraka......41 D3
Sandwich Stands......42 A3
Snacks Stands......43 D1
Taros Café......44 A3

DRINKING
Alcohol Shop......45 D1
Café Restaurant Bab Laachour......46 A3
Le Patio......47 B2
Taros Café......(see 44)

SHOPPING
Association Tilal des Arts Plastiques......48 B3
Coopérative Artisanal des Marqueteurs......49 A2
Espace Othello......50 B3
Galeries Frederic Damgaard......51 B3
Jewellery Souq......52 C2
Rafia Craft......53 D3
Spice Souq......54 C2
Woodcarving Workshops......55 A2

TRANSPORT
Local Buses......56 D1
Petits Taxis......57 D1
Residence Shahrazed......58 B3
Résidence Hôtel Al-Arboussas......59 B2

MAPS

The tourist office sells a useful map of town (Dh15) and an interesting guidebook *Essaouira – La Séductrice* (Essaouira – the Enchantress, in French, Dh40), which has information on everything from local history and arts to traditional music, festivals and architecture. Another good buy (though not always available locally) is *Essaouira de Bab en Bab: Promenades* (in French) by Hammad Berrada, a wonderful book of walking tours. It provides details of eight different walks, accompanied by descriptive text, photographs and comprehensive maps of the medina.

Information

BOOKSHOPS

Galerie Aida (Map p156; ☎ 024 476290; 2 Rue de la Skala) Run by a former New Yorker, this place stocks a small but good selection of English-language books and some funky junk.

Jack's Kiosk (Map p156; ☎ 024 475538; 1 Place Moulay Hassan) Sells foreign-language newspapers and magazines along with some English, French and German books. You can also rent apartments here (see p163).

CULTURAL CENTRES

Alliance Franco-Marocaine (Map p156; ☎ 024 476197; www.ambafrance-ma.org/institut/afm-essaouira/index.cfm; Derb Lâalaouj, 9 Rue Mohammed Diouri; 9am-12.30pm & 2.30-6.30pm Mon-Fri) Offers semester-long French classes and eight-week Arabic classes as well as regular films, exhibitions and cultural events.

EMERGENCIES

Medical Emergencies (☎ 024 475716)

Police (Map p156; ☎ 19, 024 784880; Rue du Caire) Opposite the tourist office.

INTERNET ACCESS

There are internet cafés all over town. Most open from 9am to 11pm and charge Dh8 to Dh10 per hour.

Cyber Les Remparts (Map p156; 12 Rue du Rif)

Espace Internet (Map p156; 8 bis, Rue du Caire)

Mogador Informatique (5 Ave de l'Istiqlal)

MEDICAL SERVICES

Hôpital Sidi Mohammed ben Abdallah (Map p154; ☎ 024 475716; Blvd de l'Hôpital) For emergencies.

Pharmacie la Kasbah (Map p156; ☎ 024 475151; 12-14 Rue Allal ben Abdellah)

MONEY

There are several banks with ATMs around Place Moulay Hassan and along the main road leading northeast to Bab Doukkala. Most are good for foreign exchange and credit-card cash advances.

POST

Main post office (Map p154; Ave el-Mouqawama; 8.30am-4.15pm Mon-Fri, 8am-noon Sat)

Post office (Map p156; Rue Laâlouj; 8.30am-4pm Mon-Fri)

TOURIST INFORMATION

Délégation du Tourisme (Map p156; ☎ 024 783532; www.essaouira.com; 10 Rue du Caire; 9am-noon & 3-6.30pm Mon-Fri) This helpful tourist office has lots of information and advice for travellers, as well as noticeboards with information on events and activities around town.

Sights

Although there aren't so many formal sights in Essaouira, it's a wonderful place for rambling. The medina, souqs, ramparts, port and beach are perfect for leisurely discovery interspersed with relaxed lunches and unhurried coffee or fresh orange juice.

MEDINA & PORT

Essaouira's walled **medina** (Map p156) was added to Unesco's World Heritage list in 2001. Its well-preserved, late-18th-century fortified layout is a prime example of European military architecture in North Africa. For the visitor, the mellow atmosphere, narrow winding streets lined with colourful shops, whitewashed houses and heavy old wooden doors make it a wonderful place to stroll.

The dramatic, wave-lashed ramparts that surround the medina are a great place to get an overview of the labyrinth of streets. The ramparts were famously used in the opening scene of Orson Welles' *Othello* for a panoramic shot where Iago is suspended in a cage above the rocks and sea. The easiest place to access the ramparts is at **Skala**

EMMA WILSON

How long have you lived in Essaouira? I have been coming to Essaouira for 10 years, and I have lived here for about five years. I love it but I go home to London for sanity's sake every three months, usually for three weeks.

Why did you choose Essaouira? I guess Essaouira chose me and I suited it. I bought a house here at first, because I fell in love with this white, organic architecture and the town just reeled me in. This has partly to do both with the fact that the business is just more successful with me around, but mainly because I thought life here would be less stressful than in London and boy, have I been proven very wrong!

Has the town changed a lot since you have been living here? It has changed hugely in the last five years. There has been a huge influx of tourists, so now there are a lot of hotels all built along the seafront. A lot of authenticity has been removed and with lots of foreigners buying up houses in the old city, mostly to turn them into holiday homes, the town is now too cleaned up. These days it's hard to find the true Essaouira I used to know, where the fishermen were sitting in the port mending their nets or pitching sheets of plastic anywhere they could to sell their catch. The money spent by the local authorities is all superficial I'm afraid. The infrastructure really is a mess and Morocco is a little corrupt!

How do you feel about the changes, is it good or bad? I personally have mixed views about the changes. Of course for us in some ways the changes are good because more people come to Essaouira, so we now have a successful business. But for many locals it has had a negative effect, because there is no work for them here so they have been pushed to alcohol and drugs. They are a lot more aggressive and you cannot leave a bag in a café and go back an hour later for it and expect it still to be there like you used to.

Unfortunately when a new hotel opens employees are brought in from more educated towns or cities like Marrakesh, Agadir or Casa, so there is less and less work for the people in the town. We were made to feel very welcome here at first, but there is now a lot of resentment against the foreigners like me who have bought places here and are running a business, do you get my story? It happens in so many places but is so sad to see and it is us who are to blame really. I still love the place to bits though…

What is your favourite building or monument? My favourite building in town is probably Villa Maroc from the interior, but I love walking along the ramparts at any time of the day. It is truly stunning there and I don't go often enough.

de la Ville (Map p156), the impressive sea bastion built along the cliffs. A collection of European brass cannons from the 18th and 19th centuries lines the walkway here and you'll also get great views out to sea and gorgeous sunsets.

Down by the harbour, the **Skala du Port** (Map p154; adult/child Dh10/3; 8.30am-noon & 2.30-6pm) offers more cannons and picturesque views over the fishing port and the Île de Mogador. Looking back at the walled medina from here, through a curtain of swirling seagulls, you'll get the same evocative picture that is used on nearly all official literature.

The large working port is a bustling place with plenty of activity throughout the day. Along with the flurry of boats, nets being repaired and the day's catch being landed you can see traditional wooden boats being made. It's also worth visiting the **fish auction** (Map p154; 3-5pm Mon-Sat), which takes place in the market hall just outside the port gates.

ÎLE DE MOGADOR & ELEANORA'S FALCONS

Used in Phoenician and Roman times for the production of Tyrian purple dye, and once known as the Îles Purpuraires (Purple Isles), the **Île de Mogador** (off Map p154) is actually two islands and several tiny islets. A massive fortification, a mosque and a disused prison are all that is left of what was once a thriving settlement, and today the uninhabited islands are a sanctuary for Eleanora's falcons.

These elegant birds of prey come here to breed from April to October before making their incredible return journey south to

What do you like about this place? I like the naivety of the people and the way they showed me what is really important in life – spending time with your family, watching the kids grow, while we in Europe run around like headless chickens. I am sure they have it more right than us really!

What is your favourite restaurant? My favourite restaurant was Elizir but he has closed just now, but he is going to reopen I hope. I love the fresh fish at the stalls just outside the harbour, particularly number 33 Ali. I have known the boys there for 10 years so they always really look after me, but I hate sharing a table so I normally go there around 3pm.

Your favourite bar or café? Taros is the only real bar really. It's a great place to go at sunset, with the seagulls soaring over you on the rooftop terrace. The Café France on the square is very authentic but I hate to say that the Italian Gelateria on the corner is my favourite, because they have excellent coffee and ice cream!

Where do you go to relax? Océan Vagabond on the beach is good to relax, otherwise I go further south to the beach in Sidi Kaouki.

What is your favourite word in the local darija (Moroccan dialect)? *Chuir* which means 'so so'. When someone asks 'Are you ok?' you can answer '*chuir*'.

There seem to be many characters in the streets here, do you have a favourite? You are right, there are so many, and I love or hate them all for different reasons. The tramp at the car park by the fish stalls is cool though. He sort of works there but doesn't get paid, as in he hangs out there looking filthy dirty so we all give him money. I have to say he is very helpful and speaks excellent English.

What do you do on weekends? The week and weekends are all the same to me. If I have clients staying in one of our houses, or I'm doing up someone's house, I will usually be running around with them. If not, I'll be seeing friends in the country, or off to Marrakesh or Sidi Kaouki for a couple of days.

What does Essaouira represent for you? Essaouira for me is the old Essaouira: lovely, giving, smiling people, the simplicity of their lives and they seem so content. The fact that they have time to sit and have tea with friends and chat all day (although now that drives me mad). I love the architecture and the town definitely has some magic that I will never forget.

Emma Wilson is an interior designer, who rents out houses, and girl-about-town.

Madagascar. The falcons can easily be seen through binoculars from Essaouira beach, with the best viewing in the early evening. Another viewing place (though not recommended in the evening if you're alone) is south of town, about 1km or so beyond the lighthouse, on the shore by the mouth of the river.

The islands are strictly off limits in breeding season but you can arrange a private boat trip at other times. You need to obtain a permit (free) from the port office before seeking out one of the small fishing boats at the port and negotiating the price of the trip. It shouldn't cost more than Dh300.

There is also an organised boat trip, **Ciel et Mer** (Map p154; ☎ 024 474618, 064 326493; www.mogador-iles.com; Port de Peche; adult/child Dh80/40) around the islands, but bad sailing conditions can delay departures or leave you stranded at sea unable to escape relentless folk music. In summer there are four departures between 11.30am and 6.30pm. For the rest of the year, departures are at noon and 3.30pm. It also organises fishing trips.

SIDI MOHAMMED BEN ABDALLAH MUSEUM

Essaouira's beautifully refurbished **museum** (Map p156; ☎ 024 475300; Rue Laâlouj; adult/child Dh10/3; 8.30am-6pm Wed-Mon) in an old riad, has a small but interesting collection of jewellery, costumes, weapons, amazing musical instruments and carpets of the region. There's a section explaining the signs and symbols used by local craftspeople and some interesting photographs of Essaouira at the turn of the century. Note also the Roman and Phoenician objects found in the bay.

Activities

BEACH & WATERSPORTS

Essaouira's wide, sandy beach is a great place for walking, but the strong winds and currents mean it's not so good for sunbathing or swimming. Footballers, windsurfers and kitesurfers take over the town end of the beach, while fiercely competitive horse and camel owners ply the sands further on. They can be quite insistent, so be firm and make it clear if you've no interest in taking a ride – and bargain hard if you do.

If you're walking, head south across the Ksob River (impassable at high tide) to see the ruins of the **Borj el-Berod** (off Map p154), an old fortress and pavilion partially covered in sand. Local legend has it that this was the original inspiration for the Jimi Hendrix classic 'Castles Made of Sand'; however, the song was released a year before he visited. From here you can walk inland to the village of Diabat (p166) or continue along the sands to the sand dunes of Cap Sim.

A number of outlets rent water-sports equipment and offer instruction along the beach. **Club Mistral at Sofitel** (Map p154; ☎ 024 783934; www.club-mistral.com; Blvd Mohammed V; 9am-6pm) rents windsurfing equipment (Dh170 per hour) and surfboards (Dh80 per hour). It also offers kitesurfing and surfing tuition for all levels (from Dh250 per hour). Six-hour surfing courses cost Dh1100 and 10-hour kitesurfing courses cost Dh2300.

Further along the beach, **Océan Vagabond** (off Map p154; ☎ 024 783934; www.oceanvagabond.com, in French; 8am-8pm) rents surfboards (three days for Dh500) and gives two-hour surfing lessons (Dh350). It also offers kitesurfing lessons (six hours cost Dh1950) and rental (three days for Dh1200), and windsurfing lessons (one hour/six hours costs Dh500/1200) and rental (Dh60 per hour). It has a cool café-restaurant with a laid-back terrace on the beach.

HAMMAMS

There are plenty of small hammams hidden about town;

Hammam de la Kasbah (Map p156; 7 Rue de Marrakesh; admission Dh8) For a more traditional, local experience. Women only.

Hammam Lalla Mira (Map p156; ☎ 024 475907; www.lallamira.ma; 14 Rue d'Algerie; hammam Dh15, gommage Dh60; 9.30am-7pm women) One of the oldest, this newly restored hammam is heated by solar energy and, although aimed at tourists, has a wonderful traditional interior. Good value massages with argan oil.

Hammam Riad el-Madina (Map p156; ☎ 024 475046; 9 Rue el-Attarine; admission Dh70, massage from Dh100; 9-10am & 3-4pm women, 10am-12.30pm & 4-7pm mixed) Another good place to break a first sweat.

Sofitel Mogador (Map p154; ☎ 024 479000; Blvd Mohammed V; 7am-12.30pm & 4-10.30pm women, 2.30-4pm mixed) A traditional hammam, also offering hydrotherapy, aquagym and massages. Excellent service.

RIDING

To try something more serious than the horse and camel rides on the beach, several companies offer cross-country trekking and multi-day rides in the countryside around Essaouira. Tailor-made horse trips can be arranged through Ranch de Diabat (p166), which also offers riding lessons for adults and children. **Abouda Safar** (☎ 028 271258, 062 743497; www.abouda-safar.com) offers an eight-day trek around the region or half-day/full-day local treks (Dh350/450).

For camel riding, the best place to go is the **Maison du Chameau** (off Map p154; ☎ 024 785962; maisonduchameau@yahoo.fr; Douar Al Arab; per hr Dh 110, per day incl lunch Dh380, r Dh190-330), a remote guest house that is home to eight *meharis* (white Sudanese racing camels). The guest house offers weeklong camel-riding courses, shorter excursions and a selection of peaceful rooms decked out in vibrant fuchsia-pink and electric-blue.

Festivals & Events

Essaouira has three major festivals that draw hoards of performers and spectators to town.

Printemps Musical des Alizés (May; www.alizesfestival.com) A small music festival featuring classical music and opera.

Gnaoua and World Music Festival (3rd weekend Jun; www.festival-gnaoua.net) A four-day musical extravaganza featuring international, national and local performers as well as a series of art exhibitions.

Festival des Andalousies Atlantiques (late Sep) An eclectic mix of Andalusian music, art and dance by local and international performers.

Sleeping

Accommodation in Essaouira isn't cheap but there's now a seemingly endless selection of properties to choose from at all price levels. Most hotels and riads are within the walls of the medina, so everything you need is within walking distance. In summer book ahead or at least arrive early in the day to find a room. As the medina gets increasingly crowded, hotels are being built along the coast further south and on the seafront.

BUDGET

The choice of budget accommodation in Essaouira is well above the usual Moroccan standard. Not only will you find a place where the bathrooms won't scare you, you'll probably get a character-laden room and terrace as well.

Hôtel Smara (Map p156; ☎ 024 475655; 26 Rue de la Skala; s/d/q Dh75/105/185, d/q with sea view Dh200/275) All whitewashed, the Smara has just four rooms overlooking the sea, the best ones on the roof terrace where breakfast is served. The other rooms open onto an internal room, but can be damp in winter. The communal bathrooms are tiled and clean. Popular because it's good value, especially the quadruple rooms, so book ahead or arrive early.

Dar Afram (Map p156; ☎ 024 785657; www.dar-afram.com; 10 Rue Sidi Magdoul; s Dh150, d Dh300-400, Jun-Sep s Dh250, d Dh400-450) This extremely friendly guest house has simple, spotless rooms with shared bathrooms and a funky vibe. The Aussie-Moroccan owners are musicians and an impromptu session often follows the evening meals shared around a communal table. It also has a lovely tiled hammam.

our pick **Riad Nakhla** (Map p156; ☎/fax 024 474940; www.essaouiranet.com/riad-nakhla; 2 Rue Agadir; s Dh225, d Dh325, ste Dh400-500) Riad Nakhla comes as a bit of shock. It looks like any other budget place from the outside, but inside the weary traveller is met with a friendly reception in a beautiful courtyard, with elegant stone columns and a fountain trickling, more what you'd expect from a hotel in a higher price bracket. The well-appointed bedrooms are simple but comfortable and immaculately kept, full of local flavour with shuttered windows, colourful bedspreads and great *tadelakt*-clad bathrooms. All have a TV. Breakfast on the roof terrace with views over the ocean and town is another treat. It's an incredible bargain at this price.

Hôtel Beau Rivage (Map p156; ☎ 024 475925; www.essaouiranet.com/beaurivage; 14 Place Moulay Hassan; s/d/tr Dh250/350/450, d without bathroom Dh200) As central as it gets, overlooking the main square, the Beau Rivage has bright and cheerful rooms with modern fittings and spotless bathrooms. The rooms are a bit noisy but offer the greatest spectacle in town, while breakfast is served on the charming and quiet roof terrace with views over the port and town.

Hôtel Les Matins Bleus (Map p156; ☎ 024 785363, 066 308899; www.les-matins-bleus.com; 22 Rue de Drâa; s/d/ste Dh275/420/840, Jun-Sep Dh300/460/920) Hidden down a dead-end street, this charming hotel has bright, traditionally styled rooms surrounding a central courtyard painted in cheerful colours. The rooms all have plain white walls, lovely local fabrics and spotless bathrooms. Breakfast is served on the sheltered terrace from where you'll get good views over the medina.

MIDRANGE

In this price range you'll be spoilt for choice in Essaouira. Each place is more charming than the next.

Lalla Mira (Map p156; ☎ 024 475046; 14 Rue d'Algerie;www.lallamira.net; s/d/ste Dh436/692/920; 💻) This gorgeous little place, the town's first eco-hotel, has simple rooms with ochre *tadelakt* walls, wrought-iron furniture, natural fabrics and solar-powered underfloor heating. The hotel also has anti-allergy beds, a great hammam (see p160) and a good restaurant serving a selection of vegetarian food.

Le Grand Large (Map p156; ☎ 024 472866; www.riadlegrandlarge.com; 2 Rue Oum-Rabia; r Dh495-715, half board per person extra Dh140) After the simple whitewash and muted colours of many riads in town, Le Grand Large is much more colourful with pink, green and blue walls, bright throws on cast-iron beds and buckets of character. It's a friendly, cheerful place with an excellent restaurant.

Dar Al-Bahar (Map p156; ☎ 024 476831; www.daralbahar.com; 1 Rue Touahen; d Dh550-850, ste Dh1045) The rooms at the Al-Bahar are elegantly simple, with plain white walls, wrought-iron furniture and a contrasting touch of blue, pink, green or yellow in the traditional bedspreads and curtains. Local artworks adorn the walls and the views from the terrace overlooking the ocean are magnificent.

Dar Adul (Map p156; ☎ 024 473910; www.dar-adul.com; 63 Rue Touahen; d Dh600-770, ste Dh880) This lovingly restored house has just a few comfy rooms with subtle lighting, beautiful furniture, restrained muted colours and little touches that make it feel like a home rather than a hotel. The staff is incredibly friendly – you'll feel more like family than a paying guest by the time you leave.

La Casa del Mar (Map p156; ☎ 024 475091; www.lacasa-delmar.com; 35 Rue D'Oujda; d incl breakfast Dh825/990) Delightful guest house that seamlessly blends contemporary design with traditional style and creates a stunning yet simple atmosphere where you can sit back and relax. Retire to your room, join the other guests for a communal Moroccan meal or Spanish paella, arrange a home visit from a masseur or henna artist, or just watch the sunset from the seafront terrace.

TOP END

Madada (Map p156; ☎ 024 475512; www.madada.com; 5 Rue Youssef el-Fassi; d Dh1240-1670, ste Dh1835; ❄) Sleek, stylish and very, very slick, Madada offers luxurious, contemporary rooms in a traditional house. Ivory and sand *tadelakt*, pared-back minimalism, designer furniture, neutral colours and a profound sense of calm run throughout. The spacious, bright rooms have subtle decor, brass handbasins, private terraces and rosewood furniture. The upstairs rooms have a large terrace with sweeping views of the bay.

Palais Heure Bleue (Map p156; ☎ 024 474222; www.heure-bleue.com; 2 Rue Ibn Batouta; d/ste Dh2200/3900; ❄ 🏊 💻) A decided hush falls as you walk through the doors of the Heure Bleue, Essaouira's top hotel. This swish place has everything you could ever want, from a rooftop swimming pool to its own private cinema and billiard room. Chic European style and colonial charm meet in the lounge, where a grand piano sits beneath trophy heads from a long-forgotten hunting trip, and in the bedrooms where zebra prints, dark woods and marble counter tops vie for attention.

APARTMENTS & RIADS

Essaouira has a great selection of apartments and riads to rent, most done up in impeccable style. If you're travelling as a family or in a group, they can be an affordable and flexible option. Prices range from about Dh500 per night for a one-bed apartment up to Dh3000 per night for the grand three-bedroomed former British consulate.

our pick **Dar Beida** (Map p156; ☎ 067 965386, UK 00 44 07768 352190; www.castlesinthesand.com; per week incl maid, firewood & babouches per person from Dh3300) A stunning 18th-century traditional Moroccan house, the 'White House' right in the centre of Essaouira, was lovingly restored by London interior decorator Emma Wilson (see p158) and her husband with iconic 1950 and '60s furniture found in local junk markets. The house has several bedrooms, the best one on the upper roof terrace, and two living rooms with lots of books and

CDs, and a large terrace. This is definitely the place to be in Essaouira. Dar Emma is Emma's other house for rent, more traditional but equally comfortable and funky.

Jack's Apartments (Map p156; ☎ 024 475538; www.essaouira.com/apartments; 1 Place Moulay Hassan) and **Karimo** (Map p156; ☎ 024 474500; www.karimo.net; Place Moulay Hassan) both have a good selection of rental properties. Book well in advance during the high season.

Eating

RESTAURANTS

Essaouira is packed with cafés and restaurants so there's no difficulty finding somewhere to eat. However, the standards vary substantially.

Medina

Riad Al-Baraka (Map p156; ☎ 024 473561; 113 Rue Mohammed el-Qory; mains Dh45-95, set menu Dh90-130; ⏰ noon-3pm & 6.30pm-late Mon-Sat) Set in a former Jewish school, this hip place has several dining rooms and a bar set around a large courtyard shaded by a huge fig tree. The food is mainly Moroccan with some Middle Eastern and Jewish influences, the decor cool, and there's live music by local bands at weekends.

Restaurant El-Minzah (Map p156; ☎ 024 475308; 3 Ave Oqba ben Nafii; mains Dh50-120, set menus from Dh95) Sit on the outside terrace or in the elegant dining room inside at this popular place facing the ramparts. The menu features a good selection of international dishes with specialities such as blue shark and Berber tajine with argan oil, and there's lively Gnawa music here on Saturday nights.

Restaurant Ferdaous (Map p156; ☎ 024 473655; 27 Rue Abdesslam Lebadi; mains Dh60-80, set menu Dh105; ⏰ closed Mon) A delightful Moroccan restaurant, and one of the few places in town that serves real, home-cooked, traditional Moroccan food. The seasonal menu offers an innovative take on traditional recipes, the service is very friendly and the low tables and padded seating make it feel like the real McCoy.

our pick **Elizir** (Map p156; ☎ 024 472103; 1 Rue Agadir; mains Dh80-90) The best restaurant in town by far, this place was temporarily closed at the time of research, but will hopefully reopen soon. The Elizir serves a perfectly cooked mix of Moroccan and Mediterranean dishes with an innovative twist. The owner of this old house just off the main street is super-friendly, and loves to talk about where he found all the iconic 1950s and '60s furniture he has collected from local junk markets. The decor is sublime, and if it were in London or New York, it would be voted the hippest place in town.

Restaurante Les Alizés (Map p156; ☎ 024 476819; 26 Rue de la Skala; mains Dh75-90) This popular place, run by a charming Moroccan couple in a 19th-century house, has delicious Moroccan dishes, particularly the couscous with fish and the tajine of *boulettes de sardines* (sardine balls). You'll get a very friendly welcome. Book well ahead as it fills up every night, both with Moroccans and visitors. It's above Pension Smar.

Le 5 (Map p156; ☎ 024 784726; 5 Rue Youssef el-Fassi; Dh180; ⏰ 7-11pm Wed-Mon, noon-3pm Sat & Sun) Deep-purple seating, warm stone arches and giant lampshades dominate this trendy restaurant which serves well-cooked and original Mediterranean and Moroccan dishes. One of the favourite places to head for dinner.

Beachfront

Ocean Vagabond (off Map p154; ☎ 024 783934; Blvd Mohammed V; mains Dh60-90) Although a good walk from town, this simple little café is the best of the beachfront offerings. It serves a decent but limited range of sandwiches, pizza, pasta and salads and has plenty of comfy seats in the sand from where the kids can run free.

Côté Plage (Map p154; ☎ 024 479000; Blvd Mohammed V; mains Dh150) Part of the looming Sofitel across the road, this beachfront café has a nice and elegant decked area where you can sit beneath the shade of giant white umbrellas. You can nibble on tapas (Dh35) as you look out over the ocean for the afternoon or arrive on Sunday for the all-day barbecue.

CAFÉS, PÂTISSERIES & ICE-CREAM PARLOURS

Taros Café (Map p156; ☎ 024 476407; 2 Rue de la Skala; ⏰ 8am-11pm Mon-Sat) The roof terrace at the Taros is a wonderful place for afternoon tea. The salons in this beautifully restored house are lined with artworks.

Café d'Horloge (Map p156; Place Chefchaouni) Set on the attractive square beneath the clocktower, this popular café is an excellent choice for a breakfast of *amlou* (a spread made of local argan oil, almond and honey) and crepes or bread (Dh25). It's away from the hoards of people on the main café drag and a good choice for a quiet coffee or snack.

Gelateria Dolce Freddo (Map p156; Place Moulay Hassan) With more than 30 varieties of authentic Italian ice cream on offer, you'll find it hard to resist temptation at this little place on the main square. It's just Dh5 a scoop and the best you'll find in town.

Au Bonheur des Dames (Map p156; ☎ 024 475968; Place du Marché au Grains) A new, elegant terrace on this picturesque square that serves an upmarket selection of teas, coffee, fresh juices and a good breakfast (Dh80).

For morning croissants or an afternoon pastry the best places to go are **Pâtisserie Driss** (Map p156), which has a hidden seating area, and **Café Faid** (Map p156), both near Place Moulay Hassan.

QUICK EATS

One of Essaouira's best food experiences is the **outdoor fish grills** (Map p154) that line the port end of Place Moulay Hassan. Just choose what you want to eat from the colourful displays of fresh fish and seafood at each grill, agree on a price (expect to pay about Dh40 for lunch) and wait for it to be cooked on the spot.

Alternatively, you can visit the **fish souq** (Map p156; just off Ave de l'Istiqlal), buy some of the day's catch and take it to one of the grill stands in the southern corner. It'll come back cooked and served with bread and salad for Dh30.

There are plenty of snack stands (Map p154) and hole-in-the-wall type places along Ave Sidi Mohammed ben Abdallah, Ave Zerktouni and just inside Bab Doukkala.

Drinking

Despite its popularity as a tourist destination, Essaouira isn't the hottest place for nightlife. To warm up for an evening out, you could visit the alcohol shop (Map p156) near Bab Doukkala and take your drinks to your hotel terrace to watch the sun go down. Alternatively, try the terrace at the **Café Restaurant Bab Laachour** (Map p156; Place Moulay Hassan).

One of the most atmospheric terraces in town, and the only real bar, is at the **Taros Café** (Map p156; ☎ 024 476407; 2 Rue du Skala; 🕑 8am-11pm Mon-Sat), where you can sip your drinks under giant lamps and huddle round your table to fend off the wind whipping up from the sea. The restaurant (mains Dh70 to Dh120) is a bit hit-and-miss for food, but it has live music and belly dancing most nights.

For something more sultry, the hip bar and restaurant **Le Patio** (Map p156; ☎ 024 474166; 28 Rue Moulay Rachid; 🕑 5.30-11pm Tue-Sun) is a candlelit den with blood-red furnishings and a black mirror ball. You'll need to buy some tapas (Dh35) to just sit and drink or you might even be tempted by the whiff of grilled fish coming from the canopied restaurant (mains Dh85 to Dh150).

Shopping

Essaouira is well known for its woodwork and you can visit the string of **woodcarving workshops** (Map p156) near the Skala de la Ville. The exquisite marquetry work on sale is made from local fragrant thuya wood, which is now an endangered species. Although the products are beautiful and sold at excellent prices, buying anything made from thuya threatens the last remaining stands of trees by increasing demand and therefore encouraging illegal logging. For a guilt-free conscience look for crafts made from other woods instead. For fixed-price shopping try the **Coopérative Artisanal des Marqueteurs** (Map p156; 6 Rue Khalid ibn Oualid).

Essaouira's other great product is its raffia work, made from the fibres of the doum palm. For the most stylish designs, try **Rafia Craft** (Map p156; ☎ 024 783632; 82 Rue d'Agadir), which sells much of its line to European outlets.

For herbal Viagra, Berber lipstick, cures for baldness and exotic spices, the **spice souq** (Map p156) is the place to go. You can also buy argan-oil products here as well as the traditional *amlou* (about Dh40 per bottle). Nearby is the **jewellery souq** (Map p156), a small area of jewellery shops with everything from heavy Berber beads to gaudy gold.

Essaouira also has a reputation as an artists hub, and several galleries around town sell works by local painters. It's a mixed bag of talent and you may need to look in all of them before finding something you like. **Galeries Frederic Damgaard** (Map p156; ☎ 024 784446; www.galeriedamgaard.com; Rue Oqba ben Nafi) is the best and oldest in town and features the work of local artists. Nearby, the **Association Tilal des Arts Plastiques** (Map p156; ☎ 024 475424; 4 Rue de Caire) and **Espace Othello** (Map p156; ☎ 024 475095; 9 Rue Mohammed Layachi; 9am-1pm & 3-8pm) feature up-and-coming artists.

Getting There & Away

AIR

Direct flights to Casablanca and Paris leave from **Aéroport de Mogador** (☎ 024 476709; Route d'Agadir), 15km south of town, though the schedule is unreliable.

BUS

The **bus station** (off Map p154; ☎ 024 785241) is about 400m northeast of the medina, an easy walk during the day but better in a petit taxi (Dh10) if you're arriving/leaving late at night. The **left-luggage office** (Dh7 per item) is open 24 hours.

CTM (☎ 024 784764) has several buses daily for Safi (Dh45, 2½ hours), El-Jadida (Dh85, four hours) and Casablanca (Dh125, six hours), and one to Marrakesh (Dh75, 2½ hours). The bus to Agadir (Dh70, three hours) continues to Inezgane (Dh70). It's best to book a day in advance for long-distance services.

Other companies run cheaper and more frequent buses to the same destinations as well as to Taroudannt (Dh70, six hours), Tan Tan (Dh130, six hours) and Rabat (Dh90, six hours).

Supratours (Map p154; ☎ 024 475317), the ONCF subsidiary, runs buses to Marrakesh train station (Dh80, 2½ hours, four daily) to connect with trains to Casablanca from the station near Bab Marrakesh. You should book several days in advance for this service, particularly in summer.

Local bus 5 to Diabat (Dh4) and Sidi Kaouki (Dh6) leaves from Blvd Moulay Youssef outside Bab Doukkala. There are about eight services a day.

TAXI

The grand-taxi rank (off Map p154) lies immediately west of the bus station. The fare to Agadir (or Inezgane) is Dh75.

Getting Around

To get to the airport take bus 5 (Dh10, 15 minutes) or a petit taxi (Dh150 to Dh200). The blue petits taxis are also a good idea for getting to and from the bus station (Dh10) but they can't enter the medina. If you're happy to walk but don't want to carry your bags, there are plenty of enterprising men with luggage carts who will wheel your bags directly to your hotel (about Dh20).

THE NEW OLIVE OIL

Organic argan oil is 'the new olive oil', increasingly used in hip restaurants around the world to season salads with its nutty flavour. The wrinkled argan tree is unique to this part of the world and, as a result, the argan forests of the Souss Valley and the Haha Coast south of Essaouira have recently been designated by Unesco as a Biosphere reserve.

The tree, *Argania spinosa*, is resistant to heat and survives temperatures up to 50°C, so is an essential tool in the fight against desertification in southern Morocco. It has become vital to the local economy, providing firewood, fodder for the goats – you can see them actually climb into the branches – and oil for humans. Berber women harvest the fruits in spring and then feed them to goats, whose digestive juices dissolve the tough elastic coating on the shell. The nuts are then recovered from the goats' dung, and the kernels are split, lightly toasted, pulped and pressed. To produce just one litre of oil takes 30kg of nuts and 15 hours of manual labour, solely done by women. In a recent change to this tradition, some cooperatives have decided to cut the goats out of the process and are hand-picking fruits from the trees to produce a more subtle-tasting oil. You can see this whole process in a guided tour at the **Coopérative Amal** (☎ 024 788141; www.targanine.com, in French; Tamanar; admission free; 8am-7pm Mon-Fri), 80km north of Agadir, whose organic oil won the 2001 Slow Food Award.

The Berbers have long used argan oil to heal, but modern research suggests that the oil may help reduce cholesterol and prevent arteriosclerosis. The oil also has a high vitamin E content, which makes it a great anti-wrinkle cream. In the kitchen its rich and sweet nutty flavour works wonders as a salad dressing, or added to grilled vegetables or tajine. Berbers mix it with ground almonds and honey to make *amlou,* a delicacy believed to have aphrodisiac properties.

You can hire bikes from **Résidence Shahrazed** (Map p156; ☎ 024 472977; 1 Rue Youssef el-Fassi; per day Dh80) and **Résidence Hôtel Al-Arboussas** (Map p156; ☎ 024 472610; 24 Impasse Rue Laâlouj; per day Dh80).

Cars can be hired from **Wind Car** (Map p154; ☎ /fax 024 472804; Rue Princesse Lalla Amina) for around Dh400 per day. **Avis** (☎ 024 474926) also has an office at the airport.

AROUND ESSAOUIRA

If you have your own transport, it's worth taking a trip to one of the small women's cooperatives around Essaouira that sell argan products, natural cosmetics and foodstuffs. Try **Assafar Imitaghant** (off Map p154; ☎ 061 553586) 8km from town on the road to Marrakesh or the **Coóperative Tiguemine** (off Map p156; ☎ 024 790110) 7km further on. The tourist office has a full list of places to visit. Best of all, travel south to the village of Tamanar to see the whole argan process at the **Coopérative Amal** (see p165).

Diabat الديابات

The sleepy Berber village of Diabat, just south of Essaouira, was once a dope-smoking colony made popular with hippies after a visit by Jimi Hendrix in the early '70s. Today it is the site of a major project for a new marina, golf course and tourist complex.

The main reason to visit is to hire a horse or join a trekking tour at **Ranch de Diabat** (☎ 062 297203; www.ranchdediabat.com, in French; 3-/6-day trip Dh3500/6000). You can take a lesson, ride along the beach or sign up for a multi-day trip through the surrounding countryside.

If you want to stay in Diabat, your best bet is the rustic **Auberge Tangaro** (☎ 024 784784; www.auberge-tangaro.com; d half board per person Dh700-900), a remote old house in a serene location. The rooms here are chic but spartan, each has its own open fireplace and is lit by candlelight (there's no electricity on the property). The hearty communal evening meals are romantically lit by candelabra.

To get to Diabat drive south on the coast road to Agadir and turn right just after the bridge about 7km out of town. Alternatively, local bus 5 leaves from outside Bab Marrakech (Dh5, every two hours).

Sidi Kaouki سيدي كاوكي

The constant blustery winds, wild beach and decent accommodation at Sidi Kaouki are fast turning it into one of Morocco's top windsurfing and surfing spots. It's not for the faint-hearted and the waters here can be dangerous for inexperienced surfers.

A clutch of guest houses and small stalls serving tajine, seafood and snacks stretch along the beachfront. You can rent a horse (half-hour/hour costs Dh70/120) and ride along the long stretch of beach, or try your hand at mono-gliding at **VHM** (Village Hôtel Meziane; ☎ 024 475035; per hr Dh90; 10am-6pm) at the far end of the beach. The VHM centre also has a restaurant (mains Dh30 to Dh55).

For overnight stays try **El Kaouki** (☎ 024 476600; www.kaouki.com; s/d/tr incl breakfast 210/300/410, half board extra Dh120), a lovely house with simple but comfortable rooms in white and blue, decorated with local textiles, and with good views of the ocean or country behind. There is no electricity, which makes for romantic candlelit dinners. You'll get a warm welcome. It's a good place to stay for a few days.

Alternatively, try the swish new apartments at **Windy Kaouki** (☎ 024 472279; www.wind-y-kaouki.com; apt Dh750-1150). Although it's fairly plain from the outside, the wonderful rooms display a modern take on traditional Moroccan decor, with warm colours, open fireplaces and balconies with sea views.

Sidi Kaouki is about 27km south of Essaouira. Bus 5 (Dh7) leaves from outside Bab Marrakech every two hours.

Mediterranean Coast & the Rif

شاطئ البحر المتوسط والريف البحري

Northern Morocco is like a living dream. Fantastic elements come and go, leaving you wondering, when safely back at home, if it was all real. The gateway to the region is also the historic gateway to Africa: Tangier, where the ghosts of the International Zone can still be found, among scenes straight from *The Thousand and One Nights*. Heading east, you enter the former Spanish Protectorate, beginning with its capital, Tetouan, where the medina still rings with the sound of medieval craftsmen. The wild and rocky coast contains living remnants of that time, including the autonomous cities of Ceuta and Melilla, with their impressive medieval fortifications and spectacular architectural treasures, and two island fortresses still manned by the Spanish Foreign Legion. Two undiscovered national parks, in Al-Hoceima and the Beni-Snassen mountains, add Barbary sheep and fishing eagles to the exotic mix. Heading inland, one passes through endless fields of marijuana, and finds the mountain village of Chefchaouen, with its central kasbah, set against the dramatic escarpments of the Rif, the home of tough Berber tribes.

Once you're out of Tangier, all of this unfolds with a sense of discovery. This is one of the least visited parts of Morocco, and days go by without seeing a foreign face. But go quickly: the coastline is rapidly being developed into a Moroccan version of southern Spain, with a single highway from end to end nearing completion, and resorts blooming in Martil, M'Diq, Saïdia and even Nador. Unfortunately, that's one more part of this never-ending story.

HIGHLIGHTS

- Stare into the eyes of the Moroccan Mona Lisa in **Tangier** (p176)
- See the dragons launching from the roof of an eclectic palace in **Ceuta** (p191)
- Wander amidst 900 Modernist and art-deco buildings in **Melilla** (p217)
- Smoke sheesha (flavoured tobacco) in the ancient medina of **Tetouan** (p198)
- Discover **El Peñón de Velez de La Gomera** (p214), an exotic fortress still manned by the Spanish Foreign Legion
- Explore the undiscovered **National Park of Al-Hoceima** (p214)
- Stay in a rural Berber house in the picturesque **Beni-Snassen Mountains** (p225)
- Wander the gardens of the kasbah in **Chefchaouen** (p203)

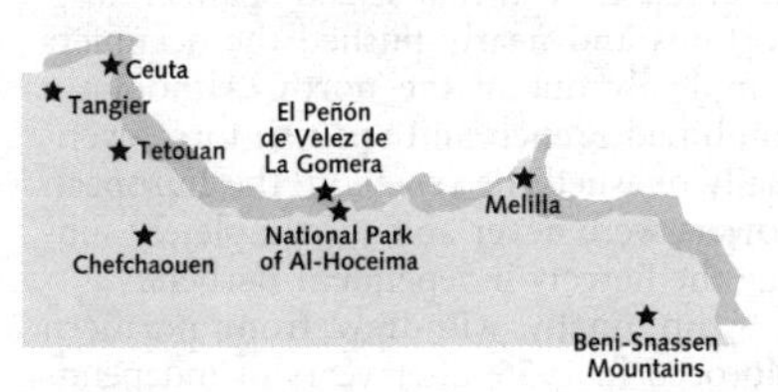

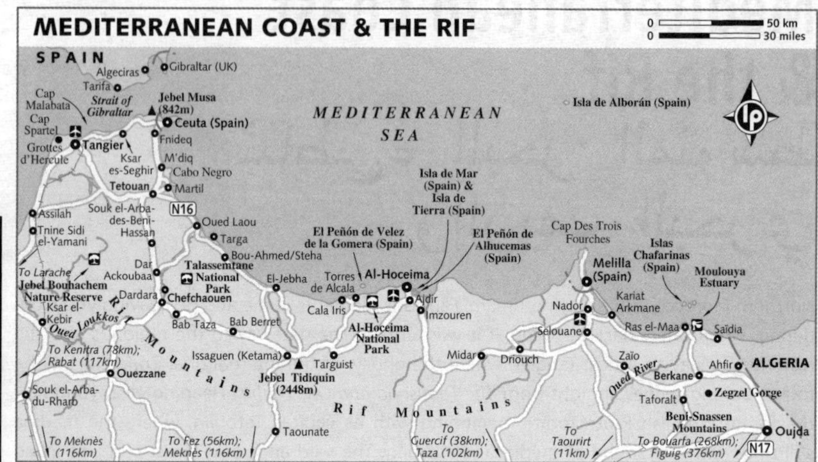

History

Due to its location just across the Strait of Gibraltar, Mediterranean Morocco has long been subject to European influences, especially from Portugal and Spain. During the 15th century, every port on the Mediterranean fell under the control of the Portuguese, with the exception of Melilla, which was Spanish. The Iberian powers were finally pushed out of Morocco in the 16th century, but not for good.

In the 19th century, Morocco was again carved up by European powers, and Spain landed 90,000 troops at Melilla. France and Spain soon came to agreement on a territorial-administrative division for Morocco, which created a Spanish Protectorate along the northern coast, with the capital at Tetouan. Meanwhile, Tangier was made into a special zone under international administration.

It did not take long for colonial rule to give rise to tribal rebellions. In the Rif War (1921–26), the Berber leader Abd al-Krim led a revolt that seized Spanish fortifications and nearly pushed the occupiers completely out of the north. Although a combined French and Spanish force eventually quashed the rebellion, the European powers were never able to completely subdue the fiercely independent Berbers.

Spain finally withdrew from northern Morocco in 1956, after years of independence movements and nationalist uprisings. The exceptions were the *plazas de soberanía,* the last vestiges of the Spanish empire, which spot the coastline (p187). In any case, the whole region still maintains a strong Spanish flavour, including the dominant foreign tongue, colonial architecture, and cuisine.

Climate

Weather along the coast is generally mild, with a tendency toward cool and wet. Average daily temperatures range from 12°C in winter to 25°C in summer. The mountains are colder, with temperatures reaching 0°C in winter. The north also has more rainfall than other parts of the country. Weather can be cloudy and rainy for days on end, as the clouds get trapped in the mountains. Only the summer months – especially July and August – are dry.

Getting There & Away

Tangier is easily the most convenient gateway into this region, as it is well connected by ferry to Europe and then by rail to the cities along the Atlantic coast. Several other cities along the coast, including Ceuta, Melilla, Nador and Al-Hoceima, have ferry connections to Spain, although some are seasonal. If you are making your way to the region from the south, Chefchaouen is accessible by road from Fez, Meknès and Rabat.

Getting Around

The northern coast is more difficult to get around than some other parts of Morocco. With the exception of Tangier, this region

TOP PICKS

- DARNA, the Women's Association of Tangier, Tangier, (p175). Profits support local women in need.
- Musée de la Fondation Lorin, Tangier, (p176). An intriguing photo museum in the Tangier Medina that also promotes cultural programs for local kids.
- Chaouen Rural, Chefchaouen, (p204). A joint Spanish-Moroccan effort aimed at developing the rural economy of the Chefchaouen region through tourism.
- Asociación Rif para el Desarrollo del Turismo Rural (Rif Association for the Development of Rural Tourism), National Park of Al-Hoceima, (p215). Another joint Spanish-Moroccan effort aimed at developing the rural tourism in the National Park of Al-Hoceima
- Gite Tagma, Beni-Snassen Mountains, (p225). A successful new rural hotel in the Beni-Snassen Mountains being used as a model for rural tourism development

is not connected by rail, so travellers are dependent on buses and taxis. Roads here weave and wind around the Rif mountains, so routes never seem to be as direct as they could be, and many feel the lack of investment and maintenance. Reaching smaller destinations can require long waits for grands taxis to fill – or hiring a vehicle yourself. Make sure you understand how long it will take to get back to your departure point.

WEST MEDITERRANEAN COAST شاطىء البحر المتوسط

TANGIER طنجة

pop 1,000,000

The amazing thing about Tangier is that it is much closer to *Casablanca* – the movie – than you ever thought possible. The rich cultural stew, the chaotic street life, the constant wheeling and dealing, the idiosyncratic expats, the corrupt officials, the anything-goes cynicism, the sense of personal fates enmeshed in political change, and even the real model for Rick's Café are all there, waiting to be rediscovered. While construction cranes loom overhead, the city has a personality resistant to change, as if it were quite sure that all attempts at reform were doomed to failure. And that is the very source of its allure. Tangier is more than just a city, it is an ancient memory, a raw part of the human mind, alternately attractive and repellent, but always fascinating, at least for a few days. As the omnipresent photos of the king will remind you, the *Arabian Nights* are still alive and well – and just a ferry ride from Spain.

Like the dynamic strait upon which it sits, Tangier is the product of 1001 currents, including Islam, Berber tribes, Western colonial masters, a highly strategic location, a vibrant port, and now, tourism. This grand mélange has suffused the city with a strange, mirage-like atmosphere, while filling it to the brim with alluring oddities, from its museums to its residents. The dominant theme is Darwinian commerce, of the most intense kind. Virtually everyone is on the make, which takes some adjustment. The call to prayer echoes amidst endless scams, while the rich rub elbows with the destitute. Anything still goes. But the astute traveller can avoid the hassles and discover ample rewards at any time of year – just remember that weather, crowds and prices all hit highs in summer.

For Westerners, Tangier has long been an alter ego, a place to retire from convention and explore the fringe, at least vicariously. After all, this was the city that attracted the founding members of the Beat Generation, that inspired Paul Bowles and William S Burroughs to write their twisted tales, and that has seen a succession of over-the-top personalities, from the Rolling Stones to Malcolm Forbes, pass through like shooting stars. While the cultural scene is long gone – this city of one million doesn't even have a public library – the aura remains, and still attracts. Meanwhile, those one million

Tangaouis face Europe, where many long to go – but cannot – keeping their back to 'the interior', the local term for the rest of Morocco. So, like the Roman God Janus, this is a city with two faces. Just don't be fooled by either one. Ultimately, the Beaux-Arts façades and Moorish arches both hide a place that is neither Moroccan nor European, but a paradoxical blend of both, making the greatest oddity in Tangier…Tangier itself.

History

Tangier's history is a raucous tale of foreign invasion, much of it driven by the city's strategic location at the entrance to the Mediterranean. The area was first settled as a trading base by the ancient Greeks and Phoenicians (who brought the traditional Moroccan hooded robe, the jellaba, with them), and named for the goddess Tinge, the lover of Hercules, whose Herculean effort separated Europe from Africa to form the Strait of Gibraltar. Under Roman rule, it was the capital of the province of Mauretania Tingitana. The Vandals attacked from Spain in AD 429, followed by the Byzantines, and then the Arabs, who invaded in 705 and quelled the Berber tribes. Tangier passed between various Arab factions before finally coming under Almohad rule in 1149. Then the Portuguese arrived, capturing the city on their second attempt in 1471, only to hand it to the British 200 years later as a wedding gift for Charles II. Its value is difficult to assess: the English diarist Samuel Pepys called it 'the excrescence of the earth'. Moroccans regained control of the city under Sultan Moulay Ismail in 1679, destroying much of the city in the process. They remained in power until the mid-19th century, when North Africa once again piqued the interest of the European powers.

The modern history of Tangier begins here. While the rest of Morocco was divided between France and Spain, strategic Tangier was turned into an 'International Zone' of various sectors, similar to West Berlin in the Cold War. France, Spain, Britain, Portugal, Sweden, Holland, Belgium, Italy and the USA all had a piece of the pie, which was managed by the sultan, at least on paper. This situation lasted from 1912 until shortly after Moroccan independence, in 1956, when the city was returned to the rest of the country. During this famous Interzone period, expats flooded in, forming half the

PAUL BOWLES IN TANGIER

Perhaps the best-known foreign writer in Tangier was the controversial American author Paul Bowles, who died in 1999, aged 88. Bowles made a brief but life-changing trip to Tangier in 1910, on Gertrude Stein's advice, then devoted the next 15 years to music composition and criticism back home. In 1938 he married Jane Sydney Auer, but they were never a conventional couple – he was an ambivalent bisexual and she was an active lesbian. After WWII Bowles took her to Tangier, where he remained the rest of his life. Here he turned to writing amidst a lively creative circle, including the likes of Allen Ginsberg and William Burroughs.

During the 1950s Bowles began taping, transcribing and translating stories by Moroccan authors, in particular Driss ben Hamed Charhadi (also known by the pseudonym Larbi Layachi) and Mohammed Mrabet. He was also an important early recorder of Moroccan folk music.

Thanks partly to Bernardo Bertolucci's 1990 film, Bowles' best-known book is *The Sheltering Sky* (1949), a bleak and powerful story of an innocent American couple slowly dismantled by a trip through Morocco. His other works include *Let It Come Down* (1952), a thriller set in Tangier; *The Spider's House*, set in 1950s Fez; and two excellent collections of travel tales: *Their Heads Are Green* (1963) and *Points in Time* (1982). *A Distant Episode: the Selected Stories* is a good compilation of Bowles' short stories.

There is a dark and nihilistic undercurrent to Bowles' writing, which appears to have reflected his life. Fellow writer Joe Ambrose, who knew Bowles well, described him as 'a murderer, a sadist, a voyeur, a poisoner, a polymath, a sexual exploiter of adolescent boys…Bowles was a great writer but his malevolence and debauchery informs that art and must not be ignored if his art is to be understood.' Bowles' autobiography *Without Stopping* (1972; nicknamed *Without Telling*) sheds little light on these matters.

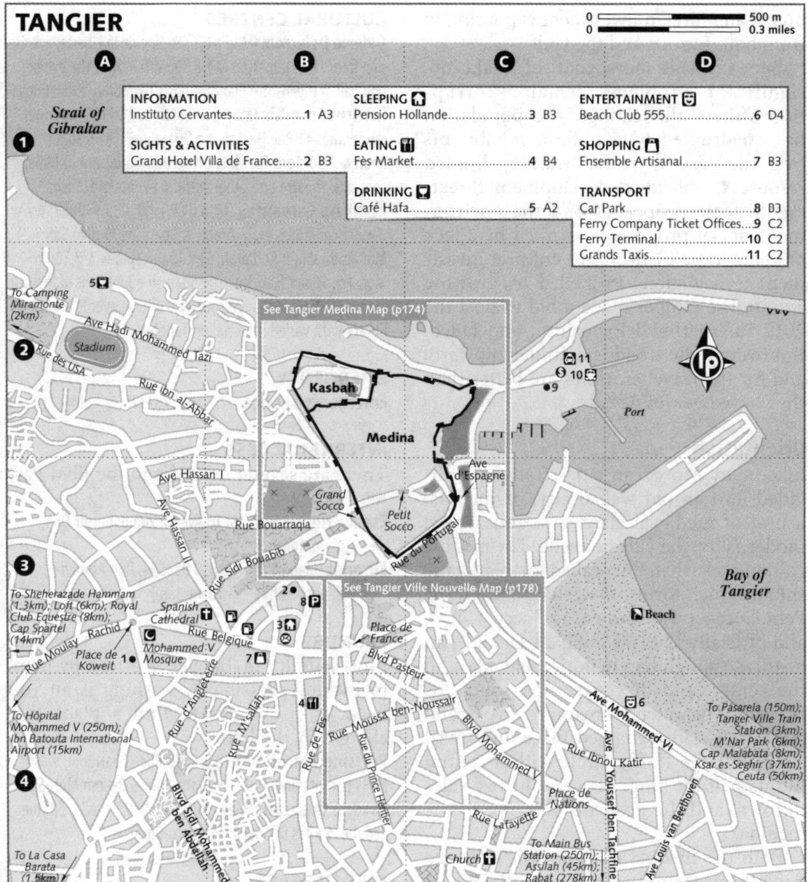

population, and a wild, anything-goes culture broke out, attracting all sorts of people, for reasons both high and low. Socialites, artists, currency speculators, drug addicts, spies, sexual deviants, exiles, eccentrics – the marginalia of mankind all arrived, giving the city a particularly sordid reputation.

When the Interzone period ended, Tangier entered a long period of decline. As the economic base moved on, so did the cultural scene. The city became a dreary port, while retaining its criminality. Having taken a dislike to it, the king of Morocco, Mohammed V, cut off access to key funds. Street hustlers multiplied, turning off tourists. The numbers of expats dwindled, until there were only a few thousand left.

In 1999, however, Tangier's fortunes once again began to change. A new king, Mohammed VI, took charge, and quickly instituted a major tourism development plan for northern Morocco, with Tangier at its hub, managed by the man credited with the development of Marrakesh. Since then the port's container facilities have relocated to a new duty-free zone down the coast, freeing space for yachts and cruise ships; classic hotels are being revived, from the Rif (complete) to the Grand Hotel Villa de France (under restoration); the first riads have taken hold, a la Marrakesh; the classic entrance to the medina, the Grand Socco, has been redone; a new corniche lines the beach; wealthy expats are slowly returning, at least for a vacation home; and foreign investment is pouring in from both Europe and the Gulf.

Beneath this new coat of make-up, significant problems remain: corruption afflicts all dealings; the population has quadrupled to a million inhabitants over the past 25 years, straining limited resources; unbridled development threatens historic properties and the environment; social progress is stymied by a lack of democratic institutions; cultural investment is negligible. Propelled by growing ambitions, Tangier made a bid to host the 2012 International Exposition and failed. But overall, the trend is definitely upward, and for the traveller, times are better than they have been in decades.

Orientation

Like many Moroccan cities, Tangier is divided into an old walled city, or medina, a nest of medieval alleyways, and a new, modern city, the ville nouvelle. The medina contains a kasbah, the walled fortress of the sultan, which forms its western corner; the Petit Socco (also known as Socco Chico, and officially as Place Souq ad-Dakhil), an historic, though barely noticeable, plaza in the centre; and of course, the souqs, or markets. The much more impressive Grand Socco (officially renamed Place du 9 Avril 1947), a large traffic circle with a central fountain, is the hinge between the two sides of town, and the postcard entrance to the medina.

Both the medina and the ville nouvelle flank the waterfront, which rings the Bay of Tangier. The heart of the ville nouvelle lies a few blocks to the west, in the area extending from the Place de France (which contains the French Consulate), down the Blvd Pasteur, and into the northern end of Ave Mohammed V (*not* VI). Here you'll find the main post office, banks, and many restaurants, bars and hotels. A further 1.5km south takes you to Place Jamia el-Arabia, where the main bus station and grand taxi rank are located.

Information

BOOKSHOPS

Librairie des Colonnes (Map p178; ☎ 039 936955; 54 Blvd Pasteur; 9.30am-1pm & 4-7pm Mon-Sat) Tangier's best bookshop, but still modest. Hardly any English-language books.

CULTURAL CENTRES

Galerie Delacroix (Map p178; 86 Rue de la Liberté; admission free; 11am-1pm & 4-8.30pm Tue-Sun) The exhibition hall of the Institut Français; hosts temporary exhibitions.

Institut Français (Map p178; ☎ 039 941054; info@iftanger.ma; 41 Rue Hassan ibn Ouazzane; 8.30am-noon & 2.30-7pm Tue-Sat) Offers a full program of films, concerts, theatre and other cultural events in French.

Instituto Cervantes (Map p171; ☎ 039 932001; www.tanger.cervantes.es, in Arabic & Spanish; 99 Blvd Sidi Mohammed ben Abdallah; 10am-1pm & 3-7.30pm Mon-Fri, 10am-1pm Sat) The Spanish equivalent of Institut Français; offers language courses, cultural events and a library with varied material on Tangier.

EMERGENCY

Emergency Service (☎ 039 373737; 24hr)

INTERNET ACCESS

There are several net cafés in the Blvd Pasteur area.

Espace Net (Map p178; 16 Ave Mexique; per hr Dh5; 9.30am-1am)

Euronet (Map p178; ☎ 039 933544; Rue Ahmed Chaouki; per hr Dh7; 10am-1am)

LAUNDRY

Most laundry in Tangier is priced by item, to include pressing. If washing is all you need, it is cheaper to find a place that charges by the kilo.

Pressing Detroit (Map p178; 10 Rue el-Jarraoui; wash/press pair of pants Dh8; 9am-1pm & 3-8pm Mon-Sat)

Laverie Ouazzani (Map p178; ☎ 039 949683; 50 Rue Zeriabe; 5 kilos Dh50-70; 9am-9pm)

LEFT LUGGAGE

Consigne (Map p174; cnr Rue Dar Dbagh & Rue du Portugal; depending on size Dh5-15; 6.30am-noon) A convenient place to leave your luggage for the day. At the southeast entrance to the medina.

MEDICAL SERVICES

Clinique du Croissant Rouge (Red Cross Clinic; Map p178; ☎ 039 946976; 6 Rue al-Mansour Dahabi)

Hopital Mohammed V (☎ 039 930856; Rue Val Fleurie) On the road to the airport.

Pharmacy Anegax (Map p174; Rue as-Siaghin)

MONEY

Blvds Pasteur and Mohammed V are lined with numerous banks with ATMs and *bureau de change* counters. Outside of working hours, try the exchange bureaus in the big hotels.

BMCE (Banque Marocaine du Commerce Extérieur; Map p178; Blvd Pasteur; ⌚ 9am-1pm & 3-7pm Mon-Fri, 10am-1pm & 4-7pm Sat & Sun) One of several in this area.

POST

Main post office (Map p178; Cnr Rue Quevada & Ave Mohammed V) Post restante is at the counter furthest to the right; parcel post is on the south side of the building.

TOURIST INFORMATION

ONMT (Délégation Régionale du Tourisme; Map p178; ☎ 039 948050; dttanger@yahoo.fr; 29 Blvd Pasteur; ⌚ 8.30am-4.30pm Mon-Fri) The recent investment in tourism infrastructure hasn't made it here. Verbal help, but hardly any printed material.

TRAVEL AGENCIES

The following all sell ferry, as well as flight, tickets.

Carlson Wagonlit (Map p178; ☎ 039 331024; 91 Rue de la Liberté)

Hispamaroc (Map p178; ☎ 039 932178; hispamaroc@mamnet.net.ma; 2 Rue el-Jabha el-Ouatania)

Dangers & Annoyances

Given the number of young men walking the street in groups, it's best to stick to the beaten path at all times, and to take cabs point to point at night. Solo women may be subject to being hassled after about 10pm, and should avoid the port area after dark. If you have a serious problem and need help of the authorities, contact the **Brigade Touristique** (Tourist Police; Map p174; Ave Mohammed VI, Tangier Port).

Many of the hassles of Tangier can be mitigated or avoided by hiring an inexpensive guide (p179). This is particularly recommended for first-time visitors; see the boxed text, below.

Don't be caught without cash. Most hotels, restaurants and shops do not accept credit cards, and you don't want to give out your card number here anyway.

Sights

GRAND SOCCO

The newly renovated **Grand Socco** (Map p174) is the romantic entrance to the medina, a

FRESH OFF THE BOAT?

For many people Tangier is a first: first time in Africa, first time in an Islamic country, first time in a developing country, or some combination of the above. The most common profile is someone arriving from Spain for the day, drawn by the exotic scent from across the strait. If any of that describes you, consider the following:

- You *will* be approached by street hustlers. Their goal is to sell you a fake Rolex, take you to their uncle's rug shop, or become your guide for the day. They are not dangerous, just annoying. If you ignore them, they will typically go away. If not, a polite *'la, shokran'* – 'no thanks' – will help, particularly when repeated. For the persistent, *'déjame en paz'* ('DAY-hah-may en pahs'), Spanish for 'leave me in peace', works wonders. Be aware that if you encourage them, they will follow you until you either pay them to go away, or the sun sets.
- Haggling can feel intimidating, but is only the local sport. The artistry that goes into it is impressive, and may involve several people, each saving you from the last. You know you have emerged victorious only when the sale takes place after the shopkeeper has trailed you down the street. Decline all offers to 'see my other store'.
- Attempts to cheat tourists are commonplace. Pay the exact amount in order to avoid being short-changed. Take a close look at anything you buy: the 'brass' is often tin, the 'fossils' are made of concrete, and those Nike sneakers, needless to say…
- Western cities tend to be segregated by income; here highs and lows exist side by side, with often abrupt transitions. A new world is often just one humble door away. Conversely, a low level of cleanliness does not necessarily mean a high-risk area.
- When dealing with cab drivers, make sure to arrange any fee up front. If a cabbie tries to elevate the fare after you have agreed on it, pay the agreed fare and walk away. If hiring a cab for sightseeing, be aware that cab drivers will often try to convince you to change your itinerary, in order to save themselves time/gas.

For more general information, see 'Dangers & Annoyances' p459.

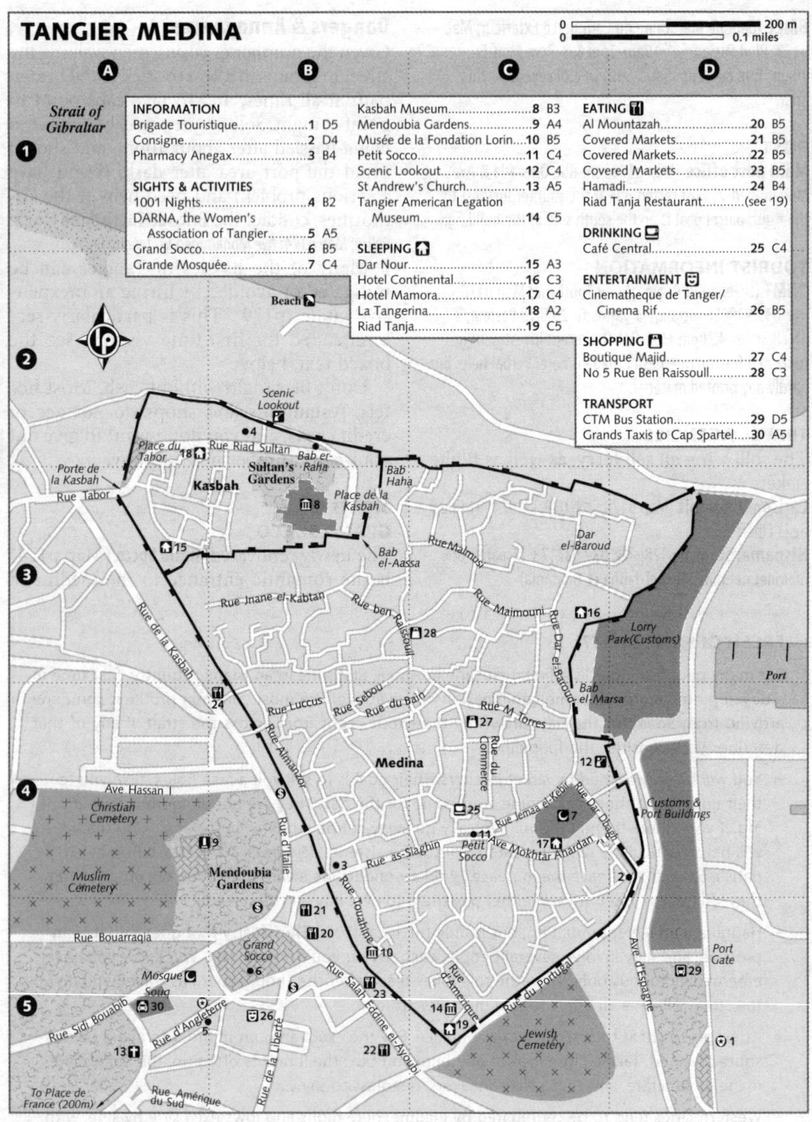

large, sloping, palm-ringed plaza with a central fountain that stands before the keyhole gate Bab Fass. Once a major market, its cobblestone circle is now the end of the line for taxis, the point at which the modern streets narrow into the past. For the best ground-floor view, climb the steps at the highest point on the circle, across from the large tan building (the police station), to what locals simply call *La Terrasse*. This is what you came for, one of those dreamy moments when you think you've entered a movie set. Alternatively, climb to the rooftop café Al Mountazah (p182), at the opposite end of the circle, and sit on the edge: a great place to while away an hour or two.

The Grand Socco is also the hub of several other sights, all visible from within it. First is the **Cinematheque de Tanger** (Map p174), also known as Cinema Rif, which stands on the circle. The brightest light on Tangier's cultural scene, it is the brainchild of artist and photographer Yto Barrada (see p176). A combination arthouse cinema, café and archive, it is the local focal point for anything having to do with film (see p184). Young Tangaouis come to soak up the ambience.

The yellow building opposite La Terrasse is **DARNA, the Women's Association of Tangier** (Map p174; lunch prix fixe Dh30-50; 9am-noon & 3-5pm), a small complex offering an inexpensive restaurant, a boutique shop with women's clothing and a sunny courtyard, making it a popular stop for lunch or just to relax. Since 2002, DARNA has served as a community house to help local women in need, such as those suffering the after-effects of divorce.

Across the Grand Socco from the Cinema Rif is the large **Mendoubia Gardens** (Map p174), a recently restored park full of strolling couples and children playing football. The gardens are flanked by an elegant line of colonial buildings, perhaps the most attractive of its kind in the city. At the top of the central hill is a monument flanked by cannons that contains the speech given by Mohammed V asking for independence.

A short walk down Rue d'Angleterre brings you to one of the more charming oddities of Tangier, **St Andrew's Church** (Map p174; services Sun 8.30am, 11am). Built from 1894 to 1905, on land granted by Queen Victoria, the interior of this Anglican church is in Moorish style, with no graven images, and the Lord's Prayer in Arabic. Behind the altar is a cleft that indicates the direction of Mecca; carved quotes are from the Koran. What were the local builders thinking?

Outside in the church graveyard, there are some fascinating wartime headstones, including the fighter pilot shot while escaping (which reads 'Good Hunting, Tim') and the moving sight of entire downed aircrews, their headstones attached shoulder to shoulder. For entrance call the caretaker, Mustapha Chergui (☎ 079 137583), who has rung the church bell over the Grand Socco for the past 45 years.

MEDINA

The medina is the top attraction of Tangier, a labyrinth of alleyways both commercial and residential, contained by the walls of a 15th century Portuguese fortress. Clean and well-lit, as medinas go, the place is full of traveller's treasures, from fleeting glimpses of ancient ways of living, to the more material rewards of the souqs. Seamlessly joined, its neighbourhoods are defined by five traditional services: a fountain, an oven, a mosque, a Koranic school and a hammam. The thing to do is to get lost and wander for a few hours, although there are a few sites you don't want to miss. Finding your way by map is often difficult, and the direct route is frequently not the best. It sometimes helps to walk around the medina before heading into it. Get as close to your destination as possible, then ask if you run into problems. Young people will be happy to take you anywhere (for a few dirhams).

From the Grand Socco, enter the medina opposite the Mendoubia Gardens, on Rue as-Siaghin, and follow the road downhill until it widens at Café Central (p183), on the left. This is the **Petit Socco** (Map p174), which would otherwise be hardly noticeable. In the past, this was the most notorious crossroads of Tangier, the site of drug deals and all forms of prostitution (rumour has it the brothels are still open). Today the facades are freshly painted, and tourists abound, but given its sordid past, it is still a somewhat eerie place to sit and drink your mint tea.

From the Petit Socco, Rue Jemaa el-Kebir (formerly Rue de la Marine) leads east past the **Grande Mosquée** (Map p174), which at one time housed a Portuguese church. Legend has it that it was built after a rich Arab Gulf sheikh sailing past Tangier noticed that St Andrew's spire overshadowed all the city's minarets. Shocked, he wrote a cheque. A little further on you reach a **scenic lookout** (Map p174) over the port.

Now to avoid getting lost, head out of the medina a moment, and circle down to its southernmost corner, where you will re-enter via the narrow gate to Rue D'Amerique/Zankat America. A dogleg brings you to a door in a covered passageway on your left. Here you will find another great local oddity, and must-visit,

YTO BARRADA

Local culture maven Yto Barrada gives her perspective on the changing identity of Tangier.

How did you end up in Tangier? I grew up here, and went to the American School. Then I moved away for 15 years, most of it in France, but also New York and Jerusalem. I've been here for years now.

How would you describe the cultural scene here? Morose, but with a glorious past. It's strange, people think there is a lot happening here when there isn't. It's all that Tangier mythology. But we're trying to bring it back. And all that mythology helps, in terms of attracting attention.

So it's improving? It has to improve. We've had a lot of infrastructure changes, but that's not enough. That's not what attracts visitors. The cultural infrastructure has to change, too. And people are starting to understand that. There's no economic development without cultural development, not when your economy is based on tourism.

What do you think of all the changes that have occurred since the new king took over? There's lots of incredible energy. Definitely. And there wasn't any before, so that's essential. But there has also been a lot of environmental damage. Our forests are going away. And we have to look out for our heritage. The developers are everywhere.

Is the old expat scene returning at all? It's hard to say. People are coming back to Tangier, and from all over the world, and that's very good to see, but I don't know how many. The ones who do come here are still quite special, though. They come for various reasons – some good, some bad – but they are all looking for that unique something we have – although we do get a lot of retirees now, too!

What's the identity of Tangier today, then? People see us as a bit rough and on the edge. This is the end of the world, a jumping-off place. Always has been. It's like *Camino Real,* which Tennessee Williams wrote here. There's a lot of fascinating characters from various places who have come to this far-away place, and strange things happen.

Sounds like the bar scene in Star Wars. Even better!

Does the anything-goes atmosphere of the past still exist? Yes – but it has moved to property development.

What's your favourite place to take visitors? La Casa Barata (p184). It's basically a huge junkyard. But if you like searching for treasures, that is the place. It is its own little world.

Yto Barrada is the artistic director and cofounder of Cinematheque de Tanger, the new arthouse cinema on the Grand Socco.

the **Tangier American Legation Museum** (Map p174; ☎ 039 935317; www.legation.org; 8 Rue D'Amerique; admission free, but donations appreciated; 🕒 10am-1pm & 3-5pm Mon-Fri, weekends by appointment). Morocco was, surprisingly, the very first country to recognise the fledgling United States, and this was the first piece of American real estate abroad (look for the letter of thanks from George Washington to Sultan Moulay Suleyman). It is also the only US National Historic Landmark on foreign soil, and undoubtedly the only one that contains an American flag in the form of a Berber rug. But you don't have to care about American history to visit the Legation. The elegant five-storey mansion holds an eclectic collection that, in classic Tangerine fashion, resists categorisation. An impressive display of paintings and prints is a dreamy trip through the Tangerine past through the eyes of its artists, most notably the Scotsman James McBey, whose hypnotic painting of his servant girl, Zohra, has been called the Moroccan Mona Lisa – her eyes will follow you around the room, as he must have her. A special room is dedicated to Paul Bowles and the Beat Generation. The romantic map room upstairs contains walls lined with ancient parchments and diplomatic mementoes, including a hilarious letter from the US consul recounting his gift of a lion from the sultan in 1839. It is at this point you realise that you have entered the plot of an exotic historical novel.

Around the corner from the Legation is the **Musée de la Fondation Lorin** (Map p174; ☎ 039 930306; fondationlorin@gmail.com; 44 Rue Touahine; admission free, but donations appreciated; 🕒 11am-1pm & 3.30-7.30pm Sun-Fri), which is another eclectic stop. Here you will find an open two-storey room with an engaging collection of black-and-white photographs of 19th and 20th century Tangier on the walls. Meanwhile there is likely a children's theatre going on in the centre, as the museum doubles as a workshop for disadvantaged kids, bringing life to the static display.

Now continue along Rue Touahine to Rue as-Siaghin, and exit the medina from where you started. Follow the perimeter all the way to the western end, to the highest part of the city, enter the Porte de la Kasbah, and follow the road to the **Kasbah Museum** (Map p174; ☎ 039 932097; Place de la Kasbah; adult/child Dh10/3; 🕑 9am-4pm Wed-Mon). The museum is perfectly sited in Dar el-Makhzen, the former sultan's palace (where Portuguese and British governors also lived) and has recently been completely redone. The new focus is on the history of the area from prehistoric times to the 19th century, most of it presented in seven rooms around a central courtyard. Placards are in French and Arabic, but English brochures are available. Some highlights are an enormous flint tool about the size of a human head; a crushed wine container with scenes of a bacchanalian feast (there must be something in the local water supply…); an extraordinary floor mosaic from Volubilis; and a fascinating wall map of trade routes past and present, superimposed on the map of 12th century cartographer Al-Idrisi (it's upside down). Before you leave, don't miss the exotic Sultan's Garden off the main courtyard, opposite the entrance.

VILLE NOUVELLE

With its Riviera architecture and colonial ambience, the area around Place de France and Blvd Pasteur still hints at the glamour of the 1930s. It's a popular place for an early evening promenade, or a few hours sipping mint tea in one of the many streetside cafés – particularly the landmark Café de Paris (p183), whose retro facade is screaming to be captured on canvas. Where is that Tangier expat Matisse when we need him?

Next door is the aptly named **Terrasse des Paresseux** (Idlers' Terrace; Map p178), which provides

YOU CAN'T BEAT TANGIER

The Beat Generation was a post-WWII American counterculture movement that combined visceral engagement in worldly experiences with a quest for deeper understanding. It reached its apotheosis in Tangier. Many Beat artists – writer Jack Kerouac, and poets Allen Ginsberg and Gregory Curso – were just passing through, while writers William Burroughs and Paul Bowles, and the multitalented Brion Gysin, spent significant parts of their lives here, further inspiring a coterie of local artists. The result was a mixed bag, from the heights of artistic creativity to the lows of moral depravity. Today Beat history can still be found throughout the city:

Hotel el-Muniria (p181) William Burroughs wrote *The Naked Lunch,* his biting satire of the modern American mind, here. Originally titled 'Interzone', the book was written in the cut-up technique developed by Brion Gysin. Ginsberg and Kerouac also shacked up here in 1957.

Tanger Inn (p181 & p184) Photos of Beat customers abound on the walls of this bar below the el-Muniria.

Café Central (p183) Burroughs' principal hangout on the Petit Socco, where he sized up his louche opportunities.

1001 Nights (Map p174) A legendary café in the kasbah established by Brion Gysin, also known for his Dreamachine, a kinetic work of art that induces a trance-like condition. The café was famous for its house band of trance musicians, the Master Musicians of Jajouka, who released a record produced by the Rolling Stones' Brian Jones. It has been 'closed for renovations' for years.

Tangier American Legation Museum (opposite) Houses a room dedicated to Paul Bowles and the Beat artists of Tangier, including the talented John Hopkins, whose overlooked *All I Wanted Was Company* deserves rediscovery.

Hotel Continental (p180) Scenes from the movie version of Paul Bowles' *The Sheltering Sky* were filmed here.

Café Hafa (p183) Paul Bowles and the Rolling Stones came here to smoke hashish.

Café De Paris (p183) The main literary salon during the Interzone, it also drew Tennessee Williams and Truman Capote.

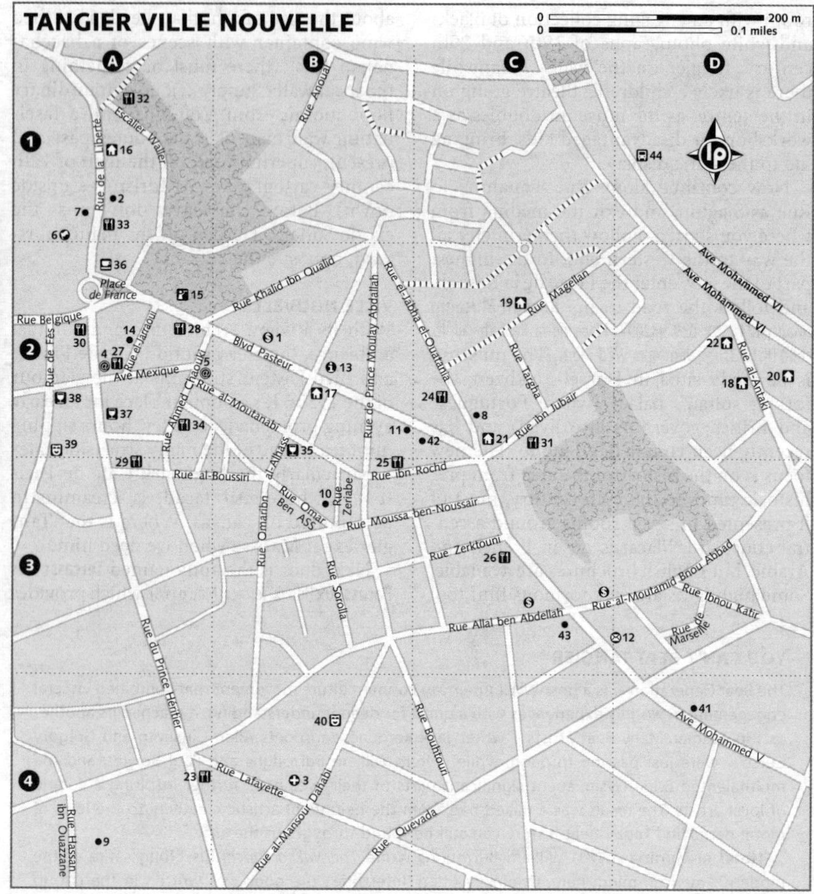

INFORMATION
BMCE (ATM) 1 B2
Carlson Wagonlit 2 A1
Clinique du Croissant Rouge 3 B4
Espace Net 4 A2
Euronet 5 A2
French Consulate 6 A1
Galerie Delacroix 7 A1
Hispamaroc 8 C2
Institut Français 9 A4
Laverie Ouazzani 10 B3
Librairie des Colonnes 11 B2
Main Post Office 12 D3
ONMT 13 B2
Pressing Detroit 14 A2

SIGHTS & ACTIVITIES
Café de Paris (see 36)
El-Minzah Wellness (see 16)
Terrasse des Paresseux 15 A2

SLEEPING
El-Minzah 16 A1
Hotel de Paris 17 B2
Hotel el-Djenina 18 D2
Hotel el-Muniria 19 C2
Hotel Rif 20 D2
Hôtel Rembrandt 21 C2
Marco Polo 22 D2

EATING
Anna e Paolo 23 A4
Casa de España 24 C2
Casa Pepé 25 B3
Champs Élysées 26 C3
Fast Food Brahim 27 A2
La Giralda 28 A2
Le Pagode 29 A3
Mix Max 30 A2
Number One 31 C2
Populaire Saveur de Poisson 32 A1
Pâtisserie La Española 33 A1
Restaurant el-Korsan (see 16)
San Remo 34 A2

DRINKING
Americain's Pub 35 B2
Café de Paris 36 A2
Caid's Bar (see 16)
Hole in the Wall Bar 37 A2
Pilo 38 A2
Tanger Inn (see 19)

ENTERTAINMENT
Cinema Paris 39 A2
Regine Club 40 B4

TRANSPORT
Amine Car 41 D4
Avis 42 C2
Hertz 43 C3
Local Buses for Train Station 44 D1

sweeping views of the port and, on a clear day, Gibraltar and Spain. A set of ancient cannons faces the bay, symbolically warding off usurpers.

TOWN BEACH

The wide **town beach** (Map p171) has been improved in recent years, although it's not as clean in the off-season as it is in the bustling summer. In any case, locals advise that it is not clean enough for swimming, particularly the section closest to the port. It works well for a seaside stroll, however, and the new corniche makes walking easy. It's not a great place late in the day, when muggings aren't unknown. Remember there are plenty of attractive beaches down the nearby Atlantic coast.

Activities

SPAS & HAMMAMS

Pamper yourself at the luxury spa **El Minzah Wellness** (Map p178; ☎ 039 935885; www.elminzah.com; 85 Rue de la Liberté; fitness room Dh150), where there's a fully equipped gym (with superb views to sea), sauna and Jacuzzi, as well as a range of both massage and therapeutic treatments.

Sheherazade Hammam (☎ 039 372828; serenity@serenityspa.ma; Rue Adolfo Fessere, in Quartier California) is a chance for women to escape the all-too-male world of Morocco, at least for a few hours, and indulge the body in luxurious surroundings. This female-only hammam gets high marks from local customers. Located west of Place de Koweit, on the road to the golf course; take a cab.

HORSE RIDING

Along the road to Cap Spartel, the **Royal Club Equestre** (☎ 039 934384; Rte Boubana Tanger; half-hr Dh75, 1hr Dh150, both incl guide; 🕑 8am-noon & 2-6pm, Tue-Sun) is set in the midst of forested hills, a pleasant place to explore on horseback. All riders must be accompanied by a guide, which is included in the price of the horse hire.

Tangier for Children

For kids, **M'Nar Park** (☎ 039 343829; www.mnarparc.ma; Cap Malabata; aquapark adult/child Dh100/50; 🕑 8am-6pm, pool 15 Jun-15 Sep) is heaven, and the only game in town. Located south of Cap Malabata, with great views across the Bay of Tangier, this cliffside resort offers a water park, an electronic game park, karting, a small train, a mini-football field, restaurants, a café and 38 residential bungalows for families.

Tour Guides

If your appetite for adventure allows it, this is one place where it makes sense to hire a local guide. Virtually all the hassles go away, as the street hustlers will leave you alone; navigation becomes effortless, saving you valuable time; you'll learn more, to include gaining access to places you might not otherwise see; and it's cheap. If you have the inclination, it is quite possible to find a young, English-speaking guide who will take you all over Tangier for Dh100 a day – a bargain for navigation alone. For more information see the Directory, p461.

To find a reputable guide, you can inquire at any hotel or the tourism information office, but this can take time. If you want to plan ahead, an excellent choice is **Said Nacir** (☎ 071 045706; www.d-destination.com). An English-speaking national guide with 20 years experience, he specialises in private tours of Tangier for small parties, from individuals to families, and at low rates, thanks to the discounts he commands from vendors. For Dh800, he offers a complete day trip from Spain including ferry tickets, pick-up, entry fees, lunch and guide services – a bargain. Itineraries can also be customised to personal taste.

Festivals & Events

The place to go for listings of events and local info is *Tanger Pocket,* a French-language brochure available at most hotels and online (www.tangerpocket.com). Also see www.maghrebarts.ma/festivals, in French.

Salon du Livre (☎ 039 941054; Institut Français, 41 Rue Hassan ibn Ouazzane) Annual week-long book festival with varying themes, held in late February/March.

Le Festival International de Théâtre Amateur (☎ 039 930306; Fondation Lorin, 44 Rue Touahine) A week of Arabic- and French-speaking theatre, traditionally held every May, run by Fondation Lorin.

TANJAzz (www.tanjazz.org) Usually held in the last week of May, this ever-popular festival hosts concerts by local and international jazz musicians, including some leading names.

Carnaval (☎ 039 321271; Association Tanger Med) Begun in 2007, this is Tangier's humble, if growing, attempt to follow in Rio's footsteps.

Festival du Court Métrage Méditerranéen (International Mediterranean Short Film Festival) Week-long festival of short films from around the Mediterranean, held end of June.

Sleeping

Tangier's sleeping options cater to all budgets and styles, spanning the spectrum from the ultracheap pensions near the port to the chic hotels along the oceanfront. Most budget accommodations are clustered around the medina and close to the port gate. They're cheap but only occasionally cheerful, so it can pay to hunt around. In addition to those listed below, you can find plenty of choice in the streets around Ave Mokhtar Ahardan and the Rue Magellan. Off-season travellers should get a reduced rate, which may even be negotiated further (like everything here). Before accepting your room, however, make sure that it has not grown musty from the sea.

MEDINA

Budget

Hotel Continental (Map p174; ☎ 039 931024; hcontinental@iam.net.ma; 36 Rue Dar el-Baroud; s/d incl breakfast Dh310/396) Nothing appears to have been touched here for decades, making this piece of faded grandeur a fascinating bit of archaeology. A seemingly endless succession of dimly lit spaces is cluttered with more antiques than a pharaoh's tomb; one is tempted to explore with a gas lamp. The rooms are bare bones. The manager, Jimmy, also dabbles in retail, as a dated sign on the way in reveals: 'Jimmy's World Famous Perfumerie, patronised by film stars and the international jet set'. How the mighty have fallen.

Hotel Mamora (Map p174; ☎ 039 934105; www.hotelmamora.site.voila.fr; 19 Rue des Postes; low season s/d with sink Dh60/120, with toilet Dh100/150, with shower Dh200/230) With a variety of rooms at different rates, this is a good bet. It's a bit institutional, like an old school, but clean, well run, and strong value for the money. The rooms overlooking the green-tiled roof of the Grande Mosquée (such as Room 39, at Dh200) are the most picturesque, if you don't mind the muezzin's call. Prices are negotiable in off-season.

Midrange

our pick **La Tangerina** (Map p174; ☎ 039 94 773119; www.latangerina.com; Riad Sultan Kasbah; d incl breakfast Dh400-1000) This is easily the best midrange choice in Tangier, a perfectly renovated riad at the very top of the kasbah, with 10 rooms of different personality, easily accessible by car (a rarity), fairly priced and with highly attentive hosts. Bathed in light and lined with rope banisters, it feels like an elegant, Berber-carpeted steamship cresting the medina. The meticulous attention to detail shows in the old radios in each room which play relaxing music. The roof terrace overlooks the ancient crenellated walls of the kasbah, while below, neighbourhood washing hangs from abandoned coastal cannons, proclaiming the passage of history. Reserve early. Dinner is available on request.

Riad Tanja (Map p174; ☎ 039 333538; www.riadtanja.com; Rue du Portugal, Escalier Américain; d Dh800-1000; ❄) On the edge of the medina, the Tanja combines modern Spain with a traditional riad to form a stylish mix. Rooms are exceedingly comfortable, with huge bathrooms, brick floors and decorations drawn from Tangier's artistic heritage. Some look over the city while the terrace (with an excellent restaurant, serving alcohol) offers grand views over the strait to Spain. However, the riad has lost some of the finer points at this price level, with evident moisture problems, and halls full of rugs that look jumbled and worn. Follow the signs from the stepped gate to the medina on Rue Portugal.

Dar Nour (Map p174; ☎ 062 112724; www.darnour.com; 20 Rue Gourna; d/tr incl breakfast from Dh650/1200). With no central courtyard, rooms here branch off two winding staircases, creating a maze of rooms and salons and terraces that threaten your navigational skills. The effect is dark romance, like exploring a cave. Once you get to the top, there is an impressive view over the roofs of the medina. The location is authentic, but a dense residential neighbourhood without a tourist in sight may not be to everyone's liking. Beware of moisture/mould issues.

VILLE NOUVELLE

Budget

Many of the unrated hotels and pensions along Rue Salah Eddine el-Ayoubi and Ave d'Espagne are little better than the cheapies in the medina. This Salah/Espange area can be dodgy at night, and questionable for women travelling alone. Following are some alternatives.

our pick **Hotel El-Muniria** (Map p178; ☎ 039 935337; 1 Rue Magellan; s/d Dh150/200) This is your best low-end option in the ville nouvelle, and an important cut above the gloomy and often dirty competition, not to mention chock-full of Beat-generation history (see the boxed text, p177). French windows and bright, flowery fabrics set it apart, revealing the careful touch of a hands-on family operation. Room 4 is a great hideaway, a quiet corner double with lots of light, as is Room 8, a quiet double with a harbour view. Noise from the bar below is the only drawback.

Pension Hollande (Map p171; ☎ 039 937838; 139 Rue de Hollande; s/d low season Dh200/250, high season Dh300/350) Tucked away in a quiet street a short walk from Place de France, this former hospital has sparkling whitewashed rooms and high ceilings, though the bathrooms can be claustrophobic. All rooms have sinks; doubles come with a shower. Hot water can be an issue – reception may ask you to give notice, to put on the heater. Of the main rooms, Room 11 and Room 6 are your best bets, but for a budget steal, don't miss the loft rooms up the hidden spiral staircase (single/double Dh100/150, shared bathroom).

Hotel de Paris (Map p178; ☎ 039 931877; 42 Blvd Pasteur; s/d with bathroom low season Dh280/350, high season Dh320/400, incl breakfast) This reliable choice in the heart of the ville nouvelle has a classy, old-world aura in its lobby, although the breakfast area is dim. There are a variety of room types and prices depending on bathroom arrangements and balconies. All are clean and modern, but those overlooking Blvd Pasteur can get noisy. The helpful front desk makes for a pleasant stay.

Midrange

Nicer hotels line the Ave Mohammed VI, offering spectacular views over the Bay of Tangier and close proximity to the attractions of the city, with a couple of options right in the centre.

Hotel El Djenina (Map p178; ☎ 039 922244; eldjenina_hotel@caramail.com; 8 Rue al-Antaki; s/d low season from Dh294/356, high season Dh357/463, breakfast Dh30; ❄) This hotel is basically a half-step below the Marco Polo, with a suitable reduction in price. The rooms are still bright and modern, albeit smaller, and the facilities less impressive, although a cosy bar/restaurant with patio views to the sea, under construction at time of research, will definitely close the gap.

Marco Polo (Map p178; ☎ 039 941124; www.marco-polo.ma; 2 Rue al-Antaki; s/d low season from Dh330/400, high season Dh420/560, breakfast Dh35) This newly renovated hotel is the perfect choice if you aren't looking for local atmosphere. Lots of light, sparkling marble floors and pastel walls make this a bright and welcoming, though generic, space. An excellent, central location across from the beach provides easy access to both the ville nouvelle and the medina, and its popular restaurant is also convenient. All 35 rooms are brand new, as is the huge fitness centre and hammam.

Hotel Rembrandt (Map p178; ☎ 039 937870; hotelrembrandt@menara.ma; Ave Mohammed V; s/d Dh500/640, high season Dh600/760, sea view add Dh100, breakfast Dh80; ❄ 🏊) Asylum-like doors provide a strange institutional ambience to the upper floors of this hotel, where plastic caramel baths don't match the rooms – in marked contrast to the downstairs lobby, with its classic elevator and spiral staircase. However, the glassed-in restaurant (set menu Dh150, alcohol served) is a welcome addition, the green garden café is a tranquil spot to relax, and the swank Bleu Pub, which overlooks the pool, is a popular night spot (beer from Dh20, wine from Dh70).

Top End

El-Minzah (Map p178; ☎ 039 935885; www.elminzah.com; 85 Rue de la Liberté; s/d incl breakfast from Dh1300/1700, high season from Dh1700/2100; ❄ 🏊) The classiest five-star hotel in Tangier proper, and a local landmark, this beautifully maintained 1930's period piece offers three excellent restaurants, three equally good bars, a fitness centre, a spa, pleasant gardens and even a babysitting service. Shaped like an enormous hollow square, with a tremendous Spanish-Moorish courtyard, it has history oozing from its walls. Portside rooms offer beautiful views, but can be noisy when the wind is blowing. The owner is currently restoring its sister ship, the Grand Hotel Villa de France.

Eating

RESTAURANTS

Medina

Hamadi (Map p174; ☎ 039 934514; 2 Rue de la Kasbah; mains Dh40-70; 🕑 9.30am-3.30pm & 7.30-11pm) This is one of the best 'palace restaurants' offering multicourse local cuisine, uniformed staff, live music and perhaps belly-dancing, all of it aimed at the next tour bus. But the price is right, the decor bright and the location pleasant. Avoid the rush hour at lunch, when they try to move tables at 25-minute intervals.

Populaire Saveur de Poisson (Map p178; ☎ 039 336326; 2 Escalier Waller; prix fixe Dh150; 12.30-4pm & 7-10pm Sat-Thu) This charming little seafood restaurant offers excellent, filling set menus in rustic surroundings. The owner, a self-described Popeye lookalike, serves inventive plates of fresh catch with sticky *seffa* (sweet couscous) for dessert, all of it washed down with a homemade juice cocktail made from 15 kinds of fruit (have a look at the vat in back). Not just a meal, a whole experience.

Riad Tanja Restaurant (Map p174; ☎ 039 333538; www.riadtanja.com; Rue du Portugal; prix fixe Dh300) With a reputation for some of the best food in the city, and a romantic view of the ville nouvelle climbing up the opposite hill, this is a great place to splurge, particularly with that special someone. The bi-level dining area feels more like a well-designed living room, with a dozen tables, high ceilings and international decor.

Ville Nouvelle

our pick **Anna e Paolo** (Map p178; ☎ 039 944617; 77 Rue de Prince Heretier; mains from Dh60) This is the top Italian bistro in the city, a family-run restaurant with Venetian owners that feels like you have been invited for Sunday dinner. Expect a highly international crowd, lots of cross-table conversations about the events of the day, wholesome food and a shot of grappa on the way out the door. Watch your head on the way upstairs.

Casa de España (Map p178; ☎ 039 947359; 11 Rue el-Jabha el-Ouatania; mains from Dh60, lunch set menu Dh60) With its attractive minimal style, this contemporary Spanish bar/restaurant is a breath of fresh air after so many mosaic interiors. Snappily dressed waiters serve up classic Spanish dishes, with some wonderful specials like lamb with summer fruits, and there's free tapas with drinks.

Number One (Map p178; ☎ 039 941674; 1 Ave Mohammed V; mains from Dh65; noon-3pm & 7-11pm) The rose walls and white windows in this renovated apartment provide the feel of a holiday cottage, while the red lighting, background jazz and exotic mementoes lend it an intimate, sultry allure. The Moroccan/French cuisine gets high marks from locals, who have been coming here for 45 years.

Le Pagode (Map p178; ☎ 039 938086; Rue al-Boussiri; mains from Dh80; Tue-Sun) If you're tired of tajines and pasta, this realistic bit of Asia is the answer. An intimate and classy dining area, with lacquered furniture, white tablecloths and low lighting is mated with a classic Chinese menu.

Restaurant el-Korsan (Map p178; ☎ 039 935885; El-Minzah Hotel, 85 Rue de la Liberté; mains around Dh130; 8-11pm) One of Tangier's top restaurants, this chic and classy place inside the El-Minzah offers a smaller, more intimate version of the palace restaurant theme – without the bus tours. Well-presented Moroccan classics are served to soft live music, and often traditional dancing. Reservations are necessary, including one day prior notice for lunch. Dress well.

San Remo (Map p178; ☎ 039 938451; 15 Rue Ahmed Chaouki; pizzas around Dh50, mains from Dh150; noon-3pm & 7.30-11pm) An international menu, long on Italian and with a slant towards fish, tables with bright cloths facing the street, Moroccan background music and a mix of clientele – expats, tourists, local businessmen – make this a lively spot with a great cultural crossroads feel.

CAFÉS, PATISSERIES & ICE-CREAM PARLOURS

Tangier's 800-plus café's are a study in local culture, and can be characterised many ways, beginning with old versus new. The former are almost exclusively male, and often shabby, while the latter (such as those listed below) are bright, modern and design-conscious, with light food, high ceilings, lots of light, and – gasp! – women. Coffee purists should see Drinking (opposite).

Patisserie La Española (Map p178; 97 Rue de la Liberté; 7am-10.30pm winter, 7am-12.30am summer) A heavily mirrored tea room, this café tempts people off the street with its pretty arrangements of cakes and pastries. Everyone seems to come here – locals and foreigners, businessmen and courting couples.

Al Mountazah (Map p174; Grand Socco; winter 7am-10pm, summer 7am-1am) While it seems more Floridian than Moroccan, you can't beat this rooftop perch for observing the activity on the Grand Socco: sip your morning coffee and watch the square come alive from the great terrace. Offers breakfast for Dh12 (7am to 10am) and ice cream in summer.

La Giralda (Map p178; ☎ 072 744941; 1st fl, 5 Blvd Pasteur; breakfast from Dh12; 6am-10pm;) The young and beautiful adore this chic and quiet café overlooking the Terrasse des Paresseux, with its plush furniture and intricately carved ceiling. Huge windows give great sea views.

Champs Élysées (Map p178; 6 Ave Mohammed V; breakfast from Dh18; 6am-10pm) This enormous café-in-the-round is high on opulence, with a huge central chandelier and red velour upholstery. The lack of a dress code is the big surprise. Great sticky pastries.

QUICK EATS

In the medina there's a host of cheap eating possibilities around the Petit Socco (Map p174) and the adjacent Ave Mokhtar Ahardan, with rotisserie chicken, sandwiches and brochettes all on offer. In the ville nouvelle, try the streets immediately south of Place de France, which are flush with fast-food outlets, sandwich bars and fish counters.

Fast Food Brahim (Map p178; 16 Ave Mexique; sandwiches Dh15-18; 11am-midnight) Great made-to-order sandwiches. You can't go wrong here with half a baguette filled with *kefta* (spicy lamb meatballs) and salad to eat on the hoof.

Mix Max (Map p178; 6 Ave du Prince Héritier; meals Dh20-45; noon-2am) One of the newer and trendier fast-food joints, with great paninis, shawarmas and other creative fast fare.

SELF-CATERING

The covered markets (Map p174) near the Grand Socco are the best places for fresh produce, particularly on Thursday and Sunday, when Riffian women descend on the city in traditional hats and candy-striped skirts to sell their agricultural products. Fez market (Map p171), to the west of the city centre, is good for imported cheese and other treats.

Casa Pepé (Map p178; ☎ 039 937039 Rue ibn Rochd; 9am-10pm) One of several general stores in this area. You can stock up at the deli here, and buy dry goods and liquor.

Drinking

CAFÉS

For coffee purists, these are three legends. For pastries or more, see those listed under Eating (opposite).

Café de Paris (Map p178; Place de France; 6am-11pm) Gravity weighs upon the grand letters of the grand Café de Paris, reminding us of its age at the crossroads of Tangier. Facing the Place de France since 1927, this is the most famous of the coffee establishments along Blvd Pasteur, most recently as a setting in *The Bourne Ultimatum*. In the past it was a prime gathering spot for literati.

Café Hafa (Map p171; Ave Hadi Mohammed Tazi; 8.30am-11pm Mon-Fri, 8.30am-2am Sat & Sun) With its stadium seating overlooking the strait, you could easily lose an afternoon lazing in this open-air café, but you need good weather. Locals hang out here to enjoy a game of backgammon.

Café Central (Map p174; ☎ 033 079283; Petit Socco; 6am-11.30pm) The premier people-watching site in the medina, newly renovated. See the local Mafiosi arrive in his new Benz, watch odd specimens of humanity drift past, hear the strange shouts echo down the alleys, and wonder what is going on upstairs. It's the perfect place to sip your coffee.

BARS

Given its hedonistic past, it's no surprise that the drinking scene is firmly entrenched in Tangerine culture. It's equally unsurprising that bars are principally the domain of men, although there are a few more-Westernised places where women can take a drink. Many only get going after midnight.

Caid's Bar (Map p178; El-Minzah, 85 Rue de la Liberté; wine from Dh30; 10am-midnight) Welcome to Rick's Café, or at least the real model for the bar in *Casablanca*. Long the establishment's drinking hole of choice, this el-Minzah landmark is a classy relic of the grand days of international Tangier, and photos of the famous and infamous adorn the walls. Women are more than welcome, and the adjacent wine bar is equally good.

Americain's Pub (Map p178; Rue al-Moutanabi; noon-2am) Don't be fooled by the name: this pub is outfitted as an authentic part of the London underground, with white tiled walls, ubiquitous red trim and signage far more authentic than the Bobbies would appreciate. It's the perfect place to hide:

there's no street number, and the phone is out of order.

Hole in the Wall Bar (Map p178; ☎ 039 932424; Rue du Prince Heretier; beer from Dh14; ⏰ 11am-midnight) For chuckles only, walk up Rue du Prince Heretier from the Terrasse des Paresseux one-and-a-half blocks and you will see a pair of swinging black doors, Old West style. Welcome to the smallest bar in Tangier, if not the world. Beer only.

Pilo (Map p178; cnr Ave Mexique/Rue de Fès) A party atmosphere pervades these two floors of local colour, underscored by some high-energy music ('mo-rockin'?) and festive lighting. Women can feel comfortable here, as the management has figured the rest of us out: ask them to show you the Freudian poster entitled 'What's On a Man's Mind'.

Entertainment

NIGHTCLUBS

Tangier's clubbing scene picks up in the summer, when Europeans arrive on the ferries. Discos cluster near Place de France and line the beach, appealing to a wide range of clientele, from grey-haired couples to sex tourists. Cover charges vary and may be rolled into drink prices. If leaving late, have the doorman call a taxi.

Loft (☎ 073 280927; www.loftclub-tanger.com; Route de Boubana) Easily Tangier's premier nightspot, this world class, state-of-the-art club holds 2000 people and feels like an enormous silver cruise ship, with upper-storey balconies, sparkling metal railings, billowing sail-like curtains, spot lights cutting through the artificial fog – and no cover. Go after midnight.

Beach Club 555 (Map p171; Ave Mohammed VI) You pass through airport-like security run by SWAT team guards, and find yourself on a faux tropical lagoon, replete with bridge and tiki huts. Inside, waiters dressed in white satin and fake afros serve visiting mafiosi. Unlike most anywhere in Tangier, the place is crawling with young women, known locally as geishas, who work freelance for the house.

Regine Club (Map p178; 8 Rue al-Mansour Dahabi; ⏰ 10pm-3am Mon-Sat) Welcome to the 1980s. This disco has stayed the same so long it is a museum piece, replete with glass-reflecting ball, purple velour couches, movie posters from *Terminator* and a musty smell. Did we mention the clientele?

Pasarela (Ave Mohammed VI; ⏰ 8pm-3am Mon-Sat, happy hour 8-11pm Sep-Jun; 🏊) This Canadian-owned seaside venue is a large complex with several bars, an attractive garden, an outdoor swimming pool and a comfortable vibe. Music is mostly Western and fairly up-to-the-minute, with live music, although the coloured lights on the dance floor are screaming for an upgrade.

GAY VENUES

Tangier was once a gay destination, but that scene has long since departed for Marrakesh, leaving no establishments behind. Concierges report that the **Tanger Inn** (Map p178; Hotel el-Muniria, 1 Rue Magellan; beer Dh10; ⏰ 10.30pm-1am, to 3am Fri & Sat) and some of the bars along the beach attract gay clientele, particularly late on weekends.

CINEMAS

Films are either in Arabic or dubbed in French.

Cinema Rif/Cinematheque de Tanger (Cinematheque de Tanger; Map p174; ☎ 039 934683; Grand Socco) Your first choice (see p176), here you'll find both indy and mainstream films, mostly American, Moroccan, Spanish or French (with Spanish and American films typically dubbed into Arabic).

Cinema Paris (Map p178; Rue de Fès; admission downstairs Dh12, balcony Dh18) Shows French, American and Bollywood films, the latter two dubbed into French or Arabic.

Shopping

VILLE NOUVELLE

La Casa Barata (Ave Abou Kacem Sebti at Ave Fayçal Ben Abdel Aziz, ⏰ 9am-8pm Sat-Thu) Literally 'the cheap house', this large arena of dealers carries everything you can imagine, from vegetables to electronics to carpets. The best opportunity to find real treasure, and an experience unto itself.

Ensemble Artisanal (Map p171; cnr Rue Belgique & Rue M'sallah; ⏰ 9am-1pm & 3-7pm Sat-Thu) This government-backed arts-and-crafts centre is a good place to see the range of local crafts and watch the artisans at work. There's no haggling, as prices are fixed, but they are also much higher than in the souqs.

MEDINA

The souqs of the medina are a wonderful place to spend hours shopping. Just be careful: there are many things of dubious quality and the novelty of exotica can get old after a while (do you really have a place for that tin lamp?). Following are some unusual places you might want to see.

Boutique Majid (Map p174; ☎ 039 938892; www.boutiquemajid.com; Rue Les Almohades) You can get lost for hours in this exotic antique shop, but the real gem is Majid himself. Straight out of central casting, to include his red fez, he will regale you with stories of the Rolling Stones and other luminaries while showing you his amazing collection of Moroccan doors. 'If you want a door,' he confides in his husky voice, 'you must talk to Majid!'.

Bazaar of Silver Jewelry (☎ 039 336231; 13 Rue Jamaa Jadida) The name says it all: two floors of glass cases full of silver jewellery from throughout Morocco, both new and antique, and great staff, too. Located in an obscure alley near the Café Central (p183), ask there or call.

No 5 Rue Ben Raissoull (Map p174) This nameless hole-in-the-wall garment factory is noted for its fascinating combinations of traditional Moroccan dress and Western women's wear. Watch them winding threads in the street using a modified hair dryer.

Getting There & Away

Tackling anywhere unfamiliar after dark is always more traumatic, so try to arrive early in the day. Remember to change money to pay cab fare.

AIR

The Ibn Batouta International Airport (formerly 'Boukhalef'; TNG) is located 15km southwest of the city centre. Recently renovated, it is now attracting a number of budget airlines (including Easyjet from Madrid, ClickAir from Barcelona, and Atlas Blue from Amsterdam, Barcelona, Casablanca, London-Heathrow and Paris-CDG) as well as British Airways, Iberia and Royal Air Maroc. Check the internet for the latest service providers/schedules, as these are constantly changing.

BOAT

You have two options for crossing the Strait of Gibraltar: the fast ferries owned by FRS and Balearia, which look like futuristic catamarans (to Algeciras Dh440, one hour; to Tarifa Dh320, 35 minutes); and the slow ferries, which take up to three hours (Dh320 to Algeciras). The former are more susceptible to weather delays, which can close the port for days, but they're lifesavers for those prone to seasickness. Tickets are available from the company ticket booths outside the ferry terminal building (Map p171), in the terminal itself, or from virtually any travel agency around town; be sure to pick up an exit form so you can avoid hassles later. The main destination is the Spanish port of Algeciras, with less frequent services to Tarifa and Málaga (Spain), Gibraltar and Sète (France; advance reservation required). The Tarifa service includes a free bus transfer to Algeciras (15 minutes). Book in advance during peak periods (particularly Easter and the last week in August), allow 90 minutes before departure to get tickets and navigate passport control, and remember the time difference with Spain (Morocco is two hours behind).

There is a left-luggage office (p172) just outside the port gates. For more details see p485.

BUS

The **CTM station** (Map p174; ☎ 039 931172) is conveniently beside the port gate. Destinations include Casablanca (Dh120, six hours), Rabat (Dh90, 4½ hours), Marrakesh (Dh210, 10 hours), Agadir (Dh300, 14 hours) Fez (Dh100, six hours), Meknès (Dh80, five hours), Chefchaouen (Dh40, three hours) and Tetouan (Dh20, one hour). Baggage is Dh5 (4kg to 10kg). Left luggage is Dh5 per day.

Cheaper bus companies operate from the **main bus station** (gare routière; ☎ 039 946928; Place Jamia el-Arabia), about 2km to the south of the city centre – the distinctly un-Moroccan-looking minarets are a useful nearby landmark. There are regular departures for all the destinations mentioned above, plus services to Al-Hoceima (Dh85, 10 hours) and Fnideq (Dh20, 1½ hours) – a small town 3km from the Ceuta border. The main bus station can be busy, but pretty hassle-free, thanks to the police office in the centre. It has a **left-luggage facility** (per item per 24hr Dh5-7; 🕑 5am-1am). A metered petit taxi to/from the town centre will cost around Dh8.

CAR

The major car rental agencies are located at the airport. The following have in-town locations:

Amine Car (Map p178; ☎ 039 944050; fax 039 325835; 43 Ave Mohammed V)
Avis (Map p178; ☎ 039 934646; fax 039 330624; 54 Blvd Pasteur; 🕒 8am-noon & 2-7pm Mon-Sat, 9am-noon Sun)
Hertz (Map p178; ☎ 039 322210; fax 039 322165; 36 Ave Mohammed V; 🕒 8am-noon & 2.30-6.30pm Mon-Fri, 9am-noon & 3-6pm Sat, 9am-noon Sun)

A reasonably secure and convenient **car park** (Map p171; 42 Rue Hollande; per hr Dh2, per night Dh15, per 24hr Dh25) is next to the Dawliz complex.

TAXI

The grand taxi rank for places outside Tangier is across from the main bus station. Grand taxis are the beige Mercedes sedans. The most common destinations are Tetouan (Dh30, one hour), Assilah (Dh20, 30 minutes) and Larache (Dh30, one hour). For Ceuta, travel to Fnideq (Dh40, one hour), 3km from the border. There are no direct taxis to the border (Bab Sebta). Grands taxis to Tetouan also frequently wait for arriving trains at Tanger Ville train station. For destinations in the outskirts of Tangier, such as the Caves of Hercules or Cap Malabata, use the grand taxi rank on the Grand Socco.

TRAIN

Tanger Ville, the new and sparkling Neo-Moorish train station, is hassle-free. Five trains depart daily for Sidi Kacem, Meknès, Fez, Rabat (Ville), Casablanca (Voyageurs) and Marrakesh, including a night service with couchettes, the famed *Marrakesh Express*, which should be reserved a day in advance (Dh269/176 for 1st/2nd class, Dh350 with couchette). If heading back to Spain, this train arrives in time for the morning ferry. From Sidi Kacem you can get connections south to Marrakesh or east to Oujda. Schedules are best checked at www.oncf.ma. Note that the **left luggage office** (per item Dh10; 🕒 7am-1pm & 2-9.30pm) only accepts locked bags. A petit taxi to/from Tangier centre should cost around Dh10.

Getting Around

TO/FROM THE AIRPORT

From the port, a grand taxi takes 30 to 40 minutes and costs Dh150 for the entire car, but if you find the cab beyond the port, the price falls to Dh100. If you want to pick up a local bus from the airport, Bus 17 and Bus 70 run to the Grand Socco, but you'll need to walk 2km to the main road.

BUS

Buses aren't really necessary for getting around Tangier, but two potentially useful services are Bus 13, which runs from the train station via Ave Mohammed VI to the port gate, and Bus 17, which links the train station and the main bus station. Tickets cost Dh5.

TAXI

Distinguishable by their ultramarine colour with a yellow stripe down the side, petits taxis do standard journeys around town for Dh7 to Dh10; they charge 50% more at night.

AROUND TANGIER

Cap Spartel رأس سبارطيل

Just 14km west of Tangier lies Cap Spartel, the northwestern extremity of Africa's Atlantic coast. It is a popular day trip with locals and tourists alike. A dramatic drive takes you through La Montagne, an exclusive suburb of royal palaces and villas, and over the pine-covered headland to the **Cap Spartel Lighthouse**. This is normally closed, but the caretaker might be convinced to let you in for a few dirhams. The beaches to the south are clean and quiet outside the summer season, so you can find your own private cove.

Below Cap Spartel, the beach **Plage Robinson** stretches off to the south – a great place for a bracing walk. Five kilometres further you reach the **Grottes d'Hercule** (admission Dh5; 🕒 8am till dark), next to Le Mirage hotel, the mythical dwelling place of Hercules. Since the 1920s these caves have been quarried for millstones, worked by prostitutes and used as a venue for private parties by rich celebrities from Tangier. A much-photographed view of the Atlantic from within resembles a map of Africa. Camel rides are available here, just before the entrance to the caves on the right. A beach ride is a special treat.

SLEEPING & EATING

Camping Achakkar (☎ 039 933840; camping per person Dh20, plus per tent/car/camper Dh20/10/45) Inland from the grotto, this shady site has

THE LAST PIECES OF EMPIRE

Some of the most fascinating places in northern Morocco are not Moroccan at all, they are Spanish. When Spain recognised Moroccan independence in 1956, it retained a collection of historical oddities that had predated the Spanish Protectorate. Known by the euphemism *plazas de soberanía* (places of sovereignty), they have a population of 145,000, and are divided into two groups.

The *plazas mayores* (greater places) contain virtually all the people, and include the coastal cities of Ceuta and Melilla. Politically these are 'autonomous cities', with governmental powers placing them somewhere between a city and a region of Spain.

The *plazas menores* (lesser places) are only inhabited by a handful of Spanish legionnaires, if that. These include three islands in the Bay of Al-Hoceima: Isla de Mar, Isla de Tierra (both deserted, apart from Spanish flags) and El Peñón de Alhucemas, a striking white fortress home to some 60 soldiers. El Peñón de Velez de la Gomera, at the end of a long canyon in the National Park of Al-Hoceima, is another ancient rock fortress, connected to the mainland by a narrow spit of sand – and a guardhouse, one of the oddest national borders you'll ever see. The Islas Chafarinas, 3km from Ras el-Mar, have three small islands: Isla del Congreso, Isla del Rey, and Isla Isabel II, the latter with a garrison of 190 troops. Spain also owns the tiny Isla Perejil, near Ceuta, which was the cause of one of the world's smallest conflicts, when Spanish troops evicted a handful of Moroccan soldiers in 2002; and the Isla de Alborán, about 75km north of Melilla, which has a small navy garrison.

While the two fortress *peñónes* are must-sees, none of the *plazas menores* can be entered, as they are military sites. Morocco claims them all, making their defence necessary. Otherwise, their strategic importance is more elusive than the Mediterranean monk seal, the last of which disappeared from the Islas Chafarinas in the 1990s.

clean facilities, but no hot water (electricity Dh25). It has a café with simple meals and a shop that stocks essentials.

Le Mirage (☎ 039 333332; www.lemirage-tanger.com; d from Dh2400, May-Nov from Dh1800;) This is one of the finest hotels in the Tangier area, with a dramatic location perched on the cliff beside the grotto, offering a view of miles of broad Atlantic beach. The bungalows are exquisite, as the price suggests. Nonguests can get a taste of the opulence in the immaculate restaurant (meals from Dh200), or just stop by for a drink beneath the pergola. From the sunny terrace you can see the Roman ruins of Cotta, where fish oil was processed.

Restaurant Cap Spartel (☎ 039 933722; Cap Spartel Rd; salads Dh40-60, mains from Dh70) This seafood restaurant next to the lighthouse is popular on weekends.

GETTING THERE & AWAY

Grands taxis from Tangier are the best way of getting to Cap Spartel. A one-way charter should cost around Dh50, and slightly more than double for a round trip including waiting time. Taxis leave from the rank in front of St Andrew's Church in Tangier. Petits taxis are reluctant to make the trip one way only – the price isn't much different to a grand taxi.

Road to Ceuta

The scenic road from Tangier to Ceuta is worth taking: green patchwork fields, alluring mountain roads, rolling hills, rocky headlands and cul-de-sac beaches reveal a different side to Morocco, now under siege by development. A complete grand taxi will cost Dh200.

The road begins at Cap Malabata, the headland opposite Tangier, which is undergoing extensive reconstruction; cranes and roadwork are everywhere. For an off-the-beaten-track moment, visit the unsigned **Casa Italiano**, the obvious coastal ruin soon after you crest the hill. While apparently an old castle, it is actually the remains of an unfinished home, c 1900. Follow the path beneath the 'Tanger–Cap Malabat' road sign to the white house of the caretaker, **Banyahim Abdelsalam** (☎ 063 593078), whose door faces the road. It's the perfect place for a picnic, with great views of passing ships.

Ksar es-Seghir, 25km further around the coast, is a small fishing port dominated by the remains of a Portuguese fort, itself surrounded by a serious fence, preventing entry. The beach here is popular with locals in summer, and there are some decent seafood restaurants, but otherwise head on. Just beyond you'll spot **Port Tanger Mediterranéa**, the new container facility relocated from Tangier proper, and an interesting bit of engineering.

The best view along the way is the great crag of **Jebel Musa**, one of the ancient Pillars of Hercules (the Rock of Gibraltar being the other), which rises 10km or so further on.

CEUTA (SEBTA) سبتة

pop 75,000

Ceuta is one of a handful of Spanish possessions on the coastline of Morocco (see p187), and a real gem. Located on a peninsula jutting out into the Mediterranean, it offers a compact dose of fantastic architecture, interesting museums, excellent food, a relaxing maritime park and bracing nature walks, with A-plus traveller support at every turn. The city is particularly beautiful at night, a skyline of artfully lit buildings and bursting palms.

If entering from Morocco, Ceuta is also an eye-opener. Like the former West Berlin, it comes across as a grand social experiment concocted by rival political systems. Leaving the beggars and street hustlers behind, you cross over a grim border zone, a 100m no-man's-land of haphazardly placed barricades, part of a €30 million fence erected by the EU to prevent illegal immigration, to find yourself blinking in the light of Spanish culture, a relaxed world of well-kept plazas, beautiful buildings and tapas bars bubbling over until the wee hours. This experience alone is worth the trip and lingers thereafter.

This cultural-island phenomenon is the essence of Ceuta. It explains the heavy Spanish military presence, the Moroccan immigrants, the duty-free shopping, the shady cross-border commerce, the tourism and the local caution towards foreigners. Many people simply pass through here to avoid the hassles of Tangier, but this small piece of Spain has more than enough charms of its own, and is the perfect weekend getaway. Don't miss it.

History

Ceuta served as one of the Roman Empire's coastal bases (its Arabic name, Sebta, stems from the Latin *Septem*). After a brief stint under the control of the Byzantine Empire, the city was taken in AD 931 by the Arab rulers of Muslim Spain – the basis for Spain's claim of historical rights to the land. For the next 500 years, however, this city at the tip of Africa was like a prized possession, fought over and ruled successively by Spanish princes, Moroccan sultans and Portuguese kings. Things began to settle down when Portugal and Spain united under one crown in 1580, and Ceuta passed to Spain by default. When the two countries split in 1640, Ceuta remained Spanish, and has been ever since.

Recent history has been focused on problems with Spain over immigration and political sovereignty. In 2002 there was a bizarre conflict over the tiny nearby isle of Perejil, after half a dozen Moroccan

SURVIVAL SPANISH

Hello/Goodbye	¡Hola!/¡Adios!
Yes/No	Sí/No
Please/Thankyou	Por favor/Gracias
Where is…?	¿Dónde está…?
hotel	hotel
guesthouse	pensíon
camping	camping
Do you have any rooms available?	¿Tiene habitaciones libres?
a single room	una habitación individual
a double room	una habitación doble
How much is it?	¿Cuánto cuesta?
What time does the next… leave?	¿A qué hora sale/llega el próximo…?
boat	barca
bus	autobús
I'd like a…	Quisiera un…
one-way ticket	billete sencillo
return ticket	billete de ida y vuelta
beer	cerveza
sandwich	bocadillo

soldiers tried to reclaim it from Spain. In 2006 youths set fire to several mosques in Ceuta, after a number of local Muslims were arrested on the Spanish mainland in connection with the Madrid bombings. In 2007 the king of Spain visited the city for the first time in 80 years, sparking protests from the Moroccan government. So far none of this has closed a single tapas bar.

Orientation

Ceuta has three distinct areas. García Aldave, a large piece of the mainland covered by forest and dilapidated military installations; the city centre, a narrow isthmus that contains most of the attractions; and Monte Hacho, the tall, rounded end of the peninsula.

The heart of the city centre is the Plaza de Africa, while its backbone is the Paseo de Revellin, a popular pedestrian street. Tourist information, paths and signage are all done very well, although little English is spoken, even among tourist staff.

Information

To phone Ceuta from outside Spain, dial ☎ 0034. Remember that Ceuta is two hours ahead of Morocco during April and May and one hour ahead at other times, and that most businesses are closed on Sunday.

INTERNET ACCESS

Cyber Ceuta (☎ 956 512303; Paseo de Colón; per hr €2.40; 11am-2pm & 5-10pm Mon-Sat, 5-10pm Sun)

MEDICAL SERVICES

Instituto Gestión Sanitario (Ingesa) (☎ 956 528400; 24hr) Two locations, one next to the Royal Walls, another east of the fishing port.

MONEY

Euros are used for all transactions in Ceuta. ATMs are plentiful; outside banking hours you can change money at the more expensive hotels. There are informal moneychangers on both sides of the border, although it's technically illegal to take dirhams out of Morocco.

POST

Correos (Post Office; 59 Calle Real; 8.30am-8.30pm Mon-Fri, 9.30am-2pm Sat)

TOURIST INFORMATION

Main Tourist Office (☎ 856 200560; www.ceuta.es, in Spanish; Baluarte de los Mallorquines; 8.30am-8.30pm Mon-Fri, 9am-8pm Sat & Sun) Very friendly and efficient, with good maps and brochures.

Plaza de Africa Kiosk (☎ 956 528146; 10am-1pm & 5-8pm15 Sep-31 May, 10.30am-1.30pm & 6-8pm 1 Jun-14 Sep) A smaller satellite office.

Estacion Marítima Kiosk (☎ 956 506275; 9am-9pm) Another satellite office.

TRAVEL AGENCIES

Avenida Muelle Cañonero Dato and the approach to the estación marítima are lined with agencies selling ferry tickets to Algeciras.

Viajes Eideres (☎/fax 956 524656; eidere@teleline.es; Plaza de Africa)

Sights & Activities

Ceuta's history is outlined by the *ruta monumenta,* a series of excellent information boards in English and Spanish outside key buildings and monuments.

PLAZA DE AFRICA

This is the charming heart of Ceuta, with manicured tropical plantings, a square of cobblestone streets and some of the city's finest architecture. Moving clockwise from the oblong **Commandancia General**, a military headquarters closed to visitors, you encounter the striking yellow **Santuario de Nuestra Señora de Africa** (9am-1pm & 5-9pm Mon-Sat, 9am-1pm & 6.30-9pm Sun & holidays) an 18th-century Andalucian-style church; the 19th-century **Palacio de la Asamblea**, with its elegant dome and clock, a combination palace and city hall; and finally the 17th century, twin-spired **Cathedral Santa Maria de la Asuncion** (☎ 956 517771; 9am-1pm & 6-8pm Tue-Sun) whose museum was under renovation at time of research. The centre of the plaza contains a memorial to soldiers lost in the Spanish-Moroccan War of 1860, a conflict over the borders of Ceuta.

ROYAL WALLS

The most impressive sight in Ceuta is the medieval **Royal Walls** (☎ 956 511770; Avenida González Tablas; free admission incl gallery; 10am-2pm & 5-8pm). These extensive fortifications, of great strategic complexity, have been beautifully restored, with information boards in English. The beautifully designed **Museo de los Muralles Reales**, a gallery that houses temporary art exhibitions, lies within the walls themselves. It's a most atmospheric space, worth visiting regardless of what's on show – although

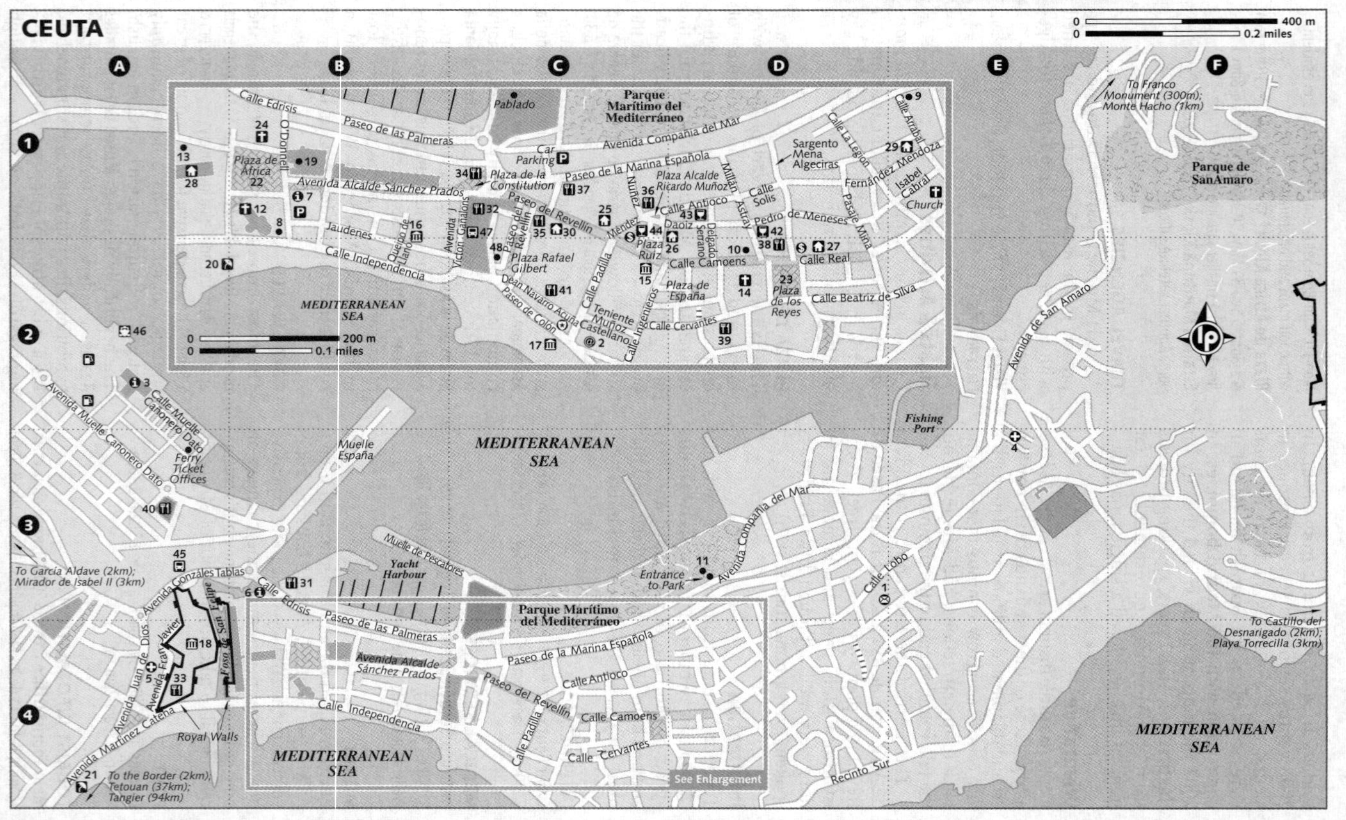
CEUTA
0 400 m
0 0.2 miles
To Franco Monument (300m); Monte Hacho (1km)
Parque de SanAmaro
Avenida de San Amaro
Fishing Port
MEDITERRANEAN SEA
Muelle España
Calle Muelle Cañonero Dato
Avenida Muelle Cañonero Dato
Ferry Ticket Offices
To García Aldave (2km); Mirador de Isabel II (3km)
Avenida Gonzáles Tablas
Avenida Juan de Dios
Avenida Fran Javier
Fosa de San Felipe
Royal Walls
Avenida Martínez Catena
To the Border (2km); Tetouan (37km); Tangier (94km)
Calle Edrisis
Muelle de Pescadores
Yacht Harbour
Entrance to Park
Avenida Compañía del Mar
Calle Lobo
Recinto Sur
To Castillo del Desnarigado (2km); Playa Torrecilla (3km)
Parque Marítimo del Mediterráneo
Paseo de las Palmeras
Paseo de la Marina Española
Avenida Alcalde Sánchez Prados
Paseo del Revellín
Calle Antioco
Calle Camoens
Calle Padilla
Calle Independencia
Calle Cervantes
See Enlargement
Pablado
O'Donnell
Plaza de África
Car Parking
Plaza de la Constitución
Jaudenes
Quepo de Llano
Avenida J Victori Goñalons
Plaza Rafael Gilbert
Dean Navarro Acuña
Paseo de Colón
Teniente Muñoz Castellano
Calle Ingenieros
Plaza de España
Plaza Ruiz
Méndez Núñez
Plaza Alcalde Ricardo Muñoz
Daoiz
Delgado Serrano
Millán Astray
Calle Solís
Pedro de Meneses
Sargento Mena Algeciras
Calle La Legión
Pasaje Mina
Calle Arrabal
Fernández Mendoza
Isabel Cabral
Church
Calle Real
Plaza de los Reyes
Calle Beatriz de Silva
0 200 m
0 0.1 miles

INFORMATION
Correos....1 D3
Cyber Ceuta....2 C2
Estacion Marítima Kiosk....3 A2
Instituto Gestión Sanitario (Ingesa)....4 E3
Instituto Gestión Sanitario (Ingesa)....5 A4
Main Tourist Office....6 A3
Plaza de Africa Kiosk....7 B2
Viajes Eideres....8 B2

SIGHTS & ACTIVITIES
Baños Arabes....9 E1
Casa de los Dragones....10 D2
Casino....11 C3
Cathedral Santa Maria de la Asuncion....12 B2
Commandancia General....13 A1
Iglesia de San Fransico....14 D2
Museo de Ceuta....15 C2
Museo de la Basilica Tardorromana....16 B2
Museo de la Legión....17 C2
Museo de los Muralles Reales....18 A4
Palacio de Asamblea....19 B2
Parque Marítimo del Mediterráneo....(see 11)
Playa de la Ribera....20 A2
Playa del Chorrillo....21 A4
Plaza de Africa....22 B2
Plaza de los Reyes....23 D2
Santuario de Nuestra Señora de Africa....24 B2

SLEEPING
Hostal Central....25 C1
Hostal Plaza Ruiz....26 D2
Hostal Real....27 D2
Parador Hotel La Muralla....28 A1
Pensión Charito....29 E1
Pensión La Bohemia....30 C1

EATING
Cala Carlota....31 B3
Central Market....32 C1
El Angulo....33 A4
El Puente Cafeteria....34 C1
Gran Muralla....35 C1
La Jota....36 C1
La Marina....37 C4
Mesón el Bache....38 D2
Mesón el Cortijo....39 D2
Supersol....40 A3
Supersol....41 C2

DRINKING
Café Central....42 D1
Dublin....43 D1
Tokio Pub....44 C1

TRANSPORT
Buses to Border....45 A3
Buses to Border....(see 47)
Estacion Marítima....46 A2
Local Bus Station....47 C1
Renfe Office....48 C2

if you're lucky enough to catch local artist Diego Canca, don't miss his work.

BEACHES

Easily overlooked, the two town beaches, **Playa del Chorillo** and **Playa de la Ribera**, lie to the south of the isthmus, beneath Avenida Martinez Catena. They are well kept and conveniently located, although the sand is a bland grey.

MUSEO DE LA LEGIÓN

This intriguing **museum** (☎ 606 733566; Paseo de Colón; admission free, donations appreciated; ⏲ 10am-1.30pm & 4-6pm Mon-Fri, 4-6pm Sat & Sun) is dedicated to and run by the Spanish Legion, an army unit set up in 1920 that played a pivotal role in Franco's republican army. Loaded to the gills with memorabilia, weaponry and uniforms, not to mention glory, pomp and circumstance, it is a fascinating glimpse into the military culture that shaped the north, from the imperious statue of Franco, to the explanation of how the legion's intrepid founder, Millan Astray, lost his right eye, to the history of the legion in cinema. They even check your passport at the door. Alternatively, you can enlist at http://lalegion.es. There are guided tours in English.

MUSEO DE CEUTA

This ageing city **museum** (☎ 956 517398; 30 Paseo del Revellín; admission free; ⏲ 10am-2pm & 5-8pm Mon-Sat, 10am-2pm Sun mid-Sep–May, 10am-2pm & 7-9pm Mon-Fri, 10am-2pm Sat Jun–mid-Sep) has a small collection showing the peninsula's pre-Spanish history, with all labels in Spanish.

PLAZA DE LOS REYES

With its green triumphal arch (inscribed 'a monument to coexistence') and fountain, this plaza borders the twin-towered yellow **Iglesia de San Francisco**. But the real treasure lies across the street: the **Casa de los Dragones** (House of Dragons) a fantastic dream that has entered the real world. Recently restored to perfection, this former home is an extraordinary example of eclectic architecture, with Moorish arches, polished brick facades, Mansard roofs, fabulous balconies, and the *pièce de résistance*, four enormous dark dragons springing from the roof. The intricate anagram of the Cerni Gonzalez Brothers, the builders, is emblazoned on the corner. Tip your hat.

MUSEO DE LA BASILICA TARDORROMANA

This superbly executed underground **museum** (⏲ 10am-1.30pm & 5-7.30pm Mon-Sat, 10am-1.30pm Sun) is integrated into the architectural remains of an ancient basilica discovered during street work in the '80s, including a bridge over open tombs, skeletons included. The artefacts become a means of branching out into various elements of local history. In Spanish, but definitely worth a lap through. Enter via c/Queipo de Llano.

PARQUE MARÍTIMO DEL MEDITERRÁNEO

This creative **maritime park** (admission Mon €3, Tue-Fri €4, Sat, Sun & hol €5; ⏲ 10am-7pm, pool Apr-

Sep) is one of several versions developed by the brilliant artist and architect Cesar Manrique of the Canary Islands. The architect borrowed the city walls theme to construct a huge pool deck on the sea, including a grand lagoon and two other saltwater pools, surrounded by 10 bars, pubs, restaurants and cafés. A central island holds a fortress **casino** (9pm-4am Sun-Thu, 9pm-6am Fri & Sat). A pictorial display of Manrique's work lies just inside the entrance, 50m to the right. This is a real hit in the summer, and perfect for families.

BAÑOS ARABES

Accidentally discovered during street work, these ancient **Arab baths** (Calle Arrabal 16; 11.30am-1.30pm & 5-7pm Mon-Fri, 11.30am-1.30pm Sat & Sun), sit on a main road, an incongruous sight. There are two of them, with barrel-vaulted roofs originally covered with marble – the high-tech spa of its time.

MONTE HACHO

A walk around Monte Hacho is an option on a nice day; maps are available at the tourist office or you can wing it and follow the coast. Since it's an uphill slog from town, a good option is to start by taking a cab (€10) to the **Mirador de San Antonio** two-thirds of the way up, which offers magnificent views over Ceuta and north to Gibraltar. The summit of the peninsula is crowned by the massive Fortaleza de Hacho, a fort first built by the Byzantines, and still an active military installation. No visitors are allowed.

Back down at the main road, you keep going clockwise until you reach the **Castillo del Desnarigado** (956 511770; admission free; 11am-2pm Sat & Sun) a small fort on the southeastern tip of the peninsula, which houses a small military museum. There is a lighthouse above, and a secluded beach, **Playa Torrecilla**, below.

GARCÍA ALDAVE

If you've done everything else, the García Aldave can be crossed from coast to coast along the N354, either by car or on foot (a hiking map from the tourist office will help). The route contains a series of circular neomedieval watchtowers, closed to visitors. Several of these are visible from the excellent **Mirador de Isabel II**, which offers great views across the isthmus to Monte Hacho. On 1 November, the Day of the Dead, there is a mass pilgrimage here to remember the deceased.

The road ends at Benzú, a small town on the northern coast, which faces the grand sight of Jebel Musa rising across the border. The mountain is known here as the Dead Woman, as it resembles one, lying on her back. Contemplate mortality here over a cup of mint tea.

Sleeping

Ceuta isn't overrun with sleeping options, so if you're arriving late in the day an advance reservation can be a good idea.

BUDGET

Most cheap places are *pensiónes* (guesthouses), some of which are identifiable only by the large blue-and-white 'CH' plaque.

Pensión La Bohemia (956 510615; 16 Paseo del Revellín; s/d €25/35) This well-run operation, one flight above a shopping arcade, offers a bright and spotless set of rooms arranged around a central court, with potted plants, shiny tile floors and a surfeit of pictures of Marilyn Monroe. Bathrooms are shared, with plenty of hot water, and communal showers. Rooms have small TVs and fans.

Hostal Real (956 511449; fax 956 512166; 1 Calle Real; s/d/tr €34/45/60;) Not quite as cosy as La Bohemia, but good, clean rooms are available. Just check to see what you're getting: Room 7 is a good streetside quad, and Room 6 an equally good triple, but others have no windows and can get musty. Guests are welcome to use the laundry facilities if vacancy is low, and the popcorn machine is a perennial favourite.

Pensión Charito (956 513982; pcharito@terra.es; 1st fl, 5 Calle Arrabal; s/d €15/20) This place is poorly signed – look for the green and cream building above the bar/café Limité. Though a bit aged, the inside is clean and homey with hot showers and a small, well-equipped kitchen. If rooms are full the staff may not be present.

MIDRANGE & TOP END

our pick **Hostal Plaza Ruiz** (956 516733; www.hostalesceuta.com; 3 Plaza Ruiz; s €34-45, d €44-60, tr €54-76, q €64-80;) Sister hotel to the Central, this place has a similar, welcoming style and a charming location. Rooms are airy, with nice pine furniture; the best have wrought-iron balconies overlooking the cafés of the plaza. Bathrooms and fridges are standard.

Hostal Central (☎ 956 516716; www.hostalesceuta.com; Paseo del Revellín; s/d/tr €34/44/54;) This good-value, centrally located two-star hotel is the next step up from a pension, but has the same cosy charm. Bright rooms are small but spotless, and all come with bathroom and fridge. Low-season discounts can tip this place into the budget bracket.

Parador Hotel La Muralla (☎ 956 514940; ceuta@parador.es; 15 Plaza de Africa; s/d from €65/90;) Ceuta's top address is this spacious four-star hotel perfectly situated on the Plaza de Africa. Rooms are comfortable, but not luxurious, with simple wooden doors and plain ceramic tile. Balconies overlook a pleasant garden overflowing with palm trees. A bar/café and gym add value, but the best asset is the bargain price.

Eating

RESTAURANTS

In addition to the places listed here, the Pablado Marinero (Seamen's Village) beside the yacht harbour is home to a variety of decent restaurants.

La Marina (☎ 956 514007; 1 Alférez Bayton; mains from €12, set menu €8; Mon-Sat, closed Feb) This smart, friendly restaurant is often crowded at lunch time. It specialises in fish dishes, but also does a great-value three-course set menu of the chicken/fish and chips variety.

Gran Muralla (☎ 956 517625; Plaza de la Constitución; mains from €5) If you've had enough local food, you'll find hearty portions of Chinese standards here. Window tables have views over the plaza and out to sea. Be careful during off-hours, as yesterday's rice will be waiting.

El Angulo (☎ 956 515810; 1 Muralles Reales; mains from €15; noon-4pm & 8.30pm-midnight Mon-Sat) Here's your chance to eat inside the Royal Walls. The local meats and seafood are as good as the unique atmosphere. White tablecloths and stone fortifications work surprisingly well together.

Cala Carlota (☎ 956 525061; Calle Edrisis; set menu from €7) This simple restaurant has a prime location in the Club Nautico overlooking the yacht harbour, with outdoor seating in season. The three-course *menú del diá* (daily set menu) is a popular choice, while the luscious fish dishes will set you back the same amount on their own.

TAPAS BARS

The best place to look for tapas bars is in the streets behind the post office and around Millán Astray to the north of Calle Camoens. In addition to tapas, they all serve more substantial *raciones* (a larger helping of tapas) and *bocadillos* (sandwiches).

Mesón el Bache (☎ 956 516642; Sargento Mena Algeciras; tapas €1.50; 9am-3pm & 8pm-midnight Mon-Sat) Have your tapas in a rustic hunting lodge. The locals love it. Just downhill from Plaza Real, looking towards the port.

Mesón el Cortijo (☎ 956 511983; 14 Calle Cervantes; tapas from €1; 10.30am-4.30pm & 7.30pm-2.30am Mon-Sat) A classic neighbourhood gathering place heavy on tapas, *cerveza* (beer) and friendliness. Catch up on football, gossip, and practice your Español.

DESSERT

La Jota (6 Calle Méndez Nuñez; breakfast €1.80, tapas €0.60) Offers a delightful array of cakes and ice creams, although the scoops are less than generous. A good place to start – or end – a day of exploring the city.

QUICK EATS

our pick El Puente Cafeteria (Plaza de la Constitución; breakfast/sandwiches from €1.50) Opening out onto a plaza made for people-watching, El Puente is a trendy and modern café-bar with great sandwiches. It's an ideal stop for breakfast. It gets busy, so work hard to catch the eyes of the staff.

SELF-CATERING

The **Supersol supermarket** (Avenida Muelle Cañonero Dato) is the best place to stock up on essentials and treats alike; there's a smaller branch in the city centre on Dean Navarro Acuña.

The cavernous **Central Market** (8am-3pm Mon-Sat) is the local spot for fresh meat and produce, and a vibrant experience as well.

Drinking

Café Central (☎ 956 510393; 3 Calle Millán Astray; 3.30pm-4am) Conviviality reigns in this sophisticated bar/coffee lounge, with subdued music and an art-deco entrance. The bronze statue of an arm lifting a tankard over the bar – a working beer pull – is an eccentric touch. An excellent place for coffee, brandy or ice cream (or all three) at any time.

Dublin (Delgado Serrano; pints until 10pm from €3, thereafter €5; 🕑 3.30pm-3am Mon-Sat) It's like every other Irish pub you've ever been in, but if you need that Guinness fix, this is the place. If the volume gets to you, you can escape to the tables outside. Go down steps where Calle Delgado Serrano takes a 90-degree bend.

Tokio Pub (Plaza Ruiz; 🕑 4pm-3am) A sticky-floor bar worthy of a frat party, although it mellows during the day.

Getting There & Away

MOROCCO

Buses and grands taxis to Ceuta often terminate at Fnideq, rather than at the border (Bab Sebta). If so, the border is a further 1km walk, or Dh3 by taxi. Although the border is open 24 hours, public transport is sparse from 7pm to 5am.

On the Moroccan side, you'll either fill out a departure form at the passport window, if on foot, or at the vehicle registration window (ignore any hustlers trying to sell you these free forms). If you're driving a hire car, you will be required to show proof of authorisation to take the vehicle out of the country. The 100m crossing is surprisingly disorganised, with multiple people asking for your passport. Pedestrians must frequently walk in the car lanes.

Coming the other way, there is a large grand taxi lot next to Moroccan border control. Departures are plentiful to Tetouan (Dh30, 40 minutes), from where you can pick up onward transport. Taxis to Chefchaouen or Tangier are rare, and you'll most likely have to bargain hard to hire a vehicle yourself (Chefchaouen Dh300, 90 minutes; Tangier Dh180, one hour). A good alternative is to take a grand taxi to Fnideq (Dh5, 10 minutes), just south of the border, from where transport to Tangier is more frequent (Dh30, one hour).

MAINLAND SPAIN

The unmissable **Estación Marítima** (ferry terminal; Calle Muelle Cañonero Dato) is west of the town centre. There are several daily high-speed ferries to Algeciras (p485). Ticket offices are around the corner. Much flashier (and far more expensive) is to take the helicopter service **Helicopteros del Sureste** (Málaga airport ☎ 952 04870; www.helisureste.com) from Ceuta to Málaga Airport.

You can purchase train tickets to European destinations at the **Renfe office** (☎ 956 511317; 17 Plaza Rafael Gilbert), or at a travel agency. Several agencies in the ferry terminal also sell Enatcar (the main Spanish coach company) bus tickets.

Getting Around

Bus 7 runs up to the border *(frontera)* every 10 minutes or so from Plaza de la Constitución (€0.60). If you arrive by ferry and want to head straight for the border, there's a bus stop on Avenida González Tablas opposite the entrance to the ramparts. There's also a taxi rank outside the terminal building.

If you have your own vehicle, street parking is restricted to a maximum of two hours (€1) during the day. If you are staying longer, use the **car park** (per hr €0.50, per 12hr €4) on Calle O'Donnell or near the Poblado Marinero.

THE RIF MOUNTAINS جبل اريف

TETOUAN تطوان

pop 320,000

Tetouan occupies a striking location at the foot of the Rif mountains, and just a few kilometres from the sea. From 1912 until 1956 it was the capital of the Spanish Protectorate, which encompassed much of northern Morocco. This and the town's long relationship with Andalucia have left it with a Hispano-Moorish character that is unique in Morocco, as physically reflected in the Spanish part of the city, known as the Ensanche ('extension'), whose white buildings and broad boulevards have recently been restored to their original condition.

Tetouan is also unlike Tangier or the Imperial Cities in that it has not been discovered by foreign tourists. There is an air of authenticity here that adds great value to a visit. The ancient medina, a Unesco world heritage site, looks like it has not changed in several centuries. There have been some recent upgrades – a new bus station, restorations to the medina wall, some public gardens – but nothing like the towns along the coast. This is partly because the city has been greatly mismanaged, leaving it disconnected from the world. But to the savvy traveller, this spells opportunity.

History

The history of Tetouan is mainly the story of its long relationship with Spain. From the 8th century onwards, the city served as the main point of contact between Morocco and Andalucia. In the 14th century the Merenids established the town as a base from which to control rebellious Rif tribes, and to attack Ceuta, but it was destroyed by Henry III of Castille in 1399. After the Rec`onquista (the reconquest of Spain, completed in 1492), the town was rebuilt by Andalucian refugees. It prospered due in part to their skills, and to thriving pirate activity.

Moulay Ismail built Tetouan's defensive walls in the 17th century, and the town's trade links with Spain improved and developed. In 1860, the Spanish took the town under Leopoldo O'Donnell, who extensively Europeanised it, but upon recapture two years later the Moors removed all signs of European influence.

At the turn of the 20th century, Spanish forces occupied Tetouan for three years, claiming it was protecting Ceuta from Rif tribes. In 1913 the Spanish made Tetouan the capital of their protectorate, which was abandoned in 1956 when Morocco regained independence. Lately the Andalucian government has provided a great cultural boost to the city by sponsoring the restoration of the Ensanche.

Orientation

The Ensanche is centred on Place Moulay el-Mehdi and the pedestrian stretch of Ave Mohammed V, which runs east to Plaza al Jala. Here you'll find hotels, banks and places to eat. The entrance to the medina is off the grand Place Hassan II, which faces the Royal Palace. The rest of the sprawling town has little to offer the visitor.

Information

CULTURAL CENTRES

Institut Français (☎ 039 961212; institutfrancais@iftetouan.ma; 13 Rue Chakib Arsalane; 🕑 8am-noon & 3-6pm Tue-Fri) Puts on films, concerts and exhibitions, as well as offering a library and café. Popular with locals, especially youth.

La Casa de España (Rue Chakib Arsalane, behind church; 🕑 bar/restaurant noon-3pm & 7-11pm) The Spanish version of the above, but more of a club. Has a TV room, café, bar/restaurant and disco. Very well done and worth a visit.

INTERNET ACCESS

Imex Media (☎ 039 961533; 19 Ave Mohammed V; per hr Dh5)

Remote Studios (☎ 039 711172; 13 Ave Mohammed V; per hr Dh9; 🕑 9am-midnight)

MEDICAL SERVICES

Clinique du Croissant Rouge (Red Cross Clinic; ☎ 039 962020; Place al-Hammama, Quartier Scolaire)

Dépot de Médicaments d'Urgence (☎ 039 965902; 7 Rue al-Ouahda; 🕑 9pm-9.30am) Nighttime pharmacy.

Main hospital (☎ 039 972430; Martil Rd) About 2km out of town.

Pharmacie Derdabi (☎ 039 991109; Fendak Najjar-Sakiat Foukia; 🕑 9am-7pm) Daytime pharmacy in medina.

MONEY

There are plenty of banks with ATMs along Ave Mohammed V.

BMCE (Place Moulay el-Mehdi; 🕑 10am-2pm & 4-8pm) Change cash and travellers cheques outside regular banking hours.

POST

Post office (Place Moulay el-Mehdi; 🕑 8am-4.30pm Mon-Fri)

TOURIST INFORMATION

ONMT (Délégation Régionale du Tourisme; ☎ 039 961915; fax 039 961914; 30 Ave Mohammed V; 🕑 8.30am-12.30pm & 1.30-4.30pm Mon-Fri) With several employees and no written information on the history of the medina, this place defies common sense. The 1951 mural of northern Morocco on the 2nd floor is the only reason to visit.

TRAVEL AGENCIES

Royal Air Maroc (☎ 039 961577; 5 Ave Mohammed V; 🕑 9am-noon & 2.30-6.30pm Mon-Sat)

Voyages Hispamaroc (☎ 039 713338; 23 Ave Mohammed V; 🕑 8.30am-12.30pm & 3-7pm, closed Sat morning & Sun)

Sights

MEDINA

The whitewashed medina of Tetouan is an authentic time machine, and very traveller-friendly, with wide, moped-free lanes, few

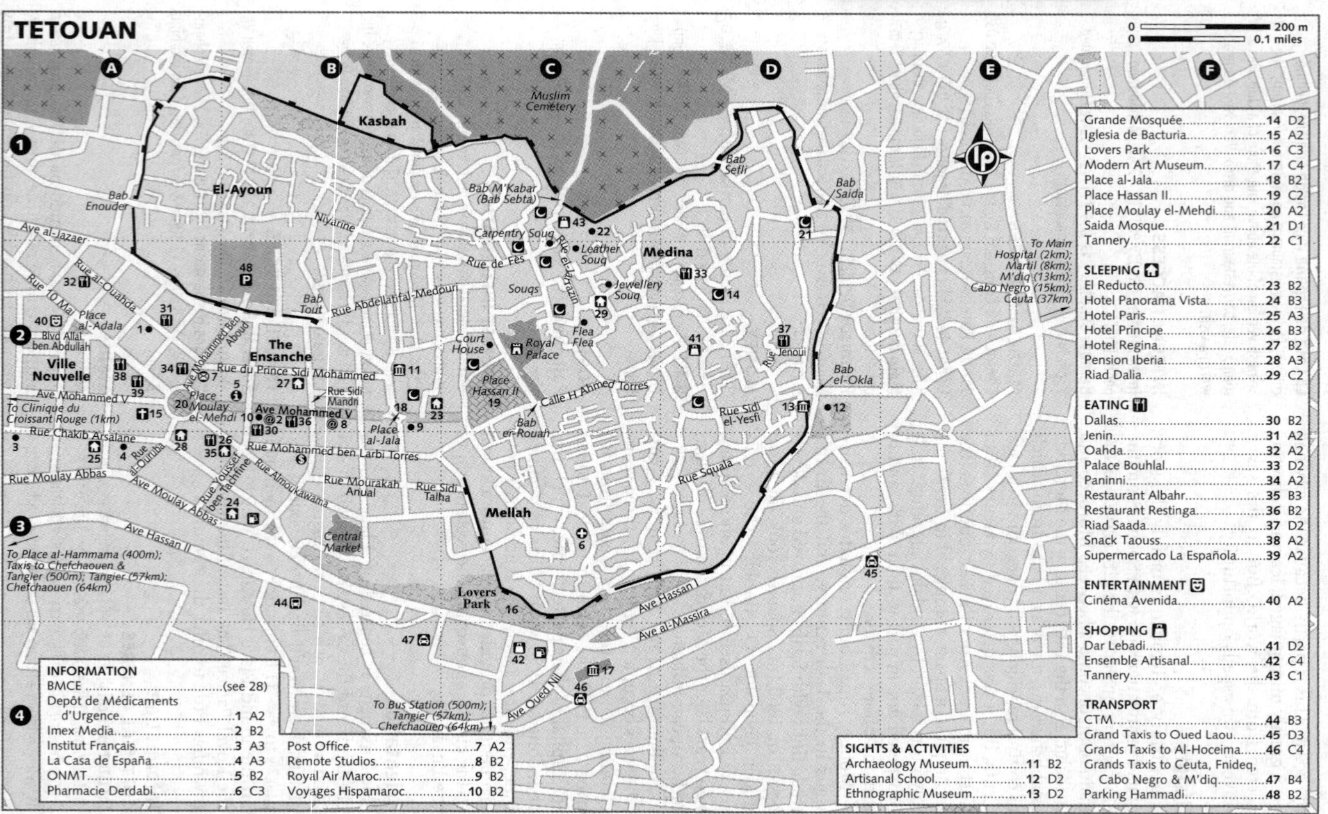
TETOUAN
0 200 m
0 0.1 miles
A
B
C
D
E
F
1
2
3
4
Kasbah
El-Ayoun
Muslim Cemetery
Medina
Mellah
The Ensanche
Ville Nouvelle
Bab Enouder
Bab M'Kabar (Bab Sebta)
Bab Sefli
Bab Saida
Bab el-Okla
Bab Tout
Bab er-Rouah
Carpentry Souq
Leather Souq
Jewellery Souq
Souqs
Flea
Flea
Royal Palace
Court House
Place Hassan II
Place al-Jala
Place Moulay el-Mehdi
Place al-Adala
Lovers Park
Central Market
Niyarine
Ave al-Jazaer
Rue al-Ouahda
Rue 10 Mai
Blvd Allal ben Abdullah
Ave Mohammed Ben Aboud
Rue du Prince Sidi Mohammed
Rue Sidi Mandri
Ave Mohammed V
Rue Chakib Arsalane
Rue al-Ouriba
Rue Moulay Abbas
Ave Moulay Abbas
Rue Youssef ben Tachfine
Rue Almoukawama
Rue Mohammed ben Larbi Torres
Rue Mourakah Anual
Rue Sidi Talha
Rue Abdellatifal-Medouri
Rue de Fès
Rue el-Jarrazin
Calle H Ahmed Torres
Rue Sidi el-Yesfi
Rue Jenoui
Rue Squala
Ave Hassan II
Ave al-Massira
Ave Oued Nil
To Clinique du Croissant Rouge (1km)
To Place al-Hammama (400m); Taxis to Chefchaouen & Tangier (500m); Tangier (57km); Chefchaouen (64km)
To Bus Station (500m); Tangier (57km); Chefchaouen (64km)
To Main Hospital (2km); Martil (8km); M'diq (13km); Cabo Negro (15km); Ceuta (37km)
INFORMATION
BMCE (see 28)
Depôt de Médicaments d'Urgence 1 A2
Imex Media 2 B2
Institut Français 3 A3
La Casa de España 4 A3
ONMT 5 B2
Pharmacie Derdabi 6 C3
Post Office 7 A2
Remote Studios 8 B2
Royal Air Maroc 9 B2
Voyages Hispamaroc 10 B2
SIGHTS & ACTIVITIES
Archaeology Museum 11 B2
Artisanal School 12 D2
Ethnographic Museum 13 D2
Grande Mosquée 14 D2
Iglesia de Bacturia 15 A2
Lovers Park 16 C3
Modern Art Museum 17 C4
Place al-Jala 18 B2
Place Hassan II 19 C2
Place Moulay el-Mehdi 20 A2
Saida Mosque 21 D1
Tannery 22 C1
SLEEPING
El Reducto 23 B2
Hotel Panorama Vista 24 B3
Hotel Paris 25 A3
Hotel Principe 26 B3
Hotel Regina 27 B2
Pension Iberia 28 A3
Riad Dalia 29 C2
EATING
Dallas 30 B2
Jenin 31 A2
Oahda 32 A2
Palace Bouhlal 33 D2
Paninni 34 A2
Restaurant Albahr 35 B3
Restaurant Restinga 36 B2
Riad Saada 37 D2
Snack Taouss 38 A2
Supermercado La Española 39 A2
ENTERTAINMENT
Cinéma Avenida 40 A2
SHOPPING
Dar Lebadi 41 D2
Ensemble Artisanal 42 C4
Tannery 43 C1
TRANSPORT
CTM 44 B3
Grand Taxis to Oued Laou 45 D3
Grands Taxis to Al-Hoceima 46 C4
Grands Taxis to Ceuta, Fnideq, Cabo Negro & M'diq 47 B4
Parking Hammadi 48 B2

street hustlers, amiable residents and a general lack of congestion, particularly in the large residential areas. In the commercial spaces, the sights and sounds of traditional life are everywhere: craftsmen pound gold, silk merchants offer thousands of spools of multicoloured thread and bakers tend the public ovens. There are some 40 mosques as well, of which the **Grande Mosquée** and **Saida Mosque** both northeast of Place Hassan II, are the most impressive, although non-Muslims are not allowed to enter. If you get lost, a few dirhams in local hands will get you to any doorstep.

Just inside the picture-perfect eastern gate, Bab el-Okla, is the **Ethnographic Museum** (admission Dh10; 9am-4pm Mon-Fri) which is worth a visit for the terrace views of the Rif (ask the caretaker to open it for you, if necessary), its pleasant garden with old cannons and the display of silk wedding gowns. Otherwise, you'll see some of the same decorative features in the palace restaurants.

Just outside Bab el-Okla is the **Artisanal School** (☎ 039 972721; admission Dh10; 8am-noon & 2.30-5.30pm Mon-Fri) the best artisan centre in northern Morocco. This is a fascinating opportunity to see masters teaching apprentices traditional arts, including ornamental woodwork, silk costumes, carved plaster, intricate mosaics and decorative rifles. A fantastic central treasury holds the best of the best – don't miss the ceiling. Staff will open it upon request. The building itself is of interest, set around a large courtyard, with fine doors upstairs.

The medina is bordered to the south by newly renovated **Lovers Park** a pleasant escape. At the time of research the old train station just south of here was being transformed into the **Modern Art Museum** projected to open by 2009.

PLACE HASSAN II

The broad and empty **Place Hassan II**, which is mostly roped off for security reasons, links the medina to the Ensanche. It looks like it houses the Wizard of Oz with guards standing in front of the long flat facade of the royal palace, and four fountains with central columns towering all around. These are not minarets, as one might suppose, but art-nouveau light towers designed by a student of Gaudí. The large decorations on the opposite wall are abstract Hands of Fatima, a common symbol used to ward off the evil eye. There are a few nondescript cafés which are good for a rest, particularly on the 2nd floor, which allows a grander view.

THE ENSANCHE

Take in the Ensanche by walking along Ave Mohammed V from **Place al-Jala** to **Place Moulay el-Mehdi**. The broad boulevard is lined by bright white Spanish colonial architecture, with a few art-deco elements, reminiscent of styles found elsewhere (eg Cuba, the Philippines) and recently restored by the Andalucian government. A few blocks from the Place al-Jala there is an **Archaeology Museum** (Ave al-Jazaer; admission Dh10; 8.30am-noon & 2.30-6.30pm Mon-Fri) with an excellent collection of artefacts from the Roman ruins at Lixus (p138). However, during research the published hours were not being adhered to; the museum had been closed for a week, and it was not clear when it would reopen. The Catholic **Iglesia de Bacturia** (Place Moulay el-Mehdi; Sunday mass 11am open to visitors at 7pm), was built in 1917 and is still active.

Sleeping

Due to the rapid development of the nearby coast the first question one must now answer is whether to stay in town or not. Tetouan's port, Martil, is only an inexpensive 10 minute cab ride away; M'Diq, the classiest option, is twice that. The contrast could not be greater between the ancient medina and these modern Floridian beachfronts, and can be either jarring or a relief.

If you choose the city, your next decision is whether to stay in the medina or not. A night or two within the ancient walls is an unforgettable adventure if you have not done so elsewhere, but longer stays can be taxing.

BUDGET

our pick Pension Iberia (☎ 039 963679; 5 Place Moulay el-Mehdi; s/d/tr Dh50/80/120) This is the best budget option, with classic high-ceilinged rooms and shuttered balconies that open out to the Place Moulay el-Mehdi – book Room 11 if possible. Views of the white city flowing over the hills and the fountain in the Place – better observed from here than the street – add a dash of romance.

Baths are shared, and hot showers an extra Dh10. Conveniently located, with public parking (Parking Hammadi; Ave al-Jazaer) 100m away.

Hotel Príncipe (☎ 033 113128; 20 Rue Youssef ben Tachfine; s/d/tr without shower Dh70/80/140, s/d/tr with shower Dh90/120/180) Another aesthetically challenged budget option, where all floor tiles, bedspreads and wallpaper appears deliberately chosen to assault the senses. The visual noise is matched by the audio from the boisterous male café below. Furniture is worn, paint is peeling, though staff are accommodating. Pay up for a room with a shower.

Hotel Regina (☎ 039 962113; 8 Rue Sidi Mandri; s/d Dh150/175) One of the larger budget choices, the Regina initially feels a bit tired, but the whitewashed walls and crazy 1970s fabrics manage to wake you up. While the attached bathrooms are sometimes worn, and cleanliness is iffy, it's decent value for the price.

Hotel Paris (☎ 039 966750; 31 Rue Chakib Arsalane; s/d Dh207/250, breakfast Dh35 summer only) Not your honeymoon suite, but performs the basic functions. The simple, uninspiring rooms are clean, but the bathrooms are small, and with no separation between shower and toilet. Institutional hallways accelerate you outdoors.

MIDRANGE & TOP END

Riad Dalia (☎ 018 025049; www.riad-dalia.com; 25 Rue Ouessaa; s without bathroom Dh150, small ste Dh400, master ste Dh600) The first riad hotel in the medina, this funky, family-run option is an eclectic adventure. The 300-year-old former Dutch consul's house has been transformed into a hotel without much renovation, so it feels like the consul may turn up at any moment. In fact, the proprietor has his ancient letters in a scrapbook at the front desk, not to mention his stamp collection. The master suite is immense and fit for royalty. In the upper levels, students smoke sheesha (a flavoured tobacco) or court furtively amid a romantic mystery-novel ambience. The mixed pricing allows a room for every budget, but do be careful of the suicide stairs to the roof, especially when wet.

Hotel Panorama Vista (☎ 039 964970; Ave Moulay Abbas; s/d incl breakfast Dh307/404; ❄) This is the best bet outside the medina. The rooms are chain-hotel style, without any local ambience, but clean and with dramatic views over the Rif. The popular café, with its wall of glass, offers a strong Moroccan continental breakfast. In the unpopulated off-season there is no heating – a challenge cured with piles of blankets. The 10 minute explanation as to why all the stoppers have been removed from the hotel baths is added entertainment value – until you want a bath.

El Reducto (☎ 039 968120; www.riadtetouan.com; Zanqat Zawya 38; s/d incl breakfast Dh425/550, half-board Dh500/700) This is the premier place to stay in Tetouan if you want an upscale medina experience at a very reasonable price. The spotless, palatial rooms are truly fantastic with big baths (one has a Jacuzzi for two), the highest quality antique furniture and beautiful silk bedspreads. Marble staircases and elegant tiled walls complete the royal ambience, the product of a two-year restoration completed in 2006. So you always wanted to be a sultan?

Eating

RESTAURANTS

Tetouan is not known for its restaurants. Aside from two excellent palace options (popular with tour groups, so reserve ahead) you are restricted to grilled food and sandwiches.

Restaurant Restinga (21 Ave Mohammed V; fish dishes from Dh50, beer Dh18; 🕑 noon-9pm) The open-air courtyard covered by a canopy of eucalyptus is this charming restaurant's primary attraction – along with the rare alcohol license. It's a great place to duck out of the crowded boulevard for a rest and a beer, as well as some seafood from the coast.

Restaurant Albahr (☎ 066 689675; 21 Rue Almoukawama; mains from Dh30; 🕑 noon-9pm) Nothing fancy here – fried foods, burgers and fish and chips – but they do it well and the price is right. Salads a plus.

Riad Saada (☎ 061 299846; 18 Rue Jenoui; set menu Dh100; 🕑 8am-late) This is a classic Moroccan experience, from the endless plates of food (soup, couscous, tajines, salads, kebabs, grilled cakes) to the entertainment (belly dancing, traditional musicians) to the superb setting, including a spectacular open ceiling with an enormous pendulum lamp, two golden throne chairs for weddings and beautiful carved plaster walls. Enter via Bab el-Okla, turn right immediately, take second left at Optique Seffar, and you will see the entrance, a very long tiled corridor.

Palace Bouhlal (☎ 039 998797; 48 Jamaa Kebir; set menu Dh100; 🕑 10am-4pm) Another sumptuous palace option with plush couches, wall rugs, intimate dining spaces (especially upstairs), gurgling fountains and a grand Moorish arch complementing the usual four-course meal. Follow the lane north around the Grande Mosquée and look for signs directing you down a tiny alley. Be sure to duck into Les Secrets des Plantes first, on the right just before the entrance, where 670 spices line the walls.

CAFÉS & PATISSERIES

our pick **Jenin** (☎ 039 962246; 8 Rue al-Ouahda; coffee Dh8; 🕑 6am-9.30pm winter, 6am-11pm summer, closed Fri afternoon) This sparkling, modern café is the trendiest in town. The 10 blends of different fruit juices are the highlight, along with the presence of courting couples and groups of young women. A world away from the smoky male cafés on the same block.

Oahda (☎ 039 966794; 16 Rue al-Ouahda; 🕑 7am-9pm, closed Fri afternoon) Another female-friendly café, not as nicely appointed as Jenin but just as popular with locals. A bit claustrophobic on the upper floor.

Dallas (☎ 039 966069; 11 Rue Youssef ben Tachfine; 🕑 5am-10pm) Yes, named after the TV show, but otherwise the name has no bearing on this place, a patisserie stacked to the rafters with plates of pastries. This is where local families come to load up on sweets. One block off Ave Mohammed V.

QUICK EATS

Snack Taouss (☎ 061 231158; 3 Rue 10 Mai; burgers Dh18; 🕑 7am-10pm) Known for its burgers and chips, this little snack bar also does decent, inexpensive pizzas, salads, *harira* (lentil soup), tajines and more. There's a small seating area upstairs (handy if you're waiting for a pizza), or you can eat on the move. If it's full, there's a similar place, 10 Mai, next door.

Paninni (☎ 039 700654; 5-6 Ave Mohammed Ben Aboud; paninni Dh18; 🕑 noon-11pm) Made to order sandwiches make this a standout option. Choose from a smorgasbord of ingredients both normal and exotic.

SELF-CATERING

There's loads of fresh fruit and veg for sale in the medina on the road leading east to Bab el-Okla. The central market (closed Friday) around the corner from Lovers Park puts on a good display, with fish brought in from the coast. **Supermercado La Española** (Rue 10 Mai; 🕑 10am-9pm) is small but easy to find. It sells alcohol and other staples.

Drinking

As is the Moroccan norm, Tetouan's drinking establishments are firmly in the male sphere. The more welcoming cafés are listed under Eating (left); for a drop of the hard stuff, head for the dark and smoky bars along Rue 10 Mai, northwest of Place Moulay el-Mehdi. If you just want a beer, Restaurant Restinga (opposite) is the place.

Entertainment

Apart from a palace meal, **Cinéma Avenida** (Place al-Adala; admission Dh20-30; 🕑 film times 3.30pm, 6pm, 8pm & 10pm) is the only game in town. Films are usually in French, with some Spanish.

Shopping

Wood and leatherwork are the local specialities; for the latter go straight to the source at the small **tannery** (Bab M'Kabar) in the north of the medina.

Dar Lebadi (☎ 039 973856; Jenoui section) The shopping palace of the medina, this 200-year-old building, a former governor's house, has been meticulously restored, and is now a clearinghouse for Berber artisans, with friendly staff. Worth a stop just to see the building, but be careful: you may be there for hours.

Ensemble Artisanal (Ave Hassan II; 🕑 8am-8pm Mon-Sat) This government-sponsored emporium is a hive of activity, with carpet weavers, leatherworkers, jewellers and woodworkers all plying their trades. Prices are fixed.

Getting There & Away

AIR

The Tetouan Airport opens for occasional charter flights from Paris (eg Club Med) but has no scheduled service. Persistent rumours that a full-fledged airport is coming may be inspired by efforts to sell foreigners real estate.

BUS

Tetouan is now blessed by a new **bus station**, which replaces its seedy predecessor. The

MEDITERRANEAN COAST & THE RIF

scrolling electronic timetable is so high-tech it's jarring. The bus touts are still in place, though – just walk past them and read the departure times on your own. You can get to any town in the north from here. The left luggage office had not yet opened during research.

CTM (☎ 039 711654) has its own station a five minute taxi ride away from the main bus station. It is a better bet for quality reasons and for any long-haul destinations. All the usual suspects are served from here, including Essaouira (Dh270, 13½ hours), Fez (Dh93, five hours), Marrakesh (Dh235, 11 hours), Rabat (Dh110, four to five hours) and many more. Buses for Martil (Dh4, 25 minutes), M'diq (Dh8, one hour), Fnideq (Dh10, 1¼ hours) and other local destinations also depart from here. Left luggage is Dh5/kg/day.

TAXI

Grands taxis to Fnideq (for Ceuta; Dh30, 30 minutes), Martil (Dh5, 10 minutes), Cabo Negro and M'diq (Dh10, 20 minutes) leave from Ave Hassan II, near Lovers Park. Occasional grands taxis to Al-Hoceima (Dh150, five hours) wait on a dusty lot 100m further east behind the new Modern Art Museum.

The taxi rank on Place al-Hammama, 2km west of central Tetouan, is the place to pick up grands taxis to Chefchaouen (Dh30, one hour) and Tangier (Dh25, one hour). If you are arriving from either of these places, the taxi driver may drop you closer to the town centre.

Grands taxis to Oued Laou are located underneath the Ave al-Massira overpass – which is easily missed.

Getting Around

Petits taxis are canary yellow but don't have meters; a ride around town should be around Dh10. If you have your own vehicle, you can keep your car at the guarded **Parking Hammadi** (Ave Al Jazaer; per 4hr daytime Dh10, per night Dh10).

AROUND TETOUAN

Martil مارتيل

Tetouan's port of Martil is a rapidly growing, modern beach town with a broad mountain view and a long corniche paralleled by streets full of cafés, ice-cream shops and restaurants. It has year-round visitors, and heaves in the summer. It's a viable base if you don't mind the 8km/10 minute cab ride to Tetouan.

SLEEPING & EATING

Camping al-Boustane (☎ 039 688822; fax 039 689682; Corniche; camping per person Dh15, per tent/car/campervan Dh30/15/30, electricity Dh20; 🅿) This secure camp site one block from the beach has excellent facilities, including a surprising gem of a restaurant and a pool in summer, but serious drainage problems in rain. Turn off corniche at fountain.

Hotel Etoile de la Mer (☎ 039 979058; Ave Moulay al-Hassan; s/d Dh176/231 summer, Dh150/177 winter) With its funky design – a central atrium crisscrossed by stairways – and central location one block from the beach, this is Martil's top sleeping option. The best rooms have balconies overlooking the sea, and the remodelled restaurant serves alcohol.

Restaurant al-Boustane (☎ 039 688822; mains from Dh50; 🕒 12.30-4pm & 7-11pm) Don't be put off by the location – this Mediterranean bistro in the back of the camper park (above) serves a tasty array of omelettes, fish, meat and tajines, and is full of talkative campers recounting their adventures.

Piccola Roma (☎ 042 353167; 202 Miramar; pizza from Dh18; 🕒 11am-3pm & 6pm-midnight) A local institution since 1992, this is your place for pizza, burgers and shawarma. Located one street back from corniche, across from the blinking ice-cream sign.

GETTING THERE & AWAY

Local buses to Tetouan (Dh4, 25 minutes) leave from the bus station near the water tower at the south end of the beach. You'll find grands taxis (Dh4, 15 minutes) near the big new mosque.

Cabo Negro & M'diq الرأس الاسود و مضيق

About 5km up the coast from Martil, the headland of Cabo Negro juts out into the Mediterranean and is clearly visible from Martil. Tucked into the lee of its north side is the surprising town of M'Diq. Once a small fishing village, it has rapidly grown into the classiest resort on the coast, with a grand entrance, excellent hotels and restaurants, a fine beach and a yacht club. There is really little to separate this place from

Florida, but if you are suffering from medina fatigue, it's the perfect stop, and only 20 minutes from Tetouan.

SLEEPING & EATING

M'diq's sleeping options tend to cater to the summer tourist trade and ignore the lower end of the price bracket. Ask for discounts outside the summer months. Given the number of new apartments, it is worth inquiring about rentals on site. There's a string of cafés and cheap eateries along the seafront, where women are more prevalent in summer.

Hotel Narijiss (☎ 039 975841; Ave Lalla Nezha; s/d Dh150/250;) This decent hotel is 200m up the hill rising from the seafront to the Tetouan road. It's a bit nondescript, but rooms have bathrooms and satellite TV, and there's a café tucked outside.

Golden Beach Hotel (☎ 039 975077; www.goldenbeachhotel.com; 84 Rte de Sebta; s/d incl breakfast Dh370/540 low season, Dh540/750 high season;) This four-star right on the beach is worth the splurge – short on charm, but well run, well-maintained and with great facilities, including a pool by the corniche and a piano bar with a most clever bar top: piano keys in marble.

Las Olas Restaurant and Café (☎ 039 664433; Corniche; mains from Dh40; 11am-midnight) You can't miss this waterfront landmark dressed up as a lighthouse, with a hopping downstairs café and an upstairs seafood restaurant. The decor is snappy, the rooftop views superb, and they don't have to go far to get fresh catch. Located directly on the corniche parking lot.

Royal Yachting Club de M'diq (☎ 039 663887; meals from Dh90) This classy place, with a pleasant outdoor terrace overlooking the port, is a private club, but the well-dressed tourist is more than welcome. Seafood is the specialty here, of course. Alcohol is also served.

GETTING THERE & AWAY

Grands taxis and buses travelling between Tetouan and Fnideq (3km short of the border with Ceuta) pass through M'diq. Grands taxis to Tetouan (Dh5, 20 minutes) depart from a stand near the Narijiss Hotel. Those for the border (Dh10) gather on the north side of town beside the Banque Populaire.

CHEFCHAOUEN شفشاون

pop 45,000

Beautifully sited beneath the raw peaks of the Rif, Chefchaouen is one of the prettiest towns in Morocco, an artsy, whitewashed mountain village that feels like its own world. While tourism has definitely taken hold, the balance between ease and authenticity is just right. The old medina is a delight of Moroccan and Andalucian influence with red-tiled roofs, bright-blue buildings and narrow lanes converging on busy Uta el-Hammam square and its restored kasbah. Long known to backpackers for the easy availability of kif, the town has rapidly gentrified, and offers a range of quality accommodation, good food, lots to do and no hassles to speak of, making it a strong alternative to a hectic multi-city tour. This is a great place to relax, explore and take day-trips in the cool green hills. Families take note.

History

Chefchaouen was originally known as Chaouen, meaning 'peaks'. Under Spanish occupation the spelling changed to Xaouen, and in 1975 the town was renamed Chefchaouen ('Look at the Peaks'). These days, the names are used interchangeably.

Moulay Ali ben Rachid founded Chaouen in 1471 as a base for Riffian Berber tribes to launch attacks on the Portuguese in Ceuta. The town expanded with the arrival of Muslim and Jewish refugees from Granada in 1494, who built the whitewashed houses, with tiny balconies, tiled roofs and patios (often with a citrus tree in the centre), that give the town its distinctive Spanish flavour. The pale-blue wash prevalent today was introduced in the 1930s by the Jewish refugees – previously windows and doors had been painted a traditional Muslim green.

The town remained isolated and xenophobic – Christians were forbidden to enter on pain of death – until occupied by Spanish troops in 1920. When the Spanish arrived they were surprised to hear the Jewish inhabitants still speaking a variant of medieval Castilian. The Spanish were briefly thrown out by Abd al-Krim during the Rif War in the 1920s, but they soon returned and remained until independence in 1956.

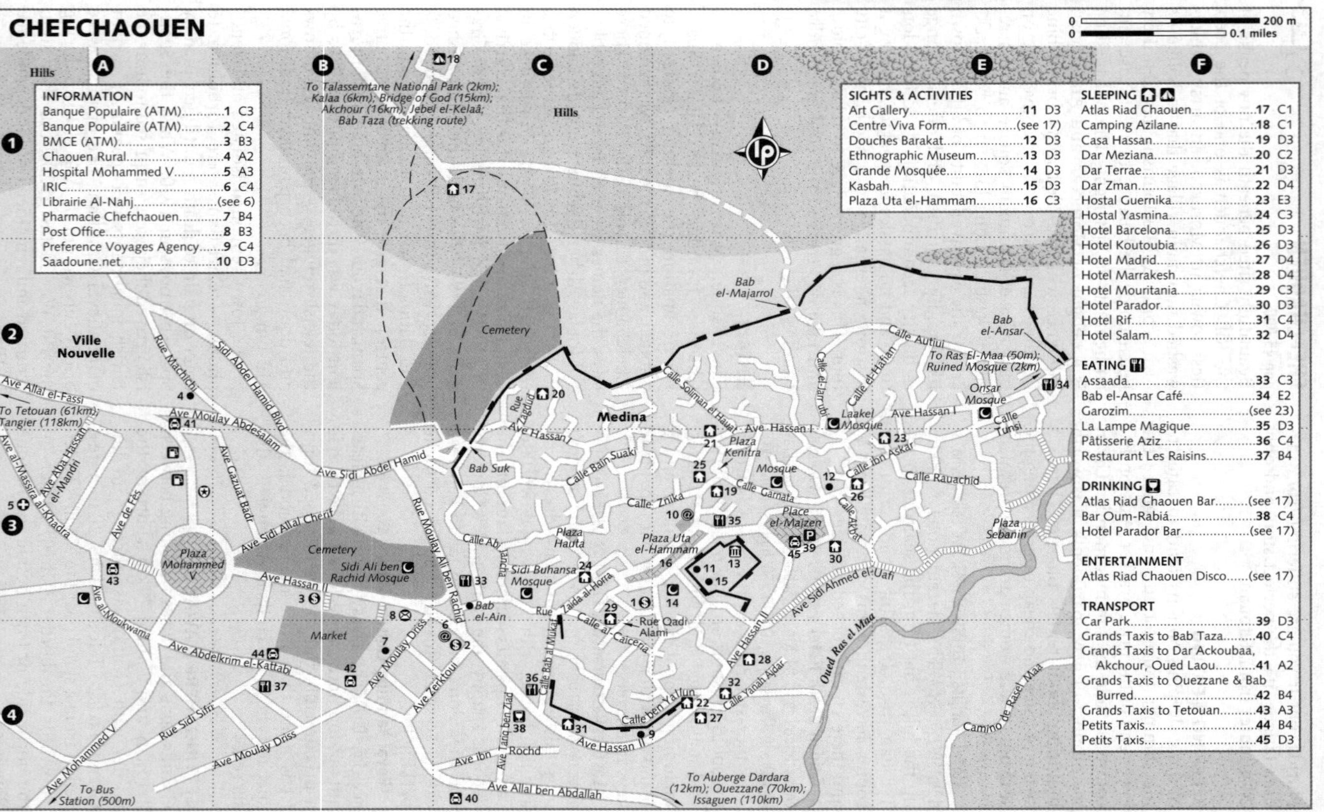
CHEFCHAOUEN
0 200 m
0 0.1 miles
INFORMATION
Banque Populaire (ATM) 1 C3
Banque Populaire (ATM) 2 C4
BMCE (ATM) 3 B3
Chaouen Rural 4 A2
Hospital Mohammed V 5 A3
IRIC 6 C4
Librairie Al-Nahj (see 6)
Pharmacie Chefchaouen 7 B4
Post Office 8 B3
Preference Voyages Agency 9 C4
Saadoune.net 10 D3
SIGHTS & ACTIVITIES
Art Gallery 11 D3
Centre Viva Form (see 17)
Douches Barakat 12 D3
Ethnographic Museum 13 D3
Grande Mosquée 14 D3
Kasbah 15 D3
Plaza Uta el-Hammam 16 C3
SLEEPING
Atlas Riad Chaouen 17 C1
Camping Azilane 18 C1
Casa Hassan 19 D3
Dar Meziana 20 C2
Dar Terrae 21 D3
Dar Zman 22 D4
Hostal Guernika 23 E3
Hostal Yasmina 24 C3
Hotel Barcelona 25 D3
Hotel Koutoubia 26 D3
Hotel Madrid 27 D4
Hotel Marrakesh 28 D4
Hotel Mouritania 29 C3
Hotel Parador 30 D3
Hotel Rif 31 C4
Hotel Salam 32 D4
EATING
Assaada 33 C3
Bab el-Ansar Café 34 E2
Garozim (see 23)
La Lampe Magique 35 D3
Pâtisserie Aziz 36 C4
Restaurant Les Raisins 37 B4
DRINKING
Atlas Riad Chaouen Bar (see 17)
Bar Oum-Rabiá 38 C4
Hotel Parador Bar (see 17)
ENTERTAINMENT
Atlas Riad Chaouen Disco (see 17)
TRANSPORT
Car Park 39 D3
Grands Taxis to Bab Taza 40 C4
Grands Taxis to Dar Ackoubaa, Akchour, Oued Laou 41 A2
Grands Taxis to Ouezzane & Bab Burred 42 B4
Grands Taxis to Tetouan 43 A3
Petits Taxis 44 B4
Petits Taxis 45 D3
To Talassemtane National Park (2km); Kalaa (6km); Bridge of God (15km); Akchour (16km); Jebel el-Kelaâ; Bab Taza (trekking route)
To Tetouan (61km); Tangier (118km)
To Ras El-Maa (50m); Ruined Mosque (2km)
To Auberge Dardara (12km); Ouezzane (70km); Issaguen (110km)
To Bus Station (500m)
Ville Nouvelle
Medina
Hills
Cemetery
Market
Plaza Mohammed V
Bab Suk
Bab el-Majarrol
Bab el-Ansar
Bab el-Ain
Oued Ras el Maa

Orientation

Chefchaouen is split into an eastern half (the medina), and a western half (the *ciudad nueva,* or new city). The heart of the medina is Plaza Uta el-Hammam, with its unmistakeable kasbah. The principal route of the ciudad nueva is Ave Hassan II, which stretches from Plaza Mohammed V, past the western gate of Bab el-Ain, around the southern medina wall, and into the medina itself. Here it dead-ends at Place el-Majzen, the main drop-off point, which faces the kasbah. The bus station is a 1km hike southwest of the town centre. The falls of Ras-el-Maa lie just beyond the medina walls to the northeast.

Information

BOOKSHOPS

Librairie Al-Nahj (☎ 039 986945; Ave Hassan II; 🕑 8am-10pm) Small, but with a decent selection of international periodicals, and a few English translations of local authors. English dailies available after 11.30am.

INTERNET ACCESS

IRIC (Institut Raouachid pour l'Information et le Commerce; Ave Hassan II; per hr Dh6; 🕑 9am-midnight)

Saadoune.net (Plaza Uta el-Hammam; per hr Dh10; 🕑 9am-2pm & 3pm-midnight)

MEDICAL SERVICES

Hospital Mohammed V (☎ 039 986228; Ave al-Massira al-Khadra)

Pharmacie Chefchaouen (☎ 039 986158; Ave Moulay Driss; 🕑 9am-1pm & 3-8pm)

MONEY

Banque Populaire medina (Plaza Uta el-Hammam; 🕑 9.30am-1pm & 3.30-9pm Mon-Fri) ATM; ciudad nueva (Ave Hassan II)

BMCE (Ave Hassan II; 🕑 8.15am-3.45pm Mon-Fri). ATM.

POST

Post office (Ave Hassan II; 🕑 8am-4.30pm Mon-Fri, 8am-noon Sat-Sun)

TOURIST INFORMATION

Due to open by 2009 in the new building next to Hotel Parador.

TRAVEL AGENT/CAR RENTAL

Preference Voyages Agency (☎ 039 987913; 39 Ave Hassan II) This extremely helpful travel agency – the first in Chefchaouen – also operates the town's only rental-car company. English-speaking and with reasonable rates.

Sights & Activities

MEDINA

Chefchaouen's medina is one of the loveliest in Morocco. Small and uncrowded, it's easy to explore, with enough winding paths to keep you diverted, but compact enough that you'll never get too lost. Most of the buildings are painted a blinding blue-white, giving them a clean, fresh look, while terracotta tiles add an Andalucian flavour.

The heart of the medina is the shady, cobbled **Plaza Uta el-Hammam** which is lined with cafés and restaurants, all serving similar fare. This is a peaceful place to relax and watch the world go by, particularly after a long day of exploration. The plaza is dominated by the red-hued walls of the **kasbah** and the adjacent **Grande Mosquée**. Noteworthy for its unusual octagonal tower, the Grande Mosquée was built in the 15th century by the son of the town's founder, Ali ben Rachid, and is closed to non-Muslims. The **kasbah** (☎ 039 986343; admission incl museum & gallery Dh10; 🕑 9am-1pm & 3-6.30pm Wed-Mon, 9-11.30am & 3-4.30pm Fri) is a heavily restored walled fortress that now contains a lovely garden, a small **Ethnographic Museum**, and an even smaller **Art Gallery**. The ethnographic museum contains some fascinating views of old Chefchaouen, including the Plaza and the kasbah; the gallery promotes the work of talented local artists.

RAS EL-MAA

Just beyond the far eastern gate of the medina lie the falls of **Ras El-Maa**. In season there is a popular café on the right, just before the bridge. The sound of the water and the verdant hills just beyond the medina wall provide a sudden, strong dose of nature. Continuing over the bridge, you can walk to the ruined mosque in the distance. It was built by the Spanish, but abandoned during the Rif War in the 1920s. From here you'll have a grand view of the entire town sprawling over the green hills below. The mosque is a popular destination, but women may not feel comfortable there by themselves.

SPAS & HAMMAMS

The **Centre Viva Form** (☎ 039 986002; Rue Sidi Abdelhamid BP 13; 🕑 noon-9pm) is a sophisticated,

CLIMBING JEBEL EL-KELAÂ

Looming over Chefchaouen at 1616m, Jebel el-Kelaâ might initially appear a daunting peak, but with an early start and a packed lunch, it can easily be climbed in a day if you're in reasonably good shape.

The hike starts from behind Camping Azilane, following the 4WD track that takes you to the hamlet of Aïn Tissimlane. Rocks painted with a yellow and white stripe indicate that you're on the right path. The initial hour is relatively steep as you climb above the trees to get your first views over Chefchaouen, before cutting into the mountains along the steady *piste*. You should reach Aïn Tissimlane within a couple of hours of setting out, after which the path climbs and zigzags steeply through great boulders for nearly an hour to a pass. Turn west along the track, which leads to the saddle of the mountain, from where you can make the final push to the summit. There's a rough path, although you'll need to scramble in places. The peak is attained relatively quickly, and your exertions are rewarded with the most sublime views over this part of the Rif.

It's straightforward and quick to descend by the same route. Alternatively, you can head north from the saddle on a path that takes you to a cluster of villages on the other side of the mountain. One of these villages, El-Kelaâ, has 16th-century grain stores, and a mosque with a leaning minaret. From here, a number of simple tracks will take you back to Chefchaouen in a couple of hours.

full-service spa located at the Atlas Riad Chaouen hotel. Prices range from a foot massage (Dh50) to the 50-minute slimming massage, which will trim your wallet of Dh400.

A traditional, and far less expensive, option is local hammam **Douches Barakat** (shower Dh6, hammam Dh8; ⌚ men 8am-noon, women noon-8pm).

TREKKING

There are numerous trekking opportunities of various durations in the Chefchaouen area, including the vast 60,000 hectare **Talassemtane National Park**, which begins just outside town (p440). Some popular destinations include the small villages of Kalaa and Akchour, and the Bridge of God, a natural formation that looks like a stone arch. The duration of these excursions depends on how much you wish to drive versus walk. For information on guides and organised tours, see below.

Tours

There are two organisations competing for travellers interested in exploring the natural environment around Chefchaouen. One is the local **Association des Guides du Tourisme** (☎ 062 113917; guiderando@yahoo.fr; half-day tour Dh120) which is run by Abdeslam Mouden, an English speaker with a wealth of local knowledge and guide experience. This group is connected to the new Tourist Information office.

The other is **Chaouen Rural** (☎ 039 987267; www.chaouenrural.org; 3 Rue Machichi; ⌚ 9am-7pm Mon-Fri) a local company sponsored by the government of Catalonia that is developing the rural tourism potential of the region. This well-run operation specialises in package trips into Talassemtane National Park that include staying in rural houses and interacting with the local culture. Prices are a very reasonable Dh150 to Dh180 per person per day, including transport, guide and half-board. The website is French/Spanish, but some English is spoken, and brochures are available in English.

Festivals & Events

The active cultural association **Rif el-Andalus** (☎ 039 986800) organises two events in July. One is a large open-air art exhibition, and the other is the Alegria Chamalia, an international music festival.

Sleeping

Chefchaouen has a large number of accommodation options, but few hotels have heating. You will be sleeping beneath plenty of blankets during cold winter nights. Some hotels also have deadly staircases, with slick stone steps – steep, tall, curving and of alternating height – under low ceilings.

It pays to be alert on that tired slog to the rooftop terrace for breakfast.

MEDINA

Budget

Most of the budget options are in the medina. The best of these are cheerful, tiled houses with interior courtyards and superb roof terraces. Facilities are mostly shared, but toilets are generally Western-style and hot showers are often included in the price.

Hotel Mouritania (☎ 039 986184; 15 Rue Qadi Alami; s/d Dh45/80) Rooms are simple here, but staff are helpful, there's a comfy courtyard lounge ideal for meeting other travellers, and the breakfasts (Dh20) are great.

Hostal Yasmina (☎ 039 883118; yasmina45@hotmail.com; 12 Zaida Al-Horra; r per person Dh70) For the price bracket, this place sparkles. Rooms are bright and clean, the location is a stone's throw from Plaza Uta el-Hammam, and the roof terrace is very welcoming. This bargain doesn't have many rooms, though, so it can fill up quickly.

Hotel Barcelona (☎ 039 988506; 12 Rue Targui; r per person Dh70 without bathroom, s/d with bathroom Dh200/300) A friendly budget option in bright Chefchaouen blue. Fixtures and fittings are pretty basic, but the hotel has recently been repainted, and the roof terrace is great.

Hotel Koutoubia (☎ 068 115358; Calle Andalouse; s/d Dh150/200) This brand new hotel does budget accommodation perfectly, with friendly and attentive management, a central location, traditional decor, spotless rooms and an open roof terrace with breakfast (Dh15) in good weather.

our pick **Hostal Guernika** (☎ 039 987434; 49 Onssar; r Dh200) This is a warm and charming place, with a very caring and attentive owner, not too far from the Plaza Uta el-Hammam. There are several great streetside rooms – large and bright, facing the mountains – but others are dark. All have showers. Reserve in summer, Easter and December.

Dar Terrae (☎ 039 987598; darterrae@hotmail.com; Ave Hassan I; s/d/tr incl breakfast Dh250/350/450) These funky, cheerfully painted rooms are individually decorated with their own bathroom and fireplace, and hidden up and down a tumble of stairs and odd corners. The Italian owners prepare a fantastic breakfast spread every day, and other meals on request. It's poorly signed – if in doubt ask for the 'Hotel Italiano'.

Midrange & Top End

our pick **Dar Meziana** (☎ 039 987806; www.darmeziana.com; Rue Zagdud; s/d/tr from Dh475/650/950; ❄) Beautifully decorated, and in a class by itself, this new boutique hotel is an artful creation, with a unique angular courtyard, lush plantings, lots of light, the highest quality furniture and extraordinary ceilings. On the edge of the medina but otherwise perfect.

Casa Hassan (☎ 039 986153; www.casahassan.com; 22 Rue Targui; s/d/tr with half-board from Dh500/650/800; ❄) A large hotel with a boutique-hotel feel, this long-established upmarket choice is showing its age a bit, but still has sizable rooms with creative layouts, including beds tucked into coves, and an in-house hammam. The terrace provides an elegant lounge, and the cosy Restaurant Tissemlal a warm hearth.

Dar Zman (☎ 039 987598; darterrae@hotmail.com; Ave Hassan II; s/d incl breakfast Dh350/450) A brand new, finely done guest house with eight brightly painted rooms and a lovely rooftop breakfast area, created by some ambitious young hoteliers. The faux artefacts revealed in the walls are a clever touch.

Hotel Parador (☎ 039 986136; parador@iam.net.ma; Place el-Majzen; s/d/tr Dh394/526/681; 🏊) This aging four-star reflects a time when aspiring to be Western was chic. Now its soulless rooms are lacking what you came for: local culture. Perks include a good restaurant, a pool in summer and one of Chefchaouen's few bars.

AROUND THE MEDINA

Budget

There's another cluster of budget hotels on Ave Hassan II, which runs south of the medina alongside the old city walls. These places are a step up from the pensions in the medina, in that they offer private bathrooms and have restaurants on site. They also offer great Rif views from one side of the building.

Hotel Salam (☎ 039 986239; 39 Ave Hassan II; s/d/tr Dh80/140/180) Another out-of-medina experience, the freshly painted Salam has perked up its bright courtyard rooms. Shared facilities are adequate, but sinks in all rooms are a bonus, as is the espresso machine in the ground-floor café.

Hotel Rif (☎ 039 986982; hotelrif@hotmail.com; 29 Ave Hassan II; s/d incl breakfast Dh150/180, with bathroom & breakfast Dh180/240; ❄) Just below the medina walls, it has some good rooms with great views, and adequate rooms without. Suffering from dark and jumbled aesthetics, it's nevertheless popular with tour groups, so advance booking is a good idea. The restaurant has the bonus of an alcohol licence.

Hotel Marrakesh (☎ 039 987774; Ave Hassan II; s/d incl breakfast Dh150/220, with shower Dh300/360) Set downhill from the action, the Marrakesh is a hotel with a bit of soul. Bright pastel rooms invite the fresh air in, the common room attracts with its central fireplace and carved plaster ceiling, and the roof terrace offers fine views over the valley. The seven-jet showers, however, are as mysterious as any medina alley.

Hotel Madrid (☎ 039 987497; Ave Hassan II; s/d/tr from Dh300/357/429;) With its jumbled rugs on floors and stairways, this hotel appears ready to trip up your visit, but the old-world lobby is cheery, and the cosy rooms a pleasant surprise, with wrought-iron canopy beds and well-appointed bathrooms packed with complimentary toiletries.

Camping Azilane (☎ 039 986979; camping per adult Dh15, plus per tent/car/campervan Dh15/20/35) A shady setting with great views makes this site popular, even if it is a stiff 20-minute walk from the medina. A small restaurant opens during the summer, and a shop sells some essentials, but otherwise facilities are pretty basic (hot showers Dh10).

Midrange & Top End

Atlas Riad Chaouen (☎ 039 986002; www.hotelsatlas.com; s/d/tr incl breakfast Dh600/750/1125;) This is the top hotel in Chefchaouen; its three-star rating only serves to lower taxes. Unmistakeably perched on the hills overlooking the town, it doubles as a decent art museum, with some fantastic works by local artist Zaidi Mohammed, including a wall-length painting of the medina. All the amenities of a European four-star are present, including a huge lobby, a full-service spa, a pool with gorgeous mountain views, the only nightclub in the area, a high-end restaurant and a jazzy bar (where a beer will set you back a record Dh40).

Auberge Dardara (☎ 061 150503; aubergedardara@gmail.com; Rte Nationale 2; s/d Dh490/790;) This is an authentic French auberge in the Moroccan countryside offering large rustic suites with Moroccan touches. The 10 hectare complex includes an active farm and gardens, pool, craft shop, hammam, fitness centre, horses and the most sophisticated kitchen in the Chefchaouen area. Guest programs include crafts, gardening and more. It's a 10-minute taxi ride (Dh5) to Bab Taza.

Eating

RESTAURANTS

A popular eating option in Chefchaouen is to choose one of about a dozen **Plaza Café-Restaurants** (Plaza Uta el-Hamman; breakfast from Dh15, mains from Dh25; 8am-11pm) on the main square. Menus are virtually identical – continental breakfasts, soups and salads, tajines and seafood – but the food is generally pretty good and the ambience lively.

La Lampe Magique (☎ 065 406464; Rue Targui; mains from Dh45, set menu Dh75; 11am-11pm) This magical place overlooking Plaza Uta el-Hammam serves delicious Moroccan staples in a grand setting. Three bright-blue floors include a laid-back lounge, a more formal dining area and a roof-top terrace. The menu – featuring favourites like lamb tajine with prunes and some great cooked salads – is better than average, but this place is really about atmosphere.

Auberge Dardara Restaurant (☎ 061 150503; aubergedardara@gmail.com; Rte Nationale 2; mains from Dh40; noon-4pm & 7-11pm;) This is the best kitchen in the area, and worth the 10-minute drive from town (to Bab Taza, Dh5). The Tangerine owner forgoes the tajine and couscous routine for cosmopolitan spice and the freshest ingredients, most grown on site, and others, like the anchovies, imported from the coast that day. The succulent goat cooked with sweet figs is a marvel.

Assaada (☎ 066 317316; Bab el-Ain; set menu Dh40) This reliable cheapie tries hard to please. Located on both sides of the alley just prior to Bab el-Ain, it offers the usual menu *complet*, but also great fruit shakes, and a funky graffiti rooftop terrace that exudes an urban charm. The staircase is not for the faint-hearted.

Restaurant Les Raisins (☎ 067 982878; www.france.com/lesraisins2001; 7 Rue Sidi Sifri; tajines Dh20, set menu from Dh40; 7am-9pm) A bit out of the way, this family-run place is a perennial favourite with locals and tourists alike, and known for its couscous royal. Late, lazy lunches are the best, with the front terrace catching the afternoon sun.

Garozim (☎ 039 988352) This is an inexpensive spot that manages to combine its setting above a medina alley, its rustic decor, and Edith Piaf crooning in the background into a single charming experience. The usual local fare is offered, but you may need to wake the waitress. Located next to Hostal Guernika (p205).

CAFÉS, PATISSERIES & ICE-CREAM PARLOURS

It's hard to get past the cafés on Plaza Uta el-Hammam for a long juice or a relaxing mint tea. From mid-afternoon, hawkers do the rounds of the cafés carrying trays laden with sticky pastries for sale. In the back rooms, local men play cards and smoke kif – worth a look, although women won't feel particularly welcome.

Bab el-Ansar Café (Bab el-Ansar) Just outside the medina, this café has a great location overlooking the falls of Ras el Maa, with three terraces tumbling down the hill. Views are particularly nice in the late afternoon, with the sun catching the mountains opposite.

Pâtisserie Aziz (Ave Hassan II) For a great selection of pastries, make your way here. They squeeze a mean juice and make good coffee too, for a quick breakfast on the run.

SELF-CATERING

The market off Ave Hassan II is excellent for fresh fish, meat, fruit and vegetables, and gets particularly busy on Monday and Thursday, when people come from outside Chefchaouen to sell produce.

Several local specialities are worth checking out, particularly the fragrant mountain honey and soft ewe's cheese – both served up at breakfast. Add fresh *dial makla* (a type of bread) and you have your picnic.

Drinking

While it's easy to find kif in Chefchaouen, it's hard to find a beer. There's just one free-standing, and very masculine, option, **Bar Oum-Rabiá** (Ave Hassan II; 10am-10pm). The small bar at the **Hotel Parador** (Place el-Majzen; beer from Dh20; 2-11pm), is better, while the jazzy bar at the **Atlas Riad Chaouen** (beer Dh40 ; 2pm-late) is the nicest but pricey and farther away.

Entertainment

The disco at the **Atlas Riad Chouen** (☎ 039 986002; www.hotelsatlas.com) is the only nightclub in the area. Hotel residents are the clientele during the week, joined by locals on weekends.

Shopping

Chefchaouen remains an artisan centre and, as such, an excellent place to shop – especially for woven rugs and blankets in bright primary colours. Many shops have looms in situ, so you can see the blankets being made. Previously silk was the material of choice: the mulberry trees in Plaza Uta el-Hammam are a legacy of these times. Most of the weaving nowadays is with wool, one of the area's biggest products.

The largest concentration of tourist shops is located around the Uta el-Hammam and Place el-Majzen.

Getting There & Away

BUS

Many bus services from Chefchaouen originate elsewhere, so are often full on arrival. Where possible, buy your ticket a day in advance to secure your seat. The bus station is 1.5km southwest of the town centre at the far end of Ave Mohammed V (Dh10 in a petit taxi from Place el-Majzen). CTM and all other buses use the same station.

CTM (☎ 039 987669) serves Rabat (Dh90, five hours), Kenitra (Dh80, 5½ hours) Ouezzane (Dh20, 1½ hours), Tetouan (Dh20, 1½ hours), Fez (Dh70, four hours), Tangier (Dh40, three hours), Al Hoceima (Dh75, six hours), Nador (Dh125, nine hours) and Casablanca (Dh120, eight hours).

Other companies run a number of cheaper services to the same destinations, including a daily departure for Oued Laou (Dh18, two hours).

TAXI

The fixed price for a grand taxi from Tangier Airport to Chefchaouen is Dh750. Unless you can find several people to split the fare with you, it is far cheaper to go to Tangier first, then hop to Chefchaouen via Tetouan. Even if you buy two places, you will save over Dh500 and add less than an hour.

Grands taxis north leave Chefchaouen from just below Plaza Mohammed V. Most just run to Tetouan (Dh30, one hour), where you must change for Tangier or Ceuta – direct taxis are rare. From Ave

Allal ben Abdallah you can catch a grand taxi to Dar Ackoubaa (Dh15, 20 minutes) from Ave Moulay Abdesalam, the junction for Oued Laou.

Grands taxis headed south gather below the central market. Catch one to Ouezzane (Dh30, 75 minutes), where you can pick up onward transport to Fez and Meknès. There is very little transport heading east to the coast. The best option is to take a grand taxi to Dardara junction (Dh8, 15 minutes) or Bab Taza (Dh15, 30 minutes) and hope for the best from there.

Getting Around

Blue petits taxis congregate on Place el-Majzen and near the market. They're unmetered; most fares shouldn't top Dh10. The safe and convenient Hotel Parador **car park** (Place el-Majzen; per night Dh10) can be used by non-guests.

OUEZZANE وزان

pop 53,000

Ouezzane is a sprawling, scruffy, industrial town of concrete construction with little to offer the traveller, although that may be changing a little. Part of the medina is under reconstruction, and it is fascinating to see what a little mortar and white paint can do. If you are driving through, it is worth it to stop and have a look at the work being done, but there is no reason to stay here unless you run out of petrol. Police checkpoints are common both entering and leaving the town.

Orientation

The centre of town is a large triangle known as Place de L'Independence. There are a few restaurants and rough hotels across the street, and behind them, the medina. The reconstruction includes the tiled Green Mosque, with its interesting octagonal minaret, though is closed to the public. Uphill are several streets that form a commercial area, with numerous stalls, which are worth a walk around.

Sleeping & Eating

If you do suffer a thrown piston, you have two acceptable choices for sleeping:

Hotel Bouhlal (☎ 037 907154; Hay el-Haddadine Qu; s/d/tr Dh80/120/150, air-con an extra Dh10-20;) This is your best budget option, although located in a nondescript industrial side street with nothing nearby. Inside, the rooms are clean, and the roof terrace a welcome oasis, but shared bathrooms have cold showers and squat toilets. Staff can rustle up breakfast with a little warning, but otherwise head to the Motel Rif for a meal.

Motel Rif (☎ 037 907172; r Dh250; 5-person apt Dh700;) This odd, sprawling blue-and-white complex on the outskirts of town – on the way to Chefchaouen, and 3km before the road to Fez – fancies itself as a drive-in resort, with tiki umbrellas by the pool, camper parking (Dh50 for two), a cavernous restaurant (set menu Dh80) and a 35 hectare farm to provide it with produce. The large proportions of the concrete block buildings makes it feel like a factory converted to hotel use.

There are several other budget hotels across from the Place de L'Independence, all of which seem to be competing for the bottom rung of a short ladder. **Restaurant des Négociants** (Place de l'Indépendence), in the Grand Hotel, is the most popular eatery, but given the flies, you may end up staying in Ouezzane longer than you wish.

Getting There & Away

BUS

Two dusty lots on Rue de la Marche Verte, 50m northwest of the main square, function as the bus station and grand-taxi stand. Get an early start when trying to leave Ouezzane, as there are virtually no buses after 5pm.

CTM has buses to Fez (Dh45, two hours, two daily) and to Tetouan (Dh40, three hours, one daily) via Chefchaouen (Dh25, 1½ hours). There are frequent non-CTM buses before 5pm to Meknès (Dh40), Fez (Dh40), Tetouan (Dh35), Chefchaouen (Dh20), Kenitra (Dh25, 2½ hours), Casablanca (Dh65, five hours) and Tangier (Dh50, four hours). Most non-CTM buses for Chefchaouen actually stop at Dardara junction, on the main road, from where you can pick up a grand taxi (Dh10) for the final 10km into town.

TAXI

There are grands taxis to Chefchaouen (Dh30, 75 minutes) and Fez (Dh60, 2½ hours). For longer-distance destinations (such as Rabat or Tangier) you may have to take a taxi to Souk el-Arba-du-Rharb

(Dh20, 45 minutes) or Ksar el-Kebir (Dh25, one hour), and change.

NORTH & EAST OF CHEFCHAOUEN

Oued Laou واد لاو

With its dusty main street lined with slapdash construction, small but growing Oued Laou looks like a Wild West town on the sea. Waterfront budget rooms, cheap beer and food, internet cafés and a very long, empty beach make it a backpacker paradise, especially in summer. There's nothing to do aside from watching the fishermen haul their boats in the morning.

INTERNET CAFÉS

Cyber Costa (per hr Dh5; 9am-midnight) Opposite the Rais Restaurant.

SLEEPING & EATING

our pick **Hotel Oued Laou** (039 670249; Blvd Massira; s/d/tr from Dh120/130/150) There are several new budget hotels to choose from, but this is the best. Located on the beach, it has a pool room, one of the better café/restaurants and an energetic young manager. Get a room with views to the sea.

Mare Nostrum (022 312218; bungalow Dh700 Sep, Dh1000 May, Dh1500 Jun-Aug;) If you are backpacking on a trust fund, this is the perfect getaway. Located 3km from town on the road to Tetouan, this small, self-contained and newly constructed resort consists of a series of bungalows hanging on the cliffs overlooking the sea, with a pool, an upscale restaurant (mains from Dh100), a charming lounge and its own private cul-de-sac beach far below. The bungalows are large, with canopy beds and offer magnificent views towards the rocky headland. Reserve ahead in summer.

Rais Restaurant (Corniche; mains from Dh10) Facing the fishing boats, this place has great sardines fresh from the boat, and filling meals of chicken and chips.

GETTING THERE & AWAY

If you're driving from Chefchaouen turn off the main Tetouan road at Dar Ackoubaa, 11km north of Chefchaouen. It's a wonderful drive past the large hydroelectric dam and through rolling hills and the stunning Laou Gorge. Coming from Tetouan, S608 hugs the dramatic coastline for 140km all the way to El-Jebha.

Three buses a day connect Tetouan and Oued Laou (Dh21, two hours). There's also one bus from Chefchaouen (Dh18, 90 minutes), which continues along the coast to El-Jebha (Dh25, five hours); the return service leaves El-Jebha early in the morning. However, at Oued Laou it dumps you out by the souq, leaving you a 45-minute walk or Dh5 grand-taxi ride to town.

Grands taxis run from beside the mosque in Oued Laou to Tetouan (Dh30, one hour) via Dar Ackoubaa (Dh15, 20 minutes), where you can pick up a passing taxi for Chefchaouen.

Targa to El-Jebha من ترگ إلى الجبهة

This stretch of the coast is very dramatic, and still remote – at least until 2010, when the coastal highway linking Tetouan to El-Jebha should be complete.

Seventeen kilometres southeast of Oued Laou, **Targa** is a little village with a history of piracy. High atop an outcrop of black rock, a stone fort overlooks the village, built during the Spanish Protectorate. The 13th-century mosque is associated with a local saint.

About 18km southeast of Targa, in the wide valley of Oued Bouchia, are the twin villages of **Steha** (an administrative centre) and **Bou-Ahmed**. Set back from the coast, the latter is the end point for a long-distance trek from Chefchaouen (see p443). There's an interesting souq every Tuesday, and a basic camping area in summer.

From here the road follows the coast on a splendid roller-coaster ride to the blue and white town of **El-Jebha**, 52km to the southeast. The rugged coastline forms a number of breathtaking and secluded bays – worth exploring if you have your own transport. Each Tuesday, the local souq draws Rif farmers from the surrounding villages. El-Jebha is the last stop before the road climbs up through the Rif to Issaguen.

Issaguen (Ketama) دازكان

pop 5000

Heading southeast out of Chefchaouen, the road N2 plunges into the heart of the Rif, running about 150km along the backbone of the mountains. The roads are rough, and the endless twists and turns make the going slow. There are few petrol stations.

The small town of Bab Berret marks the unofficial entry point to kif country, which is regarded as the largest hashish production area in the world. Marijuana fields carpet the hills in all directions, fed by the huge stacks of chemical fertiliser on sale in the markets.

Issaguen, known locally (and on many maps) as Ketama, appears unexpectedly from the middle of the pine forests. A scruffy frontier town, it is the commercial centre of kif cultivation and smuggling. Traffic moves haphazardly down its pitted dirt main street, where gutted sheep hang by the roadside and hooded men walk furtively about.

To the southeast, Jebel Tidiquin (2448m), the highest peak in the Rif Mountains, dominates the skyline.

DANGERS & ANNOYANCES

Issaguen has a notorious reputation. This is an area beyond the law, harbouring people who can no longer show their faces in other parts of Morocco. People will wonder what you are doing here, and naturally assume you are buying hashish. There is nowhere to turn if you get into trouble, and little to hold anyone back who wants some. Travellers are advised to pass through and not spend the night.

SLEEPING & EATING

The great anomaly of Issaguen is the **Hotel Tidighine** (☎ 067 255171; r from Dh300-500;), which has recently undergone an extensive renovation into a three- or four-star hotel. At the time of research it was about to reopen. With 68 modern rooms, it dwarfs all the other buildings in town, and is several steps above in quality as well, with a fully equipped hotel kitchen, a large pool and 12 bungalows set in the woods. The local economy must be booming. The only other options are a few seedy cafés on the main road that offer simple food and a bed out back.

GETTING THERE & AWAY

There is no bus station in Issaguen. Passing buses simply stop on the main road by the T-junction (next to the petrol station). The main destinations from here are Tetouan (Dh44, five hours, around six daily) via Chefchaouen (Dh38, three hours), Al-Hoceima (Dh36, three hours, at least nine daily) and Fez (Dh42, four hours, seven daily).

Almost all grands taxis are for local transport only. Occasional grands taxis leave for Al-Hoceima (Dh45) and Tetouan (Dh75), otherwise you're looking at hiring *collectif.*

THE CANNABIS INDUSTRY

The Rif is home to the largest acreage of cannabis cultivation in the world, an estimated 134,000 hectares, or 42% of global production. Cultivation has expanded rapidly since the 1980s, in part due to increasing European demand. The cannabis trade is now the region's main economic activity, involving an estimated 800,000 people, and probably Morocco's main source of foreign currency, although rural farmers reap little from it. The annual per capita income generated by cannabis production was estimated at US$267 in 2002.

Cannabis cultivation started around Ketama in the 15th century. In 1912 the right to cultivate cannabis was granted to a few Rif tribes by Spain. In 1956, when Morocco gained independence, cannabis was prohibited, but Mohammed V later condoned cultivation in the Rif after the prohibition led to conflict there.

Most large shipments of Moroccan hashish (a concentrated form of marijuana) are smuggled into Europe by boat, including small speedboats that can make a round trip to Spain in an hour. The primary departure points are Martil, Oued Laou and Bou Ahmed, although the bigger ports of Nador, Tetouan, Tangier and Larache are also used. Traffickers also export hashish concealed in trucks and cars embarked on ferries leaving from the Spanish enclaves of Ceuta and Melilla or from Tangier.

Not surprisingly, of all hashish seizures worldwide, half are made in Spain. Recent seizures of cocaine and hashish packed together suggests that Colombian drug traffickers have gotten involved. Traffickers have also branched out into human smuggling, to include smuggling hashish and migrants into Europe together.

AL-HOCEIMA الحسيمة

pop 113,000

Al-Hoceima is a great place to spend a few days, and perhaps more. Quiet, safe, relaxing and hassle-free, this modern seaside resort is full of proud and genial Berbers with a surprisingly independent, Western outlook, far more than any other town in the north. In fact, if the northern Berbers had their own country, this would be its capital. There is far more of the Berber tongue, Tarifit, spoken than Spanish (see boxed text, below).

Founded by the Spanish as Villa Sanjuro, the town was built as a garrison after the Rif Wars in the early 20th century; rebel Abd al-Krim operated nearby. Moroccan independence brought the name-change to Al-Hoceima, but Spanish influence remains strong in language, architecture and business.

In recent years many of Al-Hoceima's émigrés have returned and have ploughed money into the town, particularly into its booming tourism industry. Now a major government-sponsored facelift is underway as well. During research the large Place de la Marche Vente was being transformed into a new cliffside park named – surprise! – Plaza Mohammed VI. A new corniche was being built along the coast. The Hotel Quemado had been taken down, freeing up the beachfront, and the future of the landmark Hotel Mohammed V was in doubt. The Place du Rif is slated to be turned into a pedestrian zone. Best of all, the wonderful National Park of Al-Hoceima has been carefully opened to rural tourism – an opportunity not to be missed.

SURVIVAL TARAFIT

Hello/Goodbye	*salam/beslama*
Yes/No	*naam/alla*
Please/Thankyou	*minfadlak/shoukran*
Where is...?	*fin...?*
hotel	*hotel*
camping	*el moukhayam*
Do you have any	*wash kayan shi*
rooms available?	*bit khawi?*
a single room	*bit dyal wahad*
a double room	*bit dyad jouje danass*
How much is it?	*beshhal?*
What time does	*foukash yamshi...?*
the next... leave?	
boat	*en babour*
bus	*el car*
I'd like a...	*bghit*
one-way ticket	*warga aller*
return ticket	*warga aller retour*
beer	*bira*
sandwich	*cascrout*

Orientation

Al-Hoceima sits atop high cliffs overlooking two coves, one a beach (Plage Quemado) and the other a commercial port. Blvd Mohammed V parallels the edge from the Spanish College at one end to Place du Rif at the other. Most of the banks, hotels and restaurants are along or close to here, with budget options clustered around Place du Rif. The flat grid of wide streets is easy to walk and navigate. The three other town beaches lie further south, along with El Peñón de Alhucemas, one of the last bits of the Spanish Protectorate.

Information

INTERNET ACCESS

Cyber Club On-line (103 Blvd Mohammed V; per hr Dh5; 10am-2pm & 4pm-midnight)

MEDICAL SERVICES

Pharmacie Nouvelle (Calle Moulay Idriss Alkbar; 8.30am-9.30pm Mon-Sat, 3pm-12.30am Sun)

MONEY

Blvd Mohammed V has several banks with ATMs, including branches of BMCE, BMCI and Banque Populaire.

POST

Post office (Calle Moulay Idriss Alkbar; 8.30am-6.30pm Mon-Fri, 8am-noon Sat)

TOURIST INFORMATION

ONMT (Délégation Régionale du Tourisme; ☎ 039 981185; Ave Tariq ibn Ziad; 9am-4pm Mon-Fri)

TRAVEL AGENCIES

All sell ferry tickets from Al-Hoceima in season, and from Nador year-round.

Chafarinas Tours (☎ 039 840202; 109 Blvd Mohammed V)

Ketama Voyages (☎/fax 039 982772; 146 Blvd Mohammed V)

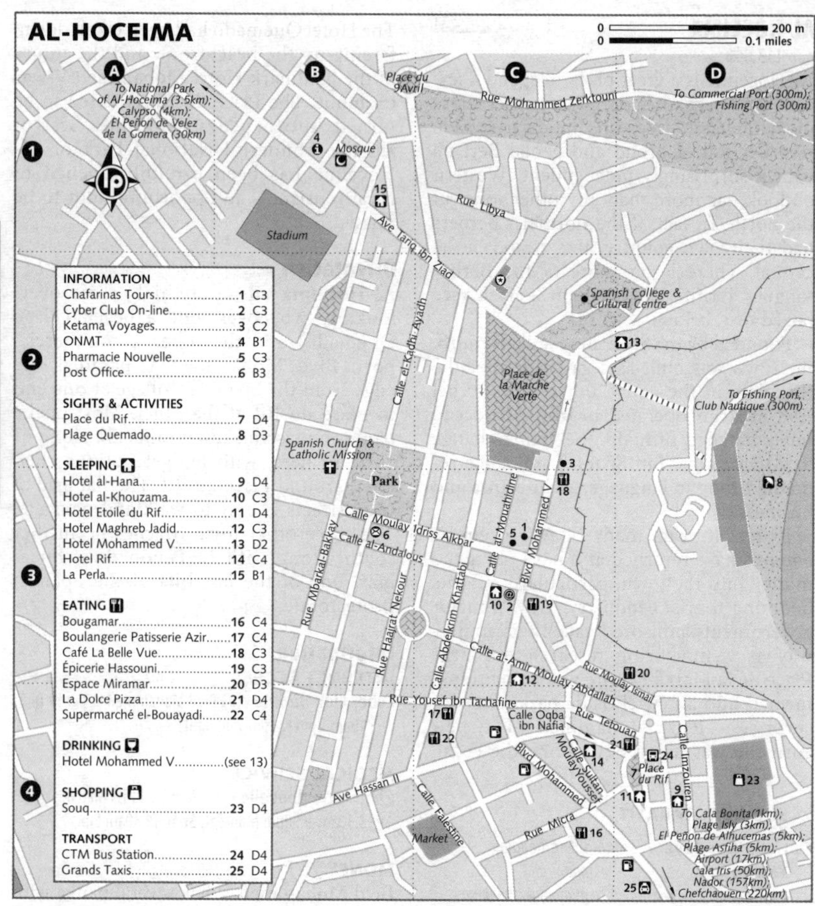

Sights & Activities

BEACHES

A pretty steep-sided bay protects the town beach, **Plage Quemado**. The beach is clean enough, but the seaside resort atmosphere is marred by the port to the north and the massive buildings towering over the cliffs.

In the summer, a better option is one of the three white sandy beaches that begin 5km south of town: **Cala Bonita**, **Plage Isly** and **Plage Asfiha**. Off-season they tend to be strewn with rubbish. Plage Asfiha has several ramshackle restaurants right on the beach serving sardines and chips, and feels the most remote. The best way to reach these beaches is by grand taxi. For the entire taxi, reckon on about Dh49 to Cala Bonita and Dh72 to Plage Asfiha. Local buses to Ajdir and Imzouren, which pass the turn-offs for these beaches (Dh2 to Dh3), leave from beside the Mobil petrol station at the south end of Blvd Mohammed V.

EL PEÑÓN DE ALHUCEMAS

One of the plazas de soberanía (see boxed text, p187) this extraordinary white island fortress can be seen a few hundred metres off Playa Asfiha, along with the uninhabited islets Isla de Mar and Isla de Tierra, which fly the Spanish flag. Spanish rule dates back to 1559, when the Saadi dynasty gave it to Spain in exchange for military assistance. In 1673, the Spanish military established a garrison there, and never left. Today, the fort hosts 60 soldiers, and cannot be visited. Spanish sovereignty has been contested by Morocco since independence in 1956.

THE PORT

The port is mainly used for a large commercial fishing operation. It is a great place to watch the catch being unloaded, and to find dinner: take your selected fish to the Club Nautique (right) for cooking.

Sleeping

The streets between the Place du Rif and the souq are packed with ultracheap hotels. Some are pretty dingy, so look around before committing.

Hotel Rif (☎ 039 982268; 13 Calle Sultan Moulay Youssef; s/d Dh40/80) If your budget is really maxed-out, you'll end up in this long hallway lined with simple rooms. Bathrooms are shared, with cold showers and squat toilets, but you do get your own sink. Keep your door locked: the staff sleeps during the day.

Hotel al-Hana (☎ 039 981642; 17 Calle Imzouren; s/d/tr Dh50/60/75) At the lower end of this price range, this simple hotel is tucked into the tiny streets east of Place du Rif. All facilities are shared, including the clean squat toilets (hot showers cost Dh10). It's well kept, but insects like the kitchen.

our pick **Hotel Etoile du Rif** (☎ 039 840848; Place du Rif; s/d/tr Dh159/185/239) This curvaceous art-deco hotel, an island in the Place du Rif, has hardly changed since 1920, and is undoubtedly the local bargain. Spotless rooms have bathrooms and satellite TV, and most have a balcony too. There's a handy café downstairs, and the hotel could hardly be better placed for buses. No need to look elsewhere.

MIDRANGE & TOP END

Hotel al-Khouzama (☎/fax 039 985669; Calle al-Andalous; s/d/tr Dh274/353/447; ❄) Just off Blvd Mohammed V, this three-star hotel is a long-time favourite for business travellers, and is suitably comfortable, with spacious rooms (though those facing away from the street are a bit dark). All come with bathroom and satellite TV, and the guys at reception are friendly and helpful.

Hotel Maghreb Jadid (☎ 039 982504; fax 039 982505; 56 Blvd Mohammed V; s/d Dh264/333; ❄) This is a reliable standby if the other hotels in this price range are booked. Rooms are spacious, and most have enclosed balconies, but the lack of any division between shower and toilet is a step down. Putting out home flags for visitors is a nice touch.

Hotel Mohammed V (☎ 039 982233; fax 039 983314; Place Mohammed VI; s/d Dh352/466; ❄) Once Al-Hoceima's top option, this hotel occupies a series of low rise concrete blocks perched above Plage Quemado – modern and bland. Rooms are comfortable enough and come with balconies giving lovely views over the bay. However, at the time of research, it was unclear whether the hotel was to be renovated or taken down.

La Perla (Ave Tariq ibn Zaid) This modern mirrored-glass high-rise luxury hotel was on the verge of opening during research. Expect three or four stars.

Eating

RESTAURANTS

Cheap restaurants cluster around Place du Rif, serving up filling tajines, brochettes and a bit of seafood to the bus-station crowd from about Dh25 per head. There are also many snack shops around town.

Espace Miramar (☎ 039 984242; Rue Moulay Ismail; mains from Dh20) It's hard to go wrong at this 5000 sq metre complex with pizzeria, two cafés, a grill and restaurant, all of it perched on the cliffs overlooking the sea, and with occasional live music as well. The nice view is marred by the strip-mined hill opposite, but this is the place to start.

Club Nautique (☎ 039 981461; Port d'Al-Hoceima; mains Dh60-90) This is the main restaurant at the port, and a good one. Buy your fish fresh off the boat and have them grill it for you. The 2nd floor overlooks the whole port and is a great place to relax and a have a beer.

La Dolce Pizza (☎ 039 984752; Place du Rif; pizza from Dh27; 🕑 5.30-11pm) This cute Italian bistro thrust out into the chaos of Place du Rif has just four tables, but lots of charm. Service is appallingly slow, and the cook is a microwave, but the decor makes it a pleasant place to sit and have some pizza, hamburgers or salads.

CAFÉS & PATISSERIES

Boulangerie Patisserie Azir (☎ 061 177142; 14 Rue Yousef Beni Tachafine; 🕑 5am-8pm) This new patisserie is already the town favourite, with great home-baked bread and tons of different sweets.

Café La Belle Vue (131 Blvd Mohammed V; 🕑 6am-8pm) This café gets its name from the terrace at the back overlooking the bay. There are several similar cafés on this stretch of Mohammed V with great views.

SELF-CATERING

Many small general food stores are dotted around town, including **Épicerie Hassouni** (Blvd Mohammed V) and **Supermarché el-Bouayadi** (Calle Abdelkrim Khattabi).

For alcohol try **Bougamar** (near cnr of Rue Micra), the local liquor store, where bottles are dispensed from behind the counter pharmacy-style.

Drinking

Hotel Mohammed V (Place Mohammed VI) This has an inviting bar, particularly as the terrace has some excellent views over Plage Quemado. A beer here will set you back Dh20.

Club Nautique (Port d'Al-Hoceima; beer Dh15) A more atmospheric option, and the bar here usually attracts quite a crowd.

Entertainment

Calypso (☎ 039 841601; Plage Tala Youssef; admission Dh80) This nightclub at Chafarina Beach Resort is the only option if you're carrying your dancing shoes; a lively place in the summer months, partly due to the professional female company.

Shopping

There is a weekly market Monday and Tuesday in the **souq**.

Getting There & Away

AIR

From June to September, Atlas Blue airlines flies from Amsterdam and Brussels twice a week to the small local airport (AHU) located 12km (Dh100 by taxi) from town. Royal Air Maroc offers sporadic service from Paris and various parts of Spain, as well as Casablanca. Otherwise the best option is a flight to Nador, 150km east.

BOAT

From June to September, Comarit runs a daily ferry to Almería in Spain (seven to eight hours). Fares are around Dh450 each way. A new service, **Reduan Ferry** (www.reduanferry.com) keeps threatening to connect Al-Hoceima to Màlaga, but at the time of research had not yet done so. Out of season the alternative remains a ferry to Nador, 150km east.

BUS

All the bus companies have offices around Place du Rif. **CTM** (☎ 039 982273) runs one daily bus to Oujda via Nador (Dh60, 3½ hours), two direct to Nador (Dh55, three hours) and three to Tetouan (Dh80, seven hours) via Chefchaouen (Dh65, six hours). There's also one evening departure for Casablanca (Dh170, 11½ hours) via Taza (Dh60, four hours), Fez (Dh90, six hours), Meknès (Dh105, 7½ hours) and Rabat (Dh140, 10 hours). This bus is timed to arrive in Taza in time to connect with the night train headed for Marrakesh.

Several small companies also serve the aforementioned destinations. There are at least three buses a day to Tetouan and Tangier (Dh80 to Dh90, nine hours). These stop in Chefchaouen only if there's enough demand. Otherwise, they'll drop you on the main road at Dardara, from where you can share a grand taxi into Chefchaouen (Dh8, 15 minutes). Heading east, there are also a couple of buses a day to Nador (Dh39, three hours) and Oujda (Dh58, seven hours).

TAXI

Grands taxis line up on the road at the southern end of Blvd Mohammed V. The most popular destinations are Taza (Dh60, 2½ hours) and Nador (Dh55, 2½ hours), although occasional taxis do go to Fez (Dh120). Taxis go through Nador to Melilla, not direct.

AROUND AL-HOCEIMA

National Park of Al-Hoceima

المنتزه الوطني للحسيمة

The undiscovered National Park of Al-Hoceima is the hidden jewel of this region. Its great mesas and dry canyons are reminiscent of the American southwest, except that they border the sea, where the limestone cliffs resemble Mallorca. Its isolation has helped preserve several at-risk species, from its tuya forests to an important colony of fishing eagle. The park's 310 sq km are spotted with Berber settlements and criss-crossed by dirt roads, making it an ideal trekking and mountain-bike territory. While a 4WD opens up your options, a 2x4 will get you through the main tracks.

While the park offers several remote and scenic beaches, the highlight is the fantastic sight of El Peñón de Velez de la Gomera, one of the plazas de soberanía (see boxed text, p187). After a long trek through a canyon, the fortress looms on the edge of a striking scythe of beach below high walls of rock. Attached by a spit of sand that ends at a guardhouse, this tiny piece of Spain is one of the world's strangest national borders. A few stone walls nearby are all that is left of Bades, a city wiped out by a flood in ancient times. This is an exhilarating travel destination, awash with the scope of human history and the flux of time.

The best way to experience the park is to go through **Asociación Rif para el Desarrollo del Turismo Rural** (Rif Association for the Development of Rural Tourism; ☎ 039 981833; www.parquenacionalalhucemas.com; riftourisme@yahoo.fr; Calle Ajdir 19) a local organisation with Spanish backing that is developing the park's rural tourism potential, to include new signage to keep you from getting lost. This energetic and helpful group will lay out an itinerary that will involve inexpensive stays in one or more rural homes (including all meals and transport) providing exposure to the unique Berber culture in the region, beaches, wildlife and more. Burros are available to help get you around in certain areas. Prices vary from Dh200 to Dh300 half-board per person depending on size of party and length of stay.

Alternatively, you can walk to El Peñón de Velez de la Gomera along the coast from Cala Iris (see below) in 1½ hours. Without your own transport, you'll need to hire a grand taxi to get there. In summer there may be enough people to share one, otherwise expect to pay Dh130 one-way. Facing inland from the beach, there is an unsigned, concrete-block rural house on the left, 100m from the sea, that rents out simple rooms with a shared bath and optional meals. Ask for the 'casa rural'. The price is Dh75 with breakfast, Dh150 with two meals, and Dh200 with three.

Cala Iris & Torres de Alcala

كالا إيريس و نهر الكالا

Cala Iris is a poor fishing village that is about to be changed forever. At the time of research the construction of a huge 10,000-bed tourist development was about to begin, with completion aimed for 2012. The previous camp ground has been closed. The scruffy port remains, and is full of sardine boats that fish at night with lamps. Locals will take you with them for Dh100. There is also a rough-looking, nameless restaurant behind the Cooperative des Marins Pecheurs that serves typical Berber food. The port is flanked by attractive beaches: Yellich (to the east) faces an island that you can walk out to; Oued Sahfa lies to the west, and an hour's hike over the hill lies Mestaza.

There are a couple of very basic shops at Torres de Alcala, 5km east. Three semi-ruined Spanish towers stand sentinel over this village, set back from a shingle beach caught between two rocky headlands. Better to focus your efforts on the adjacent National Park of Al-Hoceima.

EAST MEDITERRANEAN COAST

MELILLA مليلية

pop 65,000

Who would expect to find 900 Modernist buildings, the second largest such collection outside Barcelona, in North Africa? Yet here they are, along with one perfectly preserved medieval fortress, several fascinating museums and nearly 50 tapas bars. The result is Melilla, a nirvana for architecture and history buffs, as well as a great place to spend the weekend.

Along with Ceuta, Melilla is one of two autonomous Spanish cities on the Moroccan coast, known as the *plazas majores* (see boxed text, p187). These cultural islands have much in common: their economies are rooted in cross-border commerce, their societies are strongly multicultural and there is a significant military presence, the result of strained relations. Melilla is nearly equally divided between Christian and Muslim, with the latter being predominantly Berber. Various forces – immigrants trying to get in, Moroccan claims to sovereignty, local employment issues and more – have caused headaches in the past. In 2005 thousands of sub-Saharan immigrants tried to force their way in, and six died. One result was the construction of a €33 million fence that stretches from one side of the enclave to the other. Another was the reassuring visit of the king and queen of Spain in 2007, the first royal visit in 80 years, to great local acclaim.

Apart from a certain caution with strangers, Melilla is very easy on the traveller, and tourist infrastructure is excellent. While ferry-loads of visitors pour in during summer, in the off-season you'll have plenty of breathing room.

History

Melilla oozes with history, but it is neither as broad nor as deep as you might expect. While the area has been inhabited for more than 2000 years, the old city wasn't begun until after Spanish conquest in 1496, then built up in four stages. Up until the end of the 19th century, virtually all of Melilla was contained within a single impregnable fortress. Current borders were fixed by several treaties with Morocco between 1859 and 1894, the last following an unsuccessful siege by rebellious Rif Berbers. The method involved shooting a cannonball and seeing how far it went. More fighting with rebel Berbers broke out several times in the ensuing years, until the Spanish Protectorate consolidated its grip in 1927. In 1936, Franco flew here from the Canary Islands to launch the Spanish Civil War. Local politics still tip to the right.

Orientation

Melilla is a semicircle of 12 sq km carved out of the Moroccan coastline. The old town, Melilla la Vieja, is a highly complex, multilevel fortress that juts out into the sea. It contains numerous museums, as well as some small residential areas. The port and major beaches lie to the south, with the ferry terminal directly east.

The 'new town' is a broken grid of streets with an attractive commercial centre full of Modernist buildings. While compact, it is deficient in street signs. The heart is the long triangular Parque Hernandez, which ends at the circular Plaza de España, forming a huge exclamation point. Most of the hotels, banks and restaurants are located to the north. Like neighbouring Morocco, 4km to the south, you'll find few locals wearing shorts in the city, even when it is hot.

Information

To phone Melilla from outside Spain, dial ☎ 0034. Melilla is one hour ahead of Morocco during summer and two hours in April and May. Most shops and businesses are closed on Sunday.

INTERNET ACCESS

There are numerous internet cafés downtown.

Locutoria Dosmil (Calle Ejercito España, local 14-25; per hr €2; 9am-2pm & 4-9pm)

MODERNISME & MELILLA

Like many of the movements from which it drew its inspiration (eg the English Arts & Crafts Movement) Modernisme was a broad reaction to the material values of an industrial age, which suffused culture with a machinelike spirit. Centred in Barcelona, it was the Catalan version of art nouveau. Modernist architecture is characterised by the use of curves over straight lines, the frequent use of natural motifs (especially plants), lively decoration and rich detail, asymmetrical forms, a refined aesthetic and dynamism. Its chief proponent was Antoni Gaudí, the architect of Barcelona's famous Sagrada Familia cathedral. But in Melilla, Modernism is synonymous with Enrique Nieto.

Nieto was a student of Gaudí, who worked on his Casa Milá in Barcelona. Wanting to escape his master's shadow, however, he left for booming Melilla in 1909, in his late twenties, and stayed the rest of his life. He became the city architect in 1931, retired in 1949, and died four years later. During his long career he took part in over 1000 projects and finished 457, forever changing the face of his city. His work drew on many styles, including art deco. He also helped found one, known as Sgraffito Architecture, a blend of art deco and aerodynamic forms. His work included Melilla's main synagogue, the main mosque and several buildings for the Catholic Church, representing the diversity of the city's culture. Perhaps due to the distant location of his canvas, however, this great painter in concrete is not well-known outside of Melilla.

MEDICAL SERVICES

Urgencias Sanitarias (☎ 956 674400; 40 Alvaro de Bazan; 5pm-9am Mon-Sat, 24hr Sun & public holidays) Night pharmacy.

Hospital Comarcal (☎ 956 670000) South side of Río de Oro.

MONEY

Euros are used for all transactions in Melilla. You'll find several banks (with ATMs) around Avenida de Juan Carlos I Rey. Most will buy or sell dirham at an inferior rate to the Moroccan dealers hanging around the ferry port or the border.

On the Moroccan side of the border you can change cash at the Crédit du Maroc. There's also a Banque Populaire with an ATM 200m further into Morocco; walk straight ahead to the crossroads and it's on your left on the road to the port.

POST

Main post office (Correos y telégrafos; Calle Pablo Vallescá; 8.30am-8.30pm Mon-Fri, 9.30am-1pm Sat)

TOURIST INFORMATION

Oficina del Turismo (main) (☎ 952 976151; www.melillaturismo.com, in English; 21 Calle Fortuny; 9am-2pm & 5-8pm Mon-Fri) Offers special tours of religious sites. Website contains a comprehensive history and architectural tour.

Oficina del Turismo (kiosk) (☎ 952 976151; www.melillaturismo.com, in English; Plaza de España; 10am-2pm & 4-8pm Mon-Fri). Faces the Palacio de Asamblea.

Fundación Melilla Ciudad Monumental (☎ 952 976201; www.melillamonumental.org, in English; C/Miguel Acosta, 13;) In-depth information on local architecture.

TRAVEL AGENCIES

Viajes Melilla (☎ 952 679352; 1 Ave Duquesa de la Victoria)

Sights & Activities

MELILLA LA VIEJA (OLD MELILLA)

The fortress of Old Melilla has been restored to perfection. The main entrance is **Puerta de la Marina**, fronted by a statue of Franco, from where you ascend to the summit, passing several small museums. The first is the **Museo de Arqueología e Historia** (☎ 952 976216; Plaza Pedro de Estopiñán; admission free; 10am-2pm & 4-8.30pm Tue-Sat, 10am-2pm Sun winter, 10am-2pm & 5-9.30pm Tue-Sat, 10am-2pm Sun summer) which has a nifty little collection of architectural drawings, ancient ceramics and coins, and numerous models and archaeological finds, signed in English. The small door across the courtyard leads into the cavelike **Aljibes de las Peñuelas** (admission free; 10am-2pm & 5-9.30pm Tue-Sat, 10am-2pm Sun Apr-Sep, 10am-2pm & 4-8.30pm Tue-Sat, 10am-2pm Sun Oct-Mar), an other-worldly cistern that is still flowing. The new Berber museum across the way is due to open by 2010.

The Calle de la Concepción continues up to the 17th-century **Iglesia de la Purísima Concepción** (Parish of the Immaculate Conception; ☎ 952 681516; 10am-3pm & 4-9pm Tue-Sat, 10am-12.30pm Sun) worth a stop for its resplendent nave – and on to the adjacent **Cuevas del Conventico** (Caves of the Convent; ☎ 952 680929; admission €1.20; 10.30am-1.30pm & 4.30-8pm Tue-Sat, 10.30am-2pm Sun). These extensive and well-restored caves were used as a refuge during sieges, and pop out at a small beach below the cliffs. The guided tour (in Spanish) is excellent.

Finally you reach the summit of the fort, with its panoramic views, and the **Museo Militar** (☎ 952 685587; admission free; 10am-2pm Tue-Sun). The history of the Spanish Protectorate is dominated by military history, and this museum is the one place where you can feel the grand sweep of that violent drama, with martial music playing in the background. Don't miss the antique photographs room, where biplanes, legionnaires and Berber horsemen all fuse into a dreamy adventure novel, or the 'do not touch the cannonballs' sign, which is straight from *Dr Strangelove*.

NEW TOWN

At the turn of the 20th century, Melilla was the only centre of trade between Tetouan and the Algerian border. As the city grew, it expressed itself in the architectural style of Modernisme, the Catalan version of art nouveau (not to be confused with the cultural movement of modernism), which was then in vogue. Inspired by the Catalan architect Enrique Nieto, a disciple of Gaudí who made Melilla his home, this trend continued locally even after it went out of fashion elsewhere. The result is a living museum of some 900 Modernist and art-deco buildings. Unlike Ceuta, many of these treasures have yet to be dusted off, but the overall architectural wealth is greater.

The best way to appreciate this heritage is to stroll the area to the north of Parque

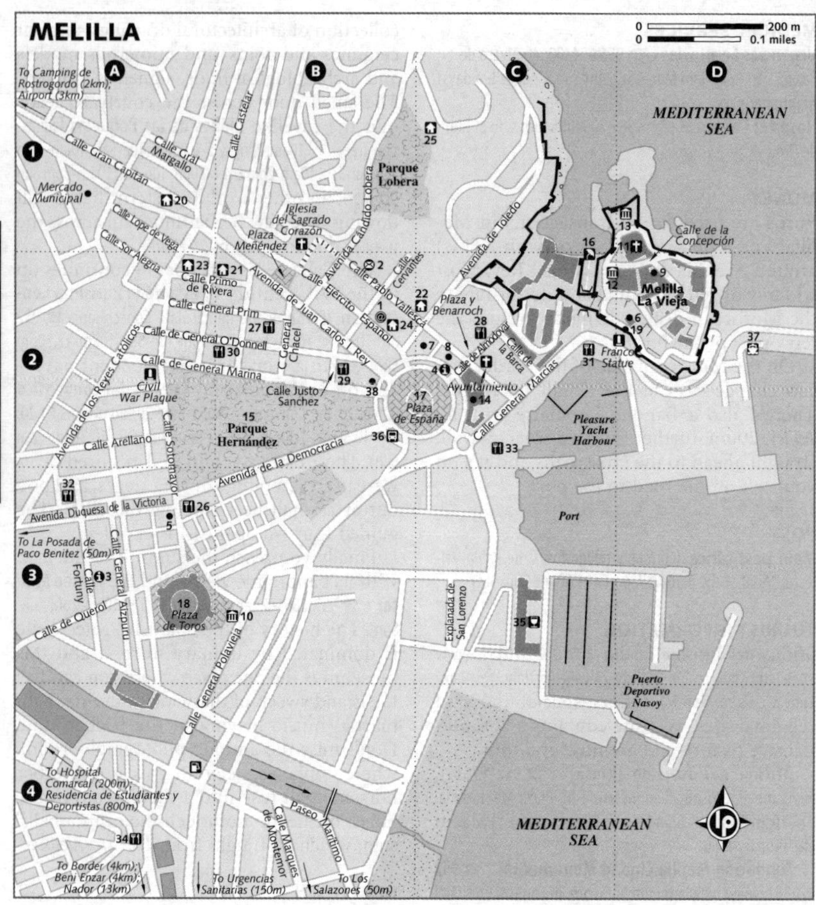

Hernandez, known as 'the golden triangle'. Several fine examples are on the **Plaza de España**, including Nieto's art deco **Palacio de Asamblea**, whose floor plan depicts a ducal crown; his **Casino Militar**, whose facade still depicts a republican coat of arms; and the **Banco de España**. Architecture fans seeking more detailed information should see the resources listed under Tourist Information, p217.

While the Palacio is an operating town hall, the staff at the entrance are willing to show tourists around upon request. Worth seeing are two rooms on the upper floor, Salon Dorado, which contains a large painting of the arrival of Spaniards in Melilla in 1497, and the Sala de Plenos, where the local congress meets.

With its central fountain, the Plaza is a pleasant place to sit. At the centre is an art-deco military monument to campaigns in Morocco. In the distance you can see Melilla's most striking contemporary building, the new courthouse, which looks like a flying saucer has landed on the roof. This observation deck is now closed to visitors.

From the Plaza you can take a pleasant stroll down the long, palm-lined **Parque Hernández**. There is a nameless café midway that serves up mint tea. At the end, turn left down Calle Sotomayor. The **Plaza De Toros** the only operating bull ring in Africa, lies straight ahead.

On the other side is the **Gaselec Museum** (☎ 952 671902; admission free; 6-9pm Mon-Fri,

11.30am-1.30pm & 6-9pm Sat & Sun) This intriguing oddity, the passion of the president of the local gas and electric company, houses a museum of Ancient Egypt completely composed of reproductions, including King Tut's mask and sarcophagus. Future plans include faux exhibitions on entirely different subjects. While many of the artefacts look fake, the unusual concept works in its own way, and could well be – ahem – reproduced elsewhere.

BEACHES

The one distressing sight in Melilla is the state of its coastline, which is everywhere strewn with plastic bottles and bags. While efforts are made to clean certain beaches, it is hard to escape this problem, particularly out of season, making you fear for the future of the Mediterranean.

There is one large beach south of the port, divided into four sections. During research there was a plastic bag visible in the water on average every 10m. The foul Rio de Oro empties into this area as well. Needless to say, stick to sunbathing.

An intriguing alternative is the secluded **Playa de la Ensanada de los Galápagos**, which is reached by taking a tunnel under the fort. It is open May to September.

Sleeping

There aren't many hotels in Melilla, so they tend to fill up even in the off-season. Prices rise 15% to 20% during peak periods.

BUDGET

Hostal La Rosa Blanca (☎ 952 682738; 7 Calle Gran Capitán; s/d €20/32) A very basic option, the rooms are clean but vary in quality, so make sure to look before you buy, and beware those tattered bedspreads. Rooms have sinks and shared baths.

our pick **Residencia de Estudiantes y Deportistas** (Residence of Students and Athletes; ☎ 952 670008; Calle Alfonso X; s/d incl breakfast €23/36, half-board €28.50/47, full-board €34/58;) This is the best budget choice if you don't mind being away from the town centre. Imagine a well-run college dormitory and you get the picture: 87 sparkling rooms, internet access, cafeteria, library and TV lounge. Rooms above the 2nd floor have balconies. Take local bus 3, which stops near Plaza España on Calle Marina every 10 minutes. The trip takes 10 to 15 minutes.

Hostal Residencia Cazaza (☎ 956 684648; 6 Calle Primo de Rivera; s/d €26/36) While the rooms here are beat up, this old building with its high ceilings and small balconies manages to be charming, and has a central location in the golden triangle. Management is friendly.

Camping de Rostrogordo (☎ 956 685262; camping per adult €4, plus per tent/car/campervan €4/5/6) With the cramped streets of Melilla, this is a decent option if you have a vehicle, 2km north of town. It's well run with good facilities; prices take a 15% hike in summer.

MIDRANGE & TOP END

Hotel Nacional (☎ 956 684540; fax 956 684481; 10 Calle Primo de Rivera; s/d €35/55;) This hotel offers similar amenities to the Cazaza, but is more expensive. The compact rooms, with quaint iron furniture and modern bathrooms, can be quite snug. Those facing inside are dark and glum, so get one looking to the street. Corner room 104 is a strong choice.

Hotel Anfora (☎ 956 683340; fax 956 683344; 8 Calle Pablo Vallescá; s/d incl breakfast €46/72;) This rather industrial-feeling two-star hotel offers standard-fare rooms with TV, fridges and balconies. The highlight is the roof terrace, offering vistas of Melilla La Vieja and the sea beyond.

Parador de Melilla (☎ 956 684940; Avenida Cándido Lobera; s/d €94/118;) This is a very classy choice with large, grand rooms, warm use of wood throughout, a high level of quality furnishings and balconies with great views to sea. The circular dining room overlooking the city is an elegant touch. The adjacent Parque Lobera is great for kids.

Hotel Rusadir (☎ 956 681240; 5 Calle Pablo Vallescá; s/d incl breakfast €66/88 low season, €86/102 high season;) This three-star hotel has been completely renovated to excellent effect, including an impressive lobby and design-conscious rooms with TV, minibars and balconies. The restaurant puts out an impressive breakfast buffet.

Eating

Many of Melilla's restaurants are associated with hotels (like the Rusadir or the Parador), but there are plenty of others around Avenida de Juan Carlos I Rey.

RESTAURANTS

Parnaso (☎ 952 684184; 30 Avenida Duquesa de la Victoria; sandwiches from €2.50; 7am-1am Mon-Sat) This hopping bistro with outdoor seating on a tree-lined avenue offers inexpensive but tasty sandwiches and tapas. Popular during lunch and with the after-work crowd.

our pick **La Pérgola** (Calle General Marcías; noon-midnight) A waterfront terrace, white tablecloths and café music make this classy spot a very pleasant place for a meal, or just a late afternoon drink. The speciality is seafood, and at €10 the prix fixe menu cannot be beaten.

Antony Pizza Factory (☎ 952 671505; Avenida de la Democracia; pizza €4-6, pasta from €5.50; 8pm-late) Less factory than cosy brasserie, its staff still works hard to dish out heavily loaded pizzas and some rich pasta sauces. Popular with Melilla's young, it has a sunken snug area for quiet dining.

La Posada de Paco Benitez (☎ 952 681629; mains from €10; 1-3.30pm & 8.30-midnight Tue-Thu) This charming restaurant is decked out like a rural Spanish cottage. The focus is on seafood and meats, Iberian-style, complemented by a strong wine menu. Following Ave Duquesa, take the second right before the bridge, and the restaurant is on your right.

Los Salazones (☎ 952 673652; Calle Conde de Alcaudete; 15; mains from €12; 1.30-4.30pm & 9pm-late) Another local favourite, this meat and seafood restaurant is located a block from the beach, and is the perfect place to end a day in the sun. Sit at the marble-topped barrels and enjoy the grilled fish.

CAFÉS

Real Club Marítimo (Yacht Harbour; 9.15am-1pm) This is a private yacht club but travellers are welcome to come and sample a croissant and coffee by the sea.

Café Rossy (5 Calle General Prim; sandwiches from €1.70; 7am-1pm & 4.30-10pm) Another reliable place to grab a quick eat or while away an hour with a book and a coffee. The *bocadillos* are a perfect lunchtime snack.

Café Toga (☎ 952 680533; Plaza y Benarroch; sandwiches €1.50; 6.30am-11pm Mon-Sat) This small bar on a broad plaza dishes out tapas and sandwiches throughout the day. Located beneath the sign for 'Academia Vetonia'.

TAPAS BARS

Casa Marta (Calle Justo Sanchez; noon-5pm & 8pm-2am) This is a rockin' tapas bar that brims with people of all ages both inside and out: outdoor seating is under a tent in the street. Each beer comes with free tapas, so three beers gets you a free dinner. Don't miss the *filetillo*, thin strips of meat with gravy.

La Cervecería (Calle de General O'Donnell; tapas from €1.50; 12.30-4pm & 8.30pm-midnight) High on decoration, this one-room bar is a green explosion of decorative tile on all surfaces, including the furniture.

SELF-CATERING

There are plenty of small grocery shops in the streets around Parque Hernández. For the complete supermarket experience, go to **Supersol** (Calle General Polavieja; 10am-10pm, closed Sun) on the road to the frontier.

Drinking

Look no further, **Puerto Deportivo Nasoy** is Melilla's bar zone, with 12 different options grouped side by side on the waterfront. Enter through the parking lot next to the courthouse.

Getting There & Away

AIR

Air Nostrum (Iberia) (902 400500; Melilla Airport; www.airnostrum.com) offers 12 daily flights between Melilla and Màlaga, as well as two daily flights to Almeria, Barcelona and Madrid, and one daily flight to Granada. The airport is a 10-minute (€5) taxi ride, and has no ATM.

CAR

Melilla is a duty-free zone, so if you're driving it's worth filling up here. Petrol is about one-third cheaper than in Morocco or Spain.

FERRY

Acciona (Transmediterranea) (956 690902; Plaza de España; 9am-1pm & 5-7pm Mon-Fri, 9am-noon Sat) serves Melilla from Màlaga and Almeria. Tickets are also available for purchase at the **estación marítima** (ferry port; 956 681633).

The ferry for Màlaga departs Melilla Monday through Saturday at midnight and arrives in Màlaga at 4pm. On Mondays it also leaves Melilla at 9am. From Màlaga it departs Monday at 11pm and arrives in Melilla at 9pm Tuesday. From Tuesday to Saturday it departs Màlaga at 2pm and arrives at 9pm. Prices begin at €35.

The ferry to Almeria departs Melilla on Monday at 10am and from Tuesday to Sunday at 2.30pm. It departs Almeria Monday at 5.30pm and Tuesday to Sunday at midnight.

BORDER CROSSING

To get to the border, you'll need to either take a taxi (€8) or catch local bus 2 (marked 'Aforos'), which runs between Plaza de España and the Beni Enzar border post (€0.60, every 30 minutes from 7.30am to 11pm). From where the buses stop, it's about 50m to Spanish customs and another 200m to Moroccan customs.

Before entering Morocco, fill in a white form and get your passport stamped at the booth. Touts may approach trying to charge you for these forms, or ask a fee to fill them out for you. If you're driving into Morocco, remember to retain the green customs slip, which you must present when you (and your vehicle) leave the country. Large queues of vehicles entering Morocco are frequent and time-consuming; procedures for foot passengers are quick and easy.

On the Moroccan side of the border, bus 19 (usually unmarked) runs hourly to Nador (Dh23, 25 minutes). Frequent grands taxis (Dh5, 15 minutes) to Nador are tucked away on a lot to the right of this crossroad.

When entering Melilla from Morocco, fill in a yellow form and get your passport stamped. Some nationalities require visas to enter Spain: if they don't stop you here, they will when you try to move on to the mainland. Bus 43 goes to Plaza España (€0.60).

Getting Around

The centre of Melilla is compact and easy to walk around. Buses ply the route between Plaza de España and the border. The local **taxi service** (956 683621) is also useful.

NADOR الناظور

pop 150,000

There is a new road from Al-Hoceima to Nador that is a delight to travel, even when squashed into a grand taxi. It passes through red cliffs, verdant gorges and, midway, an enormous sculpture of deeply eroded hills.

Unfortunately Nador itself offers little when you arrive, regardless of its size. Apart from Marchika, its pretty lagoon, there are no sights or attractions in this endless sprawl of concrete blocks. The city serves more as a transport link, with a major airport, active ferry port and sleek new train under development (with service to Fez by 2010). Like the rest of the coast, this situation is changing, with the requisite corniche and palm-lined boulevards under construction, and new hotels, restaurants and a marina coming, but for now it is best to press on.

Orientation

The centre of Nador is built on a strict grid system. The main north–south axis is Ave Hassan II, with the main bus station and taxi stand at its southern end. It is bisected by the promenade Ave Mohammed V, which runs east to west from the waterfront to the town hall. The needle-thin minaret of the Grande Mosquée is a useful landmark.

Information

Credit Maroc (64 Ave Mohammed V) One of several banks on Mohammed V with foreign-exchange services and ATM.

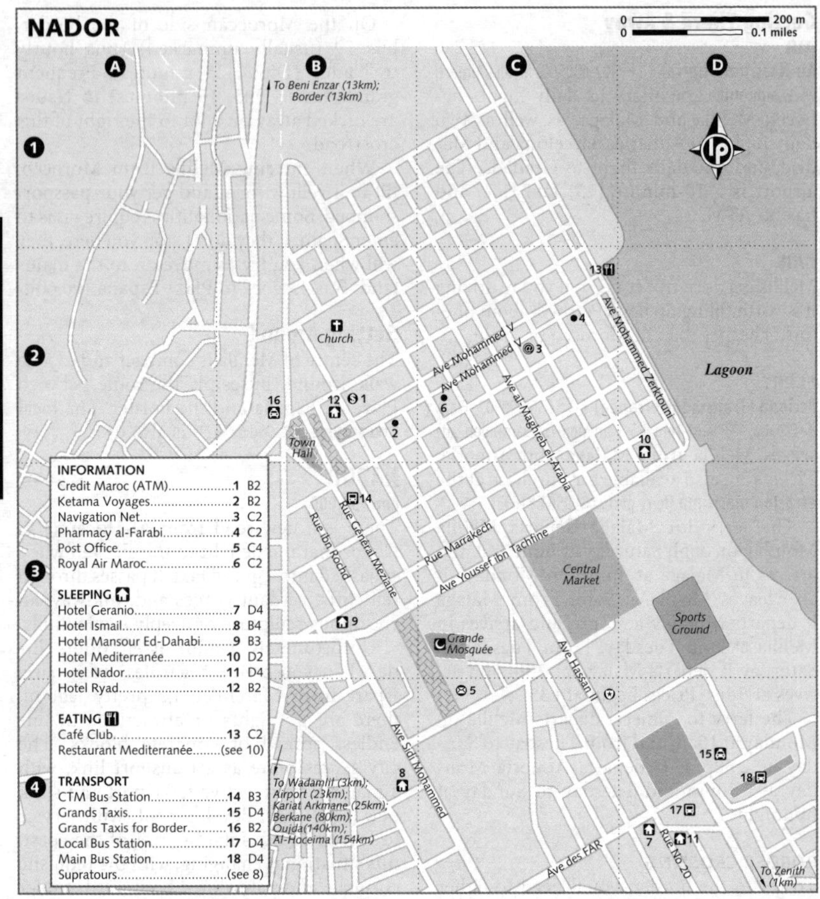

Ketama Voyages (☎ 036 606191; ketama-nador@iam.net.ma; 56 Ave Mohammed) Sells ferry tickets to Almería.
Navigation Net (Ave Mohammed V; per hr Dh8; 🕑 9.30am-11pm) Internet café.
Pharmacy al-Farabi (☎ 036 606011; Ave Mohammed V)
Post Office (🕑 8am-4.15pm Mon-Fri) Located next to Grande Mosquée.
Royal Air Maroc (Ave Mohammed V; 🕑 8.30am-12.15pm & 2.30-7pm Mon-Fri, 9am-noon & 3-6pm Sat)

Sleeping

There's no shortage of hotels of all classes in Nador. The cheaper places are near the bus and grand taxi stations.

Hotel Geranio (☎ 036 602828; 16 Rue No 20; s/d Dh70/120) Just away from the chaos of the bus station, streetside rooms here can be noisy, but a drop in prices has made this the top budget option. Clean rooms come with tiny bathrooms. There's a ground-floor cafeteria as well.

Hotel Mansour Ed-Dahabi (☎ 036 606583; 105 Rue Marrakech; s/d Dh288/348) A pleasant central location and quiet atmosphere are the advantages of this three-star hotel. It's a bit bland, but the rooms are comfortable and fully equipped, with carved plaster ceilings. Off-season discounts can be generous.

our pick **Hotel Mediterranée** (☎ 036 606495; fax 036 606611; hotel.mediterranee@gmail.com; 2-4 Ave Youssef ibn Tachfine; s/d Dh227/276) This is easily your best option in Nador. Recently renovated, with classy spaces all united by varnished trim, it occupies an excellent location overlooking the corniche and the lagoon beyond. The corner rooms have the best views and are full of light, and the restaurant is one of the best in town (below). If you need some downtime you could sleep, eat and beach right here, in high style, and at a bargain price.

Hotel Ryad (☎ 036 607717; hotelryad@hotmail.com; Ave Mohammed V; s/d incl breakfast Dh500/600; ❄) Beautiful handmade wooden furniture makes this hotel's plush modern rooms stand out. Those on the top floor have views over the lagoon. The two hotel bars and disco also make this the centre of local nightlife, which is more hopping than one might expect.

Eating & Drinking

There are numerous cheap eats around the CTM bus station, serving up quick brochettes, sandwiches and tajines. Ave Mohammed V is the place for a lazy coffee – street cafés line the road under shady orange trees.

Zenith (☎ 036 332298; 33-35 Rue 72; mains from Dh40; 🕑 8am-midnight) The new face of Nador, this swank and ever-popular café on two downtown floors is where all those construction plans are being discussed over coffee. There's a fine pizzeria upstairs, and burgers and pasta too.

Wadamlil (☎ 036 606260; 39 Rue Tawima; 🕑 8am-4am) Simple paper-covered tables on a main road disguise one of Nador's most popular restaurants, which is open nearly around the clock. Choose your own assortment of seafood and meat from a glass case and have it cooked to order. Expect a meal to run approximately Dh70 per person.

Restaurante Mediterranée (☎ 036 609494; Ave Youssef ibn Tachfine; dishes from Dh65; 🕑 noon-3pm & 7-10pm) The Hotel Mediterranée's restaurant is a swish dining room, with prompt service, an international menu and views to sea.

Café Club (Ave Mohammed Zerktouni; 🕑 6am-11pm) Jutting into the lagoon at the far end of Mohammed V, this island café is a good breakfast option and a welcome bit of maritime focus in an otherwise concrete forest.

Getting There & Away

AIR

The airport is 23km south of Nador. Royal Air Maroc operates numerous flights to Europe and Casablanca. Iberia connects Nador with Spain. Budget carriers Ryanair and Clickair have recently begun service from Marseille and Barcelona.

BOAT

Acciona has opened a new fast ferry service to Almeria. It leaves Almeria Tuesday to Saturday at night, arrives Nador early in the morning, then turns around and leaves within three hours. Comarit has a slow ferry that leaves Nador for Almeria at 10pm every day, and leaves Almeria for Nador at 10am every day. The trip takes five to six hours. Comanav also offers a service four days a week to Almeria, and services to Sete, France on Sunday.

The port of Beni Enzar is 7km from the city but traffic makes it feel much further. The quickest way to get there is by grand taxi (DH8, 15 minutes).

BUS

From the **CTM office** (☎ 056 600136; Rue Genéral Meziane) there are departures to all the usual suspects: Casablanca, Rabat, Meknès, Fez, Tangier, Larache, Sidi Kacem, Al-Hoceima, Chefchaouen and more. In the evening, several slightly cheaper Casablanca-bound coaches run by other companies leave from the same area.

The main bus station is southeast of the centre. There are frequent departures for Tetouan (Dh130, 10 hours) between 9am and 9pm. Some of these services go via Chefchaouen (Dh130, nine hours). There are hourly buses to Oujda (Dh25, three hours) via Berkane (Dh16, one hour) from 6am to 5pm, and every two hours to Al-Hoceima (Dh35, three hours) throughout the day. Buses also leave for Fez (Dh74, seven hours) every 30 minutes or so in the morning.

Other useful services include buses to Ras el-Maa (Dh15, two hours, three daily), and Saídia (Dh22, two hours). Buses leave every hour between 7am and 7pm for Beni Enzar (the Melilla border) from outside the main bus station (Dh3, 25 minutes). In theory it's bus 19 but in practice they're usually unnumbered.

Unlike elsewhere, CTM has a small office in the main bus station in addition to its main office.

TAXI

The huge grand-taxi lot next to the main bus station serves plenty of destinations including Oujda (Dh50, three hours), Al-Hoceima (Dh55, three hours), Berkane (Dh25, one hour) and Taza (Dh55). Less frequent taxis go to Fez (Dh110, five hours) and other points south. Grands taxis to Beni Enzar (the Melilla border; Dh5, 15 minutes) leave every few minutes from here and also from a junction north of the town hall.

TRAIN

Nador was nearing completion of its new rail link during research. If that proves insufficient, **Supratours** (☎ 056 607262; Ave Sidi Mohammed) runs a daily early evening bus to Taourirt (Dh40), connecting with trains to Casablanca.

EAST OF NADOR

East of Nador, on the opposite side of the lagoon, the coast is a mix of salt marsh and sand dunes, which attract a wide-variety of birdlife, including the greater flamingo. There are two scruffy towns here, **Kariat Arkmane** and **Ras el-Maa**, each with basic camping facilities in summer, that can be reached by bus, but unless you want to see birds, there is insufficient reason to make a special trip. If you are passing through anyway, stop at Ras el-Maa and walk up to the lighthouse, from where you can see the Islas Chafarinas, the last bit of Spain on the northern coast (see boxed text, p187).

BERKANE بركان

pop 80,000

Berkane is a dusty modern town about 80km southeast of Nador on the road to Oujda. It's most useful to travellers as a transit point, including the gas smugglers who blow through town like bats out of hell on their nightly runs to Algeria. It can serve as a base for exploring the Beni-Snassen Mountains, but there is also better lodging closer by.

The town is easy to navigate as it's stretched along Blvd Mohammed V, which leads from the green and white Grande Mosquée in the west (don't miss the many stork nests in the trees) to the large roundabout at the other end, dominated by a large pink courthouse. You'll find the post office and plenty of ATMs here. Halfway between is the main square, with the CTM station on the south side and a petrol station opposite.

Sights & Activities

The only site of interest in Berkane is the **French Church** (☎ 036 610289; 🕒 8.30am-noon & 2.30-6pm Mon-Sat, closed Wed afternoon). Built in 1909, it was the life project of a single priest with a very broad view of religion. The interior contains a strange amalgamation of alchemy, signs of the Zodiac and Biblical scenes transplanted to Morocco, all painted by the priest himself. From the Grand Mosquée, head down Blvd Mohammed V and turn left at Maroc Telecom. The church is straight ahead.

The church is now home to the Association Homme et Environment (Man & Environment Association), a dedicated, and rare, local environmental group. Ask for its president, Nadjib Bachiri, who speaks fluent English and enjoys giving tours. Entrance is free, but donations to the association are most welcome.

Sleeping & Eating

The main options for sleeping and eating are strung along or near Blvd Mohammed V. In addition, a new upscale hotel, the Rosalina, was slated to open on Mohammed V soon after time of research, with double rooms around Dh400.

Hotel Mounir (☎ 036 611867; 54 Blvd Mohammed V; r per person Dh50-70) This reasonable cheapie is next to the Grande Mosquée. You get a clean, self-contained room with hot shower and an early morning wake-up call from the muezzin.

Hotel Zaki (☎ 036 613743; 27 Rte d'Oujda; s/d incl breakfast Dh360/420; ❄) This three-star hotel is 400m east of the main roundabout. The 2nd floor is like a designer showroom, with each room tastefully decorated in its own style, but careful of dangerous carpets jumbled on the stairs, which have been there for years.

Café du Jardin (Blvd Mohammed V; 🕒 5am-8pm) Located in a garden opposite the main square, this place has the closest thing to atmosphere in Berkane, although the clientele is decidedly masculine.

Café Royal (Blvd Mohammed V) Near the square, this is the local place for pizza.

Getting There & Away

Berkane's bus and taxi stands are scattered all over town. The **CTM office** (☎ 056 613992) is next to Café Laetizia on the west side of the main square. There is just one early evening departure for Fez (Dh100, six hours), Meknès (Dh110, 7½ hours), Rabat (Dh150, 10 hours), Casablanca (Dh17, 11 hours) and Oujda (Dh15, one hour). Long-hauls to Spain also leave from here.

Most other long-distance buses gather in the streets behind the CMH petrol station, and serve the above destinations. The buses to Nador (Dh18, one hour) stop immediately behind the petrol station, and run hourly until mid-afternoon.

Local buses for Taforalt (Dh8, 30 minutes) depart from beside Hotel Mounir twice a day, while grands taxis for Taforalt (Dh10, 25 minutes) and Nador (Dh25, one hour) use the lot on the opposite side of the road, between the Shell petrol station and the bridge.

Grands taxis for Oujda (Dh17, one hour) leave from near the bus station; for Saídia (Dh8, 15 minutes) or Ras el-Mar (Dh8, 15 minutes) from the square in front of the pink courthouse at the end of Blvd Mohammed V; and for Nador from the lot opposite the Great Mosque.

BENI-SNASSEN MOUNTAINS
جبال بني سناسن

Far more alluring than Berkane are the beautiful Beni-Snassen Mountains that border it to the south. While technically termed a 'site of biological and ecological interest', they are for all intents and purposes a national park. This is a verdant area of scenic gorges that few imagine when they think of Morocco, and even fewer visit.

From Berkane, take the national road to **Taforalt** (Tafoughalt) which passes through beautiful mountain scenery. Taforalt is a somewhat haphazard settlement that arose around a former French military installation, but the northern end, which you come upon first, contains a charming strip of cafés and restaurants, and an excellent new hotel, **Auberge de Taforalt** (☎ 062 045119; http://taforaltclub.com; d/tr Dh300/400, Berber tents 2-people Dh300, 4-people Dh500). This wonderfully creative boutique hotel has rooms in the form of caves surrounding a well-lit central lodge, and a snazzy kitchen. For kids, or for the kid in you, there are also five Berber tents on the roof for rent as rooms.

Guests at the Auberge also receive free admission to the classy **Club Taforalt** (☎ 062 045119; http://taforaltclub.com; entrance Dh10, pool Dh50; Apr-Sep;) across the street. The humble entrance to this public facility gives way to an elegant swimming pool with breathtaking mountain views. There is also a floral garden, a children's play area and a charming stone restaurant, all of it under the boughs of the forest. If you are coming to this area to explore the park in season, the combination of the Auberge and the Club Taforalt (which have the same owner) constitutes a full-service mountain resort that is far preferable to staying in Berkane.

An equally alluring place to stay is **Gite Tagma** (☎ 036 610289; r per person incl full-board Dh200) It doesn't get any more authentic, or tranquil, than this remote, 300-year-old rural lodge midway up the mountains, with its small working farm. Five simple bedrooms surround a common compound, with wonderful views of pine-dotted canyons. From here you can easily trek to the postcard Sidi Ali Oussaidi Mosque, standing against the mountains like a Bavarian chapel, and the romantic town of Tagma, which sits in the valley below like a small Berber fortress. Or you can just kick back with a book and dream. The *gîte* ('sjeet' in French) is a joint project between the owner and Assocation Homme et Environment (opposite), and the model for rural tourism development in this region. It is signposted about 15km on the national road from Berkane to Taforalt, but don't miss the chance to be taken up by a donkey; ask the owner.

Soon after you enter Taforalt from Berkane, turn left at the post office, then immediately turn left again and follow signs to the Infokiosk, which has a small but well-done display on the natural history of the park, and an observation platform with heavenly views of a distant mesa. If you're lucky you will catch sight of a big-horned Barbary sheep from the adjacent reserve. They generally arrive around 4pm, when it is cooler.

About 2km back down the national road is a right turn signposted for two *grottes* (caves). The **Grottes des Pigeons** (1km) is the site of an active excavation by Oxford University that has revealed human remains from the Pleistocene era, including some of the earliest human jewellery (80,000 years old). Another 5km brings you to the **Grottes de Chameau**, a multistorey cave complex with three entrances that has been closed for years due to flooding damage. Three kilometres more brings you to the pretty **Zegzel Gorge** and a beautiful serpentine drive. Don't miss the chance to sample the kumquats, a local industry. Even the Romans remarked upon them.

The source of the **Charaâ River** provides a worthwhile detour. Follow signs to the tiny hamlet of Zegzel, 2km up a side road. At the end there's a popular picnic spot near where the river gushes out of the cliff. Not far from here, a spectacular ridge road cuts east to Oujda. You'll need a 4WD vehicle, a good map and an early start.

If you don't have your own vehicle, the easiest way to access the park is to hire a grand taxi from Berkane. The minimum fare will be in the region of Dh200 for two hours, although not all drivers will be willing to take their vehicles along the poor roads near the hamlet of Zegzel. A cheaper alternative is to take a bus or grand taxi to Taforalt and walk down. Two buses each morning make the journey from Berkane (Dh8, 30 minutes), with return services in the afternoons. Grands taxis cost Dh10, and are most frequent on market days (Wednesday and Sunday).

SAÍDIA السعيدية

pop 3000

At time of research most of Saídia was in flux. Fadesa, a Spanish construction company purchased by Moroccan owners, was in the process of transforming this sleepy backwater into a large resort town, similar to those at M'Diq and Martil (not to mention the Costa del Sol). It will be fed by the new road to Nador, due to open by 2009. The town has a fine beach and several pre-existing hotels now surrounded by empty boulevards of new tarmac. Hopefully it will not end up looking like the new developments west of town, which are horrific. A meaningful review will have to wait until the cranes have departed.

The adjacent border with Algeria remains closed. While Morocco would like to reopen it, Algeria has so far refused to agree. However, there is no active conflict.

Imperial Cities, Middle Atlas & the East

الأطلس المتوسط والشرق رهش ىروتاريما

If you were to look for Morocco in microcosm, this region would take the title. Its diversity runs the spectrum from ancient cities and ruins to grand mountain vistas and desert oases.

The plains of the north have acted as Morocco's breadbasket for centuries, feeding the rise of cities whose culture went on to dominate the rest of the country. The Romans were the first to get in on the act, and left remains at Volubilis as testament.

The streets of Fez's World Heritage medina rank high on the must-see list of any visitor to the country. Getting lost amid the souqs and alleys is an unforgettable (and often unavoidable) way to spend a day. Meknès, another imperial capital and near neighbour to Fez offers a more pocket-sized version of the medina experience.

To the south, the land rises into the limestone range of the Middle Atlas, which are home to the Barbary ape, Morocco's only monkey. The area is made for hiking, and in winter the wealthy still come here to ski.

Across the mountains, towns like Midelt herald drier climes, and the distinctive kasbahs of the south begin to make an appearance. The desert isn't far away, and by the time you reach the oasis of Figuig, the olive tree has long given way to the date palm.

HIGHLIGHTS

- Dive into the warren of medina streets looking for souqs and souvenirs in historic **Fez** (p228)
- Enjoy the sounds of the sublime at the **Fes Festival of World Sacred Music** (p242)
- Travel back in time in the mosaic-strewn Roman ruins of **Volubilis** (p266)
- Explore the out-sized imperial architecture of **Meknès** (p254)
- Spend a day and night on pilgrimage in the holy town of **Moulay Idriss** (p268)
- Hike out into the green wooded slopes of the Middle Atlas around **Azrou** (p272)
- Make like a troglodyte in the weird caverns of **Gouffre du Friouato** (p282)

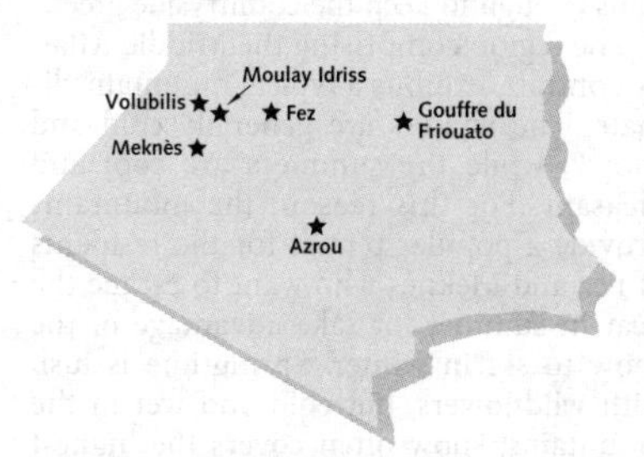

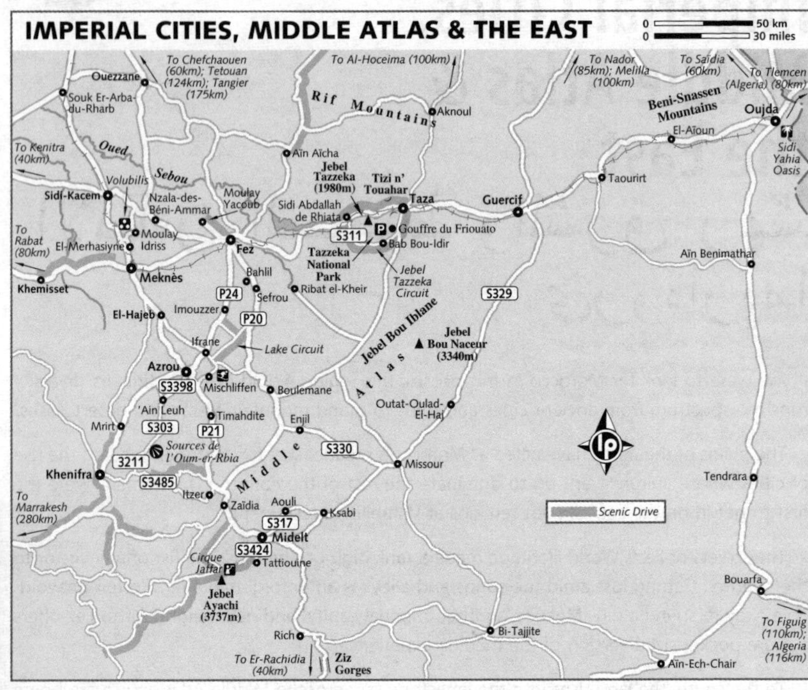

CLIMATE

The climate of this region varies widely between the mountainous area to the south and the dry flatlands of the valley (formed between the Middle Atlas and Rif Mountains) to the north and east. Around Fez and Meknès and in the east, summers are scorching hot, with temperatures averaging around 30°C in July and August. Levels of rainfall in the summer are minuscule, mimicking the climate of the desert further south. During the rest of the year, the climate is not as harsh. Winter and spring are pleasantly mild, and it rains enough to keep the countryside green.

The region comprising the Middle Atlas, by contrast, exhibits a typical mountain climate. The winters are generally cold and snowy, while the summers are cool and pleasant. For this reason, the mountains provide a popular retreat for the residents of Fez and Meknès who want to escape the heat in summer, or take advantage of the snow to ski in winter. Springtime is lush with wildflowers, but cold and wet in the mountains; snow often covers the highest peaks as late as June.

GETTING THERE & AWAY

The train line connects the region's major cities to the coast, with direct links from Tangier, Rabat and Casablanca. There are also direct flights from Europe – primarily France – to Fez and Oujda. Fez and Oujda link into Royal Air Maroc's internal flight network, via Casablanca.

GETTING AROUND

From Marrakesh and Casablanca, the train line runs east through Meknès, Fez and Taza all the way to Oujda. Travelling around the mountainous Middle Atlas, however, requires catching a bus or hiring a grand taxi.

IMPERIAL CITIES

FEZ فاس

pop 1 million

In recent years Fez has boomed as a tourist destination. Money has poured into the city, from foreigners buying up riads in the medina to new parks and fountains in the ville nouvelle. If you believe the travel and style pages of the Western media, Fez has become the new Marrakesh.

Tell a Fassi that however, and they'll laugh in your face. Fez as the new anywhere? This is an old and supremely self-confident city that has nothing to prove to anyone. Dynasties and booms have all come and gone in the city's 1200-year existence, and Fez will be around long after the next fashion has burned itself out. Fez is the spiritual and cultural centre of the country, and the pulse of life here Morocco's symbolic heartbeat.

Founded shortly after the Arabs exploded across North Africa and Spain, Fez was shaped by each of the great dynasties and by its population's roots in Muslim Spain and the Arab east. The fertile countryside allowed the city to grow quickly, and nurture a reputation for culture and learning. Any Fassi will be quick to point out that the city created the world's first university, centuries before Oxford and Cambridge were a twinkle in anyone's eye. With learning came Islamic orthodoxy. Green – the colour of Islam – is also the colour of Fez, endlessly repeated on its tiles and doors.

Such authority means that the city's allegiance, or at least submission, has always been essential to whoever held Morocco's throne. Morocco's independence movement was born here, and when there are strikes or protests, they are always at their most vociferous in Fez.

For visitors, the medina of Fès el-Bali (Old Fez) is the city's great drawcard and it has an impressive checklist of selling points: Morocco's first World Heritage site, and both the world's largest living Islamic medieval city and the biggest car-free urban environment on the planet. But statistics count for little when you first encounter the medina up close. It's an assault on the senses, a warren of narrow lanes and covered bazaars fit to bursting with aromatic food stands, craft workshops, mosques and an endless parade of people. Old and new constantly collide – the man driving the donkeys and mules that remain the main form of transport is likely to be chatting on his mobile phone, while the ancient skyline is punctuated equally with satellite dishes and minarets.

Although much work is being done to restore or consolidate parts of the medina, swathes of it remain in poor repair, and scaffolding is everywhere. Over 14,000 buildings are listed as being in need of rehabilitation, and for all the romance of medina life to visitors, many residents have been happy to sell up to foreigners to swap their sometimes medieval living conditions for a modern apartment in the ville nouvelle.

For the visitor, the trick is to dive straight in. It is initially overwhelming, but once you adjust to the pace of the city, Fez reveals its charms in most unexpected ways. Seemingly blind alleys lead to squares with exquisite fountains or filled with the rhythmic hammer-music of copper beaters, while a set of exquisite carved wooden doors might as easily lead into a *medersa* (theological school) or restored riad. Getting lost in Fez is where the fun really starts.

History

In AD 789, Idriss I – who founded Morocco's first imperial dynasty – decided that Oualili (Volubilis) was too small and drew up plans for a grand new capital. He died before the plans were implemented, however, so credit for the founding of Fez is often awarded to his son, Idriss II, who carried out the will of his father. The memory of Idriss II is perpetuated in his *zawiya* (religious fraternity based around a shrine) in the heart of Fez el-Bali.

By 809, Fez was well established. Its name is believed to come from the Arabic word for axe; one tale relates that a golden pickaxe was unearthed here at the start of construction.

The city started as a modest Berber town, but then 8000 families fleeing Al-Andalus settled the east bank of the Oued Fez. They were later joined by Arab families from Kairouan (Qayrawan) in modern-day Tunisia, who took over the west bank, creating the Kairaouine quarter. The heritages of these two peoples formed a solid foundation for future religious, cultural and architectural richness. Idriss II's heirs split the kingdom, but Fez continued to enjoy peace and prosperity until the 10th century.

Over the next centuries, the fortunes of Fez rose and fell with the dynasties. Civil war and famine – incited by Berber invasions – were relieved only by the rise of the Almoravids. When that dynasty fell from power around 1154, they fled Fez and

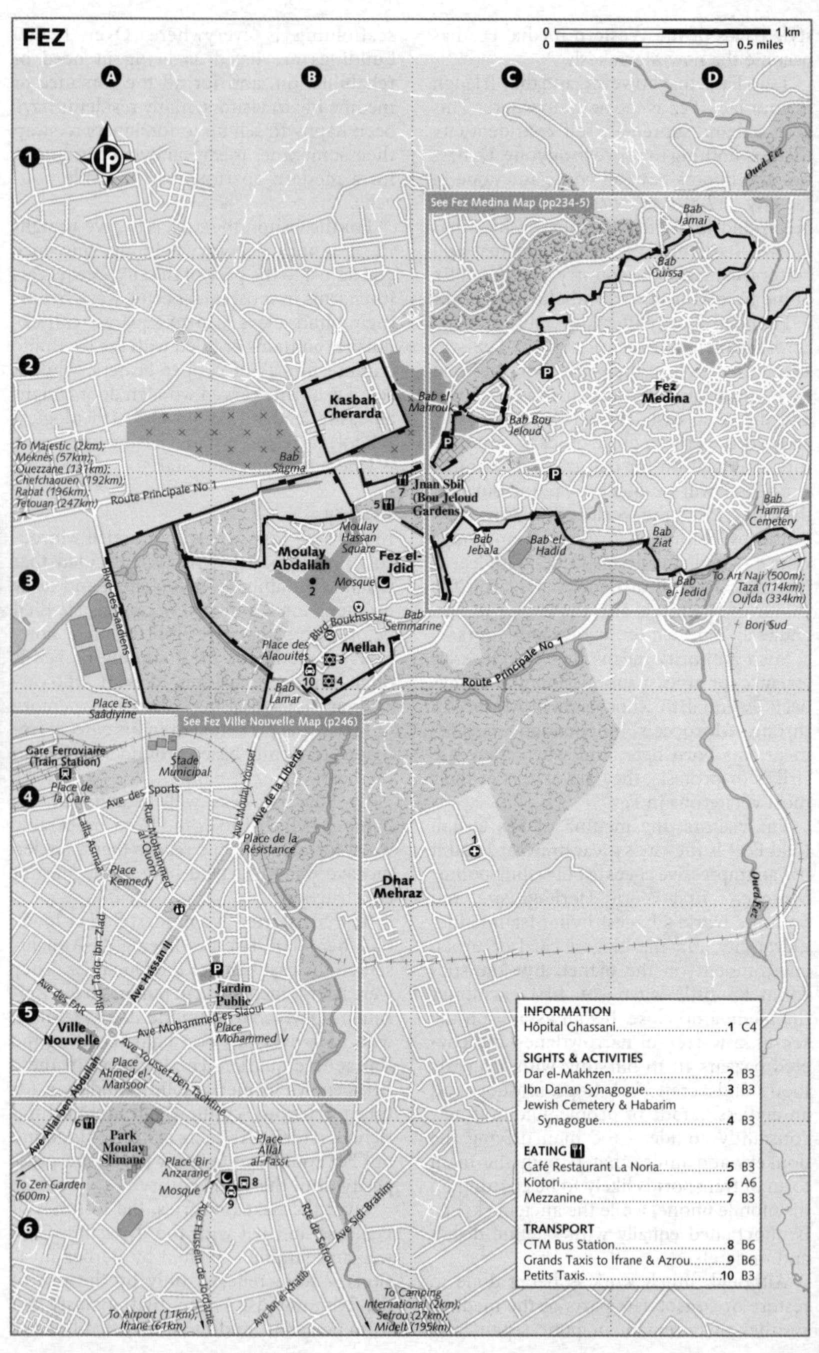
FEZ
0 1 km
0 0.5 miles
See Fez Medina Map (pp234-5)
See Fez Ville Nouvelle Map (p246)
Kasbah Cherarda
Bab el-Mahrouk
Bab Bou Jeloud
Fez Medina
Bab Jamaï
Bab Guissa
Bab Sagma
Jnan Sbil (Bou Jeloud Gardens)
Moulay Hassan Square
Moulay Abdallah
Fez el-Jdid
Mosque
Bab Jebala
Bab el-Hadid
Bab Ziat
Bab el-Jedid
Bab Hamra Cemetery
To Art Naji (500m); Taza (114km); Oujda (334km)
Borj Sud
Oued Fez
To Majestic (2km); Meknès (57km); Ouezzane (131km); Chefchaouen (192km); Rabat (196km); Tetouan (247km)
Route Principale No 1
Blvd des Saadiens
Blvd Boukhsissat
Bab Semmarine
Place des Alaouites
Mellah
Bab Lamar
Place Es-Saadiyine
Gare Ferroviaire (Train Station)
Place de la Gare
Stade Municipal
Ave des Sports
Lalla Asmaa
Rue Mohammed al-Quorri
Ave Moulay Youssef
Ave de la Liberté
Place de la Résistance
Place Kennedy
Dhar Mehraz
Blvd Tariq ibn Ziad
Ave Hassan II
Ave des FAR
Jardin Public
Ave Mohammed es Slaoui
Place Mohammed V
Ville Nouvelle
Ave Youssef ben Tachfine
Place Ahmed el-Mansoor
Ave Allal ben Abdullah
Park Moulay Slimane
Place Bir Anzarane
Mosque
Place Allal al-Fassi
To Zen Garden (600m)
Ave Hussein de Jordanie
Rte de Sefrou
Ave Sidi Brahim
Ave Ibn el-Khatib
To Airport (11km); Ifrane (61km)
To Camping International (2km); Sefrou (27km); Midelt (195km)
INFORMATION
Hôpital Ghassani 1 C4
SIGHTS & ACTIVITIES
Dar el-Makhzen 2 B3
Ibn Danan Synagogue 3 B3
Jewish Cemetery & Habarim Synagogue 4 B3
EATING
Café Restaurant La Noria 5 B3
Kiotori 6 A6
Mezzanine 7 B3
TRANSPORT
CTM Bus Station 8 B6
Grands Taxis to Ifrane & Azrou 9 B6
Petits Taxis 10 B3

destroyed the city walls as they went. Only when the succeeding Almohad dynasty was assured of the Fassis' loyalty were the walls replaced – large sections still date from this period.

Fez continued to be a crucial crossroads, wielding intellectual rather than political influence. With the Kairaouine Mosque and University already well established, it was *the* centre of learning and culture in an empire stretching from Spain to Senegal. It recovered its political status only much later, with the arrival of the Merenid dynasty around 1250.

The archaeological legacy of the Merenids is still evident today – from their exquisite *medersas* to the building of the self-contained Fez el-Jdid (New Fez). As the Merenids collapsed, successive battling dynasties were unable to retain power for any notable period, although sultans often resided here in their attempt to maintain control over the north.

During the 19th century, as central power crumbled and European interference increased, the distinction between Marrakesh and Fez diminished with both effectively serving as capitals of a fragmented country. Fez retained its status as the 'moral' capital. It was here, on 30 March 1912, that the treaty introducing the French and Spanish protectorates over Morocco was signed. Less than three weeks later, rioting and virtual revolt against the new masters served as a reminder of the city's volatility.

The French may have moved the political capital to Rabat, but Fez remains a constituency to be reckoned with. The Istiqlal (Independence) Party of Allal al-Fassi was established here; many of the impulses towards ejecting the French originated here; and the city was the scene of violent strikes and riots in the 1980s.

As one of Morocco's most traditional cities, Fez is generally regarded with a certain amount of awe, perhaps tinged with jealousy, by the rest of the country. Indeed, a disproportionate share of Morocco's intellectual and economic elite hail from here and it's a widely held belief (especially among Fassis) that anyone born in Fez medina is more religious, cultured, artistic and refined.

Fassi womenfolk, also considered to be the country's most elegant and its most gifted cooks, are much sought after as wives. When the news came out that Mohammed VI's new bride was from Fez, the locals were not in the least surprised.

Orientation

Fez can be neatly divided into three distinct parts: Fez el-Bali (the core of the medina) in the east; Fez el-Jdid (containing the Mellah – Jewish quarter – and Royal Palace) in the centre; and the Ville Nouvelle, the modern administrative area constructed by the French, to the southwest. Nowadays, the city's expanding population has filled out the ville nouvelle and has spread to the hillsides to the north and south.

Fez el-Bali is the area most interesting to visitors. The main entrances are Bab Bou Jeloud and Batha in the northwest corner. The ville nouvelle is laid out in typical French colonial style with wide, tree-lined boulevards, squares and parks. Blvd Mohammed V – interrupted by Place Mohammed V – runs north–south and bisects the main road Ave Hassan II. Most restaurants and midrange hotels, as well as the post office and banks are along these streets.

Frequent local buses connect the ville nouvelle with the medina via Ave de la Liberté, with two routes then splitting to run north and south along the old city walls, past either Bab el-Jedid or Bab el-Mahrouk. It is also possible to walk between the two – following Blvd Moulay Youssef from Ave Hassan II will take you there via the *mellah* and Royal Palace (Dar el-Makhzen). Allow about 30 minutes from Place Florence to Bab Bou Jeloud.

MAPS

Fez from Bab to Bab: Walks in the Medina by Hammad Berrada is a great book of walking tours in the Fez medina. It details 11 different walks, allowing readers to discover otherwise unknown corners and courtyards amidst this labyrinth. *Fes Medina Tourist Circuits Guide* accompanies the self-guided walking tours marked throughout the medina.

Information

BOOKSHOPS

Librarie Fikr al-Moasser (Map p246; 15 Rue du 16 Novembre) Stocks a small range of foreign-language titles, including travel guides and coffee-table books.

CULTURAL CENTRES

Institut Français (Map p246; ☎ 035 623921; www.institutfrancaisfes.com; 33 Rue Loukili) Organises a packed program of films, concerts, exhibitions and plays.

INTERNET ACCESS

Cyber Batha (Map pp234-5; Derb Douh; per hr Dh10; 9am-10pm) Has English as well as French keyboards.

Cyber Club (Map p246; Blvd Mohammed V; per hr Dh6; 9am-10pm)

Teleboutique Cyber Club (Map p246; Blvd Mohammed V; per hr Dh7; 9am-11pm) Above téléboutique on corner.

MEDIA

L'Agenda Free bimonthly listings magazine (in French) produced by the regional tourism board. Available at the tourist office and some riads and restaurants.

The View From Fez (http://riadzany.blogspot.com) Essential news and views blog for keeping up to date with what's happening in Fez.

MEDICAL SERVICES

Hôpital Ghassani (Map p230; ☎ 055 622777) One of the city's biggest hospitals; located east of the ville nouvelle in the Dhar Mehraz district.

Night Pharmacy (Map p246; ☎ 035 623493; Blvd Moulay Youssef; 9pm-6am) Located in the north of the ville nouvelle; staffed by a doctor and a pharmacist.

MONEY

There are plenty of banks (with ATMs) in the ville nouvelle along Blvd Mohammed V, virtually all offering foreign exchange. There's not much happening in the medina, with these useful exceptions:

Banque Populaire (Map pp234-5; Ave des Français; 8.45am-noon & 2.45-6pm Mon-Thu, 8.45am-noon Sat) ATM and foreign exchange.

Société Générale (Map pp234-5; Ave des Français; 8.45am-noon & 2.45-6pm Mon-Thu, 8.45-11am Fri, 8.45am-noon Sat) ATM and foreign exchange.

POST

Main post office (Map p246; cnr Ave Hassan II & Blvd Mohammed V) Poste restante is at the far left; the parcels office is through a separate door.

Post office (Map pp234-5; Place Batha) Located in the medina, also has an ATM.

TOURIST INFORMATION

There is no tourist information situated in the medina.

Syndicat d'Initiative (Tourist Information Office; Map p246; ☎ 035 623460; Place Mohammed V)

TRAVEL AGENCIES

Carlson Wagonlit (Map p246; ☎ 035 622958; fax 035 624436) Behind Central Market; useful for flights and ferries.

Dangers & Annoyances

Although Fez is safe in comparison to Western cities of the same size, it's not really safe to walk on your own in the medina late at night, especially for women. Knifepoint robberies are not unknown. Hotels and many restaurants are usually happy to provide an escort on request if you're out late.

Fez has long been notorious for its *faux guides* (unofficial guides) and carpet-shop hustlers, all after their slice of the tourist dirham. *Faux guides* tend to congregate around Bab Bou Jeloud, the main western entrance to the medina, although crackdowns by the authorities have greatly reduced their numbers and hassle.

Even many official guides will suggest visitors turn their tour into a shopping trip, and the pressure to buy can be immense. Fez's carpet sellers are masters of their game. If you really don't want to buy, it might be best not to enter the shop at all: once the parade of beautiful rugs begins, even the hardest-minded of tourists can be convinced to buy something they didn't really want (honeyed words suggesting that you could always sell the carpet later on eBay at vast profit should be treated with extreme scepticism). It's also worth remembering that, any time you enter a shop with a guide, the price of the goods immediately goes up to cover their commission. Shopping in Fez needn't be a battle – indeed it's best treated as a game – but it's worth being prepared.

The touts who used to hang about Fez train station to pick up custom have now taken to boarding trains to Fez, often at Sidi Kacem junction. Be particularly aware of overly friendly young men approaching you claiming to be students or teachers returning to Fez – they'll often have 'brothers' who have hotels, carpet shops or similar.

Sights

THE MEDINA (FÈS EL-BALI)

Travelling from the ville nouvelle to Fès el-Bali is like literally stepping back in time. The essential footprint of the medina hasn't changed in nearly a millennium, as the surrounding hills have constrained expansion – the last big growth of the traditional medina was in the 13th century with the construction of Fès el-Jdid (p237). Today, around 150,000 Fassis still call this maze of twisting alleys, blind turns and hidden souqs home, while tourists call it one of the most mind-boggling places they'll visit in Morocco.

Bab Bou Jeloud in the west is the main entrance to the old city, with two main streets descending into the medina's heart. On your left as you enter is Talaa Kebira (Big Slope), with Talaa Seghira (Little Slope) on your right. Both converge near Place an-Nejjarine, continuing to the Kairaouine Mosque and Zawiya Moulay Idriss II – the heart of the city. From here, it's uphill to reach the northern gates of Bab Guissa and Bab Jamaï, or head south towards Bab R'cif – one of the few places where vehicular traffic penetrates the old city.

While we've listed the major sights below, they're really only a small part of the charm of the medina. It pays to give yourself a little random exploration, and simply follow your nose or ears to discover the most unexpected charms of Fez's nature. Following your nose will lead you to women with bundles of freshly cut herbs, children carrying trays of loaves to be baked in the local bakery or a café selling glasses of spiced Berber coffee. Around the next corner you might find a beautifully tiled fountain, a workshop making wooden hammam buckets, a camel's head announcing a specialist butcher, or just a gang of kids turning their alley into a football pitch. Everywhere, listen out for the call to prayer or the mule driver's cry *'balak!'* (look out!) to warn of the approach of a heavily laden pack animal.

Navigation can be confusing and getting lost at some stage is a certainty, but look at this as part of the adventure. A handy tip is to note the 'main' streets that eventually lead to a gate or landmark – just follow the general flow of people. Ask shopkeepers for directions, or you can fall back on the eager kids happy to rescue confused foreigners for a dirham or two.

Kairaouine Mosque & University

Both the largest mosque in Africa, and possibly the oldest university in the world, this **mosque complex** (Map pp234–5) is the spiritual heart of Fez and Morocco itself. Established in 859 by Tunisian refugees and expanded by the Almoravids in the 12th century, it can accommodate up to 20,000 people at prayer. It's so large that it can be difficult to actually see: over the centuries the streets and houses of the Kairaouine quarter have encroached on the building so much they disguise its true shape. The mosque has recently been restored, but non-Muslims are forbidden to enter and will have to be content with glimpses of its seemingly endless columns from the gates on Talaa Kebira and Place as-Seffarine. Better still is to take the view from any vantage point over the medina: the huge green

LIFE IN THE LEATHER DISTRICT

Tanneries provide perhaps the greatest illustration of how resolutely some parts of Morocco have clung to practices developed in medieval times. Moroccan leather, and more particularly the Fassi leather produced in Fez, has for centuries been highly prized as among the finest in the world. One type of leather, a soft goatskin used mainly in bookbinding, is simply known as 'morocco'.

It's claimed that tanning leather in Morocco goes back several millennia, and little has changed since medieval times. Donkeys still labour through the narrow street carrying skins to dye pits, which are still constructed to traditional designs (with the addition of modern ceramic tiles). Tanners are organised according to ancient guild principles, with workers typically born into the job. Unfortunately, health and safety principles are similarly old-fashioned, and health problems among the workers, who are knee-deep in chemicals all day, are not uncommon.

Rank odours abound at the tanneries, and the delicate tourist who comes to view the work will often be offered a sprig of mint to hold to their nose to take the edge off the pong (rain also dampens the smell). Major components in processing the skins are pigeon poo and cow urine (for potassium) with ash; more delicate ingredients such as indigo, saffron and poppy are added later for colour.

FEZ MEDINA

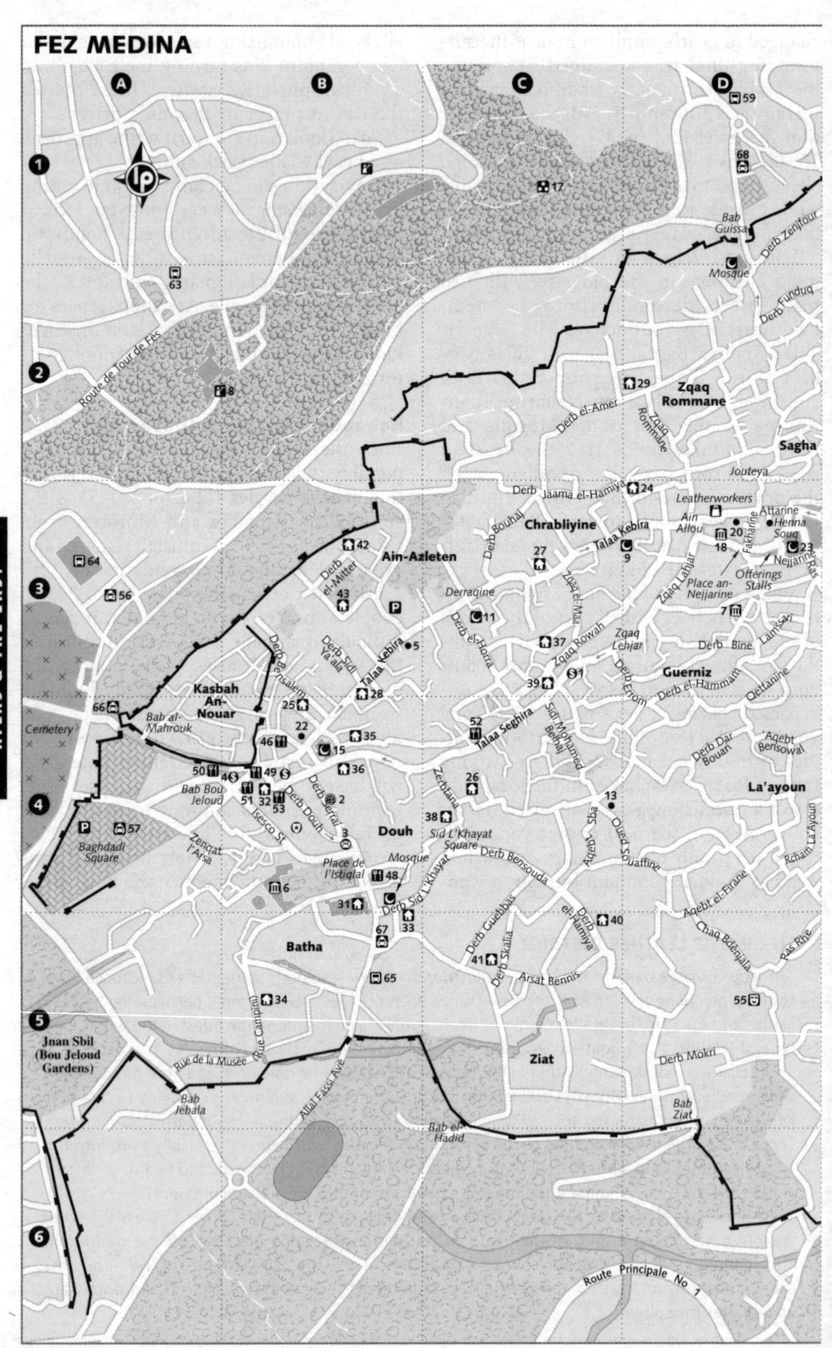
Route de Tour de Fes
Zqaq Rommane
Sagha
Chrabliyine
Ain-Azleten
Leatherworkers
Ain Allou
Attarine
Henna Souq
Place an-Nejjarine
Offerings Stalls
Talaa Kebira
Talaa Seghira
Derb Jaama el-Hamiya
Derb el-Amer
Derb Bouhaj
Derb el-Mitter
Derraqine
Derb el-Horra
Zqaq Rowah
Zqaq el-Maa
Zqaq Lehjar
Derb Bine Lamssari
Guerniz
Derb el-Hammam
Qettanine
Derb Dar Bouan
'Aqebt Bensowal
La'ayoun
Kasbah An-Nouar
Bab al-Mahrouk
Cemetery
Bab Bou Jeloud
Baghdadi Square
Derb Bensalem
Derb Sidi Ya'ala
Derb Douh
Derb Serrai
Isesco St
Zenqat l'Arsa
Douh
Place de l'Istiqlal
Mosque
Sid L'Khayat Square
Derb Sid L'Khayat
Zerbtana
Derb Bensouda
Sidi Mohamed Belhaj
Aqebt Sba
Oued Souaffine
Aqebt el-Firane
Chaq Bdenjala
Ras Rhe
Rcham La'Ayoun
Derb Guebbas
Derb Skalia
Derb el-Hamiya
Arsat Bennis
Batha
Jnan Sbil (Bou Jeloud Gardens)
Rue de la Musée
(Rue Caniptit)
Allal Fassi Ave
Bab Jebala
Bab el-Hadid
Ziat
Derb Mokri
Bab Ziat
Route Principale No 1
Bab Guissa
Derb Zenjfour
Derb Funduq
Jouteya
Fakharine
Nejjarine
Ras

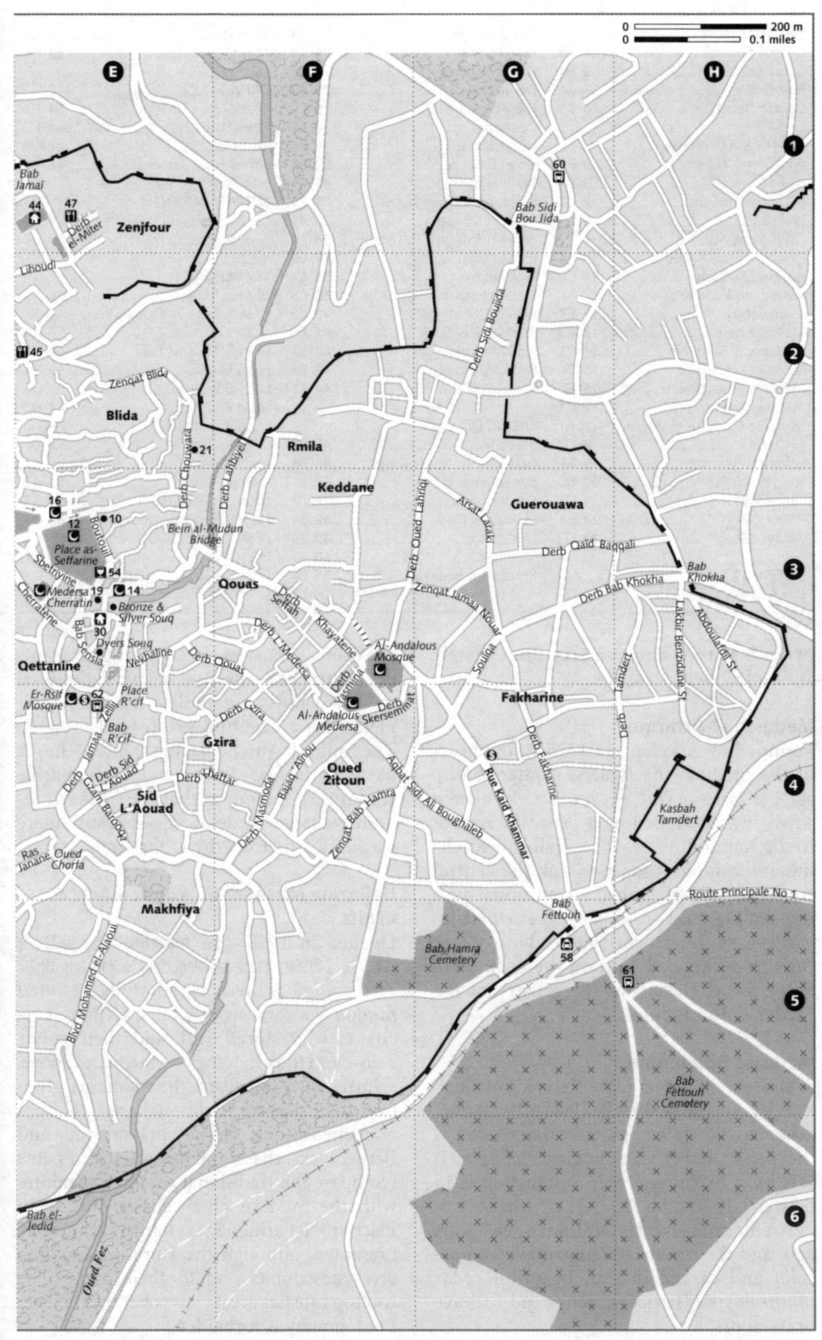
0 200 m
0 0.1 miles
Zenjfour
Blida
Rmila
Keddane
Guerouawa
Qouas
Qettanine
Gzira
Oued Zitoun
Fakharine
Sid L'Aouad
Makhfiya
Bab Jamaï
Derb el-Miter
Lihoudi
Zenqat Blida
Derb Chouwara
Derb Lahbiyel
Bein al-Mudun Bridge
Place as-Seffarine
Boutouil
Sbetriyine
Cherratene
Medersa Cherratin
Bronze & Silver Souq
Dyers Souq
Bab Sensla
Nekhaline
Er-Rsif Mosque
Place R'cif
Bab R'cif
Zellij
Derb Jamaa
Derb Sid L'Aouad
Gzam Barooq
Ras Janane
Oued Chorfa
Blvd Mohamed el-Alaoui
Oued Fez
Bab el-Jedid
Derb Qouas
Derb Gzira
Derb Lhattar
Derb Masmoda
Bajaq 'Ainou
Derb Seffah
Derb L'Medersa
Khayatene
Derb Yasmina
Al-Andalous Mosque
Al-Andalous Medersa
Derb Skersemmat
Aqbat Sidi Ali Boughaleb
Zenqat Bab Hamra
Zenqat Jamaa Nouar
Derb Oued Lahriqi
Arsat Laraki
Derb Sidi Boujida
Bab Sidi Bou Jida
Souiqa
Rue Kaid Khammar
Derb Fakharine
Derb Qaïd Baqqali
Derb Bab Khokha
Bab Khokha
Lakbir Benzidane St
Abdoulafdil St
Derb Tamdert
Kasbah Tamdert
Bab Fettouh
Route Principale No 1
Bab Hamra Cemetery
Bab Fettouh Cemetery
1 2 3 4 5 6
E F G H
10 12 14 16 19 21 30 44 45 47 54 58 60 61 62

INFORMATION
Banque Populaire ... 1 C3
Cyber Batha ... 2 B4
Post Office ... 3 B4
Société Générale ... 4 B4

SIGHTS & ACTIVITIES
Ain Azleten Hammam ... 5 B3
Batha Museum ... 6 B4
Belghazi Museum ... 7 D3
Borj Nord ... 8 A2
Chrabliyine Mosque ... 9 D3
Funduq Tastawniyine ... 10 E3
Gazleane Mosque ... 11 C3
Kairaouine Mosque & University ... 12 E3
Massage Maroc ... 13 C4
Medersa as-Seffarine ... 14 E3
Medersa Bou Inania ... 15 B4
Medersa el-Attarine ... 16 E3
Merenid Tombs ... 17 C1
Nejjarine Museum of Wooden Arts & Crafts ... 18 D3
Seffarine Hammam ... 19 E3
Souq an-Nejjarine ... 20 D3
Tanneries ... 21 E2
Water Clock ... 22 B4
Zawiya Moulay Idriss II ... 23 D3

SLEEPING
Dar Attajalli ... 24 D3
Dar Bouânania ... 25 B4
Dar Dmana ... 26 C4
Dar El Hana ... 27 C3
Dar Iman ... 28 B3
Dar Roumana ... 29 D2
Dar Seffarine ... 30 E3
Hôtel Batha ... 31 B4
Hôtel Cascade ... 32 B4
Pension Batha ... 33 B5
Pension Campini ... 34 B5
Pension Kawtar ... 35 B4
Pension Talaa ... 36 B4
Riad 9 ... 37 C3
Riad Fès ... 38 C4
Riad Laaroussa ... 39 C3
Riad Les Oudayas ... 40 C5
Riad Lune et Soleil ... 41 C5
Riad Maison Bleue ... 42 B3
Ryad Mabrouka ... 43 B3
Sofitel Palais Jamaï ... 44 E1

EATING
B'sara Stalls ... 45 E2
Café Clock ... 46 B4
Dar Anebar ... 47 E1
Dar Roumana ... (see 29)
La Maison Bleue ... 48 B4
Le Kasbah ... 49 B4
Médina Café ... 50 A4
Restaurant Bouayad ... 51 B4
Snail Stand ... 52 C4
Thami's ... 53 B4

DRINKING
Cremerie La Place ... 54 E3
Hotel Batha ... (see 31)
Riad Fès ... (see 38)
Sofitel Palais Jamaï ... (see 44)

ENTERTAINMENT
Les Musicales du Palais el-Mokri ... 55 D5

TRANSPORT
Grands Taxis ... 56 A3
Grands Taxis to Moulay Yacoub ... 57 A4
Grands Taxis to Taza ... 58 G5
Local Bus Stop ... 59 D1
Local Bus Stop ... 60 G1
Local Bus Stop ... 61 H5
Local Bus Stop & Petits Taxis ... 62 E4
Local Buses & Petits Taxis ... 63 A2
Main Bus Station ... 64 A3
No 9 Bus to Ville Nouvelle ... 65 B5
Petits Taxis ... 66 A4
Petits Taxis ... 67 B5
Petits Taxis ... 68 D1

pyramidal roof and minaret immediately announce their presence.

Medersa el-Attarine

Founded by Abu Said in 1325 in the heart of the medina, the **Medersa el-Attarine** (Map pp234-5; admission Dh10; 9am-6pm, closed during prayers) was designed as a separate annexe to the Kairaouine Mosque. Halls for teaching and a modest masjid flank the central courtyard. Displaying the traditional patterns of Merenid artisanship, the *zellij* (tilework) base, stuccowork and cedar wood at the top of the walls and on the ceiling are every bit as elegant as the artistry of the Medersa Bou Inania.

Medersa Bou Inania

A short walk down Talaa Kebira from Bab Bou Jeloud, the **Medersa Bou Inania** (Map pp234-5; admission Dh10; 9am-6pm, closed during prayers) is the finest of Fez's theological colleges. It was built by the Merenid sultan Bou Inan between 1350 and 1357. The *medersa* underwent extensive restoration a few years ago, and the results are amazing: elaborate *zellij* and carved plaster, beautiful cedar *mashrabiyyas* (lattice screens) and massive brass doors.

Whereas most *medersas* just have a simple prayer hall, the Bou Inania is unusual in that it hosts a complete mosque, complete with a beautiful green-tiled minaret. The mihrab (niche facing Mecca) has a particularly fine ceiling and onyx marble columns. It's thought that the *medersa* required a larger-scale mosque because there was none other nearby at the time.

Nejjarine Museum of Wooden Arts & Crafts

Opened in 1998, this **museum** (Map pp234-5; 035 740580; Place an-Nejjarine; admission Dh20; 10am-7pm) is in a wonderfully restored *funduq* – a caravanserai for travelling merchants who stored and sold their goods below and took lodgings on the floors above. Centred on a courtyard, the rooms are given over to displays of traditional artefacts from craftsmen's tools, chunky prayer beads and Berber locks, chests and musical instruments (compare the traditional wedding furniture with the modern glitzy chairs outside in Place an-Nejjarine). Everything is beautifully presented, although the stunning building gives the exhibits a run for their money. The rooftop café has great views over the medina. Photography is forbidden.

Batha Museum

Housed in a wonderful 19th century summer palace, converted to a museum in 1916, the **Batha Museum** (Map pp234-5; ☎ 035 634116; Rue de la Musée, Batha; admission Dh10; 🕑 8.30am-noon & 2.30-6pm Wed-Mon) houses an excellent collection of traditional Moroccan arts and crafts. Historical and artistic artefacts include fine woodcarving, *zellij* and sculpted plaster, much of it from the city's ruined or decaying *medersas*. It also has some fine Fassi embroidery, colourful Berber carpets and antique instruments.

The highlight of the museum is the superb ceramic collection dating from the 14th century to the present. These are some fantastic examples of the famous blue pottery of Fez. The cobalt glaze responsible for the colour is developed from a special process discovered in the 10th century.

The museum's Andalucian-style garden offers temporary respite from the bustle and noise of the medina, and the spreading holm oaks provide a backdrop for the open-air concerts the museum hosts during the Sacred Music and Sufi Culture festivals (p242).

Belghazi Museum

The private **Belghazi Museum** (Map pp234-5; ☎ 035 741178; 19 Derb Ghorba; admission Dh40; 🕑 9am-6.30pm), owned by the family of the same name, contains a collection that almost rivals that of the Batha Museum. The 17th-century palace in which it is housed provides a perfect backdrop for the exquisite carpets, jewellery, weapons and wedding chests on display. Much of this stuff is actually for sale if the price is right.

The palace also contains a shady courtyard café, and terrace with good views over the city. Though buried in the guts of the medina, the museum is well signposted from the Kairaouine Mosque and Place as-Seffarine.

Tanneries

The Chouwara **tanneries** (Map pp234-5; Derb Chouwara, Blida) are one of the city's most iconic sights (and smells). Head east or northeast from Place as-Seffarine and take the left fork after about 50m; you'll soon pick up the unmistakeable waft of skin and dye that will guide you into the heart of the leather district (the touts offering to show you the way make it even harder to miss).

It's not possible to get in amongst the tanning pits themselves, but there are plenty of vantage points from the streets that line them, all occupied (with typical Fassi ingenuity) by leather shops. Each shop has a terrace that allows you to look over the action. Try to get here in the morning when the pits are awash with coloured dye. Salesmen will happily give an explanation of the processes involved and will expect a small tip in return or, even better, a sale. While this might feel a little commercialised, you probably won't find a better selection of leather in Morocco, and prices are as good as you'll get.

FEZ EL-JDID (NEW FEZ)

Only in a city as old as Fez could you find a district dubbed 'New' because it's only 700 years old. The paranoid Merenid sultan Abu Youssef Yacoub (1258–86) purpose-built the quarter, packing it with his Syrian mercenary guards and seeking to isolate himself from his subjects. Even today almost half of the area is given over to the grounds of the Royal Palace, still popular with Mohammed VI. Its other main legacy is the architectural evidence of its early Jewish inhabitants.

The entrance to **Dar el-Makhzen** (Royal Palace; Map p230; Place des Alaouites) is a stunning example of modern restoration, but the 80 hectares of palace grounds are not open to the public. Visitors must suffice with viewing its imposing brass doors, surrounded by fine *zellij* and carved cedarwood. Note the lemon trees to one side – tour guides are prone to plucking the fruit to demonstrate the juice's astringent cleaning properties on the palace gates.

Mellah

In the 14th century Fez el-Jdid became a refuge for Jews, thus creating a *mellah* (Jewish quarter). The records suggest that the move was orchestrated to offer the Jews greater protection. And they certainly did enjoy the favour of the sultan, repaying him with their loyalty during conflict. Around 200 Jews remain in Fez, but all have now left the Mellah in favour of the ville nouvelle. Their old houses remain, with their open balconies looking onto the streets a marked contrast to Muslim styles.

The southwest corner of the *mellah* is home to the fascinating **Jewish Cemetery & Habarim Synagogue** (Map p230; donations welcomed; 7am-7pm), where the sea of blindingly white tombs stretches down the hill; those in dedicated enclosures are tombs of rabbis. One of the oldest, high up against the north wall, is that of Rabbi Vidal Hasserfaty, who died in 1600. On the slope below, the large tomb with green trimming is that of the martyr Solica. In 1834 this 14-year-old girl refused to convert to Islam or accept the advances of the governor of Tangier and subsequently had her throat slit.

The Habarim Synagogue, at the far end of the cemetery, now houses a museum with a whole mishmash of articles, including some poignant photos and postcards, left behind after the Jewish exodus. If the museum is locked, the gatekeeper will open it for you.

The gatekeeper can direct you to the nearby **Ibn Danan Synagogue** (Map p230; donations welcomed), which was restored with the aid of Unesco in 1999. There are no set opening times as such, but someone will usually let you in and point out the main features, including a *mikva* (ritual bath) in the basement. **Rue des Mérinides** (Map p230) is lined with houses which are distinguished by their wooden and wrought-iron balconies, as well as by their stuccowork.

Jnan Sbil (Bou Jeloud Gardens) & Baghdadi Square

These **gardens** (Map pp234-5; Ave Moulay Hassan), also known as Jnane Sbil, have been providing welcome green space for well over a century. They're a good halfway break between the *mellah* and Bab Bou Jeloud, and were undergoing extensive renovation and replanting when we visited. Continue on from here to reach **Baghdadi Square** (Map pp234–5), an open-air market on the edge of the medina.

NORTH OF THE MEDINA

Viewed from the surrounding hills, Fez's jumbled buildings merge into a palette of white-flecked sandstone. Only here and there do the green-tiled roofs of the mosques and *medersas* provide a hint of colour. For one of the best panoramas of the city, head up to **Borj Nord** (Map pp234–5). Like its counterpart on the southern hills (Borj Sud), Borj Nord was built by Sultan Ahmed al-Mansour in the late 16th century to monitor the potentially disloyal populace of Fez.

Further up, the **Merenid tombs** (Map pp234–5) are dramatic in their advanced state of ruin, although little remains of their fine original decoration. The views over Fez are spectacular and well worth the climb. Look for the black smoke in the southern part of the city, marking the potteries. It's best at dusk as the lights come on and the

THE FOUNTAINS OF FEZ

It seems like you can barely turn a corner in the Fez medina without coming across a public fountain *(seqqâya)* – Fassis have historically had something of an obsession for them. It was largely the Almoravid (1061–1147) and Almohad (1147–1248) dynasties that were the great water engineers. To supply water to their cities they diverted rivers, created lakes and constructed vast canal systems. While they did this across the country, fountain construction really reached its peak in imperial Fez.

There are said to be well over 60 public fountains inside the medina. Along with the hammam, they are usually located near the neighbourhood mosque. Many were paid for by princes and wealthy merchants. Some of these fountains are simple basins against a wall. The majority are beautifully decorative structures of coloured tiles, often under a canopy of intricately carved wood. One of the finest is the an-Nejjarine fountain. Built in the 18th century, it features *zellij* (tilework) and stucco that form patterns as delicate as lacework.

Many fountains are still used for water collection and washing widely by their neighbourhoods. Those you see abandoned are likely to suffer from a broken mains pipe somewhere beneath the city; many are directly spring fed. And if you think that a love of fountains is restricted to the medina, check out the ultramodern and sparkly fountains recently installed along Ave Hassan II in the ville nouvelle.

WHAT'S ON IN THE VILLE NOUVELLE?

Compared to the sensory assault provided by the medina, the ville nouvelle can seem boring: very modern, but with little actually going on. But for most Fassis, the ville nouvelle is the place where it's at: far more interesting and progressive than crumbling Fez el-Bali. In the last few years, huge amounts of money have been poured into the area, which can best be seen along the long boulevard of Ave Hassan II, with its manicured lawns, palm trees, flower beds and fountains. A stroll here is a favourite evening pastime, when it's packed with families with kids, trendy teenagers and courting couples. Stop for an ice cream or just sit on a bench and people-watch: this is the 'real' Morocco as much as any donkey-packed lane in the old city.

muezzins' prayer calls echo round the valley. A taxi from Bab Bou Jeloud should cost around Dh7; it's a 10-minute walk back downhill to the medina.

Activities

HAMMAMS

For more opulent hammam experiences Riad Maison Bleue (p244) and Riad Laaroussa (p244) both have excellent private spas, with treatments starting from Dh300.

Convenient, foreigner-friendly and recently renovated, **Ain Azleten Hammam** (Map pp234-5; Talaa Kebira, Ain Azleten; men 6am-noon & 8.30-11pm, women noon-8.30pm) is a good option if you want to try a public hammam. A session costs around Dh40, with attendants on hand to help you slough away the dirt.

A beautiful example of traditional bathhouse architecture, **Seffarine Hammam** (Map pp234-5; Seffarine Sq; men 6am-midnight, women 8am-10pm) was recently chosen for restoration by the Venice Institute for Urban Sustainability. Sessions cost around Dh40.

MASSAGE

Massage Maroc (Map pp234-5; ☎ 068 823040; www.massagemaroc.com in French; 9 Derb Moulay Ismail; by appointment) offers a variety of treatments, including Ayurvedic massage, reiki and reflexology, along with meditation and kundalini yoga.

Walking Tour: 'Mazing Medina

This route (Map p240) takes you from Bab Bou Jeloud to the Kairaouine Mosque, then north to the Sofitel Palais Jamaï. It could take a few hours or all day, depending on the number of distractions.

Unlike much of the rest of the city walls and gates, the main entry, **Bab Bou Jeloud (1)**, is a recent addition, built in 1913. Pass through it and you come upon a hive of activity. The touts and *faux guides* that used to pester visitors here have largely disappeared, but if you need to get your bearings, the street cafés here as the street turns towards Talaa Seghira are excellent places for people-watching.

For the tour, take the first left and then right downhill along Talaa Kebira. This part of the street is a produce market – watch out for the camel butchers displaying the heads of their wares. Where the produce ends you're at the **Medersa Bou Inania (2)**, which represents the Merenid building style at its most perfect.

Opposite the entrance to the *medersa* (above eye-level) is a famous 14th-century **water clock (3)** designed by a clockmaker and part-time magician. Carved beams held brass bowls with water flowing between them to mark the hours, but the secret of its mechanism apparently died with its creator.

About 400m from the Medersa Bou Inania, as you go around an unmistakeable dogleg, you'll catch sight of the pretty, green-tiled minaret of the **Chrabliyine Mosque** (**4**; named for the slipper-makers who can still be found working in this area) straight ahead.

Still heading downhill, past the shoe sellers and a group of leatherworkers, about 230m from the Gazleane mosque, look out for a right turn onto Derb Fkahrine and a sign indicating the entrance to a tiny tree-filled square known as the **henna souq (5)** – if you reach the Dar Saada restaurant, you've gone too far. Nowadays there are more stalls here selling blue Fez pottery than henna, which Moroccan women use to decorate their hands and feet for events such as weddings.

Exiting the henna souq the same way you entered, head south with your back to Dar Saada. After roughly 50m a right turn brings

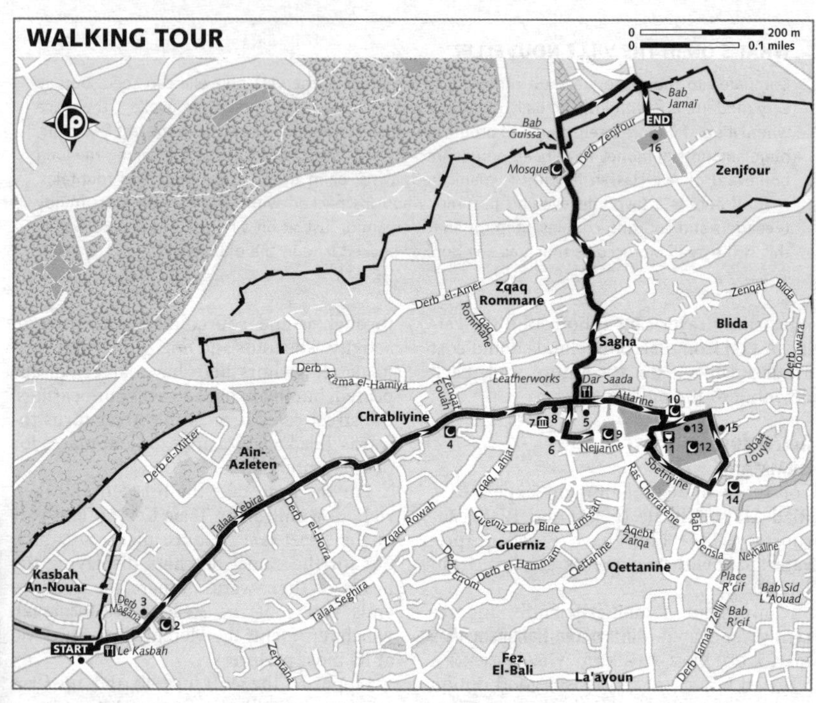

WALK FACTS

Start Bab Bou Jeloud
End Palais Jamai
Distance 3 km
Duration two to three hours

you into **Place an-Nejjarine (7)**, a larger square dominated by one of the city's most beautiful fountains and a most impressive *funduq* (hotel) – now beautifully restored and transformed into the **Nejjarine Museum of Wooden Arts & Crafts (7)**. The lanes immediately north of the museum form part of the **Souq an-Nejjarine** (**8**; Carpenters' Souq), where you'll see craftsmen putting finishing touches to glittering thrones used in wedding ceremonies.

From Place an-Nejjarine, continue south and turn left almost immediately down a lane, ducking under the bar that prevents the passage of mules and donkeys. The lane leads between stalls piled high with candles and other offerings, to the entrance of **Zawiya Moulay Idriss II (9)**. You may peer into the bright, tiled interior, although non-Muslims may not enter. Moulay Idriss II is highly revered – to Fassis this is the heart of their city.

Afterwards, the simplest thing is to backtrack to Dar Saada on Talaa Kebira. Follow the lane east – over a slight hummock and past haberdashers' stalls – until it ends at a T-intersection about 100m later, where you'll find the **Medersa el-Attarine (10)**.

On emerging from the *medersa,* turn left (south). After you've passed the **Pâtisserie Kortouba (11)** – a handy pit stop – the shops come to a sudden end at the walls of the great **Kairaouine Mosque & University (12)**. The university claims to be the world's oldest and is surpassed only by Al-Azhar in Cairo as a centre of Muslim learning. Among its many luminaries was the pre-eminent historian Ibn Khaldun, and you may catch sight of his successors hurrying to lessons.

As you proceed along the university walls anticlockwise, the sound of metalworkers leads you into another small and attractive square, **Place as-Seffarine** (**13**; Brass-makers Square). The air rings with the sound of metalwork. Look out for the huge pans and plates that are hired out for wedding parties.

With the university walls (and the entrance to its library) still on your left, there is the small **Medersa as-Seffarine (14)**, with a studded cedar door, on the square's east side. Built in 1280, it is the oldest *medersa* in Fez, but is in an advanced state of disrepair.

Still following the mosque walls anticlockwise (now heading north) keep a lookout on the right for the 14th-century **Funduq Tastawniyine (15)**, with its rickety wooden galleries. Originally the preserve of businessmen from Tetouan, it served for centuries as a hotel and warehouse for travelling merchants.

If you continue around the Kairaouine, you'll pass its ornate north door before arriving back where you started beside the patisserie. From here you can retrace your steps uphill to Bab Bou Jeloud. If you prefer an alternate route, turn south off Talaa Kebira at Ain Allou – this street turns into Talaa Seghira, the medina's other main thoroughfare.

Otherwise, return only as far as Dar Saada, then turn north to reach Bab Guissa in the northern medina. Stick to the wider streets and you'll reach a little square with a disused cinema on its north side. Take the lane heading northwest and keep going up – you'll pass plenty of donkeys carrying sacks from the local cement merchant.

As you near Bab Guissa you can see the late 19th-century **Sofitel Palais Jamaï (16)**. What is now a luxury hotel was built by Sidi Mohammed ben Arib al-Jamaï, the grand vizier to Moulay al-Hassan I. Set in well-watered gardens, the former palace is a wonderful place to rest and admire the view. You can catch an onward petit taxi from Bab Guissa.

Courses

COOKERY

If you want to pick up some culinary skills on your trip, chef **Lahcen Beqqi** (www.fescooking.com) offers a *bouquet garni* of different single- and multiple-day Moroccan cookery classes, from around Dh300 to Dh400 per person. Classes start with shopping in the souq for ingredients, and cooking your meals in a riad kitchen.

LANGUAGE

DMG Arabophon (☎ 035 603475; www.arabicstudy.com; courses Dh2100-8400) runs intensive programs in Darija and modern standard Arabic, as well as shorter courses aimed at travellers: a half-day 'Curious Explorer' (Dh325) and a one-week 'Serious Explorer' (Dh750). DMG also offers courses in Tamazight Berber.

The **Arabic Language Institute** (☎ 035 624850; www.alif-fes.com; 3-/6-week courses Dh5200/9400) offers longer courses aimed at foreigners, and can assist in finding accommodation for students in apartments or with local families. Lessons are held at the **American Language Center** (Map p246; ☎ 035 624850; 2 Rue Ahmed Hiba).

Tours

The Fassi authorities have woken to the difficulties tourists have in navigating the medina, and introduced a series of well-signed self-guided walks through the old city. There are five to choose from, each highlighting different aspects of traditional Fez:

Dark blue Monuments and souqs
Green Andalucian palaces and gardens
Orange Fès el-Jdid
Pale blue Andalucian quarter
Purple Artisanal crafts tour

The head-height signs are easy to follow, showing the direction of the next major landmark, and there are excellent English information boards at regular intervals.

An alternative is to hire a guide. As well as pointing out incredible architecture and clandestine corners, guides can answer cultural questions, help overcome language barriers, and – perhaps most importantly – ward off other would-be guides. A full-day tour with an official guide costs Dh250 – always ask to see identification.

The quality of guides can vary considerably, so communication is very important to ensure that you get the best out of the experience. If you're not interested in shopping, say so firmly at the outset, although be aware that the guide who won't take a tourist to a single shop probably hasn't been born yet. It may be necessary to pay an extra Dh50 to Dh100 as a 'no shopping' supplement. If possible, get a recommendation for a guide from other travellers; alternatively, arrange one through the tourist office, Syndicat d'Initiative or the larger hotels.

For those short of time, the tourist office offers panoramic tours of Fez, taking in all the best viewpoints of the city, including Borj Nord and Borj Sud, and the potteries. A 45-minute tour costs Dh200.

FÈS FESTIVAL OF WORLD SACRED MUSIC

Every June the **Fès Festival of World Sacred Music** (☎ 035 740691; www.fesfestival.com) brings together music groups and artists from all corners of the globe, and has become one of the most successful world music festivals going. Based on the pluralism of Moroccan Sufism, the festival has attracted big international stars such as Ravi Shankar, Youssou N'Dour and Salif Keita. Concerts are held in a variety of venues, including the Batha Museum and the square outside Bab Bou Jeloud. While the big names are a draw, equally fascinating are the more intimate concerts held by Morocco's various *tariqas* (Sufi orders). Fringe events include art exhibitions, films and talks at literary cafés. In 2001 the festival was praised by the UN as a major event promoting dialogue between civilisations. Tickets can go like hot cakes and accommodation books up far in advance – so organise as far ahead as possible if you plan on attending.

Festivals & Events

Fez has several festivals that are worth being aware of when you're planning your trip. The Fès Festival of World Sacred Music (see above) is the city's internationally famous drawcard, but there are two newer festivals that bear a visit.

The **Festival of Sufi Culture** (www.par-chemins.org) debuted in 2007 and hosts a series of events every April including films and lectures, and some spectacular concerts held in the garden of the Batha Museum with Sufi musicians from across the world. In July, the **National Festival of Berber Culture**, run in association with the Institut Royal de la Culture Amazigh, aims to promote and protect Amazigh (Berber) culture. Its program includes musical performances as well as lectures and workshops.

Fez's biggest religious festival is also one of the country's largest. The *moussem* (festival in honour of a saint) of the city's founder, Moulay Idriss, draws huge crowds. Local artisans create special tributes and there's a huge procession through the medina. Traditional music is played and followers dance and shower the musicians (and onlookers) with orange- or rosewater.

Just outside Fez, Sefrou's Cherry Festival every July is worth a daytrip (see p254).

Sleeping

Fez doesn't lack for variety in its accommodation options, with everything from simple pensions to boutique riads. Your main choice is whether to stay in the colour and chaos of the medina, or a petit taxi ride away in the ville nouvelle (where budgets tend to go further). Room rates in Fez are in the higher (city) bracket – see p450 for details. Booking in advance is advised during high season, and especially during the World Sacred Music Festival in June, when supplements also often apply. Note that although prices here are listed in dirhams, many riads actually list (and charge) rooms in euros, so be aware of currency exchange rates when booking.

The agency **Fez Riads** (☎ 072 513357; www.fez-riads.com) is a good place to find accommodation in the medina, and donates a percentage of profits to local restoration projects.

MEDINA

Budget

Most of the cheapest options are in touching distance of Bab Bou Jeloud, placing you right in the middle of the action. Unless noted, rooms have shared bathrooms at this price range – and don't expect hot water at the lower prices.

Pension Talaa (Map pp234-5; ☎ 035 633359; pacohicham@hotmail.com; 14 Talaa Seghira; s/d Dh90/120) A small but well-formed little pension right in the middle of things on Talaa Seghira. There are just handful of compact rooms so it's often full, but it gets good reviews from guests for the price and has friendly staff.

Hôtel Cascade (Map pp234-5; ☎ 035 638442; 26 Rue Serrajine, Bab Bou Jeloud; r Dh160, dm Dh80, breakfast Dh20) One of the grand-daddies of the Morocco shoestring hotels, the Cascade still keeps drawing them in. You don't expect much for the price – it's all pretty basic – but if you need to stretch your budget and want to meet plenty of like-minded travellers then this might be the place for you.

Pension Batha (Map pp234-5; ☎ 035 741150; 8 Sidi L'Khayat, Batha; r incl breakfast Dh250) Slightly downhill from the main taxi rank in Batha, this is a very likeable place to stay. It's a tall, thin building with lots of stairs leading up to a nice terrace. Rooms are simple, but the place has a homely atmosphere. Not to be confused with the nearby Hôtel Batha.

Pension Kawtar (Map pp234-5; ☎ 035 740172; pension_kaw@yahoo.fr; Derb Taryana, Talaa Seghira; s/d Dh200/300, d with bathroom Dh350, dm Dh60, breakfast Dh25) A relatively new player, and well-signed in an alley off Talaa Seghira, the Kawtar is a friendly Moroccan family-run concern, as much a home as a hostel. Amazingly, there are 10 rooms tucked into the place – those on the ground floor are a bit gloomy, but they get better the closer you get to the roof terrace. Great value for the price.

Pension Campini (Map pp234-5; ☎ 035 637342; pensioncampini@gmail.com; Rue Campini, Batha; s/d Dh200/300) A short walk away from the Batha Museum, this is a quieter location slightly outside the medina proper. Rooms are en suite and airy, and had just had a new lick of paint when we visited. There's a small terrace, with views just over the walls of Bou Jeloud Gardens.

Dar Bouânania (Map pp234-5; ☎ 035 637282; 21 Derb Bensalem, Talaa Kebira; s/d Dh200/500, s/d with shower Dh300/600, q Dh400, breakfast Dh30) A popular choice with backpackers, this is as close as tight budgets will get to a riad. A traditional house with courtyard, *zellij* tiles and painted woodwork, it has several well-sized rooms on several levels, although as all face inward they can be quite dark at times. Shared bathrooms are clean, and there's a roof terrace. Good value, although we've received several readers' letters about guides being let in to tout for business. There's a high-season supplement of Dh100 per person.

Midrange

Many midrange options in the medina, especially the riads and dars, edge close to the top-end price bracket. A few places offer simpler rooms at manageable prices. Rates here include breakfast.

Hôtel Batha (Map pp234-5; ☎ 035 741077; fax 035 741078; Place Batha; s/d Dh395/520;) The great location, room capacity and pool keep the Batha perennially busy. It's a reasonably modern set-up, with fair rooms and cool quiet areas to retreat from the hustle of the medina. It's good value, although the eccentric attitude towards providing hot water – only at particular, often inconvenient hours – has been a frustration for many years now.

Dar Iman (Map pp234-5; ☎ 035 636528; www.fes-hostel.com; 6 Derb Benazahoum, Talaa Kebira; s/d/tr Dh600/700/960;) A well-restored 400-year-old townhouse off the main drag, this is great value for the price. All the style points you'd expect are in order, from *zellij* to tall wooden doors, but it's all been put together in a laid-back manner: less is definitely more here, and the slightly creamy walls provide a more mellow backdrop than the harsh white of other places. Only the lack of views from the terrace count against this otherwise friendly, welcoming place.

Dar El Hana (Map pp234-5; ☎ 035 635854; www.moroccangetaway.com; 22 Rue Ferrance Couicha, Chrabliyine; r from Dh800; wi-fi) If there's a cosier and more intimate guest house in Fez than this dar, we'd like to know about it. There are just three rooms (sleeping a maximum of eight altogether), all charmingly finished and presented: we fell for the 'secret' windows allowing you to spy on the street, and the open-air shower on the terrace. This is a real home from home, and it's possible to rent out the entire house so you can fully indulge your own fantasies of medina life.

Riad Lune et Soleil (Map pp234-5; ☎ 035 634523; www.riadluneetsoleil.com; 3 Derb Skalia, Batha; r Dh800-1200; wi-fi) Hospitality is all at this riad, and the husband-and-wife owners will sweep you past the lemon trees in the courtyard to make you impossibly at home. Each room is a cornucopia, filled with the evidence of a lifetime of collecting everything from old postcards and embroidery to carvings and metalwork – and each item with a story behind it. It's not a museum though; there's plenty of comfort too, and some rooms have their own Jacuzzi. You might just make it downstairs for dinner – from one of the best kitchens in the medina.

Dar Seffarine (Map pp234-5; ☎ 071 113528; www.darseffarine.com; 14 Derb Sbaalouyat, Rcif; r from Dh859; wi-fi) If you check into Dar Seffarine, ask to see the photo album of its restoration – it's the only way you'll believe that such a fabulous building was ever a complete wreck. The central courtyard is positively opulent, with pillars and painted plasterwork reaching skywards, while rooms are more understated with simple plain wood and fabrics to decorate them – only the suite with the painted domed ceiling makes a palatial exception. There's a pleasant terrace, and a more intimate side courtyard off the kitchen to relax in. The dar is a short walk from Bab Rcif.

Dar Dmana (Map pp234-5; ☎ 035 740917; www.riaddardmana.net; 21 Rue Sournas; r/ste Dh1200/1800;) With 14 rooms, this dar successfully bridges the gap between traditional Moroccan house and hotel. The ground floor has decor that's stepped out of a palace restaurant, but the high covered courtyard (with fine carved cedar balustrade) keeps things airy. After all this, the rooms are more modern and restrained, but with enough Moroccan styling to remind you where you are.

Top End

Ryad Mabrouka (Map pp234-5; ☎ 035 636345; www.ryadmabrouka.com; 25 Derb el-Mitter, Ain Azleten; r Dh900-1150, ste Dh1300-1600;) An old favourite and early player on the Fez riad scene, Mabrouka is a meticulously restored, Arab-Andalucian townhouse. The courtyard, with its stucco, mosaics, magnificent cedar doors and babbling fountain, opens onto a pleasant garden of flowers and trees. There are seven rooms, decked out with tiled floors and Berber fabrics. Enjoy a simple breakfast or an all-out Moroccan feast on the veranda overlooking the medina.

our pick **Dar Attajali** (Map pp234-5; ☎ 035 637728; www.attajalli.com; Derb Qettana, Zqaq Rommane; r from Dh1000-1500; wi-fi) A relative newcomer, Dar Attajali is a magnificent testament to the art of patient and sympathetic restoration. Everything has been done to maintain the building's integrity, using a minimum of modern techniques and chemicals, while producing a supremely comfortable guest house. Decoration is set off with gently colour-themed Fassi fabrics – colours further reflected in the planting of the terrace roof garden, and all designed to get you instantly relaxing (as if the organic, locally sourced breakfasts didn't get your day off to a good enough start).

Dar Roumana (Map pp234-5; ☎ 035 741637; www.darroumana.com; 30 Derb el-Amer, Zkak Roumane; r Dh1000-1700; wi-fi) Dar Roumana continues to win fans, with its beautifully restored and subtly decorated interiors, and gorgeous roof terrace that commands the finest views over the medina (perfect for taking breakfast or sampling the well-thought-out dinner menus). Management are welcoming rather than overwhelming, with close attention to detail: there are even personalised toiletries in the bathrooms.

Riad 9 (Map pp234-5; ☎ 035 947610; www.riad9.com; 9 Derb Lamsside, Zqaq el-Maa; r Dh1200-2400; wi-fi) This is a tiny gem of a guest house, with just three rooms, but plans to extend into the property next door to double its capacity. The decoration is idiosyncratic but lots of fun – witness the room with dentist's chairs and wall full of antique luggage. At night, the many windows looking into the courtyard are lit with candles, turning the whole into a glittering jewel box.

Riad Maison Bleue (Map pp234-5; ☎ 035 741873; www.maisonbleue.com; 33 Derb el Mitter, Ain-Azleten; s/d from Dh1700/1900; P) You have to be careful not to get lost in this riad – it's four houses knocked together and even extended across the street. Start in the orange-tree-clad Andalucian-style courtyard, then find your way to any of the 13 rooms, possibly stopping en route at the private spa, bar, dining salon and fashionably dark and plush 'Blue Lounge', where there is more eating and drinking on offer. If you don't want to crash in your room, chill on the terrace with its fine views to Borj Nord.

Riad Fès (Map pp234-5; ☎ 035 947610; www.riadfes.com; Derb ibn Slimane, Zerbtana; r/ste from Dh1700/3000; wi-fi) This labyrinthine riad blends ancient and modern with impressive panache. The older section shows off the best of traditional decor, while the newer quarters wouldn't look out of place in a Parisian boutique hotel yet remain unmistakably Moroccan. It has a trendy courtyard bar, restaurant, hammam and a plethora of terraces, and an elevator makes this place uniquely convenient for disabled or elderly travellers.

Riad Laaroussa (Map pp234-5; ☎ 074 187639; www.riad-laaroussa.com; 3 Derb Bechara, Talaa Seghira; r Dh1800-2650; wi-fi) Although a garden is meant to be the defining feature of a riad, it still comes as something of a surprise to pass through the dark entrance here to meet such a large green space, with its orange trees and softly playing fountain. Instantly relaxed, you continue to fine rooms decorated with modern art and unusual furniture that makes it clear the owners haven't just stolen ideas from this month's Moroccan style magazine. Riad Laaroussa makes a point of its restaurant-quality food (dinner Dh300), but charges a hefty mark-up on drinks.

Riad Les Oudayas (Map pp234-5; ☎ 035 636303; www.lesoudayas.com; 4 Derb el Hamiya, Ziat; r Dh2400; wi-fi) The Moroccan owner of this riad is a Paris-based designer, and it certainly shows in its careful blend of traditional styles and modern design aesthetic in everything from the downstairs salons to the chic but comfortable bedrooms. Steps lead down from street level into the courtyard garden, with a plunge pool and the riad's own hammam leading off it. Up top there's a large terrace, but if you crave privacy, two of the five rooms have their own private terraces.

Sofitel Palais Jamaï (Map pp234-5; ☎ 035 634331; www.sofitel.com; Bab Guissa; s/d incl breakfast from Dh1950/2600;) Once the pleasure dome of a late-19th-century vizier to the sultan, this grand hotel is set in Andalucian gardens overlooking the medina. Its rooms have had a recent makeover to keep it in line with the trendy medina guest houses, although some parts still suffer bland international decoration. Nonguests should still visit to enjoy a sunset drink on the terrace.

VILLE NOUVELLE

In the ville-nouvelle room rates drop considerably compared to the more popular medina, so much of the time you can get midrange service at budget prices.

Budget

Hôtel Kairouan (Map p246; ☎ 035 623590; 84 Ave Soudan; s/d Dh100/120, with bathroom Dh140/150) Dark corridors make this hotel feel more claustrophobic than it really is, but the English-speaking management is helpful, rooms are decent and even those with shared bathrooms get their own sink.

Hôtel Royal (Map p246; ☎ 035 624656; 36 Ave Soudan; s/d with bathroom Dh 120/150, with shower only Dh100/130) Well-placed near Place Florence, this is one of the more reliable and popular budget options. A few of the bathrooms are a bit clunky (hot water in mornings only), but rooms are large and many come with balconies.

Hôtel Central (Map p246; ☎ 035 622335; 50 Rue Brahim Roudani; s/d Dh130/160, with shower Dh150/180) A bright and airy budget option just off busy Blvd Mohammed V. All rooms have external toilets, but even those without a shower have their own sinks. It's good value and popular so there's sometimes not enough rooms to go around.

Hôtel Olympic (Map p246; ☎ 035 932682; fax 055 932665; cnr Blvd Mohammed V & Rue 3; s/d incl breakfast Dh275/350;) A handy choice near the central market. Rooms are nondescript but comfortable, equipped with bathroom, TV, phone and stylish brass bedsteads. Its central location means it's often heavily booked (it's popular with tour groups), so call in advance.

Hôtel de la Paix (Map p246; ☎ 035 625072; www.hotellapaixfes.com in French; 44 Ave Hassan II; s/d Dh285/365;) Cast from the bland tourist-class mould, this place is nevertheless good value for the money. Rooms are solidly comfortable, with TV and bathroom; there's also a bar and a reasonable restaurant.

Hôtel Perla (Map p246; ☎ 035 943641; www.hotelperlamaroc.com; 15 Rue de la Jordannie; s/d Dh339/402;) A stone's throw from the train station, this is another good tourist-class hotel. Rooms are compact and modern, and the service is reliable. Reassuringly unexciting.

Hôtel Splendid (Map p246; ☎ 035 622148; splendid@iam.net.ma; 9 Rue Abdelkarim el-Khattabi; s/d Dh318/412;) Although in the budget category, this hotel makes a good claim for three stars. It's all modern and tidy, with good bathrooms and comfy beds, plus a pool for the heat and a bar for the evenings. There's a dining room, but breakfast is not automatically included in the price.

Grand Hôtel de Fès (Map p246; ☎ 035 932026; grandhotel@fesnet.net.ma; 12 Blvd Chefchaouni, cnr Blvd Mohammed V; s/d Dh360/450;) A top address during the French Protectorate (read the newspaper clipping in the lobby about its big 1920s opening), the Grand works hard to keep up its standards and holds its own against more modern rivals. The lobby is old-fashioned, leading to large rooms with high ceilings and stucco walls. They are simple, but spotless, with good bathrooms.

Youth Hostel (Map p246; ☎ 035 624085; 18 Rue Abdeslam Serghini; dm Dh450; gate open 8-10am, noon-3pm & 6-10pm) One of the better youth hostels in Morocco, the Fez branch is well looked after, and right in the centre of the ville nouvelle. Tidy rooms and facilities (including Western-style toilets) are superbly clean. If you're not a Youth Hostelling International (YHI) member, there's a Dh5 surcharge. Cold showers mean that you should look to hammams – particularly in winter.

Hôtel Mounia (Map p246; ☎ 035 624838; www.hotelmouniafes.ma in French; 60 Blvd Zerktouni; s/d incl breakfast from Dh399/518;) A *zellij* lobby guides you into this modern and classy hotel that's popular with tour groups. Rooms are bright and tidy, with satellite TV. The restaurant is

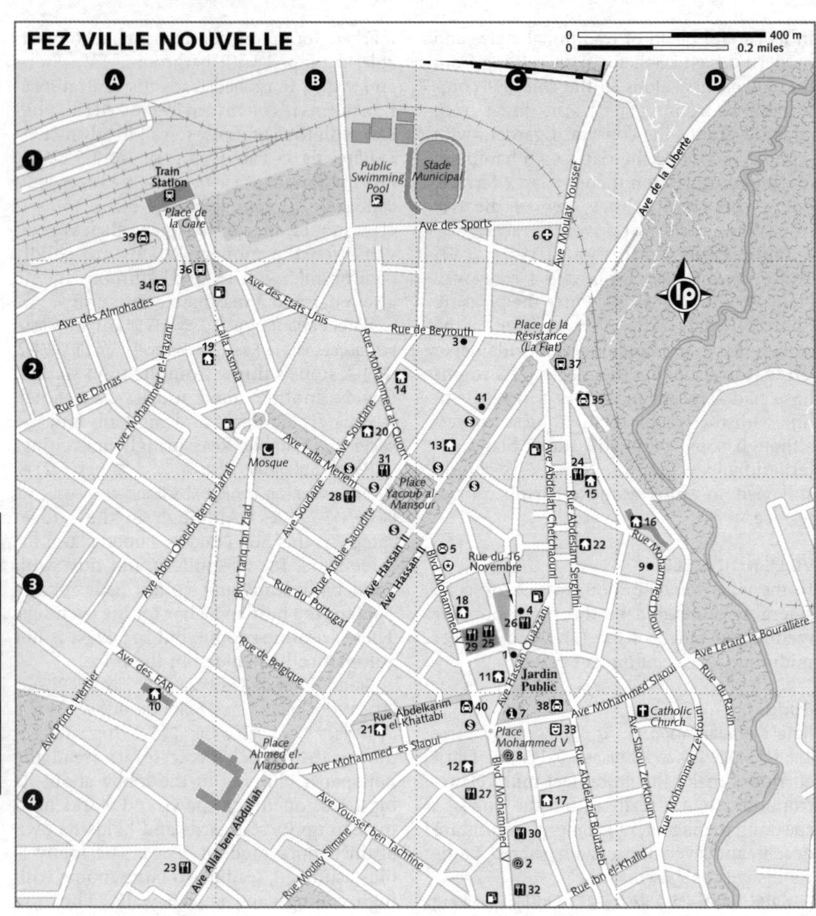

fair, and there's a smoky bar with plenty of water pipes (rooms on corridors near the bar can be noisy though). Staff are helpful, and good discounts are often available.

Midrange & Top End

Hôtel Menzeh Zalagh (Map p246; ☎ 035 625531; menzeh.zalagh@fesnet.net.ma; 10 Rue Mohammed Diouri; s/d incl breakfast Dh950/1300;) This four-star hotel has a great location, stretched along a low ridge in a sinuous wave with amazing views across to Fès el-Bali, yet convenient to the centre. Rooms are full of modern comforts with a splash of traditional Moroccan decor, and many come with balconies.

Hotel Menzeh Fes (Map p246; ☎ 035 943849; menzeh.zalagh@fesnet.net.ma; 28 Rue Abdessalam Serghini; s/d incl breakfast Dh950/1300;) Sister hotel to the Zalagh up the road, this offers virtually identical facilities, albeit with slightly smaller rooms. Not all rooms look across the old city, so ask when checking in; otherwise you'll be left just enjoying the view from the glass elevator on the side of the building.

Crown Palace Fes (Map p246; ☎ 035 948000; www.crownpalace.ma; 85 Ave des FAR; s/d from Dh1800/2100;) Its location could be better if you're into exploring on foot, but this is the best of the bunch when it comes to hotels in the ville nouvelle. Lavish but tasteful decor, natural light and spacious interiors characterise the rooms, with several restaurants, a gym and hammam, and cocktails in the bar.

INFORMATION
Carlson Wagonlit.......................1 C3
Cyber Club.......................2 C4
Institut Français.......................3 C2
Librarie Fikr al-Moasser.......................4 C3
Main Post Office.......................5 C3
Night Pharmacy.......................6 C1
Syndicat d'Initiative.......................7 C4
Teleboutique Cyber Club.......................8 C4

SIGHTS & ACTIVITIES
American Language Center.......................9 D3

SLEEPING
Crown Palace Fès.......................10 A4
Grand Hôtel de Fes.......................11 C3
Hôtel Central.......................12 C4
Hôtel de la Paix.......................13 C2
Hôtel Kairouan.......................14 B2
Hôtel Menzeh Fès.......................15 C3
Hôtel Menzeh Zalagh.......................16 D3
Hôtel Mounia.......................17 C4
Hôtel Olympic.......................18 C3
Hôtel Perla.......................19 A2
Hôtel Royal.......................20 B2
Hôtel Splendid.......................21 B4
Youth Hostel.......................22 C3

EATING
Assouan.......................23 A4
Café Jawharat Fes.......................24 C2
Central Market.......................25 C3
Cheap Eateries.......................26 C3
Chez Vittorio.......................27 C4
Chicken Mac.......................28 B3
Crémerie Skali.......................29 C3
Restaurant Marrakech.......................30 C4
Restaurant Pizza Mamia.......................31 B2
Restaurant Zagora.......................32 C4

ENTERTAINMENT
Crown Palace Fès.......................(see 10)
Le Marocain.......................33 C4

TRANSPORT
Grand Taxis to Meknès & Rabat.......................34 A2
Grand Taxis to Sefrou.......................35 C2
Local Buses.......................36 A2
Local Buses.......................37 C2
Petit Taxis.......................38 C4
Petit Taxis.......................39 A1
Petit Taxis.......................40 C4
RAM.......................41 C2

Eating

RESTAURANTS

Dining in Fez is something to be taken seriously. Fassi cuisine is famed across Morocco, and there are plenty of places in the medina to take your pick from. Popular with tour groups and their guides are the so-called 'palace restaurants' – dinner and show in lavish surroundings, usually with plain set menus and hefty price tags. A more intimate experience can be had dining at a riad, many of which are open to nonguests and offer excellent fare. A good range of cheaper places can be found around Bab Bou Jeloud. The ville nouvelle has more options, including more non-Moroccan menus.

Medina

our pick **Thami's** (Map pp234-5; Rue Serrajine; mains Dh30-70; 10am-11pm) Of the cluster of pavement restaurants leading from Bab Bou Jeloud to Talaa Seghira, this small corner place under a mulberry tree probably ranks as our favourite. The food is good and comes out bubbling hot, with filling *kefta* (spiced meatball) tajines, fried fish and bowls of stewed beans. Eat, then sit back and watch the medina parade pass before your eyes.

Restaurant Bouayad (Map pp234-5; 035 637464; Rue Serrajine; mains Dh40-60; 10am-11pm) Just inside Bab Bou Jeloud, this restaurant is more popular with tourists than locals, but still turns out a good range of Moroccan dishes – the fish tajine is particularly good. The interior is nicely cool in the hot summer months, although staff build up enough of a sweat, as the small kitchen can get overwhelmed when the place is packed out.

Le Kasbah (Map pp234-5; Rue Serrajine; mains Dh40, set menu Dh70; 8am-midnight) On several floors opposite the cheap hotels at Bab Bou Jeloud, this restaurant occupies a prime spot: the top floor looks out over the medina, making it a good place to relax over food. The menu itself isn't overly exciting – tajines, couscous and meat from the grill, but fair value. Be warned: if you only want to linger for views and a pot of mint tea – the cost of drinks is double if you're not eating.

our pick **Café Clock** (Map pp234-5; 035 637855; www.cafeclock.com; 7 Derb el-Mergana, Talaa Kebira; mains Dh55-80; 9am-10pm; wi-fi) Even we need a break from Moroccan food every now and then, and Café Clock was love at first sight. In a restored townhouse, this funky place has a refreshing menu with offerings such as falafel, grilled sandwiches, some interesting vegetarian options, a monstrously large camel burger, and delicious cakes and tarts. Better still, their 'Clock Culture' program includes calligraphy and conversation classes, a lecture program and sunset concerts every Sunday (cover charge around Dh20), attracting a good mix of locals, expats and tourists.

Médina Café (Map pp234-5; 035 633430; 6 Derb Mernissi, Bab Bou Jeloud; mains Dh70-100; 8am-10pm) Just outside Bab Bou Jeloud, this small restaurant is an oasis of serenity, decorated in a traditional yet restrained manner, with fine attention to detail. During the day it's a good place to visit for a quick bite or a fruit juice; in the evening better Moroccan fare is on offer – the lamb tajine with dried figs and apricots is a winner, while the plates of couscous are big enough for two.

Mezzanine (Map p230; 035 633430; 17 Kasbah Chams; tapas selection from Dh100 or per dish around

LET'S DO LUNCH

The restaurateurs around Bab Bou Jeloud seem to spend half their day trying to catch your eye and entice you to sit down and eat. We decided to sit down with one of them – Thami Bouziani (from Thami's, p247) – and talk.

How did you start out? My older brother taught me how to cook and he still helps me occasionally. I've never had another job. I've always been in this corner spot here looking down Talaa Seghira for 16 years. I started out making takeaway sandwiches for the people going to the cinema next door, but that closed down recently. I didn't have any tables and chairs then. It's only in the last three or four years that I've been catering to tourists. Now I have two big tables and a small one, and I've just renovated my kitchen.

But it's tiny! How do you manage? I cook everything in this kitchen. I have two gas burners, a griddle for brochettes, a fridge and a small sink, and a table for preparation. When it's busy I have a woman come to help me do the preparation. She does the 'women's food', like the couscous. I start in the morning around 10am and make the tomato sauce for the *kefta* (spiced meatball) tajine, and prepare all the vegetables. I buy all my meat, fish and vegetables in the Bou Jeloud souq around the corner. I haven't got space to squeeze juice or make coffee or tea, so I order that from the cafés around me. The same goes for bottles of water or soft drinks; I don't have enough storage space to keep stock here.

Have you noticed changes in the medina? Yes, there are lots more tourists now. The city authorities have just put up *mamounie* (wooden trellis-work) over the street which makes for more shade, and they're renovating the walls in this street. They've had to cut back the big mulberry tree over my restaurant a bit, but it's all looking good; I like the changes. One foreigner suggested I should put up a sign with my name; I think I will.

How do you attract customers? I have an article in English about my restaurant, with a photo of me, that was on *The View from Fez* blog. I've laminated it and show it to all the tourists, along with my menu. I've learned a few words of English too, like 'excellent food'!

What do the tourists want? They're often new to Morocco so they don't know. I give them a taster of *makoda* (potato fritters), or some *loubia* (beans), and they always ask for more because it's so good. They like my food because it's nicely spiced.

What food do they order? They usually ask my advice so I tell them what's best today. It could be turkey brochettes, *kefta* tajine with egg, couscous, fried fish or tajine of chicken or beef. I have a *melange* (mixture) too, a bit of everything. Sometimes a tourist has eaten something fancy in a hotel and asks me for it. I tell him to come back the next day, when the woman who helps me has shown me how to do it.

You have lots of Moroccan customers too. Do they order differently to tourists? Oh yes. Local people are more money-conscious. They'll just order something simple like a plate of *loubia* or some fried fish and eat that with one or two loaves of bread. But the tourists usually have a full meal, salad, main course and dessert, and mint tea. Sometimes very poor people come and ask me for food. I give them bread filled with fish, *makoda, loubia* or egg, but I don't charge them.

Dh30; ⌚ noon-1am) Opposite the entrance to the Jnane Sbil gardens slightly away from Bou Jeloud Sq, this new tapas bar is bringing a bit of city chic to the medina. With modern Moroccan furniture and *tadelakt* (smooth lime plaster) walls, the setting is consciously cool. Order as you like from a good selection of Moroccan- and Mediterranean-styled tapas, and wrap things up with a sweet dessert on the lovely roof terrace. Alcohol is served.

Dar Anebar (Map pp234-5; ☎ 035 635787; 25 Derb el-Miter, Zkak Roumane; mains from Dh120; ⌚ from 7.30pm) Another good riad for dining, where you'll eat in truly fine surroundings, in the splendid courtyard, or one of the cosy salons. The menu is strictly Moroccan, but of the highest standard, and you can accompany dinner with a bottle of wine.

Dar Roumana (Map pp234-5; ☎ 035 741637; 30 Derb el Amer, Zkak Roumane; mains around Dh150; ⌚ 7.30-9.30pm Tue-Sat) The menu here takes cues from the riad's name – house of pomegranates. Mediterranean with a Moroccan slant, including some interesting seafood dishes such as swordfish with pomegranates. It all works fabulously, and you eat in the courtyard or in fine weather up on the wonderful terrace. Alcohol is served.

La Maison Bleue (Map pp234-5; ☎ 035 636052; 2 Place de l'Istiqlal; set menu incl wine Dh550; dinner from 7.30pm) Reservations are necessary at this elegant riad restaurant. The setting is intimate and romantic, with diners serenaded by an oud player (replaced by livelier Gnawa song and dance at the end of the evening). You'll be treated to an array of cooked salads, tajines, couscous and *bastilla* (savoury pastries), plus filo pastry desserts. Top marks for presentation and atmosphere.

Ville Nouvelle

Chicken Mac (Map p246; Ave Lalla Meriem; mains around Dh30; 9am-11pm) Several eateries seem to run into each other along this strip in a continuously busy row of tables and chairs on the street. Chicken Mac is the last one away from Hassan II, and quickly serves up generous plates of rotisserie chicken, bowls of *harira* (soup) and other cheap, filling meals.

Kiotori (Map p230; ☎ 035 651700; 12 Rue Ahmed Chaouki; sushi Dh50-105, maki rolls Dh20-25; lunch & dinner;) Come to Fez and eat sushi? Why not? With a Japanese chef at the helm, and suitably minimalist surroundings, Kiotori carries off the challenge with aplomb. Choose individual sushi or tempura (battered seafood or vegetable) dishes from a wide selection or grab a mix through the set menus. Some Fassis shun it because it doesn't have a liquor licence, but that doesn't mean you should.

Restaurant Marrakech (Map p246; ☎ 035 930876; 11 Rue Omar el-Mokhtar; mains from Dh55;) A charming restaurant that goes from strength to strength behind thick wooden doors. Red *tadelakt* walls and dark furniture, with a cushion-strewn salon at the back add ambience, while the menu's variety refreshes the palettes, with dishes like chicken tajine with apple and olive, or lamb with aubergine and peppers (there's also a set three-course menu).

Chez Vittorio (Map p246; ☎ 035 624730; 21 Rue Brahim Roudani; mains from Dh80, salads from Dh30, pizza or pasta from Dh56) This dependable favourite covers the rustic Italian restaurant angle well, right down to the candles and checked cloths. The food is good value, and while the initial service can be a bit creaky your meal tends to arrive in a trice. Go for the pizzas or steak, as the pasta often disappoints. You can also enjoy a glass of wine with your meal.

Restaurant Zagora (Map p246; ☎ 035 940686; 5 Blvd Mohammed V; mains Dh80-100) Just off the southern end of Mohammed V, this classy restaurant is popular with tour groups and locals alike. The wine list is probably the most extensive in the ville nouvelle and the menu is equally broad, although the pleasant setting (complete with oud player) means that both food and drink attract a sizeable surcharge.

Zen Garden (☎ 035 932929; 26 Ave Omar Ibn Khattab; mains from Dh100; lunch & dinner;) Worth the taxi ride to get there, the Zen Garden is as pleasing as Majestic (below), and kinder on the bank balance. Deservedly popular, with a good line in continental-style dishes in refined surroundings. Alcohol is served.

Majestic (☎ 035 729999; Rte de Zwagha; mains Dh140-190; noon-10pm;) You'll need to grab a taxi for this upscale place, although if you make a reservation the restaurant offers a pick-up and drop-off service. The stylish open-plan layout looks to London- and Parisien-style magazines for inspiration and pulls it off, while the menu is distinctly French-leaning, with some Mediterranean influences (the fish is a high point). Service is excellent, and there's a good wine list that adds to the evening out, but pack your wallet well before dining.

QUICK EATS

In the medina, you won't have to walk far to find someone selling food – tiny cell-like places grilling brochettes or cooking up cauldrons of soup, sandwich shops or just a guy with a pushcart selling peanut cookies. Bab Bou Jeloud has quite a cluster of options, otherwise follow your nose. In the ville nouvelle, there are a few cheap eats on or just off Blvd Mohammed V, especially around the central market. You'll also find a good choice of sandwich places around Place Yacoub al-Mansour.

B'sara stalls (Map pp234-5; Acherbine; soup Dh4) The Fassi speciality of *b'sara* (garlic and butter bean soup) shouldn't be missed. Served from hole-in-the-wall places throughout the medina from huge cauldrons, our favourites are in the Acherbine area. Perfect fuel for exploring the city, the soup is ladled into rough pottery bowls and served with a hunk of bread and dash of olive oil.

our pick **Snail Stand** (Map pp234-5; cnr Talaa Seghira & Derb el-Horra; snails Dh5) This permanent stand is a good place to fill up on a molluscan snack – the ultimate in pre-packaged fast food. Grab a pin to pluck the beasts out of their shells, then slurp down the aromatic broth. Delicious!

Restaurant Pizza Mamia (Map p246; Place Florence; salads Dh20, pizzas from Dh25; lunch & dinner) Compact and cosy, this place serves good and quick pizzas from a wood-fired oven, plus salads, burgers and other fast-food options. Popular with families and young couples.

Cheap Eateries (Map p246; Aves Hassan Ouazzani & Abdellah Chefchaouni; meals around Dh35) The raft of clean and cheap eateries along this strip near the Jardin Public serve fresh salads, brochettes and tajines that could hold their own in many of the city's upmarket restaurants. The place closest to the garden is our favourite.

CAFÉS, PATISSERIES & ICE-CREAM PARLOURS

It can seem as if the main occupation in the ville nouvelle is sitting in cafés nursing a coffee and croissant. Blvd Mohammed V and Ave Hassan II have the greatest concentration, but you don't have to go far to grab a table, order a drink and watch the day unfold. In the medina, many of the restaurants around Bab Bou Jeloud double as cafés, otherwise hole-in-the-wall places are often the order of the day.

Crémerie Skali (Map p246; Blvd Mohammed V; breakfast around Dh20; 6am-10pm) With a good corner location, this is an ideal stop for breakfast – one that's popular with office workers and families alike. As well as pastries and juice, it can rustle up some mean scrambled eggs.

Café Restaurant La Noria (Map p230; Fès el-Jdid; mains Dh40-60; 7am-9pm) This café is tucked away in the Bou Jeloud Gardens next to an old waterwheel – a delightful retreat from the bustle of the city. The shady courtyard is perfect to relax in, and in addition to drinks and juices, there's a good dining menu if you're peckish.

Café Jawharat Fes (Map p246; 16 Ave Farhat Hachad; wi-fi) Handy for students in the American Language Center, this is an extravagantly decorated café with a good terrace and friendly atmosphere. Bring your laptop to use the free wi-fi.

Assouan (Map p246; 4 Ave Omar Ibnou Khattab) Come here for three things – coffee, cake and a pavement location tailor-made for people-watching. Always busy and popular.

Cremerie La Place (Map pp234-5; Seffarine Sq; 7.30am-8pm) Put a café in one of the most interesting spots in the medina, and you have a near-perfect combination. Over juice, tea, coffee and pastries, the parade passes before you, accompanied by the tapping of the square's coppersmiths.

SELF-CATERING

For fresh fruit and vegies, spices, nuts, olives or a parcel of delicious dates, you can't beat the ville nouvelle's **central market** (Map p246; Blvd Mohammed V; 8.30am-2.30pm). It also has a couple of good cheese stalls and there are alcohol shops around the outside.

In the medina, fresh produce abounds – start at the fresh fruit stalls at the top of Talaa Kebira and work your way down from there (the squeamish might care to avert their eyes as they pass the butchers' stalls, with rows of sheep and cow heads). Vendors will call out at you to offer their freshest dates and olives.

Drinking

For a drop of the hard stuff, there are more options in the ville nouvelle than the medina. As is the Moroccan norm, bars tend to be seedy, smoky places, where men are men and women are prostitutes – you have been warned! Places listed below offer a more congenial atmosphere; drinking up time is around 11pm.

Hotel Batha (Map pp234-5; Place Batha) There are a couple of options for drinks in this handily located medina hotel. Inside the hotel proper, the bar by the pool catches the overspill from the Churchill Bar, and in winter even features a log fire to warm yourself by. At the back of the hotel (side entrance), the outside Consul Bar is a more relaxed place for late-night drinks, and has its own disco until midnight (closed Monday).

Riad Fès (Map pp234-5; 5 Derb ibn Slimane) The classiest place for a drink in the whole city, the courtyard bar of Riad Fès is a delight. Stucco columns catch the light reflected off the central pool, and soft music plays

FASSI POTTERY

Ceramics seem to be everywhere in Fez – from the distinctive blue pottery to the intricate mosaics decorating fountains and riads. **Art Naji** (☎ 035 669166; www.artnaji.net; Ain Nokbi; 🕑 8am-6pm) is the place to go to buy the real deal. You can see the entire production process, from pot-throwing to the painstaking hand painting and laying out of *zellij* (tilework) – it's a joy to behold. The potteries are about 500m east of Bab el-Ftouh, an easy trip in a petit taxi – look for the plumes of black smoke produced by olive pits, which burn at the right temperature for firing the clay. You can even commission a mosaic and arrange for it to be shipped home.

while you sit at the glass bar or slump into the cushions. There's a good range of beer and spirits, plus wine available by the glass. Open to the elements, it's a little cold in winter, but fashionably cool in summer.

Mezzanine (Map p230; ☎ 035 633430; 17 Kasbah Chams; 🕑 noon-1am) Scoring highly on the fashion meter and for late-opening, this new bar is the hippest thing in the medina – more Ibiza than Moulay Idriss. The terrace overlooking Jnan Sbil gardens is a good place to chill with a beer or cocktail, and there's tapas too if you want some finger food (see p247).

Sofitel Palais Jamaï (Map pp234-5; Bab Guissa) A great place for a sundowner, the Palais Jamaï has a great terrace looking out across old Fez: an ideal way to finish up a day in the medina. Drinks are slightly more expensive before dinner, but you can help yourself to as many free bar snacks as you like.

Entertainment

Live music buffs know the best time to visit Fez is festival time (see p242). Café Clock (see p247) has regular Sunday sunset concerts worth checking out.

Les Musicales du Palais el-Mokri (Map pp234-5; ☎ 068 601791; www.lesmusicalesdefes.com in French; Mokri Palace, Chaq Bdenjala, Ziat; admission Dh60; 🕑 4-6pm Wed & Sun) Traditional music concerts held in the salons of the Mokri Palace: feast your eyes on the spectacular surroundings and imagine yourself a pasha of old. See the website for the program of events and groups performing (except in August). The entrance fee includes tea and Moroccan pastries.

Crown Palace Fes (p246; 85 Ave Des FAR; 🕑 from 6pm) When it comes to glam nightlife, Fez is no Marrakesh. Cashed-up locals usually end up partying in the downstairs piano bar or upstairs cigar and cocktail bar at the Crown Palace. When these bars close around 1am, the crowd sometimes relocates to the basement nightclub – the 'VIP' – that has a DJ between midnight and 3am each night.

Le Marocain (Map p246; 38 Ave Mohammed Slaoui; 🕑 from 9pm) The rear bar of this decidedly louche nightspot is where the city's working girls tout for trade; their male colleagues are usually found preening in the front bar. The band and resident chanteuse aren't likely to be appearing in a concert hall near you in the near future, but they're fun to listen to before you take to the dance floor. Well-priced drinks (beers Dh15) come with tapas-like snacks.

Shopping

Fez is the artisanal capital of Morocco. The choice of crafts is wide, quality is high, and prices are competitive, so take your time to shop around. As usual, it's best to seek out the little shops off the main tourist routes (principally Talaa Kebira and Talaa Seghira in the medina). For leather, the area around the tanneries unsurprisingly has the best selection of goods.

In the medina, there are many well-restored riads and *funduqs* that have been converted into carpet showrooms. While they certainly offer a great opportunity to sit with a mint tea in spectacular surroundings and look at some fabulous rugs, the hard sell is like no other place in Morocco. You can pick up some wonderful pieces, but also pay over the odds for factory-made rubbish. See also p232 to help prepare you for the Fez carpet shopping experience.

Getting There & Away

AIR

Fez airport (☎ 035 674712) is 15km south of the city, at Saïss. **RAM** (Map p246; ☎ 035 625516; 54 Ave Hassan II) operates daily flights to Casablanca; for international connections (mainly to France, see p479).

CTM

The main bus station for **CTM buses** (☎ 035 732992) is near Place Atlas in the southern ville nouvelle (Map p230). In high season buy tickets in advance, particularly to Tangier, Marrakesh and Chefchaouen.

CTM runs seven buses a day to Casablanca (Dh100, five hours) via Rabat (Dh80, 3½ hours) between 6.30am and 4.30pm, and six buses to Meknès (Dh20, one hour) between 8.30am and 8.30pm. Buses for Marrakesh (Dh160, nine hours) run twice daily (morning and evening).

Heading north and east, there are three buses for Tangier (Dh100, six hours), three for Chefchaouen (Dh70, four hours), two for Tetouan (Dh93, five hours), one for Al-Hoceima (Dh90, six hours), two for Nador (Dh74, seven hours), and a daily service for Oujda (Dh100, six hours).

International services to Spain and France with Eurolines also depart from the CTM bus station.

Other Companies

Non-CTM buses depart from the **main bus station** (Map pp234-5; ☎ 035 636032) outside Bab el-Mahrouk. Fares are slightly less than CTM and reservations can be made for popular routes. It has a **left-luggage facility** (per item Dh5, 🕑 6am-midnight).

At least six buses run daily to Casablanca, Chefchaouen, Er-Rachidia, Marrakesh, Meknès, Oujda, Rabat, Tangier and Tetouan. Less frequent buses go to Rissani (Dh120, 10 hours), Ouarzazate (Dh142, 14 hours) and Tinerhir (Dh108, 10 hours).

Locally, there are frequent departures to Azrou (Dh18, two hours), Ifrane (Dh16, 90 minutes), Moulay Yacoub (Dh8, 30 minutes), Sefrou (Dh8, 40 minutes), Taza (Dh34, three hours, hourly) and Ouezzane (Dh34, three hours, twice daily).

CAR

There are several car parks near the medina: just south of Place l'Istiqal, on Ave des Français outside Bab Bou Jeloud, and inside the medina wall north of Talaa Kebira at Ain Azleen. In the ville nouvelle is a guarded car park in front of the central market.

TAXI

There are several grand taxi ranks dotted around town. Taxis for Meknès (Dh16, one hour) and Rabat (Dh59) leave from in front of the main bus station (Map pp234–5; outside Bab el-Mahrouk) and from near the train station (Map p246). Taxis for Taza (Dh44, 2½ hours) depart from near Bab Fettouh (Map pp234–5), the medina's southeastern gate. Those going to Moulay Yacoub (Dh9, 20 minutes) leave from the open ground to the west of Bab Bou Jeloud (Map pp234–5). The rank for Sefrou (Dh12, 30 minutes) is located just below Place de la Résistance in the ville nouvelle (Map p246). Azrou (Dh30, one hour) and Ifrane (Dh21, 45 minutes) taxis wait at a parking lot to the west of the CTM bus station in the south of the ville nouvelle (Map p230).

TRAIN

The **train station** (Map p246; ☎ 035 930333) is in the ville nouvelle, a 10-minute walk northwest of Place Florence. To take advantage of the **left-luggage office** (per item Dh10; 🕑 6am-8pm), bags must be locked or padlocked.

Trains depart every two hours between 7am and 5pm to Casablanca (Dh103, 4¼ hours), via Rabat (Dh76, 3½ hours) and Meknès (Dh18, one hour). There are two additional overnight trains. Eight trains go to Marrakesh (Dh180, eight hours) and one goes to Tangier (Dh97, five hours) direct (four more via Sidi Kacem). Direct trains for Oujda (Dh108, six hours) via Taza (Dh39, two hours) leave three times daily.

Getting Around

TO/FROM THE AIRPORT

There is a regular bus service (bus 16) between the airport and the train station (Dh3, 25 minutes), with departures every half-hour or so. Grands taxis from any stand charge a set fare of Dh120.

BUS

Fez has a reliable local bus service. At certain times of day, however, the buses are like sardine cans and are notorious for pickpockets. The standard fare is Dh2.50. Some useful routes:

No 9 Place Atlas via Blvd Abdallah Chefchaouni (both in the ville nouvelle) to near the Batha Museum (Fès el-Bali); the bus returns via Place de la Résistance, Ave Hassan II and Ave des FAR.

No 10 Train station via Bab Guissa (northern Fès el-Bali) to Bab Sidi Bou Jida (northeastern Fès el-Bali).

No 19 Train station via Ave Hassan II (both in ville nouvelle) and Bab el-Jdid (southern Fès el-Bali) to Place Rcif (central Fès el-Bali).
No 47 Train station to Bab Bou Jeloud (Fès el-Bali).

TAXI

Drivers of the red petits taxis generally use their meters without any fuss. Expect to pay about Dh9 from the train or CTM station to Bab Bou Jeloud. As usual, there is a 50% surcharge after 8pm. You'll find taxi ranks outside all the gates of the medina. Only grands taxis go out to the airport (see opposite).

AROUND FEZ

Sefrou صفرو

The small Berber town of Sefrou, just 30km southeast of Fez, is a picturesque place situated on the edge of the Middle Atlas. It has a small but interesting medina, which once hosted one of Morocco's largest Jewish communities (as many as 8000 people, according to some accounts), and it was here that Moulay Idriss II lived while overseeing the building of Fez. It's an easy day trip from Fez, ideal if you need to escape the big city.

INFORMATION

BMCE (Blvd Mohammed V) Has an ATM.
Club Internet Ibn Battouta (Off Blvd Mohammed V; per hr Dh7; 9am-midnight)
Main post office (Blvd Mohammed V)
Pharmacie de Sefrou (Blvd Mohammed V; 8am-8pm Mon-Sat)
Post office (Rte de Fès)

SIGHTS & ACTIVITIES

Sefrou's medina is a manageable place to get around, especially compared to Fez. The Oued Aggaï flows through its centre, opening the place up and giving it more of an airy feeling than many old medinas. The best point of entry is the northerly **Bab el-Maqam**. Follow the main flow of people downhill to the southeast and pass two mosques. Cross over the river and continue up the main shopping street to where the road splits: straight ahead takes you to Bab Merba, in the medina's southern wall, next to another mosque; the right fork brings you to the beginning of the **mellah**,

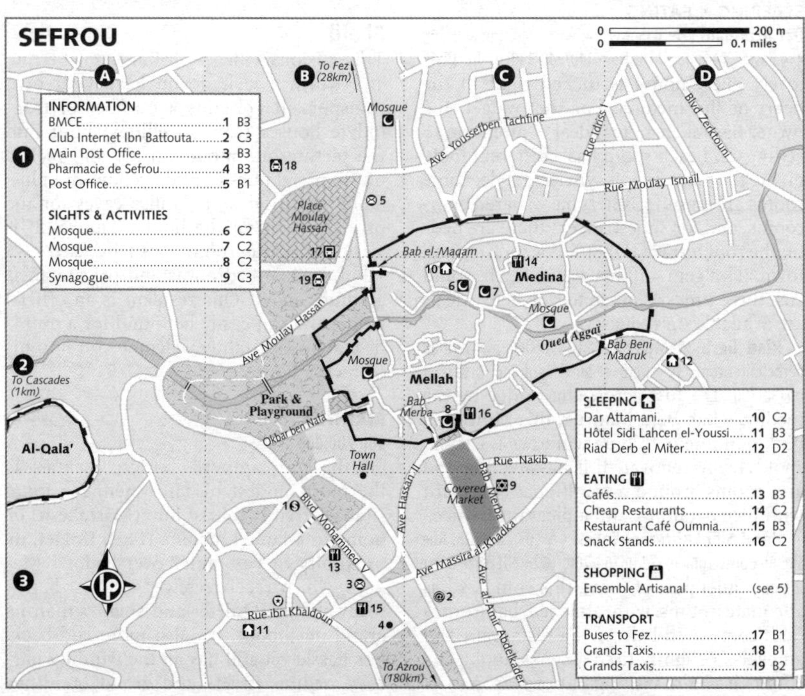

which stretches from here northwest along the river. Although its Jewish population has gone, the district still retains a few distinctive wooden-galleried houses and lanes so narrow two people can only just pass. In its heyday, the *mellah* was so dark and crowded that street lamps had to be lit even in the middle of the day. Just south of Bab Merba is a **synagogue**, which is now closed. When we visited, the king had just announced money to restore the city walls, although there were mixed feelings about a plan to pave over sections of the river in the medina.

A 1.5km walk west of town are the **Cascades**, a modest waterfall. Follow the signs from Ave Moulay Hassan around **Al-Qala'** (a semifortified village) and along the river's lush valley.

Sefrou is a sleepy place on the whole. However, things liven up on Thursday (market day) and in early June when the annual **Cherry Festival** fills the streets for three days of folk music, parades and sports events, culminating with the crowning of the Cherry Queen.

SLEEPING & EATING

Dar Attamani (☎ 035 969174; www.darattamani.com; 414 Bastna, Medina; s/d/tr from 140/240/330; wi-fi) This lovely guest house is tucked right in the heart of the medina. For the budget, the owner has taken a great deal of attention to styling, and each room has a different look, giving the place an idiosyncratic style. Some rooms are en suite, others have shared bathrooms, and for shoestringers there are beds on the roof terrace (Dh80). For such a small town, it's a gem – if this was in Fez it would cost three times as much to stay here. Meals are available on request.

Riad Derb el Miter (☎ 035 660602; www.riadderbelmiter.com; 304 Derb el-Miter; s/d incl breakfast Dh190/380; 💻) Just across the bridge by the medina's Bab Beni Madruk, this Moroccan pink building with blue windows is easy to spot. Newly renovated, it has five big and airy rooms around a traditional courtyard with nice detailing, and a pleasant terrace.

Hôtel Sidi Lahcen el-Youssi (☎ 035 683428; Rue Sidi Ali Bousserghine; s/d Dh165/200; 🍴) Situated in a very quiet part of town, this complex has adequate rooms with attached bathrooms (and some with balcony), a restaurant and an ever-so-slightly tired air. Ask about discounts if you're visiting out of season.

Restaurant Café Oumnia (☎ 055 660679; Ave Massira al-Khadka; set menu Dh65; 🕐 8am-9pm) This is Sefrou's only formal restaurant, near the post office. Set on two levels, with clean and bright restaurant decor, its daily three-course set menu is good value at Dh65, and there's a licensed bar.

There's a string of cafés and a bar along Blvd Mohammed V, all fairly masculine places to drink coffee. There are a few cheap eats with soup, kebabs and the like in the medina.

SHOPPING

You might snap up a bargain at the market held every Thursday; otherwise try **Ensemble Artisanal** (Rte de Fès), which offers the usual selection of rugs, pots, clothes and leather at fixed prices.

GETTING THERE & AWAY

Regular buses (Dh8, 40 minutes) and grands taxis (Dh12, 30 minutes) run between Sefrou and Place de la Résistance in Fez. For Azrou, take a grand taxi to Immouzzer (Dh12) and change.

Bhalil بهاليل

This curious village is 5km from Sefrou, and worth a visit if you have your own transport. It contains a number of troglodyte houses (cave dwellings) built into the picturesque mountainside and picked out in pastel hues of pink, yellow and blue. Some go so far as to utilise caves for the primary room of the house. The result is a cool, spacious room – usually used as a salon – while bedrooms and private areas are built above. One resident is an official guide, and can easily be found for a tour – he'll almost certainly welcome you into his own cave home.

MEKNÈS مكناس

pop 700,000

Of the four imperial cities, Meknès is the most modest by far – neither capital (Rabat), trendy tourist hub (Marrakesh) or home to a famed medina (Fez). In fact, its proximity to Fez rather overshadows Meknès, which receives fewer visitors than it really should. Quieter and smaller than its grand neighbour, it's also more laid-back, less hassle yet still has all the winding narrow medina streets and grand buildings

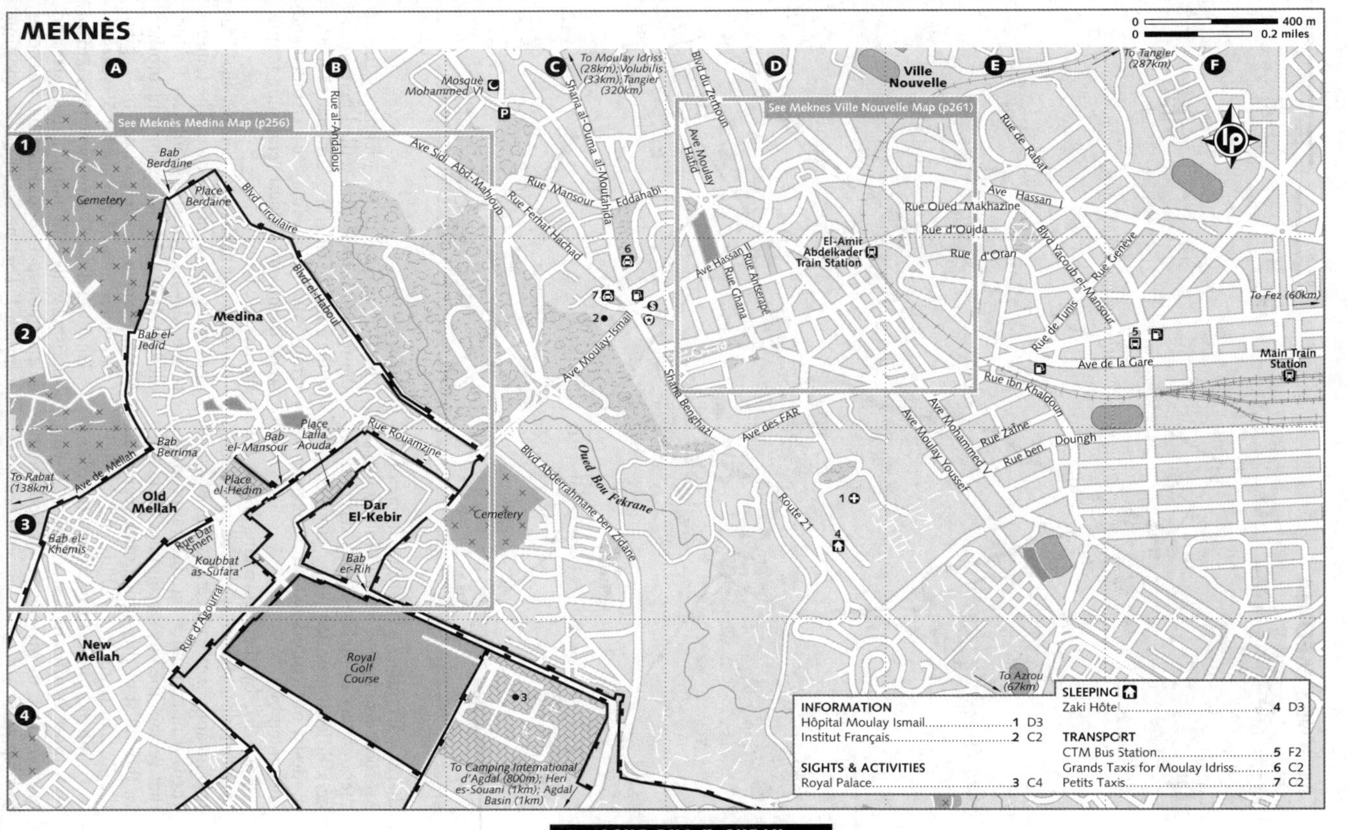
MEKNÈS
0 400 m
0 0.2 miles
Ville Nouvelle
To Moulay Idriss (28km); Volubilis (33km); Tangier (320km)
To Tangier (287km)
Mosquè Mohammed VI
See Meknès Medina Map (p256)
See Meknes Ville Nouvelle Map (p261)
Rue al-Andalous
Bab Berdaine
Place Berdaine
Gemetery
Blvd Circulaire
Blvd el-Haboul
Ave Sidi Abd-Mahjoub
Rue Ferhat Hachad
Rue Mansour Eddahabi
Shana al-Ouma al-Moutahida
Blvd du Zerhoun
Ave Moulay Hafid
Ave Hassan II
Rue Ghana
Rue Antserapé
El-Amir Abdelkader Train Station
Rue Oued Makhazine
Rue d'Oujda
Rue d'Oran
Ave Hassan I
Rue de Rabat
Blvd Yacoub el-Mansour
Rue Genève
Rue de Tunis
To Fez (60km)
Ave de la Gare
Main Train Station
Rue ibn Khaldoun
Rue Zaine
Rue ben Dough
Ave Mohammed V
Ave Moulay Youssef
Ave des FAR
Shana Benghazi
Ave Moulay-Ismail
Medina
Bab el-Jedid
Bab Berrima
Ave de Mellah
To Rabat (138km)
Old Mellah
Bab el-Khemis
Bab el-Mansour
Place Lalla Aouda
Place el-Hedim
Rue Rouamzine
Dar El-Kebir
Cemetery
Rue Dar Smen
Koubbat as-Sufara
Bab er-Rih
Blvd Abderrahmane ben Zidane
Oued Bou Fekrane
Route 21
Rue d'Agourrai
New Mellah
Royal Golf Course
To Camping International d'Agdal (800m); Heri es-Souani (1km); Agdal Basin (1km)
To Azrou (67km)
INFORMATION
Hôpital Moulay Ismail 1 D3
Institut Français 2 C2
SIGHTS & ACTIVITIES
Royal Palace 3 C4
SLEEPING
Zaki Hôte 4 D3
TRANSPORT
CTM Bus Station 5 F2
Grands Taxis for Moulay Idriss 6 C2
Petits Taxis 7 C2

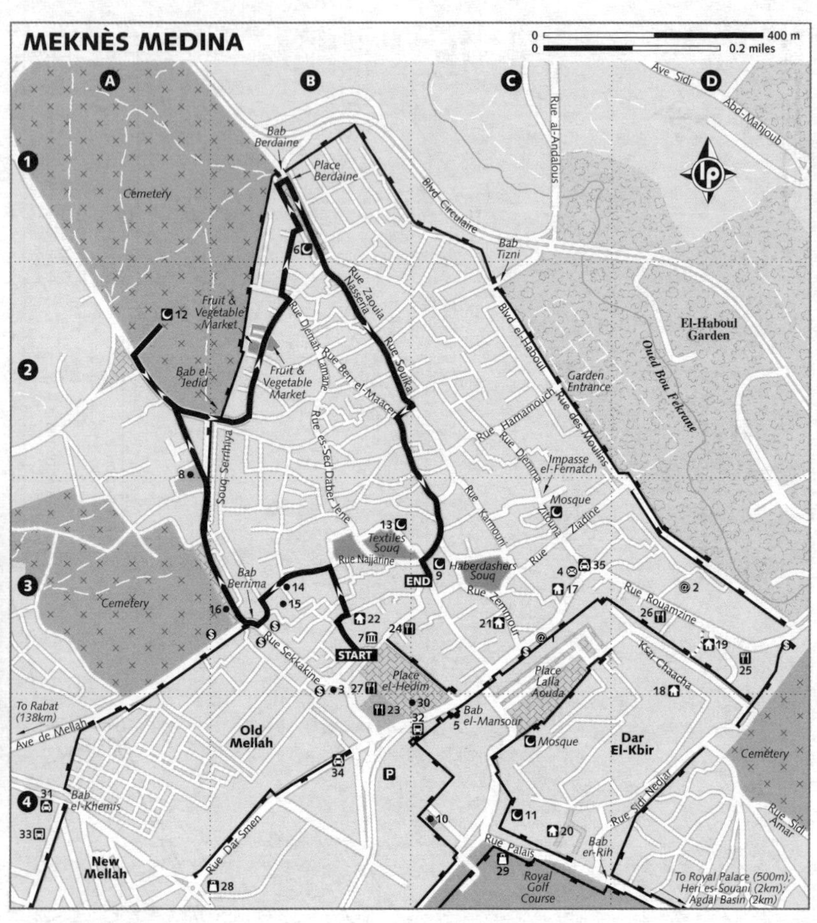

that it warrants as a one-time home of the Moroccan sultanate. Sultan Moulay Ismail, the architect of Meknès' glory days, might be a little disgruntled at the city's current modesty, but visitors will find much to be enchanted by.

Encircled by the rich plains below the Middle Atlas, Meknès is blessed with a hinterland abundant with cereals, olives, wine, citrus fruit and other agricultural products that remain the city's economic backbone. In the midst of this agricultural region sit the Roman ruins at Volubilis and the hilltop tomb of Moulay Idriss, two of the country's most significant historic sites. If you base yourself in Meknès you'll find plenty to keep you busy.

History

The Berber tribe of the Meknassis (hence the name Meknès) first settled here in the 10th century. Under the Almohads and Merenids, Meknès' medina was expanded and some of the city's oldest remaining monuments were built.

It wasn't until the 17th century that Meknès really came into its own. The founder of the Alawite dynasty, Moulay ar-Rashid, died in 1672. His successor and brother, Moulay Ismail, made Meknès his capital, from where he would reign for 55 years.

Ismail endowed the city with 25km of imposing walls with monumental gates and an enormous palace complex that was never completed. That he could devote the time

INFORMATION		
Cyber Bab Mansour	1	C3
Meet Net	2	D3
Pharmacy el-Fath	3	B3
Post Office	4	C3
SIGHTS & ACTIVITIES		
Bab el-Mansour	5	C4
Berdaine Mosque	6	B1
Dar Jamaï Museum	7	B3
Flea Market	8	A2
Grande Mosquée	9	C3
Koubbat as-Sufara'	10	C4
Mausoleum of Moulay Ismail	11	C4
Mausoleum of Sidi ben Aïssa	12	A2
Medersa Bou Inania	13	B3
Okchen Market	14	B3
Qissariat ad-Dahab	15	B3
Spices,Herbs &Nuts Souq	16	B3
SLEEPING		
Hôtel Regina	17	C3
Maison d'Hôtes Riad	18	D3
Maroc Hôtel	19	D3
Palais Didi	20	C4
Riad Safir	21	C3
Ryad Bahia	22	B3
EATING		
Covered Market	23	B4
Dar Sultana	(see 22)	
Restaurant Mille et Une Nuits	24	B3
Restaurant Oumnia	25	D3
Restaurant Riad	(see 18)	
Rue Rouamzine Eateries	26	D3
Ryad Bahia	(see 22)	
Sandwich Stands	27	B3
SHOPPING		
Centre Artisinale	28	B4
Pottery stalls	(see 23)	
Souvenir Shops	29	C4
TRANSPORT		
Calèches	30	C4
Grands Taxis	31	A4
Local Buses	32	C4
Main Bus Station	33	A4
Petits Taxis	34	B4
Petits Taxis	35	C3

and resources to construction was partly due to his uncommon success in subduing all opposition in Morocco and keeping foreign meddlers at bay, mainly because of his notorious Black Guard (see p259).

Ismail's death in 1727 also struck the death knell for Meknès. The town resumed its role as a backwater, as his grandson Mohammed III (1757–90) moved to Marrakesh. The 1755 earthquake that devastated Lisbon also dealt Meknès a heavy blow. As so often happened in Morocco, its monuments were subsequently stripped in order to be added to buildings elsewhere. It's only been in the past few decades, as tourist potential has become obvious, that any serious restoration attempts have taken place.

In 1912 the arrival of the protectorate revived Meknès as the French made it their military headquarters. The army was accompanied by French farmers who settled on the fertile land nearby. After independence most properties were recovered by the Moroccan government and leased to local farmers.

Orientation

The valley of the (usually dry) Oued Bou Fekrane neatly divides the old medina in the west and the French-built ville nouvelle in the east. Ave Moulay Ismail connects them, then becomes the principal route of the ville nouvelle, where its name changes to Ave Hassan II.

Moulay Ismail's tomb and imperial city are south of the medina. Train and CTM bus stations are in the ville nouvelle, as are most offices and banks, as well as the more expensive hotels. It's a 20-minute walk from the medina to the ville nouvelle, but regular (and crowded) local buses and urban grands taxis shuttle between the two.

Information

BOOKSHOPS

Librarie Dar al-Kitab al-Watani (Map p261; ☎ 035 521280; 10-21 Blvd Allal ben Abdallah) Mostly French books, with a few English titles.

CULTURAL CENTRES

Institut Français (Map p255; ☎ 035 515851; inst.fr.mek@aim.net.ma; Rue Ferhat Hachad; 8.30am-noon & 2.30-6.30pm Mon-Sat) The centre of Meknès' cultural life, with films, plays, concerts and exhibitions.

INTERNET ACCESS

Cyber Bab Mansour (Map p256; Zankat Accra; per hr Dh6; 9am-midnight)

Cyber de Paris (Map p261; Rue Accra; per hr Dh8; 9am-2am)

Meet Net (Map p256; Rue Rouamzine; per hr Dh8; 10am-1pm & 3-9.30pm Mon-Sat)

Quick Net (Map p261; 28 Rue Emir Abdelkander; per hr Dh6; 9am-10pm)

MEDICAL SERVICES

Hôpital Moulay Ismail (Map p255; ☎ 035 522805; off Ave des FAR)

Night Pharmacy (Map p261; Rue de Paris)

Pharmacy el-Fath (Map p256; Place el-Hedim)

MONEY

There are plenty of banks with ATMs both in the ville nouvelle (mainly on Ave Hassan II and Ave Mohammed V) and the medina (Rue Sekkakine).

BMCE (Map p261; 98 Ave des FAR; 10am-1pm & 4-7pm) An after-hours exchange office on the southeast side of the ville nouvelle.

POST

Main post office (Map p261; Place de l'Istiqlal) The parcel office is in the same building, around the corner on Rue Tetouan.

Post office (Map p256; Rue Dar Smen) In the medina.

TOURIST INFORMATION

Délégation Régionale du Tourisme (Map p261; ☎ 055 524426; fax 055 516046; Place de l'Istiqlal; ⏲ 8.30am-noon & 2.30-6.30pm Mon-Thu, 8-11.30am & 3-6.30pm Fri) Limited tourist information and pamphlets.

TRAVEL AGENCIES

Carlson Wagonlit (Map p261; ☎ 055 521995; 1 Rue Ghana) A source for air, ferry and coach tickets.

RAM (Map p261; ☎ 055 520963; 7 Ave Mohammed V) Handles tickets for all major airlines.

Sights

MEDINA

The heart of the Meknès medina is Place el-Hedim, the large square facing Bab el-Mansour. Built by Moulay Ismail and originally used for royal announcements and public executions, it's a good place to sit and watch the world go by – kids playing football, hawkers selling miracle cures, and promenading families. There's always something going on, and you get the sense that the city authorities would love for it to turn into the local equivalent of Marrakesh's Djemma el Fna. Things have recently been spruced up with the canopied seating areas for the food bars facing the old walls. Behind these there's an excellent produce market (see p264).

To the south, the impressive monumental gateway of Bab el-Mansour leads into Moulay Ismail's imperial city. The narrow streets of the old *mellah* are in the west of the medina – look for the old balconied houses so distinctive of the Jewish quarter.

Dar Jamaï Museum

Overlooking Place el-Hedim is Dar Jamaï, a palace built in 1882 by the powerful Jamaï family, two of whom were viziers to Sultan Moulay al-Hassan I. When the sultan died in 1894, the family fell foul of court politics and lost everything, including the palace, which was passed on to the powerful Al-Glaoui family. In 1912 the French commandeered the palace for a military hospital.

Since 1920 the palace has housed the Administration des Beaux Arts and one of Morocco's best **museums** (Map p256; ☎ 055 530863; Place el-Hedim; admission Dh10; ⏲ 9am-noon & 3-6.30pm Wed-Mon). Exhibits include traditional ceramics, jewellery, rugs and some fantastic textiles and embroidery. Look out for the brocaded saddles, and some exquisite examples of Meknasi needlework (including some extravagant gold and silver kaftans). The *koubba* (domed sanctuary) upstairs is furnished as a traditional salon complete with luxurious rugs and cushions. The museum also has a fine collection of antique carpets, representing various styles from different regions of Morocco.

The exhibits are well constructed; explanations are in French, Arabic and sometimes English. The museum's Andalucian garden and courtyard are shady, peaceful spots amid overgrown orange trees.

Grande Mosquée & Medersa Bou Inania

Opposite the Grande Mosquée, the **Medersa Bou Inania** (Map p256; Rue Najjarine; admission Dh10; ⏲ 9am-noon & 3-6pm) is typical of the exquisite interior design that distinguishes Merenid monuments. It was completed in 1358 by Bou Inan, after whom a more lavish *medersa* in Fez is also named. This *medersa* is a good display of the classic Moroccan decorative styles – the *zellij* base, delicate stucco midriff and carved olivewood ceiling.

Students aged eight to 10 years once lived two to a cell on the ground floor, while older students and teachers lived on the 1st floor. Anyone can climb onto the roof for views of the green-tiled roof and minaret of the Grande Mosquée nearby, but the *medersa* is otherwise closed to non-Muslims.

IMPERIAL CITY

Bab el-Mansour

The focus of Place el-Hedim is the huge gate of Bab el-Mansour, the grandest of all imperial Moroccan gateways. The gate is well preserved with lavish (if faded) *zellij* and inscriptions across the top. It was completed by Moulay Ismail's son, Moulay Abdallah, in 1732. You can't walk through the bab itself (although it's sometimes open to host exhibitions), but instead have to make do with a side gate to the left.

Mausoleum of Moulay Ismail

Diagonally opposite the Koubbat as-Sufara' is the **resting place** (Map p256; donations welcomed;

THE ALMIGHTY MOULAY

Few men dominate the history of a country like the towering figure of Sultan Moulay Ismail (1672–1727). Originating from the sand-blown plains of the Tafilalt region, his family were sherifs (descendants of the Prophet Mohammed) – a pedigree that continues to underpin the current monarchy.

Ruthlessness as well as good breeding were essential characteristics for becoming sultan. On inheriting the throne from his brother Moulay ar-Rashid, Moulay Ismail set about diffusing the rival claims of his 83 brothers and half-brothers, celebrating his first day in power by murdering all those who refused to submit to his rule. His politics continued in this bloody vein with military campaigns in the south, the Rif Mountains and Algerian hinterland, bringing most of Morocco under his control. He even brought the Salé corsairs to heel, taxing their piracy handsomely to swell the imperial coffers.

The peace won, Moulay Ismail retired to his capital at Meknès and began building his grandiose imperial palace, plundering the country for the best materials, and building city walls, kasbahs and many new towns. This cultural flowering was Morocco's last great golden age.

Moulay Ismail also considered himself a lover. Although he sought (but failed to receive) the hand in marriage of Louis XIV of France's daughter, he still fathered literally hundreds of children. Rather foolishly however he did nothing to secure his succession. When he died the sultanate was rocked by a series of internecine power struggles, from which the Alawites never fully recovered.

Nevertheless, his legacy was to be the foundations of modern Morocco. He liberated Tangier from the British, subdued the Berber tribes and relieved the Spanish of much of their Moroccan territory. Moulay Ismail sowed the seeds of the current monarchy and beneath his strong-arm rule the coherent entity of modern Morocco was first glimpsed.

8.30am-noon & 2-6pm Sat-Thu) of the sultan who made Meknès his capital in the 17th century. Moulay Ismail's stature as one of Morocco's greatest rulers means that non-Muslim visitors are welcomed into the sanctuary. Entry is through a series of austere, peaceful courtyards meant to induce a quiet and humble attitude among visitors, an aim that's not always successful in the face of a busload of tourists. The tomb hall is a lavish contrast and showcase of the best of Moroccan craftsmanship. Photography is permitted, but non-Muslims may not approach the tomb itself.

Koubbat as-Sufara'

South of Bab el-Mansour lies the *mechouar* (parade ground), now known as Place Lalla Aouda, where Moulay Ismail inspected his famed Black Guard. After bringing 16,000 slaves from sub-Saharan Africa, Moulay Ismail guaranteed the continued existence of his elite units by providing the soldiers with women and raising their offspring for service in the guard. By the time of his death, the Black Guard had expanded tenfold. Its successes were many, ranging from quelling internal rebellions, to chasing European powers out of northern Morocco, to disposing of the Ottoman Turk threat from Algeria.

Following the road around to the right, you'll find an expanse of grass and a small building, the **Koubbat as-Sufara'** (Map p256; admission Dh10; 9am-noon & 3-6pm), once the reception hall for foreign ambassadors. Beside the entrance, you will notice the shafts that descend into a vast crypt. This dark and slightly spooky network of rooms was used for food storage, although tour guides will delight in recounting the (erroneous) story that it was used as a dungeon for the Christian slaves who provided labour for Moulay Ismail's building spree. Bring a torch.

Heri es-Souani & Agdal Basin

Nearly 2km southeast of the mausoleum, Moulay Ismail's immense granaries and stables, **Heri es-Souani** (admission Dh10; 9am-noon & 3-6.30pm), were ingeniously designed. Tiny windows, massive walls and a system of underfloor water channels kept the temperatures cool and air circulating. The building provided stabling and food for an incredible 12,000 horses, and Moulay Ismail regarded it as one of his finest architectural projects.

The roof fell in long ago, but the first few vaults have been restored. They're impressive, but overly lit to rob them of much of their ambience – seek out the darker, more atmospheric corners. Those beyond stand in partial ruin, row upon row across a huge area.

Immediately north of the granaries and stables lies an enormous stone-lined lake, the **Agdal Basin**. Fed by a complex system of irrigation channels some 25km long, it served as both a reservoir for the sultan's gardens and a pleasure lake. There are plenty of benches to break your stroll around the waters, and a giant Giacometti-like statue of a traditional water seller.

In summer it's a long hot walk here from Moulay Ismail's mausoleum, so you might want to catch a taxi or calèche (horse-drawn carriage). If you do decide to walk, follow the road from the mausoleum south between the high walls, past the main entrance of the Royal Palace (no visitors) and a campsite, to find the entrance straight ahead.

Walking Tour: Saunter through the Souqs

The walk described here is marked on the Meknès Medina map (p256). The easiest route into the souqs is through the arch to the left of the Dar Jamaï Museum on the north side of Place el-Hedim. Plunge in and head northwards, and you will quickly find yourself amid souvenir stalls and carpet shops.

As you walk, notice the *qissariat* (covered markets) off to either side. A couple of these are devoted to textiles and carpets, which are noisily auctioned off on Sunday mornings. **Okchen Market**, in the last *qissaria* on the left before you reach the T-junction with Rue Najjarine, specialises in fine embroidery.

Turning right on Rue Najjarine takes you to the Grande Mosquée and Medersa Bou Inania. For now though, turn left on Rue Najjarine, passing stalls with *babouches* (leather slippers) in multicoloured rows. Just before you hit Rue Sekkakine, look out on the left for **Qissariat ad-Dahab**, the jewellery souq.

Exit the medina via Bab Berrima and follow the lane north, hugging the outside of the city wall. You'll pass a colourful souq, selling spices, herbs and nuts, and a lively **flea market**. On the other side of the lane, workshops turn out gigantic bakers' 'paddles', used for scooping bread out of the ovens.

Beyond them you'll find workers busily stuffing mattresses. A left turn here takes you northwest to the newly restored **mausoleum of Sidi ben Aïssa** (closed to non-Muslims). Sidi ben Aïssa gave rise to one of the more unusual religious fraternities in Morocco, known for their self-mutilation and imperviousness to snake bites. His followers gather here in April and July from all over Morocco and further afield (see Festivals, below).

A right turn by the mattress stuffers leads back into the medina via Bab el-Jedid, the arch that shelters a couple of musical instrument shops. Turning left up Rue el-Hanaya, through a small **fruit & vegetable market**, you will eventually arrive at the **Berdaine Mosque** and, just beyond it, the city's northernmost gate, Bab Berdaine.

From here you can wend your way back down Rue Zaouia Nasseria (which becomes Rue Souika), passing tailors and the odd carpet showroom. With luck you'll emerge near the Grande Mosquée.

Tours

Compared to Fez and Marrakesh, the Meknès medina is fairly easy to navigate. If you are short of time, or if you wish to gain some local insight, book an official guide through the tourist office for Dh250 for a day. Calèche rides of this imperial city with a guide are easy to pick up from around the Mausoleum of Moulay Ismail – expect to pay around Dh150 for a couple of hours.

Festivals & Events

One of the largest *moussems* (festivals) in Morocco takes place in April at the mausoleum of Sidi ben Aïssa, outside the medina walls. Members of this Sufi brotherhood are renowned for their trances that make them impervious to pain, but public displays of glass-eating, snake bites and ritual body piercing are no longer allowed (although you'll see pictures about town). But it's still a busy and popular festival with *fantasias* (musket-firing cavalry charges), fairs and the usual singing and dancing.

Sleeping

Most of the accommodation is located in the ville nouvelle, with the exception of a

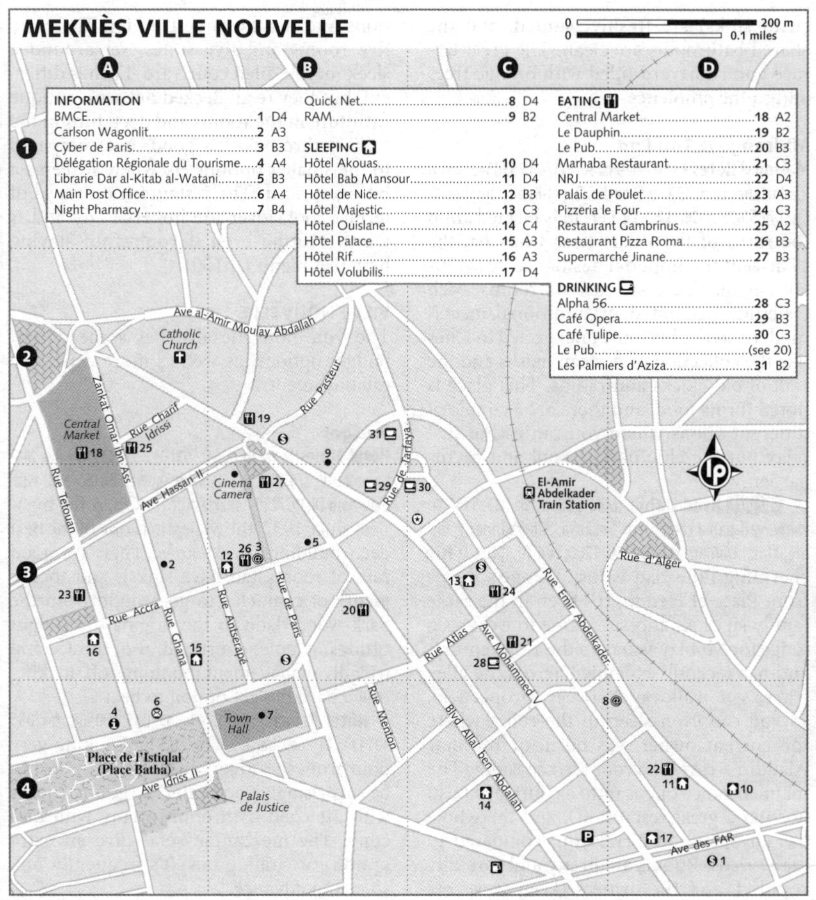

cluster of ultrabudget options and a few exquisite new riads.

MEDINA

Most of Meknès' cheapies cluster along Rue Dar Smen and Rue Rouamzine in the old city. In the high season and during festivals, they can fill up quickly. To be on the safe side, get here early in the day or reserve a room.

Budget

Camping International d'Agdal (☎ 035 551828; camping per adult/child Dh17/12, plus per tent/bicycle/car/caravan/campervan Dh10/10/17/17/20) Barely 50m from Heri es-Souani, just off the road towards Royal Palace (but poorly signed), this campsite has a great location and an attractive shady site. Hot showers are Dh7, electricity Dh15 and water Dh20. Facilities are well maintained, and it has a small shop, café and restaurant.

Hôtel Regina (Map p256; ☎ 035 530280; 19 Rue Dar Smen; s/d/tr Dh70/100/130, shower Dh5) This ultra cheapie frankly feels a bit threadbare, but it's not entirely without merit. Rooms are completely no-frills, but the central courtyard opens the place up and wards off claustrophobia. Showers cost extra, and there's no guarantee of hot water.

Maroc Hôtel (Map p256; ☎ 035 530075; 7 Rue Rouamzine; s/d Dh90/180) A perennially popular shoestring option, the Maroc has kept its standards up over the many years we've been visiting. Friendly and quiet, rooms (with sinks) are freshly painted, and the shared bathrooms are clean. The great terrace and courtyard filled with orange trees add to the ambience.

Midrange & Top End

Maison d'Hôtes Riad (Map p256; ☎ 035 530542; www.riadmeknes.com; 79 Ksar Chaacha, Dar el-Kabir; r incl breakfast Dh650-750;) This riad is located amid the ruins of the Palais Ksar Chaacha, the 17th-century imperial residence of Moulay Ismail. There are just six rooms, each tastefully decorated in traditional-meets-modern style, plus some unexpected touches like the collection of African masks and the wall of old clocks and radios. This place is noted for its food, and there are a couple of different salons where you can eat, or just relax but the chic plunge pool and cactus garden.

our pick **Ryad Bahia** (Map p256; ☎ 035 554541; www.ryad-bahia.com; Derb Sekkaya, Tiberbarine; r incl breakfast Dh670, ste Dh950-1200; wi-fi) This charming little riad is just a stone's throw from Place el-Hedim. It's been in the same family since an ancestor came to work as a judge for Moulay Ismail in the 17th century, and has recently expanded across the alley (there's a walkway between properties), so you can even sleep in the room where the current owner was born, or the new Aladdin's-cave-like roof terrace room. The main entrance opens onto a courtyard (also hosting a great restaurant), and the whole has an open and airy layout compared to many riads. Rooms are pretty and carefully restored, and the owners (keen travellers themselves) are eager to swap travel stories as well as guide guests in the medina.

Riad Safir (Map p256; ☎ 035 534785; www.riadsafir.com; 1 Derb Lalla Alamia; r/ste incl breakfast Dh1200/1500; wi-fi) With just three lovely rooms Safir offers a very intimate stay in Meknès. It's extremely homely, and instead of the imposing *zellij* and plaster of some places it presents a softer face with swathes of soft fabrics and carpets in creams and warm oranges and plenty of wood. There are plans to expand into the property next door, adding a plunge pool and self-contained apartment to rent.

Palais Didi (Map p256; ☎ 035 558590; www.palaisdidi.com; 7 Dar el-Kbir; r/ste Dh1200/1500; wi-fi) The Didi fancies itself as the *grande dame* of the Meknès medina accommodation options and it's the largest by far. There are five rooms and five suites, set around a sleek marble-tiled courtyard. Each is different, but they're all decked out with antique furniture in the rooms and deep tubs in the *zellij* bathrooms. It's good, but compared to the smaller options elsewhere it seems a bit overpriced. The restaurant on the roof terrace looks over the imperial city and is worth visiting even if you're not staying here (set menu Dh150).

VILLE NOUVELLE

The ville nouvelle also has some decent budget options, as well as more expensive establishments.

Budget

Hôtel Majestic (Map p261; ☎ 035 522035; 19 Ave Mohammed V; s/d Dh127/168, with shower Dh165/198, with bathroom Dh197/229, breakfast Dh22) Open for business since 1937, the Majestic is one of the best deco buildings in Meknès. There's a good mix of rooms (all have sinks), and there's plenty of character to go around from the dark-wood dado to the original deco light fittings. A quiet courtyard, roof terrace and friendly management top things off, making this a hard budget option to beat.

Hôtel Palace (Map p261; ☎ 035 400468; fax 055 401431; 11 Rue Ghana; s/d Dh180/230) Looking very dour from the street, this hotel turns out to be surprisingly good value: large airy rooms with attached bathrooms, many with balcony. The mezzanine sofas give an extra option for chilling out. It's frequently full, so call in advance.

Hôtel Ouislane (Map p261; ☎ 035 524828; 54 Rue Allal ben Abdallah; s/d Dh205/242) Another decent and clean option at the higher end of the budget bracket, the Ouislane has large airy rooms with attached bathrooms. It doesn't set the world alight, but for the prices it's reasonable value.

Hôtel Volubilis (Map p261; ☎ 035 525082; Ave des FAR; s/d Dh228/270) Recently spruced up, this is a decent enough option, with fair rooms, reasonably comfy beds and en suite bathrooms. Try to avoid the rooms at the front above the main road, as they can stay pretty noisy throughout the night.

Midrange & Top End

Hôtel Bab Mansour (Map p261; ☎ 035 525239; fax 055 510741; 38 Rue el-Emir Abdelkader; s/d Dh324/400, breakfast Dh40;) It's a fine line between tasteful and characterless and, while comfortable enough, the Bab Mansour never quite seems to develop much of a personality – the famous bab is depicted in tiles in the bathrooms, but it's more DIY store than Moroccan *zellij*. That said, it's well-run, with everything you'd expect in a tourist-class hotel.

Hôtel Akouas (Map p261; ☎ 035 515967; 27 Rue Emir Abdelkader; s/d/tr Dh341/422/543;) This friendly, family-run three-star has a little more local colour than its rivals. Rooms, while not huge, are modern, serviceable and very fairly priced. The place also has a decent restaurant and a nightclub.

Hôtel de Nice (Map p261; ☎ 035 520318; nice_hotel@menara.ma; cnr Rue Accra & Rue Antserapé; s/d Dh387/482, breakfast Dh46;) This hotel continues to fly the flag for quality and service. Modern, efficient and ever-so-slightly shiny, it's a surprise that room rates aren't a good Dh100 more than they actually are. Rooms are nicely decorated and well-sized, and there's a decent bar and restaurant too. Advance booking recommended.

Hôtel Rif (Map p261; ☎ 035 522591; hotel_rif@menara.ma; Rue Accra; s/d Dh402/503, breakfast Dh50;) The Rif has had quite a refit since our last visit, improving the place enormously and bringing its rooms up to a standard that better reflects the tariff. The interior still has a slightly funky modernist ambience, and we love the concrete-chocolate confection of the exterior. The courtyard pool is good for dipping toes in, but as it's overlooked by the bar, female bathers will feel enormously exposed.

Zaki Hôtel (Map p255; ☎ 035 514146; Blvd Al Massira, Rte 21; s/d Dh1318/1486;) The poshest option in Meknès, the Zaki is a short trek from the centre of town. You're rewarded for your efforts with landscaped grounds, ornate *zellij* and stucco in the lobby, a restaurant and bar, and efficient and professional service throughout. Rooms contain all the modern comforts expected by tourist and business traveller alike, with the decor adding a twist of Moroccan flavour.

Eating

RESTAURANTS

Medina

Restaurant Mille et Une Nuits (Map p256; ☎ 035 559002; off Place el-Hedim; mains Dh45-85) Easily located off Place el-Hedim, this is another converted house, whose owners have leant towards the more showy 'palace' restaurant style of surroundings. You'll find all the Moroccan standards and classics on a reasonably priced menu.

Restaurant Oumnia (Map p256; ☎ 035 533938; 8 Ain Fouki Rouamzine; set menu Dh80) This is less a formal restaurant than a few rooms of a family home converted into dining salons, and the emphasis here is on warm service and hearty Moroccan fare. There's just a three-course set menu, but it's a real winner, with delicious *harira* (lentil soup), salads and a choice of several tajines of the day.

Ryad Bahia (Map p256; ☎ 035 554541; www.ryad-bahia.com; Derb Sekkaya, Tiberbarine; mains Dh80-100) Nonresidents are welcome to eat at the restaurant of this riad, and it makes a pleasant evening dining spot with its tables around the courtyard. The menu is typically Moroccan, but all tasty and served and presented nicely.

Restaurant Riad (Map p256; ☎ 055 530542; 79 Ksar Chaacha; set menus Dh110 & Dh160) While all the riads in the Meknès medina have lovely restaurants, this is probably the pick of the bunch. Set around a lush green courtyard, it's a great place to relax, and while the menu of salads, tajines and couscous is simple, it's all delicious and served with care and attention.

Dar Sultana (Map p256; ☎ 035 535720; Derb Sekkaya, Tiberbarine; mains from Dh70, three-course set menu Dh150) Also going under the name Sweet Sultana, this is a small but charming restaurant in a converted medina house. The tent canopy over the courtyard gives an intimate, even romantic, atmosphere, set off by walls painted with henna designs and bright fabrics. The spread of cooked Moroccan salads is a big highlight of the menu.

Ville Nouvelle

our pick **Marhaba Restaurant** (Map p261; 23 Ave Mohammed V; tajines Dh25; noon-10pm) We adore this canteen-style place – the essence of cheap and cheerful – and so does everyone else, judging by how busy it is of an evening. While you can get tajines and the like, do as everyone else does and fill up on a bowl of *harira*, a plate of *makoda* (potato fritters) with bread and hard-boiled eggs – and walk out with change from Dh15. We defy you to eat better for cheaper.

Restaurant Gambrinus (Map p261; ☎ 035 520258; Zankat Omar ibn Ass; mains around Dh50, set menu Dh70) A good place for Moroccan food in colourful surroundings in the ville nouvelle, which feels like something of a surprise when you discover that the original Gambrinus was a Czech immigrant in 1914. It's perennially popular with locals, who come for the good range of tajines.

Pizzeria le Four (Map p261; ☎ 035 520857; 1 Rue Atlas; pizzas Dh40-60, mains Dh65-85) This is as good a place as any in the ville nouvelle to load up on pizza, and the dark-wood and brick surroundings take you halfway out of Morocco towards Italy. Alcohol is served, so late at night you sometimes find local men getting sloshed among the clientele. Watch out for the steep service tax added to bills.

Le Dauphin (Map p261; ☎ 035 523423; 5 Ave Mohammed V; mains Dh75-120, set menu Dh150) It might have an uninspiring exterior, but the French dining room and lovely garden give this restaurant one of the nicest dining settings in town. The menu is continental, with some good meat and fish dishes. Alcohol is served.

Le Pub (Map p261; ☎ 035 524247; 20 Blvd Allal ben Abdallah; mains Dh75-150; 🕒 11am-midnight) The dark mirrored windows and bouncers on the door make you wonder what you're letting yourself in for, but Le Pub is a welcome change if you're feeling tajine fatigue. The menu is split in two – half offering continental dishes, the other branching into a Moroccan take on Chinese and Thai dishes. We preferred the oriental dishes over the pasta, but there are some good steaks too. As befits the name, alcohol is served.

QUICK EATS

Palais de Poulet (Map p261; Rue Tetouan; mains from Dh25, salads Dh15) Looking down from the Hôtel Rif towards Ave Hassan II, this is one of several good and cheap rotisserie places where you can fill up quickly on chicken, chips, bread and salad. Although you order from the table, pay at the counter inside.

Restaurant Pizza Roma (Map p261; Rue Accra; mains from Dh20) Although the name suggests that pizzas are the speciality here, you could do far worse than load up on a filling plate of rotisserie chicken with rice and chips. An unassuming place, it's popular with female diners.

NRJ (Map p261; ☎ 035 400324; 30 Rue Amir Abdelkader; breakfast from Dh22, salads Dh20-30, pizza Dh35-60; 🕒 24hr; wi-fi) If you're a young and fashionable Meknassi, then you're going to be hanging out at NRJ. Importing a bit of big-city laptop-friendly cool, it's all glass-topped tables, under-lit seating and funky tunes on the stereo. Perfect for a light meal any time of day, and the paninis and good range of juices are particularly good.

Sandwich stands (Map p256; Place el-Hedim; sandwiches around Dh30; 🕒 7am-10pm) Take your pick of any one of the stands lining Place el-Hedim, and sit at the canopied tables to watch the scene as you eat. There are larger meals like tajines, but the sandwiches are usually quick and excellent, while a few places nearer the medina walls do a good line in sardines.

Rue Rouamzine eateries (Map p256; Rue Rouamzine; meals Dh30-50; 🕒 11am-10pm) Particularly handy for the cheap hotels on the edge of the medina proper, this street has plenty of good eating places serving up sandwiches, kebabs, tajines, grilled chicken, fruit juices and ice cream.

SELF-CATERING

Covered Market (Map p256; Place el-Hedim) This is *the* place in Meknès to get fresh produce, and is virtually a tourist attraction in itself, with its beautifully arranged pyramids of sugary sweet delicacies, dates and nuts, olives and preserved lemons in glistening piles. There's also good-quality fruit and veg here, as well as meat – the faint-hearted may choose to avoid the automated chicken-plucking machines at the rear of the hall.

Central Market (Map p261; Ave Hassan II) A good place to shop in the ville nouvelle, with a variety of fresh food stalls, alcohol shops and various imported foodstuffs.

Supermarché Jinane (Map p261; cnr Ave Mohammed V & Ave Hassan II; 🕒 7.30am-10pm) A large supermarket stocked with all the essentials.

Drinking

CAFÉS

When choosing sticky pastries in Meknès, don't overlook the *marakchia* – the local take on an éclair, full of cream and covered with gooey chocolate. The ville nouvelle is the place to go for relaxed café culture, especially on and around Ave Mohammed V and the pedestrianised area around Cinema Camera. Those following are female-friendly as far as Moroccan cafés go.

Les Palmiers d'Aziza (Map p261; 9 Rue de Tarfaya) With an exterior in bright Marrakesh pink, this popular café offers several options – sit in the sunny garden, hang at the tables near the mouthwatering cookie counter, or head upstairs to the covered terrace away from public view. The latter is a popular choice for boys and girls on dates. The ice cream and smoothies here are excellent.

Alpha 56 (Map p261; Ave Mohammed V) Popular with the young and trendy, this place has a good selection of pastries. The downstairs can be a little smoky, in which case you can retreat to the salon upstairs.

Café Tulipe (Map p261; Rue de Tarfaya) Just off the main road, the Tulipe has a large shady terrace and modern interior, it's one of the most pleasant cafés in which to kill an hour or two.

Café Opera (Map p261; 7 Ave Mohammed V) Airy and old-fashioned, this grand café is a classic – among the most popular for Moroccan men to sip their mint tea. Sitting outside people-watching is a great breakfast pastime.

BARS

It's a popular adage that Meknès has more bars than any other Moroccan city, and if all you're after is a quick bottle of Flag beer, then you won't lack for options (in the ville nouvelle at least). Many are grouped around Blvd Allal ben Abdallah, but are generally pretty seedy affairs, designed for serious drinking and smoking, with women not at all welcomed.

The hotel bars listed in the sleeping section are more amenable, as well as the restaurants listed above as licensed. Le Pub (opposite) is appropriately one of the nicer places to get a drink – slump in a comfy chair, drink at the bar itself, or head downstairs to smoke a sheesha and catch some live music on weekends.

Shopping

While the souqs of Meknès aren't as extensive as those of Fez or Marrakesh, the lack of hassle can make them a relaxed place to potter around looking for souvenirs. For details, see the walking tour, p260.

As always, the government-run **Centre Artisanale** (Map p256; Ave Zine el-Abidine Riad; 9am-1pm & 3-7pm Mon-Sat) is the place to go if you want to get an idea of what to look for and how much to spend. Quality is high but prices are fixed. Other shops are located just outside the Mausoleum of Moulay Ismail. There are also some good **pottery stalls** (Map p256) set up on the western side of Place el-Hedim.

Getting There & Away

BUS

The **CTM bus station** (Map p255; ☎ 035 522585; Ave des FAR) is about 500m east of the junction with Ave Mohammed V. The main bus station (Map p256) lies just outside Bab el-Khemis, west of the medina. It has a left-luggage office and the usual snack stands.

CTM departures include: Casablanca (Dh80, four hours, six daily) via Rabat (Dh50, 2½ hours), Fez and Marrakesh (Dh120, eight hours, daily), Tangier (Dh80, five hours, three daily), Oujda (Dh110, six hours, two daily) via Taza (Dh65, three hours), Er-Rachidia (Dh110, six hours, daily), and three buses to Nador (Dh110, six hours).

Slightly cheaper than CTM, other buses are available from the numbered windows in the main bus station:

No 5 Rabat and Casablanca (hourly 6am to 3pm)
No 6 Tangier (hourly 5am to 4pm), Tetouan (four daily), Chefchaouen (three daily), Ouezzane (five daily)
No 7 Fez (hourly 5am to 6pm), Taza (four daily), Oujda (hourly 4am to 11.30pm), Nador (five daily)
No 8 Moulay Idriss (hourly 8am to 6pm)
No 9 Marrakesh (seven daily, mostly morning departures)

TAXI

The principal grand taxi rank (Map p256) is a dirt lot next to the bus station at Bab el-Khemis. There are regular departures to Fez (Dh16, one hour), Ifrane (Dh24, one hour), Azrou (Dh32, one hour) and Rabat (Dh44, 90 minutes). Taxis leave less frequently for Taza (Dh70, 2½ hours). Grands taxis for Moulay Idriss (Dh12, 20 minutes) leave from opposite the Institut Français (Map p255) – this is also the place to organise round trips to Volubilis.

TRAIN

Although Meknès has two train stations, head for the more convenient **El-Amir Abdelkader** (Map p261; ☎ 035 522763), two blocks east of Ave Mohammed V. There are nine daily trains to Fez (Dh18, one hour), three of which continue to Taza (Dh55, 3½ hours) and Oujda (Dh124, 6½ hours). Eight go to Casablanca (Dh86, 3½ hours) via Rabat (Dh59, 2¼ hours). There are five direct services to Marrakesh (Dh162, seven hours). For Tangier, there's one daily train (Dh80, four hours), or take a westbound train and change at Sidi Kacem.

Getting Around

BUS

Overcrowded city buses ply the route between the medina and ville nouvelle. The most useful are bus 2 (Bab el-Mansour to Blvd Allal ben Abdallah, returning to the medina along Ave Mohammed V) and bus 7 (Bab el-Mansour to the CTM bus station). Tickets are Dh2.

CAR

There's a handy car park just southwest of Bab el-Mansour, and another in the ville nouvelle near the intersection of Ave Idriss II and Ave des FAR.

TAXI

Urban grands taxis (silver-coloured Mercedes Benz with black roofs) link the ville nouvelle and the medina, charging Dh2.50 per seat or Dh15 for the whole taxi. Pale-blue petits taxis use the meter: from El-Amir Abdelkader train station to the medina expect to pay around Dh8.

A more touristy way to get around the medina is by calèche, available for hire on Place el-Hedim and outside the Mausoleum of Moulay Ismail. They charge around Dh60 per hour.

AROUND MEKNÈS

Volubilis (Oualili) وليلي

The Roman ruins of Volubilis sit in the midst of a fertile plain about 33km north of Meknès. The city is the best preserved archaeological site in Morocco and was declared a Unesco World Heritage site in 1997. Its most amazing features are its many beautiful mosaics preserved in situ.

Volubilis can easily be combined with nearby Moulay Idriss to make a fantastic day trip from Meknès.

HISTORY

Excavations indicate that the site was originally settled by Carthaginian traders in the 3rd century BC. One of the Roman Empire's most remote outposts, Volubilis was annexed in about AD 40. According to some historians, Rome imposed strict controls on what could, and could not, be produced in its North African possessions, according to the needs of the empire. One result was massive deforestation and the large-scale planting of wheat around Volubilis. At its peak, it is estimated that the city housed up to 20,000 people. The site's most impressive monuments were built in the 2nd and 3rd centuries, including the triumphal arch, capitol, baths and basilica.

As the neighbouring Berber tribes began to reassert themselves, so the Romans abandoned Volubilis around 280. Nevertheless, the city's population of Berbers, Greeks, Jews and Syrians continued to speak Latin right up until the arrival of Islam. Moulay Idriss found sanctuary here in the 8th century, before moving his capital to Fez. Volubilis continued to be inhabited until the 18th century, when its marble was plundered for Moulay Ismail's palaces in Meknès, and its buildings were finally felled by the Lisbon earthquake of 1755.

INFORMATION

Less than half of the 40-hectare **site** (admission Dh20, parking Dh5; 🕒 8am-sunset) has been excavated, and archaeologists continue to make the occasional exciting discovery. Most are on display in the archaeology museum in Rabat (see p123), but an on-site museum is planned for Volubilis that will finally house all the finds together.

Although parts of certain buildings are roped off, you are free to wander the site at will. Bar a couple of vague signboards, there's little in the way of signposting or information on what you're actually seeing. It's well worth considering taking a guide, especially if you're pressed for time. If you prefer to wander on your own, allow at least two hours to see the essentials, up to a full day for the real enthusiast.

In the heat of a summer day, the sun can be incredibly fierce at Volubilis, so bring a hat and plenty of water. Spring is the ideal season, when wildflowers blossom amid the abandoned stones, and the surrounding fields are at their greenest. The best time to visit is either first thing in the morning or late afternoon, when you're more likely to have the place to yourself, with just the guardian's donkey grazing among the ruins. At dusk, when the last rays of the

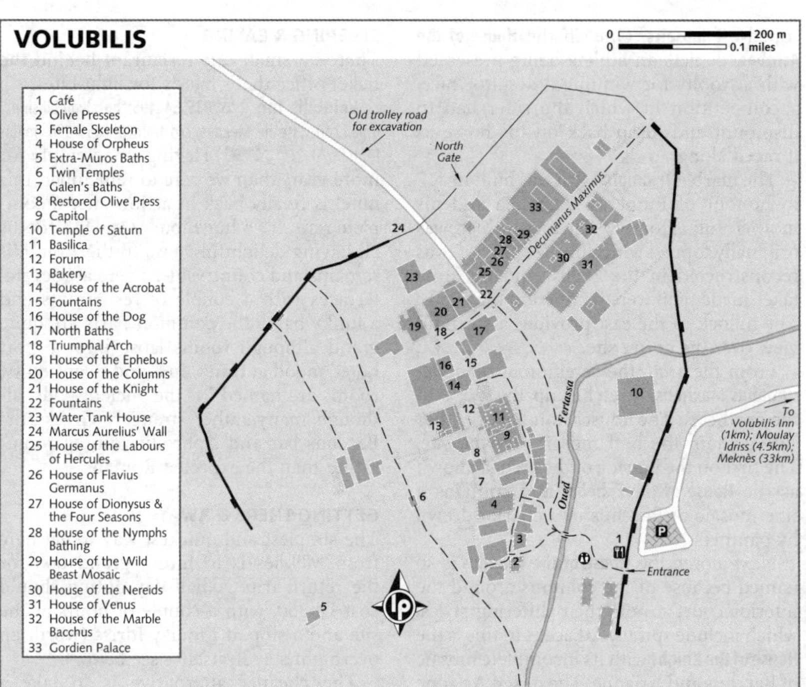

sun light the ancient columns, Volubilis is at its most magical.

Guides

Many official guides in Fez and Meknès are knowledgeable about this site, and most will be happy to accompany you for their normal daily rate. Better though are the guides that hang around the entrance who conduct good one-hour tours for around Dh140. Most speak decent enough English to explain the site in detail.

SIGHTS

The better-known monuments are in the northern part of the site, although it's more convenient to start in the south. Once over the Oued Fertassa, the path leads onto the ridge and through the residential quarter. Although the least remarkable part of the site, the **olive presses** here indicate the economic basis of ancient Volubilis, much as the plentiful olive groves in the surrounding area do today. Near the presses, the remains of a **female skeleton** (thought to be Muslim as she was buried facing Mecca) are entombed in one of the walls; she's now protected by an iron sheet.

Next to the House of Orpheus are the remains of **Galen's Baths**. Although largely broken, they clearly show the highly developed underfloor heating in this Roman hammam. Opposite the steam room are the communal toilets – where citizens could go about their business and have a chat at the same time.

The capitol, basilica and 1300-sq-metre forum are, typically, built on a high point. The **capitol**, dedicated to the Triad of Jupiter, Juno and Minerva, dates back to 218; the **basilica** and **forum** lie immediately to its north. The reconstructed columns of the basilica are usually topped with storks' nests – an iconic Volubilis image if the birds are nesting at the time of your visit. Around the forum is a series of plinths carved with Latin inscriptions that would have supported statues of the great and good. Keep your eyes out for the carved stone drainhole cover – an understated example of Roman civil engineering.

Further north again, on the left just before the triumphal arch, are a couple more

IMPERIAL CITIES, MIDDLE ATLAS & THE EAST

roped-off **mosaics**. One, in the **House of the Acrobat**, depicts an athlete being presented with a trophy for winning a desultor race, a competition in which the rider had to dismount and jump back on his horse as it raced along.

The marble **Triumphal Arch** was built in 217 in honour of Emperor Caracalla and his mother, Julia Domna. The arch, which was originally topped with a bronze chariot, was reconstructed in the 1930s, and the mistakes made then were rectified in the 1960s. The hillock to the east provides a splendid view over the entire site.

From the arch, the ceremonial road, **Decumanus Maximus**, stretches up the slope to the northeast. The houses lining it on either side contain the best mosaics on the site. The first on the far side of the arch is known as the **House of the Ephebus** and contains a fine mosaic of Bacchus in a chariot drawn by panthers.

Next along, the **House of the Columns** is so named because of the columns around the interior court – note their differing styles, which include spirals. Adjacent to this is the **House of the Knight** with its incomplete mosaic of Bacchus and Ariadne. The naked Ariadne has suffered somewhat from the attentions of admirers – or Muslim iconoclasts.

In the next couple of houses are excellent mosaics entitled the **Labours of Hercules** and **Nymphs Bathing**. The former is almost a circular comic strip, recounting the Twelve Labours. Several of Hercules' heroic feats were reputed to have occurred in Morocco, making him a popular figure at the time.

The best mosaics are saved until last. Cross the Decumanus Maximus and head for the lone cypress tree, which marks the **House of Venus**. There are two particularly fine mosaics here, appropriately with semi-romantic themes. The first is the **Abduction of Hylas by the Nymphs**, an erotic composition showing Hercules' lover Hylas being lured away from his duty by two beautiful nymphs. The second mosaic is **Diana Bathing**. The goddess was glimpsed in her bath by the hunter Acteon, who she turned into a stag as punishment. Acteon can be seen sprouting horns, about to be chased by his own pack of hounds – the fate of mythical peeping toms everywhere. A third mosaic from this house, of Venus in the waves, can be seen in the Kasbah Museum in Tangier (p177).

SLEEPING & EATING

There's a small café restaurant behind the ticket office that's handy for light bites.

Volubilis Inn (☎ 035 544405; hotelvolubilisinn@gmail.com; Rte de Meknès; s/d from Dh 856/996, mains from Dh70; P ✲) Having stood empty for more years than we care to remember, this hotel is finally back in action after a complete refit. It's a huge four-star, with rooms all having delightful views to the Volubilis remains and countryside. There are several terraces with a couple of restaurants and a funky bar – the common parts are quite grand although rooms lapse into 'airport hotel' mood at times. In a nod to antiquity, rooms are named for the ancient gods, although many rather strangely Greek (the Bacchus bar and Aphrodite dining room) rather than the expected Roman.

GETTING THERE & AWAY

The simplest and quickest way to get here from Meknès is to hire a grand taxi for the return trip. A half-day outing should cost Dh350, with a couple of hours at the site and a stop at Moulay Idriss (worth an overnight stay in itself – see below).

The cheaper alternative is to take a shared grand taxi from near Meknès' Institut Français to Moulay Idriss (Dh12) and then hire a grand taxi to take you to Volubilis (Dh40 complete hire). If the weather isn't too hot, it's a lovely 45-minute walk between Moulay Idriss and Volubilis.

There are no buses to Volubilis.

Moulay Idriss مولاي ادريس

The picturesque whitewashed town of Moulay Idriss sits astride two green hills in a cradle of mountains slightly less than 5km from Volubilis, and is one of the country's most important pilgrimage sites. It's named for Moulay Idriss, a great-grandson of the Prophet Mohammed, the founder of the country's first real dynasty, and Morocco's most revered saint. His tomb is at the heart of the town, and is the focus of the country's largest *moussem* every August.

Moulay Idriss fled Mecca in the late 8th century in the face of persecution at the hands of the recently installed Abbasid caliphate, which was based in Baghdad. Idriss settled at Volubilis, where he converted the locals to Islam, and made himself their leader, establishing the Idrissid dynasty.

Moulay Idriss' holy status kept it closed to non-Muslims until the mid-20th century, and its pious reputation continues to deter some travellers. However, the embargo on non-Muslims staying overnight in the town has long disappeared, and local family-run guest houses have started to open to cater to visitors. Those that do stay are invariably charmed – it's a pretty and relaxed town with a centre free of carpet shops and traffic and a chance to see Morocco as Moroccans experience it.

The main road leading from the bus/grands taxis stand to the square (Place Mohammed VI) has a Banque Populaire ATM, and a couple of internet cafés.

SIGHTS

Although this twin-hill town is a veritable maze of narrow lanes and dead ends, it is not hard to find the few points of interest. The first is the **Mausoleum of Moulay Idriss**, the object of veneration and the reason for the country's greatest annual *moussem* in late August. An important pilgrimage for many, including the royals, it is accompanied by *fantasias*, markets and music. It's said locally that five pilgrimages to Moulay Idriss during the *moussem* equals one haj to Mecca.

From the main road (where buses and grands taxis arrive), head uphill and bear right where the road forks. You'll quickly find yourself on the wide square of Place Mohammed VI lined with cafés and cheap food stands – a great place to sit and watch the pace of life. At the top of the square is the entrance to the mausoleum via a three-arched gateway at the top of some steps, surrounded by shops selling religious goods to pilgrims. Not far inside there's a barrier, beyond which non-Muslims cannot pass. Moulay Ismail created this pilgrimage site by building the mausoleum and moving the body of Moulay Idriss, in a successful attempt to rally the support of the faithful.

From here, head left up into the maze of streets to find your way to a couple of vantage points that give good panoramic views of the mausoleum, the town and the surrounding country. Plenty of guides will offer their services – you can get an informative, entertaining tour for as little as Dh30.

If you don't feel like being guided, head back to the fork and take the road heading uphill, signposted to the Municipalité. Near the top of the hill, just before the Agfa photo shop, take the cobbled street to the right. As you climb up you'll notice the only **cylindrical minaret** in Morocco, built in 1939. The green tiles spell out in stylised script the standard Muslim refrain: *la illah illa Allah* (there is no god but Allah). At the top of the hill ask a local for the **grande terrasse** or **petite terrasse**. These terraces provide vantage points high above the mausoleum and most of the town.

SLEEPING & EATING

Rooms are at a premium during the *moussem*, so book in advance.

Maison d'Hôte Slimani (☎ 035544793; www.maisondhote-slimani.tk; 39 Rue Drazat; s/d Dh100/200, breakfast dh30) Follow signs to the View Panoramique from the main shrine to find this cheap and cheerful backpacker-style place. A handful of en suite rooms on several levels cluster around a courtyard, simple but good value.

Hotel Diyar Timnay (☎ 035 544400; amzday@menara.ma; 7 Aïn Rjal; s/d/tr incl breakfast 160/240/300; ❄) Near the grands taxis stands, this is the town's only formal hotel. It's unexpectedly large when you get inside, with plenty of bright rooms – good but unflashy. Most are en suite, although a few have separate (but still private) bathrooms. The restaurant does a roaring lunchtime trade with tour groups visiting Volubilis, and has great views to the archaeological site (mains Dh50-60).

La Colombe Blanche (☎ 035 544596; www.maisondhote-zerhoune.ma; 21 Derb Zouak Tazgha; r incl breakfast Dh300-500) This is very much a home turned guest house – the family occupies the ground floor while guests are up above, all contributing to a very friendly atmosphere. Although it bills itself as a restaurant, home-cooked meals are really on request. In good weather eat on the terrace, with views to Volubilis. At the shrine, turn right uphill and follow the signs.

Maison d'Hôte El Kasaba (☎ 035 544354; senhab@hotmail.com; 32 Ou Bab Kasbah; per person incl breakfast Dh200) Another Moroccan home-from-home, with a handful of friendly rooms with a sprinkling of Moroccan chintz. The host's warm welcome extends to getting you stuck into preparing dinner: cookery lessons are encouraged.

Buttons Inn (☎ 035 544371; www.buttonsinn.ma; 42 Derb Zouak Tazgha; dm/s/d/tr incl breakfast Dh180/250/400/600; 💻) A new backpackers place, that's situated to the right and uphill from the main shrine, this house has been carefully restored in traditional style. There are a variety of rooms and a couple of terraces, with a friendly welcome and good amenities throughout.

Dar Al Andaloussiya Diyafa (☎ 035 544749; Derb Zouak Tazgha; r Dh600-1000; ❄) 'Dar Al Andalous' is Moulay Idriss' big attempt to import a bit of big-city riad-chic to the town. For the most part it works, with good rooms and facilities and plenty of Moroccan fabrics. It's near Colombe Blanche, a big white corner building picked out in green.

Les Trois Boules d'Or (View Panoramique) This café-restaurant has the best views over Moulay Idriss, and is a good place to finish your walking tour, with a mint tea or cold drink. It was closed when we visited, but was reportedly due to reopen under new owners as we went to press.

The cheap food stands around the main square are all good for a quick snack. The grilled chicken with salad is something of a local speciality.

GETTING THERE & AWAY

Grands taxis (Dh12, 20 minutes) to Moulay Idriss leave Meknès from outside the Institut Français, and buses (Dh6) leave from the Meknès bus station every hour from 8am to 6pm. Taxis leave Moulay Idriss from a stand at the bottom of town on the main road.

If you have your own transport, you might consider continuing to Fez via Nzala-des-Béni-Ammar, or to Meknès via the village of El-Merhasiyne. Both routes have wonderful views and eventually join back up with the main roads. As the road surfaces are very rough, these drives are really only possible in summer unless you have a 4WD.

MIDDLE ATLAS الأطلس المتوسط

IFRANE إفران

pop 10,000

As foreign tourists head to the medinas for a taste of the 'real' Morocco, Moroccan tourists find more favour with places like Ifrane. Tidy, ordered and modern, it feels more like Switzerland relocated to the Middle Atlas than North Africa.

The French built Ifrane in the 1930s, deliberately trying to recreate an alpine-style resort. It has neat red-roofed houses, blooming flower-beds and lake-studded parks, all kept impeccably tidy. Many major employers (including the government) maintain apartment complexes here for their vacationing workers, and it's a popular summer day trip for picnickers. In the winter the affluent flock here to ski, and the hoi polloi come for the pure fun of throwing snowballs at each other. Outside the holiday season, Ifrane's population is boosted by the rich, trendy students of the town's prestigious Al-Akhawayn University.

Orientation

The main road from Meknès is called Blvd Mohammed V as it runs through Ifrane from west to east. This is where you will find the bus station, west of the centre, and the tourist office, at the intersection with Ave des Tilluels. Most of the cafés and hotels are clustered in the centre along two parallel roads a 10-minute walk to the south: Rue de la Cascade and Ave de la Poste. East of the centre, they intersect with Ave Hassan II, the main road out of town to Fez (arriving from Fez, the centre of Ifrane is just after the artificial lake).

Information

BMCE (Ave de la Marche Verte) One of several banks with ATMs on this road.
Pharmacie Mischliffen (Rue de la Cascade)
Post office (Ave de la Poste)
Tourist office (☎ 035 566821; fax 035 566822; Ave Prince Moulay Abdallah; 🕓 8.30am-noon & 2.30-6.30pm Mon-Fri)

Sights

The campus of Al-Akhawayn University is at the northern end of town, and is a squeaky-clean showcase of Moroccan education. It was founded in 1995 by Morocco's King Hassan II and King Fahd of Saudi Arabia and includes in its lofty aims the promotion of tolerance between faiths. For now, only the rich and beautiful need apply – the car parks are full of flash cars, and the air trills with the most fashionable of mobile-phone ring tones. Lessons in English are based on the American system and there

IMPERIAL CITIES, MIDDLE ATLAS & THE EAST

are US staff and exchange students. You can wander into the well-kept grounds – weekday afternoons are the best, as there are plenty of students who are usually willing to show you around.

Ifrane's other landmark is the **stone lion** that sits on a patch of grass near the Hôtel Chamonix. It was carved by a German soldier during WWII, when Ifrane was used briefly as a prisoner-of-war camp, and commemorates the last wild Atlas lion, which was shot near here in the early 1920s. Having your picture taken with the lion is something of a ritual for day-trippers.

Sleeping

Hotel prices in Ifrane reflect the town's affluence, and its year-round popularity means demand for rooms runs high.

Hotel les Tilleuls (035 566658; fax 035 566079; cnr Ave des Tilluels & Rue de la Cascade; s/d from Dh260/320) The cheapest hotel in Ifrane is this comfortable, old institution on the corner of the main square.

Hôtel Chamonix (035 566028; fax 035 566826; Ave de la Marche Verte; s/d Dh359/408;) This three-star is well maintained and centrally located. Rooms are bright and clean, if a little bland, with attached bathrooms. There's a decent restaurant and bar (which turns into a nightclub on weekends), and the hotel can rent out ski equipment.

Hôtel Perce-Neige (035 566404; fax 035 567116; Rue des Asphodelles; s/d Dh387/459) Ifrane's prettiest accommodation option is situated about 200m southeast of the centre. The rooms could be a bit bigger, but they're very comfortable and come with satellite TV and bathrooms. The licensed restaurant is a good dining option (set menus Dh120). The shop in the lobby sells paintings by local artists

Hôtel Mischliffen (035 566607; P) Set in pine and oak forests overlooking Ifrane from the north, this oversized ski-lodge, owned by the king, was still closed for extensive rebuilding when we visited, and increasingly resembles a sturdy castle. With work dragging into the years, it's anyone's guess when it will finally reopen, but expect five-star rooms and prices.

If you wish to camp, the leafy **camp site** (Blvd Mohammed V; camping per person Dh7, plus per car/tent/campervan Dh8/15/30; closed winter) is just west of the bus station.

Eating

Several cafés and cheap eats cluster around the bus station area, where you'll also find the market for fresh produce.

Le Crouistillant (Rue de la Cascade; 7am-9pm) On the corner facing the square, this is a good café for a drink and a sticky pastry.

Complexe Touristique Aguelman (Ave Hassan II, meals Dh30-50; 9am-10pm) Overlooking the artificial lake on the main road, this is a huddle of options under one roof, aimed squarely at the local tourist market. There's a more formal dining room with Moroccan dishes for the evenings, a bar, and a simple diner with pizza, pasta, omelettes and sandwiches. In fine weather, eat at the tables outside overlooking the water.

Cookie Craque (055 567171; Ave des Tilleuls; pizza Dh50-60, crêpes Dh24-40; 7am-midnight) This café-restaurant has a wonderful choice of sweets, savouries and ice cream to take away or eat in. The toasted sandwiches and filled crêpes are the biggest draw, although there are plenty of more substantial meals on the menu. In winter, get in quick to nab the seats by the log fire.

Café Restaurant la Rose (055 566215; 7 Rue de la Cascade; mains around Dh45, set menu Dh70) This small restaurant has always been popular in town for its Middle Atlas trout and traditional Moroccan fare, but was closed for renovation when we visited.

Le Pain (Ave de la Marche Verte; mains around Dh60; 9am-10pm) Le Pain is situated just up from the Hôtel Chamonix. Among its features is a wide glass frontage, with different seating areas, including some for simple café drinkers and others for snacks. Another area again is set aside for full restaurant meals, including some decent pizzas.

Getting There & Away

The main bus and grand taxi stations are next to the market, west of the town centre.

Each morning, CTM buses leave for Marrakesh (Dh130, eight hours) via Beni Mellal (Dh60, four hours), and for Casablanca (Dh100, 4½ hours) via Meknès (Dh24, one hour) and Rabat (Dh65, 3½ hours).

Non-CTM buses are more frequent. There are hourly buses to Fez (Dh16, one hour) and Azrou (Dh7, 25 minutes). Less frequent are services to Beni Mellal (Dh55, four hours), Marrakesh (Dh105, eight hours) and Midelt (Dh42, 3½ hours).

There are plentiful grands taxis to Fez (Dh21), Meknès (Dh24) and Midelt (Dh55), as well as Azrou (Dh10).

LAKE CIRCUIT (ROUTE DES LACS)

A pretty diversion north of Ifrane is the lake circuit around **Dayet Aoua**. Signposted off the main Fez road 17km north of Ifrane, the route winds for 60km through the lake country between the P24 and P20. If you don't have your own vehicle, hiring a grand taxi in Ifrane for a tour of a couple of hours should cost around Dh250. That said, the joy of the area is to get out and walk along the lake shore and enjoy the tranquillity of the scenery. This is an area made for hikers and mountain bikers. For longer treks and camping, try contacting local guide **Moulay Abdellah Lahrizi** (☎ 063 772687; www.tourisme-vert-ifrane.com).

Dayet Aoua is surrounded by woodlands, and the whole area is notably rich in birdlife. Keep an eye out in particular for raptors, including booted eagles, black and red kites and harriers. The lake itself attracts significant numbers of ducks and waders, including crested coot, woodpeckers, tree creepers and nuthatches, which flit among the trees around the southeastern end of the lake.

The lake is a popular picnic destination for families at the weekend, but during the week you'll get the place largely to yourself. Beyond Dayet Aoua, the road loops east and then south, skirting past Dayet Ifrah and the even smaller lake of Dayet Hachlat. The road is decent, but is liable to be snowbound in winter.

If you want to linger longer, there are two good sleeping options at Dayet Aoua. Advance reservations for both are recommended during holiday periods.

An attractive French-run chalet sitting on the northern shore of the lake, **Hôtel Restaurant Chalet du Lac** (☎ 035 663277; fax 035 663197; s/d with half-board Dh330/570) has reasonable rooms, but the restaurant (mains from Dh80 to Dh120) is the big draw, and the reason most people come here. It's a great splurge for lunch, followed by a walk around the lake to burn it off.

Le Gîte Dayet Aoua (☎ 035 604880; www.gite-dayetaoua.com, in French; r incl breakfast from Dh300, s/d with half-board Dh400/540) is another appealingly rustic and quiet place east of Dayet Aoua. There are five pretty rooms with Berber decoration, and a cheerful licensed dining room (mains from Dh80 to Dh110) serving wholesome country cooking (there's also a Berber tent to eat in during warm weather). Prices vary according to occupancy and meals. The *gîte* (hostel) is also a great source of local information for hiking, and can hire out tents (Dh50), guides (Dh250) and horses (Dh300) if you're tempted to really get exploring (all prices per day).

AZROU أزرو

pop 50,000

The Berber town of Azrou is an important market centre sitting at the junction of the roads to Fez, Meknès, Midelt and Khenifra. Deep in the Middle Atlas it sits amid stunning scenery, with sweeping views of cedar and pine forests, and high meadows that burst into flower every spring. Thoroughly unhurried, it's a relaxing spot to wind down if you've had too much of big cities.

Azrou hosts one of the region's largest weekly souqs, and is particularly known for its Berber carpets, so timing your visit for market day (Tuesday) is a good idea. A museum of the Middle Atlas has been under construction for some years, yet its final opening seems permanently delayed. Better instead to just head out of town to enjoy the countryside; there are plenty of day walks that take in the mountain air and great views. You might even spot a few of the local Barbary apes.

Orientation

Azrou (Great Rock) takes its name from the outcrop marking the town's western boundary. The big new Ennour mosque in front of it provides another handy landmark. The bus station and taxi stands lie to the north; beyond this is the site of the weekly souq. Other hotels, banks and eateries are southeast of here on and around Place Mohammed V.

Information

BMCE (Place Mohammed V) *Bureau de change* and one of several ATMs on the square.
Cyber Abridn (Place Mohammed V; per hr Dh6; 🕒 9am-midnight)
Cyber Kawtar (Bus station; per hr Dh6; 🕒 9am-midnight)
Pharmacie Sakhra (Place Mohammed V)
Post office (Blvd Prince Héritier Sidi Mohammed)

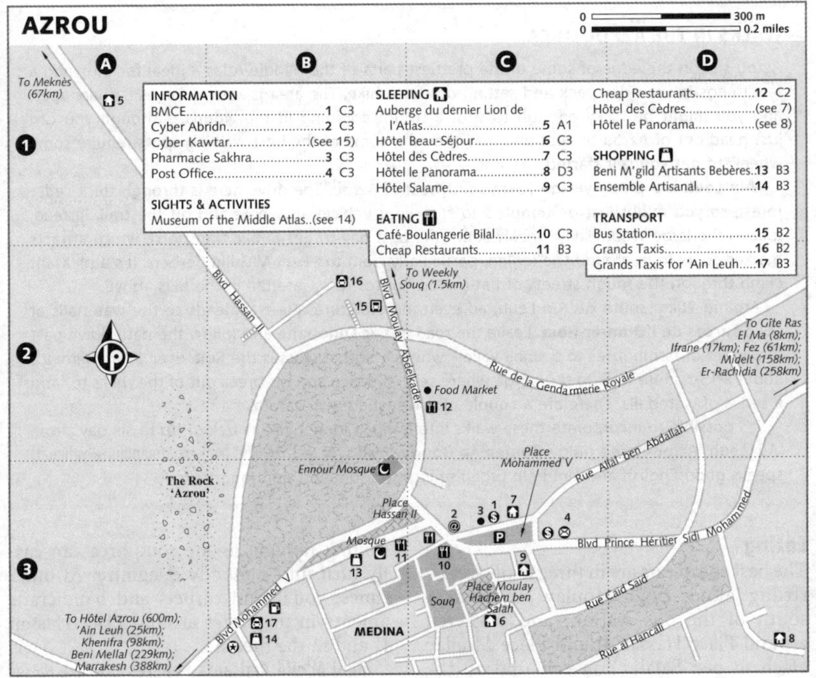

Sleeping

For its size, Azrou has a surprising number of sleeping options, with more being added out of town along the Fez road (look out for the Disneyland-esque 'castle' being built to attract Gulf Arab tourists.

Hôtel Salame (☎ 035 562562; salame_hotel@yahoo.fr; Place Moulay Hachem ben Salah; s/d Dh60/120) This small hotel is an exceedingly pleasant place to stay. Small, cute rooms are nicely presented with a smattering of traditional Berber decoration, and you will be made welcome by the friendly staff. Shared bathrooms are kept constantly clean, with 24-hour hot showers (Dh10).

Hôtel Beau-Sejour (☎ 035 560692; beau-sejour-hotel@yahoo.fr; 45 Place Moulay Hachem ben Salah; s/d/tr Dh70/100/180, cold/hot showers Dh5/10) Another decent budget option, rooms here are pretty simple and unaffected. The roof terrace has good views across Azrou.

Hôtel des Cèdres (☎ 035 562326; Place Mohammed V; s/d/tr Dh75/105/160) Built in 1925, this hotel still has plenty of interesting period features and a hint of deco styling in its fixtures. Rooms are good value – all have sinks, and though some share showers and toilets, there are plans to make all en suite.

Hôtel Azrou (☎ 035 562116; Rte de Khenifra; s/d with shower Dh109/142, with shower & toilet Dh138/163) A decent midrange place on the south side of town, this is a fair choice. It has comfy rooms – plus a bar, a restaurant and an ivy-covered terrace (although the atmosphere can be a little seedy at night. If you fancy a game, the staff are the local *petanque* champions.

Auberge du dernier Lion de l'Atlas (☎ 035 561868; a.elkhaldi@menara.ma; Rte de Meknès; s/d incl breakfast Dh150/250) The youth hostel is about 500m east of town, set back slightly from the road. The facilities are pretty basic with cold showers (what did you expect for Dh20?), and you need a YHI membership card to check in.

Hôtel le Panorama (☎ 035 562010; panorama@extra.net.ma; s/d Dh280/342) Built in aw grand alpine-chalet style, Azrou's most comfortable hotel is in a quiet wooded spot a short walk northeast of town, with pleasant garden. Staff are friendly and efficient. Rooms are compact and modern, with balconies, and the restaurant is good.

WALKS IN THE AZROU AREA

Azrou sits on the edge of some of the prettiest parts of the Middle Atlas – ideal for throwing a few things in your day pack and setting out for a hike. The area is known for its Barbary apes, and you might be lucky enough to spot a troupe foraging in the woods. Although you can just head out of Azrou by foot and into the hills, some of the best walking spots require some wheels to get yourself started.

'Ain Leuh is a pretty village 25km southwest of Azrou. The drive here is through thick cedar forest, so you might just be tempted to stop your vehicle anywhere and hit the trail. Instead, take in the large Wednesday weekly souq (the best day to get public transport), which attracts market-goers from around the region, particularly from the Beni M'Guild Berbers. It's a pleasant climb through the rough streets of flat-roofed houses to a waterfall in the hills above.

Around 20km south of 'Ain Leuh, an even more picturesque walk leads to the waterfalls at the **Sources de l'Oum-er-Rbia**. Leave the road at **Lac Ouiouane** and follow the path down past a number of farmhouses to a small valley, where a bridge crosses the Rbia river. From here, it's about a 15-minute walk to the gorge where several dozen springs break out of the rocks to form a series of waterfalls. There are a couple of cafés where you can take a rest.

It's possible to incorporate these walks into a much longer circuit trek of up to six days from 'Ain Leuh. Azrou-based guide **Boujemaa Boudadoud** (☎ 063 760825; boujemaatoumliline@yahoo.fr) speaks good English and can help organise logistics for short and long treks.

Eating

The best cheap eats are in three main areas – strung along Blvd Moulay Abdelkader south of the bus station, and clustered around Place Hassan II and Place Moulay Hachem ben Salah. You can find all the trusty favourites here – rotisserie chicken, brochettes and steaming bowls of *harira*.

Café Boulangerie Bilal (Place Mohammed V) An always-busy café with upstairs seating, good sandwich and pastry options, plus fruit juices and the occasional ice cream for the hot weather.

Hôtel des Cèdres (☎ 035 562326; Place Mohammed V; mains around Dh50) A hotel restaurant with a 1920s dining room and log fire, and our favourite eating place in Azrou. The local trout is always good, plus there are some more unusual dishes like rabbit tajine.

Hôtel le Panorama (☎ 035 562010; set menu Dh130) Another hotel restaurant, the Panorama is better in the evenings, when you can also wash down your meal with a glass of wine or beer. Some tasty tajines, and a handful of continental dishes in pleasant surroundings.

Shopping

The weekly souq is held on Tuesday about 1.5km northeast of town. Here you'll witness Berber women from the surrounding villages haggling with dealers over the flat-weave carpets, as well as fresh produce and other market goods. Take care if it's been raining though, as the souq area can easily turn into a muddy quagmire. At other times, you'll find carpets and handicrafts aplenty in the stores around Place Hassan II and in the medina.

Beni M'gild Artisants Bebères (55 Place Hassan II; 🕑 10am-6pm) This is one of several shops along this stretch of road with a good selection of Middle Atlas rugs, including those of the seminomadic Beni M'Guild Berbers.

Ensemble Artisanal (Blvd Mohammed V; 🕑 8.30am-noon & 2.30-6.30pm) Here you'll find more Berber rugs, plus some interesting carved cedar and juniper wood. The planned Museum of the Middle Atlas will be next door.

Getting There & Away

Azrou is a crossroads, with one axis heading northwest to southeast from Meknès to Er-Rachidia, and the other northeast to Fez and southwest to Marrakesh.

BUS

CTM (☎ 035 562002) offers daily departures from the bus station on Blvd Moulay Abdelkader to Beni Mellal (Dh55, three hours), Casablanca (Dh105, six hours), Fez (Dh27, two hours), Marrakesh (Dh135, seven hours) and Meknès (Dh25, 1½ hours).

Other slightly cheaper companies have frequent daily departures to Fez (Dh18), Meknès (Dh16), Ifrane (Dh7), Midelt (Dh30) and Er-Rachidia (Dh70).

TAXI

The grand taxi lot is down a stepped path below the bus station. Regular taxis go to Fez (Dh30, one hour), Meknès (Dh32, one hour), Khenifra (Dh25, one hour), Ifrane (Dh10, 10 minutes) and less frequently to Midelt (Dh47, 90 minutes). Those for 'Ain Leuh (Dh14, 20 minutes) wait beside the Shell petrol station on the main road out to the southwest.

MIDELT ميدلت

pop 35,000

Midelt sits in a no-man's land of north and the south, stuck between the Middle and the High Atlas. Coming from the north in particular, the landscape seems dry and barren but it offers some breathtaking views, especially of the eastern High Atlas which seem to rise out of nowhere.

Midelt is the sort of place people pass through, but it can make a handy break between Fez and the desert, and possibly for a spot of carpet-shopping. It's also a good base for some off-piste exploring, most notably Jebel Ayachi, which can be climbed without technical experience.

Midelt consists of little more than one main street (Ave Mohammed V in the north, which becomes Ave Hassan II to the south), a modest souq and a number of oversized restaurants, which cater to the tourist buses whistling through on their way south.

Information

BMCI (Ave Hassan II) One of several banks with ATMs on this street.

Complexe Touristique Timnay Inter-Cultures (☎ 035 360188; http://timnay-tourisme.com; Rte de Zaidia) The best source of information – including trekking guides and 4WD rental – in the eastern High Atlas, about 15km north of Midelt.

Post office (off Ave Hassan II) South of the centre.

Sawtcom (Rue Ezzerqutouni; per hr Dh6; 8am-midnight) Internet access.

Sights

KASBAH MYRIEM

If you're in the mood for carpets, this **workshop** (Atelier de Tissages et Borderie; ☎ 035 582443; 8am-noon & 2-5.30pm Mon-Thu & Sat), about 1.5km out of town, is worth a look. Run by Franciscan nuns, it assists Berber women develop their embroidery and weaving. The workshop provides looms and materials, as well as a simple place to work. Local girls – aged 15 or so – come here in order to learn these skills from more experienced women. Literacy lessons are also offered. Follow the signs from the main road, then enter behind the clinic.

While you are here, you may wish to peek into the **monastery** (services at 7.15am daily & 10am Sun), which is home to five Franciscan monks. The grounds and chapel are a peaceful place to collect your thoughts. Ring the bell at the gate to the right of the workshop.

KASBAH DES NOYERS

The village of **Berrem**, 6km west of Midelt, is also known as the Kasbah des Noyers for the ancient walnut trees shading its environs. There's not much going on here, but the quaint village, with its colourful mosque and ancient earthen walls, makes a good destination for a day-hike from Midelt. Follow the main path through the kasbah to the scenic overlook of the **Gorges des Berrem**. Hiring a grand taxi from Midelt costs about Dh40.

Sleeping

Hôtel Atlas (☎ 035 582938; 3 Rue Mohammed el-Amraoui; s/d Dh70/100) This tiny pension is a fair budget option, with home-cooked food on request. Rooms are predictably simple, but clean, as are the shared bathrooms with squat toilets (hot showers cost Dh10). Watch out for carpets though – we've had a couple of letters from travellers complaining of hard sell.

Hôtel Massira (☎ 035 361010; 11 Rue des Anciens Combatants; s/d/tr Dh50/100/200) On the Er-Rachidia side of town, this is a great new place. For the price, rooms are large and excellent, and the en suite bathrooms have gallons of hot water. There's a roof terrace with panoramic views: the perfect spot to take in the huge breakfasts (Dh20).

Auberge Jaafar (☎ 035 583415; fax 055 583514; Berrem; r Dh225;) This kasbah-style complex is about 6km west of Midelt, just past the village of Berrem. Rooms of all shapes and sizes are set up around terraces and blooming courtyards. All facilities are shared, but everything is clean, although the service can be a bit ramshackle at times. Order during the day if you're going to eat in.

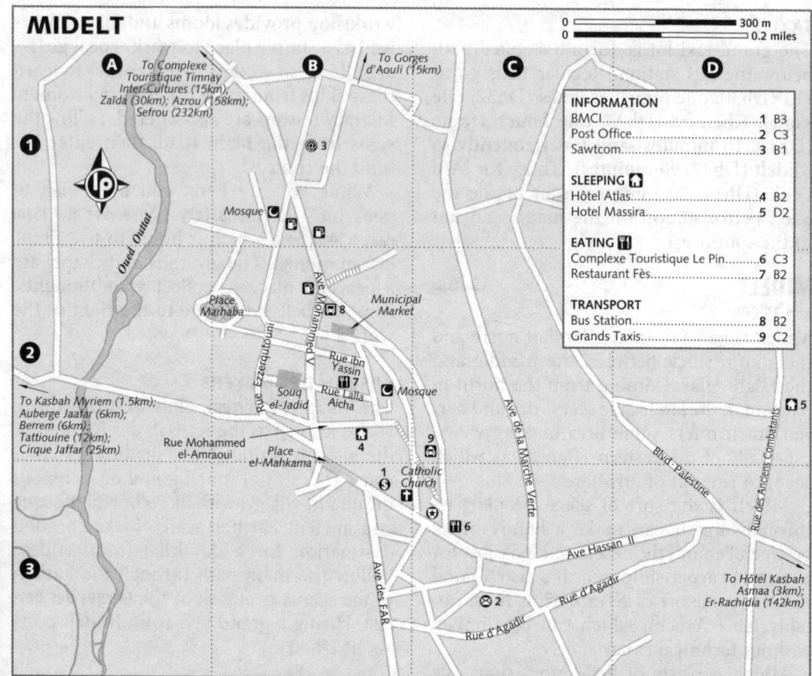

Hôtel Kasbah Asmaa (☎ 035 580405; s/d Dh300/350;) About 3km south of Midelt, this hotel is hard to miss – the kasbah-style exterior announces that you're on the road south. Another tour-group staple, it has fair rooms and an inviting pool at the bottom of the property, far away from the rooms so as not to be overlooked. The licensed restaurant, contained in several traditionally decorated salons, is, for nonguests, worth eating at.

Hôtel el-Ayachi (☎ 035 582161; hotelayachi@caramail.com; Rue d'Agadir; s/d Dh290/355) One of Midelt's older hotels, as described by its creaky 1950s styling, the Ayachi lives off the tour groups – one night only and no repeat customers. Rooms are a bit shabby, along with the slightly musty bathrooms.

Complexe Touristique Timnay Inter-Cultures (☎ 035 360188; http://timnay-tourisme.com; Rte de Zaïdia; camping per person Dh20, plus per tent/car/campervan Dh15/15/25, bungalows from Dh200, Berber tents per person Dh25;) About 15km north of Midelt, this centre is a joint Moroccan-Belgian venture aimed at developing local tourism. Accommodation is simple – it works best with your own tent or campervan – but Camping Timnay (as it's known locally) is a good base for exploring the region, as you can organise treks and guides from here. For the evenings, there's a restaurant and bar. To get here, take a grand taxi headed for Zaïdia and ask the driver to let you out at Timnay.

Eating

As usual, cheap eats and snacks are plentiful in the area around the bus station, where there's also a produce market.

Restaurant Fès (☎ 062 057754; Rue Lalla Aicha; set menu Dh70) Serving up hearty portions of traditional cooking, this place is ever-popular. The menu never seems to change – salad or soup, tajine and fruit – and is always simple but fresh.

Complexe Touristique Le Pin (☎ 035 583550; Ave Hassan II; mains Dh50-60, buffet Dh70; noon-5pm year round & 7-10pm Apr-Aug) This large restaurant draws the coach groups (beware the lunchtime crush), but you can easily escape them in the garden, and the large turnover of covers ensures fresh meals, all served in generous portions. Alcohol is served.

Getting There & Away

Midelt's bus station is off Ave Mohammed V. CTM services mostly run at night. There's an evening departure to Casablanca (Dh135, seven hours) via Rabat (Dh105, 6½ hours), and to Rissani (Dh75, five hours) via Er-Rachidia (Dh48, 2½ hours) and Erfoud (Dh59, 4½ hours). There are also night-time services for Azrou (Dh30, 90 minutes), Meknès (Dh66, four hours) and Fez (Dh77, five hours).

Other buses cover the same routes at more sociable hours for slightly less – Fez (Dh65, five hours) is serviced by six departures throughout the day.

Grands taxis run to Azrou (Dh47, 90 minutes) and Er-Rachidia (Dh55, two hours).

AROUND MIDELT

Midelt's location on the cusp of the eastern High Atlas makes it a great base for exploring. Off the main routes, roads are rough piste, with many only really negotiable between May and October and even then only by 4WD. It's heaven for mountain bikers, as well as ideal hiking country. Complexe Touristique Timnay Inter-Cultures and Safari Atlas in Midelt will rent you a 4WD (with driver) for around Dh1000 – good value if there's a group of you.

Cirque Jaffar

The Cirque Jaffar winds through the foothills of Jebel Ayachi, 25km southwest of Midelt. It's a rough piste, and regular cars will grumble on the route in all seasons but the height of summer. The scenery is wonderful though – the dramatic crests of the Atlas, carpeted in places with cedar forest, and studded with tiny Berber mountain villages. From Midelt, take the Zaïdia road for about 10km and turn off at the signpost for the village of Aït Oum Gam. Then follow the signs to Matkan Tounfit. After that the route loops back through Tattiouine and on to Rte S3424 back to Midelt. Allow a day for the whole 80km circuit. The Complexe Touristique Timnay Inter-Cultures offers this day trip for Dh350 per person including meals.

If walking is more your thing, and you have a tent, it's possible to strike out from Timnay to the Cirque Jaffar on foot. A two-day round trip gives a good taste of the area. From Timnay you can walk to the village of Sidi Amar, which is surrounded by apple orchards and is particularly colourful during the souq each Wednesday. Camp further along at Jaffar, located in the valley in the centre of the spectacular circle. On day two, return to the Timnay complex via the impressive river gorges. A guide isn't strictly necessary, but can be organised via the Complexe Touristique Timnay Inter-Cultures. An equally good companion is the guidebook *Grand Atlas Traverse* by Michael Peyron.

Gorges d'Aouli

An interesting road trip takes you 15km northeast of Midelt along the S317 road to the **Gorges d'Aouli**. A series of cliffs carved by the Moulaya, they were until recently mined extensively for lead, copper and silver. The abandoned workings can be clearly seen – many halfway up the cliff face – although the mine entrances themselves are blocked off for safety reasons. Nevertheless, the place exudes a slightly creepy ghost-

CLIMBING JEBEL AYACHI

The highest mountain in the eastern High Atlas, Jebel Ayachi (3737m) is more a massif than a single peak, stretching along a 45km ridge southwest of Midelt. Its size offers a host of trekking opportunities, not least an ascent of Ichichi n'Boukhlib, the highest peak.

The best time to tackle Jebel Ayachi is April to May or September to November, although you should be aware that snow can persist above 3400m well into July. From Midelt, take a grand taxi to the village of Tattiouine, from where you start the climb. It's a tiring but nontechnical ascent achievable in a single day. There's a simple mountain bivouac at the summit, although you'll obviously need to bring your own supplies.

A guide is definitely a good idea. The best place to arrange one is through the Complexe Touristique Timnay Inter-Cultures (p275) north of Midelt. The daily rate is around Dh300. An alternative, if you're up to the arranging, is to hire a mule and driver in Tattiouine.

town feel, especially with the dipping sun at the end of the day. Further along the road, the small village of **Aouli** sits against the spectacular backdrop of the river gorge. This would be a great stretch to explore by mountain bike (the road deteriorates to rough piste at some points); a round trip by grand taxi from Midelt should cost no more than Dh250.

THE EAST

TAZA تازة

pop 200,000

At first glance, Taza seems to fulfil all the criteria of a sleepy provincial capital. The rush of activity common in Moroccan towns of comparable size seems entirely absent here, while its sprawling layout gives it a slightly abandoned air. But it makes an interesting break in a journey: climb the crumbling fortifications of Taza Haute and the panoramic views of the Rif to the north and the Middle Atlas to the south are breathtaking. Taza also provides a handy base for exploring the eastern Middle Atlas, including Gouffre du Friouato (one of the most incredible open caverns in the world) and Tazzeka National Park.

History

The fortified citadel of Taza is built on the edge of an escarpment overlooking the only feasible pass between the Rif Mountains and the Middle Atlas. It has been important throughout Morocco's history as a garrison town from which to exert control over the country's eastern extremities.

The Tizi n'Touahar, as the pass is known, was the traditional invasion route for armies moving west from Tunisia and Algeria. This is, in fact, where the Romans and the Arabs entered Morocco. The town itself was the base from which the Almohads, Merenids and Alawites swept to conquer lowland Morocco and establish their dynasties.

All Moroccan sultans had a hand in fortifying Taza. Nevertheless, their control over the area was always tenuous because the fiercely independent and rebellious local tribes continually exploited any weakness in the central power in order to overrun the city. Never was this more so than in the first years of the 20th century, when 'El-Rogui' (Pretender to the Sultan's Throne) Bou Hamra, held sway over most of north-eastern Morocco.

The French occupied Taza in 1914 and made it the main base from which they fought the prolonged rebellion by the tribes of the Rif Mountains and Middle Atlas.

Orientation

If you arrive by train or bus, you are likely to find yourself on the main Fez-to-Oujda road, a short taxi ride north of Place de l'Indépendance. This square is the heart of the ville nouvelle (also called Taza Bas, or Lower Taza) and the site of banks, the main post office and most hotels and restaurants, as well as the CTM bus station.

The medina, ringed by its impressive walls usually referred to as Taza Haute (Upper Taza), occupies the hill 2km to the south. Local buses (Dh2) and sky-blue petits taxis (Dh6) run regularly between the ville nouvelle and Place Aharrach (opposite the post office) in the medina.

Information

Attajariwafa Bank (Map p280; Ave Moulay Youseff) Has an ATM.

BMCI (Map p280; Place de l'Indépendance) Has an ATM.

Cyber Attoraya (Map p279; Rue Allal ben Abdallah; per hr Dh5; ⏲ 24hr)

Cyber Taza Net (Map p279; Place Aharrah, Taza Haute; per hr Dh4; ⏲ 8am-11pm)

Hammam (Map p279; Place Aharrach; Dh10; ⏲ men 5am-noon & 7pm-midnight, women noon-7pm)

Main post office (Map p280; off Rue de Marché)

Pharmacy Aharrach (Map p279; Place Aharrach)

Post office (Map p279; Ave Moulay el-Hassan) Opposite the main square.

Sights & Activities

The partially ruined **medina walls** (Map p279), around 3km in circumference, are a legacy from when Taza served briefly as the Almohad capital in the 12th century. The **bastion** – where the walls jut out to the east of the medina – was added 400 years later by the Saadians. The most interesting section of wall is around **Bab er-Rih** (Gate of the Wind; Map p279), from where there are superb views over the surrounding countryside. Look southwest to the wooded slopes of Jebel Tazzeka in the Middle Atlas, and then to the Rif in the north, and it's easy to see the strategic significance of Taza's location.

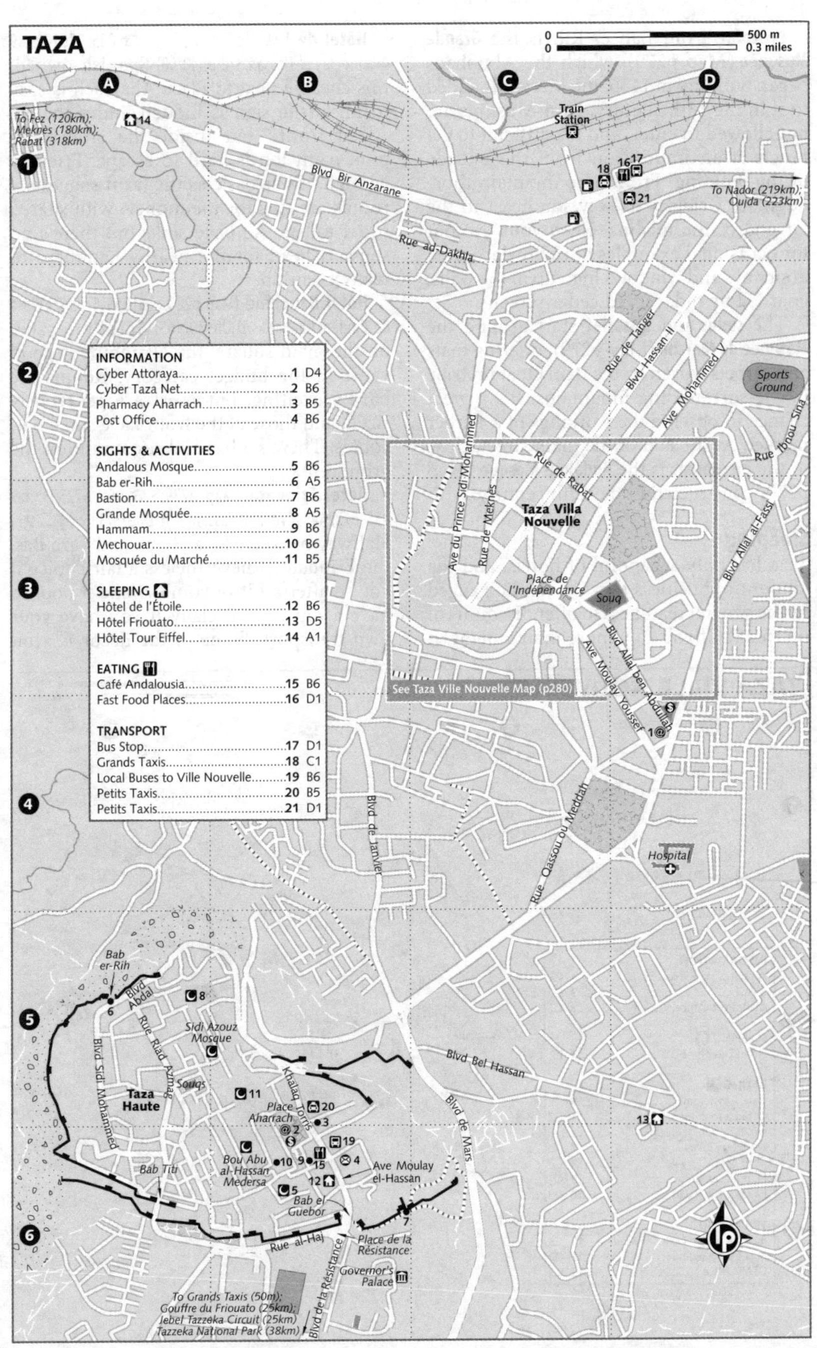

IMPERIAL CITIES, MIDDLE ATLAS & THE EAST

Not far from Bab er-Rih is the **Grande Mosquée** (Map p279), which the Almohads began building in 1135; the Merenids added to it in the 13th century. Non-Muslims are not allowed to enter, and it's difficult to get much of an impression from the outside of the building. From here the main thoroughfare wriggles its way southeast to the far end of the medina. Keep your eye out for occasional examples of richly decorated doorways and windows high up in the walls, guarded by old, carved cedar screens.

The **souqs** and **qissariat** start around the **Mosquée du Marché** (Map p279), offering mats and carpets woven by the Beni Ouarain tribe in the surrounding mountains. It's a great chance to observe the workings of a Berber market. At the end of the main street, close to the **mechouar**, is the **Andalous Mosque** (Map p279) constructed in the 12th century.

Sleeping

Taza has only a handful of hotels, and the amount of business they do can be gauged by the general readiness to offer discounts of up to 25% if you stay more than a night.

Hôtel de l'Étoile (Map p279; ☎ 055 270179; 39 Ave Moulay el-Hassan; s/d Dh40/50) Spanish-owned, this cheapie next to Place Aharrach is easy to miss (the sign is hidden under the arcaded front), but inside the strawberry pink paint job is hard to escape. Friendly enough, it's as basic as the tariff suggests – rooms are fine for the money, with shared squat toilets. All have sinks but there's no shower: head for the nearby hammam to really clean up.

Hôtel Dauphiné (Map p280; ☎ 055 673567; Place de l'Indépendance; s/d Dh130/165) Ideally located on the main square, the Dauphiné is good value in the budget category. Rooms are hardly exciting, but most are generously sized, and those at the front have small balconies. There's a bar and restaurant on the ground floor.

Hôtel Friouato (Map p279; ☎ 055 672593; fax 055 672244; Blvd Bel Hassan; s/d Dh275/315; 🏊 P) Halfway between Taza Haute and Taza Bas, the Friouato is nevertheless a fair choice if you're after a bit of comfort and a pool to have a dip in, especially if you have your own transport. Some of the decor is a bit

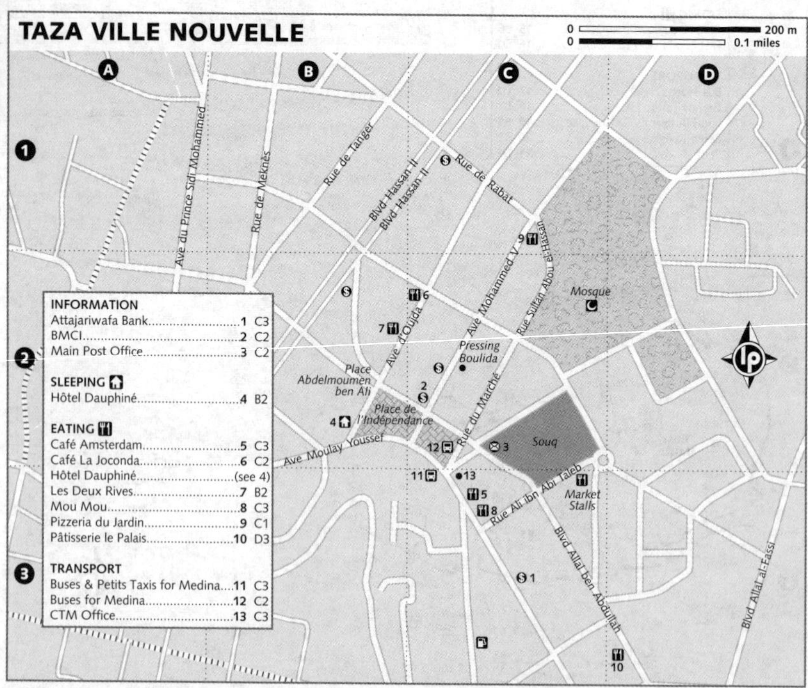

tired, but all the three-star amenities are there, including a bar and restaurant.

Hôtel Tour Eiffel (Map p279; ☎ 055 671562; tourazhar@hotmail.com; Blvd Bir Anzarane; s/d Dh316/401, breakfast Dh28; ❄) Stuck on the road out of town, the Tour Eiffel is named for its high aspirations. Past the cramped lobby, a lift swishes you up to well-sized and fairly comfy rooms, many with great views out towards the mountains. The house restaurant has good juices and is noted for its seafood.

Eating

There aren't really any restaurants in the medina, just snack stalls selling kebabs and the like, although there is plenty of fresh produce in the souqs. In the ville nouvelle, the street souq just off Place de l'Indépendance also has produce and lots of tasty snack stands that really come to life in the evening. Ave Mohammed V is well supplied for grocer stores. If you're waiting for onward transport and are in need of sustenance, there's a whole row of fast-food places where the buses stop on the Fez–Oujda road (Blvd Bir Anzarane).

Les Deux Rives (Map p280; ☎ 055 671227; 20 Ave d'Oujda; mains Dh30-60) This fresh and cosy little restaurant is a good option. The menu is a mix of Moroccan and continental – some tajines, couscous and a good *pastilla* (pie), with a smattering of pizzas and grilled meat thrown in.

Pizzeria du Jardin (Map p280; 44 Rue Sultan Abou el-Hassan; mains Dh35-40) This is a friendly place serving a few tajines, pizzas and fast-food options, with some huge salads, all overlooked by glossy photos of Bogart and Garbo. It's busy in the evenings but dead in the afternoon.

Hôtel Dauphiné (Map p280; ☎ 055 673567; Place de l'Indépendance; meals Dh80) On the ground floor of the hotel, the Dauphiné serves up the usual range of Moroccan standards (with some good fish), plus a handful of continental dishes thrown in. It's pretty tasty and efficiently served, but the big dining room could use a little atmosphere.

Mou Mou (Map p280; Ave Moulay Youssef; pizzas from Dh30, shawarma from Dh30) If you've been lulled into thinking that Taza is a sleepy place, hit this packed-out corner place, with happy customers spilling out of the door. Tasty fast-food is the order of the day here: great shawarma, paninis, pizzas and juices.

Café Amsterdam (Map p280; Ave Moulay Youssef) This is a great breakfast stop with its own patisserie so you're never short of sticky pastry options. Sadly there's no outside seating, but the interior is crisply decorated.

Café la Joconda (Map p280; Ave d'Oujda) Another good modern café with plenty of pavement seating, and one that's not threatened by the concept of female customers.

Pâtisserie le Palais (Map p280; 65 Blvd Allal ben Abdullah) The pastries available here are considered by many to be the best in Taza.

Café Andalousia (Map p279; Place Aharrach) Join the old guys sitting here overlooking the medina square making a coffee last all afternoon.

Getting There & Away

BUS

Few buses actually originate in Taza, but plenty pass through on their way between Oujda and points west of Taza such as Fez, Tangier and Casablanca, as well as to the coast.

The **CTM office** (Map p280; ☎ 055 673037; Place de l'Indépendance) is located in the ville nouvelle. There's a morning departure for Casablanca (Dh135, eight hours), stopping at Fez (Dh45, two hours), Meknès (Dh65, 2½ hours) and Rabat (Dh105, 6½ hours). Two overnight buses leave for Tangier (Dh140, eight hours). There are also morning services for Oujda (Dh55, 3½ hours) and Nador (Dh50, 2½ hours).

Non-CTM buses servicing these same destinations stop on the Fez–Oujda road next to the grand taxi lot. It's all a bit random, so ask around the day before as to what's expected – and jump in a grand taxi if the wait seems too long.

TAXI

Most grands taxis leave from the main Fez–Oujda road, near the train station. They depart fairly regularly for Fez (Dh44, 2½ hours). Less frequently, taxis head for Oujda (Dh75, 3½ hours) and Al-Hoceima (Dh65, 2½ hours). Grands taxis to the Gouffre du Friouato (Dh14) leave from a lot to the south of the medina.

TRAIN

Taza's location on the train line makes rail the best transport option. Four trains run to Fez (Dh39, two hours), two of which continue to Meknès (Dh55, three hours),

Rabat (Dh109, six hours) and Casablanca (Dh134, seven hours), and there's one service to Tangier (Dh132, eight hours), although you can also change at Sidi Kacem. In the opposite direction, three trains go to Oujda (Dh73, three hours).

AROUND TAZA

Jebel Tazzeka Circuit

It's possible to make an interesting day trip of a circuit around Jebel Tazzeka, southwest of Taza. This takes in the Cascades de Ras el-Oued at the edge of Tazzeka National Park, the cave systems of Gouffre du Friouato and the gorges of the Oued Zireg. The scenery is grand, although the road is very narrow and twisty in parts, with plenty of blind corners from which grands taxis can unexpectedly speed out.

The road is too quiet to hitch easily. If you don't have a vehicle, expect to pay around Dh500 for a grand taxi for the day from Taza, although a few direct grands taxis to the Gouffre du Friouato can sometimes be found near the medina.

THE FIRST LEG

The first stop is the **Cascades de Ras el-Oued**, 10km from Taza. A popular picnic site, they're at their grandest in the early spring, flushed with rain and snow melt – by the end of summer the flow is just a trickle. Just above the waterfalls is the village of **Ras el-Mar**, where there's a small café with great mountain views. The entry to **Tazzeka National Park** is also near here. With its stands of cork oak you could conceivably spend a day walking here.

Leaving the waterfalls, continue along the right fork onto the plateau and up to a small pass. On your left you'll see the strange depression of the **Daïa Chiker**, a dry lake bed. In early spring, however, a shallow lake often forms as a result of a geological curiosity associated with fault lines in the calciferous rock structure.

GOUFFRE DU FRIOUATO

Further along, 25km from Taza, the **Gouffre du Friouato** (☎ 067 640626; admission Dh3, guide Dh100, torch Dh100; 🕙 8am-6pm) is well signposted, up a very steep road. The cavern is the main attraction of this circuit and it's well worth coming up here simply to look into its gaping mouth.

At over 20m wide and 230m deep, it is said to be the deepest cavern in the whole of North Africa, and the cave system is possibly the most extensive. It was first investigated in 1935 and has only been partially explored to date.

Access is via 520 precipitous steps (with handrails) that lead you all the way to the floor of the cavern (it's a quite strenuous climb back up). At the bottom, you can squeeze through a hole to start exploring the fascinating chambers that are found 200 more steps below. It's dark and dirty and eerily beautiful. The most spectacular chambers, full of extraordinary formations, are the **Salle de Lixus** and the **Salle de Draperies.** The latter are the most spectacular, and do indeed resemble thin sheets of curtains, frozen and calcified. Allow at least three hours there and back. Speleologists have explored to a depth of 300m, but they believe there are more caves another 500m below.

The admission fee allows you to enter as far as the cavern mouth. Beyond that, a guide is needed to accompany you further underground to the grandest chambers. Bank on the occasional scramble, and a couple of squeezes through narrow sections: we don't recommend this for claustrophobes. A torch (available at the site entrance), good shoes and warm clothes are also recommended.

BACK TO TAZA

Beyond the Gouffre du Friouato, the road begins to climb again into coniferous forests past **Bab Bou-Idir**. Abandoned for much of the year, this village comes alive in summer when holiday-makers fill its camp site and tiled alpine-style houses. This is a good base if you wish to do some day hikes in the area. There's a national park information office, open in summer, and marked trails commencing in the village.

About 8km past Bab Bou-Idir, a rough track branches off to the right 9km up to **Jebel Tazzeka** (1980m). A piste goes to the summit, and it's a tough climb. At the top there's a TV relay station, and really great panoramic views out to both the Rif and the Middle Atlas.

The main road continues for another 38km to join the main Fez–Taza road at Sidi Abdallah de Rhiata. On the way you will wind around hairpin bends through some dense woodland and then down through the pretty gorges of the **Oued Zireg**. From the intersection at Sidi Abdallah de Rhiata, you can take the main highway back east to Taza, pausing at **Tizi n'Touahar** on the way for more views.

OUJDA وجدة

pop 880,000

Oujda is the largest city in eastern Morocco, and its modern facade belies its millennium-old age. It's a relaxed sort of a place that often seems surprised to see foreign travellers, but it wasn't always like this. A quick survey of the map and recent history gives the reason. The terminus of the train line, it has good links to the rest of the country, and once capitalised on its location near the busiest border-crossing with Algeria, making it a popular centre for traders and tourists alike. When the border closed in 1995 Oujda's economy took a major hit, from which it has arguably yet to recover. It's hoped that the plans to develop tourism along the nearby Mediterranean coast will have a positive knock-on effect for the city. In the meantime Oujda's important university remains a mainstay of the economy and the city's intellectual life.

Despite few genuine attractions for the traveller, it's a hassle-free place in which to catch your breath, after heading down from the Rif Mountains or taking the long look south to Figuig and the Sahara.

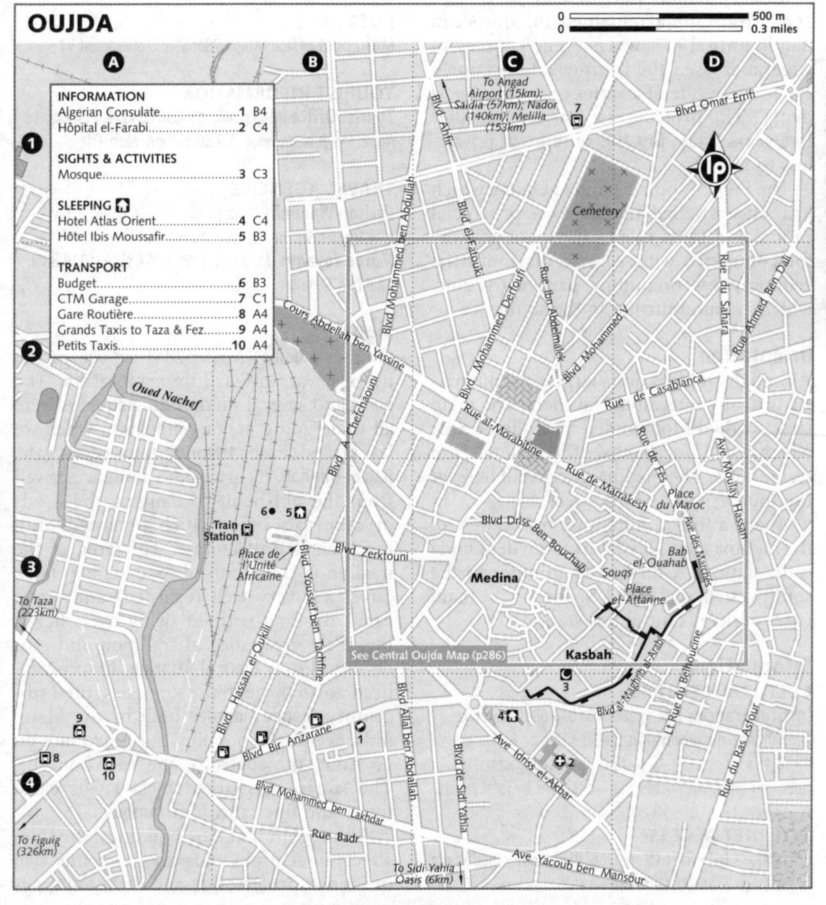

History

The site of Oujda has long been important as it lies on the main axis connecting Morocco with the rest of North Africa (the Romans built a road through here). Like Taza, it occupied a key position in controlling the east and was often seen as a vital stepping stone for armies aiming to seize control of the heartland around.

The town was founded by the Meghraoua tribe in the 10th century and remained independent until the Almohads overran it in the 11th century. Later, under the Merenids, Algerian rulers based in Tlemcen took the town on several occasions, and then in the 17th century it fell under the sway of the Ottoman in Algiers.

Moulay Ismail put an end to this in 1687, and Oujda remained in Moroccan hands until 1907, when French forces in Algeria crossed the frontier and occupied the town in one of a series of similar 'incidents'. The protectorate was still another five years away, but the sultan was powerless to stop it.

The French soon expanded Oujda, which has since swelled in size as a provincial capital and in its role as the main gateway for commerce with Algeria. Its industrial economy rests on mining, particularly zinc, which is found further to the south.

Orientation

Although Oujda is quite large, only the centre is of any interest to travellers. The main street is Blvd Mohammed V, along or near which you'll find banks, offices, hotels and restaurants. The medina lies east of here, at the southern end of the street.

About a five-minute walk to the west of the medina along Blvd Zerktouni lies Oujda train station. A further 15 minutes to the southwest, across Oued Nachef, is the main *gare routière* (central bus station).

Information

CULTURAL CENTRES

Institut Français (Map p286; ☎ 036 684404; www.ambafrance-ma.org/institut/oujda; 3 Rue de Berkane; 🕑 8.45am-noon & 1.45-6.30pm Tue-Sat) Concerts, lectures and films, with occasional exhibitions by local artists.

INTERNET ACCESS

K@ramoss Internet (Map p286; Blvd Mohammed V; per hr Dh5; 🕑 24hr) Upstairs above a café.

Surfnet (Map p286; Ave Idriss el-Akbar; per hr Dh6; 🕑 9am-11pm) In the basement.

MEDICAL SERVICES

Hôpital el-Farabi (Map p283; ☎ 036 682705; Ave Idriss el-Akbar)

Pharmacie Mouslime (Map p286; Blvd Mohammed V)

MONEY

Most banks with ATMs and *bureau de change* are located along Blvd Mohammed V in the medina and around Place du 16 Août near the town hall.

Western Union (Map p286; Blvd Mohammed V; 🕑 8am-noon & 2-6pm Mon-Thu, 8-11.30am & 2.30-6.30pm Fri, 9am-12.30pm Sat) Has a *bureau de change* where you can change cash outside banking hours.

POST

Main post office (Map p286; Blvd Mohammed V)

TOURIST INFORMATION

Tourist Office (Map p286; ☎ 036 684329; Place du 16 Août; 🕑 8.30am-noon & 2.30-6.30pm Mon-Fri)

TRAVEL AGENCIES

Carlson Wagonlit (Map p286; ☎ 036 682520; Blvd Mohammed V) For ferry and air tickets.

Maroc Voyages (Map p286; ☎ 036 683993; 110 Blvd Allal ben Abdallah)

Sights

Oujda's **medina** (Map p286) isn't large but it stills warrants a little exploration. The walls and several surrounding squares were all undergoing major renovation when we last visited. Enter through the eastern gate, **Bab el-Ouahab**, its gruesome name is derived from the old habit of hanging the heads of criminals here, which persisted until the French Protectorate. This area of the medina is chock-full of food stalls (Oujda olives are very well regarded) and street cafés. Bustling without being overwhelming, it's a great slice of tradition and modernity. From **Place el-Attarine** (Map p286), head north through the souqs past the 14th-century **Grande Mosquée** built by the Merenids, eventually popping out near Place du 16 Août, the centre of the ville nouvelle. The square is marked by a 1930s clock tower and fine sandstone **mosque**.

Although full of new buildings, the sidestreets in central Oujda are frequently rich in French protectorate and deco buildings (although often in poor condition). Walking south along Blvd Mohammed V, note the fine French neo-Moorish **Banque al-Maghrib**, before arriving at the **Cathedrale St Louis** (invariably with nesting storks on its imposing towers).

Sleeping

While the Algerian border remains closed, Oujda's hotels suffer from being filled to over-capacity. At most hotels, rates fall quickly on asking, especially if you stay multiple nights.

BUDGET

Hôtel Tlemcen (Map p286; ☎ 036 700384; 26 Rue Ramdane el-Gadhi; r per person Dh60) This friendly little place offers excellent value, and has an exceedingly grand-looking lobby for the price of the rooms. Quarters are small but bright, with bathrooms and TV.

Hôtel al-Hanna (Map p286; ☎ 036 686003; 132 Rue de Marrakesh; s/d Dh57/77, with bathroom Dh77/93) This place is very handy for bus connections. Rooms are airy (many with balconies). All rooms have their own sink, but it's definitely worth paying the extra for an attached bathroom.

Hôtel Atrah (Map p286; ☎ 036 686533; off Rue Ramdane el-Gadhi; s/d Dh113/178) The tiles and plasterwork in the lobby lend some traditional Moroccan flavour here. Self-contained rooms are a bit boxy, but otherwise this is a good budget choice.

Hôtel Angad (Map p286; ☎ 036 691451; Rue Ramdane el-Gadhi; s/d Dh90/140, high season Dh161/194) The top pick of the budget hotels is this affordable two-star. Rooms are just about essentially furnished, with large bathroom and TV, but you're better off getting a room at the back as street-side can be noisy. The downstairs café does breakfast and pizza.

Hôtel la Concorde (Map p286; ☎ 036 682328; 57 Blvd Mohammed V; s/d Dh177/206) The low-ceilinged reception – they've squeezed in a mezzanine bar upstairs – instantly makes you feel cramped in this hotel, but the rooms are better than you'd think. There's a slight impression of a good hotel fallen on hard times, but it's fine for the price and location.

MIDRANGE & TOP END

Hôtel Oujda (Map p286; ☎ 036 684093; fax 036 685064; Blvd Mohammed V; s/d Dh278/352; ❄ 🏊) According to the decor, this hotel's clock stopped in the early 1970s: there's a 'space age' lobby and funky bathroom tiles. Still, everything works, it's all comfy enough and the staff are eager to please. The restaurant offers lovely views of the nearby square and Église St Louis.

Hotel Al Manar (Map p286; ☎ 036 688855; hotelalmanara@menara.ma; 50 Blvd Zerktouni; s/d Dh360/420; ❄) Centrally located, the Al Manar is suitably towering for its name. Functional and practical seem to have been the bywords for the decor: rooms are fine value for the money, although avoid the darker, small-windowed interior rooms.

Hotel Atlas Orient (Map p283; ☎ 036 700606; www.hotelsatlas.com; Place Syrte, Ave Idriss el-Akbar; s/d Dh512/624, ste from Dh1200; P ❄ 🏊) Oujda's best hotel by some distance, the Atlas is a new and professionally run business-class outfit. Plush rooms look out either to the medina or the lovely gardens, plus there are two restaurants, a nightclub and pool if you're in need of diversions.

Hôtel Ibis Moussafir (Map p283; ☎ 036 688202; www.ibishotel.com; Blvd Abdella Chefchaouni; s/d incl breakfast Dh539/698; ❄ 🏊) Bang in front of you as you leave the train station, the Ibis has all the up-to-the-minute facilities and comfortable rooms you'd expect from this international hotel chain. Off the peg, you could be anywhere (or nowhere) in the world.

Eating

RESTAURANTS

Restaurant Nacional (Map p286; ☎ 036 703257; 107 Blvd Allal ben Abdallah; meals from Dh25) Unassuming from the outside, this is a real Oujda institution: people are virtually queuing for tables at lunchtime (there's a big – and packed – salon upstairs). The salads are great, and waiters rush in every direction with plates of grilled meat, fried fish and tajines. Recommended.

Restaurant Miami Inn (Map p286; 67 Blvd Mohammed V; meals around Dh30) Cheap, fast and popular, this is a good filler for rotisserie chicken, chips and generous plates of salad.

Ramses Pizza (Map p286; Blvd Mohammed V; pizzas around Dh40) Near the cathedral, Ramses serves up decent enough pizzas. It's divided in two – half serves as a café (very smoky), the other is the more usual restaurant fashion.

Restaurant Le Comme Chez Soi (Map p286; ☎ 036 686079; 8 Rue Sijilmassa; mains from Dh85) This licensed restaurant is as close to fancy dining

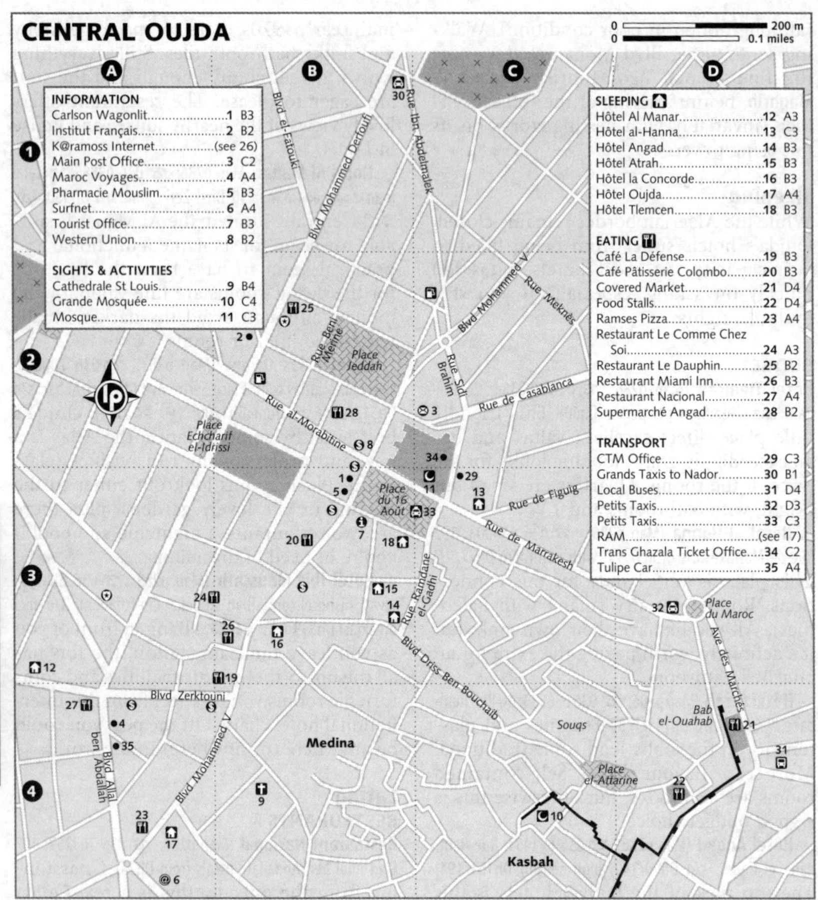

Oujda gets, and is worth the splurge. The menu leans towards the French, with some good meat and fish dishes, plus a smattering of pastas.

Restaurant Le Dauphin (Map p286; ☎ 035 686145; 38 Rue de Berkane; mains Dh75-100) The Dauphin is well regarded for its fish dishes – a reminder of how close you are to the Mediterranean. Waiters pour the wine while you work out which catch of the day is going to end up on your plate.

CAFÉS, PATISSERIES & ICE-CREAM PARLOURS

In conversation on the train to Oujda, we asked a resident the best thing about the city. 'It has plenty of cafés,' was the reply. It's impossible to disagree, and people-watching over coffee, mint tea and pastries seems to be a major occupation for locals (well, the men anyway). The most popular are along Blvd Mohammed V south of Place du 16 Août. On this stretch we like Café Pâtisserie Colombe and Café la Défense, but it's best to just wander and see what catches your eye.

QUICK EATS

In the ville nouvelle, Rue de Marrakesh and the pedestrianised area just south of Place du 16 Août are both good for kebabs, sandwiches, juice and other quick snacks. In the medina, the stalls inside Bab el-Ouahab offer more traditional fare, including *kefta*, bowls of *harira* and boiled snails.

SELF-CATERING

For those in search of picnic fodder, fresh fruit and veg is on offer in the covered market to the north of Bab el-Ouahab, while **Supermarché Angad** (Map p286; off Place Jeddah; 7.30am-noon & 3-8.30pm) is good for packaged goods.

Getting There & Away

AIR

Oujda's **Angad Airport** (off Map p283; ☎ 036 683261) is 15km north of the town off the road Saïdia. Grand taxi fares are set at Dh120, but any bus to Nador, Berkane, Saïdia etc can drop you on the main road for a few dirham.

RAM (Map p286; ☎ 036 683909; 45 Blvd Mohammed V) has two (sometimes three) daily flights to Casablanca. RAM also operates direct flights to France – for more see p481.

BUS

Just off Place du 16 Août, the **CTM office** (Map p286; ☎ 036 682047; Rue Sidi Brahim) sells tickets for its two daily buses: Casablanca (Dh170, 11 hours) via Taza (Dh55, 3½ hours), Fez (Dh100, 4½ hours), Meknès (Dh110, five hours) and Rabat (Dh155, 9½ hours); and Tangier (Dh150, 12½ hours) also via Taza, Fez and Meknès. The buses leave in the evening from the CTM garage further north on Blvd Omar Errifi.

SAT and Trans Ghazala operate from the *gare routière*. Between them they run six daily services to Casablanca via Fez, Meknès and Rabat. You can buy tickets for these services at the **Trans Ghazala ticket office** (Map p286; ☎ 036 685387; Rue Sidi Brahim), opposite CTM, or at the *gare routière*.

Numerous other companies with ticket offices in the bus station offer frequent departures for Taza, Fez and Meknès as well as Berkane (Dh12, one hour) and Nador (Dh28, three hours). There are also several buses a day to Saïdia (Dh14, 1½ hours) to Al-Hoceima (Dh58, five hours). There are also two daily buses to Tangier (Dh140, 14 hours) via Chefchaouen and Tetouan. Buses leave for Bouarfa (Dh54, five hours) and Figuig (Dh80, seven hours) in the mornings.

TAXI

Grands taxis to Taza (Dh75, 3½ hours) leave regularly from outside the main *gare routière*. You'll need to change here for onward connections. Grands taxis heading north to Nador (Dh54, three hours), Saïdia (Dh24, one hour) and Berkane (Dh18, one hour) congregate to the north of town near the junction of Rue ibn Abdelmalek and Blvd Mohammed Derfoufi.

CAR

If you want to rent a car, try **Budget** (Map p283; ☎ 036 681011; fax 036 681013) at the train station or **Tulipe Car** (Map p283; ☎ /fax 036 683861; Résidence Le Paris, Blvd Allal ben Abdallah).

TRAIN

Oujda has a fine French neo-Moorish **train station** (Map p283; ☎ 036 686737), at the west end of Blvd Zerktouni. Three daily direct trains leave for Casablanca (Dh202, 10 hours) and one for Tangier (via Sidi Kacem, Dh202, 11 hours). All stop at Taza (Dh73, 3½ hours), Fez (Dh108, six hours) and Meknès (Dh125, 6½ hours). There's a **left-luggage counter** (per item per day Dh10, 6am-9pm).

BORDER CROSSING

To Algeria

Few people anticipate the Algerian border reopening soon. Buses and grands taxis used to run constantly to the border, and onto the town of Tlemcen. We live in hope they will again, some day.

AROUND OUJDA

Sidi Yahia Oasis واحة سيدي يحيى

The oasis of Sidi Yahia, 6km south of Oujda, is venerated by Moroccan Muslims, Jews and Christians alike as being the last resting place of Sidi Yahia Ben Younes who, according to local tradition, is none other than John the Baptist.

For most of the year it's a disappointingly scruffy place that's little more than a satellite town for Oujda. But every September (dates vary according to the lunar calendar), thousands of pilgrims flock here for a week-long *moussem*. It is one of the bigger celebrations of this type in the country, complete with a *fantasia,* and is worth making a detour for. The trees around the shrine (closed to non-Muslims) are festooned with rags, tied to receive blessings – a throwback to pre-Islamic fertility beliefs.

To get to Sidi Yahia, take bus 1 (Dh4) from outside Bab el-Ouahab in Oujda. A petit taxi should cost around Dh18.

BOUARFA بوعرفة

Taking the long drive south to Bouarfa and on to Figuig can feel like a journey into limbo. The views of scrubby desert quickly fade to monotony, enlivened only by the occasional camel, and checkpoint manned by bored gendarmes (the closer you get to Figuig, the closer you are to the sensitive Algerian border).

Bouarfa is an administrative and garrison town of Bouarfa, as well as a minor transport hub for the southeastern corner of Morocco. It's a useful spot to refuel, stretch your legs and find somewhere to eat.

The **Hôtel Climat du Maroc** (☎ 036 796382; Blvd Hassan II; d/ste Dh380/500;) is the best sleeping option, easily spotted with its domed entrance and desert-pink exterior. Rooms are surprisingly good for this remote location, but order food far in advance of wanting dinner. The **Hôtel Tamlalt** (☎ 036 798799; Blvd Massira; d Dh60) south of the bus stand is very spartan, but bearable for the price.

The area around the bus station has the usual assortment of places offering brochettes, rotisserie chicken and the like. **Restaurant Elwafa** (Blvd Hassan II; meals Dh30), near the Hôtel Climat du Maroc, is the best seated option, with tajines and couscous. **Café Amsterdam** (cnr Blvd Mohammed V & Blvd Hassan II) has pastries for breakfast.

A handful of buses leave daily to Oujda (Dh54, five hours), mostly in the morning. There are also several buses to Figuig (Dh24, two hours). There's a daily morning bus to Er-Rachidia (Dh58, five hours), where you can pick up transport to the south.

A grand taxi to Figuig costs around Dh400 to hire outright.

FIGUIG فجيج

pop 15,000

In the days of cross-border tourism, Figuig (*fig-eeg*) was relatively popular with travellers. Algeria is just 2km away, but it might as well be a light year away. Few people make it here now, which is a shame because it certainly has its charms: a conglomeration of seven traditional desert villages amid 200,000 date palms fed by artesian wells. Once a historic way station for pilgrims travelling to Mecca, Figuig now sleeps its days away, only labouring into action for the autumn date harvest.

Orientation & Information

The main road from Bouarfa runs roughly north–south through the oasis and – in theory – on to Beni Ounif, on the Algerian side of the frontier. The town's petrol station, bus station, two hotels and post office are lined up along this main road, Blvd Hassan II.

Banque Populaire, Figuig's sole bank, has an ATM and exchange facilities, while **Figuig Net** (per hr Dh10) plugs the town into the web.

Where the road passes the second of the two hotels, Figuig Hotel, it drops downhill towards what is known as the 'lower town' – the basin of palms that makes up the oldest part of Figuig. This ridge provides a handy landmark as well as good views over the *palmeraie* (oasis-like area).

Sights & Activities

The parched landscape of Figuig is dotted with seven *ksour* that make up the town, all the same ochre colour as the earth they're made from. Each settlement controls an area of *palmeraie* and its all-important supply of water. In the past, feuding families would divert these water channels to wash around the foundations of their enemy's kasbah, hoping that the walls would eventually collapse.

The largest and most rewarding of the *ksour* is **Zenaga**, which stretches south below the ridge splitting the oasis. Numerous paths follow the irrigation channels through the palm trees and past neatly tended vegetable gardens. Then suddenly you're in among a warren of covered passages. As you tunnel between the houses, look out for some marvellous, ancient wooden doors; and watch out – sometimes you may find yourself in someone's backyard.

The crumbling state of many of the *ksour* enables you to see their clever construction: palm tree trunks plastered with pisé, and ceilings made of palm fronds. It's cool and dark and often eerily quiet. Occasionally you may meet married women swathed from head to toe in white robes, with the startling exception of one uncovered eye. It's very easy to get lost. Village children will happily guide you for a few dirham, or you can arrange a more formal half-day tour through the Figuig Hotel.

In the upper part of town, to the west of the main road, **Ksar el-Oudahir** is home to a lovely octagonal minaret built in the 11th century. It's known, for obvious reasons, as the *sawmann al-hajaria*, the 'tower of stone'.

There's a souq every Wednesday in the lower town, with some pretty local textiles and embroidery. There's also a very sleepy **Ensemble Artisanal** (Blvd Hassan II; 4-8pm), across the public gardens from the post office.

Sleeping & Eating

Figuig has just two hotels, patiently waiting for better and busier days. Nights can be surprisingly cold, so ask for extra bedding if needed.

Figuig Hotel (036 899309; s/d Dh160/190; camping per person Dh35;) is the town's only decent hotel, with reasonable and comfy rooms. In the *palmeraie*, rooms have views towards Algeria: there's no mistaking this hotel is in the desert. There's a restaurant (meals around Dh50), but order in advance to give staff a chance to nip to the market. You can also pitch a tent in the grounds.

Figuig's eating options are equally limited. Apart from the Figuig Hotel, your best bet is the **Café des Palmeraie** (Blvd Hassan II), opposite the bus station. Staff can rustle up a basic omelette, brochettes and chips. **Café Oasis** (Blvd Hassan II), in the public gardens by the post office, is a better option for coffee and a snack.

Getting There & Away

BUS

Arriving in Figuig, buses stop at the 'bus station' – little more than a junction and three ticket offices – at the north end of town. They then continue on to the lower town; if you're staying at the Figuig Hotel, ask the driver to drop you off.

Always try to check out transport options the day before travelling. There are just a couple of buses a day to Oujda (Dh80, seven hours) in the early morning, via Bouarfa (Dh24, two hours). There are more direct buses to Bouarfa itself – get the earliest possible connection if you want to transit and catch onward transport to Er-Rachidia.

BORDER CROSSING

To Algeria

The border with Algeria is closed, but, should it reopen, it's 3km from Figuig to Moroccan customs, another 1km to Algerian customs and a further 3km to the first Algerian town, Beni Ounif.

Marrakesh & Central Morocco

مراكش و وسط مراكش

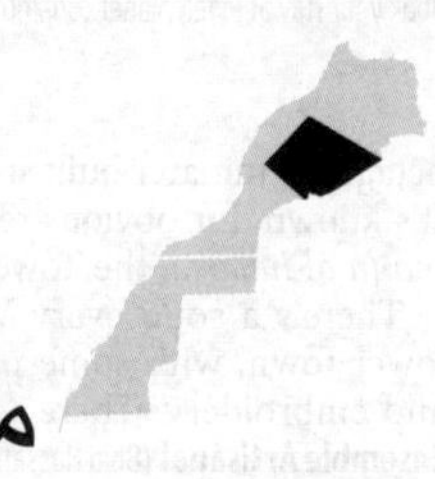

Through no fault of their own, maps can't do central Morocco justice. On a city plan, Marrakesh's walled medina looks like a neat bundle of streets, and the legendary Djemaa el-Fna like a glorified parking lot – but even the best satellite technology can't capture the meanderings of covered souqs and the mayhem of backflipping Gnawa musicians. Towering Jebel Toubkal pops up to the south, but there's no telling how those distant snowcapped High Atlas mountain ranges on both sides of Marrakesh cool the brain on a scorching summer's day. Only on trails between these peaks can you appreciate the treks kids walk to get to school in the isolated Zat Valley, or the tenacity of red-stone villages wedged into rocky crevices in the Aït Bougomez Valley.

Most of all, it seems impossible that so much life should exist so close to the expanse of desert just over the Tizi n'Tichka pass. What you can't guess from longitude coordinates is the burbling river interrupting the stony-faced Todra Gorge, or the rocks melting like wax candles into the green carpet of the Dadès Gorge. Just when all signs of vegetation seem to have dried up in the Ziz and Draâ river valleys, water seeps through fissures and erupts into oases until the landscape is taken over by the Saharan sand dunes of Erg Chebbi (Merzouga) and Erg Chigaga (M'Hamid). Mileage suggests you can return from the Sahara to Marrakesh in one day flat, but central Morocco is the place to put down the map, get lost and live a little.

HIGHLIGHTS

- Catch a command performance of the show that's played for 1000 years, and never gets old: Unesco-acclaimed street theatre in the **Djemaa el-Fna** (p298)
- Find next season's trends made with medieval tools by the crafty artisans in Marrakesh **souqs** (p321)
- Rediscover long-lost social graces behind austere pink walls at an authentic Marrakshi **riad**
- Walk through Morocco's Shangri-la, the stunning **Aït Bougomez Valley** (p329)
- Follow caravan routes on a camel and camp out in the rolling dunes at **Erg Chigaga** (p351)
- Spot red-rock villages balancing atop crags and extreme geological formations oozing into palm oases in the **Dadès Gorge** (p357)
- Witness the original monsters of rock: 300m sheer stone cliffs at **Todra Gorge** (p360)
- Hear the shifting sands sing in the magnificent rose-pink dunes of **Erg Chebbi** (p370) near Merzouga

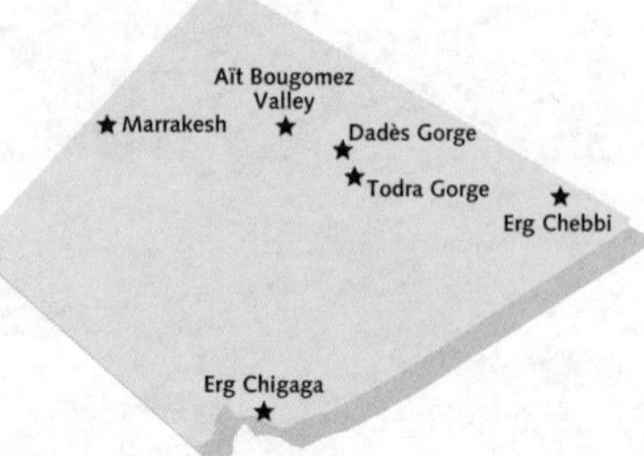

HISTORY

If Dr Who were to muck about with local timelines, there would be a gaping hole in our time-space continuum. On a map Central Morocco appears isolated by mountains and desert on three sides, but it has made African, Arab and European history as the final leg of legendary trans-Saharan trade routes. Trading contacts with southern Morocco may have helped inspire Portugal's naval exploration of Africa's riches – voyages that kickstarted the age of exploration and later European colonialism. Without the Almoravids' power base here to expand their empire into Europe, there may never have been Muslims in Spain, let alone Moorish architecture. Without the sensational Saadian sugar-dealers and Jewish salt-traders here, European meals might have remained medievally bland, and world history would certainly be a lot less spicy.

Marrakesh is often at the centre of this historical action, having served as the capital to three separate dynasties – more than the imperial cities of Fez and Meknès. But other regional players have had historical importance far out of proportion to their size or location. In the snowy High Atlas, climbers may stub their toes on petroglyphs showing signs of human civilisation from 1500 years ago. Songs and stories repeated in Berber village *moussems* (festivals) and the Unesco-recognised Djemaa el-Fna embellish histories of triumphant local heroes and tragic love affairs. In their day, mudbrick *ksour* (castles) and watchtowers along the Drâa Valley were more reliable than tracking numbers to make sure precious caravan cargo reached its destination. Tiny Glaoui mountain strongholds played huge roles in the history of French colonialism in Africa, and also in agitating for independence. Today the area is the centre of attention as Morocco's big draw for visitors and a multicultural Mid-Eastern milieu that's true to its history and promising for its future.

CLIMATE

With geography ranging from desert dunes and rocky plains to mountains rising more than 4000m above sea level, the climate of Central Morocco is one of extremes. Bitterly cold High Atlas winters start in September and last into June, and sweltering deserts will leave you panting for water by May.

Spring and autumn are the best times to explore, with temperatures averaging 20°C to 25°C. April is traditionally sandstorm season in the desert, when wind speeds of only 10km/h pick up the fine sand and dust, and whisk it across the plains. Storms often last three to four days, during which desert travel is inadvisable. If travelling in the desert in sandstorm season, allow a few extra days to ensure you get to see the dunes rather than just gritty brown haze.

LANGUAGE

In the High Atlas the main language is the Berber dialect of Tashelhit (with some pockets of Tamazight). Elsewhere Darija (Moroccan Arabic) and French are universally spoken.

GETTING THERE & AWAY

Marrakesh is the transport hub of the region, well supplied by train, bus and air links. Direct flights from London to Marrakesh's Menara airport are now offered by low-cost airlines such as Easyjet, RyanAir and AtlasBlue, and frequent flight and train services from Casablanca further expands travel options. Royal Air Maroc (RAM) also runs daily flights to Ouarzazate (via Casablanca) as well as Marrakesh. However, you could consider flying Paris–Ouarzazate directly on one of several flights weekly. Marrakesh–Ouarzazate flights go rather nonsensically via Casablanca – it's faster to drive.

A direct three-hour rail service to/from Casablanca links Marrakesh to the major cities in the north. Supratours bus services continue on to Essaouira, Agadir and right down south to Laâyoune and Dakhla. Similar services are offered by CTM and other local bus companies, although these tend to be more crowded and less comfortable.

GETTING AROUND

Except for the line from Casablanca to Marrakesh, there are no rail links in Central Morocco. Buses are still the cheapest way to get around Central Morocco, but they're becoming more expensive to operate as the price of petrol soars – according to bus company officials, all prices may be expected to rise from those quoted throughout this chapter, so pad your budget if your plans include bus travel.

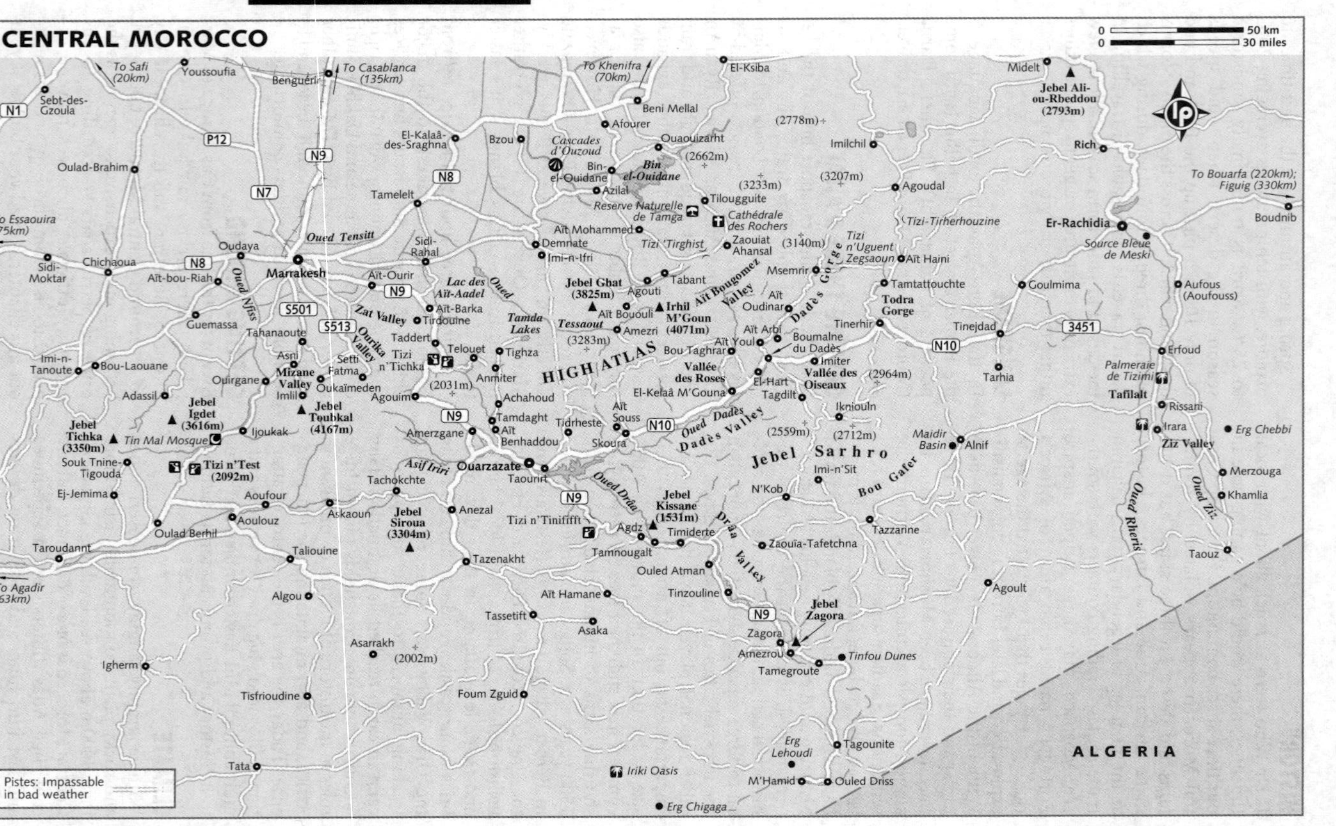
CENTRAL MOROCCO
0 50 km
0 30 miles
To Safi (20km)
Youssoufia
Benguérir
To Casablanca (135km)
Sebt-des-Gzoula
N1
P12
N9
N8
N7
Oulad-Brahim
El-Kelaâ-des-Sraghna
Bzou
Tamelelt
To Essaouira (75km)
Oued Tensitt
Oudaya
Sidi-Moktar
Chichaoua
Aït-bou-Riah
Marrakesh
Oued Nfiss
S501
Guemassa
Tahanaoute
S513
Asni
Imi-n-Tanoute
Bou-Laouane
Ouirgane
Mizane Valley
Imlil
Adassil
Jebel Igdet (3616m)
Jebel Toubkal (4167m)
Jebel Tichka (3350m)
Tin Mal Mosque
Ijoukak
Souk Tnine-Tigouda
Tizi n'Test (2092m)
Ej-Jemima
Oulad Berhil
Aoufour
Aoulouz
Askaoun
Taroudannt
Taliouine
To Agadir (63km)
Algou
Igherm
Asarrakh
(2002m)
Tisfrioudine
Tata
Pistes: Impassable in bad weather
Sidi-Rahal
Aït-Ourir
Zat Valley
Ourika Valley
Setti Fatma
Oukaïmeden
Taddert
Tizi n'Tichka
Agouim
Lac des Aït-Aadel
Oued
Aït-Barka
Tirdouine
Telouet
(2031m)
Tighza
Anmiter
Achahoud
Tamdaght
Aït Benhaddou
Amerzgane
Asif Iriri
Ouarzazate
Taourirt
Tachokchte
Anezal
Jebel Siroua (3304m)
Tazenakht
Tamda Lakes
To Khenifra (70km)
El-Ksiba
Beni Mellal
Afourer
Cascades d'Ouzoud
Bin-el-Ouidane
Bin el-Ouidane
Ouaouizarht
(2662m)
Azilal
Reserve Naturelle de Tamga
Aït Mohammed
Demnate
Imi-n-Ifri
Tilougguite
Cathédrale des Rochers
Tizi 'Tirghist'
Zaouiat Ahansal
(3233m)
Jebel Ghat (3825m)
Tabant
Agouti
Aït Bououli
Irhil M'Goun (4071m)
Aït Bougomez Valley
Tessaout
Amezri
(3283m)
HIGH ATLAS
Bou Taghrar
Vallée des Roses
El-Kelaâ M'Gouna
Tidrheste
Aït Souss
Skoura
N10
Oued Dadès
Dadès Valley
Oued Drâa
N9
Tizi n'Tinififft
Agdz
Jebel Kissane (1531m)
Timiderte
Tamnougalt
Ouled Atman
Drâa Valley
Aït Hamane
Tinzouline
Tassetift
Asaka
Foum Zguid
Iriki Oasis
Erg Chigaga
(2778m)
Imilchil
(3207m)
Agoudal
Tizi-Tirherhouzine
(3140m)
Tizi n'Uguent Zegsaoun
Aït Haini
Msemrir
Dadès Gorge
Aït Oudinar
Aït Arbi
Aït Youl
Boumalne du Dadès
Imiter
El-Hart
Vallée des Oiseaux
(2964m)
Tagdilt
Iknioun
(2559m)
(2712m)
Jebel Sarhro
Imi-n'Sit
N'Kob
Bou Gafer
Zaouïa-Tafetchna
Tazzarine
Tamtattouchte
Todra Gorge
Tinerhir
Tinejdad
Tarhia
Goulmima
3451
Maidir Basin
Alnif
Agoult
Jebel Zagora
Zagora
Amezrou
Tamegroute
Tinfou Dunes
Erg Lehoudi
Tagounite
M'Hamid
Ouled Driss
Midelt
Jebel Ali-ou-Rbeddou (2793m)
Rich
Er-Rachidia
Source Bleue de Meski
To Bouarfa (220km); Figuig (330km)
Boudnib
Aufous (Aoufouss)
Erfoud
Palmeraie de Tizimi
Tafilalt
Rissani
Irara
Erg Chebbi
Ziz Valley
Merzouga
Khamlia
Oued Rheris
Oued Ziz
Taouz
ALGERIA

CTM provides adequate service, but Supratours and other private companies are now offering more frequent departures, air-conditioned coaches and reserved seating to tourist destinations. Shared grands taxis are an alternative, since there's now good sealed roads to nearly every destination featured in this chapter. Mountain regions are best traversed on foot, mountain bike, mule or 4WD (around Dh1200 to Dh1400 per day). Desert travellers will need to hire either a 4WD or camels (Dh350 to Dh400 per person per day) for that ultimate experience at the sand dunes of Erg Chigaga and Erg Chebbi.

MARRAKESH مراكش

pop 1,608,095

From the moment you arrive in Marrakesh, you'll get the distinct feeling you've left something behind – a toothbrush or socks, maybe? But no, what you'll be missing in Marrakesh is predictability and all sense of direction. Never mind: you're better off without them here. Marrakesh is too packed with mind-boggling distractions and labyrinthine alleyways to adhere to boring linear logic. If you did have a destination, you'd only be waylaid by snake charmers, out-of-control donkey carts, trendy silver leather poufs and ancient Berber cures for everything from relationships to rent.

Start at the action-packed Djemaa el-Fna, and if you can tear yourself away from the castanet-clanging water-sellers and turbaned potion-sellers, head into Marrakesh's maze of covered market streets. Marrakesh's souqs are like a cold riad plunge pool on a scorching July day: nothing quite prepares you for the shock. Dive in headfirst at any street headed north off the Djemaa el-Fna, and with any luck you'll emerge exhilarated and triumphant some hours later, carpet in tow.

While you're in the heart of the medina, you may come upon a palace museum, stay

MARRAKESH IN...

Two Days

Get fresh with freshly squeezed orange-juice carts on the **Djemaa el-Fna** (p298), then dive right into the maze of souqs towards the Rahba Qedima where potion sellers promise cures for whatever ails you, from stubbed toes to broken hearts. Up the street, the glorious decor at **Ali ben Youssef Medersa** (p298) will raise eyebrows and lift spirits, Dar Bellarj will show you what Marrakesh's creative minds are up to lately, and the **Musée de Marrakech** (p301) crafts displays provide a point of reference for the work you'll find in the souqs. Shop your way over to **Souq Sebbaghine** (Dyers' Souq) where skeins of wool are hung out to dry, pass the gossipy **Mouassine Fountain** (p303) and unwind with a leisurely lunch at **Terrasse des Épices** (p316). Stop for a coffee or tea amid the Saadian splendours of **Dar Cherifa** (p317), then hit the **Djemaa el-Fna** to take in the sunset spectacle before dinner at stylish **Villa Flore** (p316).

The next day go for the glitz at the **Saadian Tombs** (p300) before getting royally wowed by the woodworked ceilings at the **Bahia Palace** (p299). Grab some *mechoui* (roast lamb) to go from **Mechoui Alley** (p318) and enjoy your picnic feast in the technology-assisted splendours of the **Cyberpark** (p304). Post-*mechoui,* haggle your way into a cab to chill out at the **Jardin Majorelle** (p304), then troll the **galleries** off Rue Yougoslavie (p304) and **boutiques** along Rue de la Liberté (p321). Stop for a cocktail on the rooftop at ultracool **Kechmara** (p319), before your dinner at nearby **Al Fassia** (p317), and cap off the night with a toast in the company of smooth-talking diplomats and shimmying candle-dancers at **Comptoir** (p319).

Four Days

Follow the two day itinerary, and on the third day take an easy day-trip to hike the High Atlas foothills around lovely **Imlil** (p334) wedged between snowcapped mountains and terrace-farmed hillsides. Return to Marrakesh in time for cocktail hour at **Kosybar** (p320) and finish up with an utterly memorable meal in **Djemaa el-Fna** (p298).

On the fourth day go for a **cooking course** (p307) or Palmeraie **cycling circuit** (p305), then get steam-cleaned in one of Marrakesh's legendary **hammams** (p305). Finish in style, strutting your stuff at **Pacha** (p320).

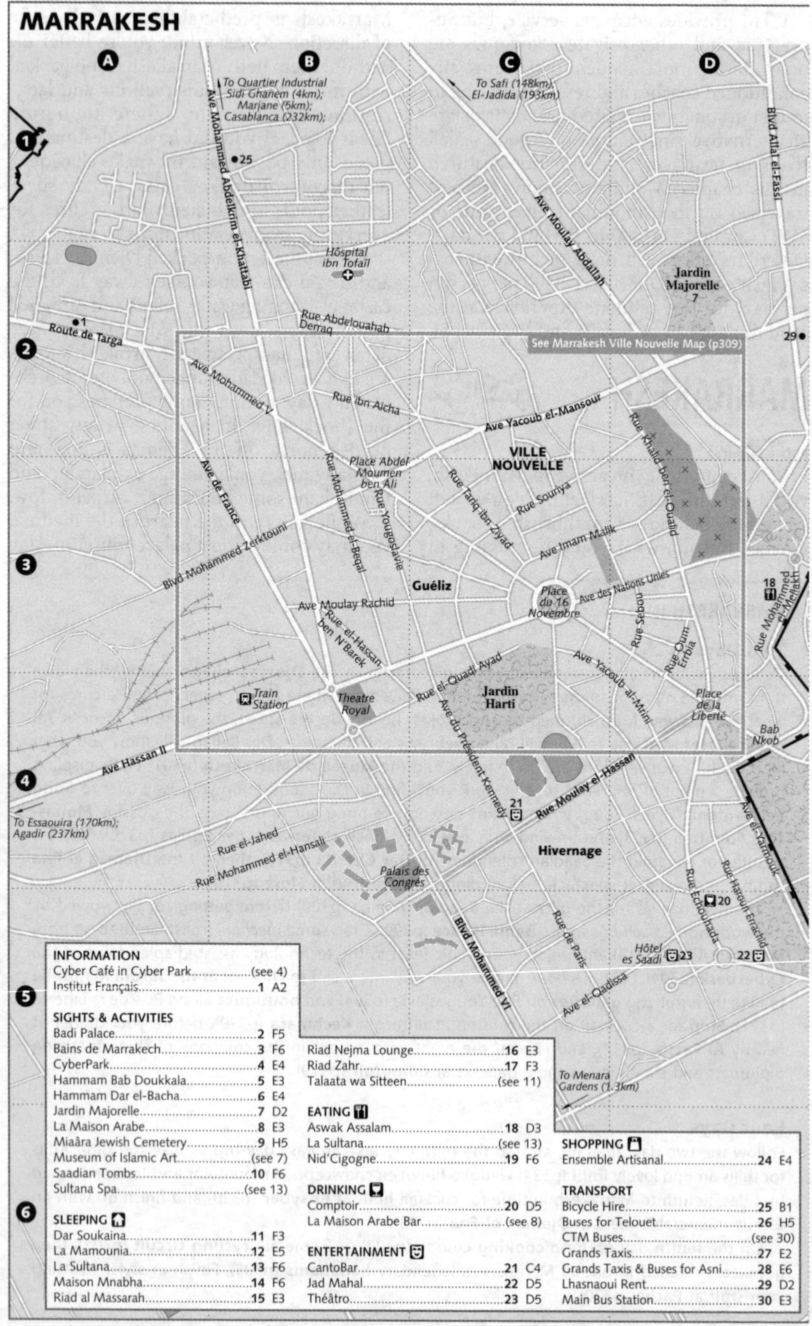
MARRAKESH
A
B
C
D
1
2
3
4
5
6
To Quartier Industrial Sidi Ghanem (4km); Marjane (5km); Casablanca (232km);
To Safi (148km); El-Jadida (193km)
Blvd Allal el-Fassi
Ave Mohammed Abdelkrim el-Khattabi
Ave Moulay Abdallah
Hôspital ibn Tofaïl
Jardin Majorelle
7
25
1
Route de Targa
Rue Abdelouahab Derraq
29
See Marrakesh Ville Nouvelle Map (p309)
Ave Mohammed V
Rue ibn Aicha
Ave Yacoub el-Mansour
VILLE NOUVELLE
Rue Khalid ben el-Oualid
Place Abdel Moumen ben Ali
Ave de France
Rue Mohammed el-Beqal
Rue Yougoslavie
Rue Tariq ibn Ziyad
Rue Souriya
Blvd Mohammed Zerktouni
Ave Imam Malik
Guéliz
Place du 16 Novembre
Ave des Nations Unies
18
Rue Mohammed el-Mellakh
Ave Moulay Rachid
Rue el-Hassan ben N'Barek
Rue Sebou
Rue Oum Errbia
Ave Yacoub al-Mrini
Rue el-Quadi Ayad
Jardin Harti
Train Station
Theatre Royal
Place de la Liberté
Bab Nkob
Ave du Président Kennedy
Ave Hassan II
21
Rue Moulay el-Hassan
Ave el-Yarmouk
To Essaouira (170km); Agadir (237km)
Rue el-Jahed
Rue Mohammed el-Hansali
Hivernage
Palais des Congrès
Blvd Mohammed VI
Rue de Paris
Rue Echouhada
Rue Haroun Errachid
20
Hôtel es Saadi
23
22
Ave el-Qadissa
To Menara Gardens (1.3km)
INFORMATION
Cyber Café in Cyber Park (see 4)
Institut Français 1 A2
SIGHTS & ACTIVITIES
Badi Palace 2 F5
Bains de Marrakech 3 F6
CyberPark 4 E4
Hammam Bab Doukkala 5 E3
Hammam Dar el-Bacha 6 E4
Jardin Majorelle 7 D2
La Maison Arabe 8 E3
Miaâra Jewish Cemetery 9 H5
Museum of Islamic Art (see 7)
Saadian Tombs 10 F6
Sultana Spa (see 13)
SLEEPING
Dar Soukaina 11 F3
La Mamounia 12 E5
La Sultana 13 F6
Maison Mnabha 14 F6
Riad al Massarah 15 E3
Riad Nejma Lounge 16 E3
Riad Zahr 17 F3
Talaata wa Sitteen (see 11)
EATING
Aswak Assalam 18 D3
La Sultana (see 13)
Nid'Cigogne 19 F6
DRINKING
Comptoir 20 D5
La Maison Arabe Bar (see 8)
ENTERTAINMENT
CantoBar 21 C4
Jad Mahal 22 D5
Théâtro 23 D5
SHOPPING
Ensemble Artisanal 24 E4
TRANSPORT
Bicycle Hire 25 B1
Buses for Telouet 26 H5
CTM Buses (see 30)
Grands Taxis 27 E2
Grands Taxis & Buses for Asni 28 E6
Lhasnaoui Rent 29 D2
Main Bus Station 30 E3

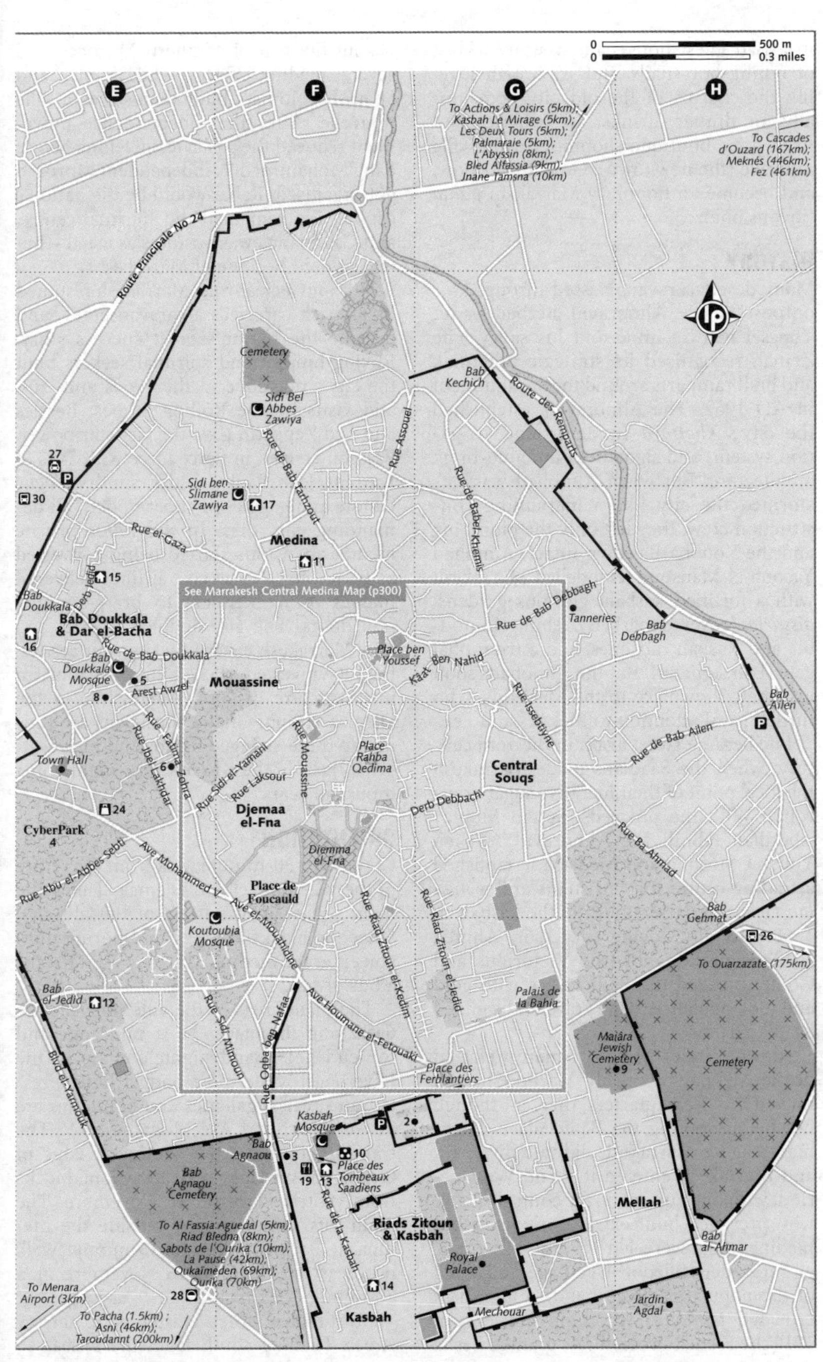
0 500 m
0 0.3 miles
To Actions & Loisirs (5km); Kasbah Le Mirage (5km); Les Deux Tours (5km); Palmaraie (5km); L'Abyssin (8km); Bled Alfassia (9km); Jnane Tamsna (10km)
To Cascades d'Ouzard (167km); Meknès (446km); Fez (461km)
Route Principale No 24
Cemetery
Sidi Bel Abbes Zawiya
Bab Kechich
Route des Remparts
Rue Assouel
Rue de Bab Tarhzout
Rue de Bab el-Khemis
Sidi ben Slimane Zawiya
Rue el-Gaza
Medina
Bab Doukkala
Derb Jedid
Bab Doukkala & Dar el-Bacha
See Marrakesh Central Medina Map (p300)
Rue de Bab Debbagh
Tanneries
Bab Debbagh
Place ben Youssef
Kâat Ben Nahid
Rue de Bab Doukkala
Bab Doukkala Mosque
Arest Awzel
Mouassine
Rue Fatima Zohra
Rue Ibel Lakhdar
Rue Isbebtiyne
Bab Ailen
Rue de Bab Ailen
Town Hall
Rue Sidi el-Yamani
Rue Laksour
Rue Mouassine
Place Rahba Qedima
Central Souqs
Derb Debbachi
Djemaa el-Fna
CyberPark
Rue Ba Ahmad
Rue Abu el-Abbes Sebti
Ave Mohammed V
Djemma el-Fna
Place de Foucauld
Rue Riad Zitoun el-Kedim
Rue Riad Zitoun el-Jedid
Ave el-Mouahidine
Koutoubia Mosque
Bab Gehmat
To Ouarzazate (175km)
Bab el-Jedid
Rue Sidi Mimoun
Rue Oqba ben Nafaa
Ave Houmane el-Fetouaki
Palais de la Bahia
Maiâra Jewish Cemetery
Cemetery
Blvd el-Yarmouk
Place des Ferblantiers
Kasbah Mosque
Bab Agnaou
Bab Agnaou Cemetery
Place des Tombeaux Saadiens
Rue de la Kasbah
Riads Zitoun & Kasbah
Mellah
To Al Fassia Aguedal (5km); Riad Bledna (8km); Sabots de l'Ourika (10km); La Pause (42km); Oukaïmeden (69km); Ourika (70km)
Royal Palace
Bab al-Ahmar
To Menara Airport (3km)
Jardin Agdal
Mechouar
Kasbah
To Pacha (1.5km); Asni (46km); Taroudannt (200km)
MARRAKESH & CENTRAL MOROCCO

in a riad guest house, and venture a dish of piping-hot snails. But it's worth leaving the charms of the old city occasionally for dinner, drinks, art galleries and fixed-price boutique shopping in the ville nouvelle (the new town). Go with the flow, and become an honorary Marrakshi *bahja* (joyous one).

HISTORY

Many desert caravans passed through this outpost before Almoravid Berber leader Youssef ben Tachfine and his savvy wife Zeinab recognised its strategic potential, and built ramparts around the encampment in AD 1062. The Almoravids established the city's *khettara* (underground irrigation system) and signature pink mud-brick architecture. But when Almohad warriors stormed the city like a marauding construction crew, they left only the plumbing and the Koubba Ba'adiyn intact. Almohad Yacoub el-Mansour remodelled Marrakesh with a fortified kasbah, glorious gardens, *qissariat* (covered markets), rebuilt Koutoubia and Kasbah mosques, and a triumphal gate (Bab Agnaou). But the Almohads soon lost their showpiece to the Merenids, who turned royal attention to Meknès and Fez.

Life became sweet again in the 16th century, when the Saadians made Marrakesh the focal point of their lucrative sugar-trade route. With the proceeds, Sultan Moulay Abdullah rebuilt the Almoravid Ali ben Youssef Mosque and Medersa, established a trading centre for Christians and a *mellah* (Jewish quarter) outside the kasbah in 1558. His glitz-loving successor, Ahmed el-Mansour Eddahbi (the Victorious and Golden), paved the Badi Palace with gold and took opulence to the grave in the gilded Saadian Tombs.

Alawite leader Moulay Ismail preferred docile Meknès to unruly Marrakesh, and moved his headquarters there – though not before looting the Badi Palace. High-maintenance Marrakesh slid into disrepair, and Marrakesh entered its Wild West period, with big guns vying for control. Those who prevailed built extravagant riads, but medina walls were left to crumble, once-grand gardens filled with garbage, and much of the population lived hand to mouth in crowded *fondouqs* (rooming houses). In 1912 the French Protectorate granted Pasha Glaoui the run of southern Morocco and several medina palaces, while French and Spanish colonists built themselves a ville nouvelle. After the independence movement reduced the pasha to snivelling before King Mohammed V, independent Morocco got organised. Rabat would be the nation's capital, Fez remained the spiritual centre, and Casablanca was business as usual – but what would become of Marrakesh?

Without a clear role, Marrakesh resumed its fallback career as a caravanserai – and became the nation's great success story. Roving hippies and spiritual seekers built the city's mystique in the 1960s and '70s, and visits by the Rolling Stones, Beatles and Led Zeppelin gave the city star power. Fashion arrived in fierce force with Yves St Laurent, Jean-Paul Gaultier, sundry *Vogue* editors and gaggles of supermodels, all demanding chic digs. In the 1990s private medina mansions started being converted as B&Bs, just as low-cost airlines delivered masses of weekenders to brass-studded riad doors. The city doubled in size, and now Marrakesh eagerly awaits your arrival: the city invested US$2 billion in tourism infrastructure in 2007. Meanwhile in the Djemaa el-Fna, Gnawa musicians are tuning up three-stringed banjos and megawatt grins, just as they have every night for a thousand years.

ORIENTATION

Count on a 30-minute walk from the centre of the ville nouvelle to Djemaa el-Fna, the main square in the heart of the old city. Since the blocks are long and boring until you enter the medina, you may want to take a bus or taxi.

The main areas of the ville nouvelle are **Guéliz** and **Hivernage**. Most midrange and top-end hotels and nightclubs are in the Hivernage, while most budget hotels, restaurants, cafés, galleries and boutiques are in Guéliz around Ave Mohammed V. The train station is at the southwest edge of Guéliz on Ave Hassan II, a few long blocks from central Place du 16 Novembre. The main bus station is just outside the medina at Bab Doukkala, a 15-minute walk northeast of Place du 16 Novembre or a 20-minute walk from Djemaa el-Fna.

Most budget hotels cluster along narrow streets heading south from the **Djemaa el-**

Fna. West of the Djemaa el-Fna is the city's major landmark and handy compass needle: the minaret of the Koutoubia Mosque. The main souqs, mosques and *zawiyas* (saints' shrines) are north of Djemaa el-Fna, while most palaces are to the south along the **Rue Riad Zitoun el-Jedid**. Continue along this street and you'll bump into the **mellah** (Jewish quarter; Map pp294–5). Turn west at the covered Mellah Market, then head south along the ramparts until you reach Bab Agnaou, the triumphal arch leading to the royal **kasbah** (Map pp294–5) containing the gilded tombs of Saadian princes, the current royal palace (closed to visitors), and 16 acres of royal gardens dating from AD 1166.

Guides

Having a guide to the souqs takes away their adventure and mystique, but if you want to cover specific landmarks in an hour or two, you may want one. Just don't go expecting any sweet deals: guides get commissions on whatever you buy, which inflates prices. Some riads and most travel agencies can also arrange guides (see Tours, p308), and official guides can be booked for Dh250/400 for a half/full day at the tourist offices (p298) and in bigger hotels.

INFORMATION

Bookshops

International newspapers can be bought from stands around town, notably those outside the main tourist office and at the Marché Municipale Ibn Toumert in Guéliz, and in front of Hôtel CTM on Djemaa el-Fna.

ACR Libraire d'Art (Map p309; ☎ 024 446792; 55 Blvd Mohammed Zerktouni, Guéliz; 🕑 10am-1.30pm & 3.30-7.30pm Mon-Fri) Splashy coffee-table books about Moroccan gardens, arts and architecture in French and English, plus handy DIY books on cookery, mosaics and *tadelakt* (lime plastering).

Café du Livres (Map p309; ☎ 024 432149; 44 Rue Tariq ibn Ziad, Guéliz; 🕑 9.30am-9pm Tue-Sun) A bookish beauty, with walls of used books in English and French to browse, with cushy seating, book events and poetry readings, plus free wi-fi and tasty food (see p318).

MarraBook Café (Map p300; ☎ 024 376448; Derb Kabada 53, off Ave des Princes; 🕑 9am-9pm) Paperback books in French and English on the ground floor, photo exhibitions upstairs, tea and coffee on the terrace and welcome calm around the corner from the Djemaa.

Cultural Centres

American Language Center (Map p300; ☎ 024 447259; http://marrakesh.aca.org.ma; 3 Impasse du Moulin, Guéliz; 🕑 9am-noon & 3-7pm Mon-Fri, 9am-noon Sat) English-language institute featuring a bookshop, lending library and café where Moroccan students greet you with Hollywood accents.

Institut Français (Map pp294-5; ☎ 024 446930; www.ifm.ma, in French; Route de Targa, Guéliz; 🕑 10am-noon & 3-6pm Mon-Sat) Offers French language courses and hosts worthwhile concerts, films and dance performances.

Emergency

Ambulance (☎ 024 443724)

Brigade Touristique (Map pp294-5; ☎ 024 384601; Rue Sidi Mimoun; 🕑 24hr)

Fire (☎ 15)

Police (Map p309; ☎ 19; Rue Ouadi el-Makhazine)

Polyclinique du Sud (Map p309; ☎ 024 447999; cnr Rue de Yougoslavie & Rue ibn Aicha, Guéliz; 🕑 24hr) Private hospital for serious cases and emergency dental care.

Internet Access

Many hotels and riads offer free internet access or wi-fi, and wi-fi is free with purchase at Café du Livres (left). Cybercafés ringing the Djemaa el-Fna charge Dh8 to Dh12 per hour; just follow signs reading 'c@fe'. Most open by 10am and close around 11pm.

Cyber Café in CyberPark (Map pp294-5; Ave Mohammed V; per hr Dh10; 🕑 9.30am-8pm) Surprise: 15 terminals with fast connections amid the olive trees in the CyberPark, near the entry across from Ensemble Artisanal (p322).

Hassan Internet (Map p300; ☎ 024 441989; Immeuble Tazi, 12 Rue Riad el-Moukha; per hr Dh8; 🕑 7am-1am) A bustling place near the Tazi Hotel with 12 terminals.

Left Luggage

The main **bus station** (Map pp294-5; Bab Doukkala; bag storage per day Dh8; 🕑 24hr) has a left-luggage facility, and there are lockers with padlocks at the **train station** (Map p309; Ave Hassan II; per day Dh10; 🕑 24hr) until the station remodel is complete.

Pharmacies

Phar (Map p300; ☎ 024 430415; Djemaa el-Fna; 🕑 9am-midnight) Central location and covers all the basics.

Pharmacie de l'Unité (Map p309; ☎ 024 435982; Ave des Nations Unies, Guéliz; 🕑 8.30am-11pm) Open late for all your imported drugs, homeopathic remedies and aromatherapy needs. Located opposite Marché Municipale Ibn Toumert.

Money

Most banks change cash or travellers cheques and there's no shortage of ATMs. *Bureaux de change* (exchange bureaus) also offer the official state-set exchange rate and don't charge commission.

Crédit du Maroc Ville Nouvelle (Map p309, 215 Ave Mohammed V); Medina (Map p300, Rue de Bab Agnaou; 8.45am-1pm & 3-6.45pm Mon-Sat) Offers after-hours exchange facilities.

Voyages Schwartz (Map p309; 024 437469; 1 Rue Mauritanie, Immeuble Moutawakil, 2nd fl, Guéliz; 8.30am-noon & 3.30-6.30pm Mon-Fri, 8.30am-noon Sat) Represents American Express.

Post & Telephone

Public card phones are widely available, especially near Rue de Bab Agnaou in the medina and Ave Mohammed V in Guéliz, and cards can be bought from news vendors and *téléboutiques* (private phone offices).

DHL (Map p309; 024 437647; www.dhl.com; 113 Ave Mohammed Abdelkrim el-Khattabi, Guéliz; 8am-6pm Mon-Fri, 8.30am-12.20pm Sat) International courier service; insurance subject to surcharge.

FedEx (Map p309; 024 448257; 113 Ave Abdelkrim el-Khattabi, Guéliz; 8am-6.30pm Mon-Fri, 8am-12.15pm Sat) International courier service.

Main Post Office (Barid al-Maghrib; Map p309; 024 431963; Place du 16 Novembre, Guéliz; 8.30am-2pm Mon-Sat) Poste restante is at window 3 and the parcel office is around the corner on Ave Hassan II. Parcels should not be wrapped as they must be inspected.

Post Office (Map p300; Rue de Bab Agnaou; 8am-noon & 3-6pm Mon-Fri) Branch office facing the Djemaa el-Fna.

Toilets

When nature calls in the medina, try the downstairs toilets at Les Terrasses de l'Alhambra (p318), or make an OJ pitstop at the Café des Épices (p317). Along Ave Mohammed V in Guéliz there are dozens of spiffy cafés where you can nip to the loo.

Tourist Information

Office National Marocain du Tourisme (ONMT) (Map p309; 024 436179; Place Abdel Moumen ben Ali, Guéliz; 8.30am-noon & 2.30-6.30pm Mon-Fri, 9am-noon & 3-6pm Sat) Offers boosterish official pamphlets and numbers of licensed guides, but not much else.

SIGHTS

Medina

Most monuments in Marrakesh are inside the medina ramparts (a 16km circuit). If you do wander off-course exploring the **souqs** (Map p300; 9am-7pm, many shops closed Fri afternoon) and palaces, ask someone to point you back towards the Djemaa el-Fna (preferably a shopkeeper – kids like to mislead tourists) or head towards the Koutoubia minaret (the tallest in town).

DJEMAA EL-FNA

Think of it as live-action channel-surfing: everywhere you look in the **Djemaa el-Fna** (Map p300; about 9am-1am daily, later during Ramadan), Marrakesh's main square and open-air theatre, you'll discover drama already in progress. Snake-charmers frantically blast oboes to calm cobras hissing at careening Vespas; water-sellers in fringed hats clang brass cups together, hoping to drive people to drink. On the upper balcony of a café, star-crossed young lovers furtively plot their next meeting, while downstairs, not-so-incognito Hollywood celebrities slurp fresh-squeezed orange juice in sunglasses and studio-logo baseball caps. But Gnaoua musicians inevitably steal the show, working groovy rhythms that get fez tassels spinning and passersby grinning. To see what comes next, you don't need to tune in tomorrow – applause and a couple of dirhams ensure an encore.

The hoopla and *halqa* (street theatre) has been non-stop in the Djemaa ever since this plaza was the site of public executions c AD 1050 – hence its name, which means 'assembly of the dead'. 'La Place' sees action from dawn until well after midnight, and though you may be wary of makeshift food stalls, pickpockets, and horse-drawn-carriage traffic, stick around at sunset to watch 100 small restaurants set up shop right in the heart of the action. Find the barbecue stall displays with the freshest raw ingredients, pull up a bench and enjoy the show.

Some of the best Djemaa dinner theatre acts haven't changed much in a millennium, including astrologers, healers and cross-dressing belly dancers. Storytellers recite ancient tales alongside dentists' booths displaying jars of teeth. For bringing urban legends and Morocco's oral history to life nightly, Unesco declared the Djemaa el-Fna a 'Masterpiece of World Heritage' in 2001.

Ali ben Youssef Medersa

When faced with something too magnificent for words, Moroccans say *allahuakbar,* meaning God is great – and *allahuakbar* describes the **Ali ben Youssef Medersa** (Map p300; ☎ 024 441893; Place Ben Youssef; admission Dh40, with Musée & Koubba Dh60; 9am-6pm). Look up in the entry hall, and feel suddenly small under intricately carved cedar cupolas and *mashrabiyya* (wooden-lattice screen) balconies. Enter the *medersa's* (theological college) courtyard, and you're surrounded by Hispano-Moresque wonders of five-colour, high-lustre *zellij* (mosaic) and ingenious Iraqi-style Kufic stucco, with letters intertwined in leaves and knots.

Founded in the 14th century under the Merenids, this Quranic learning centre was once the largest in North Africa and remains one of the most splendid. This centre is affiliated with the nearby **Ali ben Youssef Mosque** (Map p300; closed to non-Muslims), and once 900 students in 132 dorm rooms studied religious and legal texts here. A couple of 2nd-floor 3-sq-metre dorm rooms on the west side of the courtyard show how students lived. The original 10th-century marble basin that used to adorn the *medersa* courtyard has now been moved to the Dar Si Said museum (p301).

The school was updated in the 19th century, but the limited bathrooms proved a persistent problem. As it declined, the Ali Ben Youssef Medersa lost students to its collegiate rival, the Medersa Bou Inania in Fez (p236). But the *medersa* still exudes magnificent, studious calm – and now that tourists have the run of the place, the green-and-white *zellij* bathrooms are top-notch.

The Koutoubia

Five times a day, one voice rises above the Djemaa din in the *adhan*, or call to prayer: that's the muezzin calling the faithful in all four cardinal directions atop the minaret of the **Koutoubia Mosque** (Map p300; cnr of Rue el-Koutoubia & Ave Mohammed V; mosque & minaret closed to non-Muslims, gardens open 8am-8pm) The Koutoubia minaret is the ultimate Marrakshi muezzin gig. This 12th-century 70m-high tower is the architectural prototype for Seville's La Giralda in Spain and Rabat's Le Tour Hassan (p121), and it's a monumental cheat sheet of Moorish ornament: scalloped keystone arches, jagged merlons (crenellations), and mathematically pleasing proportions. Originally the minaret was sheathed in Marrakshi pinkish plaster, but experts opted to preserve its exposed stone and time-tested character in its 1990s restoration.

When the present mosque and its iconic Moorish minaret were finished by Almohad Sultan Yacoub el-Mansour in the 12th century, 100 booksellers were clustered around its base – hence the name Koutoubia, from *kutubiyyin,* or booksellers. In the recently refurbished gardens outside the mosque, you might still notice a recent excavation that confirmed a longstanding Marrakshi legend: the original mosque built by lax Almoravid architects wasn't properly aligned with Mecca, but the mistake was noticed by pious Almohads, who levelled it and built a proper one. The Koutoubia mosque is off-limits to non-Muslims, but the gardens are fair game, and a prime location to hear the Koutoubia *adhan* (call to prayer) up close.

Bahia Palace

Imagine what you could build with Morocco's top artisans at your service for 14 years, and here you have it: the **Bahia Palace** (Map p300; ☎ 024 389564; Rue Riad Zitoun el-Jedid; admission Dh10; 8.30-11.45am & 2.30-5.45pm Mon-Thu & Sat-Sun, 8.30-11.30am & 3-5.45pm Fri). Located near Place des Ferblantiers, *La Bahia* (The Beautiful) boasts floor-to-ceiling decoration begun by Grand Vizier Si Moussa in the 1860s and further embellished in 1894–1900 by slave-turned-vizier Abu 'Bou' Ahmed. The painted, gilded, inlaid woodwork ceilings still have the intended effect of subduing crowds, while the carved stucco is cleverly slanted downward to meet the gaze.

Though only a portion of the palace's 8 hectares and 150 rooms is open to the public, you can see the unfurnished, opulently ornamented harem that once housed Bou Ahmed's four wives and 24 concubines. You can also see the large Court of Honour, once packed with people begging for the despot's mercy. Enemies and wives of the grand vizier stripped the palace bare of its opulent furnishings before his corpulent body was cold. Warlord Pasha Glaoui entertained European friends at the Bahia from 1908 to 1911, when his French guests booted their host and installed the protectorate's *résident-généraux* here. King Mohammed VI is more careful about his choice of royal guests, who range from dignitaries to rapper Sean 'Diddy' Combs.

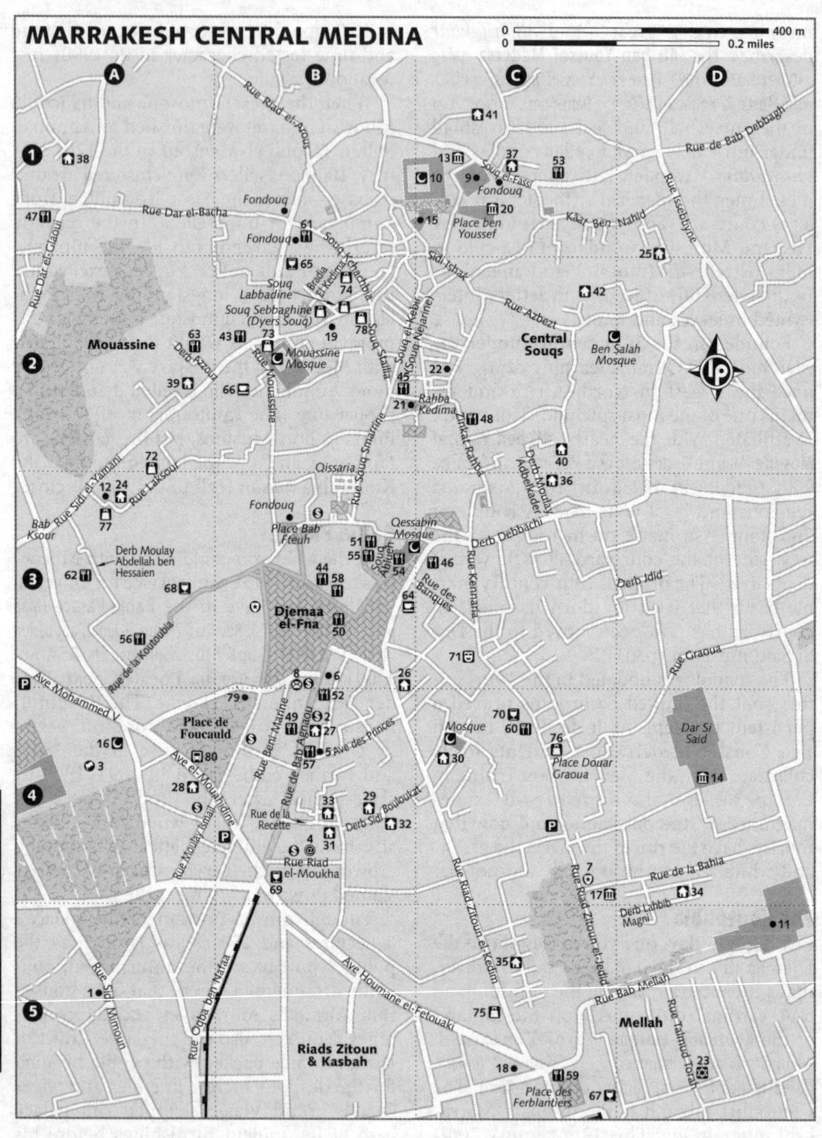

Saadian Tombs

Anyone who says you can't take it with you hasn't seen the **Saadian Tombs** (Map pp294–5; Rue de la Kasbah, near Kasbah Mosque; admission Dh10; 8.30-11.45am & 2.30-5.45pm). Saadian Sultan Ahmed el-Mansour ed-Dahbi spared no expense on his tomb, importing Italian Carrara marble and gilding honeycomb *muqarnas* (plasterwork) archways with pure gold to make the Chamber of the 12 Pillars a suitably glorious final resting place. This Marrakshi Midas played favourites even in death, keeping alpha-male princes handy in the Chamber of the Three Niches, and relegating to garden plots some 170 chancellors and wives – all overshadowed by his

INFORMATION
Brigade Touristique....1 A5
Crédit du Maroc (ATM & Bureau de Change)....2 B4
French Consulate....3 A4
Hassan Internet....4 B4
MarraBook Café....5 B4
Phar....6 B3
Police Station....7 C4
Post Office....(see 7)
Post Office....8 B3

SIGHTS & ACTIVITIES
Ali ben Youssef Medersa....9 C1
Ali ben Youssef Mosque....10 C1
Bahia Palace....11 D5
Dar Attajmil....12 A3
Dar Bellarj....13 C1
Dar Si Said....14 D4
Koubba Ba'adiyn....15 C1
Koutoubia Mosque....16 A4
Maison Tiskiwin....17 C4
Mellah Market....18 C5
Mouassine Fountain....19 B2
Museum of Moroccan Arts....(see 14)
Musée de Marrakech....20 C1
Rahba Kedima....21 C2
Souk Cuisine....22 C2
Synagogue....23 D5

SLEEPING
Dar Attajmil....24 A3
Dar Tayib....25 D1
Hotel Belleville....26 B3
Hôtel Central Palace....27 B4
Hôtel de Foucauld....28 A4
Hotel Essaouira....29 B4
Hôtel Sherazade....30 C4
Hôtel Souria....31 B4
Jnane Mogador....32 B4
Le Gallia....33 B4
Riad Akka....34 D4
Riad Eden....35 C5
Riad el Borj....36 C3
Riad Farnatchi....37 C1
Riad Julia....38 A1
Riad L'Orangeraie....39 A2
Riad Magi....40 C2
Tamkast....41 C1
Tchaikana....42 C2

EATING
Bougainvillea....43 B2
Café Argana....44 B3
Café des Épices....45 B2
Chegrouni....46 C3
Dar Moha....47 A1
Dar TimTam....48 C2
Fast Food Alahbab....49 B4
Foodstalls....50 B3
Haj Mustapha....51 B3
La Maison du Couscous....52 B4
Le Foundouk....53 C1
Les Terrasses de L'Alhambra....54 B3
Mechoui Alley....55 B3
Narwama....56 A3
Pâtisserie des Princes....57 B4
Qissaria Food Stalls....58 B3
Restaurant Place Ferblantiers....59 C5
Ryad Jama....60 C4
Terasses des Épices....61 B1
Tobsil....62 A3
Villa Flore....63 A2

DRINKING
Aqua....64 B3
Café Arabe....65 B2
Dar Cherifa....66 B2
Kosybar....67 C5
Piano Bar Les Jardins de la Koutoubia....68 A3
Restaurant/Bar du Grand Tazi....69 B4
Ryad Tamsna....70 C4

ENTERTAINMENT
Cinéma Eden....71 C3

SHOPPING
Al-Kawtar....72 A2
Assous Cooperative d'Argane....73 B2
Cooperative Artisanale Femmes de Marrakech....74 B2
Creations Pneumatiques....75 C5
Jamade....76 C4
Kif-Kif....77 A3
L'Art du Bain Savonnerie Artisanale....78 B2

TRANSPORT
Caléche Stand....79 B4
Local Buses....80 A4

mother's large mausoleum with intricate woodwork spandrels in the courtyard, exposed to the elements but vigilantly guarded by stray cats.

El-Mansour died in splendour in 1603, but a scant few decades later, Alawite Sultan Moulay Ismail walled up the Saadian Tombs to keep his predecessors out of sight and mind. Accessible only through a small passage in the Kasbah Mosque, the tombs were neglected by all except the storks until aerial photography exposed them in 1917.

The tombs are signposted down a narrow alleyway at the southern edge of the Kasbah Mosque. You can wander around the compound solo, or get a guide at the entryway to accompany you and explain what you're seeing for a modest tip (Dh15 to Dh20).

Dar Si Said

A monument to Moroccan *mâalems* (master artisans), the **Dar Si Said** (Map p300; ☎ 024 389564; signposted from Riad Zitoun el-Jedid, near Rue Kennaria; admission Dh30; 9am-noon & 3-6pm Wed-Mon) highlights Marrakesh's graceful riad architecture and local craftsmanship – though artisans from Fez must be credited for the spectacular painted woodwork in the domed wedding chamber upstairs. Grand Vizier Bou Ahmed's brother Si Said apparently didn't mind living in a construction zone, and gave his *mâalems* (master artisans) time to refine the Dar Si Said into a model of restrained 19th-century elegance.

Fittingly, this crafts showplace now houses the Museum of Moroccan Arts. Don't miss the carved door and inlaid dagger collections on the ground floor, joyous flower-painted musicians' balconies inside the 1st-floor wedding chamber, vaguely threatening kitchen implements in the 2nd-floor *douira* (kitchen), and views over the lovely *zellij* harem courtyard (currently undergoing restoration). Explanations are in Arabic and French, but Anglophones can read place names and dates and enjoy well-crafted objects d'arts on their own merits.

Musée de Marrakech

Maybe the rumours are true of a curse on the Mnebhi Palace, now home to the **Musée de Marrakech** (Map p300; ☎ 024 441893; www.museedemarrakech.ma, in French; Place ben Youssef; admission Dh30; 9am-6.30pm). These low walls and light, spacious arcaded inner courtyard left no place to hide for Mehdi Mnebhi, minister of defence during the brief, troubled 1894–1908 reign of Sultan Moulay Abdelaziz. While Minister Mnebhi was called away from home to receive a medal from Queen Victoria, sneaky England conspired with France and Spain to colonise North Africa. In Mnebhi's absence, autocrat Pasha Glaoui filched his palace – but after independence, it was seized by the state. The palace became Marrakesh's first girls' school in 1965, but upkeep and bathrooms proved a problem.

The palace's fortunes finally turned around in 1997 with an elegant restoration as a museum by the Omar Benjelloun Foundation. Rotating traditional arts displays include Rabati embroidery, Moroccan Jewish artefacts and High Atlas carpets, plus the usual orientalist artwork in the original hammam. Occasional concerts in the grand courtyard are not to be missed, the courtyard café features tasty omelettes and intriguing contemporary Moroccan art, and the bookshop offers a small but superior selection of art books, maps and postcards.

Badi Palace

As 16th-century Sultan Ahmed el-Mansour was paving the Badi Palace (Map pp294-5; near Place des Ferblantiers; admission palace/palace plus Koutoubia minbar Dh10/20; 8.30am-noon & 2.30-6pm) with gold, turquoise and crystal, his court jester wisecracked, 'It'll make a beautiful ruin'. That jester was no fool: 75 years later the place was looted. Today it's hard to guess the glories of *el-Badi* ('the Incomparable') from the stark courtyard. The main attraction here (well worth the additional Dh10 fee) is the Koutoubia *minbar* (prayer pulpit), its cedarwood steps intricately carved and inlaid with marquetry and minute gold and silver calligraphy by 12th century Cordoban artisans and a *mâalem* named Aziz – the Metropolitan Museum of Art restoration surfaced his signature under the inlay.

Check out the stork's-eye view of Marrakesh atop the pisé ramparts, and keep an eagle eye out for concerts and events held here. Bryan Ferry recently headlined a lounge music festival here, and the stately setting adds instant atmosphere to events at the Marrakesh Popular Arts Festival in July (see p464) and the Marrakesh International Film Festival (see p308).

To reach the palace entrance, head through the gate at the back of Place des Ferblantiers and turn right along the ramparts. The entrance and ticket booth are straight ahead.

Dar Bellarj

Flights of fancy come with the territory at **Dar Bellarj** (Map p300; ☎ 024 444555; 9 Toulalat Zaouiat Lahdar; Dh15 for special exhibits; 9am-1.30pm & 2.30-6pm), a stork hospital (*bellarj* is Arabic for stork) turned into Marrakesh's premier arts centre. Each year the non-profit Dar Bellarj Foundation adopts a program theme: in 2007 it was storytelling through film (the centre briefly closed to host a Moroccan film academy) and 2008 focused on women's twin traditions of textiles and storytelling. Arabic calligraphy demonstrations, art openings, crafts exhibits and arts workshops are regular draws for locals and visitors alike; mint tea is graciously offered free with admission. It's located at the corner of Ali ben Youssef Medersa. See also boxed text, opposite.

Mellah

The **mellah** (Map pp294-5; east on Rue Riad Zitoun el-Jedid), situated south of Bahia Palace, is the historic home to most of Marrakesh's Jewish community. Only a few Jewish families remain in these narrow *derbs* (alleys) – most moved to Casablanca, Israel or France in the 1950s – but you can still spot Star of David symbols proudly emblazoned on old doors, and witness cross-alley gossip in progress through wrought-iron *mellah* balconies.

Local guides may usher you into the local **synagogue** (Rue Talmud Torah; Dh20-30 donation per person requested), still in use, and the **miaâra** (Map pp294–5), or Jewish cemetery, where the gatekeeper will let you in to see bright whitewashed tombs topped with piles of rocks for remembrance (Dh10 tip expected). But to see the vibrant living legacy of *mellah* spice traders and artisans, check out the Mellah Market and artisans' showrooms in and around Place des Ferblantiers.

Maison Tiskiwin

Travel to Timbuktu and back again, via the private art collection of Dutch

MAHA EL-MADI

Dar Bellarj Foundation program director, native Marrakshiyya and cultural force to be reckoned with.

Changes in the medina: I was born and raised in these *derbs* (alleys), and I can see that everything's changing, and at the same time nothing ever changes. The souqs and *zawiyas* (religious shrines, usually dedicated to a saint) are still here, and life in the *derbs* continues with our *farnatchis* (communal ovens) and *fondouqs*. You'll see people making pilgrimages next to travellers doing their shopping, which was true hundreds of years ago too. Lots of people say the medina is changing, but really, it's us who are changing.

Watch this space: When visitors come to Marrakesh now, they want to see riads, and though they are wonderful they're not our defining features. Our main monument, the Djemaa el-Fna, isn't a building or piece of real estate: it's an open space for exchange and ideas. It belongs to Marrakesh, but it belongs to the world, too. I think we are aware of that in the medina. The history of trade, religion, art and power that you see all around you here is the world's history too.

A sense of place: Our mothers told us stories about our neighbourhoods, our local saints and heroes – ordinary people who did things no one expected of them. These were the stories that told us who we are, what we could become and about our medina. Our mothers' stories remind us that we create our own narratives every day. Now when women get together for those long hours it takes to finish a piece of embroidery or weave a piece of fabric, we repeat stories we've heard on TV – usually *telenovelas* from Spain or Hollywood movies. But what do these stories say about us? When we lose our stories, we lose our sense of place.

Weaving traditions together: This year at Dar Bellarj, we decided to focus on weaving the strands back together of women's crafts and women's storytelling traditions. We've brought in storytellers from the Djemaa el-Fna and from our neighbourhoods, and they fill in details to stories we barely remember. Even when we sell the carpet or embroidery we make, we keep the stories we listened to and told while making them. We must guard these stories carefully, because they are our children's inheritance.

anthropologist Bert Flint on display in his house, the **Maison Tiskiwin** (Map p300; ☎ 024 389192; 8 Rue de la Bahia; admission Dh15; 🕑 9.30am-12.30pm & 3-5.30pm). Each room represents a region of Morocco with indigenous crafts, from well-travelled Tuareg leather camel saddles to fine Middle Atlas carpets – the gold standard by which to judge the ones in the souqs. See if you can spot such recurring motifs as the *khamsa* (hand of Fatima) and the Southern Cross, the constellation that guided desert travellers. Flint lives in another section of the house, and Maison Tiskiwin gives the impression of a traditional Marrakshi home, complete with tantalising aromas of home cooking.

Koubba Ba'adiyn

No one knows why the Almohads spared the **Koubba Ba'adiyn** (Map p300; across from Ali ben Youssef mosque; admission Dh15, with Medersa & Koubba Dh60; 🕑 9am-7pm). They destroyed everything else their Almoravid predecessors built in Marrakesh, yet they overlooked one small, graceful 12th-century *koubba* (shrine), probably used for ablutions. This architectural relic reveals what Almohad Hispano-Moresque architecture owes to the Almoravids: keyhole arches, ribbed vaulting, interlaced carved arabesques and a domed cupola on a crenellated base.

Mouassine Fountain

The medina had 80 fountains at the start of the 20th century, and each neighbourhood relied on its own for water for cooking, public baths, orchards and gardens. The **Mouassine Fountain** (Map p300; Rue Sidi el-Yamani, near Rue Mouassine) is a classic example, with carved wood details and has continued its use as a neighbourhood wool-drying area and gossip source.

Fondouqs

Since medieval times, most Marrakshis in the medina lived not in fancy riads but **fondouqs** (Map p300; 🕑 9am-7pm generally; individual artisan's studios vary), rooming houses with artisans' studios at ground level and camel parking in the courtyard. If you ever wonder where

Marrakesh gets its wild ideas and creativity from, check out some of the 140 *fondouqs* that remain in the medina. Look for doors propped open to sprawling *fondouqs* near Place Bab Ftueh, Rue Dar el-Bacha, Souq el-Fassi (near the Ali ben Youssef Medersa) and Rue Mouassine.

Ville Nouvelle

If the medina starts to wear down both your nerves and shoe leather, escape to **Guéliz** to the art galleries around **Rue Yougoslavie**, fixed-price boutiques and hip cafés on **Rue de la Liberté**, and the perennially fashion-forward **Jardin Majorelle**. At the southwest end of the ville nouvelle, **Hivernage** offers restaurants and clubs on and around **Ave el-Qadissa** (Map pp294–5) where you can make an evening of it.

For a quick getaway just 20 minutes from the city, try a cooking class, hammam, drinks or an overnight stay in the **Palmeraie**.

Jardin Majorelle & Museum of Islamic Art

Other guests may bring flowers, but Yves Saint Laurent gave the entire **Jardin Majorelle** (☎ 024 301852; www.jardinmajorelle.com; cnr Ave Yacoub el-Mansour & Ave Moulay Abdullah; garden Dh30, museum Dh15; 🕑 8am-6pm summer, 8am-5pm winter) to Marrakesh, the city that adopted him in 1964 after a sequence of events that included in rather unfortunate order: launching hippie fashion; fame as a groundbreaking gay icon; and an obligatory stint in the French military. Saint Laurent and his partner Pierre Bergère bought the electric-blue villa and its garden to preserve the vision of its original owner, acclaimed landscape painter Jacques Majorelle, and keep it open to the public. Per his instructions, Yves Saint Laurent's ashes were scattered over the splendidly restored Jardin Majorelle upon his June 2008 passing.

Thanks to Bergère, Saint Laurent and Marrakshi botanist Abderrazak Benchaâbane, the botanical garden Majorelle began cultivating in 1924 is now a psychedelic desert mirage of over 300 plant species. Fuchsia bougainvillea explode from lemon-yellow terracotta planters, skinny cacti slouch against cobalt-blue plaster walls like wasted rock stars, and goldfish flit through pale-green reflecting pools in shocking orange flashes.

Majorelle's art-deco villa is now the Museum of Islamic Arts, which houses Saint Laurent's collection of decorative arts plus Majorelle's elegant lithographs of southern Morocco scenery. A small boutique features a fragrance inspired by the garden and developed by Benchaâbane, and a new café on the premises offers drinks and fresh lunches at high-fashion prices – but you can't argue with the view.

Other Gardens

Marrakesh has been famed for its gardens since Almoravid times, and though real-estate speculation has filled in many ville nouvelle gardens with high-rise apartment buildings, a few standouts remain besides Jardin Majorelle. Stop and smell the roses while checking email at the **CyberPark** (Map pp294-5; Ave Mohammed V, near Bab Nkob; 🕑 9am-7pm; 💻 wi-fi), an 8-hectare royal garden dating from the 18th century that now offers free wi-fi. Wait your turn for free outdoor kiosk access on park benches alongside teenagers and nervous internet daters, or pay to use the swanky air-conditioned cybercafé (per hour Dh10; see above).

Local lore tells of a sultan who seduced guests over dinner, then lovingly chucked them in the reflecting pools to drown at the **Menara Gardens** (off Map pp294-5; Ave la Menara, Hivernage; garden admission free, picnic pavilion Dh20; 🕑 5.30am-6.30pm). Nowadays dunking seems the furthest thing from the minds of couples canoodling poolside amid these royal olive groves, and clear days bring families for picnics in a stately 19th-century pavilion. Stay for sunsets against the Atlas Mountain backdrop, but skip the evening sound-and-light show, a 65-minute flag-waving version of Marrakshi history featuring lasers and interpretive dance.

Galleries

What will relentlessly creative Marrakesh dream up next? To find out, take a quick tour of the emerging Marrakesh art scene on and around Rue Yougoslavie. Start with **Galerie Noir sur Blanc** (Map p309; ☎ 024 422416; 48 Rue Yougoslavie, 1st fl; 🕑 3-7pm Mon-Fri, 10am-1pm & 3-7pm Sat), a showcase of major Moroccan talent, including elemental calligraphic paintings by Marrakshi Larbi Cherkaoui. Across the street and on the right along the Passage Ghandouri pedestrian corridor you'll spot the polished black-marble front of **Matisse Art Gallery** (Map p309; ☎ 024 448326; www.matisse-art-gallery.com; 43 Passage Ghandouri, off 61 Rue Yougoslavie; 9.30am-12.30pm & 3.30-7.30pm Mon-Sat), where you'll be greeted by ethereal figures in beeswax and natural pigments by Marrakesh's most famous artist, Mahi Binebine, and henna paintings evoking Berber *baraka* (blessings) by Farid Belkahia.

Once you've seen major Moroccan artists, head across Ave Mohammed V and down Rue ibn Toumert to check out next-generation art stars at **Galerie Ré** (Map p309; ☎ 024 432258; http://editmanar.free.fr; Résidence Al Andalous III, cnr Rue de la Mosquée and Rue Ibn Toumert; 9.30am-1pm & 3-8pm Tue-Sat, 11am-6pm Sun). Keep an eye out for Amina Benbouchta's hieroglyphically minimalist paintings, Mauoal Bouchaïb's petroglyph-inspired etchings, editions of poetry illustrated by gallery artists, and gallery opening soirées (always packed, always fabulous).

ACTIVITIES

Cycling

Bikes can be rented in Marrakesh from most budget hotels around the Djemaa el-Fna or at the large hotels along Ave Mohammed Abdelkrim el-Khattabi in the ville nouvelle for about Dh70 to Dh80 per day. For mountain bikes, racing bikes and biking trips through the High Atlas and desert, contact **Actions & Loisirs** (off Map pp294-5; ☎ 024 430931; actionsportloisirs@yahoo.fr; Tikidia Garden Hotel, Palmeraie; 2hr/half-day Dh140/350), **D&O** (☎ 024 421996) or UK-based **CycleActive** (☎ 44 1768 840 400; www.cycleactive.co.uk). To escape city traffic, head for the Palmeraie, the palm-shaded district 5km northwest of the centre where you'll spot mud-brick villages and celebrity villas.

Hammams

For the authentic experience at a bargain price, head to your local neighbourhood hammam – you'll find one near most major mosques, since hammams traditionally share a water source with ablutions fountains. Here entry costs less than Dh10, massage costs from Dh50 to Dh100 and *gommage* (scrub) Dh15 to Dh20. Two of the more impressive historic hammams are the vast **Hammam Dar el-Bacha** (Map pp294-5; 20 Rue Fatima Zohra; admission men/women Dh7/7.5; men 7am-1pm & women 1-9pm) and the 17th-century **Hammam Bab Doukkala** (Map pp294-5; Rue Bab Doukkala, southeast cnr Bab Doukkala Mosque; admission Dh7.5; women noon-7pm, men from 8pm). Bring your community hammam kit: towel, flip-flops, plastic mat and a change of knickers (you'll be expected to wear yours).

Some riads and hotels have their own private hammams in-house. You usually need to book your slot in advance, as it can take a couple of hours to heat the hammam. Community hammams are a greener option, since less water and fuel is required per person to get squeaky clean.

Marrakesh also offers more upscale spa experiences with Moroccan trappings. The best-value treatments are the hammam/*gommage* treatment for Dh160 in the sleek graphite-*tadelakt* hammam inside an art-deco villa at **Les Secrets de Marrakesh** (Map p309; ☎ 024 434848; 62 Rue de la Liberté; per couple Dh150 each; 9am-7pm) and massages run Dh350 per hour at **Bains de Marrakech** (Map pp294-5; ☎ 024 381428; www.lesbainsdemarrakech.com; 2 Derb Sedra, Bab Agnaou, medina; 9am-8pm), but treatments should be booked at least two weeks in advance.

For sheer decadence, try **La Maison Arabe** (Map pp294-5; ☎ 024 387010; www.lamaisonarabe.com; 1 Derb Assehbe, Bab Doukkala), where the basic treatment marinates you in local herbs and minerals with a hammam, *gommage* and *masque* of clay, crushed rose petals and geranium oil for Dh300; massage runs Dh600 per hour. More opulent still is the **Sultana Spa** (Map pp294-5; ☎ 024 388008; www.lasultanamarrakech.com; Rue de la Kasbah, next to Saadian Tombs; P), where you can book hammam treatments in the subterranean all-marble spa (basic hammam Dh200, cinnamon *gommage* Dh350) and four-hand amber-oil massages on the roof terrace overlooking the Saadian Tombs (starting from Dh750).

Swimming

Medina riads are restricted to plunge pools, since leakage from larger pools could endanger mud-brick foundations. Given Morocco's water shortage and the pollution caused by industrial-strength chemical pool cleaners, this is a good thing for the local environment. Olympic-sized pools and water parks in parched central and southern Morocco are emphatically discouraged by Lonely Planet.

To swim laps with a clean conscience, go for lunch and a dip at **Jnane Tamsna** (off Map pp294-5; ☎ 024 329423; www.jnanetamsna.com; Douar Abiad, Palmeraie; admission incl organic three-course lunch with wine Dh400), where the pool is filtered and shaded by aromatic organic gardens. Swimmers might also consider offsetting their 'wet footprint' with a visit and donation to a local charitable organisation (see p335).

WALKING TOUR

To discover the medina's hidden hotspots, you don't need to get hopelessly lost in the souqs (though it's highly recommended) or hit the *derbs* running at dawn. After lazing around the riad or sunning on your hotel terrace, begin your leisurely afternoon stroll at the **Bahia Palace** (**1**; p299) around 2.30pm, just as the palace reopens and before the crowds converge. After ogling the Bahia's intricately painted ceilings, head up Rue Riad Zitoun el-Jedid and follow the signs to the right under an archway for **Dar Si Said** (**2**; p301) where the painted dome of the wedding chamber will blow what's left of your Bahia-addled mind.

Head back to Rue Riad Zitoun el-Jedid and follow the road north past the broken-tile-paved entrance and Bollywood posters

WALK FACTS

Start Bahia Palace
End Terrasse des Épices
Distance 4.25 km
Duration four hours

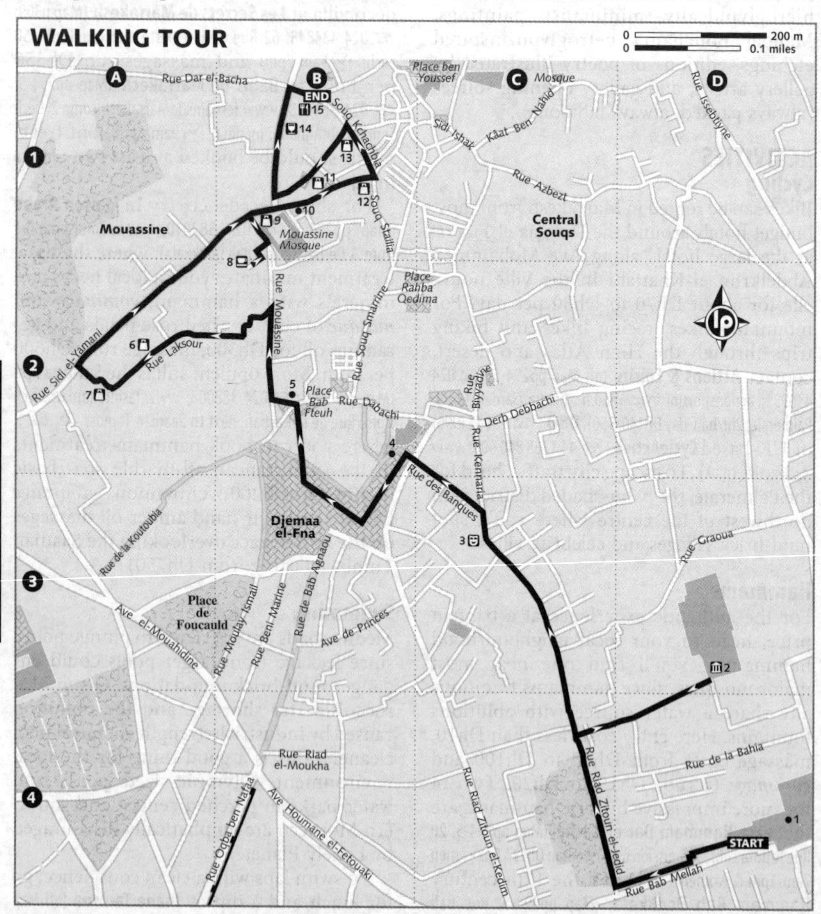

of the **Cinéma Eden** (**3;** p321) on your left to the **Djemaa el-Fna** (**4;** p298). You'll need to look sharp to dodge scooters, horse carriages, slithery snake charmers and henna tattooists who consider your hands blank-canvases begging for art. Head for the mint stalls in the northwest corner, swing right towards Place Bab Fteuh, and cross the plaza towards the covered entrance of Rue el-Mouassine. On your right is the **Bab Fteuh Fondouq** (**5;** p303) where you can glimpse jewellery and trays being hammered out in crammed artisans' studios.

Follow Rue el-Mouassine north until you reach an intersection with Rue el-Ksour, which heads left under an arch. Here you can take a shopping detour loop west along Rue el-Ksour to **Al-Kawtar** (**6;** p321) and **Kif-Kif** (**7;** p322) and back to Rue el-Mouassine via Rue Sidi el-Yamani. Otherwise, continue north past the Mouassine mosque entrance on your right and look for a sign for **Dar Cherifa** (**8;** p317) at your next left. Signs will point you left, then right under an archway to this 15th-century showplace, where you can enjoy mint tea in Saadian-stuccoed splendour. Retrace your steps to Rue Mouassine, and go left a few steps to the intersection with Rue Sidi el-Yamani.

Turn right, and the second shop on your right is **Assouss Cooperative d'Argane** (**9;** p322), tempting passersby with free samples of Fair Trade argan oil and *amelou* (argan-nut butter). Further ahead is the **Mouassine Fountain** (**10;** p303), where you can admire the woodwork or pretend to as you eavesdrop on local gossip. Head through the archway and enter the picturesque **Souq Sebbaghine** (**11**; Dyers' Souq) with skeins of yellow and red wool hung out to dry overhead against the brilliant blue sky. The right fork leads through workshops where felt is made, and just ahead on the right you can follow your nose to the fragrant artisanal soap shop **L'Art du Bain Savonnerie** (**12;** p322). Take your next left onto Souq el-Attarine, and follow this market street as it curves left until on your left you spot **Cooperative Artisanale Femmes de Marrakesh** (**13;** p321). Hook around the next corner, and follow this street to the left back towards Souq Sebbaghine and the Mouassine Fountain.

Turn right back onto Rue el-Mouassine, and just ahead you can stop for cocktail hour on the terrace at **Café Arabe** (**14;** p319), or continue north past restored *fondouqs* on your right to the intersection with Rue Dar el-Bacha. This is where you follow your rumbling stomach to the right, and heed signs for **Terrasse des Épices** (**15;** p316) on your right. Go right to the top floor, flop on a couch, and watch the sunset on your glorious afternoon in Marrakesh.

COURSES

Cooking

Many riads in the medina organise sessions with their cook, where you can learn to cook a basic tajine or couscous. Learn to cook as the *dadas* (chefs) do at **Souk Cuisine** (Map p300; ☎ 073 804955; www.soukcuisine.com; Zniquat Rahba, 5 Derb Tahtah, medina; per day incl meal & wine Dh350), where you shop in the souq for ingredients with your English-speaking Dutch hostess Gemma van de Burgt, work alongside two Moroccan women wedding-feast chefs, then sit down to enjoy the four-course lunch you helped cook.

Other hands-on cookery workshops are available at **Jnane Tamsna** (☎ 024 329423; www.jnanetamsna.com; Douar Abiad, Palmeraie; course incl meal Dh550) where you cook with organic produce from the garden; **Bled Alfassia** (off Map pp294-5; ☎ 024 329660; www.bledalfassia.com; Route de Fez, Palmeraie; rates upon request) where you'll learn the secrets of the chefs behind Al-Fassia restaurant (p317); and **Dar Attajmil** (Map p300; ☎ 024 426966, 064 235954; www.darattajmil.com; 23 Rue Laksour; courses incl meal Dh500).

Languages

The **Institut Français** (p297) offers private classes in Arabic and French any time (Dh250 per hour), an intensive French course in July (Dh850), and courses in Moroccan dialect (Dh1600) and French (Dh850) during term time. To learn the local lingo, you can also get connected with a private teacher through **Study Arabic in Marrakech** (☎ 011 921065; studyarabic@menara.ma).

MARRAKESH FOR CHILDREN

This fairy-tale city makes perfect sense to kids, and the labyrinthine layout gives their imaginations room to run wild. Harry Potter and the Hogwarts crowd might shop for school supplies from the potion-sellers in the **Rahba Qedima** (Map p300), and snake charmers and snail-sellers will give them reasons to squeal with grossed-out glee in the **Djemaa** el-Fna (see p298). Many souq stalls cater for little ones, and in a single day doting merchants might spoil your kids rotten with free treats, toys and sweets. When grown-up company gets old, steer them to the nearest park to meet and mingle with other kids.

If you have tiny tots, you might want to think twice about staying in a riad. Plunge pools and steep stairs aren't exactly childproof, and sound reverberates through riad courtyards. Most riad owners and staff dote on babies, but the same can't always be said of sleep-deprived fellow guests giving you the evil eye over breakfast.

For family adventures with built-in holiday card photo ops, go for a camel ride. Camels usually camp out in the Palmeraie; a 15-minute traipse-about is Dh30 to Dh50. **Kasbah Le Mirage** (off Map pp294-5; ☎ 024 314444; Ouahat Sidi Brahim, Palmeraie; 1½-hr camel ride Dh290) organises dromedary rides through the Palmeraie with Moroccan pancakes at the end. Marrakesh also has a wide choice of horse and pony stables, but the **Sabots de l'Ourika** (off Map pp294-5; ☎ 60 031110; Km11 Ourika Rd; 1-/3-hr walk Dh250/550) specialises in one- to three-hour horse-rides in the countryside. For a horse ride closer to the hotel, flag down a horse-drawn carriage (see p324).

TOURS

Most travel agencies have offices on or near Ave Mohammed V, west of Place du 16 Novembre in Guéliz. Most riads and hotels can arrange excursions or refer you to a reputable agency. For a good, safe time had by all, always request licensed, insured guides and specify English-speaking guides as needed.

Inside Morocco Travel (off Map pp294-5; ☎ 061 182090; Riad Bledna, Palmeraie; 9am-noon & 3-7pm Mon-Sat) Get the insider's view of Morocco on custom-designed, green-savvy adventures with Mohamed Nour, the Marrakshi eco-tourism expert and geologist who with his multilingual team knows every secret Hidden Atlas nook and hidden Sahara oasis.

Mountain Voyage (Map p309; ☎ 024 4219965; www.mountain-voyage.com; Ave Mohammed V, Immeuble El Batoul, 2nd fl, Guéliz; 9am-12.30pm & 3.30-7pm Mon-Sat) This British-owned company based in Marrakesh provides licensed, English-speaking guides for tailor-made Marrakesh tours, sustainable tourism excursions in the Middle Atlas and High Atlas excursions with stays at its own property, the Kasbah du Toubkal (p336).

Diversity Excursions (☎ 024 329423; www.diversity-excursions.co.uk) Eye-opening tours in and around Marrakesh led by Moroccan experts on local culture, history, botany and ecology are organised by the Global Diversity Foundation, and might include visits to private gardens and one of the foundation's projects.

Desir du Maroc (☎ 061 163585; www.desirdumaroc.com) Marrakshi Abdelhay Sadouk has 30 years experience introducing visitors to Moroccan culture: leading history- and culture-tours from Marrakesh to the coast, desert and mountains. Yoga and t'ai chi workshops and English-language guides available.

FESTIVALS & EVENTS

Marrakesh Marathon (www.marathon-marrakech.com; fee €25 half-marathon, €40 full marathon) Run like there's a carpet salesman after you: 5000 marathoners cross the finish line at Djemaa el-Fna at the annual road race in January.

Contemporary Dance Festival (www.maghrebarts.ma/musique.html, in French) Get inspired by this January showcase of modern dance styles from around the world, and hit the dance-floor like a Moroccan Martha Graham.

Rencontres Musicales de Marrakech (☎ 066 102729; www.maghrebarts.ma, in French) East meets West on stage in March with free concerts and events held at Palais de Bahia, Jardin Agdal and the Djemaa el-Fna.

Festival of Folklore (☎ 024 446114; www.maghrebarts.ma/musique.html, in French) Over 40 years old and proud, Marrakesh's premier festival was declared by Unesco a 'masterpiece of cultural patrimony' in 2005 for highlighting diverse dance, music and storytelling traditions from across Morocco each July.

International Film Festival (☎ 024 420200; www.festival-marrakech.com) Stars from Hollywood, Bollywood and across the Maghrib make this week-long festival in December a cosmic event (see boxed text, p61).

SLEEPING

Marrakesh has it all: you can sleep anywhere from the funkiest fleapit to the most amazing palace straight out of your orientalist Hollywood fantasy. The first decision is where you want to be: right in the heart of the souqs down a hidden medina *derb;* in the ville nouvelle, where you'll find hotels ranging from budget to business-class; or in the Palmeraie, for a villa retreat amid the swaying palms. Many people mix it up, spending a day or two in a ville nouvelle or Djemaa el-Fna budget hotel, splashing out for one of Marrakesh's unbelievable riad guest houses, then heading for the tranquility of the Palmeraie or nearby High Atlas.

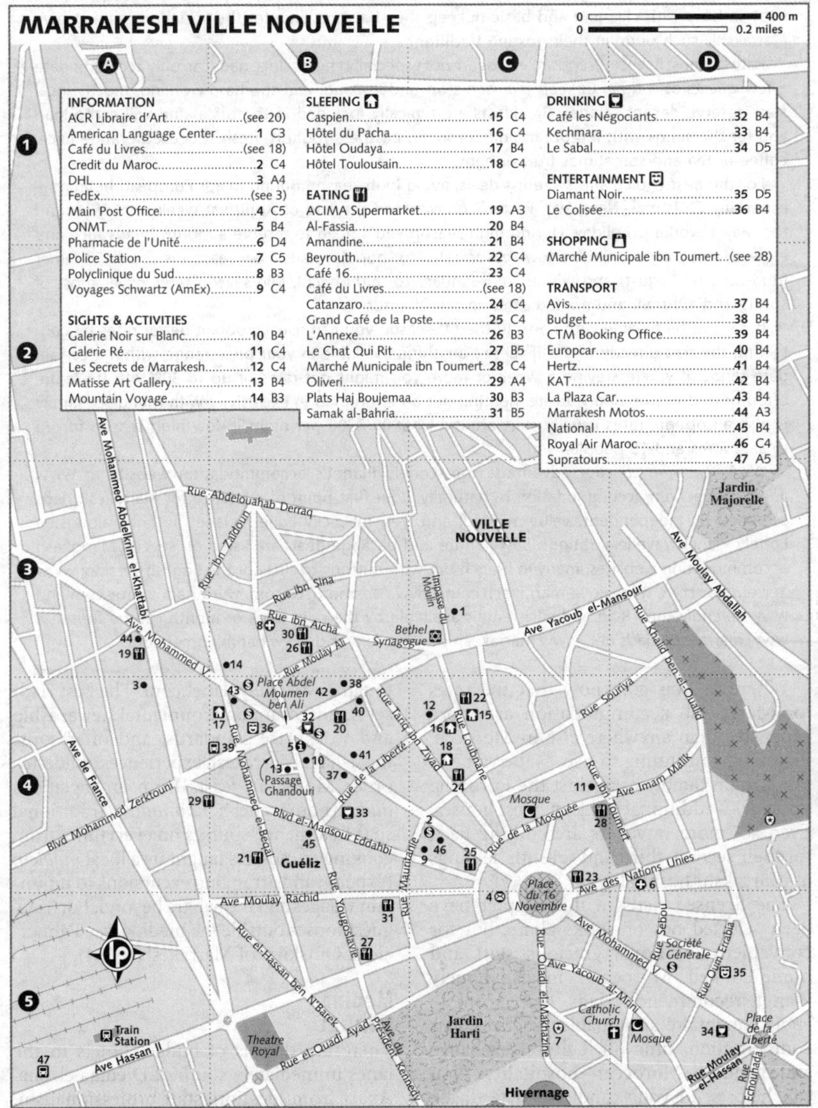

RIADS ON A BUDGET

Staying in a riad guest house lets you experience the Marrakshi art of hospitality, and gain an understanding of Marrakesh behind those brass-studded medina doors. But all is not always what it seems from websites with retouched glamour shots of candlelit riads promising locations '5 minutes' from the Djemaa el-Fna. Some are located in remote medina neighbourhoods far from restaurants, taxis and other traveller amenities, down winding, covered *derbs* (alleyways) that can seem dark and forbidding even in broad daylight. Price is also no guarantee of an idyllic riad experience. Even some high-end riads have only skeletal staffs of underpaid employees, who are kept so busy with cleaning and basic upkeep they have no time for the social graces that give Marrakshis such pride in their hosting tradition.

Rates at most licensed, reputable riads are not especially cheap, since riads can only accommodate a few guests at a time, upkeep is a non-stop undertaking, and the hard-working, mostly local staff deserve decent salaries. Breakfasts are typically included in the price, and will carbo-load you for the souqs with Moroccan and European pastries, yoghurt, fresh-squeezed orange juice, coffee or tea and sometimes fruit or eggs.

For the best choice and sweetest deals, avoid high season during major European holidays – especially Christmas–New Year, Easter/Passover, and the end of April/first week of May around the May 1 workers' holiday. During high season you'll need to reserve a month in advance and expect to pay almost double low-season rates for popular riads. Low season is usually summer (mid-June to August) and winter (mid-January to mid-March). Mid-season rates cover most of spring and autumn, and are indicated in this chapter.

It pays to be flexible with riads. In the off-season you can usually obtain better rates by contacting the riad directly to ask if there's anything available in your price range within a certain date range. If you're staying a week or more you might get rates of up to 30% off; these are often posted on the riad website. Renting out an entire riad in exclusivity with friends or family is also an option; rates usually start around Dh5000/8000 per night in low/high season for up to six rooms and 15 people.

Work the web to your advantage too. Lonely Planet's accommodation website at www.lonelyplanet.com/accommodation is, naturally, your first point of reference for Marrakesh riads screened by independent, value-minded, and, yes, nit-picky Lonely Planet authors, alongside Lonely Planet travellers' ratings. Last-minute and package deals are listed on several Marrakesh accommodation websites, many in French but with buttons to click for the English version: www.terremaroc.com, www.ilove-marrakech.com, www.riadsmorocco.com, www.riadomaroc.com and www.splendia.com. Riad and villa rentals available by the day, week or month can be found at www.marrakech-riads.net, www.marrakech-medina.com and www.habibihomes.com.

Wherever you go, know that the rates for Marrakesh accommodation are more expensive than anywhere else in Morocco. Prices are continuing to rise, as the value of the dirham fluctuates against the Euro, the state levies additional taxes on guest houses. Even so, more travellers are coming back for their second, third and seventh helpings of Marrakshi hospitality.

The licensed riads in this chapter have been selected not on looks alone, but for convenient locations, gracious staff and home-cooked Moroccan meals. Lonely Planet recommends riads that promote environmentally sustainable practices, fair compensation, time off, cultural exchange and genuine Moroccan hospitality. You can help: send your candid riad feedback to talk2us@lonelyplanet.com. The best riads set standards for environmental stewardship and workplace standards, and offer some must-have Marrakesh experiences: made-to-order Moroccan feasts from an ingenious *dada* (home chef); *hammam* (traditional spa) treatments; courses on everything from cooking to mosaics taught by a local *maâlem* (expert); and arranging excursions to mountain villages and the Sahara beyond. For 'riad' guesthouses outside the medina, see Palmeraie & Outskirts of Marrakesh (p314).

Medina

BUDGET

There are dozens of budget hotels in the lanes immediately south of Djemaa el-Fna. Apart from location, staff professionalism, degree of cleanliness and the shower situation, there's often not much difference between them. Since they are small, the best ones fill up really quickly, so it's worth calling ahead. Some will let you sleep on a mattress on the terrace for around Dh50 if you're really stuck.

Hotel Essaouira (Map p300; ☎ 024 443805; www.jnanemogador.com/hotelessaouira-marrakech.htm; 3 Sidi Bouloukat, near Jnane Mogador; s/d Dh90/140, Dh30 for mattress on roof, Dh10 extra for shower) Elusive and quite the colourful character, this 30-room hotel hides out on a *derb* off Riad Zitoun el-Qedim, just five minutes from the Djemaa el-Fna. This former family home was converted to a hotel back in the 1960s, and the original psychedelic polychrome stucco hints at its wild past. Rooms have merrily mismatched decor and the odd sink but no private bathrooms – expect a wait for showers and toilets.

Hôtel Souria (Map p300; ☎ 024 445970; 17 Rue de la Recette; s/d Dh130/170) 'How are you? Everything's good?' Even if it's been mere minutes since you last saw them, the women who run this place expertly never fail to ask. The sentiment is straightforward and so are the rooms – 10 no-frills rooms with shared bathrooms around a garden courtyard, with a patchwork-tiled terrace – but somehow it's all so heartfelt. Be sure to book ahead.

Hôtel Central Palace (Map p300; ☎ 024 440235; hotelcentralpalace@hotmail.com; 59 Derb Sidi Bouloukat; d Dh155, with shower/bathroom Dh 205/305) Sure it's central, but palatial? Actually, yes. With 40 clean rooms on four floors arranged around a burbling courtyard fountain and a roof terrace lording it over the Djemaa el-Fna, this is the rare example of a stately budget hotel. In summer, book cooler 1st-floor rooms.

Hôtel Sherazade (Map p300; ☎ 024 429305; www.hotelsherazade.com; 3 Derb Djemaa, Riad Zitoun el-Kedim; s/d with shared bathroom Dh180/230, s with private bathroom from Dh220-640, d with private bathroom from Dh270-690; ❄) Conversation comes naturally in this laid-back riad run by a Moroccan-German family, with 22 rooms and a magnetic central yellow courtyard with a trickling fountain and floor pillows. Room rates vary according to air-con, decor and bathroom – a couple have slinky *tadelakt* tubs. Between the rooftop backpacker-scene and the gruff muezzin next door, terrace rooms with shared bathrooms call for earplugs.

Hôtel de Foucauld (Map p300; ☎ 024 440806; Ave el-Mouahidine; s/d Dh220/250; ❄) One block from the Djemaa el-Fna, the Foucauld offers spacious, frayed rooms with private bathrooms and a surprisingly good restaurant at the right price. It's a good place to ask trekkers and bikers converging on the buffet breakfast (Dh25) for tips on exploring the High Atlas. Though it may seem counterintuitive, ask for rooms overlooking the street and Place Foucauld, or you'll wake up at 5am convinced you're sharing your room with the Koutoubia's muezzin.

Hotel Belleville (Map p300; ☎ 024 426481; 194 Riad Zitoun el-Kedim; s/d/tr incl breakfast Dh250/300/400) Tucked right behind the Djemaa el-Fna, but with nicer digs and more attentive service than you'd find at bigger budget hotels. What the nine rooms lack in size they make up for in personality: think bathrooms with *zellij* fixtures, curtained beds and high ceilings. Light sleeper alert: get the rooms away from the busy street, and bring earplugs.

Talaata wa Sitteen (Map pp294-5; ☎ 024 383026; www.tlaatawa-sitteen.com; 63 Derb el-Ferrane, Riad Laârouss; r per person with shared/private bathroom Dh280/445) Effortlessly charming, with stools pulled up to pine-wood tea tables, canvas-covered chaise longues on the terrace, starkly chic rooms, and straw mats and sunhats strewn about casually. Not far from Ali ben Youssef Medersa, though a hike from the Djemaa – but chatty, tasty dinners here are a highlight, and the shared *tadelakt* bathrooms are spiffier than you'd find at any Djemaa budget hotel. Breakfast is included.

Le Gallia (Map p300; ☎ 024 445913; fax 024 444853; www.ilove-marrakesh.com/hotelgallia; 30 Rue de la Recette; s/d incl breakfast Dh320/500; ❄) Sprawl out in the air-conditioned/heated comfort of one of 17 rooms around two leafy courtyards, enjoy a leisurely breakfast you could eat off the sparkling art deco–tiled floors, and soak up the rays on the tiled terrace listening to caged songbirds below. Cheerfully run by the same French family since 1929, the Gallia is constantly packed with repeat visitors, so you'll need to book at least a month ahead by fax.

Jnane Mogador (Map p300; ☎ 024 426323; www.jnanemogador.com; Derb Sidi Bouloukat, 116 Rue Riad Zitoun el-Kedim; s/d/t/q Dh360/480/580/660; 💻) An authentic 19th-century riad with all the 21st-century guest-house fixings: prime location, in-house hammam, double-decker roof terraces and owner Mohammed's laid-back hospitality. A favourite with visiting diplomats and artists; book well ahead and enjoy fascinating conversation over breakfast (Dh40 extra, and worth it).

Riad Julia (Map p300; ☎ 024 376022; www.riadjulia.com; 14 Derb Halfaoui; d incl breakfast Dh495-715;) Each room is a tribute to a Marrakesh handicraft, from mother-of-pearl inlay to chip-carved cedarwood. Five of seven rooms have AC, but all are well-kept and comfy, including bathrobes and soft Berber wedding blankets with coin fringes for good luck (wink, wink). English-speaking Ziad arranges excursions, henna tattooing, and dinners under the Berber roof tent. Babysitting service is available.

Riad Eden (Map p300; ☎ 072 046910; www.riadeden-marrakech.com; 25 Derb Jdid, Rue Riad Zitoun el-Kedim; d incl breakfast Dh490-1090;) Generous cooks, a homey living room and energetic young French family owners make the Eden a magnetic, sociable spot. Pull up a chair in the air-conditioned kitchen and watch culinary magic happen. Standard rooms are more snug and sweet than the suites, especially the African-inspired Fig room and the rooftop Orange room.

Riad Nejma Lounge (Map pp294-5; ☎ 024 382341; www.riad-nejmalounge.com; 45 Derb Sidi M'Hamed el-Haj, Bab Doukkala; d incl breakfast Dh495-795;) Lounge lizards chill on hot-pink cushions in the whitewashed courtyard, while wan club kids soak up rays on the all-red roof terrace. Graphic splashes of colour make wood-beamed guest rooms totally mod, though the rustic showers can be temperamental. Handy to ville nouvelle restaurants and shops, but don't miss tasty meals here or shopping tips from the young, hip staff.

Dar Tayib (Map p300; ☎ 024 383010; www.riad-dartayib.com; 19 Derb Lalla Azzouna; d Dh500-850, ste Dh600-950;) Marrakshi owner Latifa and French architect husband Vincent bring on the Berber charm, from good-luck-symbol carpets to winking tinwork lamps. The Yasmina room beats love potions with a canopy bed, tub and mood lighting, and clever rooftop-hideaways end writer's block. Vincent leads excursions, and Latifa organises dinners and cooking classes.

MIDRANGE

Many moderately priced riads are slightly off the tourist path in more residential sections of the medina. The best way to ensure you don't get hopelessly lost with luggage in tow en route to your riad is to make arrangements with the riad for an airport transfer, so that a representative from your riad meets you at the airport, whisks you into a taxi and delivers you to a guide with a pull cart who will lead you to your riad. This service usually runs Dh150 to Dh200, plus a small tip. If you already know your way around Marrakesh but not to your riad, ask your riad to have someone meet you at a convenient landmark; a tip for this service and any help with luggage will get your stay off on the right foot.

Riad Zahr (Map pp294-5; ☎ 024 389267; www.riadzahr.com; 14 Derb El Kori, Sidi Ben Slimane; s Dh540, d Dh870-1100;) A study in contrasts: a chrome table atop *tadelakt* floors, white Verner Panton plastic loungers on simple red Berber rugs. Not easy and something of a shock to find a mod Zen bolthole on the pilgrimage route to an ancient *zawiya*, far from any tourist landmark – but taxis are only a few minutes away.

Tamkast (Map p300; ☎ 024 384860; www.riad-tamkast.com; 10 Derb Sidi bou Amar; d incl breakfast Dh600-960) Eccentric, exclusive and eco-friendly, with just four rooms, organic vegetarian cuisine, a shoes-off policy at the front door and shockingly reasonable rates. One room has a piano and parquet floors but a bath across the hall; another has a bathroom you could live in. Tucked behind the Ali ben Youssef Mosque, but the neighbours are French pop stars and Italian *Vogue's* editor.

Riad Magi (Map p300; ☎ 053 634230; www.riad-magi.com; 79 Derb Moulay Abdelkader, Derb Debbachi; s/d incl breakfast Dh650/930;) Six rooms in shiny lime, lemon and blueberry *tadelakt* you'll be tempted to lick. The souqs are just around the corner, but the rest of the world seems miles away under the lemon trees in this serene blue-and-yellow courtyard. Ask the English-speaking manager about on-site cooking classes and restaurants; food is a favourite topic here.

Dar Soukaina (Map pp294-5; ☎ 061 245238; www.darsoukaina.com; 19 Derb el-Ferrane, Riad Laârouss; s/d/tr incl breakfast Dh790/970-1400/1150;) His'n'hers riads: the original is all soaring ceilings, cosy nooks and graceful archways, while the newer extension across the street is about sprawling beds, the grand patio and handsome woodwork. Omar keeps both houses running like clockwork and can give you insider tips on Marrakesh. A 20-minute walk from the Djemaa, and nearest gate, but worth the discovery.

Maison Mnabha (Map pp294-5; ☎ 024 381325; www.maisonmnabha.com; 32-33 Derb Mnabha, kasbah; d incl breakfast Dh830-1150, tr incl breakfast Dh1800;) Treasure-hunters seek out this 17th-century kasbah hideaway edged with stucco and brimming with elusive finds. In the antique-filled salons, the celebrity chefs, famous authors and other regulars ooh over Khadija's seasonal cuisine. English brothers Peter and Lawrence and manager Aziz are a wealth of impartial antiques advice and cultural insight (Peter holds a PhD in kasbah history), and arrange restorative massages, henna tattooing and eco-conscious desert adventures.

Dar Attajmil (Map p300; ☎ 024 426966; www.darattajmil.com; 23 Rue Laksour; d incl breakfast Dh880-1100; wi-fi) This riad is rosy and relaxed, and you will be too after a few days within these Marrakshi pink *tadelakt* walls hidden in the heart of the souqs. Lucrezia and her attentive staff offer a warm welcome and an even warmer rooftop hammam, plus scrumptious Moroccan-fusion dinners, cooking classes, *zellij* workshops and Essaouira escapes.

Riad el Borj (Map p300; ☎ 024 391223; www.riadelborj; 63 Derb Moulay Adbelkader; d Dh935-1540;) Once this was Grand Vizier Madani Glaoui's lookout, and now you too can lord it over the neighbours in the suite with original *zellij*, double-height ceilings and skylit tub, or the tower hideaway with the rippled ceiling and book nook. Loaf by the pool in the 'Berber annex', let off steam in the hammam or take advantage of mountain excursions. There's a babysitting service available.

Tchaikana (Map p300; ☎ 024 385150; www.tchaikana.com; 25 Derb el Ferrane 25; d incl breakfast Dh1100-1800) To give you a sense of the scale and sensibility here, one room has a boat hull suspended from the ceiling, and another has Tuareg tent posts. Everything is cushy, creative and eco-friendly: nubby natural fabrics, organic cuisine, and fans instead of air-con. Arriving here via the winding, dark *derb* is only intimidating the first time, but the English-speaking Belgian owners can have staff walk you at night.

TOP END

Riad Akka (Map p300; ☎ 024 375767; www.riad-akka.com; 65 Derb Lahbib Magni, near Rue Riad Zitoun el-Jedid; d incl breakfast Dh1200-1500; wi-fi) With Arabic sayings about cross-cultural understanding painted around the patio and ingenious graphite-*tadelakt*–guest rooms, the Akka's decor is impeccably hip, cosmopolitan and upbeat – and the same can be said about the staff. Trust manager Mbarka for restaurant- and shopping-recommendations, and splash out for the in-house hammam.

Riad Al Massarah (Map pp294-5; ☎ 024383206; www.riadalmassarah.com; 26 Derb Jedid; d incl breakfast Dh1200-2000; wi-fi) The ultimate feel-good hideaway: British-French owners Michel and Michael redesigned this ancient riad to maximise comfort and sunlight, and minimise electrical and water use and eco-impact. Offers top-notch hammam, massages, cooking lessons and eco-excursions – all while donating to local nonprofits and providing full benefits to a staff of five.

Riad L'Orangeraie (Map p300; ☎ 061 238789; www.riadorangeraie.com; 61 Rue Sidi el-Yamani; d incl breakfast Dh1430-1870; wi-fi) Smooth and suave, with perfectly buffed *tadelakt* walls, massaging showers (the best in town), a generous pool and sprawling rooms. This place has all the right moves, with five employees looking after seven rooms, a car and driver on call, excellent breakfasts and soothing hammam treatments.

Riad Farnatchi (Map p300; ☎ 024 384910; www.riadfarnatchi.com; 2 Derb el-Farnatchi, Ka'at Benahid; ste incl breakfast Dh3400-4750; wi-fi) Everything here aims to please: private salons aglow with skylights and fireplaces, sumptuous suede coverlets begging a snuggle, magically appearing cookies and canapés, and a jellaba and slippers in your size to lounge around the riad and take home. Before you describe your dream five-star vacation, Canadian director Lynn Perez and her expert English-speaking staff have already arranged it: chauffeured cars, personal shoppers, in-house hammam, massages, projected movies with popcorn, the works.

Ville Nouvelle

BUDGET

The ville nouvelle has a few budget options off Ave Mohammed V, near Blvd Mohammed Zerktouni, Rue Tariq ibn Ziad and Rue ibn Aicha.

Hôtel Toulousain (Map p309; ☎ 024 430033; www.geocities.com/hotel_toulousain; 44 Rue Tariq ibn Ziad; s/d with shared bathroom Dh140/190, s/d with private shower

& shared toilet Dh150/200, s/d with private bathroom Dh180/230, all incl breakfast) An easygoing budget hotel run by a kindly Moroccan-American family in the heart of Guéliz. The 31 rooms aren't glamorous and 1st-floor rooms can get stuffy in summer, so guests hang out in the tranquil patios under the banana trees. Here you're surrounded by boutiques and inexpensive, tasty restaurants, and next door to a literary café.

Hôtel du Pacha (Map p309; ☎ 024 431327; fax 024 431326; 33 Rue de la Liberté; s/d Dh275/360;) Novels practically beg to be set in this period-piece colonial hotel, with balconies and tall French windows to catch the breeze and neighbourhood gossip. Rooms are high-ceilinged and old-fashioned; the stuccoed entry, Bogart-style bar and courtyard add *noir*-novel charm. Skip the Dh30 breakfast and head down the street to gorgeous patisseries.

Hôtel Oudaya (Map p309; ☎ 024 448512; www.oudaya.ma; 147 Rue Mohammed el-Beqal; s/d/tr incl breakfast Dh380/500/690, ste incl breakfast from Dh720;) What looks like a Soviet kasbah on the outside opens into a grand courtyard draped with bougainvillea with a swimming pool and grassy knoll. All 77 rooms have hotel hammam- and pool-access plus marble bathrooms and geometric-pattern wood trim.

Caspien (Map p309; ☎ 024 422282; www.lecaspien-hotel.com; 12 Rue Loubnane; s/d Dh440/560;) Central yet quiet location, sharp staff and not so big that you get lost in the shuffle of tour groups in this newish hotel. Pointed archways, *zellij* on floors, pierced-brass lamps and balconies add Marrakesh atmosphere. For maximum quiet, choose upper-floor rooms overlooking the pool.

MIDRANGE & TOP END

On the edge of the ville nouvelle are more than enough big, gleaming, characterless hotels to keep tour groups and conference delegates under quarantine. The bulk of the midrange hotels are in Guéliz or in the quieter and more leafy Hivernage area. Most of the larger hotels with swimming pools in this category are cheaper when booked as part of a package including flights; search online for deals.

For lower rates, riads offer a much more memorable Marrakshi experience – but if you're in town strictly for business, you'll find the usual chain hotels clustered along Ave Mohammed VI (near the Palais des Congrès) and further out of town on the road to Casablanca. At the time of writing, the art-deco grande dame of swanky Marrakesh hotels, **La Mamounia** (Map pp294-5; ☎ 024 388600; www.mamounia.com; Ave Houmane el-Fetouaki;), was still closed for refurbishment despite a promised 2008 reopening date; check the websites for updates.

Palmeraie & Outskirts

When the medina seems a bit much, villas in the Palmeraie let you chill out in a palm oasis. Once your blood pressure dips and you begin to miss the madness of Marrakesh, you're within a 30-minute drive from the heart of the action. A taxi drive into town is the easiest way, but is rather costly (Dh150 to Dh250) since you often have to pay for the driver's round-trip to fetch you. The ideal combination would be to stay in a hotel or riad in the medina for a few days, then have a few days of luxurious bliss away from it all.

MIDRANGE

Riad Bledna (☎ 015396 20195; www.riadbledna.com; 2km, Route de Ouarzazate; d incl breakfast Dh600-800) A sweet eco-retreat run by a Moroccan-British family who've thought of your every comfort, as well as the environment, too. Four bright, welcoming, solar-powered guest rooms are set amid 4 acres of organic gardens, putting compost and water to use and yielding scrumptious meals. A wide range of English-language Moroccan arts courses are offered, including weaving, *tadelakt*, *zellij* and *zellij*-patchwork quilting. Stays can be combined with a day trek, river hike to remote Berber villages, or picnic in a desert ghost town.

our pick **La Pause** (☎ 061 306494; www.lapause-marrakech.com; Douar Lmih Laroussiéne, Commune Agafay; d half-board from Dh1100;) Skip off the grid to a desert getaway 45 minutes from Marrakesh (chauffeured transport to/from Marrakesh provided with rates). Play a round of turf-free golf or all-terrain disc golf using available clubs or Frisbees, or hang out in a hammock under olive trees by the filtered swimming pool. Days are for exploring the desert on foot, bike, Arabian stallion, or dromedary, and night brings starry skies and candlelit organic feasts in Berber tents.

Sleep in generous Berber tents with foam mattresses, thick carpets and outdoor showers overlooking the riverbed, or read by firelight in your own minimalist-chic, solar-powered mud-brick abode.

TOP END

Les Deux Tours (Map pp294-5; ☎ 024 329525; www.les-deuxtours.com; Douar Abiad, Circuit de la Palmeraie; s/d incl breakfast Dh2120/2240, ste s/d from Dh2620/2740; wi-fi) Tunisian architect Charles Boccara's modern Moroccan guest house started the Palmeraie villa trend and the hotel hammam craze – but few of its cookie-cutter neighbours in this oasis can match its amenities and distinctive style. Set in secret gardens are mazes of guest rooms with private balconies and hidden passageways, the legendary hammam spa and the traditional reflecting pool that makes cocktail sipping loungers seem both larger and skinnier than life.

Jnane Tamsna (off Map pp294-5; ☎ 024 329423; www.jnanetamsna.com; Douar Abiad, Palmeraie; d incl breakfast from Dh2200, ste incl breakfast from Dh3700; wi-fi) A-list celebrities like Brad Pitt, Giorgio Armani and David Bowie flock to this North African nirvana, a jigsaw of elegant patios and intimate terraces amid a 6-acre organic farm. Meryanne Loum-Martin raises the bar for responsible tourism with water-conserving plants, filtered pools, all-organic cuisine, a Fair-Trade design boutique and cultural immersion 'Diversity Excursions' run by her English ethnobotanist husband, Gary. Cooking classes, yoga retreats and literary salons here are runaway successes – Booker Prize winner Kirin Desai taught a recent workshop, with proceeds going to local literacy programs.

EATING

Slow-roasted lamb cooked in a hammam, spiced briny green olives, cumin-spiked roasted-eggplant caviar, hearty white bean soup…Marrakesh's traditional specialties are mouthwatering enough, but that's only the first page of the menu in Marrakesh. Sundrenched local produce, Mediterranean inspirations and a craze for Asian flavours have added unexpected twists to the local menu – think Corsican pizza with Atlas Mountain herbs, duck breast salad drizzled with argan oil dressing, Thai curries with Moroccan mint and more.

If you're staying at a riad, home-cooking is another tempting option. Many riad chefs are *dadas* who once cooked for Marrakesh's high society, so the meals you enjoy on your riad terrace may very well be wedding-worthy by local standards.

The least thrilling part of the Marrakesh dining experience is the arrival of the bill. Marrakshis don't eat out often, and with Dh65 to Dh80 for a scrawny chicken tajine on the Djemaa and set-price restaurant menus starting at Dh300-plus, you can see why. Good-value restaurants can be found, especially in the ville nouvelle, but they're struggling to keep prices down. Local cooking methods are labour-intensive, and ingredients are becoming more expensive as fuel prices rise.

Medina

Around sunset, donkeys descend on the Djemaa el-Fna hauling gas canisters by the cartload and all the makings of a hundred small restaurants. Within the hour, the restaurants are up and running, with chefs urging passersby to note the cleanliness of their grills, the freshness of their meat, produce and cooking oil, and their aromatic spice mixes. The grilled meats and cooked salads are cheap and often tasty, and despite alarmist warnings, your stomach should be fine if you use your bread instead of rinsed utensils and stick to bottled water. Adventurous foodies will want to try steaming snail soups, sheep's brain and skewered hearts – always go for the busiest stalls with the freshest meats.

Budget

Haj Mustapha (Map p300; east side of Souq Ablueh; tangia with bread & olives Dh35-50; 6-10pm) As dusk approaches, several stalls set out paper-sealed crockpots of *tangia* (lamb slow-cooked all day in the ashes of a hammam). This 'bachelor's stew' makes for messy eating, but Haj Mustapha offers the cleanest seating despite dire bachelor decor (eg faded photos in shattered picture frames). Use bread as your utensil to scoop up *tangia,* sprinkle with cumin and salt, and devour with olives.

Chegrouni (Map pp294-5; near Rue des Banques; tajine Dh50-70, omelette Dh25-35; 8am-11pm) You're expected to write down your own order, but your server could probably guess it anyway:

you're either a foodie here for the classic Dh50 tajine with chicken, preserved lemons and olives; a vegetarian in for flavourful vegetable-broth-only seven-vegetable couscous; or a tajine-weary traveller in dire need of a decent omelette with superior chips.

Bougainvillea (Map p300; ☎ 024 441111; 33 Rue Mouassine, cnr Rue Sidi el-Yamani; sandwiches Dh25-60; 11am-10pm) Recharge for your next lap of the souqs in this centrally located, arty fuschia riad with fresh-squeezed juices and serviceable sandwiches near the wall-o-water *zellij* fountain.

Nid'Cigogne (Map pp294-5; ☎ 024 382092; 60 Place des Tombeaux Saadiens; meals Dh40-85; 9am-9pm) Get up close and personal with the storks across the way at the Saadian Tombs in this rooftop eatery. The grilled *kefta* (meatball) sandwiches, light salads and tajines are passable, but the view is memorable and service pleasant considering those steep stairs.

La Maison du Couscous (Map p300; ☎ 024 386892; 53 Rue Bab Agnaou; couscous Dh65-85; 11.30am-10pm;) With its couscous-shaped fountain and Arctic air-conditioning, this place screams 'tourist trap' – but locals come for properly fluffy couscous infused with fragrant *smen* (seasoned clarified butter). The Atlas chicken couscous is sweet-savoury with onions, and at the risk of inflaming local rivalries, the spicy Tunisian with Merguez sausage and meatballs (Dh85) is even better.

Midrange

Ryad Jama (Map p300; ☎ 024 429872; 149 Toualat Kennaria; meals Dh70-90; 11am-4pm) À la carte lunches at realistic prices served in a family-run riad restaurant. Generous lamb tajines with prunes and almonds are graciously presented in the leafy garden for only slightly more than you'd pay for a skimpy version shoved your way in the dusty Djemaa.

Dar TimTam (Map p300; ☎ 024 391446; Zinkat Rahba, near the Rahba Kedima; salads Dh65, lunches Dh120-150; 11.30am-4pm) Head through the dim restaurant and into this 18th-century riad's innermost courtyard, where rejuvenating mint tea and a generous assortment of salads makes a fine light lunch amid the songbirds.

our pick **Villa Flore** (Map p300; ☎ 024 391700; www.villa-flore.com; 4 Derb Azzouz; mains Dh80-120; 12.30-3pm & 7.30-11pm) Dine in an art-deco-fabulous black-and-white riad on reinvented Moroccan salads and aromatic, meltingly tender lamb and duck, all presented in neat circles by stylishly suited waiters. Pull up a sofa near the French doors or sit in the sunny courtyard and unwind with a glass of wine, right in the heart of the souqs.

Le Foundouk (Map p300; ☎ 024 378190; www.foundouk.com; 55 Souq el-Fassi near Ali ben Youssef Medersa; mains Dh90-160; noon-1am Tue-Sun) An enormous, spidery iron-chandelier lit with candles sets the mood for offbeat à la carte choices, including beef with wild artichoke and orange-carrot soup. When the food lives up to the decor, it's fabulous, and when not, well, at least you got your money's worth for atmosphere. Terrace seating is scenic but chilly, and you'll need to call well in advance for sought-after downstairs seating.

Terrasse des Épices (Map p300; ☎ 024 375904; 15 Souq Cherifia; set meal Dh100-150) Head to the roof for lunch on top of the world in a mud-brick *bhou* (booth). Check the chalkboard for the Dh100 fixed-price special: Moroccan salads followed by scrawny but scrumptious chicken-leg tajine with fries, then strawberries and mint. Reservations are handy in high season.

Narwama (Map p300; ☎ 024 442510; 30 Rue el-Koutoubia, near Djemaa el-Fna; mains Dh80-140; 8pm-1am) Opposites attract at Narwama, true to its name (fire and water) with unconventional combinations: Thai green curries and almond-and-cream *bastilla* (pastry), a DJ spinning Brazilian/Italian/Arabic tunes, and the best Moroccan mint mojito in town, all in a 19th-century riad with 21st-century Zen decor. Alcohol is served here.

Top End

Dar Moha (Map p300; ☎ 024 386400; www.darmoha.ma; 81 Rue Dar el-Bacha; Dh220 lunch, à la carte dinner from Dh250; lunch noon-3pm & dinner 7.30pm-midnight Tue-Sun) Chef Mohammed Fedal gives tastebuds a tweak with clever variations on Moroccan ingredients: a '*zellij*' of grilled seasonal vegetables with Berber herbs, a pear topped with saffron sorbet and toasted almonds. The set Dh220 lunch menu is a more traditional feast, with dish after irresistible dish of orange-flower scented cucumbers and spice-rubbed grilled lamb chops. Alcohol is served here.

Tobsil (Map p300; ☎ 024 444052; 22 Derb Moulay Abdellah ben Hessaien, near Bab Ksour; 5-course menu incl wine Dh600; 7.30-11pm Wed-Mon, booking required) In this intimate riad, 50 guests max indulge in button-popping five-course menus with aperitifs and wine pairings, as Gnawa musicians play in the courtyard. No excess glitz or bellydancers distract from upstanding *mezze* (salads), *bastilla*, tajines (yes, that's plural) and couscous, capped with mint tea, fresh fruit and Moroccan pastries.

La Sultana (Map pp294-5; 024 388008; www.lasultanamarrakech.com; Rue de la Kasbah; à la carte main Dh200-plus, set meals Dh450-600; lunch & dinner) Do you dine in the intimate cloisters, or on the roof overlooking the Saadian Tombs? Would you prefer the French duck that's more tender than your last love affair, or the Moroccan *pastilla* so light it could blow away in rooftop breezes? Prices are high, service is slow and reservations essential, but the food and setting are sublime. Alcohol is served here.

VILLE NOUVELLE

The majority of restaurants in the ville nouvelle serve international cuisine, but you can also sample some fine Moroccan fare in this European oasis. All of these places serve alcohol.

Budget

Catanzaro (Map p309; 024 433731; 42 Rue Tariq ibn Ziyad, Guéliz; pizzas or pasta Dh60-80, mains Dh80-120; noon-2.30pm & 7.30-11pm Mon-Sat;) Where are we, exactly? The thin-crust, wood-fired pizza says Italy, the wooden balcony and powerful air-con suggest the Alps, but the spicy condiments and spicier clientele are definitely mid-town Marrakesh. Grilled meat dishes are juicy and generous, but the Neapolitan pizza with capers, local olives and Atlantic anchovies steals the show.

Le Chat Qui Rit (Map p309; 024 434311; 92 Rue Yougoslavie; pizzas Dh50-80, set menu Dh150; 7.30-11pm Tue-Sun;) Come here for proper pasta: al dente, tossed with fresh produce and herbs, and drizzled with fruity olive oil. Corsican chef/owner Bernard comes out to ask about everyone's pasta with the delight of a chef who already knows the answer. Seasonal seafood options are also a good bet, with fixings just in from the coast daily.

Midrange

L'Annexe (Map p309; 024 434010; www.lannexemarrakech.com; 14 Rue Moulay Ali; lunch set menu Dh80-120, mains Dh100-140; noon-3.30pm Sun-Fri & 7-11pm Mon-Sat) French lunches in a mirrored café-bistro setting, handy to all the ville nouvelle boutique action. A welcome switch to light, clean flavours after the umpteenth tajine: *duck confit* (duck slowly cooked in its own fat) atop salad, tuna tartare and a mean créme brulée.

Beyrouth (Map p309; 024 423525; 9 Rue Loubnane; mains Dh80-160) Bright, lemony Lebanese flavours, with a mix-and-match *mezze* that's a feast for two with tabouli, spinach pies and felafel for Dh160. The smoky, silky baba ghanoush (eggplant dip) here gives Moroccan eggplant caviar serious competition for the best Middle Eastern spread.

Grand Café de la Poste (Map p309; 024 433038; www.grandcafedelaposte.com; Blvd el-Mansour Eddahbi, cnr Ave Imam Malik; starters Dh75-120, mains Dh80-190; 8am-10pm;) Recently restored to its flapper-era, potted-palm glory, La Poste boasts star power in the kitchen as well as the dining room (hello Tom Hanks and Lawrence Fishburne). Mediterranean chef Cyril Lignac and Moroccan chef Sana Gamas blend cuisines in roast chicken with wild Berber thyme and olives, and a lipsmacking salad with local goat cheese and citrus-herb vinaigrette. It's located behind the main post office.

our pick **Al-Fassia** Guéliz (Map p309; 024 434060; 55 Blvd Mohammed Zerktouni, mains Dh120-180; noon-10.30pm Wed-Sun;) Zone Touristique de l'Aguedal (Al Fassia Aguedal; Map p309; 024 383839; www.alfassia-aguedal.com; MH 9 Bis, Route de l'Ourika) Glassy-eyed diners valiantly grip morsels of bread, scraping the last savoury caramelised onion from what was once a Berber pumpkin and lamb tajine. The mezze of nine starters alone is a proper feast, but there's no resisting the legendary mains, cooked Middle Atlas style by an all-women team who present the dishes with a heartfelt *B'saha!* (to your health).

Cafés, Patisseries & Ice-Cream Parlours

MEDINA

Café des Épices (Map p300; 024 391770; Place Rahba Kedima; breakfast Dh25, sandwich or salad Dh25-50; 8am-9pm) Watch the magic happen as you sip freshly squeezed OJ overlooking Rahba Kedima potion-dealers. Salads and sandwiches are fresh, but bland – all the more reason to skip to the sweets.

Café Argana (Map p300; 024 445350; 2 Djemaa el-Fna, near Place Bab Fteuh; mains Dh80-100; 7am-11pm)

Claim your seat early for the spectacular view of the Djemaa at sunset, when restaurant stalls start grilling and belly dancers begin to wriggle. The top floor is for couples sharing rather tasteless ice cream; the 1st-floor balcony has back rows for snacks, and front seats for tajines; coffee and ice-cream cones are downstairs.

Les Terrasses de L'Alhambra (Map p300; Djemaa el-Fna; meals Dh100-150; 8am-11pm) Shaded balconies offer a prime view over the storytellers and potion-sellers and respectable Italian espresso besides. The pizza is flimsy and underseasoned, but a serviceable carbo-load for your next lap of the souqs.

Pâtisserie des Princes (Map p300; 024 443033; 32 Rue de Bab Agnaou; 5am-11.30pm;) This is one of the city's most famous patisseries, and with good reason. The seductive array of local delicacies, cakes and ice creams will sate any sweet tooth. The small café at the back is a welcome respite for women, or anyone in search of a quiet coffee.

VILLE NOUVELLE

our pick Café du Livres (Map p309; 024 432149; 44 Rue Tariq ibn Ziad, Guéliz; breakfast Dh40, dishes Dh55-80; 9.30am-9pm Tue-Sun; wi-fi) A dream retreat, complete with free wi-fi, upstanding cappuccino, walls of used books in English and French to thumb through, plus gorgeous goat-cheese salads and chocolate cake (Michelin-starred chef Richard Neat consulted on the menu).

Café 16 (Map p309; 024 339670; 18 Place du 16 Novembre; cakes Dh25-50, ice cream Dh20-50; 9am-12am) The blonde-wood decor and the prices may seem European, but the welcome is Marrakshi and so are intriguing ice-cream flavours like mint tea and *kaab el-gazelle* (almond cookie). The home-made gold-leafed chocolate-coffee cream cake and raspberry-mousse cake are standouts.

Amandine (Map p309; 024 449612; 177 Rue Mohammed el-Beqal, Guéliz; breakfast Dh40-50; 6am-11pm) Observe local internet daters lingering over their coffee or knocking it back in record time at the marble-top espresso bar, and then pop over to the sunny desert salon for flaky croissants or velvety chocolate-mousse cake studded with raspberries.

Oliveri (Map p309; 024 448913; 9 Blvd el-Mansour Eddahbi; ice cream from Dh15; 7am-10pm;) Thermometers aren't necessary in Marrakesh; all you need to gauge the heat are the lines at Oliveri. Ice creams have been made on these parlour premises for 50 years, and while the seasonal fresh fruit varieties are admirable, it's the pistachio that inspires repeat pilgrimages.

Quick Eats

MEDINA

At lunch time, before the stalls on Djemaa el-Fna get going, much of the same fare is available on Rue Beni Marine and in the *qissaria* (covered market) on the north side of the square. You'll find several vendors sharing a central kitchen whip up meals for under Dh50, including such as *tangia*, fried fish, lemon chicken and French fries. Eat whatever looks fresh and tasty, even if you have to wait for a free stool. Just around the corner from the Koubba Ba'adiyn are more labyrinthine *qissariat* with stalls serving tajines, steaming snails and the occasional stewed sheep's head for lunch.

our pick Mechoui Alley (Map p300; east side of Souq Ablueh; quarter-kilo lamb with bread Dh30-50; 11am-2pm) Just before noon, the vendors at this row of stalls start carving up steaming sides of *mechoui* (slow-roasted lamb), as though expecting King Henry VIII for lunch. Point to the best-looking cut of meat, and ask for a '*nuss*' (half) or '*rubb*' (quarter) kilo. Some haggling might ensue, but should procure a baggie of falling-off-the-bone delicious lamb with fresh-baked bread, cumin, salt and olives (though you're better off picking out your own across the souq).

Fast Food Alahbab (Map p300; Rue de Bab Agnaou; salads Dh15-25, sandwiches Dh20-30; 7am-11pm) The awning boasting 'recommended by Lonely Planet' must be 25 years old now, and still we stand by our initial assessment of the Dh35 *shawarma* accompanied by four sauces and just-right French fries, though the avocado milkshake is best avoided.

Restaurant Place Ferblantiers (Map p300; west entrance Place des Ferblantier; tajines Dh45-65; lunch) Plop down on a plastic chair in the courtyard, and have whatever's bubbling away on the burner. The meat and produce are fresh from the Mellah Market across the street, and the chef whips up dishes in front of you.

VILLE NOUVELLE

For bottom-rung local food, head for a group of hole-in-the-wall places on Rue ibn Aicha, where a solid meal of rotisserie chicken or brochettes, French fries and salad will cost around Dh35 to Dh60. Check out the fresh meats at the refrigerated counter, and just point at whatever parts strike your fancy.

Another local secret hiding in plain sight is the cheerful stretch of sidewalk stalls selling fresh fish from the coast and chips on Ave Moulay Rachid near the corner of Rue Mauritanie.

our pick **Plats Haj Boujemaa** (Map p309; 25 Rue ibn Aicha; Dh35-75 noon-8pm Tue-Sun) A reliable option where you can grab a stool under a sidewalk umbrella and trust the Haj to cook the meat of your choice to perfection. But be advised that even when properly cooked until golden, sheep's testicles have a floury texture that's hard to get over, not to mention stringy bits that stick in your teeth. That said, the chips are fantastic.

Samak al-Bahria (Map p309; Ave Moulay Rachid, cnr Rue Mauritanie; seafood with chips Dh30-80; noon-10pm Tue-Sun) The best option along this stretch of sidewalk stalls, al-Bahria serves fresh fish and perfectly tender fried calamari with generous chunks of lemon, plus salt and cumin.

Self-Catering

For a solid selection of fresh produce, dried fruits and nuts, try the new **Marché Municipale ibn Toumert** (Map p309; Rue ibn Toumert, off Ave Mohammed V). The souqs are also filled with food stalls selling olives, dates and sweets, and carts loaded with fruit and vegetables; prices are better in the Bab Doukkala food souq than right off the Djemaa. For staples such as cheese, cereal and alcohol (often difficult to find elsewhere), a few markets in the ville nouvelle are useful; otherwise head for the supermarkets, **ACIMA supermarket** (Map p309; 109 Ave Mohammed Abdelkrim el-Khattabi, Guéliz) and **Aswak Assalam** (Map pp294-5; Ave du 11 Janvier, Bab Doukkala) or the huge shop **Marjane** (off Map pp294-5; Casablanca road), 4km out of town.

DRINKING

Cafés

our pick **Dar Cherifa** (Map p300; ☎ 024 426463; 8 Derb Cherfa Lakbir, nr Rue el-Mouassine; tea/coffee Dh15-25; noon-7pm) Revive souq-sore eyes at this serene late-15th-century Saadian riad, where tea and saffron coffee is served with contemporary art and literature downstairs, or terrace views upstairs.

Aqua (Map p300; ☎ 024 381324; 68 Place Djemaa el-Fna) The most romantic of the cafés ringing the Djemaa, with candles, smart modern decor and service that's attentive but not intrusive. Stick with coffee, tea and sweets, as salads and mains are oddly flavourless.

Café les Négociants (Map p309; ☎ 024 435762; 110 Ave Mohammed V; 6am-11pm) Watch all of Marrakesh stream past over espresso or *nus-nus* (half coffee, half milk) at this prime corner location across from the tourist office. The crowd is mostly male, but women are increasingly taking over the tables on the Blvd Mohammed Zerktouni side.

Bars

As elsewhere in Morocco, the traditional bars in Marrakesh are mostly male and definitely seedy. Trendy upscale bars are more accommodating and appealing for women, especially ones that offer women free entry and/or free drinks midweek or on Sundays – go now, before they do the math. Most of the women you'll see queuing up to claim their freebies will be Western, but Moroccan girls do increasingly go out on the town together. Many bars also serve food and may turn into party places later at night, such as Le Foundouk (p316) and Café de la Poste (p317).

Kechmara (Map p309; ☎ 024 434060; 3 Rue de La Liberté, Guéliz; set menu Dh80-120;) Pull up a Saarinen tulip chair and stay awhile in this smartly contemporary café with a hip Marrakshi crowd, local art, groovy music and a low-key cocktail bar on the silvery *tadelakt* terrace. The selection of reasonably priced sandwiches and Moroccan-Mediterranean mains and excellent espresso make that chair hard to leave.

Comptoir (Map pp294-5; ☎ 024 437702; Rue Echouhada, Hivernage; 8pm-1am;) Never mind the restaurant downstairs; the flash lounge upstairs is the place to be for dashing diplomats, visiting fashion designers and married Casa playboys to mingle over cocktails or bottles of wine. There's no avoiding the belly dancers, who descend en masse every other hour like scantily clad chaperones to break up all that flirting.

Café Arabe (Map p300; ☎ 024 429728; www.cafearabe.com; 184 Rue Mouassine, medina; 10am-midnight;) Gloat over souq purchases with cocktails on the roof at sunset or a glass of wine next to the Zen-*zellij* courtyard fountain.

The pasta is limp and bland, but the lamb tajines are tasty, and wine prices are down to earth for such a stylish place.

Kosybar (Map pp294-5; ☎ 024 380324; http://kozibar.tripod.com; 47 Place des Ferblantiers, medina; noon-1am;) The Marrakesh-meets-Kyoto interiors are full of plush, private nooks, but keep heading upstairs to low-slung chairs on the rooftop terrace. At the aptly named Kosybar you can enjoy wines with a side of samba as storks give you the once-over from nearby nests; skip the cardboard-tasting sushi and stick with bar snacks.

La Maison Arabe Bar (Map pp294-5; ☎ 024 387010; www.lamaisonarabe.com; La Maison Arabe, 1 Derb Assehbe, Bab Doukkala; 8pm-1am;) Could be the 20-year single-malt scotch talking, but fellow drinkers look Hemingway-esque in leather club chairs by the fireplace within these hand-carved wood walls. The fusion tapas vacillate between bland and deep-fried, but their cocktails hit the spot after your Maison Arabe hammam (p305).

Piano Bar Les Jardins de la Koutoubia (Map p300; ☎ 024 388800; www.lesjardinsdelakoutoubia.com; Les Jardins de la Koutoubia Hotel, 26 Rue de la Koutoubia; entry free with drink; 5pm-1am) You won't be the first to tell the pianist 'Play it again, Sam', but he'll gamely play 'As Time Goes By' anyway. This is a classy joint, from the natural cedar ceilings to the plush Berber carpets, and the terrace restaurant serves a decent Indian curry when you get the munchies.

Restaurant/Bar du Grand Tazi (Map p300; ☎ 024 442787; Ave el-Mouahidine, cnr Rue de Bab Agnaou; 7pm-1am) Raucous but not sleazy, serving Dh25 local beer to throngs of travellers and Marrakshis just off work in the souqs. The tales take a turn for the outrageous as the evening wears on, but then some of us enjoy that kind of thing.

L'Abyssin (off Map pp294-5; ☎ 024 328584; www.palaisrhoul.com; Palais Rhoul, Dar Tounsi, Route de Fès, Palmeraie; 8-11pm Tue, noon-3.30pm & 8-11pm Wed-Sun;) Stay cool and look cooler lounging in white canvas pavilions set in the garden of the Palais Rhoul villa and spa. Once you've made your grand entrance down the reflecting-pool runway, you'll want to make an evening of it here, and the Mediterranean and Moroccan food will see you through dinner (try the duck).

Le Sabal (Map p309; ☎ 024 422422; www.lesabal.com; Ave Mohammed V, Place de la Liberté, Guéliz; noon-2am) Days turns into nights spent in this retrofitted 1925 villa with sunny garden seating and a tent-bar downstairs, and plush, purplish nocturnal lounge upstairs. Now under hip Marrakshi management, the scene is more casual and local, drawn by reasonably priced drinks and an appealing à la carte menu.

ENTERTAINMENT

Nightclubs

Sleeping is overrated in a city where the nightlife begins around midnight. Most of the hottest clubs are in the Hivernage, or in a new zone outside the city along Blvd Mohammed VI in the new Hotel Zone Aguedal extension of the Hivernage. Admissions range from Dh150 to Dh350 including the first drink, but those who arrive early and dressed smartly midweek may get in free. Each drink thereafter costs at least Dh50. For out-of-town clubs like Pacha, remember that a taxi back can be really expensive – taxi drivers know they've got you stranded.

Pacha (Map pp294-5; ☎ 024 388405; www.pachamarrakech.com; Complexe Pacha Marrakech, Blvd Mohammed VI, Hotel Zone Aguedal, Hivernage; admission before/after 10pm free/Dh150-200 Mon-Fri, Dh200-300 Sat & Sun; 8pm-5am;) Pacha Ibiza was the prototype for this enormous clubbing complex that's now Africa's biggest, with DJs mashing up international and Magrebi hits for huge weekend influxes of Casa hipsters and raging Rabatis. The complex includes two dazzling restaurants and a pool to lounge away afternoons until the party starts. Since they charge big for drinks, savvy clubsters smuggle in water. Pacha doesn't come close to hitting its 3000-people occupancy during the week, so bring your own entourage and you might get in free.

Diamant Noir (Map p309; ☎ 024 434351; Hôtel Marrakech, cnr Ave Mohammed V & Rue Oum Errabia, Guéliz; admission from Dh100; 10pm-4am) For its rare gay-friendly clientele on weeknights and seedy charm on weekends, the gravitational pull of 'Le Dia' remains undeniable. The dark dance-floor thumps with hip hop and gleams with mirrors and bronzer-enhanced skin, while professionals lurk at the shady end of the upstairs bar. Cash only.

Jad Mahal (Map pp294-5; ☎ 024 436984; 10 Rue Haroun Errachid, Hivernage; free admission with drink/dinner; 7.30pm-2am) Through the restaurant at the far end of the courtyard, the Jad Mahal's bar is a local favourite spot to linger over cocktails by the bronze elephant until staff crank up the volume on a catchy song, the house cover-band arrives or diners break into spontaneous dance moves over an '80s tune, whichever comes first.

Théâtro (Map pp294-5; ☎ 024 448811; Hôtel es Saadi, Rue Qadissia, Hivernage; admission Dh200; 11.30pm-5am) Don't bother schmoozing the bouncer for entry to the boring VIP area, because the dance floor in this converted theatre is where the action is: packed, sweaty, carefree, fabulous. Saturdays are white nights, with white-clad clubbers grooving til dawn on the signature mix of house, techno, R'n'B and Morocco-pop.

CantoBar (Map pp294-5; ☎ 024 42335038; Ave Moulay Hassan, cnr Ave President Kennedy, Guéliz; free admission with dinner/drink; 7.30pm-4am) Located behind el-Harti Stadium within staggering distance of Le Sabal bar and Diamant Noir disco, CantoBar completes the night-out trifecta with karaoke and kitsch. Decent mojitos and dark lighting let you quit worrying about going off-key, and afterwards you can collapse on red armchairs shaped like high heels.

Cinema

For a good selection of French and sometimes Moroccan films check out the program at the Institut Français (see p297), where films are usually in French or subtitled in French.

Le Colisée (Map p309; ☎ 024 448893; Blvd Mohammed Zerktouni, nr Rue Mohammed el-Beqal, Guéliz; stall/balcony Mon Dh15/25, Tue-Sun Dh25/35; 3pm, 7pm & 9.30pm) The plushest cinema in town, Le Colisée is plenty comfortable, with great sound and a mixed male-female, Moroccan and expat crowd. Films are sometimes in the original language (including English) and subtitled in French.

Cinéma Eden (Map p300; Derb Debachi, near Rue des Banques, medina; Dh15; shows at 3pm, 6pm & 9pm) The crowd here is rowdy, local and all-male, and where Bollywood sing-alongs reign supreme. Films are usually dubbed into Darija, except for the songs.

SHOPPING

Medina

Calling all shoppers: Marrakesh will leave you cursing carry-on restrictions, especially in the medina. The souqs are crammed with household items you can't possibly live without – sand-worn Berber cedar chests, ingenious teapots with dromedary humps, dramatic iron floor lanterns – but given shipping and insurance rates (see p471), you may have to settle for some hand-carved jewellery boxes, *tadelakt* soap dishes and candle-holders made from recycled anchovy tins. More than a few stylish expats you'll meet are design fanatics who couldn't resist, and ended up buying riads as places to house their souq finds.

That said, there are plenty of knick-knacks you might not mind leaving behind – all those ceramic Koutoubia mini-minarets and uncomfortable bolster pillows fringed, tasselled and mirrored beyond all recognition. Be selective, chat before you begin bargaining for items you're sure you want and buy only from shopkeepers who are pleasant in return – that way, you'll have a great story to accompany your scores, and not wind up hot and bothered in the souqs.

SUSTAINABLE SHOPPING

No matter how you're faring elsewhere in the souqs, you can count on feel-good retail experiences from medina outlets supporting non-profit causes, boutiques that sell items made by cooperatives and businesses that engage in Fair Trade with hard-working artisans – and even better, the prices at these stores are fair and fixed.

Cooperative Artisanale Femmes de Marrakesh (Map p300; ☎ 024 378308; 67 Souq Kchachbia; 9.30am-12.30pm & 2.30-6.30pm) A hidden treasure worth seeking in the souqs. Here you'll find breezy cotton clothing and household linens made by a Marrakesh women's cooperative and a small annex packed with items made by non-profit and women's cooperatives from across Morocco, including sustainably harvested thuyya wood bowls from Essaouira, Safi tea sets and small Middle Atlas rugs.

Al-Kawtar (Map p300; ☎ 024 378293; www.alkawtar.org; Rue Laksour 57; 10am-6pm) Another wonderful nonprofit boutique, where you can find luxe household linens minutely embroidered along the edges for less than you'd pay for plain cotton back home. You can also get fabulous hand-stitched Marrakesh-mod tunics, dresses, shirts and pants off the rack or tailored to fit you –

there's no extra charge for alterations. All the items here are made by disabled women, and your purchases pay for their salaries, training programs and a childcare centre.

Assouss Cooperative d'Argane (Map p300; ☎ 061 729678; 94 Rue el-Mouassine, cnr Rue Sidi el-Yamani; 9am-1pm & 3-7pm Sat-Thu, 9am-noon Fri) For pampering and foodie finds, this is the Marrakesh retail outlet of a women's argan cooperative outside Essaouira. The all-women staff will ply you with free samples and proudly explain how their ultra-emollient cosmetic oil and gourmet salad oils are made.

L'Art du Bain Savonnerie Artisanale (Map p300; ☎ 068 445942; www.lartdubain.com; Souq Lebbadine, nr Souq Sebbaghine; 9.30-7.30pm) Also sells argan oil from an Essaouira cooperative alongside handmade soaps made with fragrant blends of local herbs, flowers and spices.

Kif-Kif (Map p300; ☎ 061 082041; www.kifkifbystef.com; 8 Rue Laksour, near Bab Ksour; 10am-8pm) A hip boutique that engages the city's most inventive artisans to come up with clever gifts. These include tote bags made of pop-art awning fabric, rings with interchangeable felt baubles and adorable striped-jersey baby jellabas – and 15% of the price on all kids' items goes to a local nonprofit organisation supporting disabled children.

Jamade (Map p300; ☎ 024 429042; 1 Pl Douar Graoua, cnr Rue Riad Zitoun el-Jedid; 10am-1.30pm & 3.30-7.30pm) Also sells locally designed items at fixed prices, including some hip, hand-sewn coasters and placemats from Tigmi women's cooperative.

Tadert Titbirine (☎ 024 377416; titbirine@menara.ma) Contact Fair Trade–design entrepreneur Brigitte Perkins for a visit to this textile atelier which brings a contemporary edge to traditional Moroccan techniques of hand-weaving and embroidery. It has been recognised by the state for raising Moroccan handicraft standards with handwoven, custom-embroidered silk wraps and limited-edition organic Rif cotton household linens for the likes of Calvin Klein.

To buy crafts directly from Marrakesh's favourite recycling artisans, head over to Riad Zitoun el-Kedim and check out the items cleverly fashioned from recycled tyres: Michelin mirrors, well-travelled footstools, man-bags with street cred. There are several to choose from, but there's usually a good selection among the framed Bob Marley posters at **Creations Pneumatiques** (Map p300; ☎ 066 091746; 110 Rue Riad Zitoun el-Kedim; 7am-10pm).

Ville Nouvelle

To get a jump start on the souqs, savvy shoppers visit the **Ensemble Artisanal** (Map pp294-5; ☎ 024 443503; Ave Mohammed V, across from Cyber Park; 9.30am-12.30pm & 3-7pm Mon-Sat) to glimpse artisans at work and see the range of crafts and prices Marrakesh has to offer. The set prices are higher than in the souqs and the selection is obviously more limited, but it's hassle-free shopping and the producer gets paid directly.

Upscale fixed-price boutiques worth checking out in the ville nouvelle for gifts, fashion and household linens are on and around **Rue de la Liberté** in Guéliz, and the nearby **Marché Municipale ibn Toumert** (Map p309; Rue ibn Toumert, off Ave Mohammed V, Guéliz; 8am-7pm) offers jewellery and ceramics at reasonable prices if you're prepared to bargain.

Modern Moroccan design fanatics hire taxis in the morning or late afternoon to scour the local designer factory outlets 4km outside Marrakesh at **Quartier Industrial Sidi Ghanem** (off Map pp294-5; km 4, Route de Safi; 9am-6pm Mon-Sat); negotiate a set rate of Dh150 to Dh250 for the ride there and back from the medina. Score a map of the quarter at an open showroom, or just troll the lanes to find which outlets are open (hours are erratic).

In the Palmeraie, one boutique featuring gorgeous design and local art is at **Jnane Tamsna** (off Map pp294-5; ☎ 024 329423; www.jnanetamsna.com; Douar Abiad, Palmeraie), which supports Fair Trade with local artisans.

GETTING THERE & AWAY

Air

Six kilometres southwest of town is the recently expanded and quite spiffy **Menara airport** (☎ 024 447865; information desk 8am-6pm). The airport has an information desk in the check-in hall and there are some banks where you can exchange currency.

Royal Air Maroc (RAM; Map p309; ☎ call centre 090 000800, 024 436205; www.royalairmaroc.com; 197 Ave Mohammed V, Guéliz; 8.30am-12.20pm & 2.30-7pm) has several flights daily to and from Casablanca (round trip from Dh650, 40 minutes), where you can pick up connections, as well as a direct weekly flight to Agadir (round trip from Dh1100, 35 minutes). It is advisable to reconfirm your flight with their 24-hour call centre. RAM also operates direct international flights to London (3½ hours) and Geneva (three hours) six days a week and daily flights to Paris (3¼ hours).

Atlas Blue (☎ 082 009090; www.atlas-blue.com; Menara airport), the sister company of RAM, has cheap flights to Marrakesh from London, Paris, Amsterdam and many other European cities. Other carriers include **Air France** (http://www.airfrance.co.ma/), which flies to Paris at least once a day. **Easyjet** (www.easyjet.com) flies to Marrakesh daily from London Gatwick and **Ryanair** (www.ryanair.com) has at least four flights from London Luton to Marrakesh weekly.

Bus

Most buses arrive and depart from the **main bus station** (Map pp294-5; ☎ 024 433933; Bab Doukkala) just outside the city walls at Bab Doukkala, a 25-minute walk or Dh5 to Dh10 taxi ride from Djemaa el-Fna. The large main building is lined with booths covering local and long-distance destinations; get tickets for early-morning departures the day before as some booths aren't open first thing. Buses leave most frequently between 4am and 7pm.

The bus station has handy **left-luggage facilities** (small/big bag per day Dh5/8; 24hr), but the smoky cafés, frightening toilets and pushy touts are all best avoided.

A number of companies run buses to Fez (from Dh130, 8½ hours, at least six daily) and Meknès (from Dh120, six hours, at least three daily).

Buses to Asni (Dh10) also leave from the southern side of the medina outside Bab er-Rob. There's at least one bus a day to Telouet (Dh50, four hours) that leaves in the afternoon from Bab Gehmat in the medina's southwest wall.

CTM (Map pp294-5; ☎ 024 434402; www.ctm.co.ma; Window 10, Bab Doukkala bus station) operates daily buses to Fez (Dh160, 8½ hours, one daily) via Beni Mellal (Dh70, 2½ hours), Ouarzazate (Dh75, four hours, one daily) and Tan Tan (Dh195, six hours, five daily) via Tiznit (Dh120, five hours). There are also daily services to Agadir (Dh90, four hours, nine daily), Casablanca (Dh85, four hours, three daily) and Laâyoune (Dh290, 14 hours, four daily). CTM services to Essaouira (Dh80, three hours) fill up quickly so it is best to purchase your ticket the day before.

Tickets can also be bought at the **CTM Office** (Map p309; ☎ 024 448328; 12 Blvd Mohammed Zerktouni, Guéliz). This is also the arrival and departure point for their international buses, including Paris (from Dh1000, 48 hours) and Madrid (from Dh900, 36 hours), on Tuesday, Wednesday and Saturday.

Supratours (Map p309; ☎ 024 435525; Ave Hassan II) is west of the train station. You can catch a bus from here to Agadir (Dh90, four hours, five daily), Dakhla (Dh420, 25 hours, one daily), Essaouira (Dh65, 2½ hours, three daily), Laâyoune (Dh280, 15 hours, two daily) and Tan Tan (Dh180, 10 hours, two daily). Supratours also offers connecting buses to trains; for schedules and connections, see p324.

Car

Local car-rental companies often offer more competitive deals than international operators, with quoted rates starting at around Dh400 per day with unlimited mileage, possibly cheaper if you take it for a minimum of three days. For 4WD rentals, count on Dh700 to Dh1000 per day with minimal insurance. However, you should be able to negotiate a 10% to 20% discount normally and even more in the low season (October to mid-December and mid-January to the end of February). If you'd rather look at the scenery than the road in the mountains or desert, you can hire a car with a driver through a local car-rental agency (see p308) starting at Dh1350 plus tip per day all-inclusive for a 4WD or a small minibus, though English-speaking drivers aren't always available.

INTERNATIONAL AGENCIES

Avis (www.avis.com; Ave Mohammed V **Map p309**; ☎ 024 432525;137 Ave Mohammed V; airport ☎ 024 433169)

Budget (www.budget.com; Blvd Mohammed Zerktouni Map p309; ☎ 024 431180; 80 Blvd Mohammed Zerktouni; airport ☎ 024 438875)

Europcar (www.europcar.com; Blvd Mohammed Zerktouni Map p309; ☎ 024 431228; 63 Blvd Mohammed Zerktouni; airport ☎ 024 437718)

Hertz (www.hertz.com; Ave Mohammed V **Map p309**; ☎ 024 439984; 154 Ave Mohammed V; airport ☎ 024 447230)

National (Map p309; www.nationalcar.com; Rue de la Liberté ☎ 024 430683; 1 Rue de la Liberté; airport ☎ 024 437846)

LOCAL AGENCIES

La Plaza Car (Map p309; ☎ 024 421801; www.laplaza car.com; Immeuble 141, 23 Rue Mohammed el-Beqal)
Lhasnaoui Rent (Map pp294-5; ☎ 024 312415; www.lhasnaouirent.com; cnr Blvd Allal el-Fassi & Yacoub el-Mansour, 15 Immeuble el-Omairi)
KAT (Map p309; ☎ 024 433581; http://membres.lycos.fr/katcar; 68 Blvd Mohammed Zerktouni)

Taxi

Departing from outside Bab er-Rob near the royal palace are grands taxis to destinations in the High Atlas, including Asni (Dh18), Ijoukak (Dh20), Ouirgane (Dh35) and Setti Fatma (Dh35).

Those serving destinations further afield gather on a dirt lot to the north of the main bus station. Destinations include Agadir (Dh120), Azilal (Dh75), Beni Mellal (Dh110), Demnate (Dh55), Essaouira (Dh130), Ouarzazate (Dh90) and Taroudannt (Dh110).

Train

From the **train station** (Map p309; ☎ 024 447768, 090 203040 information only; www.oncf.ma; cnr Ave Hassan II & Blvd Mohammed VI, Guéliz) you can take a taxi or city bus (bus 3, 8, 10 or 14, among others; Dh3) into the centre.

There are nine daily trains to Casablanca (2nd-class rapide, Dh84, three hours) and Rabat (Dh112, four hours). There are direct trains to Fez (Dh180, seven hours, eight daily), Meknès (Dh162, 6½ hours), and Safi (Dh25, three hours, one daily). Overnight trains to Tangier (Dh190, 10½ hours) leave once daily. For sleeping berths to Tangier the ticket costs Dh350, or Dh650 for a single sleeping car compartment; book at least two days in advance.

GETTING AROUND

To/From the Airport

A petit taxi to Marrakesh from the airport (6km) should be no more than Dh60 by day or Dh80 by night, but you may have difficulty convincing the driver of this. As with any taxi trip, the taxi should use the meter to determine the price. Alternatively, bus 11 runs irregularly to Djemaa el-Fna. Airport transfers arranged through hotels or riad guest houses in the medina or ville nouvelle should cost Dh150 to Dh200, or Dh150 to Dh250 to the Palmeraie.

Bus

Local buses (Map p300; ☎ 024 3433933; all fares Dh3) leave for the ville nouvelle at seemingly random intervals from Place Foucauld near the Djemaa el-Fna. Key bus lines are:
Nos 1 & 20: medina-Guéliz (along Ave Mohammed V)
Nos 2 and 10: medina-Gare Routière
Nos 3 and 8: medina-train station
No 11: medina-Menara Gardens

Calèches

These are the horse-drawn green carriages you'll see at Place Foucauld next to the Djemaa el-Fna. They're a pleasant way to get around, if you avoid the rush hours (8am, midday and 5.30pm to 7.30pm). One-way trips within the medina officially cost Dh15; otherwise, state-fixed rates of Dh100 per hour apply. Expect a tour of the ramparts to take 1½ hours, and allow three hours for the Palmeraie. In the Hivernage, calèches linger outside major hotels along Ave el-Qadissia and Rue Echouhada.

Car & Motorcycle

Your feet are the best way to get around the medina, which is mostly closed to car traffic. Driving in Marrakesh is an extreme sport, with scooters zooming from all sides and traffic roundabouts the meek may never escape – best to leave the driving to unfazed taxi drivers whenever possible. For day trips, you might rent a bike, car or a motorcycle. **Marrakesh Motos** (Map p309; ☎ 024 448359, 061 316413; 31 Ave Mohammed Abdelkrim el-Khattabi; 🕑 9am-10pm), located about 2km out of the town centre on the Casablanca road just beyond the Goodyear garage, rents out scooters and 125cc motorcycles for Dh250 to Dh300 per day.

If you do rent a car or motorcycle, there are often parking places near the gates and entrances to the medina. There are public parking lots near the Koutoubia Mosque and just south of Place de Foucauld on Ave el-Mouahidine; expect to pay Dh20/40 during the day/24 hours. If you find street parking, a guardian will expect a Dh10 tip for keeping an eye on your car; look for the guy in the blue coat, and pay your tip afterwards.

Taxi

The creamy-beige petits taxis around town charge Dh5 to Dh15 per journey. They're all supposed to use their meters, but you may need to insist, especially coming from the train station or airport. If your party numbers more than three you must take a grand taxi, which requires some negotiation.

EAST OF MARRAKESH

After a few especially hot days, Marrakesh can leave you feeling as cooked as a kebab left too long on a Djemaa el-Fna grill. For a dramatic, restorative change of scenery, head for the picture-perfect Aït Bougomez Valley and the sparkling waterfalls of Cascades d'Ouzoud.

DEMNATE دمنات

Who knew that an authentic immersion experience in Berber culture and cuisine could be found less than 1½ hours from Marrakesh? A foodie and cultural hub for centuries, Demnate is today often overlooked by bus tour hordes rushing to get to the Cascades d'Ouzoud – conveniently leaving intrepid travellers room to see, hear and taste Demnate's indigenous Berber culture. As in other towns ruled by the ruthless Glaoui, the once-grand Glaoui kasbah and mud-brick ramparts have been left to crumble and the triumphal gate has been pulled down, yet Demnate's fascinating heritage has survived and thrived against the odds.

Sights & Activities

At the heart of town is a **mellah**, with an entry about 150m on the right after the town's main gate. Hundreds of Jewish families from Morocco, France, Israel, Canada and the United States come here each July for the country's most historic **Jewish moussem** (festival), a week-long mystical event that is said to offer miracle cures for longstanding ailments. Demnate also has two *zawiyas*, making the annual **Hamdouchi Moussem** in September twice as raucous. Each *zawiya* literally follows the beat of its own drummer, dancing to different rhythms in an all-day dance-off and music festival in the centre of town before going their separate ways in 3-hour parades leading to the *zawiyas*. Sometimes the *moussem* peaks in blood purification, with dancers cutting themselves on the scalp in a dramatic act of ritual cleansing.

CULTURAL ENCOUNTERS

Between the *moussems* and raucous weddings all summer, the local music scene is quite happening. To hear for yourself, Demnate's local self-help association, **Complexe Association de l'Entreaide Demnate** (☎ 068 131304 in French, 068 909801 in English; ettajmi@yahoo.fr; Ave Mohammed V, near gate; dinner concerts requested donation of Dh300-550 per person all-inclusive, depending on number of diners; 🕑 by prior appointment), can arrange a dinner concert catered by the local women's catering cooperative, with explanations of the Berber lyrics in French or English. Proceeds underwrite an impressive range of community assistance programs, which you might arrange with kindly director Mr Mohammed Ettajami to see in action at the Complexe. Among the inspired local initiatives housed in the Complexe are literacy classes, catering training courses, women's entrepreneurship classes, community childcare and a computer lab. Donations are appreciated for any visit to the Complexe.

If you'll be passing through around teatime, you can arrange tea with a local family through **Association Attadamoun Pour les Handicapés** (☎ 068 909801; handicadem1@yahoo.fr; Demnate), another wonderful nonprofit organisation providing schooling, job training and essential life skills to disabled youth throughout the region. The association's director, Mr Hassan Khallaf, speaks fluent English and is extremely knowledgeable and proud of Demnate's mixed Muslim/Jewish heritage. By prior arrangement he gives wonderful historical tours of Demnate's *mellah*, passing through souqs and *fondouqs* and ending in a local elementary school supported by interfaith foundations. Proceeds for teas, *mellah* walking tours, and overnight stays in the association's cheerful salon (Dh100 to Dh300 per person suggested) support the association's heroic efforts to extend essential support services and educational opportunities to all.

The Association de l'Entreaide Demnate's catering cooperative have teamed with local wildlife guides to launch a new program: nature hikes and strolls through olive and almond groves surrounding Demnate, with gourmet picnics delivered to a scenic hilltop or cool riverside location. Demnate's fragrant hand-rolled couscous made of barley, corn or wheat is available upon request. Arrangements should be made at least two days in advance through the association (see p325), with proceeds funding the association's catering and women's business development programs.

NATURE & HIKING

Once you're in Demnate, detour 6km to the east to **Imi-n-Ifri** ('Grotto's Mouth' in Berber), a natural bridge over a gorge that looks like a monster's yawning mouth. You can clamber down into the gorge and pass through this toothy maw by yourself – the paths are clearly marked and recently levelled – but it's worth paying a small tip (Dh20 to Dh30) to a local guide to help you over some tricky boulders and explain the local lore associated with this travertine bridge formed some 1.8 million years ago.

The two sides of the bridge are said to represent two local lovers whose families kept them apart, so this Romeo and Juliet held hands and turned to stone. On the south side of the gorge is a spring with water rich in natural mineral salts, where brides come for pre-wedding rites; in summer you may hear women singing and playing drums and tambourines for Berber bachelorette parties. On the other side of the gorge is a freshwater spring said to cure acne, which explains the number of teens hanging out here. Pass under the bridge, and suddenly you're in a *Lord of the Rings* setting, with flocks of crows swooping down from dramatic stalactites overhead.

Along the road that forks to the left at Imi-n-Ifri is one of the most breathtaking and pristine valleys in the High Atlas foothills, leading into the Aït Bougomez Valley. It's like driving into an Impressionist painting: golden wheat fields ripple in the breeze, dotted with red poppies in spring and women in pinafores and polka-dotted kerchiefs cutting wheat with a scythe. Mountains are striped gold, green and purple with wheat growing on stone-walled terraces, and red-stone villages cling to iron-rich red cliffsides like architectural chameleons. The road here is fairly new, so the valley seems untouched by time.

Follow the road 6km from Imi-n-Ifri to the village of Iouaridene, and you're in prehistoric territory. Signs point you towards what geologists claim are **dinosaur footprints** dating from the mid-Jurassic period, about 170 million years ago. Quadruped and carnivorous dinosaurs once roamed this area, and the local kids do a mean impersonation of a T Rex. At the time of writing the bridge beyond Iouaridene was washed out, but exploration of this spectacular valley portal to Aït Bougomez may be possible on foot or with a 4WD in dry season.

The 100-year-old olive groves climbing over the hillsides around Demnate produce what is widely considered to be Morocco's best olive oil, with trace mineral salts and terrace-farming methods yielding a golden colour, and subtle flavour variations that compare favourably with Tuscan varieties. Almonds are another renowned local product, and the flowering of the local trees makes March a good time to visit.

Sleeping

Other than overnight stays at the Association Attadamoun Pour les Handicapés (p325), pleasant, good-value lodging is available 500m to the left at the fork in the road at Imi-n-Ifri at the new **our pick** **Riad Aykbalou** (☎ 023 507498; www.iminifri-riad.com; 2km Imi-n-Ifri, 8km Demnate; s half-board with shared/private bathroom Dh120/150, d half-board with shared/private bathroom Dh250/280). Rooms are simple and cheery with splashes of bright colour, pine furnishings and henna lamps, and the seasonal tajines make good on Demnate's culinary reputation with fresh herbs, flavourful vegetables and meats (nonguests pay Dh80 for tajines, Dh20 for salads). A more upscale option is the ecologically minded **Kasbah Timdaf** (☎ 023 507178; 15 min from Demnate on road to Azilal; GPS coordinates N 31°46,50 W 007°01,13; s Dh495, d Dh660-880, q Dh1650), with spacious rooms and *tadelakt* bathrooms in a stone and mud-brick farm surrounded by almond and olive groves.

Eating

The clear sign you've arrived in a foodie capital is the 40 restaurant stalls lining the main street – that's about one for every 50 people in town. The stiff competition means Demnati cooks must attempt to deliver the freshest, tastiest tajines starting at just Dh20; try whatever place seems to be winning the crowds over that day, or go with reliable **Café d'Ouzoud** (☎ 023 456087; Ave Mohammed V), a couple of hundred metres before the main gate into Demnate. For a more leisurely dining experience complete with a refreshing dip in the restaurant pool, head to **Café-Restaurant Al Jazeera** (☎ 044 458239; nr Gare Routiére, Demnate; 8am-8pm;); call ahead to try Demnate's signature fine-grain couscous drizzled with local olive oil.

Shopping

The Sunday weekly **souq** 10 minutes south of town is an opportunity to taste-test local olives, olive oils and almonds, and see Demnate's local woodwork, wool outerwear and simple pottery with Berber good-luck symbols in henna to enhance your cooking efforts. The potteries are located 2km outside town in the village of Boughlou, turning right at the mosque and heading 4km off-road; you might hire a guide through Demnate's Association de l'Entreaide (p325) to take you, and explain the painstaking process used to fire pots and glaze them a distinctive natural-yellow hue.

Getting There & Away

Grands taxis to Marrakesh (Dh55) and Azilal (Dh45) leave from the main gate. Buses leave for Marrakesh (Dh25, 1½ hours) every couple of hours until 6pm from the bus station (take the road to the right before entering the main town gate).

CASCADES D'OUZOUD

شالا لد ت أزوض

Some 167km northeast of Marrakesh and a world away from the city heat are Morocco's waterfalls, one of the most popular day trips from Marrakesh for tourists and Moroccans alike. Here the Oued Ouzoud drops 110m into the canyon of Oued el-Abid in three-tiered falls. Though drought has reduced the water lately, the view from the mouth of the falls is still impressive, and it only gets better as you descend into the cool of the canyon, past the late-afternoon rainbow mists and the pools at its base. The falls are most dramatic from March to June when there's more water, but young Moroccans often camp here in the heat of summer on terraces faceting the falls.

To reach the falls, walk past the signs for Riad Cascades d'Ouzoud (see right) towards the precipice, where converging paths wind down towards the falls. To the left of the town square is a path lined with souvenir stalls and cafés. For lunch at eye-level with the falls, stop at **Chez Amis Salah** (8am-6pm) where salad and bread accompany tajines for Dh80 or omelettes for Dh60; several other neighbouring cafés offer similar fare and prices, but the cliff's-edge seating sets this one apart. Bathrooms shared by several cafés are out back past the bleating goats, and are best braved before you have lunch.

Locals might try to 'guide' you into the gorge for a few dirham, but you can follow the well-trodden paths. At the bottom, you can hike along the riverbed or cross the river to another path leading up to the village. Barbary apes clamour for attention and food along this path, but a signpost advises not to feed them.

If you continue downstream, there are small, reasonably clean pools where you can swim. To see the picturesque Berber village of Tanaghmelt, follow the path by the lower pools up past a farmhouse and up the slopes for about 1.5km. For longer treks, follow the course of the river to caves (two hours) and the Gorges of Oued el-Abid (another two hours).

Many cafés lining the falls offer shady camp sites for Dh15 with rather dire hole-in-the-ground toilet facilities. If hygiene is a priority, camp sites and Berber tents are available with indoor toilet facilities and showers at **Dar Essalam Hotel** (☎ 015 972385; camp site without/with rented tent Dh20/40, s/d/tr Dh50/100/150) on the town square facing the falls; bare-bones rooms with shared bathrooms are available as well.

Riad Cascades d'Ouzoud (☎ 062 143804; www.ouzoud.com; s Dh510-610, d Dh710-810, tr Dh 950, ste Dh1050-1150, all incl breakfast) offers a rustically stylish retreat within view of the falls, with solar-heated showers, Berber-style carved-wood furnishings and doors, and a family-style welcome from local staff. The riad offers treks led by a local guide, who can also arrange kayaking, river-sliding, visits to rural souqs and tea with local families.

Getting There & Away

From Marrakesh, it's easiest to get transport direct to Azilal, from where grands taxis run when full to Ouzoud (Dh25 per person, or Dh250 for the whole taxi, return). Don't leave it past 4pm to try to begin your trip back to Azilal.

AZILAL أزيلال

This tidy centre for regional development is mainly of interest to travellers as a handy transport hub between Demnate, the Cascades d'Ouzoud and the Aït Bougomez Valley. A good pit stop for Dh30 lunches of tasty grilled chicken and chips is **Ibnou Ziad Restaurant** (Ave Hassan II), though football fans might be delayed by matches shown on

HAPPY VALLEY GOODWILL TOUR

Take in spectacular scenery and bring the happiness home with you after supporting 11 worthy local causes on this four-night, five-day adventure:

Day 1

- Depart Marrakesh; nature hike and picnic outside Demnate arranged by local-guide program and women's catering collective at **Association de l'Entreaide Demnate** (p325).
- Tea with local family or **mellah** tour arranged by Demnate's **Association Attadamoun Pour les Handicapés** (p325).
- Dinner concert organised by Association de l'Entreaide Demnate (p325).
- Overnight at Assocation Attadamoun Pour les Handicapés or **Riad Aykbalou** (p326) at Imi-n-Ifri.

Day 2

- Depart Demnate; lunch at **Ibnou Ziad Restaurant** (above) in Azilal.
- Optional off-road side trip for **Association Assamer** (opposite) carpet cooperative and country-style tea at **Hassan Benkoum** (opposite).
- Visit to wood carvers' studio at **Association Ighrem Atelier du Sculpture** (p330).
- Sample goat cheese, walnut-butters and mountain honey at **Cooperative Tikhiouine** (p330).
- Dinner & overnight at **Ecolodge Dar Itrane** (p330).

Day 3

- Morning hike to **Zawiya Sidi Moussa** arranged through **Association Renaissance de Aït Bougomez** (p330).
- Lunch at **Café des Amis** (p331) in Tabant.
- Teach one-hour after-school English program at Tabant girls' boarding school (p330).
- Off-road to Zaouiat Ahansal; visit women's weaving collective and training program at **Atelier du Tissages de l'Association du Zaouiat Ahsal** (p331).
- Dinner & overnight at gîtes **Sidi Ahmed Amahdar** (p321).

Day 4

- Drive to **Reserve Naturelle de Tamga** for rock-climbing at **La Cathédrale du Rocher**, a wildflower hike, or bird-watching organised by **Association Renaissance de Aït Bougomez** (p330).
- Lunch at **Gîte le Cathedrale** (p331).
- Drive to Ben Ouirgane; overnight stay at eco-friendly **Little Morocco** (p332).

Day 5

- Return to Marrakesh via Cascades d'Ouzoud; lunch at **Chez Amis Salah** (p327) in Cascades d'Ouzoud.

TV here. Market day is Thursday, and the town's **Complexe Artisanal** (on right across from town hall) occasionally hosts regional arts-and-crafts showcases.

This is the last internet outpost before heading into Aït Bougomez; email addicts can check one last time at **Cyber Adrau** (Ave Hassan II, next to Hôtel Assounfou; per hr Dh8; 8am-midnight). ATMs and credit-card machines are also scarce for miles around, so you might want to use the cash machines at **Banque Populaire** (Ave Hassan II) located next to the police station.

Across from Ibnou Ziad Restaurant is the laid-back **Hôtel Souss** (072 328495; s/d with shared bathroom Dh35/70, Dh5 hot showers), which offers a friendly welcome, spacious rooms, thick blankets and oddly endearing child-sized desks; a video arcade with Playstation is upstairs.

Buses run between Azilal and Marrakesh (Dh45, two to six daily). Plenty of grands taxis run from the taxi lot behind Marrakesh's bus station to Azilal (Dh70) and, less frequently, from Azilal to Demnate (Dh34).

AÏT BOUGOMEZ VALLEY

وادي عيت بو غومز

Arguably the best-kept secret in Morocco is the region known as the 'happy valley', which until 2001 was snowbound four months a year and largely inaccessible except on foot or mule. Though some roads are still accessible only by 4WD, paved roads have given unprecedented entry to High Atlas foothills faceted with mud-brick towers and signature *ighremt* (stone-reinforced houses) in reddish rock with windows outlined in white stone. Here you can escape the reach of mobile phones, bosses and the countless other minor irritants of modern living, and spend days happily absorbed by orchards in bloom, mysterious petroglyphs and barley rippling in the breeze. This valley is nature's answer to Prozac, especially for trekkers seeking the performance highs of climbing M'Goun Massif (see p436).

But more than just natural beauty, Aït Bougomez has a remarkable resourcefulness that never ceases to impress. Even steep mountainsides are used for terrace farming, so you'll spot tiny plots of wheat on nose-bleed-inducing high-altitude walled terraces. Villages are built with rock and clay quarried on the spot, so they often blend in mimetically with their spectacular backdrops. Since the nearest medical dispensary is in Tabant, mountain plants are collected to make wildcrafted herbal remedies.

The Aït Bougomez may be a happy place, but people here have to work hard just to make ends meet and send their children to school. To ensure the happiness of future generations, locals here have undertaken ambitious initiatives – woodworkers' collectives, girls' schools, organic farming and ecotourism – and they would be very happy indeed if you stopped by and showed your support.

Aït Bououli

From Azilal you'll arrive at Aït Mohammed, where you can follow the road leading southwest through hills marking geologic time in stripes of red, purple and white mineral deposits. Before you reach Agouti along this road, adventurers equipped with 4WD and steely nerves can detour into a steep red-clay gorge to Aït Bououli, which until a couple of years ago was inaccessible even by mule for months at a time. In this remote outpost 14km off the main road, there's a souq selling wild mountain herbs on Saturday, petroglyphs to explore with the help of a local guide and a stopping place for tea with homemade bread and butter, a cold drink or a tajine with a valley view at **Chez Hassan Benkoum** (tajine Dh70-100, tea with bread and butter donation).

Some 2.5km beyond Aït Bououli is a picturesque trio of villages built right into the two-toned rock bluff. At the far end of the triple town is a football pitch and a building housing the **Association Assamer** (8am-noon) that supports a women's cooperative that weaves carpets using some locally produced natural dyes. Enquire at the association whether you can see carpets, and you may be shown work on the premises or led to cooperative members' homes to see their work in progress.

Agouti

A trekker's haven, Agouti offers a range of *gîtes d'étape* (rustic hotels) and family-style guest houses, many with stellar views and down-to-earth Berber hospitality. The first on your left is **Flilou** (024 343796; tamsilt@menara.ma; dm with shared bathroom Dh50, s/d with private bathroom with half-board Dh120/150) with clean dorm rooms for trekkers (two with mountain views), doubles with hand-painted red beds around the rear courtyard, savoury meals and clean, updated bathrooms with blessedly hot water. Among the many more basic *gîte* options lining the road is **Chez Daoud** (☎ 062 105183; dm Dh50), a short walk down from the road beside barley fields, with rudimentary washing facilities.

Agouti is also home to a woodworkers' collective, the **Association Ighrem Atelier du Sculpture** (500m from Flilou, on left) which offers a glimpse of woodworkers honing their craft by day and the opportunity to buy spoons, bowls and honey dippers hand-carved of fragrant juniper wood directly from the artisan. Part of the proceeds goes to the collective for its vocational training outreach programs.

Another notable local initiative is **Cooperative Tikhiouine** (☎ 023 459736), 5km along the main road from Agouti in the village of Timmit (follow the signs from the road 50m downhill to the centre). Formed in 2005 by plucky young women over the protests of their parents and other naysaying locals, this women's cooperative secured EU funding to start its business cultivating organic walnuts, making mountain honey, selling locally cultivated saffron, and even making their own mild, aged goat-cheese. At the cooperative's centre, you can sample and purchase these products. 'Food-packaging companies are capitalising on our local produce, and we wanted to prove we could make better products for a fair price by producing them artisanally and packaging them ourselves', explains the dynamic, precocious president of the collective, aged 21. 'At first some people didn't want their daughters involved, but now there are 60 of us, and since we've won an award from Morocco as a model collective, every family wants to be involved'.

Tabant

The heart of the valley in more ways than one, Tabant attracts adventurers, ecotourists and visitors eager to preserve and support this spectacular remote region. This town is the sole official school for mountain guides, and though there is no official *bureau des guides* (tourist office) here, treks through the valley and to the mountains beyond can be arranged through Mr Brahim Aitsri, the tourism director responsible for the regional self-help association, the **Association Renaissance de Aït Bougomez** (☎ 061 497001, 023 459085; ausf_maroc2@yahoo.fr). Suggested treks range from two- to-three-hour valley strolls birdwatching or collecting Berber medicinal herbs, to four-day trans-mountain treks following ancient nomad routes with dromedaries. Other popular excursions include hikes up the cone-shaped hill to the *zawiya* of local *marabout* (saint) **Sidi Moussa**, which may or may not cure infertility as promised, but certainly offers stirring, romantic views over the valley. A portion of tour proceeds supports the association's projects, including women's literacy, water purification projects and a maternal and child-health program.

The association also runs a boarding school for girls who live in villages without schools. The school can be visited by prior arrangement with the school's English teacher, Merzouk Farami (☎ 072 180937; farami1982@hotmail.com; donation appreciated). Visitors can also donate basic English-language books to the school and/or volunteer to teach an after-school English lesson to the students, who are eager to practice with native speakers.

SLEEPING

In Tabant, the *gîte* of **Aït Oliqdim Mohamed** (☎ 023 459326; dm Dh50) is clean and offers cold showers and a delicious tajine if warned in advance. Of the three *gîtes* in the nearby village of Ikhf-n-Ighir, **Outagloute Benassar** (☎ 023 459175; dm Dh50) has clean dorm rooms, outside toilets and a selection of maps and books.

One highly appealing accommodation option just outside Tabant in Imelghas village is **our pick** **Ecolodge Dar Itrane** (☎ 010 086930; www.origins-lodge.com; Imelghas; half-board per person Dh440) where seemingly opposing ideas happily coexist: ecological and comfortable, rural and hip, internationally owned and locally engaged. Eighteen impeccable rooms in a former *gîte* have been kitted out with handmade Berber-style furnishings, plus bathrooms in gleaming *tadelakt* and hammered brass with solar-powered hot showers. The open organic kitchen invites the curious, the hydro-electric-powered hammam soothes the weary and downtime can be whiled away in the library of books and videos on Berber culture or browsing the boutique of locally made goods. With Dh22 donations from guests, Dar Itrane is helping to restore the Zawiya Sidi Moussa.

EATING

Among Tabant's attractions are its bustling regional **Sunday souq**, with a fresh produce market along the main street next to the used-donkey sales lot, and the **Café des Amis** (50m down main street), just across from the post office. For just Dh20, they'll whip up a scrumptious tajine in 30 minutes with garden-fresh vegetables, free-range meat and wildly aromatic mountain herbs.

Getting There & Away

Minibuses occasionally run from Azilal to Tabant (Dh40, three hours) in the morning when full, from near the central mosque. You can sometimes find a grand taxi for Dh60 per seat. There are plenty of trucks that head to Azilal on Thursday for its Friday market.

ZAOUIAT AHANSAL زاهنسال

You'll need a 4WD to head over the 40km of *piste* and the 2629m-high Tizi 'Tirghist to Zaouiat Ahansal. At the northern end of Imelghas, there's a *piste* that leads to the left towards Zauoiat Ahansal, and about 15km along atop a rocky hill, there's another fork in the road at a yellow sign where you'll take the right-hand road for Zaouiat Ahansal. Stretches of this road are currently being paved, but it's slow going along these twisting mountain roads, especially on Monday market day. Once you get to Zaouiat Ahansal, cross the bridge towards the magnificent mud-brick towers of the **ancient douar** (village) atop a steep hill; this structure once housed the entire 300-person community.

Just past this landmark on your left is the **Atelier du Tissages de l'Association du Zaouiat Ahsal** (1-6pm Tue-Sun), a women's weaving centre and after-school vocational training program. Here you can watch carpets being woven by apprentices as well as weaving *mâalems* (expert artisans) whose hands are a blur as they work with pronged antique carpet tools that could easily put an eye out in lesser hands. To give everyone a laugh, ask to give it a try yourself – just don't be offended if they take out your knot. The carpets are for sale, and part of the proceeds support the weaving training program and the village association's medical dispensary; the rest goes directly to the woman who made it, no middlemen involved.

Sleeping

The association also runs the *gîte d'étape* of **Sidi Ahmed Amahdar** (☎ 023 459393; Dh20), which offers hot showers, clean shared bathrooms and a clamorous welcome from the women who run the place; proceeds support the adjoining medical dispensary and women's weaving school. There are more *gîtes* in the surrounding villages of Agoudim, Amezrai and Taghia, the latter being two hours' walk upstream. North of town is Ouaouizarht (wah-ri-zat), which has a hotel and a Wednesday market.

Getting There & Away

If you're on a schedule, your only reliable bet is 4WD. Otherwise, there are trucks from Tabant to Zaouiat Ahansal on Sunday, and regular minivans run between Zaouiat Ahansal and Aït Mohammed (Dh40) and less frequently to Ouaouizarht via Tilougguite.

CATHÉDRALE DES ROCHER & RESERVE NATURELLE DE TAMGA

Continuing north along the main road from Zaouiat Ahansal leads you to the natural splendours of **La Cathédrale des Rocher**, the 'rock cathedral' with sheer stone faces that are a climber's ultimate challenge and delight, and the **Reserve Naturelle de Tamga**, a vast national reserve consisting of eight separate parks. Bird-watchers will have a field day (or several) observing the 107 species of birds, including some rare and endangered species. A small **botanical garden** 3km from the sign marking the park's entry offers a microcosm of the park's diverse plantlife, including fragrant North African wild thyme and medicinal herbs said to cure rheumatism. Overnight stays are possible 2km after the sign for the Cathédrale at **Gîte le Cathedrale** (per person half-board for dm or camping Dh 150; lunch/dinner Dh50/60). Bring a flashlight, because the solar-powered lighting here goes off early and the way to the shared bathroom is pitch black.

BIN EL-OUIRGANE

Once you've come as far as the Cathédrale, you can head back to Azilal via the paved road leading to Bin el-Ouirgane. Confusingly, a lake, the dam that created the lake and the town on the shores of the lake all share the same name. The dam provides the majority of the electricity available in the region, and though the water levels dropped in recent drought years, the lake is still quite a sight for dry eyes. Accommodation is available here at the eco-friendly (and just plain friendly) **Little Morocco** (☎ UK 44 0 1239 820951, Morocco 063 42373; www.littlemorocco.co.uk; outside Ben Ouidane village, see website for map & directions; s/d with half-board Dh300/600), a responsible-tourism joint venture between a British family and a local Berber family. Rooms are available in a traditional stone and mud-plaster home (cleaned without harmful chemicals) with hammam access included in the room rate. Climbing expeditions, mule rides, country souq visits, folkloric musical evenings and kayaking can be arranged through Little Morocco.

IMILCHIL املسيل

Just another striking Middle Atlas Berber village most of the year, Imilchil is flooded with visitors during its three-day September *moussem*. At this huge fair, local Berbers stock up for long months of isolation in winter, and while they're at it, scope the scene for someone to marry. Women strut their stuff in striped woollen cloaks and elaborate jewellery, and boys preen in flowing white jellabas.

The festival usually runs Friday to Sunday the third or fourth week of September; dates are posted at tourist offices throughout the country. Organised tours to the event are available from major cities in central Morocco, and the new paved road from Rich to Imilchil has brought busloads of tourists to eye prospective spouses. With hustlers, *faux guides* and souvenir stalls eyeing the tourists, onlookers are beginning to outnumber the young lovers – but there's no denying the voyeuristic fascination of the event.

During the festival, the area is covered in tented accommodation; otherwise, there are two basic hotels, a few simple refuge-style places and several café/restaurants.

To get to Imilchil from Marrakesh, head northeast by bus or a series of grands taxis to Kasba Tadla. From there you need to get another grand taxi to El-Ksiba. From El-Ksiba there is a daily bus to Aghbala. The turn-off for Imilchil is near Tizi n'Isly, about 10km before Aghbala. From there, 61km of paved road leads south to Imilchil. Around here there are a few grands taxis or souq lorries for transport, especially on Friday and Sunday market days.

If you have plenty of time, it's also possible to get to Imilchil (a breathtaking 160km by souq lorry or 4WD) from Boumalne du Dadès or Tinerhir. Minivans leave Imilchil for Tinerhir (Dh50 to Dh55) on Saturday.

SOUQ DAYS

In the Ourika Valley, around Jebel Toubkal, and towards the Tizi n'Tichka pass, local market days featuring local crafts, fresh produce and donkeys include:

- Monday: Tnine de l'Ourika
- Tuesday: Tahanaoute, Aït Ourir
- Wednesday: Tirdouine
- Thursday: El-Khemis
- Friday: Jemaa Rhemat
- Saturday: Asni
- Sunday: Setti Fatma

SOUTH OF MARRAKESH

OURIKA VALLEY وادة اوريكة

Easy on the eyes and city-stressed nerves, this bucolic blooming valley just 45 minutes by car or grand taxi from Marrakesh is the city's escape hatch. Temperatures are cooler here in the shadow east of Jebel Toubkal, and the sight of snow-capped High Atlas peaks puts the pressures of city living in proper perspective. A patchwork of fields runs downhill towards Marrakesh like a green carpet, providing places to camp, picnic or just loll and listen to your blood pressure drop. The valley is especially mood-altering February to April, when almond and cherry orchards bloom manically and wildflowers run riot.

Popular destinations in the area are the ski resort of Oukaïmeden (especially during peak snow season, November to March), the village and waterfalls of Setti Fatma further east, and the terraced town of Imlil, wedged into a crevice below Jebel Toubkal. But the area is full of hidden valleys, cliffside villages, ancient petroglyphs, moonscape plateaux and trickling mountain streams that reward travellers for packing their walking shoes. To get the lay of the land, stop by the **Centre d'Informations Touristique Ourika** (☎ 068 465545; ⏲ 8.30am-7pm Mon-Sat, 8.30am-1pm Sun), in the village of Tnine 33km from Marrakesh. This office is operated by a local NGO and provides information and a map of valley vista points. When trekking in winter, be advised that the valley has occasional flash floods; a particularly devastating flood in 1995 resulted in the loss of hundreds of lives.

If you're passing through Tnine on Monday, you can't miss the weekly souq along the main road. Another worthwhile stop in Tnine following the signs off the main road to the left before the bridge is the organic botanical garden at **Nectarôme** (☎ 024 313800; www.nectarome.com; ⏲ 10am-5pm), a Franco-Moroccan natural cosmetics and skin-care company that combines traditional Berber herbal remedies and hammam treatments with modern aromatherapy. Whether or not you're an aromatherapy believer, the garden certainly smells great, and a foot bath and foot massage with organic essential oils here (Dh100 to Dh200) is just the thing after a long trek.

Garden picnics with mountain-views await approximately 8km after Tnine towards Setti Fattma and across the bridge over the river at **Timalizene** (☎ 024 484059, 063 564656; www.timalizene.com, in French; garden entry Dh15, lunch Dh120, booking recommended), a wild aromatic garden and guest house (s/d incl breakfast Dh275/380) that also offers botanical treks and visits to Berber villages.

About 45km from Marrakesh a warm welcome awaits at the eight-room **Auberge le Maquis** (☎ 024 484531; www.le-maquis.com, in French; Aghbalou; per person half-board Dh450), a family-style getaway and launching pad/finish line for bikers and trekkers. The local management makes meals feel like casual dinners among friends, and they dote on kids: children under 12 get half-board for the cost of dinner only. The auberge arranges treks to Yaggour plateau petroglyphs and mule treks for little ones. Nonguests can use the pool for Dh80, and there's a play-yard where kids can cut loose.

Another 5km along the road to Setti Fatma is the charming **our pick** **Ourika Garden** (☎ 024 484441; www.ourika-garden.com; Aghbalou; s half-board Dh660, d half-board Dh770-960), a guest house set amid a gardener's dream: organic terraced plots of aromatic herbs, succulents and vegetables with footbridges and valley vistas in between. Breakfasts on the terrace are sumptuous feasts featuring fresh local goat-cheese and olive oil, and the attentive staff are so full of smiles it's a wonder there are no pulled muscles.

Oukaïmeden اوكيمدين

Best known as Morocco's only ski resort, Oukaïmeden (elevation 2650m, 75km from Marrakesh) is also a handy trekking base to explore local rock carvings; the Club Alpin Français (CAF) can point you towards trailheads. In peak snow season, skiers will find seven runs from nursery to black, six tows and the highest ski-lift in Africa (3243m). Gear, passes and lessons are available in town at prices that will delight skiers used to European and American rates.

Peak season has historically been late January to March, but in recent years snow has been scarce by March, and there is environmentally oblivious talk of manufacturing snow to artificially extend the season. Given Morocco's scarce water supplies and the energy output required to create snow, eco-savvy skiers are best advised to 'snowboard' the dunes in Merzouga instead (p370) when snow is low.

SLEEPING & EATING

CAF refuge (☎ 024 319036; www.caf-maroc.com; CAF or HI members/nonmembers per person Dh69/92; hot showers Dh5) offers dormitory beds, a few private rooms, a bar-restaurant (Dh18 for breakfast) and a well-equipped kitchen, but you'll need your own sleeping bag. They can arrange group pickups from Marrakesh (Dh300 to Dh400 for up to four by grand taxi or Dh700 to Dh900 for nine to 12 by minibus or 4WD), and onsite they sell a selection of French trekking- and mountaineering-guidebooks.

The **Hôtel Chez Juju** (☎ 024 319005; www.hotelchezjuju.com; full-board s/d Dh390/680) has a reliable Alpine-styled bar-restaurant and wood-ceilinged rooms with drippy showers curtained off in the corner and communal toilets. Sticking out amid the snowcapped mountains like a fake tan in winter is the orange-tinted, high-rise **Hotel Kenzi Louka** (☎ 024 319080; fax 024 319088; www.kenzi-hotels.com; s/d Dh750/900; breakfast Dh90;), with 101 bland rooms and equally bland international restaurant. Still, the place has a following among snow-bunnies who prefer their mountain views from chairs alongside the indoor swimming pool.

Your best bet to get to Ouakaïmeden is to arrange transport through CAF. Otherwise you can charter a grand taxi (Dh600 return from Marrakesh), or take a Setti Fatma– or Aghbalou-bound bus and try hitching up the mountain from there.

Setti Fatma ستي فتما

A little village that's seen a whole lot of tourist action in the past decade, Setti Fatma is still a scenic stop for lunch by the river running through town, and has hikes to the seven waterfalls in a nearby hidden valley. The village is neatly nestled in a canyon beneath the High Atlas mountains at the far end of the Ourika Valley road, 24km south of the Oukaïmeden turn-off. Prime times to visit are in early March where the cherry and almond trees are in bloom, or in August for the four-day *moussem,* with its fair and market at the *koubba* of Setti Fatma. During the summer the place is clogged with heat-struck visitors from Marrakesh gasping for air; to cool down without the crowds, head instead to the lesser-known and splendidly untrammelled Zat Valley (p337).

Waterfall hikes range from an easy 20-minute stroll to arduous stream-hikes; ignore the *faux guides* and find a licensed guide to lead the way on foot or mule at the **bureau des guides** (☎/fax 024 426113) 200m beyond the Hôtel Asgaour. The *bureau des guides* can also offer advice on treks further afield (see p433), including hikes east to Tourcht, north to Imi n'Taddert, to Anammer and Tizi n'Oucheg in the Aït Oucheg Valley, and from the Yaggour Plateau into the Zat Valley.

Kitted out colourfully as a Marrakshi water-seller, our pick **Hôtel Restaurant La Perle D'Ourika** (☎ 061 567239; d incl breakfast Dh200-450; set meals Dh80-100) is smartly run by the motherly Ammaria, who will ply you with piles of her legendary seasonal couscous dishes, including wild mushroom. **Hôtel Asgaour** (☎ 066 416419; r for up to 3 people with shared/private bathroom Dh150/100) has simple but airy, clean rooms with slightly lumpy pillows and communal showers (Dh5). The restaurant downstairs serves set-price meals with bubbling, well-caramelised tajines for Dh50 to Dh60.

Both sides of the river at Setti Fatma are lined with rustic café-restaurants offering tajines priced to move. Two of the better choices are **Café-Restaurant Imlil** (on left side near the parking at the end of town), and **Café-Restaurant Azrrabzou** (opposite river) over a rickety plank bridge in a patch of almond trees. Both offer set meals with salad, tajine and bottled water starting at Dh50, or generous tajines for Dh30 that could satisfy two famished trekkers.

Grands taxis to Setti Fatma leave frequently all day from Bab er-Rob in Marrakesh (Dh35) and there are less-frequent minibuses (Dh15 to Dh25). Transport returns when full.

JEBEL TOUBKAL جبل توبقال

For pure mountain air that cuts through the heat and makes you giddy, don't miss the highest mountain in North Africa: snow-capped Jebel Toubkal. Mountain trails, criss-crossing the High Atlas (p423) head up and away from base camps at Imlil, where there's a handy and highly informative **bureau des guides** (☎/fax 024 485626). Travel agencies in Marrakesh can also arrange multiday treks with English-speaking guides.

Asni اسني

The Saturday souq is the major draw for travellers at this junction of the Marrakesh–Taroudannt road and the Mizane Valley road to Imlil, 47km south of Marrakesh. Sellers lug fruit, vegetables and livestock over the Atlas Mountains to sell here, but increasingly you'll find jewellery, rugs and souvenirs among the donkeys. From Asni there's an old mule track running through the Mizane Valley and past tiny stone Berber villages to Imlil; the route takes about six hours.

Imlil إمليل

The sleeper hit of the Mizane Valley, tiny terraced Imlil (elevation 1740m) has become a favourite hitching post for trekkers and overheated Marrakesh escapees. The paved road ends here, and it's a five-hour trek to the base of Jebel Toubkal. You could make a day trip of it with a mountain stream

HIDDEN OASES GOODWILL TOUR

Follow your bliss and find new sources of inspiration at 1· terrific community ventures on this four-night, five-day eco-adventure:

Day 1

- Depart Marrakesh; nature hike and overnight in Zat Valley with **L'Association des Amis du Zat** (p338).

Day 2

- Zat Valley river hike; lunch provided by **L'Association des Amis du Zat** (p338).
- Head over Tizi n'Tichka pass to Telouet; tour **Glaoui kasbah** (p338).
- Plant tree in Tighza with **Baraka Community Partnerships** (p338).
- Dinner & overnight in Tighza with **Homestays Morocco** (p338).

Day 3

- Depart Tighza to Telouet and onwards to visit **Aït Benhaddou kasbah** (p339).
- Lunch overlooking kasbah at **Auberge Cafe-Restaurant Bilal** (p340).
- Ouarzazate Fair-Trade shopping excursion to **Coopérative de Tissage** (p344), **Ensemble Artisanal** (p344) and **Horizon Artisanat** (p344).
- Onwards to Agdz to visit **Association Development Hart Chaou community garden project** (p345).
- Dinner & overnight in Zagora at eco-friendly **Dar Raha** (p348).

Day 4

- Browse for crafts in **Amezrou Mellah** (p349) and **Arc-en-Ciel women's cooperative** (p349).
- Depart for desert trip to Erg Chigaga arranged through sustainable tourism agency **Inside Morocco Travel** (p308).
- Campfire dinner & overnight under the stars in **Erg Chigaga** (p351).

Day 5

- Depart desert via **Foum Zguid** (p352).
- Optional carpet-shopping at community weaving collectives **Cooperative Ahilal des Tapis** (p353)and **Iklane Association** (p353).
- Lunch at **I Rocher** (p338), or optional overnight.
- Evening return to Marrakesh.

hike, but the real attraction here is waking up in a High Atlas nook surrounded by flowering trees in spring and snowcapped Jebel Toubkal in the heat of summer.

En route to Imlil, stop for a refreshing Berber tea and visit to the nonprofit herb garden and school at **Dar Taliba** (El Hanchane near Imlil; donations appreciated & used wisely). This groundbreaking girls' school gives rural girls access to middle-school education and keeps essential Berber botanical knowledge alive.

SLEEPING & EATING

Rustic cold-water accommodation options here have gotten spiffier of late, both in Imlil proper and in *gîtes* lining the lush terrace-farmed valley to the east of Imlil. During major European holidays it's best to reserve, but otherwise you can try your luck at the *gîtes* once you get to town. Prices increase by at least 15% in high season between April and October; some places close in the cold off-season between November and February.

Budget

Hôtel el-Aïne (☎ 024 485625; rooftop beds Dh30, r per person Dh45) Get the light, pleasant upstairs rooms clustered around a tranquil courtyard with an old walnut tree; expect hot showers and shared toilets.

CAF Refuge (☎ 024 485612; www.caf-maroc.com; dm CAF & HI members/nonmembers Dh35/58, camping per person/per tent Dh6/12) A climbers' hostel offers dorm-style bunks, cooking facilities, and first-aid equipment; show your Lonely Planet guidebook to get the HI rate. CAF also offers camping.

Hotel Café Aksoual (☎ 024 485612; s/d/tr/q Dh70/80/100/120) One of the larger hotels in town, with clean comfortable rooms, hot showers and reliable trekking advice from manager/guide Hassan.

Hôtel Etoile de Toubkal (☎ 024 485618; s/d/tr Dh120/160/230, d with bathroom Dh250) Not exactly a scenic view of the parking at the village entrance, but the reasonable rooms each have a balcony and some have a bathroom.

Atlas Gîte Imlil (Chez Jean Pierre; ☎ /fax 024 485609; d with half-board Dh170; mid-Feb–end Oct) Four basic rooms with communal bathrooms, cosy sitting areas, and a bar and restaurant serving Moroccan food with a hint of Burgundy.

Dar Adrar (☎ 070 726809; http://toubkl.guide.free.fr/gite; d incl breakfast/half-board Dh220/330) Sitting on top of the world and Imlil, Dar Adrar has simple rooms that don't distract from the mountaintop views, an in-house hammam (Dh40, book ahead) and an invaluable resource in owner and expert Atlas Mountain guide Mohamed Aztat.

Café-Hotel Soleil (☎ /fax 024 485622; d incl breakfast without/with bathroom Dh170/220, per person without/with bathroom half-board Dh170/220) Spartan but clean, with beds or mattresses on the floor, hot showers and meals on the terrace overlooking the river. Located opposite the *bureau de guides.*

Top End

Kasbah du Toubkal (☎ 024 485611, 061 343337; www.kasbahdutoubkal.com; incl breakfast d/tr Dh1430/2750, ste Dh3410-4850) This converted historic kasbah (1800m) lords it over Imlil with panoramic views of snowy peaks and verdant valleys. The UK-based ownership and local Imlil staff run the place with the environment and community in mind, and levy a 5% community tariff on stays that has helped build a local girls' school and purchase an ambulance. Eleven bedrooms range from quaintly cute to kasbah cool, and three 'Berber salons' with sleeping lofts allow families and groups to bunk communally. At guests' disposal are a traditional hammam (book ahead), board games for playing fireside, local staff who seem genuinely glad to see you – no snootiness here – and excellent meals (Dh180 to Dh250).

GETTING THERE & AWAY

Frequent local buses (Dh15, 1½ hours) and grands taxis (Dh30, one hour) leave south of Bab er-Rob in Marrakesh (south of the medina) to Asni. Local minibuses and very occasional taxis travel the final 17km between Asni and Imlil (Dh15 to Dh20, one hour). Expect a car journey from Marrakesh to Imlil to take at least 2.5 hours.

TO THE TIZI N'TEST

Even with white knuckles and gritted teeth, you'll have to admire the route to Taroudannt as it winds through the High Atlas, careens over the Tizi n'Test at 2092m, then swoops down onto the Souss plain. As if the road weren't enough of an adventure, the weather is subject to sudden changes. Heavy clouds and mist often cut visibility to near zero at the top of the pass and you might find your way blocked by snow in winter, so check weather conditions before leaving.

Along the way, you might stop for an overnight stay at the pretty town of Ouirgane, 15km south of Asni, or forge onward to visit ancient **Tin Mal mosque**. Tin Mal village is on the right of the road coming from Marrakesh, just past a kasbah perched on a rocky outcrop to your left. The village's Almohad-era mosque was built in 1156 in honour of the dynasty's strict spiritual leader, Mohammed ibn Tumart, who left a trail of smashed wine jugs and musical instruments in his wake. The mosque is still used for Friday prayers, but on other days the guardian will usher you through its massive doors and rose-coloured archways into the serene prayer hall (Dh10 to Dh20 tip expected).

A former French Legionnaire's retreat, **Au Sanglier Qui Fume** (☎/fax 044 485707; www.ausanglierquifume.com; km 61, Route de Taroudannt; s incl breakfast/half-board Dh325/420, d incl breakfast/half-board Dh415/605, d ste incl breakfast/half-board Dh505-655/Dh695-845;) has been run by the same French family since 1945. All 15 rooms and 10 suites have private bathrooms, and most have fireplaces or wood stoves. The chronically restless can initiate tournaments of billiards, table tennis and darts, and take horse-riding excursions and mountain-bike trips (rental Dh100 per day).

Nature lovers flock like Barbary sheep to environmentally minded **Dar Tassa** (☎ 079 886081; www.dartassa.com; Douar Tassa Ouirgane; d Dh605, ste Dh660-770), in the mountain hamlet of Tassa Ouirgane (1300m) adjoining the Takherkhort nature preserve near Ouirgane. Ask about excursions and treks in the preserve to see Barbary sheep, Amaseen gazelles, and other rare and endangered species. Afterwards, weary trekkers will appreciate Jacuzzis in the suites, and rest easy knowing that a percentage of the room rate helps the High Atlas Foundation plant trees locally.

Romantic enough to soften the flintiest cynic, **Chez Momo** (☎ 024 485704; www.aubergemomo.com, in French; Route de Taroudannt, 62km, 150m off main road in Ouirgane town centre; d/ste half-board Dh650/880;) has six get-cosy rooms with wrought-iron beds and suggestive lighting overlooking the wildflower garden and pool; suites have fireplaces.

Grands taxis (Dh25 per person) run to Ouirgane occasionally from Bab er-Rob in Marrakesh.

TO THE TIZI N'TICHKA

Higher than the Tizi n'Test to the west but an easier drive, the Tizi n'Tichka connects Marrakesh with the pre-Sahara oases – when the weather cooperates. In winter check with the **Gendarmerie of the Col du Tichka** (☎ 024 890615) whether the pass is open; in 2005, several tourists stranded on the pass died in their car.

Soon after Aït Ourir and the road leading to the Zat Valley, the ascending road takes a turn for the scenic amid oak trees, walnut groves and oleander bushes. Past the village of Taddert, the road gets steeper and the landscape is stripped of colour, except for hardy wildflowers and kids along the road selling geodes dyed shocking red and green. At the top of the Tizi n'Tichka pass, reward yourself with a bracing espresso and views at café-restaurant **Assanfou** (☎ 061 132130; 9am-7pm). You can also reach the Tizi n'Tichka on foot through the spectacular Zat Valley.

Once over the pass, you descend into the lunar landscape of the Anti Atlas and the desert beyond. Instead of staying on the paved road from Tizi n'Tichka to Ouarzazate, those with a 4WD or mountain bike could follow the 36km of rough *piste* south from Telouet along the Ouadi Ounila through Anmiter and Tamdaght to Aït Benhaddou. Most hotels in Telouet can arrange guides and mules for the walk for around Dh250 to Dh300 per day.

Zat Valley

For decades trekkers have jealously guarded the secret of one of the most pristine hidden valleys in the High Atlas, but the Zat Valley isn't about to let fame go to its splendid trailhead. When Marrakesh is sweating it out just 50km to the northwest, breezes are rippling through barley and swaying poplar trees along the footpaths of this charmed river valley.

To get here, take the N9 to Ouarzazate until it crosses the Oued Zat at Aït Ourir, then head south towards the transport town of Tighdouine at the near end of the valley. Tighdouine has tasty roadside tajines and a peculiar frontier feel as the last stop before entering Zat's land of make-believe: gardens built right into cliff faces, stone houses with bright-blue doors and white-framed windows, and movie-star-beautiful families leaning out to say hello.

This is all best appreciated on foot or mule. There's a road winding above the valley floor, but only physicist drivers able to calculate clearance in millimetres should attempt it. Development has been further limited by the designation of airspace over the Zat Valley as a national security zone that must be left clear of electrical stations and cell towers. Time seems to have forgotten the Zat Valley, which is a mixed blessing: some small villages here are without running water or access for medical emergencies, and children walk upwards of 8km one way to reach the nearest school.

But without spoiling the local landscape, the local self-help association has come up with a home remedy: two- to five-day walking tours, with mules for anyone who gets weak in the knees from the Zat Valley's natural beauty. **L'Association des Amis du Zat** (☎ 024 485543; azat96@yahoo.fr) organises scenic walking tours of the valley for groups of six or more. Suggested donations for treks including trail guide, meals, overnight stays and mules as needed are on a sliding scale from Dh400 to Dh750 per day.

Hikers stay overnight at picturesque stopping points along the valley at any of three *gîtes* run by the association and built by local villagers with donations from the many trekkers besotted with this valley over the years. When villagers who eke out a living from tiny terrace plots invite you home for their best homemade bread, butter, walnuts and wild sage tea, the hardest hearts melt like snow on the High Atlas mountains visible from the Zat Valley. In terms of etiquette, it's fine to offer a small monetary token of appreciation, but don't press the issue if refused – and save larger donations for the association, who use it wisely on such critical community projects as bridges, reforestation, literacy programs and a medical dispensary.

Telouet تلوات

Before 1928 there was no avoiding this stop on the trans-Saharan caravan route: anyone passing through the Tizi n'Tichka paid tolls to local warlords for the privilege. But Telouet's privileged position ended in 1953, when native son and French collaborator Pasha Glaoui was ousted by the Moroccan Independence movement. Legend has it that when the imposing doors of Telouet's Glaoui kasbah were thrown open at last, locals who had mysteriously disappeared from their villages years before stumbled dazed onto Telouet streets, having spent years locked in the Glaoui basement. But the new state was ambivalent about the Glaoui clan's hometown, and with little outside investment and a paved road bypassing the town entirely, Telouet seems arrested in time half a century ago.

The once-glorious **Glaoui kasbah** (admission by donation, Dh10 suggested) has been left to crumble, and the best indication of Telouet's former position as the centre of a trading empire is the 2nd-floor receiving court. No less than 300 artisans were recruited (if that's the word) to complete salons faceted with stucco, *zellij* and painted cedar ceilings that make Marrakesh's royal Bahia Palace seem like a freshman artisan effort. See this architectural masterpiece while you can – ceilings have already collapsed in the many rooms marked with a red X.

SLEEPING & EATING

Along the narrow river valley oases beyond Telouet are more crumbling Glaoui kasbahs, ancient fortified villages such as **Anmiter** (11km from Telouet, accessible by bus) and sudden flashes of green and silver along the river below. The best way to visit these is through our pick **Homestays Morocco** (☎ 77840487; www.homestaysmorocco.net), which arranges overnight stays with local families in and around the village of Tighza to provide much-needed income to this remote subsistence farming community 21km from Telouet by *piste*. The family-welcome received by guests is that of a minor football hero, meals are farm-fresh and embarrassingly generous, and the stars seem within reach at night. Tighza native Mohamed El Qasemy and his British wife Caroline (yes, they met on vacation) run this program, and at the time of writing are finishing a new solar- and wind-powered kasbah guest house in Tighza (call ☎ 77840487 for availability and rates), and manage **Baraka Community Partnerships** (www.barakacommunity.com), which organises volunteers to build schools, plant trees and supply basic medical care (see p477).

In Telouet, **Auberge Lion D'Or** (☎ 024 888507; mattress on roof Dh25, d half-board Dh250) has 16 rooms with private bathrooms, simple pine beds and a convenient location on the kasbah's doorstep. They also make filling *panachés* (fruit smoothies), although the deluxe version with almond milk, avocado, banana and imported kiwi is perhaps too much of a good thing. For other meals, try the restaurants around Telouet's central square, where you'll find Dh40 tajines and Dh30 Berber omelettes (with tomato, olives and mountain herbs).

Halfway between the turn-off for Telouet and Aït Benhaddou is our pick **I Rocha** (☎ 067 737002; www.irocha.com; Tisseldi, Ighrem N'Oudal; d half-

MARRAKESH & CENTRAL MOROCCO

board per person Dh460;), a cliffside guest house that lifts you and your travel-worn spirits way up over the green river valley below. The 10 rooms have easygoing Berber charm, with painted ceilings, folk art on reclaimed Styrofoam and slinky *tadelakt* walls. Owners Ahmed and Katherine provide a family-style setting and terrific French-Moroccan dishes with herbs fresh from the terrace garden; guests can learn how to cook them for Dh350. To unwind after guided hikes to the Fint Oasis and nearby natural springs, go for a hammam (Dh80) and dip in the small pool.

GETTING THERE & AWAY

From the N9 Marrakesh–Ouarzazate Rd, the turn-off to Telouet is a few kilometres beyond the pass. There's a daily bus from Bab Gehmat in Marrakesh (Dh55), which returns to Marrakesh at 7am. A bus leaves Ouarzazate at noon, also returning at 7am (Dh40 to Dh50). Grands taxis may be an option for Dh50 to Dh70 per seat, but you might get stuck renting out all six seats.

AÏT BENHADDOU آيت بنحدو

Introductions aren't strictly necessary, since you'll probably recognise this red mud-brick kasbah 32km from Ouarzazate from such films as *Lawrence of Arabia*, *Jesus of Nazareth* (for which much of Aït Benhaddou was rebuilt), *Jewel of the Nile* (note the suspiciously Egyptian tapered gate towers) and *Gladiator*. Like certain Botoxed stars, this Unesco-protected kasbah seems a little too frozen in time; with the help of Hollywood touch-ups it still resembles its youthful days in the 11th century as an Almoravid caravanserai.

From the Hôtel la Kasbah, head down past the souvenir stalls and you'll see the kasbah on the other side of the parched Oued Ounila riverbed. But where are all the people? In recent years the population of the Aït Benhaddou kasbah has dwindled, giving the place the eerie feeling of a deserted stage-set around sunset. The few remaining residents make a few dirham providing you access through their family homes to the kasbah (Dh10 tip customary). Climb the kasbah to see a ruined *agadir* (fortified granary) with magnificent views of the surrounding *palmeraie* and unforgiving *hammada* (stony desert).

A less retouched kasbah can be found 7km north along the tarmac from Aït Benhaddou: the **Tamdaght kasbah** (Dh10 tip to caretaker), yet another crumbling Glaoui fortification topped by storks' nests.

Sleeping

Auberge Baraka (☎ 024 890305; fax 024 886273; mattresses on terrace Dh30, s/d Dh100/170) When convenience is paramount, the Baraka offers simple, serviceable rooms with private bathrooms and a Moroccan restaurant (set menu Dh80) in the middle of town.

Riad Maktoub (☎ 024 888694; www.riadmaktoub.com; Aït Benhaddou; d half-board Dh500, ste half-board Dh600-1100) Within these pisé walls are several rooms overlooking the garden courtyard and four with fireplaces. The suites seem a tad overdressed for the desert with fussy heavy fabrics and movie-prop knickknacks; the snug, spare doubles with comfy new mattresses are the sweet deal here.

Kasbah Ellouze (☎ 024 890459; www.kasbahellouze.com; Tamdaght; s/d half-board with shared bathroom Dh528/704, s/d half-board with private bathroom Dh737/924, ste half-board Dh1364) Situated in Tamdaght, 7km north of Aït Benhaddou, this new pisé guest house blends in with the ancient Glaoui kasbah, located within the adjacent walled village and overlooking almond orchards (*luz* means almonds). Tower rooms with shared bathrooms are great value, while the green-tiled suite is spiffy but not any more special than the stylish air-conditioned doubles in the annex across the alley.

Dar Mouna (☎ 028 843054; www.darmouna.com; s/d incl breakfast Dh480/600, s/d half-board Dh720/840, ste incl breakfast/half-board Dh780/960;) An elegant pisé guest house that threatens to steal scenes from the movie star of a kasbah directly across the valley. Light, high-ceilinged rooms facing the valley are the ones to get, though split-level suites are ideal for families. Meals feature herbs grown in the garden, home-made honey, home-baked bread and a priceless terrace view. Amenities include a bar, hammam, oversized chlorinated pool and on-site rental for bikes, mules and dromedaries.

Eating

Auberge SouSou (near the entrance to the kasbah; meals from Dh30), this roadside eatery serves a no-fuss Dh30 sandwich, Dh40 Berber omelette and variable Dh40 to Dh60 tajines on dusty yet cheerful garden furniture.

Auberge Cafe-Restaurant Bilal (☎ 068 248370) For lunch with a view, pull up a patio chair and gaze at Aït Benhaddou across the way. Set menus with salad, plat du jour and dessert are Dh90 for individuals or Dh65 for groups.

Getting There & Away

To get here from Ouarzazate, take the main road towards Marrakesh as far as the signposted turn-off (22km); Aït Benhaddou is another 9km down a bitumen road. Cycling from Ouarzazate takes around three hours.

Grands taxis run from outside Ouarzazate bus station when full (Dh20 per person) and from the turn-off (Dh120 one-way or Dh250 to Dh350 half-day with return). Minibuses run from Tamdaght to Ouarzazate in the morning when full.

OUARZAZATE ورزازت

pop 79,000

Strategically located enough that it didn't have to be scenic, Ouarzazate (war-zazat) has historically gotten by on its wits instead of its looks. The sprawling Taourirt kasbah was built on prime commercial real-estate, and for centuries it was where people from the Atlas, Drâa and Dadès valleys converged to do business. The modern town you see today was built as a French garrison town in the 1920s so that the protectorate could keep a watchful eye on its business interests. The movie business gradually took off in Ouarzazate after the protectorate left in the 1950s, and the region of Ouarzazate has since built quite a résumé as a body-double for Tibet, Rome, Somalia and Egypt.

Ouarzazate is always ready for action, with well-stocked supermarkets where you can pick up essential desert supplies from wet wipes to whisky. With scores of travel and rental agencies offering bikes, motorbikes and camels, this is an ideal launching pad for the mountains, desert and gorges. But from November to March, come prepared for icy winds that can come whipping down from the High Atlas Mountains without warning.

Business-savvy Ouarzazate has traditionally catered to captive package tourists

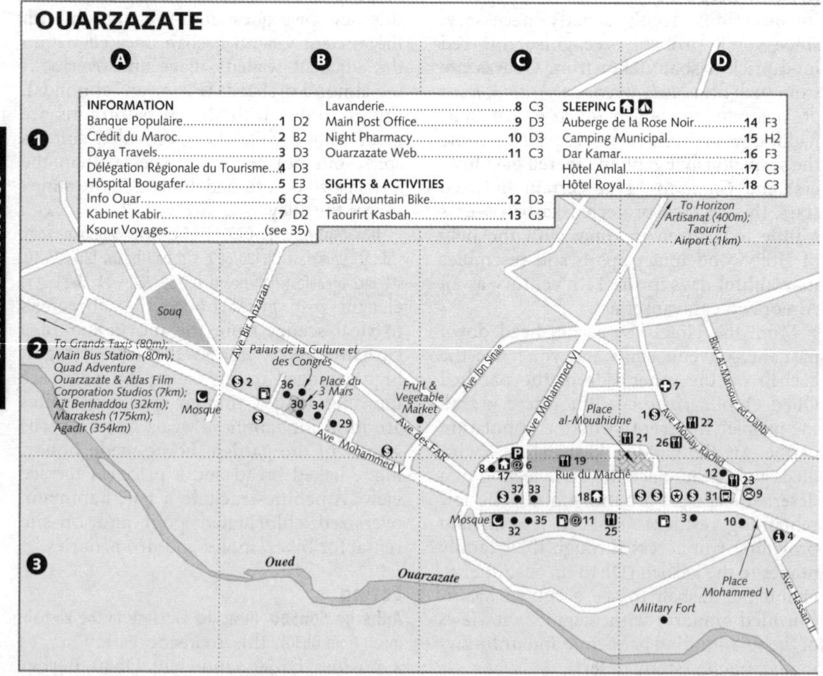

instead of independent travellers, and as a result it's been seen as a holding pen for tourists chomping at the bit to get to the dunes. But now that King Mohammed VI has been spending time here and fixing up the roads, Ouarzazate is working hard to rebuild its desert mystique. The new brick plaza at the centre of town is having its intended effect of drawing locals and visitors for balmy desert evening strolls, and the golf course on the east end of town has been wisely left to resume its life as a desert. Still, if Ouarzazate really wants to get in touch with its caravanserai roots, the generic condo-hotel complexes under construction may need rethinking.

Information

EMERGENCY

Police (☎ 190; Ave Mohammed V)

INTERNET ACCESS

Info Ouar (per hr Dh10) Around the corner from Hôtel Amlal.

Ouarzazate Web (Ave Mohammed V; per hr Dh10) Centrally located and professionally run.

LAUNDRY

Lavanderie (Rue du Marché; 9am-noon & 2-8pm; washers Dh30, dryers Dh20) Near Hôtel Amlal, has modern washers and dryers.

MEDICAL SERVICES

Hôspital Bougafer (☎ 024 882444; Ave Mohammed V) Public hospital east of the tourist office.

Kabinet Kabir (☎ 024 885276) More reliable private clinic used by resident expatriates.

Night Pharmacy (☎ 024 882490; Ave Mohammed V; 8am-1pm & 3.30-11pm)

MONEY

There are plenty of banks on the northern end of Ave Mohammed V, all with ATMs.

Banque Populaire (Ave Moulay Rachid; 8.30-11.30am & 2.30-4.30pm Mon-Fri, 3-6pm Sat, 9am-1pm Sun)

Crédit du Maroc (cnr Ave Mohammed V & Ave Bir Anzaran) At the western end of town; offers cash advances on your credit card.

POST & TELEPHONE

There are numerous téléboutiques in the centre.

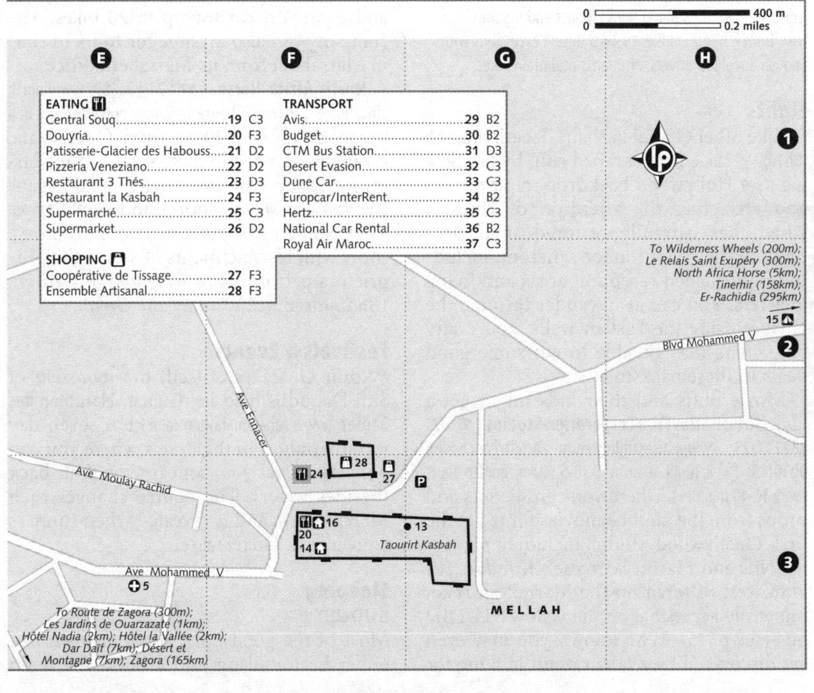

Main post office (Ave Mohammed V; 8.30am-noon & 2.30-6pm Mon-Fri, 8.30am-noon Sat) Postal services and a direct-dial international phone.

TOURIST INFORMATION

Délégation Régionale du Tourisme (ONMT; ☎ 024 882485; fax 024 885290; Ave Mohammed V; 8.30am-4.30pm) Unusually sharp and helpful tourist office.

TRAVEL AGENCIES

Daya Travels (☎/fax 024 887707; www.dayatravels.com; Ave Mohammed V) English-speaking Dutch-Moroccan owners organise desert excursions, rent mountain bikes and provide free bike-trail maps.

Desert Dream (☎ 024 885343; www.sahara-desert-dream.com; 4 Blvd Al-Mansour ed-Dahbi) Budget-minded, friendly agency offers fixed-rate, all-inclusive excursions to the desert or the gorges by camel, 4WD or on foot. Located opposite from Berber Palace Hotel.

Désert et Montagne (☎ 024 854949; www.desert-montagne.ma, in French) Morocco's first female mountain guide and her company organise trips designed for women and families to meet Berber women in the mountains. Other options include walking and 4WD trips in the High Atlas, desert trips of three to 15 days, and longer trips following caravan routes. Operates from Dar Daïf (see opposite).

Ksour Voyages (☎ 024 882840; www.ksour-voyages.com; 11 Place du 3 Mars) Books flights and organises trips from mountain hikes to 4WD desert excursions with English-speaking drivers; also rents mountain bikes.

Sights

Unlike other Glaoui kasbahs, **Taourirt Kasbah** (Dh10; 8am-6.30pm) escaped ruin by taking a gig as a Hollywood backdrop in *Star Wars* and attracting the attention of Unesco, which has carefully restored small sections of the Glaoui inner-sanctum, including unfurnished reception areas and living quarters. You can also wander through the village inside the kasbah walls, and crafty bargainers may be able to cut some good deals in these backstreet shops.

Movie buffs and their kids might get a kick out of **Atlas Film Corporation Studios** (☎ 024 882212/23; www.atlastudios.com; adult/concession Dh30/15; 8.30-11.50am & 2.30-5.50pm, guided tours every 30-40 minutes), where you can see sets and props from the famous movies filmed at the first 'Ouallywood' studio, including *Jewel of the Nile* and Martin Scorcese's *Kundun*. It's 5km west of town on the Marrakesh road, but easily accessible on the yellow STUDID bus (see p345). Who knows, you may even get discovered by a talent scout looking for extras – though as locals point out, the Dh40 to Dh100 day rates for extras aren't exactly Screen Actors' Guild pay.

Activities

Though many agencies and hotels still offer them, quad bikes cause considerable damage to the fragile local desert ecosystem and are not recommended. Already quad use is being restricted in Merzouga, and with growing awareness of the environmental issues they raise along with inevitable clouds of dust, Ouarzazate, Zagora and Mhamid may follow suit.

Saïd Mountain Bike (☎ 062 869324; www.saidmountainbike.com; Ave Moulay Rachid cnr Rue de la Poste; per day/week Dh220/990) keeps a fleet of 43 mountain bikes in top condition, and offers mountain biking–, mule- and dromedary-excursions into the mountains and desert.

For professionally guided off-*piste* motorbike tours throughout southern Morocco, contact British-run **Wilderness Wheels** (☎ 024 888128, in Marrakesh 024 330443; www.wildernesswheels.com; 44 Hay al-Qods, excursions starting at 3 days/2 nights for Dh8470) just off Ave Mohammed V. Prices include overnight stays, complete riding gear and a support car for up to 20 bikes. The company can also arrange for tours to start in Marrakesh from its Marrakesh office.

North Africa Horse (☎ 024 886689; www.northafricahorse.fr, in French; Route de Skoura, opposite Royal Golf Ouarzazate), located 20km from Ouarzazate, arranges stunts with horses and dromedaries for Hollywood productions and organises five- to six-day horse and camel trips. They sometimes put on a touristy horse show with re-enactments of stunts the proprietors performed in *Kingdom of Heaven, Gladiator* and *Alexander the Great*.

Festivals & Events

Within Ouarzazate itself, the *moussem* of Sidi Daoud is held in August. **Marathon des Sables** (www.saharamarathon.co.uk) is a seven-day ultramarathon in the desert where you can only take what you can carry on your back (besides water). The course changes each March/April, and is revealed when runners converge in Ouarzazate.

Sleeping

BUDGET

Most of the good hotel deals in town can either be found on and around the main drag of Ave Mohammed V or 1km to 2km along the Route de Zagora.

Camping Municipal (☎ 024 888322; camping per person Dh15 plus per car/tent site Dh10/5) Signposted next to the 'Tourist Complex' off the main road out of town about 3km from the bus station, alongside the Oued Ouarzazate. Mostly for motor-homes but there are spots for tents under trees, new bathrooms, hot showers (Dh6), a basic restaurant and electrical hookups for Dh20.

Hôtel Royal (☎ 024 890042; 24 Ave Mohammed V; s/d/tr no shower & shared toilet Dh45/80/100, shower & shared toilet 70/100/140, private bathroom Dh90/120/160) Central and far more pleasant than you'd expect for the price, though bring earplugs for rooms facing the street. The terrace and courtyard are traveller hangouts with fresh juices, good coffee, passable pizza (Dh 45) and tajines (Dh40).

Hôtel Nadia (☎ 024 854940; km 2 Route de Zagora; s/d incl breakfast Dh180/200;) With shiny new tiled bathrooms and guestrooms, bouncy new beds, chipper staff and a suitably modest pool, this place is a welcome switch from the usual dusty budget hotels and faux kasbahs.

Hôtel Amlal (☎ 024 884030; www.hotel-amlal.com; 24 Rue du Marché; s/d/tr/q Dh200/250/300/350;) A block north of Ave Mohammed V, Hôtel Amlal is surprisingly calm, cordial and dustless. Rooms have iron bedsteads, teensy TVs and endearingly quirky decor-schemes.

Hôtel La Vallée (☎ 024 854034; www.la-vallee.mezgarne.com; 2km on Route de Zagora; s/d 100/120 with shared bathroom, s/d/ste with private bathroom Dh160/300/350;) Trekkers, bikers and families easily fill these 41 rooms, and live musical accompaniment makes the mealtime race to the poolside Berber tent buffet even more madcap (breakfast Dh20). Stuccoed ceilings, desert murals and reliably hot showers add that something extra.

MIDRANGE

Les Jardins de Ouarzazate (☎ 024 854200; www.lesjardinsdeouarzazate.com; 1km Route de Zagora; d incl breakfast/half-board Dh440/550; wi-fi) Overlooking a *palmeraie*, this hotel is less starkly urban than its neighbours. The lobby is an overwhelming 21-gun salute to Moroccan decor schemes and there's an ostentatiously huge chlorinated pool, but the 27 rooms are more serene, and the wi-fi-enabled garden tents let you email amid bucolic splendour.

TOP END

our pick **Dar Kamar** (☎ 024 888733; www.darkamar.com; 45 Kasbah Taourirt; s Dh880-1078, d Dh1100-1320;) You'd never guess this warm, exuberant pisé guest house was a stern 17th-century Glaoui courthouse in its former life. Even the decor has a sense of humour: upturned tajines serve as sinks, rope pulleys become banisters and local ironworkers went wild on the bathrooms (a hammam is in the works). The staff delight in making cultural connections, and organise village photography excursions that benefit the village self-help association so that when cameras click, photographers really connect with their subject.

Auberge de la Rose Noir (☎ 024 882016; Quartier de la Mosquée, Hay Taourirt; d Dh850-950, ste Dh1350) Hidden inside the kasbah in a pisé house across the *derb* (alley) from her grandfather's house, owner Rose Hitti has created a romantic seven-room getaway with mood lighting, generous beds and gossamer fabrics. Bonuses include babysitting services and a direct-trade exposition of carpets by local women at prices set by the weaver (Dh200 to Dh2000).

Dar Daïf (☎ 024 854232; www.dardaif.ma, in French; Douar Talmasla; d/tr incl breakfast Dh370/814, ste incl breakfast Dh1166-1661;) Right on the edge of the *palmeraie* near the ruined Kasbah des Cigognes, this reinvented pisé kasbah is a maze of courtyards, hideaway guest rooms, private suite terraces and a terrace pool. The hammam is free, but dinner is compulsory (adults/children Dh188/110). To get here, head 1.5km along the road to Zagora, take a left turn at the sign after Hotel la Vallée, and follow signs along the 5km *piste*.

Eating

Patisserie-Glacier des Habouss (Rue du Marché; 6am-10pm) The magnetic appeal is irresistable on balmy evenings, when all strolls lead here for French éclairs (Dh7) and Moroccan pastries and ice cream. In the mornings, trekkers and locals alike line up for good fresh baguettes (Dh10), croissants (Dh2.5) and coffee.

Pizzeria Veneziano (☎ 024 887676; Ave Moulay Rachid; pizzas Dh30-45, noon-9.30pm) A bright, good-value place, Veneziano serves tasty thin-crust pizzas with some good local toppings like desert herbs and goat cheese, plus the usual pastas, real Italian espresso and a large menu of *panachés* (Dh15).

Restaurant 3 Thés (☎ 024 886363; cnr Ave Moulay Rachid & Rue de la Poste; mains Dh30-55; ⏰ lunch & dinner) The wrought-iron sidewalk seating and get-cosy interiors say Paris café, but the menu says tasty vegetarian tajines (Dh30), cheeseburgers (Dh35), meat tajines with figs, prunes and almonds (Dh55).

Restaurant la Kasbah (☎ 024 882033; Ave Mohammed V; mains Dh60-80, set menus Dh98; ⏰ lunch & dinner) With pleasant terraces overlooking the Taourirt Kasbah, this restaurant is inevitably popular with exhausted sightseers, and makes a well-spiced beef couscous.

Douyria (☎ 024 885288; 72 Ave Mohammed V; mains Dh80-110; ⏰ breakfast, lunch & dinner) Try this for romance: candlelit dinner in a nook lined with purple and green cushions, all on a terrace atop the Taourirt Kasbah. Go with the specialty couscous and vaguely sweet milk *brik* (pastry) for dinner, and come back together tomorrow for breakfast under the umbrella – ouch, those ironwork chairs get hot.

Le Relais Saint Exupéry (☎ 024 887779; www.relaissaintexupery.com; 13 Blvd Moulay Abdallah; set menu Dh90-260, dinner mains Dh90-130; ⏰ lunch & dinner, closed Wed lunch & Jul) No, that's not a desert mirage: you really do have a choice of grilled duck with wine-mustard reduction or the dromedary meat special. If you find it odd to come across such adventurous gastronomy in a suburb near the Ouarzazate airport, that's the point: this airport was an inspiration to *Little Prince* author and pilot, Antoine de Saint-Exupéry.

SELF-CATERING

The **Supermarché** (Ave Mohammed V) carries all the desert essentials: water, toothpaste, lip balm, packaged soups, cookies, film, vodka and argan anti-cellulite lotion. There's another larger **supermarket** (Ave Moulay Rachid) with imported European foods. Fresh cheese, meat and vegetables can be found at the daily **central souq** (Rue du Marché).

Shopping

Opposite the entrance to the kasbah is the **Coopérative de Tissage** (Weaving Cooperative; ☎ 024 884057; Ave Mohammed V), where you can glimpse local women artisans at work on *hanbels* (locally woven carpets) and embroidered straw mats, and take one home at fixed prices of Dh550 to Dh750 per sq metre. Next door is the **Ensemble Artisanal** (⏰ 9am-noon & 3-6.30pm), the state-run showroom with stone carvings, pottery and woollen carpets woven by the region's Ouzguita Berbers. On the north side of town, **Horizon Artisanat** (☎ 024 882415; 181 Ave de la Victoire; ⏰ 9am-6pm Mon-Fri) sells handmade pottery, metalwork and carpets produced by the local Horizon Association, which works to integrate disabled children and adults into the community.

Getting There & Away

AIR

Two kilometres north of town is **Taourirt airport** (☎ 024 882383). There is no bus into town, but a taxi should cost Dh35 to Dh60. **Royal Air Maroc** (RAM; ☎ 024 885102; 1 Ave Mohammed V) has daily flights direct to Casablanca (from Dh1690, one hour), morning flights to London via Casablanca and multiple flights daily to Paris via Casablanca, as well as regular charter flights from Belgium, France and Germany.

BUS

The most convenient way to arrive is with **CTM** (☎ 024 882427; Blvd Mohammed V), as its station is bang in the centre of town near the post office. It has buses to Marrakesh (Dh65, five hours, three daily) and Casablanca (Dh135, 8½ hours, one daily).

At the main bus station, 1.5km northwest of the town centre, Trans-Ghazala has buses to Marrakesh (Dh65, four to five hours, six daily) and Satas has a bus to Er-Rachidia (Dh75, six hours) at 11am. There are frequent departures to Agadir (Dh115, four to five hours, six daily), Boumalne du Dadès (Dh25, five daily) and Taroudannt (Dh75, five hours, five daily); one of these goes via Tazenakht (Dh20), Foum Zguid (Dh45, four hours) and Tata (Dh60, five hours). Services also go to M'Hamid (Dh70, seven hours, four daily) via Zagora (Dh45, four hours).

CAR

To stop at will at splendid *ksour* (castles) along the Drâa Valley en route to the desert, you might want to rent a car (from Dh350 per day). In a bus or grand taxi you'll simply speed past and arrive in Zagora disappointed. Most of the car-rental agencies are on Ave Mohammed V and Place du 3 Mars, and include:

Avis (☎ 024 888000; www.avis.com; cnr Ave Mohammed V & Place du 3 Mars)
Budget (☎ 024 884202; www.budget.com; Ave Mohammed V & airport)
Desert Evasion (☎ 024 888682; www.desert-evasion.net; Imm El Ghifari, Ave Mohamed V) 4WD with local drivers for custom itineraries at set rates (Dh1250 to Dh800 depending on car type). Payment due upon receipt of keys.
Dune Car (☎ 024 887391; fax 024 884901; Ave Mohammed V) Reliable and much cheaper than the international agencies; also has 4WDs.
Europcar/InterRent (☎ 024 882035; www.europcar.com; Place du 3 Mars)
Hertz (☎ 024 882084; www.hertz.com; 33 Ave Mohammed V)
National Car Rental (☎ 024 885244; Place du 3 Mars)

TAXI

Taxis leave from outside the main bus station to Agdz (Dh30), Aït Benhaddou (Dh20), Boumalne du Dadès (Dh40), Marrakesh (Dh90 to Dh110), Skoura (Dh15), Tinerhir (Dh55) and Zagora (Dh70).

Getting Around

There are shared petits taxis that run up and down Ave Mohammed V for the flat rate of Dh5 per person (based on three people sharing). The yellow STUDID bus (Dh5) runs a half-hourly service up and down Ave Mohammed V.

DRÂA VALLEY

وادة درعة

Until you see the desolate Drâa Valley, there's just no way to comprehend the amazing feat of Morocco's existence. Before the Almoravids could conquer territory from Marrakesh all the way up to Barcelona, and Saadians could seize control of the Saharan sugar and gold trades, first they had to get past unassailable gorges, mud-brick watchtowers and fiercely autonomous oases. Today a well-paved road and cushy hotels make the going considerably less rough, yet still there's something about this landscape so exposed to the elements that it seems wildly adventurous.

From Ouarzazate the N9 plunges southeast into the Drâa Valley, formed by a narrow ribbon of water from the High Atlas that carved through the rock and occasionally seeps into the sand before emerging triumphantly in a lush oasis. The lushest and most fascinating section of the valley lies between Agdz and Zagora, a stretch of about 95km. Beyond that, a road takes you 96km further south to M'Hamid, a town 40km short of the Algerian border that recently opened as a major desert tourism destination and still has a no-man's-land feel.

The drive to Zagora takes three to four hours. With a 4WD, you can take the slower, more scenic route on the *piste* that runs parallel to the road and the river from Tamnougalt to Zagora.

AGDZ اكدز

Travellers who zoom from Ouarzazate to Zagora are missing out on Agdz (ag-dez), a classic caravan oasis with a still-pristine *palmeraie,* mud-brick kasbah, clever gardens, Thursday farmers' market (October–November) and great lodgings heading east off the paved main road onto narrow *pistes.* The tajine-shaped Jebel Kissane overlooks the town, and 20km away is the 1660m Tizi n'Tinififft. Agdz crafts traditions include carving, pottery and basket-weaving, and you might find some examples along with saffron-coloured carpets, from nearby Tazenakht in shops along the main thoroughfare.

One fascinating stop for passionate gardeners on the way out of town is the **Association Development Hart Chaou community garden project** (☎ 076 872842; tasawante@hotmail.com; Hart Chaou, km 1 south of Agdz; donation appreciated; call ahead for entry). In the past decade, this small agricultural village bypassed by time and tourism faced droughts and tough times. Several families had no land, water or other means to support themselves – so the village rallied, and designated a vacant lot near a functioning well as a community garden. Villagers took turns using the water and communal compost pile, and two years later, this small organic garden provides 80% of the nutritional needs of the village's 114 families. To see this amazing oasis, call gatekeeper Mohammed Moussas (☎ 076 872842) at least a couple of hours ahead, and he'll meet you by the main road and lead you to the garden. Try some garden-ripe fava beans or a tomato, exchange gardening tips, have some tea at the nearby school the association has started and consider a donation to help buy next year's seeds (tip: Dh200 plants an entire plot of beans or onions, and Dh800 plants tomatoes).

Sleeping & Eating

Casbah Caïd Ali (☎ 024 843640; www.casbah-caidali.net; Rue Hassan II; with/without breakfast d Dh229/209, tent Dh15, Dh20 vehicle, per person plus Dh13;) Off the main road to the east is this former kasbah of the local *caid* (leader), whose descendants have opened their historic family home to guests. Salons around the partially restored kasbah courtyard have been converted to large guestrooms with Berber motifs on the curved ceilings and simple wood and wrought-iron furnishings, all quite comfortable, with shared bathrooms. Meals (set menu Dh65 to Dh85) are served in Berber tents by the small spring-water pool (water is reused for the garden). Camp sites are available in the garden under the palms.

Rose du Sable (☎ 024 886452; www.rosedusable.com; s/d/tr Dh462/627/792;) Like a rock star in the desert, this eight-room guest house keeps a low profile but can't help but stand out, with trippy yellow stained-glass windows, Flintstone-esque inlaid-granite walls, and fully wheelchair-accessible guestrooms. The Jolie-Pitts recommend this guest house, and who are we to argue?

Dar Qamar (☎ 024 843784; www.locsudmaroc.com; Agdz; s Dh440-715, d Dh550-880, tr Dh770-990;) Red-stained pisé walls, Tinherir-tiled walkways and fish in the fountain to eat mosquitoes: much about this organically chic guest house makes you wonder why no one thought of it ages ago. You can rent bikes, explore the *palmeraie,* enjoy a glass of wine and local dates in the garden, use the in-house hammam or be led to the historic community hammams nearby.

At the entry to town on the left, there's a gas station with a kasbah convenience store and café, the **Kasbah Total** (8am-9pm, sometimes closed in summer & winter), where you can fuel up on good espresso and packaged snacks galore.

Getting There & Away

CTM and several other buses stop here en route between Ouarzazate and Zagora, though you're not guaranteed a seat. Otherwise, occasional grands taxis go to Ouarzazate (Dh25) and Zagora (Dh28).

AGDZ TO ZAGORA

The mother of all *ksour* (castles) is the 16th-century fortified village at **Tamnougalt** (admission Dh 10; guide compulsory Dh50), one of the oldest mud-brick *ksar* still standing and an essential stop on any Moroccan architecture pilgrimage. The maze of rooms leads through a sizable *mellah*, dips underground with strategically placed skylights and candle nooks, and emerges into dazzlingly bright courtyard stables lined with horseshoe arches. See if you can distinguish between the Arab, Andalusian and Berber Jewish motifs that blend so seamlessly here.

To reach Tamnougalt turn left off the main road 4km past Agdz, then 2km east up a bumpy *piste*. **Chez Yacob** (☎ 024 843394; www.chezyacob.com; km 4 Route de Zagora, Agdz; half-board per person Dh250) is next door to the main *ksar,* and offers five unfussy, snug rooms arranged around a torchlit courtyard with shared bathrooms, capped by a large terrace overlooking the kasbah and the *palmeraie*. Set menu meals are Dh80.

Nearby at the edge of the *palmeraie* is **Kasbah Itrane** (☎/fax 024 843614; merrsana@gmail.com; Route de Zagora, 5km south of Agdz; per person half-board without/with bathroom Dh200/220;) with less character but clean rooms, a garden with chlorinated swimming pool and a set menu for Dh80.

If you really want to (all together now) rock the kasbahs, check out the prime specimens along the main road at Timiderte, **Kasbah Said Arabi** at Ouled Atman and the kasbah at Tinzouline, where there's also a memorable Monday souq. You'll know you're getting close to Tinzouline when you see people selling sweet local *boufeggou* dates to passing motorists. At Tansikht, about 30km before Zagora, look out for the old watchtower guarding the *palmeraie,* signposted 'Oasis Du Drâa'.

With a 4WD there are several excursions you could make along the far (north) side of the Drâa. These are signposted as *'circuits touristiques'* from the road. From Tamnougalt you can parallel to the Drâa following a dirt road through villages, fields and splendid river vistas all the way to Zagora.

ZAGORA زاكورة

pop 34,821

The iconic 'Tombouktou, 52 jours' (Timbuktu, 52 days) signpost was recently taken down in an inexplicable government beautification scheme, but Zagora's fame as a desert outpost is indelible. The Saadians launched their expedition to conquer Timbuktu from Zagora in 1591, and the many desert caravans that passed through this oasis have given this isolated spot its cool, cosmopolitan character.

This can be seen in the adjacent village of Amezrou (about 1.5km south of the Zagora city centre across the Oued Drâa), which still has a historic *mellah* where artisans work good-luck charms from African, Berber, Jewish and Muslim traditions into their designs – when crossing the desert for 52 days, you need all the luck you can get.

Jebel Zagora and a *palmeraie* make a dramatic backdrop to the rather drab French colonial outpost buildings and the splashy new town hall complex, but all this is erased when a sandstorm blows an eerie bronze-tinged haze into town. For all its modernisation of late, Zagora is still a trading post at heart, with a large market on Wednesdays and Sundays offering fruit, vegetables, herbs, hardware, handicrafts, sheep, goats and donkeys. The *moussem* of Moulay Abdelkader Jilali takes place at the same time as Moulid an-Nabi (see p466), and it brings the town to life.

Information

Banque Populaire (Blvd Mohammed V) Has an ATM.
BMCE (Blvd Mohammed V) ATM.
Placenet Cyber Center (95 Blvd Mohammed V; per hr Dh10) Internet access.
Pharmacy Zagora (☎ 024 847195; Blvd Mohammed V; 8.30am-1pm & 3-8pm Mon-Fri, 8.30am-1pm Sat)

Sights & Activities

The spectacular **Jebel Zagora** rising over the Oued Drâa is worth climbing for the views, provided you have enough stamina and sunblock and set off early. The round-trip to Jebel Zagora takes about two to three hours on foot, or 45 minutes by car along the *piste* to the right beyond Camping de la Montagne. Halfway up are the faint ruins of an 11th-century Almoravid fortress, but the military installation at the summit is off-limits.

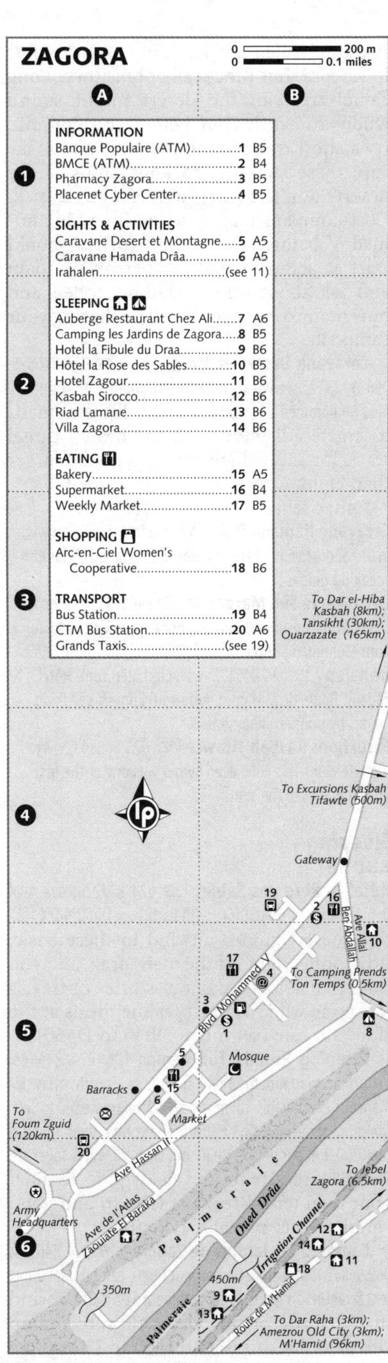

Camel rides are not only still possible in Zagora, but practically obligatory. Long camel treks in the desert might sound wildly romantic, but before you commit, try a short trek around the oasis and make sure these swaying, rocking 'ships of the desert' don't leave you sore and seasick. Cost-compare at agencies on Blvd Mohammed V before you commit (prices should start at about Dh350 per person per day) and ask about water, bedding, toilets and how many other people will be sharing your camp site.

Caravane Desert et Montagne (☎ 024 846898, 066 122312; www.caravanedesertetmontagne.com; 112 Blvd Mohammed V) partners with local nomads to create adventures off the beaten camel track for individuals and groups no larger than eight.

Other reliable agencies are:

Caravane Hamada Drâa (☎ /fax 024 846930; www.hamadadraa.com, in French; Blvd Mohammed V) English-speaking guides.

Découverte Sud Maroc (☎ 024 846115; www.geocities.com/decousudma) Run by English-speaking, Zagora-born Mohamad Sirirou.

Irahalen (☎ 024 846178; www.irahalen.com; Hotel Zagour, Route de M'Hamid, Amezrou) English-speaking guides by prior arrangement.

Excursions Kasbah Tifawte (☎ 024 848843; www.tifawte.com) This kohl-eyed owner was one of the first official guides in the south.

Sleeping

BUDGET

Hôtel la Rose des Sables (☎ 024 847274; Ave Allal Ben Abdallah; s/d Dh50/60, with bathroom Dh60/90) Off-duty desert guides unwind in these basic, tidy rooms right off the main drag, and you might be able to coax out stories of travellers gone wild over tasty tajine meals at the sidewalk café (set menu Dh40 to Dh50).

Camping Prends Ton Temps (☎ 024 846543; http://campingauberge.skyblog.com, in French; Hay El-Mansour ed-Dahabi, 300m off Blvd Mohammed V to left; camping per person Dh10 plus per tent Dh5, fixed tent s/d Dh40/60, hut per person Dh30, hut with shower & toilet s/d Dh80/100) Huts, tents and shady plots to pitch your own tent. Breakfast (Dh20) and good simple meals available (Dh60).

Camping les Jardins de Zagora (☎ 024 846971, 068 961701; Amezrou; Berber tent Dh40, camping for 2 incl tent & car Dh50, r with private bathroom d Dh150) Unwind in the shade of this clean, flowered camp site next door to the hotel Ksar Tinzouline overlooking Jebel Zagora. Beds in Berber tents come with electricity, and tajines are cooked to order (set menu Dh80).

Auberge Restaurant Chez Ali (☎ 024 846258; www.chezali.prophp.org; Ave de l'Atlas Zaouiate El Baraka; garden tents per person Dh40 & showers Dh5, r per person with breakfast/full-board Dh100/260, with terrace breakfast/full-board Dh200/360) The peacocks stalking the garden can't be bothered, but otherwise the welcome here is very enthusiastic. The skylit-rooms upstairs have new pine furnishings and tiled floors, though some mattresses are a tad lumpy. Meals are homestyle Berber cooking, and wildly popular overnight trips are run by friendly English-speaking guides Mohamed and Yusuf (book ahead).

Hotel Zagour (☎ 024 846178; www.zagour.com; Route de M'Hamid, 600m before bridge, Amezrou; d incl breakfast/half-board Dh250/400; 🏊) Ceramic castles hold remote-controls, camel reins repurposed as a towel rack, new mattresses and paint touch-ups make up for prior guests who were a tad rough on the place. Meals are by the terrace pool or in a pastel stuccoed restaurant where Marie Antoinette might feel right at home.

Hotel la Fibule du Draa (☎ 024 847318; www.zagora-desert.com; 50m to right off Route de M'Hamid, Amezrou; s/d/tr incl breakfast Dh380/430/700; 🏊) A sharp hometown team run this place like an extension of their own houses. All 24 two-tone green-cream rooms come with small fridges so you can cater your own meals and beer lugged from Ouarzazate; choose views over the pool or garden, and take full advantage of the buffet breakfast.

MIDRANGE

our pick Dar Raha (☎ 024 846993; http://darraha.free.fr; Amezrou; s/d incl breakfast Dh220/410, half-board Dh300/550) 'How thoughtful!' is the operative phrase here, from the heartfelt hello and half-price rates for kids aged five to 12 years old to oasis-appropriate details like local palm mats, recycled wire lamps and thick straw pisé walls eliminating the need for a pool or air-con. Enjoy home-cooked meals and chats in the kitchen, and check out the expo of local paintings and crafts; studio visits can be arranged here in the heart of the Amezrou *mellah*.

Kasbah Sirocco (☎ 024 846125; www.kasbah-sirocco.com; Amezrou; s/d/tr & q incl breakfast Dh425/660/957, half-board s/d Dh616/990; ❄ 🏊) The torchlit raw-pisé hall makes a dramatic entry to light, easygoing rooms overlooking the *palmeraie*. Added attractions are savoury Moroccan cooking, especially the *mechoui* (slow-cooked lamb, Dh120; mains Dh60 to Dh70) and excursions including camel treks, desert camping and trekking. Cool off with cocktails by the needlessly huge chlorinated pool or better yet, in the subterranean stone cave bar.

Villa Zagora (☎ 024 846093; www.mavillaausahara.com; Amezrou; incl breakfast Berber tent Dh220, d with shared/private bathroom Dh286/365, ste Dh495, d half-board with shared/private bathroom Dh418/506, ste Dh638;) Light, breezy, and naturally charming, with staff that fuss over you like the Moroccan aunties and uncles you never knew you had. Meals here are marathons of dishes made with the freshest ingredients; pace yourself, so the chef can show off her considerable talents. The pool is suitably small and its water is wisely used on the aromatic gardens; forget camels and read the day away on the verandah.

TOP END

Riad Lamane (☎ 024 848388; www.riadlamane.com; Amezrou; walled 'tent' half-board Dh350, bungalows per person half-board Dh600-800; wi-fi) Two-storey round mud-brick bungalows and upscale buffed-*tadelakt* 'tents' set in a pretty, wi-fi-enabled garden with a dashingly handsome African-style bar. Follow the track along the irrigation canal 100m past La Fibule.

Eating & Drinking

All hotels have their own restaurants and will provide Dh100 to Dh150 set meals to nonguests by prior reservation. Moroccan fare with less flair can be had at cheap, popular restaurants along Blvd Mohammed V. Picnic makings can be found at market produce stalls, the supermarket at the northern end of town with limited supplies (no alcohol) and a bakery. The local dates are famous in Morocco, but are becoming more scarce because of the Bayoud disease, a fungus that has killed many palms across North Africa. For a stiff drink, head to La Fibule du Draa's bar (opposite) by the pool, the wine cave at Kasbah Sirocco (opposite) or the African bar at Riad Lamane (above).

Shopping

The picturesque **Amezrou Mellah** has a few silver workshops still working in the tradition started here by Jewish artisans. At the crossroads for Amezrou, **Arc-en-Ciel Women's Cooperative** (Route de M'Hamid; 9am-noon & 2-7pm) sells folkloric tote bags, baby clothes and funky fleece jumpers made from fabric remnants.

Getting There & Away

AIR

Plans had been announced to open the new Zagora airport to domestic and international flights last year, but fuel prices have apparently delayed the plan.

BUS

The **CTM bus station** (☎ 024 847327; Blvd Mohammed V) is at the southwestern end of Mohammed V, and the **bus station** and grand taxi lot is at the northern end. There's a daily CTM bus to Ouarzazate (Dh50, four hours), which continues on to Marrakesh (Dh100, 9½ hours) and Casablanca (Dh175, 12½ hours).

Other companies have at least one run a day (either morning or around 9pm) to Boumalne du Dadès (Dh75), Casablanca (Dh175), Erfoud (Dh85), Er-Rachidia (Dh125), Marrakesh (Dh90, two daily), Ouarzazate (Dh40) and Rabat (Dh180). There are buses to Rissani (Dh80) via N'Kob (Dh 20) and Tazzarine (Dh30) three times a week. A bus passes through headed to M'Hamid (Dh20, two hours) in the morning. More frequent minibuses run to M'Hamid (Dh25) throughout the day when full.

TAXI

Grands taxis are more regular early in the morning. Destinations include Agdz (Dh30, 1½ hours), Ouarzazate (Dh62, three hours), M'Hamid (Dh30, 1½ hours), Tazzarine (Dh45, 2½ hours) and N'Kob (Dh38, 1½ hours).

SOUTH OF ZAGORA

Tamegroute تامكروت

Stressed out? You've come to the right place: Tamegroute's **Zawiya Nassiriyya** is said to cure anxiety and high blood-pressure, thanks to the post-mortem calming influence of Sidi Mohammed ben Nassir – founder of the influential and very studious Nassiri brotherhood in the 17th century. While non-Muslims can't visit his green-roofed tomb, from Saturday through Friday in the mornings and later afternoons, anyone can visit the library and enter the *medersa* for Quranic scholars, associated with Sidi Mohammed ben Nassir's shrine (donation for upkeep expected). Among the library books on these glassed-in shelves are ancient medical, mathematics, algebra and law texts, in addition to Qurans dating from the 13th century and written on gazelle hide.

Besides relieving tension, Tamegroute is known for its labyrinth of *ksour* connected by dark passageways, which you can explore by yourself to test the powers of your internal compass or with a local guide. If you look lost, locals will probably direct you towards the **collective pottery studio** (🕑 8am-6pm Mon-Fri), where the distinctive rustic green Tamegroute pottery is made and painted with *baraka*-enhancing symbols in henna. To get there by the road, just follow the signs for the *Cooperative des Potiers*. Tamegroute also has a Saturday souq.

If the *zawiya* is working its mellow charms, head across the road to **Auberge-Restaurant-Camping Jnane Dar Diafa** (☎ 024 840622; www.jnanedar.ch, in German; s/d with shared bathroom Dh125/170; s/d/tr/ste with bathroom from Dh200/300/400/600) for a leisurely lunch made with vegetables grown on the premises in the breezy gazebo restaurant amid the gardens. You can also crash overnight in the seriously scuffed but mystically winsome upstairs rooms overlooking the garden. Ask for the Comsa room with mosquito nets over the beds or the Malika with the star-patterned decor.

Tinfou Dunes كثبا

The great inland sea of dunes in Merzouga or Erg Chebbi can make this small patch of two to three big dunes seem like a kiddie sand box by comparison, but the Tinfou Dunes offer a sneak preview of Sahara sand. As you're heading 8km south of Tamegroute, you'll spot them on your left. On busy days it can feel like a playground here, but it's still fun to climb and run down the big dunes.

Tinfou to M'Hamid

If a taste of dunes at Tinfou leaves you craving more, you could head east to the mighty pink dunes of Merzouga (see p370) or make a break for the open desert at Erg Chebbi via M'Hamid. The road south disappears into the sand at M'Hamid, 96km south of Zagora and some 40km from Algeria (the southern border is still a contentious issue between the two countries). The journey to M'Hamid takes you through a dauntingly bleak landscape of sun-scorched rubble, and just as it's getting monotonous, the road ascends up and over the Tizi Beni Selmane pass. The village of Tagounite has petrol, several cafés and the *ksar* of Oulad Driss for a worthwhile pitstop before the final 5km run into M'Hamid.

M'Hamid المحاميد

pop 3000

Once it was a lonesome oasis, but these days M'Hamid is a wallflower no more. Border tensions between Algeria, Morocco and the Polisario had isolated this once-thriving caravan stop until the 1990s, when accords allowed M'Hamid to start hosting visitors again. Today the road is flanked with hotels to accommodate travellers lured here by the golden dunes at nearby Erg Chigaga, experience the perverse thrill and metallic light of sandstorms, and see the road disappear into nowhere.

This one dot on a map actually covers two towns and five different ethnic groups: the Harratine, Berber, Chorfa, Beni M'Hamid and the fabled nomadic 'Blue Men'. M'Hamid Jdid, the prematurely aged 'new' town, has a mosque, roadside café-restaurants, small, mostly grim hotels, a few hodge-podge craft shops and a Monday market. The old town of M'Hamid Bali, 3km away across the Oued Drâa, has a well-preserved kasbah.

SIGHTS & ACTIVITIES

M'Hamid's main attractions begin where the buildings end and relentless desert takes over, despite woven-palm barriers to keep it at bay. There's a frontier-town feel here, with tough guys in a *shesh* (turban) and sunglasses hanging around M'Hamid Jdid at dusty cafés, swapping stories about the tourist who got lost in the desert only to turn up years later, married with children. Have you heard the one about the tourists who declined a local guide's services, and were lost to a sandstorm just 2km from town? Stick around, and you will – sales ploys come with the territory here, but

WHICH DESERT?

Watching the sunset over rolling Sahara dunes is a once-in-a-lifetime experience that can actually be found two places in Morocco: Erg Chebbi (next to Merzouga) and Erg Chigaga (near M'Hamid). Here's how the two destinations match up on key dune-going criteria suggested by Lonely Planet traveller feedback:

- **Natural beauty**: Both. Merzouga's rose-gold dunes are set off by the sun-blackened hard-packed *reg* (hard-packed desert) that surrounds it. Erg Chigaga's dunes are yellow-gold, and surrounded by sun-bleached *reg* and sandier *sahel* (a mix of soft and hard sand) dotted with pretty, poisonous calitropis trees.
- **Dromedary trips**: Merzouga. Within half an hour's dromedary ride from downtown Merzouga, you can be inside rolling dunes, while it takes a two-hour 4WD drive to get you that close in M'Hamid.
- **Calm**: Erg Chigaga is more remote and farther from city noise. Merzouga is finally limiting the use of quad bikes on the dunes, after all the noise and dune deterioration got locals riled and turned off tourists. But both regions need to work on restricting 4WD access to the *sahel* at the dunes, since dromedary rides lose a certain magic when cars are roaring past, and 4WD arrivals after sunset rudely interrupt stargazing.
- **Romance**: Erg Chigaga has the edge here, with fires and candles setting the mood without hindering nighttime visibility in the desert. In longer-established Merzouga, some longstanding encampments actually have streetlights that affect stargazing and romantic prospects with their brash fluorescent glow.
- **Convenience**: Merzouga, but it's a close call. In Merzouga, you can stay at a comfy hotel with a fabulous view onto the dunes, and take in the scenery on a two-hour camel ride. Erg Chigaga is faster to get to from Marrakesh, but it involves a trek after you get to M'Hamid that takes at least 2½ hours by 4WD with a guide.
- **Environmental awareness**: Neither. Nothing spoils that perfect sunset dune dreamscape faster than the sight of litter blowing across the pristine sand. If every visitor who loves these dunes packed up their litter and picked up a few stray plastic bags and bottles, the sunsets and environmental outlook here would be that much rosier. But agencies must also do their part at their desert encampments to curtail waste – flush toilets are worrying, since water treatment plants are far from here.
- **Child-friendliness**: Both. Since sound travels in the desert, you'll need to switch off electronic games and anything else that bleeps to preserve the dunes' tranquil timelessness. But no matter: this is nature's own playground, where kids really cut loose and frolic. With any luck, they'll sleep the whole ride back to Marrakesh.

don't be reeled in by *faux guide* scare tactics. Treks on foot, camel or 4WD to Erg Chigaga with reliable, licensed guides can be arranged in Marrakesh, Zagora or right here in M'Hamid.

The star attraction is **Erg Chigaga**, a mind-boggling 40km stretch of golden Saharan dunes up to 300m high some 56km from M'Hamid that can take up to 2½ to three hours to reach by 4WD in good conditions on the *reg*. The best way to get there is in classic movie style: by camel, which takes five days or a week (from Dh380 per day) round-trip. If you've got the hang of camel-riding by now, you might consider the epic 12-day camel trip to Foum Zguid via Erg Chigaga.

Otherwise you'll need to shell out for a 4WD, which costs around Dh1300, plus another Dh250 for the camp. Many agencies offer guides and/or drivers, which is a good idea – even local drivers familiar with desert conditions have been known to stray off-course or get stuck in the sand. For all-inclusive trips to desert camps via camel and 4WD, local **Sahara Services** (☎ 061 776766; www.saharaservices.info; Kasbah Sahara Services, M'Hamid, 300m on right after M'Hamid entry) has the cushiest offering: round-trip to an encampment for mud-brick walled Berber tents in

Erg Chigaga with dinner and music by firelight in the dunes, dromedary rides from base camp, and unlikely mod-cons: flushing toilets, hot meals, even hot showers. This agency is not to be confused with competitor Saharia Services, a competing agency without the same reputation for professionalism. Another recommended agency is **Zbar Travel** (☎ 068 517280; www.zbartravel.com), which offers similar trips to an Erg Chigaga encampment or sleep-outs under the stars (winds permitting), sand-boarding, dromedary and walking treks to Erg Ezahar (a tall 'screaming dune' that wails eerily when the wind kicks up), and insights on Saharawi culture and botany.

Many overnight camel treks (from Dh300 per person) from M'Hamid go 10km north of town to **Erg Lehoudi** (Dunes of the Jews), which has 100m-high dunes dotted with semipermanent bivouacs and is badly in need of rubbish collection. With a 4WD, you can drive out there along a *piste* off the main road 18km before M'Hamid, but a guide is advisable. Other possible destinations include the **Iriki oasis**, a tiny plot not far from Erg Chigaga near a vast desert mirage that looks like a lake, or some of the smaller dunes at Mesouria, 8km from M'Hamid.

SLEEPING & EATING

Hotel Tabarkat (☎ 024 848688; www.tabarkat.com; Douar Ksar Bounou BP 35, M'Hamid; s Dh450, d Dh580-670;) The main kasbah is pretty enough, with art-deco posters of Morocco – but the best deals are out back in the cactus garden. 'Garden rooms' are actually freestanding mud-brick houses, with Tamegroute green-tiled bathrooms, unfussy furnishings and African mudcloth decor.

Dar Azawad (☎ 024 848730; www.darazawad.com; Douar Ouled Driss, M'Hamid; tent/d/ste half-board Dh500/700/900;) The eight 'nomad tents' here are ideal for Armani-clad nomads with cleverly designed mud-brick walls, yellow stained-glass windows and full bathrooms with hot showers. With highly original ironwork (including an iron-lung shower), palm-wood ceilings, and beige *tadelakt* walls, the 10 spacious regular rooms are as nice as the five suites, which have terraces and tubs. Bonus amenities include a spa, bar and boutique with upscale crafts.

Camping Hammada du Drâa (☎ 024 848080; camping per person Dh15 plus per car Dh20, Berber tents per person Dh50) This cheerfully run camp has clean communal facilities.

Kasbah Sahara Services (☎ 061 776766; www.saharaservices.info; Kasbah Sahara Services, M'Hamid, 300m on right after M'Hamid entry; half-board per person tent/r Dh150/240) Six cocoonlike rooms with their own bath and shower, and Berber tents out back, plus a tasty restaurant offering generous portions of salad, kebabs and chips for Dh80.

GETTING THERE & AWAY

There's a daily CTM bus at 4.30pm to Zagora (Dh25, two hours), Ouarzazate (Dh70, seven hours), Marrakesh (Dh120, 11 to 13 hours) and Casablanca (Dh205, 15 hours). Private buses to Marrakesh (via Zagora and Ouarzazate) leave at around 7am and 2pm (Dh120, 15 hours).

FOUM ZGUID TO TIZI N'TICHKA

If you go to Erg Chigaga by 4WD, instead of backtracking to M'Hamid to get to Marrakesh you can exit the desert heading north to Marrakesh via Foum Zguid. En route through the *sahel* and *reg*, you'll pass the **Iriki oasis** under an imposing plateau on your right, with a lone café offering cool drinks and tea on deck chairs with a view across a vast lake with a few thirsty birds and gazelles along the edge. But look again: 'Lake Iriki' is actually a mirage with deceptive silhouettes of poisonous calitropis bushes.

Another 30km or so from Cafe Iriki you'll turn north, and as you near a plateau on your left what you'll swear is a hotel (another illusion of geography) is the guardhouse for Foum Zguid, where you may be asked to show your passport. Foum Zguid is still a strategic military base, so you may hear reports from nearby watchtowers break through radio static. The town itself is a crossroads with all the necessities: water, petrol, a public phone, serviceable omelettes and coffee from cafés on the right after the town's major/only intersection, and a foosball table across the street.

For a more satisfying meal, head out of town north 8km towards Marrakesh to the turnoff for the *piste* to Zagora/Amezrou on your right, and you'll spot **Maison d'Hôte Hiba** (☎ 015 727282; 8km Foum Zguid) a rock-studded restaurant with cave-man charm and some very tasty set meals of tajine, salad, and fruit for Dh80 served on the scenic terrace. Follow the *piste* another 2.5km along, and you'll come to **Cooperative Ahilal des Tapis**, where you'll find carpets made on clean, well-equipped premises plus tajine-shaped baskets and *lugnâa*, a local-style wrap with graphic abstract flower patterns in bold colours on plain white-and black-fabric. Prices are set, with a small percentage going to the association for overhead, equipment, training and childcare, and the rest going directly to the women who made the item. This project provides essential support for families in this rocky Anti Atlas terrain, so any purchases you make will be met with sincere thanks.

Your next stop en route to Tizi n'Tichka is Tazenakht, the last stop for a quick bite, coffee, petrol and carpets. This town has a couple of intersections and several carpet shops that mostly sell to trade, but the best option is to buy from the source 4km outside of Tazenakht at **Iklane Association** (Irkane Village, km 4 on Tazenakht Rd). Here the association takes 8% of reasonable retail prices for initiatives like the community clean-up program (hence the immaculate village); the rest goes to the carpet maker.

ZAGORA TO RISSANI

Desert-bound travellers often make a beeline from Ouarzazate to M'Hamid, but tack on another day or two and you could take a more scenic route to the desert at Merzouga. The roads that encircle the stark mass of the Jebel Sarhro make it possible to complete a loop from Ouarzazate to Zagora over to Rissani and Merzouga, returning via the Todra and Dadès gorges. The Zagora–Rissani route with the most photo ops goes through the castle-filled village of N'Kob, heading 98km back up the Drâa Valley before turning off (by Restaurant la Gazelle) towards Tazzarine.

Grands taxis run between Tazzarine and Ouarzazate (Dh70), between Tazzarine and Alnif (Dh25), and Alnif and Rissani (Dh30), so you can cobble together transport. There's also a bus between Rissani and Zagora via Alnif, Tazzarine and N'Kob on Tuesday, Friday and Sunday. If you're driving, there are Ziz petrol stations along the way, though they sometimes run out of fuel. A full tank should easily see you through from Zagora to Rissani.

N'Kob, Tazzarine & Alnif

نيكوب تزارين و النيف

One of Morocco's best-kept secrets is the oasis village of N'Kob, where no less than 45 mud-brick *ksour* (castles) will make you stop and stare. Better still, you can stay overnight in a couple of castles converted to guest houses (see below). Wander through N'Kob's fascinating architectural or geological history on day hikes arranged by the **Bureau des Guides** (☎ 067 487509) on the main street or take a longer trek of the Jebel Sarhro region (see p446), otherwise stick around for the Sunday market: this desert detour is a destination in its own right.

Beyond N'Kob, Tazzarine (150km from Rissani) is a scruffy crossroads town where the roads from Zagora and Agdz meet and drivers brake for internet cafés, lunch, petrol and a Tuesday market. Further on, you'll reach the oasis town of Alnif and one of Morocco's richest seams of fossils: the Maidir basin, packed with trilobites, the ancestors of crabs. You'll see fossils for sale along the roadsides, but beware of convincing fakes sculpted out of resin. The genuine article is for sale at fixed prices at **Ihmadi Trilobites Centre** (☎ 066 221593; trilobites@caramail.com; Alnif), and the geologist owner also leads short trips to local fossil sites (Dh180 for the afternoon). To pack in a few more oases en route to Rissani, you could head from here onto a *piste* heading north 47km to link up with the main Ouarzazate–Er-Rachidia road (information and maps available at Ihmadi Trilobites Centre). Otherwise, the paved main road is a straight shot 100km or so across the *hammada* to Rissani.

SLEEPING

Auberge Restaurant Ennakhil (☎ 024 839719; N'Kob; s/d/tr Dh90/130/160; breakfast Dh30 mains Dh50-80) Berber *baraka* all around: cute rooms with wedding blankets and Berber good-luck symbols carved into palm ceilings, clever sinks that are upturned water jars and palm-stump seating on the terrace for views onto the village and Jebel Saghro.

Kasbah Baha Baha (☎ 024839763; www.bahabaha.com, in French; N'Kob; Berber tents s/d/tr Dh80/150/210, s/d/tr with shared bathroom Dh200/300/400, s/d with shower Dh300/400) All the makings of home, if your home happened to be a gorgeously restored kasbah with a vast garden, its own wood-fired bread oven and ethnographic museum, and a 360-degree view of an oasis and neighbouring castles. Unlike other upscale places, staff are at ease here, cracking jokes and stopping to chat with guests.

Ouadjou (☎ 024 839314; www.ouadjou.com; 2km before N'kob; tent without/with half-board Dh50/150, without/with half-board s Dh130/200, d 240/360; P) This new camping complex 1.5km before you enter N'kob has tents that are as nice as the rooms, with end tables and reading lamps plus linens and blankets. Facilities include hot showers, electrical hookups, and a clothes-washing sink and clothes line; lunchtime visitors can use the pool for an extra Dh30.

Camp Amasstou (☎ 024 839078, per person half-board Dh150; P) Follow signs pointing south into Tazzarine's oasis to the best budget accommodation in the valley. In this peaceable *palmeraie*, you'll find a gorgeous walled garden featuring four large wool Berber tents and a small pool. Pull up a goatskin bench and swap life stories with fellow travellers, or call it a night on your narrow tent bed with clean linens.

our pick **Ksar Jenna** (☎ 024 839790; www.ksarjenna.com; 2km before N'Kob; per person half-board Dh550;) Holds its own with top Marrakesh riads for style at a fraction of the price, with just seven designer-fabulous rooms, memorable meals under the splendid painted dining-room ceiling and aperitifs or excellent espresso in the garden bar (it's a Moroccan/Italian venture).

Kasbah Imdoukal (☎ 024 839798; www.kasbahimdoukal.com, in French; N'Kob; d/tr/ste Dh770/990/1100;) Berber pride meets Bordeaux cool: think Berber carved wood furnishings and luxurious pillows, Amazigh friezes atop *tadelakt* guest room walls, Berber village excursions with poolside lounging after, and dinners of *madfouna* (Berber calzone) with a glass of wine.

EATING

For meals, try your guest house or stop at a couple of worthy eateries en route:

Kasbah Meteorites (☎ 035 783809; www.kasbahmeteorites.c.la, in French; Alnif; meals Dh70-80;) A pleasant pitstop for filling set lunches and a dip in an oversized chlorinated pool. Also offers basic accommodation.

Kasbah Riad Du Sud (☎ 024 886453; www.hotelriaddusud.com; Tamsahlte via Tazzarine; set lunch Dh100; reservations essential) If you're leaving Merzouga in the morning and don't want to leave lunch to chance, call ahead for a memorable millet couscous or a goat or dromedary tajine at this gastronomical oasis. Pricey rooms are also available.

DADÈS VALLEY & THE GORGES

سهول داداس و المضايق

Nomad crossings, rose valleys, two-tone kasbahs and melting rocks: on paper, the Dadès River Valley sounds a little unbelievable. Stretching from the daunting High Atlas in the north to the rugged Jebel Sarhro range to the south, the valley is dotted with oases and mud-brick palaces that give the region its fairy-tale nickname – Valley of a Thousand Kasbahs. Some of the best views can be had only on foot, along hidden passageways between the Dadès and Todra gorges and rough *piste* nomad routes to the Middle Atlas.

SKOURA سكورة

Architectural marvels in mud-brick are hidden at every turn of this huge, labyrinthine oasis, just 39km from dusty Ouarzazate but a class apart in architecture and accommodation. The easiest kasbah to access is family-owned **Kasbah Amerdil** (admission by donation Dh15), signposted just a few hundred metres from the main road, where the owner will show you around the castle featured on Morocco's Dh50 note, plus his family's prize collection of ancient tools. To get a sense of Skoura's splendours from the inside out, stay overnight in a converted kasbah, and explore the *palmeraie* on bike tomorrow.

SLEEPING & EATING

Kasbah Aït Abou (☎ 024852234; www.chez.com/kasbahaitabou; signposted in red inside Palmeraie de Skoura; per person half-board Dh180) You don't have to be loaded to live like a *caid* at this family kasbah, built in 1825 with a 25m-high mud-brick tower that's an engineering marvel and the largest still standing in the region. Rooms are plenty big and cool, water is hot, and candlelight dinners in the courtyard and breakfast in the garden are highlights.

Chez Talout (☎ 062 498283; www.talout.com; signposted 7km northwest of Skoura; d with shared/private bathroom half-board Dh400/500, ste half-board Dh800;) This locally owned landmark makes a scenic, rejuvenating stop for lunch (Dh100) on the terrace overlooking the oasis, overnights in wood-beamed rooms featuring the work of local artisans, and outings on foot, horse and mountain bike. A percentage of proceeds support a local artisans' self-help organisation.

Maison d'Hôtes Amerdil (☎ 024 852279; next to Kasbah Amerdil; d half-board Dh400-500) Wake up overlooking the kasbah next door in the tower rooms of this new mud-brick guest house. The private bathrooms have showerheads over toilets for obsessive multitaskers; tower rooms are much nicer than dim, cavelike ones downstairs. The plasma TV downstairs detracts from the romance, but draws sports fans from miles around.

our pick **Sawadi** (☎ 024 852341; www.sawadi.ma; signposted in green on north end of Palmeraie de Skoura; s half-board Dh500-690, d half-board Dh950-1250, up to 7 people in large house Dh2800-3250;) Extravagantly friendly to guests and the planet too, with pisé bungalow hideaways and family-friendly villas among organic vegetable and herb gardens with an ingeniously salt-filtered pool. Let your hosts ply you with homegrown organic food and spoil you silly with attention here, or arrange memorable excursions exploring the region's natural wonders (including 100 bird species).

Kasbah Aït ben Moro (☎ 024 852116; www.aitbenmoro.com; s/d with shared bathroom & half-board Dh350; s/d/tr with private bathroom & half-board Dh700/1000-1100/1350;) An 18th-century kasbah given a stylish makeover in 2000 remains true to its desert roots with the original palm-beam ceilings, moody low-lit passageways, cactus gardens, naturally cool courtyards, Berber blankets, and water-conserving savvy (hence no pool). The three tower rooms are the best deal, with a shared bath and stunning views over Skoura.

Jardins de Skoura (☎ 024 852324; www.lesjardinsdeskoura.com; Palmeraie de Skoura; r/ste incl breakfast Dh880/1200;) The originator of the low-key, high-romance Skoura style, with intimate seating nooks carved from pisé walls, locally produced crafts and crossroads chic Indian sari curtains, and set-price meals (Dh130 to Dh180) featuring Moroccan mains and French desserts.

There are regular but infrequent buses from Ouarzazate and Tinerhir (Dh40), but a grand taxi from Ouarzazate (Dh25) is a better option.

KELAÂ M'GOUNA قلعة مكونة

Although it takes its name from the nearby M'Goun mountain, the small town of Kelaâ M'Gouna is famous for roses and daggers. You can tell you're approaching town some 50km from Skoura when you see pink roses peeking through dense roadside hedgerows, and once you arrive, you can't miss the bottles of local rosewater for sale in every self-respecting local establishment. You can tell the local rosewater by its pure, heady scent; the sickly-sweet synthetic stuff from Casablanca is a bottled headache. Around May harvest-time you'll see rose garlands everywhere, especially during the town's signature rose festival (first weekend of May). On Wednesday market days, you can load up on dried edible roses.

But life in Kelaâ M'Gouna must not always have been so rosy, because the region also has a long tradition of dagger-making. There's a set-price showroom with hundreds of styles at **Cooperative Artisan du Poignards Azlag** (high season 9am-5pm, some close for lunch), on the main road at the eastern edge of town, where ceremonial daggers sell from Dh200 to several thousand dirham. Enter the trinket-filled courtyard boutiques beyond at your own risk; browsers are pushed to buy and bargaining sessions here feel oddly like duels.

If you really want to stop and smell the roses with a nature walk, ask at the **bureau des guides** (☎ 061 796101, 062 132192) 1km west of town or book official guides through local hotels. For more information on trekking in the M'Goun Massif, see p436.

Sleeping & Eating

Hôtel du Grand Atlas (☎ 024 836838; Ave Mohammed V; s/d/tr Dh50/100/150) Chipped but still chipper, with dinged walls, soft beds, decent shared bathrooms, an in-house hammam (Dh10, massage Dh50), popular café/restaurant (omelette breakfast Dh25) and a cheery management who can hook you up with official hiking guides.

Kasbah Itran (☎ 024 837103; www.kasbahitran.com; El Kelaa Mgouna BP 124; d half-board shared/private bathroom Dh350/500) A maze of private terraces and nine snug rooms with fireplaces, most with views over the M'Goun river to the nearby Ang Ksar and Kasbah des Glaouis. Trekkers flock here to wolf down hearty tajines and head off on natural history hikes arranged on site with local guides. Minivans from town run past the kasbah en route to the village of Torbis (Dh5).

Rosa d'Amaskina (☎ 024 836913; www.rosadamaskina.com; meals Dh70-120) Stop and smell the roses overflowing the courtyard rose garden at this restaurant 6km before town, and enjoy seasonal Moroccan meals on the riverside terrace.

Otherwise, you grab a bite at any café-restaurants in the centre of town that looks respectably crowded, or rely on **Hôtel du Grand Atlas** (Ave Mohammed V) for a set Dh80 meal of soup, tajine, dessert and tea.

Getting There & Away

Buses run between Ouarzazate and Tinerhir and beyond, but are often full. You can catch a grand taxi to Ouarzazate (Dh30), Skoura (Dh10), Boumalne du Dadès (Dh7) and Tinerhir (Dh6).

BOUMALNE DU DADÈS بوملنه داده

At the crossroads of the Dadès Valley, Boumalne has river valley views and handy amenities like banks, internet cafés, bike rental and a public hammam. Head 24km northeast of Kelaâ M'Gouna until you reach a fork: the main road continues over the river to the hillside town of Boumalne du Dadès, while the left branch leads up the stunning Dadès Gorge. Market day is Wednesday.

If you think this place is for the birds, you're right: the *hammada* and grassy plains immediately south of Boumalne du Dadès offer some rewarding birdwatching opportunities. Take the *piste* leading off the main road beyond town south towards the village of Tagdilt and Vallée des Oiseaux (Valley of the Birds) to look for larks, wheat-ears, sandgrouse, buzzards and eagle owls.

Most visitors come to town to take care of business before plunging into the Dadès Gorge. The **Banque Populaire** (Ave Mohammed V) changes money and has an ATM. On the same street there's internet access at **Taziri Net** (per hr Dh5; 🕙 9am-11pm). Treks can be

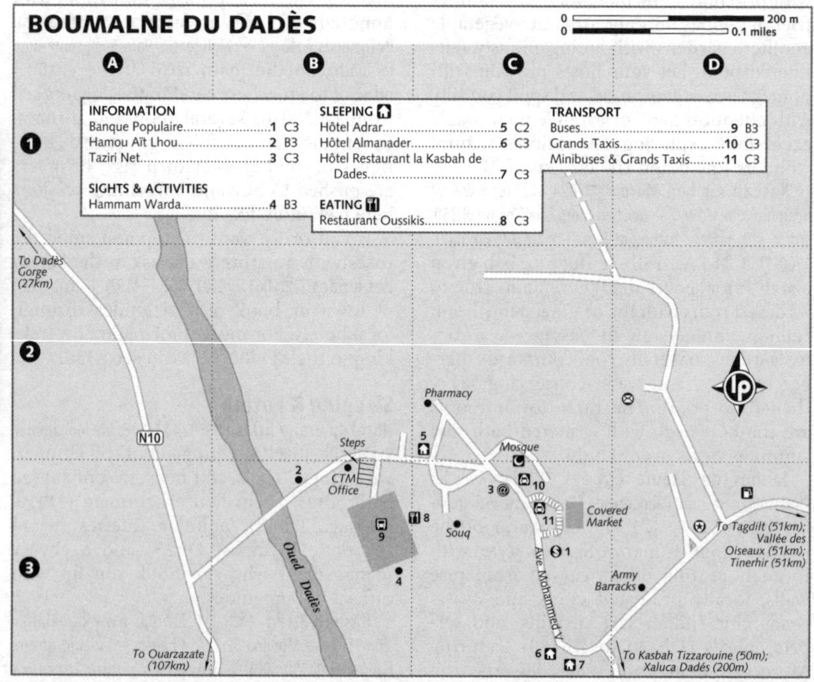

arranged through some hotels or through knowledgeable official guide **Hamou Aït Lhou** (☎ 067 593292; hamou57@voila.fr; Ave Mohammed V), who leads trips on foot or on mountain bike and rents mountain bikes (Dh120 per day).

Through the gate to the souq and at the opposite end of the plaza is **Hammam Warda** (admission Dh8 plus tip for attendant; 8am-8pm), which serves both men and women.

Sleeping

Hôtel Adrar (☎ 024 830765; Ave Mohammed V; d incl breakfast/half-board Dh150/250;) Handy to the bus station yet clean, with meals at the popular local restaurant downstairs. With all the commotion, you might want earplugs, or book one of the six air-con rooms so you can keep the windows shut.

Hôtel Almanader (☎ 024 830172; Ave Mohammed V; half-board d/tr Dh360/520) Bigger in personality and smaller in size than its neighbour la Kasbah, the Almanadar has 12 tidy, quirky rooms with tiny terraces, candy-coloured stucco decor, bare light bulbs and easygoing staff.

Hôtel Restaurant la Kasbah de Dades (☎ 024 830505; http://kasbahdedades.com; Ave Mohammed V; per person half-board Dh200;) Hanging over the valley, la Kasbah has 32 recently repainted rooms with balconies and dingy tour-trampled carpet but shiny tiled bathrooms, plus a respectable restaurant with a view and an espresso bar.

Xaluca Dadés (☎ 035 578450; signposted at top of hill on Ave Mohammed V; half-board s/d/ste Dh1054/1518/2028;) The only hotel in Boumalne that qualifies as a destination, the Xaluca turned a 1970s hilltop hotel fabulous, with African folk art and torches, a corridor remodelled into a mine shaft, and rock walls and mud-cloth bedspreads in the 106 snappy guestrooms, each with its own balcony and view over the valley. Other amenities include a hammam (Dh100), bar with a billiards table, a panoramic terrace swimming pool and Jacuzzi, and a loud, active gym.

Eating

Restaurant Oussikis (☎ 066 641421; Place de Souk, Boumalne Dades; Dh70-90) The best option for a meal is through the gate to the souq plaza and on your left at where you'll spot trained chef Fadil Faska in a spotless open kitchen turning fresh local ingredients into consistently savoury *kefta* (spiced meatballs) and tajines; call ahead for his float-away-flaky *bastilla* (pastry).

For more basic eats, the restaurant below Hôtel Adrar serves a filling meal of tajine or brochettes with salad and a drink for about Dh35 to Dh70, including local specialty of *gallia* (local hen) tajine. The restaurants of the Hôtel al-Manader and the Hôtel Restaurant la Kasbah de Dades also both have good menus (Dh70 to Dh100) and great views.

Getting There & Away

BUS

Buses leave daily to Ouarzazate (Dh40), Zagora (Dh65), Tinerhir (Dh25), Fez (Dh135), Casablanca (Dh150 to Dh190) and Rabat (Dh195), and multiple times daily to Er-Rachidia (Dh45), Erfoud (Dh60) and Marrakesh (Dh70 to Dh90).

TAXI, TRUCK & MINIBUS

You may have to wait a while for a grand taxi or minibus to fill up; fares are Dh50 to Ouarzazate, Dh30 to Tinerhir and Dh15 to Aït Oudinar (the start of the Dadés Gorge).

DADÉS GORGE مخنف ا مفيق ا دادس

Those art-deco tourism posters you'll see all over southern Morocco showing a striking pink-and-white kasbah in a rocky oasis aren't exaggerating: the Dadès Gorge really is that impressive. Some of the most impressive scenery can be seen just 6.5km into the gorge at **Aït Arbi**, where almond and fig trees provide a lush green valley backdrop for two-tone kasbahs and *ksour*.

But many of the best views in the Dadés Gorge aren't immediately visible from the road. A couple of kilometres past Aït Arbi, the road crosses an *oued*, and this river valley offers a sneaky back way to Kelaâ M'Gouna on foot. After another 5km and over a small pass, the hidden **Gorge de Miguirne** (Sidi Boubar Gorge) joins from the right. The small gorge has springs and rock pools and makes a good half-day hike involving some wading.

Another 4km brings you to extraordinary **red rock formations** that appear to be melting right into the green carpet of the *palmeraie* below. Further on where the gorge suddenly narrows, you'll find the village of Aït

Oudinar, with a few shops and a Sunday souq. About 2km beyond Aït Oudinar the road takes a turn for the harrowing, with hairpin bends inside the canyon. When the road eventually flattens out again, you might take that as your cue to turn around: you've already seen the best gorge scenery you can see without a 4WD.

The road is sealed all the way to Msemrir (63km), but you'll need a 4WD beyond that – especially for the *piste* that leads east and then south into the Todra Gorge. Many of the *pistes* are impassable in winter or after heavy rain, and even in good weather it can be rough going. If you're up for a challenge, you could travel north from Msemrir into the heart of the High Atlas and beyond to Imilchil. It's a long way, but it's feasible, thanks to the well-beaten path of market-bound trucks and minivans. Market day in Msemrir is Saturday.

Most hotels in the gorge and in Boumalne du Dadès can put you in touch with hiking guides (from Dh170 to Dh220 per day), arrange 4WD trips to the Todra Gorge and hire out bicycles (Dh70 to Dh100 per day). For more challenging walks, explore the smaller gorges west and east of the Oued Dadès, some of which lead up to nomad pastures. There's a good trail heading northwest, which begins just across the river from the cluster of hotels 28km from Boumalne du Dadès.

Sleeping

Most of the accommodation options listed here are within 28km of Boulmane du Dadès, and the kilometre markings here refer to the distance from Boumalne. Nearly all will let you sleep in the salon or on the terrace (even in summer you may need a sleeping bag) for around Dh25, or camp by the river for around Dh10. Msemrir offers a choice of two basic hotels: the cheerful **Hôtel El-Ouarda** (☎ 024 831609; r per person Dh70) or the **Café Agdal** (r per person Dh70).

Café Miguirne (☎ 068 763804; km14; mattresses on terrace Dh20, d with stand-up/sit-down toilet Dh70/100; 💻) A rosy outlook on the gorge is offered from this pinkish perch high above the gorge, where hardy trekkers converge and local staff exude enthusiasm for visitors. Rooms have straw-mat floors and soft beds with crisp sheets, but only six of the nine have sit-down toilets. Dinners are a good value (tajine/couscous Dh35/26) and internet use is available for Dh5.

Auberge des Gorges du Dadès (☎ 024 831719; www.aubergeaitoudinar.com; 25.5km; camping per person Dh15, r per person incl breakfast/half-board Dh120/200) A bubbly personality overlooking the river, the Auberge has 12 en suite rooms with splashy Amazigh motifs and big bathrooms plus a pleasantly shaded camping area. The trek leader speaks English, French and Spanish and has more than 23 years' experience.

Hôtel le Vieux Chateau du Dadès (☎ 024 831261; fax 024 830221; 27km; r per person half-board downstairs/upstairs Dh150/220) River views, good value and a terrace restaurant amid the chirping songbirds make this hotel worth going the extra mile to find. The tiled rooms upstairs have better views, but the snug pisé-walled downstairs guestrooms carved with auspicious Amazigh symbols bring on Berber *baraka*. Hikes and natural henna tattoos can be arranged at the front desk (tattoo Dh35 per hand).

Les 5 Lunes (☎ 024 830723; 23km, Aït Oudinar; d with shared bathroom incl breakfast/half-board Dh200/360, tr with private bathroom breakfast/half-board Dh300/540) Romance is in the air in this snug treehouse-style berth teetering above valley treetops, with four plain but pretty doubles and one triple and a hewn-stone bathroom. Book ahead for dinner next to the restaurant fireplace, followed by stargazing through the courtyard telescope.

our pick Kasbah de Mimi (☎ 024 830505; mimi.kasbah@laposte.net; 12km, Aït Ibrine; per person half-board Dh440; 🚗) Save yourself the trouble of cultivating friends with fabulous country houses, and book a weekend at one of four rooms in Kasbah de Mimi instead. At this painstakingly restored cliffside getaway, everything is in excellent taste: the original Berber *baraka* painted on living room walls, the paté hors d'ouevres, the water-conserving terrace gardens and grand piano in the fully stocked library. The cliff-hanger of a driveway is harrowing; leave your car at the top by the sign and walk down.

Chez Pierre (☎ 024 830267; http://chezpierre.ifrance.com; 27km; per person half-board Dh570, 2-person minimum; 🚗) This rock-climbing hotel has eight airy rooms and one apartment shimmying right up the gorge. Decor is kept simple to focus attention on what really matters: the view over the valley from flowering terraces and poolside sun decks. Picnics and hikes with official guides can be arranged.

Eating

Most hotels offer half-board rates and dinner, which may be followed by local Berber music. Since there aren't a lot of shops in the gorge, pack in some trail snacks from Boumalne or Ouarzazate.

Restaurant Isabelle (15km; menu Dh70) Enjoy your meal on the terrace with a side of stupefaction at the sight of melting rocks across the valley. Your choice of a hearty omelette or tajine comes with salad and a drink.

Restaurant Panorama (☎ 024 831555; www.auberge-panorama.sup.fr; 10km, Aït Ibrirne; mains Dh60-80) If you don't have time to stay overnight in the gorge, you can always take in the view over a meal just inside the gorge at the Panorama. Dishes include flavourful vegetarian options, a good homemade couscous, and the local specialty kebab of minced *gallia*.

Getting There & Away

Grands taxis and minibuses run up the gorge from Boumalne and charge Dh15 per person to the cluster of hotels in the middle of the gorge (near Vieux Chateau) and Dh30 to Msemrir; ask to be dropped at your chosen hotel. To return, wait by the road and flag down a passing vehicle. Hiring a taxi for a half-day trip into the gorge should cost around Dh200.

The energetic could combine the Dadès and Todra gorges by crossing between the two (a two- to three-day walk); otherwise you'll need a 4WD.

Minibuses run up to Msemrir fairly frequently; the last one back to Boumalne leaves around 4pm. Trucks go to Tamtattouchte and Aït Haini on Saturdays, and continue the next day to Imilchil. There's accommodation in Tamtattouchte (see p362) but none in Aït Haini (souq on Thursday).

TINERHIR تنرهير

Lingering in this dusty mining town doesn't make much sense when the Todra Gorge awaits just 12km away. But if you need a break after the 51km drive from Boumalne du Dadès, there are a couple of places where you can stop for a meal or an inexpensive overnight stay.

There are several banks with ATMs in the west of town, including **BMCE** (Ave Mohammed V) and **Crédit du Maroc** (Ave Mohammed V). **Tichka Internet** (Rue Zaid Ouhmed; per hr Dh6 ; 7am-9.30pm), is next to the Hôtel de l'Avenir. The old town is immediately southeast of the modern centre, with a souq and interesting old *ksar*. An enormous souq is held about 2.5km west of the centre on Monday, and there's a smaller livestock souq in town on Saturday.

Sleeping

Hôtel de l'Avenir (☎ 024 834599; www.avenir.tineghir.net; 27 Rue Zaid Ouhmed; mattress on roof Dh30, s/d/tr Dh30/100/150) A sociable spot, with cafés lining the plaza outside and 10 rooms grouped around a chatty dining area inside (breakfast Dh25). All the signs of a well-loved travel hub are here: piles of donated books, travel photos and postcards on the walls, mountain-bike hire and enough advice to last a lifetime of Todra trekking.

Hôtel l'Oasis (☎ 024 833670; Ave Mohammed V; per room without/with bathroom Dh100/150, d with half-board Dh350) Rooms are clean and surprisingly quiet, given that the Total station is next door, and the community-minded management sells crafts made to benefit the local Association des Handicapés (handicap assistance association). Meals here are a cut above other options in town, and not just because they're on the upstairs terrace – the food is so reliably tasty that many local wedding receptions are held here.

Hôtel Tomboctou (☎ 024 834604; www.hoteltomboctou.com; 126 Ave Bir Anzarane; s/d terrace room with shared bathroom incl breakfast Dh210/320, half-board Dh280/460, s/d/tr/q incl breakfast Dh500/590/780/920, half-board Dh570/730/990/1200, ste half-board Dh1400;) Quirky, rosy little rooms in a renovated kasbah built in 1936 for the local *caid*. Bathrooms are quite splashy with pink marble sinks, solar-heated water and Jacuzzis in the suites, but the big perk here is the full bar by the courtyard pool. Mountain trekking and bicycle trips can be organised.

Eating

Several simple restaurants line Ave Hassan II, including **Café des Amis** (Ave Hassan II), which serves excellent brochettes, **Café Central** (Ave Hassan II) and **Restaurant Essaada** (Ave Hassan II) – and they all serve simple Moroccan dishes. You'll find more choices along Ave Mohammed V. The restaurant at Hôtel l'Oasis offers reliable three-course meals for Dh80 to Dh100. The restaurant **l'Avenir** (27 Rue Zaid Ouhmed), in the same building, but not connected to the hotel, serves good grills and salads.

For more upscale dining, head 3km out of town on the road to Todra, and on your left you'll spot **Chez Michéle** (☎ 024 835151; www.chez-michele.com; mains Dh90-140; lunch & dinner), where dapper servers ceremoniously present dishes of game-hen with fresh morels and tender beef with quince.

Getting There & Away

BUS

In the centre of town, buses leave from the Place Principale, off Ave Mohammed V to Marrakesh (Dh105, five daily) via Ouarzazate (Dh45), and to Casablanca (Dh165), Erfoud (Dh30, three daily), Meknès (Dh115, six daily), Rissani (Dh45) and Zagora (Dh80). Anything westbound will drop you in Boumalne du Dadès (Dh15).

TAXI & MINIVAN

Grands taxis to Ouarzazate (Dh55) and Er-Rachidia (Dh45) leave from the eastern end of the gardens. This is also the place to hunt for a ride (taxis, lorries or pick-up trucks) up to the Todra Gorge (Dh8) and beyond.

An 8am minivan runs to Tamtattouchte (Dh15 to Dh20) and Aït Haini (Dh25 to Dh30) and to Imilchil (Dh30 to Dh40); check for additional departures in the afternoon.

TODRA GORGE مخنف ا مفيق ا تودرغة

Being stuck between a rock and a hard place is a fantastic experience to have in the Todra Gorge, where the massive fault dividing the High Atlas from the Jebel Sarhro is at some points just wide enough for a crystal-clear river and some trekkers to squeeze through. The road from Tinerhir passes green *palmeraies* and yellowish Berber villages, until 15km along, high walls of pink and grey rock close in around the road. The approach is thrilling and somehow urgent, as though the doors of heaven were about to close before you.

Arrivals at the Todra are best timed in the morning, when the sun briefly alights on the bottom of the gorge, providing your shining golden moment of welcome. In the

MARRAKESH & CENTRAL MOROCCO

afternoon it gets very dark and, in winter, bitterly cold. If you pass through the gorge and keep heading up the road, you'll reach the end of the tarmac at the stunning Berber village of Tamtattouchte.

Activities

TREKKING & CLIMBING

About a 30-minute walk beyond the main gorge is the Petite Gorge. This is the starting point of many pleasant day hikes, including one starting by the Auberge-Camping le Festival, 2km after the Petite Gorge.

For a more strenuous hike, you could do a three-hour loop from north of the gorge to Tizgui, south of the gorge. The walk starts after leaving the main gorge (Map p361); as the road heads right (northeast), take the track leading up the hill to the left (southwest). Regular donkey and mule traffic keep this path well-defined for most of the route. Head to the pass, and from there, ascend southeast to the next pass. This would be a good place to stray from the main route to look over the rim of the gorge – but be careful, as the winds get mighty powerful up here. From the second pass, descend to the beautiful village of Tizgui, where you can walk back through the *palmeraies* to the gorge.

With all the ruined kasbahs in the *palmeraies* to the south of here, this area is a photographer's dream. If you want to push on, you could walk back to Tinerhir through the *palmeraies* in three or four hours.

Rock-climbing on the vertical rock face of the gorge is becoming increasingly popular. There are some sublime routes here (French grade 5), some of them bolted. Pillar du Couchant, near the entrance to the gorge, offers classic long climbs; the Petite Gorge is better for novice climbers, with some good short routes. Most hotels can provide further information, but the guides with the most experience usually speak Spanish and not much English.

Assettif Aventure (☎ 024 895090; www.assettif.org, in French), located 700m before the gorge, Assettif arranges treks and horse riding (day trip Dh500), and hires out bikes (per day Dh100) and mountaineering equipment. You can also do an overnight horse trek with

FROM GORGE TO GORGE

The 42km from Tamtattouchte to the Dadès Gorge should only be attempted by 4WD during the summer months (May to September). The tough five-hour journey might threaten to shake a few teeth loose, but with a stunning landscape of twisted hills and the boulder-strewn valley of Tizgui n'Ouadda, it's certainly easy on the eyes.

In May, many nomadic Berbers with homes in Aït Haini head to this valley to pitch their tents and graze large herds of sheep. If you stop, women might invite you into their tent for tea to find out your story and tell you theirs.

About midway on this route, you'll crest the 2639m-high Tizi n'Uguent Zegsaoun before a bone-rattling descent to Msemrir. The crossing is prone to flash floods in the early spring and you should always seek up-to-date advice on the state of the *piste* before setting off. The turning for the *piste* is just after Tamtattouchte, below the auberge on the top of the hill. Since the track is very difficult to follow, a local guide is recommended.

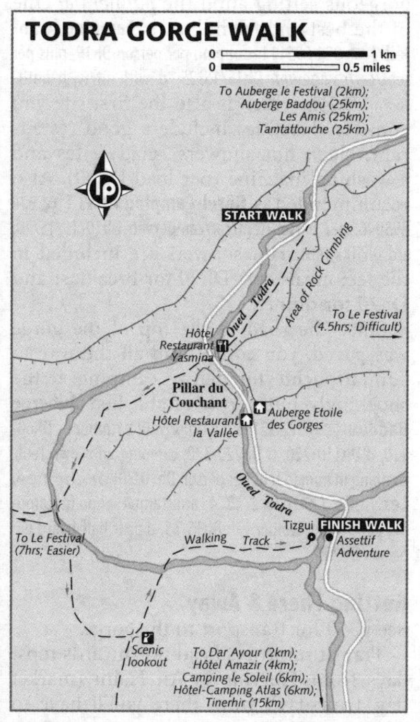

guide and food for Dh800. Advance booking is recommended, especially for overnight trips and during busy periods.

A network of difficult *pistes* heading into the High and Middle Atlas provides a lifeline to villages that are otherwise still largely inaccessible. The two most popular trips are the rough *pistes* west to the Dadès Gorge (see the boxed text, p361) and north to Imilchil. You'll need a 4WD for either trip, and it's best to ask locals about current conditions along these roads before leaving, even in spring and summer.

Sleeping & Eating

Auberge Etoile des Gorges (☎ 024 895045; fax 024 832151; s/d/tr with shared bathroom Dh50/70/100, r with private bathroom Dh120) A plucky little budget hotel in the mouth of the mighty gorge, featuring six simple rooms with orthopaedically stiff beds, solar-heated showers and minor road noise easily ignored on a roof deck with a close-up view of the gorge and reasonable meals (three-course meals Dh60 to Dh70).

Hôtel Restaurant la Vallée (☎ 024 895126; d with shared bathroom Dh120, d with private bathroom incl breakfast/half-board Dh150/300) Overlooking the river on one side and facing the gorge on the other, this simple hotel is all about the views from the 2nd-floor rooms. Nine of the 12 rooms have private bathrooms, with showers rather awkwardly over the toilet but plenty of light.

our pick Dar Ayour (☎ 024 895271; www.darayour.com; 13km Gorges du Todra, Tinghir; r with shared/private bathroom Dh100/150, r incl breakfast/half-board Dh200/350) Riads have arrived in Todra with this warm, artsy five-story guest house that's all Middle Atlas rugs, winking mirrorwork blankets and pillows, and colourful abstract paintings. The 2nd floor is a three-room suite that can sleep a family of seven, the third storey has three en suite guestrooms, and breakfast (Dh35) with a view is served up on the terrace.

Hôtel Restaurant Yasmina (☎ 024 895118; www.todragorge.com; s/d incl breakfast Dh160/250, half-board Dh250/400) Tucked beneath the sheer rock walls at the heart of the gorge, the Yasmina has fairly small, functional rooms and a good terrace restaurant (set menu Dh70 to Dh100) to take in the views. The prime location does have its downside: it's overrun by tour groups during the day.

Auberge Le Festival (☎ 061 267251; http://aubergelefestival.com; main house half-board s/d Dh300/460, tower room s/d Dh400/700, cave room d/tr Dh700/900) Get in touch with your primal instincts in a cave guestroom dug right into the hillside, or do your best Romeo and Juliet impersonation on your private wrought-iron tower balcony. Meals are tasty and innovative – who knew a tajine would be good with melted cheese? – and the charming multilingual owner can arrange trekking and climbing.

Hôtel Amazir (☎ 024 895109; d/tr incl breakfast Dh400/600, half-board Dh600/800; ❄ 🏊) Don't be fooled by its stern, stony exterior: inside, this place is relaxed, with pretty, unfussy rooms, a pool terrace surrounded by palms, and the lulling sound of the rushing river below. It's on a bend in the road at the southern end of the gorge, 5km before you enter, away from gorge-gawking crowds.

CAMPING

Along the road to the gorge, about 9km from Tinerhir, is a line of camp sites, all with basic rooms but benefiting from a gorgeous setting amid the *palmeraie*. One of the best and friendliest is **Camping le Soleil** (☎ 024 895111; camping per person Dh15, plus per tent/car/campervan Dh15/15/25, d without/with bathroom 120/240), which is also the first site you come to. Facilities include a good restaurant, clean hot showers, shady sites and a washing machine (per load Dh20). Also recommended is **Hôtel-Camping Atlas** (☎ 024 895046; per person/tent/car/campervan Dh10/15/15/20; s/d Dh100/140). Hot showers are included in the fee; meals cost Dh20 for breakfast and Dh70 for dinner.

Since the road to the top of the gorge was paved, you could head all the way to Tamtattouchte for deluxe camping at the shockingly pink, long-established **Auberge Baddou** (☎ 072 521389; with private bathroom s Dh60-110, d Dh110-220, tr Dh220-320, camping with own tent/camping in nomad tent per person Dh20/30) or the new **Les Amis** (☎ 070 234374; amistamt@yahoo.fr; camping per person/camper van Dh15/35, d or tr half-board per person Dh200).

Getting There & Away

See p359 for transport to the gorge.

Transit minivans head northwards most days from Tinerhir to Aït Haini (market day Thursday); from there you'll have to hitch. A sealed road now runs all the way to Aït Haini (paving in progress towards Imilchil) beyond which the *piste* continues over the Tizi Tirherhouzine to Agoudal (the highest village en route; basic accommodation is available) and on to Imilchil, just over 100km from the gorge.

GOULMIMA غولميما

Goulmima is a centre of Berber culture and makes a more interesting sightseeing stopover than Er-Rachidia, which has better sleeping options. Market days are Tuesday, Thursday and Saturday. Most facilities, including ATMs, internet and cafés, can be found along the main street.

The main attraction is the labyrinthine **Ksar Aït Goulmima**. Unlike many *ksour* and kasbahs in the region, this walled village is still home to several hundred people. A guide can lead you to the 500-year-old mosque and through the **mellah** into the *palmeraie*.

To get to the *ksar*, head through the main part of town and turn right at the roundabout to/from Er-Rachidia. After 500m, you'll pass the Maison d'Hôtes les Palmiers. Another 800m further along is the turn-off left to the youth hostel; the *ksar* is straight on.

The peaceful converted home of a French-Moroccan couple, **Maison d'Hôtes les Palmiers** (☎/fax 035 784004; s/d/tr/q Dh180/260/330/360, per person half-board Dh250) sits in a mature garden on the edge of the *palmeraie*. Rooms are spacious and spotless, with tiled baths; all are heated in winter, but only one has air-conditioning. The mostly Moroccan dinner menu is fabulous (dinner Dh95). Trekking information and guides for the *ksar* are available.

In another converted family home a Moroccan family runs the **Youth Hostel** (☎ 066 908442; www.aub.ht.st, in French; Hay Othmane Secteur 3, No 4 Ksar Goulmima; mattress/d per person Dh50/100). You could crash anywhere in this walled garden complex and find a soft place to land on the grass or piles of rugs, floral upholstered mattresses and mirrored pillows. It has a couple of double rooms, shared showers with off-and-on hot water, and a kitchen. Meals cost Dh20 for breakfast, Dh50 for lunch/dinner.

Grands taxis run from town when full to Er-Rachidia and Tinerhir.

ZIZ VALLEY & THE TAFILALT وادة زيز و تافلالت

The Oued Ziz brings life to this barren landscape, running past the small town of Rich and carving out a valley that continues south beyond Merzouga. Along the road to Er-Rachidia you'll see the spectacular Jurassic geography of the Ziz Gorges, beginning 20km south of Rich at the French-built Tunnel du Légionnaire and marking thousands of years of geologic time with their exposed strata. This route nips through palm-fringed towns and past several *ksour* and a series of dams, including the Barrage Hassan Adakhil with turquoise water visible from the main highway. Beyond Er-Rachidia, the road heads past the fertile Source Bleue de Meski before plunging into the desert and rolling dunes of Merzouga.

The tough Tafilalt was one of the last areas to succumb to French control under the protectorate, with tribes putting up sporadic resistance until 1932. Two years later Morocco was officially considered 'pacified', but just to be on the safe side, Erfoud was built as an administrative and garrison town to keep a watchful eye on the Tafilalt tribes.

ER-RACHIDIA الراشيدية

Garrison towns aren't generally known for their charm or culture, but Er-Rachidia is trying to change that. Along with some nicer accommodations it now has an enormous theatre, and every May since 2003 has been host to performers from throughout the Sahara at the **Festival du Desert** (www.festivaldudesert.ma). Market days are Sunday, Tuesday and Thursday.

Information

There are at least four banks in town, including a **BMCE** (Place Moulay Hassan) and a **Banque Populaire** near the main street heading out to Erfoud, both of which have ATMs.

Cyber Challenge Internet (Rue Sidi Bou Abdallah; per hr Dh5; 🕐 7am-midnight) is on a 2nd floor near the covered market. If you've taken transit this far but want to drive to the desert, one of the last agencies until Merzouga is **Camino**

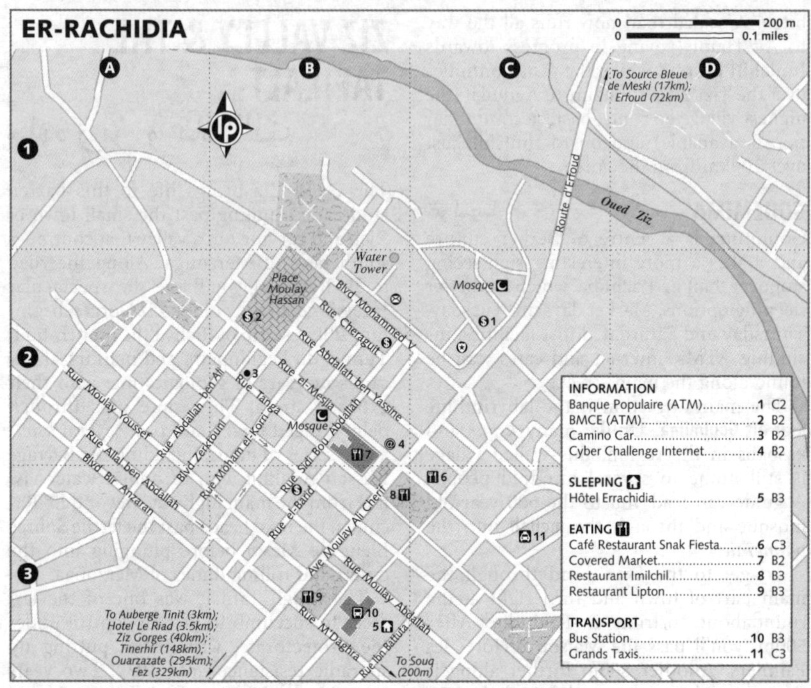

Car (☎ 035 574947; 102 Blvd Zerktouni 1st-fl, Er-Rachidia; daily rental Dh300-350).

Sleeping

Hôtel Errachidia (☎ 035 570453; hotelerrachidia@yahoo.fr; 31 Rue Ibn Battuta; s/d/tr Dh250/320/410;) Don't be fooled by the setting behind the bus station (handy for early or late arrivals), or the Soviet-style concrete exterior: inside are 26 perfectly comfortable rooms with sparkling white bathrooms, most of which face away from the street and are quite peaceful. Note that only 10 of the 21 rooms have air-con.

Hotel le Riad (☎ 035 791006; www.hotelleriad.com; Route de Goulmima, Er-Rachidia; s Dh600, d & tr Dh70;) A true business-class hotel has landed in Er-Rachidia, with all the fixings: internet access, sprawling suite guestrooms, marble bathtubs, an absurdly huge pool and suited stampedes of pharmaceutical conferences. Exceedingly comfortable and reasonably priced, given the high standard of service.

Eating

Opposite the **covered market** where you could scrounge up picnic makings, **Restaurant Imilchil** (☎ 035 572123; Ave Moulay Ali Cherif), provides a ready-made alternative: good tajines on a big terrace (set meal Dh70).

Right across Rue el-Mesjia is **Café Restaurant Snak Fiesta** (Rue el-Mesjia; lunch & dinner), which serves fresh Moroccan salads (Dh15) and sandwiches (Dh20) at the right price. Near the bus station is the faded but friendly **Restaurant Lipton** (Ave Moulay Ali Cherif).

Getting There & Away

BUS

Buses operate out of the central **bus station** (Rue M'Daghra). **CTM** (☎ 035 572024) has departures to Rabat/Casablanca (Dh140/170, 10/11 hours, one daily), Fez (Dh105, 8½ hours, one daily) and Meknès (Dh90, seven hours, six daily).

There are also private buses that run to Fez (Dh85, five daily), Marrakesh (Dh125, 11 hours, three daily), Ouarzazate (Dh65, six hours, three daily), and Rissani (Dh18, two hours, nine daily) via Erfoud (Dh15).

TAXI

Most grands taxis depart from a lot located about three blocks northeast of the main bus station. The main destinations include Azrou (Dh80, five hours), Erfoud (Dh20, one hour), Fez (Dh130, five hours), Meknès (Dh110, five hours), Tinerhir (Dh40, 1½ hours), Rissani (Dh25, 1½ hours) and Merzouga via Rissani (Dh50, 1½ hours).

AROUND ER-RACHIDIA

Source Bleue de Meski

عين مسكي الزرقاء

This natural spring spilling into a swimming pool 17km southeast of Er-Rachidia has become a weekend draw for heat-plagued locals from Er-Rachidia. During the week, it's not a bad place for a quick dip (Dh5), though you may feel self-conscious with villagers watching you strip down to your skivvies. If you want to work up a sweat before you take the chilly plunge, there's a nice hike from the camping area to the deserted Ksar Meski on the far side of the *oued*.

The spring is about 1km west of the main road and signposted. Public buses travel from Er-Rachidia to a terminal just above the spring between 7am and 9pm (Dh3). Alternatively, any bus or grand taxi to Erfoud or Aufous can drop you off at the turn-off. When leaving, you should be able to flag down a grand taxi or hitch from the main road. If you're driving south to Erfoud, there are great photo opportunities of the Ziz *palmeraies* just north of Aufous, when the road turns a corner on the desert plateau to reveal a green gorge below.

Down in this *palmeraie* is the a wonderful find: our pick **Maison d'Hôtes Zouala** (☎ 072 144633; http://labrisenet.free.fr/maison_zouala, in French; 30km on the Er-Rachidia–Erfoud road, in centre of Douar Irgroum; per person half-board Dh250). This pisé house was the owner's ancestral home, and now he's extended his family's welcome to guests in this peaceful hideaway with private and shared bathrooms, home cooking (they bake their own bread), and local touches like women's embroidered shawls for curtains, and jugs as lamp bases. Bikes are available to explore, but ask also about treks to hidden springs and visits to local homes during date and olive harvests. A portion of proceeds helps fund the village association's literacy program.

At the edge of the *palmeraie* just before the town of Aufous is **Camping Tissirt** (☎ 062 141378; tissirtziz@yahoo.fr; per person/car/car-camping/caravan Dh15/15/20/30, d half-board Dh15 plus tent/shower/electricity/water/meal Dh15/10/15/20/Dh60-70), a comfortable and scenic stopping point under the palms en route to the Merzouga dunes. The pisé bungalows are especially appealing, with tile floors and palm-stump end tables, and meal offerings include *madfouna* (local Berber calzone). While you're here, wander around Asous, which offers useful services – food, petrol and phone – and has some stunning pisé buildings and an impressive ruin of a kasbah above. The weekly souq is on Thursday.

ERFOUD ارفود

pop 24,000

Fossilised bathtubs and moist, sweet dates are Erfoud's claims to fame, but this wasn't always the case. Until recently Erfoud was the end of the road, and the boisterous staging point for desert tours. But now that the tarmac goes right up to the base of the dunes in Merzouga, you can sit at a sidewalk café here and just hear the swoosh of 4WDs gunning it past Erfoud to hotels with dune views just down the road. The Merzouga road is clearly marked, so you don't need to stop to hire a guide, but it's still worth a pause here for coffee, pizza, fossils and fresh dates during the September to October harvest.

Information

There are several banks in town but only the **BMCE** (Ave Moulay Ismail) has an ATM. Internet access is available at **Internet Moulay el Hassane** (Ave Moulay el-Hassan per hr Dh5; 10am-1am).

Sights & Activities

There's more history to Erfoud than immediately meets the eye. Just 5km north of Erfoud is the impressive **Ksar M'Aadid**, well worth a look if you have your own transport.

It takes some digging to find Erfoud's other claim to historical fame: shiny black fossilised marble, which is quarried nearby in the desert. You can watch it being cut into prehistoric sinks at **Manar Marbre** (☎ 055 578125; Route de Jouf; 9am-6pm), the marble factory between the town and Kasbah Tizimi, and scour the showroom downstairs for prehistoric bookends and

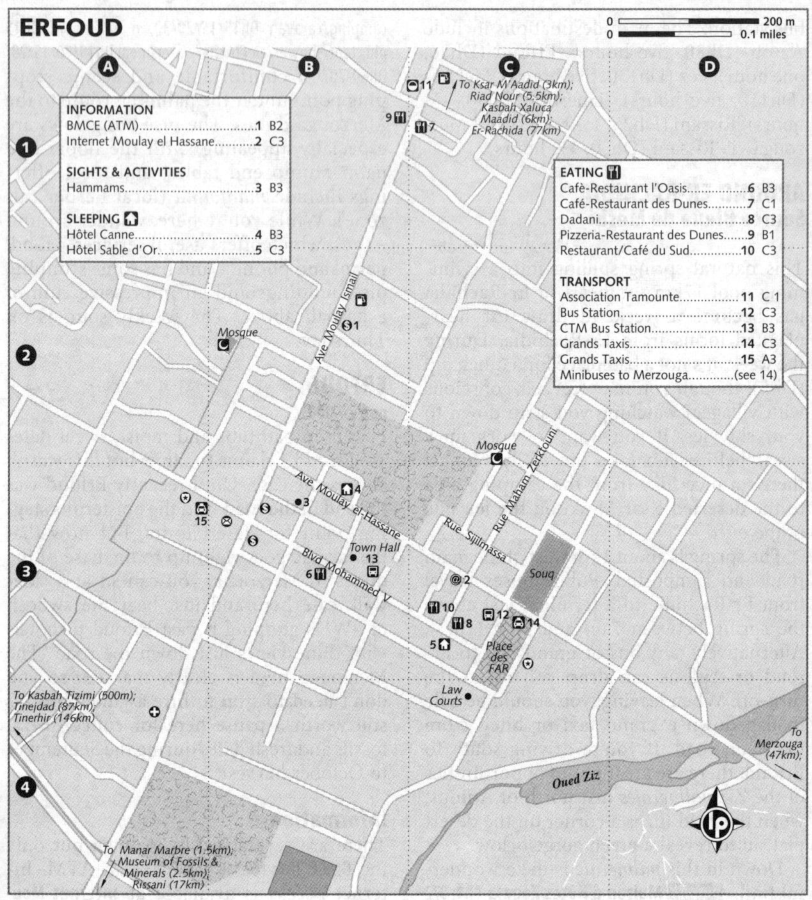

trilobite earrings. The display is more fun and the prices are better at the **Museum of Fossils & Minerals** (☎ 061 425927, 068 757563; brahimtahiri@hotmail.com; 3km on the Rissani road; 🕑 8am-7pm), which has prize fossils in museum display cases not for sale, and others in the boutique you can buy: tiny fish frozen in a final flip and ingenious carved black marble espresso cups studded with ancient ammonite fossils.

In September or October Erfoud has an increasingly well-attended **date festival**, with dancing and music. But if it's been awhile since you've had a good, juicy date and can't wait until October, the souq at the southern end of town sells some of the town's famous dates along with fresh produce.

Hammams (Dh7 entry) for men and women are located behind Hôtel Sable d'Or.

Sleeping

BUDGET

Hôtel Canne (☎ 035 578695; fax 035 578696; 85 Ave Moulay el-Hassane; s/d/tr Dh150/180/240;) The sharp team of women who run this centrally located place are rightfully proud of the reputation the Canne has earned as the best women-friendly budget hotel for miles around. Aqua-blue bathroom fixtures betray no trace of toothpaste spatter, and the clean linens are on so tightly you may have to wrestle yourself into bed.

Hôtel Sable d'Or (☎ 035 576348; Blvd Mohammed V; s/d Dh150/170) On a street lined with cafés, this easygoing place offers simple rooms with private bathrooms, peeling paint, tiled floors and clean linens.

MIDRANGE & TOP END

Riad Nour (☎ 035 577748; http://riad-nour.ifrance.com; 5km before Erfoud on right; s/d Dh240/590;) The next-door neighbour to the glitzy Xaluca, but they probably don't run in the same circles. Inner peace is the goal here, with 12 guestrooms in white with touches of blue, wrought-iron beds and framed calligraphy. There's a pool out back you can splash around in and a fully stocked bar in front, and the main garden courtyard attracts nesting songbirds and lovebirds.

Kasbah Xaluca Maadid (☎ 035 578450; www.xaluca.com; 5km before Erfoud on right; s/d Dh740/900, junior/royal ste Dh2000/2900;) Exactly the kind of flashy pool-party scene where they film music videos (and in fact a Moroccan music video request show was filming at our last visit to the Xaluca). Junior suites are the rock stars here, with fossilised marble bedsteads and mineral lamps; suites are a bit frilly with chintz dust ruffles on four-poster beds.

Eating

Don't miss the chance to try the local speciality *kalia,* minced mutton with tomato, peppers, egg, onion and 44 spices (no, you can't count them) served in a tajine.

Restaurant/Café du Sud (19 Ave Mohammed V; mains Dh30-50) Next to the Hôtel Ziz, this is one of the most popular local eateries. The *kalia* (Dh30) is excellent and *madfouna* (Dh45) is available if you order in advance.

our pick **Pizzeria-Restaurant des Dunes** (☎ 035 576793; Ave Moulay Ismail; pizza Dh40, set menu Dh80-100) Do not adjust your GPS: you're about to experience authentic wood-fired pizza right here in the desert, including a stunning pizza margherita with local anchovies, olives and fresh oregano for just Dh40. Bet you'll be heading here on your way back from the dunes, too.

Café-Restaurant des Dunes (☎ 035 576793; Ave Moulay Ismail; meals Dh60) Pull up a cushioned ironwork throne at a sidewalk table, and enjoy some rays with your fresh-squeezed orange juice at this sidewalk café for just Dh5. The same family owns the top-end Kasbah Zaluca Maadid and the pizza restaurant across the road.

Two other popular places are the new **Dadani** (Ave Mohammed V; menu Dh70, mains Dh40-45, breakfast Dh20) and **Café-Restaurant l'Oasis** (Ave Mohammed V; mains Dh35-45), both of which serve solid Moroccan dishes for reasonable prices.

Getting There & Away

BUS

The **CTM station** (☎ 035 576886; Ave Mohammed V) runs a service twice daily to Fez (Dh95, seven hours) via Er-Rachidia (Dh15, 1¼ hours), Marrakesh (Dh135, 11½ hours), Midelt (Dh59, five hours), Meknès (Dh125, 6½ hours) and Rissani (Dh5, 20 minutes).

Other busses leave from Place des FAR. There are services to Tinerhir (Dh30, twice daily), to Ouarzazate (Dh70, three daily) and Fez (Dh97, three daily).

A local bus runs to Zagora (Dh75, six hours) at 8.30am on Tuesday and Thursday. A minivan runs sporadically to Merzouga (Dh15 to Dh20) from the parking lot in Place des FAR. The driver might try to steer you towards whichever auberge pays commission, so stand by your guns if you have a particular place in mind. Minibuses can drop you off at any auberge en route.

TAXI

Grands taxis are, as a rule, a more reliable bet. Some leave from Place des FAR and others from opposite the post office for Merzouga (Dh30, one hour), Rissani (Dh7, 20 minutes), Er-Rachidia (Dh20, one hour) and Tinerhir (Dh60). Since the road was laid to Merzouga, the price of hiring a 4WD and driver, formerly the only certain way of getting over the *piste,* has dropped. **Association Tamounte** (☎ 035 577523; 5 Ave Moulay Ismail) rents car and driver for Dh450 a day, plus the cost of diesel.

RISSANI الريصاني

Many visitors are tempted to pass straight through the town of Rissani, but photographers, history buffs and architecture aficionados could spend days wandering through decrepit *ksour,* artfully crumbling kasbahs, a *zawiya* open to all and recently opened *ksar* museum along these well-worn caravan tracks. Rissani is the point where Oued Ziz quietly ebbs away, but historically fortunes flowed through here in gold and slaves from caravans from the *sahel.* Rissani was so strategic that the Filali (ancestors of the Alawite dynasty that rules today) used it as the staging ground for their epic battle to supplant the Saadians as the ruling dynasty in Morocco.

The centre of Rissani is quite small and manageable and still has a significant *ksar* at its heart, including important Alawite monuments. Travellers will find most of their practical needs satisfied along the northern edge of the souq, which becomes a bustling hive of activity every Sunday, Tuesday and Thursday.

Information

There's a post and phone office at the northern end of the medina walls, and a Banque Populaire with an ATM opposite the souq. **Info Keys Cyber Club** (per hr Dh5) is one of several internet places.

Sights & Activities

For a tour of Rissani's ancient architectural splendours, famed *palmeraie* and glimpses of life on the edge of the desert, try this 21km loop (Map p368) along a circuit south of Rissani. Look sharp: Some sights are along bumpy roads that lead you past several ruined *ksour* and the scant ruins of the fabled city of Sijilmassa.

From Rissani's centre, head north from the souq and follow the main road west. About 2km to the southeast is the cheering yellow **Zawiya Moulay Ali ash-Sharif** (open

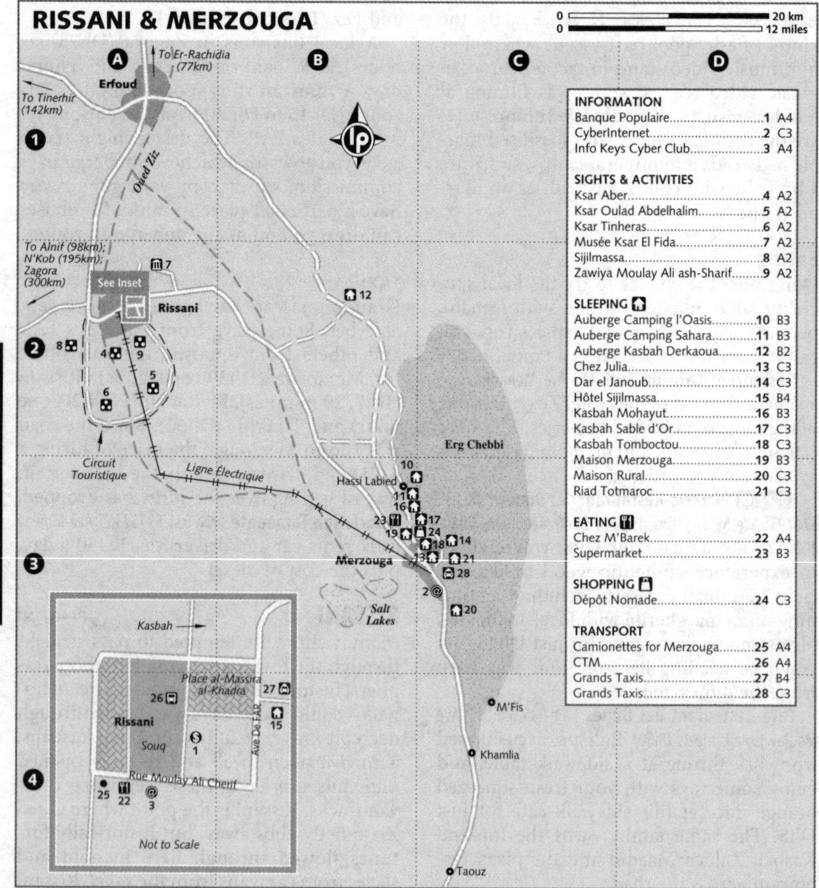

to non-Muslims; admission free; ⌚ 9am-6pm), built to honour the founder of the Alawite dynasty that still rules Morocco today. Behind the *zawiya* along a dirt track you'll see the fantastic crumbling towers of 19th-century **Ksar Aber**, which formerly housed the dynasty's disgraced or unwanted members and like those black sheep, has been abandoned to its ruination.

About 1km or so past the *zawiya* on your right is **Ksar Oulad Abdelhalim**, built around 1900 for Sultan Moulay Hassan's elder brother. Walk through the wooden door into the walled compound, then veer right, left and right again into the ruin of the palace once called the 'Alhambra of the Tafilalt'. There's little left intact beyond some painted ceiling beams and carved stucco, but plenty to fascinate a photographer – extra memory cards may come in handy here.

Back on the road, you'll continue past another group of *ksour*, some of which are still inhabited by members of the Filali. There are good views from **Ksar Tinheras**.

You come to the ruins of **Sijilmassa** just before you reach Rissani. This was the capital of a virtually independent Islamic principality adhering to the Shiite 'heresy' (see About Islam, p57) in the early days of the Arab conquest of North Africa. Sijilmassa's foundation is lost in myth – some speculate it was in AD 757 – but certainly by the end of the 8th century it played a key role as a staging post for trans-Saharan trade. Caravans of up to 20,000 camels crossed the sands to the remote desert salt mines of Taodeni and Tagahaza (in modern-day Mali), then continued to Niger and Ghana, where a pound of Saharan salt was traded for an ounce of African gold.

But as the Berbers say, where there's gold, there's trouble. The inevitable internal feuding led to the collapse of the fabled city in the 14th century, and Sijilmassa is now a ruin with little to indicate its past glories beyond two decorated gateways and a few other partially standing structures. With all this glorious decay, album cover photo shoots fairly beg to be set here.

There are other *ksour* in the region including Ksar al-Beidha, Ksar Haroun and several *ksour* on the road to Merzouga; look for signposts on your left heading south out of town. Just 2.5km south of town you'll also see signs for a Musée, which is worth the detour. **Musee Ksar El Fida** (☎ 061 847817; Rissani; entry with guide Dh10) is an enormous restored Alawaite kasbah built from 1854–72 that shows how life was lived within these walls in the 19th century, from their elaborate costumes to the contents of a 19th-century toolbox.

Sleeping & Eating

Since most tourists stay in Erfoud or Merzouga, accommodation in Rissani is limited and the standards mostly poor.

Hôtel Sijilmassa (☎/fax 035 575042; Place al-Massira al-Khadra; s Dh80, d Dh140-160; ❄) is located near the bus and grand taxi station for early/late arrivals. En suite rooms here are clean and comfortable, though the bathrooms that lead you through the shower to reach the toilet are odd. All rooms have air-conditioning except one, and the downstairs restaurant features a hearty *kalia*.

our pick **Chez M'barek** (☎ 067 501658; panorama72003@yahoo.fr; 7 Rue Moulay Ali Chrif, Rissani; breakfast Dh15, set menu Dh40) serves authentic *kalia* that is rich in tomato and meat, or a well-spiced *madfouna* that will feed at least four (Dh80) in the cool basement or breezy terrace. Call in your *madfouna* order two hours beforehand so that it will be ready when you arrive.

Shopping

If you have time on your hands, Rissani has a few carpet and jewellery shops with some interesting stock along the main square. On market days it's also worth looking around the souq for a solid-quality jellaba or burnous, plus crafts and the occasional piece of sand-worn old jewellery.

Getting There & Away

Buses leave from the new *gare routière* 400m from the square, on the road to Erfoud. There are services to Fez (Dh110, two daily, 13 hours) via Meknès (Dh100, nine hours) and Marrakesh (Dh150, one daily, 10 hours), plus an evening run to Casablanca (Dh150, one daily, 15 hours). Buses run occasionally to Zagora (Dh80, five hours) and Tinerhir (Dh50, six hours); check station for departures. There are six buses a day to Er-Rachidia (Dh20, three hours) via Erfoud.

CTM (☎ 066 367006; Place de la Marche Verte) has an office in the centre of town, and runs one bus a day at 8pm to Fez/Meknès (Dh135/125, eight to nine hours) via Er-Rachidia (Dh30, 1½ hours).

Grands taxis run frequently from opposite the Hôtel Sijilmassa to Erfoud (Dh12), Er-Rachidia (Dh28), Tinerhir (Dh65), Merzouga (Dh15) and occasionally to Taouz (Dh30).

You can also reach Merzouga by *camionette* (minivan; Dh10), which leaves hourly from outside Chez M'Barek.

ERG CHEBBI, MERZOUGA & HASSI LABIED

Of course a sight this extraordinary has to have its own local legend: when a wealthy local family didn't offer hospitality to a poor woman and her son, God was offended, and buried them under the mounds of sand 50km south of Erfoud now called **Erg Chebbi**. Erg Chebbi rises above the towns of **Merzouga** and **Hassi Labied**, where you can stay at hotels with spectacular dune views. Sunrises and sunsets alone don't reveal the versatility of the *erg* (sand dune), which is constantly shape-shifting to reach heights of 160m and even in the flat light of midday glows a stunning shade of rose gold. Imperceptible shifts in sunlight tint the dunes orange, yellow, pink or purple; silhouetted by moonlight, they look even more immense.

Sights & Activities

Most hotels offer excursions into the dunes, which can range from Dh80 to Dh200 for a couple of hours' sunrise or sunset camel trek. Overnight trips usually include a bed in a Berber tent, dinner and breakfast, and range from Dh300 to Dh650 per person. Outings in a 4WD are more expensive, up to Dh1200 per day for a car taking up to five passengers.

For birdwatchers, this is perhaps the best area in Morocco for spotting many desert species, including desert sparrows, Egyptian nightjars, desert warblers, fulvous babblers and blue-cheeked bee-eaters. Sometimes in spring (dependent on rainfall) a shallow lake appears northwest of Merzouga, attracting flocks of flamingos and other waterbirds.

But in recent years, birds and tourists have begun to stray further from the beaten path in **Merzouga**, put off by the same concern: noise. The constant pounding of quads was levelling dunes, and their reverberating vibrations were becoming a deterrent to wildlife, travellers and local residents. The town has begun to rally, posting a sign prohibiting quad use in the dunes. Better yet, the demand for quads seems to be dropping as travellers become more attuned to the issues (and dust) they raise.

On the subject of annoyances: as you may notice, Merzouga doesn't like to miss any opportunity to be of service to travellers. Surely you must need a guide? A dromedary trip? A place to stay? If you show up in town unaccompanied by a guide, you can anticipate these refrains, but try to keep it in perspective: since getting by in the desert is notoriously tough, you might get a little pushy sometimes too. Just don't get talked into anything you don't want, and if you feel like you're being pressured, step away from the interaction.

Information

Merzouga may be a tiny village, but does have *téléboutiques*, general stores, a mechanic

CAMEL QUERIES

Before you agree on a camel trek, here are a few key questions to ask the guide:

How big is your camp, and how many people are headed there tonight? The cheaper treks often congregate in the same spot, so if you have a romantic notion of being alone in the dunes under the stars, you need to find an outfit with a separate camp or set up a longer trip.

How far is it to the camp site? Not everyone is cut out for dromedary-riding – it can make some people seasick, and others chafe. If you're going on a long trek, you might bring motion-sickness pills and cornstarch or talcum powder.

Does the trek guide speak English, or another language I know? This is important in the unlikely case of emergency in the desert, and to avoid those awkward hand-gesture explanations when you need to use the bathroom.

and, of course, a couple of carpet shops. It also has an internet place at the town centre, signposted **CyberInternet** (Dh5 per hr; 9am-10pm). Even smaller Hassi Labied has the **Dépôt Nomade**, a former desert caravan trading centre turned carpet shop.

Sleeping & Eating

Purists lament the encroachment, but a string of hotels now flank the western side of Erg Chebbi from the village of Merzouga north past the oasis village of Hassi Labied. On the upside, many of these places have spectacular dune views from rooms and terraces. Most offer half-board options, and often you can sleep on a terrace mattress or in a Berber tent for Dh30 to Dh50 per person (and up at swankier resorts). Sand toys (snowboard, skis etc) and bicycles are free to use at many hotels.

In May 2006, heavy rains caused a freak flash flood in Merzouga that took six lives, 300 homes and a dozen hotels. At the time of writing, some of these hotels are still in the process of rebuilding. Sometimes a taxi driver may insist that the hotel where you want to stay was lost in the flood, but if it's in this guidebook, that's clearly not the case. There's an easy way to resolve this with a mobile phone: call and ask hotel staff to explain to the driver where you want to go.

Many hotels are reached along a series of *pistes* that run 1km or more east off the tarmac road. Since they're not all close together – Hassi Labied is 5km from Merzouga, and some of the hotels listed here are far beyond that – it's worth calling ahead to make sure hotels have space.

To pack a picnic for the desert or load up on snacks, the supermarket 2km before Merzouga on the left provides most necessities.

HASSI LABIED

This tiny village 5km north of Merzouga and a way off the tarmac has a good range of accommodation.

Auberge Camping Sahara (☎ 035 577039; s half-board Dh110, d/tr/ste half-board with bathroom Dh140/170/250, terrace camping per person Dh20) Basic but spotless rooms and Turkish toilets in a friendly Tuareg-run place backing right onto the dunes at the southernmost end of the village. The auberge organises excursions and will even help you buy your complete Tuareg outfit in the market.

Kasbah Sable d'Or (Chez Isabelle & Rachid; ☎ 035 577859; http://kasbah-sable-dor.co; half-board per person with shared/private bathroom Dh140/170) When the goat bleats welcome, you know you've come to the right place. Rachid and Isabelle offer four rooms in their home with hand-painted murals on the doors, fans instead of air-con and tasty home-cooked dinners in the family salon. You can also camp in a Bedouin tent (Dh25), have a private overnight camel trek (Dh300 to Dh500), or get up early to watch the sunrise atop a camel (Dh150).

Kasbah Mohayut (☎ 066 039185; www.mohayut.com; s/d/ste per person half-board Dh350/300/250;) Find your niche at the Mohayut in sculpted-*tadelakt* guestrooms, in the shade by a small pool, or on the roof overlooking the dunes. All the old doors, Berber rugs and painted-wood bed boards add charm, but the mattresses and showerheads need replacing. Standard rooms are nicer than the lacy suite; angle for a double with a fireplace and salon.

Maison Merzouga (☎ 035 577299; fax 035 578428; s/d incl breakfast Dh350/540, half-board Dh500/600) Unlike places nearer the dunes, this 14-room family-run guest house focuses on Berber hospitality instead of desert-themed decor. Lounging in your guestroom or the in-house hammam seems like a lost opportunity, when your hosts invite you into the open kitchen to learn how they bake bread, or to the *palmeraie* to explain how ancient irrigation systems work. The best room here is the cheapest tower room, with dune views.

our pick **Dar el Janoub** (☎/fax 035 577852; www.dareljanoub.com; d standard/large/ste per person Dh500/600/700;) Neighbouring hotels take the *1001 Nights* approach to hospitality, but Dar el Janoub is an Amazigh haiku. That splashy graphic pattern on the lobby wall is the Berber alphabet, and the architect stuck to elemental building shapes, because when you're facing the dunes, why compete? Rates are on the high end, but for the price you're getting that million-dirham view, half-board, a chlorinated pool, and pure poetry.

Kasbah Tombouctou (☎ 035 577091; fax 035 578449; www.xaluca.com; s/d & tr/ste half-board per person Dh1045/764/1014;) The statue of kissing camels by the door pretty much tells you what you're in for here: Moroccan extravagance with a wink. It's laid out like a *douar* (village), complete with signposts towards the spa and hammam, pool, and huge restaurant. Guestrooms are surprisingly plain pisé but with colourful canopied beds and *tadelakt* bathrooms; suites are pretty much the same, only bigger.

MERZOUGA

Most places are south of the scruffy village centre.

Maison Rural (☎ 035 577871; with own tent & electricity Dh20, in Berber tent in dunes with camel ride Dh250, per person half-board with shared bathroom Dh150, per person half-board with private bathroom Dh200) A rural room with a view. All 10 rooms around this sleepy courtyard have orthopaedic beds, fans and heating (no air-conditioning). Some rooms have dune views – ask for the corner room. Camping with a guided camel and tent in the dunes is a sweet deal here.

Chez Julia (☎ 035 573182; s/d/tr/q Dh160/180/200/230) Pure charm in the heart of Merzouga, Chez Julia offers nine simply furnished rooms in soft, sunwashed colours with immaculate white-tiled shared bathrooms. Every element shows signs of gracious co-existence with often harsh elements: sun-bleached doors, bristling straw-textured pisé, and lovingly worn antique mantelpieces. The Moroccan ladies who run the place can cook up a storm of delicious Moroccan meals and Austrian dishes like schnitzel and apfelstrudel, too (meals Dh100; breakfast Dh38 to Dh50).

Riad Totmaroc (☎ 070 624136; www.totmarroc.com; Merzouga; per person half-board Dh350) A mod kasbah that provides instant relief from the white-hot desert with five guestrooms in bold, eye-soothing shades of blue and green, shady patios looking right onto the dunes, an open kitchen turning out tasty meals, and dromedary overnights with an experienced official local tour leader.

NORTH OF HASSI LABIED

Auberge Kasbah Derkaoua (☎ /fax 035 577140; www.aubergederkaoua.com, in French; half-board per person adult/under 16 Dh500/275; closed Jan, some of Jun-Aug;) The furthest north of the auberges (one of the first signs when coming from Rissani), A former Sufi centre is just the place to retreat from society and contemplate the meaning of the desert in your private bungalow in this walled garden compound. When you're ready to rejoin the world, head off on intrepid excursions on camel, horse and 4WD arranged in-house. The food is a delicious combination of French and Moroccan and is served beneath the starlit sky in the gardens, or a nearby tented camp.

Getting There & Away

Thankfully, the sealed road now continues all the way to Merzouga and 25km beyond it to Taouz, releasing travellers from the clutches of *faux guides*.

Most hotels are located at least 1km off the road at the base of the dunes, but they're all accessible by car. The *pistes* can be rough and there is always a possibility of getting stuck in sand, albeit remote, so make sure you have plenty of water for emergencies and a mobile phone.

Without your own transport you'll have to rely on the grands taxis and minivans that sporadically run from Merzouga to Rissani and Erfoud and back. All minibuses will pick up or drop off in Hassi Labied – your auberge can make arrangements. Minivans run from Merzouga between 7.30am and 9.30am in high season.

Grands taxis leave from Merzouga centre, opposite Dakar Restaurant, heading north to Rissani (Dh12) and south to the end of the road at Taouz (Dh100 round-trip with 45 minutes to look around).

TAOUZ تاوز

Come to Taouz if you want to see the desert close in at the end of the road. The only sight in this desolate village, beyond the pull of rocky desert, hidden minerals and occasional dinosaur remains, is **Casa Taouz**, a house beyond the village that offers tea and occasionally food.

The village of Khamlia is between Merzouga and Taouz. Its inhabitants are thought to be descended from slaves brought from south of the Sahara who somehow evaded export and settled here. The place looks like just another frontier town, but it's home to several Gnawa musicians. The most famous of these is Les Pigeons du Sable: some of their music is available on CD in Europe, and they occasionally perform here and at the annual Festival du Desert (see p363). Ask at their house (marked by a banner) for details.

If you have a 4WD, there are several places to stay in the desert around Taouz. Signposts along the road include their GPS locations.

The Souss, Anti Atlas & Western Sahara

سو الأطلس الصغير و الصحراء الغربيّة

The fertile plains, sudden granite mountains and long stretches of pristine beach of Morocco's southwest corner announce that you are arriving somewhere different. And you are. The Souss and the Anti Atlas are the most geographically varied regions of Morocco and also the most culturally distinct. And as if the vast, challenging nature of the landscape has had a softening effect on the character of the people, the sort of hassle visitors can suffer elsewhere in Morocco, is rare here, while the hospitality is legendary.

The Souss plain, with red-walled Taroudannt at its centre, is one of Morocco's most important agricultural zones. To the south lies the Anti Atlas, not as challenging as the High Atlas, but less visited and with plenty worth visiting, including the contorted slopes of Jebel Bani, prehistoric rock carvings in the Akka Oasis and the idyllically peaceful Ameln Valley.

On the coast, Agadir is both the principal port of the south and Morocco's premier beach resort. The glorious coast runs hundreds of kilometres south, past nature reserves, the art-deco splendours of Sidi Ifni and the tiny town of Tarfaya.

Further south, the Western Sahara is a vast, desolate and lightly populated tract of *hammada* (stony desert). Inhabited by free-spirited Saharawis, fishing communities and industrious Moroccans, it is a hotly disputed territory and is watched over by the ever-present security forces. .

HIGHLIGHTS

- Ride killer waves or watch others in the ocean at Morocco's top surfing spot of **Taghazout** (p385)
- Commune with Antoine de Saint-Exupery's *Little Prince* at **Tarfaya** (p410)
- Escape the crowds and find prehistoric rock carvings around **Tata** (p407)
- Hang loose in **Mirleft** (p395), the coolest spot in the south with six fabulous beaches
- Lose yourself among the pink-hued rock faces and lush green *palmeraies* of the peaceful **Ameln Valley** (p406)
- Trek or drive through the foothills of the **Anti Atlas** (p402), concertinaed like mille-feuille
- Travel to the end of the road in the **Western Sahara** (p408) beyond the town of Dakhla

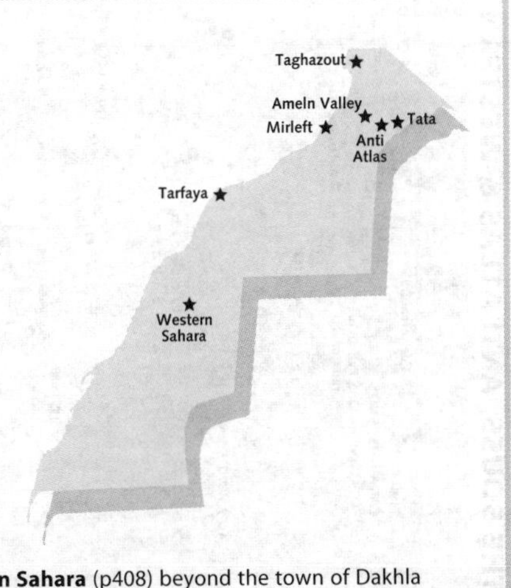

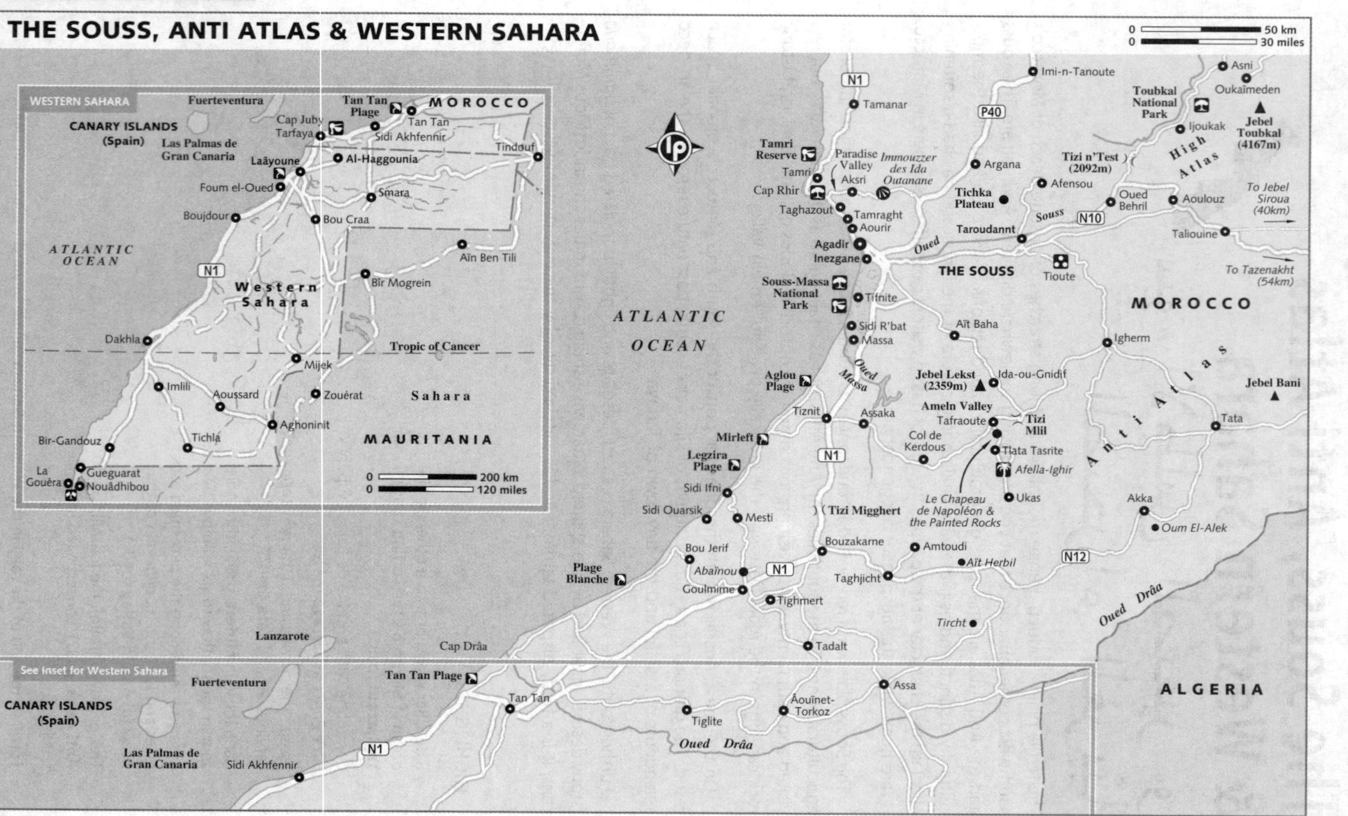
THE SOUSS, ANTI ATLAS & WESTERN SAHARA
0 50 km
0 30 miles
WESTERN SAHARA
Fuerteventura
CANARY ISLANDS (Spain)
Las Palmas de Gran Canaria
Tan Tan Plage
Tan Tan
MOROCCO
Cap Juby
Tarfaya
Sidi Akhfennir
Tindouf
Laâyoune
Al-Haggounia
Foum el-Oued
Smara
Boujdour
Bou Craa
ATLANTIC OCEAN
Aïn Ben Tili
N1
Western Sahara
Bir Mogrein
Dakhla
Tropic of Cancer
Mijek
Imlili
Aoussard
Zouérat
Sahara
Aghoninit
MAURITANIA
Bir-Gandouz
Tichla
La Gouêra
Gueguarat
Nouâdhibou
0 200 km
0 120 miles
Lanzarote
Cap Drâa
See Inset for Western Sahara
Fuerteventura
Tan Tan Plage
CANARY ISLANDS (Spain)
Tan Tan
Las Palmas de Gran Canaria
N1
Sidi Akhfennir
Tiglite
Oued Drâa
Âouïnet-Torkoz
Assa
ALGERIA
Imi-n-Tanoute
N1
Tamanar
P40
Tamri Reserve
Tamri
Paradise Valley
Aksri
Immouzzer des Ida Outanane
Cap Rhir
Taghazout
Tamraght
Aourir
Agadir
Inezgane
Argana
Tichka Plateau
Afensou
Tizi n'Test (2092m)
Toubkal National Park
Ijoukak
High Atlas
Asni
Oukaïmeden
Jebel Toubkal (4167m)
Oued Behril
Aoulouz
To Jebel Siroua (40km)
Souss
N10
Taroudannt
Oued
Taliouine
THE SOUSS
Tioute
To Tazenakht (54km)
MOROCCO
Souss-Massa National Park
Tifnite
ATLANTIC OCEAN
Sidi R'bat
Massa
Aït Baha
Igherm
Oued Massa
Aglou Plage
Jebel Lekst (2359m)
Ida-ou-Gnidif
Ameln Valley
Anti Atlas
Jebel Bani
Tiznit
Assaka
Tafraoute
Tizi Mlil
Tata
Mirleft
Col de Kerdous
Tlata Tasrite
N1
Legzira Plage
Afella-Ighir
Sidi Ifni
Ukas
Akka
Le Chapeau de Napoléon & the Painted Rocks
Sidi Ouarsik
Mesti
Tizi Mighert
Oum El-Alek
Bouzakarne
Bou Jerif
Amtoudi
Aït Herbil
N12
Plage Blanche
Abaïnou
N1
Taghjicht
Goulmime
Tighmert
Oued Drâa
Tircht
Tadalt

HISTORY

The region's history is as varied as its landscape. Taroudannt in the Souss Valley has a story that parallels Marrakesh, with its walls dating to the 11th century, and its glory years in the 16th century as part of an empire that stretched to Timbuktu. Agadir shares a story with the more northerly Atlantic ports, both formerly occupied by the Portuguese and Spanish. Meanwhile, the region's Chleuh tribes people have a long history of dissidence and independence, many of their communities remaining beyond central authority well into the 1930s.

Deeper south lay the wild frontier. The nomadic desert tribes known collectively as Saharawi (constituting the indigenous population of the Western Sahara) were even more difficult to control. Their unique independent spirit ultimately manifested itself in the 20th century in the Polisario movement. The bid for autonomy for the Western Saharan province remains a thorn in the current government's side. For a deeper understanding of the situation today, read *Endgame in the Western Sahara: What Future for Africa's Last Colony?* by Toby Shelley. An expert on resource politics, he believes there is still hope for a peaceful resolution to the conflict.

CLIMATE

The south divides into three distinct geographical areas, each with its own microclimate. The semitropical, verdant Souss Valley is hot and humid, with temperatures ranging between 22°C and a steamy 38°C, when water vapour rises like a mist from the huge citrus groves that fill the valley. The valley is also prone to heavy winds in spring. The climate of the barren Anti Atlas veers between freezing winters and hot, dry summers. The deep southern coast enjoys a more constant year-round sunny climate.

LANGUAGE

Arabic remains the lingua franca of all major cities in the south. The Chleuh tribes who dominate the Souss speak Tachelait, a Berber dialect, most noticeable in the villages of the Ameln Valley and the Anti Atlas. French is widely spoken and Spanish is still heard in some of Spain's former territories.

GETTING THERE & AWAY

Agadir is the hub airport of the south, but is now poorly served compared to Marrakesh. Most international services are European charter flights and a quirk of airline licences makes it impossible to buy a one-way ticket out of Agadir. **Royal Air Maroc** (RAM; ☎ 022 311122; www.royalairmaroc.com) operates flights to and from Laâyoune (Friday, Sunday, Tuesday) and Dakhla (Wednesday) and others via Casablanca. Direct flights from Agadir to the Western Sahara are often more expensive than via Casablanca, though none are cheap. **Regional Air Lines** (RGL; ☎ 022 536940; www.regionalmaroc.com) also operates direct flights to Dakhla and Laâyoune.

There is no train out of Agadir, but Supratours (buses run by the rail network) runs regular, fast buses to Marrakesh (four daily), Tiznit, Laâyoune and Dakhla. CTM bus services also operate to a range of destinations including Casablanca and Essaouira.

GETTING AROUND

CTM, Satas and other local bus companies operate a range of bus routes across the region, including to Taroudannt, Tiznit, Laâyoune and Dakhla. Grands taxis are the fastest means of public transport and run to most destinations in the region.

The distances involved in touring the region, particularly in the south, make it worthwhile considering car rental. Agadir is one of the better places to hire a car in Morocco and all the major agencies are represented.

THE SOUSS VALLEY

AGADIR اكادير

pop 679,000

Agadir feels unlike anywhere else in Morocco. A busy port and seaside town built around a fortified kasbah, it was completely destroyed by an earthquake in 1960. It has since been rebuilt as Morocco's premier beach resort with some 30,000 beds. Laid out as a large grid of downtown streets, surrounded by spacious residential suburbs, Agadir doesn't have the bustling street life found in so many Moroccan cities, although the new marina development may soon provide this. Its lure, for now, lies in

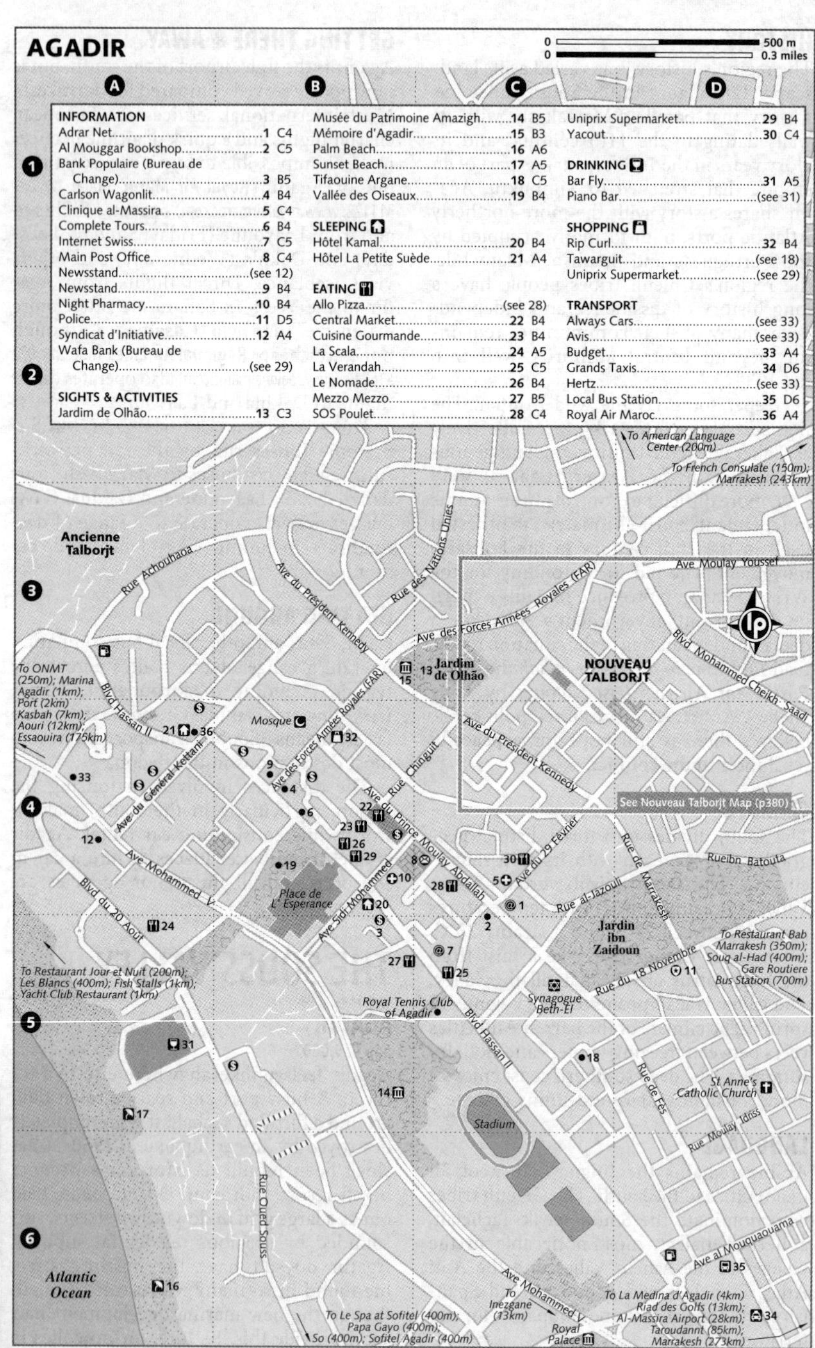
AGADIR
0 500 m
0 0.3 miles
A
B
C
D
1
2
3
4
5
6
INFORMATION
Adrar Net.....1 C4
Al Mouggar Bookshop.....2 C5
Bank Populaire (Bureau de Change).....3 B5
Carlson Wagonlit.....4 B4
Clinique al-Massira.....5 C4
Complete Tours.....6 B4
Internet Swiss.....7 C5
Main Post Office.....8 C4
Newsstand.....(see 12)
Newsstand.....9 B4
Night Pharmacy.....10 B4
Police.....11 D5
Syndicat d'Initiative.....12 A4
Wafa Bank (Bureau de Change).....(see 29)
SIGHTS & ACTIVITIES
Jardim de Olhão.....13 C3
Musée du Patrimoine Amazigh.....14 B5
Mémoire d'Agadir.....15 B3
Palm Beach.....16 A6
Sunset Beach.....17 A5
Tifaouine Argane.....18 C5
Vallée des Oiseaux.....19 B4
SLEEPING
Hôtel Kamal.....20 B4
Hôtel La Petite Suède.....21 A4
EATING
Allo Pizza.....(see 28)
Central Market.....22 B4
Cuisine Gourmande.....23 B4
La Scala.....24 A5
La Verandah.....25 C5
Le Nomade.....26 B4
Mezzo Mezzo.....27 B5
SOS Poulet.....28 C4
Uniprix Supermarket.....29 B4
Yacout.....30 C4
DRINKING
Bar Fly.....31 A5
Piano Bar.....(see 31)
SHOPPING
Rip Curl.....32 B4
Tawarguit.....(see 18)
Uniprix Supermarket.....(see 29)
TRANSPORT
Always Cars.....(see 33)
Avis.....(see 33)
Budget.....33 A4
Grands Taxis.....34 D6
Hertz.....(see 33)
Local Bus Station.....35 D6
Royal Air Maroc.....36 A4
To American Language Center (200m)
To French Consulate (150m); Marrakesh (243km)
Ancienne Talborjt
Rue Achouhaoa
Ave du Président Kennedy
Rue des Nations Unies
Ave Moulay Youssef
Ave des Forces Armées Royales (FAR)
Jardim de Olhão
NOUVEAU TALBORJT
Blvd Mohammed Cheikh Saadi
To ONMT (250m); Marina Agadir (1km); Port (2km) Kasbah (7km); Aouri (12km); Essaouira (175km)
Blvd Hassan II
Mosque
Ave du Général Kettani
Rue Chinguit
See Nouveau Talborjt Map (p380)
Ave du Prince Moulay Abdallah
Ave du 29 Février
Rue de Marrakesh
Rueibn Batouta
Ave Mohammed V
Place de L' Esperance
Ave Sidi Mohammed
Rue al-Jazouli
Jardin ibn Zaidoun
Blvd du 20 Août
To Restaurant Bab Marrakesh (350m); Souq al-Had (400m); Gare Routiere Bus Station (700m)
Rue du 18 Novembre
To Restaurant Jour et Nuit (200m); Les Blancs (400m); Fish Stalls (1km); Yacht Club Restaurant (1km)
Royal Tennis Club of Agadir
Synagogue Beth-El
Blvd Hassan II
St Anne's Catholic Church
Rue de Fès
Rue Moulay Idriss
Stadium
Rue Oued Souss
Ave al Mouquaouama
Atlantic Ocean
To Inezgane (13km)
Ave Mohammed V
To La Medina d'Agadir (4km) Riad des Golfs (13km); Al-Massira Airport (28km); Taroudannt (85km); Marrakesh (273km)
To Le Spa at Sofitel (400m); Papa Gayo (400m); So (400m); Sofitel Agadir (400m)
Royal Palace

its huge swathe of sandy beach: more sheltered than many other stretches of the Atlantic, it offers clean water, safe swimming and some 300 sunny days a year.

Although Agadir's tourism industry is mainly geared to package-tour holidaymakers, it has an increasing number of attractions for independent travellers. It's a good place to stop, not only for some good old-fashioned R&R and for its improved restaurants, but for its gentle sights – the ruined kasbah, the undeveloped nearby beaches (popular for surfing and windsurfing) and the Souss-Massa National Park.

History

Named after the *agadir* (fortified granary) of the Irir tribe, Agadir has a long history of boom and bust. It was founded in the 15th century by Portuguese merchants wanting to develop trade links with the Saharan caravans. From the mid-16th century, as the Saadian empire expanded, the port became very prosperous from the export of local sugar, cotton and saltpetre, and the products of the Saharan trade, which the Moroccans then controlled. But this prosperity came to an abrupt end in the 1760s when the Alawite Sultan Sidi Mohammed ben Abdallah diverted the trade north to Essaouira.

French colonists did go some way towards redeveloping Agadir in the 20th century, but the devastating earthquake on 29 February 1960, which killed as many as 18,000 people, around half of the population, completely destroyed the city. The authorities were unable to manage with the apocalyptic aftermath of death and disease, sprayed the area with lime and DDT, and consequently left the dead where they had been buried, in the collapsed city. The mound this created is now known as Old Talborjt, north of the modern city.

Since its reconstruction, Agadir has developed into an important port, with a large fishing fleet helping to make Morocco the world's largest exporter of tinned sardines. At the same time, Agadir has continued to grow as Morocco's top beach resort. The opening of the new luxury marina complex is a sign of plans to move the resort upmarket, as is the start of work on the huge new luxury resort at Taghazout.

Orientation

Agadir is spread over a large area, both along the coast and inland from the huge swathe of beach. From the northern end and the marina, three main boulevards – 20 Aout, nearest the ocean, Mohammed V and Hassan II – run through the main tourist area. The southern district of Founti has some of the best resort hotels. Inland in the northeast side of town, Nouveau Talborjt (New Talborjt) is the business centre and has most of the budget hotels.

Information

BOOKSHOPS

News-stands along Blvd Hassan II, particularly near the junction with Ave des Forces Armées Royals (FAR) have a good selection of international papers (usually a day or two late) and magazines.

Al Mouggar Bookshop (Map p376; ☎ 028 842712; Ave du Prince Moulay Abdallah) Just off Ave du 29 Février, there's a wide selection of French books from novels and history to travel guides, and some in English about Morocco.

EMERGENCY

Most of the larger hotels in Agadir are able to recommend reliable, English-speaking doctors.

Ambulance (☎ 15)

Police (☎ 19; Rue du 18 Novembre)

INTERNET ACCESS

There are dozens of internet places, charging Dh5 to Dh10 per hour.

Adrar Net (Map p376; Ave du 29 Février, Talborjt; per hr Dh5).

Internet Swiss (Map p376; Blvd Hassan II; per hr Dh10; 🕑 9am-11pm) The busiest, most conveniently located cybercafé.

MEDICAL SERVICES

The Syndicat d'Initiative (p378) posts a list of doctors and pharmacies on its door.

Clinique al-Massira (Map p376; ☎ 028 843238; Ave du 29 Février)

Night Pharmacy (Map p376; ☎ 028 820349; Ave Sidi Mohammed) Located in the basement of the town hall, next to the post office. A list of other night services is usually posted in the windows of all pharmacies.

MONEY

Most banks have ATMs, and there are exchange booths and ATMs at the airport. Large hotels change cash and travellers cheques. These banks have exchange offices.

Banque Populaire (Map p376; Blvd Hassan II)

Wafa Bank (Map p376; Blvd Hassan II)

POST

Main post office (Map p376; Ave Sidi Mohammed; 8.30am-6.30pm Mon-Fri, 8.30am-noon Sat)

TOURIST INFORMATION

Information booth (028 839077; Al-Massira airport; 8.30am-noon & 2.30-6.30pm)

ONMT (Délégation Régionale du Tourisme; Map p376; 028 846377; fax 028 846379; Immeuble Ignouan, Ave Mohammed V; 8.30am-noon & 2.30-6.30pm Mon-Thu, 8.30-11.30am & 3-6.30pm Fri) The best place for local and regional information.

Syndicat d'Initiative (Map p376; 028 825304; Ave Mohammed V; 9am-noon & 3-6.30pm) Useful for the list of doctors and pharmacies.

TRAVEL AGENCIES

Atlantic Sport Travel (Map p376 ; 061 387177; atlantic.sport.travel@gmail.com) Runs day treks and mountain-bike trips out of Agadir.

Carlson Wagonlit (Map p376; 028 841528; 26 Ave des Forces Armées Royales) Represents all major airlines.

Complete Tours (Map p376 ; 028 823401; Immeuble Oumlil 26, Ave Hassan II; www.complete-tours.com) Runs trips to Taroudannt, Immouzzer and elsewhere in the region.

Sights

The old **kasbah** (Map p376), on a hill 7km northwest of the centre and visible from much of Agadir, is a rare survival of the earthquake. Built in 1541 by Saadian Sultan Mohammed ech-Cheikh, it was restored in the 1740s. The inscription over the entry arch in Dutch and Arabic ('Believe in God and respect the King') is a reminder of the beginning of trade with the Low Countries. Events took a turn for the worse in the 1750s when Agadir joined in a local revolt against the Alawite Sultan Moulay Abdallah. His revenge was to garrison the kasbah, move the Jewish community to Essaouira and forbid merchants to trade here. Abandoned to the inhabitants of Agadir, the garrison once provided housing for nearly 300 people. All that remains is the outer wall, though traces of these dwellings can still be made out. But the real reason for visiting is to take in the view of Agadir, the port, marina and sprawling suburbs. The grassy area below the kasbah, **Ancienne Talborjt** (Map p376), covers the remains of old Agadir town and constitutes a mass grave for all those who died in the 1960 earthquake. The walk up to the kasbah is long, hot and uncomfortable: get a taxi up (Dh20 to Dh25) and walk back down. After a visit to the kasbah it is worth dropping in at the **port** (Map p376), to eat or just soak up some atmosphere.

The small **Musée du Patrimoine Amazigh** (Map p376; 028 821632; Passage Aït Souss, Blvd Hassan II; admission Dh20; 9.30am-5.30pm Mon-Sat) has an excellent display of Berber artefacts, especially strong on jewellery. Inspired by Bert Flint, the Dutch owner of the Maison Tiskiwin in Marrakesh (p302), this is a great place to learn about the traditional life and culture of the Berber people of the region. A free guided tour can be arranged on request (a tip is welcome). Nearby is the **Vallée des Oiseaux** (Valley of the Birds; Map p376; adult/child Dh5/3; 9.30am-12.30pm & 2.30-7pm), a shaded children's playground, with an aviary and small zoo, created in the dry riverbed that runs down from Blvd Hassan II south to Blvd du 20 Août.

Equally refreshing is **Jardin de Olhão** (Map p376; Ave du Président Kennedy; 8am-6pm), a cool, relaxing spot created in 1992 to mark the twinning of Agadir with the Portuguese town of Olhão. In the southwest corner there's **Mémoire d'Agadir** (Map p376; admission free; 9am-12.30pm & 3-7pm Tue-Sat) a small museum dedicated to the 1960 earthquake. Displays include interesting photos of Agadir since the 1920s, while others show the effects of the quake.

The newest sight in town is **Marina Agadir** (Map p376; 028 828298; www.port-marina-agadir.com), a billion-dirham pleasure port between the beach and commercial port. As well as mooring for your floating pleasure palace, the marina has a range of apartments and a hotel (still not open at the time of writing). With shops (mostly international brands), cafés and restaurants, this will increasingly become a hub of activity in the city.

Four kilometres south, on the Inezgane road, Coco Polizzi, a Rabat-born Italian architect, has created the **La Médina d'Agadir** (028 280253; www.medinapolizzi.com, in French; Aghroud Ben Sergao; adult/child Dh40/20; 8.30am-6.30pm), an idealised Berber village, built using tra-

MARIE-LUCE MILANO KRIMI

Formerly from Alsace, in the northeast of France, Marie-Luce Milano Krimi is assistant to the general manager of the Agadir Beach Club Hotel

How long have you lived in Agadir? I have been living here in Agadir for 22 years! I arrived in 1986

Why did you choose to live here? I arrived to work at Club Med for the summer season, met my future husband (Moroccan guy also working there) and we decided to try living together. Twenty-two years later we have two daughters, two dogs, two cats, several birds, a few red fishes and many friends.

Has it changed much since then? It has changed a hell of a lot! Before it was like a big village – everybody knowing each other. Now it's quite a big town, many new people, more Europeans as well, the town has become nice and clean, but it has lost its 'typical' side… Progress has its good and bad sides we all know, and having Marjane, the big supermarket is not one of the good sides. I liked the little shop next door, open all day and nearly all night, with a little man speaking hardly any other language than Arabic but knowing exactly what you were looking for in whatever language you spoke and saying 'oh don't worry, come and pay tomorrow' when you didn't have any change.

So what do you like best about the place? People's attitude. Space. The beach. I love the blue sky when I get up in the morning, birds singing, everybody saying hello when you go out. I also love the fact that IMPOSSIBLE is not a word Moroccans understand. Everything is possible if you are patient.

And your favourite restaurant? I love the Mezzo Mezzo for Jean Mi, the owner of the place, the pizza is the best in town.

What's your favourite phrase in Arabic, Berber or French? Inshallah. I used to hate it. Then I understood that in fact the whole world should use it. And now I use it a million times a day! Inshallah is a real philosophy.

How do you spend your weekends? We both work a lot, so the weekend is usually only Sunday. My daughters spend their Saturdays bodyboarding. I sometimes go to the souq for my shopping. Then we go to the beach or to Taroudannt and see friends in the evening. We certainly don't stay home in front of the TV, this is for sure.

ditional techniques and materials, with workshops for 30 independent artisans. A café-restaurant provides refreshments. Shuttle buses (adult/child costs Dh60/30) drive out to La Médina d'Agadir from the kiosk on Blvd du 20 Août, picking up at several hotels on the way.

Activities

BEACH

The glory of Agadir is its crescent **beach**, which usually remains unruffled when the Atlantic winds are blustering elsewhere. It's clean and well maintained, and during peak periods (June to September) is patrolled by lifeguards (there is a strong undertow) and police.

The beach is mostly hassle-free, but single females or families will have a more relaxed time at one of the private beaches (Dh20 for a deckchair and umbrella) such as **Sunset Beach** or **Palm Beach** (Map p376) which also have showers, toilets and a kids' play area. Many larger beach hotels and surf clubs rent out windsurfing equipment (Dh120 per hour), jet skis (Dh300 for 20 minutes), bodyboards (Dh60 per hour) and surfboards (Dh120 per hour). If you prefer to stroll, the **promenade** runs for several kilometres from the marina to the royal palace.

You can get out onto the water by sailing with **Voiles du Sud** (☎ 061 215746; www.voilesdusud.com; per person in morning Dh300, per person day trip incl lunch Dh450), who operates a 16-person ketch and 30-person catamaran out of the marina.

HAMMAMS

There are a few hammams in Nouveau Talborjt, including **Hammam Salam** (Map p380; 12 Rue de Tarfaya; from Dh10) and the very spruce, women-only **Hammam Talborjt** (Map p380; Rue de Tarfaya; from Dh10) just south of Ave du

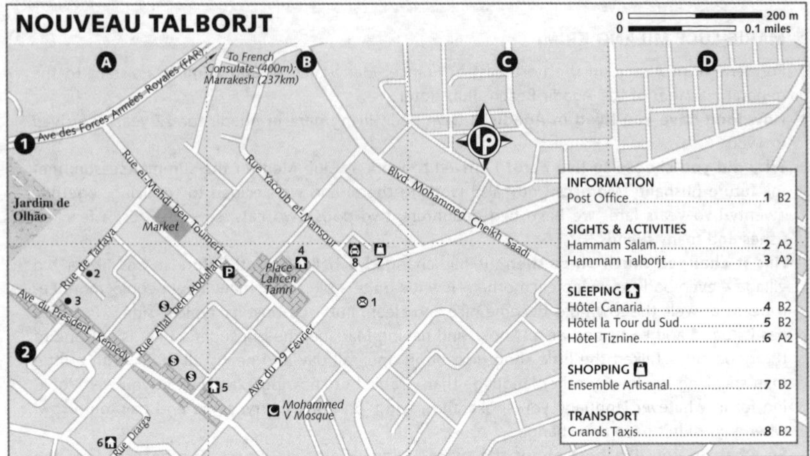

Président Kennedy. Many big hotels have more luxurious hammams where you can pamper yourself from Dh80.

If you want something more sophisticated, several hotels have spas offering hammam, massage and a range of treatments, one of the best being **Le Spa at Sofitel** (off Map p376; ☎ 028 820088; www.sofitel.com; Baie des Palmiers, Ben Sergao; massage per hr from Dh650). In the centre of town, **Tifaouine Argane** (Map p376; ☎ 028 690043; www.tifaouine-argane.com; Blvd Mahdi Ben Barka, No.8 Riad Salam; 2hr massage from Dh350) is an argan centre where you can buy oil and argan-based cosmetics and enjoy a range of massages.

Sleeping

Agadir has set its sights on the midrange and top-end visitor, but if you move away from the beach, you will find a very good selection of budget places. High season in Agadir includes Easter, summer and the Christmas period, when European holidaymakers fly out on package tours. During these months, it's best to book ahead to be sure of a room. Midrange and top-end hotels offer a discount on rooms during low season, though it's always worth checking online for rates. Prices for budget hotels remain pretty much constant throughout the year.

BUDGET

Sea views come at a price, so most budget hotels are away from the ocean in Nouveau Talborjt. The all-night bus activity and prostitution ensure that most hotel receptions here are open 24 hours, so if you've already booked a room, don't worry about arriving late.

Hôtel Canaria (Map p380; ☎ 028 846727; Place Lahcen Tamri; s/d without bathroom Dh70/90, s/d with bathroom Dh80/100) This hotel overlooks a pleasant square, although the rooms, with pine furniture and potted plants, all face into the internal upper courtyard.

Hôtel Tiznine (Map p380; ☎ 028 843925; 3 Rue Drarga; s/d Dh80/120, with shower Dh120/160) One of Agadir's best budget places, with a dozen good-sized rooms around a green-and-white-tiled flowering courtyard. Some rooms have private bathroom, but the communal ones are spotless. The manager speaks good English, and Yacout (opposite) is nearby for breakfast.

Hôtel La Petite Suède (Map p376; ☎ 028 840779; fax 028 840057; cnr Blvd Hassan II & Ave du Général Kettani; s/d/tr Dh160/244/333) Simple but perfectly located hotel, five minutes' walk from the beach, with very good, friendly service. The streetside rooms have large balconies, but the inside rooms are quieter.

Hôtel La Tour du Sud (Map p380; ☎ 028 822694; Ave du Président Kennedy; s/d Dh191/223) En-suite rooms in this solid two-star hotel, formerly the Hotel de Paris, are brightly decorated in traditional style, gathered around two courtyards dominated by trees. The good ground-floor café serves breakfast (Dh24) on the terrace.

MIDRANGE

our pick Hôtel Kamal (Map p380; ☎ 028 842817; fax 028 843940; Blvd Hassan II; s/d Dh403/462;) An extremely popular and well-run downtown hotel in a modernist white block located near the town hall. The Kamal manages to appeal to a wide range of clients, including package-tour groups and travelling Moroccans. Rooms are bright and clean, the staff are helpful and there's a pool large enough to swim laps. Streetside rooms can be noisy, and breakfast (Dh36) is dull and overpriced.

TOP END

Most luxury hotels along the seafront cater to package tours, but most of them offer deals on their published rates, so be sure to ask.

Sofitel Agadir (Map p376; ☎ 028 820088; www.sofitel.com; Baie des Palmiers, Ben Sergao; s/d from Dh750/900;) The Sofitel stands out from the large range of resort hotels. Built like a low-rise kasbah, it manages to seem smaller than its 240 rooms, all of which have had a recent upgrade. Luxury facilities include an excellent thalassotherapy spa, hammam, several swimming pools, a well-tended beach and a range of restaurants. It also boasts Agadir's most happening nightclub (see p382).

Riad des Golfs (☎ 028 337033; www.riaddesgolfs.com; Chemins des Francais; ste from Dh1760;) Tucked away to the south of Agadir, this villa, designed and run by a French architect and his wife, bucks the trend of mega-hotels. Eight large and simply elegant suites, a heated pool surrounded by olive trees and a restaurant serving some of the city's best food (only for residents) mean that this appeals to more than just golfers heading to the nearby courses.

Eating

Agadir used to be a culinary desert where you were lucky to find anything reliable outside the usual tajine or pizza. But a number of recent openings have stirred things up. Many stop serving food by 10pm, but some stay open later for drinks. Agadir restaurants serve alcohol unless stated.

RESTAURANTS

Le Nomade (Map p376; ☎ 028 841186; Blvd Hassan II; mains DH60) In a row of restaurants near the municipal market, Hadj Larbi's restaurant serves straightforward Moroccan classics: couscous, tajine and brochettes cooked on a wood-fired grill. No alcohol.

La Scala (Map p376; ☎ 028 846773; Rue du Oued Souss; meal with wine Dh350) Excellent Moroccan restaurant, popular with wealthy Moroccans, Arab tourists and Westerners, which makes for a pleasantly cosmopolitan atmosphere. The food is elegant and fresh, and beautifully presented.

our pick Les Blancs (off Map p376; ☎ 028 828388; Marina; mains from Dh90) The best-located restaurant in Agadir by a long way. At the very northern end of the beach and at the entrance to the new marina development, Les Blancs is a chilled, elegant, white-tiled bar, lounge and restaurant. A Spaniard runs the kitchen serving a mix of Andalucian and Moroccan dishes. Service can be slow.

Yacht Club Restaurant (off Map p376; ☎ 028 843708; commercial port; meal Dh200) Also known as Restaurant du Port, the fish couldn't be fresher at this modernist waterfront restaurant situated inside the commercial fishing port. The lighting and decor are plain, but the food, particularly the freshly fried and grilled catch of the day and calamari, is reliable and the service hassle-free. There's a terrace for warm days.

Mezzo Mezzo (Map p376; ☎ 028 848819; Blvd Hassan II; meal Dh200) Ask any Agadir resident for their list of favourite restaurants and this pizzeria will be on it. Why? 'Because it's always so much fun.' 'I've never had a bad meal there.' 'Worth going just to see Jean Michel, the maitre d', at work.' Classic pizzas and pastas.

Restaurant Bab Marrakesh (Map p376; ☎ 028 826144; Rue de Massa; tajine for 2 people Dh100, couscous Dh70, sandwich Dh25-35) Near Souq al-Had, this is the real thing, far removed from the tourist traps near the beach. Highly regarded by locals, it serves authentic Moroccan food at authentic prices.

CAFÉS

There's a good choice of cafés where you can start the day with coffee and pastries or recover from the rigours of Agadir beach life. Most tend to be open by 8am and run until at least 8pm.

Yacout (Map p376; Ave du 29 Février) With its shaded garden, screeching parrot and delicious Moroccan-Western pastries, Yacout wins hands down as *the* breakfast spot.

Later in the day it serves sandwiches, Moroccan sweets and ice-cream cakes. Avoid the main menu.

La Verandah (Map p376; Blvd Hassan II) Opposite the Royal Tennis Club, this Parisian-style café has a seductive array of sweet and savoury treats and is good for people-watching.

Cuisine Gourmande (Map p376; ☎ 028 821542; Central Market, Blvd Hassan II) In a corner of the Central Market's parking, this French-run café and *traiteur* serves salads and ready-made dishes, perfect for a quick meal or picnic on the beach. They also make some of Agadir's best French cakes and pastries.

QUICK EATS

The cheap snack bars in Nouveau Talborjt and around the bus stations are open after hours. **SOS Poulet** (Map p376; Ave du Prince Moulay Abdallah) and its twin, **Allo Pizza** (Map p376; Ave du Prince Moulay Abdallah), serve tasty rotisserie chickens (half chicken Dh54) and a range of pizzas (Dh45 to Dh50). For ultra-fresh, no-nonsense fish, try one of the many **fish stalls** (off Map p376; meals around Dh50) at the entrance to the commercial port.

SELF-CATERING

The large **Uniprix supermarket** (Map p376; Blvd Hassan II) sells everything from cheese and biscuits to beer, wine and spirits. The **Central Market** (Map p376) sells fresh food alongside tourist tat. At the **Souq al-Had** (off Map p376; 🕑 Tue-Sun), you can buy fresh fruit and veg from the Souss Valley. It's liveliest on Saturday and Sunday.

Drinking

There are plenty of places along the beach to chill out at midday or toast the sunset. Some of the places along Palm Beach stay open till 1am in summer. The majority of bars have happy hours between about 5pm and 8pm each night, or some offer the dubious pleasure of karaoke or crooning entertainers.

Restaurant Jour et Nuit (Map p376; ☎ 028 840610; Rue de la Plage; 🕑 24hr) is a popular spot for a sundowner, though it gets seedy as the night wears on.

Piano Bar (Map p376; Tafoukt Complex, Blvd du 20 Août) Has a real pianist under the palm trees and some of Agadir's cheapest beers. Situated in the same complex is also the Irish bar, The Pub.

Bar Fly (Map p376; ☎ 028 840123; www.tafoukthotel.com; Blvd du 20 Août) One of the happening bars of the moment, girls-only on Tuesday night and salsa on Thursday, but drinks are from Dh60.

Entertainment

Agadir's annual music festival, the **Festival Timatar** (☎ 028 820338; www.festival-timatar.com), attracts a range of top-ranking Moroccan and African musicians each July. Year-round, there is a decent range of clubs, mostly scattered along Blvd du 20 Août, or attached to the big hotels.

When bars start to close around 1am, Moroccans and tourists move to the hotel clubs. Entry ranges from Dh50 to Dh250 during weekends, including a drink. During the low season, tourists are often allowed in free of charge and clubs close around 2am.

Papa Gayo (off Map p376; ☎ 028 845400; Riu Tikida Beach, Chemins des Dunes; 🕑 10pm-4am) Still one of Agadir's most popular nightclubs, and well regarded even in fairly respectable Moroccan circles. Dance the night away and chill on the beach.

So (off Map p376; Sofitel Agadir, Baie des Palmiers; 🕑 10pm-5am) The hippest club in Agadir and one of the most expensive. So is laid out on several levels and includes a champagne bar, vodka bar, live-music stage, restaurant, dance floor and chill-out area. Guest DJs appear on Thursdays. Agadir swingers save this one for the climax of the evening's entertainment.

Shopping

Most souvenirs in Agadir are trucked in from other parts of the country and tend to be of low quality. **Uniprix supermarket** (Map p376; Blvd Hassan II) sells handicrafts at fixed prices. For some Moroccan atmosphere head to **Souq al-Had** (off Map p376; 🕑 Tue-Sun) in the southeastern suburbs, with souvenirs, household goods and a second-hand items area outside the western gate. Better-quality crafts are available at the **Ensemble Artisanal** (Map p380; ☎ 028 823872; Ave du 29 Février; 🕑 9am-1pm & 3-7pm Mon-Sat).

Tawarguit (Map p376; ☎ 028 848225; Lotissement Faiz, Rue 206) has a range of gorgeous, if pricey, homewares, crafts and paintings, including specially commissioned ranges. If you need some beachwear, **Ripcurl** (Map p376; ☎ 028 827154; Ave des Forces Armées Royales) has opened downtown.

Getting There & Away

AIR

Al-Massira Airport (off Map p376; ☎ 028 839122), 28km southeast of Agadir, is mainly served by European charter flights. There are banks with exchange booths and ATMs, car-hire offices, a tourist information office and a couple of restaurants.

Royal Air Maroc (RAM; Map p376; ☎ 028 829120; www.royalairmaroc.com; Ave du Général Kettani) has daily flights to Casablanca and Paris, as well as weekly services to Dakhla, Marrakesh and several European capitals.

Regional Air Lines (☎ 028 820330; www.regionalmaroc.com) operates services to Casablanca, Marrakesh, Ouarzazate, Laâyoune and Dakhla as well as Las Palmas in the Canary Islands.

BUS

Although a good number of buses serve Agadir, it is quite possible you'll end up in Inezgane, 13km south, the regional transport hub. Check before you buy your ticket. Plenty of grands taxis (Dh10) and local buses (Dh5) shuttle between there and Agadir.

The new *gare routière* (main bus station; Map p376) on Rue Chair al-Hamra Mohammed ben Brahim, past the Souq al-Had, looks like a work-in-progress, but this massive circular building is finally fully functioning and all major companies are running services from here. If you need to travel on a specific bus, it is worth booking ahead.

CTM (☎ 028 825341; www.ctm.co.ma) has buses to Casablanca (Dh180, eight hours, six daily). The 10.30pm continues to Rabat (Dh195, 10 hours). There are also departures for Marrakesh (Dh80, four hours, seven daily), Essaouira (Dh60, two hours, one daily), Dakhla (Dh340, 20 hours, three daily), Laâyoune (Dh190, 10 hours, five daily), Tangier (Dh300, 13 hours, one daily) and Fez (Dh235, 12 hours, one daily).

Supratours (☎ 028 224010) has fast services to Marrakesh train station (Dh90, four hours, several daily), Tiznit (Dh40, four hours, two daily), Laâyoune (Dh210, 11 hours, one daily), Dakhla (Dh340, 21 hours, one daily) and Essaouira (Dh60, three hours, several daily). **Satas** (☎ 028 842470), **Tassaout** (☎ 070 595856), **SICR** (☎ 028 214133), **Bab Salama** (☎ 028 826220) and others also run intercity services out of here.

CAR & MOTORCYCLE

Car hire is never cheap in Morocco, but you can find some of the country's best deals in Agadir. It is worth checking out the local agencies along Blvd Hassan II, where prices start at around Dh300 per day for the smallest car, though there's usually room for haggling. Always Cars is one of the most reputable of the locals, used by several foreign tour operators. Scooters and motorbikes are also available, although you should check carefully the state of the machines as we have heard of problems with the standard of maintenance.

Always Cars (Map p376; ☎ 028 846061/840760; Ave Mohammed V)
Avis (Map p376; ☎ airport 028 839244, office 028 841755; www.avis.com; Ave Mohammed V)
Budget (Map p376; ☎ airport 028 839101, office 028 848222; www.budget.com; Immeuble Marhaba, Ave Mohammed V)
Hertz (Map p376; ☎ airport 028 839071, office 028 840939; www.hertz.com; Immeuble Marhaba, Ave Mohammed V)

TAXI

The main grand-taxi rank is located at the south end of Rue de Fès. There is a smaller grand-taxi rank on Rue Yacoub el-Mansour in Nouveau Talborjt. As a rough guide, a seat on a long-distance ride (more than 50km) costs Dh4 per km. Destinations include Inezgane (Dh8), Taghazout (Dh8), Taroudannt (Dh35), Essaouira (Dh70), Marrakesh (Dh120), Laâyoune (Dh200) and Dakhla (Dh350).

Getting Around

TO/FROM THE AIRPORT

There is no direct bus between the airport and Agadir. Bus 22 runs from outside the airport (about 500m straight out on the road) to Inezgane (Dh5) every 40 minutes or so until about 8.30pm. From Inezgane, several buses run to Agadir (Dh3), or take a grand taxi (Dh8).

A grand taxi between the airport and Agadir costs Dh150 by day, and Dh200 at night for up to six people. Expect to pay more for luggage.

BUS

The main local bus station is next to the grand-taxi rank at the southern end of town. Buses 5 and 6 run every 10 minutes or so to Inezgane (Dh3). Ratag buses 12 and 14 go to Taghazout (Dh5).

TAXI

Orange petits taxis run around town. Prices are worked out by meter, so ask for it to be switched on.

AROUND AGADIR

Inezgane إنزكان

One of the region's transport hubs, Inezgane, 13km south of Agadir, is not a tourist destination, but some travellers enjoy stopping here for that very reason. There's a vast fresh-produce market across from the combined bus station and grand-taxi lot – Tuesday is the main souq.

Should you need to stay overnight, there's a clutch of cheap hotels around the bus station.

Hôtel Louz (☎ 028 331990; fax 028 331842; Ave Mokhtar Soussi; s/d with shower Dh100/160) is a cheerful hotel with modern, boxy rooms and private bathrooms. It also has a TV lounge and a restaurant, though there is better food at the stalls around the main square.

Hôtel-Restaurant La Pergola (☎ 028 271803; lapergola@menara.ma; Km 8 Rte d'Agadir; s/d Dh194/226) is a relic of another, low-key Agadir, its comfortable bungalows set in a garden full of flowers. The hotel is used by birdwatchers as it is a few minutes from the Souss estuary. The restaurant (breakfast Dh24; set menu Dh115) is old-fashioned French cuisine with some Moroccan specialities, all very comforting after a long bus journey.

You'll also find dozens of cheap cafés and restaurants around the main square and outside the market.

There are plenty of buses going in all possible directions. The bus station is just off the Agadir–Tiznit road. The CTM and Supratours offices are on either side of Ave Mokhtar Soussi.

Loads of grands taxis to Essaouira (Dh50, three hours), Tiznit (Dh20, two hours) and Taroudannt (Dh20, 2½ hours) also gather here, as well as less regular taxis for Goulimime (Dh50, 4½ hours) and Tan Tan (Dh90, six hours).

Adding to the organised chaos are regular local buses (Dh3) and grands taxis (Dh5) heading to Agadir and Al-Massira airport (bus 22).

SOUSS-MASSA NATIONAL PARK منتزه سو ماسه الوطني

Places like the Souss-Massa National Park are going to become ever more important in Morocco's future. The most significant of all the country's national parks stretches 70km south of Agadir, a block of over 33,000 hectares of protected land between the main north–south highway and the beach. It is a spectacular and wild place of cliffs, sand dunes, farmland, coastal steppes and forests.

The park was created in 1991 in recognition of its importance as a feeding ground for birds. Along with the Souss estuary near Inezgane, it has become very popular with birdwatchers, although it is also a great place for walking. The best times to visit are March to April, and October to November.

During the winter, ospreys and large flocks of pochard and other ducks are commonly seen, as well as greater flamingos. But the biggest attraction is the population of bald ibises. These birds, revered in ancient Egypt and once widespread in Central Europe, North Africa and the Middle East, are now an endangered species. A few small colonies or breeding pairs have been found around the Eastern Mediterranean, but over half of the world's total population is found in the Souss-Massa. The greatest threat, now, comes from tourism development. A few years ago Club Med was granted permission to build a massive new resort on the coast side of the park, but after pressure from BirdLife International, the global authority on bird numbers, and other concerned organisations, the plans were shelved and Club Med has retreated. For the moment, the breeding grounds remain off-limits, though you can spot the ibises around Oued Massa or at the mouth of the Tamri River .

Jackal, red fox, wild cat, genet and Eurasian wild boar are also found in the park, while a large fenced area in the north of the park contains species that have now disappeared from the south including Dorcas gazelles, addaxes, red-necked ostriches and scimitar horned oryxes. The **Souss-Massa National Park headquarters** (☎ 028 333880), which looks after the day-to-day running of the park, is located at Oued Souss. To get there, take the main Agadir–Inezgane highway past Golf des Dunes. Take the right fork and you will find the park entrance before you reach the royal palace. At the time of our visit, the centre was shut because, they said, the government had not renewed their contract. We hope this situation will have been rectified by the time of publication.

Oued Massa لويد مصا

Some 58km south of Agadir there's a second entrance to the park near the village of Massa, signposted from the main highway. Trained guides (Dh100 to Dh150) can be arranged through the forestry warden's office near the car park, as can donkey rides for kids. A track leads along the river to the estuary mouth (3km) and the village of Sidi R'bat.

The tiny village of **Sidi R'bat** has two claims to fame. Supposedly this is where the biblical Jonah was vomited up by a whale, and also where Uqba bin Nafi, the 7th-century Arab conqueror of Morocco, rode his horse triumphantly into the sea and called on God to witness the fact that he could find no land left to conquer. Spectacularly located on the gorgeous beach and in the middle of the park is **Ksar Massa** (☎ 061 280319; www.ksarmassa.com; Sidi R'bat, Oued Massa; B&B per person Dh900, full board per person Dh1350;). This wonderful guest house on the beach is a wonderful place to unwind. Luxuriously spacious rooms and suites are painted in bright colours and the pool overlooks the ocean. Management can arrange guided trips into the park and throughout the region. To get there follow the signposts from Massa.

Getting There & Away

From Agadir, 4WD tours head into the park, but both Oued Massa and Oued Souss are usually accessible by 2WD (or grand taxi). The Gab bus 17 runs from Inezgane to Massa (Dh10) every 30 minutes or so, from where it is about an hour's walk to Oued Massa river mouth. For Oued Souss and the park headquarters, take bus 40 from any stop along Ave Mohammed V in Agadir.

NORTH OF AGADIR

Most beaches near Agadir have been colonised by foreigners, who have built winter villas here. King Fahd of Saudi Arabia, who has a palace north of Agadir on the road to Taghazout, has funded the building of the road along this stretch.

If you're looking for surf and less crowded beaches, then head further north, where there are beautiful sandy coves every few kilometres.

Local bus 12 from Agadir bus station (with a stop on Blvd Mohammed V, outside the Royal Mirage Hotel) runs up the coast to Taghazout (Dh5) and beyond. The daily buses between Essaouira and Agadir also stop here.

Aourir & Tamraght طمرات و اوريد

Known collectively as Banana Village because of the large banana groves that surround them, Aourir and Tamraght lie some 12km and 15km north of Agadir, respectively, separated by Oued Tamraght. They share Banana Beach, which can be good for beginner surfers. Aourir also has a lively souq each Wednesday on the ocean side of the road.

Despite its unprepossessing location, close to the town of Aourir, **Villa Mandala** (☎ 028 314773; www.villa-mandala.com; Aourir; s/d incl breakfast Dh550/880) is a rare find. Established in 1999 to help women travel safely in Morocco, it has since morphed into a guest house that supports artisans. The villa on the beach has five airy rooms, communal showers and a large salon. Meals (Dh130) are taken communally and guests are free to wander the house, including the kitchen, where they can help prepare local dishes. There is an in-house hammam (Dh100), as well as body-therapy sessions that can be arranged, and a female staff member can also take you to Aourir hammam (Dh250). Les Amis des Artisans, the craftworkers association founded here, now has its office in Agadir, but a selection of their pottery, ironwork and other crafts is used here and is for sale.

In Tamraght, in the midst of numerous surf breaks, **Surf Marokko** (☎ 068 395124; www.surfmarokko.de) and **Dynamic Loisir** (☎ 028 314655, 061 259838; Tamraght) are both popular with the surfing crowd, and offer board rental and courses. Dynamic Loisir also runs the beach café.

Taghazout تاغزوت

Six kilometres from Tamraght, the laid-back fishing village of Taghazout, which was once famous for calamari and hippies, is now considered one of Morocco's premier surfing beaches. However soon it will be known as one of its largest resorts: at the time of our visit, bulldozers were levelling the ground between Tamraght and Taghazout villages. The first hotel and golf course are due to open at the end of 2009, though it will be some years before all 20,000 beds are ready. In the meantime, the surf is still up. Surf breaks such as Killer Point, La Source and Anka Point continue to attract experienced surfers, while beginners try out the appropriately named Hash Point. The surf is most reliable from September to May.

If you are a surfer, then the beachfront villa of our pick **Surf Maroc** (☎ 028 200368, in UK 00 44 1794 322 709; www.surfmaroc.co.uk; r per person incl half-board from Dh500) is the place to go. Run by a group of passionate British surfers, it offers a full-service surf camp for all levels, as well as yoga classes. What's more, the straightforward rooms provide an increasingly rare opportunity along this stretch of the coast to fall asleep listening to the waves break. Breakfast is served on a terrace with a good view over the surf. They have a range of packages from Dh500 per person per night half-board including surf guiding (taking you to the best waves) and from Dh200 per day for wetsuit and surfboard. They also rent nearby luxury and self-catering apartments.

There are rooms to rent in the village, and out of high season you can usually turn up and find somewhere. Otherwise, try **Résidence Amouage** (☎ 028 200006; www.residence-amouage.com; s/d Dh170/220; 💻), which has simple self-catering studios and an internet room open to the public.

There are some good places to eat on the main road, but the point of being here is to see the ocean and there are several simple café-restaurants up from the beach, of which **Panorama** (breakfast Dh18, tajine Dh40) at the south end of the beach, has the best view. Service is slow, but the fish is fresh. It's also a great place to catch the sunset.

IMMOUZZER DES IDA OUTANANE
ايموزار ادو اوتنان

This thoroughly recommended side trip takes you about 60km northeast of Agadir, into the High Atlas foothills. On the way you pass through the aptly named **Paradise Valley**, an oleander- and palm-lined gorge, and a popular picnic and swimming spot.

The famous cascades of Immouzzer, one of North Africa's most beautiful waterfalls, flow most strongly between February and August – at other times they're reduced to little more than a trickle. The site is about to change as plans have been agreed to remove many buildings close to the falls and to improve access and visitor facilities.

Water falls off the edge of the plateau in several chutes, collecting in pools at the base of the cliff. There is a cool plunge pool and second waterfall nearby – villagers will be glad to take you there, telling you how Jimi Hendrix is responsible for the peace/love symbol carved in the rock. Immouzzer, even without water pressure, is a delightful place to hang around for a few days, and walk. Steps lead down to the bottom of the falls. Also worth considering is the walk to the source of the river above the falls. Ask at Restaurant Chez Rachid for directions.

The area turns white in spring when the almond trees blossom. There is a honey harvest and festival in July/August, and around late November you may be lucky enough to witness the olive harvest, when villagers climb up into the trees to shake the olives from the branches. Thursday is souq day.

Sleeping & Eating

Hôtel Tifrit (☎ 028 826044; Paradise Valley; s/d with half board Dh250/390; 🅿) Set right by the river, this family-run auberge is about halfway along the road to Immouzzer from the coastal turn-off. Functional rooms come with clean shared bathrooms. The hotel has a pleasant terrace looking on to the river, and serves good Moroccan meals.

Auberge à la Bonne Franquette (☎ 028 823191; www.bonnefranquette-agadir.com, in French; s/d half-board Dh600/725; 🅿 💻) In the village of Aksri, 15km from Immouzzer and surrounded by argan trees, is a surprising place to find tasty and reasonably priced French cooking, served out in a flowering courtyard, weather permitting (meals around Dh120). There are also five cosy rooms with private bathrooms and a heated pool open year-round. From here you can work off that lunch with a walk through the palm groves.

Hôtel des Cascades (☎ 028 826016; www.cascades-hotel.com, in French; s/d half-board Dh600/900; 🅿) Just east of Immouzzer, in a wonderful location perched high above the valley, the hotel is set amid a riotous garden of almond and apple trees and there are tennis courts and a good restaurant (set menu Dh150) with a terrace. The hotel is built on three floors, the large rooms (the best ones are on the 3rd floor) come with a west-facing terrace or balcony. A path leads down through olive groves to the cascades and there's other excellent walking around – ask in the hotel for suggestions.

Getting There & Away

A very unreliable local bus runs from Agadir bus station to Immouzzer (Dh30, three hours), but unfortunately it doesn't run if there are not enough people. Also, you'll have to wait until the following morning for the unreliable bus back. A better option would be to share a grand taxi (Dh35), easiest on Thursday, which is market day. Many hotels and travel agencies in Agadir offer coach tours to Immouzzer.

TAROUDANNT تارودانت

pop 70,000

Taroudannt (also spelled Taroudant) is often called 'Little Marrakesh', but that doesn't do it justice: it is a place in its own right. Hidden by magnificent red-mud walls and with the snowcapped peaks of the High Atlas beckoning beyond, Taroudannt has a touch of mystery about it. Yet it is also a practical place, a market town where Berbers trade the produce of the rich and fertile Souss Valley.

There aren't any must-see sights here. Instead, it is a place to stroll and linger. The town's souqs are well worth a browse, more laid-back than Marrakesh, but with an atmosphere of activity that is missing in Agadir – many people come on a day trip (it is only 80km). Taroudannt also makes an excellent base for travellers interested in trekking up into the little-explored western High Atlas (see p445).

Some 53km east of Taroudannt is the turning for the Tizi n'Test road (see p336), one of the most spectacular and perilous passes in the country, leading you across the High Atlas and on to Marrakesh.

History

Taroudannt was one of the early bases of the Almoravides, who established themselves here in 1056 AD, at the beginning of their conquest of Morocco. In the 16th century the emerging Saadians made it their capital for about 20 years. By the time they moved on to Marrakesh, they had turned the Souss Valley, in which the city stands, into the country's most important producer of sugar cane, cotton, rice and indigo – all valuable trade items on the trans-Saharan trade routes the dynasty was so keen to control. The Saadians constructed the old part of town and the kasbah, though most of it was destroyed and the inhabitants massacred in 1687 by Moulay Ismail, as punishment for opposing him. Only the ramparts survived. Most of what stands inside them dates from the 18th century.

Taroudannt continued to be a centre of intrigue and sedition against the central government well into the 20th century, and indeed played host to the Idrissid El-Hiba, a southern chief who opposed the Treaty of Fès, the 1912 agreement that created the French Protectorate.

Orientation

Unlike many southern Moroccan towns, and perhaps because of its reputation for sedition, the French didn't use Taroudannt as an administrative or military centre, so it has no 'European' quarter or ville nouvelle.

The cheaper hotels are all on or near the two central squares: Place al-Alaouyine (still known by its former Berber name, Place Assarag) and Place an-Nasr (formerly Place Talmoqlate). Banks, restaurants and a small post office are clustered in this area.

Most buses and grands taxis terminate just outside the medina's southern gate, Bab Zorgane.

Information

Three banks have ATMs on Place al-Alaouyine (Banque Populaire, BMCE and BMCI), and all have exchange facilities and accept travellers cheques. BMCE also does cash advances.

Club Roudana (Ave Bir Zaran; per hr Dh8) Internet access.
Hospital (Ave Moulay Rachid) By the kasbah.
Main post office (Rue du 20 Août) Off Ave Hassan II, to the east of the kasbah.
Night pharmacy (☎ 028 854599) Next to Grande Mosquée.
Wafanet (Ave Mohammed V; per hr Dh8) Internet access.

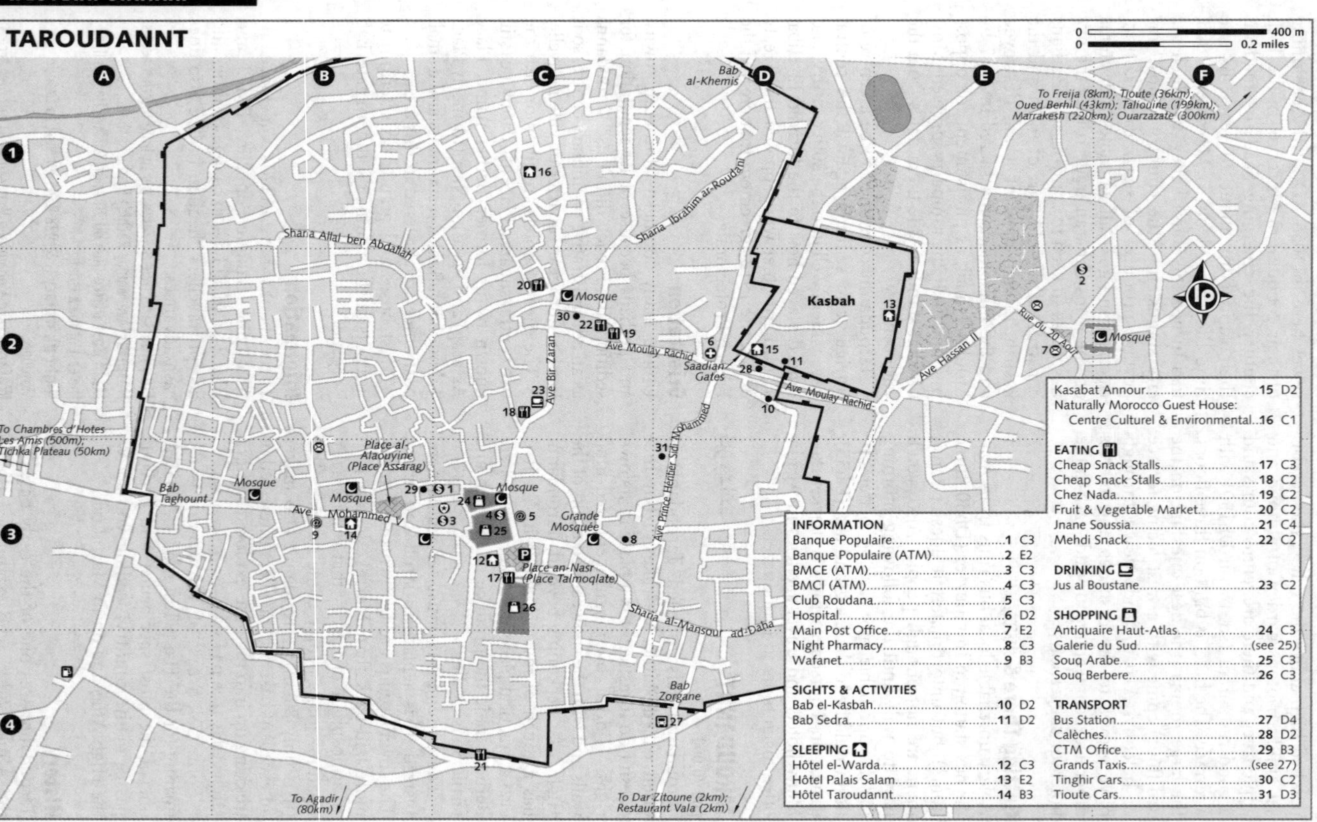
TAROUDANNT
0 400 m
0 0.2 miles
Kasbah
Bab al-Khemis
Ave Hassan II
Rue du 20 Août
Ave Moulay Rachid
Saadian Gates
Ave Prince Héritier Sidi Mohammed
Sharia Ibrahim ar-Roudani
Sharia Allal ben Abdallah
Ave Bir Zaran
Place al-Alaouyine (Place Assarag)
Ave Mohammed V
Bab Taghount
Grande Mosquée
Place an-Nasr (Place Talmoqlate)
Sharia al-Mansour ad-Daha
Bab Zorgane
To Freija (8km); Tioute (36km); Oued Berhil (43km); Taliouine (199km); Marrakesh (220km); Ouarzazate (300km)
To Chambres d'Hotes Les Amis (500m); Tichka Plateau (50km)
To Agadir (80km)
To Dar Zitoune (2km); Restaurant Vala (2km)
INFORMATION
Banque Populaire 1 C3
Banque Populaire (ATM) 2 E2
BMCE (ATM) 3 C3
BMCI (ATM) 4 C3
Club Roudana 5 C3
Hospital 6 D2
Main Post Office 7 E2
Night Pharmacy 8 C3
Wafanet 9 B3
SIGHTS & ACTIVITIES
Bab el-Kasbah 10 D2
Bab Sedra 11 D2
SLEEPING
Hôtel el-Warda 12 C3
Hôtel Palais Salam 13 E2
Hôtel Taroudannt 14 B3
Kasabat Annour 15 D2
Naturally Morocco Guest House: Centre Culturel & Environmental 16 C1
EATING
Cheap Snack Stalls 17 C3
Cheap Snack Stalls 18 C2
Chez Nada 19 C2
Fruit & Vegetable Market 20 C2
Jnane Soussia 21 C4
Mehdi Snack 22 C2
DRINKING
Jus al Boustane 23 C2
SHOPPING
Antiquaire Haut-Atlas 24 C3
Galerie du Sud (see 25)
Souq Arabe 25 C3
Souq Berbere 26 C3
TRANSPORT
Bus Station 27 D4
Calèches 28 D2
CTM Office 29 B3
Grands Taxis (see 27)
Tinghir Cars 30 C2
Tioute Cars 31 D3

Sights

The 7.5km of **ramparts** surrounding Taroudannt are among the best-preserved pisé walls in Morocco. Their colour changes from golden brown to deepest red depending on the time of day. They can easily be explored on foot (two hours) preferably in the late afternoon, or take a bike or a *calèche* (see p391) and see the walls by moonlight.

Built in the 16th and 17th century, a string of mighty defensive towers create the gates of the city. One of the most commonly used of these gates is the triple-arched **Bab el-Kasbah**, approached via an avenue of orange trees. Through here, on the right past an olive press, is another gate, **Bab Sedra**, (cyclists and pedestrians only) leading to the old kasbah quarter, a fortress built by Moulay Ismail and now the poorest part of town. The governor's palace, also in the kasbah, now forms part of the Hôtel Palais Salam (right).

Activities

Ballade Roudana des Remparts (☎ 068 395696; per hr Dh30 plus tip) will take you for a fascinating guided bike tour around the walls and city (mainly in French).

Taroudannt is a great base for trekking in the western High Atlas region, and the secluded **Tichka Plateau** (for details of treks here see p435) is a delightful meadow of springtime flowers and hidden gorges. Several agencies in town offer treks, but we recommend you insist on travelling only with a qualified guide.

Sleeping

BUDGET

Most budget hotels around Place al-Alaouyine offer basic accommodation and roof terraces, good for sunbathing and people-watching.

Hôtel el-Warda (☎ 028 852763; Place an-Nasr; s/d Dh50/70) This is the best of the ultra-cheapies, with a funky *zellij* (tilework) terrace overlooking Place an-Nasr. The rooms are basic – you get a bed and washbasin – and toilets and showers are communal. It is run by women, but single women might find the alley entrance and all-male clientele in the café difficult.

Chambres d'Hotes Les Amis (☎ 067 601686; Sidi Belkass; s/d Dh80/150) Simple but quite large whitewashed rooms with patterned tiled floors and bedspreads, a large communal bathroom, a couple of salons, a terrace and above all the owner's enthusiasm make this guest house recommended. It's a short walk out of the medina, but quieter and less hassled for that.

Hôtel Taroudannt (☎ 028 852416; Ave Mohammed V & Place al-Alaouyine; s/d/tr Dh140/160/200) The Taroudannt is faded, the en-suite rooms, though clean, have seen better days and its bar can get rowdy. And yet its jungle-style courtyard and faintly colonial public areas have a unique atmosphere – and the bar closes early. There is a good restaurant (menu Dh70) and they can organise great treks in the surrounding mountains with the excellent guide El Aouad Ali (☎ 066 637972). All told, this remains the best budget hotel in town.

MIDRANGE & TOP END

our pick **Naturally Morocco Guest House: Centre Culturel & Environmental** (☎ bookings 0044 1239 710814, 028 551628/067 297438; www.naturallymorocco.co.uk; 422 Derb Afferdou; per person half-board Dh410, 'Real Morocco' package per person 1 week Dh3500). If only there were more places like this, a medina house run by locals offering a rare glimpse into Moroccan life. Run in conjunction with UK-based Naturally Morocco, dedicated to sustainable tourism and cultural contact, they offer excursions led by skilled guides, exciting cultural experiences and delicious Moroccan meals. Sunday night dinner is followed by Berber music and dancing. Staff can arrange ecotours on birdwatching, flora and fauna, if they don't have another group.

Hôtel Palais Salam (☎ 028 852501; www.palaisalam.com; kasbah; s/d incl breakfast from Dh692/934;) This former pasha's residence should be the best hotel in town, but is sadly dilapidated, the staff demoralised and the exotic garden overly built on. Rooms in the old wing are large, but in need of refitting or at least a thorough clean. Newly refurbished rooms, a little bland but better equipped, were due to open soon after our visit.

Kasabat Annour (☎ 028 854576; www.kasabatannour.com; kasbah; s/d incl breakfast Dh880/1320;). A wonderful new addition to Taroudannt, built around a former colonel's house in the medina, right up against the kasbah walls. It features six elegant and spacious rooms around a good-sized swimming pool, and meals, hammam and treatments are available on request. There are also a couple of cheaper rooms built into the city walls which cannot, by law, have water plumbed in, so have separate facilities.

Dar Zitoune (☎ 028 551141; www.darzitoune.com; s/d/ste incl breakfast Dh900/1200/1540;) In a series of bungalows in a gorgeous fruit-filled garden, the rooms are large and simply furnished in local style, but with all the facilities one expects at this level. Suites are enormous and well priced, with working fireplaces. The pool is heated in winter and there is a hammam. The restaurant is one of the best in town (menu Dh150).

Eating

The hotel terraces on Place al-Alaouyine are good places to have breakfast, and also offer good-value set menus of couscous and salad (Dh75).

RESTAURANTS

Chez Nada (☎ 028 851726; Ave Moulay Rachid; set menu Dh70; lunch & dinner;) West of Bab al-Kasbah, this is a quiet modern family-run place, famous for its excellent and good-value tajines, including one with pigeon. There's a male-dominated café downstairs, and main dining room on the 1st-floor terrace with great views over the gardens. Food is home cooking and excellent. *Pastilla* (pie) and couscous (Dh60 to Dh95) should be ordered a couple of hours ahead.

Jnane Soussia (☎ 028 854980; set menu Dh75; dinner;) A delightful restaurant, a short walk from Bab Zorgane, with tented seating areas set around a large pool in a garden adjacent to the ramparts. The house specialities are a mouth-watering *mechoui* (whole roast lamb) and pigeon *pastilla*, which have to be ordered in advance, but everything here is good.

Restaurant Vala (☎ 028 850249; Km2, National 10; 3 courses from Dh110; lunch & dinner) You couldn't get more contemporary Moroccan than this. In a villa located 2km from the centre, this restaurant serves good, solid food to local businessmen and bureaucrats, and is packed with families on weekends. Call ahead to order couscous (Dh80 to Dh150) or *pastilla* (Dh120 to Dh150).

QUICK EATS

The best place to look for cheap eateries is around Place an-Nasr and north along Ave Bir Zaran, where you find the usual tajine, *harira* (lentil soup) and salads. Several places around Place al-Alaouyine serve sandwiches and simple grills.

Mehdi Snack (off Ave Moulay Rachid; set menu Dh25-45; lunch & early evening) Located just behind Chez Nada, and run by the same family, this is a good snack bar with cheap burgers, salads and fried sardines.

SELF-CATERING

Putting together a picnic is not a problem in Taroudannt. In addition to stalls in the souqs, there's a dedicated **fruit and vegetable market** at the northern end of Ave Bir Zaran.

Drinking

Jus al Boustane (Ave Bir Zaran; juice Dh5) Run by a cheerful chap surrounded by piles of fruit, this is a good place to stock up on vitamins with fresh juice near the Lycée Mohammed V.

Shopping

Taroudannt is the central Chleuh city of the Souss, so it is a good place to look for the good-quality silver jewellery for which this tribe is renowned. The jewellery is influenced both by Saharan tribes and by Jewish silversmiths, who formed a significant part of the community until the late 1960s.

Bab Taghount is the easiest way into the pleasant medina. South of Place an-Nasr, the **Souq Berbère** has fresh vegetables, spices, pottery and baskets. The main **Souq Arabe**, east of Place al-Alaouyine, has antique and souvenir shops hidden in the quiet streets. Look out for the **Antiquaire Haut-Atlas** (☎ 028 852145; 61 Souq el Kabir), the most reputable dealer in top-quality objects, with a huge collection of well-chosen carpets, fabulous jewellery and antique pottery. At **Galerie du Sud** (☎ 077 608260; 16 Souk el Karaza) artist Amahou Mohamed sells his striking paintings mounted in frames made out of recycled bike tyres.

A large souq on Sunday morning, just outside Bab al-Khemis, brings in people from the whole region.

Getting There & Away

BUS

All buses leave from the main bus station outside Bab Zorgane. **CTM** (Hotel Les Arcades, Place al-Alaouyine) has the most reliable buses, with one departure per day for Casablanca (Dh150, 10 hours) via Marrakesh (Dh90, six hours).

Other companies run services throughout the day to both these cities as well as to Agadir (Dh30, 2½ hours), Inezgane (Dh15, 2½ hours) and Ouarzazate (Dh80, five hours). There's one bus to Tata (Dh50, five hours).

CAR

Local agencies **Tinghir Cars** (☎ 028 850810; Ave Moulay Rachid Ferk Lahbab) and **Tioute Cars** (Ave Prince Héritier Sidi Mohammed) hire out small cars from Dh300 per day.

TAXI

Taroudannt's grands taxis also gather at the bus station outside Bab Zorgane. The main destinations are Inezgane (Dh23), and sometimes Agadir (Dh28) and Marrakesh (Dh130).

Getting Around

You can tour the ramparts in a *calèche.* The *calèches* gather just inside Bab al-Kasbah, on Place al-Alaouyine and other prominent spots. A one-way trip around town costs Dh15 to Dh20, while one-hour tours are Dh50 or more depending on your bargaining skills. Taroudannt is also a good place to cycle: reliable bikes can be rented at **Bab Tamaklat** (☎ 012 987351), near Place Talmoqlate.

TALIOUINE تالوين

The straggling village of Taliouine, halfway between Taroudannt and Ouarzazate, is dominated by hills and the impressive Glaoui kasbah. It is disintegrating fast, but the best part is still inhabited by descendants of the Glaoui's servants. A caretaker can show you around.

Taliouine is the centre for saffron, the most expensive spice in the world, which grows in a very narrow band of land. The *crocus sativus,* from which it comes flowers between late October and November, when a festival is held to celebrate the harvest. **Coopérative Souktana du Safran** (☎ 068 395215; www.safran-souktana.mezgarne.com; 🕒 7.30am-1.30pm & 2-8pm) has a small museum, saffron tasting and shop, where you need to insist that bags are weighed in front of you. Auberge le Safran (see right) also sells top-quality spice. Saffron here costs around Dh30 per gram.

The village comes to life during the Monday **souq**, behind the kasbah.

Taliouine is becoming a popular trekking centre for the nearby **Jebel Siroua** (see p445), which offers some of the finest walking in the Anti Atlas.

The N10 road east from Taroudannt to Taliouine is less dramatic than the Tizi n'Test, but provides a good alternative if you are heading to Ouarzazate. The road north of Taliouine crosses a beautiful and immense landscape, to join the main Marrakesh–Ouarzazate road near the turn-off to Aït Benhaddou.

Sleeping

Auberge le Safran (☎ /fax 028 534046, 068 394223; www.auberge-safran.com, in French; d/tr/q Dh170/200/280) Closer to the centre and currently the best in the village, the five simple but pretty en-suite rooms are decorated in bright colours. The family suites are particularly spacious and the roof terrace has great views. They harvest their own saffron, which they sell and use in the delicious cooking (meals from Dh80). They also organise a range of treks into the mountains.

Auberge Souktana (☎ 028 534075; souktana@menara.ma s/d room with shower Dh180/220, bungalow Dh100/160, tent Dh50/80) A small family-run auberge, the former Youth Hostel, 1km east of the village on the main road, with recently modernised rooms, four small bungalows with basin and space for tents. The multilingual hosts have a wealth of information on the region, and have great experience at running Jebel Siroua treks. Reservations are essential in trekking season.

Hotel Ibn Toumerte (☎ 028 534125; fax 028 534126; s/d Dh445/538; ❄ 🏊) Right next to the kasbah, a bunkerlike 1970s hotel has little character but does have some stunning retro decor, small though comfortable rooms, great views, a neglected pool and the town's only bar. Meals cost Dh169.

Getting There & Away

Buses pass through Taliouine from both Ouarzazate and Taroudannt (Dh30), but there are not always seats available. Your best chance is to wait at the main bus stop in town. Grands taxis head west to Oued Berhil, where you can change for Taroudannt, and east to Tazenakht (Dh20), where you can change for Ouarzazate (Dh27).

TIZNIT تزنيت

pop 53,600

South of the Souss Valley and beyond the western end of the Anti Atlas, Tiznit is an old walled medina town surrounded by modern development. It was originally the site of a cluster of kasbahs, which were encircled in the 19th century by some 5km of pisé wall. It quickly became a trade centre and remains the provincial capital, a central point between the coastal towns and the Anti Atlas. Good for a visit, but Tiznit is most often seen on your way through or on a day-trip from Mirleft or one of the other coastal towns.

History

In 1881 Sultan Moulay Al-Hassan (1873–94) chose Tiznit as a base from which to assert his authority over the rebellious Berber tribes of the south. To do this, he built the town's perimeter walls. Jewish silversmiths were moved into the town and gave it a reputation as a centre for silver.

However, Tiznit remained embroiled in local sedition. In 1912, it was a base for resistance to the 1912 treaty that turned Morocco into a French and Spanish protectorate. This resistance movement was led by El-Hiba, the so-called 'Blue Sultan' from the Western Sahara, who earned his nickname for always wearing his Saharawi veil.

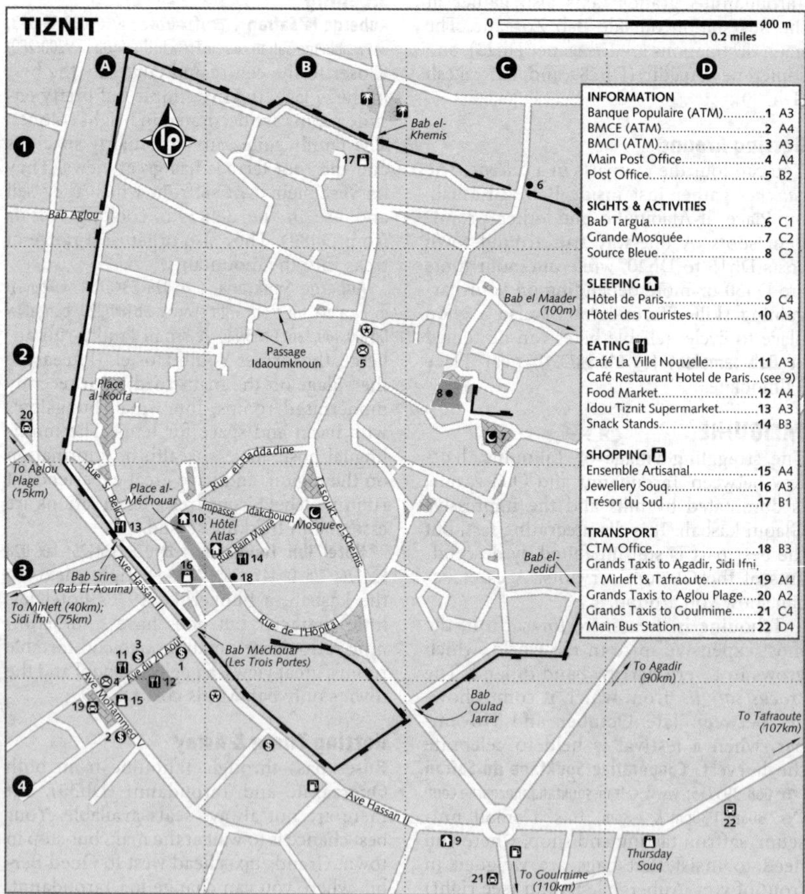

Following Sultan Moulay Hafid's capitulation to the French at the Treaty of Fés, El-Hiba proclaimed himself sultan at Tiznit's mosque in 1912. The southern tribes rose to support him and El-Hiba marched north at the head of an army of men from the Tuareg and Anti Atlas tribes. They were welcomed as liberators in Marrakesh but much of the army was slaughtered by the French as it moved towards Fez. El-Hiba retreated to Taroudannt, then Tiznit, then up into the Anti Atlas, where he pursued a campaign of resistance against the French until his death in 1919.

Orientation

Within the medina, Place al-Méchouar is where you'll find the jewellery souq and cheap hotels. Outside the main gate, Bab Méchouar, is the main grand-taxi rank, the main post office, banks, restaurants and a food market.

Midrange to top-end hotels can be found to the south of the medina.

Information

Banks in Tiznit include **BMCE** (Ave Mohammed V), **BMCI** (Ave du 20 Août) and **Banque Populaire** (Ave du 20 Août), all of which have ATMs.

The **main post office** (Ave du 20 Août) and a smaller branch in the medina are open the usual hours.

Sights & Activities

Tiznit is a sleepy place with a medina that is a fun place to wander around and with an equally sleepy jewellery souq. The Berber traders here are tough salesmen, but it is still worth trying to strike a bargain. Things liven up considerably on Thursday, which is market day.

The minaret of the **Grande Mosquée** (Great Mosque; closed to non-Muslims) is studded with jutting wooden sticks. Local legend suggests this is where the souls of the dead congregate. More likely, these are left in place by the masons who built the minaret to help them climb up and replaster. A similar arrangement is used on minarets in south of the Sahara, notably in Timbuktu.

Nearby is the **Source Bleue**, the original town spring, now a stagnant shallow pool, green rather than blue. Legend has it that a woman of ill repute, Lalla Zninia, stopped to rest here at what was then plain desert. She spent the next three days repenting her wicked ways and God was so impressed with her fervour that he showed forgiveness by having a spring gush beneath her feet. Her name was thus given to the village that preceded Sultan Moulay al-Hassan's 19th-century fortress town.

It's possible to climb onto sections of the 5km-long city walls, which have 29 towers and nine gates. From **Bab Targua**, for instance, you get a great view over the lush *palmeraie,* where there is another natural spring, used as a laundry by local women.

Sleeping

Many budget hotels are right on Place al-Méchouar, but lone women may find the area a bit off-putting late at night.

Hôtel des Touristes (☎ 028 862018; Place al-Méchouar; s/d Dh50/90) Budget doesn't have to mean slummy, as this spotless, welcoming place at the end of the Place shows. Rooms are simple, decorated in Moroccan style, and showers are free and hot. The pious staff are serious and ensure it is safe for women travellers.

Hôtel de Paris (☎ 028 862865; www.hoteldeparis.ma; Ave Hassan II; s/d Dh138/164; ❄) On a busy roundabout a short walk from the old walls, the hotel has some questionable colour schemes (pink and orange?), but en-suite rooms are bright, spacious and well run.

Bab el Maader (☎ 028 864252; www.bab-el-maader.com; Rue El Haj Ali; r Dh220-275; 🚭 💻) Hotel Idou Tiznit, across from Hôtel de Paris, is the most expensive in town, with a pool and vast marble lobby, but this is Tiznit's best address, a five-room guest house with a courtyard, plenty of great decorative touches and good use of Moroccan fabrics and materials. The laid-back owners will arrange trips in the region. Home-cooked lunch or dinner is available on request (Dh110).

Eating

Most of the budget hotels on the main square have cafés offering food, the Hôtel Atlas being one of the most popular on the Place al-Méchouar. A number of snack stands along Rue Bain Maure offer acceptable sandwiches for around Dh10.

Café La Ville Nouvelle (Ave du 20 Août; mains Dh35-55; 🕑 lunch & early dinner) An attractive restaurant serving the classic salads, brochettes

BEYOND THE GLITTER

Berber jewellery serves a much wider purpose than simple adornment. The jewellery a woman wears identifies her as a member of a clan or tribe, it is a sign of her wealth, it reflects cultural traditions and it has power beyond the visual, to protect her from the evil eye.

A woman will receive jewellery from her mother until she marries. For her marriage, her future husband will commission his mother or sister to provide jewellery for her and these will be kept by her as dowry and added to throughout her life. This jewellery will always be made of silver, as gold is considered evil. Necklaces are important, the traditional assemblage in the southern oasis valleys sometimes featuring talismans of silver, pink coral, amazonite, amber, Czech glass and West African ebony beads. A woman will also have bracelets, *fibulas* (elaborate brooches, often triangular, used for fastening garments), anklets, earrings and headdresses. Some pieces will be worn every day, others – the finest – will be saved for occasions such as festivals, pilgrimages and funerals.

The protective, medicinal and magical properties of jewellery are extremely important. The necklaces contain charms bought from magicians or holy men, which offer protection against the evil eye, disease, accidents and difficulties in childbirth. Silver is believed to cure rheumatism; coral symbolises fertility and is thought to have curative powers; amber is worn as a symbol of wealth and to protect against sorcery (it's also considered an aphrodisiac and a cure for colds); amazonite and carnelian stones are used in divining fortunes; and shells traded from East Africa symbolise fertility.

Talismans feature stylised motifs of animals, sun, moon and stars, all of which are believed to have supernatural powers. A common symbol to ward off the evil eye is the hand of Fatima, the daughter of the Prophet Mohammed. Any depiction of the hand (which represents human creative power and dominance) or of the number five is believed to have the same effect as metaphorically poking fingers into the evil eye with the words *khamsa fi ainek* (five in your eye).

and couscous, while the popular downstairs café is good for coffee and pastries.

Café-Restaurant Hôtel de Paris (☎ 028 862865; www.hoteldeparis.ma; Ave Hassan II; mains Dh40-50; ⏰ lunch & dinner) There is something wonderfully old-fashioned and correct about the bright, tiled dining room, where, true to their name, they serve a predominantly French menu, with a range of large salads (Dh12 to Dh30), simple fish and meat dishes, and fresh juices, including almond during the season. The loud TV can dampen the pleasure.

If you want food for a picnic, head for the **market** (Ave du 20 Août), or the **Idou Tiznit Supermarket** (☎ 028 602397; Carrefour de Tiznit), which sells a range of local and imported food.

Shopping

With its long history of silversmiths, the **jewellery souq** has some of the best work in the south. Some of this jewellery is made in Tiznit, some bought from Saharan tribes in the south. You will need time to look around and bargain to get the best prices.

Away from the souq, **Trésor du Sud** (☎ 028 862885; www.tresordusud.com; 27 Bab al-Khemis) is not the cheapest, but the work is good; they only deal in hallmarked solid silver and you can see a craftsman at work.

The **Ensemble Artisanal** (Ave du 20 Août; ⏰ 8.30am-1pm & 2.30-8.30pm), opposite the main post office, covers the full range of local crafts.

Getting There & Away

BUS

All buses leave from the main bus station just off the Tafraoute road, past the Thursday souq. CTM tickets are also available from the CTM office on Place al-Mechouar in town. CTM has buses for Agadir (Dh40, two hours, one daily), Casablanca (Dh220, 10 hours, one daily), Marrakesh (Dh120, five hours, one daily) and a twice-daily service south to Goulimime (Dh35), Tan Tan (Dh75), Laâyoune (Dh190) and Dakhla (Dh340).

Other companies run daily buses to the above destinations plus Sidi Ifni (Dh25, 1½ hours), Tafraoute (Dh35, four hours) and Tata (Dh80, 6½ hours).

TAXI

Grands taxis to Sidi Ifni (Dh23), Mirleft (Dh16), Agadir (Dh25) and occasionally Tafraoute (Dh40) leave from the main grand-taxi rank, opposite the post office in the western part of town.

Goulmime-bound grands taxis (Dh35) wait at a stand just south of the Hôtel Idou Tiznit roundabout. For Aglou Plage (Dh5) they leave from Ave Hassan II.

AROUND TIZNIT

Aglou Plage اكلو بلاج

Aglou Plage, 15km from Tiznit, is a long beach with good surf, but the strong undertow makes it dangerous for swimming most of the time. When Atlantic winds start blustering, it's a wild and woolly sort of place. It is still pretty undeveloped, with a raised walkway and behind it some seafront cafés, the best being **Idou Aglou** (☎ 028 613189; mains Dh50) an offshoot of the Tiznit hotel, which serves snacks (sandwiches Dh15) and a full restaurant menu. If you want to stay, **Le Chant du Chameau** (☎ 068 167255; www.chantduchameau.com; half-board per person Dh385) is a delightful French-Moroccan-run guest house at the south end of Aglou beach. A rust-red house, some fantasy tents, and a dramatic view of the beach and sea, they also offer excursions in the area and a weeklong course in *tadelakt,* the local plaster-work.

Grands taxis come out here from Tiznit (Dh5).

MIRLEFT ميرلفت

pop 6500

One of the most beautiful roads in the region runs south of Aglou Plage, with wonderful views of the ocean, rugged hills and the occasional empty cove. Then comes Mirleft, 38km southwest of Tiznit, 140km from Agadir, and one of the region's least promoted attractions. That, perhaps, explains why it remains popular with artists, musicians and people returning from some serious desert bashing, as well as Marrakshis wanting to hide away from the world. The climate is gentle, the air clear and the views magnificent. Mirleft is no longer untouched – it has a bank (with ATM) and post office – but unlike most tourism development in Morocco, all this is the doing of individuals, with not a large corporation or chain hotel in sight.

If at first the place seems uninspiring, the gentle bustle soon becomes contagious. A social morning coffee is followed by a trip to the beach – choose from Fish Beach, Camping Beach, Coquillage Beach, Aftas Beach, Plage Sauvage and Marabout's Beach, the last being the most dramatic with its *marabout*'s (saint's) tomb and savage-looking rocks. And then back to town for a walk along a short main street where you can find a billiards hall, arts and crafts, an argan product store, phone booths, cafés, restaurants and a small vegetable market.

Out of the village there are plenty of activities to keep you busy. The beach is good for surf casting (fishing) and hotels will help organise trips from fishing to desert excursions. If you have a head for heights, **Le Nid d'Aigle** (☎ 071 668505; www.nidaigle.com) is the place for hang-gliding. **Mirleft Ride** (☎ 061 441933; mirleftride.net) runs surf schools and organises both fishing trips and treks into the hills. **Anzid Quad Evasion** (☎ 077 756548; www.anzidquadevasion.com) runs a range of quad tours into the surrounding country.

Sleeping

our pick **Hôtel Resto Abertih** (☎ 028 710304, 072 225872; www.abertih.com; r per person with shared/private bathroom Dh100/150; wi-fi) This gorgeous blue-and-yellow cubist guest house has 11 rooms decorated in simple fabrics and strong colours, and is scattered around upper terraces. Below there is an atmospheric bar-restaurant, a favourite hang-out of the local expat community and where the amiable French proprietor holds court. The menu (Dh80) is simple and delicious: grilled fish, some Moroccan standards, apple tart and lobster on request.

Hôtel Atlas (☎ 028 719309; www.atlas-mirleft.com, in French; r per person without/with shower Dh120/150;) In the same vein – and the same family as Hotel Resto Abertih – is Hotel Atlas, with a great 1st-floor streetside balcony – fantastic in the early evenings. Vibrant aquamarines, yellows, terracottas and blues splash colour throughout the 17 rooms. There is also a huge roof terrace with sofas and cushions for summertime barbecues and music. Meals are usually only available on request.

Sally's Bed & Breakfast (☎ 028 719402, 061 469888; www.sallymirleft.com; d from Dh660) Created by a horse-loving Englishwoman, a gorgeous villa on the edge of the cliff above Tourga Beach, Sally's offers a home-stay feel, five rooms with private bathroom, and a sun terrace with Jacuzzi. Sally can arrange horse treks.

Les 3 Chameaux (☎ 028 719187; www.3chameaux.com; d/ste half-board Dh750/1000;) High on the hill, in a renovated 1930s military fort, is Mirleft's best address, a lovely guest house with fabulous views over the village to the sea beyond. Whitewashed wood and terracotta urns make for subdued and relaxed surroundings, the pool is heated, the restaurant relaxed and the whole place designed to help you unwind. No wonder Marrakshis come here for down time. Unusually, the suites are better value than the small rooms.

Eating

Apart from excellent restaurants at the above hotels, a number of cafés on the main street serve up some of the tonnes of caught fresh fish that end up here. On the souq street, **Restaurant Ayour** (☎ 028 719371; meals Dh85; lunch & dinner) serves reliable tajines and grilled fish. The newcomer in town, **Restaurant Tikiout** (☎ 028 719463; main street) is run by a former chef from Agadir and serves classic French dishes such as *salade de chevre* (goat-cheese salad), quiche and chicken livers.

Getting There & Away

Local buses and grands taxis between Tiznit and Sidi Ifni stop in Mirleft. There's also a daily bus to Agadir (Dh30).

SIDI IFNI سيدي إفني

pop 20,600

The eerily empty outpost of Sidi Ifni, with its fabulous decaying Spanish art-deco architecture, often shrouded in Atlantic mists in July and August, is a haunting reminder of Spanish imperial ambitions. At the heart of what was the Spanish Sahara, Sidi Ifni was once a base for slave-trading operations and later a large exporter of fish to the Spanish mainland.

Returned to Moroccan control only in 1969, the splendid esplanade and *calles* (streets) are still quintessentially Spanish in character. The town's unhurried pace of life attracts a surprising number of visitors, and it is an increasingly popular base for surfing and paragliding.

History

Spain acquired the enclave of Sidi Ifni after they defeated the Moroccan forces in the war of 1859. They christened their new possession Santa Cruz del Mar Pequeña, but seem to have been uncertain what to do with it as they did not take full possession until 1934. Most of Sidi Ifni dates from the 1930s and features an eclectic mix of faded art-deco and traditional Moroccan styles.

On Moroccan independence in 1957, Spain refused to withdraw, citing the fact that some 60% of the town's population was Spanish. The protracted dispute over territorial rights eventually ended with a UN-brokered agreement for Spain to cede the enclave back to Morocco in 1969. Santa Cruz was renamed Sidi Ifni, after a holy man buried in the town in the early 1900s. Ifni still celebrates 'Independence Day' (30 June) with a festival on the abandoned airfield.

Information

Banque Populaire (Ave Mohammed V) and **BMCE** (Ave Mohammed V) have currency exchange and ATMs. The nearby **post office** (Ave Mohammed V) still has a letterbox outside marked 'Correos – Avion/Ordinario' (Post – Air Mail/Ordinary) as well as an ATM. Internet is available at several places, including **Fabionet** (Ave Mohammed V; per hr Dh4), around the corner from the bus stands. For information on the town, check out www.geocities.com/ifnirocks.

Sights & Activities

The real draw of Sidi Ifni is its atmosphere, which has lured many a passing foreigner to settle. The small old Spanish part of town is one of the main attractions. At its heart is **Place Hassan II** (often still called Plaza de España), the colonial centrepiece consisting of a large square with a small park in the centre and surrounded by the main administration buildings: law courts (former church), royal palace, Spanish consulate and town hall, mostly in grand art-deco style.

Other interesting remnants of the colonial era include the **Hôtel Bellevue**, also on Place Hassan II, a nearby **lighthouse** and the **house in the form of a ship** on the edge of the cliff, which served as the Spanish Naval Secretariat (next to Hôtel Suerte Loca). There's also some funky art-deco architecture in the streets east of Place Hassan II.

The **beach** is big and rarely busy, though not always clean. At the south end is the port: Ifni's economy is based on small-scale fishing, most of the catch being sold in Aga-

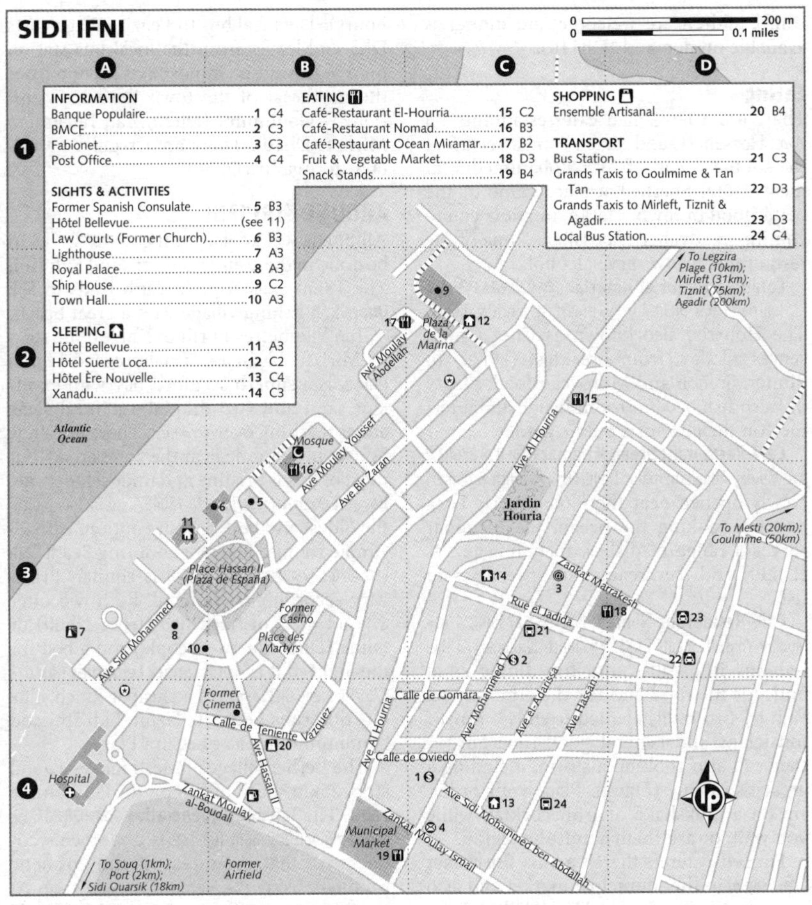

dir. The odd construction just offshore is the remains of an old land-sea conveyor that was used to take cargo from ships to the old Spanish port. There's some excellent surfing here – ask at Hôtel Suerte Loca (right) or Café Restaurant Nomad (p398) for their recommendations.

Sleeping

Like the rest of Ifni, most of the hotels have seen better days. The colonial-era **Hôtel Bellevue** (☎ 028 875072; Place Hassan II) was closed for renovation at the time of our visit.

Hôtel Ère Nouvelle (☎ 028 875298; 5 Ave Sidi Mohammed ben Abdallah; s/d Dh30/50) A centrally located cheapie, the rooms are simple but clean (go for the brighter top floor) with shared facilities. There's a terrace and a decent restaurant (mains Dh25 to Dh40).

Hôtel Suerte Loca (☎ 028 875350; fax 028 780003; Ave Moulay Youssef; s/d without shower Dh70/105, with shower Dh120/170) Stay here for the beach views, the variety of simple rooms with balconies, and the restaurant (set menu Dh56), popular for its French, Spanish and Moroccan cuisine, including paella.

our pick **Xanadu** (☎ 028 876718; www.maisonxanadu.com; 5 Rue el Jadida; r incl breakfast Dh330; 💻) The most charming address in town, a restored house in the centre, not far from Ave Mohammed V. Soothing colours, elegance and a subtlety about the many little touches in the five rooms put this French-Moroccan collaboration far ahead of anywhere else in

Ifni. Children are welcome and dinner is available on demand (Dh110).

Eating

There are a few small café-restaurants on Ave Hassan II, and snack stands set up at the southern end of Ave Mohammed V at dusk. Hôtel Suerte Loca has some of the better food in town – let them know you're coming in advance if possible. None of the restaurants below serve alcohol.

Café-Restaurant el Hourria (☎ 028 876343; Ave Al Hourria; mains Dh30-40; ⏰ breakfast, lunch & dinner) The Hourria, also known as Chez Omar, serves all day, from breakfast (Dh20) to dinner. French and Moroccan food, plenty of fresh fish, a calm room inside and a terrace on the edge of a public garden .

Café-Restaurant Ocean Miramar (☎ 028 876637; Ave Moulay Abdellah; mains Dh40-60; ⏰ lunch & dinner) Newly opened near the Hôtel Suerte Loca and overlooking the ocean, the Miramar serves a range of dishes, including pizzas (Dh30) and ice cream, but specialises in fish.

Café-Restaurant Nomad (☎ 062 173308; 5 Ave Moulay Youssef; meals Dh85; ⏰ lunch & dinner) This remains Ifni's all-round top dining spot, both for the food and for the atmosphere. Run by two multitalented friends – artists, musicians and general good-time guys – they can also cook up a storm, including a great fish tajine (Dh60). Place your order, sip on a milkshake or fruit cocktail while you wait, or ask them about the region.

For self-caterers there's a busy **fish market** (⏰ 5-8pm) in the municipal market and also a covered **fruit and vegetable market** (off Zankat Marrakesh). On Sunday, a large souq takes place 1km out of town on the road to the port.

Shopping

Crafts enthusiasts should drop in to the **Ensemble Artisanal** (Ave Hassan II). Look in the markets for *melhaf*, the very fine and colourful fabrics Saharan women use to cover themselves.

Getting There & Away

Buses depart from Ave Mohammed V, near Fabionet. Services for Agadir (Dh40, 3½ hours, one daily) and Marrakesh (Dh130, 8½ hours, one daily) both travel via Mirleft (Dh10, 30 minutes) and Tiznit (Dh25, 1½ hours). The local bus to Legzira Plage costs Dh3 and leaves from the local bus station on Ave Hassan I. Grands taxis leaving from the northeast of the town head to Tiznit (Dh23), Goulimime (Dh20), Tan Tan and to Mirleft (Dh10). There are irregular grands taxis to Agadir (Dh50).

AROUND SIDI IFNI

All hotels will advise on the many walks to be done in the countryside around Sidi Ifni. The 18km coastal path south leads to **Sidi Ouarsik**, a fishing village with a great beach.

Ten kilometres north of Ifni, on the road to Mirleft, El Gzira, usually called **Legzira Plage**, is a superb secluded bay with excellent sand and two dramatic natural **stone arches** reaching over the sea. There are a few houses in a huddle near the access road, but most of this is pristine and undeveloped. **Auberge Legzira** (☎/fax 028 780457; s/d Dh150/300) is the oldest and best sleeping option, with 20 simple rooms. The neighbouring **Beach Club** (☎ 070 522800; s/d Dh150/200) is similar. Prices vary according to demand. Both will offer a good meal of fresh fish (from Dh60) or tajine (Dh80 for two people) and a bed for the night. If it is open, **Snack Les Amies** (☎ 028 875510; menu Dh35) serves a cheaper lunch. The bus that runs between Tiznit, Sidi Ifni and Goulimime stops at Legzira Plage.

The Berber village of Mesti makes a good stop, 25km south of Ifni on the Goulimime road. The **Tafyoucht Cooperative** (☎ 028 867252; ⏰ 7am-noon & 2-6pm Tue-Sat) is a women's cooperative that produces oil and cosmetic products from the versatile argan tree. At the Mesti turnoff, the shop of **Miel Afoulki** (☎ 067 166418), a honey cooperative, sells some extraordinary local flavours, including orange and euphorbia.

GOULIMIME كلميم

pop 96,000

Once the 'Gateway of the Sahara', dusty derelict Goulimime (or Guelmim) sprang up as a border town where farmers from the fertile Souss traded with nomads from the south.

In its heyday, Tuareg, the so-called 'blue men' came in from the desert to buy and sell camels at the weekly souq. In the evenings, women performed the mesmerising *guedra* dance to the sound of a drumbeat. Nowadays you might only get a taste of this during the weeklong *moussem* (festival) and camel fair held here in July or August (the dates change).

But if you have come from the north, you will still recognise Goulimime as a border town. For the first time, you will see Saharawis in the majority. But there is little reason to stop, the only tourist sight being the unremarkable ruins of the early-20th-century Palace of Caid Dahman (admission free), in the street behind Hotel de la Jeunesse on Blvd Mohammed V. What's more, there is an undercurrent of aggression not found in places such as Tan Tan or Sidi Ifni.

The town is disturbed once a week by day-trippers from Agadir, who descend for the Saturday-morning souq, a few kilometres outside town on the road to Tan Tan. There is plenty of fruit there, and some overpriced souvenirs, but most day-trippers leave sorely disappointed.

Information

Place Bir Anazarane is the centre of town, and near here you'll find the post office, banks and the internet. The main bus and grand-taxi stations are about 1km north of here along Ave Abaynou.

The **tourist office** (☎ 028 872911; 3 Résidence Sahara, Route d'Agadir; 🕑 9am-noon & 2.30-6pm Mon-Fri) offers basic information on the town and trips further south.

Several places offer internet access, including **Anakhla Net** (Ave Youssef ibn Tachfine; per hr Dh8), next to Hôtel Salam.

Sleeping

You will only want to stay in Goulimime if necessary, as hotels are basic and some will be tricky for women (full as they are of trans-Saharan tradesmen). If you have transport, there is better accommodation outside town.

Fort Bou-Jerif (☎ 072 130017; www.fortboujerif.com; camp site Dh20 plus per person Dh30, r from Dh320, half board per person motel/hotel Dh340/440; 💻) Run by a French couple, this wonderful oasis of civilisation in the desert is about 40km northwest of town (the last 9km is rough *piste*). Built near a ruined French Foreign Legion fort, this compound has a range of sleeping options, from rooms in a motel

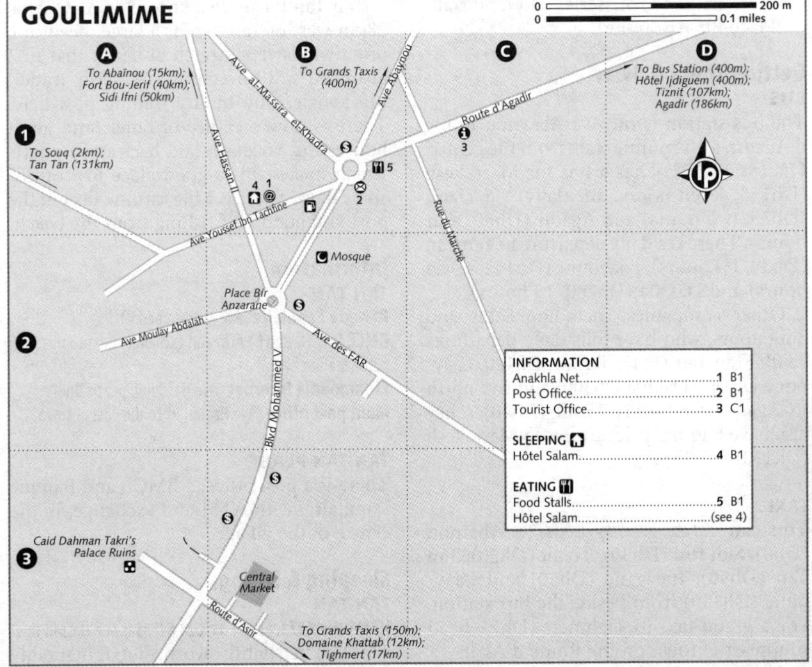

and a hotel, to nomad tents and camping spaces. There is also an excellent restaurant (menu Dh175), where you can try a camel tajine. They also offer 4WD trips to Plage Blanche, a little-visited and unspoiled stretch of beach 40km west of Bou-Jerif.

Domaine Khattab (☎ 061 176411; fax 028 873150; Km 12 Route d'Assa; camp site Dh50 plus per tent Dh25, bungalow s/d Dh150/200) A 20-hectare working farm with a tiny zoo is a little paradise for families. There are bungalow rooms and a camp site, as well as a restaurant serving simple set meals (Dh55). Bathroom facilities are spotless, and you can have a hot shower by candlelight (Dh10). The friendly owner organises treks in the region

Hôtel Ijdiguen (☎ 028 771453; Blvd Ibnou Battouta; s/d Dh75/150) Conveniently situated opposite the entrance to the bus station, this simple hotel has clean, tiled rooms (quieter at the back) and communal showers (Dh7).

Eating

The best food in town is served at **Hôtel Salam** (☎ 028 872057; fax 048 770912; Ave Youssef ibn Tachfine), where a traditional three-course Moroccan meal costs Dh85. Alcohol is available.

There are good rotisseries and food stalls on Place Bir Anzarane.

Getting There & Away

BUS

The bus station is off Ave Abaynou Route d'Agadir, a 10-minute walk from the centre. **CTM** (☎ 028 873855) has a bus for Marrakesh (Dh125, seven hours, one daily) via Tiznit (Dh35, two hours) and Agadir (Dh65, four hours). There is a daily departure to Tan Tan (Dh39, 1½ hours), Laâyoune (Dh142, seven hours) and Dakhla (Dh280, 15 hours).

Other companies, including Satas and Supratours, who have four daily departures south (Tan Tan Dh45; Tarfaya Dh120; Laâyoune Dh140; Dakhla Dh300) and five north to Agadir (Dh75) via Tiznit (Dh40). They also have four daily departures to Marrakesh (Dh130).

TAXI

You can catch grands taxis to Abaïnou (Dh8), Sidi Ifni (Dh20), Tiznit (Dh50), Tan Tan (Dh40), Inezgane (Dh50) and Laâyoune (Dh130) from beside the bus station. For a grand taxi to Tighmert (Dh7), head southeast of town on the Route d'Asrir.

TAN TAN & TAN TAN PLAGE طانطان

pop 50,000

South of Goulmime, across the dry Oued Drâa, you enter the cauldron of the Sahara proper. The 125km of desert highway to Tan Tan is impressive for its bleak emptiness and harsh *hammada* (flat, stony desert).

If you weren't stopped by security on the way in, you could probably drive along Tan Tan's main street without realising you had missed most of the town, which spreads south of the highway (known as Ave Hassan II within the town boundaries). The majority of the inhabitants are nomads who settled here, and blue robes are a big feature. The army and police presence is also noticeable, due to the disputed status of the Western Sahara (for more information, see p408).

The town was founded in the 1940s during the Spanish Protectorate, but had its moment in 1975, when it was the departure point for the Green March (see Marching to the King's Tune, p45). There's nothing much to do in Tan Tan, though a *moussem* does sometimes take place in September, or June. The Sunday souq is held 1.5km south of town.

Tan Tan Plage, also known as Al-Ouatia, 28km west of Tan Tan, is a large, beautiful, often windswept stretch of beach that first attracted a 19th-century Scottish trader, Mackenzie, who built a trading post here. There is now a choice of hotels and guest houses and a friendly laid-back atmosphere, which makes this a good place to stop for some days. There is a big sardine fleet in the port and good surf fishing from the beach.

Information

TAN TAN

Banque Populaire (Ave Mohammed V).
BMCE (Ave Hassan II) ATM and exchange, next to the Shell petrol station.
El-Hagounia Internet (Ave Hassan II; per hr Dh8)
Main post office (Ave Hassan II) To the east of town.

TAN TAN PLAGE

There is a post office, a BMCE and Banque Populaire, with ATM and exchange, in the centre of the village.

Sleeping & Eating

TAN TAN

Hôtel Bir Azzarane (☎ 028 877834; Ave Hassan II; s/d Dh50/80) A slightly worn, but remarkably

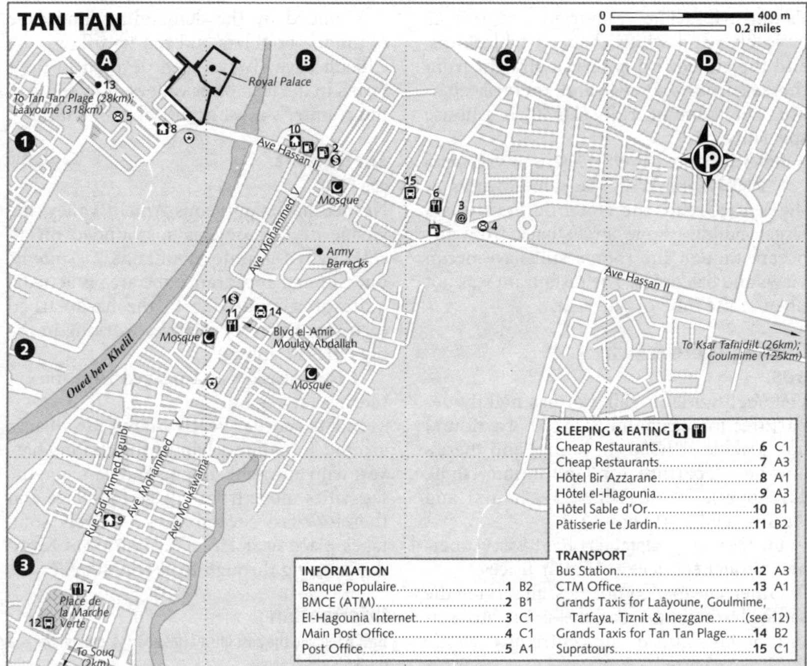

friendly place, next to the royal palace (and therefore extremely secure) on the west side of the river. Rooms are boxy and many have windows only onto the corridor but at this price…

Hôtel el-Hagounia (☎ 028 878561; Rue Sidi Ahmed Rguibi; s/d Dh50/80) The most convenient for the bus station, the rooms here are basic but clean, the showers are communal (Dh5) and the place is safe. Look out for the sign from the station.

Hôtel Sable d'Or (☎ /fax 028 878069; Ave Hassan II; s/d Dh150/200) Tan Tan's best hotel by far. The big, airy rooms come with comfy beds, TV and hot showers. There's also a popular café terrace and a rather bleak restaurant (meals Dh60 to Dh100) with too many plastic flowers.

Ksar Tafnidilt (☎ 063 233115; www.tafnidilt.com; tent per person Dh60, bivouac per person half-board Dh245, s/d half-board Dh470/740, breakfast Dh35, lunch & dinner Dh150; 🅿) If you have transport and can brave the *piste*, this large complex 6km from the road and some 20km north of Tan Tan, just before the police post, repays the effort. Tafnidilt has rooms, tents and camp space, and has an air of being very far from anywhere and plenty of ideas of ways to spend time.

There are dozens of cheap restaurants on Ave Hassan II, Ave Mohammed V and around the Place de la Marche Verte. To sip a mint tea, or for breakfast, head for the Hôtel Sable d'Or (left) or back up the hill to **Pâtisserie Le Jardin** (Ave Mohammed V).

TAN TAN PLAGE

Résidence Raja (☎ 028 879503; beside Place des Taxis; s/d Dh70/100) The best budget option in the village, the small rooms are more or less clean, the communal showers more or less hot and the welcome is friendly. Convenient location for transport.

our pick **Villa Océan** (☎ 028 879660/879641; villa ocean@menara.ma; Blvd de la Plage; s/d Dh150/200) This is a wonderful oceanfront guest house with a handful of spacious and airy rooms, some with ocean views, and clean bathrooms. It is good value, and has friendly French owners who know a huge amount about the region and can arrange trips to grottoes and other sights inland (half-day from Dh300) and fishing trips. The restaurant and terrace have blue-and-white checked tablecloths, and the grilled fish is served straight from the sea (meals Dh80) and there is alcohol. The tajine of fruits (Dh30) is a house speciality.

Hotel de France (☎ 028 879641; www.hotel-tantan.com; s/d Dh200/250) With the same owners as the Villa Ocean, the Hotel de France is a larger building, one street back from the ocean, though the rooms still have ocean views and balconies. The restaurant was not open at the time of our visit.

Getting There & Away

BUS

CTM (Ave Hassan II) in Tan Tan has nightly departures for Laâyoune (Dh120, 4½ hours) and Dakhla (Dh250, 14 hours) and there's another departure for Goulimime(Dh39, 1½ hours), Tiznit (Dh75, 3½ hours) and Agadir (Dh90, 4½ hours).

Further east, **Supratours** (Ave Hassan II) operates similar services at similar prices.

Other, cheaper companies, all serving the same destinations, use the main bus station 500m south of the centre at Place de la Marche Verte.

TAXI

You can catch grands taxis headed for Laâyoune (Dh100), Goulimime(Dh40) and occasionally Tarfaya (Dh60), Tiznit (Dh80) or Inezgane (Dh100), at the bus station at Place de la Marche Verte.

Grands taxis to Tan Tan Plage (Dh12) leave from the top of Blvd el-Amir Moulay Abdallah.

THE ANTI ATLAS الأطلس الصغير

The Anti Atlas remains one of the least visited parts of Morocco's mountainscape, which is surprising, as it is beautiful and close to Agadir. The mountains are the stronghold of the Chleuh tribes, who live in a loose confederation of villages strung across the barren mountains, some of them still far beyond the reach of any central authority. The region was only finally pacified by the French relatively recently, in the 1930s.

Moulded by the demanding landscape of granite boulders and red-lava flows, the Chleuh have always been devoted to their farms in the lush oasis valleys, now some of the country's most beautiful *palmeraies*.

TAFRAOUTE تافراوت

pop 5000

Nestled in the gorgeous Ameln Valley, the village of Tafraoute is surrounded on all sides by red-granite mountains. Despite its unassuming appearance the area is actually quite prosperous due to the hard-earned cash sent home by relatives working in the big cities or abroad.

It is a pleasant and relaxed base for exploring the region.

In late February/early March the villages around Tafraoute celebrate the almond harvest with all-night singing and dancing; the festivities move from village to village and therefore last several days. A lively souq takes place near Hôtel Salama from Monday evening through to Wednesday.

Information

BMCE (behind the post office) Has an ATM, though the system is often down.

Banque Populaire (Place Mohammed V; 🕑 Wed) Only opens for the souq.

Internet café (per hr Dh12) On the Tazekka road. Internet is also available at Hôtel Les Amandiers.

Post office (Place Mohammed V) Has pay phones outside.

Activities

CYCLING

The best way to get around the beautiful villages of the Ameln Valley is by walking or cycling. Bikes can be rented from Abid, next to Hôtel Salama, or from the shop **Artisanat du Coin** (per day Dh60). You can also rent mountain bikes or book a mountain-biking trip from **Tafraoute Adventure** (☎ 061 387173) and **Au Coin des Nomades** (☎ 061 627921). **Tafraoute Quadbikes** (☎ 070 409384) also have mountain bikes and helmets.

HAMMAMS

Tafraoute is an excellent place for a completely authentic hammam experience as most houses here still lack water. There are three hammams in the town, but locals prefer the old one, just behind the market. Second choice is the one off the main roundabout. All cost Dh10.

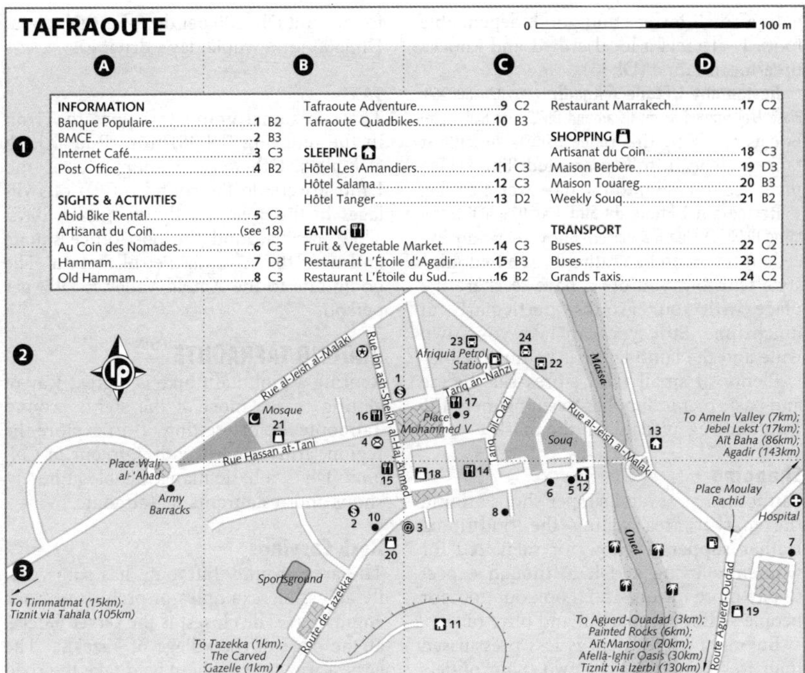

TREKKING

Tafraoute has plenty of possibilities for trekkers, though most of the walks are strenuous. Several companies and guides offer mountain-biking and trekking trips either up Jebel Lekst (2359m) or along the palm-filled gorges of Aït Mansour, leading towards the bald expanses of the southern Anti Atlas (see p444). **Tafraoute Aventure** (☎ 061 387173) has a good selection of maps, as does **Au Coin des Nomades** (☎ 061 627921) near Hôtel Salama, whose owner, Houssine Laroussi, is a respected climber. For short walks, you could get by with *Tafraout in Colours* (Dh7) a one-page brochure that shows villages and roads through the valley.

Sleeping

Hôtel Tanger (☎ 028 800190; r per person Dh30) A small, friendly nine-room hotel with very basic rooms and a communal bathrooms, situated in the centre of town near the souq. You can eat on the roof (Dh20 to Dh35) as long as the wind is blowing the right way from the *oued* (river).

Hôtel Salama (☎ 028 800026; s/d Dh199/298;) Completely renovated to higher standards, the long-established Salama mixes local materials with modern standards. The result is the best midrange hotel in town with great mountain views from the terrace, a restaurant serving full meals (Dh65) and a tea house overlooking the market square.

Hôtel Les Amandiers (☎ 028 800088; hotelles aman diers@menara.ma; s/d from Dh350/450;) Sitting like a castle on the crest of the hill overlooking the town, Les Amandiers wants to be Tafraoute's top hotel, in every sense. The kasbah-style hotel has spacious, if unglamorous rooms and a pool with spectacular views, as well as a bar and restaurant (set menu Dh120). Service, like much of the furnishings, is tired, but efficient.

Eating

Apart from the hotel restaurants, Tafraoute has a few good local places to eat.

Restaurant Marrakech (☎ 063 229250; Rue Annahda; set menu Dh55) A cheap, family-run restaurant on the road up from the bus station with a small terrace and good, dependable food. It attracts a local crowd and knocks up a mean tajine (Dh35).

Restaurant L'Étoile d'Agadir (☎ 028 800268; Place Mohammed V; meals around Dh75; 8am-6pm) Locals swear by this place for its succulent tajines, all beautifully presented. This is also *the* place to ease into the day over a coffee.

Restaurant L'Étoile du Sud (☎ 028 800038; set menu Dh90; lunch & dinner) They serve an excellent set menu in a rather kitsch Bedouin-style tent, but you often have to share the place with tour groups, particularly at lunch-time. Still, you can take your own wine and the lamb tajine is commendable.

Plenty of small food stores sell cheese and basic picnic supplies to supplement the fruit and veg available in the market.

Shopping

Tafraoute has several slipper shops around the market area selling the traditional leather slippers (yellow for men, red for women, starting at Dh75, though expect to pay more for quality). Look out, too, for people selling local argan and olive oil.

Buying a carpet here is less pressurised than in Marrakesh. The two main outlets are **Maison Touareg** (Rte Tazekka) and **Maison Berbère** (Rte Aguerd-Oudad). Alternatively you can also pick Berber carpets up from small dealers at the weekly **souq** on Rue Hassan at-Tani.

Artisanat du Coin (Sharia ibn ash-Sheikh al-Haj Ahmed), near the post office, specialises in Berber jewellery and other portable knick-knacks.

Getting There & Away

BUS

Buses depart from outside the various company offices on Rue al-Jeish al-Malaki.

Trans Balady runs buses to Agadir (Dh40, six hours, daily): the 2pm and 6.30pm departures go via Tiznit (Dh25, four hours), while the 6pm bus takes you through Aït Baha (Dh20, 2½ hours). Other companies serve these same destinations as well as Casablanca (Dh100, 14 hours, five daily) and Marrakesh (Dh90, seven hours, four daily).

CAR

You can hire a 4WD with a driver from Maison Touareg or Tafraoute Adventure for around Dh1200 per day plus fuel (about Dh3000 for a whole day's driving).

TAXI

The occasional grand taxi goes to Tiznit in the morning (Dh35) from Rue al-Jeish al-Malaki. Otherwise, station wagons and Land Rovers do the rounds of various villages in the area, mostly on market days. They hang around the post-office square and near the Afriquia Petrol Station. The going rate to the Ameln Valley is Dh7 per person.

AROUND TAFRAOUTE

Renting a mountain bike is a great way of getting to see most of the sights around Tafraoute. Before setting off to explore the region, arm yourself with *Tafraout in Colours* (Dh7), a basic map available at hotels, shops and restaurants in Tafraoute.

Rock Carvings

The area around Tafraoute has some easily accessible examples of prehistoric rock engravings. The closest is the **Carved Gazelle**, at the edge of the village of Tazekka. The easiest way to walk here is to take the road past the BMCE and the sports ground, then follow a footpath southwest through the palm groves. After about 15 minutes you reach the edge of the village. From here on you'll need a local to help you locate the gazelle, a simple engraving on the top face of a fallen block.

To find the other engravings at **Tirnmatmat**, you need to go further west towards Aït Omar (on Rte 7148). Just before the village, an unmarked *piste,* opposite a well, leads to Tirnmatmat, where you will find the *gravures* (engravings) along the riverbed (the local kids will lead you there, or engage a guide from Tafraoute). The village sits in a lovely spot and there is good walking in all directions.

Le Châpeau de Napoléon & the Painted Rocks

The village of Aguerd-Oudad, 3km south of Tafraoute, makes for a nice stroll or bike ride. On the way you pass the unmistakable rock formation known as Le Châpeau de Napoléon (Napoleon's Hat).

Take the signposted track through the village to the square, where there's a

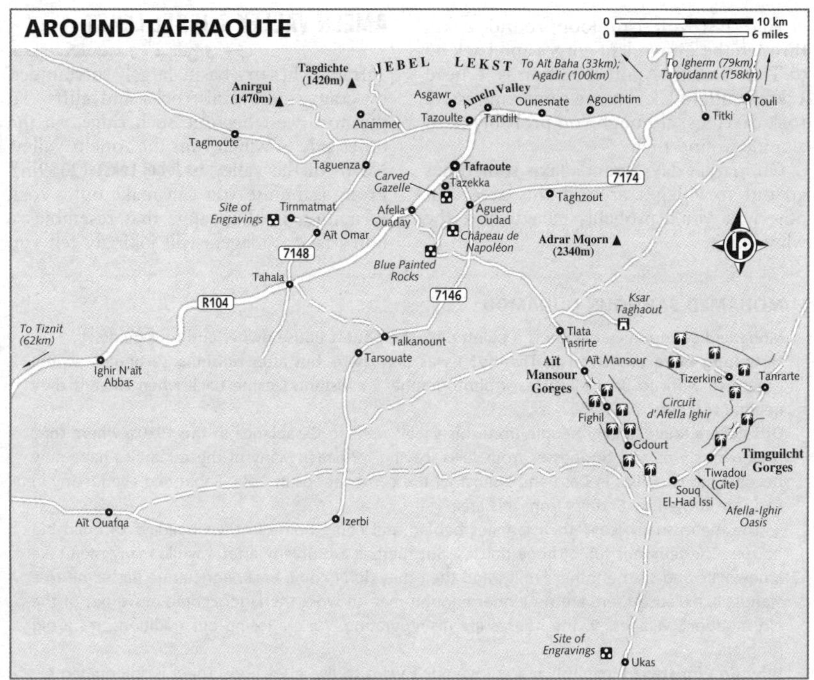

mosque. Veer right and left to get around the mosque, then follow the *piste,* power lines and river out into the flat countryside. After 1.5km you'll spot some pale-blue rocks to your left, the Pierres Bleues (Painted Rocks) – the work of Belgian artist Jean Verame.

Verame spray-painted the smooth, rounded boulders in shades of blue, red, purple and black in 1984 and, although the rocks have a faded air, they remain strange and impressive against the landscape. On a bike or driving you can follow a *piste* signposted off the new Tiznit Rd and then walk for 10 minutes.

Afella-Ighir

South of Tafraoute is the pretty oasis of Afella-Ighir. You could get there in a 4WD but it's preferable to drive part of the way, then leave the car and continue on foot or mountain bike. Alternatively make your base the village of Tiwadou, which has the wonderful **Auberge Sahnoun** (☎/fax 028 216609, 067 095376; m_sahnoun@hotmail.com; half board per person Dh150). This place has three simple rooms with shared facilities, is run by Mohamed Sahnoun, an expert mountain guide who organises three- to seven-day treks in his region but has also created his own museum – a room filled with objects that were part of local everyday life (p406). This would make an excellent remote base.

Leave Tafraoute on the new road past Aguerd-Oudad, turning left 3km south of the village, and travel roughly 19km over a mountain pass (snowed over in winter) through Tlata Tasrirte to the start of the dramatic Aït Mansour Gorges. The surfaced road continues south to the village of Aït Mansour at the bottom of the gorge, where **Chez Messaoud** (☎ 070 793567, 028 801245) serves tea and juice. If you book ahead, they will also prepare a lunch of couscous or tajine (Dh40). A little further, the river runs across the road, marking the start of the Afella-Ighir oasis. From here a track leads through a string of villages for about 10km to Souq el-Had Issi (30km from Tafraoute), a rather depressing town that has exploded with newly arrived workers for the nearby gold mine, Minas de Akka. From Souq el-Had Issi you can loop round 25km through the Timguilcht gorges and back up to Tlata Tasrite. Another option is to head 12km south to Ukas to see some impressive rock carvings, although you probably need a guide to find them.

On market days, grands taxis sometimes go out to villages around this area, but otherwise you'll probably have to hire the whole taxi.

AMELN VALLEY & JEBEL LEKST

جبل لكست و املن وادي

Tafraoute lies in a basin, largely surrounded by craggy gold-pink rocks and cliffs. To the northwest lies one such ridge, on the other side of which runs the Ameln Valley. North of the valley is **Jebel Lekst** (2359m). From Tafraoute you can make out a rock formation in this range that resembles a lion's face. Villagers will jokingly tell you

MOHAMED SAHNOUN OUHAMOU

Mohamed Sahnoun Ouhamou is a painter, teacher, guest-house owner and tour guide.

How long have you lived in Tiwado? I was born here, but after finishing secondary school I went to work in Beni Mellal as a photographer's assistant. I came back when I heard they needed teachers.

Did others leave? Many people from this valley went to Casablanca in the 1950s, where they took over shops and businesses from Jews leaving for Israel. Many of these families have now become industrialists in Casa and almost all the corner shops in Casa, Rabat and even many in Paris are owned by Berbers from this area.

The men usually leave their families behind and come home in their holidays to build big houses. The region is full of huge houses. But there is a problem: after a while many men take a new wife and start another family, and then they don't come back. Agriculture has come to a standstill, because there are no longer enough men to work the land. People move out of the old mudbrick villages, so the houses are disintegrating. We are losing our traditions, it's a big problem.

Why do you stay? I love this place; I wouldn't want to live elsewhere. There is still human exchange, and also something I value immensely: solidarity. If someone needs something, everyone helps. They have helped me build a house here and a small museum with objects from daily life as we used to know it, but which is now disappearing.

How can tourism help? Tourism and education are the only solutions. That's why I built my guest house. And that's why I work with local women who got left behind: in some villages, 90% or more are women, the rest are children and old men. The day the husband stops sending money the hardship begins. So we started a women's cooperative and now have 86 women learning about weaving and embroidery, and how to read and write. Before the women were not really valued, now they have some income as they sell their work to tourists. I'm the only man allowed to go in because I teach them. We also teach their children, so all now do at least three years primary school. But local people value 'commerce', trade, so from 14 years onwards, boys go into business. They don't care about education.

What is your favourite time? I like the *moussem* of Timguilcht in March. The tomb of the saint is in the village but people go on a pilgrimage to the nearby sacred mountain Afarkad because they believe he lives there. When you go up seven times, it is like going to Mecca. We all get together and it is a happy time.

What is your favourite area? I am fascinated by the rock carvings. I am a self-taught painter and I love what my ancestors did. I heard that the rock carvings here are the same as some found in Gabon. There are seven sites and I organise treks of three, five or seven days in the winter months to go and see them. I love introducing foreigners to this area. Going off to the mountains and total tranquillity.

What is your favourite restaurant? There are no restaurants here, but my wife cooks the best tajine. If people are walking in the area they can call us ahead, and she will cook for them as she does for me. It's simply the best.

Where do you go to relax? I love beauty, so I made this beautiful garden in the *palmeraie*: it is my little paradise.

that he is there to guard the women while their husbands are away working.

The Agadir road takes you to the valley, dotted with picturesque Berber villages. Four kilometres out of Tafraoute, the road forks with the right branch turning east up the valley towards Agadir. Shortly after, the village of **Tandilt** stands on the left of the road, across a *oued*. **Yamina** (☎ 070 523883; www.yamina-tafraout.com; half board per person Dh350) is run by a Berber woman and her French husband, who have created a unique fusion of styles, a Berber house as one rarely finds them, made of palm trees and plaster, of great beauty and comfort inside. Yamina prepares delicious and unusually light local dishes.

Another few kilometres on at **Oumesnate**, follow a signpost off to the left along a short *piste* and a footpath for the **Maison Traditionelle** (☎ 066 917768, 066 918145; maisondhote@gmail.com; admission Dh10; 8.30-sunset). This three-storey house (some 400 years old) has been open to the public since 1982. An elderly man, who was brought up in the house and was later blinded, will take you on a fascinating tour, telling tales of traditional life. Nearby, the current family home serves as a restaurant and guest house. Call ahead for a delicious lunch of couscous or tajine, served on a terrace overlooking the valley (Dh60), or to reserve a room (half board per person costs Dh200).

For trekking in Jebel Lekst and the Ameln Valley, see p444.

TATA طاطا

pop 40,000

Situated on the Saharan plain at the foot of Jebel Bani, Tata was an oasis settlement along the trade route from Zagora to Tan Tan. Close to the Algerian border, the small modern town has a garrison feel, dominated as it is by the military installations on the hill above.

The *palmeraie* is well worth exploring as is the old **kasbah**, converted into the Dar Infiane hotel (right) and a small museum.

More than anything in town, Tata is best as a base for off-the-beaten-track excursions, such as Akka oasis, desert camping and the rock engravings at Oum el-Alek, Tircht and Aït Herbil, among the finest in Morocco. Information is available from the tourist office at the **Maison du Patrimoine Tataoui** (☎ 072 130395; Ave Mohammed V) on the main road. If you are lucky enough to be staying at Dar Infiane, the staff can arrange fantastic excursions.

You'll find a post office and Banque Populaire (with an ATM) just off the main road, as well as the **Délégation de Tourisme** (Tourist office; ☎ 028 802076, 076 002699) with helpful staff.

Sleeping & Eating

Along Ave Mohammed V are several basic hotels, at around Dh40 per person.

Hôtel Renaissance (☎ 028 802225; fax 028 802042; Ave Mohammed V; d/ste Dh140/285) This big hotel is on both sides of the road, with the older part on one side and an annexe with comfortable minisuites on the other. The restaurant serves standard Moroccan dishes, but also has an alcohol license.

Le Relais des Sables (☎ 028 802302; fax 028 802300; s/d without bathroom Dh235/316, s/d with bathroom Dh375/466, ste Dh414) This is among the most comfortable accommodation options in town, and hence is popular with tour groups. It has a bar and a licensed restaurant, and rooms are arranged around flowery courtyards. It is worth the extra dirham even though the cheaper rooms are a bit poky.

our pick **Dar Infiane** (☎ 028 24437292, 061 610170; www.darinfiane.com; s/d incl breakfast Dh620/1000) Tata's old kasbah, deep in the *palmeraie*, has been turned into an extraordinary guest house by architect Latifa Maali and owner Patrick Simon. Off a carpet-strewn central courtyard lie six rooms and a fabulous terrace pool, overlooking thousands of palm trees. Excursions from Dar Infiane are carefully crafted and range from using a light aircraft to fly over the green veins of the southern oases to going with Latifa to local markets or visiting rock engravings with knowledgeable guides. Dinners (Dh200) are delicious, and evenings on the rooftop terrace are magical in the still of the Sahara night.

Café Restaurante el-Amal (Ave Mohammed V; mains Dh50) In an attractive spot next to the camp site, you can get a good square meal here of tajine or brochette.

Getting There & Away

Buses and taxis collect on Place Massira, one block east of Ave Mohammed V. A

Satas bus leaves every other day for Agadir (Dh80, eight hours, three daily) via Tiznit (Dh60, 6½ hours). Other companies operate departures to Marrakesh (Dh120, one daily), Agadir via Tiznit or Taroudannt (Dh70, five hours, one daily) and Goulimime (Dh60, six hours, one daily).

Grands taxis ply the routes to Tiznit (Dh100), Taroudannt (Dh70), Agadir (Dh90) and Goulimime (Dh80).

WESTERN SAHARA الصحراء الغربية

Ask any Moroccan about the status of the Western Sahara and they will insist it belongs to them, yet the UN is clear that this is still under dispute. Moroccan maps may show this region as part of their country, but few outside Morocco will agree.

This area largely comprises the former Spanish colonies of Spanish Sahara and part of Tarfaya. Travelling through here, one does marvel at the dispute. The towns are merely administrative centres, and the road cuts through a vast area of *hammada* – featureless, arid, inhospitable and uninviting.

Despite the 1991 ceasefire in the Polisario-backed war, the desert is still occupied by the Moroccan military. But, apart from the endless police roadblocks, going south to Dakhla is now a routine affair.

One of the benefits of the area's tax-free status is that petrol costs a couple of dirham less per litre than in the rest of the country. The first of the Atlas Sahara petrol stations is just south of Tarfaya.

History

Despite its windswept desolation, the Western Sahara has a long and violent history. Islamic missionaries started to spread Islam among the Zenata and Sanhaja Berber tribes in the 7th century, but it was only in the 13th century when a second wave of Arab settlers, the Maqil from Yemen, migrated to the desert that the whole region was Arabised.

By the 19th century the desert had new overlords again: the Spanish, who grabbed the Western Sahara and renamed it Rio de Oro, even though it had neither water nor gold. In reality, until 1934 it was Sheikh Ma

A DESERT OF DREAMS AND NIGHTMARES

The name is enough to make most of us dream. The Sahara, from the Arabic word *sahra*, meaning 'desert', is the world's largest arid zone. It is also a place of nightmares as only the well-attuned or well-prepared can survive in its 3 million sq miles of sand dunes, arid mountains and rock-strewn plains.

The 18th-century British geographer James Rennell summed up the challenge of the Sahara in his *Geographical Elucidations* (published 1790) when he wrote, 'Africa stands alone in a geographical view… its regions separated from each other by the least practicable of all boundaries, arid Desarts [sic] of such formidable extent, as to threaten those who traverse them, with the most horrible of all deaths, that arising from thirst!' The Romans never managed to cross the desert, preferring instead to patrol its northern borders. They had good reason for staying away: lucky travellers who survived the crossing described the trail of human and animal skeletons that lined the Saharan caravan routes.

European explorers of the late-18th and early-19th centuries, who struggled across the Sahara's vast expanses in search of answers to the geographical riddles of the Niger River, the legendary town of Timbuktu and the gold fields of West Africa, as often found themselves overwhelmed by the landscape as by raiders. And even in the 20th century, the desert thwarted European colonisers and idle travellers, as was so elegantly captured in Paul Bowles' novel *The Sheltering Sky*, in which a group of wealthy Americans run into increasing trouble, the further they move into the Sahara.

The dangers involved in Saharan travel give people who inhabit the wilderness a special place in society. Travel through southern towns such as Essaouira and Goulmime, both of which have depended on the desert and its trade, and you will meet some of them.

Essaouira's Gnawa people are descendants of slaves brought across the desert long ago from West Africa. While many slaves were sold in the souq and shipped across the Atlantic or north to Europe, others settled in the Atlantic port. Among them were men initiated into the mystic rites

El-Ainin and his son El-Hiba who controlled the desert and the nomadic tribes. After that, an uneasy colonial peace prevailed until Moroccan independence in 1957, when new nationalist fervour contributed to the establishment of the Polisario Front and the guerrilla war against the Spanish.

When it was abandoned by Spain in 1975, Morocco and Mauritania both raised claims to the desert region, but Mauritania soon bailed out. In November 1975 King Hassan II orchestrated the Green March – 350,000 Moroccans marched south to stake Morocco's historical claims to the Western Sahara (see boxed text, p45).

In the following years 100,000 Moroccan troops were poured in to stamp out resistance. When the Polisario lost the support of Algeria and Libya, it soon became clear that Rabat had the upper hand. The UN brokered a cease-fire in 1991, but the promised referendum, in which the Saharawis could choose between independence and integration with Morocco, has yet to materialise.

Ever since, Morocco has strengthened its hold on the territory, pouring money into infrastructure projects, particularly offshore oil exploration, and attracting Moroccans from the north to live here tax-free. The debate is still open but, to all intents and purposes, Morocco seems to have succeeded in its claim to the territory.

For the most up-to-date information on the Western Sahara, or the Saharawi Arab Democratic Republic (as they officially call themselves), log on to one of the following:

- www.un.org
- www.wsahara.net
- www.arso.org

Climate

Beyond the foothills of the Anti Atlas lies an arid hinterland starved of moisture. Here temperatures can exceed 45°C during the day and plunge to 0°C at night, while an annual rainfall of less than 125mm a year gives a suffocating aridity hovering between 5% and 30% – dry enough to mummify corpses. March to April sandstorms also plague the desert, making driving inadvisable. (The desert wind is known locally as the *chergui*, *irifi* or *sirocco*.)

Remember, it is important to carry a good supply of water. In winter it is also

of the south, often expressed through trance-inducing music. Some of these musicians – usually drummers – were pressed into service during the trans-Sahara crossing, creating rhythms to which the slave coffles moved.

No group is more closely associated with the desert than the Touareg, to whom the so-called blue men, found in places such as Goulimime, belong. Wrapped in their veils so only their eyes are exposed to the desert's withering condition, bound by strict tribal codes, Touareg have long had a reputation for toughness and independence. The 14th-century Arab traveller Ibn Battuta wrote of them, 'They wear face-veils and there is little good to say about them. They are a rascally lot.' That opinion was confirmed over the next few centuries by many who plied the Saharan caravan routes, whose goods or lives were often taken by Touareg.

If the idea of survival in such an inhospitable place is part of what makes the Saharan dream so potent, so too is the mysticism associated with its vast wastelands. It wasn't by chance that Moses found guidance in a desert. Jesus went to the desert (though not the Sahara) for 40 days to prepare himself, early Christian hermits headed there to draw themselves closer to divinity, the Prophet Mohammad brought his message of a new religion out of the desert. And in Morocco, many reformist movements came out of the desert fringes, most notably the reformist zeal of the Almoravids and Almohads.

Yet for many visitors, the main attraction is nothing more complicated than the pure beauty of the landscapes. Morocco has few true sand dunes (Algeria and Libya have some of the best of the Saharan dunes), but it does have thousands of kilometres of arid land. You need only head south of Goulimime, to Tan Tan and Tarfaya, or over to the sandier regions of the southeast, to have a sense of the Sahara, of the cool beauty of its sunrise, the terrifying brilliance of the midday sun and the extraordinary calm of dusk over a land that seems empty but is not and that stretches not just as far as the eye can see but further than most visitors can even imagine.

essential to carry a warm sleeping bag and some warm clothing as desert nights can be bitterly cold.

Dangers & Annoyances

In both Laâyoune and Dakhla you will be more aware of the military and police, both of whom remain sensitive to photography around military installations.

Similarly, they will not take too kindly to the photographing of the depressing refugee camps in both cities, where many Saharawis still live. The busy red-light district in Dakhla, opposite the military headquarters and barracks, is also off-limits to Westerners.

If you are crossing the border into Mauritania, you will need to engage a local guide (on the insistence of the Mauritanian authorities) to negotiate the off-*piste* road to Nouâdhibou due to the very real danger of landmines.

Language

In the Western Sahara, Arabic and French are spoken almost universally. As a previous Spanish Protectorate, the more common second language was, until recently, Spanish, a habit that lingers on with the older generation. English is also spoken, due to the UN presence.

Getting There & Away

There is no officially designated border between Morocco and the Western Sahara, and Morocco treats the region as an integrated part of the country.

Laâyoune is served by regular flights from Casablanca. More infrequent flights from Agadir and Dakhla are also available. There is a small airport at Dakhla, which operates one flight a week to Agadir and a few more to Casablanca.

There is talk of running buses to the border from Dakhla, but for now you need to arrange good 4WD transport. Take plenty of water and food (enough for two days), and allow at least six hours to cover the 380km. Hôtel Erraha (p415) in Dakhla is the best local source of information regarding the border. Jeep drivers can be found hanging out near the Dakhla checkpoint, and in the Hôtel Sahara, and charge around Dh500 to Dh600 per person for border crossings. During the winter season (November to March) overland trucks may consider giving you a lift.

Once you arrive at the border you will need to go through two customs points, one on the Moroccan side and the other in Mauritania.

It is possible to have a Mauritanian visa issued in Rabat, but you are strongly advised to get one before arriving in Africa.

See p484 for more on crossing into Mauritania.

Getting Around

Supratours and CTM both operate buses to Laâyoune and Dakhla, although Supratours provides the faster and more efficient service.

TAN TAN TO TARFAYA

The 225km drive from Tan Tan to Tarfaya takes you across a monotonous stretch of desert highway. The road is good and the traffic relatively light.

Along the route you'll see anglers' huts perched on the cliff tops (many of these anglers sell their catch by the roadside) and, further south, herds of camels wandering slowly through the *hammada*. Sidi Akhfennir, 110km further on, is a good place to stop, either at one of the garages or at a café serving grilled fish straight from the sea.

If you want to hang around longer, the **Auberge Pêche et Loisirs** (☎ 061 211983; http://peche.sudmaroc.free.fr, in French; per person half-board Dh330) has clean and comfortable rooms and is run by a man passionate about fishing, who organises trips on the nearby Naïla Lagoon or ocean.

The area just north of Tarfaya is extremely scenic, with wild, untouched Atlantic beaches and a series of surreal shipwrecks, clearly visible from the road, rising from the waters.

TARFAYA طرفايه

pop 4500

The tiny fishing port of Tarfaya was the second-largest town in the Spanish-controlled zone of the same name. The original settlement seems to have been created in the late 19th century by a Scottish trader, Donald Mackenzie, who built a small trading post on a rock just off-shore, which he called Port Victoria. When the Spanish took over, they appropriated the building, now known as Casa Mar (house in the sea; see below). Today Tarfaya is on the cusp of big developments, with Spanish and Jordanian developers planning projects, and rumours of a relaunch of the ferry connection to the Canary Islands.

But Tarfaya will forever be associated with the French pilot and writer Antoine de Saint-Exupéry. In 1926 he began flying the mail service down from France to St Louis in Senegal. Tarfaya, then known as Cap Juby, was one of the stops. In 1927 he was appointed station manager for Tarfaya and he spent a couple of years here, writing for *Courrier Sud* (Southern Mail) and dreaming up his most famous story, *Le Petit Prince (The Little Prince),* which features a pilot lost in the desert. In 1944 Saint-Exupéry disappeared over Corsica while on a photographic reconnaissance.

The **Casa Mar** is abandoned but still standing and can be easily reached at low tide. But like much of the deep south, Tarfaya is short on specific sights, but what there is, is predominantly dedicated to Saint-Exupéry. A **monument** was erected in his memory at the north end of the beach: a Bréguet 14 biplane, the sort of plane he used to fly. Nearby is the **Musée Saint-Exupéry** (Ave Mohammed V; 🕑 8.30am-4.30pm), which tells the story of his life and of the airmail service he helped run. The descriptions are in French.

Each year, the service is remembered in the Rallye Saint-Exupéry, when planes fly from Toulouse to Saint Louis and back. In October 2007, they landed at Tarfaya to commemorate the 80th anniversary of the writer taking up his post and the 25th year of the rally.

Tarfaya does have a couple of simple hotels, the better being the **Bahja** (☎ 028 895506; Blvd Bir Anzarane; s/d Dh100/130). The man responsible for the museum, Sadat Melainime also rents **three rooms** (☎ 061 079488; Ave Mohamed V; s/d Dh150/250). Both of these places can serve up a good fish tajine. Other food options revolve around the main street, where a couple of cafés serve up fried fish.

A new ferry service which opened in December 2007 between Tarfaya and Fuerteventura brought hope of a property boom as investors started buying in the hope of turning the sleepy place into a resort, but the ferry ran aground just offshore on 30 April 2008 and there is no word from the operators, **Armas** (www.navieraarmas.com), about relaunching the service. Until they do, transport to Tarfaya is limited to the buses and occasional grands taxis that run north up to Tan Tan and south to Laâyoune. There are daily services, but timetables are erratic at best.

LAÂYOUNE (AL-'UYUN) العيون

pop 200,000

The Spanish created Laâyoune as an outpost from which to administer the nearby Bou Craa phosphate mines. The Moroccans have had bigger ambitions and have spent more than US$1 billion turning it into the principal city of the Western Sahara. Now neither Saharawi nor Spanish, its population is mostly Moroccans, lured from the north by the promise of healthy wages and tax-free goods.

As a government centre and a military garrison, Laâyoune – let's not forget, like the rest of the region it is officially under foreign occupation – doesn't make much of a destination. But whether you're heading north or south, distances here are so great that you may have to stop.

Orientation

The town's showpiece is the vast Place du Méchouar (where bored youths hang about at night), but there is no obvious centre. The post office, banks and most hotels are along either Ave Hassan II or Blvd de Mekka.

Buses mostly gather at offices towards the southern end of Blvd de Mekka. Grand taxi stations are scattered about town.

Information

There are several banks with ATMs and exchange facilities near the intersection of Blvd Hassan II and Blvd Mohammed V.

Banque Populaire (Place Dchira). Has another branch on Blvd Mohammed.

BMCE (Place Hassan II) Has another branch at Place Dchira.

Délégation Régionale du Tourisme (ONMT; ☎ 028 891694; Ave de l'Islam; 🕑 9am-noon & 2.30-6.30pm Mon-Fri) Few handouts, but the staff are anxious to please.

Post office (Place Hassan II; 🕑 8.30am-noon & 2.30-6.30pm Sat-Thu, 8.30-11.30am & 3-6.30pm Fri) Also has public phones with international connection. There is a smaller (post only) branch on Place Dchira.

Sahar@Network (Blvd de Mekka; per hr Dh10) Internet access.

W@dernet (Blvd de Mekka; per hr Dh8) Internet access.

Wafa Bank (cnr of Ave Hassan II & Blvd Mohammed)

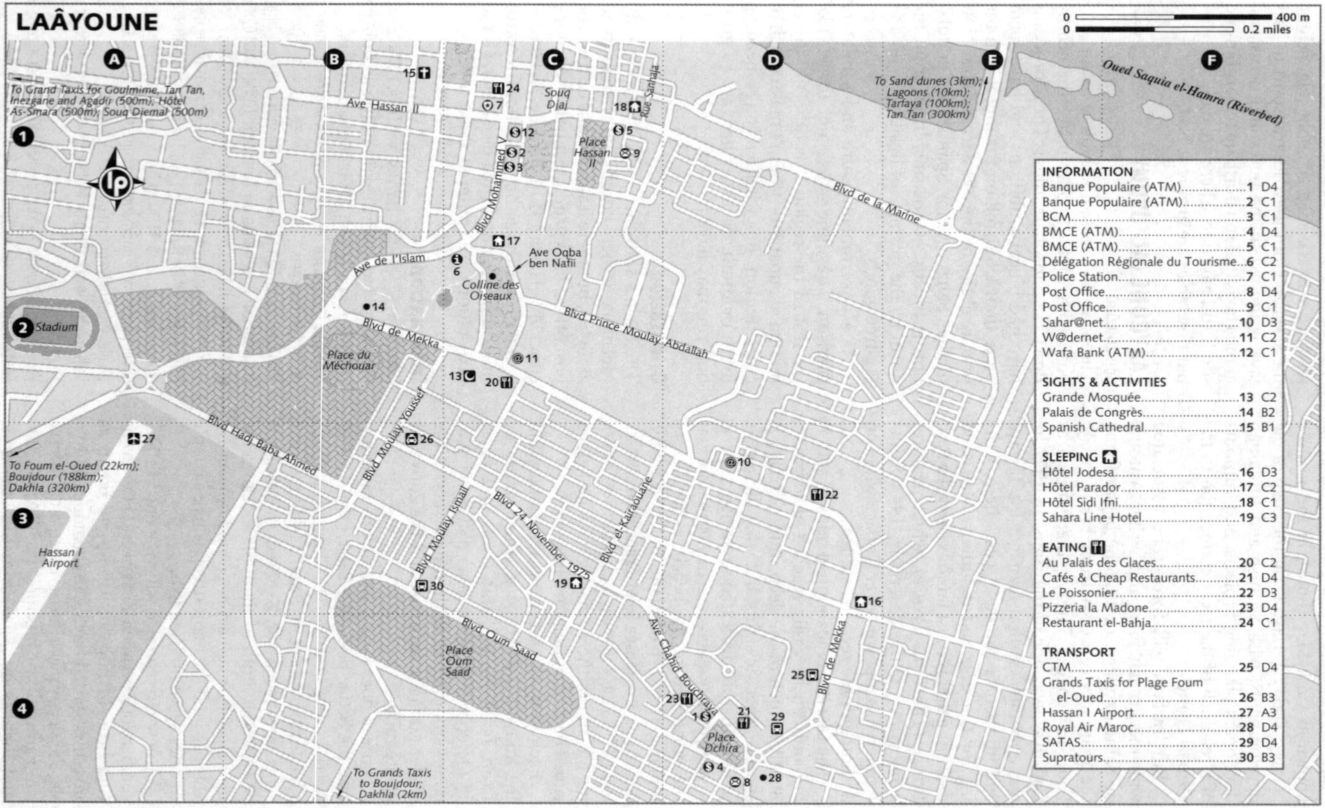
LAÂYOUNE
0 400 m
0 0.2 miles
A
B
C
D
E
F
1
2
3
4
To Grand Taxis for Goulmime, Tan Tan, Inezgane and Agadir (500m); Hôtel As-Smara (500m); Souq Djemal (500m)
To Sand dunes (3km); Lagoons (10km); Tarfaya (100km); Tan Tan (300km)
Oued Saquia el-Hamra (Riverbed)
Ave Hassan II
Souq Djaj
Rue Sanhaja
Place Hassan II
Blvd Mohammed V
Blvd de la Marine
Ave de l'Islam
Ave Oqba ben Nafii
Colline des Oiseaux
Stadium
Blvd de Mekka
Blvd Prince Moulay Abdallah
Place du Méchouar
Blvd Moulay Youssef
Blvd Hadj Baba Ahmed
To Foum el-Oued (22km); Boujdour (188km); Dakhla (320km)
Hassan I Airport
Blvd Moulay Ismail
Blvd 24 November 1975
Blvd el-Kairaouane
Blvd Oum Saad
Place Oum Saad
Ave Chahid Bouchraya
Place Dchira
To Grands Taxis to Boujdour; Dakhla (2km)
INFORMATION
Banque Populaire (ATM) 1 D4
Banque Populaire (ATM) 2 C1
BCM 3 C1
BMCE (ATM) 4 D4
BMCE (ATM) 5 C1
Délégation Régionale du Tourisme 6 C2
Police Station 7 C1
Post Office 8 D4
Post Office 9 C1
Sahar@net 10 D3
W@dernet 11 C2
Wafa Bank (ATM) 12 C1
SIGHTS & ACTIVITIES
Grande Mosquée 13 C2
Palais de Congrès 14 B2
Spanish Cathedral 15 B1
SLEEPING
Hôtel Jodesa 16 D3
Hôtel Parador 17 C2
Hôtel Sidi Ifni 18 C1
Sahara Line Hotel 19 C3
EATING
Au Palais des Glaces 20 C2
Cafés & Cheap Restaurants 21 D4
Le Poissonier 22 D3
Pizzeria la Madone 23 D4
Restaurant el-Bahja 24 C1
TRANSPORT
CTM 25 D4
Grands Taxis for Plage Foum el-Oued 26 B3
Hassan I Airport 27 A3
Royal Air Maroc 28 D4
SATAS 29 D4
Supratours 30 B3

Sights & Activities

The Moroccan government wants the grand Place du Méchouar to attract our attention, but the **Palais de Congrès** (Blvd de Mekka) and new **Grande Mosquée** (Moulay Abdel Aziz Mosque; Blvd Moulay Youssef) are unlikely to have you reaching for your camera. The original Spanish town runs along the riverbed Saquia el-Hamra over which presides the startling **Spanish cathedral**, (now closed) on Ave Hassan II, with its huge, rounded white dome mimicking the local architecture. To the southwest of the cathedral, bustling **Souq Djemal** is the liveliest area of town and has some of the best food stalls.

More alluring are the kilometres of dunes north and west of town, clearly visible from several vantage points in and around the city. To get in among them, take a 4WD off the road to Tarfaya (local travel agents can organise trips). Lagoons to the north of town are great for birdwatching.

Sleeping

The UN maintain a significant presence in Laâyoune and tend to fill the better hotels, so you would be wise to book ahead. Unsurprisingly, good accommodation in this desert outpost is relatively expensive by Moroccan standards.

BUDGET

Hôtel Sidi Ifni (☎ 028 893488; 12 Rue Sanhaja, Souq Djaj; s/d Dh35/55) By far the best of the real cheapies, this place is very local in flavour. Showers here use cold, salty bore water – luckily there are public showers opposite.

Hôtel Jodesa (☎ 028 992064; fax 048 893784; 223 Blvd de Mekka; s/d without shower Dh100/144, with shower Dh144/155) Centrally located north of Place Dchira, this modern hotel is a good cheaper option. Rooms are basic, but reasonably spacious and some have private bathroom.

MIDRANGE & TOP END

Hôtel Parador (☎ 028 892814; fax 028 890962; Ave de l'Islam; s/d Dh1100/1400;) A survivor from Spanish days, built in hacienda style around gardens, it has a faintly colonial bar and a good, if expensive, restaurant (set menu Dh200). The rooms are equipped with all the creature comforts you'd expect and each has a small terrace.

Sahara Line Hotel (☎ 028 995454; fax 028 990155; Blvd el-Kairaouane; s/d/tr Dh399/506/614;) A reliable three-star option, the swish, carpeted air-conditioned rooms have fridge, bathrooms and TV. There's a restaurant on the top floor (breakfast Dh50), but no bar.

Eating

There are many cafés and simple restaurants around Place Dchira, where Dh20 should get you a filling meal. More lively food stalls can be found at the Souq Djemal.

The hotel restaurants at the Sahara Line Hotel and the Parador offer more upmarket meals.

Au Palais des Glaces (☎ 028 980476; Blvd de Mekka; breakfast Dh10-17) A modern and very European-style tearoom, patisserie and ice-cream parlour, with the best ice creams in town. A good place to start the day, too.

Restaurant el-Bahja (Blvd Mohammed V; set menu Dh20; lunch & dinner) Simple grilled meat – lamb, certainly, camel perhaps – is served without ceremony here, but with plenty of grease and chips. A good place for when you've had enough of fresh fish.

Pizzeria la Madone (☎ 028 993252; 141 Ave Chahid Bouchraya; pizzas Dh40-60) A cosy place to eat in, though they also do a brisk takeaway trade. Thin-crust pizzas, *harira* (lentil soup), salads, omelettes are all excellent, as is the pasta marinara.

Le Poissonier (☎ 028 993262, 061 235795; 183 Blvd de Mekka; meals Dh60-90; lunch & dinner) Apart from the restaurants at the top-end hotels, this is the best restaurant in town and if you have to be in Laâyoune, there are worse ways of spending your time than over a fish soup or lobster in this friendly place.

Getting There & Away

AIR

The **Hassan I Airport** (☎ 028 893346) is located 2km south of Laâyoune. **Royal Air Maroc** (RAM; ☎ 028 894071; Place Dchira) operates three direct weekly flights to Casablanca (1½ hours) and one to Dakhla (one hour). **Regional Air Lines** (☎ in Casablanca 022 538080; www.regionalmaroc.com) has flights to Agadir (1¼ hours).

BUS

CTM (Blvd de Mekka) has a morning bus to Dakhla (Dh141, seven hours, one daily) and services to Agadir (Dh190, 10½ hours, three daily) via Tan Tan (Dh100, four hours) and Goulimime (Dh142, seven hours, three daily).

Supratours (Place Oum Essad) has buses to Marrakesh (Dh270, 16 hours, two daily), and to Dakhla (Dh150, nine hours, one daily).

Satas (Blvd de Mekka) will get you to Tiznit (Dh130, nine hours, two daily), Agadir (Dh190, two daily), Dakhla (Dh140, one daily) and Tan Tan (Dh100, two daily).

TAXI

Catch grands taxis north to Tan Tan (Dh100), Goulimime (Dh130) and Inezgane (for Agadir; Dh180) about 1.5km east of Place Hassan II along Ave Hassan II. A local red-and-white petit taxi will take you there for Dh5 or so; ask the driver for Place Tan Tan.

Grands taxis heading south to Boujdour (Dh70) and Dakhla (Dh170) leave from 'Place Boujdour' in the southern suburbs. A petit taxi there also costs about Dh4.

The taxi lot for Foum el-Oued (Dh8), the nearest beach, is more conveniently located just south of the Great Mosque.

DAKHLA (AD-DAKHLA) الداخلة

pop 40,000

'Marrakesh is for tourists', said one Moroccan blog, 'but Dakhla is for travellers'. But not for long: French newspaper *Le Figaro* didn't put Dakhla on its list of cool destinations on a whim. Things are starting to happen down here.

Established by the Spanish in 1844 and formerly called Villa Cisneros, Dakhla lies just north of the Tropic of Cancer on a sandy peninsula stretching out 40km from the main coastline. It's a very lonely 520km drive from Laâyoune (more than 1000km from Agadir) through endless *hammada*. It is the sort of journey you would think would only be worthwhile if you were en route to Mauritania or trying to get lost: after so many hours of driving, it is tempting to imagine that you are arriving at the end of the earth. And yet Dakhla is the focus of some significant and upmarket hotel projects and feels less remote than many towns in the south.

Dakhla's whitewashed, arcaded streets are rather soulless but it is a pleasant enough place and the government continues to pour money into the town. New apartment blocks are constantly stretching the town boundaries, roads are being paved, the huge new port is home to Morocco's largest fishing fleet, day-trippers from the nearby Canary Islands scuttle through town looking for Moroccan exotica and it won't be long before some of the Marrakesh set bring their private jets down for a weekend.

The old **Spanish lighthouse** at Point Durnford is good for some fantastic views. Otherwise it's out into the desert for some four-wheel driving, or down to the beach to windsurf, kitesurf, paraglide or go fishing (all hotels can help arrange these activities).

Orientation & Information

Dakhla is reasonably easy to get around, with the bus offices, central post office and most hotels and cafés situated around the old central market.

The **tourist office** (☎ 028 898228; 1 Rue Tiris; ⏰ 8.30am-noon & 2.30-6.30pm Mon-Fri) is up a side street to the east of the CTM office.

Dakhla has a number of banks with ATMs, including **BMCE** (Ave el-Walaa) and **Crédit du Maroc** (Ave Mohammed V) on the road running along the seafront. You'll also find internet cafés dotted around town charging Dh10 per hour.

There are plenty of mechanics, mostly in the newer part of town to the southwest, who can service vehicles before a trek south.

Sleeping & Eating

Café Restaurant Samarkand (☎ 028 898316; Ave Mohammed V; mains Dh40-80) The favourite place to hang out for an hour or two under the pergolas, with fairy lights, mock gaslights and stone lions. They usually serve coffee and croissants in the morning and good salads, fish and omelettes later.

Casa Luis (☎ 028 898193; 14 Ave Mohammed V; meal around Dh100) A good Spanish restaurant where you can enjoy an excellent octopus salad, a decent paella and beer or wine to wash it down.

Hôtel Aigue (☎ 028 897395; Ave Sidi Ahmed Laaroussi; s/d Dh60/80) Peach paintwork, hot water and standards of cleanliness above the norm make this hotel, just south of the CTM office, one of Dakhla's better budget deals. Rooms are bright; facilities are communal.

Sahara Regency (☎ 028 931555; www.sahararegency.com; Ave al-Walae; s/d/ste incl breakfast Dh660/880/1100; ❄ 🏊 💻) Some time soon there will be a Marrakesh-style five-star hotel, but for now this modern four-star resort hotel, 100m from the gorgeous bay, is Dakhla's best. The colourful spacious rooms have all the modern amenities, and all kinds of water sports, including fishing and kitesurfing, are available. The hotel has no less than three bars and a good rooftop restaurant. Like elsewhere in Dakhla, bathrooms don't always have water.

Hôtel Erraha (☎ /fax 028 898811; Ave Beuchekroune; s/d Dh180/220) This spick-and-span hotel boasts 24-hour hot water and spacious rooms, some with kitchenettes. Its location about 1km southwest of the centre, near the new Edderhem Mosque, is a pain if you want to hang out in town, but convenient for grand taxi and the SAT and Supratour stations.

Hôtel Doumss (☎ 028 898046; fax 028 898045; Ave el-Walaa; s/d Dh250/300) Large rooms have bathrooms and balconies, but are somewhat dull and functional. Unexpectedly, there is also a bar, which closes at 7pm. To find it, head north to the water tower and keep going for another 200m.

Getting There & Away

Aéroport Dakhla (☎ 028 897049) is just west of town; a petit taxi to a hotel costs Dh4, although most are within walking distance. **RAM** (☎ 028 897049; Ave des PTT) operates three flights a week to Casablanca, one of them stopping in Agadir and two in Laâyoune. **Regional Airlines** (☎ 082 000080) has four flights a week to Casablanca, three to Laâyoune, two to Las Palmas in the Canaries, and one to Agadir.

CTM (Blvd 4 Mars), **Supratours** (Ave Mohammed V), and **Satas** (Blvd de Walae) have daily services to Laâyoune (Dh141, eight hours), Tan Tan (Dh250, 14 hours) and Agadir (Dh340, 21 hours); tickets should be booked ahead.

Grands taxis for Laâyoune (Dh170) leave from an area called Al-Messira at the southwest end of town.

Trekking

Not so long ago, trekking in Morocco was the preserve of dedicated climbers and a few intrepid amateurs on their way to the top of Jebel Toubkal, which at 4167m is North Africa's highest peak. But things have changed and now there are treks for all times of year and all levels of fitness: treks to test the fittest athletes and others where you can have your bags carried, arrive to find your lunch laid out for you and sleep in luxury.

Morocco is blessed with some of the world's most dramatic and beautiful mountains, many of which only see a handful of travellers every year; others remain totally unexplored by foreigners. Morocco's broad range of climates is also a blessing for trekkers. When December snows make Jebel Toubkal impossible to trek, Jebel Sarhro, on the southern side of the Atlas and at the edge of the Sahara, is passable. When the summer sun makes the Rif too hot to trek, it also melts the snow off Toubkal, enticing crowds up to the summit.

Not every trekking area or mountain range is covered in this chapter. Instead we have selected some of what we think are the most exciting and interesting treks in a country overendowed with walking possibilities. Some are obvious – the ascent of Toubkal, for instance. Others, such as the M'Goun walk, are less so, but no less extraordinary.

As trekking in Morocco has grown in popularity, so have the options available to the walker. You could buy a package from home, including flights and transfers, guides and food. Or you could turn up at the trailhead, find a guide, hire mules and head off into the Berber heartland. Whichever you choose, trekking is often the highlight of any visit to Morocco.

HIGHLIGHTS

- Head for the heights and the summit of **Jebel Toubkal** (p431), the highest mountain in North Africa
- Opt for the gentler walking on offer in the little-visited cedar forests of the **Rif Mountains** (p440)
- In **Jebel Sarhro** (p446) you will find some of the most rugged and stunning scenery in Morocco, perfect for winter walking
- Get away from the crowds in the remote **M'Goun Massif** (p437) and be inspired by its spectacular valleys and beautiful villages
- Climb to the remote **Tichka Plateau** (p435) in spring and find yourself wading through meadows of wild flowers

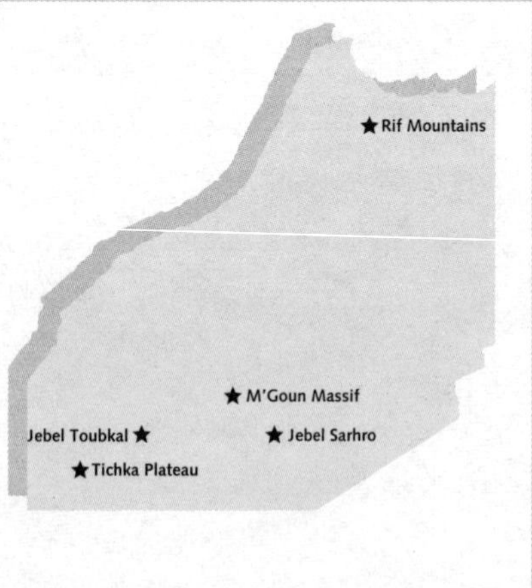

GETTING STARTED

MAPS

Morocco is covered by a 1:100,000 and also a 1:50,000 topographical map series. Some of the 1:50,000 series are unavailable to the public (the coverage of the Jebel Sarhro, Eastern High Atlas and Middle Atlas is patchy). Due to the restrictions placed upon map purchases, travellers exploring wide areas are advised to stick to the 1:100,000 series. The Soviet military also made 1:100,000 maps of Morocco, and although marked in Cyrillic script these maps are as topographically accurate as any available.

Division de la Cartographie (☎ 037 708935; cnr Ave Moulay Youssef & Ave Moulay Hassan I, Rabat; www.acfcc.gov.ma, in French; 🕑 9am-3.30pm Mon-Fri), of the Moroccan Survey, stocks a range of topographical Moroccan maps and town plans, many prepared by the French Institut Géographique National (IGN). Staff can be reluctant to sell maps to regions they consider to be sensitive. For some of these, you may need to make a written request (in French), explaining who you are and why you want the maps. A panel meets on Friday, so you'll get a decision on Friday afternoon or (more likely) Monday morning. You may need your passport for ID. Maps of the Toubkal region of the High Atlas are usually available over the counter

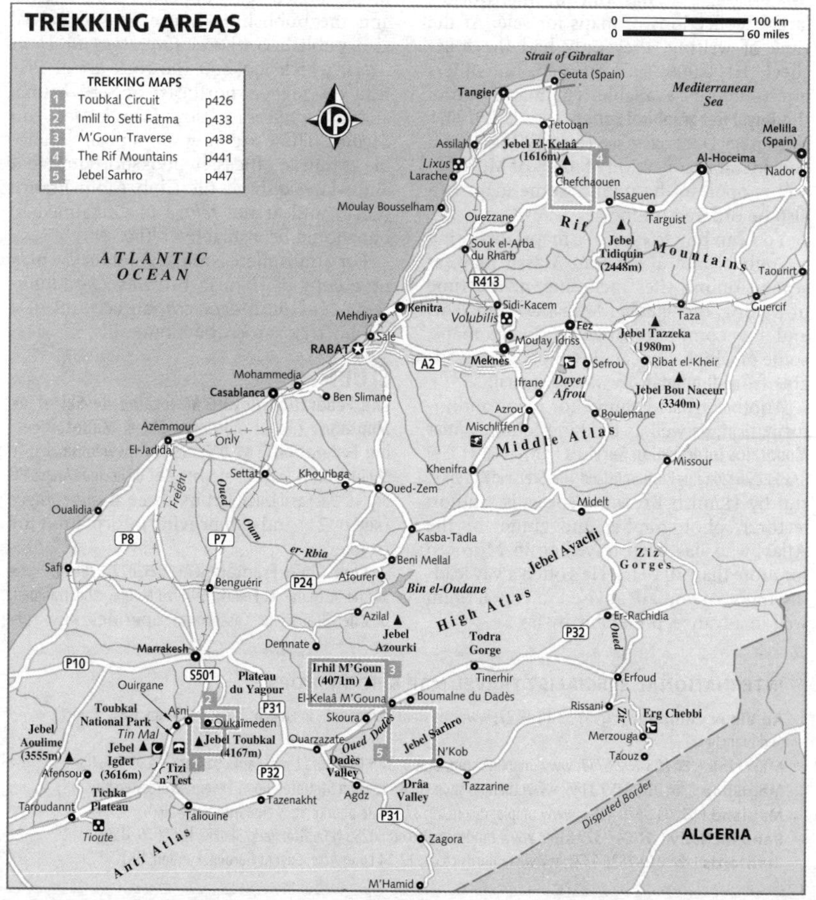

and the four-sheet, 1:100,000 *Toubkal Massif* walking map is now also available online at Stanfords (www.stanfords.co.uk) and elsewhere. There is now also a free phone number for the Division de la Cartographie (French and Arabic only): ☎ 0800 02929.

If you get no joy in Rabat, you may find maps of the Toubkal area, the M'Goun Massif and Jebel Sarhro in shops in Marrakesh, Imlil and elsewhere. Photocopies of maps of some parts of the High Atlas are sometimes available at the reception of **Hôtel Ali** (☎ 024 444979; www.hotel-ali.hostel-marrakech.co.uk; Rue Moulay Ismail) in Marrakesh, at the marked-up price of Dh140 or more.

Several sources in the UK may be able to supply maps. **Stanfords** (☎ 020-7836 1321; www.stanfords.co.uk) has one of the world's largest collections of maps for sale. At the time of writing, they only had the four-sheet, 1:100,000 *Toubkal* map, but others are sometimes available. The map room of the **Royal Geographical Society** (☎ 020-7591 3050; www.rgs.org; 1 Kensington Gore, London SW7 2AR) has a considerable collection of maps of Morocco and is open to the public. Some maps can also be ordered online.

You can buy West Col's maps, including a Toubkal and a M'Goun Massif map, at several online sites including, at the time of writing, on **Amazon** (www.amazon.co.uk). This and the complete range of Soviet maps, some of which you can download, are available from **Omnimap** (www.omnimap.com).

Another trusted source for maps and information, as well as trekking tours, is **Atlas Mountains Information Services** (☎/fax 00 44 1592 873 546; 26 Kirkcaldy Rd, Burntisland, Fife, Scotland KY3 9HQ), run by Hamish Brown, a specialist author, lecturer, photographer and guide for the Atlas, who has been travelling in Morocco for more than 40 years. He's often away leading treks, so you are advised to contact him well in advance, preferably by fax.

BOOKS

The Moroccan tourist office, Office National Marocain du Tourisme (ONMT), publishes an extremely useful booklet called *Morocco: Mountain and Desert Tourism* (2005). A French edition should also be available. The booklet has a good introduction to trekking in Morocco and then lists car hire, *bureaux des guides* (guide offices), tourist offices, lists of *gîtes d'étape* (trekkers' hostels), huts, *refuges,* camp sites, *souq* (market) days and other useful information. You should be able to pick them up at the office of the Association of Guides in Imlil, at the ONMT office in Marrakesh or in other major cities, or at Moroccan tourist offices overseas.

Some trekking guidebooks are listed in the boxed text, opposite. The ONMT and the publishing house Edisud/Belvisi also publish *Gravures Rupestres du Haut Atlas,* which looks at the rock art of Plateau du Yagour, northeast of Setti Fatma, and *Randonnées Pédestres Dans le Massif du Mgoun*. These are only sporadically available at tourist offices, in bookshops in Rabat and Marrakesh, at the Club Alpin France (CAF) and at the *refuge* in Oukaïmeden, but should be available online.

For atmosphere – and a good read – pick up a copy of Hamish Brown's *The Mountains Look on Marrakech*, an account of a 96-day trek across the mountains.

CLUBS

The Fédération Royale Marocaine de Ski et de Montagne (Royal Moroccan Ski & Mountaineering Federation) (☎ 022 203798; www.frmsm.ma; Le Ministère de la Jeunesse et Sport, Parc de la Ligue Arabe, PO Box 15899, Casablanca;) runs three basic *refuges* (see p421) and can provide information for trekkers.

Club Alpin Français (CAF; ☎ 022 270090; www.cafmaroc.co.ma, in French; 50 Blvd Moulay Abderrahman, Quartier Beauséjour, Casablanca) operates key *ref-*

INTERNATIONAL SPECIALIST TRAVEL MAP & BOOKSHOPS

Au Vieux Campeur (☎ 01 53 10 48 27; www.au-vieux-campeur.fr, in French; 2 Rue de Latran, Paris, France and branches)
Map Link (☎ 805-692 6777; www.maplink.com; Unit 5, 30 S La Patera Lane, Santa Barbara, CA 93117, USA)
Map Shop (☎ 016-8459 3146; www.themap shop.co.uk; 15 High St, Upton upon Severn, Worcestershire, UK)
Mapland (☎ 03-9670 4383; www.mapland.com.au; 372 Little Bourke St, Melbourne, Australia)
Rand McNally (☎ 847-329 8100; www.randmcnally.com; 8255 N Central Park, Skokie, IL 60076, USA)
Stanfords (☎ 020-7836 1321; www.stanfords.co.uk; 12-14 Long Acre, Covent Garden, London, UK)

TOP TREKKING GUIDEBOOKS

- *Great Atlas Traverse* by Michael Peyron. Peyron lived in Morocco for decades and his two-volume work is the definitive text (volume one covers the Toubkal region) for the great traverse. Less useful for the casual trekker.
- *Le Massif du Toubkal* by Jean Dresch and Jacques de Lépiney; published by Edisud/Belvisi in French, it is primarily of use to mountaineers concentrating on the high peaks around Toubkal.
- *Trekking in the Atlas Mountains: Toubkal, Mgoun Massif and Jebel Sahro* by Karl Smith. A guide from the walkers' guidebook publisher Cicerone, intended for experienced trekkers, with route descriptions and a weatherproof cover, but minimal mapping.
- *Trekking in the Moroccan Atlas* by Richard Knight. The most recent guide, with coverage of Jebel Sarhro and Jebel Siroua, and detailed sketch maps of each part of the route. Likely to be the most useful of all for inexperienced trekkers, although also the bulkiest.

uges in the Toubkal area, particularly those in Imlil and Oukaïmeden and on Toubkal (see p430). The club website is a good source of trekking information, including links to recommended guides.

ORGANISED TREKS

For details of foreign and Moroccan operators offering trekking tours in Morocco, see p488.

CLOTHING & EQUIPMENT

There are some essentials you are advised to attend to whatever the season: strong, well-broken-in walking boots are the key to happy trekking, as is a waterproof and windproof outer layer – it's amazing how quickly the weather can change. Light, baggy, cotton trousers and long-sleeved shirts are best in summer (June to August), but prepare for very cold weather during winter (November to March) wherever you trek in the country. Outside the height of summer, pack warm clothing, a woollen hat and gloves for trekking in the High Atlas. In summer, even at 1800m, it's cold enough at night to require a fleece or jumper. At the same time, you will need a sunhat, sunglasses and high-factor sunscreen year-round.

The key decision to make, when planning a route, is whether or not to sleep in tents. A good tent opens up endless trekking possibilities and will get you away from the crowds, but you don't necessarily have to bring your own, as most tour operators will rent one. It is also possible to rent them from some guides and from trailheads such as Imlil. If you would rather not camp, in most regions you can choose to stay in villages, either in *gîtes d'étape* or *chez l'habitant* (in someone's home). In both of these and especially in remote areas, rooms may not even have a mattress on the floor, although in places such as Imlil they often come with the luxury of a bed.

Whether you are camping or staying in houses, from September to early April a four-season sleeping bag is essential for the High Atlas and Jebel Sarhro – temperatures as low as -10°C are not unknown at this time. In lower mountain ranges, even in high summer, a bag comfortable at 0°C is recommended. A thick sleeping mat or thin foam mattress is a good idea since the ground is extremely rocky. These can usually be supplied by guides.

If you want to go above 3000m between November and May, you will need to have experience in winter mountaineering and be equipped with crampons, ice axes, snow shovels and other essential equipment. Again, this equipment is available for hire through most tour operators or in Imlil.

Many *gîtes* have cooking facilities, but you may want to bring a stove if you are camping. Multifuel stoves that burn anything from aviation fuel to diesel are ideal. Methylated spirits is very hard to get hold of, but kerosene is available. Pierce-type butane gas canisters are also available, but not recommended for environmental reasons. Your guide will be able to advise you on this.

Bring a basic medical kit and a supply of water-purification tablets or a mechanical purifier – all water should be treated unless you take it from the very source.

HAPPY FEET

Mountain Berbers manage to walk and often even run up and down mountains in sandals. How do they do it? Practice makes perfect and they have had a lifetime to achieve this happy state. Should you copy them? Not if you want to carry on walking. The most common difficulty that visitors experience on a trek is blisters from ill-fitting boots or ill-chosen footwear. If you want to do more than stroll across a valley, you will greatly enhance your pleasure by buying a pair of properly fitted, waterproof (preferably Gore-Tex) boots and give yourself time to break them in. Even then you may get blisters. Many trekkers carry 'second skin', a plastic layer that can be put over blisters and usually stops them hurting. Happy feet make for a happy walker.

If you are combining trekking with visits to urban areas, consider storing extra luggage before your trek rather than lugging around unwanted gear. Most hotels will let you leave luggage, sometimes for a small fee. Train stations in larger cities have secure left-luggage facilities, although many of these offices will only accept luggage that is locked, so make sure you have a lock for your suitcase.

GUIDES

However much experience you have at trekking and at map reading, we strongly recommend that you hire a qualified guide. Why? If for no other reason than to be your translator (how is your Berber?), your chaperone (*faux guides* won't come near you if you are with a guide), deal-getter and vocal guidebook. A good guide will enhance your cultural experience. For one thing, they will know people throughout the area, which will undoubtedly result in invitations for tea and food, and richer experiences of Berber life. And then, if something does go wrong, a local guide will be the quickest route to getting help. Every year foreigners die in the Moroccan mountains. Whatever the cause – a freak storm, an unlucky slip, a rock slide – their chances of survival would invariably have increased with the presence of a guide. So however confident you feel, we recommend that you never walk into the mountains unguided.

Choosing a guide can be a problem. A flash-looking, English-speaking *faux guide* (unofficial guide) from Marrakesh is no substitute for a gnarled, old, local mountain guide who knows the area like the back of his hand. All official guides carry photo-identity cards. Guides should be authorised by the Fédération Royale Marocaine de Ski et Montagne (Royal Moroccan Ski & Mountaineering Federation) or l'Association Nationale des Guides et Accompagnateurs en Montagne du Maroc. They should be credited as *guides de montagnes* (mountain guides), which requires study for at least six months at the Centre de Formation aux Métiers de Montagne, a school for mountain guides at Tabant in the Aït Bou Goumez valley. Note that *accompagnateurs* (escorts) will have had only one week's training and will not be insured to lead mountain trips. It is also worth pointing out that a *guide de tourisme* (tourist guide) is not qualified to lead treks.

Official mountain guides, who can always show an identity card as proof of their status, have been trained in mountain craft, including first aid. In times of uncertain weather or in an emergency, they will be infinitely more efficient than a cheaper guide lacking proper training. If a guide you are thinking of engaging is reluctant to show their photo card, it probably means they either don't have one or it has expired (they should be renewed every three years).

There are more than four hundred accredited mountain guides working in Morocco and many of them can be found through the *bureaux des guides* in Imlil, Setti Fatma, Tabant (Aït Bou Goumez Valley) and El-Kelaâ M'Gouna.

Some *guides de montagne* will have additional training in rock climbing, canyoning and mountaineering. All guides speak French and some also speak English, Spanish or German. In the past few years several young Moroccan women have succeeded in breaking into the previously all-male world of mountain guiding. Their services are in high demand.

At the time of writing, the minimum rate for official guides was Dh300 per day (per group, not per person). This rate can vary according to season and location. Rates do not include food and accommodation expenses. Guides generally get free accommodation in *refuges* and *gîtes,* but you may be asked to cover expenses for meals. If you embark on a linear route you'll also be expected to pay for their return journey.

Negotiate all fees before departure and count on giving at least a 10% tip at the end, unless you have been very unhappy with the service. If your guide is organising your trip (rather than a tour operator), be sure to go through all aspects of the trek ahead of time: discuss where each day will start and end, whether tents will be shared (most guides have a tent or sleeping bag), how many mules will be hired, who will be cooking (if there are enough of you, the guide may insist on hiring a cook, usually at Dh100 a day), food preferences, water provision, and the division of food and equipment between the group.

MULES

Mules (and the odd donkey) are widely used in Morocco for transporting goods through the mountains, and you can easily hire one to carry your gear. If you are relying on heavy local supplies, or are in a large group, hiring a mule (which can carry the gear of four people) makes especially good sense. As a rough guide, mules can carry up to 120kg, although, if the route is very steep or demanding, the muleteer may insist upon carrying less. He will have the well-being of his meal ticket in mind, although Moroccans are rarely sentimental about their pack animals.

Some trekking routes are not suitable for mules, although detours (for the mule) are often possible. If high passes are covered in snow, porters may have to be used instead of mules (one porter can carry up to 18kg). A mule and muleteer usually charge a standard Dh100 per day.

As with guides, if you embark on a linear route you'll also be expected to pay for the muleteer's return journey.

ON THE TREK

ACCOMMODATION

The bulk of trekking accommodation in the High and Middle Atlas are *gîtes*. In the Rif and little-walked Anti Atlas, *gîtes* are uncommon, and accommodation is more often in local homes or in tents.

Gîtes provide basic accommodation, often offering little more than a foam mattress in an empty room, or on a roof terrace or balcony. They have basic bathrooms and toilets, although the better ones will have hot showers. Given notice, the proprietor can rustle up a tajine. The standard rate is now Dh50 per person per night, although prices can vary according to season and location. Meals are extra (usually Dh30 to Dh50 per person), as are hot showers (usually Dh10 to Dh15 per shower). The more upscale, privately owned *gîtes* charge as much as Dh100 for accommodation and the same for meals, while one luxury lodge charges Dh2000 a night for a double room (see p336).

CAF has five *refuges* in the Toubkal/Oukaïmeden area, and officially bookings should be made in advance through the **Oukaïmeden Refuge** (☎ 024 319036; ouka@cafmaroc.co.ma). However, in practice you can usually find out if space is available at the other *refuges* in the Toubkal region by asking in Imlil. Be warned, though, that *refuges* are often packed in July and August. Members of CAF and other affiliated and recognised alpine organisations (eg the Alpine Club in the UK) get the cheapest price for a bed, followed by HI members. Children aged between five and 15 years get a 50% reduction.

The Fédération Royale Marocaine de Ski et de Montagne has *refuges* (per person Dh50, Dh20 breakfast) at Oukaïmeden (well maintained and comfortable) and in the Jebel Bou Iblane (less comfortable, but with a guardian) in the Middle Atlas, 60km south of Taza. Their *refuge* at Ain Aflafal, on the southern face of Irhil M'Goun, was abandoned and it is now a summer shop selling water and soft drinks.

FOOD

The choice of dry rations is limited in rural Morocco and you cannot be sure of finding much beyond powdered milk, a range of dried fruit and sachets of soup, biscuits, some tinned fish and dates. Supermarkets in larger towns and cities are a much better option, and if you take a mule, you will be able to plan a more varied diet.

Bread, eggs, vegetables and some basic supplies (eg tea and tinned tuna) may be available in some mountain villages, but you cannot count on it. Meals can also be arranged in some villages (Dh30 to Dh50 per person is standard), especially at *gîtes* and *refuges,* although they usually need to be ordered in advance. Again, do not rely on local suppliers as your only source of food unless you have made previous arrangements.

Change money in the nearest major town and ensure that you have plenty of small notes. If you do get stuck, euro notes may be accepted.

RESPONSIBLE TREKKING

Morocco's potential as a walking destination is now being developed, but many regions remain remote and are extremely susceptible to the cultural and environmental impact of tourism. Many travellers return home warmed and heartened by the hospitality of the Berber people, but as visitor numbers increase so too does the pressure on the inhabitants. In response, travellers should adopt an appropriate code of behaviour.

WORDS TO TREK BY

Even just a few words in a foreign language can make a big difference to your experience. The following words may be helpful on these treks – '(A)' indicates Arabic, '(B)' indicates Berber. Other useful Arabic and Berber words can be found in the Glossary, p513.

adfel (B) – snow
adrar (B) – mountain (plural *idraren*)
afella (B) – summit
agdal (B) – pasture (also *aougdal*)
aghbalu (B) – water spring
'ain (A) – water spring
aman (B) – water
anzar (B) – rain
argaz (B) – man
asserdoun (B) – mule
assif (B) – watercourse, river
azaghar (B) – plane, plateau (also *izwghar*)
azib (B) – seasonal shelter for shepherds
brhel (A) – mule
châba (B) – ravine
iferd (B) – lake
ifri (B) – cave
jebel (A) – mountain or hill
kerkour (B) – cairn
taddart (B) – house
talat (B) – dried-up ravine or watercourse
tamada (B) – lake
tigm (B) – house
tizi (B) – mountain pass

Cross-Cultural Considerations

The way you dress is very important, especially among remote mountain people, who remain conservative in their habits. In villages travellers should wear buttoned shirts or T-shirts and not sleeveless vests, which villagers use as underwear. Above all, trousers should be worn rather than shorts. This applies equally to men and women. The importance of dress in the villages cannot be overemphasised (as many a frustrated and embarrassed trekking tour leader will affirm). However much you might disagree with this conservatism, respecting local traditions will bring greater rewards, not least by way of contact, hospitality and assistance.

Invitations for tea and offers of food are common in the mountains. By taking a guide, who may have friends in many villages, you'll open yourself to even more offers of genuine hospitality. While these offers are unconditional, it is worth bearing in mind that the mountain economy is one of basic subsistence farming. No-one has large supplies and in outlying villages there may be no surplus food. Being able to offer your hosts some Chinese gunpowder tea and some sugar (preferably in cones) is a very welcome gesture. Dried fruits are also appreciated, as is a taste of any imported food you may have. For this reason, it is important to be generous when buying provisions for yourself and guides.

In remote areas, people along the way will often ask for medicine, from a disinfectant and bandages to painkillers or cream for dry skin (which many children have). Always make sure that the guide explains what to do with what you offer, and how and how often to take it.

For considerations on alcohol, taking photos and giving gifts to children see the boxed text, p456.

Environmental Considerations

RUBBISH

Carry out all your rubbish; never bury it or burn it (Western-style packaging never burns well). Your guide may be happy to bag up all your rubbish then hurl it over a cliff, but that approach is simply unsustainable, especially given that more and more people are now trekking in Morocco. So if you have carried it in, then you should carry it out. Minimise the waste you'll carry out by taking minimal packaging and by repackaging provisions into reusable containers when appropriate. If you want to make a gesture, think about making an effort to carry out rubbish left by others.

Don't rely on bought water in plastic bottles. Disposal of these bottles is creating a major problem in Morocco. Use iodine drops or purification tablets with locally sourced water.

HUMAN WASTE DISPOSAL

Contamination of water sources by human faeces can lead to the transmission of hepatitis, typhoid and intestinal parasites. This is a particular problem in more populated trekking areas.

Where there is a toilet, it is a good idea to use it; where there is none, bury your waste. Dig a small hole 15cm (six inches) deep and at least 100m from any watercourse – something important to remember, given how many trekking routes follow rivers and streams. Consider carrying a lightweight trowel for this purpose: in the arid Atlas Mountains, digging without one can be difficult. Cover the waste with soil and a rock. Use toilet paper sparingly, burn it when possible or bury it with the waste. In snow dig down to the soil; otherwise, your waste will be exposed when the snow melts.

WASHING

Don't use detergents or toothpaste in or near watercourses, even if they are biodegradable. For personal washing use biodegradable soap and wash at least 50m away from any watercourse. Disperse the waste water widely to allow the soil to filter it fully before it finally makes its way back to the watercourse. Use a scourer, sand or snow to wash cooking utensils rather than detergent. Again, make sure you're at least 50m from any watercourse.

EROSION

Hillsides and mountain slopes, especially at high altitudes, are prone to erosion. Stick to existing tracks and avoid short cuts that bypass a switchback. If you blaze a new trail straight down a slope, it will turn into a watercourse with the next heavy rainfall, eventually causing soil loss and deep scarring.

LOW-IMPACT COOKING & CAMPING

Don't depend on open fires for cooking. As you will see on your walk, the cutting of wood for fires in Morocco has caused widespread deforestation. Ideally, cook on a lightweight multifuel or kerosene stove and avoid those powered by disposable butane gas canisters. If you do make a fire, ensure it is fully extinguished after use by spreading the embers and dousing them with water. A fire is only truly safe to leave when you can comfortably place your hand in it.

Vegetation at high altitude is highly sensitive. When camping minimise your impact on the environment by not removing or disturbing the vegetation around your camp site. In order to avoid aggravating the persistent and serious problem of overgrazing in many of the regions, sufficient fodder (barley) for all baggage mules and donkeys should be brought in. It is a good idea to enquire carefully about this before setting off.

THE HIGH ATLAS

الأطلس الكبير

The highest mountain range in North Africa is a trekker's paradise. The High Atlas runs diagonally across Morocco, from the Atlantic coast northeast of Agadir all the way to northern Algeria. Running for almost 1000km, the range includes several summits higher than 4000m and more than 400 above 3000m. This makes a spectacular setting for walks and offers the possibility of bagging a few summits as you go. The Toubkal region contains all the highest peaks and is the most frequently visited area of the High Atlas, partly because it is only two hours from Marrakesh and easily accessible by public transport.

The Berbers call the High Atlas 'Idraren Draren' (Mountains of Mountains) and their presence here will be one of the most memorable aspects of a walk. Although wild and harsh, the area has long been inhabited by Berbers, whose flat-roofed, earthen villages seem to have grown out of the mountainsides, above terraced gardens and orchards of walnuts and fruit trees.

The first road, up the Tizi n'Test, was only cut through this remote region in the early 20th century. Before then, the only way to travel was via the well-worn mule trails that criss-cross the mountains and once carried trade caravans and pilgrims between the Sahara and the northern plains. Walking along them now often gives the sense of stepping back into an earlier time.

WILDLIFE

Spectacularly rugged and sparsely vegetated, these mountains contain terraced cliffs, enormous escarpments, deep gorges and flat-topped summits. Where the rock is exposed you can see a thick sequence of sedimentary and volcanic rocks, most often Jurassic limestone, cut through by layers of granite. The oldest rocks are the 610-million-year-old granites and granodiorites of the Ourika region (near Setti Fatma). Some minor glaciation also took place around 45,000 years ago.

The slopes and valleys have been transformed over centuries by the work of Berber farmers, who have cut terraces high up on the steep mountainsides and irrigated them with ingenious systems of small channels, called *targa* in Berber, which bring water from rivers and streams.

In spite of the harsh climate, icy in winter and scalding in summer, the Atlas Mountains are extremely fertile and productive. The lower valleys are full of almond and apricot orchards, as well as carob, quince, pomegranate, apple, cherry and fig trees. Vegetable plots include potatoes, carrots, turnips, onions, lentils and beans. In October much of the terraces is ploughed for a winter crop of barley, which is harvested in late May or June. Walnuts are also a major crop in higher villages, and are harvested in late September.

Overgrazing, agriculture and the collection of wood for fuel has had a tremendous impact on the High Atlas and much of its indigenous vegetation has disappeared. In the subalpine zone (2400m to 3200m) you'll see thickets of Spanish juniper *(Juniperus thurifer)*. These thick, gnarled trees are often blasted into extraordinary shapes by the wind, their exposed roots clinging like fingers to the rock. Higher up, the main sight is 'hedgehog plants', spiny, domed bushes that burst into flower for a short time in the spring. Wild herbs including lavender, rosemary and thyme are common – you will smell them underfoot as you walk.

Big mammals are not common in the High Atlas, though mouflons (mountain sheep with big horns), wild boars and gazelles are found in some areas. Other wildlife includes Moorish geckos, Iberian wall lizards and painted frogs. Small snakes are quite common, but will usually be dealt with by guides before you get a chance to look at them closely.

Birds of the subalpine zone include Moussier's redstarts, crimson-winged finches and, in wooded areas, Levaillant's green woodpeckers. Crows are omnipresent, and you'll sometimes catch a glimpse of majestic raptors such as lammergeiers, Egyptian vultures and golden eagles.

PLANNING

When to Trek

You can trek throughout the year in the High Atlas, but different seasons offer some very different experiences. Above 2000m, temperatures often drop below freezing between November and May, when snow covers the higher peaks and passes. Only lower-valley walking is possible during this season, unless you are prepared to bring ropes and crampons. Late April to late June is one of the ideal times to visit because in April and May the alpine flowers will be in bloom and by June, when Marrakesh is already simmering, daytime temperatures are usually pleasantly warm.

Midsummer guarantees long daylight hours and snow-free passes (though not always a snow-free Toubkal), but in the lower valleys temperatures can be extremely hot and water nonexistent. Rivers have maximum flow in autumn (November) and in late spring (April or May), after the winter snows have melted. Though many rivers are reduced to a trickle by midsummer, the area can still be subject to flash flooding in summer after tremendous thunderstorms, something to bear in mind when deciding where to camp. Despite the heat, July and August are the busiest months for visitors to Marrakesh and the High Atlas: trekking at this time can be wonderful, but is best done early morning and later in the afternoon, leaving plenty of time for a shady lunch and rest in between.

Guides & Mules

Imlil is by far the best place to engage a guide and hire a mule if necessary. There is a **bureau des guides** (☎/fax 024 485626) on the village square, which has a list of official guides, complete with mugshots, which eliminates the risk of impostors. Guides work in rotation, so if you have specific needs try to organise a guide in advance. Of the 60 official guides based in the Toubkal area, only 10 or so may be in Imlil at any one time. Some of the more successful guides are also attached to the Kasbah du Toubkal.

It's rarely a problem to organise mules, usually done once a guide has been hired and with the guide's help. Trekkers should be aware that mules have problems crossing Tizi n'Ouanoums, east of Lac d'Ifni, or Tizi n'Taddate, between the Toubkal and Tazaghart *refuge,* from November to May. As the mules will then have to take lengthy detours, you may need to carry one day's kit and food. Talk this through with your guide and muleteer. Allow a day or so to hire a guide and make the required trekking arrangements.

Accommodation

Imlil is the most convenient and best-equipped trailhead for the High Atlas and Toubkal. For accommodation and eating in Imlil see p335.

Three kilometres above Imlil, and now also accessible by a drivable *piste* (track), **Aroumd** (or Armed), at 1960m, is a growing village surrounded by orchards and terraced fields at the beginning of a broad valley that leads up towards Toubkal. Several trekking companies use Aroumd as a base for group treks around the Toubkal area and, with four *gîtes,* it makes a good stop on the Toubkal ascent.

Gîte Atlas Toubkal (☎ 024 485664, 068 882764; dm Dh30) A large *gîte* run by the family of veteran mountain guide Mohamed Id Balaïd, the clean, basic dorm rooms are a good deal. They can also cook you a good walker's breakfast or dinner. Hot showers are extra (Dh10).

Les Roches Armed/Chez Lahcen (☎ 067 644915; dm Dh30) Like all the places in Aroumd, Lahcen's house, up at the top of the village, has grown and grown. It's a steep climb to get there, but worth it for the mountain views and the neat and clean rooms with mattresses on the floor. A hot shower costs Dh10. Meals are available on request.

Hôtel Armed (☎ 024 485745; idbelaid@menara.ma; s/d incl breakfast Dh150/300) Now in its second generation, this hotel-restaurant was the first officially to offer accommodation in Aroumd and remains one of the best. Continued expansion means they now have a range of straightforward rooms, with mattresses, hot showers, a terrace with panoramic terrace and good solid Moroccan cooking in the restaurant. Highly recommended for family tours. The owners also arranges treks.

Camping-Auberge Atlas Toubkal/Chez Omar le Rouge (☎ 024 485750, 066 936488; omar_id_mensour@hotmail.com; s/d Dh50/100, camping per tent Dh10) Omar's Atlas Toubkal has basic rooms with mattresses and communal facilities, including hot showers (Dh10). He also runs a basic camp site across the road, with the possibility of using the showers. Meals are available (breakfast Dh15, tajine Dh30).

TOUBKAL CIRCUIT VIA LAC D'IFNI جولة جبل توبقال عبر دحيرة إفني

You get the best of both worlds on this circuit: the majestic peaks and fabulous views of the Jebel Toubkal and a fascinating glimpse into Berber life in some remote High Atlas villages. You will need tents and camping gear for this particular route, though with short detours you could use basic village accommodation and mountain *refuges,* a good option early or late in the season, when temperatures can plummet.

The trek is fairly strenuous so you might want to include an extra rest day, or consider the options for making the trek a little shorter. Indeed, if the following seems too much, there is always the simple and popular two-day ascent of Toubkal from Imlil (see p431).

Most of the route is above 2000m, with several high passes over 3000m. The ascent of Jebel Toubkal takes place on the sixth day, allowing five days of acclimatisation to altitude, which can be an issue over 3000m. The circuit detailed below is best done in late spring or summer. Numerous other trekking routes emanate from this outline.

Planning

The best place to organise this trek is in Imlil (p334). The walk described requires seven days, but the circuit can be shortened

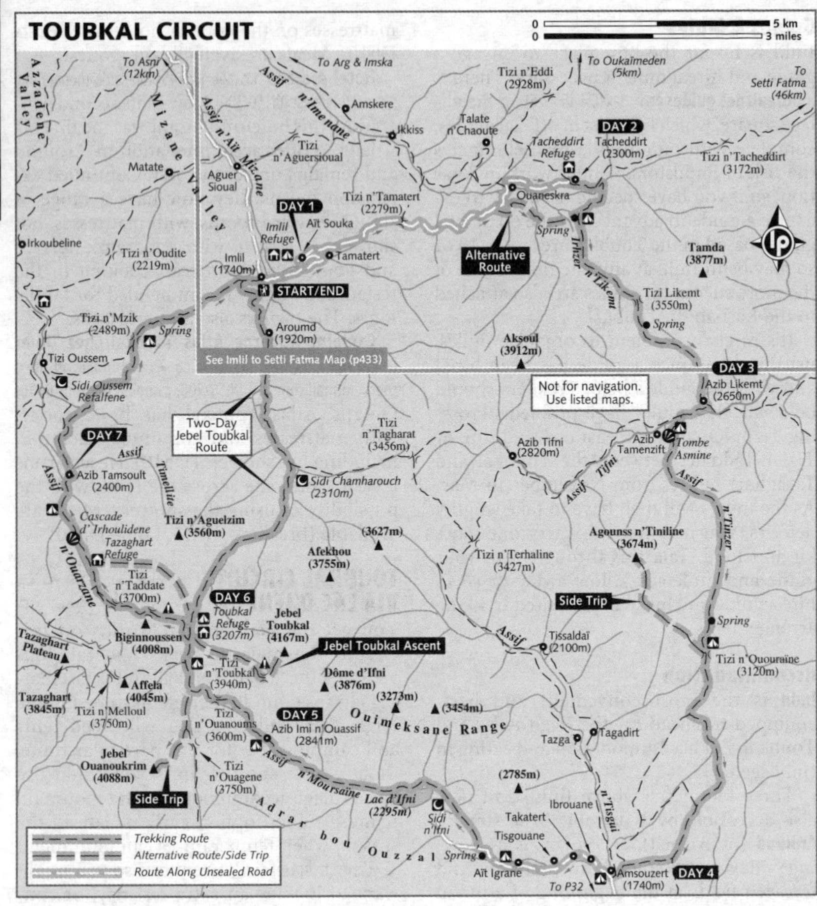

or lengthened. From Azib Likemt, for instance, you could head west to Sidi Chamharouch via Tizi n'Tagharat (3465m), which would make a three-day circuit from Imlil (spending the second night at Azib Tifni). Alternatively, you could save two days by skipping the trek over Tizi n'Taddate to the Tazaghart *refuge* after you've ascended Toubkal. There are options for extending the trek, either by peak-bagging or exploring side routes, such as the Tazaghart plateau. Mountain guides can customise routes to suit time, ability and conditions.

Maps

The 1:50,000 sheet map *Jebel Toubkal* covers the whole Toubkal Circuit and is sometimes available through the Bureau des Guides in Imlil. Occasionally you can get hold of the 1994 edition, which is both clearer and more accurate.

The four-sheet 1:100,000 topographical *Toubkal Massif Walking Map*, which also covers the circuit, is produced by the Division de la Cartographie (Moroccan Survey) and can usually be obtained from their office in Rabat or from Stanfords in London (for both see p417).

Government-produced 1:100,000 *Cartes des Randonnées dans le Massif du Toubkal* marks trekking routes but is less useful because it includes less topographical detail.

The newest map, Orientazion's 1:50,000 *Toubkal and Marrakech*, is clear and hand-

THE TREK AT A GLANCE

Duration seven to nine days
Distance 60.2km
Standard medium to hard
Start/Finish Imlil village
Highest Point Jebel Toubkal (4167m)
Nearest Large Town Marrakesh
Accommodation camping, village *gîtes* and mountain *refuges*
Public Transport yes
Summary Easily accessible from Marrakesh, this circuit around (and up) Jebel Toubkal passes through a variety of landscapes, ranging from lush, cultivated valleys and Berber villages to forbidding peaks and bleak high passes. This is a demanding trek, with long, gruelling climbs over rocky terrain. A guide is highly recommended, fitness essential.

ily water-resistant, but has misspellings and does not show all gullies and cliffs.

Day 1: Imlil to Tacheddirt

3½ to 4½ hours/9.5km/560m ascent

For much of this relatively gentle first day, the route follows the 4WD track that links **Imlil** (1740m) to the village of **Ouaneskra**, 2km west of Tacheddirt (2300m).

Follow the track up through the centre of Imlil and take the left-hand fork over the river, **Assif n'Aït Mizane**. The *piste* climbs gently eastwards through fields of barley and orchards of walnuts, apple and cherry trees before zigzagging up to **Aït Souka**.

After an hour or so, just past a stream known as Talat n'Aït Souka, a fairly well defined but rocky path heads east, skirting the village of **Tamatert**. The rocky path continues eastwards for about 15 minutes, passing through a small pine grove and crossing the road. It then climbs steeply northeast to the pass, **Tizi n'Tamatert** (2279m). The walk up takes 30 to 45 minutes. At the pass is Bivi Thé, a weather-beaten tin shed that sells soft drinks and mint tea only when there is enough business. To the northeast there are great views of **Tizi n'Eddi** (2928m), the pass that leads to the ski resort of Oukaïmeden, and **Tizi n'Tacheddirt** (3172m), northeast of which is the beautiful **Ourika Valley**.

The path rejoins the dirt road at Tizi n'Tamatert, from where it's an easy 45-minute walk to the village of Ouaneskra. All along this stretch you will be treated to great views across the valley to the neat Berber houses and lush terraces of Talate n'Chaoute, Tamguist and Ouaneskra.

A little before reaching Ouaneskra, the path divides. The mule track to the right traverses the southern side of the valley. This is a short cut to the best camping place, near the track and close to **Irhzer n'Likemt**, a stream and reliable water source. This is the starting place for the next day's climb.

If you would rather take the longer route via Ouaneskra and Tacheddirt, then take the northern side of the valley after crossing Tizi n'Tamatert. There are three *gîtes* in Ouaneskra, and a pleasant little restaurant, so it is tempting to stop here for the night. But the second day's walk is fairly long, so it's best to have lunch here and then carry on. The village of **Tacheddirt** is 2km further along the well-defined mule trail or by the 4WD road that runs along the north side of the slope. In Tacheddirt, 50 people can sleep at **Tigmmi n Tacheddirt** (☎ 062 105 169; per person from Dh50), the new *gîte* from the owner of Hôtel Armed in Aroumd. You may also be able to stay at the CAF Refuge, *chez l'habitant* in the house of the *refuge gardien* (attendant) or elsewhere in the village (Dh30 to Dh50).

From Tacheddirt, the hiking track then loops south to the camp site near Irhzer n'Likemt.

Day 2: Tacheddirt to Azib Likemt

five to six hours/9km/1200m ascent/900m descent

There is a lot of climbing on this day, but the rewards are all around you. From Tacheddirt you can either head straight down and across the **Assif n'Imenane** and then up past the camp site, or wind around the head of the valley on a more gentle route to the start of the climb. Either way, you will want to leave Tacheddirt as early as possible to make the two- to three-hour walk up to **Tizi Likemt** (3550m). Though the majority of the walk should be shaded, it's still a hard climb, especially for the 'unaclimbatised'. Halfway up it gets steeper and then turns into a very steep scree slope towards the top. The doyen of Atlas climbers Michael Peyron calls this 'the grandfather of all Atlas scree slopes'. He also points out that skiers would be challenged to manage skiing down it when the snow falls.

Close to the camp site, a well-defined rocky path heads up the centre of the gully on the east side of the river bed (though it crosses over twice). It climbs for about 50 minutes before bearing left (southeast) up to the col (pass). From the top of the Tizi Likemt there are great views of jagged peaks and verdant valleys, up to Oukaïmeden and, on clear days, as far as Jebel Toubkal.

The path leading down the other side (southeast) is quite rocky. You'll pass a semi-permanent water source on the left after 30 minutes, and the first of the irrigated pastures above **Azib Likemt** after another hour. An *azib* is a summer settlement and Azib Likemt (2650m) is occupied from the first week of May usually to the last week of October, during which time local people grow crops on the irrigated terraces and fatten their cattle in lush summer pastures. Their rudimentary stone dwellings, the well-worked terraces and sheer natural beauty of the valley provide an amazing vista.

You may be offered shelter or a place to pitch your tent in Azib Likemt, but if not then walk through the terraces down to the **Assif Tifni**, cross the river, turn right and then walk upstream to a group of large boulders, where you'll find some flat ground close to the river on which to pitch your tent.

Day 3: Azib Likemt to Amsouzert

six to 7½ hours/15.2km/470m ascent/1380m descent

This direct route south to **Amsouzert** is less demanding than yesterday's walk and is packed with contrasts, from precipitous valleys to stunning peaks and some good ridge walking too.

From Azib Likemt, the well-worn trail leads south from behind the camp site, up the mountainside and into the tremendous gorge formed by **Assif n'Tinzer**. Well above the river's eastern bank, the trail snakes above what at certain times of the year is the thundering **Tombe Asmine waterfall** and an alternative camp site, before descending close to the river. Follow the river for about two hours, past stunning cliffs and through wide pastures, until an obvious track leads up the side of the valley to **Tizi n'Ououraïne** (3120m; also known as Tizi n'Ouaraï).

From here you are treated to some brilliant views of the eastern face of Toubkal, as well as of **Dôme d'Ifni** (3876m) and the rest of the jagged Toubkal massif. By way of contrast, **Agounss n'Tiniline** (3674m), 90 minutes away to the northwest, and other lesser peaks and ridges to the east are softer and rounded. (There's huge potential for sustained ridge walking or a long circuit back to Azib Likemt from Tizi n'Ououraïne.)

Continue over the col, where the trail traverses around the head of the valley to a spur and the crossroads of trails. Heading southwest, a trail leads down the ridge to **Tagadirt** (after 50m there's a fantastic viewpoint looking south to **Jebel Siroua**), but turn left (southeast) and follow the mule track south. Traverse around the head of another valley and then along the side of a spur, finally gaining the ridge after about 90 minutes. **Lac d'Ifni** is visible to the west. After a further 15 minutes, just before two pointed outcrops, the path forks. Turn right and continue descending slowly southwards to a large cairn (another good viewpoint). Descend southwest, then west down the end of the spur to arrive in Amsouzert (1740m) in 30 minutes.

Amsouzert is a relatively large, prosperous village (with one mosque and a handful of satellite dishes at last count), spread on both sides of the river. If you're planning a rest day, this is an excellent place to take it. Next to the school you'll find an outdoor tearoom shaded by an enormous walnut tree. You may be able to **camp** (per tent Dh20) here or else stay at **Gîte Himmi Omar** (dm Dh40, tajine Dh30) or at the same family's new *gîte* just a little further down the road. Above the village, just below the track to Lac d'Ifni, is Hotel Igroute, closed at the time of writing.

There are a number of small shops in Amsouzert, and a couple of cafés near the village school, just west of the river. There's also early morning transport to the Taroudannt to Ouarzazate N10 road, with connections to Marrakesh and Ouarzazate. About 3km south of Amsouzert is another village called Imlil (not to be confused with the Imlil trailhead on the northern side of the range), which hosts a *souq* each Wednesday.

SIDE TRIP: AGOUNSS N'TINILINE

From Tizi n'Ououraïne the easiest side trip is the straightforward 1½-hour trek up to **Agounss n'Tiniline** (3674m), which lies to the northwest. The summit is reached after crossing a number of lesser peaks, and it affords tremendous views of the Toubkal ridge.

Day 4: Amsouzert to Azib Imi n'Ouassif

5½ to six hours/10.5km/1100m ascent

Unfortunately for those with mules, between November and May your beasts of burden will not be able to make it more than 2km west of Lac d'Ifni. The muleteer will have to take the animal around to the Toubkal Refuge via Sidi Chamharouch, which means you will have to carry your necessary kit to **Azib Imi n'Ouassif**, over **Tizi n'Ouanoums** (3600m) to Toubkal Refuge. But there are consolations, among them Lac d'Ifni, the largest lake in the Atlas and a welcome contrast to the barren landscape of the approach.

From Amsouzert follow the level, well-used 4WD track that continues northwest towards Lac d'Ifni above the north side of the river. The path takes you through the villages of **Ibrouane**, **Takatert** and **Tisgouane** before reaching **Aït Igrane**, where there are a couple of cafés and, should you need it, basic accommodation at **Gîte Belaïde** (dm Dh40). There is also a shady **camp site** (Dh30) on a flat, stony site just beyond the Café Toubkal, with a rudimentary shower (cold) and toilet block.

Follow the 4WD track along the riverbed northwest out of Aït Igrane. Pick up the narrow rocky mule path at the end of the river valley, where the vegetation ends abruptly and the 4WD track crosses the river (there's a spring to the north) then turns sharp left. The mule path then leads around the north side of Lac d'Ifni (2295m), across an incredibly sharp, rocky, barren and inhospitable terrain. The climb is steep at first, but there is relief as it descends to the northeastern corner of Lac d'Ifni, a surprisingly large, and very inviting expanse of still, green water. The walk to the lake should take two to three hours. After you have seen the lake, but before you reach the shore, you will pass somewhere marked as a café. No coffee here, but if it is attended you should be able to buy water and soft drinks and, if no one else has ordered before you, a tajine.

On the small beach on the northern shore are a few stone shelters where you can seek shade – they make a good, if at times fly-filled, spot for a lakeside lunch. The ground is rocky and there is no vegetation to speak of, but the lake is safe – and very refreshing – to swim in.

Every October, villagers from the surrounding area gather at Lac d'Ifni for a three-day *moussem* (festival) in honour of a local *marabout* (saint), whose tomb sits in splendid isolation high above the southeastern corner of the lake. A track leads around from the northeast shore of the lake up to the tomb. At other times, anglers come to fish for the lake's celebrated trout.

From the northwestern side of the lake the track crosses the wide, dry part of Lac d'Ifni and then makes a long snaking trudge of more than 1km towards **Tizi n'Ouanoums**. Once clear of the lake, the path climbs through a rocky gorge, keeping to the south side of the river. It's a hot, sweaty climb in the afternoon sun, but relieved somewhat by the cooling sound of running water. About 3.5km from the lake, you'll reach **Azib Imi n'Ouassif** (2841m; marked on the 1:100,000 map by altitude only), situated at a crossing of dramatic gorges. Beyond this point the path climbs steeply to Tizi n'Ouanoums. There are some small waterfalls (freezing even in the height of summer) nearby. You'll find several flat but rocky areas for pitching tents, as well as natural shelters in the surrounding cliffs, which local shepherds have probably used for centuries.

Day 5: Azib Imi n'Ouassif to Toubkal Refuge

three to four hours/4km/759m ascent/393m descent

The path to Tizi n'Ouanoums (3600m) is immediately to the northwest of the camp site, leading up into a particularly rocky, rugged landscape. It's a steep, demanding climb for pretty much the entire way, but the views from the top over **Assif n'Moursaïne**, which is hemmed in by the jagged ridges of **Adrar bou Ouzzal** and **Ouimeksane**, are spectacular. The path crosses the river several times after leaving the camp. A stone shelter and water source is reached after an hour. It can take another hour to get to the col from here. Even in midsummer it's likely to be cold and blustery at the top, and with a fair bit of snow in shady crevices.

Coming down the other side, there's lots of treacherous loose rock and snow until July. From here you can see Jebel Toubkal and, to the west, the path up to **Tizi n'Melloul** (3850m). After the descent the track levels out and heads due north to the Toubkal Refuge (3207m), which is about two hours from Tizi n'Ouanoums.

The CAF'S **Toubkal Refuge** (☎ 064 071838; dm CAF members/HI members/nonmembers Dh46/69/92), formerly known as Neltner, was completely rebuilt in the 1990s but suffers from overcrowding and damp, as well as a lack of facilities: queues for showers (Dh10) and toilets are unacceptable in busy periods. Meals are available and there's a small shop selling chocolate, cola, biscuits and other limited supplies. You can also make reservations through the **Oukaïmeden Refuge** (☎ 024 319036; ouka@cafmaroc.co.ma). The new privately owned **Refuge Mouflon** (☎ 061 213345; afoud@wanadoo.net.ma; dm Dh75), next to Toubkal Refuge, provides a welcome choice. The lounge can be chilly, but otherwise this is the preferable option, with more facilities (shower Dh10), a better-stocked shop and good meals (Dh50).

You can also camp downstream from the *refuge* or pick a spot 20 minutes south of the *refuge* on a flat area of pasture. The latter is preferable, but you won't have access to the *refuge's* facilities.

Assuming you reach the *refuge* before lunch, there are a number of trekking options to keep you busy in the afternoon, including the three- or four-hour descent directly north back to the starting point, Imlil, if you don't want to climb Jebel Toubkal. You might tackle the tough climb up and over Tizi n'Taddate to the Tazaghart *refuge*, which lies at the head of the Azzadene Valley, or ascend Jebel Ouanoukrim, which is best attempted straight after descending from Tizi n'Ouanoums. However, the best option (especially if you've got three days of trekking ahead of you) is to rest all afternoon to prepare for the climb up Jebel Toubkal the following morning (see opposite).

If you intend to complete the Toubkal circuit with your mules via the Tazaghart *refuge*, you should send your mules ahead on the day that you climb Toubkal. However, you might consider releasing your mules once you've been resupplied at the Toubkal *refuge*, or even at Lac d'Ifni, as with two high passes ahead that mules cannot climb, and with supplies run down, this may be the wiser course of action. You will have to pay for the time it takes your mules and muleteers to return to Imlil.

SIDE TRIP: JEBEL OUANOUKRIM ASCENT

The final stages of the circuit are fairly demanding, but if you still have itchy feet it's possible to spend the afternoon climbing Jebel Ouanoukrim (4088m, five to six hours return), the second-highest mountain in the region.

To do this, after descending from Tizi n'Ouanoums, turn left as you hit the river and head south up the valley. As ever, it is a good idea to take a guide, or at least get some advice before setting off for this peak. Take the valley path back beyond the turn-off to Tizi n'Ouanoums and continue to climb up to Tizi n'Ouagene (3750m); from there follow the ridge to the summit.

Day 6: Toubkal Refuge to Azib Tamsoult

5½ to six hours/6km/493m ascent/1300m descent

From the *refuge* pick up the mule track that heads northwest then gently climbs north across the slope. Pass the first jagged, narrow gully; then, from a position high above a stream, turn left along a ridge west into the second valley. Initially keep to the southern side of the gully. The rough trail soon switches to the northern side and the route becomes rougher, requiring considerable scrambling.

After about 80 minutes, and having passed a couple of flat areas and a spring, you'll reach a wide and rather difficult scree slope: it's an unpleasant climb with a heavy pack. Follow the rough, zigzagging trail up to a small cliff face to the northeast, then turn left and traverse across to the rocky and exposed **Tizi n'Taddate** (3700m). To the left of the col is **Biginoussen** (4008m), while straight ahead the trail traverses the head of **Assif n'Timellite** to another col. (This area is covered in snow until mid-June, and sometimes even later.) From this second col is a steep, tricky descent down the northern side of the narrow, rocky gully. Some scrambling is required for the first hour, until the cliffs part, leaving a simple descent to 3000m and the small but homy **CAF Tazaghart Refuge** (☎ 067 852754 or via the CAF Chalet in Oukaïmeden 024 319036; dm CAF/HI members/nonmembers Dh42/63/83), which sits beside a stunning waterfall.

An alternative route has recently been opened between the Toubkal and Tazaghart *refuges*. From the Toubkal *refuge*, head down the mule trail for about 15 minutes. You will come to a fork near a small rounded wall, used as a sheepfold. Turn left, westwards, up the zigzagging mule path, which will bring you to **Tizi n'Aguelzim** (3560m) after two hours. There are amazing views on all sides at the pass: east to the Toubkal summit, northeast to the Imlil valley, northwest to Azzadene and west to the Tazaghart plateau. From here the track drops down in some 72 hairpins bends, at the bottom of which it crosses a stream. Twenty minutes further on, at a fork, take the left-hand track, and again 15 minutes later. Here the track leads uphill for around 10 minutes to the Tazaghart *refuge*.

Booking at the *refuge* is made complicated by the fact that the *gardien* is based in Tizi Oussem. You need to phone ahead, or else try passing a message to him via the muleteers or shepherds who pass. This will be easier if you are coming from the north. You'll probably find the place closed unless you've made a reservation. There are mattresses for 22 people, gaslights and a basic kitchen (there is a charge for using their gas). Campers can pitch tents beside the *refuge,* or on flat ground above the falls.

The *refuge* is mostly used by climbers drawn to the cliffs of Tazaghart, whose summit (3845m) is accessible to trekkers, who also have the chance to explore the wonderful **Tazaghart plateau** to the west.

Tizi n'Melloul (3850m), southeast of Tazaghart *refuge,* not only offers a harder route to and from the Toubkal Refuge, but also provides access to **Afella** (4045m), to the southeast of the pass, and to the jagged ridge leading north to Biginoussen.

The route down to **Azib Tamsoult** (2400m) is straightforward. Shortly after passing the impressive **Cascades d'Irhoulidene**, vegetation and tree cover increase. A five-minute walk from the base of the falls brings you to a pleasant wooded area, ideal for camping. To reach the village walk north for 10 to 15 minutes.

Day 7: Azib Tamsoult to Imlil

4½ to five hours/6km/89m ascent/749m descent

If you have made good time and you have the legs, you could continue down to Imlil at the end of day six. From the vegetable patches of Azib Tamsoult, with the **Assif n'Ouarzane** down to the left, a mule track traversing the forested slopes of the valley is visible to the north. Head towards it through the village and over the stream, and stay on it, avoiding left forks into the valley.

Climbing slightly and heading steadily northeast, with **Tizi Oussem** due west, you arrive at **Tizi n'Mzik** (2489m), where there's a possible camp site. Imlil is a 90-minute descent along a well-worn mule track; there's a spring to the right of the trail after 20 minutes.

JEBEL TOUBKAL ASCENT تساق جبل توبقال

North Africa's highest mountain is a big crowd-puller and every year, summer and winter, thousands of people come to climb the big one. Part of the reason for its popularity is that in summer Jebel Toubkal does not require any climbing experience, and anyone in good physical condition can get to the summit. Mountain runners can jog up from Imlil in a few hours, while overnighters from Marrakesh will take longer to plod up in trainers. Although the ascent isn't technically difficult, it is made challenging by Toubkal's notoriously extreme and fast-changing climate and by its long, steep slopes of brooding deep-brown, red and almost black volcanic scree. The other issue here can be altitude sickness: at 4167m, Jebel Toubkal is high enough to make this a possibility, which means you should factor in sufficient time to ascend slowly and steadily.

The route described is the standard walk undertaken by most visitors to Jebel Toubkal, but there are plenty of variations. An ascent of Toubkal can be combined with satellite peaks, and many (very fit) people squeeze in an ascent of Ouanoukrim (4088m) as well. Alternatively, the ascent can be made more leisurely by spending a night en route between Imlil and the Toubkal Refuge, either camping or lodging the night at Sidi Chamharouch. As elsewhere, it is recommended that you hire a guide for the ascent.

Maps

The same maps are recommended for the ascent as for the Toubkal Circuit (p426).

THE TREK AT A GLANCE

Duration two days
Distance 22km
Standard medium to hard
Start/Finish Imlil village
Highest Point Jebel Toubkal (4167m)
Nearest Large Town Marrakesh
Accommodation camping and mountain *refuges*
Public Transport yes
Summary The ascent of Jebel Toubkal is the most popular walk in the High Atlas. The views are magnificent. The route is straightforward and, outside winter and spring, usually easily achieved without mountaineering experience or a guide. However, it should not be taken lightly as the trek up the scree slope is hard, trekkers can be struck down with altitude sickness and the mountain's climate can be extreme: there can be snow even in June.

Day 1: Imlil to Toubkal Refuge

four to six hours/10km/1467m ascent

Toubkal rears above you when you leave the trailhead at Imlil (see p334). Try for a departure as early as possible for the walk up to the Toubkal *refuges*. It's not a particularly steep climb, but it is uphill all the way, there is little shade once past Aroumd and it can be very tiring, especially if you haven't done any previous warm-up walks or spent time acclimatising. Follow the dirt track that leads through Imlil towards **Aroumd (Armed)**. At the top of the village, a mule track on your left wends its way steeply through barley fields and apple and walnut trees and past the imposing Kasbah du Toubkal (see p336). Beyond the kasbah the path zigzags steeply upwards to rejoin the road at Aroumd, where the broad valley floor is hemmed in by towering slopes.

Once past Aroumd, heading up the valley, cross the broad, stony valley floor. On the other side follow the well-defined mule trail, which climbs up to a very large rock (you can see this from the valley floor) above the eastern side of the Assif Reraya, which leads to the hamlet and *marabout* (saint's mausoleum) of Sidi Chamharouch. The origins of **Sidi Chamharouch** (2310m) may be pre-Islamic, but the *marabout* is now a place of pilgrimage for Muslims, so not everyone travelling this way is going to the summit. The number of pilgrims and peak-baggers has given birth to a hamlet, a cluster of stalls just under halfway between Imlil and the Toubkal *refuge* selling soft drinks, some food and sometimes jewellery and souvenirs. Just beyond the *marabout*, which is out of bounds to non-Muslims, and to the left of the track, there are a couple of nice cascades and pools that make a great place to have lunch, with shade in the overhang of the rocks.

After crossing the river by the bridge at Sidi Chamharouch, the rocky path veers away from the river for a couple of kilometres and zigzags above the valley floor. It then levels off a bit, before rejoining the course of the river. The *refuge* (p430) is visible for a good hour or so before you reach it, situated immediately below the western flank of Jebel Toubkal.

Day 2: The Ascent

seven to eight hours/12km/960m ascent & descent

There is usually an air of excitement at the *refuge* as trekkers consider the prospects ahead. Two cwms (valleys formed by past glacial activity) run down the western flank of Toubkal, divided by the west-northwest ridge, which leads down from the summit. The southern cwm is the more usual route, and starts immediately below the refuge. Set off as early as possible to avoid climbing in the sun – there is no shade apart from the rocks – and be sure to have more than enough water and snacks. Warm clothing is also essential as a strong, bitter wind often blows across the summit.

If you have come up on a one-day trek from Imlil you may not be properly acclimatised, which means that altitude sickness is a real possibility. Be sure to walk at a steady, slow pace. If you do experience more than mild symptoms (serious symptoms may include a severe headache or vomiting) you should descend immediately. However tempting, do not lie down to sleep for a while on the slope.

The southern cwm track starts behind the *refuge*, where you need to cross the river and head eastwards to the clearly visible scree slope. Start to climb on the well-defined path that moves to the left of the slope. Cross the 'field' of boulders and then follow the straightforward path that zigzags up to **Tizi n'Toubkal** (3940m), straight ahead on the skyline. From there the path turns left (northeast) and follows the ridge to the summit (4167m). Provided there is no heat haze, you should be rewarded by superb views in all directions, especially early in the morning. Allow up to four hours to reach the top, depending on your fitness and weather conditions.

Stick to the same route coming down, bearing left when the *refuge* comes into view. The descent to the *refuge* should only take an hour or two, after which you can return directly to Aroumd or Imlil. If you are planning on spending a second night at the *refuge*, you could come down the longer route via the Ihibi sud, or south circuit. It is a straightforward two- to three-hour walk down to the refuge.

IMLIL TO SETTI FATMA

إمليل إلى ستي فاطمة

You get a taste of just about everything the mountains have to offer on this walk: high, windswept passes, wild and rocky landscapes and lush valleys that support a way of life that seems to have changed little in centuries. The route crosses a widely varied terrain and passes through a dozen or more Berber villages, some of which have yet to be connected with electricity. What's more, the trailhead is only two hours from Marrakesh and is easily accessible by public transport.

THE TREK AT A GLANCE

Duration three days
Distance 30km
Standard easy to medium
Start Imlil village
Finish Setti Fatma
Highest Point Tizi n'Tacheddirt (3172m)
Nearest Large Town Marrakesh
Accommodation camping and *gîtes*
Public Transport yes
Summary A superb and relatively leisurely three-day walk through some of the most spectacular country in the High Atlas. The route leads over only one rocky high pass, which is followed by a long descent into the upper Ourika Valley, a heavily cultivated area where countless green terraces and shady walnut groves cascade down the steep mountainsides.

Planning

This walk can be done comfortably in three days and could feasibly be completed in two by a very fit walker, although they might prefer taking in some of the many possible side trips and variations, especially around Timichi. If you're planning a longer stay, you'll need to bring extra supplies. This area of the High Atlas is covered by the 1:100,000 *Oukaïmeden-Toubkal* government survey sheet.

Setti Fatma has a **bureaux des guides** (☎/fax 024 426113), several small hotels (with hot

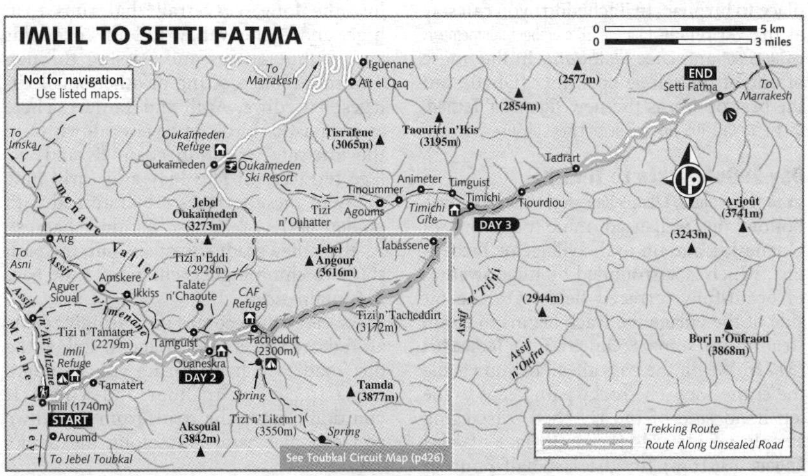

showers) and plenty of cafés; see p334. Buses and grands taxis (Dh30) travel pretty frequently between Setti Fatma and Bab er-Rob in Marrakesh (67km).

Day 1: Imlil to Ouaneskra

three to 3½ hours/7km/560m ascent

The first section of this trek is almost the same route as for the first day of the Toubkal Circuit (see p425), walking out of the trailhead and into the mountains. Once at **Tizi n'Tamatert** (2279m), it's an easy 45-minute walk to the village of **Ouaneskra** along a track that gives lovely views across the valley.

Ouaneskra now has three well-run **gîtes** (per person Dh50, meals Dh30, hot shower Dh10). You will pass the first one just before you cross the river, outside the village. The other two are at either end of the village. Where you stay will probably depend upon whom your guide has family connections with.

If you have walked to Ouaneskra in the morning, you could spend the afternoon in the **Imenane Valley**, which stretches from Ouaneskra and Tacheddirt northwest towards Asni. As the land is fertile and well watered and therefore heavily cultivated, the valley is dotted with Berber villages.

Alternatively, you could make a head start on the next day's walk by continuing another 2km to **Tacheddirt** (2300m), following the new road as it veers off to the right before Ouaneskra and crossing the Amagdoul plateau, which in summer is a popular place to bivouac. In Tacheddirt you can stay at the **CAF refuge** (dm CAF/HI members/nonmembers Dh30/45/60) and *chez l'habitant,* in the house of one of the refuge operators (Dh40), but the best option is the new **Tigmmi n' Tacheddirt** (☎ 062 105 169; per person from Dh50).

Day 2: Ouaneskra to Timichi

six to seven hours/12km/900m ascent/1300m descent

Follow the well-used mule path out of Ouaneskra and on to the village of Tacheddirt, which is surrounded by huge swathes of beautifully terraced fields. On the far side of the village the track begins to climb steadily up some 850m to **Tizi n'Tacheddirt** (3172m), with the pass ahead of you visible the entire way. The rocky path keeps to the left-hand side of the riverbed, zigzagging steeply up towards the south face of **Jebel Angour** (3616m) for the last half-hour or so. The pass is exposed and windy, but as ever has some stunning views. There is then an exhilarating and very long descent (at least three hours) down to **Timichi**. There is a welcome sheltered spot for lunch some 30 minutes' walk beyond Tizi n'Tacheddirt.

The path continues down past ancient, gnarled juniper trees and around the sloping eastern flank of Jebel Angour, where sheep and goats are brought to graze from early spring – you may not see the shepherds, but they will certainly see you. Though fairly well defined, this part of the trail is very rocky and at times clings precariously to the mountainside. The colour of the landscape gradually changes from a pale coffee colour to red and then to green. Finally, the cascading terraces of **Iabassene** village come into view. Head now for the huge old walnut tree that stands guard outside the village, and then follow the path that leads past the village houses. The path veers northeast from here and Timichi is just another 2km further on.

There are two *gîtes,* **Chez Ali Ouhya** (dm Dh30) in Iabassene and another, Chez Oussalem Brahim, in Timichi. The latter is outside the village proper, on the south side of the river, and has a great terrace from which to watch village activities. Basic meals are usually available at both places.

Day 3: Timichi to Setti Fatma

four to 4½ hours/11km/370m descent

Cross the river bed and turn right to follow the long, easy trail that runs east, high above the valley full of cornfields and walnut groves and passing through Tiourdiou and a string of other small villages: Tiwediwe, Anfli and Tadrart. There are fantastic, bird's-eye views down onto the intricate irrigation channels and village terraces. In late May and early June many of these terraces are crammed with golden barley, ready for summer harvest. As the valley gradually opens out, the path starts to climb higher, clinging to the bare mountain-sides.

As the path becomes increasingly rocky, at Tadrart you might prefer to follow the dirt road, which will bring you into **Setti Fatma** (p334) in an hour and a half. If you don't fancy the road, from Tiwediwe you can pick your way along the river's course.

WESTERN HIGH ATLAS الأطلس الكبير الغربي

You don't have to go too far west of Jebel Toubkal to find a very different landscape and some very different trekking conditions. The lower ranges to the west, running down towards the Souss plains, are generally warmer and greener but can still offer great walking in a magical area where jagged mountains and deep gorges are mixed with considerable forests, fertile valleys of date, almond, olive and walnut trees, and distinctive Berber villages. The terrain may make for gentler trekking, but it still offers some challenges and plenty of rewards.

Highlights

The gem here is the Tichka plateau, a bewitching area of highland meadows that are particularly delightful in spring, when they are covered in wildflowers. Although much of the walking here is less demanding than in the Toubkal area, the Tichka is still cut through by hidden gorges, thick with forests, edged with peaks and studded with stunning Berber villages.

Information

This area has some of the most remote walking Morocco has to offer. Some of the villages are very isolated and will not have seen the number of foreigners who pass through the villages of the Toubkal area or even the M'Goun.

While being off the beaten track is its strength, it also presents difficulties. There are, for instance, very few places to stay here, no official *refuges,* and almost no hotels outside the two bases, Taliouine (see p391) and, nearer Taroudannt, Tioute, although there is a delightful riad-style place now in Afensou and it is possible to stay in houses in other mountain villages. For most treks in this area you will need to carry camping equipment as well as all your necessary supplies. Although there are Berber villages up in the mountains, travellers cannot rely on finding food, water or anything else.

While these issues can be problems for visiting trekkers, they are not for the local experts, so, as ever, we recommend you travel with a guide. Alternatively, consult the UK-based **Atlas Mountain Information Service** (☎/fax 00 44 1592-873546; 26 Kirkcaldy Rd, Burntisland, Fife, Scotland KY3 9HQ). As well as being able to offer advice and make recommendations, they are also experts at running treks right across the plateau.

The best map for this area is the 1:100,000 *Tizi n'Test and Igli,* available from the Division de la Cartographie in Rabat or try www.omnimap.com and Hotel Ali in Marrakesh.

Guides & Mules

There is no *bureau de guide* in Taroudannt or any of the other towns that you might visit in this area. If you are not travelling with an organised tour, you can arrange a trek with guides from the Imlil's **Bureau des Guides** (☎/fax 024 485626).

As elsewhere in the mountains of Morocco, mules and muleteers are often easy to find and happy to travel, usually with a day's notice. Your guide will be able to arrange this.

Routes

If you don't want to camp then your options are limited, but using Afensou as a trailhead (and taking advantage of its hotel), you can make several varied circular day walks – to Imoulas, for instance, which has a Sunday *souq* and is a 9km round trip. You can also make a two-day trek out of Afensou to the village of Zawyat Tafilalt, where you can sleep in village houses, returning the next day via Tazoudot.

The Tichka plateau can be crossed in a leisurely week on a route that starts at Afensou and could run like this: Day 1, walk to Tazoudot and sleep *chez l'habitant*; Day 2, walk to Imamarn, then up the Medlawa Valley to the plateau, where you camp; Day 3, cross the plateau and camp; Day 4, spend the day peak-bagging by walking up Jebel Amendach (3382m); Day 5, descend from the plateau down the spectacular Nfis Gorge, camping near the village of Imi n'Oksar; Day 6, walk down to Souq Sebt Talnakant, from where you should find transport out, especially after the weekly Saturday market.

The Tichka plateau is riven by the Oued Nfis, which can be followed all the way to Imlil and then on to Jebel Toubkal. This is a long trek (12 days), but five or six days will get you to Tin Mal and the Tizi n'Test road.

Transport

You can get into the west of the range via **Imi n'Tanoute**, **Timesgadiouine** or **Argana**, on the Agadir-to-Marrakesh road, and also from **Taroudannt** to the south.

If you come from the west, you can get along the dirt roads to **Afensou** (not to be mistaken with another village of the same name to the south) on transport heading for the nearby mines or, on Wednesday, heading for the Thursday *souq*. **Souq Sebt Talnakant**, which is closer to Timesgadiouine and Argana, is an alternative, more westerly, trailhead. Transports head up there on Friday for the Saturday *souq*.

Heading south from Taroudannt things are a little easier, as *camionettes* (pick-up trucks) ply the route beside the Oued Ouaar up to **Tasguint** and **Imoulas** (with a Sunday *souq*) and up to **Tagmout** and **Souk Tnine-Tigouga** (with a Monday *souq*).

CENTRAL HIGH ATLAS – M'GOUN MASSIF الأطلس الك - جبل المكون

While the crowds flock to Jebel Toubkal, attracted by its 'highest mountain' tag and proximity to Marrakesh, a growing number of trekkers are moving over to the central High Atlas and the **M'Goun Massif**. The M'Goun offers great scope for trekkers, arguably more so than the Toubkal as it is remote and, so far, relatively unexploited. There is just as much drama here as around Toubkal: sedimentary rock forms, dramatic ridges and escarpments, tremendous gorges displaying deep-red and orange walls carved by erosion. These gorges are some of the highlights of the area and some can be walked and/or waded through (they're sometimes waist deep with water), making for a memorable, if chilling, experience. One of the great pleasures of this walk is the chance to follow one river up to its source, cross the mountain and then follow another river down into its valley.

Planning

MAPS

The 1:100,000 survey sheets *Azilal, Zawyat Ahannsal, Qalat M'Gouna* and *Skoura* cover all of the major trekking areas. The government also produces the 1:100,000 *Carte des Randonnées de Zaouiat Ahancal* map, which covers everywhere from Agouti in the east to Zaouiat Ahansal in the west, but its scope is of limited use for most trekkers.

More easily found and more useful is West Col Productions' 1:100,000 *Mgoun Massif* (occasionally available in Morocco, but otherwise usually stocked by **Stanfords** (www.stanfords.co.uk) and **Omnimap** (www.omnimap.com), which, although devoid of contours, is a good trail reference and useful for planning.

The German-produced *Kultur Trekking im Zentralen Hohen Atlas* shows the trek from Aït Bou Goumez to El-Kelaâ M'Gouna, and usefully marks and grades the many *gîtes* throughout the range.

Randonnées Pédestres Dans le Massif du M'Goun is a French trekking guidebook to the region, usually available in major Moroccan cities.

EQUIPMENT & SUPPLIES

All basic food supplies (meat, fruit, vegetables and bottled water) are available in Tabant. For anything else, including gas canisters, the hypermarket in Marrakesh is the best bet; otherwise, petrol, diesel and kerosene can be bought in Azilal.

Bottled water is widely available, but purifying locally sourced water is a more responsible alternative (see Rubbish, p422).

There is no *gîte* in Rougoult, but there is excellent camping beside the river. Your guide should be able to arrange tents. But if not, you will need to spend the night in Sebt Aït Bou Wlli, making the second-day walk much longer.

If you are walking in spring, and perhaps at other times of the year, a stick or trekking pole will be useful to help you vault over the many streams and to balance as you skip stones across rivers. If the river is high you may need to wade and, as the riverbed is too stony to walk barefoot, you may need plastic or waterproof sandals, or be prepared to get your boots wet.

GUIDES & MULES

Perhaps because the Centre de Formation aux Métiers de Montagne, the guide school, is in Tabant, many guides have good knowledge of the M'Goun. Guides from the Dadès and Sarhro area to the south and from further west in Imlil and in Marrakesh are all likely to have the knowledge and the enthusiasm to lead a trip through the M'Goun.

All guides can sort out local muleteers and mules for you.

THE M'GOUN TRAVERSE سلسلة جبال المكون

The M'Goun Massif has a reputation for being tough – it is home to some of Morocco's highest peaks and toughest trekking. But this walk will suit all grades of trekkers, including families, assuming children will enjoy riding the mules on the steeper section and through the rivers. The landscape is incredibly varied, with lush valleys and bare rock walls. Some of the Berber architecture styles you will see are found only in this valley, Yemen and Afghanistan.

Arrival Day

If you have come from Marrakesh the chances are you will be longing to stretch your legs and, if you have camping equipment, you could start by strolling down the valley to Agerssif, where there is an ideal camping spot beside the river, shaded by walnut trees, just near the bridge. Alternatively, you could make the hour-long walk along the quiet road from Agouti to Tabant, where you can stock up at the shops and where there is a basic café. If you have walked to Tabant, then continue on to the *marabout* and *agadir* (fortified communal granary) of Sidi Moussa, which sits on top of an unmistakable pyramid-shaped hill northwest of the village. Sidi Moussa is said to be effective in helping girls marry and bear children. The Aït Bougomez Valley (p329) is so beautiful here, especially in spring, and the views from the *marabout* so stunning that you will soon forget the long and winding drive to get here.

There are several gîtes in Agouti and neighbouring Talsnant village, the quietest being **Chez Daoud** (☎ 062 105183; Dh50), a short walk down from the road, beside barley fields, with rudimentary washing facilities. **Flilou** (☎ 024 343796; tamsilt@menara.ma; dm/d Dh50/150), on the road, has clean dorms and considerably more expensive doubles in a neat Berber house with spotless washing facilities.

Day 1: Agouti to Rougoult

six to seven hours/17km/326m descent & ascent

Agouti sits at the head of the Aït Bou Goumez Valley and the walk out of the village along the road has delightful views of the Happy Valley, the reasons for its name soon becoming obvious. After a leisurely hour and a half, a *piste* leads off left down from the road. A little further on there is a choice of following the *piste* or taking a steeper, shorter path that zigzags down into the valley, rejoining the *piste* at the village of **Agerssif** (1489m), which you should reach in less than three hours from Agouti. Agerssif sits at the confluence of the Lakhdar and Bou Goumez Rivers, where there is a bridge. The river here is a good place to rest and a great spot to camp.

The Lakhdar Valley narrows considerably as the *piste*, wide enough to be used by vehicles, climbs its south side. A half an hour or so upstream is the picturesque village of **Taghoulit** (1519m), surrounded by juniper trees, and with a simple **gîte** (per person Dh45). The *piste* continues up the gorge and then out into the broadening and more fertile upper valley, until it reaches **Sebt Aït Bou Wlli**, (pronounced Ait Bouli), a sizeable village above the river with a school (marked by flags), a Saturday market and, since 2005, electricity. The **Gîte d'Etape Adrar** (☎ 023 458479; per person Dh50, half board Dh120) is on the main *piste* and if you don't want to camp this is one option, the other being a homestay in Rougoult.

Several valleys meet at this village: Jebel Rat heads straight up on another good walk past the village of Abachkou to Jebel Rat (3797m). Our *piste* heads left, south, the valley becoming ever more beautiful as it winds up above wheat and barley fields, and juniper, wild fig and almond trees. The

> **THE TREK AT A GLANCE**
>
> **Duration** four days
> **Distance** 57km
> **Standard** medium
> **Start** Agouti
> **Finish** Aït Alla
> **Highest Point** Tizi n'Rougoult (2860m)
> **Accommodation** camping and *gîtes*
> **Public Transport** yes
> **Summary** This walk through the heart of the M'Goun will suit most grades of trekkers, even younger ones. There is one long day of walking, but this varied trek crosses some stunning mountain landscapes, passes through river gorges, and leads up one river and down another into valleys blessed by beauty and fertility.

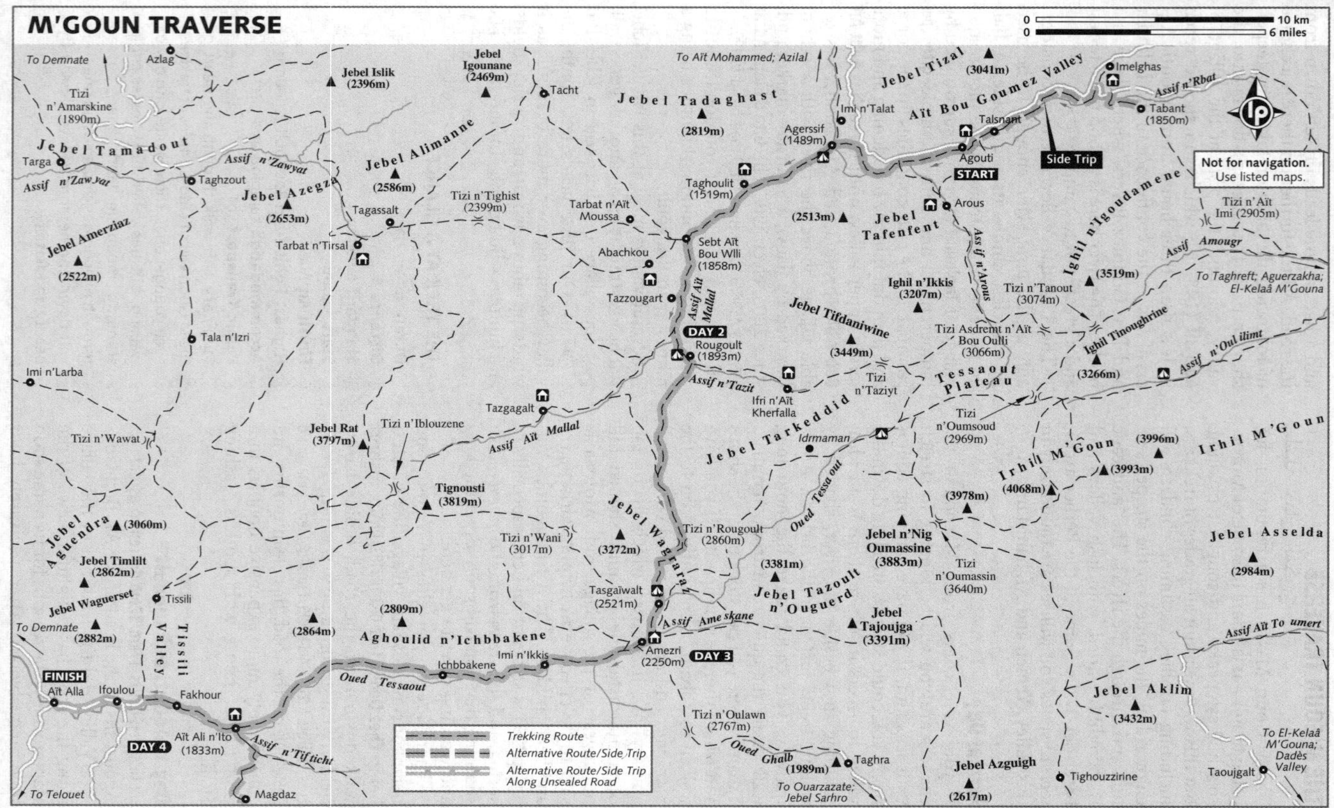
M'GOUN TRAVERSE
0
10 km
0
6 miles
Not for navigation.
Use listed maps.
Trekking Route
Alternative Route/Side Trip
Alternative Route/Side Trip Along Unsealed Road
START
FINISH
DAY 2
DAY 3
DAY 4
Side Trip
To Demnate
To Aït Mohammed; Azilal
To Taghreft; Aguerzakha; El-Kelaâ M'Gouna
To El-Kelaâ M'Gouna; Dadès Valley
To Ouarzazate; Jebel Sarhro
To Telouet
To Demnate
Azlag
Tizi n'Amarskine (1890m)
Jebel Tamadout
Targa
Assif n'Zawyat
Assif n'Zaw yat
Taghzout
Jebel Islik (2396m)
Jebel Igounane (2469m)
Tacht
Jebel Alimanne
(2586m)
Jebel Azegza
(2653m)
Tizi n'Tighist (2399m)
Tagassalt
Tarbat n'Tirsal
Jebel Amerziaz
(2522m)
Tala n'Izri
Imi n'Larba
Tizi n'Wawat
Jebel Aguendra
(3060m)
Jebel Timlilt (2862m)
Jebel Waguerset
(2882m)
Tissili
Tissili Valley
Jebel Tadaghast
(2819m)
Tarbat n'Aït Moussa
Abachkou
Tazzougart
Sebt Aït Bou Wlli (1858m)
Taghoulit (1519m)
Agerssif (1489m)
Imi n'Talat
Jebel Tizal
(3041m)
Aït Bou Goumez Valley
Talsnant
Agouti
Imelghas
Assif n'Rbat
Tabant (1850m)
Arous
Jebel Tafenfent
(2513m)
Assif n'Arous
Ighil n'Igoudamene
(3519m)
Tizi n'Aït Imi (2905m)
Assif Amougr
Ighil n'Ikkis (3207m)
Tizi n'Tanout (3074m)
Tizi Asdremt n'Aït Bou Oulli (3066m)
Ighil Tinoughrine
(3266m)
Assif n'Oul ilimt
Assif Aït Mallal
Rougoult (1893m)
Jebel Tifdaniwine
(3449m)
Tizi n'Taziyt
Tessaout Plateau
Assif n'Tazit
Ifri n'Aït Kherfalla
Tazgagalt
Assif Aït Mallal
Jebel Rat (3797m)
Tizi n'Iblouzene
Tignousti (3819m)
Jebel Tarkeddid
Idrmaman
Tizi n'Oumsoud (2969m)
Irhil M'Goun
(4068m)
(3993m)
(3996m)
Irhil M'Goun
(3978m)
Oued Tessa out
Jebel Wagraraz
(3272m)
Tizi n'Wani (3017m)
Tizi n'Rougoult (2860m)
Jebel n'Nig Oumassine (3883m)
Tizi n'Oumassin (3640m)
Jebel Asselda
(2984m)
(3381m)
Jebel Tazoult n'Ouguerd
Jebel Tajoujga (3391m)
Tasgaïwalt (2521m)
Assif Ameskane
Amezri (2250m)
(2809m)
(2864m)
Aghoulid n'Ichbbakene
Imi n'Ikkis
Ichbbakene
Oued Tessaout
Assif Aït Toumert
Jebel Aklim
(3432m)
Aït Alla
Ifoulou
Fakhour
Aït Ali n'Ito (1833m)
Assif n'Tifticht
Magdaz
Tizi n'Oulawn (2767m)
Oued Ghalb
(1989m)
Taghra
Jebel Azguigh
(2617m)
Tighouzzirine
Taoujgalt

village of **Tazouggart**, on the opposite side of the valley, marks a more-than-halfway point between Sebt Aït Bou Wlli and the day's end. From here, the landscape becomes ever more fantastic, with a hint of Shangri-la about it, until after two to 2½ hours you reach **Rougoult** (1893m). There is excellent camping just below the village beside the Tifra River. If you don't want to camp, there is the possibility of staying **chez l'habitant** (per person Dh30) in village houses, though you will need to ask around to see who has space.

Day 2: Rougoult to Amezri

six to seven hours/14km/600m descent/970m ascent

For two hours, the morning walk follows the Tifra, the stony path criss-crossing the river. There are terraces wherever there is space on the banks, although in places the valley is simply too narrow to cultivate. As it climbs, so the landscape becomes more barren. The mule path is well trodden and although it occasionally is forced to climb above gorges, it does follow the course of the river, roughly due south.

The source of the Tifra, no more than a trickle at the best of times, sits just below the pass of **Tizi n'Rougoult** (2860m). At this point, even the juniper trees are below you and only alpine plants and bushes above. From the broad saddle beneath the pass, a path leads left (east) to a ridge that climbs to over 3500m. The Rougoult pass is well worn, straight ahead. From the pass, the summit of Ighil M'Goun – at 4068m, just under 100m lower than Jebel Toubkal – is due east. Ahead of you there are long views across the southern M'Goun Massif and, more immediately, across the **Tessaout River**, a vast primordial scene that looks as though it has just been formed, the mountain slopes showing great gashes of rust, green and grey rocks.

From the Rougoult pass, the mule path is clearly marked, winding down in front of you and leading, after two hours to the first village, **Tasgaïwalt**. From here, keeping the river to your left, in all likeliness being followed by curious village children looking for entertainment, it is a gentle walk – 40 minutes, though you could easily spend longer – along the track to the village of **Amezri** (2250m). The 24-bed (mattress) **Gîte d'Etape Agnid Mohamed** (per person Dh50, breakfast Dh20, meals Dh50) has several large sleeping rooms, some of which look down onto the valley, a rudimentary shower and toilets, and the possibility of camping (around Dh20).

Day 3: Amezri to Aït Ali n'Ito

six hours/18km/427m descent/150m ascent

The third day is one of gentle pleasures as the path follows the Tessaout River, shelving gently from 2250m to 1833m. The valley is hemmed in by some impressive cliffs, particularly by the Ichbbakene escarpment, which rises a sheer 1000m above the river.

The river has few or no fish since a large flood flushed them out a few years back, but it does irrigate some exceptionally fertile farmland which the Berbers, here of the Aït Atta tribe, use to grow a range of seasonal crops. In the spring, the valleys are carpeted with wildflowers, while the fruit and nut trees add their blossoms to the spectacle. In this part of its course, the Tessaout flows more or less due west and is fed by a series of smaller streams that bring melted snow off the higher mountains.

At several places along the day's walk, the path crosses the river. For much of the year, it should be possible to hop over stones. But in spring, when the valley is at its most beautiful, the river may be too high and you may have to wade, as at the village of **Imi n'Ikkis**, some 5km from Amezri. The village is no more than a cluster of houses, but does have a shop (no sign) that usually stocks water and soft drinks, may also have the lurid green plastic shoes villagers wear to wade in the rivers, and occasionally has some tinned food.

As the path passes beneath the larger village of **Ichbbakene**, an hour and a half further downstream and backed by the sheer escarpment, you will see the significant building of the Hotel Edare. Built by a villager who worked in France, it was not operating at the time of our visit.

Two and a half hours further on, having crossed the river at several places, the path narrows and squeezes itself beneath the stone and mud houses of the village of Aït Hamza. At the bottom of the village is a working **water mill**. Powered by water diverted from the river, it's used to grind the annual wheat crop. Another hour of delightful walking leads to the village of Aït Ali n'Ito. The **Gîte d'Etape Assounfou** (☎ 066

075060, 024 385747; fax 024 385744; per person Dh50, breakfast Dh25) is one of the best in the region, with great views over the valley, not to mention hot showers (Dh10), a boutique and electricity.

If you have time, there is a good side trip to the village of **Magdaz**, a three-hour round trip to the south of Aït Ali n'Ito, but well worth the effort as this is one of the most beautiful villages in the Atlas Mountains. Apart from the beauty of the place, check out the village's extraordinary architecture, where tower-houses have been built in steps using stone and wood, a technique only known here, in Fakhour (see tomorrow's walk), and in Yemen and Afghanistan.

Day 4: Aït Ali n'Ito to Aït Alla

2½ to three hours/8km/150m descent

A dirt road leads alongside the river on a gentle walk down to the end of the trek. Occasionally the route does climb a little before it reaches the beautiful little village of **Fakhour**, where the houses climb up the hillside. Fakhour is noted for its *agadir*, which can be visited. There's no entry fee, but the *gardien* should be tipped (Dh10 would be welcome).

Less than an hour beyond Fakhour, the village of Ifoulou sits on a bend of the river and the road. This village seems to sleep for most of the week, there being little other than a drinks stand open, but on Monday it is the site for a large *souq*, when villagers from along the valleys come to trade and talk. Half an hour beyond the village, the *piste* joins the main Demnate–Skoura road by the new road bridge over the Tessaout River, below the village of Aït Alla. From here it should be possible to find transport in either direction, although there is no certainty as to how long you will need to wait.

THE RIF MOUNTAINS

جبل اريف

Why don't more people come to walk in the Rif Mountains? The first and lowest of the mountain ranges that ripple south through Morocco, they make perfect trekking country, blessed as they are with magnificent ranges, gorges and valleys, clothed in forests of cedar, cork oak and fir. Being close to the Mediterranean, the Rif are also the greenest of Morocco's mountains and springtime, with its riot of wildflowers, is one of the most delightful times to walk here.

One thing that does deter trekkers is the region's reputation as an area of drug production. But although kif (marijuana) production takes up over three quarters of cultivatable land east of Chefchaouen, trekkers have little reason to feel threatened, especially if travelling with a guide – villagers will be genuinely interested and surprised to see you. The trek detailed here, setting out from Chefchaouen, is well trodden and unproblematic in this respect.

The Rif Mountains rarely top more than 2500m in height, with most treks only occasionally venturing over 2000m, so altitude sickness isn't the worry it can be in other parts of Morocco.

WILDLIFE

The Rif's climate and proximity to Europe endows it with a Mediterranean climate – the area closely resembles the sierras of southern Spain. Cedars make up the majority of tree species, including a rare local species *Abies maroccana*, a variant of the Spanish cedar that is only found above 1500m. It's a relict of an older, cooler period in Morocco's history. In addition, cork oak, holm pine and wild olive dot the limestone mountains. The stony land is hard to cultivate and thin in nutrients; deforestation is an issue here as in other parts of Morocco.

Locals may tell you that there are wolves in the mountains, but you shouldn't believe the stories – the closest you'll get is spotting a red fox or feral dog near a village. Wild boar are also native, but have a retiring nature that makes them hard to spot. The Rif's most famous mammals are the Barbary apes (known locally as *mgou*), whose range extends south into the Middle Atlas.

You'll have better luck with birdlife. Raptors easily spotted wheeling on thermals include black-shouldered kites, golden eagles and long-legged buzzards. Ravens can also be seen against the limestone cliffs.

Scorpions present a small risk in the Rif, although less so than further south. Be wary of the red scorpion; stings are extremely painful. The venomous *fer à cheval* viper (named for the horseshoe-like mark on its head) is more likely to flee from you than vice versa.

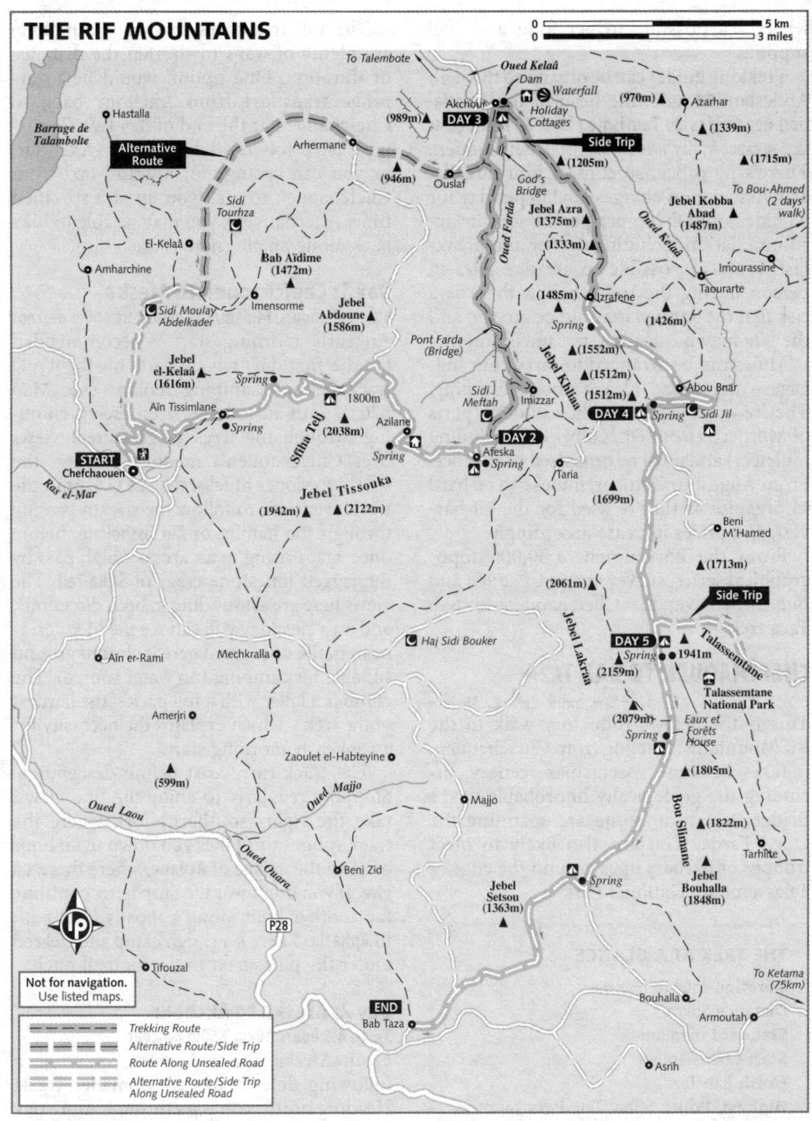

PLANNING

You can trek year-round in the Rif Mountains, though it can be bitterly cold between November and March, when snow is common. It rains frequently between late September and June, while during high summer it is fiercely hot, even on the peaks, and some water sources dry up.

Trekking is relatively undeveloped in the Rif, but in many villages there are simple *gîtes* where it's possible to sleep for the night. Otherwise, a tent is extremely worthwhile. A decent sleeping bag is essential whatever the season, as is a light waterproof jacket – rain showers are common. Most treks originate in Chefchaouen, where it's possible to get food and fuel supplies.

Trekking guides can be organised through Abdeslam Moude, the head of the **Association des Guides du Tourisme** (☎ 062 113917; guiderando@yahoo.fr; day tour Dh350) in Chefchaouen. There's no office, so contact him directly. The Association charges Dh350 per day for a guide, and Dh200 per person for *gîte* accommodation including dinner and breakfast. It's also possible to arrange *gîtes* in person during the trek, though there is a risk that the *gardien* may not be around and the *gite* may be closed – not uncommon.

Mules can be arranged to carry your luggage – not a bad idea if you're camping. They're more expensive than in other parts of Morocco (from Dh200 per day including muleteer) and must be organised in advance. From August to October, mules can be hard to organise as they're used for the kif harvest, and prices increase accordingly.

From the government 1:50,000 topographical series, survey sheets *Chaouen* and *Bab Taza* cover the Chefchaouen-to-Bab Taza trek.

CHEFCHAOUEN TO BAB TAZA

شفشاون إلى باب تازة

This is the best introductory walk to the Rif Mountains. Starting from Chefchaouen, it takes in some spectacular scenery, including the geologically improbable God's Bridge, a natural stone arc spanning the Oued Farda. You are also likely to meet troupes of Barbary apes around the edge of Talassemtane National Park.

THE TREK AT A GLANCE

Duration four to five days
Distance 56km
Standard medium
Start Chefchaouen
Finish Bab Taza
Highest Point Sfiha Telj Pass (approximately 1800m)
Accommodation camping and *gîtes*
Public Transport yes
Summary The walking here is relatively undemanding but the mountain scenery is spectacular, the tiny Riffian villages worth a detour, and the gorges and weird geology fascinating.

The full trek takes five days, but there are plenty of ways to shorten the distance or duration. One option would be to arrange transport from Akchour back to Chefchaouen at the end of day two. Transport isn't too hard to find in Akchour, or you can arrange for a grand taxi from Chefchaouen to pick you up at a specified time. Alternatively, you may be able to hike back along an alternate route.

Day 1: Chefchaouen to Afeska

5½ to 6½ hours/14.5km/1200m ascent/600m descent

An early morning start is recommended for the first day, which starts on the 4WD track behind Camping Azilane (see Map p202), with an initially steep ascent climbing through the trees to give great views over Chefchaouen's medina. Skirting the southern slopes of **Jebel el-Kelaâ** (1616m), the track evens out to follow the stream passing through the hamlet of **Aïn Tissimlane**, before once again rising in an arc to a high pass by the jagged limestone crags of **Sfiha Telj**. The views here are astounding in both directions, and on a clear day you can see the Mediterranean in the distance. There is cleared ground suitable for camping (no water source). The climb is a killer with a full pack – the hardest of the trek – which explains the necessity for a cool early morning start.

The track turns east before descending. Stopping regularly to enjoy the fine views, take the right (southern) fork where the track splits – this takes you down in an hour or so to the village of **Azilane**, where there's a *gîte*. If you don't want to stop here, continue for another hour along a mostly level path to **Aphasia**. There's a rough camp site cleared under the pines next to the football pitch.

Day 2: Afeska to Akchour

3½ to 4½ hours/10km/860m descent

From Afeska, the wide *piste* you've been following deteriorates to a smaller track. Heading north, you pass through more oak and pine woods to **Sidi Meftah**, where there's a *marabout* and spring, before leaving the woods and descending the switchbacks to **Imizzar** on the **Oued Farda**. Once beside the river, turn left (away from the village, northwest), then cross the river below some impressive overhanging cliffs and continue heading northwest. You'll join a well-worn mule track that eventually leads down to

Pont Farda, an ancient bridge over Oued Farda.

Cross to the west bank of the river and continue north, dwarfed by the surrounding scenery. After an hour, the trails bears left away from the river towards **Ouslaf**, which is overshadowed by a giant rock buttress, but keep on the same path while it bears right, descending to rejoin the river on the outskirts of **Akchour** (398m), which sits on the **Oued Kelaâ**.

Akchour is strung out along the river. As you approach it, you first come to a small café with very welcome river-cooled soft drinks, and a dam with a deep pool that seems made for swimming, although the water temperature means short dips only! Upstream from the dam is a pleasant camping spot at the confluence of the Oued Kelaâ and Oued Farda.

Akchour has a couple of other cafés that can throw together a basic tajine, and offer even more basic rooms for the night, for a negotiable Dh50.

From Akchour, it's usually possible to get transport back to Chefchaouen – most likely one of the rugged vans or 4WDs that battle it out on the *piste*. If there's nothing going from Akchour, try **Talembote**, 2km further north, which has a market on Tuesdays with regular transport to Chefchaouen (Dh15). Most passing vehicles will stop to pick you up if they have space – a case of paid hitchhiking. They may drop you at Dar Ackoubaa, the junction town 10km north of Chefchaouen on the P28 highway.

SIDE TRIP: GOD'S BRIDGE

With an early start from Afeska, you can reach Akchour by lunchtime, giving time for the short hike (1½ hours, 3km return) to **God's Bridge** – an unlikely geological structure that shouldn't be missed.

The path south from Akchour's dam up the Oued Farda is rough in places, but well worth any scrambling. You'll also have to cross the river twice but this is quite easy where it's not deep – if you don't mind the occasional splash. (However, if you're trekking in spring, check in Afeska that snow melt hasn't made the river impassable.) God's Bridge is about 45 minutes from Akchour. A huge red stone arch towers 25m above the river and it almost beggars belief that it was carved by nature and not by human hand. Over countless millennia, the river flowed as an underground watercourse, eroding the rock and carving a path deeper and deeper, leaving the bridge high and dry.

Day 3: Akchour to Pastures above Abou Bnar

4½ to six hours/12km/977m ascent

An early morning start (with full water bottles, since there are no springs on the route until you reach Izrafene) sees you leaving Akchour by heading to the north, crossing the bridge over the Oued Kelaâ and then cutting right (southeast) along the track to Izrafene. It's a particularly picturesque walk as you climb up and around **Jebel Azra** (1375m). Your eyes lift from the steep gorges you've trekked through and out over the sweep of open mountains. If you're up for some scrambling, add half an hour to attain the peak, from where you can drink in further gorgeous views.

Having cut around the mountain, the countryside becomes gentler – rolling even – as the trail heads south. The village of **Izrafene** marks the halfway point of the day's trek. Just before the village, a track bears east at a col, tempting the adventurous to abandon the Bab Taza hike and walk to Taourarte and on to **Bou-Ahmed** on the coast, a further two days' walk.

From Izrafene, the track turns into a 4WD *piste* – the first since Afeska. It follows a narrow valley, gradually turning east up onto a ridge with gentle views. Where it forks, turn left, and then, just 25m later, turn right onto a trail that heads southeast to **Abou Bnar** through a pretty stretch of oak wood. There's little to detain you here, so continue alongside the river (not the 4WD track) through the open, grassy country to the *marabout* of **Sidi Jil**. This is a pretty area for camping, but if you continue for another 30 minutes, you'll come to an even more beautiful spot, set in wide pasture near a spring – an idyllic place for a night's rest.

ALTERNATIVE ROUTE: RETURN TO CHEFCHAOUEN

It's possible to trek back to Chefchaouen from Akchour in a day by an alternate route. The route goes via the villages of **Ouslaf**, **Arhermane** and **El-Kelaâ**. El-Kelaâ is the site of fascinating **Mosquée Srifiyenne**, with its strange leaning tower. This route takes a quick six hours and avoids any major climbs or descents.

Day 4: Pastures Above Abou Bnar to Talassemtane National Park

two to 2½ hours/6km/352m ascent

From the camp site southwest of Abou Bnar, walk back to the 4WD track. Turn left and cross the river, and walk south into the pine woodland. You will quickly come to a T-junction, where you should keep on the right (the left goes downhill to Beni M'Hamed) where the path starts to ascend again.

Keep on the main track, ignoring further side tracks and junctions. As you rise and go through several mini-passes, the views return. To the west, the huge mass of **Jebel Lakraa** (2159m) dominates the countryside.

By late morning you'll reach the edge of **Talassemtane National Park**. A small sign indicates that you should turn left off the 4WD track to the house of the park's Eaux et Forêts *guardien*. You can camp outside his house and draw water, and he can advise on short hikes into the park.

SIDE TRIPS

The short walking day allows plenty of time to explore the area and watch wildlife. Talassemtane National Park is where you are most likely to see Barbary apes.

Head north, back along the 4WD track above the *guardien's* house to a clearing and junction. Turn right and follow the track east into *mgou* country. Troops are relatively common here, although quickly retreat into the safety of the trees if you get too close. The track bends south, giving great views out across the valley to the long ridge of **Jebel Taloussisse** (2005m), before turning briefly east again. Here a trail on the right leads south over the spur of **Talassemtane** (1941m) to a football pitch – strange, but true! – on an area of flat land. From here it's possible to make a rocky traverse west, back to the camp site.

Climbing **Jebel Lakraa** is another alternative for gung-ho trekkers. The best approach is from the north of the mountain, trekking along the ridge to descend one of the stream gullies southeast of the summit. However, there's no fixed path and it's a scramble in places. Allow around 3½ hours return.

Day 5: Talassemtane National Park to Bab Taza

2½ to 3½ hours/13.5km/825m descent

The final day is a quick descent along the 4WD track to Bab Taza, where local kif cultivation is much in evidence. The trail swings through a wide pasture and on through the cork woodland of **Jebel Setsou** (1363m) before revealing the sprawl of **Bab Taza** (or so it seems after a few days in the mountains) below.

In Bab Taza, there are quite a few cafés and a couple of grotty-looking hotels strung along the main road. The main business seems to be in huge sacks of fertiliser used for growing kif. Grands taxis leave regularly throughout the day for Chefchaouen (Dh12, 30 minutes) from the western end of town.

THE ANTI ATLAS
الأطلس الصغير

The last significant mountains before the Sahara, the arid, pink-and-ochre-coloured chain of the Anti Atlas is less visited by trekkers and yet offers some wonderful trekking opportunities. **Tafraoute** is the ideal launching point, with the quartzite massif of **Jebel Lekst** (2359m, see p406), the 'amethyst mountain', lying about 10km to the north, and the twin peaks of **Adrar Mqorn** (2344m) 10km to the southeast. Beneath the arid, jagged mass of these peaks lie lush irrigated valleys and a string of oases.

At the eastern end of the Anti Atlas, almost due south of Jebel Toubkal, **Jebel Siroua** (3305m) raises its bleak bulk above the landscape. This dramatic volcano makes an excellent centrepiece to a varied long-distance trek. See Tafraoute (p402) for more general information on this region.

AROUND TAFRAOUTE

Morocco has such a wealth of trekking options that perhaps it is not surprising that an area with the potential of Tafraoute has not yet been fully exploited. The adventurous trekker will find here, as elsewhere in the Moroccan south, many challenging and rewarding treks because the Anti Atlas around Tafraoute has rugged, barren rocks and lush green valleys aplenty.

Jebel Lekst is the star attraction. The 'amethyst mountain' is a massive ridge that stretches away northwest of Tafraoute. In spite of the harshness of the landscape, the Berbers who live in villages such as Tagoudiche still manage to grow the mountain staples of wheat, barley, olives, figs and almonds. The latest area to be trekked in this region is around Jebel Aklim (2531m), northeast of Tafraoute. Easily reached from Taroudannt and Agadir, Jebel Aklim has the advantage of sitting in an even more remote area than Jebel Lekst, yet still surrounded by Berber villages in valleys guarded by old kasbahs. From the top of Jebel Aklim, there are great views over to the High Atlas and to Jebel Siroua.

This is a tougher region than the M'Goun or Tichka plateau and trekkers need to cope with a lack of facilities and the harsh climate. This close to the Sahara, the summers are blisteringly hot, and winter sees the occasional snowfall on the high passes and peaks, so the area is best walked at the end of winter – late February is ideal. Daytime temperatures may be 20°C, but at night it can drop below freezing.

Other than the odd small store, you won't find many supplies in the area, so the great challenge is how to carry enough food and water to keep you going. As with other remote areas in Morocco, it is often possible to stay in village houses, but you still need to be prepared to camp and to carry food and water.

The best way of doing this is by hiring a guide and mules. There is no *bureau de guide* in Taliouine, or Taroudannt for that matter, although there are guides in town – and many more *faux guides*. As ever, insist on seeing a guide's ID card before you waste your time talking through possibilities. As a rule, trained mountain guides do not tout for business in the street. Mules are not commonly used in the Anti Atlas, but you may be able to arrange this through your guide.

Jebel Lekst and the approaches from Tafraoute are covered by the 1:50,000 map sheets *Had Tahala* and *Tanalt,* while the whole area is covered by 1:100,000 sheets *Annzi, Tafrawt, Foum al-Hisn* and *Taghjijt*.

There are some 26 villages neatly spaced out through the Ameln Valley, the valley that runs along the south side of **Jebel Lekst**, and they make for a great walk. You'd need weeks to do a full circuit, but a stunningly beautiful and suitably stretching five-day walk would start in **Oumesnate**, take in several villages, and head up to the village of Tagdichte, the launching point for a day ascent of Jebel Lekst. It's a tough scramble, and the ascent is best seen as part of a gentle trek east through the valley from, say, Tirnmatmat – where there are some excellent day walks – to Oumesnate (both villages lie just off the 7148 road). This is an enchanting area to trek.

Southeast of Tafraoute the possibilities are equally exciting. The scramble up **Adrar Mqorn** is hard but worthwhile. Due south of its twin peaks are the palm-filled gorges of **Aït Mansour** and **Timguilcht**, which make up the oasis of **Afella-Ighir**. There is plenty to explore.

Jebel Aklim makes a great focal point for a four or five-day walk out of Irghem, with its copper mines. From here the route leads to the mountain, which dominates the landscape.

Transport is an issue throughout this part of the Anti Atlas. *Camionettes* provide a reliable though infrequent service to some villages and grands taxis will run on *souq* days, though at other times you may need to hire one to get you to the trailheads.

JEBEL SIROUA جبل السروة

Some way south of the High Atlas, at the eastern edge of Anti Atlas, the isolated volcanic peak of **Jebel Siroua** (3304m) offers unique and exciting trekking. Isolated villages, tremendous gorges, a tricky final ascent and some dramatic scenery all make this an excellent place for trekkers in search of solitude, stark beauty and a serious walk.

The ascent of Jebel Siroua is the most obvious walk to make, but, as ever in Morocco, lasting memories will be found elsewhere – in the beauty of lush valleys, in the hospitality shown in Berber homes, in the play of light on rock and the proximity of the Sahara. So if you don't fancy the climb to the summit, the mountain circuit will still make a wonderful trek.

The **Auberge Souktana** (p391), a couple of kilometres east of Taliouine on the main road, is the best place to seek advice. Owned by a Franco-Moroccan couple, it has become the trailhead – here you can arrange guides, mules and gear for the circuit. The 1:100,000 *Taliwine* and 1:50,000 *Sirwa* maps cover the route. In winter it can be fiercely cold in the region, so the best time to trek is spring. See Taliouine (p391) for further general information.

If you need supplies, regional markets take place at Taliouine and Aoulouz on Wednesday, Askaoun on Thursday and Tazenakht and Igli on Sunday.

Mules, as ever, can be hired at short notice (often the next day) at villages around the mountain

There's a challenging, weeklong trek which allows you to walk out of Taliouine along a gentle dirt trail that heads eastward up the **Zagmouzine Valley** to **Tagmout**. It then heads northeast through **Atougha**, from where it is a six-hour trek to the summit of Jebel Siroua. Walking at a regular pace, you'll be ascending the summit on the morning of the fourth day. After descending into the gorges for the night, you'll pass the extraordinary cliff village of **Tisgui** before reaching **Tagouyamt** on the fifth day. Tagouyamt has limited supplies and, in case you can't find a room, a good place to camp in the amazing **Tislit Gorge**. From Tagouyamt, the valley continues to **Ihoukarn** from where you can either head south to the Taliouine–Ouarzazate road at Tizi n'Taghatine (you'll be able to pick up passing transport here) or else complete the circuit by walking west back to Taliouine.

An alternative circuit that is even less trekked starts at the village of Tamlakout, where there is a classified *gîte*, and takes in Aït Tigga, the Assif Mdist and the foot of Jebel Siroua. It then ascends the mountain, continues to Aziouane and exits via the Amassines. Some of the trek is strenuous but no one day should involve more than six hours' walking.

Taliouine and Anezale (for Tamlakout) are both on the main Agadir–Taroudannt–Ouarzazate road and are regularly served by grands taxis and buses.

JEBEL SARHRO

جبل صغرو

The starkly beautiful **Jebel Sarhro** range of mountains continues the line of the Anti Atlas, rising up between the High Atlas and Dadès Valley to the north, with the Sahara stretching away to the south.

Little-visited and relatively undeveloped for the tourist market, it offers a landscape of flat-topped mesas, deep gorges and twisted volcanic pinnacles softened by date palms and almond groves. This wild, arid, isolated country is inhabited by the Aït Atta tribe, great warriors famous for their last stand against the French here, on **Jebel Bou Gafer**, in 1933.

PLANNING

Jebel Sarhro throws up so many options that it can be hard to settle on a route. Wherever you go is likely to be eye-poppingly gorgeous, but be sure to choose a route that touches the heart of the range, between **Igli** and **Bab n'Ali**. The Sarhro is a winter trekking destination, although don't let that fool you: it can still freeze, and snow falls as low as 1400m. But unlike some of the higher Atlas treks, it doesn't always snow in winter and even when it does, it is usually possible to trek. In spring there is still water around and night-time temperatures no longer fall well below zero. In late autumn you might see Berber clans moving their camps down from the higher mountains. Summer is scorchingly hot (above 35°C), water sources disappear, and snakes and scorpions are two a penny. Dehydration is common at any time of the year.

Jebel Sarhro has three trekking centres, the towns of **Kelaâ M'Gouna** (p355) and **Boumalne du Dadès** (p356) on the north side of the range, and the southern village of **N'Kob** (p353). A number of foreign tour operators (such as Explore, Exodus and Walks Worldwide) run good-value trips here, but all three of the Sarhro trekking centres have **bureaux des guides** (☎/fax El-Kelaâ 061796101/062132192, ☎ Boumalne 067 593292, ☎ N'Kob 067 487 509) which charge around Dh300 a day for a guide and Dh100 for a mule.

Supplies should be bought beforehand in Ouarzazate or Marrakesh, although you will find tea, tinned fish, biscuits and bread in these three towns and may find eggs, dates, almonds, bread and tinned fish in some villages. In this environment, and with the amount of water that must often be carried, mules are a worthwhile investment and are usually easy to find.

The 1:100,000 *Boumalne* and *Tazzarine* maps cover the region, but the most useful trekking map is the 1:100,000 *Randonnée culturelle dans le Djebel Sarhro* by Mohamed Aït Hamza and Herbert Popp, published in Germany, written in French and available

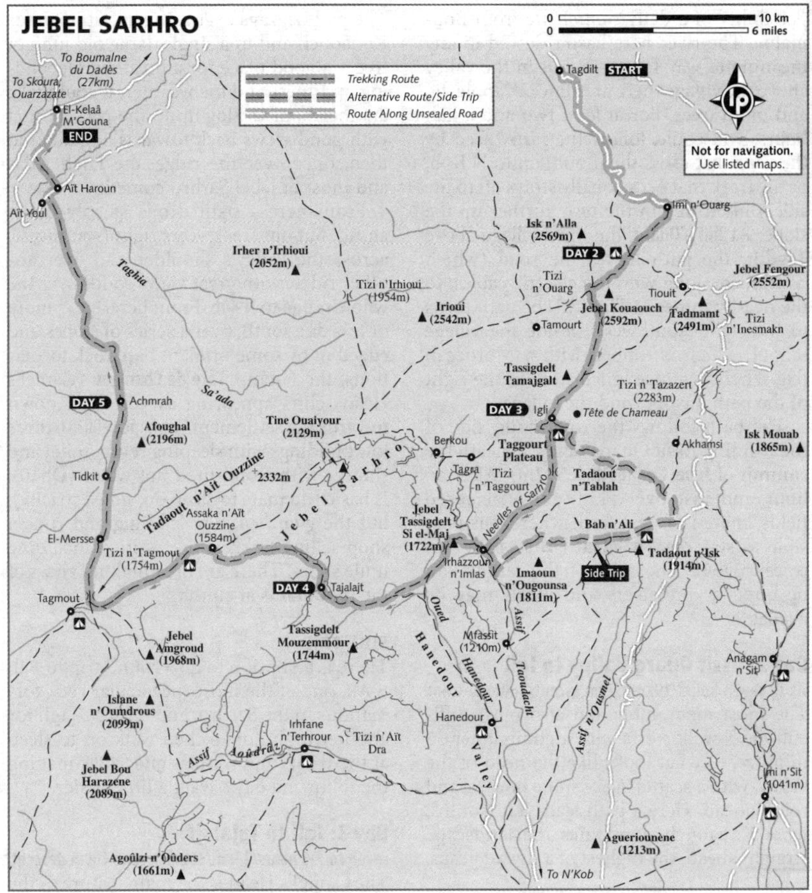

in Morocco. Expensive (Dh150), but worth the price for the history and information on the back as well as for the map.

Minibuses run from Boumalne du Dadès to Ikniouln (Dh25), at the northern edge of the range, departing around noon and returning to Boumalne early the next morning. Ikniouln has its market on Wednesday.

THE SARHRO LOOP

The classic Sarhro walk cuts right through the middle of the range, starting from Boumalne du Dadès or El-Kelaâ M'Gouna and proceeding to N'Kob. It is a great walk and one that many agencies, both local and international, now feature.

The Sarhro Loop is just as varied and interesting, but has one big advantage over the traverse route: it ends up on the same side of the mountains as it starts, allowing you to trek and then carry on into the Dadès gorges or to Merzouga and the dunes. You can walk it in either direction. Tents could be used, but the route offers the possibility of staying in *gîtes* or *chez l'habitant*, which can be very welcome in winter when you can wake in the morning to find that a metre of snow fell during the night.

Day 1: Tagdilt to the Assif Ouarg Valley

four hours/17km/200m ascent

Tagdilt is an uninspiring village but a very useful trailhead, with three *gîtes* and the possibility of a daily *camionette* from Boumalne. The river here hasn't flowed in any meaningful way for years, but in the valley above the village there are almond, apple, fig and plum trees. For at least two and a half hours, you could follow the *piste*, used by the vans that cross the mountain to N'Kob, or the track that occasionally strays off to the side, only to rejoin the *piste* further up the slope. At **Imi n'Ouarg**, the third village above Tagdilt, the path leaves the road (which continues, along with the electric cables, to the nearby mines at Tiouit). The path turns to the right (southwest) beside the village school, which is topped with a Moroccan flag. There is a nice lunch stop, to the right of the path, just beyond the village.

The path follows the right-hand side of the winding Assif Ouarg valley, beneath the summit of **Jebel Kouaouch** (2592m). After an hour and just over 3km, above terraced fields, there is a neat farm where it is possible to stay **chez l'habitant** (☎ 061 082321; per person Dh30-50). The sons of the family can be hired as muleteers and meals may be available.

Day 2: Assif Ouarg Valley to Igli

six to seven hours/19km/620m ascent/860m descent

The most memorable and also most difficult day's walk starts with a climb, after 35 minutes, to what looks like the head of the valley, with a scattering of stone houses, and rocks ahead. Here a path leads left (south). Jebel Kouaouch dominates the landscape straight ahead, the highest of a row of peaks.

THE TREK AT A GLANCE

Duration five days
Distance 56km
Standard medium to hard
Start Boumalne du Dadès
Finish El-Kelaâ M'Gouna
Highest Point Tizi n'Ouarg (approximately 2300m)
Accommodation camping and *gîtes*
Public Transport yes
Summary This is a great alternative to the classic Sarhro traverse and gives a taste of the staggering and varied beauty of the range. There are some demanding climbs and long days of walking, so there is the option of adding another night to the route.

The path zigzags over a stream, up towards Kouâouch and to a single, large old juniper tree – a good place for a breather. Depending on fitness and the weather, it could take another hour to slog up to the pass, at first with good views back towards Tagdilt; and then, once over the ridge, the High Atlas and most of Jebel Sarhro come into view.

From here a path drops steeply down ahead, but our track veers right (southwest) across the valley's shoulder and over another ridge, with great views south over the whole range to **N'Kob**. From here, **Igli** is more or less due south, over a series of slopes and edged in by some brilliant bare rock formations, the famous **Tête de Chameau** (Camel's Head) cliffs appearing as you walk down towards the settlement. The **gîte** (Dh30), three low buildings with sleeping room, toilet and shower with wood-fired hot water (Dh10), is basic (no mats to sleep on, no electricity), but the *guardien* is welcoming and runs a shop selling trekkers' necessities, including mule shoes. There are breathtaking views of the mountains at sunset.

SIDE TRIP

There is an option to do a round trip to Bab n'Ali, one of the most spectacular rock formations in the Sarhro, and return to Igli for another night, or to then walk on to sleep at the Irhazzoun n'Imlas **gîte** (Dh30), making the following day's walk a little easier.

Day 3: Igli to Tajalajt

seven to 7½ hours/24km/350m ascent/400m descent

The Camel's Head is the main feature of the first part of the walk, looming on the right-hand side, the peak of **Jebel Amlal**, sacred to the Aït Atta Berbers, some of whom meet there each August. The morning's walk is gentler than the previous day's, leading through wide, rocky valleys. After some 1½ hours, beneath a small village (Taouginte), the path curves around an Aït Atta cemetery, the graves marked with piles of stone. Beyond here, the path leads below the **Needles of Sarhro**, a long dramatic cliff that slopes down after another 1½ hours to the Amguis River. Several valleys meet in this beautiful spot, which would be a great place to camp, with palms and oleander. Half an hour southwards down the valley takes you to **Ighazoun**, a small village above well-tended fields with a good lunch place beside the river.

At Ighazoun the path joins a motor *piste* which runs left to N'Kob, right towards the Dadès. Take the right track (northwest) towards a sheer cliff on the left, the rocky path leading beneath it and up to a broadening valley. The *piste* loops around the north side of Jebel Tassigdelt Si el-Haj (1722m) and then south again towards Tiguiza, where there is a basic **gîte** (☎ 071 728006; Dh 30). Before you reach Tiguiza, another *piste* leads right (west) to Akerkour village and then into a narrowing fertile valley dotted with palms and up an increasing incline to the beautifully sited village of **Tajalajt**, where it is possible to stay **chez l'habitant** (per person Dh30-40) and obtain basic meals if there is food.

Day 4: Tajalajt to Achmrah

eight to 8½ hours/26km/200m ascent/300m descent

A long day, but another day walking in splendour, starting up the valley *piste* from Tajalajt, above the terraced fields of corn, and palm and almond groves. Less than 1½ hours brings you to **Assaka n'Aït Ouzzine** (1584m), which has a large ruined kasbah just above the beautiful valley. From here the *piste* leads out of the valley into a very different landscape, a rocky steppe that might have been lifted out of Central Asia, often complete with howling wind. One and a half hours from Assaka, wedged between 2000m ridges, brings you to **Tagmout**, also sometimes called Amgroud after one of the mountains overlooking you, where there is a well-kept **gîte** (per person Dh30, breakfast Dh25) with electricity, mattresses and blankets. A simple lunch is usually available (Dh25 to Dh30).

From Tagmout the motor *piste* leads northwest to the Dadès Valley and south to N'Kob, and you may find transport moving along it to Boumalne's Wednesday *souq* and N'Kob's on Sunday. The trek heads due north, climbing for more than an hour to the top of the Tizi n'Tagmout (1754m). There are stunning views from here to the M'Goun, Jebel Siroua and Toubkal. The track leads in another hour to **El-Mersse**, where there are the twin essentials of shade and a year-round spring.

The track continues due north, mostly a gentle descent, but with the occasional climb. Under 1½ hours after El Mersse, there is another camp site at **Tidkit**, set beside a river and with shade trees. There are a couple of houses here, so it may be possible to sleep *chez l'habitant*, or in **Achmrah**, another hour down the track. However, the Berbers on this side of Jebel Sarhro are seminomadic and may be absent. If the houses are empty, the animal shelters will be as well, a less glamorous but still effective place to sleep.

Day 5: Achmrah to the Dadès Valley

four hours/14km/slight ascent/450m descent

The best parts of this morning walk are at the beginning and the end. The track runs north of Achmrah in a short climb that suddenly reveals more views of the M'Goun and Siroua. Less than half an hour later, it crosses a well-made motor track, which leads to an anthracite mine and should not be followed. Instead continue north, occasionally northwest, on a well-worn track that leads down a gully towards the Dadès valley. As you get closer, you will see the villages of Aït Youl on your left, and Aït Haroun on the right. The valley here is studded with old kasbahs. Head for Aït Haroun, where there is a bridge over the Dadès River. The Boumalne–El-Kelaâ M'Gouna road is nearby.

Directory

CONTENTS

ACCOMMODATION

In this book, we have defined budget as up to Dh400 for doubles, midrange as Dh400 to Dh800 for doubles and top end above Dh800. The exceptions to this are the pricier towns of Casablanca, Essaouira, Fez, Rabat and Tangier. For these towns, we have defined budget as up to Dh600, midrange as Dh600 to Dh1200 and top end as more than Dh1200.

Accommodation in Morocco ranges from friendly budget homestays or hostels to expensive, top-of-the-market luxury riads (traditional courtyard houses), country estates and grand converted palaces. In between are charming midrange *maisons d'hôtes* (small hotels) and riads that predominate in the larger cities such as Fez and Marrakesh. Like anywhere that caters to a European summer-holiday crowd, the Moroccan coast also has its fair share of oversized tourist complexes, while budget travellers may also come across individuals' houses converted in the dead of night without the appropriate licenses.

In this book the official, government-assigned rates (including taxes) are quoted, although these are intended as a guide only. Many hotels will offer significant 'promotional discounts' from their advertised rates, especially in large resorts like Agadir or during the low season (May to October). It is always worth asking when you book.

Accommodation is often scarce during Easter week and August, when half of Spain and the whole of France seem to be on holiday in Morocco. Another very busy time in the south, particularly in Marrakesh, is Christmas and New Year. Finding a room in Fez at short notice in June can also be a challenge due to the increasingly popular World Sacred Music Festival.

To make a reservation, hotels usually require confirmation by fax or email plus a credit-card number.

Apartments

If travelling in a small group or as a family, consider self-catering options, particularly in low season, when prices can drop substantially. Agadir, El-Jadida, Assilah and the bigger tourist centres along the Mediterranean and Atlantic coasts have a fair number of apartments with self-catering facilities. The riad agencies (p453) also rent apartments.

Camping

You can camp anywhere in Morocco if you have permission from the site's owner. There are also many official camp sites. Most of the bigger cities have camp sites although they're often some way from the main attractions. Some are worth the extra effort to get to, while others – usually consisting of a barren and stony area offering little shade – are often the domain of

PRACTICALITIES

- **Newspapers & Magazines** Although censorship has decreased, newspapers still practise a degree of self-censorship. Among the French-language papers, *L'Opinion* (www.lopinion.ma, in French), which is attached to the opposition Istiqlal Party, airs some of the points of contention in Moroccan society. *Libération* (www.liberation.press.ma, in French), the Union Socialiste des Forces Populaires' daily, is similar if less punchy. *Al-Bayane* (www.albayane.ma), another opposition French-language daily, isn't too bad for foreign news. For a full list of Moroccan newspapers online, go to www.onlinenewspapers.com/morocco.htm. A selection of European newspapers (including some British dailies) and the *International Herald Tribune* are available in most of the main cities. *Le Monde* is the most common. The British *Guardian Weekly* is also usually available, as occasionally is *USA Today* and more commonly, *Time, Newsweek* and the *Economist*.
- **Radio** Moroccan radio encompasses only a handful of local AM and FM stations, the bulk of which broadcast in either Arabic or French. Midi 1 at 97.5FM covers northern Morocco, Algeria and Tunisia, and plays reasonable contemporary music.
- **TV** Satellite dishes are everywhere in Morocco and pick up dozens of foreign stations. There are two government-owned stations, TVM and 2M, which broadcast in Arabic and French. TV5 is a European satellite import from the Francophone world, while 2M is the primary household station.
- **Video & DVD Systems** Morocco and France use the Secam video system, which is incompatible with both the PAL system used in Australia and most of Western Europe, and the NTSC system used in North America and Japan. Like Western Europe (but not the NTSC system of the Americas), Morocco runs on the PAL DVD system, but Moroccan DVDs share region 5 with Eastern Europe (Western Europe is region 2 while Australia is region 4), which means Moroccan DVDs may not play on all machines elsewhere.
- **Electricity** Moroccan sockets accept the European round two-pin plugs so bring an international adaptor if your device comes from elsewhere. The electric current is 220V/50Hz but older buildings may still use 110V. Electricity is generally reliable and available nearly everywhere travellers go.
- **Weights & Measures** Use the metric system for weights and measures; conversion charts are on the inside front cover of this book.

enormous campervans, to whom the basic facilities make no difference. If you're really lucky, you may have a swimming pool.

Most sites have water, electricity and, in summer, a small restaurant and grocery store. At official sites you'll pay around Dh10 to Dh20 per person, plus Dh10 to Dh20 to pitch a tent and about Dh10 to Dh15 for small vehicles (parking your campervan or caravan costs around Dh20 to Dh30, although this can go as high as Dh45). Electricity generally costs another Dh10 to Dh15 and a hot shower is about Dh5 to Dh10. As with most things, prices rise the closer you are to Marrakesh.

Gîtes d'Étape, Homestays & Refuges

Gîtes d'étape are homes or hostels, often belonging to mountain guides, which offer accommodation (often just a mattress on the floor) around popular trekking routes in the Atlas. They have basic bathrooms and sometimes hot showers. Official rates begin at Dh30 but prices do vary according to the season and location. You may also pay extra for meals (Dh30 to Dh50) and hot showers (Dh10 to Dh15) depending on the availability of facilities, such as hot-water showers and meals. You may also come across more comfortable privately owned *gîtes* that charge as much as Dh100 for accommodation and the same for meals.

Larger than *gîtes,* mountain refuges (mostly run by the Club Alpin Français, CAF) offer Swiss chalet–style accommodation. Sleeping is in dormitories with communal showers and there is usually a lively communal dining/living room.

BOOK YOUR STAY ONLINE

For more accommodation reviews and recommendations by Lonely Planet authors, check out lonelyplanet.com/hotels. You'll find the true, insider lowdown on the best places to stay. Reviews are thorough and independent. Best of all, you can book online.

Similarly, if you are trekking in the High Atlas or travelling off the beaten track elsewhere, you may be offered accommodation in village homes. Many won't have running water or electricity, but you'll find them big on warmth and hospitality. You should be prepared to pay what you would in *gîtes d'étape* or mountain refuges.

Hostels

The Federation Royale Morocaine des Auberges de Jeunes (☎ 022 470952; fax 022 227677; frmaj@iam.net.ma) runs eight reliable youth hostels at Casablanca, Fez, Goulmima, Marrakesh, Meknès, Plage Mehdiya, Rabat and Tangier. Some hostels have kitchens and family rooms. If you're travelling alone, they are among the cheapest places to stay (between Dh20 and Dh45 a night) but many are inconveniently located.

Hotels

You'll find cheap, unclassified (without a star rating) or one-star hotels clustered in the medinas of the bigger cities. Some are bright and spotless, others haven't seen a mop for years. Cheaper prices usually mean communal washing facilities and squat toilets. Occasionally there is a gas-heated shower, for which you'll pay an extra Dh5 to Dh10. Where there is no hot water at all, head for the local hammam (see opposite).

Many cheap hotels in the south offer a mattress on the roof terrace for Dh25 to Dh30, while others also have traditional Moroccan salons, lined with banks of seats and cushions, where budget travellers can sleep for a similar price.

Midrange hotels in Morocco are generally of a high standard, and range from imitation Western-style rooms, which are modern if a little soulless, to *maisons d'hôtes,* which capture the essence of Moroccan style with both comfort and character. In this price range, you should expect an ensuite room with shower. Top-end hotels are similar to midrange places but with more luxurious levels of comfort and design. Some hotels in more isolated regions offer half-board *(demi-pension)* options, which means breakfast and dinner is included, and can be a good deal.

You'll need your passport number (and entry-stamp number) when filling in a hotel register. For registered hotels, there's a government tax (included in quoted prices throughout the book). This floats around Dh25 per head, the exact amount depending on the hotel's rating.

If you're a resident in Morocco, you're entitled to a 25% discount on classified hotel rates on your third night in some establishments.

Riads, Dars & Kasbahs

For many guests, the chance to stay in a converted traditional house is a major drawcard for a trip to Morocco. They're the type of accommodation that the term 'boutique hotel' could have been invented for, and no two are alike. Service tends to be personal, with many places noted for their food as much as their lodgings. Room rates are comparable to four- or five-star hotels. Marrakesh is the most famous destination for riad aficionados (there are several hundred), with Fez coming a close second. Essaouira, Rabat, Tangier and Assilah are also popular. With their popularity seemingly unassailable you can increasingly find riads in the most unexpected corners of the country.

Although the term riad is often used generically for such places, a riad proper is a house built around a garden with trees. You'll also come across plenty of *dars* (traditional houses with internal courtyards). Kasbahs (old citadels), which often function as hotels, are found throughout the major tourist centres of the south. Rooms in kasbahs are small and dark, due to the nature of the building, but are lovely and cool in summer.

Most riads operate on advance bookings, and it's worth planning ahead, as most only have a handful of rooms and can fill quickly. Advance booking often means that someone from the riad will be sent to meet you outside the medina when you arrive: labyrinthine streets often conspire against finding the front door on your first attempt.

Many riads list their online rates in euros, rather than dirhams, at exchange rates favourable to themselves, so always double check the prices when booking.

For an idea of properties and prices, visit the websites of these agencies:

Fez Riads (☎ 072 513357; www.fez-riads.com) A percentage of profits are donated towards restoration projects in the Fez medina.

Marrakech Riads (☎ 024 391609; www.marrakech-riads.com) Well-established and respected agency.

ACTIVITIES

Morocco is a magnificent trekking destination offering an array of landscapes and treks to suit all abilities. Trekking is not the only activity on offer, however, with birdwatching enthusiasts, golfers, cyclists, climbers, riders and spa devotees all catered for in a bewildering selection of activity holidays. See also the courses section (p458) for more ideas.

Birdwatching

Morocco is a birdwatcher's paradise. A startling array of species inhabits the country's diverse ecosystems and varied environments, especially the coastal wetlands. Around 460 species have been recorded in the country, many of them migrants passing through in spring and autumn when Morocco becomes a way station between sub-Saharan Africa and breeding grounds in Scandinavia, Greenland and northern Russia, while others fly to Morocco to avoid the harsh northern-European winters. Early winter months at the wetlands are particularly active, but the most pleasant time of year is March through May, when the weather is comfortable and the widest variety of species is usually present. For more information on Morocco's birdlife, see p94.

In Merdja Zerga National Park, a well-regarded local birding guide is Hassan Dalil (see p134). Tour companies (all UK-based) that offer birding tours to Morocco include the following:

Birdfinders (☎ 01258 839066; www.birdfinders.co.uk)

Birdwatching Breaks (☎ 01381 610495; www.birdwatchingbreaks.com)

Naturetrek (☎ 0196 273 3051; www.naturetrek.co.uk)

Wildwings (☎ 0117 965 8333; www.wildwings.co.uk)

Camel Treks & Desert Safaris

Exploring the Moroccan Sahara by camel is one of the country's signature activities and is one of the most rewarding wilderness experiences in the country, whether on an overnight excursion or a two-week trek. The most evocative stretches of Saharan sand include Zagora (p347) and Tinfou (p350) in the Drâa Valley; M'Hamid and the dunes of Erg Chigaga (p350), 95km further south; and the dunes of Erg Chebbi (p370) near Merzouga, southeast of Rissani.

Autumn (September and October) and winter (November to early March) are the only seasons worth considering. Prices start at around Dh300 per person per day (or Dh350 for an overnight excursion), but vary depending on the number of people, the length of the trek and your negotiating skills. The agency will organise the bivouac (temporary camp), which may be a permanent camp for shorter trips, and may offer Berber music and *mechoui* (barbecued lamb).

Many places offer camel treks. Travellers with lots of time can arrive in places such as Zagora, M'Hamid and Merzouga and organise a local guide and provisions while there; this benefits the local community and counters the trend towards young guides leaving home to look for work in the more popular tourist cities. If you do this, try to get recommendations from other travellers and count on spending Dh300 to Dh350 for an overnight excursion. M'Hamid is probably the most hassle-free of the three towns, although the choice is wider at Zagora (which has three professional operators) and Merzouga.

If you've neither the time nor the inclination to spend time cooling your heels while you wait for negotiations to be completed, you could also organise it in advance, either through an international tour company or a local company based in Ouarzazate or Marrakesh. For more information on tour companies, see p488, and the Zagora (p347) and Ouarzazate (p342) sections of the book.

Hammams

Visiting a hammam (traditional bathhouse) is infinitely preferable to cursing under a cold shower in a cheap hotel. They're busy, social places where you'll find gallons of hot water and staff available to scrub you squeaky clean. They're good places to meet

HAMMAM KNOW-HOW

For affluent Western travellers, the communal bathhouse can be a cultural shock. Where do you look, where do you sit, are you sitting too close, what do you wear? All that naked flesh appears a minefield of social disaster and embarrassment.

For Muslims however, there is nothing shameful or embarrassing about the body among your own gender, and attitudes to nakedness are a lot less prudish than those of their Western counterparts. It may seem surprising in a society where modesty on the street is so important that women will think nothing of enquiring curiously after why you don't shave your pubic hair! On a more practical level, in houses where there is often no water, the hammam is the only place to get clean.

Most 'good' public hammams in cities tend to be modern, white-tiled and spacious affairs. Moroccans come prepared with an *el-kis* (coarse glove), black soap made from the resin of olives (which stings if you get it in your eyes), henna (which is used by women) and *ghassoul*.

After undressing to your underwear, head straight for the hot room and stake out your area with your mat and toiletries. If in doubt, follow what everyone else is doing, which usually means covering yourself with black soap and sweating a while to soften up your skin for the pummelling it will later take. After about five minutes get a friend, or masseur/masseuse from the hammam, to scrub you down. It's by no means a tender process as rolls of dead skin peel away with the black soap. Nor is it for the modestly inclined, as arms are raised, breasts and inner thighs scrubbed and ears rinsed out with as much ceremony as a childhood bathtime.

Once all the dirt has been rinsed away most people move to the tepid room to apply the reddish-brown henna (in the women's hammam only) and then *ghassoul*, which is also used to wash your hair. These products soften and smooth the skin, and no self-respecting Moroccan would swap them for any fancy commercial product.

Once your inhibitions have been stripped away, the hammam is a thoroughly relaxing and enjoyable experience, and it's easy to see why it is so beloved. It is intimate and friendly, a place to relax and talk about your problems and, for Moroccan women especially, a welcome break from tedious chores and difficult spouses. Afterwards you feel thoroughly wrung out and totally relaxed. You'll probably never be so clean again.

the locals and, especially for women, somewhere to relax away from the street hassle.

Every town has at least one hammam. Often there are separate hammams for men and women, while others are open to either sex at different hours or on alternate days. They can be difficult to find; some are unmarked and others simply have a picture of a man or woman stencilled on the wall outside. Local people will be happy to direct you to one. Most hammams are very welcoming, but a few (often those close to a mosque) are unwilling to accept foreign visitors.

Bring your own towels (in a waterproof bag), a plastic mat or something to sit on, and flip-flops (thongs). You'll be given a bucket and scoop – remember to use the communal bucket when filling yours with water. Toiletries can be bought at some hammams, as can *ghassoul* (handfuls of clay mixed with herbs, dried roses and lavender).

A visit to a hammam usually costs around Dh10, with a massage costing at least an extra Dh15. Most hammams also have showers. A few midrange or top-end hotels have hammams, which normally require advance notice (up to 24 hours) to heat up, and which cost up to Dh100 per person for a minimum of four or five people.

Horse Riding

The south of Morocco is popular for horse riding, be it along the southern beaches of Diabat (p160) and Agadir, through the lush valleys of the Souss and Ouirgane, in the Middle and High Atlas, or exploring the dramatic Todra Gorge and the desert landscapes of the south.

A couple of specialist travel companies offer guided horse-riding trips in Morocco.

Club Farah (☎ 035 548844; www.clubfarah.com) Has excellent horse-riding tour operator based outside Meknès, running individual and group trips in the Middle Atlas.

Unicorn Trails (☎ 01767 600606; www.unicorntrails.com) UK-based operator with a selection of riding trips in the High Atlas and Atlantic Coast.

Motorbiking, Quads & Karts

The wide, open spaces and stunning scenery of south-central Morocco are attracting a growing number of roadsters. The only Moroccan-based off-road biking agency is **Wilderness Wheels** (☎ 024 888128; www.wildernesswheels.com; 44 Hay al-Qods, Ouarzazateh; half-/1-/2-day expedition Dh800/1400/3500). Itineraries cover the Dadès and Drâa Valleys and even the desert as far south as Merzouga.

Quad biking and karting are also becoming popular in adventure bases such as Ouarzazate, Merzouga, Zagora and Erfoud.

Mountain Biking

Ordinary cycling is possible in Morocco, but mountain biking opens up the options considerably. Roads are well maintained, although often very narrow. For the very fit, the vast networks of *pistes* (dirt tracks) and even the footpaths of the High Atlas offer the most rewarding biking, although the Anti Atlas, Jebel Sarhro plateau and the Drâa Valley offer some excellent trails. There are also possibilities at Oualidia (p149). A few travel agencies and midrange hotels hire out mountain bikes for around Dh100 but the quality isn't really high enough for an extended trip. Serious cyclists can contact one of the adventure tour companies listed on p488.

Rock Climbing

Rock climbing is increasingly a feature of the Moroccan activities scene and there are some sublime opportunities for the vertically inclined. Anyone contemplating routes should have plenty of experience under their belt and be prepared to bring all their own equipment.

Areas in the Anti Atlas and High Atlas offer everything from bouldering to very severe mountaineering routes that shouldn't be attempted unless you have a great deal of experience. The Dadès (p357) and Todra (p360) Gorges are both prime climbing territory.

It's worth contacting the following if you're keen to hook up with other climbers:

Nicolo Berzi (☎ +39 0335-6535349; nicolobe@tiscalinet.it) Italian climbing guide organising trips to Todra Gorge.

Royal Moroccan Ski & Mountaineering Federation (☎ 022 474979; www.frmsm.ma; Casablanca) This group runs climbing competitions in the Todra Gorge.

Serac Outdoors Sports (www.seracoutdoorsports.co.uk) UK operator that runs climbing trips in the Anti Atlas.

Skiing

Although Morocco's ski stations are somewhat ramshackle in comparison with Europe's alpine offerings, skiing is a viable option from November to April.

Ski trekking *(ski randonné)* is increasingly popular, especially from late December to February when the Aït Bougomez Valley (p329) promises Morocco's prime ski-trekking routes.

Oukaïmeden (p333), about 70km south of Marrakesh, is a popular downhill ski resort that boasts the highest ski lift in North Africa. You can hire equipment here. There are a few other spots dotted around the Middle Atlas, including Mischliffen, but the last few years have seen barely enough snow for a proper season.

Surfing

Morocco has thousands of kilometres of ocean coast making it a fine, if underrated, surfing destination. Plage Mehdiya (p133) has reliable year-round breaks, and there are a few other places further up the coast towards Larache.

Anchor Point in Agadir has been recommended, although it can be very inconsistent. Taghazout (p385), close by, is a laid-back spot popular with surfers. **Surf Maroc** (www.surfmaroc.co.uk) runs a great surf camp here for all levels.

Essaouira has been singled out by some surfers, though it's a far better windsurfing destination.

Perhaps the best breaks in the country are just north of Safi. The Lalla Fatna beach (p153) is the point of access and has drawn some of the biggest names in surfing for some of the longest tubular right-handers in the world. Other beaches in the vicinity of Safi are also worth checking out. For reliable information contact **Surfland** (☎ 023 366110; ⌚ Apr–mid-Nov) in Oualidia or **Dream Surf Oualidia** (☎ 061 817817, 041 291838; ⌚ year-round) on the beach in town. Surfland is also a great place for beginners' lessons, which take place in the sheltered bay. For further details see p149. There's also good surf to be found around Rabat (p132) and El-Jadida (p147).

Trekking

For the definitive guide to Morocco's world-class trekking possibilities, see above.

TREKKING THE WAY ALLAH INTENDED

Morocco, beloved for its casual 'God-willing, now-pass-another-cup-of-tea' charm, does not provide its trekking guests with much in the way of resources for safe and responsible exploration, or protection of the Moroccan environment. The following suggestions should lend a hand.

- Dress appropriately according to custom (p51).
- Use current topographical maps and run them by a local if you can: someone who lives in the area can verify water sources and indicate rivers that are now dry.
- Camp only in designated camp sites; fields are a private source of business for local families.
- Buy or collect firewood (do not chop) and use it sparingly to respect its scarcity.
- Scorpions hide under rocks and potentially in shoes and sleeping bags, so you'll want to shake these out occasionally. They will not sting unless provoked.
- Understand that laundering and bathing in rivers and streams pollutes a village's primary water source.
- Carry out rubbish to the nearest town or city.
- Be aware that some villages consider photography blasphemous and in others a camera makes you the Pied Piper. It is always inappropriate to photograph someone without permission and cameras can cause particular offence when pointed at women.
- Refrain from feeding or handling animals - even Barbary macaques, who will tease you with their charisma!
- Hitchhike at your own risk and remember: if you flag down a grand taxi then you're no longer hitchhiking – expect to pay the fare to the next town.
- Consider the impact of 4WDs before embarking on any off-*piste* adventures (see the boxed text, p91)
- Give a warm smile and some kind words to the friendly children who live in rural areas. Handing out money, candy and other gifts to kids teaches them to beg and harass tourists. If you wish to give something to children in a local community, it's better to give a donation to a local charity or school.
- Don't drink alcohol in remote villages where the practice is considered offensive.

White-Water Rafting

White-water rafting is very underdeveloped in Morocco, although the rivers in the High Atlas near Bin el-Ouidane Dam in the area around Azilal and Afourer have stunning scenery.

Only a few specialist adventure companies organise rafting trips to Morocco. Try the reputable **Water by Nature** (www.waterbynature.com), which has outlets in the UK and the USA. They cater for all levels of experience, and run family rafting trips.

Windsurfing & Kitesurfing

The conditions at self-styled 'Windy City' Essaouira (p160) and even more so at Sidi Kaouki (p166) make them fantastic spots for windsurfers and kitesurfers. You can hire boards on these beaches (Dh170 per hour for windsurfing equipment). You'll also be able to tap into a reasonable windsurfing community here year-round. The area around El-Jadida (p147) is also good while Surfland in Oualidia (see p149) runs kitesurfing classes.

BUSINESS HOURS

Although a Muslim country, for business purposes Morocco follows the Monday to Friday working week. Friday is the main prayer day, however, so many businesses take an extended lunch break on Friday afternoon. During Ramadan the rhythm of the country changes and office hours shift to around 8am to 3pm or 4pm.

For details of opening hours for shops, banks, post offices and restaurants, see the Quick Reference inside the front cover.

Banking hours can vary a little, with some banks closing at 11.30pm on weekdays. In the main tourist cities, *bureaux de change* (foreign-exchange bureaus) keep longer hours (often until 8pm) and open over the weekend.

Medina souqs and produce markets in the villes nouvelles (new towns) of the bigger cities tend to wind down on Thursday afternoon and are usually empty on Friday, so plan your shopping trips accordingly. Souqs in small villages start early and usually wind down before the onset of the afternoon heat.

Government offices open from 8.30am to noon and 2pm to 6.30pm, Monday to Thursday. On Friday, the midday break lasts from about 11.30am to 3pm.

Tourist offices are generally open from 8.30am to noon and 2.30pm to 6.30pm from Monday to Thursday, and from 8.30am to 11.30am and 3pm to 6.30pm on Friday.

Téléboutiques (private telephone offices) and internet cafés often stay open late into the night, especially in cities.

CHILDREN

Your children have a decided advantage – having yet to acquire the stereotypes about Africa or the Middle East to which many of us are exposed, their first impression of the continent is likely to be the warmth and friendliness of the people. Indeed, many Moroccans have grown up in large families and children will help break the ice and open doors to closer contact with local people who are generally very friendly, helpful and protective towards children (conversely, couples travelling alone may frequently be asked why they don't have any kids). The result is that travelling with children in Morocco adds a whole new dimension to your journey. Or, as one of our authors wrote: 'Travelling in Morocco with kids is a great thing to do. Done it often and loved it all.'

For more information and hints on travelling with children, Lonely Planet's *Travel with Children* by Cathy Lanigan is highly recommended.

PRACTICALITIES

Most hotels will not charge children under two years of age. For those between two and 12 years sharing the same room as their parents, it's usually 50% off the adult rate. If you want reasonable toilet and bathroom facilities, you'll need to stay in midrange hotels.

If you look hard enough, you can buy just about anything you need for young children, although you should bring any special foods required and high-factor sunscreen. Disposable nappies are a practical solution when travelling despite the environmental drawbacks. International brands are readily available and cost about Dh25 for 10.

To avoid stomach upsets, stick to purified or bottled water. UHT, pasteurised and powdered milk are also widely available. Be extra careful about choosing restaurants; steer clear of salads and stick to piping-hot tajines, couscous, soups and omelettes. Moroccan markets are full of delicious fruit and vegies, but be sure to wash or peel them.

Avoid travelling in the interior during midsummer, when temperatures rise to 40°C plus. Beware of dehydration and sunburn, even on cloudy days.

Morocco has a great rail infrastructure and travel by train may be the easiest, most enjoyable option – children can stretch their legs and the tables are handy for drawing and games. Kids under four travel free, while those aged between four and 12 years get a reduction of 10% to 50%, depending on the service.

Grands taxis and buses can be a real squeeze with young children who count not as passengers in their own right but as wriggling luggage - kids have to sit on your lap. The safety record of buses and shared taxis is poor, and many roads are potholed. Hire-car companies rarely have child seats, so bring your own, and check that they clip into the seat belts.

There are few formal babysitting services but it can usually be arranged through top-end hotels or by tapping into the expat network, which is particularly active in Marrakesh. If you want an English-speaking babysitter, be sure to request that specifically as it's not a given.

One reader has reported that letting your kids run amok in carpet shops proved to be an excellent bargaining technique!

SIGHTS & ACTIVITIES

Successful travel with children can require a special effort. Above all, don't try to overdo things. Make sure activities include the kids (older children could help in the planning of these) and try to think of things that will capture their imagination – the latter shouldn't be difficult in Morocco. The sensory explosion and barely controlled chaos of the souqs in Fez and Marrakesh are endlessly fascinating and will supply many exciting (and possibly exasperating) moments. A night around a campfire with Berber music is unforgettable, although at the end of a hot day, a hotel pool may be all you need for hours of contented fun.

Camel or horse rides along the beaches of Essaouira (p160) and Agadir or among the sand dunes at M'Hamid (p350) or Merzouga (p370) are sure to be a big hit, as is quad biking or karting with older children in Ouarzazate (p342).

Another popular activity is the calèche (horse-drawn carriage) ride around the ramparts of cities like Marrakesh (p324) and Taroudannt (p391).

Other organised attractions of particular interest to younger kids include Yasmina Amusement Park in Casablanca (p108); Surfland (p149) in Oualidia; Parque Marítimo del Mediterráneo (p191) in Ceuta; Vallée des Oiseaux (p378) in Agadir; and the Atlas Film Corporation Studios (p342) in Ouarzazate.

Sights appropriate for children are covered throughout this book, with dedicated sections in Marrakesh (p307), Casablanca (p108) and Rabat (p123).

CLIMATE

Morocco's weather reflects its distinct geographical zones. Coastal Morocco is generally mild, but can become cool and wet in the north. Rainfall is highest in the Rif and northern Middle Atlas, where only the summer months are dry. As you go higher into the Middle and High Atlas mountains, expect bitterly cold, snowy winters and cool, fresh summers. Elsewhere, rain falls mostly between November and March but is unpredictable, and drought remains a perennial problem. Blustery winds are common along the Atlantic seaboard. The Moroccan interior can become stiflingly hot in summer, easily exceeding 40°C. Fronting the desert, these plains are also subject to particulalrly uncomfortable springtime sandstorms (which are known as the sirocco, *chergui* or *irifi*) and usually occur around April.

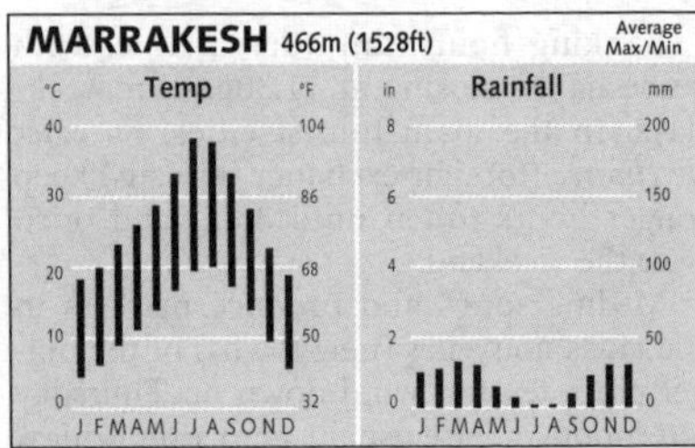

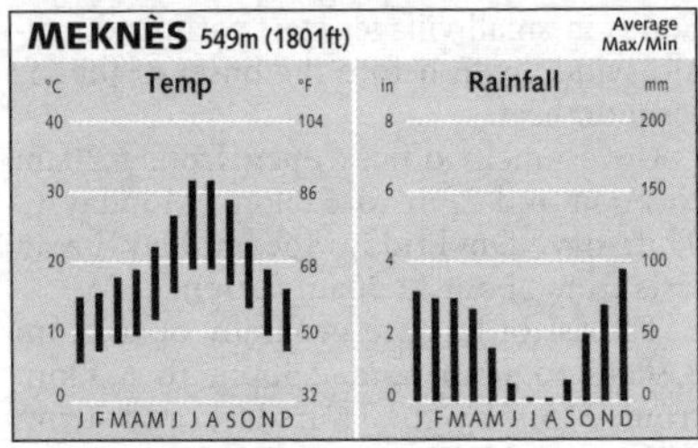

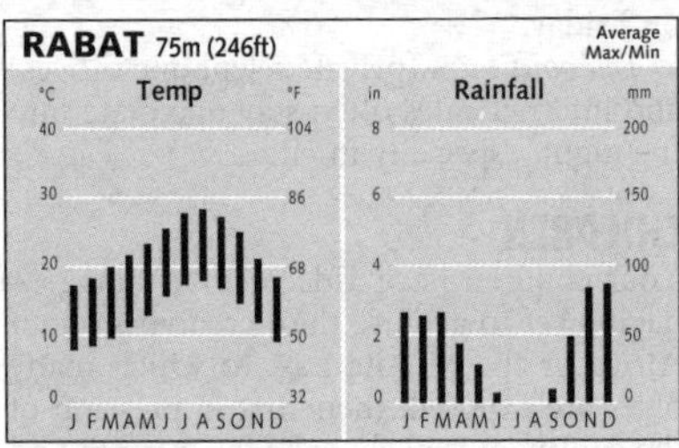

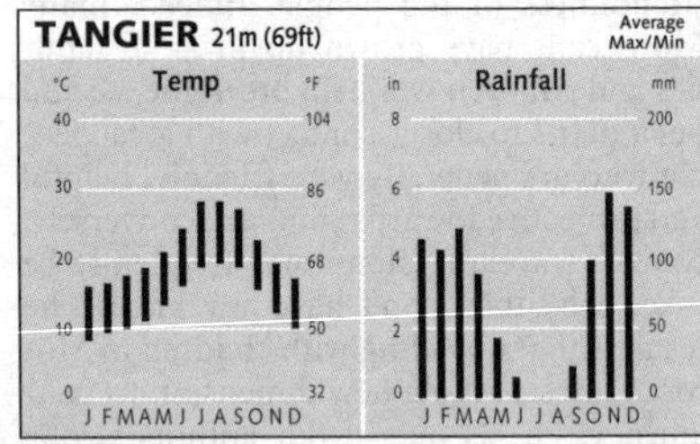

For information on when to go to Morocco, see p21.

COURSES

There are some great short and long courses on offer if you want to learn to write, cook like a Moroccan, or just talk like one.

Cooking

Marrakesh has the widest selection of courses in Moroccan cooking. Souq Cuisine (p307) is among the best. Fez also has a handful of courses (p241) worth investigating.

Language

There are courses in modern standard Arabic in most of the major towns in Morocco, with an especially high concentration in Rabat (p123) and Casablanca (p107) offering both long- and short-term programs.

The most romantic choice however is Fez. The **Arabic Language Institute** (www.alif-fes.com; 3-/6-week course Dh5200/9400) is the possibly the most renowned language institute in Morocco. As well as longer courses aimed at foreigners (assistance is given in finding accommodation with local families), it can offer individual private study. Another excellent choice in Fez is **DMG Arabophon** (www.arabicstudy.com; courses Dh2100-8400) which offers a variety of courses, as well as classes in Tamazight Berber.

Writing

Morocco is just the place to get the creative juices flowing. If you fancy marshalling your ideas into something more coherent, **Traveller's Tales** (www.travellerstales.org) runs a travel-writing course in Marrakesh, led by Anthony Sattin, one of the authors of this guide.

CUSTOMS

Duty-free allowances are up to 200 cigarettes, or 50 cigars, or 400g of tobacco, plus 1L of spirits and one bottle of wine.

There are no restrictions on bringing foreign currency into the country, but importing or exporting dirhams is forbidden.

DANGERS & ANNOYANCES

Morocco is a relatively safe place to travel and the great majority of people are friendly and honest. Nevertheless, the country does have a few traps for the unwary.

In the large cities there are some desperate people, and while physical attacks on foreigners are rare, they not unheard of. Treat the medinas with particular caution at night.

Drugs

Morocco's era as a hippie paradise, riding the Marrakesh Express and all that, was long ago consigned to history. Plenty of fine dope (known as kif) may be grown in the Rif Mountains, but drug busts are common and Morocco is not a place where you'd want to investigate local prison conditions from the inside.

The vast majority of all Moroccan stories of extortion and rip-offs are drug related. A common ploy is to get you stoned, force you to buy a piece of hash the size of a house brick and then turn you over to the police (or at least threaten to). Of course, once you've been tainted with a little hash, you're unlikely to call the cops, and the hustlers know it.

Associating with Tangier's lowlife is for the initiated only. New arrivals should ignore late-night offers of hashish and grass – these dealers have a sixth sense for greenness, and won't miss an opportunity to squeeze ridiculous amounts of money out of frightened people. Tetouan is another popular venue, and watch out for similar scams in Assilah, Casablanca and Marrakesh. Hashish is sometimes referred to as 'chocolate', the Spanish slang, or more often just as 'something special' or 'shit', which you will definitely be in if you get caught.

You may occasionally find someone offering you *majoun*, a kind of sticky, pasty mass (not unlike molasses) made of crushed seeds of the marijuana plant. A small ball of this can send you reeling (see Paul Bowles' *Their Heads Are Green* or *Let It Come Down* for descriptions). Anyone with a slight tendency to paranoia when smoking dope should be aware that this is a common reaction among first-time *majoun*-munchers.

Issaguen and the Rif Mountains are Morocco's kif-growing heartland. Issaguen in particular can be a bag-load of trouble and is best avoided unless you're accompanied by a reliable guide.

Recent legislation and a hard government line may have forced dealers to give up their more aggressive tactics, but the hassle has by no means disappeared and although locals continue to smoke as a recreational pastime, as a tourist you're rather more vulnerable. Always bear in mind that it's illegal to sell or consume hashish in Morocco. If caught, you may be looking at a fine and, in the worst case, a prison sentence of up to five years. See p468 for more information.

Although the police attitude in Spain is relaxed in respect to small amounts of cannabis for private use, Spanish customs will come down hard on people entering the country from Morocco if they find any, and you may be done for trafficking. If you're taking a car across, the chances that it will be searched are high. *Never* carry parcels or drive vehicles across borders for other people.

Getting Lost

A minor irritation is the ever-changing street names in Moroccan cities. For years, there's been a slow process of replacing old French, Spanish and Berber names with Arabic ones. The result so far is that, depending on whom you talk to, what map you use or which part of the street you are on, you're likely to see up to three different names.

The general Arabic word for street is *sharia*, or *derb* in medinas (*zankat* for smaller ones). In the north you'll still find the Spanish *calle* and *avenida,* and more commonly, the French *avenue, boulevard* or *rue.*

In some cases the Arabic seems to have gained the upper hand. This is reflected in this guidebook, in which some streets appear as *sharia* or *zankat* if local usage seems to justify it.

Street names won't help much in the labyrinthine medinas, although a compass might. If you feel you're getting lost, stick to the main paths (which generally have a fair flow of people going either way) and you'll soon reach a landmark or exit.

Plumbing

Patience is required when it comes to Moroccan plumbing. In the cheap, unclassified hotels that don't have star ratings, trickling cold water and squat toilets are often the norm.

Sometimes hot water is enthusiastically promised, but before you start dreaming of that powerful, steaming hot shower, remember that it may be tepid at best and is often only available at certain times of the day. In country areas, water is sometimes heated by a wood fire, but this comes at an environmental cost – wood is expensive, water is often in short supply and deforestation is a major problem in Morocco. In small towns and rural areas the hammam may be a better bet.

Smoking

Smoking is a national pastime in Morocco and nonsmoking restaurants and hotels are almost unheard of.

However, this generally affects popular places rather than top-end or exclusive restaurants and hotels, where you may find nonsmoking areas. Most of the popular eateries are cafés with outdoor seating, so the problem is somewhat reduced.

Only the very top-end hotels (mainly Sofitel) have a nonsmoking policy.

In Muslim countries, it is generally considered unacceptable for women to smoke, and outside the big cities (and even within most of these) you'll seldom see women smokers. This is a cultural rather than religious dictate, although most religious leaders have condemned smoking, like drinking, as *haram* (forbidden). In practice, the only time the habit is seriously eschewed is during daylight hours of the holy month of Ramadan.

This shouldn't affect foreigners too much, although women may wish to refrain from smoking within local homes and be discreet elsewhere.

Theft

On the whole, theft is not a huge problem in Morocco. Travellers can minimise any risk however by being particularly vigilant in the major cities and by following a few basic precautions.

When wandering around the streets, keep the valuables you carry to a minimum and keep what you must carry around with you well hidden. Be particularly careful when withdrawing money from ATMs. External money pouches attract attention, but neck pouches or moneybelts worn under your clothes do not; that's where you should keep your money, passport and other important documents.

In some of the medinas – such as those in Marrakesh, Casablanca and Tangier, which have a particular reputation for petty theft –

a common tactic is for one person to distract you while another cleans out your pockets. There's no point walking around in a state of permanent alert, but keep your eyes open.

Other valuables such as cameras can be left with the hotel reception when you don't need them. If you prefer to keep things in your room (preferably locked inside your suitcase), nine times out of 10 you'll have no trouble. Leaving anything in a car, even out of sight, is asking for trouble.

Touts, Guides & Hustlers

The legendary hustlers of Morocco remain an unavoidable part of the Moroccan experience.

A few years ago special *brigades touristiques* (tourist police) were set up in the principal tourist centres to clamp down on Morocco's notorious *faux guides* and hustlers. Any person suspected of trying to operate as an unofficial guide could face jail and/or a huge fine.

This has greatly reduced, but not eliminated, the problem of *faux guides*. These people are often desperate to make a living, and they can be persistent and sometimes unpleasant. You'll generally find them hanging around the entrances to the big cities' medinas, and outside bus and train stations. Those disembarking (and embarking) the ferry in Tangier should expect at least some hassle from touts and hustlers (see p173). However, there's no point having a siege mentality. When arriving in a place for the first time, you might even benefit from the services of a guide, official or otherwise. Although high unemployment rates drive the numbers of *faux guides*, not all are necessarily complete imposters. Many are very experienced and speak half a dozen languages, and sometimes their main interest is the commission gained from certain hotels or on articles sold to you in the souqs. Be sure to agree on a price before setting off and set some parameters on what you expect to see and the number of shops you're taken to. Unofficial guides charge around Dh50 to Dh100 per day (rates should always be per guide not per person); a few dirham will suffice if you want to be guided to a specific location (like a medina exit). Whatever you give, you'll often get the you-can't-possibly-be-serious look. The best reply is

GAUCHE, GREEN & GULLIBLE

Many Moroccans genuinely believe that Westerners, though perhaps more sophisticated than themselves, are infinitely more naive, gullible and even plain stupid. Some, including the notorious *faux guides* (unofficial guides), may try to exploit this.

Very early on in your encounter with these guides, you'll be sized up for what you're worth. Apart from the physical indications such as your watch, shoes and clothes, you'll be assessed from a series of questions: how long you've been in Morocco, whether you've visited the country before, what your job is, whether you have a family (an indication of wealth) etc. Always be suspicious of these unsolicited enquiries and pretend that you know the city or country well. A few words of Arabic will convince them of this.

Considered to be the most lucrative nationalities, in descending order, are the Japanese, Americans, Canadians, Australians, the British, northern Europeans, southern Europeans, and Middle-Eastern Arabs. Considered the least lucrative are sub-Saharan Africans and Arabs from other North African countries.

Apart from the more obvious starting point of claiming to want nothing more than friendship (such as showing you around town, taking you to a cheap shop and helping you find a hotel), other classic approaches include wanting to practise English or help with the reading or deciphering of official documents and letters from friends. If you turn them down, some will try to play on your conscience by suggesting you are racist for not liking Moroccans or Muslims.

If you feel you're being categorised, you can always cause confusion by pretending you're from some very obscure land. Sometimes it's useful just to play plain stupid and control the situation that way. Be warned, though: Moroccans have a real aptitude for languages and it could be you who looks stupid as your new friend starts spouting away in the fluent Ukrainian you claim to speak, or just happens to be the brain surgeon you've claimed to be.

THANKS BUT NO THANKS

To avoid being hounded to within an inch of your life, and to help prevent nervous breakdowns and embarrassing incidents of 'medina rage', the following tips may come in handy:

- Politely decline all offers of help, and exchange a few good-humoured remarks (preferably in Arabic), but don't shake hands or get involved in lengthy conversation.
- Give the impression that you know exactly where you're going or explain that you employed a guide on your first day and now you'd like to explore the town on your own.
- Wear dark sunglasses and retreat to a café, restaurant or taxi if you're beginning to lose your cool. In extreme situations, use the word 'police' and look like you mean it.

the I've-just-paid-you-well-over-the-odds look. Maintain your good humour and after a couple of days in a place, the hassle tends to lessen considerably.

Official guides can be engaged through tourist offices and some hotels at the fixed price of around Dh250 to Dh300 per day (plus tip) for a local/national guide. It's well worth taking a guide when exploring the medinas of Fez and Marrakesh. Their local knowledge is extensive and they'll save you from being hassled by other would-be guides. If you don't want a shopping expedition included in your tour, make this clear beforehand.

Drivers should note that motorised hustlers operate on the approach roads to Fez and Marrakesh. These motorcycle nuisances are keen to find you a hotel, camp site and so on, and can be just as persistent as their colleagues on foot. Arriving by train in cities like Fez and Marrakesh you may also run into 'students' or similar, with the uncanny knowledge that your preferred hotel is closed or full, but they just happen to know this great little place…

DISCOUNT CARDS

You can stay at most Hostelling International (HI) hostels without a membership card (usually for a few dirham extra), so it's hardly worth getting a card especially for your trip.

International student cards don't open many magic doors, but they do entitle those under 30 to discounts of up to 60% on internal travel (plus on some flights *out* of the country) with Royal Air Maroc (RAM). If you plan on doing a lot of train travel, there are a variety of discount cards available including ones for (but not exclusively) students and senior travellers. Over-60s can also usually get reductions on ferry tickets to/from Spain.

EMBASSIES & CONSULATES

For details of Moroccan embassies abroad, go to the Moroccan Ministry for Foreign Affairs and Cooperation website at www.maec.gov.ma.

Embassies & Consulates in Morocco

Most embassies and diplomatic representation are in Rabat. Unless otherwise noted, all of the embassies are open Monday to Friday, from 9am until noon.

Algeria Rabat (Map p118; ☎ 037 661574; algerabat@iam.net.ma; 46-48 Ave Tariq ibn Zayid; 🕑 8.30am-4pm Mon-Fri); Oujda (Map p283; ☎ 056 710452; Blvd Bir Anzarane)

Australia The Australian embassy in Paris has consular responsibility for Morocco. Consular services to Australian citizens in Morocco are provided by the Canadian embassy.

Belgium Rabat (Map p118; ☎ 037 268060; info@ambabel-rabat.org.ma; 6 Ave de Marrakesh); Consulate in Casablanca (Map p102; ☎ 022 223049; 9 Rue al-Farabi); Tangier (☎/fax 039 941130; 2nd fl, 41 Blvd Mohammed V)

Canada (Map p118; ☎ 037 687400; www.rabat.gc.ca; 13 Rue Jaafar as-Sadiq, Agdal, Rabat; 🕑 8am-noon & 1.30-5.30pm Mon-Thu, 8am-1.30pm Fri)

France (Map p118; ☎ 037 689700, www.ambafrance-ma.org; 3 Rue Sahnoun, Agdal, Rabat); Consulate-general (Map p122 ☎ 037 268181; Rue Alla Ben Abdallah, Rabat; 🕑 8.30-11.30am Mon-Fri visa applications, 1.30-3pm Mon-Fri visa pick-up). Consulates-general are also in Agadir (off Map p376); Casablanca (Map p110); Rabat (Map p118); Tangier (Map p178); Marrakesh (Map p300); and Fez.

Germany (Map p122; ☎ 037 709662; www.amballemagne-rabat.ma; 7 Rue Madnine, Rabat)

Ireland The nearest Irish embassy is in Lisbon. Consular services to Irish citizens in Morocco are provided by the Canadian embassy.

Italy Rabat (Map p118; ☎ 037 706598; ambaciata@iambitalia.ma; 2 Rue Idriss el-Azhar); Consulate-general in Casablanca (☎ 022 277558; fax 022 277139; cnr Rue Jean Jaures & Ave Hassan Souktani)
Japan (off Map p118; ☎ 037 631782; fax 037 750078; 39 Ave Ahmed Balafrej Souissi, Rabat; 9am-1pm Mon-Fri)
Mali (off Map p118; ☎ 037 759125; fax 037 754742; 7 Rue Thami Lamdaouar, Soussi I, Rabat; 8.30am-noon & 2.30-5.30pm Mon-Fri)
Mauritania (off Map p118; ☎ 037 656678; ambassadeur@mauritanie.org.ma; 7 Rue Thami Lamdaouar, Soussi I, Rabat; 8.30am-3pm Mon-Thu, 8.30am-noon Fri)
New Zealand The closest embassy is in Madrid, Spain. The UK embassy provides consular support in Morocco.
Netherlands (Map p118; ☎ 037 219600; nlgovrab@mtds.com; 40 Rue de Tunis, Rabat)
Spain (Map p118; ☎ 037 633900; emb.rabat@mae.es; Rue Ain Khalouiya, Route.des Zaers, Km 5.300 Souissi, Rabat) Consulates also located in Agadir, Casablanca (Map p102); Nador, Rabat (Map p118); Tangier and Tetouan.
Switzerland (☎ 037 268030; fax 037 268040; Place Berkane, Rabat)
Tunisia (Map p118; ☎ 037 730636; fax 037 730637; 6 Ave de Fès, Rabat; 9am-noon & 2pm-5.30pm Mon-Fri)
UK Rabat (Map p118; ☎ 037 633333; www.britain.org.ma; 28 Ave SAR Sidi Mohammed; 8am-4.15pm Mon-Thu, 8am-1pm Fri); Consulate-general in Casablanca (Map p102; ☎ 022 857400; british.consulate2@menara.ma); Consulate in Tangier (☎ 039 936939; uktanger2@menara.ma)
USA Rabat (Map p118; ☎ 037 762265; http://rabat.usembassy.gov; 2 Ave de Marrakesh, Rabat; 8am-5.30pm Mon-Fri); Consulate in Casablanca (Map p102; ☎ 022 264550; acscasablanca@state.gov; 8 Blvd Moulay Youssef; 8am-5.30pm Mon-Fri)

FESTIVALS & EVENTS

Moussems (festivals) that honour *marabouts* (local saints) pepper the Moroccan calendar. Although some are no more than an unusually lively market day, others have taken on regional and even national importance. These festivals are common among the Berbers and are usually held during the summer months.

Moussems exist on the frontier where Islamic orthodoxy and local custom have met and compromised. Although the veneration of saints is frowned upon by more orthodox Sunni Muslims, these festivals take their inspiration from a mix of pre-Islamic Berber tradition and Sufi mystic thought. Some of the more excessive manifestations, such as self-mutilation while in an ecstatic trance, were once a common sight at such gatherings. Today they have all but disappeared in the face of official disapproval of such 'barbarism'.

It's worth making enquiries at tourist offices to determine when *moussems* and other such festivals are due to happen. Some of the most important festivals and events, in chronological order, are as follows.

February

Almond Blossom Festival A very pretty festival held in late February to early March in the Ameln Valley near Tafraoute when the valley is awash with blossom (p402).

March/April

Marathon des Sables (www.saharamarathon.co.uk) A six-day foot race 243km across the desert, held in March or April. It starts and finishes in Ouarzazate (p58).

YOUR OWN EMBASSY

It's important to realise what your own embassy can and (more often) can't do to help if you get into trouble. Generally, it won't be much help in emergencies if the trouble you're in is remotely your own fault. Remember that you're bound by the laws of the country you are in. Your embassy will not be sympathetic if you end up in jail after committing a crime locally, even if such actions are legal in your own country.

In emergencies you might get some assistance, but only if all other channels have been exhausted. For example, if you need to get home urgently, getting a free ticket home is exceedingly unlikely – the embassy would expect you to have insurance. If all your money and documents are stolen, it may assist with getting a new passport, but a loan for onward travel is out of the question.

Some embassies used to keep letters for travellers or have a small reading room with home newspapers, but these days the mail-holding service has usually been stopped and even newspapers tend to be out of date.

Nomad Festival A celebration of nomadic culture in M'Hamid every March or April, with street performances, food, crafts and camel trips .
Moussem of Sidi Abdallah ibn Hassoun A procession of huge wax candle lanterns, carried by local brotherhoods to the Grand Mosque amid music and dancing. Held on the eve of Mouloud, the Prophet's birthday.
Festival of Sufi Culture A spin-off from the Sacred Music Festival, this new Fez outing has concerts, workshops and cultural exchanges (p242).

May/June

Rose Festival A colourful local festival celebrating the huge harvest of Persian roses in the valley around Kelaâ M'Gouna, close to Ouarzazate. Dancers are showered with rose petals and children sell fragrant garlands at the roadside. Usually held in May (p355).
Festival du Desert (www.festivaldudesert.ma) A celebration of music and dance held in May between Er-Rachidia, Merzouga and Rissani, with musicians from all across the Sahara.
Gnaoua and World Music Festival (www.festival-gnaoua.co.ma) A passionate celebration held in Essaouira on the third weekend of June, with concerts featuring international, national and local performers, and art exhibitions (p161).
Moussem of Sidi Mohammed Ma al-Ainin Held at Tan Tan, in late May or early June, this is an occasion where you may see Tuareg nomads from the Sahara; it also acts as a commercial gathering for tribes people.
Moussem of Ben Aïssa Held at Meknès' Koubba of Sidi ben Aïssa; one of the country's largest *moussems*, full of medieval pageantry with illusionists and daredevil horsemen (p260).
Festival of World Sacred Music A huge nine-day festival in Fez with great (and deserved) international attention. Concerts are held at the Dar Batha Museum, Grand Mechouar and Volubilis (p242).
Cherry Festival Sefrou's annual festival held in early June lasting three days with lots of folk music and dancing. Culminates in the picturesque crowning of the Cherry Queen (p254).

July

Festival International de Rabat Features musicians from all over Africa as well as some traditional theatre. The festival is also the venue for an annual film festival (p123).
Moussem of Sidi Bousselham Held in Moulay Bousselham near Larache, this is another large-scale *moussem* commemorating the local saint, in a beautiful location overlooking the sea.
Festival of Casablanca City festival focusing on street theatre, music and cinema.
Marrakesh Popular Arts Festival (www.maghrebarts.ma, in French) A hugely colourful festival held in Marrakesh, celebrating Berber music and dance, and attracting performers from all over the country.
Moussem & Camel Market A large camel-traders fair that brings Goulmime to life; it is as much a trade event as a religious get-together.
International Cultural Festival An arts festival held in Assilah celebrating contemporary art with public art demonstrations and workshops (some for children), and other theatrical and musical performances (p141).
Timitar Agadir's annual day in the musical sun, with Moroccan and international performers.

August

Moussem of Moulay Abdallah Held south of El-Jadida in the small village of Sidi Bouzid, this huge festival is a full-on fantasia with people gathering from all the surrounding villages.
Moussem of Sidi Ahmed Held in Tiznit, this largely religious celebration sees devotees dedicating themselves to pilgrimage and prayer.

September/October

Marriage Festival A famous three-day festival held in late September at Imilchil, where thousands of people gather for the serious business of wedlock: women at this festival get to choose prospective husbands (p332).
Moussem of Moulay Idriss II The largest city *moussem* in holy Fez, held in late September or early October, when thousands gather to watch the processions to the saint's tomb (p242).
International Film Festival (www.festival-marrakech.com) A weeklong festival held in September or October that showcases Arab and African cinema, as well as films from elsewhere (p308).
Date Festival Held in Erfoud late in October to celebrate the date harvest, the lifeblood of the oases villages. Lots of music and dancing bring this corner of the desert to life (p365).

FOOD

In this book, restaurants have been organised according to location first and then categorised into the different price ranges. In general, most midrange and top-end restaurants can be found within the ville nouvelle of large cities, with a few notable exceptions in Fez and Marrakesh. Within each section, restaurants are listed in order of budget.

Eating together and communally from the same bowl has important social connotations in Morocco. Most families will rush home for the shared midday meal, which reinforces strong family relationships. Thus it is that the culture of eating out in restaurants is still alien for many working-class Moroccans, explaining the epic divide between the cheap popular café (frequented by Moroccans for drinks and on-the-hoof sandwiches) and the expensive fancy restaurant (usually the domain of French expatriates, wealthy Moroccans and tourists).

Sandwich bars and popular cafés can serve up sandwiches and brochettes for around Dh20 to Dh40, whereas the cheapest menus in budget restaurants and outside major cities tend to hover between Dh70 to Dh150. Sit-down meals in a midrange restaurant within a major city will cost between Dh150 and Dh250 per person (depending on if you have wine). At the top end of the spectrum, possibilities range from palace and riad restaurants to some very fancy French establishments. Meals in one of these places will set you back around Dh400 to Dh600 per person including wine, more in Marrakesh. Wine is comparatively expensive in Morocco and will usually add an extra Dh100 to Dh250 to the bill.

A service charge may automatically be added to your bill in better restaurants; in addition to this, a TVA tax (similar to value-added tax), usually around 10%, may be charged, but generally this is built into the price of your meal.

For detailed information about Moroccan cuisine and local customs pertaining to food, see p79.

GAY & LESBIAN TRAVELLERS

Homosexual acts (including kissing) are officially illegal in Morocco – in theory you can go to jail and/or be fined. In practice, although not openly admitted or shown, sex between men remains relatively common, even if few people engaging would actively identify themselves as gay. Platonic affection is freely shown, more so among men than women. In most places, discretion is the key and public displays of affection should be avoided (aggression towards gay male travellers is not unheard of), advice which applies equally to homosexual and heterosexual couples as a means of showing sensitivity to local feelings.

Some towns are certainly more gay-friendly than others, with Marrakesh winning the prize, followed by Tangier. That said, gay travellers generally follow the same itineraries as everyone else and although 'gay' bars can be found here and there, Moroccan nightlife tends to include something for everybody.

Lesbians shouldn't encounter any problems, though it's commonly believed by Moroccans that there are no lesbians in their country. Announcing that you're gay probably won't make would-be Romeos magically disappear. For Moroccan men it may simply confirm their belief that Western men don't measure up in the sexual department.

It is also worth bearing in mind that the pressures of poverty mean than many young men will consider having sex for money or gifts. Needless to say, exploitative relationships form an unpleasant but real dimension of the Moroccan gay scene.

Useful websites that give the lowdown on local laws and attitudes to homosexuality include the following:

Behind the Mask (www.mask.org.za/) Detailed information and related news stories for every African country.

Gay & Lesbian Arab Society (www.glas.org) Resources on homosexuality in the Arab world.

Global Gayz (www.globalgayz.com) A useful resource with good links on Morocco.

Spartacus International Gay Guide (www.spartacusworld.com) Renowned guide to gay travel around the world with information on Morocco.

HOLIDAYS

All banks, post offices and most shops shut on the main public holidays, although transport is rarely affected. Of more significance to the majority of people are the principal religious holidays, which mean interruptions and changes of time for many local bus services.

As in Europe, the summer holiday period can be intensely busy along the Atlantic Coast as many Moroccan families flock to the sea, especially the resorts around Assilah, El-Jadida, Oualidia, Safi and Essaouira. Over Easter and Christmas the influx of European holiday-makers also has a big impact on hotel availability – booking ahead is essential.

Public Holidays

New Year's Day 1 January

Independence Manifesto 11 January – commemorates the publication in Fez of the Moroccan nationalist manifesto for independence.

Labour Day 1 May
Feast of the Throne 30 July – commemorates the accession to the throne of King Mohammed VI.
Allegiance of Oued Eddahab 14 August – celebrates the 'return to the fatherland' of the Oued Eddahab region in the far south, a territory once claimed by Mauritania.
Anniversary of the King's and People's Revolution 20 August – commemorates the exile of Mohammed V by the French in 1953.
Young People's Day 21 August – celebrates the King's birthday.
Anniversary of the Green March 6 November – commemorates the Green March 'reclaiming' the Western Sahara on November 1975.
Independence Day 18 November – commemorates independence from France.

Islamic Holidays

Although most business hours and aspects of daily Moroccan life are organised around the Gregorian calendar, the religious rhythms of society are firmly tied to the lunar Hejira calendar. The word *hejira* refers to the Prophet Mohammed's flight from Mecca to Medina in AD 622 – the first year of the Muslim calendar. The lunar calendar is slightly shorter than its Gregorian equivalent, so the Muslim calendar begins around 11 days earlier each year.

Dates run from sunset to the next sunset, with each month beginning with the sighting of the new moon. The religious authorities in Fez declare the sighting, so while future holy days can be estimated, the precise dates are in doubt until a few days before the start of that month. Ask an anxious Moroccan what date the Ramadan fast is going to end and you'll understand the frustrations. For this reason, the dates given here are only approximate. Offices and businesses all shut on these days, except for the first day of Ramadan.

The following Islamic holidays are celebrated countrywide.

RAS AS-SANA

The Muslim New Year's Day is celebrated on the first day of the Hejira calendar year, 1 Moharram, the first month of the Muslim lunar calendar.

MOULID AN-NABI

Sometimes also spelled Mouloud an-Nabi, this is a lesser feast celebrating the birth of the Prophet Mohammed on 12 Rabi al-Awal, the third month of the Muslim calendar. Children are often given presents on this day.

RAMADAN

Ramadan is the auspicious holy month of sunrise-to-sunset fasting, marking the period when the Prophet Mohammed received the revelations that form the Quran. No eating, drinking or smoking is permitted during daylight hours, although children, pregnant women, the sick and the elderly are exempt. Fasting during this month (one of the five pillars of Islam) is only one aspect of Ramadan, which is a time for renewing one's relationship with God. Ramadan is also traditionally a time for *zakat* (the giving of alms, another pillar of Islam), and reading the Quran.

The Arabic for fasting is *sawm*. You may find yourself being asked *'Inta sa'im?'* ('Are you fasting?') and encouraged to do so if your answer is *'La, ana faatir'* ('No, I am breaking the fast'). Non-Muslims are not expected to participate, even if more pious Muslims suggest you do, but in practice you end up adapting to some degree.

The implications of travelling during Ramadan are many. The most obvious is that many restaurants close during daylight hours. For more information on eating during Ramadan, see p86. Equally importantly, the entire rhythm of the country changes as most offices and many shops shift to open around 8am to 3pm or 4pm, and don't reopen for the evening. Public transport runs, although often on a much-reduced timetable, which is product of both supply (fewer drivers keen to work) and demand (with many Moroccan travellers inclined to delay travel until Ramadan ends). Most tour and trekking companies continue tours during Ramadan, but if it's a pre-booked tour, contact them in advance to make sure. If you arrive in a small village during Ramadan, you may find guides less than enthusiastic about taking to the trails, even though travellers are exempt from the dictates of the fast. Normally polite Moroccans can also become decidedly sullen during the fast and everything seems to take longer than it should; this is especially the case when Ramadan falls during the interminable daylight hours of summer (as it will during the lifetime of this edition

ISLAMIC HOLIDAYS

Holiday	2009	2010	2011	2012
Ramadan begins	22 Aug	11 Aug	1 Aug	20 Jul
Eid al-Fitr	20 Sep	9 Sep	30 Aug	19 Aug
Moulid an-Nabi	9 Mar	27 Feb	16 Feb	5 Feb
New Year begins (year)	31 Dec (1430)	20 Dec (1431)	7 Dec (1432)	27 Nov (1433)
Eid al-Adha	30 Nov	19 Nov	6 Nov	26 Oct

of the guidebook). The closer you get to sunset, the itchier people become. Traffic can be particularly terrible, with everyone clamouring to get home –hungry taxi drivers don't appreciate being flagged down at this time.

That said, the celebratory aspects of Ramadan can almost compensate for the hardships of the day just passed. *Iftar* (the breaking of the fast), is a time of great activity, when people come together to eat, drink and pray. If you're fortunate enough to be invited into the home of a local family for the nightly feast, you'll be embarking on a night that you'll never forget. Take a gift of dates – traditionally the first food to be eaten after the fast.

EID AL-FITR

The end of Ramadan – or more accurately the first days of the following month of Shawwal – mark Eid al-Fitr (the Feast of the Breaking of the Fast), also known as Eid as-Sagheer (the Small Feast). The fast is traditionally ended with a meal of *harira* (lentil soup), dates and honey cakes known as *griwash*. The Eid generally lasts four or five days, during which everything grinds to a halt. This is not a good time to travel, as whole families jam the transport network to visit relatives, but it can be a great experience if you are invited to share in some of the festivities with a family. It is a very family-oriented feast, much in the way Christmas is for Christians.

THE HAJ & EID AL-ADHA

The fifth pillar of Islam, the sacred duty of all who can afford it, is to make the pilgrimage to Mecca (the haj). It can be done at any time, but at least once it should be accomplished in Zuul-Hijja, the 12th month of the Muslim year. The haj culminates in the ritual slaughter of a lamb, in commemoration of Ibrahim's sacrifice, and marks the beginning of Eid al-Adha (Feast of the Sacrifice), also known as the Eid al-Kabeer (Grand Feast). Throughout the Muslim world the act of sacrifice is repeated and the streets of towns and cities seem to run with the blood of slaughtered sheep, with the meat often distributed to the less fortunate. The holiday runs from 10 to 13 Zuul-Hijja (the 12th month of the Muslim calendar).

INSURANCE

A travel-insurance policy to cover theft, loss and medical problems is strongly recommended – the national health service in Morocco isn't always great and the few good private hospitals are expensive. Some policies offer lower and higher medical-expense options; the higher ones are chiefly for countries such as the USA, which have extremely high medical costs. Check that the policy covers ambulance or an emergency flight home, and carry proof of your insurance with you; this can be vital in avoiding any delays to treatment in emergency situations.

Buy travel insurance as early as possible. Buying just before you leave home may mean that you're not covered for delays to your flight caused by strike action that began, or was threatened, before you took out the insurance. If you need to extend your cover on the road, do so before it expires or a more expensive premium may apply.

Paying for your airline ticket with a credit card often provides some travel-accident insurance and you may be able to reclaim the payment if the operator doesn't deliver.

Some policies specifically exclude 'dangerous activities', which can include scuba diving, motorcycling, and even trekking, so discuss this with your broker. A locally acquired motorcycle licence is not valid under some policies.

You may prefer a policy that pays the medical facility directly rather than you having to pay on the spot and claim later, although in practice many Moroccan doctors and hospitals insist on payment upfront. If you have to claim later, make sure you keep all documentation. Some policies ask you to call back (reverse charge) to a centre in your home country where an immediate assessment of your problem is made, so bring your insurer's emergency telephone number and keep a copy separate from your main baggage. Find out also which private medical service your insurer uses in Morocco so that you can call them direct in the event of an emergency.

Make sure that you have adequate health insurance and any relevant car insurance if you're driving (see p494). Worldwide travel insurance is available at www.lonelyplanet.com/travel_services. You can buy, extend and claim online anytime – even if you're already on the road.

INTERNET ACCESS

It's not difficult to get online in Morocco. Internet access is widely available, efficient and cheap (Dh4 to Dh10 per hour) in internet cafés, usually with pretty impressive connections speeds – witness the many teenagers talking with their friends by webcam. One irritant for travellers is the widespread use of French or Arabic (non-qwerty) keyboards, which will reduce most travellers to one-finger typing and fumbled (and mumbled) searches for hidden punctuation marks.

Wi-fi is increasingly available in hotels, as indicated throughout the review sections of the guide. Most top-end and many midrange hotels offer wi-fi, and it's more or less standard in most riads and *maisons d'hôtes*. If you're bringing your laptop, check the power-supply voltage and bring a universal adaptor.

For useful internet resources see p25.

LEGAL MATTERS

Moroccan law prohibits the possession, offer, sale, purchase, distribution and transportation of cannabis and the penalty will most likely include a prison sentence ranging from three months to five years and/or a fine from Dh2400 up to Dh240,000. Acquittals in drugs cases are extremely rare. The UK-based **Fair Trials Abroad** (FTA; ☎ 020-8332 2800; www.fairtrialsabroad.org; London, UK) provides assistance and legal advice to nationals of EU countries imprisoned abroad.

If you get into trouble, your first call should always be to your consulate; remember that it's not unknown for the local police to be in on the scam. If you find yourself arrested by the Moroccan police, you won't have much of a legal leg to stand on and it's unlikely that any interpreter on hand will be of sufficient standard to translate an accurate statement that will, nonetheless, play a vital part in subsequent judicial proceedings. According to some human-rights groups (Human Rights Watch and L'Organisation Mondiale Contre la Torture), physical abuse while in custody is not unknown.

MAPS

Few decent maps of Morocco are available in the country itself, so get one before leaving home.

Michelin's No 742 (formerly No 959) map of Morocco is arguably the best. In addition to the 1:4,000,000 scale map of the whole of Morocco, including the disputed territory of the Western Sahara, there is a 1:1,000,000 enlargement of Morocco and 1:600,000 enlargements of Marrakesh and the High Atlas, Middle Atlas and Meknès areas. Sites of weekly markets, kasbahs and *marabouts* (holy mausolea of local saints) are also shown, and particularly scenic roads are also noted. You can buy this in major Moroccan cities.

Preferred by many and with similar, often clearer, detail (and occasionally available in Morocco) is the GeoCenter World Map *Morocco,* which shows the country at a handy 1:800,000 scale. Hildebrand's *Morocco* covers the entire country at a scale of 1:900,000, includes seven small city maps and is good for the Western Sahara.

Regionally, several maps include Morocco as part of northwestern Africa. The Michelin map No 741 (formerly Nos 953 and 153) covers all of west Africa and most of the Sahara, has a scale of 1:4,000,000 and is something of an overlanding classic. Also on the same scale is Kümmerley & Frey's *Africa, North and West*.

It's also possible to get hold of 1:200,000 Russian survey maps and air charts of Morocco from good map shops worldwide, although these usually have to be ordered and can take up to six weeks to arrive. For advice on tracking down more detailed topographical maps for trekking, see p417.

Most of these maps are available online from **Stanfords** (☎ 0044 20 7836 1321; www.stanfords.co.uk), the world's largest map shop.

MONEY

The Moroccan currency is the dirham (Dh), which is divided into 100 centimes. You will find notes in denominations up to Dh200 and coins of Dh1, Dh2, Dh5 and Dh10, as well as, less frequently, 10, 20 and 50 centimes.

The dirham is a restricted currency, meaning that it cannot be taken out of the country and is not available abroad. That said, the currency is fairly stable and there are no wild fluctuations in exchange rates. Euros, US dollars and British pounds are the most easily exchanged currencies.

Exchange rates are given on the inside front cover of this book and a guide to costs can be found on p22.

ATMs

ATMs (*guichets automatiques*) are a common sight even in the smallest towns. Virtually all accept Visa, MasterCard, Electron, Cirrus, Maestro and InterBank systems, making them by far the easiest way to access your money in Morocco. BMCE (Banque Marocaine du Commerce Extérieur), Crédit du Maroc, Banque Populaire, Banque Marocaine pour le Commerce et l'Industrie (BMCI), Societé Générale and Attajariwafa Bank also offer reliable service. Some banks charge you every time you make a withdrawal from a foreign cash machine, others don't. Ask your bank back home. The amount of money you can withdraw from an ATM generally depends on the conditions attached to your particular card, although the daily ATM limit on most cards is around Dh2000. ATMs sometimes run dry on weekends.

Black Market

The easy convertibility of the dirham leaves little room for a black market, but you'll find people in the streets asking if you want to exchange money, especially in Tangier, Casablanca and on the borders of (and just inside) the enclaves of Ceuta and Melilla. Avoid these characters; there's no monetary benefit to be had from such transactions and scams are common.

Cash

Nothing beats cash for convenience…or risk. If you lose it, it's gone forever and very few travel insurers will come to the rescue. Nonetheless, you'll certainly need to carry some cash with you. Keep a handful of notes of small denomination in your wallet (never in a back pocket) for day-to-day transactions and put the rest in a money belt or another safe place. If you're travelling in out-of-the-way places, make sure you have enough cash to last until you get to a decent-sized town. Having a secret stash of euros in small denominations is also a good idea.

The endless supply of small coins may be annoying but they're handy for the payment of taxis, tips, guides and beggars.

Credit Cards

Major credit cards are widely accepted in the main tourist centres, although their use often attracts a surcharge of around 5% from Moroccan businesses.

The main credit cards are MasterCard and Visa, and if you plan to rely on plastic cards, the best bet is to take one of each. Better still is a combination of credit and debit cards, and travellers cheques so that you have something to fall back on if an ATM swallows your card or the banks in the area are closed.

Most large bank branches will allow you to get cash advances on Visa and MasterCard. See the list of banks in the ATM section, left.

Money Changers

The importation or exportation of Moroccan currency is prohibited, but any amount of foreign currency may be brought into the country. In the Spanish enclaves of Ceuta and Melilla the currency is the euro. Most currencies are readily exchanged in banks, but Australian, Canadian and New Zealand dollars are not recognised.

If you're arriving from, or heading for, the enclaves of Ceuta and Melilla, the Moroccan banks on the borders will exchange cash only. The banks in Melilla and Ceuta deal in dirham, but at rates inferior to those in Morocco.

Banking services inside Morocco are reasonably quick and efficient. Rates vary little from bank to bank, but it doesn't hurt to look around. Branches of BMCE and Crédit du Maroc are generally the most convenient, and often have separate *bureau de change* sections that are open on weekends. Major branches of the main banks open on Saturday morning.

You'll need your passport to change travellers cheques (plus the travellers cheque receipt in some places) and to get cash advances; some banks want to see it when you change cash, too.

As exporting Moroccan currency is illegal, wind down to nothing as you approach the end of your trip and hang on to all exchange receipts – you'll need them to convert leftover dirham at most Moroccan banks.

Tipping

Tipping is an integral part of Moroccan life. Almost any service can warrant a tip, but don't be railroaded. The judicious distribution of a few dirham for a service willingly rendered can, however, make your life a lot easier.

A tip of 10% of a restaurant bill is about right (unless the service has been poor, of course), and a couple of dirham suffices at a café. Museum guides, *gardiens de voitures* (car-park attendants), porters, baggage handlers and petrol-pump attendants expect to be tipped (between Dh3 and Dh5, or Dh10 for overnight parking). It's worth bearing in mind that unskilled workers in Morocco earn somewhat less than Dh80 per day.

Travellers Cheques

Travellers cheques are so old news, and more travellers opt simply to withdraw money from ATMs or get cash advances on credit cards as they go. They do, however, offer some protection against theft.

Amex, Visa and Thomas Cook cheques are widely accepted and have efficient replacement policies. Keeping a record of the cheque numbers and those you have used is vital when it comes to replacing lost travellers cheques. Make sure you keep this record separate from the cheques themselves.

Almost all banks charge commission on travellers cheques (around Dh10 to Dh20 per cheque), though some banks charge Dh10 per transaction, so ask around before changing. Smaller banks may refuse to change travellers cheques,

PHOTOGRAPHY & VIDEO

Morocco is a photographer's dream, but never point your camera at anything that's vaguely military or could be construed as 'strategic'. This includes airports, bridges, government buildings and members of the police or armed forces. This becomes more of an issue further south, in the Western Sahara, or near the Algerian border

It is common courtesy to ask permission before taking photographs of people. Urban Moroccans are generally easygoing about it, but in the countryside locals are not so willing to have cameras pointed at them. In particular, women and older people very often don't want to be photographed. Respect their right to privacy and don't take photos.

Memory cards and batteries for digital cameras are quite easy to find in photography shops in major cities (especially Casablanca and Marrakesh), although for a short visit there's no reason not to bring your own. A USB memory stick is useful for backing up photos, but most Moroccan internet cafés will burn you a CD if needed.

For nondigital shooters, Kodak and Fuji colour negative film (35mm and APS), as well as video tapes, are readily available in bigger cities and towns, but are marginally more expensive than in Europe. Slide film is more difficult to come by. If you buy film in Morocco, be sure to check expiry dates. Professional photo labs also offer the most professional processing services.

For comprehensive advice on taking terrific photos, Lonely Planet's *Travel Photography*, *Landscape Photography* and *People Photography* have been designed to take with you on the road.

POST

Post offices are distinguished by a yellow 'PTT' sign or the 'La Poste' logo. You can sometimes buy stamps at *tabacs,* the small tobacco and newspaper kiosks you see scattered about the main city centres.

The postal system is fairly reliable, if not terribly fast. It takes at least a week for letters to get to their European destinations, and two weeks to get to Australia and North America. Sending post from a city normally gives mail a head start. Worldwide postcards cost around Dh13 to send, and letters around Dh18.

Express Mail & Couriers

There is usually an Express Mail Service (EMS), also known as Poste Rapide, in the same office as parcel post. In Morocco the service is run by **Chronopost** (☎ 022 202121; www.chronopost.com). A 500g package will cost around Dh320 to send to the UK and Europe, DH420 to North America and Dh575 to Australia.

Private courier companies have offices in the major cities that are both faster and more expensive. These include **DHL** (☎ 022 972020; www.dhl-ma.com) and **TNT** (☎ 022 272724; www.tnt.com).

Receiving Mail

Having mail addressed to 'Poste Restante, La Poste Principale' of any big town should not be a problem. Generally reliable, some offices only hang on to parcels for a couple of weeks before returning them. You'll need your passport to claim mail and there may be a small charge on collection.

An alternative way to receive mail is through Amex, which is represented by the travel agency Voyages Schwartz and has branches in Casablanca, Tangier and Marrakesh. To qualify for the client mail service, you're supposed to have Amex travellers cheques or an Amex card. In practice, you're usually asked only to produce a passport for identification and there's no charge.

Sending Mail

The parcel office, which is indicated by the sign 'colis postaux', is generally in a separate part of the post-office building.

To ship your goods home, buy a box and a shipping form at the post office and take them to the shop where you bought your wares; they know the product and can wrap and pack the pieces well with newsprint and cardboard. If you've purchased carpets, the vendor should have rolled and bound them in plastic sacks; if not, return and ask them to do so. There is a 20kg limit and parcels should not be wider, longer or higher than 1.5m. Label the outside of the boxes or carpets in several places with a waterproof pen and be very clear about the destination country. Indicate the value of the contents if you like, but you may be charged taxes at the receiving end. Don't seal the box! Customs offices at the post office need to review the contents. Your packages will be weighed and you will be charged the Par Avion (air) freight rates unless you specify that that you prefer the items shipped by land (considerably less expensive but can take three months).

Valuable speciality items such as large furniture may involve customs clearance. The shopkeeper should arrange this, plus shipping, for you but at your own cost; just make sure you keep copies of all documentation.

SHOPPING

To come to Morocco as a tourist is to shop, and the shop owners in the souqs know this only to well. An enthusiastic souvenir hunter could spend weeks trawling through the souqs of Morocco. From silver jewellery to copper and brassware, and myriad rugs and carpets, there is an enormous range. Obviously, items of inferior quality are produced in addition to higher-quality objects – it pays to take your time before buying. Many cities have a government-run Ensemble Artisanal, where crafts are sold at fixed prices. They're often good places to get an idea of prices and quality. For more information on the myriad things to browse and buy, see the Arts & Architecture chapter, p65.

Other popular items include herbs and spices, old-fashioned French-style tourism posters and Moroccan clothes. Many die-hard shoppers buy a large woven shopping basket as a souvenir and also use it to pack and transport souvenirs.

Always get a receipt for larger purchases, especially carpets, as you may be required to show this to customs on your departure from Morocco; otherwise you may have to pay an export tax, especially if you have more than one carpet. You may also have to pay a duty on taking carpets into your home country.

Markets

Moroccan towns and villages have weekly or twice-weekly markets (*souq hebdomadaire*) where people from the surrounding area

RULES TO REMEMBER

There are three rules for shopping in Morocco's souqs: patience, patience and patience. Bargaining is an essential element in Morocco's commercial culture and, through a mix of guile, persistence and silky sales techniques, Moroccan shop owners are a world-class act. For them, bargaining is entertainment and social interaction, a game seasoned with performance and rhetoric. You'd do well to see it in the same way.

Preparation

Visiting the Ensemble Artisanal, a government-run craft shop found in most cities and where they sell quality goods with fixed prices, is ideal for discovering what constitutes a fair price. Hotel receptionists or local friends can also give you an idea of what a local would pay. Armed with this information, set yourself an upper limit and stick to it.

Foreplay

Learn the art of wandering through the souqs and scanning your surrounds – sunglasses are the perfect aid in this devious pursuit. Once you've spotted your prey, engage the shop owner and score points with a *salam ou alekum* (peace be with you). His questions will follow: Where are you from? He will doubtless discover (what a coincidence!) that he has a brother/cousin/friend who lives in your home town. How long have you been in Morocco? Far be it for us to advocate lying, but the less time you've been here, the more the shop owner will be licking his lips. Then you can start to browse uninterestedly – a spark of interest means the bargaining begins (though not if you're with a guide, as a commission will have to factored in).

come to sell their wares and buy goods they don't produce themselves. These markets are different from the permanent covered markets you'll find in most towns, and usually provide a lively opportunity to observe the distinctive customs and clothing of local people.

All types of markets are called souqs. These are some of the more interesting ones:

Location	Market days
Agadir	Sat, Sun
Azrou	Tue
Chefchaouen	Mon, Thu
Figuig	Wed
Larache	Sun
M'Hamid	Mon
Midelt	Sun
Moulay Idriss	Sat
Ouarzazate	Sun
Ouezzane	Thu
Oujda	Wed, Sun
Sefrou	Thu
Tafraoute	Wed
Taroudannt	Sun
Tinerhir	Mon
Tinzouline	Mon
Tiznit	Wed
Zagora	Wed, Sun

SOLO TRAVELLERS

Morocco is a great destination for solo travellers. Popular with independent travellers and backpackers, Morocco has plenty of budget accommodation where it's easy to find a travel buddy should you be in need of one (Fez and Marrakesh are particularly good centres for this). Moroccans are also open, inquisitive and friendly, which means you will seldom be lonely, although locals may be baffled (to the verge of pitying) as to why you'd choose to travel alone, rather than with friends or (especially) family. Outside the cities, the rates in many places are per person rather than per room and single occupancy of rooms is rarely a problem. However in riads, the limited accommodation means that discounts on single occupancy are fairly minimal.

Lone female travellers to Morocco will find it more tiresome than solo male travellers, although the overwhelming consensus from readers is that the rewards far outweigh the hassles. Be cautious but don't be paranoid because if you close off all contact with local people you could end up missing one of Morocco's greatest rewards.

For more information on women travellers, see p475.

The Main Event

Whatever the vendor quotes you, offer one-third. If that's insultingly low (and even if it isn't), he'll laugh, shake his head then look pained. If you truly have insulted him, or he figures that a tour bus (filled with tourists with loads of money) is headed his way, the bargaining will end. More likely, he'll tell you that he can drop the price by a few dirhams because (a) you are his friend; (b) he likes British/American/Insert-country-here people; (c) business has been bad and what else can he do; or (d) because you are the first/last customer of the day. Play hard to get and counter with your own sob story, tell him you've seen the same item down the road for a fraction of the price or make him laugh and he will lower again. Perhaps give a little ground, even walk away, and if you are with someone, try the 'good cop, bad cop' routine (eg husband wants the souvenir, cautious wife controls the purse strings). Whatever you do, don't let on how much you *really* want the piece. If it means enough to him, he won't let you leave; if not, swallow your pride and try again. But never, ever lose your temper – Dh10 probably means more to a Moroccan trader than it does to you. If you end up paying 60% of the opening price, you've done well.

The Aftermath

After the purchase is sealed, other travellers will surely tell you that you paid too much, but bargaining depends on a wonderfully simple concept: the price is one that both parties have accepted as fair. It doesn't matter what anybody else thinks.

And one final thing: unless you're leaving on the next bus out of town, pass by the shop on the days that follow, stopping even for a mint tea. Freed from the pressure of a looming transaction, you might even get to know the man behind the salesman, which may be worth more than money can buy.

TELEPHONE & FAX

Morocco has a good telephone network and Moroccans are as obsessed with mobile (cell) phones as the rest of the world.

There are three GSM mobile-phone networks: **Meditel** (www.meditelecom.ma), **Maroc Telecom** (www.iam.ma) and **Wana** (www.maroccon nect.ma). Countrywide coverage is generally excellent, although much of the Atlas and Sahara remain, unsurprisingly, mobile-free zones. Your home mobile operator is likely to have a local agreement with one of the Moroccan operators, although roaming services tend to attract hefty charges. It may be cheaper to buy a prepaid Moroccan mobile or SIM card at a *téléboutique* (private telephone kiosk/office). A local SIM card should cost around Dh30. *Téléboutiques*, news-stands and grocery stores all sell top-up scratch cards to buy more credit. Moroccan mobile numbers start with 01, 06 or 07. Calls cost around Dh2 per minute for domestic calls, and Dh10 per minute for international calls, depending on the network.

To make a call within Morocco, you must dial the local three-digit area code even if you are dialling from the same town or code area. For local-directory enquiries dial ☎160. To make an international call, you must add the prefix ☎00 to all numbers, then the country code (it's important to remember this if dialling the Spanish enclaves of Melilla and Ceuta – the country code for Spain is ☎34.

If you're not using a mobile, you can make a call at a *téléboutique* or a public payphone. The former will usually change small notes into coins to make your call. Most payphones are card-operated, and you'll need to buy a *télécarte* (phonecard) from a *tabac* or *téléboutique*. Payphones have easy-to-follow instructions for use. Calling from a hotel normally doubles the cost of your call.

Most *téléboutiques* offer fax services, but they're often expensive – between Dh20 and Dh50 per sheet for international faxes, depending on the destination, and around Dh12 to Moroccan numbers. It normally costs Dh5 to receive a fax.

TIME

Morocco is on GMT/UTC, with the clock moved forward one hour for daylight saving between 1 June and 27 September. If you're travelling via Spain (or the enclaves of Ceuta and Melilla) take particular care with the clock, as in the summer, spring and autumn Spain is two (not one) hours ahead, which can affect plans for catching ferries and the like. For a comprehensive guide to time zones, see p534.

Time is something that most Moroccans seem to have plenty of and they're not in nearly as much of a hurry to get things done as most Westerners. Rather than getting frustrated by this, learn to go with the flow a little. It may even lengthen your life, a sentiment reflected in the Moroccan saying, 'He who hurries has one foot in the grave.'

TOILETS

Outside the major cities, public toilets are rare. If you do find one, you'll need to bring paper *(papier hygiénique)*, a tip for the attendant (Dh2 to Dh3), stout-soled shoes, and very often a nose clip. Flush toilets are a luxury in a country struggling with water shortages.

Toilets are mostly of the squat variety (referred to by Moroccans as 'Turkish toilets') with a tap, hose or container of water for sluicing – the idea being to wash yourself (with your left hand) after performing. There's seldom any toilet paper so keep a supply with you. Don't throw the paper into the toilet as the plumbing is often dodgy; instead discard it in the bin provided. Women who have their period will need to take along a plastic bag for disposing of used tampons and pads.

TRAVELLERS WITH DISABILITIES

Morocco has few facilities for the disabled, and the awkward nature of narrow medina streets and rutted pavements makes mobility even for the able-bodied something of a challenge. But that doesn't necessarily make it out of bounds for those who do have a physical disability and a sense of adventure. Not all hotels (and certainly very few of the cheaper ones) have lifts, so booking ground-floor hotel rooms ahead of time is one essential. Only a handful of the very top-end hotels have rooms designed for the disabled. Travelling by car is probably the best transport, though you'll be able to get assistance in bus and train stations (a tip will be required). Many tour operators can tailor trips to suit your requirements.

Vision- or hearing-impaired travellers are also poorly catered, for with hearing loops, Braille signs and talking pedestrian crossings nonexistent.

Organisations that disseminate information, advice and assistance on world travel for the mobility impaired include the following:

Access-able Travel Source (☎ 303-232 2979; www.access-able.com) A US-based information provider for travellers with mobility problems.

Disabled Travelers Guide (www.disabledtravelersguide.com) Comprehensive information and general guide for travellers with disabilities.

Mobility International USA (☎ 541-343 1284; www.miusa.org)

Royal Association for Disability & Rehabilitation (Radar; ☎ 020-7250 3222) This UK organisation publishes a useful guide called *Holidays & Travel Abroad: A Guide for Disabled People*.

VISAS

Most visitors to Morocco do not require visas and are allowed to remain in the country for 90 days on entry. Exceptions to this include nationals of Israel and many sub-Saharan African countries (including South Africa). These people must apply in advance for a three-month, single-entry visa (about US$30). They also have the option of applying for a three-month, double-entry visa (about US$50). In all cases, your passport must be valid for at least six months beyond your date of entry. Applications are normally processed in 48 hours.

In Spain, visas are available at Moroccan consulates in Madrid, Barcelona, Algeciras, and Las Palmas in the Canary Islands. In Mauritania, you can get a visa at the Moroccan embassy in Nouakchott within 48 hours.

As visa requirements change, it's a good idea to check with the Moroccan embassy in your country or a reputable travel agency before travelling.

Visa Extensions

Should the standard 90-day stay be insufficient, you can apply for an extension or even for residence (a *Carte de Sejour*), but the latter is difficult to get and usually requires proof of employment. Go to the nearest police headquarters *(Préfecture de Police)* with your passport, three photos and a letter from your embassy requesting a visa extension on your behalf. Applications can take hours or days, and different police

VISAS FOR NEIGHBOURING COUNTRIES

Embassies for the following countries are in Rabat - see p462 for address details.

- **Algeria** The Morocco–Algeria border remains closed, and Algeria prefers visa applicants to apply in their country of residence.
- **Mali** Visas are required for everyone except French nationals and are valid for one month (Dh250), but are renewable inside Mali. Two photographs and a yellow-fever vaccination certificate are required and the visa is usually issued on the spot. Malian visas are available at Malian border posts but by no means count on that if you're crossing at a remote desert crossing.
- **Mauritania** Everyone, except nationals of Arab League countries, needs a visa, which is valid for a one-month stay. Get these at the Mauritanian Embassy in Rabat – apply in the morning and pick up in the afternoon the following day. Visas cost Dh200 and you need two photos. It's currently quick and easy to obtain three-day transit visas (extendable in Nouakchott) at the border for €10. Good up-to-date information is available online at www.sahara-overland.com.
- **Tunisia** Citizens of EU countries, the USA and Japan can stay up to three months in Tunisia without a visa. Australians, New Zealanders and South Africans can get a three-month visa upon arrival at the airport.

headquarters use slightly different red tape to hold up proceedings.

In practice, most travellers requiring an extension find it easier to head to mainland Spain or even one of the Spanish enclaves in Morocco, and re-enter after a few days. Although this generally presents few problems other than cost, it can leave you to the mercies of individual immigration officers on re-entry, and some travellers have occasionally come unstuck this way.

Visas for Ceuta & Melilla

These two Spanish enclaves have the same visa requirements as mainland Spain. Under the 1995 Schengen agreement, one visa now covers all EU-member countries except the UK, the Republic of Ireland and Denmark, and replaces those previously issued by individual nations. Australian citizens travelling to Spain as tourists, for a maximum period of three months per calendar year, do not require a Schengen visa prior to arrival in Spain. On arrival their passports will be stamped with a Schengen Stamp (valid for three months) at the first port of entry.

South Africans and Israelis still need to obtain a visa before they travel to Europe.

For those who must apply for a visa, you'll need three photos, and you may also be asked for photocopies of passport details, credit cards and/or bank statements. The Spanish prefer you to apply for a visa in your country of residence – this is only rarely waived.

International Health Certificate

If you're coming to Morocco from certain parts of Asia, Africa or South America where yellow fever is endemic, you'll need to show you've been vaccinated by producing either a international health certificate or separate yellow-fever certificate. In practice this is usually only required if you've travelled overland up through Mauritania, or arrived on one of Royal Air Maroc's extensive connections through Africa. See p498 for general information on immunisations.

WOMEN TRAVELLERS

Prior to marriage, Moroccan men have little opportunity to meet and get to know women, which is a major reason why Western women receive so much attention. Not bound by the Moroccan social structure and Islamic law, these women are seen as excitingly independent and generally available.

Around 70% of Morocco's population is under the age of 30, and by the end of their trip most Western women may think they've met every male in this group. The constant attention soon becomes wearing and, no matter what tactic is employed, impossible to shake off.

If it's your first time in Morocco, the first few days may be something of a shock, although you'll quickly develop a thick skin to deal with the comments and unwanted looks of men. The key to not spending the rest of your trip feeling hassled is remain wary but not paranoid – it's extremely rare for any of this low-level harassment to go any further. If it does all get too much, look for the ever-increasing number of places accustomed to having the business of single Moroccan women. The upper floor of a *salon de thé* (tea house), a café, restaurant or a hotel terrace are good bets. Hammams are good male-free zones for a relaxing reprieve.

The common attitude that a Westerner is a walking visa out of a country where unemployment is rife can also impact upon the experience of women travellers. Bored youngsters (and the not so young) may have little to lose by wooing someone who can offer them an opportunity in another country or, failing that, a sexual liaison unavailable from Moroccan women. In fairness, we should point out that it isn't uncommon for Western women to come to Morocco and pick up local guys for holiday romances. That's not to say this is the basis for all relationships of mixed nationality (of which there are many success stories), but be aware that some locals could be juggling several relationships at any one time.

Women travelling with male companions are unlikely to experience much of the hassle that solo women will inevitably encounter, although it may be better to claim to be a married couple rather than just friends (the latter concept is usually greeted with disbelief).

If you are a Moroccan woman (or Moroccan in appearance) and you're travelling with your non-Moroccan spouse, it may be advisable to carry a copy of your marriage certificate. This is because premarital sex for Muslims is forbidden and Morocco has a real problem with prostitution. If your partner is thought to be Muslim you may meet with some uncomfortable situations at hotel reception desks, though it has to be said that in larger cities this is not really an issue.

For all the problems, there is one huge benefit of travelling as a woman in Morocco: unlike men, you'll have plenty of opportunities to meet local women and thereby enjoy a fascinating window into one of the least-known aspects of Moroccan society. For more information on women in Morocco see p56.

Safety Precautions

Moroccans would have to be among the most hospitable people in the world. Genuinely welcoming, they are eager to help any traveller and there are times when being a woman is a distinct advantage, especially when lost or in some form of distress. Moroccans tend to be genuinely concerned for the 'weaker sex' and will offer protection and support if you feel you're in a potentially dodgy situation.

Crimes against women remain extremely rare. More common is verbal abuse from both men and women. However, in places that have seen a large influx of tourists in recent years, problems can occur, and we've received reports of physical harassment at music festivals in Essaouira.

Women travellers should always take a few sensible precautions:

- Don't hitchhike.
- Be aware that some budget hotels double as brothels; any cheap hotel above a popular locals' bar is a likely contender. Don't compromise your safety for the sake of economy.
- On public transport try to sit next to a woman, especially in grands taxis where you're squeezed in far too closely for comfort, and trains where you could potentially be trapped inside a compartment. In grands taxis consider paying for two seats and get a ride by yourself in the front. It must be said however, that many women travel in grands taxis without the slightest problem, regardless of where they sit.
- Don't wander about alone at night as there's an attitude that all 'good women' should be at home after dark – take a taxi.
- Avoid walking alone in remote areas such as isolated beaches, forests and sand dunes.
- If you need a drink, head for a large hotel rather than a 'bunker-style', all-male preserve – any woman here is without doubt a prostitute. Then again, so are many of those in the posher places.

- Wearing dark glasses is good for avoiding eye contact, but don't spend your entire Moroccan journey hiding behind them.
- Don't react with aggression - it could be returned in kind. A good-humoured *non merci* or *la shukran* ('no thank you') is much more effective than abuse.

A wedding ring may be useful and a photo of your 'husband' and 'child' could help, although the fact that you're travelling without them will attract suspicion. Counter this by saying you'll be meeting them at your next destination. It has to be said, however, that many Moroccan men aren't too concerned whether you're married or not and may still insist they're just being friendly and could even invite you home to meet their mother.

One traveller reported that the key word to use is 'respect', a concept that most Moroccans hold dear. It's worth a try, but remember the advice of one female Lonely Planet author: 'Asking men to respect me did a fat lot of good in ending any unwanted attention I was getting.'

Always dress modestly and be aware that hotel and public swimming pools usually attract groups of men, whether they be swimming themselves or drinking at a poolside bar. Bikinis will always attract attention. The push to increase tourism numbers increasingly brings visitors unprepared (or simply unaware) that cultural mores in Muslim countries are different from the West. Although you might see tourists so-dressed, hot pants and cleavage in the Marrakesh medina is never appropriate, and we were as shocked as the locals to see a tourist sunbathing topless on a recent trip to Essaouira.

At the other end of the scale, sporting a head scarf or even a *jellaba* (Moroccan-style flowing cloak) will earn you respect, particularly in the countryside, as well as a million questions as to why you're wearing it: Are you Muslim? Are you Moroccan? Are you married to a Moroccan?

For further suggestions about what to wear (and what not to wear) while in Morocco, see p51.

WORK

With huge unemployment and a largely out-of-work youthful population, Morocco isn't the most fertile ground for digging up work opportunities. A good command of French is a prerequisite and some Arabic would certainly help. If you secure a position, your employer will have to help you get a work permit and arrange residency, which can be a long and involved process. There are some limited opportunities for doing volunteer work or teaching English, although this is not terribly well paid. Try the websites: www.workingabroad.com and www.idea list.org.

Teaching English

There are a few possibilities for teaching English as a foreign language in Morocco, and Rabat is one of the best places to start looking. First, you could approach the **British Council** (www.britishcouncil.org.ma), but you need a Diploma in Teaching English as a Foreign Language (TEFL) and openings are not all that frequent. Another possibility is the **American Language Center** (www.aca.org.ma), which has offices around the country.

The time to try is around September and October (which is the beginning of the academic year) and, to a lesser extent, early January.

Volunteering

There are many international and local organisations that arrange voluntary work on regional development projects in Morocco. They generally pay nothing, sometimes not even providing lodging, and are aimed at young people looking for something different to do for a few weeks over the summer period. Some of these organisations are really summer camps and international exchange programs.

Baraka Community Partnerships (www.barakacommunity.com), near Telouet, organises volunteers to build schools, plant trees, supply basic medical care and work on initiatives to improve local food security between partnerships.

Volunteer Abroad (www.volunteerabroad.com/Morocco.cfm) is a good place to start looking for volunteer places, as it provides links to NGOs with Morocco-specific programs. Also worth getting hold of is Lonely Planet's *The Gap Year Book*, which lists hundreds of NGOs that organise volunteer and other work and study programs around the world. Your embassy may also be able to put you onto other projects and NGOs, but unless you have a working knowledge of Arabic or Berber, or have specific specialist skills, many will not be interested.

International or local NGOs that sometimes have Morocco placements or camps include:

Chantiers Sociaux Marocains (☎ 037 262400; csm@wanadoo.net.ma; Rabat) Local NGO engaged in health, education and development projects, with international volunteers aged 18 to 30.

Jeunesse des Chantiers Marocains (http://perso.menara.ma/youthcamps) A nonprofit group open to 18 to 30 year olds, promoting cultural exchange through three- to four-week courses in Moroccan Arabic, during which you stay with local families and take part in cultural events.

International Cultural Youth Exchange (www.icye.org) Allows you to search for upcoming Moroccan volunteer opportunities.

Peace Corps (www.peacecorps.gov) Long-established US volunteer scheme with deep roots in Morocco; volunteer programs lasting two years.

United Planet (www.unitedplanet.org) Mainly long-term volunteering placements that sometimes include Morocco.

Transport

CONTENTS

GETTING THERE & AWAY

Transport reform has been central to the recent explosion of visitor numbers to Morocco. The government's 'open skies' policy has allowed the European budget airlines into the country, improving access. At the same time, overland options shouldn't be ignored – there are numerous ferry services from southern Spain and France that also link Morocco to the European rail network – a more low-carbon way of arriving in the country.

Flights, tours and rail tickets can be booked online at www.lonelyplanet.com/travel_services.

ENTERING THE COUNTRY

When entering the country through an airport, formalities are fairly quick and straightforward, but you'll have to fill in an entry form stating the purpose of your visit and your profession.

If you're entering Morocco with a vehicle, you'll need a Green Card as proof of insurance (a requirement of Moroccan law that also applies to rental vehicles). These are obtainable from your insurer at home or at the border – see p492 for more information.

THINGS CHANGE...

The information in this chapter is particularly vulnerable to change. Check directly with the airline or a travel agent to make sure you understand how a fare (and ticket you may buy) works and be aware of the security requirements for international travel. Shop carefully. The details given in this chapter should be regarded as pointers and are not a substitute for your own careful, up-to-date research.

Passport

To enter Morocco, your passport must be valid for six months from the date of entry. If you need to renew your passport, allow plenty of time, as it can take up to several months.

If you lose your passport, notify the police immediately (make sure you get a statement for insurance purposes) and contact your nearest consulate.

AIR

Airports

Morocco's main international entry point is the **Mohammed V International Airport** (☎ 022 539040), 30km southeast of Casablanca. It's conveniently linked by regular shuttle trains to Casablanca and Rabat.

Marrakesh's **Ménara Airport** (☎ 044 447865) is also well served with direct flights from most European capitals with both scheduled and budget airlines. Fez's **Saïss Airport** (☎ 035 674712) has flights to France, but flights to the UK ceased while this guide was being researched, and it's unknown when they'll restart.

Other important international airports in Morocco are **Rabat-Salé Airport** (☎ 037 808090), Tangier's **Ibn Batouta Airport** (☎ in Ibn Batouta 039 393720) and Agadir's **Al-Massira Airport** (☎ 048 839112). There are also occasional international flights from Ouarzazate to Paris; Nador to Amsterdam, Brussels, Düsseldorf and Frankfurt; Al-Hoceima to Amsterdam and Brussels; and Oujda to Paris, Marseille, Amsterdam and Brussels.

For comprehensive information about all airports in Morocco, their facilities and customs regulations and procedures, log on to the website of **Office National des Aéroports** (www.onda.org.ma, in French).

Airlines

For flights to Morocco, the high seasons are from July through to the end of August, and from mid-December to the end of December. The lowest seasons are November to mid-December, and January to mid-February.

Direct flights are possible to arrange from cities across Europe, the Middle East, West Africa and North America, and they mostly arrive in Casablanca and Marrakesh. Morocco's national carrier, Royal Air Maroc (RAM) and Air France take the lion's share of flights, with there being increasing competition from the budget airlines (including RAM's own subsidiary Atlas Blue).

INTERNATIONAL AIRLINES IN MOROCCO

Air Algérie (☎ 022 314181; www.airalgerie.dz)
Air Europa (www.air-europa.com)
Air France (☎ 022 294040; www.airfrance.com)
Alitalia (☎ 022 314181; www.alitalia.it)
Atlas Blue (☎ 082 009090; www.atlas-blue.com)
British Airways (☎ 022 229464; www.ba.com)
CorsairFly (www.corsairfly.com)
EasyJet (www.easyjet.com)
Edelweiss Air (☎ in Switzerland 044 277 4100; www.edelweissair.ch)
EgyptAir (☎ 022 315564; www.egyptair.com)
Gulf Air (☎ 022 491212; www.gulfairco.com)
Jet4You (www.jet4you.com)
Iberia (☎ 022 279600; www.iberia.com)
KLM-Royal Dutch Airlines (☎ 022 203222; www.klm.com)
Lufthansa Airlines (☎ 022 312371; www.lufthansa.com)
Regional Airlines (☎ 022 536940; www.regionalmaroc.com)
Royal Air Maroc (☎ 022 311122; www.royalairmaroc.com)
Royal Jordanian (☎ 022 305975; www.rja.com.jo)
Ryanair (www.ryanair.com)
Thomsonfly (www.thomsonfly.com)
Tunis Air (☎ 022 293452; www.tunisair.com.tn)

Tickets

Your plane ticket is traditionally the most expensive item in your budget, but prices have tumbled if you travel with any of the European budget airlines – book as far in advance as possible to get the cheapest deals. Reputable online agencies for scheduled carriers include www.travelocity.co.uk,

CLIMATE CHANGE & TRAVEL

Climate change is a serious threat to the ecosystems that humans rely upon, and air travel is the fastest-growing contributor to the problem. Lonely Planet regards travel, overall, as a global benefit, but believes we all have a responsibility to limit our personal impact on global warming.

Flying & climate change

Pretty much every form of motorised travel generates CO_2 (the main cause of human-induced climate change) but planes are far and away the worst offenders, not just because of the sheer distances they allow us to travel, but because they release greenhouse gases high into the atmosphere. The statistics are frightening: two people taking a return flight between Europe and the US will contribute as much to climate change as an average household's gas and electricity consumption over a whole year.

Carbon offset schemes

Climatecare.org and other websites use 'carbon calculators' that allow travellers to offset the level of greenhouse gases they are responsible for with financial contributions to sustainable travel schemes that reduce global warming – including projects in India, Honduras, Kazakhstan and Uganda.

Lonely Planet, together with Rough Guides and other concerned partners in the travel industry, support the carbon offset scheme run by climatecare.org. Lonely Planet offsets all of its staff and author travel.

For more information check out our website: www.lonelyplanet.com.

DEPARTURE TAX

There is no departure tax upon leaving Morocco. Departure formalities are quite straightforward – you just fill in an exit card and have your passport stamped before exiting.

www.cheaptickets.com, www.expedia.com, www.travelcuts.com (in Canada) and www.travel.com.au (in Australia).

Morocco is a small market for flights, so little or no discounting takes place. This means prices offered by travel agencies will be much the same as the airlines. Oddly, the cheapest fares are not one-way tickets, but one-month returns. In either direction the bulk of traffic is with Royal Air Maroc.

Direct flights will cost you the most. Many airlines have code-share agreements and the cheapest deals can often entail a change of plane (and carrier) in a European city. As a rule, the cheapest fares are for flights into Casablanca. Cheaper student and under-26 tickets are sometimes available.

INTERCONTINENTAL (RTW) TICKETS

With its uncompetitive airline industry, Morocco is not an easy destination to work into a round-the-world ticket. Journeying east from Morocco, you will probably need to stop over in the UAE to get a connecting flight to Asia or Australia. Heading west to the USA, you will probably need to reroute through a European city or London. Most round-the-world tickets allow a maximum of 10 stopovers, although you can buy extras. It may be better and cheaper to buy your flights in and out of Morocco separately.

Africa

RAM has an extensive network of flights throughout North and West Africa from Casablanca, and is one of the better African carriers. North African destinations are Algiers and Oran (Algeria), Tunis (Tunisia), Tripoli (Libya) and Cairo (Egypt). Direct flights to West Africa include Bamako and Ouagadougou (Mali), Nouakchott (Mauritania), Dakar (Senegal), Douala and Yaoundé (Cameroon), Niamey (Niger), Abidjan (Ivory Coast), Libreville (Gabon), Cotonou (Benin), Kinshasa (DR Congo) and Monrovia (Liberia).

Australasia

There are no direct flights between Australia or New Zealand and Morocco. All flights go via the Middle East (eg Bahrain on Gulf Air) or Europe. It can make more sense to fly to London, Paris or Madrid and then make your own way down to Morocco.

Continental Europe

The picture with flights between Europe and Morocco is constantly changing, with the budget airlines ever adding, amending and sometimes cancelling routes. Further to listings below, RAM flies to most European capitals from Casablanca.

FRANCE

France is comprehensively connected by air to Morocco.

RAM has several daily flights from Paris to Casablanca. There are further Paris connections to Tangier, Marrakesh, Fez, Oujda, Rabat, Agadir and Ouarzazate. RAM also flies from Casablanca to Bordeaux, Lille, Lyon, Marseille, Nantes, Nice, Strasbourg and Toulouse.

Air France flies to Casablanca from Paris, Lyon, Bordeaux, Nantes, Nancy, Nice and Marseilles. Air France has flights to Casablanca from Paris, Lyon, Marseilles, Nantes, Nice, Toulouse and Bordeaux, as well as a Paris–Rabat connection. At times, Air France has also operated direct flights from Paris to Ouarzazate and Oujda.

Atlas Blue flies between Marrakesh and Paris, Lyon, Bordeaux, Marseille, Nice and Nantes. French budget airlines Jet4You and Corsairfly have flights from both Paris and Lyon to Marrakesh and Fez. Corsairfly also has a Paris–Agadir connection.

Easyjet flies from Marrakesh to Paris and Lyon, and from Casablanca to Lyon. Ryanair links Marseilles to Marrakesh, Fez, Nador, Tangier and Agadir. An Oujda flight is planned.

GERMANY

RAM offers flights from Casablanca to Frankfurt. Ryanair has better connections with flights from Marrakesh to Frankfurt,

Bremen and Dusseldorf, as well as Fez to Frankfurt. Lufthansa flies Frankfurt–Casablanca. **Air Berlin** (www.airberlin.com) flies to Agadir from most major German cities. Ryanair flies between Frankfurt and both Fez and Marrakesh.

SPAIN

Iberia has excellent connections from Madrid to Morocco, with flights to Casablanca, Fez, Marrakesh, Tangier, Oujda, Ouarzazate, Agadir and Laâyoune. To Tangier, there are flights from Malaga and Barcelona. Melilla is part of Iberia's domestic network, with 12 daily flights to Malaga, as well as two daily flights to Almeria, Barcelona and Madrid, and a daily flight to Granada.

RAM flies from Casablanca to Madrid, Malaga, Barcelona, Valencia and Gran Canaria, and from Marrakesh to Madrid and Barcelona.

Easyjet flies from Madrid to Marrakesh, Casablanca and Tangier. Air Europa also flies Marrakesh to Madrid. Regional Airlines flies Valencia to Casablanca and Malaga to Tangier. Ryanair flies from Nador to Barcelona.

Middle East

The Middle East is the connecting hub for travellers from Australia, New Zealand and the Far East. RAM has direct flights to Dubai and Beirut while Gulf Air offers similar prices from Abu Dhabi. Sharjah-based budget airline **Air Arabia** (www.airarabia.com) is reportedly planning a new service to Morocco, tying the country in to its extensive Middle Eastern and South Asian network.

UK

There is a good choice of flights from the UK to Morocco. Of the scheduled airlines, RAM flies direct from London Heathrow to Casablanca (with onward connections from here), and from London Gatwick to Marrakesh. British Airways flies direct from Heathrow to Casablanca, Marrakesh and Tangier. There are currently no direct flights from the UK to Fez.

Budget airlines are well represented. Both Easyjet and Atlas Blue fly from London Gatwick to Marrakesh. Ryanair has Marrakesh flights from Bristol and Luton. Thomsonfly have a Manchester to Marrakesh connection, as well as Bristol and London Gatwick to Agadir.

For more connections, it's possible to build an itinerary with the budget airlines flying through other European hubs – see above for ideas.

USA & Canada

RAM flies direct from Casablanca to New York, and code-shares onward flights in the US with **Delta Airlines** (www.delta.com). From Canada, RAM fly from Montreal to Casablanca direct.

A cheaper alternative is often a return flight from North America to Continental Europe, and an onward ticket from there, possibly with a budget airline.

LAND

Border Crossings

Despite its lengthy border with Algeria, the only open land crossing into Morocco is the Morocco–Mauritania border between Dakhla and Nouâdhibou. Once a complicated game of permits and military convoys, this crossing is now fairly straightforward and remains the most popular overland route to West Africa. For further details of this route, see p484.

Extensive ferry links between northern Morocco and southern Europe (mainly, but not exclusively, Spain) make entering the country 'overland' a popular option, either by bus, train or your own vehicle. For information on specific ferry connections, see p485.

Bus

The main point of entry for buses into Morocco is via the ferries from Spain. All passengers have to disembark for customs and immigration. Ad hoc public-transport links exist between Dakhla and Nouâdhibou for crossing the Mauritania border.

Car & Motorcycle

Drivers will need the vehicle's registration papers, liability insurance and an international driver's permit in addition to their domestic licence. All vehicles travelling across international borders should display the nationality plate of the country of registration. A warning triangle to use in event of breakdown is also useful, and is compulsory in Europe.

Your local automobile association can provide specific details about all documentation, in particular the Green Card for insurance. For more information on paperwork, see p492.

Pre-booking a rental car before leaving home will enable you to find the cheapest deals (multinational agencies are listed on p493). No matter where you hire your car, make sure you understand what is included in the price and what your liabilities are (this is particularly important if you are planning any off-*piste* driving, which probably won't be covered). Note the European hire companies do not usually permit their vehicles to be driven to Morocco.

Morocco is a country made for touring, and you'll see plenty of campervans on the road, and pouring off the ferries in Tangier. Motorcycle touring is also becoming popular, but many bikes are unfamiliar in Morocco (particularly those with larger capacity engines), so repairs can be tricky. Some basic maintenance knowledge is essential and you should carry all necessary spares, including cables and levers, inner tubes, puncture repair kit, tyre levers, pump, fuses, chain, washable air filter, cable ties – and a good tool kit. As with a car, double-check insurance liabilities before setting off.

Morocco is well served with petrol stations, although these become few and far between south of Tan Tan towards the border of Mauritania (for more information, see Mauritania p484). Diesel is considerably cheaper than leaded fuel. If you're entering Morocco via Ceuta or Melilla, take the opportunity to fill up on duty-free fuel.

Algeria

Morocco closed its border with Algeria in the early 1990s, and despite the end of the civil war there, it shows no sign of being in a hurry to reopen it – Algeria has refused overtures to open the border until a resolution of the status of Western Sahara. Keep an eye on possible developments at **Sahara Overland** (www.sahara-overland.com), the essential online resource for Saharan travel.

Continental Europe

BUS

It's possible to get a bus ticket to destinations in Morocco from as far away as London, but journeys are long and not much cheaper than scheduled airfares. **Eurolines** (www.eurolines.com) is a consortium of European coach companies that operates across Europe and to Morocco. It has offices in all major European cities. You can contact them in your own country or via the website, which gives details of prices, passes and travel agencies where you can book tickets. In Morocco, services are run in conjunction with the Compagnie de Transports Marocains (CTM), Morocco's national line.

CTM (☎ in Casablanca 022 458080; www.ctm.co.ma) operates buses from Casablanca and most other main cities to France, Belgium, Spain, Germany and Italy. Most leave from or go via Casablanca and cross to Europe at Tangier, but a few cross from Nador to Almería.

Buses to Spain leave Casablanca daily except Sunday. Book a week in advance, or further ahead if your plans clash with major holidays in Spain or France, as the buses fill up quickly with Moroccans working abroad.

Another reliable bus service with good links from Morocco to Span is **Tramesa** (☎ 022 245274; http://perso.menara.ma/tramesa07, in French).

TRAIN

Despite the popularity of the budget airlines, getting to Morocco by train from Europe is a viable and civilised way to travel. The granddaddy of planners for rail travel is *Thomas Cook European Timetable*, published monthly with updated schedules since 1883 (see www.thomascookpublishing.com for more information). Probably the best online resource for continent-wide train travel is **Seat 61** (www.seat61.com), which has comprehensively and regularly updated information on getting to Morocco by train.

Morocco is no longer part of the Inter Rail train-pass system, so if you are adding Morocco onto a longer European trip you will have to buy tickets locally. However, train travel in Morocco is inexpensive and good value, and if you are planning a lot of travel you can get discount rail cards on arrival (see p497 for more information).

Taking a direct train from France is one option. The most comfortable and popular alternative is to take the Francisco de Goya

TUNNEL VISION

Mythology states that it was Hercules who first prised apart the European and African continents but his labour is now, it seems, under threat. Plans are on the table to dig a 24km-long, and 300m-deep underwater tunnel from Cap Malabata, east of Tangier, to Punta Paloma, 40km west of Gibraltar, creating a passage that backers say will reconnect Europe and Africa. The estimated €10 billion rail tunnel opens up the possibility of a train ride from London to Marrakesh.

The idea has been around since the 1970s, but it wasn't until 2004 that the two countries took serious steps towards making it a reality. A feasibility study was launched in 2007 that involved digging a 300m shaft into bedrock near Tangier. Assuming the project goes ahead, the EU is expected to be asked to put its hands in its pockets for much of the funding, with the backing of public companies.

The challenges are daunting. The tunnels (one running in each direction, linked by a service tunnel) would have to be around six times deeper than the Channel Tunnel linking France and England, which was in itself one of the biggest and most expensive civil-engineering projects of the 20th century. Even more challenging is the movement of the Earth's crust, with the slow movements between the separate African and European tectonic plates. While both countries stand firm behind the project for now, even the Greek heroes themselves might have baulked at such a Herculean project.

Trainhotel from Paris (Austerlitz) to Madrid, run by a consortium of the French and Spanish railways called **Elipsos** (www.elipsos.com). The train departs Paris early evening and arrives in Madrid at 9am in the morning. You can book a four-berth tourist-class sleeper (one way €165) or one- and two-berth 1st-class sleepers, and there is a restaurant and a café-bar. ISIC card holders can get a 15% discount, and all tickets can be booked online.

Alternatively, you can take the TGV from La Gare Montparnasse to Algeciras or Málaga via Madrid (around €172 one way with couchette, 25 hours), which can be booked through the **SNCF website** (www.voyage-sncf.com) or **RailEurope** (www.raileurope.co.uk). From North America and Australia, you can also order tickets online through **Rail-Europe** (www.raileurope.com in North America, www.raileurope.com.au in Australia).

The onward trip to Algeciras can be done on the **Renfe** (www.renfe.es) 'Estrella del Estrecho', which leaves from Madrid Chamartin (€37 one way, five hours). The train station is about 10 minutes' walk from the ferry terminals – if you arrive during the day you should be able to hop almost straight onto a boat (see p486).

Mauritania

CAR & MOTORCYCLE

The trans-Saharan route via Mauritania is now the most popular route from North Africa into sub-Saharan Africa, and hundreds of adventurous souls do it every year. While this route is generally regarded as safe, check safety advice before travelling: the murder of a family of French tourists near Nouakchott in 2007 and related Al-Qaeda threats led to the cancelling of the 2008 Paris–Dakar rally through Mauritania.

The route into Mauritania from Dakhla runs south along the coast for 460km, across the border to Nouâdhibou and then south along the coast to the Mauritanian capital Nouakchott. At the close of 2005 this route became entirely paved, making it the only sealed road across the Sahara (barring a short stretch in the no-man's-land between the two border posts). While this makes things vastly easier for drivers, you should still respect the desert, and it makes sense to travel with other vehicles and set off early in order to reach the border before dusk (particularly advisable if you are travelling in a 2WD). It's also advisable to fill up with petrol at every available station. Some stations south of Dakhla may be out of fuel, in particular the last station 50km before the border.

Moroccan border formalities are processed in the basic settlement of Guergarat. The border, about 15km from the settlement, is heavily mined, so stay on the road.

Mauritanian visas can be bought without hassle at the border for €20. Currency declaration forms are no longer required. Alcohol is illegal in Mauritania and vehicle searches are common. As well as getting stamped in, you need to buy a 30-day temporary-vehicle-import form (€10) and register with the police. Mauritanian currency (ouguiya, UM) is available at the border. From the border it's a short drive to the first major Mauritanian town of Nouâdhibou, 50km away.

MINIBUS & JEEP

There are ad hoc transport links from Dakhla to the Mauritania border and beyond. Minibuses and 4WDs leave from the military checkpoint on the road out of Dakhla (the Hotel Sahara has also been reported by travellers as a good place to arrange transport from). Expect to pay between Dh200 and Dh400 for a seat in a vehicle going to Nouâdhibou. A few grands taxis also run to the border, but you'll still need to hitch to get to the Mauritanian checkpoint, as walking across the border is forbidden.

From Nouâdhibou, bush taxis cost around UM1750 to the border, although it's also worth asking around the hotels and camp sites (Camping Abba is popular with overlanders) for places in departing vehicles.

For information about trans-Saharan travel, see Chris Scott's *Sahara Overland*, both a book and website (www.sahara-overland.com). **Horizons Unlimited's Sahara Travel Forum** (www.horizonsunlimited.com) has a useful bulletin board with regularly updated information on travel between Morocco and Mauritania.

SEA

Catching a ferry is a perennially popular way of getting to Morocco. In the summer the most popular route from Algeciras to Tangier is packed with both day-trippers and holidaymakers with campervans. Alternative crossings are Tarifa to Tangier, Algeciras to the Spanish enclaves of Ceuta and Melilla, and even a longer voyage from Sète in France. All the port cities (and most cities in Morocco) have numerous travel agencies and ticket offices, or you can literally turn up and buy one at the dock.

There are plenty of ferry options, but it's worth noting that Acciona, Transmediterranea, Euroferry and Ferrimaroc are all in fact the same company, operating slightly different services and timetables.

If you're sailing from Europe to Morocco, discounts for students (with ISIC cards), Inter Rail or Eurail pass-holders and EU pensioners are frequently advertised. They're less commonly available in Morocco, but it's still worth asking. All ferry tickets purchased in Morocco are subject to Dh20 tax.

High season for ferries is generally the European summer (June to August), Christmas and New Year. More ferries run to cope with demand – foot passengers are often safe to buy a ticket on arrival at the port, but it's worth booking in advance if you're driving a vehicle.

France

France is linked to Morocco by the Sète–Tangier ferry route. It's more luxurious than those linking Spain and Morocco and it needs to be, as the voyage takes 36 hours (over two nights). You may be thankful for the onboard swimming pool and 'disco bar'. Sète is two hours by train from Marseilles.

Two companies are operating on this route, **Comarit** (www.comarit.com, in French & Spanish) and **Comanav** (www.comanav.ma, in French). Both sail around every fourth or fifth day, leaving port between 6pm and 7pm in both directions. Advance booking is strongly recommended. Comanav also operate a weekly Sète–Nador route for similar prices. Advance reservations are recommended.

Fares cost from €165 per person in a four-bed cabin in high season (mid-July to mid-September), plus €5 port tax (payable twice on return journeys). Meals are included. Children aged between two and 12 travel for half-price. Low-season (November to February) fares start from €120. A car costs €265/205 in high/low season. Comarit also offers chair seats for around €72, but they might be a bit of an endurance test by the end of the voyage.

Discounts of up to 20% can be had for students and those under 26 years of age, Moroccan residents abroad and groups of four travelling together with a car.

In Tangier, **Comanav** (☎ 039 940504; 43 Ave Abou al-Alâa el-Maâri) and **Comarit** (☎ 039 320032; Ave des FAR) sell tickets and have detailed timetables, as do their booths at Tangier dock.

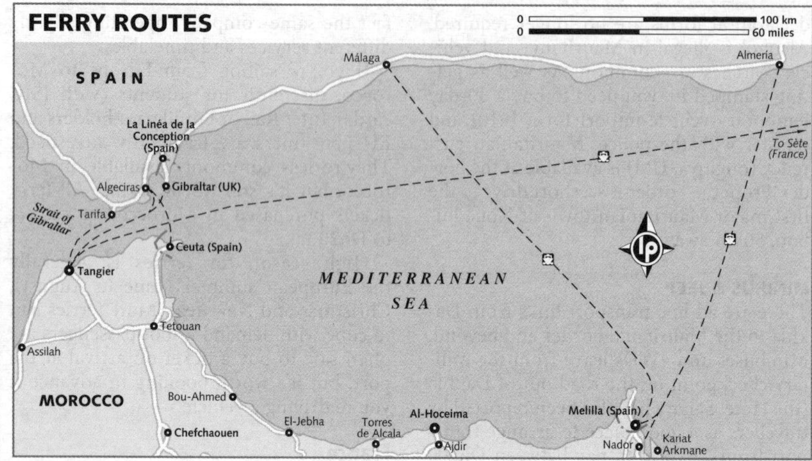

Gibraltar

The catamaran ferry company **FRS** (www.frs.es) is meant to sail weekly between Tangier and Gibraltar (or more specifically La Línea across the border in Spain). Should it resume, prices should be around €32/99 per passenger/car. The trip takes 75 minutes.

Spain

Ferries from Spain to Morocco are plentiful. The Spanish government-run company Trasmediterránea runs regular sailings, as do Buquebus, Comanav, Comarit, EuroFerrys and FRS. Hydrofoils and catamarans (also referred to as fast ferries) are used extensively, but are more expensive and can be disrupted by rough seas.

The most popular and frequent service is the Algeciras to Tangier route. It's traditionally been known for its hassle and hustlers, but these have largely been cleared out of the port, and entering Morocco here should no longer fill the traveller with dread (see p173). Car owners may find the Algeciras to Ceuta route to be more worthwhile because of the availability of tax-free petrol in the Spanish enclave. The other routes are Tarifa to Tangier, Almería to Melilla or Nador, and Málaga to Melilla. Heading into Morocco via Melilla (and then Nador) is easily the most hassle-free way to arrive from the Spanish mainland, though crossings can take eight hours, cost twice as much as crossing from Algeciras to Ceuta or Tangier and are much less frequent.

On most routes, more boats are scheduled in the high season (mid-June to mid-September). During August and Easter, when demand is highest, those with vehicles should book well in advance. At other times you're unlikely to have problems getting a convenient passage.

As well as in Madrid, **Trasmediterránea** (☎ in Spain 902 45 46 45; www.trasmediterranea.es) has offices at many Spanish ports, including Almería, Algeciras, Ceuta, Melilla and Málaga.

Tickets for most companies can be reserved online (see specific route details). Alternatively **Direct Ferries** (www.directferries.co.uk) is a useful European-wide booking site, with mirror sites in most European languages.

Surcharges are exacted on cars not conforming to the standard 6m length and 1.8m height. Charges for campervans also vary. Rates for motorbikes depend on engine capacity, while bicycles are normally charged the minimum motorbike rate.

Spanish passport control is quite uncomplicated, but non-EU citizens should make sure they get an exit stamp before boarding the ferry. Once on board you need to fill in an embarkation form and get your passport stamped before disembarking. Customs can be slow on the Spanish side if you're coming from Morocco.

ALGECIRAS TO TANGIER

This is by some stretch the busiest sea crossing between Spain and Morocco, with ferries at least every 90 minutes between these ports, and hourly in the summer. Services typically run from 7am (or 6am in summer) until 10pm, but during peak demand in August some 24-hour services aren't unknown. The crossing takes 80 minutes to 2½ hours, depending on the ship.

All the ferry companies operate this route: Trasmediterránea, Buquebus, Comanav, Comarit, EuroFerrys, FRS and Limadet. Competition keeps the prices uniform between them. You can expect to pay around €31 one way, standard class. Children up to four years old travel free, while children aged from four to 12 pay 50%. Cars cost between €60 and €80, and campervans are €105. Some ferry companies offer 1st class for an extra 20%, but it's barely worth it for the short trip.

Ticket offices line up outside the ferry terminal in Tangier, so it's easy to walk between them and pick the best sailing for you. There are more ticket offices inside the terminal building itself. In Tangier itself, touts will try and guide you towards their favourite travel agency for their bit of commission, but can be safely disregarded. In Algeciras, try the **Trasmediterránea office** (☎ 956 58 34 07; Recinto del Puerto) or any of the ferry offices port-side.

ALGECIRAS TO CEUTA

Trasmediterránea, EuroFerrys, Buquebus and Balearia offer over 20 high-speed ferry crossings (35 minutes) from Ceuta between 7am and 10pm, and the same number from Algeciras between 6am and 10pm. Extra services are added on demand on Sunday evening and during August.

At the time of writing, fares were €25 per person without a car (local residents pay about 50% less), and €30 per car. Children aged between two and 12 travel for half the fare, and those aged under two travel free.

In Ceuta, there are dozens of private ticket offices close to and inside the ferry terminal (Estación Marítima). The ferry companies have offices in the main building – this is often the best place to get tickets (from specific companies only) at the last minute.

ALMERÍA TO AL-HOCEIMA

This is probably the quietest route from Spain to Morocco, and is highly seasonal. Comarit serves Al-Hoceima from Almería (along with Redouene and Malaga) daily from late June to the end of September. The voyage takes seven or eight hours, with deck-class tickets costing around €45 one way.

There are no ferries outside this season, so travellers take the ferry to Nador. A new ferry service called Reduan has been threatening to start a route between Al-Hoceima and Málaga, but has yet to announce dates.

ALMERÍA TO MELILLA

Melilla is a less popular destination than Tangier or Ceuta, but Acciona (Trasmediterránea) offers a service, with daily departures. The trip takes six to eight hours. The base fare is €35 each way. You can also get beds in two- or four-person cabins, some with toilets, for around €100 per person. Higher-class *(preferente)* berths cost around €110 per person. Children aged from two to 12 travel for half-price (infants go free).

A normal-sized car costs €160, campervans range from €230 depending on their length, and motorbikes from €55. Bicycles are free.

Buy your tickets at the Estación Marítima (a 10- to 15-minute walk from the train and bus stations), from travel agencies or from the **Trasmediterránea office** (☎ 956 690902; Plaza de España), in the centre of town.

Services are added on demand during the high season. Fares rise by up to 25% and fast ferries also operate at this time.

ALMERÍA TO NADOR

An alternative to sailing to Tangier is at Nador, further east along the coast. It's much quieter, although it has poorer transport links to the rest of the country. On top of that, it's next door to Melilla, where you can fill up on duty-free fuel if you're driving (and booze if you're not).

Several companies sail from Nador's Beni Enzar port to Almería, taking up to six hours depending on the vessel. Acciona has a fast-ferry service running every Tuesday to Saturday at night. Comarit has a daily slow ferry, while Comanav sails four times a week. Further services are added in the summer. Deck fare costs €28.50, with other prices similar to the Melilla crossing. Fares rise by roughly 15% in high season.

MÁLAGA TO MELILLA

Acciona (Trasmediterránea) runs a daily service from Málaga to Melilla, which takes around seven hours. In the high season (June to September), there is also a high-speed service, which takes four hours. Prices are around €35/160 per passenger/car.

As in Almería, you can purchase tickets most easily at the Estación Marítima, which is more or less directly south of the town centre. In Melilla, buy tickets from **Trasmediterránea** (☎ 956 690902; Plaza de España) or at the Estación Marítima.

TARIFA TO TANGIER

Tarifa is now a regular destination for ferry crossings, with a catamaran making the trip in a nippy 35 minutes (making it both the fastest and most practical way to get across the strait). **FRS** (www.frs.es; ☎ Tarifa port 956 681830, ☎ Tangier port 039 942612) operates the service, with two to five sailings a day according to the season. If you're travelling by foot, the ticket includes a free bus transfer from Tarifa to Algeciras (15 minutes) – making it the fastest way to get across the strait.

Fares are €39 per passenger (children aged from three to 12 travel for half-price), €99 per car, €180 per caravan and €15 per bike/motorbike.

Italy

If you really want to enjoy the ocean blue, the longest sea route to Morocco is from Genoa to Tangier.

Grandi Navi Veloci (GNV; www.gnv.it) has a weekly sailing every Saturday, returning from Tangier every Monday throughout the year. The voyage takes 45 hours and stops briefly at Barcelona. Costs start from €45 for a berth in a four-person cabin, and €183 for a car.

Comanav (www.comanav.ma) has four sailings a week in July, August and September only. Prices are comparable to GNV.

TOURS

There is no shortage of tour operators running organised trips to Morocco. Perusing the adverts of travel pages in weekend newspapers or travel magazines like **Wanderlust** (www.wanderlust.co.uk) can quickly overwhelm you for choice.

Organised trips can be especially good if you have a particular interest – see also Activities on left for specialist operators from horse riding to rafting.

Atlas Sahara Trek (☎ 044 393901; www.atlas-sahara-trek.com; 6 bis rue Houdoud, Marrakesh) Winter camel-treks to Erg Chigaga and summer hikes into the remote M'Goun valley.

Best of Morocco (☎ in UK 01380-828533; www.morocco-travel.com) Over 30 years' experience with UK-based tailor-made tours and holidays including everything from camel trekking and skiing to cultural tours and beach holidays.

Bike Morocco (☎ in UK 07940 296711; www.bikemorocco.com) Popular and nimble UK mountain-biking operator, running vehicle-supported tours in the Atlas Mountains, from weekend breaks to longer trips.

Equatorial Travel (☎ in UK 0133 534 8770; www.equatorialtravel.co.uk; Ashbourne, Derbyshire, UK) Trekking, 4WD and camel trips off the beaten track run by a small agency based on a fair-trade concept.

Heritage Tours (☎ in USA 800-378 4555; www.heritagetoursonline.com) US-based customised travel with a real emphasis on culture and the arts. Good city tours and classic itineraries.

Ibertours Travel (☎ in Australia 03-9670 8388; www.ibertours.com.au) Australian Moroccan specialist, running camel treks, city tours and the like, highlighting Morocco's Andalusian links with cross-border trips to Spain.

Journeys Elite (☎ in UK 01983-853064; www.journeyselite.com) Excellent UK-based newcomer on the block, offering tailor-made trips including riad-based city tours, desert safaris and dedicated photography tours, with fine attention to individual needs.

KE Adventure Travel (☎ in UK 0176 877 3966; www.keadventure.com; Keswick, Cumbria, UK) Trekking, climbing and mountain-bike specialists with treks to Toubkal, an Atlas traverse and Jebel Sarhro.

Marrakesh Voyage (☎ in USA 1-888-990 2999; www.morocco-travel-agency.com) US-based company with extensive list of itineraries covering all bases, as well as special tours aimed at Morocco's various music festivals.

Mountain Voyage (☎ 024 421996; www.mountain-voyage.com; Marrakesh) The Moroccan arm of UK-operator Discover, owner of the Kasbah du Toubkal. Mountain Voyage use reliable guides and equipment on tailor-made treks.

Naturally Morocco (☎ in UK 0709-2343879; www.natural lymorocco.co.uk) Sustainable, ecotourism deeply involved in local communities, especially in and around Taroudannt. Special-interest tours include trekking, biking, wildlife and even geology.

Nature Trekking Maroc (☎ 024 432477; www.maroctrekking.com; Marrakesh) Very well-organised treks by an experienced team of mountain guides.

Sahara Expédition (☎ 044 427977; www.saharaexpe.ma; Marrakesh) Camel treks in the Drâa Valley and beyond, and trekking in the High Atlas.

Sherpa Expeditions (☎ 020 8577 2717; www.sherpa-walking-holidays.co.uk; Hounslow, UK) A well-respected trekking company that organises escorted and self-guided treks in the High Atlas and Jebel Sarhro.

Wilderness Travel (☎ 01-800 368 2794; www.wildernesstravel.com; Berkeley, USA) Well-established specialists offering three top-notch trekking or camel itineraries in Morocco.

Yallah (☎ 044 431338; www.yallahmorocco.com) Reliable Moroccan operator running desert safaris, city tours and trekking, either for groups or tailor-made.

Other local tour operators specialising in trekking or desert safaris can be found in Ouarzazate (p342) or Marrakesh (p308).

GETTING AROUND

Getting around Morocco is pretty straightforward – transport networks between towns are good, and even off the beaten track there's often something going your way. Internal flights operate out of Casablanca, the rail network is excellent in linking the major cities, while large bus companies like CTM are comfortable and efficient. Local networks are cheaper and more cheerful but do the job. Good sealed roads are generally the order of the day, with much investment being poured into areas like the Rif to improve their connectivity. Roads in remote mountain and desert areas are often just *piste*. Car hire is comparatively expensive, but gives you the most freedom, although navigating the big cities can be stressful.

AIR

Royal Air Maroc (RAM; ☎ head office 022 912000; www.royalairmaroc.com) dominates the Moroccan air industry, with mild competition from one other domestic airline, **Regional Airlines** (☎ in Casablanca 022 536940; www.regionalmaroc.com). Both airlines use Casablanca as a hub so internal flights are routed through Mohammed V. The country is crying out for a direct Fez–Marrakesh flight. RAM's safety record is good, with tight security at airports.

Internal airports serviced by RAM are Agadir, Al-Hoceima, Casablanca, Dakhla, Essaouira, Fez, Laâyoune, Marrakesh, Nador, Ouarzazate, Oujda, Rabat and Tangier. Popular routes such as Marrakesh, Tangier and Agadir all have several flights per day. You can pick up a free timetable at most RAM offices; timetables are also online.

Domestic flights can be booked online or through any travel agency as well as Royal Air Maroc offices. Remember that you should always confirm flights 72 hours before departure. Student and under-26 youth discounts of 25% are available on all RAM domestic flights, but only if the ticket is bought in advance from one of its offices. Children aged from two to 12 travel at half-price.

In general, flying isn't really worthwhile, except for long-distance routes such as to Laâyoune or Dakhla in the Western Sahara, when it can save you a lot of time. A flight from Casablanca to Laâyoune would set you back around Dh2300 and take just over an hour and a half, compared to 19 hours by bus.

BICYCLE

If you've the energy, mountain biking can be a great way of travelling in Morocco. There are no special road rules pertaining to cyclists and they are afforded little consideration by drivers. Although surfaced roads are generally well maintained, they tend to be narrow and dusty, which can be hairy given the kamikaze drivers.

However, there's plenty of opportunity for getting off the beaten track if you choose, with thousands of kilometres of remote *pistes* to be explored. You do need to be pretty fit, though. Distances are great and you'll need to carry all supplies with you, and plenty of drinking water. Useful spares to bring include spokes, brake blocks and inner tubes.

Unfortunately, cyclists in remote areas have reported being besieged by gangs of stone-throwing children, so be sure to watch your back.

Bus companies are generally happy to carry bikes as luggage for an extra Dh10 or so, although it's generally only possible to transport your bike on trains if they travel in the goods wagon. Prices depend on the distance and are about 40% of the passenger fare. Most camp sites charge around Dh10 for bicycles.

There are a few external tour operators that offer organised mountain-biking trips (see opposite). The UK-based **Cyclists' Touring Club** (☎ 0870 873 0060; www.ctc.org.uk) is a mine of information and has a comprehensive members' library of routes, including Morocco, written up by cyclists.

Hire

Moroccan cities and towns are better explored on foot, though you will find bicycles for hire in cities like Marrakesh (from around Dh60 to Dh100 per day), and cycle parks where your bike can be parked and watched over for the day. Don't expect the latest model of mountain bike, as you will be sorely disappointed.

BUS

Anyone in Morocco for any length of time will undoubtedly make considerable use of the local bus networks. The cheapest and most efficient way to travel around the country, buses are generally safe, although the same can't necessarily be said for the driving. On some older buses, legroom is extremely limited and long journeys can be rather an endurance test for taller travellers.

Most bus trips longer than three hours will incorporate a scheduled stop to stretch your legs and refuel your body. When travelling during the day, pay attention to where you're sitting, to avoid melting in the sun. Heading from north to south, this means sitting on the right in the morning, on the left in the afternoon. Travelling east to west, sit on the right, or on the left if going from west to east. Many buses also have rather meagre curtains. Night buses operate on many intercity routes, which can be both quicker and cooler, although not necessarily more sleep-inducing.

There's no state bus company, but this role is fulfilled by the effective national carrier, Compagnie de Transports Marocains (CTM; see right), which operates throughout the country. After CTM, a host of smaller local companies fight it out for custom, although outfits like Supratours and Satas are well respected nationally.

Some Moroccan bus stations are like madhouses, with touts running around screaming out any number of destinations for buses about to depart. In most cities or towns there's a single central bus station *(gare routière)*, but in some places CTM maintains a separate terminal. Occasionally, there are other stations for a limited number of fairly local destinations. Touts can happily guide you to the ticket booth (and take a small commission from the company), but always double-check that their recommended service really is the most comfortable, direct and convenient option.

Bus stations in the main cities have left-luggage depots (*consigne*), sometimes open 24 hours. Bags must be padlocked. You can transport bikes on buses, but they'll be charged as freight (around Dh10 per bike for an average journey).

Bus Operators

COMPAGNIE DE TRANSPORTS MAROCAINS

CTM (☎ in Casablanca 022 458080) is the best and most reliable bus company in Morocco, and serves most destinations of interest to travellers. Established in 1919, it's Morocco's oldest bus company.

On CTM buses, children aged four years and over pay full fares, which tend to be 15% to 30% more expensive than other lines, and are comparable to 2nd-class fares on normal trains. Tickets can be purchased in advance. Intercity timetables often seem to have a penchant for late-night departures.

Many CTM buses are modern and comfortable, and some 1st-class buses have videos (a mixed blessing), air-conditioning and heating (they sometimes overdo both).

There is an official baggage charge on CTM buses (Dh5 per pack). Once you have bought your ticket, you get a baggage tag, which you should hang on to, as you'll need it when you arrive.

CTM also operates international buses (in conjunction with Eurolines) from all the main Moroccan cities to Spain, France, Italy and northern Europe (see p483).

SUPRATOURS

The ONCF train company runs buses through **Supratours** (☎ 037 686297; www.supratourstravel.com) to complement its train network. Thus Nador, near Melilla on the Mediterranean coast, is linked to the Oujda–Casablanca rail line by a special bus to Taourirt station.

Tetouan is linked to the main line from Tangier by bus to Tnine Sidi Lyamani. Train passengers heading further south than Marrakesh link up at Marrakesh station with buses for Essaouira, Agadir, Laâyoune and Dakhla. It's possible to buy a ticket to cover the complete trip (including the bus journey) at the railway ticket office.

Supratours services are more expensive than regular buses, but are comparable to CTM fares. They do not use the main bus stations, but depart from outside their own town-centre offices (explained in individual town sections throughout this book). Through tickets to and from connecting train stations are available (Nador through to Fez, for example), and travellers with rail tickets for connecting services have priority.

OTHER COMPANIES

Morocco's other bus companies are all privately owned and only operate regionally. The biggest of them is Satas, which covers Casablanca and everywhere further south, and is just as good as CTM. In the north, Trans Ghazala is equally reliable. Both have modern, comfortable buses.

At the cheaper end of the scale, and on the shorter or local routes, there are a fair number of two-bit operations with one or two well-worn buses, so don't expect comfortable seats or any air-conditioning. Unlike CTM buses, these services tend to stop an awful lot and only depart when the driver considers them sufficiently full. They're dirt cheap and good fun for shorter trips. The cheaper buses rarely have heating in winter, even when crossing the mountains, so make sure that you have plenty of warm clothing

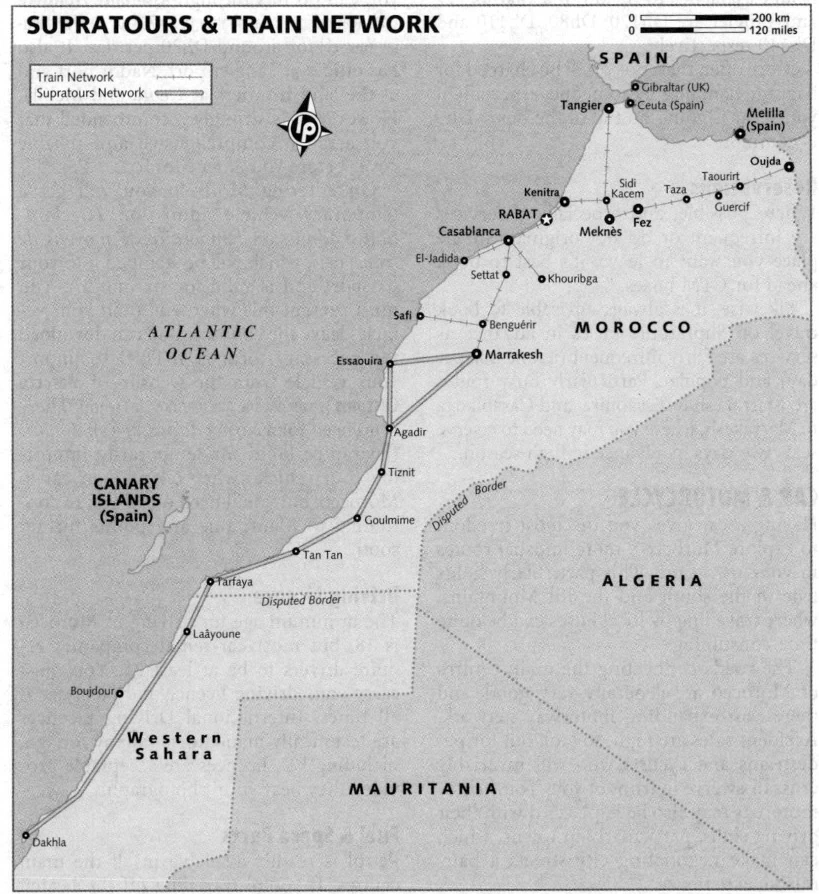

with you. If traffic is held up by snowdrifts in the mountain passes, then you'll really feel the cold. The Marrakesh to Ouarzazate road is particularly prone to this.

Classes

Some companies offer 1st- and 2nd-class, although the difference in fare and comfort is rarely great. On the secondary runs (ie if you're not getting on the bus at the start of the route) you can often buy your tickets on the bus, but if you do, you might end up standing.

Costs

Bus travel is cheap considering the distances that have to be covered. Typical fares from Casablanca to Agadir, Marrakesh, Fez and Tangier are Dh170, Dh80, Dh110 and Dh140 respectively.

More often than not you'll be charged for baggage handling by someone, especially if your gear is going on top of the bus – Dh5 is common.

Reservations

Where possible, and especially if services are infrequent or do not originate in the place you want to leave, it's best to book ahead for CTM buses.

Likewise, it is always advisable to book travel on Supratours buses in advance as services are fairly infrequent (ie one bus per day) and popular. Particularly busy routes are Marrakesh to Essaouira, and Casablanca to Marrakesh, where you may need to reserve seats two days in advance in high season.

CAR & MOTORCYCLE

Having a car gives you the most freedom to explore Morocco's more unusual routes in your own time. This particularly holds true in the south and the Rif Mountains, where travelling by local buses can be quite time-consuming.

The roads connecting the main centres of Morocco are generally very good, and there's an expanding motorway network. Accident rates are high, so look out for pedestrians and cyclists who will invariably cross or swerve in front of you. Your fellow motorists may also be haphazard with their driving skills, particularly in towns, which can make negotiating city streets a hair-raising experience.

Bring Your Own Vehicle

Taking your own vehicle to Morocco is comparatively easy. In addition to your vehicle registration document (*carte grise* in Morocco) and International Driving Permit, a Green Card *(carte verte)* is required from the car's insurer (you may be covered in your current car insurance policy, especially if you live in Continental Europe, so check with your insurance company). These are relatively inexpensive, though often only provide third-party, fire and theft protection. Not all insurers cover Morocco.

If you cannot get a Green Card in advance, temporary insurance must be arranged at Spanish or Moroccan ferry ports; you can do this through **Assurance Frontière** (☎ head office in Casablanca 022 470810; 28 Blvd Moulay Youssef) for around Dh20 per day. It also has offices at Tangier port, Nador port and at the land frontiers at Ceuta and Melilla. However, it is strongly recommended that you arrange comprehensive and reliable cover before you enter Morocco.

On entering Morocco you will get a temporary vehicle admission *(Declaration d'admission temporaire de moyens de transport)*, which will be stamped into your passport and is valid for six months. You must present this when you (and your vehicle) leave the country. You can download the necessary form (D16TER) to import your vehicle from the website of **Morocco Customs** (www.douane.gov.ma/mre/, in French). There is no need for a *carnet de passage en douane* (guarantee bond for temporarily importing your vehicle) when taking your car to Morocco, but you'll need one if you're continuing to Mauritania and points further south.

Driving Licence

The minimum age for driving in Morocco is 18, but most car-rental companies require drivers to be at least 21. You must carry your driving licence and passport at all times. International Driving Licences are technically mandatory – many foreign, including EU, licences are acceptable provided they bear your photograph.

Fuel & Spare Parts

Petrol is readily available in all the main centres. If you're travelling off the beaten

ROAD DISTANCES (KM)

	Agadir	Al-Hoceima	Casablanca	Dakhla	Er-Rachidia	Essaouira	Fez	Figuig	Marrakesh	Meknès	Nador	Ouarzazate	Oujda	Rabat	Safi	Smara	Tan Tan	Tangier	Tarfaya	Tetouan
Agadir	---																			
Al-Hoceima	1091	---																		
Casablanca	511	536	---																	
Dakhla	1173	2264	1684	---																
Er-Rachidia	681	616	545	1854	---															
Essaouira	160	887	351	1346	745	---														
Fez	756	275	289	1920	329	640	---													
Figuig	1076	669	920	2249	395	1081	719	---												
Marrakesh	273	758	232	1448	510	170	461	905	---											
Meknès	740	335	229	1913	346	580	57	741	446	---										
Nador	1095	175	628	2260	510	979	339	516	822	399	---									
Ouarzazate	354	992	442	1548	295	380	687	701	175	652	816	---								
Oujda	1099	293	632	2272	514	983	334	326	826	403	104	820	---							
Rabat	602	445	91	1775	482	442	196	877	321	139	535	528	541	---						
Safi	294	792	256	1467	683	129	545	1078	148	486	884	361	888	347	---					
Smara	551	1642	1062	746	1232	724	1307	1627	824	1291	1646	926	1650	1153	845	---				
Tan Tan	331	1422	842	842	1012	504	1087	1407	504	1071	1426	705	1430	933	625	220	---			
Tangier	880	323	369	2053	608	720	303	988	598	287	1086	811	609	278	625	1431	1211	---		
Tarfaya	544	1635	1055	633	1225	517	1300	1620	817	1284	1639	919	1643	1146	838	331	213	1424	---	
Tetouan	892	278	385	2065	604	736	247	931	675	258	437	820	555	294	641	1443	1223	57	1436	---

track, however, fill up the tank at every opportunity. Super (leaded) and unleaded *(sans plomb)* cost around Dh14 per litre and diesel *(gasoil)* is around Dh9. Premium is the standard fuel for cars; unleaded is only available at larger stations, including most of the Afriquia stations.

Costs rise the further you go from the northwest of the country. The big exception is the territory of the Western Sahara, where petrol is sold by the Atlas Sahara service station chain and is tax-free, so is about 30% cheaper. Keep a close eye on fuel in the southern desert and fill up wherever you get an opportunity, as stations don't always have supplies of fuel. Spare jerry cans are a good idea for emergencies.

Fuel is also very reasonably priced in the duty-free Spanish enclaves of Ceuta and Melilla, so drivers heading to Morocco and mainland Spain via the enclaves should fill up there.

Moroccan mechanics are generally extremely good and all decent-sized towns will have at least one garage (most with an extensive range of spare parts for Renaults and other French cars). If you need replacement parts and can fit them yourself, try to get a Moroccan friend to help with buying parts as this may help to keep the price closer to local levels.

Hire

Renting a car in Morocco isn't cheap, starting from Dh3500 per week or Dh500 per day for a basic car like a Renault Clio with unlimited mileage, and up to Dh10,000 per week for a 4WD. Most companies demand a (returnable) cash deposit (Dh3000 to Dh5000) unless you pay by credit card, in which case an impression is made of your card (make sure you get this back later). However, some travellers using smaller, less-reputable firms have been stung after paying by credit, realising they've been charged 10 times the agreed fee after returning home.

The best cities in which to hire cars are Casablanca, Agadir, Marrakesh, Fez and Tangier, where competition is greatest. The cheapest car is the Fiat Uno, though older Renault 4s are sometimes available. If you're organised, however, it usually works out cheaper to arrange car rental in advance through the travel agent who arranges your flight. International firms such as **Hertz** (www.hertz.com), **Budget** (www.budget.com), **Europcar** (www.europcar.com), **National** (www.nationalcar.com) and **Avis** (www.avis.com) have facilities for booking from home on toll-free or cheap-rate numbers or via the internet. Rates can vary substantially between them and there is little room for bargaining. Ordering your car over the internet can get you discounts of up to 30%.

There are also numerous local agencies and many have booths beside each other at airports – this is an excellent place to haggle. Details for these are given in regional chapters.

International agencies do not necessarily offer better vehicles than local companies, but usually provide better service in the event of a breakdown or accident, as they have a network of offices around the country. Often a replacement car can be sent out to you from the nearest depot. Always check your car's condition before signing up, and make sure that the car comes with a spare tyre, tool kit and full documentation – including insurance cover, which is compulsory for all rentals.

With larger agencies you can hire the car in one place and leave it elsewhere, although this usually involves a fee if you want to leave it in a city where the company has no branch.

Note that your rental agreement will probably not cover you for off-road *(piste)* driving, so if you damage the car or break down on a *piste* you will not be covered for damages. It might be worthwhile to OK your route with the rental company before setting off.

All companies charge per hour (Dh35 to Dh100 is common) for every hour that you go over time on the return date. If you intend to drive from Morocco to the Spanish enclaves of Ceuta or Melilla, you must have a letter from the car-hire company authorising you to take the car out of the country. Europe-based companies do not normally permit cars to be taken to Morocco. Keep receipts for oil changes and any mechanical repairs, as these costs should be reimbursed.

Some companies offer motorcycle (Dh300 per day for a DT 125cc Yamaha) and scooter (Dh200 per day) hire. Agadir is a good place to look – you'll find a number of rental booths near the big hotels.

Insurance

Insurance must, by law, be sold along with all rental agreements. You should take out Collision Damage Waiver insurance (between Dh80 and Dh110 a day). Even with this there is often an excess of between Dh3000 and Dh5000 (depending on the company), meaning that if you have an accident that's your fault, then you are liable to pay damages up to this amount. You can opt to take out a Super Collision Damage Waiver for an extra Dh50 or so a day to get rid of this excess. It's also a good idea to take out personal insurance (around Dh30 a day). When bargaining, make sure that prices include collision damage, insurance and tax (20%).

Parking

In many towns, parking zones are watched by *gardiens de voitures* (car-park attendants) in characteristic blue coats. The going rate is Dh3 for a few hours and Dh10 overnight. The parking attendants are not a guarantee of safety, but they do provide some peace of mind and will no doubt offer to wash your car for you.

In an increasing number of big city centres, parking tickets are issued from blue kerbside machines (Dh2 per hour for a maximum stay of 2½ hours). Parking is free on Sundays.

Parking is not allowed on kerbsides painted in red and white stripes. Stopping is not allowed on green and white stripes. Fines for illegally parked cars can reach Dh1500.

Roadblocks

Police control points manned by the *Gendarmerie Royale* are common on main roads in and out of most sizable towns, although as a foreigner driving you're unlikely to be stopped. It's still a good idea to slow down and put on your best smile – you'll probably get a smile in return and be waved through. Roadblocks are more common in sensitive areas like the Western Sahara, in the Rif mountains around the cannabis-producing region of Ketama and the road to Figuig near the Algerian border. At most, you may be asked to show your passport and driving licence, the purpose of your visit and where you're heading.

Intercity buses are usually delayed at checkpoints more than grands taxis, whose local drivers usually know the police.

Road Hazards

Driving at night is particularly hazardous: it's legal for vehicles travelling under 20km/h to drive without lights, and roads are often very busy with pedestrians (including large groups of schoolchildren), bicycles, horse and carts, donkeys and so on. Treat all as vehicles ready to veer out at inopportune moments.

Many minor roads are too narrow for normal vehicles to pass without going onto the shoulder. You'll find yourself hitting the dirt a lot in this way. Stones thrown up by oncoming vehicles present a danger for windscreens. In the *hammada* (stony desert), tar roads frequently disappear without warning, replaced suddenly by stretches of sand, gravel and potholes. Take care with your speed on such roads. If a strong *chergui* (dry, easterly desert wind) is blowing and carrying a lot of dust, you'll have to wait until it eases off if you don't want to do your car considerable damage.

In contrast, driving across the mountain ranges in winter can easily involve driving through snow and ice. The High Atlas passes can often be closed altogether due to snow in the winter. Check the road signs along the routes out of Marrakesh or call the **Service des Travaux Publiques** (☎ in Rabat 037 711717) before travelling.

Some of the *pistes* in Morocco can be negotiated by ordinary car, many are passable in a Renault 4 with its high suspension, but some are 4WD territory only. Whatever vehicle you have, the going will be slow. Many stretches of mountain *piste* will be impassable in bad weather: the Michelin No 742 map (formerly No 959) generally has these sections marked.

Whatever the season, enquire about road conditions with locals before setting off on a journey, check your tyres, take a usable spare and carry an adequate supply of water and petrol.

Road Rules

In Morocco you drive on the right hand side of the road, as in Continental Europe. Daylight driving is generally no problem and not too stressful, though in the bigger cities getting constantly cut off is par for the course.

In the event of a traffic accident, especially accidents involving injuries, drivers are officially required to remain at the scene and vehicles cannot be moved until the police have arrived – this may take hours.

In towns, give way to traffic entering a roundabout from the right when you're already on one. No one seems to pay much attention to striped (zebra) crossings. The speed limit in built-up areas is 40km/h.

Outside the towns there is a national speed limit of 100km/h, rising to 120km/h on the motorways. There are two main sections, from Tangier along the Atlantic coast to Casablanca, and from Rabat to Fez via Meknès. The motorway has also been extended along the Mediterranean coast from Tangier to Nador, and plans are underway to extend the network to Marrakesh, Agadir and Oujda. Tolls apply on the motorways – for example from Rabat to Tangier is Dh60 and Rabat to Casablanca is Dh20. You take a ticket upon entering the motorway and then pay at the end.

Yellow road signs implore drivers to follow the law and wear seatbelts, but in practice few people do, preferring instead to put their trust in Allah to reach their destination safely. Not doing so leaves you open to fines however, so we'd advise belting up.

LOCAL TRANSPORT

Bus

The bigger cities, such as Casablanca, Rabat, Marrakesh, Fez and Meknès, have public bus services. They're often handy for crossing from the ville nouvelle (new town) of a city to the medina (old town), but can be ludicrously overcrowded, and routes often hard to discern. Tickets are typically Dh2 to Dh3.

Grand Taxi

The elderly Mercedes vehicles you'll see belting along Moroccan roads and gathered in great flocks near bus stations are shared taxis (*grands taxis* in French or *taxiat kebira* in Arabic). They're a big feature of Morocco's public transport system and link towns to their nearest neighbours in a kind of leapfrogging system. Taxis sometimes ply longer routes when there's demand, but these services are few and usually leave first thing in the morning. Grands taxis take six extremely cramped passengers (two in the front, four in the back) and leave when full. It can often be to your advantage to pay for two seats to get the taxi going earlier (and give yourself more space). This is particularly useful for lone women as you should get the front seat to yourself.

The fixed-rate fares (listed in individual city entries) are generally a little higher than bus fares, but are still very reasonable. When asking about fares, make it clear you want to pay for *une place* (one spot) in a *taxi collectif* (shared taxi). Another expression that helps explain that you don't want to hire a taxi for yourself is that you wish to travel *ma'a an-nas* (with other people).

Touts and taxi drivers sometimes try to bounce tourists into hiring the whole taxi (*complet*). Smile and stand your ground if you're not interested, but for some routes hiring an entire grand taxi can actually be a great way to travel, especially if you're travelling with a small group – you can take your time on the road and stop whenever you want.

Before setting off, negotiate patiently for a reasonable fare (if you're hiring the whole taxi, aim for six times the fare for one place) and make sure plans for stopping en route are clear. The Ziz and Drâa Valleys, the Tizi n'Test and the Rif Mountains are particularly good to visit in a shared taxi.

Grand-taxi drivers often have something of the boy-racer about them. Overtaking on blind corners can be a badge of honour, and speed limits only adhered to when there's a police roadblock in sight. Many accidents involve overworked grand-taxi drivers falling asleep at the wheel, so night-time journeys are best avoided. Seatbelts are a rarity – and suggesting otherwise may be taken as a slur on your driver's road skills.

Petit Taxi

Cities and bigger towns have local petits taxis, which are a different colour in every city. Petits taxis are not permitted to go beyond the city limits. They are licensed to carry up to three passengers and are usually, but not always, metered. To ask in French for the meter to be switched on say *'tourne le conteur, si'l vous plaît'*. Where they are not metered, agree to a price beforehand. If the driver refuses to use the meter or won't give you a price, ask to stop and get out. Most petit-taxi drivers are perfectly honest, although those in Marrakesh are notoriously greedy with tourists.

Multiple hire is the rule rather than the exception, so you can get half-full cabs if they are going your way (for the same price). From 8pm (often 9pm in summer) there is normally a 50% surcharge.

Pick-up Truck & 4WD

In more remote parts of the country, especially in the Atlas Mountains, locals get from village to village by Berber *camionettes* (pick-up trucks), old vans or in the back of trucks. This is a bumpy but adventurous way to get to know the country and people a little better, but can mean waiting a considerable time (even days) for the next lift. When travelling between remote towns and villages, the best time to travel is early on market days (generally once or twice a week). It's common for 4WD taxis to oper-

TRAVELLERS' CODE OF ETIQUETTE

When travelling on public transport, it's considered both selfish and bad manners to eat while those around you go without. Always buy a little extra that can be offered to your neighbours. A bag of fruit makes a great choice.

Next comes the ritual. If you have offered food, etiquette dictates that your fellow passengers should decline it. It should be offered a second time, this time a little more persuasively, but again it will be turned down. On a third more insistent offer, your neighbours are free to accept the gift if they wish to.

If, conversely, you are offered food, but you don't want it, it's good manners to accept a small piece anyway. At the same time, you should pat your stomach contentedly to indicate that you are full. In return for participating in this elaborate ritual, you should be accorded great respect, offered protection and cared for like a friend.

ate on the more remote *pistes* that would destroy normal taxis.

TRAIN

Morocco's excellent train network (see Map p491) is one of Africa's best, linking most of the main centres. It is run by the **Office National des Chemins de Fer** (ONCF; www.oncf.ma, in French). There are basically two lines that carry passengers: from Tangier in the north down to Marrakesh, and from Oujda in the north-east, also to Marrakesh, joining with the Tangier line at Sidi Kacem. Plans to extend the railway south to Agadir and on to the Western Sahara seem perennially doomed never to leave the drawing board, although as we went to press work on a high-speed TGV line from Tangier to Casablanca was due to commence. Supratours runs buses linking many destinations to the rail network south and east of Marrakesh (including Essaouira and Laâyoune), and along the Mediterranean coast (including Tetouan and Nador).

Trains are comfortable, fast and run closely to their timetables. Reasonably priced, they're far preferable to buses where available. Drinks and snacks are available on the train. Smoking is not allowed in compartments. Stations aren't usually well signposted and announcements (in both French and Arabic) are frequently inaudible so keep an eye out for your station.

Most of the stations are located in the ville nouvelle. They usually have left-luggage depots, though these only accept luggage that can be locked.

Timetables for the whole system are posted in French at most stations, and ticket offices can print out mini-timetables to individual destinations. ONCF's website (in French) also has full timetables and prices.

Classes

There are two types of train, *ordinaire* (Train Navette Rapide, TNR) and *rapide* (Train Rapide Climatisé, TCR). *Rapide* trains are standard for intercity services, with *ordinaire* trains now reduced to a handful of late-night and local services. The main difference between the two is comfort and air-conditioning, rather than speed. Prices given in the guide are for rapide trains (ordinaire trains are around 30% cheaper).

There are different 1st- and 2nd-class fares on all these trains, though there's not much difference in actual comfort – 1st-class compartments have six seats, 2nd-class have eight. Second-class is more than adequate on any journey.

Shuttle services operate regularly between Kenitra, Rabat, Casablanca and Mohammed V International Airport, and supplement the rapide services on this line. There are hourly services between Casablanca and the airport (35 minutes) running roughly between 5am and 10pm, making them a convenient way to catch most flights. For more details, see the Getting Around sections under Casablanca (p116) and Rabat (p129).

Costs

Couchettes are available on the overnight ordinaire trains between Marrakesh and Tangier, and Oujda and Casablanca. The compartments fold up into six bunks (couchettes) and they're well worth the extra Dh90. There's also a more expensive overnight rapide train from Oujda.

Sample 2nd-class fares include Casablanca to Marrakesh (Dh84, three hours), Rabat to Fez (Dh76, 3½ hours) and Tangier to Marrakesh (Dh190, eight hours).

Children aged under four travel free. Those aged between four and 12 years get a reduction of 10% to 50%, depending on the service.

Reservations

You are advised to buy tickets at the station, as a supplement is charged for buying tickets on the train. Tickets can be bought up to a month before travel, and are worth getting in advance for couchettes on overnight services (particularly Tangier–Marrakesh), or if you're travelling around the Eid holidays.

Always hang on to tickets, as inspectors check them on the trains and they are collected at the station on arrival.

Train Passes

Two types of rail discount cards are available. The Carte Fidelité (Dh149) is for those aged over 26 and gives you 50% reductions on eight return or 16 one-way journeys in a 12-month period. If you're under 26, the Carte Jaune (Dh99) will give you the same discounts. Those aged over 60 can buy a Carte Retraités (Dh50), giving a 40% discount on tickets. To apply you need one passport-sized photo and a photocopy of your passport.

Health

CONTENTS

Prevention is the key to staying healthy while travelling in Morocco, and a little planning before departure will save you trouble later. With luck, the worst complaint you might come down with on your trip is a bad stomach; while infectious diseases can and do occur in Morocco, these are usually associated with poor living conditions and poverty, and can be avoided with a few precautions. A more common reason for travellers needing medical help is as a result of accidents – cars are not always well maintained and poorly lit roads are littered with potholes. Medical facilities can be excellent in large cities, but in remoter areas may be more basic.

BEFORE YOU GO

Health matters often get left to the last minute before travelling. A little planning is advisable, however – some vaccines don't ensure immunity for two weeks, so visit a doctor four to eight weeks before departure.

Travellers can register with the **International Association for Medical Advice to Travellers** (IAMAT; www.iamat.org). The website can help travellers find a doctor with recognised training. Those heading off to very remote areas may like to do a first-aid course (Red Cross and St John's Ambulance can help), or attend a remote-medicine first-aid course such as that offered by the **Royal Geographical Society** (www.rgs.org) – a particularly good idea if you're going trekking.

Bring medications in their original, clearly labelled, containers. A signed and dated letter from your physician describing your medical conditions and medications, including generic names, is also a good idea. If carrying syringes or needles, be sure to have a physician's letter documenting their medical necessity. See your dentist before a long trip; carry a spare pair of contact lenses and glasses (and take your optical prescription with you).

INSURANCE

Adequate health insurance is vital when travelling to Morocco. Check in advance that your insurance plan will make payments directly to providers or reimburse you later for overseas health expenditures – in Morocco, doctors usually expect payment on the spot. Your policy should ideally also cover emergency air evacuation home or to a hospital in a major city, which may be essential for serious problems.

RECOMMENDED VACCINATIONS

Although no specific vaccinations are required for Morocco, the World Health Organization nevertheless recommends that all travellers should be covered for diphtheria, tetanus, measles, mumps, rubella and polio, as well as hepatitis B. When making preparations to travel, en-

TRAVEL HEALTH WEBSITES

The following government travel health websites are useful resources to consult prior to departure.

Australia (www.smartraveller.gov.au)
Canada (www.hc-sc.gc.ca/english/index.html)
UK (www.doh.gov.uk/traveladvice/)
United States (www.cdc.gov/travel/)

sure that all of your routine vaccination cover is complete. Ask your doctor for an International Certificate of Vaccination, which will list all the vaccinations you've received.

MEDICAL CHECKLIST

Following is a list of other items you should consider packing in your medical kit when you are travelling.

- antibiotics (if travelling off the beaten track)
- antibacterial hand gel
- antidiarrhoeal drugs (eg loperamide)
- paracetamol (eg Tylenol) or aspirin
- anti-inflammatory drugs (eg ibuprofen)
- antihistamines (for hay fever and allergic reactions)
- antibacterial ointment (eg Bactroban) for cuts and abrasions
- steroid cream or cortisone (for allergic rashes)
- bandages, gauze, gauze rolls
- adhesive or paper tape
- scissors, safety pins, tweezers
- thermometer
- pocket knife
- DEET-containing insect repellent for the skin
- permethrin-containing insect spray for clothing, tents, and bed nets
- sun block
- oral rehydration salts
- iodine tablets (for water purification)
- syringes and sterile needles (if travelling to remote areas)

INTERNET RESOURCES

There is a wealth of travel-health advice on the internet. For further information, **Lonely Planet** (www.lonelyplanet.com) is a good place to start. **The World Health Organization** (www.who.int/ith/) is an excellent resource for travel health information, along with **MD Travel Health** (www.mdtravelhealth.com), which provides complete travel-health recommendations for every country.

FURTHER READING

Lonely Planet's *Healthy Travel* is packed with useful information including pretrip planning, emergency first aid, immunisation and disease information and what to do if you get sick on the road. Other recommended references include *Travellers' Health* by Dr Richard Dawood (Oxford University Press) and *The Travellers' Good Health Guide* by Ted Lankester (Sheldon Press), an especially useful health guide for volunteers and long-term expatriates working in the region.

IN TRANSIT

DEEP VEIN THROMBOSIS (DVT)

Deep vein thrombosis occurs when blood clots form in the legs during plane flights, chiefly because of prolonged immobility. The longer the flight, the greater the risk. Though most clots are reabsorbed uneventfully, some may break off and travel through the blood vessels to the lungs, where they may cause life-threatening complications.

The chief symptom of DVT is swelling or pain in the lower leg, usually but not always on just one side. When a blood clot travels to the lungs, it may cause chest pain and difficulty breathing. Travellers with any of these symptoms should immediately seek medical attention.

To prevent the development of DVT on long flights you should walk about the cabin, regularly contract your leg muscles while sitting and ensure that you drink plenty of fluids. Recent research also indicates that wearing flight socks, which gently compress the leg from the knee down, encourages blood to flow properly in the legs and reduces the risk of DVT occurring by up to 90%.

JET LAG & MOTION SICKNESS

Jet lag is common when crossing more than five time zones; it results in insomnia, fatigue or nausea. To avoid jet lag, set your watch to your destination's time zone when you board your plane, drink plenty of (nonalcoholic) fluids and eat lightly. Upon arrival, seek exposure to natural sunlight and readjust your eating and sleeping schedule as soon as possible.

Antihistamines such as dimenhydrinate (Dramamine) and meclizine (Antivert, Bonine) are usually the first choice for treating motion sickness. Their main side-effect is drowsiness. A herbal alternative is ginger, which works like a charm for some people.

IN MOROCCO

AVAILABILITY & COST OF HEALTH CARE

Primary medical care is not always readily available outside major cities and large towns. Pharmacies are generally well stocked, however, and pharmacists can provide valuable advice (usually in French) covering common travellers' complaints, and sell over-the-counter medication, often including some drugs only available on prescription at home. They can also advise when more specialised help is needed.

If you are being treated by a doctor or at a clinic – particularly outside the major cities – you will often be expected to purchase medical supplies on the spot. This can even include sterile dressings or intravenous fluids. Your hotel may be able to locate the nearest source of medical help. In an emergency, contact your embassy or consulate.

Standards of dental care are variable. Keep in mind that your travel insurance will not usually cover you for anything other than emergency dental treatment. The pliers of the street dentists around the Djemaa el-Fna in Marrakesh aren't recommended!

INFECTIOUS DISEASES

Hepatitis A

Hepatitis A is spread through contaminated food (particularly shellfish) and water. It causes jaundice, and although it is rarely fatal, can cause prolonged lethargy and delayed recovery. Symptoms include dark urine, a yellow colour to the whites of the eyes, fever and abdominal pain. Vaccination against Hepatitis A is recommended for travel to Morocco. The vaccine (Avaxim, VAQTA, Havrix) is given as an injection: a single dose will give protection for up to a year, while a booster 12 months later will provide a subsequent 10 years of protection. Hepatitis A and typhoid vaccines can also be given as a single dose vaccine (Hepatyrix or Viatim).

Hepatitis B

Infected blood, contaminated needles and sexual intercourse can all transmit hepatitis B. It can cause jaundice, and affects the liver, occasionally causing liver failure. All travellers should make this a routine vaccination (Morocco gives hepatitis B vaccination as part of routine childhood vaccination). The vaccine is given singly, or at the same time as the hepatitis A vaccine (Hepatyrix). A course will give protection for at least five years. It can be given over four weeks, or six months.

HIV

Morocco has an HIV infection rate of around 0.1%, primarily found in the main urban centres. Although recent education efforts have improved, AIDS awareness (SIDA in French) is relatively poor, in part due to Muslim taboos on openly discussing sexual matters.

HIV is spread via infected blood and blood products and through sexual intercourse with an infected partner, so practising safe sex is essential. There is a small risk of infection through medical procedures, such as blood transfusion, and improperly sterilised medical instruments.

Leishmaniasis

Spread through the bite of an infected sandfly, leishmaniasis can cause slowly growing skin lumps or sores. It may develop into a serious life-threatening fever usually accompanied with anaemia and weight loss. There is no vaccine, but treatment with the antimonial drugs Glucantime or Pentostam is straightforward. Infected dogs are also carriers of the infection. Sandfly bites should be avoided whenever possible. In Morocco, leishmaniasis may be found in rural areas in the Atlas Mountains, with sandflies more prevalent between June and October.

Rabies

Spread through bites or licks on broken skin from an infected animal, rabies is fatal and endemic to Morocco. Animal handlers should be vaccinated, as should those travelling to remote areas where a reliable source of post-bite vaccine is not available within 24 hours. Three injections are needed over a month. If you have not been vaccinated you will need a course of five injections starting within 24 hours or as soon as possible after the injury. Vaccination does not provide you with immunity, it merely buys you more time to seek appropriate medical help.

Tuberculosis

Tuberculosis (TB) is spread through close respiratory contact and occasionally through infected milk or milk products, and is guarded against by the BCG vaccine. This is more important for those visiting family or planning on a long stay, and those employed as teachers and health-care workers. TB can be asymptomatic, although symptoms can include cough, weight loss or fever months or even years after exposure. An X-ray is the best way to confirm if you have TB. BCG gives a moderate degree of protection against TB. It causes a small permanent scar at the site of injection, and is usually only given in specialised chest clinics. As it's a live vaccine, it shouldn't be given to pregnant women or immunocompromised individuals.

Typhoid

Typhoid is spread through food or water that has been contaminated by infected human faeces. Local outbreaks are unusual but well publicised by the local media. The first symptom is usually fever or a pink rash on the abdomen. Septicaemia (blood poisoning) may also occur. Typhoid vaccine (Typhim Vi, Typherix) will give protection for three years. In some countries, the oral vaccine Vivotif is also available.

Yellow Fever

There is a small risk of yellow fever, borne by mosquitos, in rural Chefchaouen province, but this is so small that the World Health Organization does not recommend vaccination.

Travellers arriving in Morocco from a yellow-fever-endemic area will need to show proof of vaccination before entry. This normally means if arriving directly from an infected country or if the traveller has been in an infected country during the last 10 days. We would recommend, however, that travellers carry a certificate if they have been in an infected country during the previous month to avoid any possible difficulties with immigration. Note that yellow fever is endemic to Mauritania, so your documentation must be in order if entering Morocco overland from here (although anecdotal evidence disputes how rigorously the order is enforced at the land border). For a full list of these countries visit the websites of the **World Health Organization** (www.who.int/ith/en/) or the **Centers for Disease Control and Prevention** (www.cdc.gov/travel/). There is always the possibility that a traveller without a legally required, up-to-date certificate will be vaccinated and detained in isolation at the port of arrival for up to 10 days, or possibly repatriated. The yellow-fever vaccination must be given at a designated clinic and is valid for 10 years. It is a live vaccine and must not be given to immunocompromised or pregnant travellers.

TRAVELLER'S DIARRHOEA

The strains of travel – unfamiliar food, heat, long days and erratic sleeping patterns – can all make your body more susceptible to upset stomachs.

To prevent diarrhoea, eat only fresh fruits or vegetables if they are cooked or if you have washed or peeled them yourself. Water is generally safe to drink in cities but elsewhere you should only drink treated water (see p503). Buffet meals, which may have been kept sitting warm for some time, can be risky – food should be piping hot. Meals freshly cooked in front of you (like much street food) or served in a busy restaurant are more likely to be safe. Be sensible, but not paranoid – the food is one of the treats of visiting Morocco, and you shouldn't miss out for fears of an upset stomach.

It's also very important to pay close attention to personal hygiene while on the road. Many Moroccan meals are eaten with the hand, so always wash before eating (even the smallest restaurant will have a sink and soap) and after using the toilet. Antibacterial hand gel, which cleans without needing water is a real travellers' friend.

If you develop diarrhoea, drink plenty of fluids, preferably an oral rehydration solution – all pharmacies stock these inexpensive *sels de réhydration orale*. Avoid fatty food and dairy products. A few loose stools don't require treatment, but if you start having more than four or five stools a day, you should start taking an antibiotic (usually a quinolone drug) and an antidiarrhoeal agent (such as loperamide). If diarrhoea is bloody, persists for more than 72 hours, is accompanied by fever, shaking chills or severe abdominal pain, you should seek medical attention.

ENVIRONMENTAL HAZARDS

Altitude Sickness

Lack of oxygen at high altitudes (over 2500m) affects most people to some extent. The effect may be mild or severe and occurs because less oxygen reaches the muscles and the brain at high altitudes, requiring the heart and lungs to compensate by working harder. Symptoms of Acute Mountain Sickness (AMS) usually (but not always) develop during the first 24 hours at altitude. Mild symptoms include headache, lethargy, dizziness, difficulty sleeping and loss of appetite. AMS may become more severe without warning and can be fatal. Severe symptoms include breathlessness, a dry, irritative cough (which may progress to the production of pink, frothy sputum), severe headache, lack of coordination, confusion, irrational behaviour, vomiting, drowsiness and unconsciousness. There is no hard-and-fast rule as to what is too high: AMS has been fatal at 3000m, although 3500m to 4500m is the usual range.

If you're trekking, build time into your schedule to acclimatise and ensure that your guide knows how to recognise and deal with altitude sickness. Morocco's most popular trek, to Jebel Toubkal, reaches the 4167m summit relatively quickly, so many people may suffer even mildly. The longer treks in the M'Goun Massif also reach heights of around 4000m. Treks in the Rif Mountains and Jebel Sarhro are considerably lower, so don't carry the same risks. See the trekking chapter (p416) for more specific information.

Treat mild symptoms by resting at the same altitude until recovery, or preferably descend – even 500m can help. Paracetamol or aspirin can be taken for headaches. If symptoms persist or become worse, however, immediate descent is necessary. Drug treatments should never be used to avoid descent or to enable further ascent.

Diamox (acetazolamide) reduces the headache of AMS and helps the body acclimatise to the lack of oxygen. It is only available on prescription, and those who are allergic to the sulfonamide antibiotics may also be allergic to Diamox.

The **British Mountaineering Council** (www.thebmc.co.uk) has an excellent series of downloadable fact sheets with information on altitude sickness.

Heat Illness

Morocco's sun can be fierce, so bring a hat. Heat exhaustion occurs following heavy sweating and excessive fluid loss with inadequate replacement of fluids and salt. This is particularly common when taking unaccustomed exercise before full acclimatisation. Symptoms include headache, dizziness and tiredness. Dehydration is already happening by the time you feel thirsty – aim to drink sufficient water such that you produce pale, diluted urine. The treatment of heat exhaustion involves fluid replacement with water or fruit juice or both, and cooling by cold water and fans. The treatment of the salt-loss component involves consuming salty fluids such as soup or broth, and adding a little more table salt to foods than usual.

Heat stroke is much more serious. This occurs when the body's heat-regulating mechanism breaks down. Excessive rise in body temperature leads to sweating ceasing, irrational and hyperactive behaviour and eventually loss of consciousness and death. Rapid cooling by spraying the body with water and fanning is an ideal treatment. Emergency fluid and electrolyte replacement by intravenous drip is usually also required.

Insect Bites & Stings

Bites from mosquitoes and other insects are more likely to be an irritant rather than a health risk. DEET-based insect repellents will prevent bites. Bees and wasps only cause real problems to those with a severe allergy (anaphylaxis). If you have a severe allergy to bee or wasp stings, you should carry an adrenaline injection or similar. Sandflies are found around the Mediterranean beaches. They usually cause only a nasty, itchy bite but can carry a rare skin disorder called cutaneous leishmaniasis.

Scorpions are common in southern Morocco. They can cause a painful sting that is rarely life threatening.

Bedbugs are sometimes found in the cheaper hotels. They lead to very itchy lumpy bites. Spraying the mattress with an appropriate insect killer will do a good job of getting rid of them.

Scabies are also frequently found in cheap accommodation. These tiny mites live in the skin, particularly between the fingers.

They cause an intensely itchy rash. Scabies is easily treated with lotion available from pharmacies; people with whom you come into contact with also need treating to avoid spreading scabies between asymptomatic carriers.

Snake Bites

The chances of seeing a snake in Morocco, let alone being bitten by one, are slim. Nevertheless, there are a few venomous species found in the southern desert areas, such as the horned viper. Snakes like to bask on rocks and sand, retreating during the heat of the day. Avoid walking barefoot, and the temptation to stick your hand into holes or cracks. Half of those bitten by venomous snakes are not actually injected with poison (envenomed). If bitten by a snake, do not panic. Immobilise the bitten limb with a splint (eg a stick) and apply a bandage over the site, using firm pressure, similar to a bandage over a sprain. Do not apply a tourniquet, or cut or suck the bite. Get the victim to medical help as soon as possible so that antivenin can be given if necessary.

Water

Tap water is chlorinated in Morocco's cities and generally safe to drink (and clean your teeth with). Elsewhere, stick to treated water – either filter it or use water-purification tablets. Bottled water is available everywhere as an alternative, although there is a high environmental cost through the mountains of discarded (and unrecycled) plastic bottles. Off the beaten track, water drawn from wells or pumped from boreholes should be safe, but never drink water from rivers or lakes, as this may contain bacteria or viruses that can cause diarrhoea or vomiting.

TRAVELLING WITH CHILDREN

All travellers with children should know how to treat minor ailments and when to seek medical treatment. Make sure the children are up to date with routine vaccinations, and discuss possible travel vaccines well before departure as some vaccines are not suitable for children aged under a year.

Upset stomachs are always a risk for children when travelling, so take particular care with diet. If your child is vomiting or experiencing diarrhoea, lost fluid and salts must be replaced. It may be helpful to take rehydration powders for reconstituting with sterile water. Ask your doctor about this. In Morocco's often-searing heat, sunburn, heat exhaustion and dehydration should all be guarded against.

Children should be encouraged to avoid dogs or other mammals because of the risk of rabies and other diseases – although there isn't likely to be a risk on camel rides in the desert, or with donkeys and mules working in places like Fez medina. Any bite, scratch or lick from a warm blooded, furry animal should immediately be thoroughly cleaned. If there is any possibility that the animal is infected with rabies, immediate medical assistance should be sought.

WOMEN'S HEALTH

Emotional stress, exhaustion and travelling through different time zones can all contribute to an upset in the menstrual pattern. If using oral contraceptives, remember some antibiotics, diarrhoea and vomiting can stop the pill from working and lead to the risk of pregnancy, so remember to take condoms with you just in case. Condoms should be kept in a cool dry place or they may crack and perish.

Emergency contraception is most effective if taken within 24 hours after unprotected sex. Condoms, tampons and sanitary towels are all widely available in Morocco.

Travelling during pregnancy is usually possible but there are important things to consider. Have a medical check-up before embarking on your trip. The most risky times for travel are during the first 12 weeks of pregnancy, when miscarriage is most likely, and after 30 weeks, when complications such as high blood pressure and premature delivery can occur. Most airlines will not accept a traveller after 28 to 32 weeks of pregnancy, and long-haul flights in the later stages can be very uncomfortable. Antenatal facilities vary greatly between countries in the region and you should think carefully if you're planning on getting off the beaten track. Taking written records of the pregnancy including details of your blood group, is likely to be helpful if you need medical attention while away. Ensure your insurance policy covers pregnancy, delivery and postnatal care, but remember insurance policies are only as good as the facilities available.

Language

CONTENTS

LANGUAGES IN MOROCCO

The official language in Morocco is Arabic, although French, the legacy of the protectorate, is still widely used in the cities (much less so among rural Berbers). Morocco's close ties to France help to explain the continued importance of French in education, business and the press.

Berber is spoken in the Rif and Atlas Mountains. Modern means of communication have left only a minority of Berbers monolingual – most speak at least some Arabic. See p512 for some Berber basics.

To a lesser extent than French, Spanish has maintained some hold in northern parts of the country, where Spain exercised administrative control until 1956. You may also come across Spanish in the territory of the former Spanish Sahara – over which Madrid relinquished control in 1975 – and the former enclave of Sidi Ifni. In towns like Tetouan, for instance, Spanish is more likely to be understood than French.

Reforms to Morocco's education system include the introduction of English into the curriculum for younger students, so it may become more widely spoken. However, English speakers will find that a smattering of French (and a little Spanish) can be a great asset; we've included some French basics in this language guide (p510), In the main cities and towns you'll find plenty of people (many of them touts that you may not necessarily want to hang around with), who speak various languages, including English, German and Italian.

MOROCCAN ARABIC

Written and spoken Arabic are often two very different languages. Moroccan Arabic (Darija) is a dialect of the standard language, but is so different in many respects as to be virtually like another tongue. It is also the dialect that differs most from those of other Arabic-speaking peoples. More specialised or educated language tends to be much the same across the Arab world, although pronunciation varies considerably. An Arab from Jordan or Iraq will have little trouble discussing politics or literature with an educated Moroccan, but might have difficulty ordering lunch.

Written Arabic in Morocco uses what is known as Modern Standard Arabic (MSA). MSA, which has grown from the classical Arabic of the Quran and poetry. It is the written and spoken lingua franca (common language) of the Arab world, and in fact not so far removed from the daily language of the Arab countries of the Levant. It's the language of modern Arabic literature and most media – there are no Darija newspapers or television programs in Morocco.

Foreign students of Arabic constantly face the dilemma of whether first to learn MSA (which could mean waiting some time before being able to talk with shopkeepers) and then a chosen dialect, or simply to acquire spoken competence in the latter.

If you learn even a few words and phrases, you'll discover and experience much more while travelling through the country. Just making the attempt implies a respect for local culture that Moroccans all too infrequently sense in visitors to their country.

There are many courses in both Darija and MSA available throughout Morocco (see p459), and these can be an excellent way to connect with the local people and gain a greater insight into their history and culture.

If you'd like a more comprehensive guide to the Arabic spoken in the Maghreb, get a copy of Lonely Planet's compact and comprehensive *Moroccan Arabic Phrasebook*.

PRONUNCIATION

Pronunciation of Arabic can be daunting for someone unfamiliar with the intonation and combination of sounds. This language guide should help, but bear in mind that the myriad rules governing pronunciation

LANGUAGE

THE STANDARD ARABIC ALPHABET

Final	Medial	Initial	Alone	Transliteration	Pronunciation
ـا			ا	**aa**	as in ‘father’
ـب	ـبـ	بـ	ب	**b**	as in ‘bet’
ـت	ـتـ	تـ	ت	**t**	as in ‘ten’
ـث	ـثـ	ثـ	ث	**th**	as in ‘thin’
ـج	ـجـ	جـ	ج	**j**	as in ‘jet’
ـح	ـحـ	حـ	ح	**H**	a strongly whispered ‘h’, like a sigh of relief
ـخ	ـخـ	خـ	خ	**kh**	as the ‘ch’ in Scottish *loch*
ـد			د	**d**	as in ‘dim’
ـذ			ذ	**dh**	as the ‘th’ in ‘this’; also as **d** or **z**
ـر			ر	**r**	a rolled ‘r’, as in the Spanish word *caro*
ـز			ز	**z**	as in ‘zip’
ـس	ـسـ	سـ	س	**s**	as in ‘so’, never as in ‘wisdom’
ـش	ـشـ	شـ	ش	**sh**	as in ‘ship’
ـص	ـصـ	صـ	ص		emphatic ‘s’ (see below)
ـض	ـضـ	ضـ	ض		emphatic ‘d’ (see below)
ـط	ـطـ	طـ	ط		emphatic ‘t’ (see below)
ـظ	ـظـ	ظـ	ظ		emphatic ‘z’ (see below)
ـع	ـعـ	عـ	ع	**’**	the Arabic letter *‘ayn*; pronounce as a glottal stop – like the closing of the throat before saying ‘Oh-oh!’ (see Other Sounds on p506)
ـغ	ـغـ	غـ	غ	**gh**	a guttural sound like Parisian ‘r’
ـف	ـفـ	فـ	ف	**f**	as in ‘far’
ـق	ـقـ	قـ	ق	**q**	a strongly guttural ‘k’ sound; also often pronounced as a glottal stop
ـك	ـكـ	كـ	ك	**k**	as in ‘king’
ـل	ـلـ	لـ	ل	**l**	as in ‘lamb’
ـم	ـمـ	مـ	م	**m**	as in ‘me’
ـن	ـنـ	نـ	ن	**n**	as in ‘name’
ـه	ـهـ	هـ	ه	**h**	as in ‘ham’
ـو			و	**w**	as in ‘wet’; or
				oo	long, as in ‘food’; or
				ow	as in ‘how’
ـي	ـيـ	يـ	ي	**y**	as in ‘yes’; or
				ee	as in ‘beer’, only softer; or
				ai/ay	as in ‘aisle’/as the ‘ay’ in ‘day’

Vowels Not all Arabic vowel sounds are represented in the alphabet. For more information on the vowel sounds used in this language guide, see Pronunciation on p504.

Emphatic Consonants To simplify the transliteration system used in this book, the emphatic consonants have not been differentiated from their non-emphatic counterparts.

and vowel use are too extensive to be fully covered here.

Vowels

a as in 'had'
e as in 'bet'
i as in 'hit'
o as in 'note'
u as in 'put'
aa as the 'a' in 'father'
ee as the 'e' in 'ear', only softer
oo as the 'oo' in 'food'

Consonants

Pronunciation for all Arabic consonants is covered in the alphabet table on the preceding page. Note that when double consonants occur in transliterations, both are pronounced. For example, hammam (bath), is pronounced 'ham-mam'.

For those who can already read some Arabic, it's worth noting that written Moroccan Arabic has an extra letter. This letter is the *kaf* with three dots above it and transliterated as **g**, which represents a hard 'g' (as in *Agadir*).

Other Sounds

Arabic has two sounds that are very tricky for non-Arabs to produce, the *'ayn* and the glottal stop. The letter 'ayn represents a sound with no English equivalent that comes even close. It is similar to the glottal stop (which is not actually represented in the alphabet) but the muscles at the back of the throat are gagged more forcefully – it has been described as the sound of someone being strangled. In many transliteration systems 'ayn is represented by an opening quotation mark, and the glottal stop by a closing quotation mark.

To make the transliterations in this language guide easier to use, we haven't distinguished between the glottal stop and the 'ayn, using the closing quotation mark to represent both sounds. You should find that Arabic speakers will still understand you.

ACCOMMODATION

Where is a ...? *feen kayn ...?*
campground *shee mukheyyem*
hotel *shee ootayl*
youth hostel *daar shshabab*
I'm looking for a cheap hotel. *kanqelleb 'ala shee ootayl rkhays*
What is the address? *ashnoo hoowa l'unwan?*
Please write down the address. *kteb l'unwan 'afek*
Is there a room available? *wash kayn shee beet khaweeya?*

I'd like a room ... *bgheet shee beet ...*
for one person *dyal wahed*
for two people *dyal jooj*
with a bathroom *belhammam*

Can I see the room? *wash yemkenlee nshoof lbeet?*
Where is the toilet? *fin kayn lbeet lma?*
How much is a room for one day? *bash hal kayn gbayt l wahed nhar?*
This room is too expensive. *had lbeet bezzaf ghalee*
This room is good. *had lbeet mezyana*
We'd like to check out now. *bgheena nemshee daba*

air-conditioning *kleemateezaseeyun*
bed *namooseeya*
blanket *bttaaneeya*
full *'amer*
hot water *lma skhoon*
key *saroot*
room *beet*
sheet *eezar*
shower *doosh*
toilet *beet lma*

CONVERSATION & ESSENTIALS

When Arabic speakers meet, they often exchange more extensive and formalised greetings than Westerners are used to. Any attempt to use a couple (whether correctly or not) won't go astray.

When addressing a man the polite term more or less equivalent to 'Mr' is *aseedee* (shortened to *see* before a name); for women the polite form of address is *lalla*, followed by the first name. You may be addressed as 'Mr John' or 'Mrs Anne'. To attract the attention of someone on the street or a waiter in a café, the expression *shreef* is used.

The abbreviations 'm/f/pl' refer to 'male/female/plural'.

Hi. *la bes* (informal greeting)
(response) *bekheer*
Hello. *es salaam alaykum* ('peace upon you')
(response) *wa alaykum salaam* ('and peace upon you')

Goodbye.	*bessalama*
Goodbye.	*m'a ssalama* ('with peace')
Good morning.	*sbah lkheer*
Good evening.	*mselkheer*
Please.	*'afak/'afik/'afakum* (to m/f/pl)
Thank you (very much).	*shukran (bezzef)*
You're welcome.	*la shukran 'la wejb*
Yes.	*eeyeh/na'am* (*na'am* can also mean 'I'm sorry, could you repeat that, please')
Yes, OK.	*wakha*
No.	*la*
No, thank you.	*la shukran*
Excuse me.	*smeh leeya*
How are you?	*keef halek?*
Fine, thank you.	*bekheer, lhamdoo llaah*
If God wills.	*ensha'llaah*
Go ahead/Come on!	*zid!*
What's your name?	*asmeetek?*
My name is ...	*esmee ...*
How old are you?	*shhal f'merek?*
I'm (20).	*'andee ('ashreen) 'am*
Where are you from?	*mneen nta/nti/ntooma?* (m/f/pl)
I'm/We're from ...	*ana/hna men ...*

SIGNS

Entrance	مدخل
Exit	خروج
Open	مفتوح
Closed	مغلق
Prohibited	ممنوع
Information	معلومات
Hospital	مستشفي
Police	شرطة
Men's Toilet	حمام للرجال
Women's Toilet	حمام للنساء

DIRECTIONS

Where is (the) ...?	*feen kayn ...?*
beach	*laplaje*
mosque	*jame'*
museum	*al-matHaf*
old city	*lmdeena lqdeema*
palace	*al-qasr*
park	*'arsa*
How do I get to ...?	*keefesh ghaadeenuwsul l ...?*
How far?	*bshhal b'ayd?*
Go straight ahead.	*seer neeshan.*
Turn ...	*dor ...*
left/right	*'al leeser/'al leemen*
at the corner	*felqent*
at the traffic lights	*fedo elhmer*
here	*hna*
there	*hunak*
next to	*hedda*
opposite	*'eks*
behind	*men luy*
north	*shamel*
south	*janoob*
east	*sherq*
west	*gherb*

EMERGENCIES – ARABIC

Help!	*'teqnee!*
Help me please!	*'awennee 'afak!*
Call the police!	*'ayyet 'la lbùlees!*
Call a doctor!	*'ayyet 'la shee tbeeb!*
Thief!	*sheffar!*
I've been robbed.	*tsreqt*
Where's the toilet?	*feen kayn lbeet lma?*
Go away!	*seer fhalek!*
I'm lost.	*tweddert*
There's been an accident!	*uq'at kseeda!*

HEALTH

I'm sick.	*ana mreed*
It hurts here.	*kaydernee henna*
I'm ...	*ana ...*
diabetic	*feeya merd ssukkar*
asthmatic	*feeya ddeega*
I am allergic to ...	*'andee lhsaseeya m'a ...*
penicillin	*lbeenseleen*
bees	*nhel*
dairy products	*makla llee feeha lhleeb*
antibiotics	*'anteebeeyoteek*
aspirin	*aspereen*
condoms	*kapoot*
contraceptives	*dwa dyal lhmel*
diarrhoea	*sshal*
headache	*rras*
medicine	*ddawa*
sunblock cream	*lomber*
tampons	*fota dyal dem lheed*

LANGUAGE DIFFICULTIES

Do you speak (English)?
wash kat'ref (negleezeeya)?
Does anyone here speak English?
wash kayn shee hedd henna lee kay'ref negleezeeya?

How do you say ... in Arabic?
keefash katgooloo ... bel'arabeeya?
What does this mean?
ash kat'anee hadhee?
I understand.
fhemt
I don't understand.
mafhemtsh
Please write it down for me.
ktebha leeya
Please show me on the map.
werri liya men l kharita 'afak

NUMBERS

Arabic numerals are simple enough to learn and, unlike the written language, run from left to right across the page.

Due to the fact that it was colonised by France, Morocco uses standard Western numerical systems rather than those normally associated with Arab countries.

0	*sifr*
1	*wahed*
2	*jooj*
3	*tlata*
4	*reb'a*
5	*khamsa*
6	*setta*
7	*seb'a*
8	*tmenya*
9	*tes'ood*
10	*'ashra*
11	*hdaash*
12	*tnaash*
13	*teltaash*
14	*rba'taash*
15	*khamstaash*
16	*settaash*
17	*sbe'taash*
18	*tmentaash*
19	*tse'taash*
20	*'ashreen*
21	*wahed oo'ashreen*
22	*tnayn oo'ashreen*
30	*tlateen*
40	*reb'een*
50	*khamseen*
60	*setteen*
70	*seb'een*
80	*tmaneen*
90	*tes'een*
100	*mya*
200	*myatayn*
300	*teltmya*
400	*rba'mya*
1000	*alf*
2000	*alfayn*
3000	*telt alaf*

first	*loowel*
second	*tanee*
third	*talet*
fourth	*rabe'*
fifth	*khames*

PAPERWORK

address	*'unwaan'*
name	*smeeya*
nationality	*jenseeya*
passport	*pasbor*
visa	*t'sheera*

I'm here on ...	*jeet l lmaghreeb fe ...*
business	*felkhedma*
holiday	*fel'otla*

QUESTION WORDS

Who?	*shkoon?*
Why?	*'lash?*
How?	*keefash?*
Which?	*ashmen?*
Where?	*feen?*
Is there ...?	*wash kayn ...?*
What's that?	*ash dak shee?*

SHOPPING & SERVICES

Where is (the) ...?	*feen kayn ...?*
bank	*shee baanka*
bookshop	*shee mektaba*
barber	*shee hellaq*
... embassy	*ssifaara dyal ...*
market	*souk*
pharmacy	*farmasyan*
police station	*lkoomeesareeya*
post office	*lboostaa*
restaurant	*ristura/mat'am*
souvenir shop	*baazaar*
travel agency	*wekaalet el aasfaar*

I want to change ...	*bgheet nserref ...*
some money	*shee floos*
travellers cheques	*shek seeyahee*

Can I pay by credit card?	*wash nkder nkhelles bel kart kredee?*
How much is it?	*bshhal?*
That's very expensive.	*ghalee bezzaf*

I'm only looking. *gheer kanshoof*
I don't like it. *ma'jebatneesh*
Can I look at it? *wakhkha nshoofha?*

I'd like to buy ... *bgheet nshree ...*
Do you have ...? *wash 'andkom ...?*
stamps *ttnaber*
a newspaper *jaarida*

big *kabeer*
small *sagheer*
open *mehlool*
closed *masdood*
enough *kafee*

TIME & DATES

What time is it? *shal fessa'a?*
When? *fuqash/eemta?*
today *lyoom*
tomorrow *ghedda*
yesterday *lbareh*
morning *fessbah*
afternoon *fel'sheeya*
evening *'sheeya*
day *nhar*
night *felleel*
week/month/year *l'usbu'/shshhar/l'am*
after *men b'd*
on time *felweqt*
early *bekree*
late *m'ettel*
quickly *bizerba/dgheeya*
slowly *beshweeya*

Monday *nhar letneen*
Tuesday *nhar ttlat*
Wednesday *nhar larb'*
Thursday *nhar lekhmees*
Friday *nhar jjem'a*
Saturday *nhar ssebt*
Sunday *nhar lhedd*

January *yanaayir*
February *fibraayir*
March *maaris*
April *abreel*
May *maayu*
June *yunyu*
July *yulyu*
August *aghustus/ghusht*
September *sibtimbir/shebtenber*
October *uktoobir*
November *nufimbir/nu'enbir*
December *disimbir/dijenbir*

TRANSPORT

Public Transport

When does the ... leave/arrive? *wufuqash kaykhrej/kaywsul ...?*
boat *lbaboor*
bus *ttubees*
intercity bus *lkar*
train *tran*
plane *ttayyyaara*

I'd like a ... ticket to (Casablanca). *'afak bgheet wahed lwarka l ddar lbayda (kasablanka)*
return *bash nemshee oo njee*
1st class *ddaraja lloola*
2nd class *ddaraja ttaneeya*

Where is (the) ...? *feen kayn ...?*
airport *mataar*
bus station *mhetta dyal ttobeesat*
ticket office *maktab lwerqa*
train station *lagaar*

What's the fare? *shhal taman lwarka?*
Which bus goes to ...? *ashmen kar ghaadee til ...?*
Is this bus going to ...? *wash had lkar ghaadee l ...?*
Please tell me when we arrive at ... *'afak eela wselna l ... goolhaleeya*
I want to pay for one place only. *bgheet nkhelles blaasaawaheda*
Stop here please. *wqef henna 'afak*
Please wait for me. *tsennanee 'afak*
Is this seat free? *wash had lblaasaa khaweeya?*

street *zenqa*
city *medeena*
village *qerya*
bus stop *blasa dyal ttobeesat*
station *mhetta*
number *raqem*
ticket *werqa*

Private Transport

Where can I hire a ...? *feen yimkin li nkri ...?*
bicycle *bshklit*
camel *jmel*
car *tumubeel*
donkey *hmar*
horse *'awd*

How do I get to ...?
keefesh ghaadee nuwsul l ...?
Where's the next petrol station?
fin kayna shi bumba dyal lisans griba?

I'd like ... litres.
bgheet ... itru 'afak

Please check the ...	*'afak shuf ...*
oil	*zzit*
water	*lma*

Can I park here?	*wash nqder nwakef hna?*
How long can I park here?	*sh-hal men waket neqder nstatiun hna?*
We need a mechanic.	*khesna wahed lmikanisyan*
The car broke down at ...	*tumubeel khasra f ...*
I have a flat tyre.	*'ndi pyasa fruida*

TRAVEL WITH CHILDREN

I need a car with a child seat.
bgheet wahed ttomobeel belkorsee dyal draree sghar?
Are there facilities for babies?
wesh kayn tsheelat dyal ddraree sghar?
I'm travelling with my family.
ana msafer m'a l'alla dyalee
Is it suitable for children?
wesh mnaseb l draree sghar?
Are there any activities for children?
wesh kayn shee tansheet dyal draree sghar?
Are children allowed?
wesh mesmuh l draree?
Is there a playground nearby?
wesh kayn shee ssaha dyal ll'eb qreeba?

FRENCH

PRONUNCIATION

The pronunciation guides included with each French phrase should help you in getting your message across.

ACCOMMODATION

Do you have any rooms available?
Est-ce que vous avez des chambres libres?
e·sker voo·za·vay day shom·brer lee·brer

I'd like (a) ...	*Je voudrais ...*	zher voo·dray ...
single room	*une chambre à un lit*	ewn shom·brer a un lee
double-bed room	*une chambre avec un grand lit*	ewn shom·brer a·vek un gron lee
twin room (with two beds)	*une chambre avec des lits jumeaux*	ewn shom·brer a·vek day lee zhew·mo
room with a bathroom	*une chambre avec une salle de bains*	ewn shom·brer a·vek ewn sal der bun

EMERGENCIES – FRENCH

Help!
Au secours! o skoor
I'm ill.
Je suis malade. zher swee ma·lad
I'm lost.
Je me suis égaré/e. (m/f) zhe me swee·zay·ga·ray
Leave me alone!
Fichez-moi la paix! fee·shay·mwa la pay

Call ...!	*Appelez ...!*	a·play ...
a doctor	*un médecin*	un mayd·sun
the police	*la police*	la po·lees

How much is it ...?	*Quel est le prix ...?*	kel e ler pree ...
per night	*par nuit*	par nwee
per person	*par personne*	par per·son

CONVERSATION & ESSENTIALS

Hello.	*Bonjour.*	bon·zhoor
Goodbye.	*Au revoir.*	o·rer·vwa
Yes.	*Oui.*	wee
No.	*Non.*	no
Please.	*S'il vous plaît.*	seel voo play
Thank you.	*Merci.*	mair·see

You're welcome.
Je vous en prie. (pol) zher voo·zon pree
De rien. (inf) der ree·en
Excuse me.
Excusez-moi. ek·skew·zay·mwa
Sorry. (forgive me)
Pardon. par·don
Do you speak English?
Parlez-vous anglais? par·lay·voo ong·lay
I don't understand.
Je ne comprends pas. zher ner kom·pron pa
What's your name?
Comment vous appelez-vous? (pol) ko·mon voo·za·pay·lay voo
Comment tu t'appelles? (inf) ko·mon tew ta·pel
My name is ...
Je m'appelle ... zher ma·pel ...
Where are you from?
De quel pays êtes-vous? (pol) der kel pay·ee et·voo
De quel pays es-tu? (inf) der kel pay·ee e·tew

I'm from ...	*Je viens de ...*	zher vyen der ...
I like ...	*J'aime ...*	zhem ...
I don't like ...	*Je n'aime pas ...*	zher nem pa ...
Just a minute.	*Une minute.*	ewn mee·newt

LANGUAGE

DIRECTIONS

Where is ...?
Où est ...? oo e ...
Can you show me (on the map)?
Pouvez-vous m'indiquer (sur la carte)? poo·vay·voo mun·dee·kay (sewr la kart)
Go straight ahead.
Continuez tout droit. kon·teen·way too drwa
Turn left.
Tournez à gauche. toor·nay a gosh
Turn right.
Tournez à droite. toor·nay a drwat
near (to)/far (from)
près (de)/loin (de) pray (der)/lwun (der)

NUMBERS

0	*zero*	zay·ro
1	*un*	un
2	*deux*	der
3	*trois*	trwa
4	*quatre*	ka·trer
5	*cinq*	sungk
6	*six*	sees
7	*sept*	set
8	*huit*	weet
9	*neuf*	nerf
10	*dix*	dees
11	*onze*	onz
12	*douze*	dooz
13	*treize*	trez
14	*quatorze*	ka·torz
15	*quinze*	kunz
16	*seize*	sez
17	*dix-sept*	dee·set
18	*dix-huit*	dee·zweet
19	*dix-neuf*	deez·nerf
20	*vingt*	vung
21	*vingt et un*	vung tay un
22	*vingt-deux*	vung·der
30	*trente*	tront
40	*quarante*	ka·ront
50	*cinquante*	sung·kont
60	*soixante*	swa·sont
70	*soixante-dix*	swa·son·dees
80	*quatre-vingts*	ka·trer·vung
90	*quatre-vingt-dix*	ka·trer·vung·dees
100	*cent*	son
1000	*mille*	meel

SHOPPING & SERVICES

I'd like to buy ...
Je voudrais acheter ... zher voo·dray ash·tay ...
How much is it?
C'est combien? say kom·byun
It's too expensive.
C'est trop cher. say tro shair
Can I pay by credit card?
Est-ce que je peux payer avec ma carte de crédit? es·ker zher per pay·yay a·vek ma kart der kray·dee

I'm looking for ...	*Je cherche ...*	zhe shersh ...
a bank	*une banque*	ewn bonk
the hospital	*l'hôpital*	lo·pee·tal
an internet café	*un cybercafé du coin*	un see·bair·ka·fay dew kwun
the market	*le marché*	ler mar·shay
the post office	*le bureau de poste*	ler bew·ro der post
a public toilet	*les toilettes*	lay twa·let

TIME & DATES

What time is it?	*Quelle heure est-il?*	kel er e til
It's (8) o'clock.	*Il est (huit) heures.*	il e (weet) er
It's half past ...	*Il est (...) heures et demie.*	il e (...) er e day·mee
in the morning	*du matin*	dew ma·tun
in the afternoon	*de l'après-midi*	der la·pray·mee·dee
in the evening	*du soir*	dew swar

Monday	*lundi*	lun·dee
Tuesday	*mardi*	mar·dee
Wednesday	*mercredi*	mair·krer·dee
Thursday	*jeudi*	zher·dee
Friday	*vendredi*	von·drer·dee
Saturday	*samedi*	sam·dee
Sunday	*dimanche*	dee·monsh

TRANSPORT

What time does ... leave/arrive?	*À quelle heure part/arrive ...?*	a kel er par/a·reev ...
boat	*le bateau*	ler ba·to
bus	*le bus*	ler bews
train	*le train*	ler trun

I want to go to ...
Je voudrais aller à ... zher voo·dray a·lay a ...

the first	*le premier* (m)	ler prer·myay
	la première (f)	la prer·myair
the last	*le dernier* (m)	ler dair·nyay
	la dernière (f)	la dair·nyair

I'd like to hire a/an...	*Je voudrais louer ...*	zher voo·dray loo·way ...
car	*une voiture*	ewn vwa·tewr
motorbike	*une moto*	ewn mo·to
bicycle	*un vélo*	un vay·lo

BERBER

There are three main dialects commonly delineated among the speakers of Berber, which in a certain sense also serve as loose lines of ethnic demarcation.

In the north, in the area centred on the Rif, the locals speak a dialect that has been called Riffian and is spoken as far south as Figuig on the Algerian frontier. The dialect that predominates in the Middle and High Atlas and the valleys leading into the Sahara goes by various names, including Braber or Amazigh.

More settled tribes of the High Atlas, Anti Atlas, Souss Valley and southwestern oases generally speak Tashelhit or Chleuh. The following phrases are a selection from the Tashelhit dialect, the one visitors are likely to find most useful.

CONVERSATION & ESSENTIALS

Hello.	*la bes darik* (m) *la bes darim* (f)
Hello. (response)	*la bes*
Goodbye.	*akayaoon arbee*
Please.	*barakalaufik*
Thank you.	*barakalaufik*
Yes.	*yah*
No.	*oho*
Excuse me.	*samhiy*
How are you?	*meneek antgeet?*
Fine, thank you.	*la bes, lhamdulah*
Good.	*eefulkee/eeshwa*
Bad.	*(khaib) eeghshne*
See you later.	*akranwes daghr*
Is there ...?	*ees eela ...?*
big	*mqorn*
small	*eemzee*
today	*(zig sbah) rass*
tomorrow	*(ghasad) aska*
yesterday	*eedgam*
Do you have ...?	*ees daroon ...?*
a lot	*bzef*
a little	*eemeek*
food	*teeremt*
mule	*aserdon*
somewhere to sleep	*kra lblast mahengane*
water	*arman*
How much is it?	*minshk aysker?*
no good	*oor eefulkee*
too expensive	*eeghla*
Give me ...	*fky ...*
I want ...	*reegh ...*

LANGUAGE

Also available from Lonely Planet: *Moroccan Arabic Phrasebook*

NUMBERS

1	*yen*
2	*seen*
3	*krad*
4	*koz*
5	*smoos*
6	*sddes*
7	*sa*
8	*tem*
9	*tza*
10	*mrawet*
11	*yen d mrawet*
12	*seen d mrawet*
20	*ashreent*
21	*ashreent d yen d mrawet*
22	*ashreent d seen d mrawet*
30	*ashreent d mrawet*
40	*snet id ashreent*
50	*snet id ashreent d mrawet*
100	*smoost id ashreent/meeya*

TRANSPORT & DIRECTIONS

I want to go to ...	*addowghs ...*
Where is (the) ...?	*mani gheela ...?*
village	*doorwar*
river	*aseef*
mountain	*adrar*
the pass	*tizee*
Is it near/far?	*ees eeqareb/yagoog?*
straight	*neeshan*
to the right	*fofasee*
to the left	*fozelmad*

Glossary

This glossary is a list of Arabic (A), Berber (B), French (F) and Spanish (S) terms that are used throughout this guide. For a list of trekking terms, see Words To Trek By, p422. For food-related terms see Eat Your Words, p88.

agadir (B) – fortified communal granary
'ain (A) – water source, spring
aït (B) – family (of), often precedes tribal and town names
Al-Andalus – Muslim Spain and Portugal
Alawite – hereditary dynasty that has ruled Morocco since the late 17th century
Allah (A) – God
Almohads – puritanical Muslim group (1147–1269), originally Berber, that arose in response to the corrupt Almoravid dynasty
Almoravids – Muslim group (1054–1147) that ruled Spain and the Maghreb
assif (A) – watercourse, river

bab (A) – gate
babouches (F) – traditional leather slippers
banu (A) – see *beni*
baraka (A) – divine blessing or favour
Barbary – European term used to describe the North African coast from the 16th to the 19th centuries
ben (A) – (or ibn) son of
bendir (B) – single-headed Berber drum
beni (A) – 'sons of', often precedes tribal name (also *banu*)
Berbers – indigenous inhabitants of North Africa
bidonville (F) – slum area, especially in Casablanca
borj (A) – fort (literally, 'tower')
brigade touristique (F) – tourist police
bureau de guide (F) – guides' office
burnous'(A) – warm woollen cloak with hood

caliph – successor of Mohammed; ruler of the Islamic world
calle (S) – street
camarade (F) – West-African migrant
camionette (F) – minivan or pick-up truck
capitol – main temple of Roman town, usually situated in the forum
caravanserai – large merchants' inn enclosing a courtyard, providing accommodation and a marketplace (see also *funduq*)
casa de huéspedes (S) – guest house
chergui (A) – dry, easterly desert wind
Compagnie de Transports Marocaine – CTM; national bus company
corniche (F) – coastal road
corsair – 18th-century pirate based at Salé

dar (A) – traditional town house with internal courtyard
Délégation Régionale du Tourisme – tourist office
derb (A) – lane or narrow street
douar (A) – generally used for 'village' in the High Atlas
douche (F) – public showers (see hammam)

Eaux et Forêts – government ministry responsible for national parks
eid (A) – feast
Ensemble Artisanal – government handicraft shop
erg (A) – sand dunes

fantasia (S) – military exercise featuring a cavalry charge, now performed for tourists
Fatimids – Muslim dynasty that rose to prominence in the 10th century
faux guides (F) – unofficial or informal guides
foum (A) – usually mouth of a river or valley (from Arabic for 'mouth')
frontera (S) – border
funduq (A) – caravanserai (often used to mean 'hotel')

gîte, gîte d'étape (F) – trekkers' hostel, sometimes a home stay
gardiens de voitures (F) – car-park attendants
gare routière (F) – bus station
ghassoul (A) – type of clay mixed with herbs, dried roses and lavender used in hammams for removing grease and washing hair
glaoua (A) – rug with combination of flat weave and deep fluffy pile (also *zanafi*)
Gnaoua – bluesy Moroccan musical form that began with freed slaves in Marrakesh and Essaouira
grand taxi (F) – (long-distance) shared taxi

haj (A) – pilgrimage to Mecca, hence 'haji' or 'hajia', a male or female who has made the pilgrimage
halqa (A) – street theatre
hammada (A) – stony desert
hammam (A) – Turkish-style bathhouse with sauna and massage, also known by the French word *bain* (bath) or *bain maure* (Moorish bath)
hanbel (A) – see kilim

haram (A) – literally 'forbidden', the word is sometimes used to denote a sacred or forbidden area, such as the prayer room of a mosque
Hejira – flight of the Prophet from Mecca to Medina in AD 622; the first year of the Islamic calendar

ibn (A) – son of (see also *ben*)
Idrissids – Moroccan dynasty that established a stable state in northern Morocco in the 9th century
iftar (A) – breaking of the fast at sundown during Ramadan; breakfast (also 'ftur')
imam (A) – Muslim cleric
Interzone – name coined by author William Burroughs for the period 1923–56, when Tangier was controlled by nine countries
irifi (A) – dry, desert wind, also called *chergui*

jami' (A) – Friday mosque (also *djemaa*, *jemaa* and *jamaa*)
jebel (A) – hill, mountain (sometimes *djebel* in former French possessions)
jedid (A) – new (sometimes spelled *jdid*)
jellaba (A) – popular flowing garment; men's jellabas are usually made from cotton or wool, while women's come in light synthetic fabrics

kasbah (A) – fort, citadel; often also the administrative centre (also *qasba*)
khutba – Friday sermon preached by the imam of a mosque
kif (A) – marijuana
kilim (A) – flat-woven blankets or floor coverings (also *hanbel*)
koubba (A) – sanctuary or shrine (see also *marabout*)
ksar (A) – fort or fortified stronghold (plural *ksour*)

Maghreb (A) – (literally 'west') area covered by Morocco, Algeria, Tunisia and Libya
maison d'hôtes (F) – guest house, often a restored traditional Moroccan house
majoun (A) – sticky paste made of crushed seeds of the marijuana plant
marabout – holy man or saint; also often used to describe the mausoleums of these men
masjid (A) – another name for a mosque, particularly in a *medersa* (see also *jami'*)
mechouar (A) – royal assembly place
medersa (A) – college for teaching theology, law, Arabic literature and grammar (also called *madrassa*)
medina (A) – old city; used to describe the old Arab parts of modern towns and cities
mellah (A) – Jewish quarter of the medina
mendeel (A) – brightly coloured striped cloth
Merenids (A) – Moroccan dynasty (1269–1465), responsible for the construction of many of Morocco's *medersas*

mihrab (A) – prayer niche in the wall of a mosque indicating the direction of Mecca (the *qibla*)
minbar (A) – pulpit in mosque; the imam delivers the sermon from one of the lower steps because the Prophet preached from the top step
moulay (A) – ruler
Mouloud – Islamic festival period celebrating the birth of the Prophet
moussem (A) – pilgrimage to *marabout* tomb; festival in honour of a *marabout*
muezzin (A) – mosque official who sings the call to prayer from the minaret
muqarna (A) – decorative plasterwork
musée (F) – museum

ONMT – Office National Marocain du Tourisme, national tourist body, sometimes called Délégation Régionale du Tourisme
ordinaire (F) – less comfortable train, slightly slower than a *rapide*
oued (A) – riverbed, often dry (sometimes *wad* or *wadi*)
oulad (A) – sons (of), often precedes tribal or town name

palais de justice (F) – law court
palmeraie (F) – palm grove
pastilla – a rich, savoury-sweet chicken or pigeon pie made with fine pastry; a dish of layered pastry with cinnamon and almonds served as dessert at banquets
pasha – high official in Ottoman Empire (also *pacha*)
pensiónes (S) – guest house
petit taxi (F) – local taxi
pisé (F) – building material made of sun-dried clay or mud
piste (F) – unsealed tracks, often requiring 4WD vehicles
place (F) – square, plaza
plage (F) – beach
plazas de soberanía (S) – 'Places of sovereignty', the name given to the Spanish possessions in North Africa.
Polisariou – Western Sahara rebel group
pressing (F) – laundry
Prophet (Mohammed), the – founder of Islam, who lived between AD 570 and AD 632

qaid (A) – local chief, loose equivalent of mayor in some parts of Morocco (also *caid*)
qibla (A) – the direction of Mecca, indicated by a *mihrab*
qissaria (A) – covered market sometimes forming the commercial centre of a medina
Quran – sacred book of Islam

Ramadan (A) – ninth month of the Muslim year, a period of fasting
rapide (F) – type of train more comfortable and slightly faster than an *ordinaire*

Reconquista (S) – the Christian reconquest of the Iberian peninsula from the Moors
refuge (F) – mountain hut, basic hikers' shelter
riad (A) – traditional town house set around an internal garden
ribat (A) – combined monastery and fort
Saadians – Moroccan dynasty that ruled in the 16th century
sharia (A) – street
sharia'a (A) – Islamic law
shedwi (A) – flat-woven rug of black and white bands
sherif (A) – descendant of the Prophet
Shiites – one of two main Islamic sects, formed by those who believed the true imams were descended from the Prophet's son-in-law Ali (see also Sunnis)
sidi (A) – honorific (equivalent to 'Mr'; also *si*)
skala (A) – fortress
ski randonnée (F) – ski trekking
souq hebdomadaire (F/A) – weekly market
souq (A) – market
Sufism – mystical strand of Islam that emphasises communion with God through inner attitude
Sunnis – one of two main Islamic sects, derived from followers of the Umayyad caliphate (see also Shiites)
Syndicat d'Initiative (F) – government-run tourist office
tabac (F) – tobacconist and newsagency
tadelakt (A) – waterproof lime plaster mixed with pigments and polished with a stone to give it a smooth, lustrous finish, originally used for the walls of hammams but now a favourite of interior designers
tariq (A) – road, avenue
téléboutique (F) – privately operated telephone service
télécarte (F) – phonecard
terz Fezzi (A) – intricate geometric embroidery originating in Fès
tizi (B) – mountain pass
Tuareg – nomadic Berbers of the Sahara, also known as the Blue Men because of their indigo-dyed robes

ville nouvelle (F) – new city; town built by the French alongside existing towns
vizier – another term for a provincial governor in Ottoman Empire, or adviser to the sultan in Morocco

wali (A) – Islamic holy man or saint
Wattasids – Moroccan dynasty (mid-15th to mid-16th centuries)

zawiya (A) – religious fraternity based around a *marabout*; location of the fraternity (also *zaouia*)
zellij (A) – ceramic tilework used to decorate buildings

The Authors

PAUL CLAMMER **Coordinating Author, Destination Morocco, Getting Started, Itineraries, Environment, Imperial Cities, Directory, Transport**

As a student, Paul had his first solo backpacking experience when he took a bus from his Cambridgeshire home all the way to Casablanca. Morocco instantly enchanted him. After an interlude when he trained and worked as a molecular biologist, he eventually returned to work as a tour guide, trekking in the Atlas and trying not to lose passengers in the Fez medina. He returns on a regular basis both for Lonely Planet and recreation, and is currently fighting the temptation to buy an old medina town house to restore into a more permanent bolthole.

ALISON BING **History, Culture, Arts & Architecture, Crafts, Food & Drink, Marrakesh & Central Morocco**

Alison's first crush was on the Sufi poet Rumi, after visiting his shrine in Turkey and being favourably impressed with the architecture and all that whirling. Not much has changed since she was five, taste-wise, but now that she's studied Islamic art, architecture and political economy at the American University in Cairo and Bryn Mawr College, she can explain her predilections in complete sentences.

Alison also holds a Master's degree from the Fletcher School of Law and Diplomacy, a joint program of Tufts and Harvard Universities, and regularly undermines those diplomatic credentials with opinionated travel, art, food and culture commentaries for newspapers, magazines and radio.

ANTHONY SATTIN **Atlantic Coast, The Souss, Anti Atlas & Western Sahara, Trekking**

Anthony is a writer and broadcaster with a love of literature, travel and North Africa. A Fellow of the Royal Geographical Society, he has travelled widely and has written for many national and international publications. He is a regular contributor of features and criticism to the *Sunday Times* and was recently voted one of the 10 key influences on travel writing. He has written several books on North Africa, the most recent being *The Gates of Africa,* an account of early European exploration. His radio work has included several documentaries about Morocco, the most recent being about Marrakesh for BBC Radio 4.

LONELY PLANET AUTHORS

Why is our travel information the best in the world? It's simple: our authors are passionate, dedicated travellers. They don't take freebies in exchange for positive coverage so you can be sure the advice you're given is impartial. They travel widely to all the popular spots, and off the beaten track. They don't research using just the internet or phone. They discover new places not included in any other guidebook. They personally visit thousands of hotels, restaurants, palaces, trails, galleries, temples and more. They speak with dozens of locals every day to make sure you get the kind of insider knowledge only a local could tell you. They take pride in getting all the details right, and in telling it how it is. Think you can do it? Find out how at **lonelyplanet.com**.

PAUL STILES

Mediterranean Coast & the Rif

Paul lives in the Canary Islands, beneath Mt Teide, the tallest peak in the Atlantic Ocean. On a clear day, it is possible to see the roof of Morocco from the summit. When he climbed up there, however, it was not a clear day, so he had to jump on a plane and see for himself, something he has wanted to do ever since driving a motorcycle around Tunisia. When not escaping modern life, Paul writes about it. His latest book, *Is the American Dream Killing You?*, was more than a little related to his current choice of domicile – where the answer is 'no'.

Behind the Scenes

THIS BOOK

This 9th edition of Morocco was researched and written by Paul Clammer (Coordinating Author), Alison Bing, Anthony Sattin and Paul Stiles. The 8th edition was the work of Anthony Ham, Alison Bing, Paul Clammer, Etain O'Carroll and Anthony Satin, and the 7th edition was the work of Paula Hardy, Mara Vorhees and Heidi Edsall. The Health chapter of the 7th, 8th and 9th editions was based on text written by Dr Caroline Evans; it was updated for this edition by Paul Clammer.

This guidebook was commissioned in Lonely Planet's Melbourne office, and produced by the following:

Commissioning Editors Holly Alexander, Lucy Monie
Coordinating Editor Trent Holden
Coordinating Cartographer Erin McManus
Coordinating Layout Designer Carlos Solarte
Managing Editor Geoff Howard
Managing Cartographers Shahara Ahmed, Adrian Persoglia
Managing Layout Designer Laura Jane
Assisting Editors Laura Gibb, Victoria Harrison, Dianne Schallmeiner, Kate Whitfeld
Assisting Cartographer Lyndell Stringer
Assisting Layout Designers Jim Hsu, David Kemp, Wibowo Rusli
Cover Designer Pepi Bluck
Project Manager Debra Herrmann
Proofers Simone Egger, Helen Koehne
Thanks to Quentin Frayne, Evan Jones, Lisa Knights, Katie Lynch, Katie O'Connell, Sarah Sloane, Celia Wood

THANKS

Paul Clammer

At Lonely Planet thanks to Lucy Monie, who is always a delight to work with, and to my co-authors Anthony, Alison and Paul. A special thanks also to Fez resident and fellow LP author Helen Ranger, who smoothed several crooked medina pathways. Also in Fez, thanks to Mike, Max, Jess and the rest of the Café Clock crew, Ricky Martin for the riad, David Amster for lunchtime conversation, and again to Jen and Sebastian. *Multumesc* to Alexa Radulea. *Shukran bezzef* to Boujemaa Boudaoud. And of course, thanks and love to Jo, for looking after the home front.

Alison Bing

Shukran bezzef (many thanks) to editors Lucy Monie and Holly Alexander, editorial *maâlem* (master artisan) Trent Holden, and dauntless cartographers Shahara Ahmed and Erin McManus. To sustainable tourism innovators Mohamed Nour, Amal Mouklisse, Brendan Sainsbury and Andy McKee: *tbarakallalekum*

THE LONELY PLANET STORY

Fresh from an epic journey across Europe, Asia and Australia in 1972, Tony and Maureen Wheeler sat at their kitchen table stapling together notes. The first Lonely Planet guidebook, *Across Asia on the Cheap,* was born.

Travellers snapped up the guides. Inspired by their success, the Wheelers began publishing books to Southeast Asia, India and beyond. Demand was prodigious, and the Wheelers expanded the business rapidly to keep up. Over the years, Lonely Planet extended its coverage to every country and into the virtual world via lonelyplanet.com and the Thorn Tree message board.

As Lonely Planet became a globally loved brand, Tony and Maureen received several offers for the company. But it wasn't until 2007 that they found a partner whom they trusted to remain true to the company's principles of travelling widely, treading lightly and giving sustainably. In October of that year, BBC Worldwide acquired a 75% share in the company, pledging to uphold Lonely Planet's commitment to independent travel, trustworthy advice and editorial independence.

Today, Lonely Planet has offices in Melbourne, London and Oakland, with over 500 staff members and 300 authors. Tony and Maureen are still actively involved with Lonely Planet. They're travelling more often than ever, and they're devoting their spare time to charitable projects. And the company is still driven by the philosophy of *Across Asia on the Cheap*: 'All you've got to do is decide to go and the hardest part is over. So go!'

(congratulations on your accomplishment) for making desert-travel greener. *Allahyhrem waldikum* (blessings on your parents' heads) to beloved fellow travellers Sahai Burrowes and my parents Tony and June Bing, whose deep admiration for Morocco is a proud family trait. And as always: to Marco Flavio Marinucci, for being my home at the end of every dusty desert road.

Anthony Sattin
In the UK, thanks to Mr Ali el Kasmi, and Malika Lamane of the Moroccan National Tourist Office, Jane Bayley and Janine Hewett. In Morocco, thanks to Emma Wilson, Hassan Dalil, Ingeborg Steenbeke and Titoff Gerard, Marie-Luce Milano, Ben O'Hara, Meryanne Loum-Martin, Stephen Skinner, Kamal Laftimi, and Rosena and Fred at Boutique Souk,

Paul Stiles
I was very lucky to have many people support the research process all along the way, and generally without any prior notice. My thanks goes out to Said and Yto in Tangier, Ruth and Mounaim in Al Hoceima, Najib in Berkane, Salhi in Chefchaouen, Abdeslam and Hassan in Chefchaouen, and the Ayuntamiento of Melilla, which gives out the best trinkets.

OUR READERS

Many thanks to the travellers who used the last edition and wrote to us with helpful hints, useful advice and interesting anecdotes:
Matthew Abbott, Said Abu-Aishah, Susana Afonso, Kairo Alloja, Jj Almanza, Remy Alnet, Monika Alpoegger, Ramona Altfeld, Amy Anderson, Arta Antonovica, Diane Archer, Almudena Gotor Arellano, Jenny Arkell, Jennifer Arnold, Julie Aucoin, Elizabeth Augustine, Katie Baddeley, Arnd Baechler, Christopher Baer, Amy Baker, Corina Bakhos, Michael Baldwin, Greg Banks, Ruth Banks, Tim Banks, Jean-Pierre Barral, Penny Barron, Jemma Barzey, Kim Baxter, Brent Beadle, Elena Bernardis, Marie Berteau, Christine Bertsch, Laurabi Bierer, Ola Biernacka, Amei Binns, William Bliss, Hans Bogstad, Franz Bonsema, Chris Boryer, Ania Bothe, Rein Boumans, Melissa Branfman, Karen Breuer, Francis Breyer, Eric Brouwer, Christine Buzzi, El Mahfoud Chaboun, Marie Charpentier, Sarah Cheung, Parveen Choudhry, Dori Chouhad, Erwin Christensen, Jon Clarke, Aodhagan Collins, Frank Cottle, Tasha Cowap, Ben Crewe, Casey Cross, Alan Curragh, Justin Curran, Maciej Czajkowski, Paolo Dardanelli, Natalie Davies, Monique Dehaese, Michael Dempsey, Tiana Diep, Mark Dolomount, Karla Driemeier, Eelco Edink, Donald Eischen, David Elphinstone, Georgina Esch, Joshua Eveland, Jacques Feldfeber, Marry Fermont, Jan Fiete, Manuel Fischer, Alison Flawith, Katherine Forrest, Sandra Francis-Love, Tjetske Gerbranda, Lorenzo Giacci, Marica Giessen, Pierre Gilbert, Tristan Gissing, Gerard Glennon, Sabrina Goldstein, Hannah Goodall, Philip Goulding, Willy Grandsard, Sarah Gretton, Skorpen Gro, Martin Gruenewald, Goulier Géraldine, Ida Hagen, Sbai Halim, Claire Hamilton, Roland Handel, Holli Harcey, James Harman, Thomas Hefti, Karin Helmreich, Cornelia Hendry, Joanna Hindley, Margaret Hogan, John Houde, Sue Hunt, Edward James, Emily Jamieson, Farrah Jaufuraully, Peter & Michael Johnson, Gan Jordan, Pierre Jouhaud, Aini Kamarul, Sharon Keld, Sarah Kesenne, Peter Kibble, Tanja Klein, Richard Knochenmuss, Oliver Krause, Emily Krug, Petra Kälin, Moyez Ladhani, Fabrice Lambert, Daniel Lamppinen, Marita Larsson, Jayne Lee, Valerie Lehouck, Daniel Levenson, Ian Lewis, Ann Llane, Anna Lloyd, Hans Loes, Julie Lohela, Paula Lopes, Ann Von Lossberg, Pérez Lugo, Christopher Maclellan, Heather Mak, Dorit Maoz, Vivien Marasigan, Koos Remmert Marinus, Bill Martin, Chris Martin, Sandra Martin, Karl Matson, Veronica Matthews, Eamon Mccafferty, Jeffery Mclaren, Ged Mcphail, Ciara Mcquaid, Lucas Meagor, Jennifer Milsom, Gemma Mitchell, Judith Mitsschke, Rita Montalvao, Scott

SEND US YOUR FEEDBACK

We love to hear from travellers – your comments keep us on our toes and help make our books better. Our well-travelled team reads every word on what you loved or loathed about this book. Although we cannot reply individually to postal submissions, we always guarantee that your feedback goes straight to the appropriate authors, in time for the next edition. Each person who sends us information is thanked in the next edition – and the most useful submissions are rewarded with a free book.

To send us your updates – and find out about Lonely Planet events, newsletters and travel news – visit our award-winning website: **lonelyplanet.com/contact**.

Note: we may edit, reproduce and incorporate your comments in Lonely Planet products such as guidebooks, websites and digital products, so let us know if you don't want your comments reproduced or your name acknowledged. For a copy of our privacy policy visit lonelyplanet.com/privacy.

Mooney, Adrian Moore, Lucy Moran, Eckehard Fozzy Moritz, Myron Morris, Richard Mott, Richard Munn, Jo Murphy, Ishay Nadler, Sally Norris, Jason Northcott, Bartek Nowicki, Greg O'Hern, David O'Mahony, Ros O'Maolduin, Nick O'Neil, Helen Ochyra, Geralda Oliveira, Barbara Paganoni, Glenn Palmer, Hils Pamph, Alice Pater, Matt Pepe, Uli Pfeiffer, Derek Phillips, Martina Polley, Giles Prichard, Isabelle Pronovost, Norrie Provan, Leo Rabelo, Gordon Rae, Naeema Rashid, Eric Reuland, Emily Richardson, Nils Riecken, Anton Rijsdijk, Jill Riley, Jan Doeke Rinzema, V Roberts, Daniel Robinson, Petra Roest, Kathryn Rosenbaum, Koosje Ruijgrok, Elizabeth Russell-Smith, Franca Sacco, Archie Sample, Lisa Sawyer, Gunter Schumann, Ann Scott, David Scott, Arthur Segal, Mahnaz Shaikh, Amelia Smith, Karen Stafford, Jill Stanley, Constantin Stéphane, Laura Sutcliffe, George Swann, Melissa Addey Ryan Taylor, Nadine Tiefenbach, Georg Troost, Catherina Unger, Pauline Vahl, Beau Vallance, Joan van Bussel, Marijke van Gerwen, Geert van Gestel, Carolien van Ham, Mike Verbeeck, Laura Verburg, Bart Verdeyen, Nikos Ververidis, Heidi Viney, Jean Vranic, Jan Vyjidak, Hans-Werner Wabnitz, Tom Walsh, Daniel Wang, Tony Wheeler, Andrew Whiting, Helena Wilde, Matt Willson, Angela Wilson, Kristina Wilson, Adolf Wimmer, Eva Wimmer, Stuart Winder, Matthew Wright, Jane Young, Manuele Zunelli, Sietske Zwiebel.

ACKNOWLEDGMENTS

Many thanks to the following for the use of their content:

Globe on title page ©Mountain High Maps 1993 Digital Wisdom, Inc.

Index

C

INDEX

INDEX

000 Map pages
000 Photograph pages

INDEX

INDEX

000 Map pages
000 Photograph pages

GreenDex

It seems like everyone's going green these days, but how can you know which businesses are actually eco-friendly and which are simply jumping on the sustainable-travel bandwagon?

The following Moroccan attractions, tours and accommodation choices have been selected by the authors because they demonstrate an active sustainable-tourism policy. Some are involved in environmental or wildlife protection, and many are community-owned or make a point of employing local people, thereby maintaining and preserving local identity and culture, and alleviating poverty.

We want to keep developing our sustainable-tourism content. If you think we've omitted someone who should be listed here, or if you disagree with our choices, email us at talk2us@lonelyplanet.com.au and set us straight for next time. For more information about sustainable tourism and Lonely Planet, see www.lonelyplanet.com/responsibletravel.

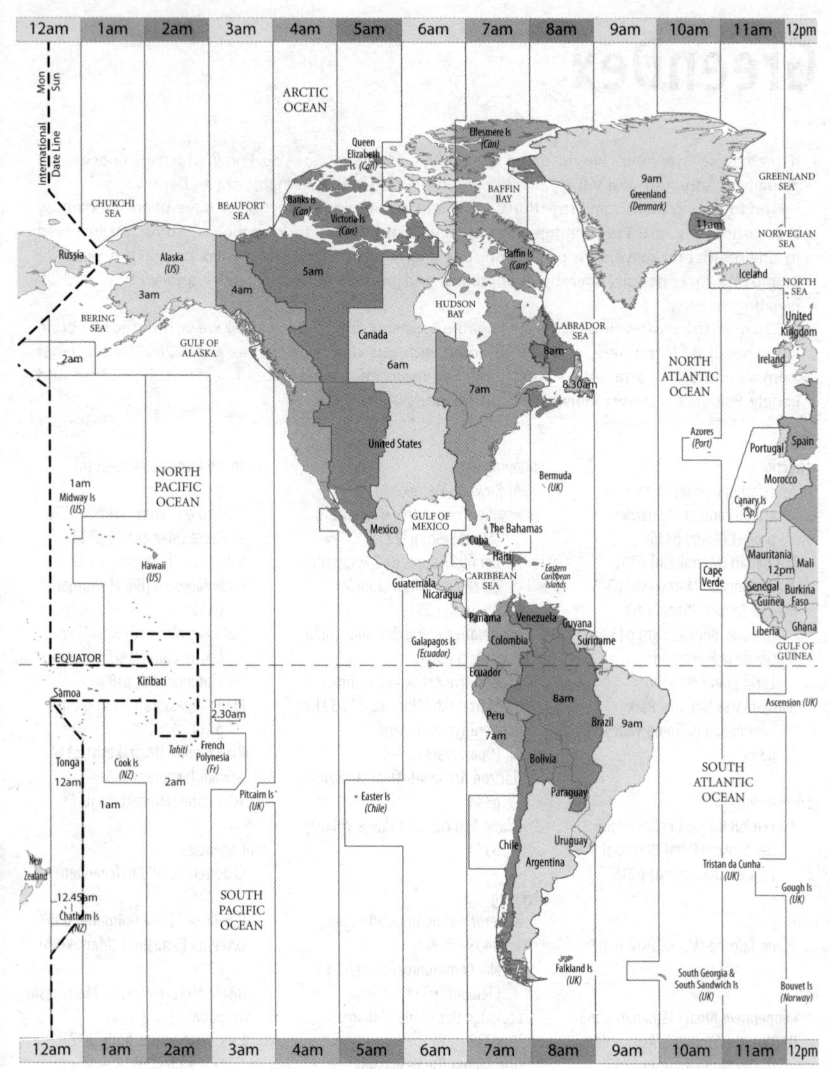
12am
1am
2am
3am
4am
5am
6am
7am
8am
9am
10am
11am
12pm
Mon
Sun
International Date Line
ARCTIC OCEAN
Queen Elizabeth Is (Can)
Ellesmere Is (Can)
Greenland (Denmark)
GREENLAND SEA
CHUKCHI SEA
BEAUFORT SEA
Banks Is (Can)
Victoria Is (Can)
BAFFIN BAY
NORWEGIAN SEA
Russia
Alaska (US)
Baffin Is (Can)
Iceland
NORTH SEA
BERING SEA
HUDSON BAY
United Kingdom
GULF OF ALASKA
Canada
LABRADOR SEA
Ireland
8.30am
NORTH ATLANTIC OCEAN
United States
Azores (Port)
Portugal
Spain
NORTH PACIFIC OCEAN
Midway Is (US)
Bermuda (UK)
Morocco
Canary Is (Sp)
GULF OF MEXICO
Mexico
The Bahamas
Cuba
Haiti
Hawaii (US)
CARIBBEAN SEA
Eastern Caribbean Islands
Mauritania
Mali
Cape Verde
Guatemala
Nicaragua
Senegal
Guinea
Burkina Faso
Panama
Venezuela
Guyana
Suriname
Colombia
Liberia
Ghana
Galapagos Is (Ecuador)
GULF OF GUINEA
EQUATOR
Ecuador
Kiribati
Samoa
Ascension (UK)
Peru
Brazil
2.30am
Tahiti
French Polynesia (Fr)
Tonga
Cook Is (NZ)
Bolivia
SOUTH ATLANTIC OCEAN
Paraguay
Pitcairn Is (UK)
Easter Is (Chile)
Chile
Uruguay
Argentina
Tristan da Cunha (UK)
New Zealand
Gough Is (UK)
12.45am
Chatham Is (NZ)
SOUTH PACIFIC OCEAN
Falkland Is (UK)
South Georgia & South Sandwich Is (UK)
Bouvet Is (Norway)

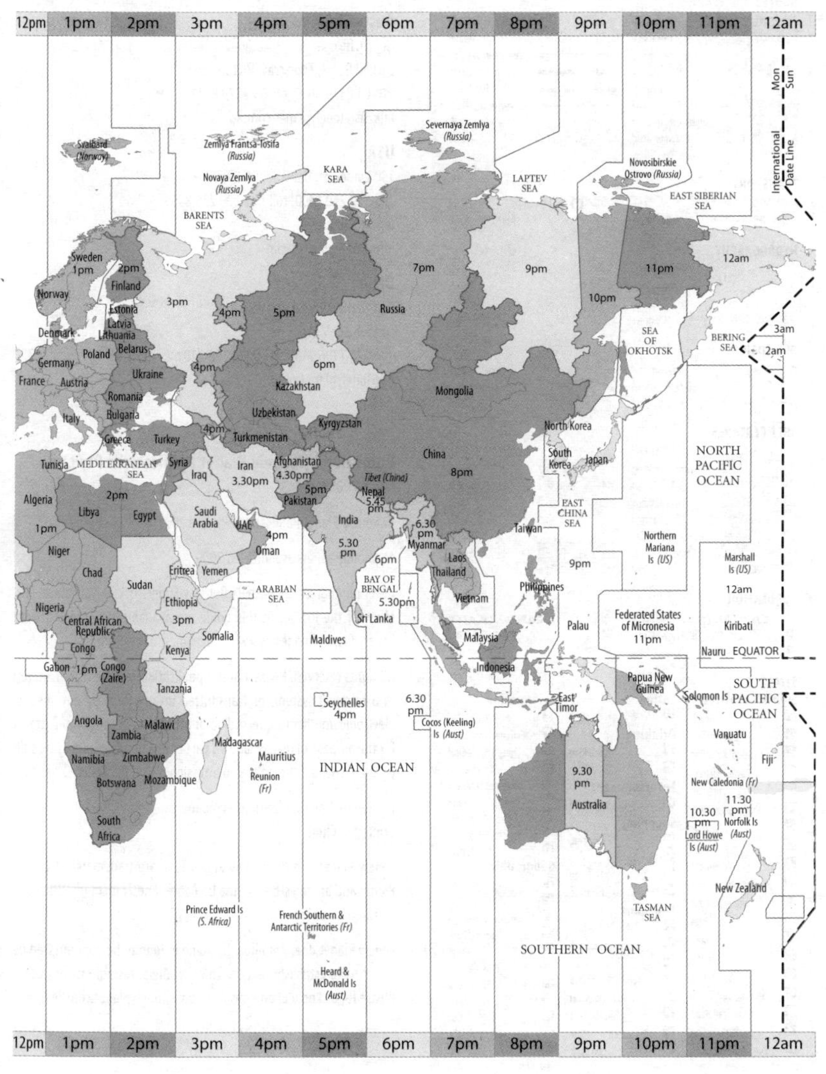
12pm 1pm 2pm 3pm 4pm 5pm 6pm 7pm 8pm 9pm 10pm 11pm 12am
International Date Line
Mon
Sun
Svalbard (Norway)
Zemlya Frantsa-Iosifa (Russia)
Severnaya Zemlya (Russia)
Novaya Zemlya (Russia)
KARA SEA
LAPTEV SEA
Novosibirskie Ostrovo (Russia)
EAST SIBERIAN SEA
BARENTS SEA
Sweden 1pm
2pm
Finland
Norway
3pm
7pm
9pm
11pm
12am
10pm
4pm
5pm
Russia
Estonia
Latvia
Lithuania
Denmark
Belarus
Poland
Germany
Ukraine
France
Austria
Romania
Bulgaria
Italy
Greece
Turkey
4pm
6pm
Kazakhstan
Uzbekistan
Turkmenistan
Kyrgyzstan
Mongolia
SEA OF OKHOTSK
BERING SEA
3am
2am
North Korea
South Korea
Japan
China
8pm
Tibet (China)
Nepal 5.45 pm
NORTH PACIFIC OCEAN
Tunisia
MEDITERRANEAN SEA
Syria
Iraq
Iran 3.30pm
Afghanistan 4.30pm
5pm
Pakistan
Algeria
2pm
Libya
Egypt
Saudi Arabia
UAE
4pm
Oman
India
5.30 pm
6.30 pm
Myanmar
EAST CHINA SEA
Taiwan
1pm
Niger
Chad
Sudan
Eritrea
Yemen
ARABIAN SEA
6pm
BAY OF BENGAL
5.30pm
Laos
Thailand
Vietnam
Philippines
Northern Mariana Is (US)
9pm
Marshall Is (US)
12am
Nigeria
Ethiopia 3pm
Somalia
Sri Lanka
Maldives
Central African Republic
Congo
Kenya
Malaysia
Palau
Federated States of Micronesia 11pm
Kiribati
Nauru EQUATOR
Gabon
1pm
Congo (Zaire)
Tanzania
Seychelles 4pm
6.30 pm
Cocos (Keeling) Is (Aust)
Indonesia
Papua New Guinea
Solomon Is
East Timor
SOUTH PACIFIC OCEAN
Angola
Zambia
Malawi
Madagascar
Mauritius
Reunion (Fr)
INDIAN OCEAN
Vanuatu
Fiji
Namibia
Zimbabwe
Botswana
Mozambique
9.30 pm
Australia
New Caledonia (Fr)
11.30 pm
Norfolk Is (Aust)
10.30 pm
Lord Howe Is (Aust)
South Africa
New Zealand
TASMAN SEA
Prince Edward Is (S. Africa)
French Southern & Antarctic Territories (Fr)
Heard & McDonald Is (Aust)
SOUTHERN OCEAN
12pm 1pm 2pm 3pm 4pm 5pm 6pm 7pm 8pm 9pm 10pm 11pm 12am

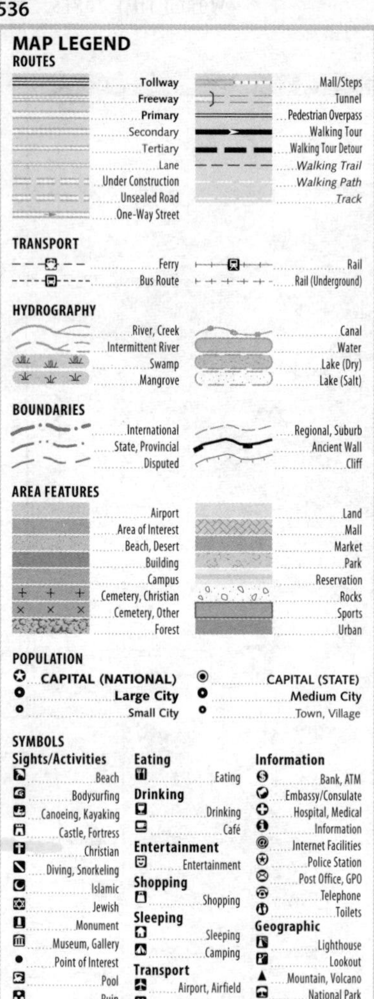

LONELY PLANET OFFICES

Australia

Head Office
Locked Bag 1, Footscray, Victoria 3011
☎ 03 8379 8000, fax 03 8379 8111
talk2us@lonelyplanet.com.au

USA

150 Linden St, Oakland, CA 94607
☎ 510 250 6400, toll free 800 275 8555
fax 510 893 8572
info@lonelyplanet.com

UK

2nd fl, 186 City Rd,
London EC1V 2NT
☎ 020 7106 2100, fax 020 7106 2101
go@lonelyplanet.co.uk

Published by Lonely Planet Publications Pty Ltd
ABN 36 005 607 983

Cover photograph by Michele Burgess/Superstock: Royal Palace, Fez. Many of the images in this guide are available for licensing from Lonely Planet Images: www.lonelyplanetimages.com.

Printed by Hang Tai Printing Company.
Printed in China.